THE COMPLETE GUIDE TO A+ CERTIFICATION

Michael W. Graves

THOMSON

DELMAR LEARNING

Australia • Canada • Mexico • Singapore • Spain • United Kingdom • United States

THOMSON
DELMAR LEARNING ™

The Complete Guide to A+ Certification

by Michael W. Graves

Vice President, Technology and Trades SBU:
Alar Elken

Editorial Director:
Sandy Clark

Senior Acquistions Editor:
Stephen Helba

Senior Channel Manager:
Dennis Williams

Senior Development Editor:
Michelle Ruelos Cannistraci

Marketing Director:
Dave Garza

Marketing Coordinator:
Stacey Wiktorek

Production Director:
Mary Ellen Black

Production Manager:
Andrew Crouth

Art/Design Coordinator:
Francis Hogan

Senior Editorial Assistant:
Dawn Daugherty

COPYRIGHT © 2006 by Delmar Learning, a division of Thomson Learning, Inc. Thomson Learning' is a trademark used herein under license.

Printed in Canada
3 4 5 6 XXX 07 06

For more information contact Thomson/Delmar Learning
5 Maxwell Drive
Clifton Park, N.Y. 12065

Or find us on the World Wide Web at
www.delmarlearning.com

ALL RIGHTS RESERVED.
No part of this work covered by the copyright hereon may be reproduced in any form or by any means—graphic, electronic, or mechanical, including photocopying, recording, taping, Web distribution, or information storage and retrieval systems—without the written permission of the publisher.

For permission to use material from the text or product, contact us by
Tel. (800) 730-2214
Fax (800) 730-2215
www.thomsonrights.com

Library of Congress Card Number:
2005925896

The Complete Guide to
A+ Certification/
Michael W. Graves

ISBN: 1418005665

NOTICE TO THE READER

Publisher does not warrant or guarantee any of the products described herein or perform any independent analysis in connection with any of the product information contained herein. Publisher does not assume, and expressly disclaims, any obligation to obtain and include information other than that provided to it by the manufacturer.

The reader is expressly warned to consider and adopt all safety precautions that might be indicated by the activities herein and to avoid all potential hazards. By following the instructions contained herein, the reader willingly assumes all risks in connection with such instructions.

The publisher makes no representation or warranties of any kind, including but not limited to, the warranties of fitness for particular purpose or merchantability, nor are any such representations implied with respect to the material set forth herein, and the publisher takes no responsibility with respect to such material. The publisher shall not be liable for any special, consequential, or exemplary damages resulting, in whole or part, from the readers' use of, or reliance upon, this material.

TABLE OF CONTENTS

PART 2
A+ GUIDE TO PC OPERATING SYSTEMS

PREFACE

Welcome to *The Complete Guide to A+ Certification*! Within this book, you will find everything you need to know to pass both the Core Hardware and the Operating Systems Technologies Exams of CompTIA's A+ Certification Program. You will discover that additional material above and beyond the scope of the exam is provided, so in addition to being a good training manual, *The Complete Guide to A+ Certification* will serve as a valuable reference long after your certification is hanging on your wall.

In this day and age, there aren't a lot of jobs that one can achieve without a college education that pay a living wage. One key exception to that rule of thumb is the job of computer repair technician or help desk technician. Many people find either one of these jobs attractive not only for the pay, but because it's actually a fun job!

There are a lot of other reasons for wanting to work with computers as well. It's also one of the fastest-growing career fields in America and the rest of the world. But for those of us who believe that variety is the spice of life, the sheer diversity of responsibilities and people that you work with is every bit as rewarding as the money.

Whatever your reasons for wanting a book of this nature may be, there is a lot in this book that will benefit virtually every level of reader. The concept of this book is to provide a textbook for PC hardware and operating systems classes. The simplified writing style makes it ideal for the beginning student with little or no background in hardware and operating systems, whereas the depth of content provides even the advanced reader with detailed information about how different components and software works.

ORGANIZATION

The book is divided into two sections. Part 1 deals with the Core Hardware Exam. This is where you will be tested on your knowledge of installing, configuring, and troubleshooting hardware devices. Part 1 starts with the basic fundamental concepts that anyone dealing with computers needs to know instinctively. Chapter 1 deals with PC basics, and Chapter 2 covers basic concepts of operating systems, and how they interface with the hardware.

In the next couple of chapters, the basics of electricity are covered and the reader is given an overview of all the components that make up a computer. From there, each of the major components is discussed, starting with the motherboard, BIOS, CPUs, and memory. These discussions cover not only the function of these components, but their history as well. Upgrading and troubleshooting techniques top off the discussion of each component. Each chapter covers a different component, following the data from the inside of the computer to the final output stage.

Part 2 takes a similar approach to operating systems and prepares you for the Operating Systems Exam. Starting with an overview of the venerable MS-DOS, the author follows the evolution of Microsoft operating systems all the way through to XP.

Part 2 starts off with the underlying concepts of operating systems and how they work. This is followed by chapters that cover DOS and Windows 3.x versions. Don't be too anxious to skip them by, however, because much of the material presented in these chapters comes into play in later chapters.

The text provides systematic coverage of the operating systems covered on the exam, in the order in which they were released. Each new OS is introduced by discussing what is new and different from the preceding operating system. After that comes a detailed discussion of the OS in general, including material concerning the user interface, OS architecture, and any relevant material surrounding configuration issues.

The last few chapters cover networking, troubleshooting, and connecting computers to the Internet. In addition, the reader is given a brief introduction to Linux. Although that operating system will not be covered on the exam, Linux has gone from being the resident operating system on under two percent of desktops to nearly ten percent, so there's a good chance you'll run into it in the real world.

FEATURES

As you browse through *The Complete Guide to A+ Certification*, a few key qualities should pop out at you right away. In Part 1, chapters are organized in a way that enables readers to understand how data moves through the PC from creation to output. In Part 2, readers are taken on a tour of operating systems from the early days of the PC all the way to the current day of Windows XP.

The author's light-handed approach to presenting information makes the material easy to read and much easier to learn. There are hundreds of high-quality illustrations that supplement the text and dozens of tables that organize information into an easy-to-understand format. Advice on troubleshooting is supplemented by the field experiences of the author himself.

The text includes the following features:

1. A+ Objectives mapped to the textbook are placed in the Introduction preceding Part 1 and Part 2.

2. Each chapter begins with a list identifying the **Objectives** to be covered for the A+ Core Hardware and Operating Systems Technologies Exams.

3. Computer technology is full of acronyms and technical terms that you need to understand, so each chapter integrates **Buzz Words**, **Tricky Terminology**, and **Acronym Alerts** to introduce and reinforce key terminology.

4. **Exam Notes** for the student are given throughout the text providing helpful hints in preparing for the A+ Exam.

5. A **Chapter Summary** provides a quick refresher and review key points from the text.

6. Each chapter concludes with two sets of questions, called **Brain Drain** and **64K$ Questions**. The first set is a series of challenging, essay-oriented questions, and the second set consists of multiple-choice and true/false review questions.

7. A comprehensive **Glossary** and **Answers to Odd-Numbered Questions** are placed at the end of the book.

8. A CD in the back of the book includes **sample video clips** from the *Mastering the A+ Exam DVD Series* and **additional practice test questions**.

9. **View the Video** icon at the end of selected chapters identifies when to refer to the accompanying CD, which reinforces concepts learned through animations and demonstrations.

SUPPLEMENTS

Lab Manual. The lab manual includes a set of twenty-nine lab exercises. Lab exercises range from installing IDE devices to setting up a peer-to-peer network. Lab exercises also include the installation and/or configuration of WIN9X, WIN2K, and WINXP. In addition, students will explore the various tools provided by Microsoft for OS management and troubleshooting.
(ISBN: 1418005673)

e.resource CD. The following instructional aids are available all on one CD.

- **Textbook Solutions** includes answers to all end-of-chapter review questions.

- **Lab Manual Solutions** includes answers to all lab exercise review questions.

- **ExamView Testbank** includes over 1400 questions in a variety of formats, including multiple-choice, true/false, matching, and more.

- **PowerPoint Presentation Slides** highlight key concepts from each chapter and can be used as handouts or as a springboard for lecture and discussion.

- **Image Library** includes all images from the textbook so instructors can customize handouts, tests, and PowerPoint presentations.

(ISBN: 1418005681)

A+ DVD Series: Mastering the A+ Exam. This comprehensive, five-part DVD series of twenty videos has been designed to assist viewers in preparing for the current A+ Exam. All topics presented are correlated to the A+ Certification Exam objectives and span the spectrum, from electronics fundamentals through preventive maintenance, basic troubleshooting techniques, wireless networking, and Windows 9X, NT 4.0, Me, 2000, and XP.

Each DVD consists of four twenty-minute videos and features numerous demonstrations and step-by-step techniques, plus professional-quality graphics and animations to illustrate concepts and aid in retention of essential information. Additional instructor elements include Assessment Questions, Discussion Topics, Applied Academics Questions, Glossary, and Answers to Assessment Questions.
(ISBN: 1401858880)

The Complete Guide to A+ Certification Study Guide. This study guide is designed to be used as a supplement to assist students in preparing for A+ certification. This

concise study guide provides twenty sample questions for each CompTIA Core Hardware and OS Technologies exam objective.
(ISBN: 1418016969)

The PC Technician's Pocket Field Guide. This pocket guide is designed to be used by both novices and experienced users who simply do not want to commit everything they have to know to memory. This pocket guide is a handy reference and includes everything you need to work in the field, including common trouble-shooting situations and general error messages.
(ISBN: 1418016977)

Online Companion. The Online Companion features an A+ Arcade with free electronic flash cards, online quizzes, and an Ask the Author section. Please visit www.delmarlearning.com/certification.

ACKNOWLEDGMENTS

The author and Thomson Delmar Learning would like to thank the following reviewers:

Shaikh Ali, City College, Fort Lauderdale, FL
Russ Davis, Pittsburgh Technical Institute, Midland, PA
Raj Desai, Southeast Missouri State, Cape Girardeau, MO
Billy Graham, Northwest Technical Institute, Springdale, AR
Kyle Muldrow, DeVry University, Long Beach, CA
David Patzarian, Albany Vo-Tech Center, Albany, NY
Roger Peterson, Northland Community and Technical College, Thief River Falls, MN
Jack Williams, Remington College, Tampa, FL

PART 1

A+ GUIDE TO PC HARDWARE

INTRODUCTION

WHO IS COMPTIA, AND WHY SHOULD I GET CERTIFIED?

Just what is certification? Look at it this way. Everywhere you go in life, you constantly have to prove yourself. You may be one of those people who can take apart a computer and put it back together with your eyes closed and one hand tied behind your back. When you're done, your old 486 outperforms your neighbor's brand new Athlon 64 FX-55. The only problem is, when you enter the job market, not many employers are willing to listen to your success stories. All they want to know is how much paper you carry. In other words, are you certified?

Virtually every professional field has some sort of certification program in place. Every state has building codes that require a certified electrician to install wiring in new houses or to make wiring changes during a remodel. Likewise, furnace installers, carpenters, heavy equipment operators, and even beauticians all require certificates. State and local authorities won't let them pick up their tools until they show their paper.

As of yet, I know of no states that *require* certification from computer professionals. As technical as computers are, one would not think that could be the case. Therefore, just anybody can hang out a shingle and call himself or herself a pro. Employers, on the other hand, expect a bit more. The computer industry has many, many certification programs—probably more than any other singular career field. Fortunately, for you, however, there is only one certification dealing with your expertise in matters of hardware that anybody pays any attention to. And that is CompTIA's A+ Certification.

CompTIA stands for the *Computing Technology Industry Association*. CompTIA is an organization of companies and professional consultants who get together and agree on various standards for the industry to follow in a valiant effort to keep things consistent. The A+ Certification exam is one of the things that they administer. Groups of hardware specialists from various areas of the industry provide input on the materials that should be covered on the exam, review and approve the questions. Then they make sure that what you are tested on adequately demonstrates that you have sufficient knowledge to successfully pursue a career as a hardware technician. Once you are awarded your certificate, you have all the proof you need to show a potential employer that you are fit for the job.

THE EXAMS

To receive your certification, you must pass two separate exams. It does not matter in what order you take them, but it is important that you finish them both within ninety days of each other. Today's exams are in linear format. Once a candidate has been processed and validated by the examiner, a bank of questions averaging eighty questions is downloaded to a computer. The number of questions a candidate sees in any given objective is based on the formula seen in the lists below.

The two tests consist of what are called the "Core Hardware Exam" and the "Operating Systems Technologies Exam." The core exam tests your knowledge of how the hardware in a computer actually works. While not targeted specifically as an exam prep book, everything you need to pass the core exam can be found in these pages. To pass this exam you need to be able to troubleshoot situations, interpret problems, and know how the parts of your computer work together to make the whole thing functional.

The Operating Systems Exam deals with Windows 9x, NT, and Windows 2000, with some emphasis on Unix and Linux as well.

CompTIA has a massive database of questions that it draws from in the administration of these exams. When your examiner schedules an exam for you, he or she will make a request through CompTIA's authorized exam provider (currently Thomson Prometric or Pearson Vue). The questions for your particular exam will then be assembled and transmitted over the Internet. You could take the exam a hundred times and not see the same question twice. However, there is a standardized approach to assure that the core material is covered on each exam.

Earlier I mentioned that each exam is broken down into knowledge categories. CompTIA has a formula it follows for setting the proportions of questions on any given exam. The proportions it uses for assembling the questions on the Core Exam are listed here.

Core Exam:
- 35% = Installation and configuration and upgrading
- 21% = Diagnosing and troubleshooting
- 5% = Preventative maintenance
- 11% = Motherboards, processors, and memory
- 9% = Printers
- 19% = Basic networking

The second test that you are required to take covers your proficiency in operating systems. In this respect, you will need to know some basic fundamentals of DOS and the personal Windows applications, including WIN95, WIN98, and WINME. You'll need to be able to navigate Windows NT 4.0 and Windows 2000, and CompTIA expects you to have a fundamental understanding of Unix and Linux. On the latter two systems, only a brief overview is covered. Here is a pretty good idea of how CompTIA breaks down the questions you'll be asked from its database.

Operating Systems Exam
- 28% = OS fundamentals
- 31% = Installation, configuration, and upgrading
- 25% = Diagnosing and troubleshooting
- 16% = Networks

Questions you might expect to see would include things of this nature:
Memory mapping is controlled by:

1. The memory mapping module
2. The CPU
3. The 8087 chip
4. The memory control chip

Which is *not* a common memory package?

1. SIPP
2. DIMM
3. DIPP
4. RISC
5. SIMM

You also might be presented with a scenario from which you will be asked specific questions. The following is an example.

A technician is charged with the task of installing memory on a batch of older 486DX computers at a client's site. Upon opening the case, she detects that the motherboard is equipped with eight 30-pin memory sockets. She knows from her work order that all the PCs are equipped with 4MB each. She was provided with a supply of 4MB 70ns SIMMs. Upon examining the SIMMs already installed she finds that they are all 80ns.

Because of the difference in speed she knows she cannot use the 4MB SIMMs.

1. True
2. False

She knows that the four sockets the 1MB SIMMs came out of are:

1. Bank 0
2. Bank 1
3. Bank 2
4. She can only tell what bank they're in by referring to the motherboard manual.

Taking the exam need not be a stressful ordeal. Proper preparation so you feel comfortable with the material, a good night's sleep the night before, and a relaxed attitude can help matters immeasurably. Another key is to avoid second-guessing yourself. When the day arrives, show up at the testing center early so you can relax for a few minutes before diving right in. Remember this: even if you fail your first attempt, it will give you a good idea of where you need to strengthen your knowledge.

THE EXAM OBJECTIVES

As I mentioned earlier, The CompTIA A+ Core Hardware Exam, which is the subject of Part 1, is broken down into six different domains of knowledge, and the exam is structured around those domains. This format allows for a more structured approach to preparing for the exam. Table I.1 lists the various domains and their relative importance to the exam.

Table I.1   The Objective Domains

Domain	Percentage of Exam
1.0 Installation, Configuration, and Upgrading	35%
2.0 Diagnosing and Troubleshooting	21%
3.0 Preventative Maintenance	5%
4.0 Motherboard/Processors/Memory	11%
5.0 Printers	9%
6.0 Basic Networking	19%
Total	100%

The CompTIA A+ Core is broken down into six domains.

The individual domains are further broken down into specific objectives that you must demonstrate that you have achieved in preparing for the exam. The next few pages discuss each domain.

DOMAIN 1: INSTALLATION, CONFIGURATION, AND UPGRADING

1.1 IDENTIFY THE NAMES, PURPOSE, AND CHARACTERISTICS OF SYSTEM MODULES. RECOGNIZE THESE MODULES BY SIGHT OR DEFINITION.

Examples of concepts and modules are:

Motherboards (Chapter 1, Chapter 3, and Chapter 6)

Firmware (Chapter 6, Chapter 10, and Chapter 16)

Power supplies (Chapter 3 and Chapter 4)

Processors/CPUs (Chapter 3, Chapter 7, and Chapter 8)

Memory (Chapter 3, Chapter 9, and Chapter 16)

Storage devices (Chapter 3, Chapter 12, and Chapter 13)

Display devices (Chapter 3, Chapter 16, and Lab Manual)

Adapter cards (Chapter 3, Chapter 10, Chapter 15, Chapter 16, Chapter 17, Chapter 32, and Lab Manual)

Ports (Chapter 3, Chapter 5, Chapter 6, Chapter 10, and Lab Manual)

Cases (Chapter 3, Chapter 5, and Lab Manual)

Riser cards (Chapter 3 and Chapter 6)

1.2 IDENTIFY BASIC PROCEDURES FOR ADDING AND REMOVING FIELD-REPLACEABLE MODULES FOR DESKTOP SYSTEMS. GIVEN A REPLACEMENT SCENARIO, CHOOSE THE APPROPRIATE SEQUENCES.

Desktop components:

Motherboard (Chapter 3 and Chapter 6)

Storage devices

    FDDs (Chapter 12 and Lab Manual)

    HDDs (Chapter 14 and Lab Manual)

    CD/CD-RW (Chapter 17 and Lab Manual)

    DVD/DVD-RW (Chapter 17)

    Tape drives (Chapter 12)

    Removable storage (Chapter 12 and Lab Manual)

Power supplies

    AC adapters (Chapter 4)

    AT/ATX (Chapter 4 and Chapter 6)

Cooling systems
 Fans (Chapter 8)
 Heat sinks (Chapter 8)
 Liquid cooling (Chapter 8)
Processors/CPUs (Chapter 8 and Lab Manual)
Memory (Chapter 9 and Lab Manual)
Display devices (Chapter 16)
Input devices
 Keyboards (Chapter 11)
 Mouse/Pointer devices (Chapter 11)
 Touch screens (Chapter 11 and Chapter 16)
Adapters
 Network Interface Cards (Chapter 32 and Lab Manual)
 Sound cards (Chapter 17 and Lab Manual)
 Video cards (Chapter 16)
 Modems (Chapter 20 and Lab Manual)
 SCSI (Chapter 15 and Lab Manual)
 IEEE 1394/FireWire (Chapter 15)
 USB (Chapter 10)
 Wireless (Chapter 32)

1.3 IDENTIFY BASIC PROCEDURES FOR ADDING AND REMOVING FIELD-REPLACEABLE MODULES FOR PORTABLE SYSTEMS. GIVEN A REPLACEMENT SCENARIO, CHOOSE THE APPROPRIATE SEQUENCES.

Portable components:

Storage devices
 FDDs (Chapter 19)
 HDDs (Chapter 14 and Chapter 19)
 CD/CD-RW (Chapter 19)
 DVD/DVD-RW (Chapter 19)
 Removable storage (Chapter 19)
Power sources
 AC adapter (Chapter 19)
 DC adapter (Chapter 19)
 Battery (Chapter 19)

Memory (Chapter 9 and Chapter 19)

Input devices

  Keyboard (Chapter 19)

  Mouse/Pointer devices (Chapter 11 and Chapter 19)

  Touch screen (Chapter 11 and Chapter 19)

PCMCIA/Mini PCI Adapters (Chapter 10 and Chapter 19)

  Network Interface Card (Chapter 32)

  Modem (Chapter 20 and Chapter 19)

  SCSI (Chapter 15)

  IEEE 1394/FireWire (Chapter 15)

  USB (Chapter 10 and Chapter 19)

  Storage (memory and hard drives) (Chapter 9, Chapter 14, and Chapter 19)

Docking stations/Port replicators (Chapter 19)

LCD panels (Chapter 16 and Chapter 19)

Wireless

  Adapters/Controllers (Chapter 32)

  Antennae (Chapter 32)

1.4 IDENTIFY TYPICAL IRQS, DMAS, AND I/O ADDRESSES AND PROCEDURES FOR ALTERING THESE SETTINGS WHEN INSTALLING AND CONFIGURING DEVICES. CHOOSE THE APPROPRIATE INSTALLATION OR CONFIGURATION STEPS IN A GIVEN SCENARIO.

Content may include the following:

Legacy devices (e.g., ISA sound cards) (Chapter 6 and Chapter 17)

Specialized devices (e.g., CAD/CAM) (Chapter 3 and Chapter 10)

Internal modems (Chapter 3, Chapter 20, and Lab Manual)

Floppy drive controllers (Chapter 3, Chapter 6, and Chapter 10)

Hard drive controllers (Chapter 3, Chapter 6, and Chapter 14)

Multimedia devices (Chapter 3, Chapter 6, and Chapter 17)

NICs (Chapter 32)

I/O ports

  Serial (Chapter 10 and Lab Manual)

  Parallel (Chapter 10 and Lab Manual)

  USB (Chapter 10 and Lab Manual)

  IEEE 1394/FireWire (Chapter 15 and Lab Manual)

  Infrared (Chapter 32)

1.5 IDENTIFY THE NAMES, PURPOSES, AND PERFORMANCE CHARACTERISTICS OF STANDARDIZED/COMMON PERIPHERAL PORTS, ASSOCIATED CABLING, AND CONNECTORS. RECOGNIZE PORTS, CABLING, AND CONNECTORS BY SIGHT.

Content may include the following:

Port types
   Serial (Chapter 10 and Lab Manual)
   Parallel (Chapter 10 and Lab Manual)
   USB (Chapter 10 and Lab Manual)
   IEEE 1394/FireWire (Chapter 15 and Lab Manual)
   Infrared (Chapter 32)
Cable types
   Serial (Straight through versus null modem) (Chapter 3 and Chapter 10)
   Parallel (Chapter 3 and Chapter 18)
   USB (Chapter 10)
Connector types
   Serial
         DB-9 (Chapter 3 and Chapter 10)
         DB-25 (Chapter 3 and Chapter 10)
         RJ-11 (Chapter 3 and Chapter 32)
         RJ-45 (Chapter 3 and Chapter 32)
   Parallel
         DB-25 (Chapter 3 and Chapter 18)
         Centronics (Lab Manual)
   PS2/MINI-DIN (Chapter 3 and Chapter 10)
   USB (Chapter 3 and Chapter 10)
   IEEE 1394 (Chapter 3 and Chapter 15)

1.6 IDENTIFY PROPER PROCEDURES FOR INSTALLING AND CONFIGURING COMMON IDE DEVICES. CHOOSE THE APPROPRIATE INSTALLATION OR CONFIGURATION SEQUENCES IN GIVEN SCENARIOS. RECOGNIZE THE ASSOCIATED CABLES.

Content may include the following:

IDE interface types
   EIDE (Chapter 14)
   ATA/ATAPI (Chapter 14)

Serial ATA (Chapter 14)

PIO (Chapter 14)

RAID (0, 1, and 5) (Chapter 15)

Master/Slave/Cable select (Chapter 14)

Devices per channel (Chapter 6 and Chapter 14)

Primary/Secondary (Chapter 6 and Chapter 14)

Cable orientation/Requirements (Chapter 3 and Chapter 14)

1.7 IDENTIFY PROPER PROCEDURES FOR INSTALLING AND CONFIGURING COMMON SCSI DEVICES. CHOOSE THE APPROPRIATE INSTALLATION OR CONFIGURATION SEQUENCES IN GIVEN SCENARIOS. RECOGNIZE THE ASSOCIATED CABLES.

Content may include the following:

SCSI interface types

Narrow (Chapter 15)

Fast (Chapter 15)

Wide (Chapter 15)

Ultra-wide (Chapter 15)

LVD (Chapter 15)

HVD (Chapter 15)

Internal versus External (Chapter 15)

SCSI IDs

Jumper block/DIP switch settings (binary equivalents) (Chapter 15)

Resolving ID conflicts (Chapter 15)

RAID (0, 1, and 5) (Chapter 15)

Cabling

Length (Chapter 15)

Type (Chapter 15)

Termination requirements (Active, Passive, Auto) (Chapter 15)

1.8 IDENTIFY PROPER PROCEDURES FOR INSTALLING AND CONFIGURING COMMON PERIPHERAL DEVICES. CHOOSE THE APPROPRIATE INSTALLATION OR CONFIGURATION SEQUENCES IN GIVEN SCENARIOS.

Content may include the following:

Modems and transceivers (Dial-up, Cable, DSL, ISDN) (Chapter 20 and Lab Manual)

External storage (Chapter 12, Chapter 14, and Chapter 17)

Digital cameras (Chapter 10)

PDAs (Chapter 19)

Wireless access points (Chapter 20)

Infrared devices (Chapter 20)

Printers (Chapter 18)

UPS (Uninterruptible Power Supply) and suppressors (Chapter 4)

Monitors (Chapter 16)

1.9 IDENTIFY PROCEDURES TO OPTIMIZE PC OPERATIONS IN SPECIFIC SITUATIONS. PREDICT THE EFFECTS OF SPECIFIC PROCEDURES UNDER GIVEN SCENARIOS.

Topics may include:

Cooling systems
  Liquid (Chapter 8)
  Air (Chapter 8)
  Heat sink (Chapter 8)
  Thermal compound (Chapter 8)
Disk subsystem enhancements
  Hard drives (Chapter 14)
  Controller cards (RAID, ATA-100, etc.) (Chapter 14 and Chapter 15)
  Cables (Chapter 3)
NICs (Chapter 32)
Specialized video cards (Chapter 16)
Memory (Chapter 9)
Additional processors (Chapter 7)

1.10 DETERMINE THE ISSUES THAT MUST BE CONSIDERED WHEN UPGRADING A PC. IN A GIVEN SCENARIO, DETERMINE WHEN AND HOW TO UPGRADE SYSTEM COMPONENTS.

Issues may include:

Drivers for legacy devices (Chapter 10 and Lab Manual)

Bus types and characteristics (Chapter 10, Chapter 15, and Chapter 16)

Cache in relationship to motherboards (Chapter 6 and Chapter 9)

Memory capacity and characteristics (Chapter 6)

Processor speed and compatibility (Chapter 7)

Hard drive capacity and characteristics (Chapter 14)

System/firmware limitations (Chapter 6 and Chapter 31)

Power supply output capacity (Chapter 4)

Components may include the following:
Motherboards (Chapter 6 and Chapter 20)

Memory (Chapter 9 and Chapter 20)

Hard drives (Chapter 13 and Chapter 20)

CPUs (Chapter 7 and Chapter 20)

BIOS (Chapter 6)

Adapter cards (Chapter 10)

Laptop power sources

 Lithium ion (Chapter 20)

 NiMH (Chapter 20)

 Fuel cell (Chapter 20)

PCMCIA Type I, II, III cards (Chapter 20)

DOMAIN 2: DIAGNOSING AND TROUBLESHOOTING

2.1 RECOGNIZE COMMON PROBLEMS ASSOCIATED WITH EACH MODULE AND THEIR SYMPTOMS, AND IDENTIFY STEPS TO ISOLATE AND TROUBLESHOOT THE PROBLEMS. GIVEN A PROBLEM SITUATION, INTERPRET THE SYMPTOMS AND INFER THE MOST LIKELY CAUSE.

Content may include the following:

I/O ports and cables

 Serial (Chapter 10 and Chapter 31)

 Parallel (Chapter 10 and Chapter 31)

 USB (Chapter 10 and Chapter 31)

 IEEE 1394/FireWire (Chapter 15 and Chapter 31)

 Infrared (Chapter 31 and Chapter 32)

 SCSI (Chapter 15 and Chapter 31)

Motherboards

 CMOS/BIOS settings (Chapter 6, Chapter 14, Chapter 17, and Chapter 31)

 POST audible/visual error codes (Chapter 6, Chapter 31, and Appendix G)

Peripherals (Chapter 6 and Chapter 31)

 Computer cases

  Power supplies (Chapter 4 and Chapter 31)

Slot covers (Chapter 5)

Front cover alignment (Chapter 6)

Storage devices and cables

FDDs (Chapter 3, Chapter 6, Chapter 12, and Chapter 31)

HDDs (Chapter 14 and Chapter 31)

CD/CD-RW (Chapter 17 and Chapter 31)

DVD/DVD-RW (Chapter 17 and Chapter 31)

Tape drives (Chapter 12 and Chapter 31)

Removable storage (Chapter 12 and Chapter 31)

Cooling systems (Chapter 14 and Chapter 31)

Fans (Chapter 5, Chapter 8, and Chapter 31)

Heat sinks (Chapter 8 and Chapter 31)

Liquid cooling (Chapter 8)

Temperature sensors (Chapter 8)

Processors/CPUs (Chapter 8 and Chapter 31)

Memory (Chapter 9 and Chapter 31)

Display devices (Chapter 16 and Chapter 31)

Input devices

Keyboards (Chapter 11 and Chapter 31)

Mouse/Pointer devices (Chapter 11 and Chapter 31)

Touch screens (Chapter 6, Chapter 11, and Chapter 31)

Adapters

Network Interface Cards (NIC) (Chapter 32 and Chapter 31)

Sound cards (Chapter 17 and Chapter 31)

Video cards (Chapter 16 and Chapter 31)

Modems (Chapter 20 and Chapter 31)

SCSI (Chapter 15 and Chapter 31)

IEEE 1394/FireWire (Chapter 15 and Chapter 31)

USB (Chapter 11 and Chapter 31)

Portable Systems

PCMCIA (Chapter 11 and Chapter 31)

Batteries (Chapter 19 and Chapter 31)

Docking stations/Port replicators (Chapter 19 and Chapter 31)

Portable unique storage (Chapter 19 and Chapter 31)

2.2 IDENTIFY BASIC TROUBLESHOOTING PROCEDURES AND TOOLS, AND HOW TO ELICIT PROBLEM SYMPTOMS FROM CUSTOMERS. JUSTIFY ASKING PARTICULAR QUESTIONS IN A GIVEN SCENARIO.

Content may include the following:

Troubleshooting/Isolation/Problem determination procedures (Chapter 31)
Determining whether a hardware or software problem (Chapter 31)
Gathering information from user (Chapter 31)
   Customer environment (Chapter 31)
   Symptoms/Error codes (Chapter 31 and Appendix F)
   Situation when the problem occurred (Chapter 31)

DOMAIN 3: PC PREVENTATIVE MAINTENANCE, SAFETY, AND ENVIRONMENTAL ISSUES

3.1 IDENTIFY THE VARIOUS TYPES OF PREVENTATIVE MAINTENANCE MEASURES, PRODUCTS, AND PROCEDURES AND WHEN AND HOW TO USE THEM.

Content may include the following:

Liquid cleaning compounds (Chapter 18)
Types of materials to clean contacts and connections (Chapter 18)
Nonstatic vacuums (chassis, power supplies, fans) (Chapter 3 and Chapter 4)
Cleaning monitors (Chapter 16)
Cleaning removable media devices (Chapter 11)
Ventilation, dust, and moisture control on the PC hardware interior (Chapter 5)
Hard disk maintenance (Defragging, ScanDisk, CHKDSK) (Chapter 14 and Chapter 31)
Verifying UPS (Uninterruptible Power Supply) and suppressors (Chapter 4 and Chapter 31)

3.2 IDENTIFY VARIOUS SAFETY MEASURES AND PROCEDURES, AND WHEN/HOW TO USE THEM.

Content may include the following:

ESD (electrostatic discharge) precautions and procedures
   What ESD can do, how it may be apparent or hidden (Chapter 4 and Chapter 31)
   Common ESD protection devices (Chapter 4)
   Situations that could present a danger or hazard (Chapter 4, Chapter 6, and Chapter 18)

Potential hazards and proper safety procedures relating to:

High-voltage equipment (Chapter 4, Chapter 6, and Chapter 18)
Power supplies (Chapter 4 and Chapter 18)
CRTs (Chapter 6 and Chapter 18)

3.3 IDENTIFY ENVIRONMENTAL PROTECTION MEASURES AND PROCEDURES, AND WHEN/HOW TO USE THEM.

Content may include the following:

Special disposal procedures that comply with environmental guidelines.
Batteries (Lab Manual)
CRTs (Lab Manual)
Chemical solvents and cans (Lab Manual)
MSDS (Lab Manual)

DOMAIN 4: MOTHERBOARDS/PROCESSORS/MEMORY

4.1 DISTINGUISH BETWEEN THE POPULAR CPU CHIPS IN TERMS OF THEIR BASIC CHARACTERISTICS.

Content may include the following:

Popular CPU chips (Pentium class compatible) (Chapter 8)
Voltage (Chapter 6 and Chapter 7)
Speeds (actual vs. advertised) (Chapter 6)
Cache level I, II, III (Chapter 6, Chapter 7, Chapter 8, and Chapter 9)
Sockets/Slots (Chapter 3, Chapter 6, Chapter 7, and Chapter 9)
VRM(s) (Chapter 6)

4.2 IDENTIFY THE TYPES OF RAM (RANDOM ACCESS MEMORY), THEIR FORM FACTORS AND OPERATIONAL CHARACTERISTICS. DETERMINE BANKING AND SPEED REQUIREMENTS UNDER GIVEN SCENARIOS.

Content may include the following:

Types
    EDO RAM (Extended Data Output RAM) (Chapter 9)
    DRAM (Dynamic Random Access Memory) (Chapter 9)

SRAM (Static RAM) (Chapter 9)

VRAM (Video RAM) (Chapter 16)

SDRAM (Synchronous Dynamic RAM) (Chapter 9 and Chapter 16)

DDR (Double Data Rate) (Chapter 9 and Chapter 16)

RAMBUS (Chapter 9)

Form factors (including pin count)

SIMM (Single In-line Memory Module) (Chapter 9)

DIMM (Dual In-line Memory Module) (Chapter 9)

SODIMM (Small outline DIMM) (Chapter 9 and Chapter 19)

MicroDIMM (Chapter 9)

RIMM (Chapter 9)

Operational characteristics

Memory chips (8-bit, 16-bit, and 32-bit) (Chapter 9)

Parity chips versus nonparity chips (Chapter 9)

ECC versus non-ECC (Chapter 9)

Single-sided versus double-sided (Chapter 9)

4.3 IDENTIFY THE MOST POPULAR TYPES OF MOTHERBOARDS, THEIR COMPONENTS, AND THEIR ARCHITECTURE (BUS STRUCTURES).

Content may include the following:

Types of motherboards

AT (Chapter 3 and Chapter 6)

ATX (Chapter 3 and Chapter 6)

Communication ports

Serial (Chapter 3 and Chapter 6)

USB (Chapter 3 and Chapter 6)

Parallel (Chapter 3 and Chapter 6)

IEEE 1394/FireWire (Chapter 3 and Chapter 6)

Infrared (Chapter 3 and Chapter 6)

Memory

SIMM (Chapter 3, Chapter 6, and Chapter 9)

DIMM (Chapter 3, Chapter 6, and Chapter 9)

RIMM (Chapter 3, Chapter 6, and Chapter 9)

SODIMM (Chapter 3, Chapter 6, and Chapter 19)

MicroDIMM (Chapter 3 and Chapter 6)

Processor sockets
    Slot 1 (Chapter 3, Chapter 6, and Chapter 7)
    Slot 2 (Chapter 3, Chapter 6, and Chapter 7)
    Slot A (Chapter 3, Chapter 6, and Chapter 7)
    Socket A (Chapter 3, Chapter 6, and Chapter 7)
    Socket 7 (Chapter 3, Chapter 6, and Chapter 7)
    Socket 8 (Chapter 3, Chapter 6, and Chapter 7)
    Socket 423 (Chapter 3, Chapter 6, and Chapter 7)
    Socket 478 (Chapter 3, Chapter 6, and Chapter 7)
    Socket 370 (Chapter 3, Chapter 6, and Chapter 7)
External cache memory (Level 2) (Chapter 6 and Chapter 7)
Bus Architecture
    ISA (Chapter 3 and Chapter 10)
    PCI (Chapter 3 and Chapter 10)
    PCI 32-bit (Chapter 3 and Chapter 10)
    PCI 64-bit (Chapter 3 and Chapter 10)
AGP
    2X (Chapter 3, Chapter 10, and Chapter 16)
    4X (Chapter 3, Chapter 10, and Chapter 16)
    8X (Pro) (Chapter 3, Chapter 10, and Chapter 16)
USB (Chapter 3 and Chapter 10)
AMR (audio modem riser) slots (Chapter 3 and Chapter 6)
CNR (communication network riser) slots (Chapter 3 and Chapter 6)
Basic compatibility guidelines
IDE (ATA, ATAPI, ULTRA-DMA, EIDE) (Chapter 14)
SCSI (Narrow, Wide, Fast, Ultra, HVD, LVD) (Chapter 13)
Chipsets (Chapter 6 and Appendix F)

4.4 IDENTIFY THE PURPOSE OF CMOS (COMPLEMENTARY METAL-OXIDE SEMICONDUCTOR) MEMORY, WHAT IT CONTAINS, AND HOW AND WHEN TO CHANGE ITS PARAMETERS. GIVEN A SCENARIO INVOLVING CMOS, CHOOSE THE APPROPRIATE COURSE OF ACTION.

CMOS Settings: (Chapter 6, Chapter 20, and Chapter 31)
    Default settings (Chapter 6 and Chapter 20)
    CPU settings (Chapter 6)
    Printer parallel port (Uni., bidirectional, disable/enable, ECP, EPP) (Chapter 6 and Chapter 20)

COM/Serial port (Memory address, interrupt request, disable) (Chapter 6)

Floppy drive (Enable/disable drive or boot, speed, density) (Chapter 6)

Hard drive (Size and drive type) (Chapter 6)

Memory (Speed, parity, nonparity) (Chapter 6)

Boot sequence (Chapter 6)

Date/Time (Chapter 6)

Passwords (Chapter 6)

Plug 'n Play BIOS (Chapter 6)

Disabling onboard devices (Chapter 6)

Disabling virus protection (Chapter 6)

Power management (Chapter 6)

Infrared (Chapter 6)

DOMAIN 5: PRINTERS

5.1 IDENTIFY PRINTER TECHNOLOGIES, INTERFACES, AND OPTIONS/UPGRADES.

Technologies include:

Laser (Chapter 18)

Dot Matrix (Chapter 18)

Ink Dispersion (Inkjet)

Solid ink (Chapter 18)

Thermal (Chapter 18)

Dye sublimation (Chapter 18)

Interfaces include:
Parallel (Chapter 10 and Chapter 18)

Network (Chapter 20)

USB (Chapter 18)

Infrared (Chapter 20)

Serial (Chapter 18)

IEEE 1394/FireWire (Chapter 15)

Wireless (Chapter 20)

Options/Upgrades include:
Memory (Chapter 18)

Hard drives (Chapter 18)

NICs (Chapter 18)

Trays and feeders (Chapter 18)

Finishers (e.g., stapling, etc.) (Chapter 18)

Scanners/fax/copier (Chapter 18)

5.2 RECOGNIZE COMMON PRINTER PROBLEMS AND TECHNIQUES USED TO RESOLVE THEM.

Content may include the following:

Printer drivers (Chapter 18)

Firmware updates (Chapter 18)

Paper feed and output (Chapter 18)

Calibrations (Chapter 18)

Printing test pages (Chapter 18)

Errors (printed or displayed) (Chapter 18)

Memory (Chapter 18)

Configuration (Chapter 18)

Network connections (Chapter 32)

Connections (Chapter 18)

Paper jams (Chapter 18)

Print quality (Chapter 18)

Safety precautions (Chapter 18)

Preventative maintenance (Chapter 18)

Consumables (Chapter 18)

Environment (Chapter 18)

DOMAIN 6: BASIC NETWORKING

6.1 IDENTIFY THE COMMON TYPES OF NETWORK CABLES, THEIR CHARACTERISTICS AND CONNECTORS.

Cable types include:

Coaxial

RG-6 (Chapter 32)

RG-8 (Chapter 32)

RG-58 (Chapter 32)

RG-59 (Chapter 32)

Plenum/PVC

UTP

    CAT3 (Chapter 32)

    CAT5/e (Chapter 32 and Lab Manual)

    CAT6 (Chapter 32)

STP (Chapter 32)

Fiber

    Single mode (Chapter 32)

    Multimode (Chapter 32)

Connector types include:

    BNC (Chapter 32 and Lab Manual)

    RJ-45 (Chapter 3, Chapter 32, and Lab Manual)

    AUI (Chapter 3, Chapter 17, Chapter 32, and Lab Manual)

    ST/SC (Chapter 32)

    IDC/UDC (Chapter 32)

6.2 IDENTIFY BASIC NETWORKING CONCEPTS INCLUDING HOW A NETWORK WORKS.

Concepts include:

Installing and configuring network cards (Chapter 32 and Lab Manual)

Addressing (Chapter 32 and Lab Manual)

Bandwidth (Chapter 32)

Status indicators (Chapter 32 and Lab Manual)

Protocols

    TCP/IP (Chapter 32)

    IPX/SPX (NWLINK) (Chapter 32)

    AppleTalk (Chapter 32)

    NETBEUI/NETBIOS (Chapter 32)

Full-duplex/Half-duplex (Chapter 20)

Cabling—Twisted pair, Coaxial, Fiber optic, RS-232 (Chapter 32)

Networking models

    Peer-to-peer (Chapter 32)

    Client/server (Chapter 32)

Infrared (Chapter 32)

Wireless (Chapter 32)

6.3 IDENTIFY COMMON TECHNOLOGIES AVAILABLE FOR ESTABLISHING INTERNET CONNECTIVITY AND THEIR CHARACTERISTICS.

Technologies include:
LAN (Chapter 32)
DSL (Chapter 20)
Cable (Chapter 20)
ISDN (Chapter 20)
Dial-up (Chapter 20)
Satellite (Chapter 32)
Wireless (Chapter 32)

Characteristic include:
Definition (Chapter 32)
Speed (Chapter 32)
Connections (Chapter 32)

CHAPTER 1

PC Basics

Before I get started in on discussions of the individual components, there are a few basic concepts I'd like to go over. In addition, a few concise definitions are going to be necessary for those just beginning in the field of computer hardware. This chapter is targeted at the beginning student.

A+ Core Hardware Exam Objectives

CompTIA exam objectives introduced in this chapter include the following:

1.1 Identify the names, purpose, and characteristics of system modules.

1.5 Identify the names, purposes, and performance characteristics of standardized/common peripheral ports, associated cabling, and their connectors. Recognize ports, cabling, and connectors by sight.

4.1 Distinguish between the popular CPU chips in terms of their basic characteristics.

4.2 Identify the types of RAM (Random Access Memory), form factors, and operational characteristics. Determine banking and speed requirements under given scenarios.

4.3 Identify the most popular types of motherboards, their components, and their architecture. (Bus structures)

The Raw Basics

First thing I ought to do is get one thing out of the way right off the bat. Just what is a computer? The first thing a complete beginner might think is that it is the thing that looks like a TV sitting on top of the desk. Somebody that's one step beyond the beginner stage might point to the box on the floor that everything plugs into and identify that as a computer. They'd be a little closer to correct. However, the definition of a computer is far more basic than all that. A *computer* is simply this:

It is a device that performs three basic functions.

■ It accepts input of data.

Table 1.1 The Standard Computer Model

Central Processing Unit (CPU)	Sometimes called the "brain" of the computer. I'll be arguing that point later in this book.
Random Access Memory (RAM)	Used for temporary storage of data.
Input/Output (I/O)	Conduit through which data is exchanged between CPU and outside.
Storage	Long-term storage of data for when computer is turned off.

The standard computer model defines the minimum components required to make up a computer system.

- It processes that input according to a specific set of instructions (either through the execution of requests or the manipulation of data).
- It provides output of processed data.

With that in mind, it's relatively easy to construct a standard computer model. While these components in no way comprise everything that makes up a computer, without them, you wouldn't have a computer. **Table 1.1** outlines the essential components that constitute the basic recipe for a barebones computer system.

Each of the aforementioned components of the computer model (illustrated in **Figure 1.1**)

BUZZ WORDS

Computer: Any device that can accept the input of user data, process that data according to a specific set of instructions, and then provide the results of that processing in the form of output to the end user.

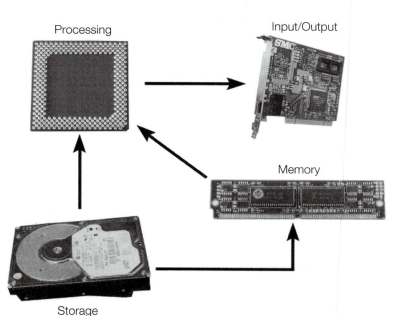

Figure 1.1 The standard computer model at a minimum calls for central processing, memory for short-term storage, some form of long-term storage, and an input/output path for data.

Processing

Input/Output

Memory

Storage

will be covered in great detail in the general body of this book. However, I would like to start with an overview of what's going on inside the system before I tackle system components in detail. With this model in mind, take a look at the three basic functions of the computer, as laid out in the "definition" of a computer.

BUZZ WORDS

Input: Any data that is intended and/or ready to be sent to the CPU for processing.

EXAM NOTE: Make sure you can explain the Standard Computer Model, as defined by CompTIA.

INPUT

Input is defined as any form of information that is ready for entry into the system. Without data, the system has nothing to do. Information can enter the system in the form of raw data or as instructions. This data is presented to the system by way of any one of a variety of devices. Some common input devices are listed in **Table 1.2**.

Input devices come in either internal or external incarnations. Some of them are cards that you install; others sit on your desk waiting for your attention. Some devices, such as a modem, are available as either an internal or an external device. Be able to recognize various input devices. And be aware that many devices can have split personalities, functioning as both an input device and an output device. The hard drive in **Figure 1.2** is an example of just such a device.

Figure 1.2 You don't often think of a hard drive as providing either input or output. But in reality, as a mass storage mechanism, it functions as both at the same time.

Table 1.2 Standard Input Devices

Floppy diskette	Hard drive	Joystick
Keyboard	Modem	Mouse
CD-ROM	Scanner	Touchpad
Touchscreen	Trackball	Voice
Digital camera	Network	Proprietary device

A collection of common devices used to input data.

PROCESSING

Processing occurs whenever data or instructions are executed, manipulated, updated, or in any way altered. Simply through-putting data from an input device, such as a keyboard, to an output device, such as a monitor, constitutes processing. It would be an easier job to understand computers if the CPU (**Figure 1.3**) was the only device in the system that was involved in processing data. Unfortunately, data is getting massaged, manipulated, recalculated, and crunched practically the entire time it is in the computer. Every device I'll look at throughout this book has its own little collection of integrated circuits (ICs) that have certain functions to perform. An IC is an electronic chip onto which specific instruction sets have been "burned." These instructions tell the device what to do with all those signals that are traveling through it.

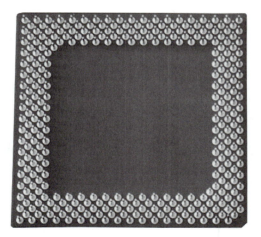

Figure 1.3 A typical microprocessor. As powerful as it is, it only does a fraction of the total processing that goes on in a computer system.

OUTPUT

If users are going to be able to take advantage of the results of the actions of processing, those results must somehow be exported from the computer to the world in which people actually live. It doesn't do a whole lot of good if the CPU simply lets the information it created float to digital heaven when it needs to make room for more data. *Output* can be printed, transmitted, displayed, stored, or played back. There are literally hundreds of devices on the market that collect the output of your computer and put it into some useable form. **Table 1.3** shows just a small number of output devices on the market today.

BUZZ WORDS

Processing: Any manipulation of data that can occur between the time the data has been input into the computer and the time that it is provided as output. Processing can consist of calculations performed on the data, replication of that data to alternative locations, and the comparison of one data set to another. Not all processing is done by the CPU.

Output: Data that is being transmitted by one device to another once that data has been processed.

Table 1.3 Typical Output Devices

Floppy diskette	Hard disk drive	Modem
Monitor	Network	Printer
Sound	Tape	Tactile

Some of the output devices found on a typical system.

EXAM NOTE: There is likely to be a list of devices for you to identify as to whether they are input devices or output devices. Some will be both. Examine the question carefully.

HOW YOUR COMPUTER EATS DATA: ONE BYTE AT A TIME

Of course, data doesn't just magically move from your fingertips or from the lens of that fancy digital camera you just bought. The various components of your system, as well as the peripheral devices you choose to employ, must provide data in a form that the CPU can understand. And contrary to what manufacturers would have you believe, CPUs are basically stupid. They are nothing more than a very complex collection of transistors crammed into a tiny package. They know ON and they know OFF. In written form, this is expressed as 0 or 1. On its most basic level, all computer data can be broken down into a series of 0s and 1s. This is *binary.* The counting method used by humans is *decimal,* a Base10 system consisting of the characters 0 through 9.

Binary is based on the principles of George Boole, who in 1854 developed an entire branch of algebra based on "true/false," "yes/no," and "on/off." This fit the concept of the transistor perfectly. Numerically, you could consider OFF to be the equivalent of zero, while ON could equal one. Therefore, machine language is a stream of zeros and ones. To translate this language of zeros and ones, programmers have various languages for writing programs. Fortunately, as a hardware technician, there are only a few basic concepts of binary you need to understand. There are also some basic terms.

> **BUZZ WORDS** ────────────
>
> **Binary:** A Base2 counting system that consists of the two characters 0 and 1.
>
> **Decimal:** A Base10 counting system that consists of ten characters, 0 through 9.

- *Bit:* a single zero or one
- *Byte:* any combination of eight zeros or ones
- *Nibble:* Four bits
- *Word:* Two to four bytes
- *Page:* One to twenty kilobytes
- *Kilobyte:* Two to the tenth power bytes, or 1024 bytes
- *Megabyte:* Two to the twentieth power bytes, or 1,048,576 bytes

The most basic unit of data is the bit. A single bit is represented as either 0 or 1. As you will see later on, a single bit can be significant.

EXAM NOTE: Know intimately the vocabulary of binary, and be able to perform a simple binary-to-decimal or decimal-to-binary conversion.

As defined in the previous list, a byte consists of eight individual bits, or eight different switches that can be turned on or off. A byte is treated by the system as a single entity and allows programmers to create values greater than 0 or 1. The number of values a byte can represent can be determined by taking the number of positions the switch can occupy (2) and multiplying it by the number of switches (8). $2 \times 2 \times 2 \times 2 \times 2 \times 2 \times 2 \times 2$ (or two to the eighth power) = 256. Therefore, from an 8-bit byte, 256 different combinations can be achieved. Counting in binary can be interesting, too. It looks like this: 0, 1, 10, 11, 100, 101, 111, 1000, 1001, 1010, 1011, 1100, and so forth. This isn't just theoretical material I'm discussing here. Later in the book, when I discuss configuring addresses to network interface cards, certain types of addresses consist of four 8-bit binary values, literally connected by dots. To configure the IP address, you type in the decimal alliteration.

The order of bits in a byte is significant as well. Programmers refer to this order by way of *least significant bit* and *most significant bit.* The most significant bit of a single byte has a mathematical value of 256, whereas the least significant bit has a value of zero. **Figure 1.4** illustrates the value of each position. It's actually easy to calculate the mathematical value of a byte. Everywhere there is a one in the position, multiply the relative value of that position by one. Everywhere there is a zero, you have a value of zero. Now add the numbers up.

Therefore, while having to deal with numbers like 1010 1101 might seem a little intimidating at first, it needn't be overwhelming. All you really have to do is start from the right, and everywhere the bit is set to 1, add the relative value for that position. So, as **Figure 1.5** illustrates, the decimal value for 1010 1101 would actually be 173. To achieve numbers higher than 256, you simply use more bytes.

128	64	32	16	8	4	2	1

Most Significant Bit   Least Significant Bit

Figure 1.4   Relative values of bits in a byte

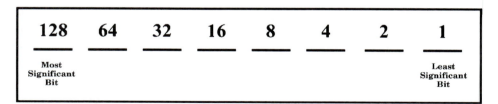

Actual Bit Values

1	0	1	0	1	1	0	1
128	64	32	16	8	4	2	1

Relative Value in Bytes
Multiply the actual bit value by its relative value. Add the totals.

$$(1 \times 128) + (0 \times 64) + (1 \times 32) + (0 \times 16) + (1 \times 8) + (1 \times 4) + (0 \times 2) + (1 \times 1) = 173$$

Figure 1.5   Calculating the relative value of a byte

HEXADECIMAL

Dealing with binary by itself can be a little cumbersome. If you had eight bytes of data you wanted to communicate to another technician, you might finding yourself writing something along the lines of 0110 1111, 1100 0000, 0001 1010, 1110 0000, 1011 0001, 0000 0001, 1001 0001, 1111 0000.

Needless to say, there must to be a better way. That way is called *hexadecimal.* Hexadecimal is a way of counting in Base16.

BUZZ WORDS ─────────

Hexadecimal: A counting system that uses Base16 as it root. As such, this system requires a total of sixteen different characters to represent base values.

Character Set: The code used to generate printable symbols that human users can understand.

EXAM NOTE: You can almost count on having some hexadecimal thrown your way on the exam. Be comfortable with the basics of hex.

A byte consists of eight bits. If you divide a byte into two nibbles, there will be two four-bit chunks to deal with. Hexadecimal provides a single character that represents each possible combination of four bits. Two raised to the fourth is sixteen, so a character set based on Base16 must have a total of sixteen symbols. The numerical symbols 0-9 cover the first ten, and the remainder is represented as the alphabetic symbols A-F. Therefore, in Base16 you count 0, 1, 2, 3, 4, 5, 6, 7, 8, 9, A, B, C, D, E, and F.

There are several different places where the computer provides information in hex, so having a good understanding of the concept is important. **Table 1.4** translates numerical values into hex.

DIGITAL CODE FORMATS

All this would be wonderful as long as all you ever had to deal with was numbers. However, people don't communicate exclusively with numbers. They also use letters and punctuation marks. This collection of letters, numbers, punctuation marks, and other symbols that humans use in order to read is known as a *character set.* People also don't communicate in binary. While it's not difficult to translate the value of a byte, it is obvious that communicating in binary is cumbersome.

In order to translate the stream of zeros and ones into something humans could understand, a common data format had to be developed that all computers could work with. 0010 1000 couldn't mean one thing for one computer and another for someone else's system. Way back in the earliest days of computers a basic character set was developed to transliterate binary into a written language. As computer technology has advanced, so has the need for a more complex character set.

ASCII   The American Standard Code for Information Interchange (ASCII), was the first set of characters that translated binary into something mere mortals could understand. However, ASCII wasn't exclusively a character set. The eight bits of the byte were used to generate 256

Table 1.4 The Hexadecimal Chart

Dec	Hex	Dec	Hex	Dec	Hex	Dec	Hex	Dec	Hex	Dec	Hex	Dec	Hex	Dec	Hex
0	0	32	20	64	40	96	60	128	80	160	a0	192	c0	224	e0
1	1	33	21	65	41	97	61	129	81	161	a1	193	c1	225	e1
2	2	34	22	66	42	98	62	130	82	162	a2	194	c2	226	e2
3	3	35	23	67	43	99	63	131	83	163	a3	195	c3	227	e3
4	4	36	24	68	44	100	64	132	84	164	a4	196	c4	228	e4
5	5	37	25	69	45	101	65	133	85	165	a5	197	c5	229	e5
6	6	38	26	70	46	102	66	134	86	166	a6	198	c6	230	e6
7	7	39	27	71	47	103	67	135	87	167	a7	199	c7	231	e7
8	8	40	28	72	48	104	68	136	88	168	a8	200	c8	232	e8
9	9	41	29	73	49	105	69	137	89	169	a9	201	c9	233	e9
10	a	42	2a	74	4a	106	6a	138	8a	170	aa	202	ca	234	ea
11	b	43	2b	75	4b	107	6b	139	8b	171	ab	203	cb	235	eb
12	c	44	2c	76	4c	108	6c	140	8c	172	ac	204	cc	236	ec
13	d	45	2d	77	4d	109	6d	141	8d	173	ad	205	cd	237	ed
14	e	46	2e	78	4e	110	6e	142	8e	174	ae	206	ce	238	ee
15	f	47	2f	79	4f	111	6f	143	8f	175	af	207	cf	239	ef
16	10	48	30	80	50	112	70	144	90	176	b0	208	d0	240	f0
17	11	49	31	81	51	113	71	145	91	177	b1	209	d1	241	f1
18	12	50	32	82	52	114	72	146	92	178	b2	210	d2	242	f2
19	13	51	33	83	53	115	73	147	93	179	b3	211	d3	243	f3
20	14	52	34	84	54	116	74	148	94	180	b4	212	d4	244	f4
21	15	53	35	85	55	117	75	149	95	181	b5	213	d5	245	f5
22	16	54	36	86	56	118	76	150	96	182	b6	214	d6	246	f6
23	17	55	37	87	57	119	77	151	97	183	b7	215	d7	247	f7
24	18	56	38	88	58	120	78	152	98	184	b8	216	d8	248	f8
25	19	57	39	89	59	121	79	153	99	185	b9	217	d9	249	f9
26	1a	58	3a	90	5a	122	7a	154	9a	186	ba	218	da	250	fa
27	1b	59	3b	91	5b	123	7b	155	9b	187	bb	219	db	251	fb
28	1c	60	3c	92	5c	124	7c	156	9c	188	bc	220	dc	252	fc
29	1d	61	3d	93	5d	125	7d	157	9d	189	bd	221	dd	253	fd
30	1e	62	3e	94	5e	126	7e	158	9e	190	be	222	de	254	fe
31	1f	63	3f	95	5f	127	7f	159	9f	191	bf	223	df	255	ff

Hexadecimal Conversion Table. Note that all leading 0's are dropped.

values. As I've emphasized before, a combination of eight zeros and ones constitutes a single character. In the original ASCII, that one set of characters had to deal with both the human interface and also be used to send commands to graphics devices, such as printers. In the original ASCII, there were actually only 128 printable characters. The remainder of the set was used as commands. You can check out both sets of characters in the ASCII Character Set tables in Appendix G.

Without going into a lot of programming detail, in ASCII the same byte can represent a number or it can represent a character or it can represent a command. This is dictated by programmers and the language or program they are working in. The decimal value of each character is used to express the text in numeric code. For example, the capital A is the decimal character 65, or binary 0100 0001.

Extended ASCII   Extended ASCII eliminated the need for putting control characters into the character set. All available 256 characters became printable symbols. This allowed for more characters than the standard alphabet in upper- and lowercase, numbers, and punctuation. Popular symbols could now be included, such as the trademark symbol. The makers of font sets put Extended ASCII to use when they want to create specialty symbols.

ISO Latin-1   ISO Latin-1 is a set of printing characters that specify European characters and symbols in addition to the 128 printing characters of ASCII. Because of the international nature of the Internet, this has been adopted as the character set of choice for some Web sites and Web browsers. See the ISO Latin Character Set table in Appendix G for a complete listing.

ANSI   The ANSI character set is the one used in Windows 3.x and Windows 9x versions. This is a 256-character set that uses the 128 printing characters of ASCII as the base and then adds another set of printing characters similar to that of ISO Latin-1. However, Microsoft extended this set somewhat, so it is not one hundred percent compatible with ISO Latin-1.

UNI Code   UNI increased character depth to 16 bits, allowing for a much greater number of characters. These additional characters were mapped out to include the character sets from all the major languages of the world, allowing for the first multilingual character set. This is the character set used by Windows NT and Windows 2000 as well as Unix. Most of the Web servers that provide international support these days provide support for UNI code.

DATA COMMUNICATIONS

Knowing what makes up bits and bytes and why character sets are necessary is very important. But the computer needs to be able to move that data around. The data that a computer system processes has to come from somewhere. In fact, data frequently has to be brought in from remote sources before you can use it. While there are many different methods of packaging data for transmission across a network, or even just from a disk drive to a hard drive, there are really only two ways of sending it over a wire. Those two ways are parallel communication and serial communication.

PARALLEL COMMUNICATION

While it may not seem like it at first glance, *parallel communication* is the simplest, most basic, and most primitive communication used by computer systems today. It is also the slowest.

With parallel communications, a byte is broken down into its individual bits and each bit travels over a different wire. For this to work, the timing and synchronization between devices must be extremely precise. All eight of the bits that are part of a single byte must arrive at their destination at the same time. Otherwise the bits from different bytes may get scrambled together.

Parallel communications is used internally on the majority of motherboard components. It's also still a popular form of hooking up printers. And even though it isn't called parallel when your hard drives do it, they do, in fact, for the most part, communicate in parallel.

SERIAL COMMUNICATIONS

When a computer connection makes use of *serial communications,* it is basically lining all the bits in a row and then sending them over the wire, one right after the other. It may sound like parallel communications would be faster, because the data is moving over eight separate wires, and not just one. It doesn't work that way, however.

Serial communications can be either synchronous or asynchronous. *Synchronous communication* is the fastest form of serial hookup. Large amounts of data are collected into chunks called packets and sent out that way; therefore, a lot of data moves on a single transfer. A header, which consists of additional control data, is added to the front of the packet, and a trailer, which contains error correction information, is added to the end. These headers and trailers tell the receiving device where one packet ends and the next begins. Synchronous communications are used by modems, network controllers, and some forms of hard drive controller.

Asynchronous communication bundles together the individual bits of a single byte and moves data

BUZZ WORDS

Serial communications: The act of transferring data a single bit at a time over a single connection.

Parallel communications: The act of transferring an entire byte of data on a single cycle, using eight separate conductors.

Synchronous communication: A form of serial communication that transmits large amounts of data at once in packets.

Asynchronous communication: A form of serial communication that transmits data a byte at a time over a single conductor.

Starting delimiter: A single bit at the beginning of a data byte being transmitted asynchronously that marks the beginning of the byte.

Ending delimiter: A single bit at the end of a byte of data being transmitted asynchronously that marks the end of a byte.

Parity: A form of error detection used by serial communications and some forms of memory to detect the presence of a single-bit error.

over the wire a single byte at a time. To separate the bytes, a *starting delimiter* and an *ending delimiter* are added to each of the eight bits. A form of error correction called *parity* may or may not be added, depending on how a particular device is configured. Parity is discussed in detail in Chapter Nine, Searching Your Memory.

PC SYSTEM ARCHITECTURE

Computers are very complex, very complicated devices. Face it. You're looking at a device that is capable of performing as many as several million instructions per second (IPS). The CPU may be performing several billion IPS. Since the CPU is working faster than the rest of the system, it relies on the components on the motherboard to keep it fed with data.

The motherboard acts as the base plane for the entire system. It is on this surface that all electronic impulses travel between input devices and CPU and then to output devices. A motherboard consists of several layers (usually four), not just one. If you look closely at a motherboard, you'll see fine paths of copper covering both the front and back surface in nice little geometric patters (**Figure 1.6** shows the back surface, so that the motherboard components won't be distracting). These are called traces. Traces aren't just on the front and back surfaces. If you were to peel back the layers, you'd also find them in between the layers.

These traces provide the path that data takes to move from Point A to Point B. The path itself is called the bus. The term bus can get a little confusing because it's used in so many different ways. To keep things simple, just remember that it is the path data takes. Computers are considered to have five primary busses. The traces are the physical incarnation of those

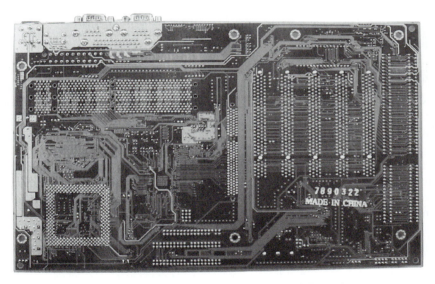

Figure 1.6   The system busses can be seen in all of those tiny copper paths you see on a motherboard.

busses. They carry the data, or in the case of the power bus, raw electricity, from its source to its destination. The motherboard is like a big city. There are lots of places where data can live and other places where it must go to work. Just like in a real city, different busses move data in different ways, to different places.

THE FIVE BUSSES

The five primary busses of the computer system consist of the CPU Bus, the Address Bus, the Local Bus, the I/O Bus, and the Power Bus. Each one of these has a specific role to fulfill and a good understanding of what each one does is critical to understanding the basics of computer hardware. Be aware, however, that throughout the course of your career, and throughout this book, you'll see many other busses discussed. Try not to let that confuse you. There are more than just the five primary ones listed here. Don't let the theory get you down, though. These busses are actually simpler than they appear at first.

CPU Bus

This is the information path between the CPU and other primary controller chips in the system. As you'll learn as you move through this book, different chips perform different functions. By itself, the CPU can't talk to the keyboard. It has no idea what the signals coming from that device mean. Located among the chips you see planted here and there along the surface of the motherboard is one that holds a program that does nothing but translate keyboard signals into pure binary code that the CPU can digest. All the chips that perform functions of this nature are located along the CPU Bus. These are the devices that can communicate directly with the CPU, at the CPU's speed.

Address Bus

Data that is stored either in memory or on a device must be available for the CPU to access. Otherwise how would the system work properly? Since the motherboard is like a big city, all the places where data lives, as well as the places where it must go, need to have addresses, so everything can find each other. When a device is installed, the operating system will assign an I/O address. When data is stored in memory, it is given an address that identifies exactly where on the memory chip the data is physically located. These addresses are generally listed as hexadecimal numbers.

The Address Bus is a bus directly from the CPU to the rest of the system that keeps track of everybody's location. Using the analogy of the Motherboard City, this is more like the Post Office than part of the transportation system.

Local Bus

Like every other big city in the world, some data is in a bigger hurry to get where it's going than other data. If a peripheral or component is designed to make use of the Local Bus, then data can move from that component to its destination (which can either be the chipset of the motherboard or L2 cache) at the same speed as the CPU itself. Data moves along this bus, not only at a higher speed, but also in a more direct route. Consider this to be the Express from the suburbs to downtown.

I/O Bus

The problem with computer users is that they don't live in Motherboard City. They live outside of town. Therefore, there has to be a bus system that moves data from the computer's town to your location and vice versa. This would be the I/O Bus, or Input/Output, as it were.

Power Bus

Here's where the analogy of the bus routes breaks down. Few busses are designed to carry nothing but raw electricity. But that's what the Power Bus does. Every component in the system needs electricity to run. This includes the CPU, RAM chips, logic chips—everything! Without electricity, you have no computer. So this is more like the power company than it is a bus line. But you get the idea.

Chapter Summary

This chapter may have been on the basic side for the more advanced readers. But then, that is why the chapter is titled "PC Basics." There is no way that anyone can call him- or herself a professional hardware technician if the information in this chapter isn't as firmly imbedded as name, age, and social security number.

Don't make the mistake of assuming that because you've been working on computers for a while that you will know all the material that is contained here. If you're planning on pursuing the A+ Core Exam, there are some details specific to CompTIA here.

Brain Drain

1. List and explain each of the basic functions that define a computer.
2. Given an IP address of 192.168.0.115, convert that address to its decimal form.
3. You have a hexadecimal address of 02FE:CCC0. Convert that address to binary.
4. Describe in as much detail as you can the differences between ASCII and UNI Code.
5. Describe the five primary systems busses and their functions.

The 64K$ Questions

1. Which of the following is not a basic function of a computer?
   a. Provide user data for input
   b. Accept the input of user data
   c. Provide output of processed user data
   d. Process user data

2. An IC is:
   a. Instruction Code
   b. Internal Circuit
   c. Informational Control
   d. Integrated Circuit

3. A byte that consists of the bits 0111 0010 has a decimal value of:
   a. 256
   b. 114
   c. 122
   d. 124

4. The hexadecimal value 03FF:26FF looks like _____ in binary.
   a. 0000 0010 1111 1111:0010 0110 1111 1111
   b. 0000 0011 1111 1111:0010 0110 1111 1111
   c. 0000 0110 1111 1111:0010 0110 1111 1111
   d. 0000 0010 1111 1111:0010 0100 1111 1111

5. Which character set included control codes as part of the basic set?
   a. ASCII
   b. Extended ASCII
   c. ANSI
   d. UNI Code

6. How many possible combinations can be made of a 16-bit binary value?
   a. 1024
   b. 16,384
   c. 65,536
   d. 1,048.576

7. Which of the primary system busses provides direct communications between the CPU and the chipset?
   a. The CPU Bus

b. The Local Bus
   c. The I/O Bus
   d. The Address Bus

8. Which of the primary system busses provides direct communications between an installed device and the chipset?
   a. The CPU Bus
   b. The Local Bus
   c. The I/O Bus
   d. The Address Bus

9. Which of the primary system busses is responsible for locating data in the system?
   a. The CPU Bus
   b. The Local Bus
   c. The I/O Bus
   d. The Address Bus

10. Which primary system bus provides electrical power to the various components in the system?
    a. The CPU Bus
    b. The Power Bus
    c. The I/O Bus
    d. The Address Bus

TRICKY TERMINOLOGY

Asynchronous communication: A form of serial communication that transmits data a byte at a time over a single conductor.

Binary: A Base2 counting system that consists of the two characters 0 and 1.

Bit: A single zero or one, resulting in a single transition between off and on.

Byte: Any combination of eight zeros or ones.

Character set: The code used to generate printable symbols that human users can understand.

Computer: Any device that can accept the input of user data, process that data according to a specific set of instructions, and then provide the results of that processing in the form of output to the end user.

Decimal: A Base10 counting system that consists of ten characters, 0 through 9.

Ending delimiter: A single bit at the end of a byte of data being transmitted asynchronously that marks the end of a byte.

Hexadecimal: A counting system that uses Base16 as it root. As such, this system requires a total of sixteen different characters to represent base values.

Input: Any data that is intended and/or ready to be sent to the CPU for processing.

Nibble: Any combination of four zeros or ones.

Output: Data that is being transmitted by one device to another once that data has been processed.

Page: The amount of data that can be moved on a single memory read/write cycle; usually between 1 to 20KB.

Parallel communications: The act of transferring an entire byte of data on a single cycle, using eight separate conductors.

Parity: A form of error detection used by serial communications and some forms of memory to detect the presence of a single-bit error.

Processing: Any manipulation of data that can occur between the time the data has been inputted into the computer and the time that is provided as output. Processing can consist of calculations performed on the data, replication of that data to alternative locations, and the comparison of one data set to another. Not all processing is done by the CPU.

Serial communications: The act of transferring data a single bit at a time over a single connection.

Starting delimiter: A single bit at the beginning of a data byte being transmitted asynchronously that marks the beginning of the byte.

Synchronous communication: A form of serial communication that transmits large amounts of data at once in packets.

Word: The amount of data that can move across the CPU's external data bus in one clock cycle; usually between two and four bytes.

ACRONYM ALERT

ANSI: American National Standards Institute. This term refers to an organization charged with establishing standards for several different industries, including the computer industry. It also refers to an early character set developed by that organization.

ASCII: American Standard Code for Information Interchange. An early character set used by computers.

CPU: Central Processing Unit. The primary microprocessor used by a computer in order to perform calculations or otherwise manipulate data.

I/O: Input/Output. The process of sending or receiving data between devices.

IC: Integrated Circuit. A single microchip onto which the code necessary to provide several different functions has been burned.

IPS: Instructions per Second. An early measurement of CPU performance that was based solely on how many times in one second the device could execute commands.

RAM: Random Access Memory. A device used for short-term storage of data or instructions that are or will soon be required by the CPU in order for it to do its job.

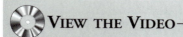 VIEW THE VIDEO

A video clip on PC System Review is available on the accompanying CD.

CHAPTER 2

AN INTRODUCTION TO OPERATING SYSTEMS

In this chapter, I'll be going over the fundamental basics of what an operating system (OS) is, what it does, and how it does what it does. Even though I won't be dealing with the OS until the second half of this book, I think it's necessary for the student to have some comprehension of the role the OS plays in making the computer run.

A+ OPERATING SYSTEM TECHNOLOGIES EXAM OBJECTIVES

I'm going to introduce a few topics covered on the CompTIA OS Exam. But trust me when I tell you, you'll be seeing these topics again in much greater detail in Part II of this book.

1.1   Identify the major desktop components and interfaces and their functions. Differentiate the characteristics of Windows 9x/Me, Windows NT 4.0 Workstation, Windows 2000 Professional, and Windows XP.

1.2   Identify the names, locations, purposes, and contents of major system files.

2.3   Identify the basic system boot sequences and boot methods, including the steps to create an emergency boot disk with utilities installed for Windows 9x/Me, Windows NT 4.0 Workstation, Windows 2000 Professional, and Windows XP.

JUST WHAT IS AN OS?

One of the first things I ask students coming into a class on operating systems is to define an operating system (OS). About ninety percent of the answers I get are variations on "It's what makes the computer work."

At first blush, this may seem like a fairly accurate answer. But consider this. If you install a newly formatted hard drive into a system, with no OS installed, and attempt to boot the machine, you will receive some variation on the message "Operating system not found." The very existence of this message proves that the computer is working. It knows enough to tell you that the OS doesn't exist.

Therefore, although the computer may not be doing what you want it to do, it is indeed working. So a more accurate reply to my question would be "The OS is what makes the computer do what you want it to do." Of course, CompTIA and the rest of the world want technicians to be a wee bit more technical than that when spewing out definitions, so the technical definition I'll offer is this:

An *operating system* is the program running on the computer that manages all of the services required by applications that are to run on the system and interfaces with the hardware. These services include:

- The file system
- Processor control
- Memory management
- Device control
- Security

EXAM NOTE: Make sure you can spout off the major functions of the OS when it comes time to take the exam!

Different OSs handle these functions in different ways, and these factors become part of my later discussions. For now, I'd like to give brief descriptions of each one before I move on.

FILE SYSTEMS

File systems will be covered in some detail in my discussion of hard disk drives (see Chapter Thirteen: Hard Disk Drive Structure and Geometry). What I'd like to point out in this section is that the file system is not just under the control of the hard disk controller, but is actually managed by the OS. One of the steps taken by the OS during installation is to write a short piece of executable code into the MBR of the hard disk. From that point forward, the OS and the hardware know to use a command set based on that specific file system. To briefly view file systems, **Table 2.1** lists the various file systems and some of their characteristics.

PROCESSOR CONTROL IN THE OS

A key concept to keep in mind is that operating systems are written to specific microprocessors. While it is true that various OSs have been written to multiple platforms (Linux is a good example), the version written for Intel processors doesn't run on Power PC processors and vice versa. There are a number of powerful reasons this is the case, but

BUZZ WORDS

Operating system: A program running on a computer system that manages all of the services required by applications that are to run on the system and interfaces with the hardware.

Table 2.1   A Comparison of File Systems

Feature	FAT16	FAT32	NTFS
File name convention	DOS 8.3	LFN system	LFN unicode
File size	232 bytes	232 bytes	264 bytes
Maximum volume size	2GB	2TB	16 exabytes
Directories	Unsorted	B-tree[1]	B-tree[1]
Compression	No	No	Yes
Security	None	None	Yes
Management	None	None	Disk quotas

[1]B-tree is a data searching algorithm that uses a storage architecture similar to a tree, with "branches" and "leaves" representing paths and objects.

Comparing the file systems

two primary reasons are the command structure built into the processor itself and how many threads of code a processor is capable of handling. A thread is any particular series of instructions that must be run from beginning to end. There may be quite a number of different instructions that make up a thread, and once the thread is complete, it is likely to be deleted from memory. When an application is running on the system, the entire OS is not running along with that entire application all at the same time. That wouldn't be possible. Instead, a program runs in a series of smaller strings of code called processes. A process is simply a single grouping of code that must be run from beginning to end. Processes can include strings of code from the application, device driver routines, strings of data, or even commands issued by the firmware of devices installed on the system. A process might run in the background the entire time the system is running.

When multiple applications are running simultaneously on a system, the processor is going to be bombarded with many different requests to process this line of code or that. It is up to the OS to decide what processes are going to run at any given time. The OS is capable of initiating a process, canceling a process, or suspending one until a later time. In the event that two processes start to repeatedly call one another, it is up to the OS to break the infinite loop that will result if nothing is done.

> **EXAM NOTE:** Know the difference between a thread and a process. Even if you don't see any related questions on the exam (which you might), these concepts will serve you in good stead later on down the road.

MEMORY MANAGEMENT

A modern computer system is equipped with massive amounts of memory these days. And not all of it is conventional RAM. In addition to RAM, the OS has to keep track of video memory, cache, and buffer memory installed on devices. From the mechanical side of memory management, it is up to the OS to allocate memory for each application or process that starts, and when each one is finished that space must be freed for use. This is one area where some OSs have been notoriously inefficient and is the cause of many system crashes.

In order to accomplish the above task, the OS needs to keep track of what memory is being used for what process and what memory addresses are available for use. Another area of "memory" managed by the OS is something called a swap file (or paging file by some OSs). Since this isn't really memory, another term is virtual memory. This is an area of hard disk space that is treated by the OS as if it were memory. If physical RAM fills up and a new process needs to be opened, then processes not currently running on the system will be moved over to the swap file, freeing physical RAM for the new process.

A critical function of the OS is to protect the memory space allocated to specific processes. Individual processes running on the system need to think that they're the only process running. If another process or application invades their space, both processes will crash and burn.

But memory mechanics isn't the only thing the OS has to be concerned with. It also needs to set and enforce certain rules for memory usage. The OS will dictate when a process can be loaded into memory and how much memory that process will be allowed to use. And when the process is no longer needed by the application, the OS needs to unload it from memory.

Device Control

Now let's take a look at all those fancy new toys you installed on your system. How does the OS deal with those? The answer to that question is two-fold. It gets some of its instructions from the computer hardware and other instructions from the device driver installed on the system.

For a device to work, it must be supported by the system BIOS and the chipset on the motherboard. If the computer won't support a device, it doesn't matter how many device drivers you install on the OS, it won't work.

The device driver provides the advanced command set specific to that particular device. The OS will have a set of files that are general command sets for specific types of drivers. Windows makes use of an Application Programming Interface (API) for each device type. For example, most modern IDE hard disks, CD-ROMs, CD-RWs, DVDs, and the like are all under the control of ATAPI. For some devices, such as a simple CD-ROM, this is all that is needed. For more sophisticated devices, like an IDE tape drive, a device driver may need to be installed. The device driver, as stated earlier, provides the command set specific to that device.

When an application running in the OS has need of the services of a particular device, the application will initiate a *system call* to the OS. A system call is simply a request for a service not directly provided by the application. The OS will then initiate an I/O operation to the specific device.

In order to keep track of where specific devices are located, the OS and the hardware make use of IRQs and DMA channels. These concepts were discussed in detail in Chapter Ten, Examining the Expansion Bus.

Buzz Words ────────

System call: A request for a service not directly provided by the application.

■ **EXAM NOTE:** Know what APIs are and what their function in the OS is.

SECURITY

Security really amounts to who gets to do what and when they get to do it. Different OSs offer vastly different levels of security. Some security measures are OS specific and some are dependent on the file system in use.

The types of security that are available include the following:

- Password authentication
- File access restrictions
- Application access restrictions
- OS control and management
- System control and management

Since the levels and degree of security vary from OS to OS, I'll defer the discussions of security to the chapters on each specific OS.

OPERATING SYSTEM STRUCTURE

That's a lot of responsibility for just one program. As such, the programmers of an OS must make sure that the OS gets priority over all system resources. Over the years, a layered approach to designing OSs has emerged. And in fact, you can effectively say that your entire computer is a layered structure. Before breaking the OS down, I think it would be a good idea to examine how the system structure works.

The first thing that you need to understand is that the average user isn't the least bit interested in running the OS. For them, the OS is a minor convenience running in the background that occasionally comes in handy, but usually gets in the way. The average user is only interested in running programs.

But as I pointed out earlier, the programs depend on the OS in order to run. Each program needs the hardware on the system in order to do its thing, and it kind of needs the OS to help it out in that respect. In fact, in most modern OSs, the applications aren't allowed to access the hardware at all. They must pass their requests on to the OS, which in turn manages hardware functions. **Figure 2.1** shows the basic model of a computer system broken down from the applications down to the basic hardware.

A modern OS such as Windows 2003 is broken down into several layers:

- User interface
- Executive kernel
- Microkernel
- Hardware abstraction layer

The user interface these days is that pretty little screen that appears when your machine boots up. The term generally used for this is the graphical user interface (GUI). When the user interfaces with the GUI, either by clicking an icon or typing something into a command line, the OS will issue a series of instructions to the OS kernel. In the old days of MS-DOS, the kernel consisted of three very small files. Modern OSs are much more sophisticated. The kernel is broken down into two layers. There is the executive kernel and the microkernel. The execu-

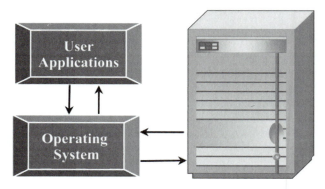

Figure 2.1   A computer system is a complex interaction between the applications, the OS, and the hardware.

tive kernel derives its name from the fact that it is the portion of the OS executing commands. When the executive kernel receives a command, it will issue a system call to one or more of several of its subcomponents. While the names and variety of these subcomponents vary from OS to OS, there will inevitably be components that manage I/O, memory, process and processor control, and security. More sophisticated OSs add additional components.

The subcomponent processes the requests it has received and passes the request on to the microkernel. The microkernel on most OSs is a single file (or a very small set of files) that provides basic I/O functions and command interpretation. If those requests are requests for more services to be provided on the OS level, they are passed on to the appropriate component. If it is a hardware request, then the appropriate device driver is called upon for its services.

In the days of DOS, this amounted to a direct access of the hardware by the application. Of course, DOS was not a multitasking OS. There were, however, programs written for DOS that emulated multitasking and provided more attractive and (sometimes) more efficient user interfaces. These were referred to as DOS shells. If two programs attempted to access the hardware at the same time, there was a complete and total system crash.

Today's OSs are all multitasking, so they can't let that happen. Therefore, the application isn't allowed to directly access the hardware. Hardware requests are passed onto the hardware abstraction layer (HAL). HAL is the only layer of the OS allowed to communicate with the hardware.

Defining HAL is more complex than a simple one-line description. HAL is a very complex layer of any modern OS. It consists of a collection of virtual device drivers, the APIs that I described earlier in the chapter. The virtual device driver is a file native to the OS that is designed to interface with a particular piece of hardware. In Microsoft OSs, the virtual device drivers are easily recognized by the fact that they end in a .vxd extension.

SEEING THE OS AT WORK

In order to show how the OS interfaces with the PC hardware, I am going to provide a brief overview of the Windows XP architecture. However, for some of the new features in XP to be truly appreciated, the reader will have to have some understanding of the evolution of OS/ hardware interfaces.

In the "good old days" of MS-DOS, the hardware, the OS, and the applications quite literally exchanged chatter among themselves. While the OS was predominately in control, firmware embedded in device drivers was able to make direct calls to the applications and vice versa. Device drivers interfaced with the OS, and the OS was responsible for making or fulfilling requests for data. But it was not at all uncommon for some devices to issue commands directly to hardware.

This did not provide for the most stable of operating environments. Starting with Windows 95, Microsoft started employing the HAL that I discussed earlier in the chapter, and with each subsequent version the technology has gotten more and more sophisticated.

Today's OSs are built in layers. XP is derived from the Windows 2000/NT architecture and consists of two primary layers, with the bottom layer subdivided into further layers (**Figure 2.2**). The two primary layers are defined as User mode and Kernel mode. As the names imply, User

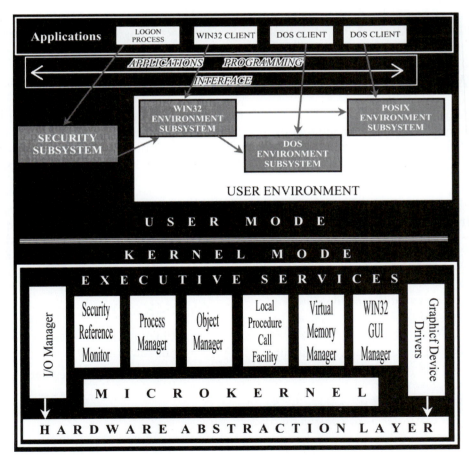

Figure 2.2   The layers of XP

mode is where all the functions dealing with logons, the user interface, running applications, and accessing the network occur. Kernel mode handles security, I/O requests and executions, and hardware interfaces.

In XP, when an application or user request involves making a hardware call, XP does not allow direct access to the hardware. The software running on the user's desktop may *think* it's accessing the hardware. In reality, it's accessing a group of files that make up the hardware abstraction layer. There are two basic pipelines for hardware requests. Those involving a graphical device, such as the video card or monitor, or perhaps a printer, will pass through the graphics device driver's interface. All other hardware calls go through the I/O manager.

These two pipelines hand off the request for hardware services to a set of files associated with the specific device. Each device installed on the system will have an associated virtual device driver. In addition to the .vxd file, groups of devices that share a common command set will have one or more dynamic link library (DLL) files that manage the common commands. These files carry a .dll extension.

The .vxd file and the .dll files associated with a specific device are what the applications running on the system "see" as being the actual hardware. These files communicate with the actual hardware device driver to control the specific device being called on for service.

CHAPTER SUMMARY

While it is not the intent of Part I this book to discuss operating systems in detail, the OS and the computer are so tightly intertwined that it is virtually impossible to discuss either subject without having to make frequent references to the other. This chapter offers a very brief look at how the OS and the hardware interact with one another. For a more detailed discussion of various operating systems, see Part II of this book.

BRAIN DRAIN

1. List the five primary functions of the OS as they relate to the hardware and applications on the system.

2. List as many different file systems supported by Microsoft OSs as you can. What are some of the differences?

3. What are some of the responsibilities of the OS in terms of controlling the microprocessor?

4. What are some of the responsibilities of the OS in terms of controlling memory?

5. Describe how HAL fools the applications into thinking they're talking to the hardware, while all the while it is actually blocking direct access.

THE 64K$ QUESTIONS

1. Which of the following is not a function of the OS?

    a. Memory management

    b. BIOS control

    c. Security

    d. Device management

2. The file name portion of a FAT16 filename could be up to _____ characters long.

   a. 8

   b. 11

   c. 32

   d. 255

3. What was the largest partition allowed by FAT16?

   a. 512MB

   b. 1GB

   c. 2GB

   d. 64TB

4. An individual line of code from within an application that is running on the processor is called a _____.

   a. String

   b. Process

   c. Thread

   d. Stream

5. A part of the hard disk treated as if it were physical memory is called _____.

   a. Virtual memory

   b. The swap file

   c. The paging file

   d. All of the above

6. Which of the following notifies the CPU that the OS wants to communicate with a specific device?

   a. System call

   b. IRQ

   c. DMA

   d. I/O address

7. Which of the following is not an example of an OS?

   a. MS Word

   b. MS-DOS

   c. Windows 3.1

   d. OS2

8. Which of the following is NOT used by the OS to identify or locate a specific device?

   a. An IRQ

   b. An I/O address

   c. An FAU

   d. All of the above are used.

9. Windows uses a(n) _____ to prevent the applications from directly accessing the hardware.

   a. InF

   b. RPG

   c. .vxd

   d. DLL

10. The two operating modes in XP are _____ and _____.

    a. System

    b. User

    c. Kernel

    d. Executive

TRICKY TERMINOLOGY

Device driver: A piece of software running on the system that provides the command set for a specific piece of hardware.

Kernel: The microcode running on the system that provides the most fundamental OS services.

Kernel mode: OS functions dealing with security, I/O requests and executions, and the hardware interface.

Microkernel: A single file (or a very small set of files) that provides basic I/O functions and command interpretation.

Operating system: A program running on a computer system that manages all of the services required by applications that are to run on the system and interfaces with the hardware.

Paging file: A file on the hard disk that holds the information stored in virtual memory. Also called a swap file.

Process: A single section of code from an application that must run from beginning to end.

System call: A request for a service not directly provided by the application.

Swap file: A file on the hard disk that holds the information stored in virtual memory. Also called a paging file.

User mode: OS functions dealing with the user interface, logons, services needed to run applications and provide network access.

Virtual device driver: A set of files that intercepts hardware calls from applications in order to prevent direct access of hardware by the applications.

Virtual memory: A section of hard disk space that is set aside and used by the OS as though it were memory. Also called a swap file or a paging file.

ACRONYM ALERT

API: Application Programming Interface. A collection of files used by Microsoft OSs that maintains and translates the basic command set required by all devices of a particular type.

ATAPI: Advanced Technology Application Programming Interface

DLL: Dynamic Link Library. A file that contains shared code that can be used by more than one application.

GUI: Graphical User Interface. The pretty point-and-click interface common to OSs today.

HAL: Hardware Abstraction Layer. A set of files that plays the part of hardware for applications running on the system so that those applications never have direct access to the hardware.

OS: Operating System

RAM: Random Access Memory. The physical memory installed on a computer system.

 VIEW THE VIDEO

A video clip on the Operating System Functions is available on the accompanying CD.

CHAPTER 3

THE BASIC COMPONENTS

Key to your success as a computer technician is going to be your ability to properly identify the primary components of the average computer system using the correct terminology. Communication is one of the biggest problems a technician faces when trying to troubleshoot a problem over the telephone. True knowledge will come with time. You'll pick up a lot of it in this book, but the buzz words sometimes seem to change by the hour. This chapter will deal with identifying the different ports, sockets, chips, wires, cables, and various bells and whistles that were used to build your system.

A+ CORE HARDWARE EXAM OBJECTIVES

CompTIA exam objectives that will be either introduced or covered include the following:

1.1   Identify the names, purpose, and characteristics of system modules. Recognize these modules by sight or definition.

1.5   Identify the names, purposes, and performance characteristics of standardized/common peripheral ports, associated cabling, and their connectors. Recognize ports, cabling, and connectors by sight.

3.2   Identify various safety measures and procedures, and when/how to use them.

3.3   Identify environmental protection measures and procedures, and when/how to use them.

4.1   Distinguish among the popular CPU chips in terms of their basic characteristics.

4.2   Identify the types of RAM (Random Access Memory), form factors, and operational characteristics. Determine banking and speed requirements under given scenarios.

4.3   Identify the most popular types of motherboards, their components, and their architecture (bus structures).

5.1   Identify printer technologies, interfaces, and options/upgrades.

INTERNAL COMPONENTS

You have to open the case in order to see most of the critical components that make a computer system work. These are the internal components. If you have a computer at your side that you can dig into as you work through this chapter, you will get a lot more out of it. If not, make use of the illustrations provided as best you can. Unfortunately, while it may be true that one picture is worth a thousand words, there's no substitute for the real thing. These days, it's pretty easy to locate used computers at extremely low prices. Many colleges have surplus outlets where they unload older technology. Online auction houses are another good source. Having a system that you don't mind poking around in as you read this book can only help, even if it happens to be older technology.

CAUTION: Before poking around inside a computer that actually *works*, make sure you provide the system with some sort of protection against *electrostatic discharge*. This is ordinary static electricity. A spark you can't even feel has the potential to destroy the delicate circuitry contained in a computer chip. Either use an antistatic wrist strap specifically designed for this purpose, or frequently ground yourself onto a large piece of metal you know goes to ground, such as a radiator for your furnace.

THE MOTHERBOARD

The average person looking inside of a computer case for the first time might not consider this to be the logical place to start at all. For many people it won't even be the first thing they notice. It's buried under all those wires and hidden behind the drives. With all those cards sticking out of it, you can barely see anything on the board itself. At least, that's the way it is on many computers. However, because the system board is the core to the whole system, it is indeed the place to start. As you can see from the one illustrated in **Figure 3.1**, it is a very complex device. Fortunately, it isn't all that hard to figure out.

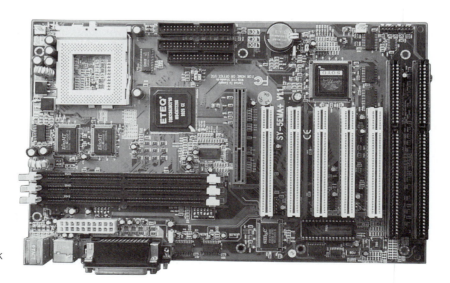

Figure 3.1 While motherboards may differ from brand to brand, most will look pretty similar to this.

FORM FACTOR

There are two different form factors (the way it's built) that you will see in motherboards. I'll get into a more detailed discussion of form factors in Chapter Five, Computer Enclosures. For now, suffice it to say that in this day and age, the most common form factor is some variation on ATX (Advanced Technology Extended). Some older ones will fall under the designation AT (Advanced Technology).

BUZZ WORDS

Form factor: A preconfigured size, orientation, and design layout for a particular component used in order to assure compatibility among manufacturers.

EXAM NOTE: Make sure you know the difference between form factors before you take the exam. In Chapter Five, Computer Enclosures, we will revisit the form factor and how it relates to computer cases.

The original AT board itself measured 12″ × 13″ and provided fairly uniform layout of expansion cards, location of memory chips, and so forth. Another form of AT-style motherboard is the more common "Baby" AT. This board measures 8.5″ × 13″, keeping the proper orientation of expansion slots, plugs, and things like that. About the only externally accessible port on an AT-style motherboard is the keyboard port. Ports such as serial and parallel ports in AT-style systems were installed using expansion cards, so they weren't directly accessible on the system board.

The majority of computers built in recent years have been based on one of several variations on the ATX theme. ATX differs from AT in several important respects. First, the board is oriented differently. Key components on the board are rotated approximately ninety degrees off the original AT design specifications. The intent of this was to reduce the overlap of key motherboard components with other major system components, such as power supplies and drives.

ATX boards also incorporate quite a few more of the peripheral components onto the motherboard. Constructed into the board itself you will find the parallel port, serial ports, keyboard and mouse port, and connections for the Universal Serial Bus. On many boards you

NONSTANDARD FORM FACTORS

In the course of performing upgrades on existing systems, you are likely to run into a number of proprietary designs. Not all manufacturers have consistently used the "standard" form factors in every line of computers they've produced. Older LBX systems were famous for being unique to the system they housed. Finding replacement motherboards for these systems is not always possible. Also note that a common source of failure in these systems is in the *riser card*. LBX systems do not have their expansion slots on the motherboard, but rather have a proprietary slot into which a single card fits, rising above the system board. Hence the name, riser card. While some manufacturers maintain a supply of replacement parts longer than others, even if you find the parts, they are likely to be more expensive than can be justified for repairing a system of that vintage.

may also find video, sound, and network cards and even modems built into the system board itself. As this book unfolds, I'll be discussing the advantages and disadvantages of using onboard peripherals.

POWER CONNECTORS

Another major difference between AT and ATX is in the connection between the system board and the power supply. AT-style computers have two plugs coming off the power supply that provide juice to the system board, frequently called the P8 and the P9 (see **Figure 3.2**). It is relatively easy to plug these in backward from how they're designed, and the results can be disastrous. The ATX form factor incorporates a single 20-pin connector that is notched and only plugs in one way.

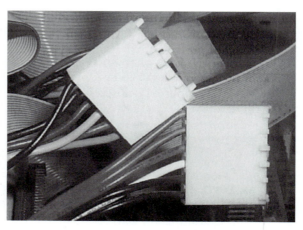

Figure 3.2   Incorrect placement of P8 and P9!!!
When working with AT-style motherboards, it is critical that the P8 and P9 power plugs go in correctly. Plugging them in with the color sequence in the order illustrated here will fry the board!

A more subtle advantage ATX power supplies provide over their AT counterparts is that of more advanced power management. "Soft" power-down of the system can be controlled more efficiently by the operating system.

EXAM NOTE: The next several pages are going to introduce you to features of the motherboard. Even if you think you know this like the back of your hand, go over the material at least once for review. A popular feature of the Core Exam is to give you a very rough illustration of a motherboard with numbered arrows pointing at key components. Your task is to identify those components. This one exercise can be worth several points.

THE EXPANSION BUS

Early in the development of computers, engineers realized that people were going to want to add new toys. Therefore, they designed in a way of expanding the machines. If you examine the rear half of the computer you will see different slots for mounting adapter cards onto the board. These are the slots that make up a large portion of the *expansion bus*. In fact, they're called expansion slots.

The astute reader may think back to Chapter One, PC Basics, when I spoke of the five primary busses, and won't recall that I ever mentioned the expansion bus. That's because, while every computer has an expansion bus, the expansion bus is

> **BUZZ WORDS**
>
> **Expansion Bus:** A circuit on a motherboard that allows accessory devices to be added to the system. The expansion bus straddles several of the primary system busses.

not a primary bus. In fact, it straddles several of the primary busses. That will be covered in greater detail in Chapter Ten, Examining the Expansion Bus.

The number of expansion slots on a system can range from as few as one to as many as eight (or even more on some full-sized AT boards). On many boards, you'll see some longer ones out toward the edge. On most boards these slots are either black or very dark gray. If you look closely, they actually appear to be two different connectors, back to back. (In fact, they are. More on that in Chapter Ten, Examining the Expansion Bus). There is a front slot with sixty-two connectors, backed up by another, shorter one with thirty-six connectors. These are your ISA slots. ISA

Figure 3.3   Here is a typical expansion bus using PCI and ISA slots.

stands for Industry Standard Architecture, and was developed by IBM years ago. Not all boards have these. If your board or computer system says anywhere on it "PC-2000 Compliant," it will not have these expansion slots.

There will also be anywhere from one to who knows how many shorter slots. These are nearly always white in color. These are your PCI slots. PCI stands for Peripheral Components Interconnect, and is the slot of choice for virtually every device made today, except the video card. If your board (and anything less than a couple of years old will have one, unless the motherboard sports onboard video) has a shorter slot that is seated a bit farther back from the edge than the rest of the slots, this is the AGP slot, or the Advanced Graphics Port. The motherboard illustrated in **Figure 3.3** offers the user the choice of ISA or PCI slots.

Collectively, these slots constitute the Expansion Bus. This little collection of connections is of sufficient importance that Chapter Ten is dedicated exclusively to a detailed discussion of the expansion bus.

MEMORY SOCKETS

Typically, computer manufacturers currently make use of one of two types of *Dual Inline Memory Modules* (DIMM). The first of these sockets to come along had 168 pins and clips on either side that lever the chip out of the socket when the need arises. Motherboards vary in how many of these are present. I've seen a few that only have a single socket. Providing only two sockets is relatively common, but this provides only a minimal upgrade capability. The majority of boards provide three or four sockets.

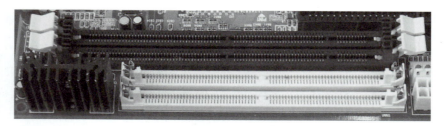

Figure 3.4 DIMM and SIMM sockets can exist on the same board. Check with your manual before you attempt using them both at the same time.

The second style of DIMM that is becoming more common, and now outpacing 168-pin production, is the 184-pin socket required by *double data rate* (DDR) memory. These sockets are larger than the earlier style socket and are keyed differently. Therefore, the memory modules are not interchangeable. There are, however, motherboards that are equipped with both 168-pin and 184-pin sockets.

DIMM sockets aren't all you will see, however. Several manufacturers still make boards that support older-style Single Inline Memory Modules (SIMM). These boards will have two different types of memory sockets, like the one shown in **Figure 3.4** (really old ones can get more complicated, and I'll cover them in more detail in Chapter Nine, Searching Your Memory). If this is the situation for you, there will be anywhere from two to four 72-pin connectors with a ridge directly in the middle of the socket for the SIMMs. These sockets will have small spring clips on each end for holding the SIMM in place.

CPU SOCKETS

First and foremost among the things you need to be able to identify and recognize on a motherboard is the Central Processing Unit (CPU). The CPU is an important consideration in your form factor. CPUs come in four different flavors as of this writing. There are two different competing versions of Slot CPUs and several versions of socket CPUs as well. The sockets are recognized by the hundreds of holes for the CPU pins, while the slots look like overgrown memory slots.

Other, more proprietary sockets you might bump into would include the Socket 8 on older Pentium PRO-based computer systems. Also, AMD uses a Socket A for its Duron line of CPUs as well as some of the Thunderbirds. These are 453-pin ZIFs. Proposed sockets as of this writing (which may well be out by the time you read this) include the Socket 423 by Intel. This is a 423-pin socket designed to support its Tehama, Tulloch, and Willomette chips, when (and if) they're ever released. Other proposed chips by Intel will require the Socket 603. Containing 603 pins, as the name suggests, this is likely to be the socket of choice for the socket-based CPUs with speeds exceeding a gigahertz.

THE CHIPSET

A critical component of your system board is the *chipset*. Throughout the course of this book, I will be referring back to these very critical chips. Several different companies manufacture excellent chipsets, and as this book un-folds, I will make a case that the chipset, in conjunction with the CPU, makes up the "brains" of your computer, not the CPU alone. The chipset illustrated in **Figure 3.5** is one of those made by ETEQ which supports a number of onboard peripherals.

Figure 3.5   The chipset is easily distinguished by the brand name emblazoned on the chips.

The chips that constitute the chipset are sophisticated microprocessors that are preprogrammed to handle the hardware functions of your computer. It is your chipset that will determine what speed front-side bus your computer supports. What's a front-side bus, you ask? That's a very good question, and I'll go into it in more detail in Chapter Seven, Understanding CPUs. For now suffice it to say that the term describes how quickly data moves back and forth between the CPU and motherboard components.

The chipset also determines, to a very great extent, what hardware your computer is capable of supporting. For example, Rambus memory is extremely fast, but operates in a fashion completely foreign to most chipsets. You must have a chipset specifically designed to support it.

You can identify the components of the chipset more easily than most of the other chips on the board (except the CPU, of course), because the name brand will be emblazoned on each of the chips that are part of it. These brands include ALI, Intel, Opti, SiS, and VIA, among others.

> **BUZZ WORDS** ——————
>
> **Chipset:** Two (possibly three on some older boards) ICs that provide hardware support and control all system speeds on a motherboard.

BIOS

Another chip you need to be able to recognize on sight is the BIOS chip. This stands for *Basic Input Output Services,* and along with the chipset, determines your computer's capabilities. Generally, this will be a chip that has either a foil or paper label pasted onto it with a brand name and a copyright date. This is one of the few components on your system board that you might be called on to replace, so knowing what it looks like is useful. Major BIOS manufacturers include AMI, Award, and Phoenix. The one in **Figure 3.6** is quite obviously made by Award.

Like the chipset, the BIOS will determine your computer's overall capabilities. Unlike the chipset, though, if something new comes along, most modern motherboards make it possible to replace an older version of BIOS with a newer version, thereby upgrading your system. This process is called *flashing* the BIOS.

Figure 3.6   The BIOS used to be easily recognizable. It was the one with the foil label. Modern BIOS chips aren't always so easy to identify.

ONBOARD CONNECTORS

Now let's move on to the common connectors that exist on your motherboard. Nearly all boards produced today include several different connectors where ribbon cables of varying widths can be attached. While each connector performs its own function, some commonality exists among them. For example, if you look closely at a ribbon cable, you'll see that one edge is colored, usually red or pink (**Figure 3.7**). The colored wire is the "number one" conductor.

Each of the connectors on your motherboard has an associated "number one" connector. This is always labeled in some manner. It just isn't always easy to figure out how it's labeled. Sometimes, the manufacturer will have the number "1" printed on the board next to the socket. Another equally common and easier-to-read, method is to put a white dot or triangle next to number one. One other way is to have a rectangle with one corner filled in with white. That corner indicates conductor number

Figure 3.7 Ribbon cables always have one wire over which the insulating material is given a different color, usually pink or red. This denotes the number one conductor on the cable.

one. However they do it, one thing remains common. Once you've properly mounted one cable, the rest will line up in the same manner.

> **EXAM NOTE:** Get to know the various connectors very well. As with the motherboard illustration I mentioned earlier, examinees are frequently given a block of illustrations with numbered arrows and asked to identify the connector to which the arrow points.

Two of those sockets will be 40-pin connectors. These are your *Integrated Drive Electronics* (IDE) ports (**Figure 3.8**). Don't fall into the habit of calling them the IDE controllers. IDE devices, by their nature, have their own controller embedded in the device itself. The connector on the system board where you connect the ribbon cable is simply a port. There will be a Primary IDE and a Secondary IDE port. Some motherboards actually ship with four of these ports. On some versions of BIOS, putting the boot drive on the primary port is necessary, because many boards require that the bootable IDE device be the master device on the primary port. Many newer BIOS versions allow you to set virtually any device as the primary boot device. I'll discuss that in more detail in Chapter Thirteen, Hard Disk Drive Structure and Geometry.

The 34-pin socket that looks very similar to the IDE ports is the floppy drive connector. There will only be one of these. Some sockets that exist on AT-style boards, but not ATX, include a 25-pin connector for your parallel port and two 9-pin connectors for the serial ports. ATX-style boards will have these ports built directly onto the back edge of the board for direct connection. Older AT boards shipped with something called a "dongle" that consisted of the appropriate ribbon cable snaking up to a backplane (one of those little metal tabs that fits into the slots in back of the computer case).

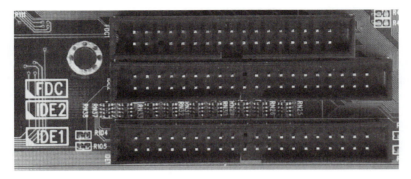

Figure 3.8   In this illustration, you can see the 40-pin connector for IDE and the 32-pin connector for the floppy drive controller side by side. On this board, they are clearly labeled. That is not always the case. Note that on each of the connectors, there is a "missing" pin. This is a null cable and not used.

Figure 3.9   This illustration shows the basic assortment of I/O connectors on the back of an ATX motherboard. Depending on brand and model of motherboard, there may be others as well. Use this illustration in the following discussions of the different connectors.

BACKPLANE CONNECTORS

I can cover the AT really quickly, because, with a few exceptions, it will have only a single externally accessible port directly embedded on the board. That will be a round 5-pin plug, about three-eighths of an inch across. That would be the AT-style keyboard connector, and the plug itself is called a DIN connector.

The I/O backplane on ATX boards (**Figure 3.9**), on the other hand, can have a plethora of connections. There will be two mini-DIN connectors, one for the keyboard and one for the mouse. These are not always as clearly labeled as one might like either. Convention places the keyboard connector closest to the edge of the case and the mouse connector toward the inside.

In addition, there will be the two 9-pin male DB connectors I discussed earlier, which are the serial ports. You might want to do yourself a favor from the start and not get into the habit of calling those ports the COM ports, as is so common. COM ports are predesignated IRQs and IO addresses. Serial ports are places to plug cables. This will be discussed in greater detail in Chapter Ten. On older PCs you may also see a 25-pin male connector. This is also a serial port. Even though it has twenty-five pins, only nine of them actually carry a signal.

The parallel port is the longer 25-pin female DB connector. It is the one with two rows of pin sockets. Also on the ATX board will be two small connectors that look like a couple of little slits, rather than plugs. These are the places to plug Universal Serial Bus (USB) devices. Few, if any, AT-class boards have the USB ports directly on the board. They generally hook up by way of a dongle that you usually have to purchase separately.

Figure 3.10 The 15-pin VGA connector is the only connector on the back of your motherboard with three rows of pins.

Figure 3.11 The outputs for sound are the same, whether they're onboard or on a separate sound card.

Those are the external peripherals that you generally will see on all ATX boards. Many boards, however, will also ship with other embedded peripherals, as well. For example, it is very common to see onboard video adapters. If so, the board will have a 15-pin female DB (**Figure 3.10**) with three rows of pins instead of the two rows we've been seeing. This is to hook up VGA (Video Graphics Array) monitors.

It's also not unusual to see onboard sound. The illustration in **Figure 3.11** is actually from a sound card, but the connectors will be the same either way. Sound cards or boards that have onboard sound will have the one-eighth-inch miniplugs for line in, microphone, and speaker out. You might also have a fourth one for line out. There is also usually a 15-pin female DB connector. This is easily differentiated by the VGA in that it is significantly longer and has only two rows of pins.

Other devices that have been known to be coupled with ATX boards include modems and network adapters. Boards that have both can cause minor confusion for the beginner because the RJ-45 connector and the two RJ-11 connectors of the modem are similar. The RJ-11s, however are the smaller ones with only four connectors. The big one with 8 connectors is the RJ-45 (**Figure 3.12**).

Figure 3.12 RJ-45 connectors look just like telephone jacks, only bigger. They feature eight connectors, but on most network interfaces only four are "live."

EXPANSION CARDS

Identifying the different boards that go into machines might take a little practice, but for the most part the ones you see will be the expansion card equivalents of some of the devices I discussed above. In addition, many proprietary devices are available only as expansion cards. The majority of cards you'll see these days will consist of PCI and AGP, with a few examples of ISA cards still running around. Chapter Ten will deal with the individual busses in great detail. For now, I'll stick to the physical characteristics.

RECOGNIZING THE BUS

All expansion cards you see today are going to fall under one of three categories. They will be ISA, PCI, or AGP. ISA is becoming more uncommon with each passing day. Later on in the book, when I discuss the expansion bus in detail, I'll cover some other types that are now obsolete. But for now, I'll only consider the ones you'll actually use in your lifetime.

PCI: Devices designed for the PCI bus, similar to the one shown in **Figure 3.13**, are easy enough to distinguish from most cards. They have an edge connector on the bottom that starts $1^3/4''$ from the backplane. The actual conductor tabs are small; twenty-two per inch to be exact. There will be a notch, $1/8''$ wide, whose center is $2^1/2''$ from where the edge connector starts, or $4^1/4''$ from the backplane. Looking from the top down, the backplane offsets to the left of the printed circuit card.

ISA: To the beginner, 8-bit ISA cards can be difficult to distinguish from PCI, but it won't take long before you can tell them apart. Compare the ISA card in **Figure 3.14** to the PCI card in Figure 3.13 and you'll see why. The edge card connector starts only $1''$ back from the backplane. The conductor tabs are quite a bit larger, allowing only ten per inch. They're nearly twice as deep as the tabs on PCI cards as well. The 16-bit ISA is a lot easier to distinguish. It has the same edge card as the 8-bit ISA, and behind that is an extension that is $1^5/8''$ long. This extension is separated by a notch that is $1/4''$ wide.

Figure 3.13 A typical PCI card.

Figure 3.14 A typical ISA card (16-bit).

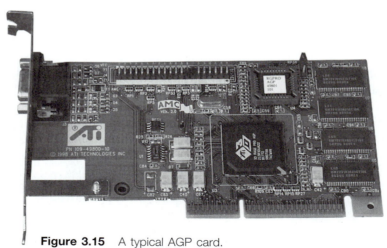

Figure 3.15 A typical AGP card.

AGP: AGP is used only for video cards like the one in **Figure 3.15**. An AGP card is easily differentiated from all other devices. The edge card sits $2^1/2''$ from the backplane. This makes the slot on the motherboard easy to distinguish as well. It sits farther back from the other slots on the board. The edge card is $2^9/16''$ wide, divided by a $^1/8''$ notch about a third of the way back.

TYPES OF EXPANSION CARDS

The cards you have to deal with when repairing, upgrading, or building computers may look pretty confusing at first. Fortunately for the beginner, there are relatively few types that are used on a day-to-day basis.

VGA Cards Video Graphics Array (VGA) cards are primarily available in PCI (increasingly rare) and AGP (the most common). In the event that you absolutely had to have an ISA video card, you could have a problem finding one. It has been several years since ISA video cards were produced on a regular basis. VGA cards have the same 15-pin connector shown in Figure 3.10. This is the most distinguishing mark. Some more advanced cards will also have a coaxial connector, just like the ones on your VCR, and possibly a round plug for SVHS output. I'll go over some of these different connectors in Chapter Sixteen, Your Computer and Graphics, and provide more detailed discussion as to their function.

You will also see a lot more chips on video cards than many other connectors. As with motherboards, video cards will have their own chipset. The chipset for a video card is easily recognized by the brand name etched on the chips. Typical chipsets include ATI, Cirrus Logic, S3, and several others. Also unique to the video card is a 24-pin accessory plug.

Sound Cards As far as the number of chips, sound cards can be the most sparsely populated of all. Many inexpensive cards have only two or three chips on board. The connectors are what make the sound card easy to identify. On the backplane there will be either three or four $^1/_8$″ audio connectors like the one shown in **Figure 3.16**. These are simply holes in the back of the card. Another plug on the back of sound cards is a 15-pin female connector with only two rows of pins. This is typically a game port and/or MIDI (Musical Instrument Device Interface) connector.

The sound card is one of the devices most commonly built into the ATX motherboards. If this is the case, then those connectors will be a part of the motherboard and will line up to specific openings in the computer case.

Figure 3.16 A typical sound card.

Modems The modulator-demodulator, more commonly known as simply the modem, is also easy to identify. The modem is the device that converts serial data to parallel and digital signals to analog signals so that they can be sent out over a telephone wire. There are two standard four-conductor RJ-11 telephone ports on the back. These are easily seen in **Figure 3.17**. One of the ports is for the line input. The modem has to be able to dial out and bring data in. The second is for plugging a real telephone in. Most people only have one telephone jack available in the room where they keep their computers, and they don't want to sacrifice voice services for data.

Modems are another device that commonly show up on "all-in-one" motherboards. As with the sound card, you will get all of the same connections. They'll simply have a spot on the backplane of the motherboard. It is also increasingly common for a motherboard to support a modem riser. A motherboard that supports this function will have a short 46-pin slot for the riser, which may be sold separately.

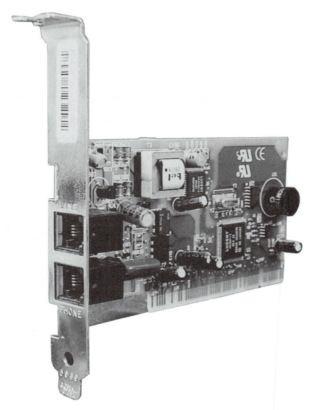

Figure 3.17 Modems will always have two RJ-11 sockets. One is to hook up to the incoming line, and the other is for your telephone.

Network Cards The network card in **Figure 3.18** is superficially similar to a modem, but not close enough to cause much confusion. The network card has a connector called the RJ-45 that resembles a telephone connector. The RJ-45 is an eight-conductor terminal that is physically larger than the RJ-11.

Older network cards might make use of something called the Bayonet Neil-Conselman (BNC) connector. This looks a little like a coaxial connector, like the one on your VCR. They differ in one major respect. The connector locks on with a twist, whereas coaxial cable has a screw-on connector. Also seen on older cards is a 15-pin Attachment Unit Interface (AUI) connector. This is a connector that can cause some confusion. It makes use of precisely the same DB-15 connector that the sound card uses for the MIDI port. There is absolutely no visible difference. When you're attempting to hook up a computer by touch, this is an easy one to mess up. Fortunately, confusing the two will do no permanent harm. The device hooked up simply won't work.

SCSI Adapters The Small Computer Systems Interface (SCSI) was invented with the purpose of hooking seemingly unlike devices together on a single chain of devices. Without prematurely worrying about precisely what SCSI means or how it works, for now lets stick to a description of what it looks like. Chapter Fifteen, The Many Faces of SCSI, has a detailed overview of the technology involved.

A SCSI adapter will usually have a 50-pin high-density connector on the back for hooking up external peripherals. Inside, depending on the type of adapter it is, it will have either one or two connectors for ribbon cables. Nearly all will have a 50-pin cable. More recent ones will also be equipped with a 68-pin or 80-pin high-density connector. These internal connectors are commonly located toward the back of the card, facing upward. Some designs have the connector facing into the computer from the back edge. Once a card is installed, it can be very difficult to attach a cable to an adapter of the latter design.

Figure 3.18 While the port on a network card is similar to that of a modem, it is physically larger, with eight conductors instead of four, and there is only one place to plug a cable into.

SCSI cards have their own BIOS chips as well. These can be identified by brand and will generally be imprinted with the version number. Some SCSI cards provide sockets for adding memory chips. The purpose of this will be discussed in Chapter Fifteen.

Specialty Cards These are rather difficult to describe, because there is a plethora of them out there, and they're all different. A few devices ship with their own hardware controller cards. Certain DVD players are examples of this. Other cards, like video accelerators, can be purchased separately and interface with an existing video card. That is the reason for the accessory plug on the video card that I mentioned earlier in this chapter.

Specialty cards can be difficult to identify if somebody simply places one in your hand and says, "What's this?" I'm including them here only as a warning that there will be some cards you'll encounter that do not lend themselves to ready identification unless you happen to either already be familiar with them from experience, or have some documentation available that describes them. Usually, there will be some form of model number etched onto the circuit board. You can use this number as a search string and look up what kind of card it is on the Internet.

THE POWER SUPPLY

That silver-colored box you see in **Figure 3.19** is usually located up toward the top of the case and to the back, or perhaps to one side in desktop designs. This is the power supply. It's what brings the juice out of the wall socket and into the computer to power everything that goes on inside. Coming out of the box will be a number of cords with two or maybe three different terminations, depending on the power supply. There is a separate section in this book on power supplies; therefore, I will discuss the finer details when the time comes. For now, I'll stick to making sure you can identify the plugs as the power plugs, the Molex, and the mini.

Figure 3.19 This ubiquitous silver box is the power plant of your computer system. Don't take it lightly.

Power supplies are made specific to their form factor. There are AT and ATX power supplies, and the two are not interchangeable. The ATX power supply will only have a single 20-pin power connector that hooks to the motherboard, usually labeled P1 (although this can vary from manufacturer to manufacturer). The AT power supply will have two 6-pin plugs for bringing power to the motherboard. These are usually labeled P8 and P9, but like the ATX connector, labeling can vary among manufacturers. It is critical that the power plugs from an AT power supply are properly oriented or you'll fry the board. The easy way to tell is that the black conductors should always be on the inside once the plugs are in place.

CAUTION: A couple of times throughout the book, I have either already mentioned, or will mention, that if you work on a computer system while it's plugged in, static electricity can drain either from the system or from your body, through the chassis and out to the ground. For the most part, this is safe enough. There is never more than 12V of low-amperage current flowing through the system even if you forget to power it off (won't do the system much good if you drop a metal part on the motherboard while it's powered up, though!)

DO NOT EVEN THINK of working on a power supply while it is plugged in. The amount of current moving across some of the circuitry is potentially lethal. If you're wearing a wrist strap, it can be worse. Most people wear the strap on their left hand, and that would direct the current right through the heart.

The plugs that bring power to internal peripherals are the Molex and the miniplug. The Molex is the larger of the two and can be recognized by the fact that two of the corners have been beveled to prevent the plug from going in backward. It has four conductors, two black and two colored. The miniswitch also has four conductors, but is substantially smaller. This plug has grooves on one side and a ridge on the other. This is the plug that powers your floppy disk drive. Some power supplies also provide a micro-miniplug for CPU fans. This is the one with only two conductors, one black and one red.

THE BOX ITSELF

Far too many people underestimate the importance of the case itself. This is one component that is frequently purchased on the basis of aesthetics rather than function. While having a pretty case is certainly important, there are other, more important factors to consider. Having a box that doesn't cut your hands to shreds every time you poke around inside is a nice feature also.

In most cases, when you select a computer case, by default you have now selected your power supply. Therefore, that is something that you need to factor into the equation. Does the case you're considering have sufficient power for your needs? Some manufacturers, on the other hand, allow you to purchase their case *sans* power supply and then select the one you need from a generous list of those available. This is a more expensive approach, but in general, not only do you have the opportunity to decide how much power you need, but the cases themselves are of better quality.

THE DRIVE BAYS

Computer cases feature both internal and external drive bays. Both are equally important. The number of drive bays that you as a user can access without opening the case varies considerably from box to box. The Micro-ATX cases so popular with the makers of those so-called Internet machines may have as few as two, while a Super Server case might have eighteen or more. As you might imagine, a Micro-ATX isn't all that good if you need to build a computer with half a dozen different drives. The following list describes the most common varieties of enclosure and how they can be recognized.

- *Minidesktop:* ~65W power supply, two 5.25″ plus one 3.5″ external drive bays and one 3.5″ internal drive bay
- *Full desktop:* 200–250W power supply, two 5.25″ plus two 3.5″ external drive bays and two 3.5″ internal drive bays
- *Minitower:* ~65W power supply, two 5.25″ plus one 3.5″ external drive bays and one 3.5″ internal drive bay
- *Midtower:* 200–250W power supply, two 5.25″ plus two 3.5″ external drive bays and two 3.5″ internal drive bays
- *Full tower:* 250–300W power supply, four to six 5.25″ plus two 3.5″ external drive bays and three to five 3.5″ internal drive bays
- *Server case:* 300–600W power supply, 10-24 5.25″ plus two 3.5″ external drive bays; rarely any internal drive bays, as it is assumed that hot-swappable devices will be employed

THE BACKPLANE

The back of the computer is the section that requires the most discussion. This is where everything hooks up. The older AT-style cases differ somewhat from the ATX cases of today, as I pointed out earlier in this chapter. The onboard peripherals I discussed when describing ATX motherboards will protrude through openings in the back of the case. While you had the motherboard in your lap it was pretty easy to pick out the VGA connector from the serial port. Now that you're leaning over the back of the box looking at everything upside down it isn't so easy, is it?

The computer in **Figure 3.20** is pretty typical for today's systems. Get to know the connectors back here so well you can identify them by touch. It makes life a whole lot easier when you're working on computers for a living. Many a time I've had to disconnect and then reconnect a computer while lying on the client's floor, all because the cables for external peripherals snaked through channels in the office furniture and/or the network cable extended about six inches from the wall. Since the cables won't stretch out to you, you have to go to the cables.

Figure 3.20 The back of your computer is where everything hooks up. Get to know it well. This particular computer is different than many in that it has two network cards.

CHAPTER SUMMARY

The purpose of this chapter is to introduce the novice to the physical components that make up a system. How these components work will be discussed in various chapters later in the book. However, being able to physically pick up a device and identify it is a basic skill that you must develop. Going back to something I said earlier, it's a very good idea for someone training to work inside of computers to get his or her hands on one or more older machines just for puttering around with. An exercise I strongly recommend is to completely dismantle a computer down to the barest essentials, then wait a day or two. After you've had plenty of time to forget what went where, go back and put it back together. But you might want to take some notes during the teardown process as to what wires went where.

BRAIN DRAIN

1. List as many onboard components as you can that will be found on both AT-style and ATX-style motherboards.

2. Now come up with as many externally accessible connectors as you can that would be found on an ATX board, but not typically on an AT board.

3. Put together a list of as many expansion devices as you can think of that would require a slot on the expansion bus.

4. From what you have learned in this chapter, what are several considerations to think about when selecting a new motherboard?

5. This task should be accomplished with a partner. Place a fully assembled computer on the table in front of you. Without looking at the back and using the sense of touch only, reach around to the back of the computer and identify as many connectors as you can.

THE 64K$ QUESTIONS

1. A key precautionary measure to take before working inside a computer system is to:
   a. Protect the carpet against dust and debris that may fall out.
   b. Protect yourself against severe electrical shock.
   c. Protect vital components from ESD.
   d. Protect the CPU from EMI.

2. Two key differences between an ATX-style motherboard and an AT-style motherboard are: (select two)
   a. Physical size of CPU sockets.
   b. The number of memory slots installed.
   c. The number of externally accessible connectors protruding from the rear.
   d. The orientation of onboard connectors and memory slots relative to the backplane.

3. On an AT-style power supply the correct orientation of the P8 and P9 connectors is:
   a. Black wires to the inside, colored wires to the outside.
   b. Black wires to the outside, colored wires to the inside.
   c. The clip holder on the P8 faces the front of the computer, while that of the P9 faces the back.
   d. It doesn't matter.

4. Modern motherboards can be adapted to new technology because they incorporate _____.
   a. Replaceable chipsets
   b. Bootblock
   c. Flash BIOS
   d. ZIP BIOS

5. A DIMM socket is equipped with _____ pin connectors.
   a. 133
   b. 168
   c. 186
   d. 184

6. The two components common to all contemporary motherboards that determine the hardware and speed capabilities of a computer are: (pick two)
   a. The CPU

    b. The BIOS

    c. The memory

    d. The chipset

7. A 40-pin connector is the hookup for _____.

    a. The parallel port

    b. The floppy disk drive

    c. Serial ports

    d. The IDE port

8. A 25-pin male connector with two rows of male pins is _____.

    a. A serial port

    b. A VGA port

    c. A parallel port

    d. An external SCSI port

9. A 25-pin male connector with two rows of female pins is _____.

    a. A serial port

    b. A VGA port

    c. A parallel port

    d. An external SCSI port

10. A 15-pin female connector with three rows of pin sockets is _____.

    a. A serial port

    b. A VGA port

    c. A parallel port

    d. An external SCSI port

TRICKY TERMINOLOGY

Chipset: Two (possibly three on some older boards) ICs that provide hardware support and control all system speeds on a motherboard.

Form factor: A preconfigured size, orientation, and design layout for a particular component used in order to assure compatibility among manufacturers.

Expansion bus: A circuit on a motherboard that allows accessory devices to be added to the system. The expansion bus straddles several of the primary system busses.

ACRONYM ALERT

AGP: Advanced Graphics Port. A high-speed bus designed exclusively for graphics.

AT: Advanced Technology. A form factor promoted by IBM in the early days of personal computing.

ATX: Advanced Technology Extended. An improvement of the older AT form factor that provided greater accessibility to components and far more efficiency in the use of space.

AUI: Attachment Unit Interface. A 15-pin female connector used by some early network cards and sound cards.

BIOS: Basic Input Output System. Basic instruction, usually (but not always) loaded onto a Read Only Memory chip that leads the system through the process of startup and provides instructions as to how to communicate with different forms of hardware.

BNC: Bayonet Neil-Conselman. A barrel-shaped connector named after the two engineers involved in the design.

CPU: Central Processing Unit. The primary microprocessor on a modern computer that is responsible for executing programs and processing user data.

DIMM: Dual Inline Memory Module. A 168- or 184-pin memory module that allows the connection on either side of the base to perform disparate functions.

IDE: Integrated Drive Electronics. A method of managing hard drives and other devices that takes the controller circuitry off the motherboard or separate controller card and places it on the device itself.

ISA: Industry Standards Architecture. An 8- or 16-bit expansion bus designed by IBM.

PCI: Peripheral Components Interconnect. A 32- or 64-bit expansion bus designed by Intel.

SCSI: Small Computer Systems Interface. An interface that allows several differ-ent types of device to hook up to the same controller circuit.

SIMM: Single Inline Memory Module. A 30- or 72-pin memory module on which two opposing pins on the base perform the same function.

USB: Universal Serial Bus. A moderate speed bus that allows 127 devices to share a single chain and a 12Mb/s bandwidth.

VGA: Video Graphics Array. The most commonly used video display in use today.

CHAPTER 4

BASIC ELECTRICITY AND THE POWER SUPPLY

A fundamental knowledge of electricity is important if you expect to have any hope of understanding how computers work. Computers run off of electricity just like your body runs off food. Having a basic comprehension about what it is that powers your computer will accomplish two things. Hopefully, it will keep you from getting killed or seriously injured. Second, knowing how electricity works is essential in understanding how electronic signals can be used to convey information.

A+ CORE HARDWARE EXAM OBJECTIVES

CompTIA exam objectives covered in this chapter include the following:

1.1 Identify the names, purpose, and characteristics of system modules. Recognize these modules by sight or definition.

1.2 Identify basic procedures for adding and removing field-replaceable modules for desktop systems. Given a replacement scenario, choose the appropriate sequences.

2.1 Recognize common problems associated with each module and their symptoms, and identify steps to isolate and troubleshoot the problems. Given a problem situation, interpret the symptoms and infer the most likely cause.

3.3 Identify environmental protection measures and procedures, and when/how to use them.

THE BASICS OF ELECTRICITY

Electrical circuits have a number of measurable identifying characteristics. Knowing what they are, what impact they have on everything around you, and how to accurately measure them is a key ingredient to success in any field that even touches on electricity. There are three fundamental characteristics I'm going to look at in this chapter. Those are voltage, current, and resistance.

VOLTAGE

Voltage is probably the most confusing term in electricity. Common household circuits are either 110-120V or 220V. I say 110-120, because the current we all receive from the power company is hardly pure and rarely 100 percent consistent. This is considered the acceptable range. 220V is generally reserved for the heavy-duty appliances in your house. If you have an electrical water heater, chances are extremely good it's 220V. Your computer, television, VCR, and such will invariably be 110-120V.

BUZZ WORDS

Voltage: The difference in charge between two objects or surfaces. This is sometimes referred to as electrical pressure.

Current: The number of electrons that flow through a circuit in a fixed amount of time.

Voltage refers to a differential charge between two objects. So when you set up a 110V circuit, the difference between the charge in your television circuit and that of the power box is basically 110V. The technical term for this is electromotive force. This is how much electrical "pressure" you have. You measure air pressure in pounds per square inch; you measure electrical pressure in volts.

There is a common misconception that just because a circuit carries high voltage, it is dangerous. Most of the time they are. It isn't, however, the voltage that makes them dangerous. People get zapped by charges in excess of 50,000 volts on a regular basis and only jump a bit. You see, that's about how much voltage is in one of those sparks that jumps from your fingers to a brass doorknob after you walk across new carpet. But there isn't much current in that little spark.

CURRENT

It's the *current* that will kill you. Current is measured in amperes, or more commonly, amps. It describes the flow of electrons through the medium. And it's the number of unwanted electrons in your body that makes an electrical shock uncomfortable. The static spark I described in the previous section was carried over an extremely low current.

One amp is a pretty hefty amount of current. The technical definition of one amp is equal to the transfer of one coulomb of charge per second. A coulomb is a fixed quantity of electrons—specifically, 6.26×10^{18} electrons. When that many electrons try to fit into your body all at once (especially considering your nervous system uses the transfer of electrons in order to function), there's generally a reaction.

> **EXAM NOTE:** Make sure you can define each one of these different measurements. You aren't likely to see them all, but you can count on seeing at least one of them. The question is, which one?

RESISTANCE

Those electrons don't just jump across the ether of nothingness, however. They have to move from one atom to the next, on down the line, until they can't move any more. Not all substances are as willing to give up the electrons they've got just so a few decillion homeless electrons can crowd their way in. When electricity, which is nothing more than an expression for the flow of electrons, encounters a substance of this nature it encounters *resistance*. A substance with a great deal of electrical resistance, such as rubber, is an *insulator*. A substance that freely contributes to the flow of electrons is a *conductor*. Most metals are good conductors.

Technically speaking, there is no such thing as a perfect conductor (although I know a few musicians who would say they've met conductors who *think* they are perfect...). Every substance known to science exhibits resistance to greater or lesser degrees. The physical number of electrons that comes out of the end of a 100-foot length of copper wire won't be the same as the number that tried to go in. A few billion filled in some areas that didn't have enough electrons to begin with (this creates something called ionization), a few billion more were sent back from whence they came.

> **BUZZ WORDS**
>
> **Resistance:** The tendency for a substance to block the flow of electrons.
>
> **Insulator:** Any substance that tends to resist the flow of electricity.
>
> **Conductor:** Any substance that encourages the flow of electricity. Also the man at the podium that waves a white stick in front of the musicians.

Likewise, there is no such thing as the perfect insulator. Even rubber allows some juice to pass. Therefore, you should not assume that, just because an electrical wire has a thick layer of insulation over it, it is safe to pick it up off your yard while standing in a mud puddle. That may well be a mistake from which you are unable to learn anything.

The measure of resistance is in a unit called an ohm (Ω). As you might imagine, voltage, current, and resistance have relationships that are meticulously intertwined. They all interact with each other, and each has an effect on the other. Ohm's Law is rather neatly described by the following three formulae.

> $V = IR$ states that Voltage is a function of Current (in amperes) multiplied by Resistance (in Ohms).
>
> $R = V/I$ tells us that Resistance, on the other hand, is arrived at by dividing Voltage by Current.
>
> $I = V/R$ is the converse of the above. In this equation, Current is derived by dividing Voltage by Resistance.

EXAM NOTE: As with the terms of measurements, you should know the three formulae listed about.

AC/DC

When it comes to electrical current, it can be either *alternating current* (AC) or *direct current* (DC). In an AC circuit, the flow of current changes direction a specific number of times each second. The number of times each second that the current changes direction is measured in hertz. When you turn on your DVD player so you can soothe your battered nerves with a couple hours of the *Matrix*, that device is plugged into a 110-120V, 60Hz AC circuit. 60Hz is pretty standard.

An AC outlet (**Figure 4.1**) in a modern building will consist of three sockets. The smaller of slotted openings is the hot lead. This is the current coming into your building from the power company. The larger slit is the return. As its name implies, this is the conductor that returns current to the power company. The rounded socket is the ground. In the event of a short circuit, the ground wire will carry unwanted current to a copper spike pounded into the ground outside the building. Under normal circumstances, there should be no measurable current on this wire.

Direct current flows in one direction only. Therefore, a DC circuit will have to deal with issues of *polarity*. The current has to flow from the positive end of the circuit to the negative side. This will be measured with little symbols. A plus sign (⊕) tells you you're dealing with the positive electrode while the minus (–) indicates negative.

A computer system relies on DC current for its power. It is the job of the power supply to convert the AC current coming out of the wall socket to DC. Therefore, in truth, power supply is actually an inaccurate name for this component. It's actually a power converter. It steps the 110-120V AC current from your outlet down to 5V and 12V DC current. And there's a very good reason it has to do that.

One of the things that will repeatedly be emphasized in later chapters is just how transient the information in a computer system really is. If current is lost for as few as 7.5ns, all information stored in memory is lost as well. If AC is changing directions sixty times per second, there's a whole lot more time during the transition than 7.5ns that a RAM chip is going to be without power. You'll be losing data more than sixty times per second. Current that is delivered to computer circuits must not only be constant; it must be stable. DC is the only type of current that will work.

Figure 4.1   An AC outlet consists of the hot, the return, and the ground.

BUZZ WORDS

Alternating current: An electrical current that reverses the direction of current flow many times each second.

Direct current: An electrical current that exhibits a steady directional flow from a source of relative positive voltage to a target of relative negative voltage.

Polarity: The characteristic of an electrical circuit to have one point of relative positive charge (or pole) and another point of relative negative charge (or pole).

Spike: A sudden transient increase in voltage.

Sag: A sudden transient decrease in voltage.

SPIKES AND SAGS

Just what do I mean by the current being stable? If you think back to when you went into the computer store to buy your system, the salesperson probably tried to convince you to purchase a surge suppressor as well. Hopefully, he or she was successful. Household current is far from pure. If it were, you would be able to say, "I have 112V coming into my house." Not 110-120. That variation would not exist. Fact of the matter is, 110-120 is only the "average" acceptable range.

A *sag* in current is when voltage takes a significant drop. This can happen as a result of many things, and in fact happens thousands of times each day. Your refrigerator goes on, voltage drops for a second or so until it stabilizes. Somebody turns on the vacuum cleaner and voltage drops.

Spikes occur when, for whatever reason, voltage suddenly increases. Lightening hitting a power line a few blocks away can cause intense voltage spikes. The refrigerator that caused that sag a few minutes ago has cooled down to the preset temperature and the thermostat tells it that it's time to shut off. For a few thousandths of a second, voltage spikes.

That's just what's going on inside your own house. There are hundreds or even thousands of houses on the grid from which you draw your power. It would be impossible for the electric company to provide pure voltage. The things you can blame them for (to a certain extent, anyway) are brownouts and blackouts. A *brownout* is a sag in voltage that lasts for more than a second or so. A *blackout* is when you lose power all together. Another outside influence that can affect the purity of electrical current is radio frequency interference (RFI), also known as electromagnetic interference (EMI). This will be discussed in greater detail in the next section.

There are a number of hardware devices on the market to protect your computer from this malfeasance. Some handle the little variations while others handle the big ones. *Surge suppressors* (**Figure 4.2**) handle the minor spikes that occur on a regular basis. They work by clamping voltage to a certain level. If a spike hits, a device called a metal oxide varistor (MOV) absorbs the differential and sends it to ground. The better ones handle bigger spikes and more of them. Each time the MOV takes a hit, a little more of its life span is used up. It's like the character in the computer games that people play. Every hit takes away some of its health points. When all the health points have been used up, the surge suppressor is no longer a surge suppressor. It's now an outlet strip that provides no protection. Get the best you can afford.

Line conditioners clean up a couple of other forms of current pollution. They deal with the sags and filter out RFI from the incoming current. In most

> **BUZZ WORDS**
>
> **Brownout:** A drop in voltage that lasts a noticeable period of time.
>
> **Blackout:** A complete loss of power to an entire area.
>
> **Surge suppressor:** A device that is able to filter out voltage surges and prevent them from reaching the devices plugged into their outlets.
>
> **Line conditioner:** A device that is able to filter out transient noise, such as EMI, from the current.

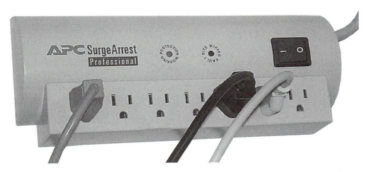

Figure 4.2   A good surge suppressor can keep your computer system alive and well even after a number of electrical spikes have come its way.

cases a good surge suppressor also has a line conditioner built in, so it is taking on both tasks.

Standby power supplies and *uninterruptible power supplies* take care of the brownouts and blackouts. They perform similar functions, just in slightly different ways. The SPS kicks in only when power is disrupted. Any other time, the computer draws its power directly from the wall. The UPS, on the other hand, provides current to the computer 100 percent of the time.

With the UPS (**Figure 4.3**), electricity comes in from the wall and passes through a rectifier circuit. A *rectifier circuit* converts the power from AC to DC. This DC current charges the batteries in the UPS. The batteries feed power to a circuit called an *inverter*, which turns it back to AC again. This AC current powers the computer. It has to revert to AC because that is the current the power supply requires. The power that feeds the computer is now filtered power. All sags and spikes have been filtered out and there is no residual EMI or RFI.

It sounds from this description like the UPS would be the only way to go, and that the SPS should have been provided a mercy death by now. In critical installations, however, this is not the case. They'll have both. The SPS is an off-line generator powered by gasoline or kerosene. It can be in another section of the building and provide current for the entire building for extended periods of time.

BUZZ WORDS

Uninterruptible power supply: A device that uses batteries to provide electrical current to another device in the event of a total power failure.

Standby power supply: A device that uses a generator to provide electrical current to a room or building in the event of a total power failure.

Rectifier circuit: A specialized series of components that converts AC current to DC current.

Inverter: A device or circuit that converts DC current to AC current.

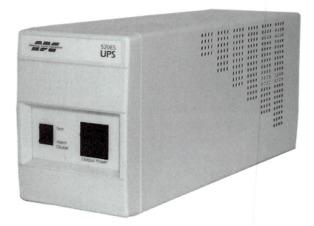

Figure 4.3   A UPS is a valuable asset for any computer, but it is essential that critical servers be equipped with one.

RFI, EMI, AND ESD

In a perfect world, electricity would be electricity, radio would be radio, and light would be light. Unfortunately, the planet earth is a miniscule speck in a universe governed by its own set of rules. Energy of all forms has a tendency to interact. Go into any physics lab and it'll have a poster of the electromagnetic spectrum hanging on the wall somewhere. One version I've seen overlaps all light waves, and magnetic, electronic, and radio frequencies onto a single chart.

I mentioned earlier that power lines could pick up radio waves the same way an antenna does. If the energy it picks up is strong enough, it will have an effect on all of your electrical appliances. For example, if you happen to live very near a transmission station for your local talk radio, you might have a hard time getting decent TV reception. Wavy lines creep all over the screen, and if it's really bad, the audio portion breaks up a bit. This is the result of Radio Frequency Interference (RFI).

RFI has some pretty nasty effects on computers and networks. If it creeps past the power supply and into the computer, it can cause some pretty oddball problems. Potentially it can cause cells within memory chips to alter their charge. This could result in corrupted data. This explains a tendency for computers in or near radio stations to lock up with far greater frequency than normal. Unshielded network cable can pick it up and start sending corrupted packets all over the place. This slows down network traffic dramatically, because all of those bad packets have to be resent.

If, for any reason, you suspect RFI to be a problem that you have to deal with, about the only solution is to invest in shielded cables. For RFI coming in off the AC, there are inline filters you can purchase at most electrical supply houses that are similar to a surge suppressor, except that they filter RFI instead of surges.

Electromagnetic Interference (EMI) is actually the same thing as RFI, except that the frequencies do not necessarily fall in the range used to transmit radio and television signals. Air-conditioning compressors generate huge amounts of EMI. Many older appliances throw out quite a bit of EMI, and your computer itself is a heavy contributor. In corporate America, a big source of EMI are the ballasts that power fluorescent lights in office buildings. When running network cable, it is essential for cable that runs through the *plenum* (that's the area between your ceiling and the floor upstairs) to be properly shielded.

In Chapter Three, The Basic Components, I introduced the concept of electrostatic discharge (ESD). It's one of the biggest thorns a technician has to deal with, because it's everywhere. You create it simply by passing through your environment. It is easy to assume that lightning storms are the biggest source of ESD, but that assumption is wrong. People are the biggest source. Every time you reposition yourself in that nice comfy fabric chair, every time you scoot your feet across the carpet, and every time you comb your hair, you generate enough static electricity to kill every chip in your computer twice over. That's why it is critical that you take steps to protect the equipment on which you work from ESD.

There are several steps you can take. If you're setting up a shop, do it right from the start. There are specially designed floor mats that drain static away, as well as bench mats. Invest in both. It's money well spent. Also, pick up a good antistatic wrist strap. These wrap around your wrist and clip to any piece of metal that goes to ground. Don't waste your money on one of those cheap plastic ones. They don't do a very good job and can be uncomfortable enough that you wind up not using them anyway.

CAUTION: When you're working on an open computer system, it is generally safe to keep the power supply plugged into the wall while you work. This keeps the system grounded and you can clip your wrist strap onto the metal chassis of the enclosure. There is very little current even when the system is turned on, and

> **BUZZ WORDS**
>
> **Plenum:** An architectural term referring to the space between the ceiling of one floor in a building and the floor of the one above it.

voltages are less than 12V. However, if there is any cause to work with the power supply, you should ground yourself to something other than the computer. Power supplies can deliver a shock of up to 15 amps at 110-120V. This is potentially fatal, although it generally stops at delivering a nasty shock. However, most people work with the wrist strap on their left hand. This would direct the current through the heart, greatly enhancing the chances that an electrical shock could be fatal. Also, never work on laser printers or monitors while they are plugged in. Unless you have received specific training, monitors should be left completely alone.

ELECTRICAL PARTS

This is a technical world we live in. There are a number of different electrical parts that any hardware technician must be able to recognize. There are not, however, very many in a computer (if any at all) that you would be wise to attempt to fix or replace.

Capacitors (**Figure 4.4**) are electrical storage devices that act as a sort of warehouse for electricity. Incoming electrical current charges the capacitor the way a battery charger revitalizes a rechargeable battery. The capacitor then provides current to the downstream circuit as it's needed. Capacitors also act as filters for electrical current. They are valuable components in your PC and show up all over the motherboard, and are a huge part of the reason the power supply works as well as it does. Capacitors are measured in *farads* (*f*) and *microfarads* (m*f*).

Figure 4.4 In a way, capacitors act as storage batteries for an electrical circuit.

Coils, such as the one shown in **Figure 4.5**, are another form of electrical filter. Instead of filtering out noise, spikes, and sags the way a capacitor does, it filters out AC. DC current passes through a coil with virtually no interruption. AC, on the other hand, has a really hard time getting through it. Therefore, one or more coils will generally protect any component that shows ill effect in the presence of AC current (such as a RAM stick). Coils can also be used to filter out specific frequencies below a certain range.

Diodes are very small devices that exhibit a very useful characteristic. They freely permit the flow of electrons in one direction, but act as a resistor when it tries to go the opposite way. The one-way streets found in so many downtown locations are traffic rectifiers. It isn't impossible for a car to go the

BUZZ WORDS

Capacitor: An electrical component that stores electrical current and provides it to the circuit as needed.

Farad: The major measurement of a capacitor's ability to store energy.

Microfarad: The minor measurement of a capacitor's ability to store energy.

Coil: An electrical component consisting of tightly wound wire that is used to filter out AC current and low frequency signals.

wrong way. Happens all the time. But travel is certainly restricted for the vehicle going the wrong way. Diodes are one-way streets for electrons.

Fuses really aren't used as much in computers as they used to be. Most power supplies may still have them installed. They are used to make sure that current flow in a circuit doesn't exceed a certain point. The filament consists of a conductive material that will vaporize above a certain point. Therefore, if you have a circuit protected by a 5A fuse, and something happens that causes 10A of electricity to flow, the conductor inside the fuse will vaporize and current flow will stop. If you can't see the filament inside a fuse, you can always test it with a multi-meter to see if it's good. A good fuse will generally register as 0.0000 ohms if you set the meter to impedance and put it in the range closest to the value of your fuse. It'll register infinite resistance if the fuse is blown.

Resistors are devices that resist the flow of electricity. That makes the name conveniently easy to remember. They are measured in ohms. Since they're so tiny, the manufacturers couldn't really expect to be able to print their value on the side. Therefore a color-coding scheme was adopted by the industry. The manufacturer paints little colored stripes around the outside of the tube, and as long as you've memorized the code, you can use the colored stripes to calculate the value of any given resistor. The code consists of four stripes. The first two are "significant" digits. The third stripe represents a multiplier, while the fourth indicates tolerance. In more simple terms, the first two are real numbers, 0 through 9. The third will represent a value, starting with 1 and going up in multiples of 10. 1, 10, 100, 1000, etc. Tolerance values (or the fourth stripe) will only be red, gold, or silver. You need to be able to determine that it's a 10,000,000 ohm, +/– 5% resistor just by looking at four colors. One of the CompTIA exam objectives is to be able to calculate the value of a resistor using color codes. **Table 4.1** outlines the industry standard color-coding scheme for resistors.

BUZZ WORDS ─────────────

Diode: An electrical component that freely permits the flow of electrons in one direction, but resists electron flow in the opposite direction.

Fuse: An electrical component that consists of a filament that vaporizes when more than a certain amount of current tries to pass.

Resistor: An electrical component that restricts the flow of current by a precisely measured amount.

Figure 4.5 Coils are useful for filtering out spurious AC as well as low frequency noise.

THE POWER SUPPLY

As I said before, the power supply is somewhat inappropriately named. It doesn't supply power to the computer. The power company does that. The power supply draws AC current from the wall and then converts it to something the computer can make use of—nice, clean DC current.

Table 4.1   Industry Standard Color Coding for Resistors

Color	Number	Multiplier	Tolerance Value
Black	0	1	Not Used
Brown	1	10	Not Used
Red	2	100	+/- 2%
Orange	3	1,000	Not Used
Yellow	4	10,000	Not Used
Green	5	100,000	Not Used
Blue	6	1,000,000	Not Used
Violet	7	10,000,000	Not Used
Gray	8	100,000,000	Not Used
White	9	Not Used as Multiplier	Not Used
Gold	Not Relevant	Not Used as Multiplier	+/– 5%
Silver	Not Relevant	Not Used as Multiplier	+/– 10%

CONVERTING AC TO DC

As I've already pointed out, the primary difference between AC current and DC current is that AC changes direction sixty times every second. This occasionally leads the beginner into believing that AC current does not exhibit polarity. Quite to the contrary, it is every bit as polarized as DC current. It's just that polarity is changing sixty times per second, along with current flow.

The fundamental job of a computer's power supply is to take that AC current and make it DC. There are three basic stages to that conversion that I am going to take a look at.

The first is the rectifier circuit. I covered what a rectifier circuit does earlier in the chapter. It consists of a series of diodes wired in series with one another. As I said earlier, a diode freely allows the flow of current in one direction, but resists flow in the opposite direction. If you pump AC current through enough diodes, backflow of current will cease to exist. Therefore, AC current is piped into the rectifier circuit with current flowing in both directions, trading sides sixty times a second. It comes out the other end going in only one direction.

Unfortunately, it's still pulsing at sixty cycles. This is because you've only filtered out electricity traveling in the reverse direction. There's what amounts to a "hole" in the current where it used to flow the other direction. Now you have a flow of electrons that is 120V for a few nanoseconds and 0V for a few nanoseconds. CPUs and RAM aren't going to like that any more that they would AC.

So the next step is to dump the electricity into capacitors. Since capacitors act somewhat like a storage battery, the incoming current charges the capacitor, and then the device releases

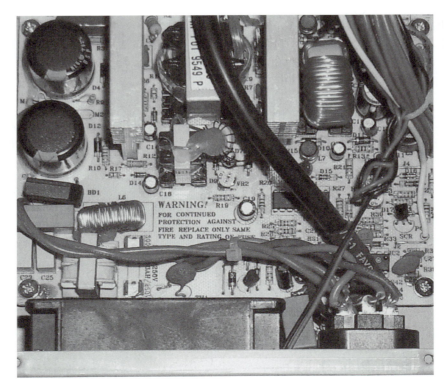

Figure 4.6 Looking at the inside of a power supply, it is actually pretty easy to see the basic components of the unit. The large cylinders are the capacitors, and the circles of coiled wire are the coils. The rectifier circuit is the only part that is not easily seen in this illustration.

current in a relatively steady flow out the other end of the circuit. **Figure 4.6** shows you what the inside of a power supply looks like.

At this point in time, you have predominantly DC current. However, even now, not all reverse flow has been completely eliminated. To filter out any residual AC current that may still exist, the current now flows through a series of coils. The nature of coils is to filter AC current, so what comes out of the power supply is now relatively clean.

AT, ATX, AND SFX POWER SUPPLIES

Currently there are only two basic types of power supplies for computer systems on the market that you'll have to deal with. Those are the older-style AT power supplies and the more recent ATX. In Chapter Three I touched on the basic differences between the two. Here, I'll go into a little more detail.

AT POWER SUPPLIES

All power supplies used in modern PCs evolved from the original PC-XT. The primary change between the XT and AT was in form factor. The PC-AT was modified in many respects for easier accessibility to internal parts. The power supply was reduced in size and redesigned to accommodate the newer case.

The first AT power supplies were 5.9" high × 5.9" wide × 8.35" deep. They ranged in power from a low of about 85W to as high as 800W, with most of them being in the 200W–250W range. When the "baby-AT" form factor became popular, a power supply to fit that case became very popular. Those were 5.9" × 5.9" × 6.5" in size.

The AT power supply delivers +12V, –12V, +5V, and –5V current. +/–12V isn't used for much of anything these days. Some devices made in the early days of PCs required this current, but about the only voltage used in AT-style computers now is the +5V current. The ISA bus calls for –5V to be routed through the slots, so that particular voltage is required for ISA cards. All other devices will operate off of +5V.

On the majority of AT power supplies you will only find two types of connector for powering components coming off the power supply. These will each have four conductors leading to the plug. In addition to those, there will be two power plugs for the motherboard. Generally, these are labeled P8 and P9, although a few manufacturers have deviated from that standard.

The larger of the component feeds, the one with two of the corners beveled, is called the *Molex*, after the manufacturer that developed it. These are the plugs you will use for hard drives, CD-ROMs, and other devices you install in your machine that draw their power from the power supply. **Figure 4.7** illustrates the voltages your multimeter should read were you to take a reading from the Molex. If that voltage varies by more than 10 percent, it is time to consider buying a new power supply.

There will also be a smaller plug called a *miniconnector* (sometimes there are two). The voltages of the conductors are the same as with the Molex. These smaller plugs power the floppy drives.

Coming off the power supply are two other connectors with six conductors each. These are the P8 and P9 mentioned earlier. Once again, keep in mind that some manufacturers have used their own numbering system. These plug into the power connector on the motherboard, and on AT-style

BUZZ WORDS

Molex: The larger four-pin connector coming off a power supply that delivers current to devices such as CD-ROM drives or hard drives. Technically speaking, it is the name of the company that invented the plug.

Miniconnector: A smaller four-pin connector coming off a power supply that delivers current to devices such as floppy disk drives.

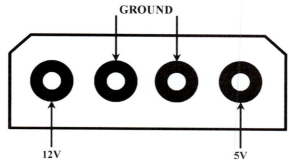

Figure 4.7 Current carried by the connectors of a Molex plug.

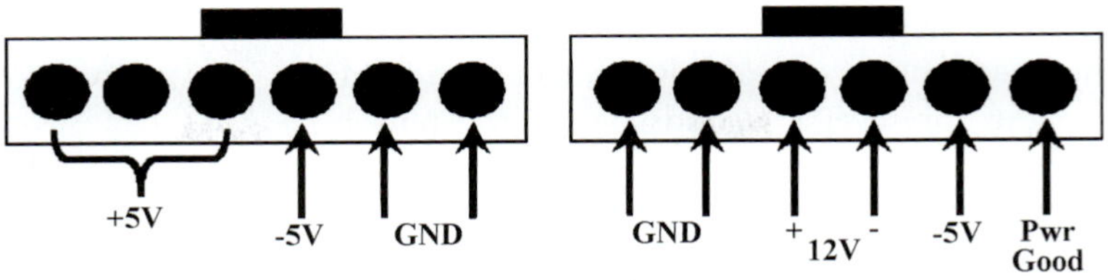

Figure 4.8   Voltage levels of conductors on the motherboard power supply cables of an AT power supply.

systems it is critical that these be plugged in correctly. The conductors carrying voltage will be brightly colored, usually shades of red, yellow, and orange. The ground cables will be black. The black ground cables must go on the inside as the connectors line up in the socket. Reversing power and ground will destroy the motherboard. **Figure 4.8** outlines the voltages coming from each conductor.

AT-style power supplies are hard-switched. By that, I mean that the on-off button on your computer case is directly coupled to the power supply. When you switch the computer on or off, you are directly interfacing with the power supply. There are three different methods that manufacturers use to provide an interface for the user. Some have a rocker switch installed directly on the power supply. It is located on the back facing of the power supply and the user turns the system on and off by reaching to the back of the machine.

This is not the most convenient approach in the world to take, and most manufacturers have moved the switch to the front of the case. On the majority of these, there is a pigtail that comes off the power supply with the switch attached to the end. This reaches around to the front of the case and couples to a button. Others keep the switch on the case and have a plastic extension arm that reaches from the button to the power supply. You see these on desktops for the most part. That particular design isn't terribly efficient to begin with and is very difficult to configure into a tower model. If you ever find yourself in the position of having to replace an AT power supply, make sure you know which type of switch you need. Otherwise, you'll be making another trip back to the store.

ATX and SFX

Electrically, these two form factors are very similar. The primary difference is in size. The ATX is for full-size towers, midtowers, and desktops, while the SFX was designed for the micro-ATX cases. SFX cases are physically smaller and generally use power supplies that deliver lower wattages.

ATX power supplies differ from AT in several respects. A significant change is that the ATX power supply supports soft switching. By this, I mean that the power switch from your case connects to the motherboard where logic circuitry handles power functions. When you turn your ATX machine off, one of two things will happen, depending on how the BIOS is configured.

If soft power is selected in the CMOS (See Chapter Six, Motherboards, BIOS, and the Chipset), the machine will not turn off simply by your pressing the button. This prevents an inadvertent switch-off in the middle of an application. In order to turn the power supply completely off, you must hold the power button in for several seconds before the power supply will switch off.

Operating systems such as Windows 9x and later take advantage of this soft power switching. When you select Shut Down from the Start menu, and then select Shut Down, your computer appears to turn off. What you really did was put it to sleep. A minimal supply of current keeps the CPU, RAM and BIOS operational.

Power management settings, both in the BIOS and in the operating system, also make use of soft power logic to control the shutdown functions of various components. Different time settings can be selected for different components, like the monitor or the hard drive, and when that amount of time has elapsed, the device turns off. However, the CPU and RAM stay active and your program will be right where you left it when you come back and reactivate your machine (usually, anyway).

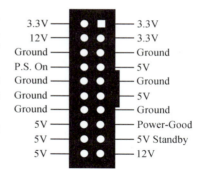

Figure 4.9 Voltage levels of conductors on the motherboard power supply cables of an ATX power supply.

Another big difference is in how the power supply hooks up to the motherboard. ATX and SFX power supplies have added +3.3V to the voltage options, and also require additional circuitry to support the soft power options. When Intel designed the ATX power supply, it also wanted to eliminate the human-error factor of feeding power to the motherboard. It replaced the P8 and P9 with a single 20-pin connector (**Figure 4.9**), which is keyed in such a fashion that it can only plug in one way.

TROUBLESHOOTING POWER SUPPLIES

Depending on how exacting you want to be, troubleshooting power supplies can either be the most difficult part of your job, or the easiest. Power supplies are like people in one respect. When they die, it's either a sudden death, or a long, drawn-out ordeal. Unfortunately, with power supplies, if it's the latter type of death, it can be a real pain to diagnose.

Many of the books I've read tell you to test a power supply by checking output voltage with a multimeter. If the voltage is plus or minus 10 percent of rated voltage, the power supply is good. I'm going out on a limb and arguing with that technique. If a power supply constantly provides output that deviates that far from the norm, it's safe to assume the power supply is dead.

The problem I see with the plus or minus 10 percent theory is that if the power supply is already that far gone, your machine is already not working and it's pretty easy to see that the power supply is the culprit. For the other 299 machines, it won't be that easy. Power supplies usually die slowly.

When this happens, output voltage will be fine 99.99999 percent of the time, and then for a few milliseconds deliver either a massive spike or a big sag. Either deviation is equally harmful. A severe spike can damage ICs on the motherboard or even drives that are plugged into it. A sag can cause memory to lose its charge, resulting in all of your RAM dumping its contents. This can result in program crashes or blue screens.

Generally if you have a machine that's been working great up until recently, and is now starting to hang a lot—or if the machine has suddenly started blue-screening on you in Windows, these may be symptoms of a failing power supply.

Blue screens are a lot more informative than many people imagine. Every time it happens, the screen provides a memory address at which the "exception" occurred, along with which CPU register was in use at the time. Any time a machine is starting to blue-screen a lot, start recording those addresses. It makes a great troubleshooting tool. I will bring this up again a couple of times in this book.

A failing power supply will generally deliver random addresses. CPU registers will rarely be the same, although since there are a lot fewer of those than there are memory addresses, you're bound to see some duplication. If it's never the same program running when the system fails, and never the same addresses, that is a strong indication of a power supply problem.

On AT power supplies, another indication of a failing power supply appears when turning the machine on for the first time in a day. If the machine routinely hangs during the POST process, but then after you turn it off and back on again, it boots fine, that's a symptom of a failing power supply. What is happening is that the capacitors in the power supply aren't charging fast enough, and a critical component in the system isn't powering up in time for POST. On the second attempt, there is more juice in the capacitors and the machine boots fine.

In theory, this isn't supposed to happen. One of the leads on the connectors powering the motherboard is the power good (PG) circuit. When the power supply is up and running, it sends a signal down the PG wire telling the motherboard that it is now okay to start the boot process. A failing power supply may start sending a PG signal before the power supply capacitors are fully charged.

The problem with failing power supplies is that they mimic the problems of other components, such as failing RAM or a bad CPU. All too often, a technician replaces the RAM, then the CPU, and then the motherboard, only to find out it was the power supply all along. I've made it a habit of keeping an AT and an ATX power supply on hand and trying that first any time my diagnostics software can't pinpoint an exact reason for the system to be malfunctioning. Pop in a new power supply and try it for a few hours. See if the problem goes away.

CHAPTER SUMMARY

The computer hardware technician doesn't need to store an encyclopedia of knowledge about electricity in his or her head. However, there are three good reasons for having a good understanding of how electricity works. First off, you need that knowledge to pass the A+ Exam. Second, that knowledge can help you troubleshoot problems that occur with computer systems. And finally—although there are some people who might consider this to be the primary reason—understanding electricity can keep you alive.

Power supplies were discussed in this chapter because they are the component that provides electrical current to all the devices in your computer. They can be very entertaining to try and troubleshoot and all but impossible to fix when they break. So if they do, just toss the old one and install a new one.

BRAIN DRAIN

1. Discuss the three primary measurements of electricity covered in this chapter and how they relate to one another.

2. Open a computer and find the following devices on the motherboard: a capacitor, a resistor, and a coil.

3. Discuss why those three components would be needed by a motherboard.

4. Jot down the color pattern you find on one of the resistors and use the chart found earlier in this chapter to calculate its value.

5. Talk about why a power supply can be such a problem to troubleshoot when it fails slowly.

THE 64K$ QUESTIONS

1. Which of the following devices is used to reduce the amount of amperage on a circuit?
   a. A capacitor
   b. A diode
   c. A resistor
   d. An MOV

2. Which two of the following are critical components in converting AC current to DC current?
   a. A capacitor
   b. A resistor
   c. An MOV
   d. A coil

3. Which of the following devices would be measured in microfarads?
   a. A capacitor
   b. A resistor

   c. An MOV
   d. A coil

4. Which of the following components would be measured in ohms?
   a. A capacitor
   b. A resistor
   c. An MOV
   d. A coil

5. What device will keep an individual computer running for a few minutes after a total power failure?
   a. A surge suppressor
   b. A line conditioner
   c. A standby power supply
   d. An uninterrupted power supply

6. Which of the following devices can keep an entire room operational during a total power failure?
   a. A surge suppressor
   b. A line conditioner
   c. A standby power supply
   d. An uninterrupted power supply

7. Power is provided to the motherboard from an AT power supply by way of _____.
   a. A single 20-pin connector
   b. A pair of 8-pin connectors
   c. A pair of 6-pin connectors
   d. A single 24-pin connector

8. One feature supported by ATX power supplies that was not supported by AT power supplies was _____.
   a. The power good signal
   b. Soft-switching
   c. Built-in surge suppression
   d. Self-diagnostics circuitry

9. Which of the following could be signs of a failing power supply?

    a. Reported memory errors

    b. Intermittent "blue screens of death"

    c. Intermittent and unexpected reboots

    d. All of the above

10. It is critical that you wear your wrist strap at all times when working on a power supply.

    a. True

    b. False

TRICKY TERMINOLOGY

Alternating current: An electrical current that reverses the direction of current flow many times each second.

Blackout: A complete loss of power to an entire area.

Brownout: A drop in voltages that lasts a noticeable period of time.

Capacitor: An electrical component that stores electrical current and provides it to the circuit as needed.

Coil: An electrical component consisting of tightly wound wire that is used to filter out AC current and low-frequency signals.

Conductor: Any substance that encourages the flow of electricity. Also the man at the podium that waves a white stick in front of the musicians.

Current: The number of electrons that flow through a circuit in a fixed amount of time.

Diode: An electrical component that freely permits the flow of electrons in one direction, but resists electron flow in the opposite direction.

Direct current: An electrical current that exhibits a steady directional flow from a source of relative positive voltage to a target of relative negative voltage.

Farad: The major measurement of a capacitor's ability to store energy.

Fuse: An electrical component that consists of a filament that vaporizes when more than a certain amount of current tries to pass.

Insulator: Any substance that tends to resist the flow of electricity.

Inverter: A device or circuit that converts DC current to AC current.

Line conditioner: A device that is able to filter out transient noise, such as EMI, from the current.

Microfarad: The minor measurement of a capacitor's ability to store energy.

Miniconnector: A smaller four-pin connector coming off a power supply that delivers current to devices such as floppy disk drives.

Molex: The larger four-pin connector coming off a power supply that delivers current to devices such as CD-ROM drives or hard drives. Technically speaking, it is the name of the company that invented the plug.

Plenum: An architectural term referring to the space between the ceiling of one floor in a building and the floor of the one above it.

Polarity: The characteristic of an electrical circuit to have one point of relative positive charge (or pole) and another point of relative negative charge (or pole).

Rectifier circuit: A specialized series of components that converts AC current to DC current.

Resistance: The tendency for a substance to block the flow of electrons.

Resistor: An electrical component that restricts the flow of current by a precisely measured amount.

Sag: A sudden transient decrease in voltage.

Spike: A sudden transient increase in voltage.

Standby power supply: A device that uses a generator to provide electrical current to a room or building in the event of a total power failure.

Surge suppressor: A device that is able to filter out voltage surges and prevent them from reaching the devices plugged into its outlets.

Uninterruptible power supply: A device that uses batteries to provide electrical current to another device in the event of a total power failure.

Voltage: The difference in charge between two objects or surfaces. This is sometimes referred to as electrical pressure.

ACRONYM ALERT

AC: Alternating Current. Current that reverses direction many times in a second.

DC: Direct Current. A unidirectional current that flows from the positive side of the circuit to the negative side.

MOV: Metal Oxide Varistor. An electrical component that can absorb abrupt spikes in current.

SPS: Standby Power Supply. A device that uses a generator to continue to provide power to an entire room or building after a total loss of electricity.

UPS: Uninterruptible Power Supply. A device that uses a bank of batteries to continue to provide current to the devices plugged in when there has been a total loss of electricity.

CHAPTER 5

COMPUTER ENCLOSURES

Okay, you've made the decision. You're going to build your own computer from the ground up. You've put together a list of components and you're ready to go shopping. The biggest problem you face is budget. You want to build the ultimate power station, but your pocketbook has other ideas. All too often, the first component that designers look to in order to shave a few bucks off the bottom line is the enclosure.

For a low-end machine that will never do much more that format a few letters to Mom and spend a couple of hours a day browsing the Internet, an inexpensive case might just be the solution. Conversely, a system being designed with the idea of future expansion in mind will suffer greatly from an inferior case. As this chapter unfolds, I'm going to make the case (sick pun intended) that the enclosure (**Figure 5.1**) should really be the first component you decide upon when designing a system.

The enclosure truly needs to follow the concept of "form follows function." Computer cases perform several functions. First and foremost, they house the components that make up your system. But their job doesn't end there. They also do all of the following:

- Act as the interface between the system and peripherals
- House the power supply that keeps your system fed with energy
- Direct the flow of fresh air over internal components
- Provide user access to all internal components
- Provide adequate space for future expansion
- Reflect the designer's aesthetic taste

That's a load of responsibility to place on the component you are most likely to try and skimp on, isn't it? A good understanding of how computer enclosures are designed can go a long

Figure 5.1 The computer enclosure isn't just another pretty face. This important component has several key functions to perform.

way in helping you make an informed decision. There is really only one stated CompTIA exam objective that is touched on in this chapter. Despite that, there are a few issues I'll point out as the chapter unfolds.

A+ CORE HARDWARE EXAM OBJECTIVES

There is only one CompTIA exam objective introduced in this chapter:

1.1   Identify the names, purpose, and characteristics of system modules. Recognize these modules by sight or definition.

FORM FACTOR

Form factor is a term that defines the physical layout of a specific component. Form factor is not the exclusive domain of the enclosure. The motherboard and computer enclosure must share the same form factor or they won't work together. Aspects of form factor that the motherboard and enclosure must agree upon include:

> **BUZZ WORDS**
>
> **Form factor:** Preset design specifications regarding size, orientation of components, and screw positions that allow different manufacturers' motherboards to fit into other manufacturers' enclosures.

- Physical size and logical orientation of motherboard within the enclosure
- Physical and electrical design of the interface between the power supply and the motherboard
- Interface between the power switch and system board (or power supply, in the case of older designs)
- Size and shape of the circuit board used to manufacture the motherboard
- Positioning of screw holes used to position the motherboard (and other components)
- Positioning of externally accessible motherboard components to the enclosure's backplane

There are some aspects of form factor that are the exclusive domain of the enclosure. These features do not affect the choice of motherboard used, beyond the parameters listed above. These include whether the case is a desktop or tower model and which of several relative sizes the case happens to be. The various case sizes and configurations were covered in Chapter Three, The Basic Components.

In the early years of personal computing, there was little or no agreement on any of these issues. Shortly after the release of the IBM PC in 1981, the market was flooded with PC clones from a variety of manufacturers. While there were similarities among the different brands, they weren't similar enough that one manufacturer's motherboard could be used in another's case. Starting with the release of the PC-AT, IBM published standards for other manufacturers to follow, and the AT form factor was born, the first standardized form factor to be adopted by a large number of different manufacturers. Since then, there have been a large number of form factors over the years. Some were more readily accepted by the industry than others. The majority of issues directly related to form factor are more commonly associated with motherboard design than with cases. Therefore a detailed discussion of the different form factors will be reserved for Chapter Six, Motherboards, BIOS, and the Chipset. For now, I will simply list some of the more common form factors, along with a brief description.

- *PC/XT:* Very little consistency or compatibility among manufacturers. Cases large, heavy, and bulky.

- *AT/Baby AT:* IBM defined strict standards for orientation of components of the motherboard, as well as placement for mounting screws. AT defined a 12″ width for the board. Length varied, but averaged around 13″. Baby AT boards were reduced to an 8.5″ width, allowing for smaller cases. Power switches connect directly to the power supply and power to the motherboard is routed through a pair of 6-connector plugs. The only externally accessible port on most AT-style boards is a full-sized 6-pin DIN (short for Deutsches Institut fur Normung) keyboard connector.

- *ATX/Mini ATX:* Overall size varies from manufacturer to manufacturer, but placement of screws is consistent. Motherboards are rotated 90º in relationship to I/O slots. The power switch connects to the motherboard rather than the power supply, and power management is a function of the motherboard. Electricity is fed to the motherboard through a keyed 20-pin connector. A variety of ports are externally accessible, including built-in serial and parallel ports, onboard sound, and, in many cases, onboard video.

- *LPX/Mini LPX:* LPX is an acronym for Low-Profile Extended. In order to reduce space, expansion slots are taken off the motherboard. Instead, a single slot exists on the motherboard onto which a riser card is installed. This riser card holds the expansion slots and cards are installed parallel to the motherboard. As with ATX, a variety of common ports are built onto the board and are externally accessible. Power switching and feed to the motherboard were frequently proprietary designs, and there was little compatibility among manufacturers.

- *NLX/Mini NLX:* This is short for New Low-Profile Extended. This form factor is an evolution of LPX. Intel has attempted to standardize a form factor based on the concept of the riser.

- *ITX:* If it's an acronym, VIA, the company that developed the form factor, isn't telling us what it means. It's a computer in a shoebox. All system components fit into a very small enclosure. Most system components, including sound, video, modems, NIC, the CPU, and many others, are soldered right onto the system board

EXAM NOTE: While CompTIA includes form factor as an objective covered in the Motherboard domain, it should be clear by now that form factor is not exclusive to motherboards. There are questions in the database that relate to the form factor of enclosures as well.

STRUCTURE OF THE ENCLOSURE

While the structure of a computer case can vary widely among manufacturers and among form factors, there are certain necessary commonalities. For the purposes of this discussion, I'll be looking at a typical ATX midtower enclosure.

THE FRAME

The key to making a cheap computer case is making a cheap *frame* (**Figure 5.2**). By using thinner-gauge substrate material and streamlining the manufacturing process, manufacturers can shave quite a few dollars off the bottom line. What kind of impact does this have on the final product? Nothing is lost in terms of overall system performance. Therefore, cheap cases make for improved cost/performance ratios. These shortcuts lead to other types of problems later on down the road, however.

There are two metals commonly used to manufacture computer cases these days. For years, steel has been the material of choice. In recent years there has been a surge in the popularity of cases made of aluminum. Both materials have their advantages and their disadvantages.

Plain old steel is substantially less expensive than aluminum. It is also easier to shape, drill, and cut. One quality of steel that should be carefully considered in some situations is that it is far more efficient than aluminum in blocking EMI (see Chapter Four, Basic Electricity and the Power Supply). On the downside, steel cases are heavier and, well, face it, they're just plain ugly! Steel cases are generally resplendent in fancy plastic faceplates and paint jobs that completely

BUZZ WORDS

Frame: The metal skeleton that provides the primary support for a computer enclosure.

Figure 5.2   With the varnish and plastic veneer stripped away, the enclosure frame is a one-piece metal bracket for holding the rest of the system together.

conceal the frame itself. In general, the sheet metal used in manufacturing steel cases is measured in thickness. The term used is *gauge*. When measuring gauge, smaller numbers mean thicker steel. For example, 14-gauge is thicker than 18-gauge.

Now, a nice brushed aluminum enclosure needs no cosmetic embellishments. Elegant—almost stately—appearance is combined with lighter weight for an appeal that's hard to resist. Add to that the fact that aluminum dissipates heat much more efficiently than steel, and it becomes a natural material for today's multi-gigahertz systems equipped with tons of peripherals. The downside is primarily cost. Aluminum is much more expensive than steel. To offset some of this cost differential, many manufacturers create shortcuts in their manufacturing process.

CASE COVERS

The actual covers that allow access to the interior of a computer enclosure, such as the one in **Figure 5.3**, tend to draw as much attention as any other feature. There are good reasons for that. They're like the front door to your house. A beautifully designed entrance with elegance in both form and function draws positive comments. If someone trips over a jutting transom and breaks an arm, the comments tend to run to the contrary.

Different styles of enclosures require different approaches to opening them. Manufacturers frequently like to camouflage cover screws or access latches. They think that somehow these relatively important components of a computer case detract from the design, and they go to great lengths to hide them.

I was once working on a rack-mount server that completely baffled me. There were no apparent screws to hold the cover on anywhere to be seen. On the surface of the top cover was a series of wide V shapes that appeared to be pointing to the back panel of the system. After puzzling over this enclosure for far more time than it deserved, I brought in a couple of my coworkers to see if they had serviced this particular model. It was brand new and they hadn't seen it yet either. Neither one of them had any better luck than I had.

We finally swallowed our pride and called tech support for that particular manufacturer. We were directed to two panels on the front of the case. They had to be pried off with a flat-blade screwdriver. When removed, they revealed two screws. Once these screws were removed, the top panel slid forward. The V shapes on the top panel meant nothing. They were only there for aesthetic reasons. (And to confuse technicians!) Once the panel was removed, taped to the inside of the top panel were instructions on how to open the case!

Fortunately, most enclosures will follow one of the following standardized designs. Some of them require the correct screwdriver for the job while others are "tool-free."

The U-shaped (**Figure 5.4**) design can be found in both desktop and tower models. It consists of a single cover for the top

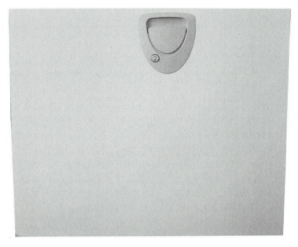

Figure 5.3 This cover from an Antec case illustrates beautiful execution of both form and function. A single latch holds it in place. Opening the case is simply a matter of lifting up on the handle, but the hinged mechanism makes sure the fit is smooth and secure.

and both sides. On either the front or the back of the cover will be a lip that wraps around the frame. Designers frequently incorporate some form of tongue-in-groove mechanism to assure that the cover securely fits over the frame. If you don't get these properly aligned, the cover will not fit over the frame. Generally, if the case screws fit onto the back of the case, they will be in plain sight. Front-mounted covers hide the screws behind the faceplate, so it must be removed prior to removing the cover.

Some of the more proprietary designs (especially the older LPX and some current NLX cases) rely on a complex tongue-in-groove fit with only a single screw holding the cover in place. Then the manufacturer hides the screw. Once again, if the screw is on the back, it will usually be in plain sight. Front-mounted screws might be behind a removable faceplate, but don't count on it. If there doesn't appear to be any logical method of removing the faceplate, start looking for small panels on the front cover.

The majority of current enclosures utilize side panels as covers. Some provide access only to the top surface of the system board. This is generally adequate as long as drive bays are removable (more on that later). Others have both left and right side panels.

Figure 5.4 The U-shaped cover is gradually giving way to single access panels. Still, there are a number of manufacturers that use this design for both desktop and tower models.

A NOTE ON SELECTING ENCLOSURES

Several enclosure manufacturers have lately been cashing in on the newest fad that entails putting a computer into a "custom" case. Of course, since their cookie cutters are stamping out several hundred copies of each so-called custom enclosure each day, it doesn't really seem right to call them custom, does it? Before shelling out two to three times as much for one of these computer cases as you would for a more conventional design, there are a couple of things to consider. Cost is obviously one of them. If your pocketbook is deep enough that you can afford to spend that much money just for cosmetics, that won't be an issue. One thing that is definitely an issue, however, is the ability of some of these cases to block EMI. Many of them include little windows so you can peek in and see the lovely components that make up the computer. They even include colorful cables, lighted fans, and case lights to add to the effect. These windows don't just let light pass. They are also a gateway for EMI. Your computer becomes a source of EMI that can affect other computers in the area as well as other electronic components such as television sets and radios. The lights themselves emit a certain amount of EMI, although probably not enough to affect the system, but they also add more heat to the inside of the enclosure that must be dissipated.

These panels will either be affixed with screws or by one of several tool-free designs. Some manufacturers use thumbscrews that, as long as they aren't tightened down too aggressively, can be removed without a screwdriver. With other designs, you never know from model to model whether you need a flathead screwdriver, a Torx, or a Phillips.

The more pleasant enclosures to work with are the tool-free designs. A single latch, or in some U-shaped designs, a latch on either side, holds the cover in place. Release the latch and lift the cover off.

TEMPERATURE CONTROL

Today's high-performance components generate much more heat than did the computers of yesteryear. In the old days, a single fan in the power supply and some strategically located ventilation holes were all that was needed to keep a computer running cool. These days computers need much more. The enclosure used for **Figure 5.5** comes standard with two case fans and has room to install two more.

The power supply fan continues to be a key component in temperature regulation. But it needs a lot of help. Nearly all CPUs these days must be equipped with an appropriate heat sink/fan combination. The more recent releases of chipsets have started running so hot that they are coming equipped with heat sinks as well. High-end video cards also now need heat sinks and fans to keep them running cool.

All that heat has to go somewhere. A decent case will come with at least one auxiliary case fan to supplement the power supply fan. The case fan blows cool air in and the power supply fan evacuates hot air. Some models of enclosure allow up to six fans, or even more, to be added as options.

Two other features of case design that were not simply added to make the case prettier are the ventilation holes (**Figure 5.6**) and the backplane fillers (**Figure 5.7**). The ventilation holes generally are designed to work with the case fan to provide more efficient heat dissipation than the power supply fan alone can provide. Backplane fillers make sure air follows the path the designers intended it to follow. When you remove an expansion card from your computer, make sure you install a filler to cover the empty slot opening. Otherwise air

Figure 5.5 Modern enclosures generally provide at least one case fan to supplement the fan in the power supply. This particular case ships with two fans installed and has room for two more.

Figure 5.6 Ventilation holes are not simply there to add aesthetic appeal. This is where cool air can get sucked into the interior of the case. This example, shown with the front panel removed, shows how these holes can serve double duty. I don't know if the detail will survive reproduction, but in the original image, you can see that the PC speaker projects its sound through these same holes.

from the case fan may simply exit through the backplane without ever passing over critical components, such as CPUs and chipsets. This defeats the purpose of having the extra case fan to begin with.

DRIVE BAYS

Every enclosure sold comes with a certain number of spaces designed for the installation of additional devices (usually disk drives of some sort). These are the *drive bays.* Drive bays come in two forms: accessible and hidden. Another set of terms frequently used is internal and external drive bays. They also come in two sizes: $3^1/2''$ and $5^1/4''$. With most modern enclosures it is safe to say that all $5^1/4''$ drive bays are externally accessible. There will generally be at least one $3^1/2''$ bay that is accessible as well as one or more $3^1/2''$ drive bays that are hidden.

The $5^1/4''$ drive bays found in conventional computer cases are referred to as *half-height* drive bays. A half-height bay is 1.62'' in height. $3^1/2''$ drive bays are nearly always 1'' high. **Figure 5.8** clearly shows the difference in size. The term half-height is a throwback to the early years of computing technology when a hard disk drive was 8'' wide × $3^1/2''$ high.

Figure 5.7 The function of the backplane filler is to keep dust out and to regulate airflow within the enclosure. If for any reason you remove an expansion card, make sure that you insert a new filler.

BUZZ WORDS

Drive bay: A metal frame within a computer enclosure (that may or may not be removable) that supports disk drives.

Full–height bay: A term that describes a disk drive that is $3^1/2''$ from top to bottom.

Half–height bay: A term that describes a disk drive that is 1.62'' from top to bottom.

Figure 5.8 Here is a half-height drive seen side by side with a 1″ high drive. There are still some tape drives on the market that are full-height. These drives take up two of your 5¹/₄″ bays.

Sometimes you might run into a situation where all available 3¹/₂″ accessible drive bays are filled and you have just acquired a new device that needs to be installed. Don't panic. There are step-down adapters that securely fit 3¹/₂″ drives into 5¹/₄″ bays. Some device manufacturers are even kind enough to provide one with the new drive. If not, they're generally available for around five dollars at most computer stores. Another thing to look for is removable hard drive bays. Fixed bays, such as the ones seen in **Figure 5.9**, make it very difficult to swap and/or install new drives.

Some server models incorporate hot-swappable drive bays. A *hot-swappable* bay will be an externally accessible 5¹/₄″ drive bay that is specially designed to allow a disk drive to be removed while the computer continues to run. The drives themselves must be mounted in a hot-swap frame to accommodate the enclosure's drive bay. This type of drive bay can add considerable cost to the case. But for a server designed to run 24/7 they are an essential addition.

Drive rails are frequently incorporated into the drive cage structure as a replacement for screws to hold drives in place. Drive rails are available in two different incarnations. There are those whose rail guides simply snap into place on the sides of the drive and those that need to be screwed on. Once the rail guides are in place, you simply line the guides up to the rails and slide the drive in until it snaps into place.

I say "simply," but this is an area where the concept of fit really comes into play. If alignment between the rails and the guides is even the tiniest fraction of an inch off, properly mounting the drive becomes a chore. This is rarely a problem with the major manufacturers, but can become an issue when price is the overall design parameter.

> **BUZZ WORDS**
>
> **Hot swap:** The ability to replace or remove a device from a computer system without having to shut the system down.
>
> **Drive rails:** Devices that attach to the side of a disk drive that allow the user to install or subsequently remove it without needing any tools.

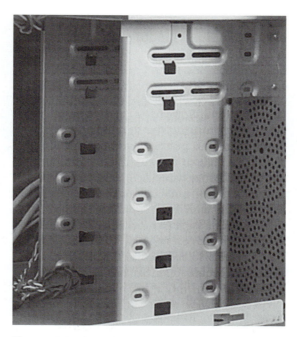

Figure 5.9 The number of drive bays in this enclosure allows for a great deal of expansion. However, the fact that all drive bays are fixed, increases the complexity and difficulty of mounting a new device.

NAVIGATING THE FRONT PANEL

The front of most enclosures will be adorned with buttons and lights. Some manufacturers prefer to keep it simple, like the one in **Figure 5.10**, while others seem to be competing with your neighbors for the annual Christmas display award.

There will generally be two switches on the front of your case. Some older enclosures feature a third. The two main ones are Power and Reset. Power, as its name implies, provides the means for turning your computer on and off. Reset provides the means for restarting your computer when it locks up.

The third button occasionally seen on older computers is the Turbo button. This may well be the most inappropriately named component in computer history. On those computers where it performs any function at all, its function is to slow the speed of the CPU down to 8MHz. Some earlier software, especially games, was designed with a specific CPU in mind. A faster machine made your game run too fast. Once you pressed Start, before you could even react, your car, or your spaceship, or whatever, had already crashed at the other end of the course. So the Turbo button was really a brake pedal. These days, algorithms within the software automatically detect system speed and make the appropriate adjustments. This button has disappeared from most machines.

Figure 5.10   The front panel of most enclosures is designed with simplicity in mind.

Figure 5.11   This particular enclosure sports sound ports and USB ports accessible from the front, but hidden by a flip-down door when not in use.

At a minimum, your enclosure will have two LEDs on the front of the case. One is the power indicator and the other is the hard drive activity light. Properly hooked up, the power indicator provides a steady glow whenever power is applied to the machine. The hard drive activity light flickers whenever the hard disk is active. Wiring them backward does no harm. Simply tell people you have a very erratic power source coming into your house and that your hard drive is always active.

It is becoming more and more common to see other amenities moved to the front of the case for the sake of convenience. In the example shown in **Figure 5.11**, sound and USB ports are accessible from the front.

Another feature found on some, but not all, enclosures is a key lock. When enabled, a key lock allows you to secure your system from casual unauthorized access. When somebody tries to power up a system that is locked, this condition is detected during the boot process and the system won't boot. Before you get lulled into a false sense of security, however, you should be aware that disabling the key lock is simply a matter of unplugging one pair of wires from the motherboard.

THE BACK PANEL

The back panel of a computer is less familiar to many users simply because, well, it's on the back! Whoever looks there except computer technicians? Most of what you see on the back is actually not related directly to the enclosure. The power supply will have one or possibly two switches, and any expansion cards that have external ports can be accessed here. These will be discussed in the appropriate chapters in this book. Before those accessories are added, the back of the case will be very similar to what you see in **Figure 5.12**.

The things that I'll be examining that are related to the enclosure are mostly structural. Different form factors will have different features.

On older PC/XT- and AT-style enclosures, there were punch-outs for DB9 and DB25 connectors. These allowed the more conscientious manufacturer to properly mount the serial and parallel ports on the back panel in a location that was easier for the end user to access. Most manufacturers simply used multi-IO cards, so these punch-outs were rarely used.

ATX, LPX, and NLX motherboards sport all of these peripherals, and usually several others, as integrated features of the circuit board. These protrude through a single rectangular opening on the back of the enclosure. To control airflow, these ports line up to an I/O template that fills this opening.

Expansion cards installed on the motherboard need a slot that allows access to any ports they sport. Along the backplane are a number of removable covers, one for each expansion slot. In order to install an expansion card, you remove the backplane cover for the appropriate slot, mount the card, and screw the backplane of the expansion card into place.

Figure 5.12 Once a computer has been assembled, the back panel can be a fairly complex forest of ports. Before assembly, it's a featureless plane.

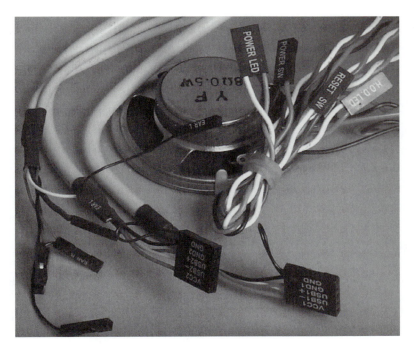

Figure 5.13   The wiring harness of many enclosures can make you think you're trying to manage a pot of boiled spaghetti. Most enclosure manufacturers are kind enough to label each lead. Unfortunately, not all motherboard manufacturers show the same courtesy.

In the old days, these backplane covers were nicely machined and shaped strips of metal that screwed into place when there was no expansion card installed. A recent development in the industry that I find distressing is an increasing propensity to cover unused slots with metal punch-outs. When it comes time to install a new device, the technician must knock out the cover for the chosen slot. Should it become necessary to uninstall that device, the old cover cannot be reused.

THE WIRING HARNESS

Earlier in the chapter, while discussing the front panel, I provided a tour of the various switches and LEDs adorning the front of the computer. For those to properly function, there must be some way of interfacing these devices with the system. That imposing cluster of wires dangling from the inside of the front panel (**Figure 5.13**) is that way.

Usually, the leads to each wire are clearly labeled as to what device they hook up to. At least it is clear as long as you understand the abbreviations that most manufacturers use. The most commonly seen leads include:

- PWR – Power
- RST – Reset
- SPK – Speaker
- TRB – Turbo (when present)
- HDD – Hard drive LED

On the motherboard, there will be wiring pins associated with each of these wires. Usually, these jumpers are labeled with similar abbreviations, so it's pretty easy to tell what wire goes where. Unfortunately, there are manufacturers to this day that give the motherboard informative labels such as J-11, J-12, J-13, and so on and so forth. When you stumble across one of these boards, have the manual ready.

CHAPTER SUMMARY

Hopefully, by now you understand that the computer enclosure is not just another pretty face. It not only has to provide a secure and safe environment for your system components, it has other tasks to perform as well. It must block spurious EMI, provide a path for cool air from the outside to follow across heated components, and provide safe and convenient access to the inside.

When shopping for a new enclosure, you'll find that enclosures range in price from under $20 to well into four digits. There are many reasons for this disparity in price. These include the type and gauge of materials used in the manufacturing process, the size of the enclosure, the number of drives, and the type of drive bays used.

Another key component housed in the enclosure that frequently ships already installed is the power supply. This was discussed in detail in Chapter Four, Basic Electricity and the Power Supply, and I did not feel it was necessary to repeat that material. The point I'm making here is that, if the overall cost of your enclosure includes a power supply, you need to ask a critical question. Is it possible to get the quality of enclosure that is required along with the quality of power supply needed for the price that the manufacturer is asking? Can a $20 case, with a 300W power supply, really be of sufficient quality?

I suppose that all goes back to a key question you should always ask before building your own computer. What is the computer going to be used for? For the Internet surfer who fires up a word processor once every six months, whether he or she needs to or not, very likely the answer will be yes. That person is unlikely to be going in and out of the case a lot, adding drives and experimenting with new toys several times a month. But for a server or a more powerful and/or complex workstation, such as a gaming box or an audio/video workstation, you'll probably want to invest a bit more into this very critical component.

BRAIN DRAIN

1. Discuss why the computer enclosure might be the first decision a designer makes when putting together a new model of computer.

2. What are the critical functions that a computer enclosure must successfully perform?

3. What are the pros and cons of using aluminum versus steel in designing a computer case?

4. Discuss some of the pitfalls of selecting an inferior enclosure.

5. List as many individual components that make up the enclosure as you can think of.

THE 64K$ QUESTIONS

1. Which of the following is a low-profile form factor?
   a. AT
   b. ATX
   c. LBX
   d. Desktop

2. LBX cases differ from ATX cases primarily in that _____.
   a. They use a different connector for motherboard power.
   b. LBX cases use a unique power supply.
   c. LBX cases were only available in desktop designs.
   d. LBX was designed around the concept of a riser that supported all the expansion cards.

3. An advantage of aluminum over steel in enclosure construction is _____. (Choose all that apply.)
   a. Light weight

b. Blocks EMI better
   c. Easier to machine
   d. Dissipates heat better

4. 24-gauge steel is 33 percent thicker than 18-gauge steel.
   a. True
   b. False

5. Failing to replace the backplane filler after removing an expansion card is not a good idea, because _____.
   a. It disrupts air flow inside the case.
   b. It releases more EMI.
   c. It allows dust to get inside the computer case more easily.
   d. All of the above.

6. Internal (hidden) drive bays are almost always _____.
   a. $5^1/4''$ half-height bays.
   b. $3^1/2''$ half-height bays.
   c. $1''$ half-height bays.
   d. $3^1/2''$ 1-inch height bays.

7. Hot-swappable drives are designed to fit into a ____ bay.
   a. $5^1/4''$ half-height
   b. $3^1/2''$ half-height
   c. $1''$ half-height
   d. $3^1/2''$ 1-inch height

8. Which of the following are buttons that can be found on the front of an older AT-style case? (Choose all that apply.)
   a. Power
   b. Voltage Select
   c. Reset
   d. Turbo

9. Which of the following is not likely to be a part of a typical wiring harness found in an enclosure?
   a. PWR

    b. RLL

    c. RST

    d. HDD

10. Which of the following is a good feature of an enclosure?

    a. Stamped metal structure

    b. Removable drive cages

    c. 28-gauge steel frame

    d. tongue-in-groove covers

TRICKY TERMINOLOGY

Drive bay: A metal frame within a computer enclosure (which may or may not be removable) that supports disk drives.

Drive rails: Devices that attach to the side of a disk drive that allow the user to install or subsequently remove it without needing any tools.

Form factor: Preset design specifications regarding size, orientation of components, and screw positions that allow different manufacturers' motherboards to fit into other manufacturers' enclosures.

Frame: The metal skeleton that provides the primary support for a computer enclosure.

Full-height bay: A term that describes a disk drive that is $3^{1}/_{2}''$ from top to bottom.

Gauge: A measurement of the thickness of a substance such as sheet metal or wire. Larger numbers indicate smaller sizes.

Half-height bay: A term that describes a disk drive that is 1.62″ from top to bottom.

Hot swap: The ability to replace or remove a device from a computer system without having to shut the system down.

ACRONYM ALERT

LPX: Low-Profile Extended. A form factor designed to take up a minimum of desktop real estate that puts the expansion slots onto a single riser card that supports the cards parallel to the motherboard. Most LPX designs were proprietary.

NLX: New Low-Profile Extended. An industry-supported form factor that took the concept of the riser card, but established strict standards for development.

CHAPTER 6

MOTHERBOARDS, BIOS, AND THE CHIPSET

The motherboard may well be the most complex device in the entire computer system. Since it controls everything that goes on in the computer, that shouldn't be much of a surprise. Just how complex is it? Take a look at the circuit board itself. It looks like a single thick layer of fiberglass. In reality, a motherboard consists of four to eight layers of substrate. Each of these layers acts as a surface upon which the engineers can apply traces.

Traces are those copper paths that cover the front and the back of the motherboard in pretty geometric patterns. Now examine all the chips, slots, switches, jumpers, sockets, capacitors, resistors, and so on and so forth. All of those have to be interconnected to the components with which they interact. That is the function of those traces. The reality of the situation is that there are far too many traces on a motherboard to apply to a single layer. Therefore, the traces you see on the front and back of a four-layer motherboard constitute approximately half of the total number of traces present on the motherboard. The remainder are applied between the layers.

In Chapter One, PC Basics, I talked about the five primary busses of the computer system. These traces are the physical implementation of those busses on the motherboard. The job of the motherboard is to integrate these five disparate functions into one. Each component of the motherboard is directly soldered to the appropriate traces, at whatever layer they reside, and connected to one (or more) of the five busses. Motherboard manufacturers have some very sophisticated manufacturing processes that they use to make the solder connections. All of the devices that are connected to the computer, either through ports on the back of the PC or through the various connectors on the motherboard, link either directly or indirectly to the motherboard in some fashion. If they didn't, they wouldn't be able to communicate with the rest of the computer.

> **BUZZ WORDS** ————
>
> **Trace:** The fine copper path seen on printed circuit boards that acts as a conductor for a signal.

A+ CORE HARDWARE EXAM OBJECTIVES

There's going to be a lot of material covered on the exam in this chapter, and if you're perusing the objectives lists too superficially, some of them might not strike you as being related to this chapter. In this chapter, I will either introduce or discuss in detail the following objectives:

1.1 Identify the names, purpose, and characteristics of system modules. Recognize these modules by sight or definition.

1.2 Identify basic procedures for adding and removing field-replaceable modules for desktop systems. Given a replacement scenario, choose the appropriate sequences.

1.5 Identify the names, purposes, and performance characteristics of standardized/common peripheral ports, associated cabling, and their connectors. Recognize ports, cabling, and connectors by sight.

1.10 Determine the issues that must be considered when upgrading a PC. In a given scenario, determine when and how to upgrade system components.

2.2 Identify basic troubleshooting procedures and tools, and how to elicit problem symptoms from customers. Justify asking particular questions in a given scenario.

4.3 Identify the most popular types of motherboards, their components and architecture (bus structures and power supplies).

4.4 Identify the purpose of CMOS (Complementary Metal-Oxide Semiconductor) memory, what it contains, and how and when to change its parameters.

AN OVERVIEW OF THE MOTHERBOARD

Take a look at the motherboard shown in **Figure 6.1**. As you can see, this is a complicated device. A computer technician must be able to identify the key components on the board just

Figure 6.1 This motherboard is based on the ATX form factor. One of the ways you can tell is that most of the I/O ports are soldered directly onto the board.

Figure 6.2 The AT-style motherboard differs from the ATX in several aspects. The feature most easily recognized is that the only peripheral directly attached is the keyboard connector.

by sight. In this section, I'll give you the grand tour. The remainder of the chapter will cover some of these components in greater detail.

Throughout this chapter, I'll be pointing out differences between two different styles of motherboard—the AT and the ATX. Later in the chapter, I will provide a complete discussion of the differences between them, but to make sure you're on the right track visually, I suggest that you examine the board in **Figure 6.2** carefully and pick out the differences as the chapter progresses.

CPU Sockets and Slots

The CPU socket or slot dictates the type of CPU that the motherboard supports. Obvious factors, such as the number of pins, represent some of the physical differences, but there are also aspects of the CPU socket that must be considered, such as whether it supports variable voltage configurations.

There are basically two forms of CPU form factor. The most common is the *socket*. Sockets are designed to accommodate the CPUs that have hundreds of pins protruding from their base. There have been a large variety of different sockets developed over the years to accommodate different families of CPUs. **Figure 6.3** illustrates a Socket 7. The Socket 7 is just one of several variations on the zero insertion force (ZIF) socket. Sockets over the years have been released as pin grid array (PGA) and staggered pin grid array (SPGA). Other terms you will see include low insertion force (LIF) and very low insertion force (VLIF). These are merely variations on the ZIF.

Buzz Words

Socket: A mounting assembly designed to support pin-mounted devices.

Slot: A mounting assembly designed to support edge card-mounted devices.

Figure 6.4 is the *slot* into which a Single Edge Contact Cartridge (SECC), or slot-mounted CPU would be mounted. Slot-mounted CPUs are built around an edge card design and mount accordingly. While the SECC is falling out of favor, there are still a lot of computers in the field today that use this form factor.

Exam Note: While it is highly unlikely the A+ exam will go into extensive detail about processor sockets and slots, you are expected to be able to identify each type. This may be done with an accompanying diagram of a motherboard.

Figure 6.3 The ZIF socket is one of the most common CPU sockets in use today, although there are a wide variety of forms it will take.

Figure 6.4 CPU slots are easily recognized by the large number of pins and sockets that need to be properly aligned. There are generally two large retaining clips that need to be installed before the CPU can be mounted. In this illustration, those clips are in place.

As I will cover in greater detail in Chapter Eight, The Evolution and Development of the CPU, different brands of CPUs, and even different models by the same manufacturer, use different voltages and run at different speeds. Some sockets are designed to work with an onboard voltage identifier, voltage regulator module (VID VRM), while some earlier styles of socket were either fixed voltage or made use of DIP switches or jumpers to allow the user to manually set voltage. **Table 6.1** is a detailed list of different slots that have been released since the days of the 486 processor.

Memory Slots

The three memory slots visible in **Figure 6.5** are 168-pin Dual Inline Memory Module (DIMM) slots. Chapter Nine, Searching Your Memory, has a detailed discussion on different memory packages that have been used over the years. As of now, the popular favorite is the DIMM. Another form that is appearing on a vast number of newer motherboards is the 184-pin DIMM.

Table 6.1 CPU Sockets and Slots, Past, Present, and Future

Socket/slot	# Pins	Voltage	Multiplier variations	CPUs supported
486 Socket	168	5v	1.0x, 2.0x, 3.0x	80486DX, 80486DX2, 80486DX4
Socket 1	169	5v	1.0x, 2.0x,3.0x	80486DX, 80486DX2, 80486DX4, 80486SX
Socket 2	238	5v	1.0x, 2.0x, 3.0x	80486DX, 80486DX2, 80486DX4, 80486SX
Socket 3	237 ZIF	3.3v 5v	1.0x, 2.0x, 3.0x	80486DX, 80486DX2, 80486DX4, 80486SX
Socket 4	273 ZIF	5v	none	Pentium
Socket 5	296 ZIF	STD VR VRE	1.5x, 2.0x	Pentium
Socket 6	235 ZIF	3.3v	2.0x, 3.0x	80486DX4
Socket 7	321 ZIF	Split STD VR VRE VRT	1.5x, 1.75x, 2.0x 2.33x, 2.5x, 2.66x 3.0x, 3.33x, 3.5x 4.0x, 4.5x, 5.0x 5.5x, 6.0x	Pentium, K5, K6, 6x86
Socket 8	387 ZIF	VID VRM (2.1v~3.5v)	2.0x, 2.5x, 3.0x 4.5x, 5.0x, 5.5x 6.0x, 6.5x, 7.0x 7.5x, 8.0x	Pentium Pro
Socket 370	370 ZIF	VID VRM (1.3v~2.1v)	4.5x, 5.0x, 5.5x 6.0x, 6.5x, 7.0x 7.5x, 8.0x	Celeron, Pentium III
Socket 423	423 ZIF	VID VRM	13.0x, 14.0x, 15.0x, 16.0x, 17.0x, 18.0x, 19.0x, 20.0x	Intel P4 Willamette, Northwood, and Celeron Willamette
Socket 478	478 ZIF	VID VRM	15.0x, 16.0x, 17.0x, 18.0x, 19.0x, 20.0x, 22.0x, 24.0x, 25.0x, 26.0x	Intel P4 Willamette, Northwood, Prescott, and Celeron Willamette and Northwood
Socket 603/604	603/602 ZIF	VID VRM	14.0x, 15.0x, 17.0x, 18.0x, 20.0x, 22.0x	Intel Foster, Prestonia, Nocona, Gallatin
Socket 754	754 ZIF	VID VRM	4x, 5x, 6x, 7x	Athlon Clawhammer, San Diego
Socket 940	940 ZIF	VID VRM	Not Available	Opteron, Sledgehammer
PAC418	418 VLIF	VID VRM	5.5x. 6.0x	Intel Merced
PAC611	611 VLIF	VID VRM	4.5X, 5.0X	Intel McKinley, Madison, Deerfield, Montecito, Shavano
Socket A	462	VID VRM (1.3v~2.05v)	6.0x, 6.5x, 7.0x, 7.5x, 8.0x	Athlon, Duron
Slot A	242	VID VRM (1.3v~2.05v)	5.0x, 5.5x, 6.0x, 6.5x , 7.0x, 7.5x, 8.0x	Athlon
Slot 1	242	VID VRM (1.3v~3.3v)	3.5x, 4.0x, 4.5x, 5.0x, 5.5x, 6.0x, 6.5x	Celeron, Pentium Pro, Pentium II, Pentium III
Slot 2	330	VID VRM (1.3v~3.3v)	4.0x, 4.5x, 5.0x, 5.5x, 6.0x	Xeon

An overview of different CPU sockets and slots

That slot is used for a more recent form of memory called Dual Data Rate (DDR) memory. Once again, for a detailed description, refer to Chapter Eight.

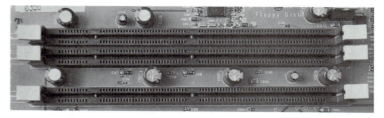

Figure 6.5   168-pin DIMM slots are still seeing a lot of action these days, but they are rapidly giving way to the newer 184-pin variety.

Even though it's been a while since new systems have shipped with them, there are still a number of machines on desktops that use the Single Inline Memory Module (SIMM). As of this writing, replacement boards can still be found that make use of SIMMs.

> **EXAM NOTE:** It is not uncommon for an examinee to be presented with a very crude diagram of a motherboard with arrows pointing to specific devices. The candidate is then asked to identify what motherboard components each arrow points to. It wouldn't be a bad idea to have a motherboard available for examination while you read this chapter.

IDE PORTS

Most motherboards typically have two ports designed for hooking up Integrated Drive Electronics (IDE) devices (**Figure 6.6**). IDE devices come in a variety of forms. Hard drives, CD and CD-RW drives, DVD drives, and tape drives can all be acquired in IDE form. Some newer boards sport four IDE ports. There can be compatibility and configuration issues that arise when trying to make all four ports work, so the majority of manufacturers keep it simple. They only give you two. Chapter Thirteen, Hard Disk Drive Structure and Geometry, will cover this matter in detail.

As I mentioned in Chapter Three, The Basic Components, these are not controllers. They are merely an interface. As the term Integrated Drive Electronics implies, on an IDE device, the electronics that control the device are imbedded into the device itself. Every IDE drive has its own controller built right in.

THE FLOPPY DRIVE CONTROLLER

Unlike the IDE port, the 34-pin floppy disk connector (it's the smaller of the three ports illustrated in Figure 6.6) is actually the interface

Figure 6.6   Zooming in on the IDE ports of an ATX motherboard, you can see that the IDE ports are directly adjacent to the floppy disk connector.

to a controller circuit. So far, all PC motherboards on the market still support the floppy disk drive. Apple has dropped this device from most of the computers in its Macintosh line. While there has been talk of the PC market following suit, so far the floppy is still alive and well.

Figure 6.7   The motherboard's chipset has more to do with how well the computer functions than the CPU does.

THE CHIPSET

Finding the *chipset* on a motherboard usually isn't too difficult. **Figure 6.7** makes that readily apparent. Recent boards make it even easier because the newer chipsets require protection from thermal overload. Like the CPU, they will be fitted with at least a heat sink, and some manufacturers make cooling fans designed for the chipset. One of the chips is very likely to be labeled with its maximum speed, or it may be covered with a heat sink. You may recall that I mentioned in Chapter Three that the microprocessor has two speeds: its internal processing speed and its front-side bus. The maximum speed of the chipset is the maximum speed at which you can set the front-side bus.

> **BUZZ WORDS**
>
> **Chipset:** A matched set of two (three on some of the older systems) ICs that control critical system functions, including bus speeds, memory types and capacity, and the type of hardware supported by a motherboard.

Modern chipsets consist of two chips, as you can see here. Later in this chapter I'll examine each of the chips and see what its functions are. However, the fact that one of these chips is equipped with its own heat sink tells you one thing. Of the two, it runs at the highest speed.

THE AMR, THE CNR, AND ACR

A slot that has recently begun to appear on inexpensive system boards is the audio-modem riser (AMR). AMR is a specification developed by Intel for packaging the audio functions required by modems together with a chip called a *codec* that converts data back and forth from analog to digital. These are combined on a small board that plugs directly into a computer's motherboard. The term riser refers to the fact that it rises above the motherboard instead of being an embedded circuit. This design means that it doesn't have to be part of the motherboard itself. It can be provided as an optional accessory and not add to the cost of the motherboard when the circuit is not required.

It isn't just modems that benefit from this technology. With AMR design, the slot can now be used for other purposes. The AMR card can also provide the foundation for higher-quality audio solutions such as 3D positional audio and better MIDI music production.

There are a few issues that arise with AMR. One is that if an AMR is installed, it utilizes motherboard resources instead of providing its own. System performance can be degraded by up to 25 percent. Another factor that degrades performance is the amount of noise that an AMR device can generate. Also, the AMR slot reduces the number of available PCI slots by one.

To counter these complaints, Intel released the Communications and Networking Riser (CNR) standard. CNR was designed to incorporate not just audio and modem functions, but could work as a network interface as well. It did not consume a PCI slot. Instead, it "shares" a PCI slot. The system designer can choose to either use the CNR slot or the adjacent PCI slot, but not both. CNR is not backwardly compatible with AMR.

The Audio-Communications Riser (ACR) specifications were developed by a coalition of manufacturers whose members include 3COM, AMD, VIA Technologies, and Lucent Technologies. Like CNR, it defines a form factor and interfaces for a variety of communications and audio subsystem designs. Building on the concept of AMR, ACR expands the riser card definition beyond the limitation of audio and modem to include networking technologies, including broadband capability. But just as with AMR, both CNR and ACR use quite a bit of system resources, and will slow the machine down significantly.

> **BUZZ WORDS**
>
> **Codec:** A coined term derived from two other terms, coder and decoder. A Code C is an IC that has been programmed to convert data from one form to another. An example of this would be a chip that takes analog signals and converts them to digital, and vice versa.

FORM FACTOR

In Chapter Three, The Basic Components, and again in Chapter Five, Computer Enclosures, I introduced the concept and the importance of form factor. Here, I will explore the different form factors as they relate to motherboards and go into a little more detail.

The most common form factor in use today is the ATX, although technicians still run into a number of computers out there that are using the older AT style. Two other styles that you see pop up from time to time are a couple of low-profile form factors known as NLX and WTX. The ones you'll really love are the LPX-based machines, because each individual design is proprietary. Still, there are enough machines out there sitting on people's desktops using LPX that a discussion of the form factor is in order. There are significant differences among these different formats that you'll need to understand.

THE ORIGINAL AT

First off, let it be said that the AT form factor was far from being the first to be used by early computers. IBM's first release was the Personal Computer (PC). Early PC motherboards were large ungainly things that often required huge cases. There were hundreds of chips spread across the surface and making any changes whatsoever required major surgery. The few companies that did spring up to mimic the IBM PC generally came up with their own designs for both case and motherboard. By the time the PC XT was released, there were a lot more companies making IBM-compatible clones. Despite this, there wasn't anything that could really be called a standard. As a result, it would be difficult to come up with anything anyone would agree on as the "PC" or "XT" form factor.

With the release of the IBM PC-AT, IBM made significant improvements to the layout of both the motherboard and the case. The layout used by IBM was embraced by the industry as a new "standard." For many years, virtually every PC manufactured used the AT form factor.

Physically the motherboard didn't shrink that much, if any. However, by changing the location and orientation of the power supply inside the case, the motherboard could be redesigned to allow easier access to the individual components. The original AT form factor was 12″ wide × 13.8″ deep. The "Baby AT" was reduced to 8.5″ × 13″, but kept the orientation and positioning of components the same. Both AT and Baby AT were marketed side by side. Large server cases benefited from the larger size of the AT, allowing for easier access to components.

Most early AT systems did not have onboard serial or parallel connectors, nor did they offer onboard connectors for hard drives. A device called the I/O controller provided all these functions. This controller occupied a single ISA (later moved to PCI) slot. Toward the end of the effective life of the AT design, these functions migrated to the motherboard, but they still did not provide the interconnects for external access. A cable with these connectors, called a dongle, hooked up the motherboard. It snaked around to the backplane of the case, where there was an appropriately shaped opening for the port.

On most AT boards, the only connector that will be accessible from the outside is a full-sized 5-pin DIN connector coming off the back of the board, as you can see in **Figure 6.8**.

Processor and SIMM slots were located on the front of the motherboard for easier access. Unfortunately, this had the adverse affect of interfering with the expansion slots. Full-length cards either had to be installed in slots away from processor or memory, or the card itself must be designed in such a way to fit over them without interfering with the heat sink/fan or the memory chips.

ATX

ATX motherboards integrate many more connectors directly to the board. The keyboard, mouse, serial ports, and parallel ports will almost always be soldered directly to the motherboard. These are called

Figure 6.8 An AT-style motherboard is easily recognized by the fact that the only part of it exposed to the outside world is the 5-pin DIN connector that the keyboard plugs into.

integrated or embedded ports or controllers (see **Figure 6.9**). Most ATX systems today will also have either two or four Universal Serial Bus (USB) ports, and some may include game connectors for sound and joystick devices.

The ATX form factor emerged in 1995, a product of Intel design.

Figure 6.9   The backplane of the ATX motherboard supports a number of I/O ports. Make sure you don't try to cram one of these into an AT-style case. They don't fit very well.

This form factor made several changes, both physically and electrically. Intel incorporated these changes with the goal of reducing overall system size without interfering with access to critical components. ATX was the initial design to take advantage of newer power management technologies. On the physical side ATX made the following changes:

- Orientation of the board was rotated 90°, relative to the AT. Lengthwise, the board extended from the front of the case to the back. The AT design went from right to left. As a result, the drive cages on the case don't block as many key components.

- Standard I/O connectors such as serial, parallel, USB, keyboard, and mouse ports were integrated into the structure of the motherboard. These ports slide through openings specifically designed into the case. Two mini-DIN connectors (PS/2) provide the interface for keyboard and mouse.

- Processor sockets and memory slots were moved from the front to the back. In addition, they were relocated to the right side close to the power supply. Full-length expansion cards can now be used in virtually any slot.

- The old AT had been designed around CPUs that didn't run that hot. They worked by pushing hot air out of the machine. New CPUs needed more efficient thermal control. The fans were turned around and moved cool air from outside into the machine. Fans were relocated to stream air over critical components.

- ATX supports additional peripherals, including network interface cards, video, sound, and even modems by soldering those components directly onto the system board.

The ATX form factor also made several modifications on the electrical side. Some of these changes were made to improve efficiency and safety. Others were made to support advancements in power management techniques. Electrical changes include the following:

- Power connectors from the power supply to the motherboard were changed from two 12-pin plugs to a single 20-pin plug. The 20-pin plug can only plug in one way, preventing a user from inadvertently putting it in backward, which could destroy a motherboard.

- The power supply can deliver 3.3V power to the motherboard, reducing the amount of circuitry required to step 5V down to 3.3V (or lower).

- Soft-power support. Instead of the power switch being purely on or off, a "sleep" mode is provided.

BUZZ WORDS —————————

Riser: A specialized expansion card that supports other expansion devices such as PCI or ISA cards horizontally, parallel to the motherboard, in order to save space.

ATX motherboards come in full-sized ATX and micro-ATX to accommodate different cases. It is important to make sure that the case and motherboard are compatible. Full-sized ATX boards will not fit in micro-ATX cases. With the exception of the very few cases designed to accept both styles, no ATX board can be used in an AT-style case. An ATX motherboard also requires the use of an ATX power supply.

Low-Profile Form Factors

There has always been a demand for computers that fit into tiny spaces. Not everybody needs a gargantuan device that holds hundreds of toys. Schools and corporations, and sometimes regular people like you and me, frequently want something simple and small that can be tucked out of the way. Manufacturers came up with a couple of approaches to this over the years.

The problem with many of the earliest low-profile designs was that they had a tendency to be proprietary. Manufacturers had boards built to their specifications and most were not interchangeable. If you fry one of these boards, you go back to the original manufacturer and pay its price.

LPX   Like the NLX that I will discuss next, LPX computers put expansion slots onto a specialized card called a riser. The *riser* supported the expansion cards horizontally, parallel to the motherboard. Installing or replacing a device could be a lot of fun.

Some computer manufacturers continue to have cases and motherboards that are made to their specifications that would fall under this category. If called upon to service one of these units, be prepared to pay large sums of money for replacement motherboards and risers.

NLX   Like the LPX design, these boards have no expansion slots directly on the board. Instead, there is a riser card that plugs into a dedicated, and usually proprietary, slot on the motherboard. Generally, this design only provides for two or three slots. The design does, however, allow for a very slim case. Because so few cards fit into a low-profile system, there are usually more ports and controllers integrated onto the motherboard than you would typically see on a Baby-AT or ATX system. The majority of low-profile boards integrate, at the very minimum, sound and video. Many include a network interface and/or a modem as well.

EBX and ITX   EBX hasn't seen a lot of success on the market as of this writing, whereas ITX is starting to become quite popular. ITX may or may not be an acronym for something, but if it is, VIA Technologies, the company that developed the form factor, isn't telling us what it means.

Unconfirmed articles have defined it as meaning Integrated Technology Extended. In most respects, ITX is identical to EBX in design philosophy. Cram everything you can onto the board.

All functions, including video, audio, telecom (including broadband), networking, and even SCSI are integrated onto a board that is 215mm × 191mm (that's 8.46″ × 7.52″, if you want to compare it to the other boards I've discussed) in size. The CPU is soldered on some boards, so you select your motherboard based on the CPU you want as well as the features you desire. Other boards, including models offered by VIA, use a Socket 370, so other CPUs that fit in that socket can be used.

WTX A new technology introduced by WTX is the flex slot. A flex slot is a standard PCI slot that happens to allow an expansion card to be twice as thick. Flex cards could be multifunction devices, with multiple ports embedded into the backplane. Such cards would allow for significant expansion without tying up as many precious resources.

WTX specifications provide for motherboards up to 14″ × 16.5″. As you might imagine, this board will not fit in standard cases. Therefore, in addition to providing for motherboard specifications, the WTX advisory committee also defined case and power supply specifications. Because WTX is designed to support more devices, and more robust devices, the board is designed for a somewhat larger power supply. WTX specifies two different power supplies for this standard. The "nominal" power supply is a mere 350W unit with only one fan installed. The second power supply defined is a dual-fan 850W job designed to power major workstations. The power supplies mount on a swing-out panel situated on the side of the case for easy access.

BIOS

A critical component of the motherboard is the Read Only Memory-Basic Input Output Services (ROM BIOS). On most machines, this chip is easily recognized by the fact that it is labeled with the manufacturer's name, the BIOS version, and a copyright date. All of this is important information if you ever find yourself having to break down and call technical support for help.

So what does the BIOS do? A few things, actually. A key function is supplying device support for the CPU. By itself, the CPU is actually pretty stupid. As sophisticated as it is, there are only so many commands it is capable of handling. Most devices have a completely different set of commands that control them. The BIOS contains a collection of very small programs, permanently stored on a read only memory (ROM) chip, which the CPU has been programmed to access on startup. These programs interpret the data coming from other devices and convert it into the commands the CPU can use.

There are also three programs on the BIOS chip that are critical to the functioning of the computer. These are the power on, self-test (POST), the CMOS setup, and the bootstrap loader. Without these programs, you would not be able to start your computer.

The Address Bus and BIOS

Needless to say, the CPU has to be able to find the information stored on the BIOS when it needs it. It does so the same way it addresses any other information in the computer. That is through the address bus. In the chapter on RAM, I'm going to discuss the address bus in much greater detail. So for now, suffice it to say that, in the old days of computers, the maximum amount of memory the 8088 CPU could address was 1MB (1,048,576 bytes). A chunk of that memory was set aside for use by hardware. In the early days of computers when IBM and Microsoft worked together on the first business-class PC, engineers allocated 384K for video memory and hardware. That left 640K of *conventional memory*. These days, the first 640K of memory in any computer system is still called the conventional memory. But in those days, the conventional memory was the only place where programs could run. The way memory was allocated at that time can be seen in **Figure 6.10**. Many early XTs actually had a total of 512K on the system board and let the BIOS fend for itself. These computers read the BIOS instructions directly off the chip.

Regardless of how the PC chooses to access the BIOS during normal operation, the CPU requires its services in order to start the computer. Therefore, it was necessary to standardize the address for the POST program and preprogram the CPU to search for that address as the initial command when it is first turned on.

For the most part, BIOS is stored on a Read Only Memory (ROM) chip. Over the years the form of this chip has changed quite a bit. The first ROM chips had to be manufactured at the factory with the code already burned onto the chip. A later version, called the Programmable ROM (PROM), allowed the chip to be programmed in the field as long as the technician had a programming device called a PROM burner available. Once programmed, the PROM chips assumed their permanent form. One form of PROM that was popular for a long while was the Erasable Programmable ROM (EPROM), which could be erased and then reprogrammed. These were easily recognized because of the foil label that covered a small glass window on the chip. Ultraviolet light was used to erase the data. This was supplanted by the Electronically Erasable Programmable ROM (EEPROM), which could be erased using the PROM burner. Today's computers almost all ship with Flash ROM. Flash ROM can be reprogrammed by the end user using a program that runs from a floppy diskette.

BUZZ WORDS

Conventional memory: The first 640K of any computer system. In the old days of DOS, the only place where programs could run was in conventional memory.

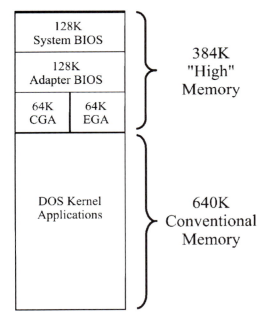

Figure 6.10   The first megabyte of physical memory was originally mapped out to specific functions.

THE PROGRAMS OF **ROM BIOS**

I mentioned earlier that there are three critical programs that run from BIOS. These are programs that, if they can't be run from BIOS, can't be run at all, because they're the ones you need when the computer is not fully functional yet. Here is a look at those programs and what they do.

POWER ON, SELF TEST

POST is the program the CPU first accesses on startup. When the user first applies power to the motherboard, a special wire in the CPU acts as an on/off switch. The CPU is programmed to jump to the address FFFF:FFF0h and run the code it finds there. This is the first line of POST. This program does a diagnostic on the computer and checks to see that everything is in working order. POST signals each device it is programmed to control and waits for a reply. Any device that fails to reply causes POST to generate an error message. Error messages occur either as a series of beeps or, if the video infrastructure has already tested out, a numerical or text message that appears on the screen. Having the chart of beep codes available will assist in diagnosing any problem. The speaker test is performed by sending a signal to it. Therefore on every POST, you will hear a single beep. Any subsequent beeps you hear after that first one can be considered a bad sign. A detailed list of commonly used beep codes can be found in Appendix F.

Once video has been tested and determined to be functional, subsequent errors may or may not be issued in numeric error codes on old computers. Newer computers actually provide a full text message describing the problem, such as "Keyboard not found. Press any Key to Continue." However, there are still plenty of machines out there using numeric codes. Once again, having a chart of these readily available is a good idea for any service bench. Such a chart appears in Appendix F along with the beep codes.

After the hardware tests are completed, POST handles the Plug 'n Play scans. First it does the recognition scan where devices identify themselves as to what IRQs they are capable of running on. Next, the allocation scan doles out resources to PnP capable devices. Any device that cannot identify itself, or be configured by the BIOS, might find itself left out in the cold. I'll be covering that in more detail in Chapter Ten, Examining the Expansion Bus.

CMOS SETUP

Some of the instruction sets loaded into BIOS are fixed. They never change. These would include information concerning the location and type of chipset installed or other support chips that may be present. Serial and parallel ports are controlled by BIOS as well. Their location never changes, although you might change their IRQ or their I/O address. Chapter Ten, Examining the Expansion Bus, will cover that in more detail.

There are other things in the computer that might require changes throughout the life of the system. Details concerning the amount of memory installed or the size and number of hard drives installed will change with the user's needs. That's where the *CMOS setup* (**Figure 6.11**) comes into play.

CMOS stands for Complimentary Metal-Oxide Semiconductor. That actually refers to the kind of chip used to store the information. CMOS chips resemble conventional memory in

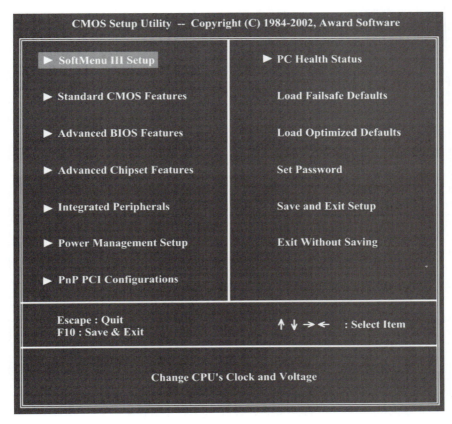

Figure 6.11   Here is the opening screen for an Award BIOS. Refer to this illustration while trying to navigate Table 6.2.

some ways and ROM in others. You can write information to the chip whenever you want without having to completely change all of the information stored within. Also, unlike the BIOS chip, the CMOS requires a constant supply of electrical current. On the motherboard is a battery that provides the current when the machine is turned off. Without this battery, the information you write to the chip would be lost when you shut your computer down. This is what is referred to as *volatile* information. Most, if not all, motherboards also have a capacitance circuit in line with the battery. These little capacitors can provide anywhere from several seconds to a couple of minutes worth of current to the CMOS while you're changing the battery. The idea is to keep your CMOS settings from being erased while you change a battery.

BUZZ WORDS

CMOS setup: One of the programs loaded on the BIOS chip. This particular program allows user-defined parameters relating to BIOS settings to be configured.

Volatile: Unstable or changeable. Requires constant power in order to continue to exist.

Table 6.2

Standard CMOS Setup

Setting	Options	Description
Date	Page Up/Page Down	Changes system date
Time	Page Up/Page Down	Changes system time
Hard Disks/Type	Auto/User/None	Settings for IDE HDD
Hard Disks/Mode	Normal/LBA/Large/Auto	HDD translation method
Drive A	Various settings	Enables/disables floppy A
Drive B	Various settings	Enables/disables floppy B
Video	EGA/VGA, CGA-40, CGA-80, Mono	Establishes type of video used
Halt On	Various options	Stops POST on selected errors

BIOS Features Setup

Setting	Options	Description
Boot Virus Detection	Enabled/Disabled	Warns of any attempt to write to the boot sector
CPU Level 1 Cache	Enabled/Disabled	Enables read/write operations to L1 cache built into CPU
CPU Level 2 Cache	Enabled/Disabled	Enables read/write operations to L2 cache built into CPU
CPU Level 2 Cache ECC Check	Enabled/Disabled	Turns on/off ECC mode
Quick Power On Self Test	Enabled/Disabled	Full Test/Tests only selected system components on cold boot
HDD Sequence	IDE/SCSI	Where to look for MBR
Boot Sequence	Options vary	Determines the order of devices in which POST looks for the MBR
Boot Up Floppy Seek	Enabled/Disabled	Tests floppy drive to see if it has forty or eighty tracks
Floppy Disk Access Control	R/W, Read Only	Security access for floppy drive
HDD Block Mode Sectors	Options vary	

HDD S.M.A.R.T Capability	Enabled/Disabled	IDE SMART capable?
PS2 Mouse Function Control	Enabled/Auto	Looks to PS2 for mouse
OS2 Onboard Memory	Enabled/Disabled	Use OS2 memory mapping
PCI/VGA Palette Snoop	Disabled/Enabled	Allows video adapters to directly access RAM looking for video information
Video ROM/BIOS Shadowing	Enabled/Disabled	Allows copying of BIOS routines to upper memory for enhanced performance
C8000-DFFFF Shadowing	Enabled/Disabled	Allows copying of Supplemental BIOS to specific addresses (multiple entries)
Boot Up NumLock Status	On/Off	Determines whether number lock on keyboard is on or off after system boots
Typomatic Rate Setting	Disabled/Enabled	Disabled turns off Typomatic Rate and Typomatic Delay
Typomatic Rate	Options vary	Sets speed at which characters repeat when a key on the keyboard is held down.
Typomatic Delay	Options vary	Sets time that elapses before keys begin to repeat when a key on the keyboard is held down.
Security Option	System/Setup	Determines where security is controlled

Chipset Features Setup

Setting	Options	Description
EDO Autoconfiguration	Enabled/Disabled	Allows chipset to control EDO timing functions
EDO Read Burst Timing	Options vary	Sets number of clock cycles for Burst Mode read operations
EDO Write Burst Timing	Options vary	Sets number of clock cycles for Burst Mode write operations
EDO RAS Precharge	3T, 4T	Sets number of clock cycles for RAS Precharge
EDO RAS/CAS Delay	2T, 3T	Sets number of clock cycles for RAS/CAS Delay
SDRAM Configuration	Options vary	Sets clock speed of SDRAM
SDRAM RAS Precharge	Auto, 3T, 4T	Sets number of clock cycles for RAS Precharge

Table 6.2 (Continued)

Chipset Features Setup

Setting	Options	Description
SDRAM RAS/CAS Delay	Auto, 3T, 2T	Sets number of clock cycles for RAS/CAS Delay
SDRAM Banks Close Policy	Arbitration, Page-Miss	
Graphics Aperture Size	Options vary	
Video Memory Cache Mode	UC, USWC	Determines how Video Memory addresses cache
PCI 2.1 Support	Enabled/Disabled	Disabled setting drops system back to PCI Version 1.0
Memory Hole at 15M-16M	Enabled/Disabled	Enables/disables use of these memory addresses
Onboard FDC Controller	Enabled/Disabled	Allows you to disable the floppy disk drive
Onboard Floppy Swap A/B	Enabled/Disabled	Switches drives A and B
Onboard Serial Port 1	Various settings/Disabled	Allows reconfiguring or disabling Serial Port 1
Onboard Serial Port 2	Various settings/Disabled	Allows reconfiguring or disabling Serial Port 2
Onboard Parallel Port	Various settings/Disabled	Allows reconfiguring or disabling Parallel Port
Parallel Port Mode	Normal, ECC, ECC/ECP	Sets up parallel communications
ECP DMA Select	Options vary	Sets DMA channel used by ECP Parallel mode
UART2 Use Infrared	Enabled/Disabled	Sets infrared port to UART2
Onboard PCI/IDE Enable	Both, Primary, Secondary, Disabled	Enables/disables IDE ports
IDE DMA Mode	Auto/Disable	Disables, autoselects Direct Memory Access
IDE 0/1 – Master/Slave	Options vary	Sets PIO mode and DMA channel for specific device

Power Management Setup

Setting	Options	Description
Power Management	User Defined, Disabled, Min, Max	Determines PM method
Video Off Option	Suspend → Off, Always On	Determines how the monitor is managed
Video Off Method	Options vary	Determines method by which monitor is shut down
HDD Power Down	Options vary	How long before hard drive shuts down
Suspend Mode	Options vary	How long before hard drive goes into suspended mode
PWR Button	Soft-off, Suspend, No Function	Determines how the power button affects power supply
Power Up on Modem ACT	Enabled/Disabled	Modem wakes machine?
AC Power Loss Restart	Enabled/Disabled	Automatically restarts machine when AC power is restored
Wake on LAN	Enabled/Disabled	NIC wakes machine?

PNP and PCI Setup

Setting	Options	Description
PNP OS Installed?	Yes/No	Is the operating system PnP compliant?
Slot 1-? IRQ (several entries)	Auto, various settings	Manually assign an IRQ to a specific slot or let PnP handle allocations?
PCI Latency Timer	Various settings	Number of clock cycles for PCI latency
IRQ 3-15 Used by ISA (several entries)	Yes/No	Is this IRQ assigned to a legacy ISA device?
Force Update ESCD	Enabled/Disabled	Forces reallocation of resources on POST
LOAD BIOS DEFAULTS?	Reloads factory Settings. No internal settings.	
SUPERVISOR PASSWORD	Allows entry of supervisor password	
USER PASSWORD	Allows entry of user password	
IDE HDD AUTODETECT	Automatically detects and configures devices on primary and secondary IDE ports	

Going into the CMOS setup for the first time can be a little intimidating for a beginner. In order to get there, the manufacturer will have provided a specific keystroke combination, which varies from one manufacturer to the next. So watch the splash screen that comes up as the system boots, or check the documentation to find out which key(s) to press.

BOOTSTRAP LOADER

The third critical program that your BIOS runs is the *bootstrap loader*. Without this small but rather important routine, your computer wouldn't be able to get past POST. Bootstrap loader scans all of the drives that you configured as possible boot devices in the setup program looking for something called

BUZZ WORDS

Bootstrap loader: A program that resides on the BIOS chip that is responsible for locating and initializing the Master Boot Record.

Boot block: A feature present on most modern system boards that allows the system to boot to a minimal configuration, including floppy drive support, in the event that the BIOS is corrupted or destroyed by a virus.

the Master Boot Record (MBR). I will talk more about the MBR in Chapter Thirteen, Hard Disk Drive Structure and Geometry. For now, suffice it to say that the MBR is 512 to 1024 bytes of some of the most important data on your computer. There is information stored there that is prerequisite for making the machine work.

Older machines can only look to hard disk drives or floppy drives for an MBR. That is not the case in most current machines. Bootstrap loaders are now smart enough to consider CD-ROMs, Zip drives, and many other storage devices as capable of containing a viable MBR.

It is possible for you to have multiple devices in your computer containing an MBR. In this case, how would the computer know which one to boot to? That's where the CMOS setup comes into play. In the BIOS Features setup section, there is a setting for Boot Sequence. Here, you will tell the computer in what order you want it to look for an MBR. Once it finds one, it stops looking.

TROUBLESHOOTING **BIOS**

The BIOS chip contains fixed, read only memory. It is very difficult to accidentally lose it. CMOS settings, on the other hand, can be lost in several ways. As far as the BIOS is concerned, exposure to high levels of magnetic energy, an electrical surge, or a spark of static electricity from your finger can either destroy it completely or simply damage bits and pieces of code stored on the chip. If it is destroyed completely, POST won't even run. Unfortunately, it is far more common for the BIOS to be damaged than it is to be destroyed. In this case, the machine may or may not make it past POST. If it makes it past POST, the machine performs erratically. Another thing that can destroy the BIOS code is peeling the foil label off to see what's underneath. If your BIOS chip happens to have a foil label, it isn't there just for looks. It covers a window to the chip itself. Exposure of UV radiation to that cell will erase the data on the chip.

Some newer motherboards have a new feature known as *boot block* that allows you to boot the machine in the event of failed BIOS. If the corruption isn't too serious, sometimes boot block can either fix it on the fly or in some cases bypass the problem component. In most cases, boot block works by booting the machine to a bootable floppy diskette that contains a flash utility and a copy of the BIOS data file. This allows you to restore the BIOS.

As I said before, the CMOS is volatile information. If power to the chip is discontinued for a significant amount of time, the information on it is lost. It is essential that this information be made nonvolatile. This is done through an onboard battery. When you turn off a computer, the battery on the motherboard keeps it and the real time clock (RTC) alive. If the battery goes dead, so does the CMOS. Other ways of losing the CMOS include electrostatic discharge, surges or dips in power from a faulty power supply, and physical impact or a short circuit caused by dropping something across its leads while the computer is powered up. Simply removing an expansion card while the computer is running has been known to kill the CMOS.

Normally, in all of the aforementioned circumstances, the CMOS can be restored. On a heavily configured and/or altered machine this can be time consuming. Running a utility such as CMOSSAVE.EXE is a good idea if you administer a lot of computers.

Changing the battery on most motherboards is a relatively simple thing. Modern motherboards use a coin-style battery. Simply flip the old one out with your fingernail and pop the new one in, oriented in the same direction for correct polarity. Some modern machines also have an RTC/battery chip, however, and these can be a bit more problematic. On older machines, you frequently have rechargeable batteries that are soldered onto the motherboard. Consider these motherboards disposable unless you're a really good practitioner of the soldering arts.

CHIPSETS

On the earliest computers, every function on the motherboard required a separate chip. There was a chip for managing IRQs, one for managing DMA channels (managing resources will be covered in detail in Chapter Ten, Examining the Expansion Bus), and one for every other function you can think of. The more functions you added the more chips you needed. The more chips you added, the more complex addressing became. And production costs increased accordingly. It was a vicious cycle. As technology advanced, and as production levels rapidly increased, it was quickly becoming apparent that there had to be a better way. The chipset is that better way. It interacts with all hardware on the system, dictates the abilities and limitations of a system, determines system bus speeds, and handles all addressing functions for the CPU.

COMPONENTS OF THE CHIPSET

Traditionally, modern chipsets are a two-chip set, the northbridge and the southbridge, although Intel's more recent designs are departing from that tradition. There is also a third chip that is integrated with many chipset designs called the Super I/O chip. Since this chip is not designed along with the other two, and frequently motherboard manufacturers get the Super I/O chip from different manufacturers, it is not technically considered part of the chipset. However, since its functions are so similar, I have chosen to include it in this section.

Choice of the chipset directly impacts the performance of the machine. All system functions are either directly or indirectly controlled by the chipset. These functions include, but are not limited to the following:

- Advanced device support
- Amount of memory supported
- Types of memory supported
- Bus speed
- Type and number of expansion busses supported
- Number of processors
- Processor speeds supported
- Processor voltage
- Power management

> **BUZZ WORDS**
>
> **Northbridge:** The faster of the ICs in the chipset that is responsible for managing RAM, cache, and AGP functions.

NORTHBRIDGE

The faster of the two chips in the chipset is the System Controller Chip. This is the one frequently known as the *northbridge.* It handles the high-speed components of the system. It is the northbridge that directly connects the CPU's front-side bus (see Chapter Seven, Understanding CPUs) to RAM, the AGP port, and other high-speed peripherals. It also sets the pace for the FSB. You just bought yourself a new 3.1GHz CPU? Congratulations, but if the chipset on your motherboard only supports up to 2GHz—it isn't going to do you a whole lot of good. And if your CPU is designed with a 133MHz FSB and you put it on a board that only supports 100MHz, then 100MHz is what the CPU's data bus will run at. In many cases, an incorrect setting will prevent the machine from booting properly.

The northbridge also decides how much RAM you're going to be able to use in your machine. Theoretically, all Pentium-based systems should be able to address up to 4GB of RAM. Pentium IIs and higher should be able to address 64GB. The sad truth is that no chipset ever manufactured has taken advantage of more than a fraction of that capability. Current motherboards are designed to support anywhere from as little as 384MB to 2GB on boards designed for desktop machines. Those designed for servers are more generous, and there are models available that support up to 16GB.

The Memory Controller Chip (MCC) is a key function absorbed by the chipset. The original MCC did the actual job of mapping data to memory, as well as directing the functions that dictated refresh cycles and timing of RAS and CAS (see Chapter Nine, Searching Your Memory). This is now handled by the northbridge component of the chipset. This also determines the kinds of memory you can use on any given system.

SOUTHBRIDGE

The Peripheral Bus Controller, also known as the *southbridge,* takes care of communication between the CPU and the slower components of the system. The southbridge takes care of things like the ISA bus, IDE ports, USB ports, and any other devices not specifically handled by the Super I/O chip. All expansion bus platforms prior to PCI are under the control of this chip as well.

SUPER I/O CHIP

This is the chip that, technically speaking, is not part of the chipset. As I said earlier, in many cases, the super I/O doesn't even come from the same manufacturer as the chipset. What makes this possible is that the super I/O controls the I/O functions that are typically found in all motherboards. These would include the floppy drive controllers, serial ports, parallel ports, IDE ports, and so on. Some super I/O chips also provide keyboard controller functions and the real time clock.

BEYOND THE BRIDGES

It is Intel's stated goal to eliminate everything on the system that slows it down. That includes the ISA bus. With the release of the 820 chipset, Intel began doing just that. They are starting to move away from the traditional northbridge/southbridge design. The 820 is similar to the old design only in that both make use of two separate chips. However, they handle system resources in a completely different manner. In place of the northbridge component is a device called the *Memory Controller Hub*. As its name infers, this device controls all system memory. It also has the responsibility for managing the AGP bus. The second chip, the *Enhanced I/O Controller Hub* handles all other functions.

Intel has made this a modular design. Engineers who design motherboards can make a simple system based on the chipset's bare essentials. However, more advanced systems can be designed with some of the optional components available. If the manufacturer wants to build a board that supports 64-bit 66MHz PCI slots, the optional P64H PCI controller hub can be implemented. Manufacturers who wish to add an additional memory channel can make use of the 862803AA memory repeater hub. This design philosophy was carried over into the 850 chipset for the Pentium 4 and most likely represents the future of Intel chipsets.

Other manufacturers aren't quite so eager to see an early funeral for ISA or any of the other slower busses. People still use it. And as long as people still use it, manufacturers can continue to make money off of the technology. Therefore, manufacturers such as VIA continue to crank out traditional chipsets.

> **BUZZ WORDS**
>
> **Southbridge:** The slower of the ICs that make up the chipset. The southbridge manages serial and parallel communications, USB, and most of the expansion slots.
>
> **Memory Controller Hub:** The IC in the newer Intel chipsets that manages RAM and AGP bus.
>
> **Enhanced I/O Controller Hub:** The IC in the newer Intel chipset that manages all function other than memory and AGP.

MOTHERBOARD REPLACEMENT

One thing every technician is eventually going to have to do is replace a motherboard. A heavy surge, lightening striking the electric pole outside the customer's house, any number of things can kill a motherboard. Even plugging the P8 and P9 cables in with the black wires on the outside. As a computer technician, changing the motherboard needs to become second nature to you.

At first it might look a little intimidating. A novice looking inside the case sees nothing but a tangle of cables and cards sticking out of the board. On top of that, the power supply and all those drives are in the way. You're going to have to take the whole computer apart just to replace the motherboard!!!

In many situations, that's the case. Then again, sometimes it's not quite so complicated. Taking a systematic approach will make it a lot easier. A little practice doesn't hurt.

Step 1: Know what kind of case you're working with. ATX motherboards do not go in AT cases. It doesn't matter how big a hammer you use. They line up in the case in different manners, and they use different types of power supplies. If you are replacing an AT-style motherboard, then you need to find an AT-style motherboard with which to replace it. And vice versa. Size is no longer an issue. For years, cases have been designed to take varying sizes of boards.

Step 2: Make sure the motherboard comes with the manual!!! Every motherboard has anywhere from a few to a multitude of jumpers and/or DIP switches and wiring connectors. There's no such thing as a universal standard. If you don't have the manual for the motherboard you're working on and try to get by with a "similar" model, it'll be like trying to make chicken teriyaki from a chili recipe. If you don't have hardcopy of the manual, then before you start removing the old board carefully note where every single cable was plugged in. Later on, while the two boards are out on the bench, make sure all jumpers and/or DIP switches are configured identically from the old board to the new.

Step 3: First, remove all cards from the expansion slots. Set them aside (preferably in static-free bags) and then remove all cables. IDE, floppy, serial, and parallel cables (if present) are all ribbon cables and you should be able to readily identify them by sight. Remove the CPU fan from the CPU and the wires connecting LEDs, the PC speaker, CD-ROM audio, and others. If you don't have the manual, make careful note of where these wires plug in! Frequently, the wires coming out of the case are clearly labeled "HD LED," "TURBO," "SPKR," and "RESET." All too often, however, the motherboard is labeled J12, J13, J14, and J27, or something like that.

Step 4: Once you have everything removed from the motherboard, remove the screws that hold it on. There are usually three to five of them. If the power supply is in the way, you're better off removing it. They're not that hard to pull and replace. Drop the new board in place, put the screws in to hold it in and reverse the procedures of removing the board. The one thing to remember here is that, on AT-style computers, it is essential that you get the P8 and P9 plugs properly aligned.

Before you put the case back together, double-check all the cables to make sure they are connected, and connected properly. Then check again. Once you're reasonably confident that everything is hooked up right, fire the machine up while it's still open. That way you can put the floppy cable back on correctly and reconnect that Molex that fell off the hard drive when you weren't looking. If the machine boots fine, then wrap it up.

One potential problem you might encounter after a motherboard replacement is related to the operating system. If the board you replaced was not an identical duplicate, OSs that support Plug 'n Play will detect that the device list has changed. It will reinstall all system device drivers. Most of the time, this is simply an inconvenience. It requires that the system reboot as many as three times before the procedure is complete. Once in a great while, you may encounter a situation where the OS must be reinstalled. Unless there is critical data and/or settings on the machine that prevent you from doing this, I would recommend that you do this anyway.

CHAPTER SUMMARY

If you've gotten this far, you now realize the importance of the motherboard to the computer system. It is the very heart of the system. All system busses pass through the motherboard and all critical functions are under its control.

In Chapter One, PC Basics, I told you that I would make a case for the CPU not truly being the brains of the computer. I made the first installment of my case in this chapter when I pointed out how many vital system functions were under the control of the chipset and not the CPU. I'll continue making my case in the next two chapters, when I discuss CPUs.

Troubleshooting motherboard issues is one of those things that take up a great deal of the lives of most computer hardware technicians. Understanding the different errors reported by the board and being able to identify them need to be second nature to the tech.

BRAIN DRAIN

1. Discuss as many differences between an AT-style motherboard and an ATX-style motherboard as you can think of.

2. List at least five features of a motherboard that will be common to all motherboards, regardless of form factor.

3. Give an overview of the functions of the system BIOS.

4. List as many functions of the chipset as you can.

5. Discuss why there needs to be a separate expansion bus.

THE 64K$ QUESTIONS

1. A typical motherboard consists of _____ layers of substrate.
   a. One
   b. Two
   c. Four
   d. Six

2. Which of the following is not an example of a pin-mounted CPU socket?
   a. PGA
   b. SECC
   c. SPGA
   d. ZIF

3. How many IDE controllers typically reside on an ATX-style motherboard?

   a. Two

   b. Four

   c. One

   d. Zero

4. Which of the following form factors makes use of a riser? (Choose all that apply.)

   a. AT

   b. NLX

   c. ATX

   d. LPX

5. POST is a function of _____.

   a. The CPU

   b. The chipset

   c. The BIOS

   d. RAM

6. Which BIOS program locates and initializes the Master Boot Record?

   a. POST

   b. Setup

   c. Startup

   d. Bootstrap loader

7. CMOS stands for _____.

   a. Common Motherboard Operational Settings

   b. Common Master Operating System

   c. Complimentary Metal-Oxide Semiconductor

   d. Creative Metaphors for Our Supervisor

8. AGP is typically under the control of _____. (Choose all that apply.)

   a. The southbridge chip

   b. The northbridge chip

   c. The memory controller hub

   d. The Super I/O controller

9. The Plug 'n Play Recognition Scan is a part of _____.

   a. Loading the OS

   b. POST

   c. Bootstrap loader

   d. Device installation

10. All computer systems, past and present, load BIOS instructions on a ROM chip.

   a. True

   b. False

TRICKY TERMINOLOGY

Boot block: A feature present on most modern system boards that allows the system to boot to a minimal configuration, including floppy drive support, in the event that the BIOS is corrupted or destroyed by a virus.

Bootstrap loader: A program that resides on the BIOS chip that is responsible for locating and initializing the Master Boot Record.

Chipset: A matched set of two (three on some of the older systems) ICs that control critical system functions, including bus speeds, memory types and capacity, and the type of hardware supported by a motherboard.

CMOS setup: One of the programs loaded on the BIOS chip. This particular program allows user-defined parameters relating to BIOS settings to be configured.

Codec: A coined term derived from two other terms, coder and decoder. A codec is an IC that has been programmed to convert data from one form to another. An example of this would be a chip that takes analog signals and converts them to digital, and vice versa.

Conventional memory: The first 640K of any computer system. In the old days of DOS, the only place where programs could run was in conventional memory.

Enhanced I/O Controller Hub: The IC in the newer Intel chipsets that manages all function other than memory and AGP.

Memory Controller Hub: The IC in the newer Intel chipsets that manages RAM and AGP bus.

Northbridge: The faster of the ICs in the chipset that is responsible for managing RAM, cache, and AGP functions.

Riser: A specialized expansion card that supports other expansion devices such as PCI or ISA cards horizontally, parallel to the motherboard, in order to save space.

Slot: A mounting assembly designed to support edge card-mounted devices.

Socket: A mounting assembly designed to support pin-mounted devices.

Southbridge: The slower of the ICs that make up the chipset. The southbridge manages serial and parallel communications, USB, and most of the expansion slots.

Trace: The fine copper path seen on printed circuit boards that acts as a conductor for a signal.

Volatile: Unstable or changeable. Requires constant power in order to continue to exist.

ACRONYM ALERT

ACR: Audio Communications Riser. A specialized card that takes the concept of the AMR and adds networking functionality as well.

AMR: Audio Modem Riser. A specialized card found on certain motherboards that supports either a modem, a sound card, or a device that combines both functions.

CMOS: Complimentary Metal-Oxide Semiconductor. The type of chip that houses the user-configurable parameters needed by BIOS.

CNR: Communications Network Riser. A specialized card that takes the concept of the AMR and adds networking functionality as well.

DDR: Dual Data Rate. A form of memory that is capable of executing two transfers of data on each clock cycle.

EBX: Embedded Board Expandable. One of several form factors whose objective was to keep the system as small as possible.

EEPROM: Electronically Erasable Programmable Read Only Memory. A more modern implementation of an IC that can be wiped clean and rewritten if necessary.

EPROM: Erasable Programmable Read Only Memory. An IC that can be wiped clean and rewritten if necessary.

LPX: Low-Profile Extended. One of several form factors whose objective was to keep the system as small as possible.

MBR: Master Boot Record. The first one or two sectors of a bootable medium that contains information about the file system, the partition tables, and a pointer to the OS.

MCC: Memory Controller Chip or Memory Controller Circuit. The chip or circuitry on the chipset that manages memory mapping and refresh functions.

NLX: New Low-profile Extended. One of several form factors whose objective was to keep the system as small as possible.

PGA: Pin Grid Array. A pin-mounted CPU on which the pins are arranged in perfectly symmetrical patterns of squares.

POST: Power On, Self Test. A program run from the BIOS chip that initializes system hardware and handles the Plug 'n Play scans.

PROM: Programmable Read Only Memory. An IC that can be programmed once.

ROM BIOS: Read Only Memory-Basic Input Output Services. A chip on the motherboard that contains all the necessary code for jumpstarting a computer from a dead off condition to the point where the OS can take over.

RTC: Real Time Clock. The chip that keeps actual time, as humans keep track of it, on the systems.

SECC: Single Edge Contact Cartridge. A type of CPU package that makes use of an edge card connector and mounts in a slot.

SPGA: Staggered Pin Grid Array. A pin-mounted CPU on which the pins are arranged in offsetting rows of pins that results in a pattern of diagonal rows.

UV: Ultraviolet. Wavelengths of light beyond the upper range of the visible light spectrum.

VID-VRM: Voltage Identifier, Voltage Regulator Module. A device that automatically locks on to the correct voltage of the installed chip and configures the device accordingly.

WTX: Workstation Technology Extended. One of several form factors whose objective was to keep the system as small as possible.

 VIEW THE VIDEO

A video clip on Motherboard Components is available on the accompanying CD.

CHAPTER 7

UNDERSTANDING CPUs

In this chapter, I will discuss what many refer to as the "brain" of the computer. However, as I pointed out in the previous chapter, the central processing unit (CPU) really does not deserve to claim that title exclusively. In reality, it is nothing more than an overgrown calculator. It basically shuffles 0s and 1s at an incredibly high rate of speed. It is a device that has evolved over the years, and each generation has assumed new responsibilities. So in a sense, it is creeping in on the title of main brain.

Even in its infancy, the CPU was a complicated device. Those that power today's computers transcend complexity and border on the world of magic. Because of the amount of information centering around the CPU, I have chosen to break it up into two separate chapters. In this chapter I will examine the structure and function of the CPU as well as some of the technologies that improve performance. In Chapter Eight, I will discuss the chronology and evolution of the microprocessor.

A+ CORE HARDWARE EXAM OBJECTIVES

CompTIA exam objectives covered in the chapter include the following:

1.1 Identify the names, purpose, and characteristics of system modules. Recognize these modules by sight or definition. (CPU)

1.9 Identify procedures to optimize PC operations in specific situations. Predict the effects of specific procedures under given scenarios.

1.10 Determine the issues that must be considered when upgrading a PC. In a given scenario, determine when and how to upgrade system components.

TRANSISTORS, BINARY, AND LOGIC GATES

The only language the computer speaks is binary. Binary is a simplified computer language consisting of 0s and 1s. Therefore, the commands native to the CPU can be no larger than its internal data bus (I'll be taking this up in detail in a few moments). The programs that you run consist of extremely detailed sets of instructions that consist of several words. If you recall from Chapter One, PC Basics, a word generally consists of the amount of data the CPU can swallow in one gulp. These instructions tell the CPU what to do every step of the way in order to achieve a specific objective. Even a single step left out of the flow of logic will cause the program to either malfunction or to stop functioning altogether. On a machine level, all these commands are really doing is telling the computer which of the CPU's wires to light up, and which to leave dormant. Turning little devices called *transistors* on and off does all of this. These combinations of on and off cascade through the computer, creating a series of logic gates.

A *logic gate* is nothing more than two or more transistors working together. The relative position of these transistors (on or off) determines how the next pair of transistors in the circuit will be switched.

A transistor is a semiconductor that acts as a switch, existing in either an on position, or an off position. A *semiconductor* is any substance that conducts electricity well enough to be considered a conductor, and resists electrical flow well enough to be considered an insulator. In other words, it's a

> ## BUZZ WORDS
>
> **Transistor:** A microscopic on/off switch that uses the electrical characteristics of a semiconductor to reverse positions.
>
> **Logic gate:** Two or more transistors whose position will direct the positioning of the next bank of transistors downstream.
>
> **Semiconductor:** A substance that exhibits the characteristics of both a conductor and a resistor, depending on the amount of voltage passing through.
>
> **Threshold voltage:** The amount of electrical differential required to move a semiconductor from a state of resistance to a state of conductance.
>
> **Register:** A bank of transistors grouped together to perform a specific function.

substance with an identity crisis. But that property makes it an ideal substance for the manufacture of transistors. Any electrical current that reaches a certain strength is allowed to flow. This is the semiconductor's *threshold voltage*. Any current less than threshold voltage is blocked. Therefore, current either flows or it doesn't, depending on how much current there is. The transistor is either on or off. Inside the CPU, transistors are grouped together as registers. A *register* is one of a series of transistor banks that will provide a pathway for the processing of data.

The binary language can be credited to work originally done by George Boole in the mid-1800s. His paper, "An Investigation Into the Laws of Thought, on Which Are Founded the Mathematical Theories of Logic and Probabilities," was published in 1852, a culmination of several years' worth of work. In this paper, he defined a new form of algebra based exclusively upon the numbers 0 and 1. These ideas would be the basis of binary as it is used by computers today. I discussed binary in Chapter One, PC Basics, and provided some key terms.

THE MICROCOMPONENTS OF THE CPU

Examine a CPU closely, and consider this. That little device that nestles easily into the palm of your hand can perform anywhere from several hundred million to a few billion transactions per second. What is even more impressive is that the actual microprocessor is only a fraction of what you're holding. The ceramic device in your hand includes the circuit board and wires necessary to interconnect the chip to the rest of the system. The chip itself is a trifle larger than your thumbnail. That tiny piece of silicon has been subdivided into several smaller sections called subcomponents. Each one of those subcomponents has a specific job to do. Understanding how a CPU works is a lot easier if you understand the purpose of each of the internal devices. As you read through the next few sections, keep referring back to the diagram in **Figure 7.1**.

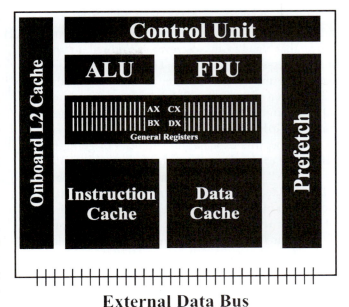

Figure 7.1   The CPU is subdivided into several sub-components, each of which has a specific task to perform.

The various subcomponents of the CPU along with their basic functions include the following:

- *The Control Unit:* The component that directs the activities of all other components in the CPU
- *The Prefetch:* The component that locates and retrieves data as the CPU requires it
- *External Data Bus:* The wires that bring data into the CPU from the outside world
- *The Instruction Cache and the Data Cache:* Storage areas for instructions that have been brought in the by the prefetch, but not yet used by the CPU
- *The Arithmetic Logic Unit:* Performs basic math functions
- *The Floating Point Unit:* Performs advanced math functions
- *Registers:* A storage point for data and/or instructions that are in current use by the CPU

Also shown in the figure is the Onboard L2 Cache; it is often included on the die of CPUs these days, but it is not part of the primary CPU circuitry. I'll discuss this later in the chapter.

THE EXTERNAL DATA BUS

I have no intention of going over each and every component of the CPU in this book. It is not an engineering text, and the average hardware technician does not need that information either in real life or on the exam. I do feel that a discussion of the *external data bus* (EDB) is in order, though.

If the data required by the CPU is located outside of the CPU, there must be some way to move that data from wherever it's stored to the internal registers of the CPU. The EDB is the front door that moves information in and out of the CPU. It is a part of the CPU that, despite the huge advances in technology over the past few decades, has seen little change.

To keep the explanation simple, I'm going to refer back to the first microprocessor used by IBM in the IBM PC. This particular CPU had an 8-bit EDB. Modern CPUs have far more than eight bits, but I'll get into that a little later. The EDB consists of a series of switches that can be either on or off. These switches are turned on and off at regular intervals, called the clock cycle. Eight switches permits 256 combinations of on/off that can be understood by the CPU on any given clock cycle.

BUZZ WORDS

External data bus: The wires that move data from outside the CPU to the internal registers of the CPU.

Front-side bus: A portion of the EDB. It is the path that data takes from outside locations to make its way into the CPU.

Back-side bus: A portion of the EDB. It is the path that data takes as it moves from cache loaded on the CPU's die into the CPU's registers.

The EDB actually exists in two different places on the CPU. One term used frequently is the *front-side bus* (FSB). The FSB is the path that data takes from the chipset and/or memory to get to the CPU. The *back-side bus* (BSB) is the channel that data located in Level One cache takes. Level One is a fancy name for the instruction and data caches discussed earlier. In the early days of CPUs, the speed of the FSB and BSB were the same. This is no longer the case.

In the early days of computing, the first CPU used by IBM possessed a 4.77MHz EDB. It had no Level One cache, so there was only an FSB. This CPU could examine the switches of the EDB 4,770,000 times per second, interpret the on/off pattern as a byte of data, and move it onto the internal registers. On today's CPUs, the FSB begins at 100MHz and has reached 466MHz on some of the new Athlons and 533MHz on the Pentium 4. Intel describes in its literature CPUs that will exceed a 1GHz FSB, perhaps by the time this book has come

to print. The BSB can function at the same speed of the FSB on some CPUs and much higher speeds on others. I will examine this in more detail a bit later.

Now, how does the CPU use the EDB to move data onto the CPU? That's actually pretty simple. Remember that there is a pin on the CPU that represents each individual data bit (**Figure 7.2**). Current on a pin during any given clock cycle represents a 1, while a lack of current is interpreted as a 0. On both the internal and external sides

Figure 7.2 The external data bus is nothing more than a series of wires. They are but a few of the pins you see protruding from the base of a CPU. The presence or absence of current on any given wire during a specific clock cycle is interpreted as data.

of the bus are microswitches that control the state of the wire. As you might imagine, for this to work properly, on any given clock cycle, both switches must be set to the same position.

THE CLOCK

Technically speaking, the clock is not part of the CPU. However, understanding what is going on inside of the CPU is difficult without knowing what the clock does and how its role affects every-

BUZZ WORDS ————————

Clock cycle: A timing signal generated by an electrical current that synchronizes data movement throughout the system. As an electrical current, a clock cycle resembles a sine wave with a rising half of the signal and a falling half.

thing else. There has to be some sort of mechanism that tells the CPU when to check for incoming data. This mechanism is the CPU clock. This is also the derivation of the term *clock cycle*. The clock ticks, and the CPU turns to the telegraphs, takes note of which switches are on, which are off, and promptly takes action. What makes the clock tick is electrical current. On earlier computers, the clock consisted of nothing more than a crystal. When hit with current, it vibrated. The nice thing about nature is that, while on the outside it looks like pure chaos, on a molecular level, things are pretty predictable. The crystal used in the early PC vibrated 4,770,000 times per second when excited by electricity. That was its clock cycle. The CPU requires a minimum of two clock cycles to act on any given command.

The clock cycles are measured in Hertz (Hz). 1Hz is equal to 1 clock cycle. 1 million clock cycles = 1MHz. 1 billion clock cycles = 1GHz. Early CPUs, up until the 80486 DX-2 series, had external data busses that operated at the same speed as the CPU. A 33MHz chip was a 33MHz chip inside and out. With the advent of "clock doubling" technology, manufacturers started making CPUs that could execute instructions internally faster than they were able to communicate with the rest of the computer. The first example of this was the Intel DX2 25/50. The external bus ran at 25MHz, but inside the CPU processed data at twice that speed.

Modern computers run on 100MHz, 133MHz, 200MHz, 266MHz, and 400MHz external data busses. Yet the chips themselves run much faster than that. Therefore, your 1.3GHz CPU is capable of processing instructions internally at 1.3 billion clock cycles per second. The FSB, however, is limited to its own speed. For example, the Athlon Thunderbird has an FSB of 266MHz. So, while the CPU is executing commands or moving data 1.3 billion times each second, the external data bus puts data on the telegraph wire, or retrieves processed data from it, only 266 million times per second. That means that, for every tick of the clock that the CPU is being fed data or instructions, it has another five ticks to act upon it while the prefetch locates more data.

THE CPU AND MEMORY

Because programs do consist of so many lines of code, it is necessary to have some fast method of feeding the instructions to the CPU. Even the 8088 could execute instructions at a rate of 4.77 million per second. You can't type them in that fast. In the early days of computing, holes were punched in cards and these were fed to the computer. Early card readers were capable of several thousand cards per second, or less than one tenth of one percent of the speed of the slowest CPU ever used on a PC. Magnetic tape was fast enough to feed data to these earlier CPUs, but a program needed to be able to jump from one section of code to another. IF/THEN statements were a good example of that. If the user or the program returned a YES, one section of the program would be executed; if a NO was returned, a completely different section of code was run. Magnetic tape could not be accessed in this way very efficiently. Even if it could, the life span of the machine would be very short. So random access memory was invented.

ACCESSING RAM

Random Access Memory (RAM) is not only extremely fast, but any line of code stored within it can be accessed at any time. By itself, the CPU is incapable of addressing RAM directly. The MCC that I discussed in Chapter Six, Motherboards, BIOS, and the Chipset, keeps track of the data stored in RAM. The MCC treats RAM like a giant spreadsheet with a column for each bit the CPU can access per clock cycle and as many rows as there are bytes of RAM. A 1MB 8088 would have eight columns and 1,048,576 rows. (This is, of course, a very simplified logical explanation of how information is stored in RAM. For more detail, refer to Chapter Nine, Searching Your Memory.) The CPU could scan up and down this spreadsheet as though it were a menu and grab the byte it needed.

THE ADDRESS BUS

In order to find whatever byte is needed, the CPU needs a roadmap to all that memory. Well, this is more work than the registers in the CPU were designed to handle. In the original IBM PC, a separate chip, called the Memory Control Chip, assumed this responsibility. As I said earlier, current PCs count on the chipset for this task. The MCC is the master of the RAM spreadsheet. To communicate with the MCC, the CPU's prefetch circuit uses its address bus. The address bus is a collection of wires that allows the CPU to tell the MCC exactly which line of code in the RAM spreadsheet, or which byte in RAM, it currently needs. The 8088 CPU was developed with twenty wires on the address bus. Subsequent CPUs increased this number, but for now, let's stick with the twenty of the 8088. While technology has changed the amount of memory that can be addressed, the method by which it does its job is fundamentally the same.

With twenty wires available, that was a collection of twenty switches that could be either on or off, or twenty switches that were either open or closed. The number of possible combinations of on/off or open/closed that is offered by twenty wires is 2^{20}. Use your scientific calculator, and you'll see that 2^{20} will always total 1,048,576. That is the total number of bytes that the 8088 can address. This became the infamous *megabyte*. Therefore, any

BUZZ WORDS

Address bus: A bank of wires running throughout the system and into the CPU that identifies specific locations. The total addressable space is calculated as 2x, where x represents the total number of wires in the bus.

time you hear the term megabyte in reference to memory, it does not refer to 1 million bytes. It refers to 1,048,576 bytes. (This can get little confusing because to hard drive manufacturers, a megabyte is an even million bytes. More on that in Chapter Thirteen, Hard Disk Drive Structure and Geometry.) If we should carry that out a little further, we see that sixteen megabytes is 16 × 1,048,576, or 16,777,216 bytes. 128MB is 128 × 1,048,576, or 134,217,728 bytes.

The combination of ON/OFF that the CPU lights up on any given clock cycle on the Address Bus tells the MCC which of the 1,048,576 rows of the RAM spreadsheet from which to extract the byte of data it seeks.

> **BUZZ WORDS**
>
> **Megabyte:** Depending on whether you are calculating a value in binary or decimal, a megabyte is either 1,000,000 bytes (decimal) or 1,048,576 bytes (binary). A binary megabyte is used in virtually every circumstance except when calculating hard drive capacity. Hard drive manufacturers typically define capacity in decimal values.

Which pattern goes to which line of RAM? That's pretty easy. The operating system controls how memory is used. It tells the CPU where everything is loaded. The "cells" in our imaginary spreadsheet are numbered from 0000 0000 0000 0000 0000 to 1111 1111 1111 1111 1111. Remember, in binary, you don't count 0, 1, 2, 3, etc. You count 0, 1, 10, 11, 100, 101, etc. To see the 20-bit address space of the 8088, simply keep counting like that until you get to 1111 1111 1111 1111 1111. Take your time. I'll wait. So it doesn't matter how many bytes of information are stored in the 1,048,576 available rows. The CPU only requires twenty wires to find what it needs. Remember, however, that later CPUs increased the size of the address bus in subsequent generations of CPUs, so they use a few more wires.

CACHE

One thing that has remained constant throughout the history of computing has been that the CPU is faster than the rest of the system. RAM can be a bottleneck, but mass storage is much worse. In the event that the CPU has to go out to the hard drive for data, there can be several hundred, or even several thousand, clock cycles in which the CPU sits idle waiting for data. Designers sidestepped this issue by adding very fast SRAM memory (see Chapter Nine, Searching Your Memory) to the motherboard as an area to store data that the CPU will probably need next. Code is accessed sequentially, and generally, so is data. With this in mind, as the system accesses the piece of data or code actually requested by the CPU, it will also retrieve the next few lines and store it in cache until the CPU requests it. Programmers developed several algorithms for predicting what data or code will be needed next. Now, the prefetch unit has an additional place to look for data before it hits the RAM or hard drive.

Starting with the 80486, CPU designers started putting small amounts of cache onboard the CPU itself. Data can be retrieved from there even quicker. The two areas of cache that are found on CPUs are Level One (L1) and Level Two (L2). Some motherboard designers have gone so far as to provide Level Three (L3) cache. Early CPUs didn't have L2 cache. However, engineers discovered that, working in conjunction with L1, L2 cache provided such a substantial

Table 7.1 CPU Onboard Cache Comparison

CPU	L1	L2	L3
Intel or AMD 80486DX and DX2	8K	N/A	N/A
Intel or AMD 80486DX4	16K	N/A	N/A
Intel Pentium	16K	N/A	N/A
Intel Pentium Pro	16K	256K, 512K, or 1M	N/A
Intel Pentium MMX	32K	N/A	N/A
Intel Pentium II and III	32K	256K	N/A
Intel Celeron	32K	0K, 32K, 128K or 256K	N/A
Intel Itanium	32K	96K	2MB or 4MB
Intel Itanium II	32K	256K	1.5MB or 3MB
Intel P4 Xeon	8K*	256K	N/A
Intel Pentium III CopperMine	32K	256K, 512K	
Intel Pentium 4	*	12K data + 8K ETC*	256K
AMD K5	16K Instruction, 8K Data	N/A	N/A
AMD K6 and K6-2	64K	N/A	N/A
AMD K6-3	64K	256K	N/A
AMD K7 Athlon	128K	512K	N/A
AMD Duron	128K	64K	N/A
AMD Athlon Thunderbird	128K	256K	N/A
AMD Athlon XP	128K	256 or 512K	N/A
AMD Athlon XP-MP	128K	256K	N/A

Different models of CPU have different amounts of cache loaded onboard. Many include L2 cache.

*The Pentium 4 and the P4 Xeon replace conventional L1 cache with something they call Execution Trace Cache. Because of its low latency of only two clock cycles, engineers dropped the cache size down to accommodate this change.

boost in performance that the major CPU manufactures began putting L2 on the CPU as well. Because the amounts of L1 and L2 cache vary among the manufacturers, and indeed among models by the same manufacturer, this is a factor that should be carefully considered when selecting CPUs. See **Table 7.1** for a comparison of the cache of various models of CPU.

The effect of L2 cache should not be underestimated. A couple of years back I performed some tests to see how much gain I actually got from adding cache to the system. I started with a motherboard that shipped with 0K L2 cache, but that allowed the user to add cache using 256K, 512K, or 1MB COAST (Chip on a Stick) modules. The basic system was a Pentium 166 CPU with 32MB of RAM. I chose such an old architecture because this was the only way I could keep the CPU constant and make sure that any differences I obtained were a result of differences in cache.

I made the measurements using Winstone. Performance with 0K of L2 cache was acceptable for a CPU of that vintage, but nothing to write home to Mom about. Adding a 256K module increased performance by a full 42 percent. Going from 256K to 512K boosted it by another 22 percent. Yet bumping it to 1MB provided only negligible gains. Admittedly, this was not a scientific process, and these results should not be construed as anything conclusive. CPU speed, the chipset used, and the amount of physical RAM installed in a machine will all have an impact on these results. However, I do feel that the results give a realistic view of the impact cache can have on performance.

CPU FORM FACTOR

In Chapter Three, I talked about how motherboards and cases came in specific form factors in order to assure that one manufacturer's product worked with another's. As with these devices, CPUs come in different form factors as well. Traditionally, CPUs have been available in either PGA (Pin Grid Array) or SPGA (Staggered Pin Grid Array). Other terms you might see tossed around on occasion are IPGA (Interstitial Pin Grid Array) and FC-PGA (Flip-Chip PGA). These are simply variations on SPGA. The only difference between PGA and SPGA is that PGA utilized perfectly arranged pins, laid out in a square grid as shown in **Figure 7.3**.

SPGA "staggered" the rows of pins across the chip. This allowed for tighter placement of pins, nearly doubling the number of pins that could be fit onto the same size package. This became necessary with the Pentium CPU because of the number of pins needed to support its wider busses and its advanced features. **Figure 7.4** shows the base of an SPGA chip very clearly.

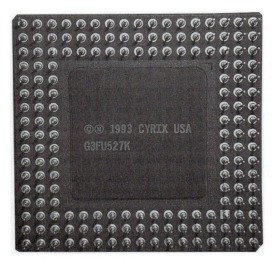

Figure 7.3   The PGA package has a perfect grid of pins extruding from the base of the chip.

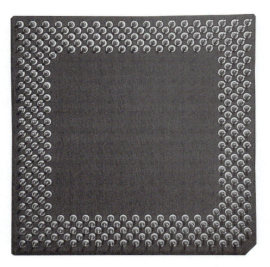

Figure 7.4   SPGA chips cram more pins onto the base of the chip by alternating the rows. Not only can the pins be placed closer together, but the rows can also be tightened up.

Intel introduced a new form factor with the release of the Pentium II called the SECC (discussed in Chapter Six, shown here in **Figure 7.5**, top). This CPU was mounted on an edge card connector, not at all dissimilar to an expansion card. Intel felt that this design would provide for better cooling. Its more recent CPU design has gone back to the PGA form factor in one it calls PPGA, or Plastic Pin Grid Array. Essentially, it is an SPGA chip using a plastic housing instead of a ceramic one.

Naturally, the form factor of the CPU must match that of the motherboard. Specifically, the CPU must fit the appropriate socket. A complete discussion of CPU sockets can be found in Chapter Six, Motherboards, BIOS, and the Chipset.

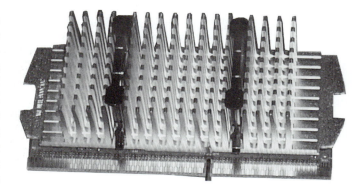

Figure 7.5 When you see them side by side like this, it's pretty hard not to be able to tell the difference between a Slot One CPU and a Socket 7 CPU.

CAUTION: Just because a motherboard says that it's for a Pentium 4, or supports a Celeron processor, is no clear-cut indication that it supports specific models. For example, there were two different versions of the FC-PGA 370 socket used by the Celeron processor, and more recent Celerons fit on a 478-pin socket. Pentium 4s have been manufactured for both 423-pin sockets and 478-pin sockets. Make sure your processor and motherboard match before confirming an order.

ADVANCED CPU CAPABILITIES

When the microprocessor first hit the scenes, it was amazing enough that it could do what it did. Here was a device that not only could add, subtract, multiply, and divide several million operations per second, but you could actually give it orders and it would follow them! The thought that a CPU could see into the future, and to a certain extent, read your mind (or at least the programmer's mind) was inconceivable. Yet, to a very great extent, many modern chips do just that. The best of CPU advances come about when the manufacturers teach them new tricks.

PROTECTED MODE

The first CPUs to come out could work only in Real Mode. What this means is that data could only be accessed across a 20-bit address bus, which was derived from joining two 16-bit registers. The end result of that was that programs operating in real mode could only "see" a total of 1MB of total memory space, and could only access data in chunks that were a maximum of 64K (a limit imposed by the 16-bit

BUZZ WORDS

Protected mode: A function of a CPU that prevents two separate programs from seeing each other's code or from attempting to use overlapping memory addresses. Should either event occur, the CPU would lock up.

registers used). In order to allow programs to use the full capacity of larger address busses, operating systems had to be modified as well as the electronics. Older programs written to access the 20-bit address bus had to work differently than the newer ones that could move into the extended space offered by a larger bus. And the CPU had to process the data accordingly.

Protected mode makes use of additional registers by allowing applications and operating systems to make use of the extended space without allowing legacy programs that can only operate in real mode to blow up the rest of the system. An older DOS program that needs to run in real mode gets its own address space that is protected from all other applications.

The real protection, however, occurs because a misbehaving application won't necessarily bring down the rest of the system. If it crashes, other applications, each running in their own protected space, continue blithely along neither knowing, nor caring, that some poor legacy app just bit the bullet.

FLOATING POINT OPERATIONS

I've already made mention of the FPU and described what it does. However, many chips optimize performance simply in redefining how this particular portion of the CPU does its job. In the 80486, simply the fact that a separate Math Coprocessor was no longer required (the circuitry was part of the CPU) was a huge advantage. It simplified the design of motherboards and shaved a few dollars off the average price of systems that required this function.

Some newer models of CPUs improve performance by reducing the number of clock cycles required to perform an FPU operation. Enhanced instruction sets provide most of this performance increase. Another method used by manufacturers is to increase the amount of circuitry dedicated to the FPU. Most modern CPUs provide multiple FPUs so that several operations can be going on at once.

In terms of overall system performance this has a minimal impact on the system. Unless you happen to be running very complicated programs requiring complex mathematical operations, changes in FPU design have only nominal affect.

INSTRUCTION PIPELINING

Another limitation of the first CPUs was that once an instruction or set of instructions was submitted to the CPU for processing, everything else in the computer sat back and waited until it was finished before submitting any more requests. Complex instructions could take many clock cycles to pass through the various stages of the CPU before the results finally made their way out the external data bus.

Instruction pipelining, generally just called pipelining, moves the next instruction onto the external data bus while the one before it is still going through its processes. Therefore, during any given clock cycle, multiple instructions can be in varying stages of completion, while others are waiting in the instruction cache for their turn at bat.

You could compare this to two different methods of emptying an aquarium. In the days before pipelining, you had to empty the fish tank with a cup. You'd fill the cup, move it over to the sink and dump the water, then go back and fill it again. You'd have to repeat this process until the tank was empty. Pipelining allowed you to put several siphon hoses into the tank, hang the other end of each one of them into the sink and start the instructions flowing through.

The impact of pipelining can depend heavily on a couple of factors. The first of these is in how linear the code being processed happens to be. If one instruction follows the other in precise order, or if the correct instructions happen to reside in L1 cache as the prefetch is lining up commands, then it works very well. As soon as the cycle is broken and the CPU has to go out looking for commands or data to process, the effect is lost. You've thrown off its groove.

> ## BUZZ WORDS
>
> **Instruction pipelining:** The ability of certain CPUs to be loading the next set of instructions or data at the same time they process the current set.
>
> **Superscalar architecture:** A microprocessor design that provides multiple pathways for data to take as it is being processed. This allows several lines of code to be processed simultaneously.

SUPERSCALAR ARCHITECTURE

Superscalar architecture was introduced to the world of CPUs with the fifth generation of microprocessors (more on the processor generations later in this chapter). This technology opens up more than just one path for instructions to follow through the processor. While there is still only a single external data bus bringing data into the CPU, once it's inside, there are two different layers of circuitry to process the data. Multiple lines of code can be processed simultaneously. In a way, it is similar to having a second CPU on board. There are some limitations, however. The second execution unit can't handle the full load of commands. Also, programs have to be written specifically to take advantage of this architecture as well. Otherwise, all that fancy new circuitry goes ignored.

To understand how this benefits most applications, consider the following scenario. If you've ever tried to get into the parking lot at the State Fair, you've seen an example of the effect this can have on the speed of throughput. When you first arrive, only a single lane is open, and the cars move through very slowly. Then somebody starts showing signs of intelligence and opens a second gate. The parking lot now fills twice as fast. This scenario is doubly accurate because the prefetch even allows instructions to slip in from the back of the line and scoot in ahead of those that have been waiting a while. A good fair attendant won't do that.

BRANCH PREDICTION

Writing computer programs is an art. I've always had the greatest respect for good programmers. They have to anticipate every possible event and accommodate that event in the code. However, code is written in blocks. And sometimes the block of code that needs to be run will be determined by the outcome of what's going on inside the CPU.

The purpose of adding cache memory to a computer system was to try to minimize the amount of time required for the CPU to find the instructions or data it needs. The more often the prefetch finds what it needs in cache, the faster the system runs overall. Of course, programs frequently run into forks in the road, situations where if the user answers "YES" to a query, it runs one routine, and conversely, a "NO" will require loading a different section of code. When this happens, the CPU will stall because the prefetch has no idea which direction to go for code. Or it can gamble by picking a direction and going there. Some programmers chose the latter method, because there was at least a fifty-fifty chance of the CPU finding what it needed in cache.

Unfortunately, the fifty-fifty-ninety rule usually applied. This rule states that if there is a fifty-fifty chance of making the correct choice, there's a ninety percent chance you'll choose wrong. *Branch prediction* allows the prefetch to bring in several lines of code from either branch, so whichever way the CPU winds up heading, there are commands there for it to process.

> ### BUZZ WORDS
>
> **Branch prediction:** The ability of certain CPUs to be able to predict a situation where either one of two separate subroutines may be run, depending on the results of processing code not yet completed. A CPU capable of branch prediction will load a few lines of code from each subroutine.
>
> **Speculative execution:** When two different subroutines have been loaded by branch prediction, speculative execution will actually process the lines of each branch loaded.

SPECULATIVE EXECUTION

Speculative execution takes branch prediction to the next level. The CPU takes a wild guess about which way the code is going and preprocesses the first few lines of code. When it guesses right, it's got a head start in running the subroutine. If it's wrong, it simply dumps the registers and starts over, using the data provided by the prefetch. No harm, no foul. That isn't any slower than it would have been had it not even tried. When it's right, a trip to the hard drive is avoided. As I will discuss in Chapter Thirteen, Hard Disk Drive Structure and Geometry, this shaves hundreds, or even thousands of clock cycles off of the total processing time.

OUT-OF-ORDER EXECUTION

Computers being what they are, it is pretty easy to assume that data always arrives at the CPU in precisely the order in which it is needed. Instructions always arrive in the right sequence and data is always there when you need it. Right?

And your spouse is always ready when you are, and you're never late for work either. Right?

The fact of the matter is, data is not always there when the processor needs it and the more complex programs become, the more the CPU starts seeing sets of instructions it is going to eventually need before it gets the ones it needs now. In the old days, the CPU just waited. If you were lucky, instructions waited in cache until the CPU was ready, and would be there when the processor was ready for them. The control unit would then make sure that those instructions ran in the correct order. More often, too many clock cycles would elapse and the instructions would be flushed from cache.

> **BUZZ WORDS** ——————
>
> **Hyperthreading:** The ability of certain CPUs to execute multiple lines of code at the same time.
>
> **Streaming SIMD:** The ability of certain CPUs to execute an instruction only once, but apply that instruction to several sets of data.

Modern CPUs employ a process knows as out-of-order execution to keep busy and minimize dead time. A CPU can run certain types of instructions in advance and store the results in the data cache. Then when the data or instructions it was waiting for arrive, it processes those instructions.

HYPERTHREADING

One of the limitations of all the technologies discussed above is that they assume that only one line of code, or thread, as it is called, will be running on the CPU at any instant in time. In today's world of multitasking operating systems and multitasking users, this is rarely the case. *Hyperthreading* allows the CPU to process two (or more) threads of code simultaneously. In the past, multiple threads could be processed, but they did so by "time-sharing" the CPU.

STREAMING SIMD EXTENSIONS

SIMD is an acronym for Single Instruction, Multiple Data. A processor frequently has a single instruction that will be executed on multiple data sets. Prior to the incorporation of *streaming SIMD extensions* (SSE), in order to do this the CPU would have to process the instruction separately for each data set to be run. SSE allows the CPU to process the instructions once and simply apply them to each data set in turn. This can reduce processing time by several clock cycles per data set.

CPU COOLING

When computers first came out, there was no need to take any special measures in order to keep the CPU running cool. At 4.77MHz, the fan in the power supply kept the air moving inside the case well enough. These days, thermal issues take the forefront. CPUs running at several gigahertz, combined with chipsets running several hundred megahertz and video cards that run at several hundred megahertz create a major problem. The CPU, without some form of cooling mechanism, can actually heat up enough to fry your eggs for you in the morning. The problem is that it's hard to keep the computer running when that happens.

CONVECTIVE COOLING

Starting with the 80486, it became necessary to add some form of device that would dissipate the heat from the CPU and expel it from the enclosure. The earliest CPU heat sinks, such as the one seen in **Figure 7.6**, simply consisted of metal fins. Heat from the CPU was moved into the fins and a cooling fan in the case sucked the warm air out of the enclosure. This process of moving heat from one metal object to another is called convection.

When the Pentium was first released, it was quite obvious that a simple passive heat sink would not be sufficient. Those babies cranked out some temperature! Innovative designers came up with various designs of heat sink that incorporated a fan built right in. This allowed the heat sink/fan combination to suck the heat out of the CPU and actively blow it away. Enclosure fans evacuated the hot air from inside the case.

LIQUID COOLING

These days, it is possible to install liquid cooling systems into computers. These elaborate systems work exactly like the radiator in an automobile. A small pump moves liquid through tubes that run in direct contact with the CPU. The cooled liquid in the tubes draws the heat away the chip and carries it to fins that are located near the outside of the case. The fins draw the heat from the liquid and a fan blows across the fins keeping them cool. The cooled liquid circulates back to the CPU to pick up more heat.

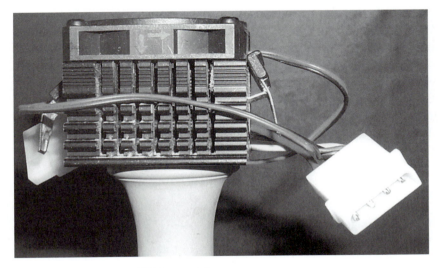

Figure 7.6 A simple CPU heat sink.

Liquid cooling has a couple of advantages over convective cooling. For one thing, it's much more efficient. Components on liquid-cooled systems run far more coolly than do those of convective systems. An advantage that often gets overlooked is the fact that since the fans don't have to spin nearly as fast in a liquid-cooled system as they do in convective systems, the system also runs more quietly.

CHAPTER SUMMARY

Okay, I've now completed my case that the CPU cannot stand alone as being the "brains" of the computer. Still, as you saw, it is a very complicated device and a technological marvel. And each year they get faster and more complex.

As a device, the CPU predates the PC by several years, having served in devices such as pocket calculators and mainframes. It is important that you have a good understanding of the history and evolution of microprocessors as they developed, and it won't hurt to have a good understanding of how they work.

BRAIN DRAIN

1. Describe how a semiconductor works, and explain why it is such a useful material in making CPUs.

2. List the key subcomponents of a CPU and briefly describe their function.

3. Explain why the 8088 CPU was only capable of recognizing 1MB of memory.

4. Just what do engineers mean by "protected mode" and why is it important today?

5. Describe in as much detail as you can how the system moves data into the CPU after you press a certain key on your keyboard.

THE 64K$ QUESTIONS

1. The binary language is an offshoot of the work of _____.
   a. George Boole
   b. Frederick Hoffner

   c. Ted Hoff
   d. Al Shugart

2. When the microprocessor is processing a thread of code and realizes it need additional data, the _____ instructs the _____ to locate that data.
   a. Prefetch, External data bus
   b. Prefetch, Control unit
   c. Control unit, Prefetch
   d. Control unit, Data cache

3. The address bus of the 8088 was _____ bits wide.
   a. 8
   b. 16
   c. 20
   d. 32

4. A microprocessor is running a line of code and comes to a place where either one of two different subroutines will be run next, depending on whether the user selects "Yes" or "No." What technology allows the

CPU to load a few lines of each subroutine even before the user makes a selection?

   a. Protected mode

   b. Instruction pipelining

   c. Branch prediction

   d. Speculative execution

5. In the example used in Question 4, what technology would allow the CPU to actually process those lines of code before the user made a selection, discarding any data generated by the wrong subroutine?

   a. Protected mode

   b. Instruction pipelining

   c. Branch prediction

   d. Speculative execution

6. The first CPU used in an IBM PC ran at _____ MHz.

   a. 2.77

   b. 4.77

   c. 8

   d. 12

7. It is not possible for a CPU to have more than one FPU.

   a. True

   b. False

8. Why is the 64K block of data so important to CPU operations?

   a. Because all registers are only 16 bits wide.

   b. It is a throwback to the days of 16-bit CPUs.

   c. Because the Pentium CPU is limited to a 64-bit external data bus.

   d. It is a throwback to the pre-PC days when microprocessors only had a 16-bit address bus.

9. The following is a collection of very useful circuits that appear on all modern CPUs, but was not a part of the original 8088.

   a. Decode unit

   b. Instruction cache

   c. Control unit

   d. L2 cache

10. Superscalar architecture is a technology that allows _____.

   a. Multiple lines of code to be processed simultaneously.

   b. Multiple processors to be installed on a single die.

   c. Multiple processors to be installed on a single system board.

   d. Merged audio/video streams to be processed as a single stream of code.

TRICKY TERMINOLOGY

Address bus: A bank of wires running throughout the system and into the CPU that specifies specific locations. The total addressable space is calculated as 2x, where x represents the total number of wires in the bus.

Arithmetic logic unit: A subcomponent of a microprocessor responsible for executing simple mathematical calculations, such as add, subtract, multiply, and divide. It cannot perform floating point calculations.

Back-side bus: A portion of the EDB. It is the path that data takes as it moves from cache loaded on the CPU's die into the CPU's registers.

Branch prediction: The ability of certain CPUs to be able to predict a situation where either one of two separate subroutines may be run, depending on the results of processing code not yet completed. A CPU capable of branch prediction will load a few lines of code from each subroutine.

Clock cycle: A timing signal generated by an electrical current that synchronizes data movement throughout the system. As an electrical current, a clock cycle resembles a sine wave with a rising half of the signal and a falling half.

Data cache: A set of registers used for storing data loaded by the prefetch until such time as the CPU is ready to use it.

Decode unit: The subcomponent of a microprocessor that takes complex instructions and breaks them down into a series of simpler instructions that the CPU is able to understand.

External data bus: The wires that move data from outside the CPU to the internal registers of the CPU.

Floating point unit: A subcomponent of a microprocessor that is responsible for more complex mathematical calculations.

Front-side bus: A portion of the EDB. It is the path that data takes from outside locations to make its way into the CPU.

Hyperthreading: The ability of certain CPUs to execute multiple lines of code at the same time.

Instruction cache: A set of registers used for storing instruction code loaded by the prefetch until such time as the CPU is ready to use it.

Instruction pipelining: The ability of certain CPUs to be loading the next set of instructions or data at the same time they process the current set.

Linewidth: The actual thickness of traces used within the CPU.

Logic gate: Two or more transistors whose position will direct the positioning of the next bank of transistors downstream.

Megabyte: Depending on whether you are calculating a value in binary or decimal, a megabyte is either 1 million bytes (decimal) or 1,048,576 bytes (binary). A binary megabyte is used in virtually every circumstance except when calculating hard drive capacity. Hard drive manufacturers typically define capacity in decimal values.

Prefetch: The subcomponent of a microprocessor that is responsible for retrieving data and moving it into the CPU.

Protected mode: A function of a CPU that prevents two separate programs from seeing each other's code or from attempting to use overlapping memory addresses. Should either event occur, the CPU would lock up.

Register: A bank of transistors grouped together to perform a specific function.

Semiconductor: A substance that exhibits the characteristics of both a conductor and a resistor, depending on the amount of voltage passing through.

Speculative execution: When two different subroutines have been loaded by branch prediction, speculative execution will actually process the lines of each branch loaded.

Streaming SIMD: The ability of certain CPUs to execute an instruction only once, but apply that instruction to several sets of data.

Threshold voltage: The amount of electrical differential required to move a semiconductor from a state of resistance to a state of conductance.

Transistor: A microscopic on/off switch that uses the electrical characteristics of a semiconductor to reverse positions.

ACRONYM ALERT

ALU: Arithmetic Logic Unit. The subcomponent of a CPU that handles rudimentary mathematical functions.

BSB: Back-Side Bus. The portion of the EDB that moves data back and forth between onboard cache and the CPU.

CPU: Central Processing Unit. The primary microprocessor that executes program code and processes user data in a computer system.

EDB: External Data Bus. The path that data uses to move from the CPU to an outside circuit, or vice versa.

FC-PGA: Flip Chip Pin Grid Array. A CPU socket designed for easy CPU installation or replacement used in modern machines.

FPU: Floating Point Unit. The subcomponent of the CPU that handles more advanced mathematical functions.

FSB: Front-Side Bus. The portion of the EDB that moves data in and out of the CPU from external locations.

Hz: Hertz. A measurement for frequency, or the number of times during any given timing cycle that the measured event occurs.

L1: Level 1. A small amount of extremely fast memory used to store data or instructions that the CPU expects it will need within a few clock cycles, or that it uses frequently.

L2: Level 2. A secondary level of slower cache memory. This is usually a larger amount of memory than the L1 and is the second place the CPU looks for needed instructions or data.

L3: Level 3. A third layer of cache supported only by a select few CPUs.

MB: Megabyte. In binary, this would be 1,048,576 bytes. In decimal, it would be 1 million bytes.

SIMD: Single Instruction, Multiple Data. A process by which a CPU can execute an instruction once, but apply that instruction to several sets of data simultaneously.

SSE: Streaming SIMD Extensions. The set of instructions that supports the execution of a single instruction on several sets of data at once.

CHAPTER 8

THE EVOLUTION AND DEVELOPMENT OF THE CPU

Now that you have a grasp of how the CPU works and some of the things going on underneath the hood, let's take a look at a detailed timeline of CPU evolution. This may not seem like such critical information at the outset, but two things make it important. First of all, knowing what CPU powers a particular computer will tell you whether or not it can run certain OSs or applications. Second, you need it to pass the A+ Core exam.

A+ CORE HARDWARE EXAM OBJECTIVES

Some of the material covered in this chapter includes the following:

1.1   Identify the names, purpose, and characteristics of system modules. Recognize these modules by sight or definition.

1.2   Identify basic procedures for adding and removing field-replaceable modules for desktop systems. Given a replacement scenario, choose the appropriate sequences.

1.10 Determine the issues that must be considered when upgrading a PC. In a given scenario, determine when and how to upgrade system components.

4.1   Distinguish among the popular CPU chips in terms of their basic characteristics.

THE EVOLUTION OF THE CPU

Of all the components in a computer system, none gets more publicity than the CPU when it comes time for a new release. It seems that everyone is waiting on the sidelines in anticipation of each new generation of CPU. Some new releases are based on speed alone, while every once in a while an actual new technology emerges. Examples of technology improvements would

Table 8.1   A Timeline of Intel CPUs

CPU	Year Intro	Clock Speeds (MHz)	Ext. Bus	Int. Bus	RAM	Transistors
8086	1978	4.77, 8, 10	16-bit	16-bit	1MB	29,000
8088	1979	4.77, 8	8-bit	16-bit	1MB	29,000
80286	1982	6, 8, 10, 12	16-bit	16-bit	16MB	134,000
80386	1985	20, 25, 33	32-bit	32-bit	4GB	275,000
80386SX	1988	16, 20, 25, 33	16-bit	32-bit	16MB	275,000
80486DX	1989	25, 33, 50	32-bit	32-bit	4GB	1.2M
80486SX	1991	16, 20, 25, 33	32-bit	32-bit	4GB	900,000
80486DX2	1992	25/50, 33/66	32-bit	32-bit	4GB	1.2M
80486DX4	1994	25/75, 33/100	32-bit	32-bit	4GB	1.2M
Pentium	1994	60,66	64-bit	32-bit	4GB	3.1M
Pentium MMX	1997	166, 200, 233, 266	64-bit	32-bit	4GB	3.1M
Pentium PRO	1995	150, 166, 180, 200	64-bit	32-bit	64GB	5.5M
Pentium II	1997	233-450MHz	64-bit	32-bit	64GB	7.5M
Pentium III	1999	450MHz to 1.4GHz	64-bit	32-bit	64GB	28M
Pentium 4	2000	1GHz and up	64-bit	32-bit	64GB	42M

Evolution of Intel CPUs

include an FSB, new instruction sets moved onboard, or a new process added to chip functions. Also, from time to time, CPU manufacturers encode certain instructions into the CPU. As a result, when the prefetch goes looking for those instructions, it finds them waiting in the parlor, ready to serve.

For the first several years of PC evolution, it was Intel putting the vast majority of CPUs into PC-compatible computers (**Table 8.1**). However, a number of other chip manufacturers, including Advanced Micro Devices (AMD), Texas Instruments, Cyrix, and others, entered the fray with competing clones. Since there is not room in this book to discuss every chip ever made, I'll limit my discussions to the primary CPU families from the major manufacturers.

AMD entered the fray early with a competing line of CPUs, even though it would be several years before it would begin to give Intel any serious competition. For many years, its CPUs were identical to those of Intel. Then, after a well-publicized lawsuit between Intel and AMD, AMD began developing significant new technologies of its own (**Table 8.2**).

EXAM NOTE: Before going in to take the exam, make sure you know order in which the different models of CPU came out. Also be able to describe key differences among models, such as bus speed and width.

Table 8.2   A Timeline of AMD CPUs

CPU	Year Intro	Clock Speeds (MHz)	Ext. Bus	Int. Bus	RAM	Transistors
AM5x86[1]	1995	133	32-bit	32-bit	4GB	1.6M
K5	1996	75, 90, 120, 133, 166	64-bit	32-bit	4GB	4.3M
K6	1997	166, 200, 233, 266, 300	64-bit	32-bit	4GB	8.8M
K6-2	1998	266, 300, 333, 350, 366, 380, 400, 450, 475, 500, 533, 550	64-bit	32-bit	64GB	9.3M
K6-3	1998	400, 450, 500, 550	64-bit	32-bit	64GB	N/A
Athlon	1999	500, 550, 600, 650, 700, 750, 800	64-bit	32-bit	64GB	22M[2]
Duron	2000	600MHz to 1.3GHz3	64-bit	32-bit	64GB	25M
Thunderbird	2000	700MHz to 1.3GHz	64-bit	32-bit	37M	
Athlon XP	2001	1.7GHz to 3GHz[3]	54-bit	32-bit	64GB	37.5M

Evolution of AMD CPUs

[1] The 5x86 was not AMD's first CPU. However, all prior CPUs were manufactured using technology acquired under a cross-licensing agreement with Intel, and are therefore identical to equivalent Intel CPUs.
[2] Transistor count does not include L2 cache.
[3] CPU in current production as of this writing. Speeds are likely to exceed these before their life cycle ends.

PROCESSOR GENERATIONS

Over the years, as CPUs have evolved, there have been relatively few drastic breakthroughs in technology. Manufacturers will produce lengthy runs of various models of CPU based on the technology of the day. When a new breakthrough occurs, a new generation is launched. Thus begat the generations of the modern CPU.

FIRST-GENERATION PROCESSORS

The first Intel CPU used by IBM in its Personal Computer was the 8088. An optional math coprocessor, the Intel 8087, was available for motherboards that supported these chips. The 8088 was actually a revision of an existing chip, the 8086. The 8086 had a 16-bit external data bus (EDB), a 16-bit internal data bus (IDB), and a 16-bit address bus. IBM wanted to make use of the 8-bit devices already on the market, so the 16-bit EDB was a problem. It also wanted to address more than the 64K of RAM that a 16-bit address bus accommodates.

It approached Intel, who agreed to produce a modification of the 8086 that it called the 8088. This chip had an 8-bit EDB, 16-bit internal registers, and a 20-bit address bus. The

Table 8.3 First-Generation Processors

Chip	Date Released	Ext. Bus	Voltage	Die Size	MIPS
8088-4.77	1979	8-bit	5V	3 μ	.3
8088-8	1980	8-bit	5V	3 μ	.4
NEC V20	1984	8-bit	5V	Unknown	Unknown
80186-8/16	1982	8/16 hybrid	5V	3 μ	N/A

First-generation CPUs

20-bit address bus was achieved by combining two 16-bit registers onto a 20-bit register. A 16-bit register can basically address 64K of memory. By using two 16-bit registers, programmers could slice programs and data into 64K chunks. This also allowed for backward compatibility to earlier systems.

Intel was to see the start of competition with this first "IBM-compatible" release. Within months, American Micro Devices, Inc. (AMD) had come out with its own 8088, and NEC released a chip called the V20. Of the three major manufacturers, NEC's was probably the best performer and showed up on a number of clones.

SECOND-GENERATION PROCESSORS

This level of CPU is really only populated by a single family of chips. That is the 80286 along with its various clones. The biggest improvements in this chip line were the address bus and the ability to work in protected mode. The address bus was extended to 24-bit, allowing up to 16MB addressable physical memory.

I discussed protected mode in detail in Chapter Seven. But to review, protected mode allowed the CPU to run multiple programs in "time slices," first focusing on one program for a few lines of code, and then allowing another program access to the CPU. In addition to time-sharing the CPU, individual programs could be given their own slice of the memory pie. Each program running on the PC had its own memory address, which was "protected" from invasion by other programs, hence the name.

Protected mode, of course, required an operating system that supported it. Windows did not yet exist as we know it, and MS-DOS had no built-in provision for either protected mode or managing memory beyond 1MB. During the life of the 286, a version of UNIX, a version of OS2, and one of Novel Netware was written to work in this mode. They allowed you to work in protected mode. However, in order to return to working in real mode, you had to reboot the machine.

The real can of worms that the 286 opened up was all that extra memory. It was invisible to MS-DOS, which was the operating system of choice for well over 80 percent of the computers being manufactured. In order to take advantage of it, certain third party companies wrote extensions to DOS that accommodated the extra addressable memory in other ways.

Table 8.4 Second-Generation Processors

Chip	Date Released	Ext. Bus	Voltage	Die Size	MIPS
80286-6	1982	16-bit	5V	1.5 μ	.9
80286-10	1982	16-bit	5V	1.5 μ	1.5
80286-12	1983	16-bit	5V	1.5 μ	2.66
80286-16	1983	16-bit	5V	1.5 μ	N/A
80286-20[1]	1990	16-bit	5V	N/A	N/A

Second-generation CPUs

[1] Clones of the 80286 series of CPUs were manufactured by AMD, Harris, and Siemens. There are no notable differences among the brands. Intel never manufactured the 80286-20. Harris and Siemens produced these after Intel had discontinued the line for use in PCs.

Expanded memory allowed data to be stored in available memory above 1MB. This required loading the EMM device driver in lower memory (taking up a big chunk of conventional memory needed by DOS programs). Out of necessity, the program ran in conventional memory. Data could be stored in expanded memory. Data from expanded memory was fed to the program in 64K chunks.

For this to work, you needed, first of all, the expanded memory installed on your computer. Then you needed to install a program designed specifically to manage expanded memory. Finally, you could run programs that had been written specifically to address expanded memory.

BUZZ WORDS

Expanded memory: Memory beyond the first megabyte of RAM that can be used for storing data. Expanded memory could not be used for executing programs.

Virtual memory: A slice of hard drive space that is reserved for the OS for temporary storage of data needed by dormant programs that is treated as if it were system memory.

THIRD-GENERATION PROCESSORS

Intel's 80386 represents this generation of microprocessors. These CPUs incorporated the first true 32-bit registers. Internal, address, and external busses were all 32-bit. This allowed for up to 4GB of addressable physical RAM and an unthinkable 64TB of addressable virtual memory. Virtual memory was an entirely new concept introduced by the 386. In addition, an advanced instruction set known as the x86 instruction set was introduced into the CPU. These core instructions continue to be the basis for Intel-based CPUs to this very day. An often-overlooked attribute of the 80386 is its ability to pipeline instructions.

The 32-bit registers allowed for twice as much data to be processed in a single clock cycle. More importantly, they allowed for commands to be 32 bits wide. Instructions could be more complex and the operating systems were subsequently more powerful. When more work can be done in a single clock cycle, everything speeds up.

> **EXAM NOTE:** The 80386 microprocessor represented a major breakthrough in personal computing. As a result, it is not at all uncommon to see questions specific to this processor on the exam.

Virtual memory is a way of convincing the programs running on the computer that there is more memory installed than there really is. It reserves a portion of hard disk space for a *swap file*. This file takes program data, user data, and so on, and loads it onto the hard drive in the same way it would have been loaded into RAM, had there been sufficient physical memory to support it. The operating system reports this swap file as memory to the applications. The release of Windows 3.0 and all subsequent versions made full use of this technology.

BUZZ WORDS

Swap file: The file on the hard disk that stores the data reserved in virtual memory.

Virtual real mode: A technique of creating separate address spaces and time slicing the CPU time so that legacy applications think they're the only programs running on the machine, even though there may be several running at once.

Another advanced operating mode that the 386 offered was called *virtual real mode* (sometimes called Virtual 8086). In this mode, "bubbles" of 1MB memory spaces are created in which separate DOS programs could run. An operating system, such as Windows, that supported virtual real mode could load all the necessary device drivers and core program files into one of these address spaces and convince DOS programs that this memory constitutes the entire machine. As a result, the DOS program thinks it's the only program running and more than one DOS program at a time could be running.

A performance enhancement that began with the 386 and that is now a part of all CPUs is the process of pipelining instructions. As one set of instructions is being executed, the CPU is already in the process of lining up the next set to send through the "pipeline." This process not only enhanced the performance of the then-present lines of chips, it also opened the door to the dual-speed CPUs of today that have faster internal processing speeds than their external data bus.

The only problem with the 80386 was that, since it utilized a 32-bit external data bus, the CPU required newly designed 32-bit motherboards. There were several manufacturers that weren't tooled up to build these boards, but there were millions of 16-bit motherboards being built. In order to increase the acceptance of the 386 family, the 80386SX was released with a 16-bit external data bus. It was basically a crippled 386. It had all the advanced functions of the 386, however, and was therefore able to run Windows.

The 386SL was the first line of CPUs to be developed for the lower voltages required for laptop computers. There had been a number of 286 laptops, but they required about three hours of charging for every half hour of use. By running at 3.3V instead of 5V, the life of the portable computer's battery was greatly enhanced. Other brands, including AMD and Cyrix, released lower-voltage CPUs.

Table 8.5 Third-Generation Processors

Chip	Date Released	Ext. Bus	Voltage	Die Size	MIPS
80386DX-16	1985	32-bit	5V	1.5 μ	5-6
80386DX-20	1987	32-bit	5V	1.5 μ	6-7
80386DX-25	1988	32-bit	5V	1.5 μ	8.5
80386DX-33	1989	32-bit	5V	1.5 μ	11.4
80386DX-40[1]	1989	32-bit	5V	1.5 μ	
80386SX-16	1988	16-bit	5V	1.5 μ	2.5
80386SX-20	1989	16-bit	5V	1.5 μ	2.5
80386SX-25	1988	16-bit	5V	1.5 μ	2.7
80386SX-33	1992	16-bit	5V	1.5 μ	2.9
80386SL-20[2]	1990	16-bit	3.3V	1 μ	4.2
80386SL-25	1991	16-bit	3.3V	1 μ	5.3

Comparison of 80386 microprocessors. While these numbers are based on Intel CPUs, it should be noted that equivalent CPUs were also manufactured by AMD and Cyrix.

[1] The 80386DX-40 was never manufactured by Intel. This was a product that was put out by both AMD and Cyrix.
[2] Other variations on the SL CPU included the SLC and the SLX. These chips were manufactured by AMD, Cyrix, IBM, and Intel.

FOURTH-GENERATION PROCESSORS

The 80486DX was basically an evolution of the 386. None of the registers or busses was altered. The real advances were in other forms. The biggest real advance of the CPU was an advanced instruction set. The most commonly used instructions were permanently loaded into the CPU and instantly available when those instructions were called upon. This prevented the CPU from having to load and unload those instructions from memory each time they were called upon.

One of the key limitations of CPUs prior to the 80486 is that the only arithmetic functions they could perform were basic addition, subtraction, multiplication, and division. Also, they could only handle full-integer mathematics. Anything more advanced required programmers to break the formulae down to their basic steps. The other option was to install the MathCo specific to the CPU. The 486DX was the first CPU to have a coprocessor built right in.

Another improvement of the 486 was to add 8K of L1 cache right on the CPU. It could also make use of L2 cache installed on the motherboard. In order to make the L2 cache faster, a special form of memory called *static RAM* (SRAM) was used. SRAM was designed differently than DRAM and did not require frequent refreshes.

BUZZ WORDS

Static RAM: A form of very high-speed memory that is frequently used for cache.

There are actually two varieties of cache. Write-through cache sends data directly out of the CPU to RAM, whether the MCC is ready or not. If not, the CPU simply sets up a wait state. In other words, the data waits in line for a seat on the external data bus. Write-back cache will store the data in L2 cache until a clock cycle comes along that can transmit it back to RAM.

The 486 had the capability of talking to the local bus at either 25 or 33MHz, depending on the CPU. ISA devices were still limited to 8.33MHz for backward compatibility, but VESA Local Bus and the Peripheral Components Interconnect (PCI) both came out during the 486 reign. I'll be discussing these busses in detail in Chapter Ten, Examining the Expansion Bus. VESA stands for Video Electronic Standards Association, which was the organization that defined the 32-bit VESA standard popular in 486s. PCI allowed for even faster bus speeds. Both tapped into the local bus to allow components to operate at the external bus speed of the CPU in order to overcome the 8.33MHz limitation of ISA.

> **NOTE:** Just changing the speed of a CPU is no guarantee of a noticeable performance gain. A rule of thumb is that to achieve a barely perceivable gain in performance, you must double CPU speed. On the other hand, new technologies, such as on-chip instruction sets that relate to the type of work you do or a faster front-side bus, can provide substantial gains.

Under earlier technology, the maximum speed of the CPU was limited to that of the external data bus. That was before Intel developed a technology called clock doubling that allowed the CPU to operate at twice the EDB speed. This allowed for a 66MHz microprocessor. These CPUs were called DX2s. Then came the DX4. DX-4 CPUs processed data internally at a speed three times that of the EDB. Therefore, the 25MHz 486 DX-4 ran internally at 75MHz, and the 33MHz DX-4 ran at 100MHz. (Note that the actual speed of the CPU was 33.32MHz.)

The 486SX was released as an "economy" 486. The official version of how this chip was different than other 486s was that it lacked a math coprocessor. This was purely marketing hype. Intel never bothered to retool for a different CPU. It simply disabled the math coprocessor. Therefore, a product that actually had to go through an extra manufacturing step was sold at a lower price simply to appease the public.

FIFTH-GENERATION PROCESSORS

Now for a quick history lesson. Throughout the reign of the 386s and 486s Intel kept a pretty tight grip on the market. It had the marketing clout, it had the engineering clout, and it had the best research and development. What it lacked was sufficient production capabilities to keep up with increasing demand for its chips. To pick up the slack, Intel signed into a cross-licensing agreement with Advanced Micro Devices, Inc. (AMD). Intel would provide the R&D, cross-license the patents to AMD, and the two companies would outsource chips to each other.

This worked out pretty well for both companies for a while. It was an almost-perfect symbiotic relationship. Unfortunately, somewhere along the line, relations between the two companies began to deteriorate. Intel had opened two new production facilities and no longer needed the services of AMD. There followed a rather unpleasant legal battle, with decisions being reversed and then restored and then being reversed again as the case was passed from one

Table 8.6 Fourth-Generation Processors

Chip	Date Released	Ext.Bus	Voltage	Die Size	iCOMP (version)	MIPS
80486DX-25	1989	32-bit	5V	1 μ	122 (1.0)	20
80486DX-33	1990	32-bit	5V	1 μ	166 (1.0)	27
80486DX-50	1991	32-bit	5V	1 μ	249 (1.0)	41
80486DX2-50	1992	32-bit	5V	.8 μ	231 (1.0)	41
80486DX2-66	1992	32-bit	5V	.8 μ	297 (1.0)	54
80486DX4-75	1992	32-bit	5V	.6 μ	319 (1.0)	53
80486DX4-100	1992	32-bit	5V	.6 μ	435 (1.0)	70.7
80486SX-16[1]	1991	32-bit	5V	1 μ	63 (1.0)	13
80486SX-20[2]	1991	32-bit	5V	1 μ	78 (1.0)	16.5
80486SX-25[2]	1991	32-bit	5V	.8 μ	100 (1.0)	20
80486SX-33[2]	1992	32-bit	5V	.8 μ	136 (1.0)	27
Blue Lightening-75[3]	1993	32-bit	5V	.8 μ	?	?

Comparison of 80486 microprocessors. AMD, Cyrix, and IBM also made competing chips.

[1] SX chips differed from DX models primarily in the fact that the onboard math coprocessor was disabled.
[2] An SL version of these chips was available in a low-power version for notebook computers.
[3] The Blue Lightening was manufactured only by IBM and could not be purchased separately. Intel's licensing agreement with IBM stated that the chip could be sold only on a board.

judge to another. While, theoretically, Intel won, it ended in a decision not entirely favorable to Intel. It was decided that the cross-licensing agreements did indeed allow AMD to continue to produce CPUs based on technology that had been licensed to it. Unfortunately for AMD, this only included technology up to the 80386. In another related case, the courts determined that the terms 80486, 80386, and so forth, had come to be generic terms for a type of CPU, in that Intel, AMD, and Cyrix had produced chips using this nomenclature without challenge from Intel. Therefore, Intel could not copyright the trade name 80486.

Of course, Intel hadn't been sitting back on its heels doing nothing the whole time the courts were deciding the outcome of the lawsuit. The 80586 was already behind the curtains, waiting for its debut. Intel had been procrastinating release of the CPU until it knew what impact the ruling may have on its intellectual property rights. The resultant release, the Pentium, was so named because it was a trademark that could be copyrighted. In addition, a few engineering tweaks used technology that had not been cross-licensed to AMD.

THE P5

The first Pentiums to be released were 5V chips. There were two speeds of the P5 made available, the 60MHz and the 66MHz. In actuality, the original design called for all P5s to be

66MHz. Unfortunately, manufacturing yields were resulting in a lot of chips that just couldn't run at 66MHz without overheating. They could, however, run at 60MHz. They were labeled as 60MHz and shipped out.

This CPU was redesigned to have a 64-bit EDB. This was passed through to two internal 32-bit data busses. Therefore, internally, data could be processed only in 32-bit chunks, but two chunks could be sent along two different pipelines in a single clock cycle. This process is known as superscalar architecture. Operating systems were only using 32-bit code; many still contained large amounts of 16-bit code. Therefore, this new architecture was a more efficient method for processing data as long as it was 32-bit code. Intel named these pipelines the U pipeline and the V pipeline. Neither available literature nor Intel's representative was able to tell me why.

Changes made to the Pentium make it quite a bit faster than the fourth-generation processors aside from raw speed and bus width. The speed of the EDB was increased as well. The fastest EDB on any 486-class CPU was 33MHz. For the Pentiums, this was increased to 60MHz for the P5-60 and 66MHz for the remainder of the fifth-generation CPUs. Another technological improvement was an ability to perform branch predictive processing. This is the same branch prediction I discussed in Chapter Seven, Understanding CPUs.

The L1 cache was divided into two sections. 8K of L1 cache was set aside specifically for instructions, while another 8K was there for data. Each cache section was specifically designed for the unique requirements of each function.

The P5s were not without their problems. A 5V chip running at this speed ran very hot. They all had to be cooled very efficiently or they would fry. The most infamous defect was a design flaw in the FPU. Certain patterns resulted in mathematical calculations that were off. At first, Intel tried to play the issue down, but as more and more demonstrations of the error emerged, it finally acknowledged it as an issue.

THE P-54C AND P-55

The P5 endured a very short life and was quickly replaced by 3.3V versions, often referred to as the P-54Cs. As the P-54C went through its life span it eventually reached a speed of 200MHz. Starting with the 200MHz, Intel began incorporating a technology it named MMX. The MMX eventually reached a top speed of 266MHz. Unlike the 486 with internal clock doublers, the Pentium made use of circuitry on the motherboard to set the internal clock speed. The 66MHz EDB on most motherboards allowed for 100MHz (1.5x), 133MHz (2x), 166MHz (2.5x), 200MHz (3x), 233MHz (3.5x), and 266MHz (4x). On earlier Pentium-class computers, this multiplier circuit was something that had to be set. If you set the multiplier too slow, the CPU would simply run at the speed you assigned it. For example, if you purchased a 233MHz CPU and set the multiplier at 3x, it would simply run at 200MHz. Likewise, if you purchased, the 200 and set it at 3.5x, it would run at 233MHz. This was a technique called *overclocking*. This practice had an inherent risk of overheating the CPU and has been blamed for data processing errors as well.

BUZZ WORDS

Overclocking: A technique of forcing a CPU or system bus to run faster than its rated speed in order to extract maximum performance.

MMX technology was developed in answer to increasing demand for improved multimedia performance. Chips incorporating MMX are known as P-55s. It incorporated four new registers and fifty-seven internally programmed commands that greatly enhanced multimedia technology. When a program called for one of these instructions, the CPU didn't have to go out onto the address bus looking for it. It was right there at home, where it belonged. MMX also extended the i386 instruction set to allow multiple bytes of data or instructions to be stored in a single set of registers. All manipulations performed on the set simultaneously affected all instructions or data stored within. This further enhanced performance.

> **BUZZ WORDS**
>
> **P-rating:** Short for performance rating, this was a labeling method that, instead of designating a CPU by its clock speed, labeled it as the Intel CPU that it could be compared to, even though the actual clock speed and bus speed of the non-Intel chip were both lower.

While MMX was not exclusive to multimedia, software had to be written to take advantage of it. The person who spent his or her entire existence poring over text documents or pounding numbers into a spreadsheet saw little or no performance gain. Also, Intel's design called for the MMX decoder and the FPU to share the same sets of registers. As a result, processing routines that require the simultaneous usage of the MMX unit and the FPU exhibited extreme slowdown.

Cyrix also released some product lines that it claimed (and others confirmed) were faster than Intel's offerings at the same clock speed. It shared with the AMD K5 the ability to reorder instructions prior to executing them. Unique to the Cyrix CPU was a feature known as speculative processing. This was when the CPU executed an instruction it thought was going to be required even before the programming code confirmed it. Some of the features that were common with the Intel processor were improved upon. For example, Cyrix's branch predictive processing was capable of multiple branches, not just a single branch. Cyrix chose to design in seven integer execution stages, compared to Intel's five stages.

As a result of these enhancements, Cyrix's 6x86, while only clocking out at 133MHz, could keep up with, and in some circumstances outperform, an Intel Pentium 166. As a result, it joined with AMD to begin using something it called *P-ratings* for its CPUs. P-ratings do not represent true clock speeds. This can make setting the multiplier on older motherboards that are still set manually a little problematic. You would definitely want to have a copy of the manual for the motherboard before attempting to configure one of these non-Intel CPUs.

EXAM NOTE: The subject of P-ratings is no longer of concern to the modern technician. CompTIA, however, still expects candidates to be able to define the concept.

Other companies quickly stepped up to the table with their "586" offerings. They weren't allowed to call them "Pentium" or even "Pentium-class." The word Pentium is a registered trademark, and Intel is righteously (and rightfully) protecting its intellectual property. AMD's first offering, the K5, was not warmly embraced by the technical community. Many complained of significant compatibility issues, claiming frequent lockups in Microsoft Windows. Others praised its virtues and called it the "Intel-killer."

Table 8.7 Intel Fifth-Generation CPUs

Chip	Date Released	Ext.Bus	Voltage	Die Size	iCOMP (version)	MIPS
Pentium 60	1993	64-bit	5V	.8 μ	510 (1.0)	100
Pentium 66	1993	64-bit	5V	.8 μ	567 (1.0)	112
Pentium 75	1994	64-bit	3.3V	.6 μ	67 (2.0)	127.5
Pentium 90	1994	64-bit	3.3V	.6 μ	81	149.8
Pentium 100	1994	64-bit	3.3V	.6 μ	90	166.3
Pentium 120	1995	64-bit	3.3V	.35 μ	100	203
Pentium 133	1995	64-bit	3.3V	.35 μ	111	218.9
Pentium 150	1996	64-bit	3.3V	.35 μ	114	N/A
Pentium 166	1996	64-bit	3.3V	.35 μ	127	N/A
Pentium 200	1996	64-bit	3.3V	.35 μ	142	N/A
Pentium 150MMX	1997	64-bit	3.3V	.35 μ	~118	N/A
Pentium 166MMX	1997	64-bit	2.8V	.35 μ	160	N/A
Pentium 200MMX	1997	64-bit	2.8V	.35 μ	182	N/A
Pentium 233MMX	1997	64-bit	2.8V	.35 μ	203	N/A

Fifth-generation CPUs from Intel

Table 8.8 AMD Fifth-Generation CPUs

Chip	Date Released	Clock Speed	Bus Speed	Multiplier	Norton SI Rating[1]	Die Size
K5-PR75	1995	75MHz	50MHz	1.5x	286	.35 μ
K5-PR90	1995	90MHz	60MHz	1.5x	359	.35 μ
K5-PR100	1996	100MHz	66MHz	1.5x	390	.35 μ
K5-PR120	1996	90MHz	60MHz	1.5x	380	.35 μ
K5-PR133	1996	100MHz	66MHz	1.5x	407	.35 μ
K5-PR150	1996	116.5MHz	60MHz	1.75x	435	.35 μ
K5-PR166	1997	116.5MHz	66MHz	1.75x	470	.35 μ
K5-PR200	Never released	133MHz	N/A	1.5x	N/A	.35 μ

Fifth-generation CPUs from AMD

[1] AMD never adopted the Intel iCOMP Rating system, and chose to compare their CPUs on the basis of Norton SI standards.

In many respects, the K5 was superior to the Pentium on a technological level. It was closer akin to a Reduced Instruction Set Computing (RISC) processor than it was to the old i386 code. It used a front-end decoder to make it i386 compatible (which may well have been the source of many of the issues reported). It also possessed the ability to process instructions outside of the order in which they were delivered. Overall, it could be argued that it was a better processor (on paper, anyway). Unfortunately, whether earned or not, it carried with it a bit of a bad reputation.

SIXTH-GENERATION PROCESSORS

The CPUs that fall under the category of Sixth Generation is quite a mixed bag. They emerged at a time when technological developments had picked up their pace rather dramatically. As a result, there are a number of different microprocessors from different companies with radically different designs and specifications. The diversity of processors that exist in this category leads to a little confusion and some disagreement as to where a couple of the processors should really fall. Where possible, I've let the manufacturer dictate.

THE PENTIUM PRO

Intel marked the introduction of its P6 with the Pentium PRO 150. This was the first of Intel's CPUs that was designed specifically to run pure 32-bit operating systems. Therefore, users running Windows NT 4.0 or pure 32-bit UNIX enjoyed noticeably faster performance. It employed a process of superpipelining. This increased the number of execution steps the CPU could process on an instruction set to a total of fourteen. L1 cache was divided into two independently addressable areas. There were separate instruction and data caches of 8K each.

This was the first chip into which Intel placed L2 cache directly onto the die. Depending on model, 256K, 512K, or 1MB of L2 cache was available. Placement of L2 cache directly onto the CPU increased performance rather dramatically. Onboard L2 cache also made the CPU the perfect candidate for servers or workstations designed for multiprocessor capability. As each processor maintained its own cache, they weren't competing for whatever cache may be available on the motherboard.

The address bus was bumped from 32-bit to 36-bit, increasing addressable memory to 64GB. This was another feature that made it the perfect choice for servers in its day.

INTEL PENTIUM II AND PENTIUM III PROCESSORS

With these CPUs, Intel combined the technology of the Pentium PRO and MMX. One of the key complaints of the Pentium PRO was that, since it was designed exclusively to handle 32-bit code, it had a tendency to bog down when forced to run OSs such as Windows 95 or Windows 98 that contained a mixture of 32-bit and 16-bit code. Through the use of *segment register caches*, 16-bit and 32-bit code could be run independently through the pipelines. Like the Pentium PRO, the II and III incorporate 512K L2 cache onboard. One significant change

Table 8.9 Pentium Pro

Chip	Date Released	Ext. Bus	Voltage	Die Size	iCOMP (version)
Pentium PRO 150	1995	32-bit	3.3V	.6/.35 μ^1	N/A
Pentium PRO 166	1995	32-bit	3.3V	.6/.35 μ^1	N/A
Pentium PRO 180	1995	32-bit	3.3V	.6/.35 μ^1	197
Pentium PRO 200	1995	32-bit	3.3V	.6/.35 μ^1	220

Pentium PRO Processors

Pentium PRO processors were available in versions with either 256KB or 512KB of L2 onboard the CPU.
[1] Die size was .6 for 256KB modules and .35 for 512KB

here, however, was that the onboard L2 cache was designed onto an independent back-side bus that ran at one-half the clock speed of the processor itself. Still, this is somewhat of an improvement over L2 cache on the motherboard, which can only be addressed at the speed of the front-side bus. The amount of L1 cache was doubled as well. Each of the L1 registers was increased to 16K, for a total of 32K L1 cache. All of the MMX commands and registers were incorporated onto the CPU as well.

BUZZ WORDS

Segment register cache: Separate cache locations maintained by Pentium II (and later) for keeping 16-bit code running separately from 32-bit code.

Differences between the Pentium II and III were primarily feature-oriented. The Pentium III added extensions to the instruction set that permitted the CPU to execute 3D graphics functions more efficiently. (The impact of this improvement might have been slightly hampered by the fact that AMD had been shipping CPUs with that feature for nearly a year already.) One controversial feature that Intel added to the chip was an electronic serial number (ESN).

The ESN was a number, unique to each CPU that was manufactured, that would identify that particular chip. This ESN could be used for many different purposes, some good, some not so good. On the positive side, a network administrator could use it to manage networks more efficiently with systems management software designed to take advantage of ESNs. However, it also could be used to track Internet usage and to gather information about users' activities while on the Internet. Consumer advocacy groups protested this potential invasion of privacy, and just prior to shipping, Intel reversed its philosophy and shipped the chip with the ESN disabled by default. As it currently stands, in order to make use of the ESN, network administrators have to run a control utility that allows them to enable or disable the ESN.

The first generation of Pentium II and some models of the Pentium III CPU brought with them a significant design change as well. Intel incorporated the chip onto an SECC. This proprietary design was intended to keep all other manufacturers from designing anything directly like it. Later releases would revert back to a conventional socketed CPU using variations on the Socket 370.

Table 8.10   Pentium II Processors

Chip	Date Released	Ext. Bus	Voltage (Core/IO)	Die Size	L2 Cache Speed	iCOMP (version)	Cacheable RAM
PII-233	1997	66MHz	2.8/3.3	.35 μ	116MHz	267 (2.0)	512MB
PII-266	1997	66MHz	2.8/3.3	.35 μ	133MHz	303 (2.0)	512MB
PII-300K	1997	66MHz	2.8/3.3	.35 μ	150MHz	332 (2.0)	512MB
PII-300D	1997	66MHz	2.0/3.3	.35 μ	150MHz	860 (3.0)	4GB
PII-333	1998	66MHz	2.0/3.3	.25 μ	166MHz	366 (2.0) 940 (3.0)[1]	4GB
PII-350	1998	100MHz	2.0/3.3	.25 μ	175MHz	1000 (3.0)	4GB
PII-400	1998	100MHz	2.0/3.3	.25 μ	200MHz	1130 (2.0)	4GB
PII-450	1998	100MHz	2.0/3.3	.25 μ	225MHz	1240 (3.0)	4GB

Pentium II CPU comparisons

[1] The Pentium II-350 was the one microprocessor for which I could locate accurate results for both iCOMP 2.0 and iCOMP 3.0 ratings. The drastically different numbers indicate the disparity in results, demonstrating why it is impossible to make accurate comparisons using different versions of the rating method.

AMD K6, K6/2, AND K6/3 PROCESSORS

AMD's excursion into the sixth generation included three different versions of the K6. I've decided to lump them all together as a group, because the technical differences were minimal. With these processors, the P-rating system was abandoned. The CPUs are rated at their actual clock speeds. AMD incorporated a full 64K in L1 cache onto these chips, 32K data and 32K instruction. To further enhance performance, a total of four instruction decoders keep data flowing through the pipelines. And, since it was adding extra components to the processor, AMD decided it might be a good idea if there was more than a single arithmetic logic unit (ALU). Six integer execution units were added. All AMD K6 series CPUs fall into the Socket Seven form factor.

The K6 series improved performance slightly over the equivalent Pentium II CPUs by Intel when running certain types of applications. However, the Pentium II instruction set seemed to give it a slight advantage when running 32-bit code. The K6/2 series added a dedicated set of forty-five instructions for handling 3D rendering of graphics that it called 3DNOW! This was a feature that enthralled the gaming crowd, and the AMD chip took its first steps into becoming a serious competitor for Intel.

Prior to the release of the K6/3, the AMD chips had taken the approach of putting the L2 cache onto the motherboard. This put the choice of how much L2 cache to use onto the motherboard manufacturer's lap. A typical Socket Super 7 board to support the AMD K6 would have anywhere from 512K to as much as 2MB of L2 cache.

The K6/3 put 256K of L2 cache onto the chip die. Still, it could be used on the majority of motherboards that supported the K5/6 CPU (though many required a BIOS upgrade) and would use the motherboard cache as a third level, or L3 cache. As a result, it was possible to have a system with up to 2.3MB of total cache.

Table 8.11 AMD K6, K6/2, and K6/3 Processors

Chip	Date Released	EDB Speed	Voltage (core/IO)	Die Size
K6-166 through 233	1997	66MHz	2.9/3.3	.35 μ
K6-233L through 300	1997	66MHz	2.2/3.3	.25 μ
K6/2-266	1998	66MHz	2.2/3.3	.25 μ
K6/2-300 Model 8	1998	100MHz	2.2/3.3	.25 μ
K6/2-300 Model 8 CXT	1998	100MHz or 66MHz	2.2/3.3	.25 μ
K6/2-333 Model 8	1998	95MHz	2.2/3.3	.25 μ
K6/2-333 Model 8 CXT	1998	95MHz or 66MHz	2.2/3.3	.25 μ
K6/2-350 Model 8 or CXT	1998	100MHz	2.2/3.3	.25 μ
K6/2-366	1998	66MHz	2.2/3.3	.25 μ
K6/2-380	1998	95MHz	2.2/3.3	.25 μ
K6/2-400	1998	100MHz	2.2/3.3	.25 μ
K6/2-450	1999	100MHz	2.2/3.3	.25 μ
K6/2-475	1999	95MHz	2.2/3.3	.25 μ
K6/2-500	1999	100MHz	2.2/3.3	.25 μ
K6/2-533	1999	97MHz	2.2/3.3	.25 μ
K6/2-550	2000	100MHz	2.2/3.3	.25 μ
K6/3-400	1999	100MHz	2.4/3.3	.25 μ
K6/3-450	1999	100MHz	2.4/3.3	.25 μ

AMD K6 sixth-generation microprocessors

The K6/2 series was available in the K6/2+ for notebook computers in speeds of 450, 475, 500, 533, and 550MHz. These differed from the standard K6/2s primarily in that they used a .18 circuit width.

SEVENTH-GENERATION PROCESSORS

It was with the Seventh-Generation processors that AMD managed to take the lead in microprocessor technology away from Intel, if but for a short while. It was first with its K7, or Athlon, processors. AMD initially followed Intel's lead in that the first few releases shipped in a Slot A form factor that was cosmetically identical to Intel's Slot 1. This was its first foray into a cartridge design (although it would later revert to producing the CPUs in a newer Socket A form factor).

AMD ATHLON AND DURON

The first Athlons to be released, the Model 1, were based on .25-micron technology. This began to be a bit of a problem as AMD started pushing the envelope of speed for transistors that size, and it made the move to .18-micron manufacturing with the Model 2.

The Thunderbird series of Athlon CPUs is its flagship line of processors. It was the first to break the gigahertz barrier and the first to hit the market with a commercially available CPU using copper instead of aluminum for the interconnects between the layers of the chip.

The Athlon chips can credit much of their superior performance not to the high processing speed but rather to a 200MHz FSB. This is a full 50 percent faster than equivalent Intel products (except for the Pentium 4, which I will get to next). More recently, supported by its own AMD 760 chipset, it has achieved a 266MHz FSB. Processors using this technology are available in 1GHz and up.

The new Athlon bus is divided into three channels. Controlling the bus is the universal processor request channel and a universal snoop channel. Data moves back and forth across the bus on a 72-bit bidirectional data channel. The data channel provides 32 bits of bandwidth in each direction plus an additional 8 bits for error-correction code.

Realizing there was a market for higher-end, low-priced chips, it came out with a line of CPUs it labeled the Duron. Following Intel's lead (when it made the Celeron), it is a scaled-down version of the Athlon. It maintains the clock speeds, but drops back to a lower 64K of on-chip L2 cache. Still, with its 128K of L1, evenly divided between instruction and data registers, performance manages to maintain very high levels.

THE PENTIUM 4

Half the fun of working in the computer industry is watching companies such as AMD and Intel play leapfrog with each other. The spirit of competition, in my opinion, is more prevalent in this industry than anywhere else in the world. Intel proves that with its Pentium 4.

The first release of the CPU was based on Intel's new 400MHz FSB and supported only by the i850 Willamette chipset. The only memory supported by this chipset is Rambus memory. This turned out to be a bit shortsighted on Intel's part, in so much as the perceived superiority of the first generation of Rambus memory was overrated. (Subsequent generations are markedly superior, but that will be discussed in Chapter Nine, Searching Your Memory.)

Subsequent chipsets were designed that could either use conventional PC-133 memory or, more recently, double data rate (DDR) memory. (These two different technologies will also be discussed in greater detail in Chapter Nine.) They also provide a 533MHz FSB.

The first P4s to hit the streets were based on the same .18-micron technology used by Pentium III CPUs. However, in 2001 the Northwood became Intel's first copper-based chip using .13-micron technology. Subsequent CPUs have followed suit.

One note on the actual FSB speeds of the Pentium 4 is this. These CPUs use something called *quad-pumped* technology. The actual clock speeds of the bus are 100MHz × 4 on the chips with a 400MHz rating and 133MHz × 4 on the 533MHz chips. What quad-pumping does is to move data four times on every clock cycle.

> **BUZZ WORDS**
>
> **Quad-pumped:** A technique of moving four bits of data over each wire on each clock cycle of the front-side bus.

CHAPTER SUMMARY

In Chapter Seven, I discussed in detail how CPUs were manufactured and what makes them tick. This chapter goes into more detail on the development of CPUs over the years and the evolution of all the bells and whistles you've come to expect. If your purpose in reading this book is to pass CompTIA's Core Exam, then there is actually more exam material in this chapter than there was in Chapter Seven.

Here I covered the generations of microprocessors and the different bus speeds and widths used by each subsequent generation. As the CPUs get more advanced, knowing the different technologies employed that I discussed in Chapter Seven is essential in understanding the differences among generations discussed in Chapter Eight. I just figured that two twenty-page chapters were going to be easier on the reader than a single forty-page chapter.

BRAIN DRAIN

1. Briefly describe the processor generations and how they differ in speed and bus width.

2. Discuss as many differences as you can between the 386 and the 486 CPUs.

3. Discuss why raw processor speed has far less impact on system performance than other factors, such as the amount of L1 cache or the amount of system memory installed.

4. Why did Intel suddenly stop using numerical designations for its CPUs?

5. The fifth-generation CPUs showed a rather remarkable diversity of characteristics. Discuss some of the Generation 5 CPUs and how they differed from each other.

THE 64K$ QUESTIONS

1. Which of the following saw no change in the migration from the 8086 to the 80286?

   a. The address bus

   b. The IDB

   c. The EDB

   d. The ALU

2. The 80286 CPU was capable of addressing _____ of RAM.

   a. 1MB

   b. 4MB

   c. 16MB

   d. 64MB

3. Which CPU was the first to support protected mode?

   a. 8088

   b. 8086

   c. 80286

   d. 80386

4. Two changes IBM wanted to make on the 8086 microprocessor before it used it in its computers was _____.

   a. The width of the address bus

   b. Core speed

   c. Voltage

   d. The width of the external data bus

5. The 80286 microprocessor has a
   _____-bit address bus.
   a. 16
   b. 20
   c. 24
   d. 32

6. The 80386 microprocessor has a
   _____-bit EDB.
   a. 16
   b. 20
   c. 24
   d. 32

7. The address bus of the 80486 was
   twice that of the 80386.
   a. True
   b. False

8. The 80486SX differed from the
   80486DX in that the SX had
   _____.
   a. A wider EDB
   b. A larger address bus
   c. It lacked an FPU
   d. It had to be soldered onto the
      board

9. The AMD series of 80386 CPUs
   suffered several compatibility issues
   when using Microsoft operating
   systems.
   a. True
   b. False

10. The Pentium 4 CPU sports either a
    _____ FSB or a _____ FSB.
    a. 400, 533
    b. 100, 133
    c. 266, 333
    d. 100 x 4, 133 x 4

TRICKY TERMINOLOGY

Benchmarking: A method of measuring the base performance of a device or system before any load is placed on it.

Expanded memory: Memory beyond the first megabyte of RAM that can be used for storing data. Expanded memory could not be used for executing programs.

Extended memory: Memory beyond the first megabyte of RAM that can be used for data storage and the execution of program code.

i386 instruction set: The basic CPU-level instructions embedded in the 80386 microprocessor. These instructions went on to become the core instructions for subsequent generations of Intel-compatible microprocessors.

Overclocking: A technique of forcing a CPU or system bus to run faster than its rated speed in order to extract maximum performance.

P-rating: short for performance rating, this was a labeling method that, instead of designating a CPU by its clock speed, labeled it as the Intel CPU that it could be compared to, even though the actual clock speed and bus speed were both lower.

Quad-pumped: A technique of moving four bits of data over each wire on each clock cycle of the front-side bus.

Segment register cache: Separate cache locations maintained by Pentium II (and later) for keeping 16-bit code running separately from 32-bit code.

Swap file: The file on the hard disk that stores the data reserved in virtual memory.

Virtual memory: A slice of hard drive space that is reserved for the OS for temporary storage of data needed by dormant programs that is treated as if it were system memory.

Virtual real mode: A technique of creating separate address spaces and time slicing the CPU time so that legacy applications think they're the only programs running on the machine, even though there may be several running at once.

ACRONYM ALERT

DDR: Double Data Rate. A technology that allows two bits of data to move over each wire on every clock cycle.

ESN: Electronic Serial Number. On Pentium III CPUs (and later) this is a number embedded by Intel at the factory that identifies that specific CPU.

iComp: Intel Comparative Microprocessor Index. A benchmarking method developed by Intel.

MMX: Multi-Media Extensions. A set of instructions targeted specifically at multi-media.

SRAM: Static RAM. A form of very high-speed memory typically used for cache.

CHAPTER 9

SEARCHING YOUR MEMORY

One of the smallest components that you'll find in a computer system is actually one of the most complex. For some people, understanding how memory works can be more difficult even than understanding the workings of the CPU. Yet a computer's memory (**Figure 9.1**) is among the simplest upgrades to perform, and that upgrade can have a more noticeable impact on overall system performance than even changing the speed of the CPU. In Chapter Seven, Understanding CPUs, I introduced the concept as well as the importance of RAM.

RAM isn't the only kind of memory your computer uses, however. Computers use all kinds of different memory. I talked about how the CPU uses cache memory in Chapter Seven. Video cards have anywhere from a few megabytes to 256MB (or even more) of memory. Many of the accessories you plug into the expansion slots have memory of their own. The list goes on and on.

Without memory, a computer is incapable of doing anything. If the RAM modules are missing, POST will return an error and the system will not boot. And even if it could boot, it

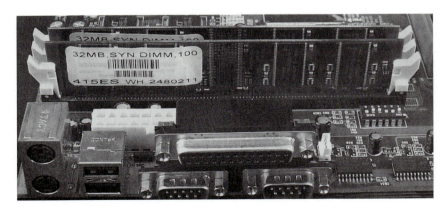

Figure 9.1 Your RAM is the central access point from which the CPU accesses all programs and data. Not too long ago, the 64MB shown here would have been sufficient for most anything. With today's OSs and applications it's a bare minimum!

wouldn't be able to accomplish anything. Until a file is loaded into memory, the CPU cannot access it. While the performance of conventional memory has improved dramatically over the past few years, it still isn't as fast as a CPU. Therefore, it can act as a bottleneck for system performance. To at least partially overcome this, today's CPUs contain anywhere from 8KB to as much as 128KB of L1 cache. Nearly all contain varying amounts of L2 cache as well. Some CPUs even provide support for L3 cache. In addition, cache memory is installed on hard drives, SCSI adapters, and even some sound cards. Somehow, the system needs to be able to keep track of all that memory, and precisely what is stored where.

A+ CORE HARDWARE EXAM OBJECTIVES

CompTIA exam objectives that will be introduced or covered in this chapter include:

1.1 Identify the names, purpose, and characteristics of system modules. Recognize these modules by sight or definition. (Memory)

1.2 Identify basic procedures for adding and removing field-replaceable modules for desktop systems. Given a replacement scenario, choose the appropriate sequences. (Memory)

1.3 Identify basic procedures for adding and removing field-replaceable modules for portable systems. Given a replacement scenario, choose the appropriate sequences. (Memory)

1.9 Identify procedures to optimize PC operations in specific situations. Predict the effects of specific procedures under given scenarios.

1.10 Determine the issues that must be considered when upgrading a PC. In a given scenario, determine when and how to upgrade system components.

2.1 Recognize common problems associated with each module and their symptoms, and identify steps to isolate and troubleshoot the problems. Given a problem situation, interpret the symptoms and infer the most likely cause.

4.2 Identify the types of RAM (Random Access Memory), form factors, and operational characteristics. Determine banking and speed requirements under given scenarios.

4.3 Identify the most popular types of motherboards, their components, and their architecture (bus structures).

HOW MEMORY WORKS

Memory, until recent years, was actually a passive device, surrendering itself to the manipulations of the chipset. In the first generations of personal computers, memory was managed by a chip called the memory controller chip (MCC). Once the MCC was absorbed by the chipset, this became a function of the northbridge, or more recently the memory controller hub. Therefore, as you're reading these next few pages, keep in the back of your mind that until I tell you otherwise, the chipset, and not the memory chip itself, will actually perform most of the active functions I'll discuss. The circuit itself is now known as the memory control circuit, and therefore is still simply the MCC.

DYNAMIC RAM

If you were to look at an actual memory chip under a microscope, you would see what looks like a grid etched into the chip. You might even compare that grid to the cells you see in a spreadsheet, complete with rows and columns. And that is exactly how the MCC treats it. The cells that make up this grid consist of microscopic transistors, each one of which is coupled with an associated microcapacitor (**Figure 9.2**). When fully charged, one of these capacitors acts to open the associated transistor. This is interpreted as a one in binary. A discharged cell fails to open the transistor and is interpreted as a zero.

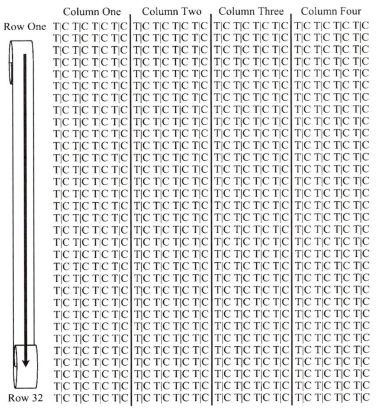

Figure 9.2   A typical memory chip is comprised of a vast number of individual cells consisting of a transistor (T) coupled with a capacitor (C). The cells are laid out in rows and columns, just like a spreadsheet.

The pattern of rows and columns is what the MCC uses for addressing purposes. How many rows there are available to the chip determines how many bits "deep" a particular chip is. Columns aren't as easily counted under a microscope because design engineers frequently embed more than a single bit into a column. An example of an early DRAM chip was designated 4 × 4. It had four columns of cells with 1,048,576 cells in each column. Into each cell was incorporated four bits. The refresh rate then determines how many columns the array has. A typical 256MB module is manufactured with either 32 × 16 or 32 × 64 chips.

The chips themselves are designed with their refresh requirements in mind. *Refresh* is a necessary process that standard DRAM must go through. All those little capacitors that activate the transistors are constantly leaking out their charge. Unless something is done to correct this, all the ones will turn into zeros. In order to prevent this from happening, an additional circuit was added to periodically recharge those little capacitors. That is what is meant by refresh.

Of course, if a cell is supposed to represent a zero you don't want to add a charge to it. This would corrupt data just as surely as losing an existing charge. Therefore, the first phase of the refresh cycle consists of determining the relative charge of a particular cell. Essentially, if the cell is less than half charged the MCC assumes it to contain a zero. That cell is not recharged. Any cells containing charges greater than half will receive a fresh charge.

Refresh rate is specified as to how many thousands of columns are affected by a single refresh cycle. Early RAM refreshed 1000 columns in a sweep, and the refresh rate was designated 1K. Subsequent generations of RAM have included 2K, 4K, 8K, and 16K. *Capacity* of a chip is therefore determined by three factors. The formula is as follows: Capacity = bit width × columns × rows. This is how manufacturers determine chip density.

In order for a computer to properly address memory, the chipset and the RAM must be marching to the same drum. Synchronizing the chipset and RAM is achieved by properly setting the timing of the memory. On the most basic level, that of the DRAM chip itself, there are two fixed parameters that constitute timing. These two measurements are Row Access Strobe (RAS), and Column Access Strobe (CAS). As you now know, memory access on the chip level is controlled in a spreadsheet-like manner. When the CPU first initializes a request for data, it will initialize a RAS cycle in order to locate the particular row that holds the information it's looking for. Once RAS has found the row, the MCC will order a CAS cycle. First, CAS has to lock onto the row address. Once it finds that, it moves across the rows until it finds out what column holds the first bit of data it is looking for.

One of the bottlenecks in RAM has always been something called the *RAS to CAS delay*. This is an interval of between two and four clock cycles (on earlier forms of RAM) between the completion of the RAS cycle and when CAS can next initiate its cycle. Another term you'll see for this delay is *CAS latency*. Memory that is advertised as CL2 has a CAS latency of two clock

BUZZ WORDS

Refresh: The process of recharging the capacitors that link to the transistors of each memory cell on a chip.

Refresh rate: The number of columns of memory cells per cycle that the MCC will recharge.

Capacity: The total number of bits a memory chip holds.

cycles. Reducing the RAS/CAS delay can have a significant effect on memory performance.

The key to understanding memory access is this. Even though the CPU can only access data 32 bits or 64 bits at a time, it is accessing that data from cache whenever possible. Since the CPU can absorb more than a single byte, memory delivers information in double words, or dwords. Since that data doesn't move directly across the CPU bus, but is rather stored in cache, on any single read operation more than one dword at a time will be retrieved. A single memory I/O operation might deliver anywhere from two to eight dwords on a single cycle. Anything the CPU can't use immediately will be stored in cache. By nature, data is most often read sequentially. The next time the prefetch goes out looking for data, the CPU is likely to find what it needs in cache.

> **BUZZ WORDS** ─────────
>
> **CAS latency:** The delay that occurs between RAS and CAS. Also known as RAS/CAS delay.
>
> **RAS/CAS delay:** The delay that occurs between RAS and CAS. Also known as CAS latency.

STATIC RAM

Static RAM (SRAM) is built differently than DRAM. SRAM is a whole lot faster than DRAM, but requires much more space. It ends up eating up more of the motherboard's precious real estate. Specifically, a 512KB SRAM is approximately the same size, if not slightly larger than a 32MB × 8 SDRAM (256MB). Therefore, in order to fit 256MB of SRAM into a computer, you're going to need a really big motherboard.

One of the things that makes SRAM so much faster is that it uses only transistors. There are no capacitors in its circuitry. On the plus side, this eliminates the necessity for a refresh cycle. Electricity moves at its own rate through the chip, and the individual transistors act like on/off switches to direct the flow. However, between four to six transistors are needed for each bit of data an SRAM chip can store. A single transistor can't affect a bit by itself. The end result is that a whole lot more electricity is used to operate the transistors. The side effect of this is that the chip runs a lot hotter.

SRAM is also substantially more expensive than DRAM. That 512K chip that was the size of a 256MB chip also costs about four times as much. If a manufacturer were to design a computer that used only SRAM in its design, the cost of the computer would be prohibitive. Therefore, a primary use for SRAM is the L2 or L3 cache on those motherboards that support secondary cache.

DRAM TIMING AND MEMORY TYPES

The evolution of memory has occurred predominantly through improvements in, or in some cases elimination of, timing cycles. Improvements in die-making technology have certainly helped, but overall, the basic design of RAM hasn't changed a whole lot. You still have DRAM made from transistors coupled with capacitors, and SRAM, which is only capacitors.

Some more recent types of DRAM have made some significant advances in how they address certain timing issues, however.

DRAM AND FAST PAGE MODE

The first generation of PCs used a form of memory called fast page mode. While primitive by today's standards, it was a step up from the conventional dynamic random access memory (DRAM) used prior to that. The steps for retrieving data from the first memory chips were cumbersome and slow. Every time the CPU made a request for data, the MCC would initiate a RAS in order to find the appropriate row. Then it would hand off the search to the CAS, which would then locate the required data. The chip would then hand over one bit of data. The other chips in the bank would hand over their bits, and the CPU had a byte to chew. On computers that ran at 4.77MHz, this didn't create much of a bottleneck. Just having a computer delighted most people. They had yet to cultivate the demand for raw speed. However, as CPUs began to run faster, the number of clock cycles wasted waiting for data from memory increased accordingly. The first major improvement in DRAM to come along was Fast Page Mode (FPM).

FPM found data in memory exactly the same way that the original DRAM found it. However, engineers made a change in the way it transferred that data. Working on the assumption that data is retrieved sequentially, they designed the chip so that, once the first bit of data was found, a new RAS cycle was not required for data that resided in the same row as the previous memory I/O operation. Since that RAS/CAS delay that I discussed earlier is one of the biggest bottlenecks in the system, eliminating a few of those made memory less of a bottleneck. Once data was located, the memory controller could move more than a bit at a time across the bus. The idea was that if the data was coming off the chip in streams, the CPU could process it accordingly.

FPM memory was used on computer systems from the days of the 80286 until well into the days the 80486. Many chipsets designed for Pentium machines supported FPM, although by that time few manufacturers chose to shoot themselves in the foot by actually using it. It has been released as DIPPs, 30-pin SIMMs, and 72-pin SIMMs. Other technologies came along to supplant FPM prior to the release of DIMMs; therefore, it is not found in that package. FPM is still alive and well, however. Some computerized circuits that require small amounts of memory where speed is not a critical issue will use a few FPMs.

EDO

FPM was king of the hill until 1994, when a new breed of memory took center stage. Extended Data Out (EDO) is actually pretty similar to FPM in many ways. What gave it a slight advantage was that there was no delay between read operations. As with FPM, if the next few bytes of data the CPU needs are located in the same row as the previous block, the RAS operation is eliminated. However, EDO also either reduces or eliminates the cycle required by CAS in order to lock on to the row address provided by RAS. RAS is still having to do its job.

It's just that the chipset can order a new RAS cycle while the data is still being read from the previous search. Therefore, by the time the MCC has finished the transfer of data from one read operation, RAS and CAS have already lined up data for the next.

EDO, like FPM, was available in both parity and nonparity modules. This is something I've had to teach some of the sales reps of otherwise excellent memory suppliers. It is true that EDO in parity form was extremely rare (and priced accordingly), however, it has been manufactured in the past. If you do happen to stumble across a box built with parity EDO, don't bother trying to upgrade with the same stuff. Before you waste a lot of time on a long, drawn-out search, consider this. First off, there will be no performance gain. Differences between parity and nonparity, regardless of what kind of memory it may be, have nothing to do with how well a system performs. Second, if you do accidentally stumble across some, and the company that has it knows what it has, it's likely to charge you through the nose. Save yourself the time and effort, and just install nonparity.

EDO hit the streets somewhat toward the end of the 80486 cycle. Therefore, pretty much any Pentium-based machine will support it. There are a few exceptions to this, so if in doubt, check the chart on chipsets provided in Appendix F. You can also find 80486-based machines that use it. The reason this becomes an issue is that, unless the module has been labeled, it is virtually impossible to tell the difference between FPM and EDO simply by looking at it. Mixing the two on the same machine is a recipe for disaster.

SDRAM

Up until now, none of the improvements I've discussed required changing the basic architecture of the DRAM chip itself. With the release of Synchronous Dynamic Random Access Memory (SDRAM), users began to see improvements in the circuitry of the module. I've repeatedly emphasized that a basic bottleneck in the system is the number of clock cycles that the CPU sits idle if it fails to find information that it needs in cache and has no other code to process. Additional clock cycles are wasted because the CPU has to use some of them in order to issue requests to the MCC.

With the development of SDRAM, designers moved a significant portion of the MCC circuitry onto the memory module itself. In effect, this means that the CPU can now access RAM directly. More importantly, data stored in RAM is available to the CPU on every single clock cycle. This provided a substantial gain in performance, but also required a chipset designed to address the memory. You would need to own a machine equipped with Intel's 440EX, VIA's VP, an OPTi Viper, an SIS 5171, or any of these companies' later chipsets to do this. Otherwise, SDRAM was actually treated in much the same way as EDO.

Even on advanced chipsets, there is little or no performance gain any time the CPU is accessing data a word at a time. EDO could find data in as few as four clock cycles on some of the newest releases, with the data being moved to the cache in bursts requiring two clock cycles each after that. SDRAM actually requires between five and seven clock cycles to set up a single read. After that, it sends more data on each burst, and sends a burst on each clock cycle. As a result, single word access is actually slower but burst mode is much faster. Since data moves in large chunks a vast majority of the time, SDRAM was the preferred memory for several years.

A newer type of SDRAM, called Virtual Channel Memory (VCM), has recently hit the market and reduces this latency to two clock cycles. Therefore, it's faster in every respect. It will be covered later, in its own section.

Since SDRAM operates in synchronization with the CPU's front-side bus, you need to make sure your memory equals the CPU bus speed. If the CPU has an external data bus of 133MHz, it will not be possible to use 66MHz memory. There is generally no problem using the faster memory on machines with slower busses. However, it is not a good idea to mix speeds on the same machine. The computer will probably boot up fine. On many motherboards, there won't be any problems at all. On some, however, mixing speeds leads to substantial increases in the number of "blue screens of death" and "fatal exceptions" in Windows. Save yourself some headaches. Just don't do it to start with.

RDRAM

Rambus DRAM (RDRAM), developed by Rambus Technologies, takes a completely different approach to the storage and retrieval of data. Intel believed in this technology so much that it invested heavily in co-developing products with Rambus. It also provided engineering support for developing the bus and chipsets to support the memory. RDRAM operates on its own direct bus to the CPU. The first generation of Rambus worked on a 400MHz operating frequency. The more recent releases feature up to 1.06GHz.

A big change is in how RDRAM moves data across that bus. Conventional memory can either transmit or receive data only on the rising end of the clock cycle. RDRAM can do so on both the rising and falling edge (see **Figure 9.3**). In effect, this doubles throughput without increasing speed.

It's also moving data in 16-bit chunks, rather than the 64-bit bandwidth of SDRAM (and other forms I'll discuss later). Since the CPU possesses a 64-bit FSB, something has to piece that 16-bit data back together into 64-bit slices. That is the job of the chipset. Intel learned the hard way that making a board that supports both SDRAM and RDRAM probably wasn't going to be feasible.

On the 820 chipset, Intel added a circuit it called the Memory Translator Hub (MTH) to handle the data path conversions. Some boards with this chipset shipped with both 168-pin DIMM sockets and 184-pin RIMM sockets. The theory was that the user could choose which memory to use. It worked fine with RDRAM. It quickly became apparent that there was a problem using SDRAM. Any form of electronic noise, whether it came from inside the computer system or got picked up from external sources, caused severe memory errors. People reported a wide range of problems. The most common were system hangs for no apparent reason, and intermittent and unexpected system reboots. Many people reported data corruption.

Once the problem became obvious, Intel initiated a voluntary recall. Customers were given several options as far as replacing their boards. In all, between 900,000 and 1 million boards based in the i820 chipset were affected.

Intel's 840 chipset uses an SDRAM Memory Repeater Hub (MRH-S) instead of an MTH. It is a far superior alternative and does not suffer from the problems described above. It does, however, have the limitation of supporting only RDRAM.

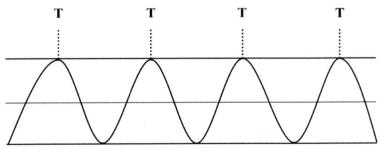

Until recent years, most memory, including EDO and SDRAM, could only move data on the rising wave of the carrier signal.

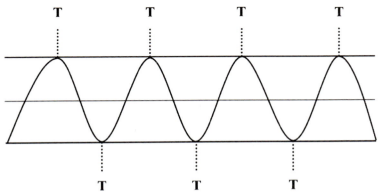

Recent memory technologies allow data to be moved on both the rising wave and the falling wave, effectively doubling throughput.

Figure 9.3   While conventional memory can only move bits of information on the rising edge of the cycle, many of the advanced memory types make use of both the rising and falling edge.

The first generations of Rambus memory met with a great deal of skepticism. Benchmark tests by several different organizations routinely reported performance gains, but they were minimal, ranging from as little as five percent to around fifteen percent. Nobody reported anywhere near the performance boost Rambus claimed. Since these earlier versions cost up to two times more than more conventional types, the cost/performance ratio made Rambus a questionable choice.

All that changed with the release of the Pentium 4, with its quad-pumped FSB. This CPU was designed to take advantage of the Rambus technology. More efficient production methods and greater acceptance of Rambus memory resulted in price drops that brought it in line with the cost of other technologies. The new 1.06GHz Rambus memory matches well with the 533MHz bus of the most recent Pentium 4 CPUs. Of all different forms of memory tested, 1.06GHz RDRAM provided the fastest benchmarks.

DDRAM

The biggest obstacle RDRAM faced in the non-Intel world was that there is a royalty assessed by Rambus on every stick of RDRAM used and on every RIMM socket installed on a motherboard. Ours is an industry that does not like paying royalties if it can avoid it.

Working with VIA Technologies (the chipset people), AMD invented its own technology that addresses the issue of memory bottleneck without the problems it insists are presented by RDRAM. Double Data Rate SDRAM (DDR or DDRAM) takes the best of RDRAM and melds it with the best of SDRAM. From RDRAM, it borrows the ability to move data across the bus on both the rising and the falling edge of the clock cycle. It doesn't claim the 1.06GHz speed of RDRAM, but on the other hand, it works in the 64-bit increments of SDRAM. Therefore, it doesn't need any fancy circuitry to reconstruct the data path. Not only does this reduce the complexity of the circuitry, but it also doesn't require retooling for manufacturers who want to make the chips. The same machines that manufacture SDRAM DIMMs can also put out DDRAM DIMMs.

DDRAM has a slightly different method of labeling its modules based on overall memory bandwidth. DDRAM is marketed as PC1600 through PC3700. PC1600 DDRAM has a maximum theoretical burst rate of 1,600MB/s and PC3700 boasts a throughput of 3,700MB/s. Each of these different types of DDRAM is rated to run a different bus speed as well. Another note is that since data moves twice on each clock cycle, DDRAM speeds are generally twice as fast as the actual clock speed. **Table 9.1** lists currently available forms of DDRAM with their appropriate bus speeds and bandwidths.

Table 9.1   A Comparison of Different DDRAM Types

JEDEC Name	Bus Speed	Burst Bandwidth
PC1600	200MHz	1.6GB/s
PC2100	266MHz	2.1GB/s
PC2700	333MHz	2.7GB/s
PC3200	400MHz	3.2GB/s
PC3500	433MHz	3.5GB/s
PC3700	466MHz	3.7GB/s

When shopping for DDRAM, make sure you purchase the correct type.

Note that the bus speeds of DDRAM are double the actual clock speed of the system bus for which they are designed. That is because this is how the manufacturers describe them in their literature.

DDRAM is getting support from a number of manufacturers at this point in time. At least half a dozen have thrown their support behind DDRAM, including Hitachi and Hyundai, two of the world's largest DRAM fabricators. It remains to be seen which of the two, RDRAM or DDRAM, will pick up the lion's share of the market.

VC SDRAM

One bottleneck that none of the previous technologies has addressed has to do with how the CPU must manage the multitasking of several programs at once while working with memory that can read only a single string of data at a time. I as a user might be working on my computer

BUZZ WORDS

Channel: A dedicated path for data to take that prevents other data from competing for time on the bus.

hardware book and playing some boogie-blues MP3s at the same time. My email client is open in the background, checking my ISP for more comments from my editor every fifteen minutes. Meanwhile, the playoff game between the Patriots and the Dolphins is playing in a window in the lower corner of the screen. The CPU has no problem with this at all, although *I* was a bit put out by the Patriots going for it on fourth and fifteen. My system does, however, spend a lot more time waiting for data than it needs to, because the memory can only be retrieving data for one program at a time. Virtual Channel SDRAM (VC SDRAM) is the first step in solving that problem.

One of the improvements of VC SDRAM is in requiring fewer clock cycles to set up a memory read operation. Its key claim to fame, however, is that it can establish up to sixteen different address lines, or *channels*, and store the instructions and/or data for each specific program in a separate channel. The memory module can then stream data from all of those locations at once. Therefore, VC SDRAM can be feeding the CPU data for any given application on any given clock cycle. Obviously, VC SDRAM requires a chipset that supports these advanced functions, and the memory is more expensive.

THE PACKAGING OF MEMORY

In the years that the PC has been on the market, probably no single component has gone through more changes in its physical packaging than the memory module. It started out as single chips that populated the motherboard like high-priced spiders, and over the years has evolved into the sophisticated modules in use today. Thanks to an organization called the *Joint Electron Device Engineering Council* (JEDEC), this evolution has been reasonably orderly. Manufacturers who design a new memory package submit it to JEDEC for approval.

EXAM NOTE: For the exam, be able to describe each and every one of the memory packages described in this section. Even the venerable old DIPP has its occasional day in the sun on the exam.

Changes in packaging have predominantly kept up with the evolution of the CPU. Each generation of microprocessor was taking a bigger byte out of memory, so to speak, and was doing so at faster and faster clock rates. Therefore, in addition to improvements in memory design, which will be discussed later in this chapter, improvements also had to be made in the way memory was assembled. For the technophiles among you, the pinouts for many of these modules can be found in Appendix G.

WHO THE HECK IS JEDEC?

Long before the personal computer was released on the public, electronics manufacturers recognized a need to standardize the packaging of certain electronic components. This became particularly critical with computers. Imagine the confusion, if every manufacturer of computers came up with its own design for memory chips. In 1960 an organization was created solely for the purpose of maintaining standards for the manufacture of semiconductor devices in general. This group, the Joint Electron Device Engineering Council (JEDEC) was handed the additional responsibility of overseeing memory packaging in 1970. For nearly three decades, if a memory manufacturer had a better idea for a design, that design had to undergo the scrutiny of JEDEC. Will it continue to hold the power it has enjoyed in the past? We can only hope that **somebody** maintains control.

DUAL INLINE PIN PACKAGE

In the earliest days of computers, memory was installed a single chip at a time, using a module called a Dual Inline Pin Package (DIPP). Individual memory chips were encased in a ceramic enclosure with pins extruding from the base. These days, DIPPs are not used in conventional PC designs, although computerized circuits requiring small amounts of memory occasionally make use of them. Many BIOS manufacturers still use the DIPP to package their product. **Figure 9.4** is an example of BIOS on a DIPP.

Early PCs used CPUs with an 8-bit data bus. Each of these chips could only generate a single bit of data per clock cycle. Therefore, to give the CPU the eight bits it required, eight chips worked in unison. This was called a bank.

Most computers actually required a ninth chip because earlier computers made use of an error-checking mechanism known as parity. Parity required an additional bit of data. Eight of the chips generated a byte of data to put onto the address bus, with the ninth being the parity bit.

Figure 9.4 This Award BIOS chip is a good example of a DIPP chip.

Increasing memory requirements were creating design problems for the engineers. Motherboards have to be made to a preordained size. There are only so many chip sockets that can fit into this space, and many of them are reserved for system-critical chips. As a result, memory expansion cards became popular. These were cards you fit into a slot on your expansion bus that were filled with as much memory as they could hold (or, as was more often the case, as you could afford). The downside to this was that you only have so many expansion slots as well. More importantly, when you put memory on an expansion card, you were now clocking that memory at the speed of the bus onto which it was installed and not the speed of the rest of the RAM on the system. As a result, computer manufacturers stopped using the DIPP shortly after release of the 80286 microprocessor.

SIPP

The Single Inline Pin Package (SIPP) was the first attempt at combining multiple DRAM chips into a single module. It was a disaster. The designers that came up with this design soldered an entire bank of chips onto a single circuit board that had one row of pins extruding from the bottom edge. This design accomplished its goal, in that it took up substantially less space on a motherboard than an entire row of DIPPs. Still, it didn't receive the acclaim its inventors would have liked. Planting one of these things into its socket was actually more difficult than mounting DIPPs, and they were easier to damage. The only real advantage was that you had fewer of them to break.

SIMM

Single Inline Memory Modules (SIMM) very quickly replaced SIPPs. SIMMs resemble tiny little expansion cards. DRAM chips are soldered onto small edge card connectors. The interface of the card is lined with the termination pads for the traces that interconnect the chips. The first SIMMs had thirty of these connectors and were referred to as 30-pin SIMMs, despite the fact that the concept of true pins had thankfully been abandoned. To this day, memory modules continue to be designated by the number of their "pins."

The 30-pin SIMM worked fine with the 286 and 386 computers of the day. It provided an 8-bit data path, which, while not ideal for the 80386, was sufficient for the 80286. Shortly after the release of the 80386, the 72-pin SIMM (**Figure 9.5**) was put on the market to accommodate the 32-bit EDB of that CPU. This module provided a 32-bit data path as well. Oddly enough, there were relatively few 386 motherboards with 72-pin sockets. The 72-pin SIMM hit the market about the same time that the 80486 microprocessor was released. Still, it would be a couple of years before the 30-pin SIMM was phased out. As a result, there were a number of 486-based motherboards that supported 30-pin memory.

Over the years, several different kinds of memory have been distributed as SIMM modules. You'll find FPM, EDO, and ECC. Therefore, make sure you don't make the mistake of confusing the memory package with the memory type. Earlier in the chapter, when I discussed the different types of memory, I pointed out several compatibility issues that can arise.

Unfortunately, manufacturers rarely labeled their products as to what type of memory they were. You might see a label with a part number, but that was about it. You would have to cross-reference that number in the manufacturer's catalog to find out what you had. As far

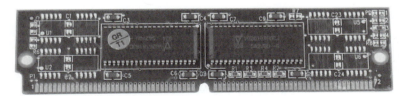

Figure 9.5 For several years, the SIMM was the memory module of choice for most motherboard manufacturers. This 72-pin SIMM replaced earlier 30-pin versions shortly after the release of Intel's 80386 microprocessor.

as just looking at a stick of RAM and being able to tell what it is? Forget it. EDO looks, feels, smells and tastes just like FPM. Unfortunately, it doesn't work the same.

There are some factors that are consistent with packaging regardless of the type of chip that was soldered onto the SIMM. For example, all 30-pin SIMMs are 8-bit memory. All 72-pin SIMMs are 32-bit memory. It doesn't matter whether it is a 72-pin FPM or a 72-pin EDO module, it is still a 32-bit piece of memory. What this means is that on any given read cycle, a 30-pin SIMM will transfer 8 bits of data, while a 72-pin SIMM will move 32 bits. Remember this. You're going to need to know it when I move on to talking about memory banking.

Physically, the circuit board that a 30-pin SIMM is built onto is about 3.5″ long and slightly less than an inch high. 30-pin SIMMs were available in 256K, 512K, 1MB, 4MB, and 16MB modules. It is unfortunate that very few motherboard chipsets supported the 16MB module. 30-pin SIMMS were notched slightly differently on one vertical edge than on the other. Unfortunately, not all SIMM sockets were made equally, and it was actually pretty easy to mount a 30-pin SIMM onto a motherboard backward. It wouldn't work that way.

Each pin in the SIMM is responsible for a separate function. For those of you with a driving need to know, those functions are defined in Appendix G.

72-pin SIMM modules were keyed with a notch in the middle and one cut into one vertical edge. They are there to prevent you from inserting the stick backward. The center notch fits over a ridge built into the SIMM socket located on the motherboard. The module installs into the socket by lining up the notch with the ridge, tilting the stick about fifteen degrees forward, and then levering it up to a vertical position. Spring clips located on either end of the socket snap into place, holding the module securely in the socket.

A 72-pin SIMM is about 4.25″ long, but they tend to vary in height. This can become an issue if a SIMM socket is positioned under a nonmovable part. Also, 72-pin SIMMs come in single-sided and double-sided modules. In other words, the DRAM chips themselves were mounted either on just one side or on both sides. Some motherboards did not support double-sided SIMMs. In many cases, the sockets were positioned so close together, the double-sided chips just didn't fit into the space they had available. In addition, there were certain versions of BIOS that had difficulty recognizing double-sided SIMMs.

As with the 30-pin SIMMs, each pin has a separate function. The same pinouts are used whether the chip is parity or nonparity; manufacturers simply don't hook up the connections used for parity if the SIMM does not generate parity. The relative pinouts for the SIMM are detailed in Appendix G.

DUAL INLINE MEMORY MODULES

Time marches on and so did CPUs. The Pentium provided the CPU with a 64-bit path to the outside world, so now two SIMMs were needed to fill a bank. The Dual Inline Memory Module (DIMM) was designed to overcome that issue. Designers improved more than just the data path while they were at it. Certain functions of the MCC were transferred over to the memory chip itself. To accommodate the extra bit width and the new functions, a few more electrical connections were required. Currently, DIMMs are manufactured in a 168-pin (**Figure 9.6**) and a 184-pin form factor. The 184-pin DIMM is used for DDR.

Figure 9.6   A 168-pin DIMM.

Those pins are symmetrically aligned along either side of the base of the module. This isn't that much different than how the 30-pin or 72-pin SIMMs were designed. What makes the DIMM different is that the terminators on each side of the module are able to perform different functions. On the SIMM, any two connectors opposite of each other had to be wired for the same function.

> **EXAM NOTE:** Be able to describe the physical and electronic differences between the DIMM and the SIMM.

The module also mounts into its socket differently. Unlike the spring clips that held the SIMM in place, a DIMM snaps down into its socket and is secured by levers. There are two notches cut into the base of the card, not just one. These notches perform two different functions. First, they prevent you from mounting the DIMM in the socket backward. Second, since there were 5V and 3.3V DIMMs, the position of the second notch varies according to the voltage. It keeps you from mounting a 5V chip into a 3.3V board, and vice versa.

Just like with the SIMM, different kinds of memory ship on DIMMs. You can get EDO, ECC, SDRAM, DDRAM, and VC SDRAM on a DIMM. And once again, getting these to work together is an exercise in futility. Fortunately, with DIMMs, it is more common for manufacturers to actually label their product so that you know what it is you're getting when you buy it.

RAMBUS INLINE MEMORY MODULE

A little earlier, I introduced the memory that was developed by Rambus, with a little help from Intel. When Rambus first published the specs on its new memory and revealed the details of its involvement with Intel, the company's stock skyrocketed. It was an overnight success.

It was an overnight success that took eight years to materialize. The company started corporate life making memory for video games. But the PC world didn't care about that type of memory. RDRAM was the memory that interested it.

RDRAM doesn't ship on a standard module. The module that supports it is known as the Rambus Inline Memory Module (RIMM) as seen in **Figure 9.7**. It is a 184-pin module with two notches located toward the center of edge card. A single Rambus channel can support only two RIMMs. To prevent this from being a limiting factor, Intel's i840 and i850 chipsets offer an optional 862803AA Memory Repeater Hub that allows a motherboard designer to pop in another pair of slots.

Figure 9.7 A 184-pin Rambus module. (Photo Courtesy of Rambus, Inc.)

One thing you need to keep in mind is that on motherboards that use RDRAM, all RIMM sockets must be filled. If you plan on using a single bank you need to fill the empty socket with a *continuity module*. Many motherboards that use RIMMs ship with one or more of these as a standard accessory. However, if your board doesn't, or if you lose it, it is something you'll need to purchase. The system will not boot with only a single RIMM installed.

Buzz Words ────

Continuity module: A null memory module that fills the empty banks on a system using Rambus memory.

Small Outline DIMM

Not too long after the DIMM became popular, memory designers released a smaller version of the chip specifically for notebook computers. The DIMM was just a trifle large for installing into the small form factor these computers use. This module is called the Small Outline Dual Inline Memory Module (SO-DIMM), as seen in **Figure 9.8**. These devices not only come in a much smaller package, but they also consume less power than a standard DIMM.

The first SO-DIMMs to ship were 72-pin modules that provided a 32-bit data path. These were eventually phased out in favor of a 144-pin, 64-bit SO-DIMM. They snap into a socket

Figure 9.8 The 144-pin SO-DIMM is a type of memory frequently used in notebook computers and on some types of video card.

(**Figure 9.9**) specially designed to endure the jarring and bumping to which notebook computers are constantly exposed without being knocked out.

There are different variations on the types of memory installed on SO-DIMMs. Depending on what kind of memory it is, there are minor variations on the functions of the individual connections.

Figure 9.10 provides a visual overview of the way that memory packages developed alongside CPUs.

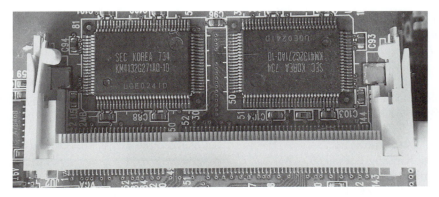

Figure 9.9   The SO-DIMM socket is a bit different than the other sockets discussed so far. It is designed to hold the memory module flat against the circuit board.

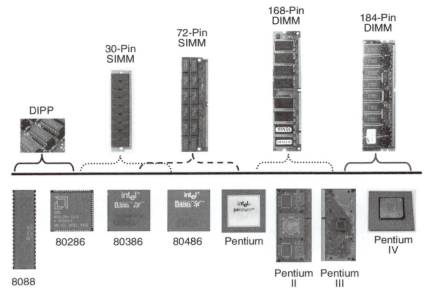

Figure 9.10   A comparison of a timeline of CPU development to the development of memory packages

MODULE SIZES AND BANKS OF MEMORY

I've taught computer hardware courses on both a college level and a professional level, and one subject that seems to provide a whole lot more stress than it really should is *memory banking*. Understanding the concept shouldn't be that difficult. The real problem exists with individual chipsets that have their own special needs.

BUZZ WORDS

Memory bank: The total number of memory modules required to assure that the bit width of available memory matches the bit width of the CPU in use.

The math is simple. If you have a CPU with a 32-bit bus, then you need 32 bits worth of memory. And by that, I don't mean quantity, but rather bit width. How big of a piece of data can move across the memory bus? If you have a 64-bit bus, then you need memory that is 64 bits wide. **Table 9.2** shows you how wide the external data bus of several popular CPUs happens to be. Unless there is a full bank of memory for the CPU to access, the computer will not boot. A bank must contain enough chips to equal the external data bus of the CPU in use.

EXAM NOTE: The concept of memory banking doesn't affect us as much now as it did in the past. Still, there are plenty of older machines out there that people want supported for which it can be an issue. It's also a concept that's emphasized on the exam.

Earlier in the chapter, I pointed out that the different memory packages have their own unique bit widths (see **Table 9.3**). That CPU I was talking about that had the 32-bit external data bus needs a 32-bit path to memory or the computer won't even try to finish the boot process. Anything with a 64-bit bus needs two 72-pin SIMMs to complete a bank, whereas a single 168-pin DIMM does the job all by itself. It's easy.

Table 9.2   Evolution of the External Data Bus

CPU	External Data Bus
80286	16-bit
80386DX	32-bit
80386SX	16-bit
80486 (all)	32-bit
Pentium (all)	64-bit
AMD K5	64-bit
AMD K6	64-bit
AMD Athalon	64-bit

Each generation of CPU, up to and including the Pentium, increased the width of the EDB. It is essential that the bank of memory be the same bit width.

Take the bus width of the CPU, divide it by the bus width of the memory you're using, and that's how many modules you need to fill a bank.

If only that's all there was to banking. There's always something that has to crop up to make life a little more difficult. So let me discuss a few basic rules.

■ *Never put sticks of a different size into the same bank.* If you need two SIMMs to fill a bank, then you need two SIMMs that are exactly the same size. You cannot put one 32MB SIMM and one 64MB SIMM into the same bank. It just won't work.

- *Never put two different speeds in the same bank.* If one SIMM is 60ns, then the other must be 60ns. You can usually get away with having different speeds of memory in different banks, although some boards get finicky as to which bank you should put the faster memory into. On the other hand, mixing speeds, even between banks, has been known to result in increased memory errors. You're better off avoiding it if you can.

Table 9.3   Evolution of the Memory Data Bus

Memory Package	Bit Width
DIPP	1-bit
30-pin SIMM	8-bit
72-pin SIMM	32-bit
168-pin DIMM	64-bit
184-pin RAMBUS	64-bit

As with the generations of CPU, each different memory package incorporates a specific bit width.

- *Never mix different types of memory.* I've said that over and over again, but it's worth repeating. On any machine, mixing types of memory is a very bad idea. In most cases, it will not work at all. Put SDRAM and EDO into the same computer, and you'll get those awful beeps telling you there is bad or missing memory, and the boot process halts. Those are the easy ones to diagnose. The hard ones to figure out are when the computer boots fine and all appears to be well on the Windows of the world. But as you work, one of two things begins to happen. Either you start getting lots and lots of blue screens and memory-related errors, or your data starts going corrupt on you. Neither situation is fun.

Now, here are some situations that, while they're not hard and fast rules, are good bits of knowledge to possess. Following a few simple guidelines will save you hours of headaches.

- *Larger memory should go in the first bank.* On some older computers, that's not just a good idea, it's a rule. On many 486 and earlier Pentium computers, if the smaller memory modules were located in the first bank, the following banks wouldn't even be recognized.

- *Try not to mix brands of memory in the same bank.* Generally, this doesn't cause problems. However, minor differences in capacitance values can theoretically lead to data corruption.

- *Avoid mixing memory with tin leads with gold-plated sockets, and vice versa.* On some machines this doesn't cause any problems with data, but interfacing the two metals will lead to faster corrosion of the tin component. On some motherboards, it simply doesn't work. The memory won't be recognized.

Another issue you should be careful of is mixing SIMMs and DIMMs. It isn't that the two packages aren't interchangeable. They frequently are. It's knowing what kind of memory each stick is equipped with that matters. The most common memory type shipping on the DIMM happens to be SDRAM. As far as I've been able to ascertain, SDRAM never shipped on 72-pin SIMMs.

Therefore, if you open a box and find the computer is using SIMMs, it's a safe bet the memory is not SDRAM. If it is a Pentium-class machine, it's probably a safe bet that you've got EDO. EDO and SDRAM doesn't mix. Therefore, you have two choices. Either you can sacrifice the EDO and upgrade to SDRAM, or you can go out looking for EDO on a DIMM. That is possible to find.

The thing to consider is this. If the computer has a chipset that supports SDRAM, performance will be significantly faster if you go that direction. Also, pricing might become an issue. Because EDO is now only being manufactured in small quantities, it is a bit pricier than SDRAM. You'll probably find that the EDO will set you back three to four times as much as SDRAM in terms of cost per megabyte. It's probably cheaper to swap it out.

ERROR CORRECTION METHODS

On your personal computers running typical desktop applications, the importance of error correction isn't quite as critical as it used to be. It used to be a major problem. When I talked about how memory worked, I pointed out that a DRAM chip basically consists of a collection of microscopic capacitors linked to transistors. Whether any given capacitor is charged or discharged determines whether it is read as a one or as a zero in binary. Should a capacitor lose too much of its charge between refresh cycles, the MCC will not recharge that cell on the next cycle. What was once a one is now a zero.

When you consider how many hundreds of billions of zeros and ones zip through your computer every second, it may not seem important if you drop an occasional bit here and there. And in many situations, it isn't. A picture you download off the web might have tens of thousands, hundreds of thousands, or even millions of bits that define the individual pixels that make up the image. Even if you were to lose more than one bit on the same pixel, color definition would not be seriously affected.

On the other hand, you're going to be a trifle upset if that lottery check for $1,000,000 you just won shows up in the mail made out for $0,000,000. Dropping a bit in an executable can make the program hang or even go so far as rendering the system unstable. Therefore, it doesn't matter how rare memory errors may be. You can't take a chance on one occurring in a critical situation. Errors must be detected, and if possible, corrected.

Over the years, two methods have evolved to prevent memory errors from resulting in disaster. The one users suffered with for several years was called parity. This was a simple error checking mechanism. It let you know something had screwed up. It just didn't do anything to fix the problem. Error Correction Code (ECC), as its name implies, not only detects the error, but also is able to dynamically correct it.

PARITY VERSUS NONPARITY

Memory wasn't always as reliable as it is today. Nor was the MCC as effective in doing its job. Therefore, it was not at all uncommon for bits to be dropped on a regular basis. *Parity* was developed as a mechanism to prevent these dropped bits from resulting in corrupted data.

The way it works is pretty simple and a bit crude, and, in many cases, the cure was worse than the disease. The memory bank had to include eight bits for data, and those bits would make up a collection of zeros and ones. Engineers added an additional bit for parity for each full byte of information generated. Now there are nine bits for each byte. Standard PCs used

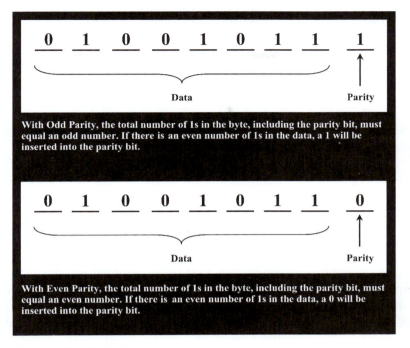

Figure 9.11   Parity in action.

a method known as odd parity. If you count up the number of ones in each byte, including the parity bit, you will have either an even number of ones or an odd number of ones.

Parity checking can be either even or odd. Any time odd-parity checking finds an even number of ones the parity bit gets set for one. If an odd number is found, the bit gets set for zero. When the CPU receives the byte and does its own count, including the parity bit, it should always find an odd number of ones. Even parity should always create an even number of ones (**Figure 9.11**). Either way, if the CPU is presented with an incorrect number, counting the parity bit, it generates a signal called a nonmaskable interrupt (NMI), which brings the system screeching to a halt with one of several equally dismaying messages on the screen.

BUZZ WORDS

Parity: An error checking mechanism that simply counted the number of 1s in a byte of data. A ninth bit is available on a parity chip for the parity bit. With odd-parity checking, if an even number of 1s is found in the byte, a 1 is placed in the parity bit to keep the number of 1s odd. With even-parity, a 0 would be placed in that position to keep the number of 1s even.

There are two things wrong with this picture. First of all, it isn't out of the question for the memory chip to drop two ones in the same byte. In this event, even though the data was twice as corrupted, parity checking can't detect this, and lets it pass. The other problem is that when an error is detected, the method of dealing with it is a bit abrupt. The parity circuit knows one of the bits is wrong; it just doesn't know which one. The designers of this scheme figured that killing the computer, a situation of which you would immediately be aware, was better than killing the data, something you might not discover until it was way too late.

BUZZ WORDS

Faux parity: A null chip that fooled a system into thinking parity memory was installed, when in fact it was not.

EXAM NOTE: It is essential that you be able to describe how parity works and the effect of a memory parity error on the computer system.

Even in the bad old days of computing, not all computers supported parity checking. Those that did had settings in the CMOS to either enable or disable the check. It should be obvious that the memory itself had to be parity memory. On the old XTs and their clones, there needed to be nine sockets in each bank. You're not likely to stumble across many of those these days.

On most 30-pin and 72-pin SIMMs, you can usually determine whether the chip is parity or nonparity by counting the number of individual DRAM chips installed on the SIMM. Three or nine chips (six or eighteen on double-sided SIMMs) would tell you that it is a parity chip. Two or eight chips (four or sixteen on double-sided) is a sure sign that you have nonparity memory. Unfortunately, none of this tells you whether the chip uses FPM or EDO.

The type of memory wasn't actually any different between parity and nonparity SIMMs. The actual memory chips themselves were FPM, or, in some rare cases, EDO. Some SIMMs used higher density memory for the data chips along with a "nibble chip" for parity. Others used *faux parity,* which was a fancy way of saying fake parity. These chips didn't use a real memory chip for parity and returned a zero, regardless of the contents of the chip. In other words, they did nothing positive. All they accomplished was to provide cheaper memory to use on computers that required parity checking.

The fact that the DRAM used was identical whether parity was built in or not was something that could be used to a technician's benefit. If a computer that provides for optional parity checking needs to have the memory upgraded, and you can't find anything but nonparity memory, you can install the nonparity memory into a separate bank and then go into the CMOS Setup and disable parity checking. In most cases the computer will work fine. Don't try to mix parity and nonparity memory in the same bank, however. I doubt you'll like the results. The machine won't boot.

ERROR CORRECTION CODE

Error Correction Code (ECC) expands upon the concept of parity, taking it to the next level. It only works with 72-pin and 168-pin modules. You can purchase special ECC memory or, on some older computers, standard parity SIMMs can be configured to use ECC. The way it works is that a 72-pin SIMM will deliver four full bytes of data, along with half of a byte of parity information. A 168-pin ECC module moves eight bytes of data and a full byte of parity. The bits of information that would have once been parity bits are grouped together as an ECC cluster.

The chipset runs an algorithm on the entire block of information being handled by the chip and stores the results of that calculation in the ECC cluster. In the event that a bit is dropped, when that algorithm is run once again on the receiving end, the equation will come up with a different answer. Instead of crashing the computer, that group of four or eight bytes is simply sent once again. The user never knows anything happened.

> **NOTE:** Even in this day and age, it is possible for multiple bits of data to be lost from the same cluster of information. If this happens, the system will react in the same way parity checking did when it encountered an error. The CPU generates an NMI and the system shuts down. These days, however, memory errors occur at a rate of less than one per every several million reads. Multiple drops are incredibly rare. If you have a system configured to use ECC and it is repeatedly generating NMIs, you've got problems other than simple memory errors on your hands. You might want to check and see if a "less-than-ept" integrator took a system that shipped with ECC and upgraded it with either EDO or SDRAM. This would result in a system that was performing ECC checks on non-ECC memory, and you would therefore see a lot of mistakes.

For ECC to work, the system BIOS must support ECC, and the CMOS settings must be configured properly. Some systems require that you make two adjustments. There will most likely be a place where you turn on parity checking, and another where you tell the system to use ECC mode. On systems that have both of these settings, both must be configured. Most computers don't make you jump through as many hoops. You simply enable ECC, and the system works fine.

TROUBLESHOOTING MEMORY

When memory begins to fail, trying to figure out what is wrong can literally drive you nuts. Understanding how memory works and being able to figure out the problems it may cause are two different issues altogether. A big problem is that a number of symptoms that sick computers exhibit can indicate issues with memory, CPUs, or motherboards. Also, memory problems are frequently intermittent. Which basically means they'll never show their face in the presence of a technician. Do yourself a favor and develop a systematic approach to all troubleshooting. With memory, you can start with the fact that there are three basic guises in which memory errors generally appear.

MEMORY NOT DETECTED

One of the first diagnostics run by the POST program is a memory test. Failure to detect memory during POST can happen in two different ways. Each failure has a different impact on the boot process. If the system finds no memory at all, the speaker will emit a series of beeps and the boot process will halt. The other situation is when the system finishes the boot process successfully, but reports an amount of memory you know to be incorrect.

If the machine is unable to boot, analyze the situation a step at a time. Is this the first time a new computer has ever been turned on? If so, first check and see if the manufacturer installed any memory. Don't laugh! It's rare, but it happens.

If there are memory chips installed, make sure they are properly seated. If they're not, don't automatically call the company and start screaming. SIMM and DIMM modules alike sometimes come loose due to the rigors of ground shipping. Simply reseat the memory and try again. If the memory is securely seated and still not working, it is possible that you have a bad module.

What if you're trying to diagnose an older machine that's been around a while? The first thing to do is to try and figure out what, if anything, changed since the last time the computer worked properly. Was service recently done on the computer? Maybe the memory got knocked loose. It can happen.

Perhaps you just completed a memory upgrade, and things aren't working as planned. If the machine was working fine before attempting the upgrade, there are a couple of things to look at. Once again, is all the memory seated properly in the sockets? Mounting memory into sockets is not always as easy as the makers of boards would have you believe, especially if they used lower-grade sockets. Run your fingers along the top edge of the modules. If there is more than one, then the edges should be perfectly parallel. If one seems to be either tipping or sinking, it isn't seated. Try again. If any of the conductors fail to make contact, the memory won't be recognized.

Once it has been confirmed that the memory is properly seated, verify that the right kind of memory is being used. At the risk of sounding like a broken record, it is very rare that two different types of memory will work together in the same computer. If SDRAM is installed in a machine alongside of EDO, you're going to have problems.

Okay, the memory's all seated properly and you know they're all the same. If you have any empty sockets, check the numbering of the sockets. Memory sockets need to be filled from Bank 0 (or 1, depending on how the sockets are numbered) on up. On some computers, if the initial bank is empty, the system won't see the memory that is installed. The computer will not boot.

If it's not a new computer, and you haven't performed any upgrades, you now ask, "What changed since the last time it worked?" Were any other components either added or replaced? As I mentioned before, it is possible for a stick of memory to get dislodged from its socket any time you're poking around inside the case.

Sometimes, however, the computer boots up just fine, but only a fraction of the memory is available to the user. On some computers, this is not an error. Motherboards with video adapters built right on frequently grab a portion of system RAM to be used as video memory. This memory is reserved by the CMOS and is neither seen nor tested during POST. Only the memory left over after video RAM has been allocated will be reported. This doesn't qualify as a memory error. The system is doing its job correctly.

If a lack of memory is causing programs to not run, or making them run too slowly, go into the CMOS and allocate a smaller amount of memory for video. Some boards allow as much as 64MB (or more) of system memory to be used for video. On a computer that only has 64MB to start with, assigning 32MB for video probably isn't the wisest choice.

Once you've determined that the problem is really a problem, reread the first half of this section. Everything I wrote about concerning a computer that fails to boot due to memory errors also applies to computers that report memory incorrectly. However, there's another problem that might occur after an upgrade. If the first bank is recognized, the machine might recognize only that memory and continue the boot process. Memory installed in other sockets might go ignored. Therefore, check all the memory installed for poor seating or incorrect memory type.

It's easy to get spoiled by working only on computers that use nothing but DIMMs. One stick is always one bank. That's not the case with earlier Pentium-class machines that use

SIMMs. You need two to fill a bank. If you try to get away with using just one, the machine will not boot at all. Also, trying to mix two sizes of memory in the same bank will halt the machine on boot up. In many cases, using two different speeds of memory in a bank will cause a boot failure. That's if you're lucky. Other times, the boot process is successful, but you end up with excessive numbers of memory errors while running applications.

MEMORY ERRORS IN APPLICATIONS

Much of the process of troubleshooting memory starts when the applications or operating system starts reporting errors. Some of these are the result of situations I discussed above. Others are the result of how the application manages the memory it has available. Most of these errors can be resolved by restarting the system.

Some messages that suggest hardware failure overstate their case. Parity errors would suggest a bad memory module, yet frequently those errors are software related. The same holds true of General Protection Faults (GPF). I have seen so-called parity errors show up on machines using nonparity EDO.

"Out of Memory" errors don't always mean that you're actually out of memory. In Windows, that can simply mean that a particular application has used up the resources available to it. Another frequently seen message is "Stack Overflow." For the most part, these are errors generated by the OS, not the hardware. As such, I don't want to go into a whole lot of detail as to what a stack overflow is or why it is bad. Any good book on operating systems can explain that. However, applications installed by the user can generate some of these same errors. Even the best-designed application suffers from amnesia from time to time.

However, if the frequency of these error messages seems to be increasing, that's a good indication of hardware failure, either pending or imminent. Some good information hangs out in those error messages you've been roundly cursing. For example, in Windows, a *fatal exception* error will report a memory address and a CPU register address where Windows thinks the fault occurred. Fatal exceptions occur when the CPU is asked to do the impossible, such as divide by zero, or when it is faced with an NMI it can't resolve. The address reported is usually right. If you've got a machine that is starting to come up with a lot of these messages, start keeping a log of those addresses. They're not as useless as they might look.

If the memory address is the same time and again, the next step is to find out what occupies that address. This isn't as impossible as it may sound. If the system is running Windows, click on Start, go up to Settings, and select Control Panel. Down toward the bottom you'll find an icon labeled System. One of the folders here is Device Manager. There are two selections here that can help you find what memory addresses are in use by the system. All the I/O addresses in use are listed here. The address in the error message is in hexadecimal. Compare it to the ranges of addresses listed in Device Manager and see if the address reported by the error falls within any of these ranges. If so, you have found the piece of hardware causing the failure.

BUZZ WORDS ——————

Fatal exception: Any event that stops the CPU completely. These can include programming errors, such as a request to divide any number by zero, or a hardware event that returns a nonmaskable interrupt.

Another section is Memory. Some files, such as device drivers, load to the same address each time the system starts. Once again, you're reading in hex. Does your address show up here? If so, find out what that file relates to (if you can). If it is a device driver, reload the driver. If it is a system file, try getting a new copy of that file and copying over the one in your system. If the address does not appear, or the errors seem to occur randomly, it might be time to replace a memory module.

If you're got more than one memory module installed in your system, figuring out which one to replace can be a lot of fun. You can do it through trial and error. Replace one and see if the problem goes away. If not, move on to the next one and try again. If you're a practicing professional, you'll probably want something a little more sophisticated. Applications such as *CheckIt Professional Edition* by Touchstone Software or Ultra-X's *Professional Diagnostics* include a utility for running diagnostics on the memory and locating the problem for you.

Memory errors don't always occur in main system memory. In the very first part of this chapter, I mentioned that add-on cards frequently are equipped with their own memory. Many of these devices use standard SIMM or DIMM modules. If that memory should fail, it will generate error messages just like the main system memory will. The best way to determine if this is the source of your problem is to start logging those errors all over again and try to determine if a particular piece of hardware is being accessed every time the error occurs.

Regardless of where the memory is located, memory does fail. The biggest reason any IC fails is electrostatic discharge. In Chapter Four, Basic Electricity and the Power Supply, I discussed the damage ESD can cause. If a chip had to be handled at any time, for any reason, a spark might have killed it. Just remember, for you to even feel a spark of static electricity, that spark needs to be between 10,000 and 20,000 volts. Less than 2,000 volts can kill an IC. You can kill a memory chip or CPU and never even know it. If you actually feel a spark move from you to the chip, you can assume its dead, even if it appears to work on the outset.

Electrical surges in power can also damage memory. Too much current can destroy any circuit. And in fact the memory can quite simply be getting old. You'd think that something with no moving parts would be immune to that. However, every substance in the world contains minute traces of radioactive elements called isotopes. When a single molecule of an isotope decays, it will emit a burst of energy sufficient to destroy one or more of the individual memory cells in a RAM chip. This is going on every day of the chip's life. You don't miss one or two cells from a row or column in a single DRAM. But it's like your brain cells. When enough are gone, you can't remember if it's doing any harm or not. Unfortunately, it is.

I mentioned at the outset of this section that memory errors frequently mimicked those created by other devices. Every once in a while, the memory tests fine (you had it tested in a professional DIMM checker), applications errors are ruled out (you had Microsoft tech support on the phone for hours), and the errors are still occurring on a regular basis. It is now time for you to look at something besides memory for the source of the problem.

The CPU itself is a good source of memory-related issues. After all, it is the device that initiates virtually all memory I/O operations. Try to keep at least one or two current CPUs hanging around that you know to be good. Use a CPU you trust for a while and see if that makes the errors go away. If they do, the problem is solved.

If not, it's possible that the motherboard itself could be at fault. By now, it should be pretty clear that the chipset is arbitrating memory operations. If the chipset starts to fail, it can generate all kinds of eerie problems. Memory problems are high on the list. A bad chipset can almost make you think the computer is haunted.

A problem that can drive you completely insane, and that you can never truly isolate, is when another chip, completely unrelated to memory, begins to fail. Dying ICs can spill a lot of electronic noise out onto the circuit. This can be interpreted as random data, and can result in memory read errors.

In cases such as I've just described, a failing chipset or other IC, the only solution is to replace the system board. On most system boards, a failing CPU can be replaced.

CHAPTER SUMMARY

I realize this was a long chapter. And there was a lot of vital information in it. Some of the most important things that I hope you take away from this chapter are some of the things you're least likely to be tested on when you take the exam. One of those subjects I feel is important is how RAM actually works. A good understanding of the workings of a memory chip help immensely when trying to troubleshoot problems.

Some of the things that I covered in this chapter can almost be put down as historical artifacts. Memory banks are an example of this. It has been several years since any new systems have been released that require an intimate knowledge in this regard. On the other hand, if you're trying to fix an older machine, that knowledge will serve you in good stead.

Troubleshooting memory can be one of the most challenging issues you will face. A good diagnostics utility is in order here. There are some out there that can save you hours of trial and effort troubleshooting. And remember to log those error messages!

BRAIN DRAIN

1. In as much detail as you can recall, describe a typical memory I/O operation, from beginning to end.

2. You have an old 486-based machine that the customer insists on keeping in operation, despite your advice to the contrary. The customer has acquired four new 16MB SIMMs. They look like they should fit, but you can't seem to get the system to recognize them. What are some of the issues that could cause this problem?

3. What were some key differences that made SDRAM so much faster than EDO?

4. Describe how parity worked as a memory error checking mechanism, and why it was a less than desirable option.

5. Describe how ECC differs from parity and what makes it a superior error checking mechanism.

THE 64K$ QUESTIONS

1. Memory I/O operations are controlled by _____.
   a. The CPU
   b. The operating system
   c. The MCC
   d. BIOS

2. The process of adding a fresh charge to the memory cells in DRAM is called _____.
    a. Precharge
    b. Refresh rate
    c. Flush
    d. Refresh

3. A SIMM differs from a DIMM in its design in that _____.
    a. All SIMMs are faster than DIMMs
    b. The terminating tabs on either side of the base of a DIMM can be assigned a separate function
    c. The DIMM moves some of the MCC circuitry from the chipset to the DIMM
    d. Physical size is the only difference.

4. SO-DIMM is an acronym for _____.
    a. Stand-Off Dual Inline Memory Module
    b. Switched Output Dual Inline Memory Module
    c. Small Outline Dual Inline Memory Module
    d. None of the above

5. A typical DRAM cell consists of a transistor paired with _____.
    a. Other transistors
    b. A diode
    c. A microscopic resistor
    d. A microscopic capacitor

6. Refresh rate is measured in _____.
    a. Milliseconds
    b. Nanoseconds

    c. How many thousands of columns refreshed per cycle
    d. Megahertz

7. Once the MCC has determined that the data being sought actually resides in RAM and resolves the address, the next thing to happen is a _____.
    a. Prerefresh
    b. CAS
    c. RAS
    d. RAS/CAS delay

8. SRAM differs from DRAM in that it consists of a transistor coupled with _____.
    a. Other transistors
    b. A diode
    c. A microscopic resistor
    d. A microscopic capacitor

9. DDRAM is so named because it _____.
    a. Operates at twice the clock speed of the FSB
    b. Operates at twice the clock speed of conventional SDRAM
    c. Moves two bits of data for each clock cycle
    d. Only requires two clock cycles to set up an I/O operation

10. Which of the following memory types move parts of the MCC circuitry onto the die of the memory module?
    a. FPM
    b. EDO
    c. SDRAM
    d. RDRAM

TRICKY TERMINOLOGY

Capacity: The total number of bits a memory chip holds.

CAS latency: The delay that occurs between RAS and CAS. Also known as RAS/CAS delay.

Channel: A dedicated path for data to take that prevents other data from competing for time on the bus.

Continuity module: A null memory module that fills the empty banks on a system using Rambus memory.

Fatal exception: Any event that stops the CPU completely. These can include programming errors, such as a request to divide any number by zero, or a hardware event that returns a non-maskable interrupt.

Faux parity: A null chip that fools a system into thinking parity memory was installed, when in fact, it was not.

Latency: The delay that occurs from the time the CPU makes a request for data and the time that information can be accessed from the device holding the data. All devices, including memory and hard drives, exhibit latency.

Memory bank: The total number of memory modules required to assure that the bit width of available memory matches the bit width of the CPU in use.

Parity: An error checking mechanism that simply counted the number of 1s in a byte of data. A ninth bit is available on a parity chip for the parity bit. With odd-parity checking, if an even number of 1s is found in the byte, a 1 is placed in the parity bit to keep the number of 1s odd. With even parity, a 0 would be placed in that position to keep the number of 1s even.

RAS/CAS delay: The delay that occurs between RAS and CAS. Also known as CAS latency.

Refresh rate: The number of columns of memory cells per cycle that the MCC will recharge.

Refresh: The process of recharging the capacitors that link to the transistors of each memory cell on a chip.

ACRONYM ALERT

CAS: Column Access Strobe. A circuit that is part of the MCC, responsible for locking onto the first column in a memory module in which the target data is located.

DDRAM: Double Data-rate RAM. A form of memory that moves two bits of data for each clock cycle.

DRAM: Dynamic Random Access Memory

Dword: Double Word

ECC: Error Correction Code. An error correction method that stored a mathematical image of data being moved on a nibble chip and could correct single-bit errors as they were detected.

EDO: Extended Data Out. A form of memory that replaced FPM and that allowed the RAS/CAS operations for the next I/O operation to be performed at the same time as data from the previous operation is being moved out of the chip.

FPM: Fast Page Mode. An early form of memory that eliminated the RAS cycle from any read operation retrieving data from the same row as the previous operation.

GPF: General Protection Fault. A failure of an application (and possibly the CPU) that results from one program invading another program's address space.

JEDEC: Joint Electron Device Engineering Council. An organization that oversees standards for many of the electronic devices in use, including memory modules.

MRH-S: SDRAM Memory Repeater Hub. A chip in newer Intel chipsets used to arbitrate memory requests between multiple banks of memory.

MTH: Memory Translator Hub. A chip in newer Intel chipsets that replaces the northbridge chip used by contemporary chipsets.

NMI: Nonmaskable Interrupt. Similar to the IRQs used by devices, an NMI is an interrupt to the CPU indicating that immediate action is required. If the CPU cannot resolve the issue, the NMI will cause the CPU to lock up.

RAS: Row Access Strobe. A circuit that is part of the MCC responsible for locking onto the first row in a memory module in which the target data is located.

RDRAM: Rambus Dynamic Random Access Memory. A specialized form of memory manufactured by Rambus, Inc.

SDRAM: Synchronous Dynamic Random Access Memory

SIPP: Single Inline Pin Package. An earlier memory module that put eight or nine DRAM chips on a single IC and mounted into the system board by way of a single row of pins protruding from the base.

SO-DIMM: Small Outline Dual Inline Memory Module. A compact form of memory used primarily in notebook computers, but also seen in some video cards.

VC-SDRAM: Virtual Channel SDRAM. A newer form of memory that gives each operational application its own address space and path to move data back and forth, so that they don't compete for bandwidth.

CHAPTER 10

EXAMINING THE EXPANSION BUS

A function of the computer system most often visited by technicians is unfortunately also an area that is all too frequently the least understood. That is the expansion bus (see **Figure 10.1**). A vast percentage of upgrades and/or replacements involve devices that reside on this all-important bus.

In Chapter One, PC Basics, I discussed the five primary busses of the computer system. Those were the CPU bus, the address bus, the I/O bus, the local bus and the power bus. Not once did I mention the expansion bus. Why? Because the expansion bus straddles several of the primary busses. Without the services of each of the primary busses, the expansion bus ceases to exist. Without the expansion bus, you lose the important ability of being able to add new devices to a computer once it leaves the factory.

Figure 10.1 The expansion bus on a modern motherboard typically allows for different types of expansion cards.

A+ CORE HARDWARE EXAM OBJECTIVES

There's quite a bit in this chapter that you can expect to see on the A+ Core exam. Among the objectives introduced or covered in this chapter are the following:

1.1   Identify the names, purpose, and characteristics of system modules. Recognize these modules by sight or definition.

1.2   Identify basic procedures for adding and removing field-replaceable modules for desktop systems. Given a replacement scenario, choose the appropriate sequences.

1.4   Identify typical IRQs, DMAs, and I/O addresses, and procedures for altering these settings when installing and configuring devices. Choose the appropriate installation or configuration steps in a given scenario.

1.5   Identify the names, purposes, and performance characteristics of standardized/common peripheral ports, associated cabling, and their connectors. Recognize ports, cabling, and connectors by sight.

2.1   Recognize common problems associated with each module and their symptoms, and identify steps to isolate and troubleshoot the problems. Given a problem situation, interpret the symptoms and infer the most likely cause.

4.3   Identify the most popular types of motherboards, their components, and their architecture (bus structures).

WHY DO YOU HAVE AN EXPANSION BUS?

The very nature of a personal computer is that it is personal. No manufacturer can possibly come up with a design that will perfectly suit every user. Most people wouldn't buy a computer without sound. Others prefer to live without it. Many people live on the Internet. To them, a modem is a standard feature. Yet for a networked office system this may not only be unnecessary, it might be a security risk. The expansion bus allows the user to customize his or her computer to fill specific needs.

The expansion bus is not unique to PC-compatible computers. Macintosh computers and mainframes all sport an expansion bus. Even computers made prior to the release of the IBM PC were equipped with a form of expansion bus. One earlier bus that enjoyed some popularity was the S100. Computers equipped with this bus used a series of 100-pin connectors through which edge cards could be inserted into the system.

IBM wasn't strictly looking to launch a product line when it came out with the PC. It was trying to launch an industry. There were already a number of computing systems on the market aimed at the end user by several manufacturers and confusion reigned. The devices that were designed for an Altair were no good for you if you later decided to move over to a Commodore 64.

IBM realized that a stable market was a healthy market and invested a lot of time and money into engineering a "standard" that it hoped other companies would follow. The folks at IBM had several issues to address. First off, they knew that CPUs would not remain the same speed forever. The first CPUs used in the IBM PC operated at 4.77MHz. Within two years, other processors hit the streets that operated at 8MHz, 10MHz, and 12MHz. Therefore, devices couldn't be designed to communicate on the CPU bus. Imagine being a modem manufacturer and having to change your product line every time CPU speeds bumped up another notch. To address this problem, IBM put the expansion bus on its own clock crystal and ran it at a speed independent of that of the CPU.

Another issue designers faced was how to incorporate existing technology into their designs so that existing manufacturers of expansion cards would not rebel. After all, these companies had invested huge sums of money tooling up their plants to make edge card circuit boards. They weren't likely to start all over simply because IBM told them they should. IBM borrowed heavily from existing technology in designing its bus. A primary source of inspiration was the Multibus designed by Intel in 1974.

When IBM launched its first line of personal computers, it also released the specifications for its expansion bus to the rest of the industry at no charge. This display of generosity was not completely altruistic in nature. It had precisely the effect that IBM wanted. Its design became the industry standard.

THE FUNCTIONS OF THE EXPANSION BUS

Because the expansion bus is not directly linked to the CPU, it needs to be able to fulfill the needs of both the device that plugs into it and the CPU. And it needs to make sure that those needs don't conflict. First off, it has to be able to properly utilize system resources, which would include interrupt requests (IRQ), input/output (I/O) addresses, and direct memory access (DMA) channels. It also needs to be able to synchronize the transfer of data across the bus. To do that, it needs to be able to interface with the address bus and the I/O bus. **Figure 10.2** illustrates the way that the expansion bus depends on four of the five primary busses on the system. Since it works at a different speed than the CPU, timing issues need to be resolved and the flow of data must be synchronized. To do all this, it needs power. So let me break down the job description of the expansion bus, task by task.

DEALING WITH SYSTEM RESOURCES

Interfacing a device with the computer system is no easy task. The fact that installing new devices in a computer system has become so simple is a tribute to the engineers who design the expansion busses you use. Devices built onto the system board are configured by the manufacturer, via the BIOS, to deal with issues such as addressing memory and communicating with the CPU.

Newly installed devices must be configured before they will correctly interface with the system. In the old days, configuration was done manually. For the most part, modern devices

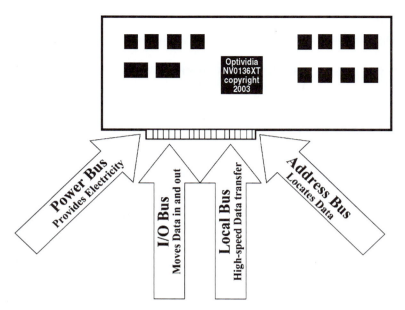

Figure 10.2 The expansion bus requires the services of the primary system busses in order to function.

do a lot of this work for you by way of Plug 'n Play (PnP). However, since PnP is known to occasionally have its ups and downs, it is necessary to have an understanding of system resources in order to deal with issues that do arise. Things that generally need to be configured include IRQs, DMA channels, and I/O addresses. A conflict in any one of these between two devices will result in one or both of the devices not working.

INTERRUPT REQUEST LINES

The interrupt request line (IRQ) is the element of configuration that is most frequently adjusted by the user. The nature of the microprocessor prevents any device from being able to initiate communication between itself and the CPU. Only the CPU can do that. Therefore, if a device needs to transmit data, it needs a way to get the processor's attention. When visitors come to your door, they get your attention by ringing the doorbell. When a device wants to attract the attention of the CPU, it makes use of its own doorbell—the IRQ.

> **EXAM NOTE:** Be prepared to explain the concepts of IRQs, I/O addresses, and DMA channels, and not simply parrot off what device uses what resource.

The IRQ consists of a wire that connects from the expansion card (or onboard device) to the motherboard. When the device needs to notify the CPU that it needs to transmit data, it sends an electrical signal along that path. In other words, it rings the doorbell. Now, if every device on the system rang the same doorbell, the CPU would have no way of knowing which device needed attention. So each device is assigned its own doorbell. When a particular wire lights up, the CPU knows exactly which device is trying to get its attention.

The original IBM PC used a chip called the 8259 to manage IRQs. This chip directed traffic for eight different IRQs, numbered 0 through 7. This was a bit of a problem, because system devices required most of them (see **Figure 10.3**). Users found that they had an extremely limited number of options for adding new devices. They clamored for more.

When the AT was released, an additional 8259 was added to the system. Since the CPU only wants to deal with a single IRQ controller, these two chips were *cascaded* together. The chips are wired from the first 8259 through what had originally been IRQ2, into IRQ9 of the second 8259. The result is that there are two chips controlling eight IRQs each, and there are fifteen usable IRQs. Because IRQ2 and IRQ9 are physically on the same wire, they provide a single interrupt. Systems using the cascaded 8259s by necessity had to reallocate system IRQs. **Figure 10.4** shows the conventional IRQ allocations of a modern computer system. Even though the 8259 chips have been absorbed by the chipset in today's motherboards, the IRQ allocations haven't changed.

Conventional wisdom is that two devices cannot share the same IRQ. That would, in theory anyway, result in the system locking up. This is, in fact, not the case. It is quite possible to have multiple devices on a single IRQ, as long as only one device is ever active at a time. You will see an example of that process at work later in this chapter when I discuss the concept of COM ports.

However, for the most part, when dealing with expansion cards, it is a good idea to follow the conventional wisdom. The first ISA cards all used a method called *edge-triggered* interrupt sensing. The card has a specific connector on its interface that generated its interrupt requests. The system could

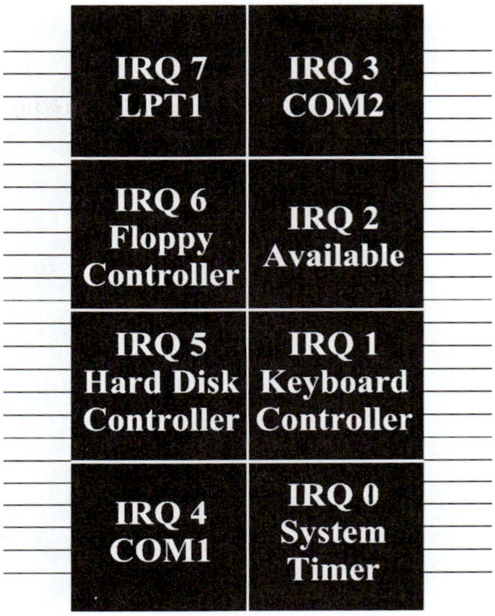

IRQ 7 **LPT1**	**IRQ 3** **COM2**
IRQ 6 **Floppy** **Controller**	**IRQ 2** **Available**
IRQ 5 **Hard Disk** **Controller**	**IRQ 1** **Keyboard** **Controller**
IRQ 4 **COM1**	**IRQ 0** **System** **Timer**

Figure 10.3 The first IBM PC possessed a mere eight IRQs for the entire system. A whopping total of one of those was available.

Buzz Words

Cascade: A process by which multiple circuits are linked together in such a way that they appear to the system as a single device.

Edge triggered: Any response that elicited and/or was controlled by a direct electrical signal coming from a pin or wire on a device. The voltage is applied, and the device depends on the interrupt controller to "remember" that it sent the signal.

Level triggered: A response that is arbitrated by a control circuit and/or device driver that allows the same device to make use of one of several interrupt channels. The level-triggered interrupt raises the voltage on the appropriate wire and holds it until the expected response is received.

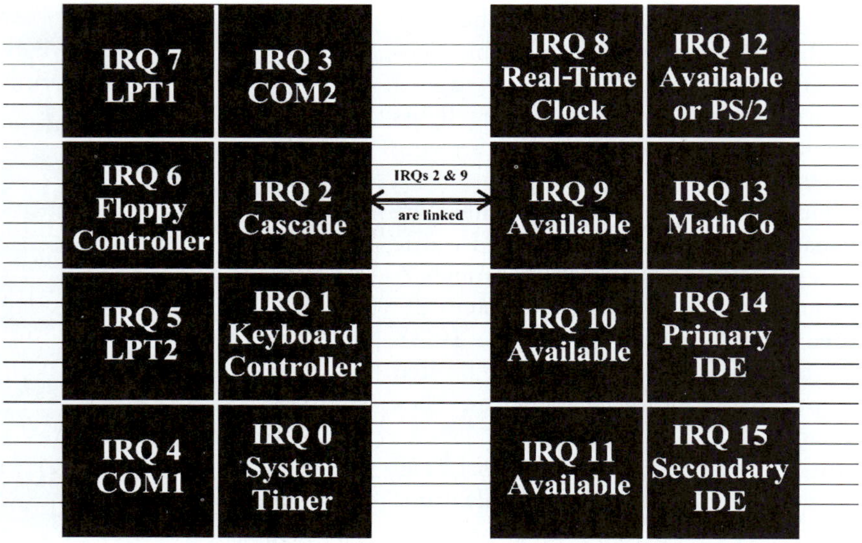

IRQ 7 LPT1	IRQ 3 COM2		IRQ 8 Real-Time Clock	IRQ 12 Available or PS/2
IRQ 6 Floppy Controller	IRQ 2 Cascade	IRQs 2 & 9 are linked	IRQ 9 Available	IRQ 13 MathCo
IRQ 5 LPT2	IRQ 1 Keyboard Controller		IRQ 10 Available	IRQ 14 Primary IDE
IRQ 4 COM1	IRQ 0 System Timer		IRQ 11 Available	IRQ 15 Secondary IDE

Figure 10.4 A second 8259 didn't quite double the number of IRQs. IRQs 2 and 9 are linked in a cascade, leaving a total of fifteen physical IRQs.

tell what device a signal was coming from by way of its IRQ. It couldn't, however, determine which physical slot in which a card was installed. Therefore, the only way to avoid confusion was to make sure that no two cards shared the same IRQ, even if they weren't active on the bus at the same time.

PCI devices incorporate *level-triggered interrupts*. The device is designed to operate at any one of several different IRQs, which can either be assigned by the BIOS, or through a setup program. A chip on the device manages four different interrupt channels. Once the IRQ is assigned, when the device needs to communicate, it simply raises the voltage on the appropriate connector.

Another concept that you should be aware of is that IRQs are numbered in order of priority. If two devices both signal the CPU at exactly the same moment, the device with the higher priority will have precedence. Therefore, critical system devices are given the highest priority. Also take note that the order of priorities does not directly map to the IRQ number. **Figure 10.5** shows the fifteen physical IRQs and their relative priorities.

INPUT OUTPUT ADDRESSES

Input output addresses (I/O addresses) can get a little confusing to the beginner. They look, feel, smell, and taste just like a memory address, because that is exactly what they are. In order to communicate with a particular piece of hardware, the system creates a little drop box in memory at a specific location. This address correlates to the address in memory of the first instruction of a device driver or BIOS instruction. In order to keep track of what device is using what

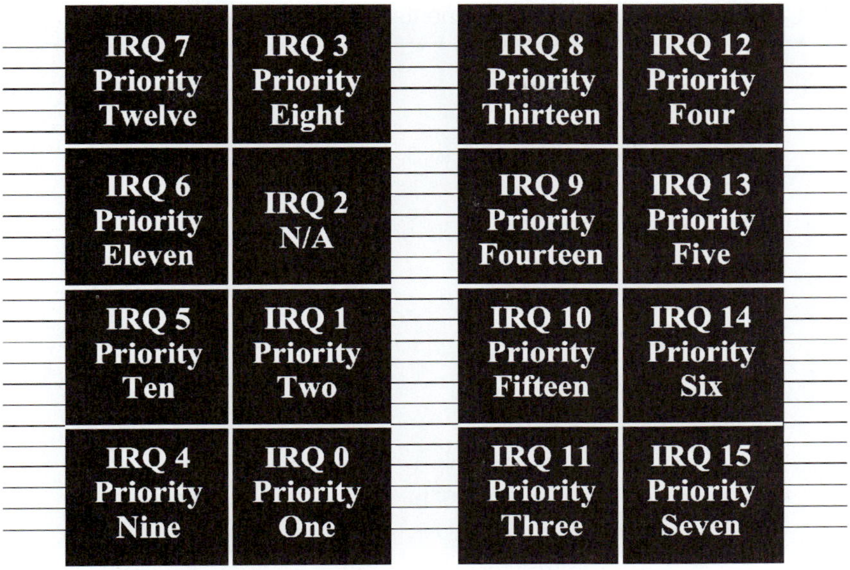

IRQ 7 Priority Twelve	IRQ 3 Priority Eight	IRQ 8 Priority Thirteen	IRQ 12 Priority Four
IRQ 6 Priority Eleven	IRQ 2 N/A	IRQ 9 Priority Fourteen	IRQ 13 Priority Five
IRQ 5 Priority Ten	IRQ 1 Priority Two	IRQ 10 Priority Fifteen	IRQ 14 Priority Six
IRQ 4 Priority Nine	IRQ 0 Priority One	IRQ 11 Priority Three	IRQ 15 Priority Seven

Figure 10.5   The physical IRQs and their relative priorities

address, an I/O address table is maintained by the CPU. When a device needs to communicate with the CPU, it first lights up its IRQ channel. When the CPU is ready to interface with that device, it looks up the IRQ in the address table and then knows where to go looking for the device driver or BIOS instruction that manages the device.

The number of available I/O addresses is limited. They consist of one or more 8-bit ports. There are 256 of these 8-bit ports, or 65,536 available 16-bit ports. Any two contiguous 8-bit ports can be combined to form a single 16-bit port, and any four contiguous 8-bit ports can be combined to form a single 32-bit port. Many of these ports are assigned by IBM for specific functions, and others have been claimed by other companies to support their devices.

EXAM NOTE: For the exam and in the real world, understand that while it may be possible for peripherals to share an IRQ, attempting to share an I/O address is sure to result in a conflict.

Most devices possess more than one I/O address. Depending on the needs of a particular piece of hardware, it may receive an I/O address range of anywhere from an address a single byte wide to one as much as 32 bytes wide. In general, I/O addresses are not something that a technician assigns manually. However, for many devices, it is possible to change the I/O address of a particular device, either through a CMOS setting or from the OS. This sometimes becomes necessary when two devices compete for the same address range. A couple examples of this would be a system that was equipped with a second parallel port and a certain brand of network interface card. The default I/O addresses of these devices frequently overlap. **Table 10.1** lists a few of the most common I/O addresses.

Table 10.1   Common I/O Address Assignments

I/O Address Range	Device
000-00Fh	DMA controller, channels 0 to 3
010-01Fh	(System use)
020-023h	Interrupt controller #1 (020-021h)
024-02Fh	(System use)
030-03Fh	(System use)
040-043h	System timer
044-04Fh	(System use)
050-05Fh	(System use)
060-063h	Keyboard & PS/2 mouse (060h), speaker (061h)
064-067h	Keyboard & PS/2 mouse (064h)
068-06Fh	Free to use
070-073h	Real-time clock/CMOS, (Non-maskable Interrupt - 070-071h)
074-07Fh	(System use)
080-083h	DMA page register 0-2
084h	DMA page register 3
089-08Bh	DMA page register 4-6
08Fh	DMA page register 7
090-09Fh	(System use)
0A0-0A3h	Interrupt controller #2
0A4-0BFh	(System use)
0C0-0CFh	DMA controller, channels 4-7 (0C0-0DFh, bytes 1-16)
0D0-0DFh	DMA controller, channels 4-7 (0C0-0DFh, bytes 17-32)
0E0-0EFh	(System use)
0F0-0FFh	Floating point unit (FPU/NPU/Math coprocessor)
100-12Fh	(System use)
130-15Fh	Commonly used for SCSI controllers
160-167h	Free to use
168-16Fh	Quaternary IDE controller, master drive
170-077h	Secondary IDE controller, master drive
178-1E7h	Free to use
1E8-1EFh	Tertiary IDE controller, master drive
1F0-1F7h	Primary IDE controller, master drive

(Continued)

Table 10.1 *(Continued)*

I/O Address Range	Device
1F8-1FFh	Free to use
200-207h	Joystick controller
208-20Bh	Free to use
20B-20Fh	(System use)
210-21Fh	Free to use
220-22Fh	Sound card
230-23Fh	Some SCSI adapters
240-24Fh	Some sound cards, some SCSI adapters, some NE2000 network cards
250-25Fh	Some NE2000 network cards
260-26Fh	Some NE2000 network cards, some non-NE2000 network cards, some sound cards
270-273h	(System use)
274-278H	Plug and Play system devices
279-27Fh	LPT2
280-28Fh	Some sound cards, some NE2000 network cards
290-29Fh	Some NE2000 network cards
2C0-2E7h	Free to use
2E8-2EFh	COM port 4
2F0-2F7h	Free to use
2F8-2FFh	COM port 2
300-301h	MIDI port
300-30Fh	Some NE2000 network cards
310-31Fh	Some NE2000 network cards
320-323h	Some non-NE2000 network cards
320-32Fh	Some NE2000 network cards
320-327h	PC-XT hard disk controller
330-333h	MIDI port
330-33Fh	Some NE2000 network cards, some SCSI controllers
340-34Fh	Some SCSI controllers
350-35Fh	Some NE2000 network cards, some SCSI controllers
360-363h	Some tape backup controller cards
360-36Fh	Some NE2000 network cards

(Continued)

Table 10.1   *(Concluded)*

I/O Address Range	Device
370-373h	Some tape backup controller cards
370-37Fh	Some NE2000 network cards
378-37Fh	LPT1 (or LPT2 on monochrome systems)
380-387h	Free to use
388-38Bh	FM synthesizer
38C-3AFh	Free to use
3B0-3BBh	VGA or monochrome video
3BC-3BFh	LPT1 on monochrome systems
3C0-3CFh	VGA or CGA video
3D3-3DFh	VGA or EGO video
3E0-3E3h	Some tape backup controllers
3E8-3Efh	COM port 3
3EC-3Efh	Tertiary IDE controller
3F0-3F7h	Floppy disk controller
3F8-3FFh	COM port 1
3f6-3F7h	Primary IDE

Common I/O address assignments

Note: While it may appear on this table that some devices overlap in their I/O address range, in fact, this is not possible. These indicate devices that may potentially occupy the range. If one device already possesses an address within the range, no other device may share it.

DIRECT MEMORY ACCESS CHANNELS

Some devices don't need a lot of help from the CPU just to transfer data between themselves and RAM. Forcing the CPU to arbitrate every byte that moves between them would be a waste of CPU time and bog the system down. Those devices should be able to learn to move data directly to memory without CPU intervention. Devices that can make use of a direct memory access (DMA) channel are able to perform this feat. An example of this is a floppy drive transfer, or a .wav file playing over your sound card.

As was the case with IRQs, originally DMA channels were under the control of a specific chip. Early computers used an 8237 chip to handle DMA functions. One of these chips was able to direct traffic for four channels. When IBM doubled the number of IRQ controllers in the PC-AT, it also doubled the number of 8237 chips. As with the 8259, the two chips were linked through two of the channels: DMA0 and DMA4. Therefore, these two DMA numbers constitute the same channel. The 8237s joined the 8259s in being swallowed by the chipset.

There is 8-bit DMA access and 16-bit DMA access. DMA channels are also directly linked to the ISA bus, and therefore can run only at the 8MHz speed of the ISA bus. Therefore, DMA is used only on devices that require relatively slow throughput. Such devices would include floppy disk drives and some sound cards. Also, if you elect to configure your parallel port to Extended Capabilities Port (ECP) mode when configuring your parallel port, you will need to select a DMA channel.

To configure an 8-bit device on a DMA channel, you need to use either one of channels DMA1 or DMA3. DMA0 and DMA2 can't be used because they are reserved by the system. DMA0 is allocated to the memory refresh circuit, while DMA2 is tied to the floppy disk drive. 16-bit devices need to be configured on DMA5, DMA6, or DMA7. DMA4 can't be used because it's the cascaded channel. **Table 10.2** summarizes DMA channel usage in a more visual way.

Table 10.2 Common DMA Channel Usage

DMA Channel	Usage
8-bit Channels	
DMA0	Memory Refresh
DMA1	Available
DMA2	Floppy Disk Drive
DMA3	Available
16-bit Channels	
DMA4	Cascade
DMA5	Available
DMA6	Available
DMA7	Available

Available and assigned DMA channels

COM AND LPT PORTS

One thing I want to emphasize right off the bat is that COM ports and serial ports are not the same things. Nor are LPT and parallel ports the same. Serial and parallel ports are physical places into which you plug cables. COM and LPT ports are preconfigured combinations of IRQ and I/O addresses.

BUZZ WORDS

COM port: A predefined combination of an IRQ and an I/O address configured for communications devices.

LPT port: A predefined combination of an IRQ and an I/O address configured for line printers.

When IBM was first writing the book on the personal computer, it decided that serial devices would be easier to configure if the user had a fixed I/O and IRQ to use. Likewise, printers would be easier to deal with if you just put them on LPT1 rather than having to fight with individual parameters. The engineers defined two COM ports and two LPT ports.

> **EXAM NOTE:** Know the resource settings for all the COM and LPT ports backward and forward. You may be asked to identify them directly. Or worse yet, you may be given a detailed configuration that includes the use of COM ports and be expected to know what resources are still available for allocation.

Early on, IBM realized that two COM ports weren't enough. There were just too many devices that worked off of a serial port. Rather than tie up an additional two IRQs, the designers at IBM made a tactical decision. How often would somebody be trying to access two different external devices at the same time? (Keep in mind, this was in the days of DOS, when a computer couldn't climb stairs and chew gum at the same time.) Therefore, when they added COM ports 3 and 4 to the mix, they used the same IRQs as COM ports 1 and 2. They simply gave the ports different I/O addresses so the CPU would know it was talking to a different device. However, if the user did hit both devices simultaneously, the system would freeze. A classic example of this was putting the modem on COM3 and a serial mouse on COM1. The system works great as long as you don't try to use the modem and the mouse at the same time. Then, both devices hit IRQ4 at the same time and the system freezes.

Table 10.3   COM and LPT Port Assignments

Port Name	IRQ	I/O
COM1	4	3F8h
COM2	3	2F8h
COM3	4	3E8h
COM4	3	2E8h
LPT1	7	378h
LPT2	5	278h

The standard COM and LPT ports, as defined by IBM

Another example is putting a parallel scanner in line with your printer on the same parallel port. One parallel port will have one LPT port. This won't matter as long as you scan when you scan and you print when you print. If you try to scan when you print, you'll have a problem. **Table 10.3** lists the COM and LPT ports as defined by IBM.

SERIAL AND PARALLEL PORTS

Two interfaces frequently overlooked by novices as being part of the expansion bus are the serial and parallel ports. Yet these ports are commonly used to interface with external devices. Many of the toys you go out and buy today hook up to one of these ports.

SERIAL PORTS

The initial IBM PC shipped with two serial ports. At the time, that was considered sufficient. However, in the years before USB and FireWire (see the section immediately following this one), those were the only places to put devices such as external modems. Some printers also hooked up to the serial port as well. On most PCs of that era, the serial and parallel ports were on an expansion card called the I/O card. Once IBM had defined an additional two COM ports, it was relatively easy for the user to add additional ports.

On most of the earlier computers, the two serial ports consisted of a single DB-9 and a single DB-25. The DB-9 connector on a computer consists of a 9-pin male connector about a half an inch long by a quarter of an inch high. The matching cable would be a nine-socket female connector. **Figure 10.6** shows a close-up of a DB-9 connector.

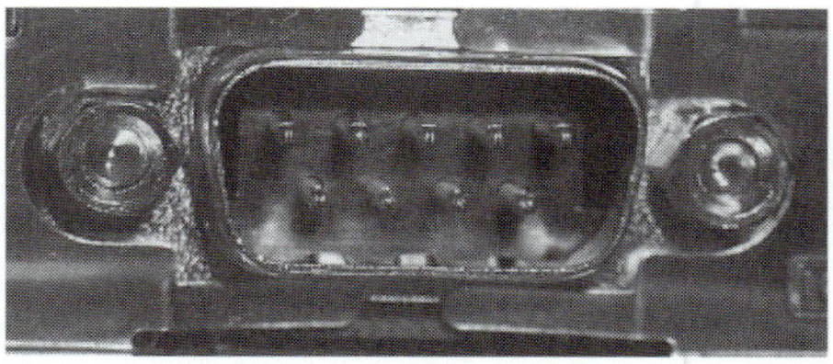

Figure 10.6   A DB-9 connector

The DB-25 serial ports (**Figure 10.7**) used on older machines differed from their 9-pin counterparts only in cosmetics. The DB-25 doesn't use any more conductors than the DB-9. The remaining pins are null. Serial ports, whether DB-9 or DB-25, sometimes get referred to as RS-232 ports, after the standards that described the port.

Figure 10.7 The 25-pin serial port actually doesn't use any more pins than the 9-pin port. It just uses bigger plugs.

Most current computers have a single DB-9. A few models still sport a pair of DB-9s. It is pretty rare to stumble across DB-25 ports on recent machines. This particular interface has become a historical artifact.

PARALLEL PORTS

Parallel ports are also DB-25 connectors. This shouldn't, however, cause any confusion with the 25-pin serial ports that may exist on the same machine. Serial ports are always male plugs on the back of the computer; the parallel port is female. Unlike the 25-pin serial port, parallel ports make use of nearly all of the conductors available. They have to transmit eight bits of data on each cycle, and on the more modern parallel modes, need to send and receive. In Chapter Eighteen, Printing Technologies: Getting it All on Paper, I will go over the various parallel port modes and how they have differed over the years.

THE UNIVERSAL SERIAL BUS

While not the most recent of the technologies to emerge, the Universal Serial Bus (USB) still enjoys immense popularity. The USB interface is 100 percent Plug 'n Play, and devices are hot-swappable. This means that the user can add and remove USB devices on the fly without having to shut the computer down. It also only loads drivers for those devices that are attached. It is theoretically possible to string together up to 127 devices in a single chain and still only tie up one IRQ.

The first commercial release of USB, Version 1.0, provided a shared bandwidth of 12Mb/s. With one device hooked up, that device enjoyed the entire 12Mb/s to itself. A second device added to the bus dropped the respective speed of each by half. A third device caused the bandwidth to be shared three ways, and so on and so forth. A USB 1.0 cable run could be as long as 100'.

USB 2.0 added a new device class called high-speed and upped total bandwidth to 480Mb/s. This added speed takes its toll in terms of cable length. A USB 2.0 cable can only be as long as 15'. USB 2.0 is completely backwards compatible to 1.0. Therefore all manufacturers are currently shipping nothing but Version 2.0 product.

BUZZ WORDS

USB hub: A device that manages the I/O for two or more USB device chains.

USB host: Any computer or other device equipped with USB-compatible BIOS, firmware, and controller.

USB device: Any component designed to be operated on the USB.

USB requires three different components to be active in order to work. Those are the host, the hub, and the device. The *host* would be any computer equipped with a USB-compatible BIOS, chipset, and controller. This would be practically any computer built since about 1998. The *hub* is the actual USB port where the cable connects. On the back of the computer, the USB hub would be the one or two USB ports provided by the manufacturer. A hub located on the computer itself is the root hub. Most electronics stores also provide devices that allow additional connections. These are external hubs. The *device* completes the chain. Devices, in USB terminology, are also known as the function.

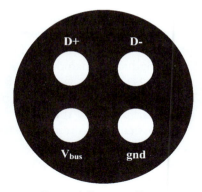

D+ and D− carry Data.
V$_{bus}$ and gnd provide power.

Figure 10.8   A cross-section of a USB cable.

EXAM NOTE: Make sure you know the number of devices that can be managed by USB and the maximum throughput of both USB 1.0 and USB 2.0.

A USB cable (**Figure 10.8**) consists of two pairs of 28-gauge wire. One pair transfers data between the device and the computer. The second pair provides power to the devices in either low-power or high-power mode. In low-power mode, it will provide up to 100mA of electricity to the device. High-power mode can provide up to 500mA. If a device requires more current than either mode provides, it must provide its own power supply. These are self-powered devices. Printers and scanners need a place to be plugged in. Anything that can operate on 500mA or less is bus-powered and won't need an outlet. Keyboards and modems fall into that category.

The nice thing about many USB devices is that they are able to double as an external hub. I am currently using a CTX USB monitor. On the back is an external hub built into the monitor that has an additional four plugs. I can plug my USB keyboard into the monitor and not have to worry about stringing the cable around the back of the desk and all the way to the computer.

FireWire   *FireWire* was originally the brainchild of Apple Computer Corporation, released in 1986. The Institute of Electrical and Electronic Engineers (IEEE) assumed development of the technology and formalized the standards as IEEE-1394 in 1995. Technically, FireWire is a form of the Small Computer Systems Interface (SCSI), which will be discussed in Chapter Fifteen, The Many Faces of SCSI. However, because it competes directly with USB as an I/O bus, I've decided to include a discussion of FireWire in this chapter.

Long a popular favorite on Macintosh Computers, it is rapidly picking up interest in the PC world as well. FireWire is everything you could want in a bus. It is auto-configuring. A new device introduced to the bus sends out its information and the FireWire protocols load all the appropriate drivers. Once the device is shut down, drivers can be shelled out of memory. Like USB, FireWire

BUZZ WORDS ─────────

FireWire: A high-speed serial SCSI connection originally developed by Apple Computer Corporation that is capable of 400Mb/s throughput.

is hot-pluggable. Devices can be put in or taken out at will, without shutting the system down. FireWire requires no termination or device ID configuration.

A standard FireWire cable consists of six conductors (**Figure 10.9**). There are two sets of 28-gauge twisted-pair wire for data transmission, plus two 22-gauge wires for carrying current. IEEE-1394 specifications call for FireWire cable to be capable of carrying up to 40V at 1.5A. However, relatively few devices actually make use of the power lines. This cable can be up to 14′ long.

Current standards support up to 400Mb/s data transfer and up to sixty-three devices on a chain. Proposed standards increase throughput to 800Mb/s. The real beauty of FireWire is that it is platform independent. In fact, it is device independent. It works on Macs as well as PCs and

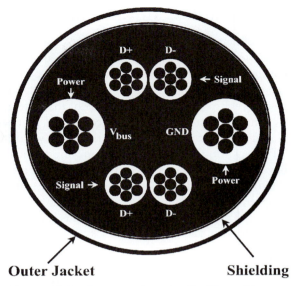

Outer Jacket   **Shielding**

Figure 10.9   Cross-section of a FireWire cable

could easily be ported to mainframes. Two FireWire-enabled devices could be linked directly together, without even requiring an intervening computer to handle data transfer. This makes it an ideal interface for digital consumer electronic devices, including audio-visual equipment.

At this point in time, FireWire practically owns the Apple market. While it's gaining headway in the PC world, it still hasn't overcome the perceived advantages of the Universal Serial Bus, and USB 2.0 is actually faster. **Table 10.4** compares both versions of USB to FireWire.

FireWire does require that both the system BIOS and the OS support IEEE-1394. All Microsoft operating systems released from Windows 98, 2nd Edition and later support FireWire. Microsoft does have supplemental files posted on its Web site for enabling Windows 98. Previous operating systems will not support it. Various Linux support sites, including most companies that provide Linux distribution packages, have patches that will enable FireWire in Linux as well.

Table 10.4   A Comparison of USB to FireWire

Specification	USB 1.0	USB 2.0	FireWire
Data transfer rate	12Mb/s	480Mb/s	400Mb/s
Cable length	100′	15′	14′
Number of devices on a chain	127	127	63

Both versions of USB and FireWire support hot-swapping devices and are capable of powering peripherals by way of their respective connectors.

THE DATA BUS: MOVING DATA ACROSS THE BUS

The primary reason for having an expansion bus is to be able to add new devices to a system. Your new computer didn't arrive with all the toys you wanted. So you went down to the computer store and bought that high-end sound card you just couldn't live without. Now you can play back all the fancy sounds your game can generate, but until you get those sounds moved from RAM to the sound card, none of that information is going to do you a whole lot of good.

In a perfect world, the devices would all operate at the same speed as the processor and would have data busses exactly the same width. You've already seen why that isn't possible. CPUs just don't stay the same from one generation to the next. As new generations of CPUs have been released, new expansion busses are also developed. Many computers (in fact most of them) have at least two separate types of expansion bus. Some even have three. Later in this chapter, I will provide a detailed description of each of the busses. To help you get through this section, **Table 10.5** outlines the various busses that have appeared over the years and ties them together with the release of CPUs.

EXAM NOTE: Make sure you know the order in which the different expansion busses evolved, along with details such as bit width and maximum bus speeds.

Table 10.5 The Evolution of the Expansion Bus

BUS	Year Released	Bus Width	Maximum Speed	Address Space	Available Memory	Bandwidth	CPU Release
PC1	1981	8-bit	4.77MHz	8-bit	1MB	7.9MB/s	8088
ISA	1984	16-bit	8MHz	20-bit	16MB	15.9MB/s	80286
MCA	1987	32-bit	10MHz	20-bit	16MB	~38.6MB/s	80386
EISA	1988	32-bit	8MHz	32-bit	4GB	31.8MB/s	80386
PC Card	1990	16-bit	8MHz	24-bit	64MB	~15.8MB/s	80386
VLB	1991	32-bit	33MHz	32-bit	4GB	127.2MB/s	80486
PCI 1.0	1992	32-bit	33MHz	32-bit	4GB	127.2MB/s	80486
PCI 2.1	1995	32- or 64-bit	66MHz	32-bit	4GB	~510MB/s	Pentium
AGP 1.0	1996	32-bit	66MHz	32-bit	4GB	254MB/s	Pentium
AGP 2.0	1998	32-bit	66MHz	32-bit	4GB	~533MB/s	Pentium
PCI-X 1.0	2000	64-bit	133MHz	64-bit	N/A	~1.2GB/s	Pentium II
PCI-X 2.0	2002	64-bit	<533MHz	64-bit	N/A	~4.3GB/s	Pentium 4

Each new release of a PCI bus is not only faster, but can also have increased bit-width and more efficient transfer of data in each clock cycle.

So how does the CPU deal with 16-bit chunks of data coming off the ISA bus, and not choke on the 64-bit data that the PCI-X devices are delivering? For one thing, if the bus is not of equal size to the CPU, delivery of data must occur over multiple bus cycles. For example, if you have a CPU that has a 133MHz front-side bus (see Chapter Seven, Understanding CPUs), and is moving data from a conventional PCI device, the bottleneck created is two-fold. First off, the CPU has a 64-bit external data bus; the PCI has 32-bit. This means that it will require two cycles of the PCI bus to move enough data to fill the CPU's bus for just one of its cycles. Second, the CPU cycle is 133MHz while the PCI bus is 33MHz. That means each cycle for the CPU represents 7.5 nanoseconds (ns), while a cycle for PCI is a hair over 30ns. Therefore, it's taking 60ns, or eight CPU clock cycles, for each chunk of data moved from the bus to the CPU.

In order to arbitrate this transfer, a special circuit is required. As you may have already guessed, this is another function of the chipset in most cases. In the case of the older ISA bus, the southbridge chip (see Chapter Six, Motherboards, BIOS, and the Chipset) is in control. Faster busses, such as AGP, will link to the northbridge chip. As I shall explain later in this chapter, PCI can be arbitrated by either the northbridge or the southbridge.

THE MEMORY BUS: ADDRESSING RAM

When I discussed the CPU in Chapter Seven, I pointed out that one of the limitations of a CPU is how much memory it can "see." This is a limitation imposed by its address bus. Expansion cards interconnect to the expansion bus and address memory in a similar manner. However, with many bus devices, greater limitations are imposed.

The ISA bus is enabled with a 24-bit address bus. Therefore, even if the CPU has a 32-bit address bus, the device installed in the slot can't see as much memory as the CPU can. It will be limited to the lower 16MB of RAM. Devices attached to the ISA bus, by default, have to locate their memory buffers in this area. DMA access can occur only with data located in the lower 16MB, which means that when the data is located elsewhere, the device driver needs to relocate the information. This adds to the many reasons why ISA is not a suitable bus for most devices communicating with modern CPUs.

TIMING ISSUES

As I discussed earlier, one of the key reasons for having a separate expansion bus is so that there doesn't have to be a new device made every time CPU speeds move up. Therefore, the expansion bus will most likely be running at a rate different that that of the CPU. On the original IBM PC, that wasn't a problem. The expansion bus and the CPU ran at the same speed. Once they started to move apart, the issue had to be faced.

While the system clock paces the CPU, the expansion bus has its own signal, generated by a bus clock. For a successful transfer of data to occur, that data has to be paced to arrive on the CPU bus at intervals in which the CPU can receive it. Early computers made use of *synchronous timing*. CPUs were developed at speeds that were either a multiple or a submultiple of the clock speed. For example, the 12MHz 80286 was 1.5× that of the 8MHz bus. Data was easily buffered. *Asynchronous timing* works by letting the bus move data however it sees fit, and then delivering that data at a rate optimal to the CPU. This does require more complex circuitry and a buffer area for the data to be held, but it also allows for better efficiency in data transfer. Most modern CPUs are designed to operate either synchronously or asynchronously. The chipset controls timing.

COMMUNICATING ACROSS BUSSES

Timing, data access, and data transfer are all complicated enough issues when there is only a single bus on the system. However, most computers have different types of expansion bus available. The computer I'm working on right now has two ISA slots, five PCI slots, and an AGP slot. Each one of those operates at a different speed, transfers data in different sized chunks, and has to handle timing issues in different manners. As a result, the system needs some way of refereeing among the different busses for them to be able to communicate among themselves.

> **BUZZ WORDS**
>
> **Synchronous timing:** Bus speeds are a submultiple of the CPU's clock speed, and data is delivered at a steady rate based on that speed.
>
> **Asynchronous timing:** A device on a bus can deliver its data at any speed it sees fit to a reserved area of memory called a buffer. Data is then fed to the CPU at a rate optimal to the CPU.
>
> **Bridge:** A specialized circuit that moves data between two disparate devices or busses in a such a manner that both devices become compatible.

This becomes particularly problematic when the busses don't even interface with the same part of the chipset. For example, the AGP bus doesn't see the southbridge chip at all. ISA doesn't communicate with the northbridge chip. Yet both have to coexist with each other, and neither operates at the speed of the CPU. To solve this problem, designers incorporated *bridges* into the circuitry. These bridges act as translators between busses.

Another place where bridges become necessary is across PCI busses. By design, as I'll discuss a little later in this chapter, a PCI bus is limited to only four slots. It can use even less than that if there are PCI devices incorporated onto the board. Yet we all know that motherboards come with more than four PCI slots. As I just said, the one I'm working on has five. This is possible because of something called the PCI to PCI Bridge (PPB). In theory, a designer could incorporate as many as 256 different PPBs onto a motherboard, supporting over a thousand slots. That would be one big motherboard!

THE EVOLUTION OF THE EXPANSION BUS

By now, it should be clear that as the CPU became faster and more complicated, the expansion bus had to be redesigned to keep up. When IBM first designed the PC bus in the postpartum days of the personal computer, it took a major step forward by making the bus available to one and all. This provided a certain degree of compatibility, which was precisely what IBM had in mind. With a few notable exceptions, this compatibility has been the mainstay of the computer industry. In fact, the task of maintaining those standards has fallen under the strict control of IEEE. Table 10.5, earlier in this chapter, provides an overview of the different busses. Here, I

Figure 10.10   Compared to modern computers, a system based on the old XT design was a very simple thing.

will take you on a more detailed bus tour. For those of you interested in specific pinouts of some of the busses discussed here, refer to Appendix G.

THE PC BUS

The bus shown in **Figure 10.10** is often called 8-bit ISA. This isn't technically correct, because the ISA standards that I will discuss next wouldn't be defined for a couple of more years. IBM called it the PC bus or sometimes the XT bus. Once the PC-AT was released in 1984, IBM referred to the 16-bit bus as the AT bus. However, those were trademarked names, so the term ISA, for Industry Standard Architecture, was coined. Nothing would officially become labeled ISA until 1987 when IEEE would formalize the standards. Writers who have fallen into the 8-bit ISA trap can be forgiven, because it was from this bus that the ISA standards were drawn. Nothing in the physical structure magically changed simply because IEEE had given it its blessing. The difference is purely semantic (and in most cases, purely bureaucratic).

The original PC bus consisted of a 7.66MHz 8-bit slot designed to accommodate the external data bus of the Intel 8088 CPU. The speed of the bus would be bumped to 8.33MHz the following year. The slot was a 62-pin edge card connector. It supported only the 20-bit address bus of the 8088. The PC bus only addresses a total of eight IRQs. Since computers of this era only made use of a single DMA controller chip, the 8-bit slot only had four conductors dedicated to DMA channels. The PC bus had a relatively long life span, despite the fact that the PC-AT rendered it virtually obsolete a year later. For the most part, most ISA devices of the day continued to be made in 8-bit versions. 8-bit "ISA" slots would continue to appear in machines all the way into the era of computers based on the 80486 CPU.

INDUSTRY STANDARD ARCHITECTURE

When IEEE released the official standards for the ISA bus in 1987, it took the design, as implemented by IBM, and strictly defined it. It was at this point in time that the industry had an "official" ISA bus. In a publication released as IEEE Draft Standard P996, the committee strictly defined signal and timing specifications that all companies had to follow. It also defined the specifications for the 16-bit extensions (see **Figure 10.11**).

BUZZ WORDS

Key: A null space on an edge card connector or memory module that is used for properly aligning the device into its slot.

The 8-bit incarnation of the bus remained as described in the section on the PC bus. The 16-bit version was extracted directly from IBM's schematics for the AT bus. The only real differences were in the strict definitions of electrical signals, something IBM had not been as informative about. For reasons of backward compatibility, the 8.33MHz speed was retained.

The 16-bit bus had to address issues other than simply a wider data path. The AT had also incorporated a second 8259 chip, enabling seven additional IRQs, and a second 8237 chip, adding three more DMA channels. Also, because of the newer CPU used in the PC-AT, the 80286 had a 24-bit address bus, and the 16-bit ISA was modified to enable it to use the extended address space as well.

In order to make sure that this new bus didn't make all those 8-bit devices that had been manufactured over the previous years obsolete, the added pins required for the changes were implemented in an extension to the original 8-bit design. This consisted of a 36-pin connector added onto the back of the 62-pin 8-bit slot. This extension is separated by a null space known as the *key*. The end result is that an 8-bit device will occupy only the front section of the slot and the system will recognize it as an 8-bit device. The 16-bit card fills the whole slot.

Figure 10.11
IBM kept the 16-bit ISA slot compatible with the 8-bit PC slot by adding the additional wires onto an extension hung off the end

The 16-bit ISA became the de facto standard for many years and continues to appear on motherboards manufactured today. It was only recently that Intel and Microsoft banded together to end the days of the ISA reign. According to their PC2002 standards, motherboards will no longer support ISA. Judging by the number of systems still appearing with ISA in 2003, I would have to assume that many manufacturers are finding other uses for the papers written by these two companies on the subject. However, as hard as the bus is to kill, there is good logic in what Intel and Microsoft are trying to do.

The ISA bus never made it past the 8.33MHz level. The newer chipsets by Intel no longer have a southbridge component, and therefore cannot support anything that slow. Other manufacturers will eventually have to follow suit. Also, the 24-bit address space is still an inherent limitation of the bus, as I discussed in the section on addressing. Therefore, I think it's safe to say that the days of ISA are dwindling rapidly.

MICRO CHANNEL ARCHITECTURE

When Intel released its 80386 microprocessor, the ISA bus first started becoming a bottleneck. On this CPU, Intel increased both the external data bus and the memory address bus to 32 bits.

Figure 10.12   Micro Channel devices have a unique interface that won't fit into any other slot.

At this same time, VGA video adapters were taking the world by storm and replacing all previous video standards (see Chapter Sixteen, Your Computer and Graphics). These devices seriously challenged the ISA bus in its throughput requirements, even with standard MS-DOS applications. Microsoft's nearly simultaneous release of Windows 3.0 exacerbated that problem greatly with its graphical interface. An MCA video card, like the one in **Figure 10.12**, could significantly improve performance.

It wasn't just graphics that were seeing the bottleneck either. Network operating systems were demonstrating that a group of PCs attached to a server could be a more attractive option than simple dumb terminals getting all their data from a mainframe. Network cards would also benefit from a faster, wider bus. Basically, the world was clamoring for something that could more easily keep up with the 386.

IBM came to the table first in 1987 with its Micro Channel Architecture (MCA). MCA was an elegant design. In many respects it established the minimum standards that subsequent bus designs would later emulate. One of the changes IBM was to make was to increase bus speed from 8.33MHz to 10MHz (it would later release a 20MHz version in a belated attempt to fend off the challenge of EISA), and to double the data path from 16 bits to 32 bits.

The most user-friendly change IBM made was that an MCA device was software-configurable. With every Micro Channel device IBM included a configuration diskette that made installation of the device nearly idiot-proof. On this disk was a program called the Programmable Option Select. When the user ran this program, it scanned the system to determine what resources might be available. Any MCA device already installed on the system simply reported its own resources. The program would scan existing config.sys and autoexec.bat files (key configuration files for the older MS-DOS and Windows 3.xx operating systems) for information on legacy devices.

Another aspect in which Micro Channel was far superior to ISA was in its handling of IRQs. When IBM first designed the PC bus, it had been the intent all along that IRQs be shared when possible. Unfortunately IBM never provided any defined standards by which this could be done. Since the devices being manufactured all used edge-triggered signaling, it was difficult (although not impossible) to implement IRQ sharing. Manufacturers of ISA devices simply didn't bother to try. That was where the rule "one device, one IRQ" came from. MCA design specifications required that MCA devices negotiate use of the data path. This prevented the IRQ line from being used simultaneously and allowed IRQs to be successfully shared.

Micro Channel pioneered a technology still in use called *bus mastering*. By adding a circuit known as the *Central Arbitration Point*, the CPU could be relieved of the duties of managing the expansion bus. A bus master was any device that was able to take control of the bus. Obviously, the CPU was the primary bus master. Also, any MCA device could be designed as a bus master. Two bus-mastering devices could transfer data directly back and forth between themselves without needing the CPU to act as a referee.

You would think that, with all these technological advancements, the computer world would have beaten a path to IBM's door. As it turned out, this wasn't the case. IBM had not been overly ec-static with the way the rest of the industry had profited from ISA. Many of these companies had actually surpassed IBM in total sales of personal computers. IBM decided not to make this technology publicly available, instead charging royalties for its use. This was an industry that had gotten spoiled by the concept of something for nothing. They flocked away from MCA in droves. Scant few companies outside of IBM ever integrated this technology onto their motherboards, and the number of card manufacturers that anted up wasn't that much greater. It turned out to be a short-lived architecture as far as the PC world was concerned. It enjoyed a long life, however, as the bus of choice for many of IBM's mini-mainframe computers.

> **BUZZ WORDS**
>
> **Bus mastering:** A technology that allows two compatible devices to exchange data directly without requiring arbitration or processing of that data by the CPU.
>
> **Central Arbitration Point:** A circuit that offloads the responsibility for refereeing and processing the transfer of data between two bus-mastering devices.

ENHANCED ISA

The failure of MCA didn't mean the industry wasn't interested in a faster bus. It only meant that they weren't willing to pay for it. There was still a driving need for a technology more advanced than that offered by ISA. Compaq Computer Corporation along with eight other companies cooperated in a joint effort to design a new industry standard that could be used without having to pay royalties. In 1988, they released the Enhanced Industry Standard Architecture (EISA) standards.

With the aid of a little reverse engineering, they managed to assemble a collection of technologies not patented by IBM. Their design incorporated many of the best features of MCA, yet managed to keep it backward compatible with ISA. EISA was a 32-bit bus operating at 8.33MHz. Like MCA, it could be configured through software.

Despite being the same speed as ISA, the designers achieve performance gains over and above simply doubling the data path. By drastically reducing the number of clock cycles involved in the average transaction, EISA devices were able to boast throughput by up to an additional 50 percent.

The biggest feat that the "gang of nine" managed was that they maintained backward compatibility with ISA. IBM didn't even attempt this with MCA. This compatibility was achieved by converting the slot into a two-story condo, as opposed to the single-floor apartment that ISA represented. There were two layers of connectors, one on top of the other. The top layer was identical to a 16-bit ISA slot and directly replicated the functions. The bottom layer of conductors could only be engaged by an EISA device. With this design, a user was able to use either a 16-bit ISA device or a 32-bit EISA device.

VESA LOCAL BUS

MCA and EISA were both significant improvements over ISA. However, neither one of them was particularly adept at handling graphics loads. Companies that made video cards realized that if anybody was going to address their particular needs, it was going to have to be them. An organization of these manufacturers, the Video Electronics Standards Association (VESA), got together and created the first bus that actually tapped into the computer's local bus and communicated directly with the CPU at the speed of its external data bus. It called its brainchild VESA Local Bus (VLB).

By tapping the local bus, video card manufacturers could add a processor to the video card and offload some of the processing load to the device itself. This design obviously favored video cards, but could also allow for advanced I/O controllers as well. High-end VESA Local Bus video cards had ROM chips that contained many of the elements of the Windows interface, and could pop them onto the screen without having to go through the process of drawing them anew each time. Examples of these elements would include scroll bars, buttons, icons, and other items of that nature.

VLB slots were designed as an extension of the 16-bit ISA slot. The cards themselves made use of only the 8-bit portion. The pinout of the front half of the card was identical to an 8-bit card in every respect. This portion of the slot handles I/O functions and power requirements. Directly behind this ISA slot was an extension which tapped into the local bus. This is where 32-bit data transfers and the advanced functions of VLB were controlled.

VESA advertised its new bus as being capable of bus mastering. In reality, it was somewhat limited in this respect. Timing issues prohibited more than three devices on a system, and, in fact, the majority came equipped with only one or two.

PERIPHERAL COMPONENTS INTERCONNECT

Intel had a slight advantage when it was designing the Peripheral Components Interconnect (PCI) bus. It had been busy at work for some time designing the CPU it was to support. Not too long after its release, Intel turned over further development of the design to an organization called the PCI Special Interest Group (PCI-SIG).

The first PCI design was based on a 33MHz, 32-bit bus. In other words, it wasn't a whole lot different from VLB in terms of speed. It directly supported the 80486 CPU. Later revisions of PCI standards, however, included definitions for a 64-bit slot and bus speeds of 66MHz. PCI 2.1 will be discussed in greater detail later in this section. The slots shown in **Figure 10.13** are typical of the 32-bit devices that flood the market.

One of the advantages Intel enjoyed was that it had designed the Plug 'n Play standards as well. By default, PCI is a Plug 'n Play device. This means that part of its core design is the ability to be software-configured. Each PCI card manufactured is equipped with a ROM chip that reports to the BIOS its *class code* and its *extended capability ID* (ECI). The class code tells the BIOS precisely what kind of device it is. The ECI reports any additional features it supports beyond the minimal standards.

The PCI bus has its own method for dealing with IRQs as well. PCI devices address IRQs through four interrupt channels, INTA#, INTB#, INTC#, and INTD#. Despite this, there are a few PCI devices that only address a single IRQ. Under PCI-SIG specifications, these devices must operate on INTA#. The other channels allow manufacturers to cascade multiple devices onto a single circuit board and dole out interrupts accordingly.

A limitation of the PCI bus shows up in how it handles electrical loads. A single PCI bus is only able to handle ten loads. As for what constitutes a load—any single-chip PCI device, either onboard or in a slot, adds one load. Any PCI card with a connector adds two loads. The end result is that there is a limitation of four PCI slots on a single circuit. Each slot will require two loads, and the interconnecting circuitry will add additional loads.

BUZZ WORDS

Class code: Information programmed onto a PCI device that tells the BIOS precisely what it is.

Extended capability ID: Information programmed onto a PCI device that defines any enhanced features beyond the basic features of its device class that it may support.

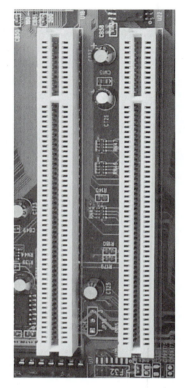

Figure 10.13 The PCI slots are the shorter (usually white) slots that make up the majority of slots on your system.

Of course, you know that systems support more than four PCI slots. In the section Communicating Across Busses I touched on this issue. Designers install a PPB between each of the PCI busses they want on the system. Properly designed and implemented, this circuit connects two PCI busses together, treating one of the busses as primary, the other as secondary. As I mentioned, it is mathematically possible to cascade up to 256 of these busses. Unfortunately, the bandwidth and higher speed of the 64-bit 66MHz PCI bus described by the PCI 2.1 standards does not allow cascading multiple busses. In fact, a 66MHz, 64-bit bus is limited to a maximum of two slots per board.

Any PCI device is capable of bus mastering. Whether or not that capability is exploited is entirely up to the designer. Bus mastering is actually a very simple concept to understand. The CPU is only required to initiate the session between two devices. Once the "handshaking" has been completed, the devices can transfer their data directly between themselves. They don't need further help from any of the other system busses, including the CPU bus and the address bus, in the process. The way this works is that one device acts as an *initiator*. This is generally the device that acts as the data source. It is also the device that will assume the role of master during the data transfer. The other device becomes the *target*, or the slave. It is up to the master device to determine the type of data transfer that is to occur. Will it be a memory read/write operation, an I/O read/write operation, or some other type of signal transfer?

Once the process has been initiated, the transfer of data happens in two stages. The first stage is the *address phase*. This is where the master device tells the target device what kind of transfer is about to occur. Once the target device acknowledges the transfer, the data will move from master to target in one or more *data phases*. The beauty of having two bus mastering devices is that all of the data will be transferred in a single data phase in one big chunk. This is known as *burst mode*. Read or write operations to memory or I/O operations to any non-bus-mastering device may require several data phases.

BUZZ WORDS

Initiator: The device in a bus-mastering chain that is to act as the source of the data being transferred.

Target: Any device that is to be the intended recipient of data.

Address phase: The portion of an I/O operation that identifies the type of transaction that is about to occur.

Data phase: The portion of an I/O operation that performs the actual transfer of data from device to device.

Burst mode: The ability of a device to transfer a large chunk of data in a single data phase.

Sometimes one device is intrinsically capable of higher speeds than another is. If the data is streaming into the target device faster than it is capable of handling, it can initiate a wait state at any time. It tells the master to chill out a bit and give it time to swallow some of the data it already has before it has to take another byte.

PCI 2.1 added several capabilities to the PCI bus. I've already mentioned that this version supports 64-bit 66MHz devices. Now, the 64-bit isn't a problem. The first PCI slots were designed to support up to 64-bit data paths. It's just that most manufacturers didn't always take advantage of this data path. You can tell if your system supports 33MHz 64-bit devices. The slot is longer. Intel borrowed from the ISA book in designing the slots. The 32-bit slots consist of two segments, divided by a key. The front section will consist of forty-nine pairs of conductors (although they're so small, it's hard to count them). Behind that section will be a smaller collection of eleven pairs. This is a relatively short slot. The 64-bit slot adds another key, followed by thirty-two pairs of conductors. It's a bigger slot.

> **EXAM NOTE:** Be prepared to differentiate between PCI 1.0 and PCI 2.1. Later in the chapter, I'll be discussing PCI-X in detail as well. Since this technology is new to the exam, you might want to make sure you understand that as well.

Implementing the 66MHz speed, on the other hand, can be a problem. Putting a 33MHz device into a 66MHz slot will illustrate the problem far more eloquently than I ever could. That fragrance of frying circuitry will explain everything. To prevent this, the 66MHz slot is keyed differently. The slot contains the same number of conductors as the 64-bit 33MHz slot, except that the order is different. The 11-pair section goes up front, followed by a key. Behind this is the 49-pair conductor followed by its key. After this is the 32-pair section. The location of the keys prevents you from inserting a 33MHz device into a 66MHz slot or vice versa.

BUZZ WORDS

Sideband addressing: The ability of a device to send and receive data in a single memory access.

The extra speed also provides bandwidth issues. A 66MHz PCI bus can support only two devices per bus, not four as I discussed earlier. A system that provides 66MHz PCI support will have two slots isolated in their own bank, separate from the rest of the PCI slots.

Devices that take advantage of the greater bandwidth would include things like gigabit Ethernet adapters and the newer high-speed SCSI interfaces. Chapter Fifteen, The Many Faces of SCSI, will take a closer look at a device known as a RAID controller that is a perfect candidate for the interface.

ACCELERATED GRAPHICS PORT

For the last several years, the bus of choice for graphics adapters has been the Accelerated Graphics Port (AGP). AGP is a dedicated 66MHz port (**Figure 10.14**), designed specifically for graphics adapters. That in and of itself greatly increases performance over the 33MHz PCI bus. On the basis of speed alone, you wouldn't expect much improvement over a 66MHz PCI card. However, Intel wove in some technological enhancements when it drew up the specifications in 1996.

Figure 10.14
The AGP slot sits a bit farther back from the other slots on the

EXAM NOTE: Know that regardless of whether an AGP bus is 2x, 4x, or 8x, it always operates at a clock speed of 66MHz.

AGP texturing is one of these enhancements. In order to speed up the rendering of images on the screen, programmers usually separate images into a minimum of two components. The basic outline of the image, called the vector, is stored as one data source, while the textures are managed independently. The video card is only equipped with so much memory, so textures can be stored in system memory. However, to access this data, the AGP card has to know where to find it. The AGP protocol uses the PIPE# command to access system memory directly for the complex operation of texture mapping.

The only method by which previous video cards could retrieve textures was through a technology called local texturing. Under this method, the card had to move the information from the computer's memory to local memory on the graphics adapter before the textures could be processed. AGP provides the graphics card with two methods of directly accessing texture maps in system memory: pipelining and sideband addressing. Pipelining is the same technology I introduced in Chapter Seven, Understanding CPUs. In addition to pipelining, AGP enhances performance through *sideband addressing*. This allows the device to concurrently receive and request data during a single bus or memory access. Earlier technologies, such as PCI, would make one request and could not make another until the data it requested had been transferred.

Another way in which AGP cards dramatically speed up throughput is the way in which they utilize the bus signal. All devices on the system bus, regardless of which technology is being used, must keep time with the clock that controls them. Conventional devices, including PCI, can execute an instruction set or retrieve data in synch with the rising end of the clock cycle (see **Figure 10.15**). PCI was a little more efficient in using the clock cycle in that it places the timing signals on the falling edge, but still could only move data in the rising edge. AGP-2x is capable of reading or writing data on both the rising edge and the falling edge. AGP-4x is actually able to either execute instructions or transfer data on each of the cycle's edges. New standards recently introduced by Intel include AGP-8x and 8x PRO. **Table 10.6** covers the different speeds of AGP and compares them to PCI.

A key limitation of AGP is that you can only have a single AGP device per computer. That is why if you purchase a motherboard with AGP graphics built into the board most of them have no separate AGP slot.

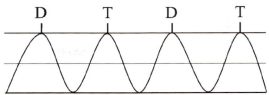

Earlier signaling methods could transfer data or timing signals on the rising crest of the wave.

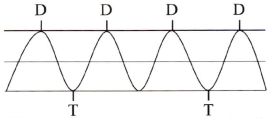

PCI improved on earlier methods in that timing signals could move on the falling end, and each transfer didn't require a separate timing signal.

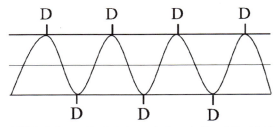

AGP took the next logical step and allowed either data or timing to move on both the rising and falling end, and one timing signal could manage a large burst of data. 2x, 4x, and 8x AGP simply moves multiple bits on each wave.

Figure 10.15   Improvements in bus signaling were not based exclusively on speed. Efficiency in timing and use of the bandwidth played a vital role.

Those that have both onboard AGP graphics and an AGP slot allow only the use of one or the other; you can't use both. Also, if you're designing a high-speed graphics workstation and want dual video capability, you can't do it the easy way and just add two video cards, if you want the cards to be identical. And for the sake of your sanity, you **do** want the cards to be identical. Some of your top-of-the-line graphics adapters have dual monitor capability built right in. This feature will assure that the graphics speed of both monitors is identical.

EXAM NOTE: Know that there can be only one AGP device active on a computer at any given time. If a computer is equipped with an AGP slot as well as onboard AGP graphics, you can use either one or the other, but not both.

Table 10.6 Comparison of AGP vs. PCI in Graphics Adapters

AGP	PCI
Single access/clock cycle	Multiple accesses/clock cycle
Pipelined requests	Nonpipelined requests
Address/data demultiplexed	Address/data multiplexed
533Mbps peak in 32-bit	133Mbps peak in 32-bit
Single target, single master	Multitarget, multimaster
Comparison of AGP-2x and PCI data transfer	

The most recent of AGP Standards is AGP-PRO. This might get a little confusing at first, but don't assume a video card is faster just because is carries the "PRO" label. It probably will be, because there is no point in putting slower chips on a Pro card. But the Pro designation refers to the slot's ability to handle power, and not to its relative speed.

The faster the video cards become, the hotter their processors run. Also, the type of memory used on high-end video cards tends to run hotter as well. When you start piling on more and more memory, power consumption and heat dissipation both become major issues. The original AGP slot was designed to deliver a maximum of 25W of power to the device. AGP-PRO adds additional connectors to the slot to access more power. An AGP-PRO50 is capable of calling on the power supply for 50W, while AGP-PRO110 can demand 110W.

Alas, you never get something for nothing. If you change a 25W lightbulb immediately after it pops, you might comment on how warm it is. Try that with a 110W bulb and you'll burn your fingers. Video cards are no different. When they burn more electricity, they run hotter. Therefore, AGP-PRO cards require supplementary cooling that standard cards don't. An AGP-PRO50 only needs a decent-sized heat sink to keep it cool. However, that heat sink is sufficiently large that you'll lose the PCI slot directly next to it in order to make room for it. AGP-PRO110 cards consume even more space. They need a heat sink and a cooling fan, and TWO PCI slots must be left open.

PCI-X

The developers of PCI have responded to the challenge of AGP with PCI Extended (PCI-X). The first release of PCI-X, Version 1.0, was a 64-bit 133MHz bus that was designed to be backwardly compatible with standard PCI cards. PCI-X, Version 2.0 now provides effective bandwidths of 266MHz and 533MHz as well. The latter speeds are running at an actual clock speed of 133MHz. Their effective bandwidth is derived from the fact that on each clock cycle the devices can move two and four bits of data, respectively.

All PCI-X slots and PCI-X devices are backwardly compatible with 64-bit PCI 2.1 slots and devices. That means that a conventional PCI device has no problem plugging into a PCI-X 533 slot, and a PCI-X 533 device works comfortably (albeit much more slowly) in a 33MHz PCI slot.

This is because PCI-X supports something called *speed mismatch compatibility*. Both slots and devices are designed to be able to clock down to the speed of its partner. The faster of the two simply throttles down to the speed of the slower device. This occurs transparently and seamlessly with no active intervention or configuration required by the user or technician installing the device.

There are some limitations that motherboard manufacturers need to observe. If a device is installed on the system that runs at 133MHz, it is the only device that will run on the PCI-X bus. Two 100MHz devices could be installed, and up to four 66MHz devices. However, multiple PCI-X busses can be linked by way of PPBs.

> **BUZZ WORDS** ——————
>
> **Speed mismatch compatibility:** A technology that allows two devices on the same bus to operate at different speeds and still successfully communicate with one another.

Look at it as if a single PCI-X bus is a four-gallon bucket. You can only put four gallons in it, and each of the PCI-X devices represents an amount of liquid. A 66MHz device puts a gallon of data onto the bus, so the bus doesn't fill up until there are four devices installed. A 100MHz device has two gallons of data, so two of them fill the bucket. The 133MHz is four gallons of data all by itself. Add one and you're done.

Since PCI-X does support bridging of multiple PCI-X busses with a PPB, you can stack up several of these slots across multiple busses and provide support for several 133MHz devices. The user doesn't have to know that the 133MHz slot is on a bus all by itself and that the two 100MHz slots occupy a separate bus. Since the slots are color-coded, the end user or technician knows in which slot a particular device should go for maximum performance. But again, since all slots and devices are interchangeable, the only thing that will happen if a device is put in the wrong slot is that it might suffer a performance loss, or that a high-speed slot is being wasted on a slower device.

Even if all you ever use are 66MHz devices, you should still see a significant performance increase. At its maximum speed of 133MHz, PCI-X 133 has a total bandwidth of around 1.2GB/s. Standard PCI limits throughput to 133MB/s, while 66MHz PCI approaches 512MB/s. A system that employs a gigabit Ethernet card, a PCI video card, and one or two other devices is seriously pushing the envelope of PCI. PCI-X will expand that envelope rather significantly.

THE DIFFERENT BUSSES IN REVIEW

One of the primary advances that has occurred with each subsequent generation of expansion bus has been an increase in speed. In fact, that increase has been practically exponential. **Figure 10.16** gives an overview of the relative speeds of the different busses I have discussed in this chapter.

That speed has come about in part because of increases in clock speed. As I pointed out earlier, the speed of the first PC bus was only 7.66MHz, and not all devices took advantage of the maximum speed. Now there are busses that operate at clock speeds of 133MHz.

Raw clock speed is actually a relatively small part of the overall speed equation. Increased efficiency in the use of available bandwidth has contributed greatly. Reducing the amount of

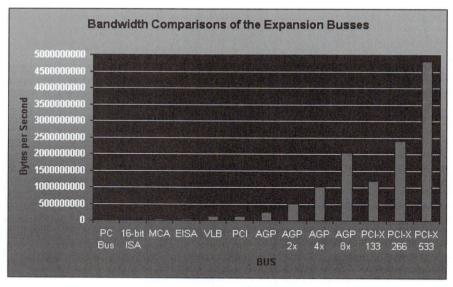

Figure 10.16 The speeds of the different expansion busses have increased at a nearly exponential rate since the PC was first developed. Notice that ISA and the PC bus speeds can't even be seen in this chart!

control data needed by each transfer means more user data is being transferred on each I/O cycle. And increasing the number of bits than can move on each clock cycle makes an even greater contribution to efficiency. **Table 10.7** summarizes the clock speed and actual data transfer rates of the various busses.

Table 10.7 An Overview of the Expansion Busses

BUS	Width (bits)	Bus Speed	Bus Bandwidth
8-bit ISA	8	7.66MHz/8.33MHz	7.9MB/s
16-bit ISA	16	8.33MHz	15.9MB/s
EISA	32	8.33MHz	31.8MB/s
MCA	32	10MHz	38.2MB/s
VLB	32	33MHz	127.2MB/s
PCI	32	33MHz	127.2MB/s
64-bit PCI 2.1	64	66MHz	508.6MB/s
AGP	32	66MHz	254.3MB/s
AGP (x2 mode)	32	66×2MHz	508.6MB/s
AGP (x4 mode)	32	66×4MHz	1017.3MB/s

Bus speed and bit width both contribute to the overall data rate of the expansion bus.

TROUBLESHOOTING THE EXPANSION BUS

Your future as a computer professional may well hinge on how well you diagnose and fix problems related to the expansion bus. For certain, you'll have your share of other problems. You'll find, however, that failures in the core system are far less frequent than those encountered when adding or changing peripheral devices.

The original intent of Plug 'n Play was to eliminate any problems that might occur in this respect. In Chapter Six, Motherboards, BIOS, and the Chipset, I went over the PnP process in some detail, and I pointed out some ways of troubleshooting the process.

Most problems are a result of resource conflicts. IRQ conflicts are increasingly rare as PnP has become more efficient. Still, they occasionally raise their little heads. I/O address problems also appear occasionally, but PnP is able to handle I/O addressing far more efficiently than it does IRQs. This isn't a function of PnP so much as it is the way I/O addresses are mapped. The final conflict you might encounter relates to use of DMA channels.

There are several symptoms that might point to a resource conflict. And unfortunately, not all of them result in the device failing to work. Two devices arguing with each other can cause many computer malfunctions that don't appear to have anything to do with the expansion bus. Some of these symptoms include the following:

- System hangs or locks up
- An erratic mouse pointer, or one that intermittently freezes
- Sound cards generating spurious noise
- Errors and crashes of applications for no apparent reason
- Your printer starts spewing out garbage
- Error messages such as "device not responding"

The key to most of these symptoms is that they will occur sporadically. Some are easier to detect than others are. An older computer that still uses a serial mouse might freeze every time the modem starts to dial. This is an obvious conflict between those two devices. And in fact, since a mouse requires a COM port the same way a modem does, it is a fairly common problem.

For some of the others, you might need to do a little detective work. The first question you might ask is, "What changed?" Take the example of the printer suddenly spewing out junk. If you decided to move from EPP or Bidirectional mode (see Chapter Eighteen, Printing Technologies: Getting it All on Paper) to ECP, ECP claimed a DMA channel. If that happens to be the same DMA your sound card was using, you'll get some interesting aftereffects. If the sound card is active, for example, if you're playing MP3s while you work, and you send a job to the printer, your system will most likely lock up like a stone. Both devices tried to actively use the channel at the same time. Even if the sound card isn't active, it can cause problems such as described above.

If you're getting system crashes, you need to ascertain if something new was added to the system. Sometimes sound cards and network cards don't like each other. This might be one of those cases where I/O addressing is actually the culprit. While the majority of sound cards default to I/O 220h for their address, there are other addresses that are frequently used. Several of these supplemental addresses fall within the range of addresses frequented by certain types of network cards. You might need to do some manual tweaking to resolve this issue. A good place to start is in Device Manager if you're running Windows. This little applet not only detects that the conflict exists, but offers suggestions for its resolution.

IRQ conflicts generally prevent one of the devices from being recognized. The card that gets the IRQ first is there and most likely works fine. The other device simply isn't seen. Windows users can once again use Device Manager for detection and resolution. The application is not always as successful here, though. If a new device has been added and can only use an IRQ owned by another device, it will be necessary to force one of them to change IRQs. This might be as easy as simply having the devices switch slots. As I pointed out earlier, PCI slots are prioritized, and PCI devices have only a fixed number of resources they can use. If one card is more limited than another, give it priority. Let it take its IRQ first, and the other card will simply have to pick another. **Table 10.8** provides a listing of the most common devices you'll have to contend with and the resources they most commonly use.

What happens if you start to run out of IRQs? Is there a way around this? The answer to that is a definite maybe! Look back in the section on COM ports. Two serial devices can be put on the same IRQ, with a different I/O address, as long as the two devices are never active on the bus at the same time.

The PCI bus is far more forgiving in this respect. Since PCI devices are able to share, sometimes PnP will tie two of them together onto a single IRQ by way of the IRQ Holder for PCI Steering. This is a virtual device that owns the IRQ and time-shares it with the devices it manages. If both devices try to hit the IRQ at the same time, IRQ Holder arbitrates the access.

CHAPTER SUMMARY

So now you understand why the expansion bus is so important. Without it, you can't add new toys. And who wants a computer that won't let you add new toys?

I showed you in this chapter just how the system makes use of four of the five primary busses to create an expansion bus. And I introduced the all-important concepts of IRQs, I/O addresses, and DMA channels. Many books choose to discuss these issues along with the motherboards, because they're considered to be motherboard resources. I chose to include the discussion in the same chapter as the components for which you as a technician will be dealing with them.

The CompTIA exam puts heavy emphasis on the history and development of the different busses over the years. That includes the ones which were short-lived, such as EISA, MCA, and VLB. Be ready to identify the characteristics of each.

Finally, I provided the basic information you need for trying to troubleshoot issues surrounding the expansion bus. This is an area where a technician spends a lot of his or her time. Be very familiar with the problems that might arise and be ready to deal with them.

Table 10.8 Commonly Used IRQ and I/O Combinations

Device	IRQ	I/O Range	DMA
		System Devices	
System timer	0	040-04Fh	N/A
IRQ cascade	2	0A0-0AFh	N/A
Real-time clock	8	070-071h	N/A
Math coprocessor	13	0F0-0FFh	N/A
		Parallel Ports	
LPT1	7	378-37Fh	1 or 3 (ECP)
LPT2	5	278h	1 or 3 (ECP)
		Serial Ports	
COM1	4	3F8-3FFh	N/A
COM2	3	2F8-2FFh	N/A
COM3	4	3E8-3FFh	N/A
COM4	3	2E8-2EFh	N/A
		Video	
VGA	11 or 12	3B0-3BBh	N/A
EGA	9	3C0 to 3CFh	N/A
		Sound	
Sound card	5 (or any available)	220-22Fh, 240-24Fh, 280-28Fh, 330-33Fh, 388-28Bh	1,3,4,6 or 7
Voice modem	May use multiple IRQs		
		Input Devices	
Keyboard	1	060-064h	N/A
PS2 mouse	12	060-064h	N/A
Joystick	N/A	200-207h	N/A
		Disk Drives	
Floppy	6	3F0-3F7h	2
IDE primary	14	1F0-0F7h AND 3F6-3F7h	N/A
IDE secondary	15	170-177h AND 376-377h	N/A
IDE tertiary	11 or 12	1E8-1Efh AND 3EE-3EFh	N/A
IDE quaternary	10 or 11	168-16Fh AND 36E-36Fh	N/A
SCSI host	May use any	130-14Fh, 140-05Fh, 220-23Fh, 330-34Fh, 340-35Fh	1, 3 or 5

Here's a list of the most common devices you'll have to contend with, and the resources they most commonly use.

BRAIN DRAIN

1. Discuss how IRQs, I/O addresses, and DMA channels are critical to configuring a device on the expansion bus, and list some of the problems you might encounter.

2. A computer system has been configured as follows: The system board has two serial ports (both active), a parallel port, and a USB hub that has been made active. There is a VGA card on IRQ 9, a network card on IRQ 11, and a sound card that is taking both IRQ 10 for normal usage and IRQ 5 for legacy applications. Both IDE channels are active and have devices hanging off of them. Assuming that IRQ steering is not being used, what IRQs remain available?

3. What is the purpose of an I/O address?

4. You have two PCI devices installed in a machine. Either one will work by itself, but when you install Device A into PCI slot 1 and Device B into PCI slot 2, Device B won't work. When you swap slots, there is no problem. Explain what is going on here.

5. List the different expansion busses used by computer systems over the years in the order that they appeared.

THE 64K$ QUESTIONS

1. An I/O address is _____.

    a. An electrical channel that notifies the CPU (or allows the CPU to notify a device) that there is data ready to be moved

    b. A buffer area used by DMA to make sure data moves smoothly

    c. A direct transfer of data from a device to memory

    d. A specific memory location that the CPU uses to locate data from a specific device

2. A DMA channel is _____.

    a. An electrical channel that notifies the CPU (or allows the CPU to notify a device) that there is data ready to be moved

    b. A buffer area used by DMA to make sure data moves smoothly

    c. A direct transfer of data from a device to memory

    d. A specific memory location that the CPU uses to locate data from a specific device

3. An IRQ is _____.

    a. An electrical channel that notifies the CPU (or allows the CPU to notify a device) that there is data ready to be moved

    b. A buffer area used by DMA to make sure data moves smoothly

    c. A direct transfer of data from a device to memory

    d. A specific memory location that the CPU uses to locate data from a specific device

4. A computer system has been configured as follows. The system board has two serial ports (both active), a parallel port, and a USB hub that has been made active. There is a VGA card on IRQ 9, a network card on IRQ 11, and a sound card that is taking both IRQ 10 for normal usage and IRQ 5 for legacy applications. Both IDE channels are active and have devices hanging off of them.

You try to install a PCI modem and the system will not recognize it. What is the most likely culprit?

a. A conflicting DMA channel

b. A conflicting IRQ

c. A conflicting I/O address

d. A faulty modem

5. Which of the following busses were backwardly compatible with ISA? (Choose all that apply.)

a. PCI

b. VLB

c. EISA

d. MCA

6. Which of the following busses was developed specifically by the video industry to address the issues of moving large amounts of graphics data?

a. PCI

b. VLB

c. EISA

d. MCA

7. At what speed does an AGP 8x video card run?

a. 33MHz

b. 66MHz

c. 133MHz

d. 533MHz

8. A circuit that interconnects two unlike busses is called _____.

a. A PCB

b. A bridge

c. A PPB

d. A Bryston Circuit

9. When two devices on two different busses that operate at completely different speeds need to communicate, the process that allows this is _____.

a. Data arbitration

b. Speed mismatch compatibility

c. Buffering

d. Flow control

10. You have a motherboard that has onboard AGP graphics as well as an AGP 8x compatible slot. A video card occupies that slot and is working perfectly. You decide you want to set up a dual-monitor system and plug the second monitor into the onboard connector. It doesn't work, so you go into the CMOS and enable onboard support. Now your original monitor doesn't work. Why?

a. An IRQ conflict exists between the onboard video and the graphics adapter.

b. Both display adapters require the same I/O address ranges.

c. You can only have one AGP device on a system at once.

d. There shouldn't be a problem. They should both work.

TRICKY TERMINOLOGY

Asynchronous timing: A device on a bus can deliver its data at any speed it sees fit to a reserved area of memory called a buffer. Data is then fed to the CPU at a rate optimal to the CPU.

Bridge: A specialized circuit that moves data between two disparate devices or busses in a such a manner that both devices become compatible.

Burst mode: The ability of a device to transfer a large chunk of data in a single data phase.

Bus mastering: A technology that allows two compatible devices to exchange data directly without requiring arbitration or processing of that data by the CPU.

Cascade: A process by which multiple circuits are linked together in such a way that they appear to the system as a single device.

Central Arbitration Point: A circuit that offloads the responsibility for refereeing and processing the transfer of data between two bus-mastering devices.

COM port: A predefined combination of an IRQ and an I/O address configured for communications devices.

Data phase: The portion of an I/O operation that performs the actual transfer of data from device to device.

Edge triggered: Any response that elicited and/or is controlled by a direct electrical signal coming from a pin or wire on a device. The voltage is applied and the device depends on the interrupt controller to "remember" that it sent the signal.

FireWire: A high-speed serial SCSI connection originally developed by Apple Computer Corporation that is capable of 400Mb/s throughput.

Initiator: The device in a bus-mastering chain that is to act as the source of the data being transferred.

Key: A null space on an edge card connector or memory module that is used for properly aligning the device into its slot.

Level triggered: A response that is arbitrated by a control circuit and/or device driver that allows the same device to make use of one of several interrupt channels. The level-triggered interrupt raises the voltage on the appropriate wire and holds it until the expected response is received.

LPT port: A predefined combination of an IRQ and an I/O address configured for line printers.

Sideband addressing: The ability of a device to send and receive data in a single memory access.

Speed mismatch compatibility: A technology that allows two devices on the same bus to operate at different speeds and still successfully communicate with one another.

Synchronous timing: Bus speeds are a submultiple of the CPU's clock speed, and data is delivered at a steady rate based on that speed.

Target: Any device that is to be the intended recipient of data.

USB device: Any component designed to be operated on the USB.

USB host: Any computer or other device equipped with USB-compatible BIOS, firmware, and controller.

USB hub: A device that manages the I/O for two or more USB device chains.

ACRONYM ALERT

ECI: Extended Capabilities ID. Information programmed onto a PCI card that defines any enhanced functions that device can perform beyond the basic functions defined by its device class.

EISA: Enhanced ISA. A 32-bit 8.33MHz bus released by a coalition of manufacturers led by Compaq. VLB was designed to be backwardly compatible with ISA.

MCA: Micro Channel Architecture. A proprietary 32-bit 12MHz bus released by IBM shortly after Intel's release of the 80386 CPU.

PCI-X: PCI Extended. A recently released 133MHz version of the PCI bus.

PPB: PCI to PCI Bridge. The circuitry that arbitrates data transfer between two different PCI busses on the same system.

VESA: Video Electronics Standards Association. The organization charged with maintaining standards surrounding graphics adapters and monitors.

VLB: VESA Local Bus. A 32-bit 33MHz bus designed by VESA to address issues surrounding the transfer of large amounts of graphics data. VLB was designed to be backwardly compatible with ISA.

 VIEW THE VIDEO

A video clip on System Resources and a video clip on Buses and I/O Ports are available on the accompanying CD.

CHAPTER 11

INPUT DEVICES

Okay. You now have a good idea about how data is processed, stored, and shuffled around in the system. Now I'll discuss how that data gets into the machine to begin with. The applications you run don't come on preprogrammed chips soldered onto the motherboard (although Tandy Corporation did that successfully when it shipped its 2000TL computer with DeskMate software installed on a PROM). You need disk drives that can read data from external sources before that data will appear on a hard disk drive. A large percentage of data processed by the computer has to come from the user. (This book certainly didn't come preprogrammed on a chip!) For that to happen there needs to be a way for the user to communicate with the computer. This chapter deals with the various devices designed for the purpose of getting information from the outside world moved into the digital world of the computer.

The problem I see with a chapter of this nature is that the variety of input devices is so vast; it would be impossible to cover them all in a single chapter. Since the primary focus of this book is on PC systems, I will cover only the basic input devices common to all systems.

A+ CORE HARDWARE EXAM OBJECTIVES

Candidates for the A+ Core Exam will find the following topics introduced or covered in this chapter:

1.2 Identify basic procedures for adding and removing field-replaceable modules for desktop systems. Given a replacement scenario, choose the appropriate sequences.

1.5 Identify the names, purposes, and performance characteristics of standardized/common peripheral ports, associated cabling, and their connectors. Recognize ports, cabling, and connectors by sight.

1.8 Identify proper procedures for installing and configuring common peripheral devices. Choose the appropriate installation or configuration sequences in given scenarios.

2.1 Recognize common problems associated with each module and their symptoms, and identify steps to isolate and troubleshoot the problems. Given a problem situation, interpret the symptoms and infer the most likely cause.

3.1 Identify the various types of preventive maintenance measures, products, and procedures, and when and how to use them.

THE KEYBOARD

The computer industry has probably seen more changes, new technology, and new products emerge than any other. Yet, as the old adage goes, the more things change, the more they stay the same. The primary device through which we enter data on a daily basis is still the humble, but ever so productive, keyboard (**Figure 11.1**). All the

Figure 11.1 Without the venerable old keyboard sitting at my desk, typing this manuscript would be a completely different job altogether.

data that goes into your spreadsheets; all the emails you send to friends, family, and coworkers; and this very manuscript are all accomplished though the simple technology of the keyboard.

One thing I won't discuss in this chapter is how to fix a keyboard. They're far too inexpensive to justify paying a technician for his or her time. I will go over some basic maintenance issues, but my primary goal is to show you how they work.

HOW THE KEYBOARD DOES ITS JOB

Just looking at the outside of the thing, you expect the keyboard to be a complicated device. Some are, some aren't. It all depends on how well made the model in question actually is. We all know how to use a keyboard. You press a key and a letter appears. It's that simple, right?

Well, not really. If you press the <Shift> key while holding down the letter, it goes from being a lowercase letter to an uppercase. So how does it know to do that? Also, those buttons that you seen running across the top of the keyboard with the letter F followed by a number don't type anything at all. Those are the function keys and they actually run programs for you. And, depending on what you're running as software, the <Ctrl> key, pressed in conjunction with one or more other keys will activate functions within that program. For example, when I press <Ctrl>+B, the text goes from normal to bold-faced. <Ctrl>+I makes it italics. So as you see, there is more going on inside the keyboard than simply typing letters.

KEYCAPS AND KEYSWITCHES

The button you push to activate a particular key is called the *keycap*. This is what most people simply call the key. The keycap on modern keyboards is removable, just like the A shown in **Figure 11.2**, allowing you to replace a worn-out keycap. In most cases, they simply pop off with a little prying by a flat-head screwdriver. Most of them are equally easy to get back on. However, that isn't always the case. The <Space> key can be particularly difficult. It requires getting the springs and clips properly aligned, then holding them in place and simultaneously snapping the keycap into position. On some keyboards, <Shift> and <Enter> are equally entertaining.

Figure 11.2 Even the lowly keycap is governed by predefined industry standards to make sure that keyboards have a uniform feel from one brand to the other.

You wouldn't think of a keyboard as necessarily being under the control of any particular standard. On the other hand, think how difficult typing would be if, every time you moved from one computer to the next, the amount of space between keys changed or the rows were separated by different distances. If you've ever moved from a "standard" keyboard to one of those ergonomic models, you know that there is a period of adjustment before typing seems natural.

Aside from the function keys, there are four rows to a standard Qwerty keyboard. From the bottom up, you have the Z row, the A row, the Q row, and the Number Row. With the exception of the distance between the A-row and the Q-row,

BUZZ WORDS —————————

Keycap: The plastic button the user presses down when typing on a keyboard.

Keycap travel: The actual distance a user must press a key on a keyboard in order to produce results.

Keyswitch: The electromechanical connection that informs the keyboard controller circuitry that a key has been pressed.

these rows are .375″ apart. The A and Q rows are separated by a space of .188″. Spacing between keys is .75″ from center to center.

What about the "feel" of a keyboard? Anyone who works on multiple computers knows that there is no "standard" feel. Some are soft and mushy and other have a crisp click when you press down on them. This is where the human factor comes in. I like a keyboard that clicks when I press down on it. Makes me feel like I'm really typing. Other people like the quieter approach. How a keyboard feels is a function of two different things. First is how far the keycap travels in order to make contact, and second is the type of keyswitch used.

Keycap travel can range anywhere from a tenth of an inch to as much as .20″. Unless there's a decent amount of travel, the keyboard has a very stiff feel. Too much travel and you feel like your fingers are treading water. What you get accustomed to is what will be better for you. Most touch typists find they work faster on keyboards with a longer throw.

The kind of *keyswitch* you use will determine if your keyboard is clicky or mushy. The keycap snaps into place over the keyswitch. Depending on the model of keyboard, the keyswitch is a component that is either impossible to replace or simply so difficult as to be practically impossible. On some particularly inexpensive models, there are no switches. There is simply a pad of rubber nipples, called a membrane, that provide the keypad resistance (**Figure 11.3**). When you press down on the keycap, it makes contact with a circuit grid laid out on a piece of plastic (**Figure 11.4**). These wouldn't be that difficult to repair if the replacement parts didn't cost nearly as much as a new keyboard! Better keyboards have individual switches. These can be replaced, but the cost of the parts plus labor time doesn't really make it worthwhile.

When designing a keyboard, manufacturers take a number of factors into consideration. Some are user-oriented while others are business decisions.

■ *Cost:* How much is the anticipated resale price of the keyboard. This will affect the type of switching mechanism used in the construction. If the keyboard is to be a minimally priced Original Equipment Manufacturer's (OEM) model, there's not going to be a lot of money poured into fancy switches. These are the keyboards that generally use membrane switching. A nicely designed tactile switch can cost $.05 to $.15 per switch.

On a 104-key device, this adds up pretty quickly. Factor in the cost of assembling such a board, and you have a pricey keyboard for most OEMs.

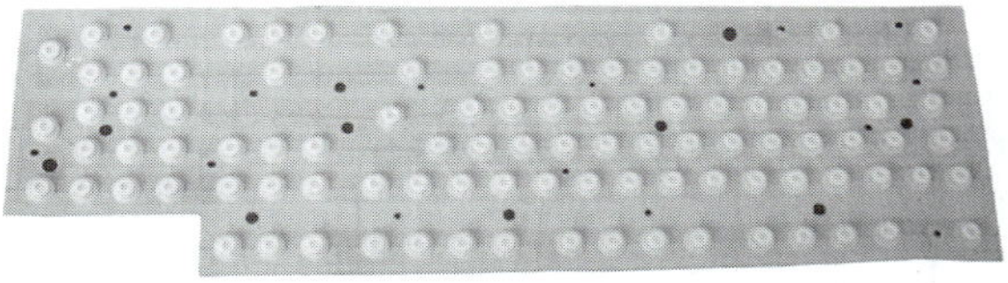

Figure 11.3 The little rubber "bubbles" keep the keycaps away from the circuit board until the user presses down on one.

- *Durability:* How long can you expect your keyboard to last? End users are going to answer this question differently than computer manufacturers. For most OEMs, the answer to this question is another question. How long is the warranty, and is the keyboard going to be covered under that warranty? Read the fine print of many computer warranties and you find out that it isn't. If the keyboard has to last for a while, then higher-quality keyswitches must be used.

Figure 11.4 When the user does press down on a keycap, it will come into contact with the appropriate circuit on the grid beneath.

- *Feel:* This is a combination of two different factors, as I mentioned. Travel and tactile feedback are strong contributors to how a keyboard feels to the typist. Neither of these factors necessarily impacts cost. One company that manufactures high-quality keyswitches, Alps, Inc., makes all levels of switch in both tactile-click and soft designs.

Keyswitches have one task to do. They complete a circuit, sending a signal to the controller that a particular key has been depressed. These switches come in several forms. The older style keyboards all used mechanical contact switches. You'll generally know if you have one of these. The keycap is not removable. Or if it is, it is so difficult to remove that replacing it might be even more so. These switches perform the actual completion of the circuit internally. When you press down, you're activating the switch. A spring returns the switch to the open position when you release it.

The next type of switch is the Foam and Foil Switch. This is the first of two variations I'll discuss on keyboards using membrane circuits. The keypad presses down on a plunger. Beneath the keys, a foam pad with a foil surface on the bottom is placed over the circuit pad. The circuit for any given key consists of two copper contacts. When the key is depressed, it forces the foil into contact with the copper conductors and the circuit is completed. A spring pushes the plunger back into position. The foam acts as a shock absorber and return mechanism for the foil. These are your generally cheap keyboards which have a very soft and spongy feel.

A better variation on this theme is the Rubber Dome Switch shown in Figure 11.3. These still make use of a membrane over which the copper circuitry is embedded. A plunger presses a button down onto the copper contacts (Figure 11.4) and the circuit is completed. Rubber dome switches use a sheet of rubber into which a dome-shaped elevation has been formed. This rubber dome forces the key back into place when it is released. These are the most prevalent OEM keyboards on the market today, as they have a much nicer feel than the older foam and foil units. They provide a semblance of tactile feedback, as well as a higher resilience to pressure. People actually feel like they're typing.

INTERNAL CIRCUITS

Now that you know how the signal gets generated, I'll take a look at how the computer knows it's getting the word "elevator" and not the <Shift>. If you're daring enough to take your keyboard apart and peek inside, you'll see a small circuit board with some chips on it. Before you do this, however, I feel morally and legally obligated to tell you that some keyboards were designed to be disposable. Taking them apart will be easy enough. But they don't go back together when you're done, and you'll have that excuse you were looking for to go out and buy a newer and nicer unit. The ones with screws can usually be disassembled and put back together. If they snap apart, I wouldn't count on it. Either way, be careful.

Now, back to that circuit board. Your keyboard will have one, with two or three main chips soldered onto the board along with some other minor components, as shown in **Figure 11.5**. One of these chips is a microprocessor. It does the keyboard's "thinking." On older keyboards, this was frequently an Intel 8048 or a Motorola 6805. There will also be a ROM chip that holds the program that translates the keyboard's signals. New keyboards use an IC that has an integrated CPU and ROM. Examples of this chip would include the 8049 and the 8255. Programmable keyboards, the kind that let you make a single key run an entire series of keystrokes, will also have an EEPROM (see Chapter Six, Motherboards, BIOS, and the Chipset) built in for holding those instructions. The 8255 is an example of a CPU/EEPROM. There is also a 16-byte buffer for streaming data in a controlled manner.

This board does require electricity to perform, as do those little LEDs that tell you the status of NUM Lock, CAPS Lock, and Scroll Lock. Therefore, one of the functions of the keyboard is to get electricity from somewhere. Power is supplied through the cable from the computer's power supply. On most keyboards, this is a 5V current.

To know what specific key has been pressed, the keys on the keyboard are laid out in a series of rows and columns called the *key matrix*. Each key holds a position related to a row and column. When a key is depressed, the keyswitch in that position closes a circuit, sending a signal

Figure 11.5 This small circuit board with only a couple of chips does all the work of translating the user's keystrokes into electrical signals the computer can use.

to the circuit board inside the keyboard. Each key sends two separate signals. The first, called the *make code*, is sent the instant the keyswitch closes the circuit. The second signal, the *break code*, occurs when the key is released. It is because of these two signals that you can make your software repeat letters just by holding a key in place. It is also why one key can be held down while another is depressed. If only a single signal was generated, neither of those features would be possible. The one signal would be sent, and that would be that.

Every key has a unique make/break code. This is true even between two keys with the same name. For example the right <Shift> and the left <Shift> generate their own specific codes. So do the right <Ctrl> and the left <Ctrl>, or the right and left <Alt>. This is why some games can use the left <Alt> key for firing a weapon and the right for another game function.

When you press a key, the position of the key that was pressed is denoted by its position in the matrix. Once that position is established the program that resides in ROM generates the make/break code for that key. The 8048 (or later) chip then translates that code into digital signals that the computer can use. The translated signal travels along the keyboard cable to the computer.

BUZZ WORDS

Key matrix: The specific geometric layout of the keyswitches on a keyboard.

Make code: A signal generated by a keyswitch when the key is first pressed down.

Break code: A signal generated by a keyswitch when the key is released.

THE KEYBOARD CABLE

The cable (**Figure 11.6**) consists of four conductors that are actually used. One of these is the 5V signal previously mentioned, while a second comprises the ground. One of the other wires provides the keyboard data signal, and the fourth carries the keyboard clock signal.

Keyboards send data across the wire in serial form. They also use asynchronous communication. What more do you need? You're not sending data across the wire very fast at all. The buffer makes sure it goes in the right order. Therefore only a single conductor is needed for carrying data. The keyboard clock makes sure the keyboard stays in synch with the rest of the system. Clock signals travel over a separate wire. Then, to provide power, two other cables provide power and ground.

The purpose of the clock signal is to properly synchronize the data coming in

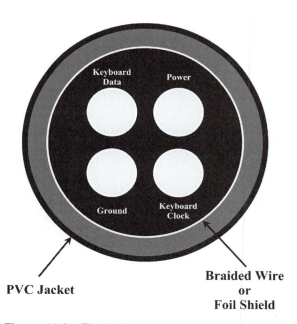

Figure 11.6   The keyboard cable is very simple. Only four wires are needed, while a layer of shielding material deflects interference.

from the keyboard with the rest of the system functions. That isn't as easy as it sounds. A very fast typist can type approximately eighty words per minute. That is barely over 5KB of data. Add the make/break codes, and that person can push about 16K of data over the keyboard wires every minute. If you recall, the bus speed of most modern motherboards is a minimum of 100MHz. The job of the clock is to see that the data from the keyboard gets there in a timely manner without slowing the rest of the computer down.

THE KEYBOARD CONTROLLER

On the receiving end, the computer has a special circuit just for interfacing with the keyboard. Not surprisingly, this circuit is called the keyboard controller. On older computers, this was the 8042 keyboard controller chip. This chip was a mini-microprocessor that had a 2KB ROM and about 128 bytes of RAM to act as a buffer. More recent computers use an 8255, which is reprogrammable, and on some motherboards, the task is handled by the chipset.

The keyboard controller receives the signals sent by the 8048 chip and translates scan codes into data the CPU can use. It also has the responsibility for generating the interrupt over IRQ1 to let the CPU know there's data coming in. In addition, periodically the system checks the status of the keyboard. The keyboard controller maintains I/O port 64h for the purpose of status checks.

KEYBOARD MAINTENANCE AND REPAIR

As I said before, for the most part, you're not going to fix a broken keyboard. But as we all know, nobody's ever written a rule that didn't have exceptions. And there are some simple maintenance routines that can delay the inevitable day of replacement. I'll start with some basic maintenance.

First rule of thumb: no matter how much you like coffee, your keyboard doesn't like it at all. It is not a good idea to have drinks near your keyboard (he sanctimoniously typed as he took a sip from his coffee). Since we all break that rule on a regular basis, spills are going to happen. Oddly enough, it's the cheapest keyboards that survive liquid exposure the best. When this happens, shut down immediately and shake out as much of the liquid as you possibly can. Better keyboards are inside of a clamshell-style case held together by screws. If the affected keyboard is of this type, open it up and use some cotton swabs to clean out as much of the rest as you can. Now's as good a time as any to clean out the dust, potato chip crumbs, and other debris that has accumulated since you first set up the machine. A can of compressed air can be used, but it's probably better if you can get your hands on a miniature vacuum cleaner.

Worn keycaps are fairly easy to replace as long as you're not dealing with an older board with mechanical contact switches. A small flat-head screwdriver is a good tool for prying them off the keyswitch. It might be worth replacing a worn or broken key on a particularly expensive keyboard or one that happens to have a feel to it that you've not found elsewhere.

While it is rare for a keyboard cable to fail before the keyboard dies of either junk poisoning or plain old wear and tear, it does happen. Once again, it would have to be a particularly special keyboard to justify the effort, but the cable can be replaced if you are reasonably adept with a soldering gun. Pop open the keyboard and follow the cable to where the leads are soldered on. Desolder the old leads and solder on the new. Be careful not to allow the solder joints to overlap.

If you're wondering where to find a replacement keyboard cable, there are two ways to go about it. Most electronics parts warehouses will sell a replacement for a moderate cost. However, practically any place that repairs computers would sell you a broken keyboard a whole lot cheaper. They might even give you one just to save them the trouble of discarding it. The chances of the problem with that keyboard also being the cable are pretty slim.

THE MOUSE

The second most common input device is the mouse. Douglas Englebart invented this innocuous little device when he worked at the Stanford Research Institute. Initial reaction to Mr. Englebart's invention could best be described as skeptical. Apple Computer Corporation incorporated the device into the graphical interface of its OS, and then PC users began to ask why they couldn't have a toy like that. These days you probably take the mouse for granted until it starts to give you trouble. Only then do you really notice it that much. Mice come in two different forms—mechanical and optical. In each of those forms you can also get standard and cordless versions. This section will deal with how these devices work and how to configure and troubleshoot them.

THE MECHANICAL MOUSE

When you use a mouse, you move the device across a surface, usually a mouse pad, and the arrow on the screen follows the direction of your movements. It seems simple enough until you realize what all is going on to make that seemingly simple procedure work right.

First of all, the mouse has to be able to detect your motions. If you look at the base of your mouse (assuming you use a mechanical mouse), you will see a small rubber ball protruding from a window on the base of the device, just like in **Figure 11.7**. This ball rolls along the surface of your mouse pad.

Now open the retaining plate that holds the ball in place. It's probably past time to clean your mouse anyway. I know it sure was for this one! Peek inside and you should see three rollers, just like the ones you see in **Figure 11.8**. One is located directly toward the front or back of the mouse and one is located on one side or the other. A third roller is positioned at 45 degrees.

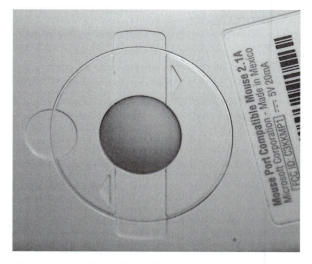

Figure 11.7   That little ball on the bottom of your mouse is what tells the cursor on your screen where to go.

Figure 11.8 As the ball moves across the surface of your mouse pad, these three rollers keep track of the direction that you're moving the mouse.

Figure 11.9 The LED shown at the base of the image shines a light through the teeth on the end of the wheel. A photosensitive receptor turns the flickering light into electronic pulses.

As the ball rolls along the surface, it moves these rollers. Direction and angle of movement directly affect the speed at which the rollers rotate. As they rotate, they move a wheel attached to one end of the roller. That wheel has a bunch of teeth cut into it. An LED shines a light past the wheel. On the other side of the wheel, a photosensitive receptor picks up the light from the LED (see **Figure 11.9**). When one of the teeth is in the way, no light hits the receptor. The space between the teeth lets the light through. As a result, the wheel generates a flickering light. In turn, that flickering light causes the receptor to generate a series of electronic pulses, which are sent to the computer. The mouse driver installed in the computer keeps track of the number of pulses generated by each roller and uses the information to move the cursor across the screen.

So let's break this down into the individual parts needed to make a mouse work. Along with that, I'll discuss how they perform their function.

- The ball rolls along the desktop, changing direction of rotation every time you change the direction in which you're moving the mouse. The ball is in contact with...

- The rollers, which change the speed at which they rotate based on the direction that the mouse is moving. If you are moving the mouse straight up, with no right/left motion whatsoever, then the side roller and diagonal roller aren't moving at all, while the up/down roller is moving at whatever speed you happen to be moving the mouse. If there is very slight right/left motion, then the other two sensors will be moving at their own speed. Each roller is attached to its own...

- Shaft, which turns a small wheel. Here is where two different technologies diverge. A few mice use a magnetic sensor, but by far the majority use an LED (as in Figure 11.9).

The LED shines its light onto an optical sensor. The wheel has thirty-six small slits cut into it. As it rotates between the path of the LED and the sensor, the light is alternately shielded and allowed to pass. In effect, the motion of the wheel is creating what appears to the sensor to be a pulsating light. The speed at which the light pulsates is determined by the speed at which the wheel is turning. These signals are transmitted to the...

- Logic chip, which translates the pulses of light into binary data, which is sent to the mouse driver. The mouse driver uses that data to position the cursor.

This is the method by which a large majority of mechanical mice work. These are known as *optomechanical mice.* There are a few out there that use a magnetic sensor on the wheel in place of an optical sensor. Aside from this difference, the function is the same.

THE OPTICAL MOUSE

The optical mouse differs significantly from its mechanical counterpart in that it has no ball. Instead of this physical interface, an optical mouse uses a pair of LEDs, a pair of optical sensors, and a mouse pad that has a distinct pattern. The LEDs shine down on the mouse pad and reflect back to photoreceptors on the base of the device. As you move the device across the pad, the reflections of light coming back from the mouse pad provide the light pulses that the mouse drivers use for tracking.

> ### BUZZ WORDS
>
> **Optomechanical mouse:** A mouse that uses perforated wheels passing in front of an LED to generate pulses of light that are used to track movement along the X and Y axis.

This is good in that there are no moving parts to get dirty or to break. This is bad in that I can't use my Queen Amidala mouse pad.

SENDING DATA

In terms of the number of conductors needed, the mouse is virtually identical to the keyboard in its requirements. There needs to be a +5V carrier, a ground, a data cable, and a clock cable. They all perform exactly the same function as their counterparts on the keyboard. It doesn't matter whether you have an older serial mouse or a PS2. Only four conductors are being used. The data that is actually sent, however, differs significantly.

The keyboard has hundreds of different signals it must send. There are only two or three buttons on most mice. Manufacturers are now tripping over each other to add new buttons and functions to confuse the user even more, but generally you're either clicking a button once or double-clicking it. There aren't a whole lot of options here. So what happens when you click a button on a mouse is that three bytes of data get sent. The first byte of data carries eight bits indicating the status of the mouse. These bits carry information as shown in **Table 11.1**.

The next two bytes provide values that indicate the total movement along the X and Y-axes, respectively. They include information that indicates precisely how many pulses were detected in each

Table 11.1 Status Byte of Mouse Signal

Bit Number	Indicates
Bit 0	Left button state. 1 = ON, 2 = OFF
Bit 1	Right button state. 1 = ON, 2 = OFF
Bit 2	0
Bit 3	1
Bit 4	X coordinate = Positive or X coordinate = Negative
Bit 5	Y coordinate = Positive or Y coordinate = Negative
Bit 6	X Overflow indicates excessive movement along the X-axis
Bit 7	Y Overflow indicates excessive movement along the Y-axis

For each click of a mouse, the first byte returns information concerning the status of the mouse.

direction since the last data was sent. Programmers do the rest of the magic, which is why different operating systems and different applications respond to the mouse in their own unique ways.

TRACKBALLS

A trackball is basically a stationary mouse. It performs the same function as a mouse while staying in one place. Many people do not like the repetitive motion involved in using a mouse. In fact, it has caused medical problems with many people. Also, a mouse is rarely where you need it when you need it there. The mouse will be at the top of the mouse pad, but the cursor will be at the bottom of the screen. You're always having to make adjustments.

The trackball is an upside-down mouse. It performs in the same manner, except that the ball is positioned at the top of the device and you move it with your thumb and/or fingers. Manufacturers seem unable to agree on how you should move the ball, so when shopping for one of these toys, try them all until you find one that feels right to you.

MOUSE MAINTENANCE

In terms of physical maintenance, cleaning is about the only thing that you can do to help your mouse. The balls pick up small particles of dust and lint, potato chip crumbs, and other debris as they move along the surface of your mouse pad. This sticks to the rollers and once enough junk accumulates, the rollers and ball won't be in synch with each other. As a result, you get erratic movement of the cursor as it moves across the screen. The fix here is simple. Clean it. Remove the ball and you'll see debris buildup on the rollers.

Many of the problems people report that are mouse-related have to do with the mouse setting in their operating system. You can adjust the sensitivity of your mouse. If it is not set sensitively enough for your taste, the mouse will require excessive movement across the pad in order to get the cursor where you want it. Conversely, if you use your mouse to make extremely minute corrections, then you might need to increase sensitivity.

GAME CONTROLLERS

As you probably already realize, most of us do not own computers. We own $2000 decks of cards and $4000 home video arcades. Playing games can frequently introduce input requirements that the more mundane functions, such as word processing, don't present. As a result, there is a booming business in producing specialized input devices whose exclusive domain is that of making games easier and more enjoyable.

Some people are perfectly happy committing mayhem on aliens using a keyboard and mouse combination. But armchair jet pilots and virtual racecar drivers like something with a little more control, and that gives them a greater sense of reality. For those folks, there are joysticks, game paddles, steering wheels, and other assorted gaming controls to make computer fun more realistic. One company even has a nicely upholstered tactile feedback interactive recliner for the avid gamer. My wife was supposed to get me one of those for Christmas, but I guess she forgot.

JOYSTICKS, GAME PADDLES, AND STEERING WHEELS

Since these all work functionally the same way, I'll group them together in a single discussion and simply refer to joysticks. The joystick has a rather unique feature that endears it to many technicians. It requires no IRQ. The system polls the device to determine when and if there is data to be moved across the bus. Physically, the joystick consists of a handle onto which buttons have been installed. That handle is seated into a base and connects to the computer by way of a 15-pin D-shell connector (**Figure 11.10**).

A pair of devices called variable resistors generates the data sent to the computer by the joystick. These consist of a strip of insulating material that varies in thickness across its length; the thicker the material is, the greater the resistance. In joysticks, these variable resistors cover a range from slightly less than one ohm to a value in excess of 100,000 ohms. One variable resistor changes values as you move along the X-coordinate, the other keeps track of the Y-coordinate. The joystick driver translates resistance values into screen coordinates. The button or buttons are simple switches. When you press down on one, it merely closes a circuit. The game you're playing determines what effect closing the circuit has.

A greater sense of realism is attained when the joystick in use is capable of tactile feedback. Tactile feedback controllers are equipped with small motors that make use of data provided by the game in play to vibrate, kick back or forward in the hand, or provide resistance to the user when he or she tries to move the joystick. This technology moves a step forward with data gloves. These are devices that users wear on their hands. Position and flexure of the hand provides input to the computer. Games and other programs that support this little toy interact far more directly with the user.

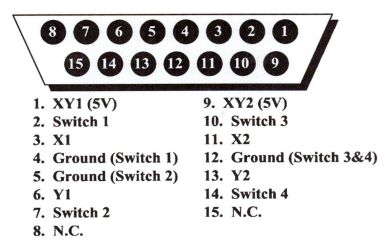

1. **XY1 (5V)**
2. **Switch 1**
3. **X1**
4. **Ground (Switch 1)**
5. **Ground (Switch 2)**
6. **Y1**
7. **Switch 2**
8. **N.C.**

9. **XY2 (5V)**
10. **Switch 3**
11. **X2**
12. **Ground (Switch 3&4)**
13. **Y2**
14. **Switch 4**
15. **N.C.**

Figure 11.10   Pinouts for 15-pin joystick connector

DIGITAL CAMERAS

Of all technology products used by consumers today, digital cameras have probably enjoyed the most significant widespread growth. While plummeting prices certainly haven't hurt this growth, perceived need has probably had a greater effect. While scanners make it relatively easy to convert a paper print into a digital file, it's still a cumbersome process. On top of that, you have the expense of film and developing, and you have to find the time to drop it off to get it developed.

A digital camera eliminates all of these inconveniences. A 16MB memory chip allows the equivalent of a whole roll of film, even in high-resolution mode. When you get home, you upload the images you want to the computer, erase the camera's memory and start all over! Not only that, but while you're taking pictures, you can preview what you've got. If a shot doesn't come out the way you'd like, delete it and do another one. Each of the photos in this book was made with a digital camera.

A lens captures an actual scene and directs light waves to a chip called the charge coupled device (CCD). The resolution of a camera is dictated by the number of sensors built into the CCD and is measured in dots per inch. The camera I own is kind of middle-of-the-road. It was relatively inexpensive, but is still a good performer. It has a maximum resolution of 2048 × 1536. Advertising slicks refer to it as a 3.2-megapixel camera. More recent cameras have exceeded the 10-megapixel range, and in the world of professional photography resolutions go far beyond these listed. I have the choice of saving files in JPEG, Tagged Image File Format (TIFF), or in a proprietary native format.

One of the biggest differences among models of digital cameras lies in how they react to color. Computers allow for extremely accurate color management. Unfortunately, the camera is not a computer. It grabs the shot based on certain settings that the user can change and others that the user can't. One of the things the user has no control over is the CCD that the manufacturer uses in the camera. These devices must be calibrated to something called *white balance* for them to accurately portray color. Typical white balance settings include daylight, fluorescent, and tungsten. Some may also include "9300K." This is in deference to a Macintosh default color setting. What all this boils down to is a lot simpler than the last few lines make it sound. Some cameras record colors *warm* and other record them *cool*. Warm color reflects a tendency for the overall image balance to be biased toward yellow and red, while cool refers to a slightly bluish shift. Which you prefer will dictate your choice in a camera. And keep in mind that this is also something that is easily correctable by most photo-editing packages.

BUZZ WORDS

White balance: A measurement of how pure the reproduction of white is accomplished in an image.

Cool: A shift in the color of an image toward the blue side.

Warm: A shift in the color of an image toward the red side.

The biggest complaint that consumers had about digital cameras was that the image did not resemble that of one taken with a conventional film camera. Film tends to render colors more naturally and does not contain the digital noise so many digital cameras are notorious for producing. Recently, some manufacturers of digital cameras have taken to substituting a CMOS (see Chapter Six, Motherboards, BIOS, and the Chipset) for the CCD.

A CMOS chip more closely approximates the size of a standard 35mm negative or transparency, whereas a CCD is rarely much larger than the nail on your left pinky. As a result, if you're simply comparing cameras on the basis of raw resolution, you might mistakenly assume that a CMOS-based camera is inferior. In fact, a CMOS imaging chip that is only rated at 3.2 megapixels is capable of rendering an image that many professional photographers acknowledge is better than what they can achieve with conventional film.

Probably the biggest choice you'll have to make is how your camera interfaces with the computer. You have to get those images from the camera to the computer somehow. Might as well make it as easy as possible. In this respect, manufacturers have been incredibly creative. The cameras themselves can directly link to the computer by way of either a serial cable or a USB cable. As you will recall from the section on data busses, USB is going to be a lot faster. There are also devices that let the user plug the actual memory card from the camera into a reader that can be installed into the computer, just like a floppy disk drive or other externally accessible drive. The data can then be read directly off the chip. These are available in both internal and external models. Finally, printer manufacturers have included a memory card reader as a feature of some of their models of color printers. Plug the memory cartridge directly into the printer and send the image straight from memory to page. Of course, this precludes any ability to alter the image.

Throughout this discussion, I have made constant mention of photo-editing packages. For the professional, this choice will have as much, if not more, impact than the choice of hardware. Most cameras, scanners, and printers come bundled with some rudimentary software that will allow limited editing. For many people that's about all they'll ever need. The imaging professional, however, needs professional tools. You'll find the capabilities of almost any piece of imaging hardware greatly enhanced by a collection of software tools that are up to the task at hand.

VIDEO CAPTURE

Once the process of capturing still images was mastered, the next logical step was to digitize motion pictures. However, a computer is not, by default, equipped with a device for generating live video. And even if it was, who would want to carry a computer around with them just to film his or her child's softball game? A more logical step at the beginning was to import the images created by existing devices. For this to happen, there needed to be an interface between the device and the computer, and then the appropriate software to convert the images into digital form.

Like everything else in this industry, at first video capture devices were very expensive and could be problematic to install and configure. Most were add-on cards that worked alongside the existing video card. What they did was allow the user to hook up any video camera, video tape recorder, or television tuner to the computer and "film" the output into a digital file. Modern technology has allowed single cards to perform all of the user's video functions, including capture.

To do this properly, there are several considerations that must be taken into account. Not only do you have to have the necessary hardware to do the actual capture, but also the rest of your system has to keep up. Graphic images require a lot more horsepower than processing text files. Assume that as you filmed the softball game mentioned earlier, you ended up with a sixteen-minute clip you wanted to preserve. You select a file format developed by the Motion-picture Joint Photographic Experts Group (MJPEG). The conversion of this clip is going to result in a file that is approximately 1.2GB in size. Therefore adequate free hard disk space is a critical factor. But just processing that image puts a lot of stress on the system. The conversion is extremely processor intensive and memory intensive. Anyone who plans on doing a lot of video capture will want a very powerful system with as much memory as he or she can afford. Most software designed for processing streaming video supports multiple processor systems. Having multiple processors will provide a dramatic improvement in performance.

The type of file system you select will determine two things—throughput requirements and storage requirements. MJPEG file compression has by far the least compression capability of any of the motion picture formats. It requires that your graphics subsystem be capable of pretty high performance, and you'd best have some heavy-duty storage space available. However, it allows for frame-by-frame editing, claims smoother bit streaming, and allows real-time compression/decompression. A file format developed by the Motion Picture Experts Group (MPEG), called MPEG II, allows for far greater file compression, but limits the user's ability to manipulate the data. What most professionals will do is create the file in MJPEG, perform their digital wonders, then convert the file to MPEG II for the rest of the world to enjoy. While each manufacturer of video cards handles the file formats in a slightly different way, for the most part, MJPEG and MPEG II can be considered standards. **Table 11.2** compares some of the conventional video compression formats in terms of file size and bandwidth needed for transmission.

Table 11.2 Bitstream and Storage Requirements for Streaming Video

File Format (by brand)	Bitstream (Kb/s)	Storage needed for 1 hr.	Video that will fit CDR
Low Resolution			
Matrox MJPEG (HQ)	1425	4.9GB	8 minutes
Matrox MJPEG (LQ)	715	2.5GB	16 minutes
Elsa MJPEG	822	2.8GB	14 minutes
ATI MPEG II	420	1.4GB	28 minutes
3D/fx MPEG II	305	1.0GB	39 minutes
High Resolution			
Matrox MJPEG (HQ)	2734	9.4GB	4 minutes
Matrox MJPEG (LQ)	1585	5.4GB	8 minutes
Elsa MJPEG	1606	5.5GB	7 minutes
ATI MPEG II	550	1.9GB	22 minutes
3D/fx MPEG II	NOT POSSIBLE		

Different file formats offer varying degrees of compression. As a result, storage and data transmission requirements can vary as well.

TOUCHSCREEN MONITORS

We've all seen them work. You order your hamburger, fries, and a large drink and the attendant simply touches the picture of the burger and a price pops up. She touches the picture of fries and another price pops up. Then she touches the large cup of soda on the screen and that price shows up on the register. Then, she touches "TOTAL" and tells you how much it's all going to cost you. The computer tells her how much change to give you so she doesn't even have to think about that. She counts out your change and then the guy bagging your order still manages to get it wrong. But that's not the computer's fault now, is it?

Touchscreen monitors are no doubt miracles of modern technology. But just how do they work? There are actually three ways of making touchscreen monitors. They all involve putting a special coating over the surface of a standard cathode-ray tube and then wiring it through the controller circuitry. Finally, a software driver interprets the position of where the touch occurred and processes the commands. These methods include an analog-resistive surface, a capacitive surface, and a surface acoustive wave surface.

- *The Analog-Resistive Monitor:* The touchscreen panel is coated with a conductive surface below the glass surface of the monitor. Contact with the screen causes an electrical charge to be sent to the controller circuitry. Monitors that use this form of technology don't care what touches them. The person using it can use bare fingers, or can wear gloves. Sometimes, the monitor is equipped with a special stylus that the user presses against the screen. The beauty of this technology is that it doesn't really matter how big or small somebody's finger is. The monitor calculates the center point of the area being touched and generates the signal accordingly.

- *The Capacitive Monitor:* These monitors use a super-thin conductive coating on the outside surface that is transparent to the naked eye. At all four corners of the screen, a circuit applies a uniform voltage. When somebody touches a finger to the screen, it draws voltage from all four corners in direct proportion to the distance at which the touch occurs. The closer to the corner, the more current its drawn. Based on how much current is drawn from each of the four corners, the touchscreen controller is able to calculate the exact position that the touch occurred. The controller communicates this information to the application, which in turn executes the appropriate commands. The only shortcoming to this technology, if you could call it that, is that only the tip of a finger or a conductive object works here. If someone is wearing gloves, the fabric insulates the screen from the touch and it doesn't work.

- *The Surface Acoustive Wave Monitor:* To make this technology work, electrical signals are converted into ultrasonic sound waves. The glass surface of the monitor is linked to two piezoelectric transducers, one for the X-axis and one for the Y-axis. By touching the monitor, you absorb some of those waves. When that happens, the controller circuitry calculates where the disruption of the signal occurred. Based on a mathematical calculation, considering the X and Y axes, the position of the disruption is determined. Any object that doesn't damage the screen can be used for touching.

Regardless of the technology employed, the touchscreen monitor works by determining precisely where somebody or something touched the surface of the cathode-ray tube (CRT). Once it does this, the device driver sends the coordinates of where the touch occurred. The software takes that information and uses it to call a specific set of instructions or input a predefined set of data. Properly programmed, this approach limits the amount of information that actually has to be provided by the operator. Any time you do that, you limit the number of errors of which we humans are capable.

Unfortunately nobody has managed to migrate this technology over to the guy bagging the order.

CHAPTER SUMMARY

The last fifteen pages or so covered a number of different ways by which the user can import data from the outside world into the digital realm of the computer. I discussed everything from the basic keyboard to more evolved technologies, such as digital cameras and touchscreen monitors.

One thing I should point out here is that the devices covered in this chapter do not represent an all-encompassing list. Many other devices that will be covered in other chapters are also input devices. Modems, network cards, and sound cards are examples of other specialized devices that provide input.

BRAIN DRAIN

1. Briefly describe how pressing the W key on a keyboard generates data and moves it to the CPU for processing.

2. How does an optical mouse differ from a mechanical mouse?

3. Briefly describe how a mouse does its job.

4. What are the three different types of touchscreen monitor, and how do they differ from one another?

5. Describe a method by which computerization will assure that the person bagging your order does not give you onion rings instead of fries.

THE 64K$ QUESTIONS

1. When you press down on a key, data is generated by two signals. These are the _____ and the _____. (Select two.)
   a. Timing
   b. Break
   c. DMA
   d. Make

2. Another channel that the keyboard will activate is the _____.
   a. DMA
   b. IRQ
   c. DSP
   d. Timer

3. The type of mouse that uses a perforated wheel that spins in front of an LED is called a _____ mouse.
   a. Optical
   b. Mechanical
   c. Photoresisive
   d. Optomechanical

4. The one device that can be installed on a computer system that does NOT use an IRQ is_____.
   a. A video card
   b. The mouse
   c. A joystick
   d. A NIC

5. A CCD is a _____.
   a. Color coupling device
   b. Capacitive charge developer
   c. Central computing device
   d. Charge coupled device

6. CCDs are used by _____.
   a. Scanners
   b. Digital cameras
   c. Touchscreen monitors
   d. Display drivers

7. The file format frequently used by video editors is _____.
   a. MPEG-III
   b. JPEG
   c. TIFF
   d. MJPEG

8. The characteristic of a digital camera that has the most impact on color accuracy is _____.
   a. The lens
   b. The file format chosen
   c. Light balance
   d. White balance

9. Which of the following is not a form of touchscreen monitor?
   a. Resistive interpolative monitor
   b. The analog-resistive monitor

c.   The capacitive monitor

d.   The surface acoustive wave monitor

10. Which touchscreen technology does not allow the use of a gloved hand?

a.   Resistive interpolative monitor

b.   The analog-resistive monitor

c.   The capacitive monitor

d.   The surface acoustive wave monitor

TRICKY TERMINOLOGY

Break code: A signal generated by a keyswitch when the key is released.

Cool: A shift in the color of an image toward the blue side.

Digital noise: Unwanted color artifacts introduced into a digitized image during capture and/or by imaging software during the processing of that image.

Key matrix: The specific geometric layout of the keyswitches on a keyboard.

Keycap travel: The actual distance a user must press a key on a keyboard in order to produce results.

Keycap: The plastic button the user presses down when typing on a keyboard.

Keyswitch: The electromechanical connection that informs the keyboard controller circuitry that a key has been pressed.

Make code: A signal generated by a keyswitch when the key is first pressed down.

Optomechanical mouse: A mouse that uses perforated wheels passing in front of an LED to generate pulses of light that are used to track movement along the X and Y axis.

Warm: A shift in the color of an image toward the red side.

White balance: A measurement of how pure the reproduction of white is accomplished in an image.

ACRONYM ALERT

CCD: Charge Coupled Device. A sensor consisting of an array of cells that interpolates a physical image and coverts it into a digital file.

MJPEG: Motion-picture Joint Photographic Experts Group. An organization that develops and maintains standards for digitizing images. Also a file format used for compressing and storing editable versions of motion pictures developed by that group.

MPEG: Motion Picture Experts Group. An organization that developed a standard for compressing and storing digital video. Their format is not as editable as MJPEG.

TIFF: Tagged Image File Format. An image file format used for storing digital images that does not result in any loss of quality.

CHAPTER 12

WORKING WITH REMOVABLE DISKS

In the first generation of the PC, there was no hard disk installed. In fact, it wasn't until the second generation that a hard disk was even supported. Information was stored on 8″ floppy disks and stored carefully away in cabinets.

These days, you would almost think the devices such as the floppy diskette could be donated to the historical society and life could move on. One simply saves the great American novel to hard disk, and when ready, it can spew out on the printer in perfectly formatted form. The fact of the matter is, most of us work with information that either travels with us or needs to travel to others that will work with it. In the modern age, this is frequently done over the Internet or by email.

Once in a while, however, there is simply no substitute for Sneakernet. Copy to a floppy and hop on over. Modern technology now offers far more sophisticated options than the floppy diskette for removable media, however. In this chapter, I'll take a look at some of the various options, how they work, and what might be the right choice for a given set of circumstances.

A+ CORE HARDWARE EXAM OBJECTIVES

Those who are taking CompTIA's Core exam can look for the following items in this chapter.

1.1   Identify the names, purpose, and characteristics of system modules. Recognize these modules by sight or definition.

1.2   Identify basic procedures for adding and removing field-replaceable modules for desktop systems. Given a replacement scenario, choose the appropriate sequences.

1.4   Identify typical IRQs, DMAs, and I/O addresses and procedures for altering these settings when installing and configuring devices. Choose the appropriate installation or configuration steps in a given scenario.

2.1 Recognize common problems associated with each module and their symptoms, and identify steps to isolate and troubleshoot the problems. Given a problem situation, interpret the symptoms and infer the most likely cause.

BUZZ WORDS

Diskette: A term typically applied to the 3.5″ floppy disk in order to distinguish it from the 5.25″ floppy disk.

THE FLOPPY DISK

The floppy disk drive was not actually invented as a device for the PC. The first floppy disk drives appeared as a storage device for IBM's mainframe computers in 1967. Alan Shugart led the team of engineers that developed the drive and after two years of development came out with the 8″ floppy. Following up on the suggestions of David Noble, they designed a fabric sleeve that enveloped a flexible mylar base coated with magnetic medium. A few years later, having established his own company, Al released the first 5.25″ drive as a product of Shugart Associates. The floppy disk drive went through several incarnations before it finally arrived at the 3.5″ drive common to computers today (see **Figure 12.1**). The 3.5″ medium is commonly known as the *diskette*. This was so that in the old days, when 5.25″ drives were still common, people could easily differentiate between the two.

There have been several variations on the various designs of floppy disk drives that have emerged through the years. However, a few things remain constant. The basic parts that make them work haven't changed a lot, and neither have the methods they use to access data. Conventional floppy drives contain the following basic components:

- A clamping mechanism holds the disk in place as it spins. Floppy disks have a tendency to be unstable at high rotational speeds.

- A spindle motor spins the disk. With the exception of the 5.25″ double-sided, high-density (DS-HD) drives, this motor spins at 300rpm. The 5.25″ DS-HD spins at 360rpm.

- One or two magnetic read/write (R/W) heads are mounted on an actuator arm that moves the heads over surface of the medium. The initial R/W head is positioned to read the bottom surface of the disk.

- A head actuator consisting of a stepper motor coupled to the floppy controller moves the actuator arm, positioning the R/W heads to the appropriate track and sector on the disk.

- A sensor detects the rotational position of the disk. 5.25″ drives use an index hole cut in the sleeve, while 3.5″ drives have a magnetic sensor inside.

Figure 12.1 The floppy diskette drive continues to be an important component in today's computer systems.

HOW THE FLOPPY DRIVE WORKS

When the drive is formatted, the magnetic medium is mapped out in circular paths known as *tracks*. These tracks get subdivided into 512-byte *sectors*. Diskettes make use of a hidden file stored on the first sectors of the diskette surface called the file allocation table (FAT) to keep track of where each file is located on the diskette. FAT records the starting track and sector number of each group of contiguous sectors used by the file. Unless a user has access to specialized software known as a *disk editor* (which allows the user to write directly to the disk on a bit-by-bit basis), FAT is invisible to the user and is seen only by the OS.

The recording head lays down data using a method known as *tunnel erasure*. Data is recorded in much the same manner as audiocassette recorders record music. Magnetic energy realigns magnetic particles embedded in the surface of the medium. As information is written to the surface, the erase heads, positioned directly behind the recording head, trim the track cleanly on the disk. This forces the data to reside within its specified track. This helps eliminate the possibility of cross talk between tracks, which could lead to corrupted data. It also provides for a method of organizing data on the diskette.

When it's time to retrieve that data from the diskette, the computer system's floppy controller generates a signal that directs the R/W heads to the appropriate area of the diskette, using FAT as a guideline. The first time you turn your computer on, the R/W heads of the drive position themselves to track 0, sector 1. An improperly calibrated drive might be slightly off kilter when this happens. If this happens, and the heads are not properly positioned over track 0, then every read/write operation that occurs from then on will be inaccurate.

Disks written by an improperly calibrated drive are usually readable by that same drive, because the read heads are off by the same degree as the write heads. However, when that disk or diskette is moved over to another drive, it can't be read.

When a request for data is made, a stepper motor attached to the actuator arms moves the heads across the diskette surface where they latch on to the appropriate track. *Stepper motors* work by ticking off small increments rather than moving smoothly across the platter. These increments are calibrated to the width of the track. Therefore each position of the motor will move the arms to the next track. Once the track is latched onto, the R/W heads can then begin streaming data over the controller to the I/O bus.

BUZZ WORDS

Sector: The smallest readable unit of data on a magnetic disk drive. A sector consists of 512 bytes.

Track: A virtual circle of sectors on a magnetic drive that makes a complete ring around the disk surface.

Disk editor: A piece of specialized software that allows a user to examine and alter the contents of a disk drive bit by bit. Disk editors even allow access to parts of the drive not normally accessible by the user, such as FAT.

Tunnel erasure: A technique of erasing the magnetic charge from the edges of a recorded track on a magnetic disk.

Stepper motor: A motor that has been designed in such a way that, rather than rotating smoothly, it jumps from one position to another in precisely measured increments.

FLOPPY FORMATS

Over the years, the floppy disk has seen service in several different sizes. The first of Mr. Shugart's floppy drives was the 8″ floppy. It stored a massive 250 kilobytes of data. As I mentioned earlier, this drive was originally developed while he was at IBM as an add-on to mainframe computers. However, it also appeared on several different computers aimed at the home market, including the venerable Radio Shack TRS-80. Despite this, the floppy disk drive didn't really achieve respectability until the release of the 5.25″ floppy in 1976. That's where I'll start.

BUZZ WORDS

Index hole: A small opening in the covering of a floppy disk that allows the R/W heads to properly align to Track 0, Sector 1.

Write protect: A process or mechanism that prevents the data on a disk or other medium from being erased or overwritten.

THE 5.25″ FLOPPY DISK DRIVE

The first 5.25″ drive that appeared in the IBM PC could store 360KB. With the release of the PC-AT, the 360K drive was replaced with a 1.2MB drive. Either one of them used a disk similar to the one in **Figure 12.2**. This drive had a remarkably long lifespan. In fact, it is possible that you'll still occasionally stumble across a computer with one of these installed.

On the original 360K drives, there were forty tracks on each side of the disk. On the 1.2MB drive, this got bumped to eighty tracks per side. Additional capacity was made possible by increasing the number of sectors per track from nine to fifteen.

The magnetic media for these drives is encased in a flexible plastic sleeve that the user inserts into the drive. On the front bezel of the drive is a lever that moves the clamping mechanism into place, holding the disk firmly in position. This lever was euphemistically referred to as the door, and the name has stuck. If this lever is not positioned, the disk will not seat and you will get the message "Drive B: not ready."

The 5.25″ disk has a spindle hole in the center for aligning the disk to the spindle motor. Adjacent to that is another smaller hole called the *index hole*. This is what allows the actuator arm to locate Track 0, Sector 1. The write access window is what allows the R/W head access to the media. This is a narrow slot opening that exposes a small section of the disk surface the entire width of usable surface. If you are looking at the side of the disk with these openings exposed, there will be a notch cut into the plastic sleeve on the upper right-hand corner. This is the *write-protect* mechanism. As crude as it may sound, placing a small piece of transparent tape over this notch prevented you from accidentally overwriting the data on the disk.

Connectors on a 5.25″ floppy disk drive are pretty straightforward. The power is derived from a standard

Figure 12.2 A 5.25″ floppy disk

Molex connector, just like your hard drive or CD-ROM. The data cable connector is unique in that on the back of the drive there is an edge card connector. The data plug slips over that. It is notched off-center to prevent the cable from being applied backwards.

3.5″ DISKETTE DRIVES

Several things make the 3.5″ diskette a significant improvement over the 5.25″ disk. For one thing, more data can be stored on a smaller disk. Second, a rigid plastic housing keeps the media more secure. Someone transporting a diskette from home to work in a pocket is less likely to do permanent damage. The smaller size assures that it can fit right into a shirt pocket. Now you won't be sitting on your sales presentation while you drive to work.

Figure 12.3   A 3.5″ diskette

The drive itself doesn't differ all that much from the original 5.25″. Differences center on the media used. 3.5″ diskettes pack more sectors into each track, and as a result hold more data. The original 3.5″ floppy first developed by IBM in 1984 had a capacity of 720K. A couple of years later, its engineers upped that capacity to 1.44MB, and that's where it has stayed until today. Teac developed and introduced a 2.88MB version, but it never really caught on.

If you look carefully at a diskette (if you don't have one handy, look at **Figure 12.3)**, you'll see that on the diskette itself, the spindle hole exposes a metal disk embedded in the center of the medium. This disk has a small rectangular hole notched in it for the spindle to engage. A plastic (or sometimes metal) sliding door covers the access opening for the R/W heads. On the top edge, opposite the sliding door, are either one or two square holes punched into the plastic cover. If there is only one, your diskette is one of the older 720K types. The presence of two holes identifies a 1.44MB diskette. One of these holes is fitted with a sliding cover. This is your write protection. You can flip that closed to prevent overwriting your diskette. The theory is that you can permanently write-protect a diskette by snapping this cover off. Of course, a piece of scotch tape judiciously applied over the opening will override the write protection. The second hole indicates to the drive that it is a 1.44MB diskette and not 720K.

Table 12.1 summarizes the specifications for 5.25″ and 3.25″ floppies.

THE FLOPPY CABLE

The connector that hooks the drive to the controller is a 34-pin ribbon cable. It is easy to distinguish the floppy cable from the hard drive cable. Not only is it narrower (the cable for hard drives generally has forty conductors, unless it's a SCSI drive), but there is a twist in the cable that is very difficult to miss. This twist is clearly visible in **Figure 12.4.**

As with all ribbon cables, the pink or red conductor on the cable is the "number one" conductor. On older cables, there might be three different types of connectors. The connector

Table 12.1   Floppy Disk Formats, Past and Present

5.25″ Format		
Specification	Double Density	High Density
Bytes per sector	512	512
Sectors per track	9	15
Tracks per side	40	80
Tracks per inch	48	96
Number of sides	2	2
Capacity	360K	1.2MB
Track width	.33mm	.16mm
Default cluster size	1	2
FAT length (sectors)	2	7
Root directory length (sectors)	7	14
Total sectors per disk	720	2,400

3.5″ Format			
Specification	Double Density	High Density (1.44MB)	2.88MB
Bytes per sector	512	512	512
Sectors per track	9	18	36
Tracks per side	80	80	80
Tracks per inch	135	135	135
Number of sides	2	2	2
Capacity	720K	1.44MB	2.88MB
Track width	.115mm	.115mm	.115mm
Default cluster size	1	2	2
FAT length (sectors)	3	9	9
Root directory length (sectors)	7	14	15
Total sectors per disk	720	2,400	5,760

A comparison of floppy disk formats, past and present

at one end plugs into the motherboard controller. One of the other types is a rectangular connector with holes for pins to plug in to. Those are for 3.5″ drives. The third kind has a larger connector that is designed to fit over an edge card, for 5.25″ drives. Most cables currently manufactured no longer have connectors for a 5.25″ drive. Since people rarely use two floppy

Figure 12.4 In order for a floppy disk drive to be a bootable device, it needs to be on the end opposite of the twist in the cable.

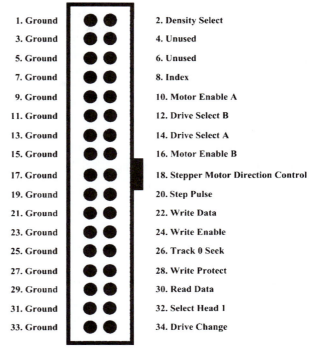

1. Ground	2. Density Select
3. Ground	4. Unused
5. Ground	6. Unused
7. Ground	8. Index
9. Ground	10. Motor Enable A
11. Ground	12. Drive Select B
13. Ground	14. Drive Select A
15. Ground	16. Motor Enable B
17. Ground	18. Stepper Motor Direction Control
19. Ground	20. Step Pulse
21. Ground	22. Write Data
23. Ground	24. Write Enable
25. Ground	26. Track 0 Seek
27. Ground	28. Write Protect
29. Ground	30. Read Data
31. Ground	32. Select Head 1
33. Ground	34. Drive Change

Figure 12.5 Standard pinouts for 34-pin floppy cable

drives anymore, it's also becoming more common to see floppy cables with only two connectors. One is for the motherboard controller and the other is for a single drive.

The reason for the twist is to identify the bootable drive. If there are two floppy drives on a system, the system BIOS identifies which is the bootable drive by its position relative to the twist. The drive on the side of the twist opposite of the controller is always the bootable drive. By default, this becomes Drive A. If you inadvertently plug your floppy into the connector on the same side of the cable as the controller, you will have no bootable floppy drive.

In the BIOS settings, there is a place where you can "swap floppies." Changing this setting from the default will make the drive on the controller side of the cable Drive A and the drive on the opposite end Drive B. It will not, however, change which device is bootable.

The thirty-fourth conductor, or the one on the opposite side of the color-coded wire, is the diskette change line. When a diskette is inserted into the drive, a signal called the drive change pulse will travel down this wire and tell the computer that a new diskette has been inserted into the drive. Naturally all the other conductors have a purpose, or they wouldn't be there. The pinouts for a standard floppy disk cable and its associated port are illustrated in **Figure 12.5**.

TROUBLESHOOTING FLOPPY DISK DRIVES

Floppy drive problems are probably misdiagnosed more often than any other device. Every time somebody inserts a diskette into the drive and the system returns some sort of error message, they automatically the drive is assumed to be defective. Much of the time, however, it's not the drive's fault. There are several different issues that will result in customers calling for help, claiming their floppy disk drive has failed.

DISKETTE PROBLEMS

Most of the time, when individuals are unable to read data from their floppies, it is the diskette itself that is to blame. Diskettes are notoriously vulnerable to environmental conditions. Excess temperature variation, exposure to magnetic radiation, or high doses of electromagnetic interference (EMI) can wipe out portions of the data on the surface of the medium. Any contamination, such as dumping your coffee on your desk while a bunch of floppies are scattered about, will damage the diskette. A piece of lint from your shirt pocket working its way past the door can scratch the surface of the medium.

The type of error message generated by your computer when trying to access data will give you a good idea of where to start. You'll often see errors like these:

Data error reading Drive A:

Seek error writing Drive A:

Sector not found reading Drive A:

Abort, Retry, Fail?

Abort, Retry, Fail, Ignore?

These are all signs of defective diskettes, not defective drives. On these diskettes, if you're a Windows user, try running Scandisk in Thorough Mode. If there is sufficient free space on the diskette, many of them can be recovered.

The floppy cable itself might be the culprit. If you are working with a brand-new computer that just arrived and the floppy drive is not detected on bootup, one of two things might have happened. Is the drive light on the floppy drive constantly glowing? If so, whoever assembled your computer got the cable on backwards. One would like to think that a mistake like this would never happen, but one would be wrong. You'll also see this same symptom if, after doing some work on the system, you happen to plug it in backwards yourself.

If the light does not glow, and during the boot process, you don't hear the actuator arm trying to latch onto Sector 1, Track 0, then you have the second problem, and it's time to open the case. Floppy drive cables are good at coming off during shipping. If that's the case, simply put it back on and your computer should work.

Another diskette issue that occasionally appears is the repeating directory syndrome. You click the A: icon in Windows Explorer and get a list of files on that diskette. Since it didn't have the file you were looking for, you pop the next one in and click the icon once again. And get the same list of files. "Hmmm," you say. "I don't recall making a copy of that disk." So you pop in a third floppy and Explorer delivers the same list again.

Here's what is happening. When you run the first directory of the diskette, the file list is stored in the computer's cache memory. That way, if you need to review the list again, it's already there. The thirty-fourth wire on the floppy cable carries the drive change signal. When you replace the diskette in the drive with a new one, an electrical signal travels up that wire to a sensor in your drive, and a new directory is generated the next time the user requests it. If that wire gets crimped or broken, the signal never arrives, and the same directory listing appears over and over again. The solution is simple. Replace the floppy cable. In the meantime, you can force a directory update by alternating between drives while doing your search. After each search of a floppy, hit the C: drive. When you try the next floppy, your computer will have to do a new search.

Sometimes your problem lies in the CMOS. One of the settings you can change is what kind of floppy disk drives you have installed. Many versions of BIOS ship with the default setting of "None" for drive A. If the battery goes dead, your CMOS will revert to factory defaults. When this happens, if your default is "None," then the computer will not see a floppy drive on the next boot. Another thing that has been known to reset the CMOS is changing expansion cards. A sign that this might have happened is if you get error messages along the lines of "Not ready error reading Drive A:", "General failure reading Drive A:", and "Insert diskette for Drive A: and press any key when ready."

If all else checks out well, and you're still having problems, it's possible that the floppy drive has failed. They do have a relatively high failure rate, compared to other components, simply because of the nature of the abuse they receive. They are exposed to the elements more than any other device, and they're purely mechanical. Therefore, they fail. You will get most of the same messages as you get with CMOS issues, along with "Drive not Ready" and "FDD Controller Failure." Floppy drives are cheap. Don't try to fix it. Simply replace it.

OTHER REMOVABLE DISK DRIVES

It's been a long time since the floppy disk could claim to be the only removable medium. In fact, for the most part, it has found itself relegated to the role of an emergency boot drive, or simply a convenient method for moving small files from home to the office. For real data storage, there is any number of other technologies that have come along to make the floppy all but obsolete. These drives hold more data (by a long shot), but they also sit on faster interfaces. That's something you can't help but appreciate the next time you try running a PowerPoint presentation from a floppy disk.

ZIP DRIVES

The Zip drive very likely leads the way in removable media. Developed by Iomega, they are also available from numerous other manufacturers. These drives are available in 100MB (being phased out, but still available as of this writing), 250MB, and 750MB formats, so they offer a reasonable amount of space for storage. As far as users are concerned, these are nothing more than high-capacity floppy disks. They insert a Zip disk into the drive and copy their files over.

The drives have been available over the years in both internal and external versions. The internal drive mounts into your computer case no differently than a floppy. It's about the same size as a floppy and the opening differs only that it is wider to accept the thicker disk. (Even after all these years, I still try to stick a floppy disk into my Zip drive from time to time!) Internal drives are available with either an IDE or SCSI interface.

External drives can be picked up that hook up to a parallel port, to the external port of a SCSI adapter, or to a USB port. For the fastest data transfer, one of the newer releases with a FireWire interface will be preferable. (For a detailed explanation of the advantages of SCSI or FireWire, see Chapter Fifteen, The Many Faces of SCSI.)

There are some trouble-shooting issues that might arise when you're dealing with Zip disks. External drives that mount onto the parallel port, like the one in **Figure 12.6**, work best if the port is set to Enhanced Parallel Port (EPP) or Enhanced Capabilities Port (ECP) mode (see Chapter Eighteen, Printing Technologies, for detailed information on these modes and how to set them). The drives are built with pass-through par-

Figure 12.6 External Zip drives are great if you need to move from one computer to another on a regular basis.

allel ports for hooking up your printer. Some computers have been known to generate I/O errors in standard bidirectional mode because they think they're printing to themselves. I/O errors are almost a guarantee if you send a job to your printer and then decide you want to load a file from the Zip. Also, if you have other devices, such as a scanner or a copy-protection software key that plugs into a parallel port, performance can drop to a crawl if you try stacking more than three devices on the parallel port.

Another issue that has been repeatedly reported is the infamous "click of death." You insert a disk into the drive and it repeatedly clicks, over and over again. You can't make it stop and you can't abort the operation. The only solution is to restart your machine. Later on, the problem will spread to other disks that you use in that same drive. It acts just like a virus, except that it's hardware related and not a software issue. Therefore, if you are working with a Zip drive and it develops the click of death, whatever you do, don't insert a new disk to test the drive. The only thing you'll accomplish is that you'll now have two destroyed disks instead of one.

So what causes that to happen?

Haven't got a clue. (I was dying to say that somewhere in this book). Neither does Iomega. It suggests that a broken R/W head or torn media within the disk might cause the problem, but that's only a theory. Several other suggestions have been offered. The one that's easiest to believe is that the first disk to fail somehow throws the R/W head out of alignment. Subsequent disks then cannot be read and are damaged by the head coming in actual contact with the surface of the medium.

JAZ DRIVES

Jaz drives are another offering by Iomega. For the most part, Jaz and Zip drives are very similar. The interfaces are comparable; both are available in parallel, USB, or SCSI, with a FireWire option. Both use disks that go in and out of the computer with the ease of a floppy disk.

Jaz drives hold a lot more data, though. The drive supports up to 2GB disks, and the disks are available in either 1GB or 2GB densities. They're also somewhat faster than Zips. Jaz drives deliver access times in the vicinity of 10ms, which compares to some hard drives (good hard drives hover around 6.5ms to 10ms).

SUPER FLOPPY DRIVES

The so-called Super Floppy is a product that has been made by several manufacturers. For the most part, these are drives that support high-capacity removable disks, but will also read and write standard 1.44MB floppy diskettes.

The major player was the LS120 or SuperDisk, a format put out in a cooperative effort by Imation and Panasonic. Mitsubishi also made a line of these drives. They were available in internal and external versions, and there's even one for notebook computers. Interface options include parallel, SCSI, and USB.

The SuperDisk got its increased capacity by dramatically increasing the number of tracks per inch embedded on the media. A metal particle coating was used instead of the metal-oxide coating used by standard floppy diskettes. Onto this metal coating a laser beam etched 1736 tracks onto which data could be stored. Externally, the diskette didn't look that much different than a standard floppy diskette.

These drives weren't known for their blazing speed. Most users would consider them too slow for running an application from the disk. However, the convenience of having one drive read and write both 120MB disks and 1.44MB diskettes was something to be considered.

For a while, it looked like the death of the SuperDisk was imminent. Both Matsushita Corporation and Imation discontinued the manufacture of these drives in the waning months of the year 2000. However, when Apple Computer Corporation stopped installing floppy diskette drives into all of its computers, there was a sudden resurgence of interest. Their popularity today has surpassed what it was before they were "discontinued."

HiFD

A drive that lost its fight for recognition was Sony's HiFD (High Capacity Floppy Disk) drive. These drives supported a proprietary 200MB disk as well as standard 1.44MB diskettes. They offered decent performance, in the range of 3.6MB/s throughput, but did not have much to offer for interface options. They were only available in external form in the choice of either parallel or USB.

The HiFD diskette packed 2822 tracks per inch onto the tiny little diskette, and yet the same drive could read standard 1.44MB diskettes as well as 720KB versions. Needless to say, it wasn't possible to try to read the HiFD diskette in a standard drive. To prevent this from happening, the HiFD diskette was designed in such a way as to not fit into a standard 3.5" drive.

The format was co-developed by Sony and Fuji Film Corporation and for a while looked like it might catch on. It received support from Sony, Teac, and Alps as far as the manufacture of drives was concerned. Fuji and Sony both offered media. However, heavy competition from Iomega in the form of the Zip drive was too much for the technology to overcome.

TAPE SOLUTIONS

Disks aren't the only domain of removable media. Tape drives have long been the primary choice of medium for the network administrator looking for a (relatively) fast and convenient way to back up servers and workstations. Tape drives were, in fact, the original "hard drive" of many computers that preceded the IBM PC. Commodore 64s, Radio Shack's TRS-80, the Texas Instruments TI-99, and many other home computing devices offered cassette tape storage mechanisms for both programs and data. Current product offerings are a bit more sophisticated than the cassette tapes used on these early machines.

BUZZ WORDS ————

Native capacity: How much data any given medium can store without benefit of compression. Various compression techniques allow data beyond native capacity to be recorded.

QIC

For many years, the drive of choice for someone looking for a reasonably high-capacity storage mechanism for backup was Quarter Inch Cartridge (QIC). The cartridge itself was of a fixed size, and in order to increase capacity, manufacturers increased the length of the tape wound onto the spools and how much data could be crammed onto an inch of tape. This is known as the data density. Standards by which tapes and drives are manufactured are under the strict control of an organization called The Quarter Inch Committee. They make sure that tapes made by one manufacturer will work in the drives made by another.

Figuring out all those different numbers in the names of QIC tapes might look a little intimidating at first, but it's actually pretty straightforward. I'll take for an example a DC-9120 tape manufactured by Maxell. The number 9120 is Maxell's part identification number. The way it does it is to use the last three numbers as the native capacity of the tape. *Native capacity* is how much data the tape can hold if you do not use any compression. The 120 in the number tells me it is a 1.2GB tape. Now what does the DC mean?

There are actually two different formats for the tape used by QIC drives. There is the QIC-DC, or data cartridge, and the QIC-MC, or mini-cartridge. The data cartridge is a tape housed in a shell that measures 4″×6″×0.625″. The mini-cartridge measures 2.5″×3.5″×0.60″. Therefore, the DC-9120 is a Data Cartridge 1.2GB tape.

Data is encoded onto magnetic media in a manner similar to floppy disk drives. An iron oxide coating is written over by magnetizing the particles. Where a particle is magnetized, you have a 1; where it is not, you have a 0. The data is laid down onto the tape in tracks. Data density is derived by two methods. The first involves increasing the number of tracks that can be recorded onto a strip of tape. The other is simply squeezing more data onto each track. Between the tracks a thin strip of unrecorded medium insulates the data.

For a while, it looked like QIC was a dead technology. It was slow and didn't provide for much native storage capacity. A good QIC drive measured its data throughput in megabytes per minute, and not per second. Backing up a 36GB hard drive onto QIC tape was a job nobody volunteered for! However, the Quarter Inch Committee has revitalized the standard and is in the process of ratifying standards that would put it back onto a competitive level with some of the other "more modern" technologies. As of this writing this is now a 25GB native/50GB compressed drive capable of approximately 2Mb/s backup speeds.

While there were several dozen standards that developed over the years, relatively few became generally popular. While by no means an all-inclusive list, **Table 12.2** lists the most common QIC formats.

Table 12.2   Common QIC Formats

Format	Interface	Recording Method	Native Capacity	Tracks per Inch	Data Throughput	Data Density	Tape on Roll
QIC-40	Floppy or optional controller card	MFM	40MB/60MB	20	2MB-to-8MB/minute	10,000bpi	205ft to 307.5ft
QIC-80	Floppy or optional controller card	MFM	80MB/120MB	28	3MB-to-9MB/minute	14,700bpi	205ft to 307.5ft
QIC-120	SCSI or QIC-02	MFM	125MB	15	3MB-to-9MB/minute	10,000bpi	600ft.
QIC-150	SCSI or QIC-02	MFM	150MB/250MB	18	3MB-to-9MB/minute	10,000bpi	600ft.
QIC-525	SCSI or SCSI-2	MFM	320MB/525MB	26	12MB/minute	16,000bpi	1,000ft.
QIC-1000	SCSI or SCSI-2	MFM	1GB	30	18MB/minute	36,000bpi	760ft.
QIC-1350	SCSI-2	RLL	1.35GB	30	18MB/minute	51,000bpi	760ft.
QIC-2100	SCSI-2	RLL	2.1GB	30	18MB/minute	68,000bpi	875ft.
QIC-3010	Floppy or IDE	MFM	255MB	40	9MB/minute	22,000bpi	300ft.
QIC-3020	Floppy or IDE	MFM	500MB	40	9MB/minute	42,000bpi	400ft.
QIC-2GB	SCSI-2	MFM	2.0GB	42	18MB/minute	40,640bpi	900ft.
QIC-5GB	SCSI-2	RLL	5GB	44	18MB/minute	96,000bpi	1,200ft.
QIC-5010	SCSI-2	RLL	13GB	144	18MB/minute	68,000bpi	—

Some of the more common QIC formats, along with their capacity and transfer rates

DAT

Digital audiotape (DAT) has enjoyed a relatively long reign as the format of choice for most high-end tape backup units, although it is starting to feel the pressure of DLT (which I'll discuss in the next section of this chapter). DAT uses a different recording method than QIC. Unlike QIC, which laid data down in tracks, DAT records information using a *helical-scan* record head. The tape wraps around the head, much the same way your video recorder handles tape. Then the data is recorded onto the entire width of tape, treating it as one really wide track. The result is that a significantly larger amount of data can be recorded per square inch of tape. Because the same technology is used in both the computer industry and the audio industry, it is necessary for us to be technically correct in our terminology.

The first thing I need to do is try to eliminate some confusion as to what constitutes data and what constitutes audio. If you're recording a digital audio signal, it is correct to call it a DAT drive. However, when that same drive is put into a computer it becomes a data recorder, a digital data storage (DDS) drive. As with any other technology, DAT has evolved in the years that it has been out. With each new generation of DAT drive, more data could be squeezed onto the tape. These different generations appear as DDS numbers. The first DAT drives to come out were DDS-1. Current drives are now up to DDS-4. A comparison of these formats can be seen in **Table 12.3**.

DAT comes in both 4mm DAT and 8mm DAT. Since the latter is identical to the tape used in audio recorders, the inevitable question arises. Can I use DAT tape in a DDS drive? And the answer is a definitive maybe! Technically speaking, in order for a tape to be used in a DDS drive the tape must be manufactured to specifications outlined in the ISO-10777 standards and the ISO-12247 standards ratified by the International Standards Organization (ISO). Unless the tape you use meets those standards, many drive manufacturers will refuse to offer support. Tapes manufactured for use in audio systems is theoretically of lower quality.

Now, can you really do it or not? And once again, the answer is a definitive maybe. If the audio tape is of excellent quality, you will probably experience no difficulties. However, a tape

> ## BUZZ WORDS
>
> **Helical scan:** A recording technology that places data in diagonal tracks along the tape, as opposed to a linear track that follows parallel to the tape edge.

Table 12.3 DDS Standards

Standard	Native Format	Compressed Format	Tape Length	Data Transfer
DDS-1	2GB	4GB	90M	~1.35MB/s
DDS-2	4GB	8GB	120M	~1.35MB/s
DDS-3	12GB	24GB	125M	~2.65MB/s
DDS-4	20GB	40GB	150M	~2.65MB/s

A comparison of DAT formats

of lower quality will result in signal dropouts. In a musical tape, if you lose a bit of data here and there, it is of little or no consequence. Losing a few bytes of a Windows 2000 Service Pack would be a different issue altogether. I suggest that if you wish to save a couple of bucks here and there by using audio-grade tape that you test it thoroughly before you entrust your company's critical data to it.

DLT

A more recent technology to emerge in tape drives is the digital linear tape (DLT) drive. Developed by Digital Equipment Corporation, DLT abandons the helical-scan head in favor of a linear-record head. DLT drives use a pure metal tape coating rather than an oxide coating.

> **BUZZ WORDS** ─────────
>
> **Signal saturation:** The maximum strength of a recording signal that a device can handle before the recording becomes unusable.

In a way, it almost looks as if DLT has taken a step backward in technology. Like the older QIC, it lays data down in parallel tracks. Instead of using a unified R/W head, though, as did QIC, the DLT drive has independent elements for read and write operations. Data throughput is significantly improved as a result. One of the advantages of DLT over DAT is a direct result of using linear technology. Because the tape does not have to be wrapped around the heads, far less tape tension is required. With less tension, there is less friction generated between the tape and the heads. As a result, both tape and drive last longer.

The use of metal tape, as opposed to metal-oxide tape, provides for significantly higher signal saturation. *Signal saturation* is the strength of signal that the tape can accurately record before distortion becomes so great that the recorded version of that signal becomes unusable. What this means to the engineer is that the signal used to record all those tiny little 1s can be much stronger than the signal used to record all the 0s. This allows for higher recording accuracy as well as faster recording speeds.

Another advantage of metal tape over metal-oxide tape is that the metal tape is far less susceptible to flaking off after extended use. It bonds more strongly to the base. When you combine this with the aforementioned fact that there is also less friction between the tape and the heads, a DLT tape lasts much longer than a DAT tape.

AIT

In some ways, the Advanced Intelligent Tape Drive (AIT) by Sony is just an extension of DAT. It uses the same helical scan R/W technology, but it adds a couple of new twists. A new technology called Memory-in-Cassette (MIC) architecture teaches the drive (and the tape) new tricks. The MIC chip consists of an EEPROM embedded in an 8mm cassette. Data access time and seek times in the event of specific file retrieval are reduced by as much as half that of either DAT or DLT. Data can be stored on the tape in partitions utilizing multiple load points (MLP). And a new write-once-read-many (WORM) feature allows data to be written to a drive permanently, with no ability to erase or write over that specific tape.

One of these features that deserves some extra attention is MLP. All tapes require a specific *load point*, which is the physical location where the actual data begins to be copied. Previous technologies allowed only one load point. If the load point was at the beginning of the tape, and a user wanted to

BUZZ WORDS

Load point: The physical location on a tape where data begins to be stored.

restore a specific file, the drive would have to start searching for that file from the very beginning of the tape. This could take several minutes. Some manufacturers sped up the process by using mid-load points (unfortunately also called MLP). Mid-load points placed the load point in the center of the tape, so searches could be done in either rewind or fast-forward mode. Multiple load points allow the user to preselect a specific point on the tape from which to start a search.

AIT native formats start at 25GB, with a theoretical potential of 2TB compressed. Higher compression ratios are made possible on AIT drives using adaptive lossless data compression (ALDC) technology. ALDC compresses data on an average of 2.6:1. Conventional compression technology is having a good day if it achieves 2:1.

Since one of the primary objections to helical scan technology was the wear and tear imposed on the media, AIT format makes use of metal-evaporated media with a proprietary Diamond Layer Coating to extend the life of the tape. In addition to a longer life, developers of AIT claim that much higher recording density can be achieved.

AIT-1

AIT-1, as the name implies, was the first generation of AIT tape drives and tapes. These drives were capable of a 35GB native capacity, and using ALDC could achieve 90GB compressed. Data throughput in native format was around 4MB/s (10MB/s compressed) on drives with an Ultra-SCSI LVD interface (see Chapter Fifteen, The Many Faces of SCSI). As of this writing, AIT-1 is still available. It can be considered the "entry level" AIT. In the event that a user should upgrade to one of the later generations of AIT somewhere down the line, media recorded by the AIT-1 drive can be read or written by all subsequent AIT generations.

AIT-2

The second generation of AIT drives increased both the capacity and the speed of the format. This was achieved through improvements in the quality of the recording heads, channel coding, and in how the media is manufactured. While remaining backwardly compatible with AIT-1, AIT-2 increases data transfer rates to 6MB/s (15MB/s compressed) and native capacity to 50GB (130GB compressed).

AIT-3

The most recent AIT offering boasts a native capacity of 100GB (260GB with compression) and a native data transfer rate of 12MB/s (31MB/s compressed). The increased capacity of AIT-3 was accomplished by doubling the number of recording tracks per inch of tape over the previous generations. Increased throughput is a result of improvements in the recording heads and controller circuitry.

Super-AIT

Super-AIT (SAIT) ups the ante in the AIT arena in areas of storage capacity, data transfer rate, and technological marvels. As of this writing, only the first generation of SAIT has reached the market. These drives offer the network administrator or user 500GB of native capacity, and when compressed, up to 1.3TB! Throughput in native mode approaches 30MB/s. By the time this book reaches the streets, SAIT-2 will most likely be available with a native capacity of 1TB (2.6TB compressed) and throughput of 60MB/s. On the drawing board is SAIT-3 and SAIT-4.

If initial research and development figures hold out, you can expect drives that store 4TB of data in native format, 10.4TB when compressed, and move it from your hard drive to tape, or vice versa, at 240MB/s.

SLR

Scalable Linear Recording (SLR) tape drives take the DLT to the next level. By incorporating multiple record channels across the breadth of the tape, storage capacity and throughput are increased. In order to assure that the heads are reading the correct tracks, a separate recording channel maintains channel synchronization.

When originally introduced, SLR drives were available as small as 525MB. Needless to say, today's drives are a bit larger. Current drives are available to 50GB in native mode, or 100GB compressed. Tandberg Data, the company that developed this technology, claims that a 30GB hard drive can be backed up in an hour our less. The small tape size allows for tape auto-changers to take up far less space than some of the competitors.

CHAPTER SUMMARY

A lot of the information presented in this chapter is actually targeted more toward the "real world" than it is the exam. Still, there is much exam material to be found here. Especially important is the section of floppy disk drives. Know their history and their evolution.

Don't, however, discount the importance of knowing about some of the other devices described in this chapter. Even some of the devices that have been discontinued are likely to show up on your bench someday after you become a professional. It wouldn't be all that impressive to have to ask the customer, "What in the world is that?"

BRAIN DRAIN

1. List as many forms of removable media as you can.

2. How did the Super Floppy drive differ from a Zip drive?

3. If you have an application that consists of 245MB worth of files, and you want to run it from removable media, what options would be best?

4. Describe how a helical-scan recording mechanism works.

5. Discuss as many differences as you can between DAT and DLT tape drives.

THE 64K$ QUESTIONS

1. 5.25″ floppy disk drives were available in _____ and _____ sizes. (Choose two)
   a. 360KB
   b. 720KB
   c. 1.2MB
   d. 1.44MB
   e. 2.88MB

2. 3.5″ floppy diskettes were available in what sizes?
   a. 360KB
   b. 720KB
   c. 1.2MB
   d. 1.44MB
   e. 2.88MB

3. Double-density floppies featured _____ sectors per track.
   a. 9
   b. 15
   c. 20
   d. 40

4. High-density floppies featured _____ sectors per track.
   a. 9
   b. 15
   c. 20
   d. 40

5. How many bytes are there per sector on a floppy disk?
   a. 9 (8 for data and 1 for parity)
   b. 256
   c. 512
   d. 1024

6. Repeating directories from multiple disks is most likely a result of _____.
   a. A bad diskette
   b. A stuck actuator arm
   c. A faulty cable
   d. Corrupted drivers

7. The "click of death" is a failure that appears on _____.
   a. Zip drives
   b. Syquest cartridges
   c. Floppy disk drives
   d. Tape drives

8. Two tape drives that use helical scan recording technology are _____ and _____.
   a. QIC
   b. DAT
   c. DLT
   d. AIC

9. Two tape drives that use linear recording technology are_____ and _____.
   a. QIC
   b. DAT
   c. DLT
   d. AIC

10. You just changed the battery on your motherboard and now the floppy drive isn't recognized. Why might this be?
    a. You accidentally unseated the cable.
    b. You damaged an IC with ESD.
    c. The CMOS reverted to default settings.
    d. A spurious electrical charge damaged the drive.

TRICKY TERMINOLOGY

Disk editor: A piece of specialized software that allows a user to examine and alter the contents of a disk drive bit by bit. Disk editors even allow access to parts of the drive not normally accessible by the user, such as FAT.

Diskette: A term typically applied to the 3.5″ floppy disk in order to distinguish it from the 5.25″ floppy disk.

Helical scan: A recording technology that places data in diagonal tracks along the tape, as opposed to a linear track that follows parallel to the tape edge.

Index hole: A small opening in the covering of a floppy disk that allows the R/W heads to properly align to Track 0, Sector 1.

Load point: The physical location on a tape where data begins to be stored.

Native capacity: How much data any given medium can store without benefit of compression. Various compression techniques allow data beyond native capacity to be recorded.

Sector: The smallest readable unit of data on a magnetic disk drive. A sector consists of 512 bytes.

Signal saturation: The maximum strength of a recording signal that a device can handle before the recording becomes unusable.

Stepper motor: A motor that has been designed in such a way that, rather than rotating smoothly, it jumps from one position to another in precisely measured increments.

Track: A virtual circle of sectors on a magnetic drive that makes a complete ring around the disk surface.

Tunnel erasure: A technique of erasing the magnetic charge from the edges of a recorded track on a magnetic disk.

Write protect: A process or mechanism that prevents the data on a disk or other medium from being erased or overwritten.

ACRONYM ALERT

AIT: Advanced Intelligent Tape. A tape format that incorporates a linear recording mechanism in conjunction with a memory chip embedded in the tape cartridge to allow for advanced features.

ALDC: Adaptive Lossless Data Compression. An advanced data compression algorithm that allows a greater degree of compression without any loss of data.

DAT: Digital Audiotape. A tape format that uses an 8mm recording tape and a helical scan recording mechanism very similar to that used by digital audio recorders.

DDS: Digital Data Storage

DLT: Digital Linear Tape. A tape format that records data in a straight line along the tape, parallel to the tape's edge.

ECP: Enhanced Capabilities Port. One of several different methods of configuring a parallel port.

EPP: Enhanced Parallel Port. One of several different methods of configuring a parallel port.

FAT: File Allocation Table. A file on a disk, hidden from the user, that identifies what file is using each sector on the disk. It is the disk's roadmap, if you will.

MIC: Memory In Cartridge. The embedded memory chip of an AIT.

MLP: Mid-Load Point. A tape drive technology that places the load point in the center of the tape.

MLP: Multiple Load Point. A tape drive technology that allows a single tape to be mounted from several different locations on the tape.

QIC: Quarter Inch Cartridge. A tape format so named because of the size of the tape used (not the size of the cartridge).

SLR: Scalable Linear Recording. A tape drive technology that uses linear recording technology and allows multiple channels of data to be stored across the width of the tape.

WORM: Write Once Read Many. A recording technology that write protects the contents of the medium in order to prevent that data from being erased or overwritten.

 VIEW THE VIDEO

A video clip on Floppy Disks is available on the accompanying CD.

CHAPTER 13

HARD DISK DRIVE STRUCTURE AND GEOMETRY

The hard disk drive is one of those devices that has a good excuse if it suffers from a complex. Of all the devices in the system, the hard drive has seen as rapid and dramatic a pace of improvement as any other, including the CPU. Yet it never gets the fanfare. It does more physical work than any other component, and yet the user complains when it makes too much noise.

From the time the Winchester Hard Disk Drive was introduced in 1975 to the present, experienced computer users have considered a hard disk drive a necessity. A hard drive is the fundamental form of mass storage in use today. While all systems of today ship with one installed, this has not always been the case. Most early computers, such as the Timex Sinclair, the Commodore series of computers, and Radio Shack's TRS-80s used a tape drive for storage. Even after the release of the PC, hard disks remained an option (and an expensive one at that) for many years.

The Winchester was far from being the first hard disk, however. IBM developed the first true hard disk drive in 1956. It called it the 305 RAMAC. The letters stood for Random Access Method for Accounting and Control. It possessed fifty disks that were two feet in diameter, and stored a mind-boggling **five megabytes** of data.

To help you understand hard drives, I'll be taking you though a few other parts of the computer as well. I'll be discussing certain BIOS instructions as well as hard drive geometry. A key issue that impinges heavily on computer performance is how a particular computer deals with I/O operations.

A+ CORE HARDWARE EXAM OBJECTIVES

Some exam objectives to be covered in this chapter include the following:

1.1 Identify the names, purpose, and characteristics of system modules. Recognize these modules by sight or definition.

1.2 Identify basic procedures for adding and removing field-replaceable modules for desktop systems. Given a replacement scenario, choose the appropriate sequences.

1.4   Identify typical IRQs, DMAs, and I/O addresses, and procedures for altering these settings when installing and configuring devices. Choose the appropriate installation or configuration steps in a given scenario.

1.5   Identify the names, purposes, and performance characteristics of standardized/common peripheral ports, associated cabling, and their connectors. Recognize ports, cabling, and connectors by sight.

1.6   Identify proper procedures for installing and configuring common IDE devices. Choose the appropriate installation or configuration sequences in given scenarios. Recognize the associated cables.

1.9   Identify procedures to optimize PC operations in specific situations. Predict the effects of specific procedures under given scenarios.

1.10 Determine the issues that must be considered when upgrading a PC. In a given scenario, determine when and how to upgrade system components.

2.1   Recognize common problems associated with each module and their symptoms, and identify steps to isolate and troubleshoot the problems. Given a problem situation, interpret the symptoms and infer the most likely cause.

3.1   Identify the various types of preventive maintenance measures, products, and procedures, and when and how to use them.

BASIC HARD DRIVE GEOMETRY

Every hard drive in use today traces its ancestry back to a form of design based on the CHS parameters. CHS stands for Cylinders, Heads, and Sectors per track. It is through this configuration that the system determines the storage capacity of the drive, and it is through this geometry that the file allocation table is able to properly map the information stored on the device. IBM first introduced CHS on the IBM PC.

I discussed the concepts of sectors and tracks in Chapter Twelve, Working with Removable Disks. With hard drives comes a new geometric structure. Hard drives also have cylinders. Hard drives are generally equipped with more than one disk onto which data is stored. These are called *platters*. On most hard drives, each platter also has two surfaces on which data is stored. (Some of the less expensive models save a few dollars per drive in production costs by not equipping the bottom surface of the platter closest to the drive's base with an actuator arm and R/W head.) If you take every track that is vertically aligned across every surface of each platter, you have a *cylinder*. **Figure 13.1** shows you the relationships between sectors, tracks, and cylinders.

BUZZ WORDS

Platter: One of two or more physical disk structures installed in a typical hard drive.

Cylinder: A virtual structure created by the tracks that line up vertically on the surface of each of the platters.

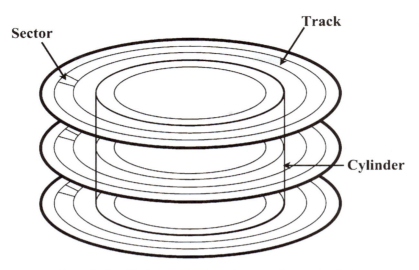

Figure 13.1   A simplified example of sectors, tracks, and cylinders

CHS reads are initialized by a routine in the BIOS known as Int13H. INT stands for interrupt and 13h is simply the hexadecimal for the number 19. Therefore, you could simply call it Interrupt 19, and you would be still correct. The Int13h routine provides for a three-dimensional address space. This space allocates a 10-bit address for tracking cylinders, an 8-bit address for heads, and a 6-bit address for sectors per track. As a result, Int13h supports 1024 cylinders, 256 heads, and 63 sectors per track. All hard drive calls must, in some way, shape, or form, conform to these parameters.

Herein lies the problem. If you do the math, you'll see that Int13h is limited to reading 16,515,072 sectors. Multiply that by 512 for the number of bytes in a sector and you see that Int13h provides support for hard drives up to and including 8GB hard disk drives. That's all, folks.

Now, obviously there are much bigger drives than this. Most computers shipping today have drives in the 40-80GB range. These larger drives are made possible through one of the drive translation methods that I will discuss later in this chapter. *Drive translation* takes disk space beyond what Int13h would typically be able to read and converts those locations into something it does understand. This is made possible by adding the *Int13h extensions* to the BIOS.

So why not just get rid of the Int13h altogether and replace it with something more modern and up to date? The problem there is that it isn't just hardware that addresses this interrupt. Any software that wants to read to the disk, which is any software written in the past twenty-five

> **BUZZ WORDS**
>
> **Drive translation:** A technique by which an address space beyond what Int13h can read is converted into something that it can understand.
>
> **Int13h extensions:** Additional instructions added to the BIOS that intercept hard disk I/O operations and provide the drive translation required by hard disks larger than 8GB.

years or so, also addresses the Int13h call. If Int13h suddenly disappears, none of that software will work. For some reason people get upset when they find the new computer they just bought won't run several thousand dollars' worth of software they've bought over the past few years.

To make sure this didn't happen, engineers simply added the extensions. Hardware and software make their calls to the to Int13h. The extensions intercept these calls and engage whatever drive translation method has been chosen. Newer extensions replace the 24-bit address space of Int13h with a 64-bit space. As a result, drives in the nine and a half trillion-gigabyte range are theoretically possible.

BUZZ WORDS

Zone bit recording: A technology that allows the sectors on the outer tracks of a hard disk to be the same physical size as those toward the center. This allows for far more sectors per track on the outer tracks.

The long and short of it is that, no matter what kind of hard drive you have, it needs to be able to somehow translate all I/O operations into something that the antiquated concept of Int13h can comprehend. When data is requested from the hard drive, the controller will first locate the cylinder that holds the data. Then it will determine which specific track has the data so that the correct R/W head is activated. Once the track is located it will lock on to the first sector that holds the data the system needs.

Early hard drives also were afflicted by the requirement that each track has the same number of sectors, regardless of their position on the platter. The tracks toward the spindle had no fewer sectors than the outermost track. As a result, the tracks toward the outside consisted of wide, sweeping sectors, while the ones toward the inside were all bunched together. Western Digital developed a technology called *zone bit recording* that allowed the sectors to be approximately the same size. The outside tracks could contain a greater number of sectors than those near the spindle. This is illustrated in **Figure 13.2**.

HOW A HARD DRIVE IS CONSTRUCTED

The physical structure of the hard drive makes it one of the most complicated devices in your system. It is an electromechanical device that requires a large number of moving parts and a fair amount of logic circuitry to work. While the platters and read/write heads are the core of the hard drive, there is a lot

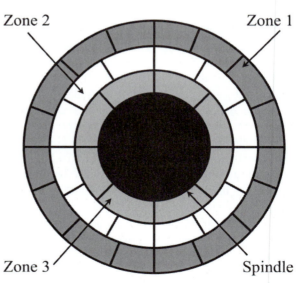

Figure 13.2   Zone bit recording permits much more efficient management of the platter surface. Without this technology, hard drives would be nowhere near the size they are today.

going on that makes them work together. And, as with any other chain, the whole thing falls apart at the weakest link.

DISK PLATTERS

The flat disks onto which data is stored are the platters. These consist of a rigid substrate material coated with some form of magnetic medium. Aluminum is the most common metal used for the substrate, although there are some companies who have taken to using glass. The platters must be very light and very rigid. Also, the surface of a hard disk must be machined to extremely tight tolerances, and aluminum is one of the easiest metals to work with. The magnetic medium has gone through a few changes over the years.

The magnetic medium is what actually holds the information you store on your drive. Zeros and ones are registered simply by the amount of magnetic charge stored by the magnetic particles. In a way, ours is an industry of sand and rust. The first material used was ferrous oxide, or plain old rust. Admittedly it was very refined rust, but when all the fancy terms are put aside, rust it was. Into the ferrous oxide was mixed an adhesive material, and it was applied to the platter using a spin-coating method. While the disk was rapidly spinning on a platter, the medium was applied. What managed to stick in spite of the forces of inertia was an incredibly even and extremely thin layer of the material.

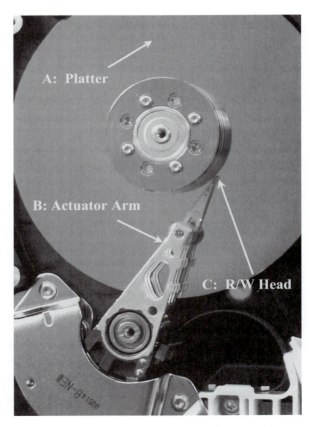

Metal oxides had their problems though. The particles were somewhat large and didn't provide as smooth a surface as might be desirable. Read/write heads had to be positioned farther away in order to prevent impact with particles that might protrude slightly from the surface. The size of the particles meant that there could only be so many per square inch. This limited how much data could be stored on any given platter.

Newer drives, like the one in **Figure 13.3**, use *thin-film metal* media. This allows for greater storage capacities and a thinner surface. A thinner surface allows read/write heads to float closer to the surface. Between the refined media and this closer proximity less magnetic energy is required to magnetize the particle.

Figure 13.3 Thin-film metal platters have a surface as reflective as any mirror.

Thin-film media is also more efficient for the manufacturers. The material is applied to the platter in a process called *vapor deposition*. This process vaporizes the metal in a chamber. The aluminum platter attracts the molecules of the metal vapors until the surface has all it can hold. The end result is the thinnest and most uniform coating that, until recently, technology was able to offer.

Prior to selling its hard drive division to Hitachi, IBM developed a technology using glass platters instead of aluminum. It claims that glass allows for higher information density and tighter head-to-surface tolerances. IBM's designers must be onto something. One of their first releases was a tiny drive that housed 1.7GB of data per square inch.

It wasn't just the substance of the platter they changed. They also came up with a new technology for platter coatings. This new surface promises a surface that is far more uniform and holds up to a hundred times more data per square inch than conventional materials. To do this, they heat a mixture of iron and platinum. When deposited on the platter the mixture forms a nearly perfect matrix of submicroscopic crystals. These crystals are much smaller than the clusters of molecules conventional magnetic media requires to hold a single bit, and each crystal can store a bit.

BUZZ WORDS

Thin-film metal: A metalized magnetic medium applied by evaporating metal and allowing it to "condense" back onto the surface being coated.

Vapor deposition: The process of applying a metal coating by the process of evaporation.

Bit cell: The collection of magnetized particles that comprise a single bit on magnetic media.

READ/WRITE HEADS

Now that you have a surface on which to store your data, you need a way to put that data on and get it back off. For every advance in coating technology, there has to be a corresponding advance in read/write (R/W) heads. Their job is to take bits of information from the computer and convert them into magnetic pulses, which in turn magnetize the surface of the medium. When the computer asks for information to be returned, they have to read the magnetic patterns embedded on the platter and convert that energy into digital information.

The term read/write is actually a misnomer on modern hard drives. In the old days, a single head performed both read and write operations. Those days are long gone. Current drives have one transducer that handles write operations and another that reads data back. They are assembled into a composite assembly that is so small as to look like a single unit to the naked eye.

One of the problems that designers face in the rapidly advancing technologies of hard drives is that, the more data that gets packed onto the drive, the smaller the individual bit cells become. A *bit cell* is the tiny collection of magnetic particles that house a single bit. The size of the bit cell will determine the track width. As tracks become narrower, the R/W heads must focus on a correspondingly smaller target.

Also, as the bit cells become smaller, they form tighter clusters with much less distance between cells. It is rather important that the magnetic energy of one bit cell not interfere with that of its neighbor. To prevent this, modern drives put a substantially weaker charge into each bit cell. An amplifier boosts that signal to a level that the controller can convert into digital signals.

For each surface of a disk platter that stores information, there must be an R/W head. When I get to the section that discusses how data is actually located on a drive I will discuss a situation where an extra head is employed. But for now, I'll stick to the one surface/one head scheme.

A critical issue relating to R/W heads is their floating height. In operation, the head does not actually come in contact with the platter. It floats on a cushion of air just a few nanometers above the surface of the platter. That distance is called the *floating height.* To put this in perspective, if the head were the size of an average two-story house that floated above the ground (and just try getting that to happen!), you wouldn't be able to slip a sheet of paper between the house and the ground.

In fact, in the event that the head and platter should come in contact with one another, this results in the infamous *head crash.* Head crashes are disastrous in that not only is the medium damaged; the head, and therefore the hard drive, will almost certainly be destroyed. There are two things that can cause a head crash. The most common is the irate user kicking a misbehaving computer. The impact of foot against computer while the disk is spinning kills the drive. A more uncommon cause is a piece of foreign material that somehow makes its way into the drive. Modern drives are so well sealed that this is an extremely rare event.

BUZZ WORDS

Floating height: The distance above a hard drive's platter that the R/W heads hover as the platter spins beneath.

Head crash: A disastrous event caused by the R/W head in a drive coming into physical contact with the platter while it is spinning.

Voice coil: An extremely fast and highly accurate motor that works by applying an electrical current to a tightly wrapped coil of wires surrounding, but not touching, a permanently magnetized cylinder. When current is applied to the coil, the cylinder rotates. Negative voltage rotates the cylinder one direction, positive the other. The amount of voltage determines how far the cylinder moves.

ACTUATOR ARMS AND THE ACTUATOR MECHANISM

R/W heads can't move themselves across the platter. They've got to ride on something, and that is the job of the actuator arm. As I've pointed out, each platter has two surfaces, and each surface needs its own R/W head. If you look at **Figure 13.4**, you will see how all the actuator arms are mounted in as a group. All platters are mounted to the same spindle. There is one pair of arms associated with each platter. When the controller needs to locate information on a different track, it directs the actuator arms to move the heads to that track.

In the old days, the same type of stepper motor I described in Chapter Twelve was used to control the actuator arms. Newer hard drives use a *voice coil*

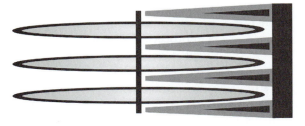

Figure 13.4   The actuator arms are responsible for getting the R/W heads where they need to be.

mechanism. This consists of a magnetic coil that moves the arm in a distance proportionate to how much energy is applied to the coil. It gets its name from the fact that this is the same technology that moves the diaphragm of a loudspeaker in a stereo system. The advantage of a voice coil mechanism is that it is more accurate and has few moving parts. Therefore, not only does it work better, it lasts longer.

A key reason manufacturers made the change from stepper motors to voice coils was because of how much data gets packed onto today's hard drives. I discussed earlier about the sectors on a hard drive being laid out in tracks. How much data can be squeezed onto a drive is directly related to the number of tracks per inch (TPI) the manufacturer can fit onto an individual platter. The first hard drives had only a couple of hundred TPI. Modern drives have now exceeded 28,000 TPI. Accurately positioning an R/W head over tracks that small would be impractical using a stepper motor.

The voice coil has no rigid steps over which it must move. Also, by providing some form of feedback mechanism, if the first attempt to position the head turns out to be inaccurate, a device called the servo dynamically repositions it in just a few milliseconds.

HEAD PARKING

Earlier, I mentioned that the head floats on a microscopically thin layer of air above the spinning platter. I pointed out that if the head should come into contact with the platter, it would cause a head crash.

When you turn your PC off, and the platter stops spinning, that head is going to sit down on the platter no matter what you do. Manufacturers have accordingly created a *head parking* system, designing into the drive platters an area reserved solely for the purpose of providing the head a safe place to sit when the PC is not in operation. This is the *landing zone*. The location of the landing zone is one of the hard disk configuration settings of the BIOS. However, all modern hard drives are designed in such a way that the BIOS can automatically detect the necessary parameters.

In the early days of computer technology, it was up to the user to properly park the heads when the PC was powered down. MS-DOS had a head-parking utility just for that purpose. Fortunately for us, it has been many years since that's been necessary. Hard drives now automatically park themselves as part of their shutdown procedure. This is good, but IBM's approach is better.

It uses a process called load/unload. When a power-down is in process, the heads are lifted into the air. Instead of dropping the heads onto the surface of the platter, IBM drives slide the actuator arms onto a restraining mechanism, which prevents the heads from ever coming into contact with the platter.

> **BUZZ WORDS**
>
> **Head parking:** A process of positioning R/W heads on a hard drive in a place where contact with the platter will do no harm.
>
> **Landing zone:** An area on the hard disk's platter where the R/W heads can be safely parked.

HARD DRIVE PERFORMANCE AND I/O OPERATIONS

Manufacturers provide all kinds of specifications to show you just how fast their drives are and why they are so much better than the competition's. The specifications provided are indeed very valuable bits of information to use when selecting a drive. I will discuss in detail the most commonly advertised specs in detail. A important limitation of hard drive performance that is rarely, if ever, mentioned by hard drive manufacturers is the amount of time required to actually perform an I/O operation from beginning to end. But since I/O operations per second are a direct corollary of the basic specifications, I'll discuss those first.

ROTATIONAL SPEED

The easiest way to improve a hard drive's overall performance is to make it spin faster. In the next two sections I will be discussing the factors of latency and data transfer rate. Both of these are directly affected by how fast the disk is spinning.

Early disks spun at 4800rpm. However, recent technologies have pushed the limit to an amazing 15,000rpm. To put that in perspective, let's go back to the analogy of the R/W head being the size of a two-story house. I also said that if it were that large, the floating height was so minute, you wouldn't be able to fit a sheet of paper between the house and the ground. Now factor this into the equation. At 10,000rpm, the ground is moving beneath the house at a speed the equivalent of approximately 6000 miles per second!

Which brings us to one of the problems design engineers had to face when designing drives this fast. It is critical that the surface be as absolutely smooth as possible. Also, significantly more heat is generated by these drives, both from the more powerful motor and from friction, which needs to be dissipated. This is something that you need to consider when designing a system for yourself or a client. If you wish to use one of these faster drives, efficient cooling of the case isn't just an option. It's an absolute necessity. This is further exacerbated when several of these drives are used together for a drive array.

The impact of rotational speed on performance is rather critical. The faster a disk rotates, the faster the R/W heads can latch onto the first sector of data during a seek operation. Once data begins to be read from the surface of the disk, faster rotational speeds mean that data is moving beneath the heads that much faster. Therefore data transfer rates are improved as well.

AVERAGE ACCESS TIME

Frequently, manufacturers will advertise their average seek time. This is all fine and good, and it's a wonderful thing to know. However, average seek time is only half of the equation that yields average access time. *Average access time* is the time that

BUZZ WORDS

Average access time: The amount of time required by a disk drive to lock on to the first sector that contains data requested by the controller.

Table 13.1 Average latency measurements based on rotational speed

Rotational Speed (rpm)	Rotations/sec	Milliseconds/ rotation	Latency
15,000	250	4ms	2ms
10,000	166.666	6ms	3ms
7,200	120	8.33ms	4.16ms
5,400	90	11.111ms	5.555ms
4,800	80	12.5ms	6.25ms

The impact of rotational speed is seen both in how many tracks per second can be read and in how long it takes to complete a single rotation.

elapses between a request for data and the instant that the first bit in information is picked up by the R/W head. The other half of the equation is the drive's latency.

Average seek time is a guess at how long it will take to move the R/W heads into position to lock onto the correct track. When the manufacturers make these measurements, they are based on moving the heads a distance equal to one third of the diameter of the platter. Obviously, if the actuator arm has to move from the first track to the last, this time will be longer. Conversely, if it is only moving from track one to track five, it will be much shorter. Still, this average provides a good comparison between two competing drives.

> **BUZZ WORDS**
>
> **Average seek time:** The amount of time it takes to locate and lock on to the first track that contains data requested by the controller.
>
> **Latency:** The amount of time that elapses between the instant the R/W heads lock onto the first track that contains information requested by the controller and then lock onto the first sector.

Latency is how long it takes for the R/W heads to lock onto the sector once the track has been located. This specification is calculated by taking rotational speed and calculating how much time one half of a complete rotation will take. Therefore a hard drive with a rotational speed of 10,000rpm will have a published latency of three milliseconds.

Of course, this is an inaccurate assessment of reality. Should the actuator arm lock onto the track a fraction of a rotation before the sector shoots past in its rotational path, it won't have time to lock onto the sector on that rotation. In effect, it would take in excess of a full rotation to actually locate the sector. **Table 13.1** compares rotational speed to latency.

DATA TRANSFER RATE

Once the data has been located and begins to move from the surface of the platter, across the drive electronics, and finally into memory, the concept of data transfer rate (DTR) comes into play. As I mentioned earlier, this is directly affected by the rotational speed of the drive.

Unfortunately for the world of consumers, there are several different methods by which DTR is measured. Most commonly cited is *burst mode*. This is how fast data can move from the R/W head to the drive's buffer in a perfect world when the data is moving downhill with a tail wind. In other words, you're never going to see those speeds. You might see this listed as the *internal host transfer rate* as well. The *external host transfer rate* is a far more critical measurement, because this tells you how fast data gets moved from the controller to RAM.

Transfer rates are provided in megabytes per second (MB/s) ratings. In the next chapter, as I discuss the different interfaces hard drive use, I'll take a closer look at some of these ratings.

> **BUZZ WORDS** ————————
>
> **Burst mode:** The speed at which data moves from the R/W heads to a drive's buffer memory. Also known as internal host transfer rate.
>
> **Internal host transfer rate:** The speed at which data moves from the R/W heads to a drive's buffer memory. Also known as burst mode.
>
> **External host transfer rate:** How fast data moves from a drive's controller to RAM.

HARD DRIVE I/O OPERATIONS

Hard disk I/O operations result in one of the biggest bottlenecks of system performance, simply because of their complexity and how often they occur. When data that does not exist in memory is requested by the CPU, a very convoluted process begins in order to locate that data on the hard drive and transfer it to memory where it can be used. There are actually four steps to a hard drive I/O operation.

- *The Queuing Phase:* This is where all the commands required by the hard disk controller are issued and, when possible, lined up in the correct order for execution.
- *The Command Phase:* The commands are executed in the order in which they exist in the controller's cache memory.
- *The Access Phase:* The R/W heads locate and lock on to the first sector containing the requested data.
- *The Data Transfer Phase:* Data is copied from the surface of the drive, moved to the controller's cache RAM, and then to system RAM.

I/O OPERATIONS/SEC

After reading the previous section, it should be obvious that the number of clock cycles for a single I/O operation can be quite substantial. And remember that transferring even a small file may result in multiple I/O operations. When files get fragmented on the hard disk, they require multiple I/O operations. This is the key reason a badly fragmented disk hurts system performance so badly. **Table 13.2** summarizes I/O operations, providing a crude estimate of how long transferring a single burst of data can actually take.

Table 13.2   Estimating I/O Operations Per Second

I/O Phase	Est. Time (ms)	Est. Time (cc)[1]	Total CC Elapsed
Queuing Phase	30 to 10,000[2]	30,000 to 10,000,000	30,000 to 10,000,000
Command Phase	.001 to .003	1 to 3	30,001 to 10,000,003
Access Phase[3]	14.2ms	14,200	44,201 to 10,014,203

Hard Drive I/O operations of a typical 7200rpm hard drive

[1] CC = clock cycles: based on a 100MHz front-side bus
[2] Time required for the queuing phase is dependant on the number of commands required to perform a specific I/O request.
[3] Access phase is one of the few delays you'll see published in the manufacturer's specs. This shows up as average access time.

DATA ENCODING MECHANISMS

The data that is stored on your hard drive isn't really data at all. You can't put a hard drive platter under a microscope and read off the zeros and ones stored there. The information is encoded into patterns of magnetically charged particles. The controller coverts a digital signal into electronic pulses which, in turn, magnetize the metal or metal-oxide particles on the platter. When the heads read data back, it is their task to interpret the pattern of charged particles and convert the magnetic fluxes into an electrical signal the controller can turn back into data. This is all part of the *data encoding mechanism*. All devices need some encoding mechanism.

Binary data moves across the bus as positive and negative electrical charges. Moving from a positive to a negative state is known as a *flux reversal*. The hard drive has a chip on board known as the encoder-decoder (ENDEC) that has the job of taking these digital waveforms and converting them into electrical signals that get sent to the R/W heads. The heads apply the magnetic charges to the media surface. A single bit of data requires tens of thousands of molecules of media to create one of the bit cells discussed earlier

One of the limiting factors that determine the maximum capacity of a hard drive is how many times it is possible to change the magnetic polarity of individual particles in a square inch of drive surface. If the polarity changes overlap, they will impact on one another. Try this little experiment. Take two magnets and some iron filings. Sprinkle the iron filings onto a sheet of paper and put one of the magnets underneath the paper and watch the pattern that the filings assume. I'm sure you did this in grade school at some time or the other. Now take the other magnet and place it alongside the first magnet under the paper. Watch what happens to the

BUZZ WORDS

Data encoding mechanism: The method used by a device to convert digital information into an electronic format recognizable by the target device.

Flux reversal: A transition of magnetic charge from a positive to a negative state, or vice versa.

filings. Rotate one of the magnets 180 degrees and see how this affects your little patterns. The closer you move the magnets to one another, the greater the confusion.

This is pretty close to what is going on when the R/W heads apply flux reversals to the media surface, except on a submicroscopic level. If the charged particles are too close to one another, the integrity of your data can be affected.

Another thing that can impact data integrity is the synchronization between the read heads and the write heads. In order to make sure that data is read back in exactly the same way as it was recorded, an accurate timing mechanism must be employed to assure synchronization. Then all read and write heads on the drive march to that same beat.

As data is written to the drive, it goes down in a series of electrical pulses that create transition cells. A *transition cell* is the minimum number of particles that can be affected by a single magnetic flux. Now if all data alternated evenly between zeros (-) and ones (+), then on playback, the data would look like -+-+-+-+ and there would be no issues. However, that would be like having a dictionary that read ABABABABABABAB from beginning to end. It wouldn't be interesting, informative, or accurate. In other words, it would be useless.

Real data will have varying numbers of zeros and ones clumped together. Therefore, the R/W head will encounter varying amounts of time in which is sees nothing but negative polarity, followed by equally varying amounts of time in which it sees nothing but positive polarity. Without a clocking mechanism in place it would appear to the controller as a -+-+-+ pattern, except that individual bits would take up widely varying amounts of hard drive space.

The clock ticks off read/write intervals. If eight zeros in a row come down the pipe, the clock counts off eight transition cells for the write head to mark down. When the read head comes along to read that data back, the clock will tick though the transition cells, and the read head will find eight zeros. It is critical that clock mechanisms be incredibly accurate. If, for any reason, the read heads were out of synch with the write heads, the results would be disastrous. **Figure 13.5** shows you what would happen. The arrows represent individual ticks of the clock. The square waves in the top half of the diagram represent positive and negative magnetic pulses. Since this is an analog electrical event, a timing mechanism needs to be in place to assure that consecutive identical bits are properly read. In order to have the system accurately interpret the magnetized surface as encoded data, read and write operations must be synchronized. If the clock ticks off four cycles while applying a negative pulse (rendering four zeros), and on the read cycle, it ticks off five cycles (rendering five zeros) all the data from that point forward will be corrupt.

The encoding mechanism determines how binary data is converted into charged particles, and then when read back, how the charged particles tell the controller to create a binary signal. The two encoding mechanisms used over the years have been modified frequency modulation (MFM) and run length limited (RLL).

MFM

MFM was one of the first methods of data encoding used in hard disk drives. An earlier method of simple frequency modulation continues to be used on floppy drives, but has never been used

BUZZ WORDS

Transition cell: The minimum number of particles that can be affected by a single magnetic flux.

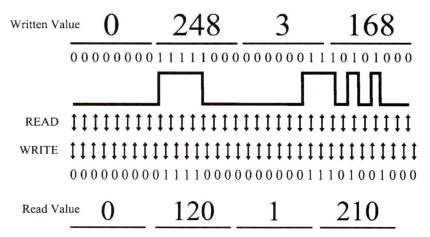

Figure 13.5 Were is possible for the read and write heads to get out of synch with one another, the results would be disastrous.

on hard drives. Using simple frequency modulation, each bit of data stored on the drive is generated by an individual flux reversal. A graphics image that sent 5000 ones in a row would send across 5000 flux reversals. For each bit, a separate clock transition would be recorded along with the bit of data.

MFM minimized the usage of clock transitions by only requiring one when a zero was preceded by another zero. That reduced the amount of physical space on the platter that was being used by timing information, and made more room available for data. Since less timing data was being generated, the clock frequency could be doubled. In other words, twice as many bits of data could be stored to surface medium per flux transition.

Many books on the subject include MFM as a form of interface. This is not entirely inaccurate, nor is it entirely accurate. MFM is an encoding mechanism, not an interface. However, it requires its own separate interface. The controller that reads and writes data based on MFM encoding will work with no other device. Therefore, the MFM controller could effectively be considered to be the MFM interface.

RLL

RLL encoding is a far more efficient means of encoding large amounts of data. Because of this, it is the method used by virtually all hard drives manufactured over the course of about twenty years. Instead of encoding and decoding data a bit at a time, it takes a cluster of data and encodes it all at once. A single flux transition can write a large block of data.

Two parameters are used to define RLL sequences. Those are run length and run limit. A run is simply the number of clock cycles (of the hard drive's controller) that data can be written to the drive without a flux reversal. The run limit represents the maximum number of bits the controller would allow to be written in a single flux without embedding a clock signal. The run length is the actual number of bits written.

Since data is moved in blocks, rather than a bit at a time, the timing that I discussed earlier is easier to maintain. Also, since there are significantly fewer clock transitions that needed to be recorded, much greater data densities were made possible. All else being equal, an RLL drive can hold twice as much data as an MFM drive using exactly the same medium.

PRML AND EPRML

Even RLL imposed some severe limitations on the amount of data that could be stored on the hard drive. Recent disk drives have been manufactured using an encoding mechanism called partial response/maximum likelihood (PRML). PRML doesn't try to read every single flux reversal that occurs. Instead, it uses a very sophisticated digital sampling algorithm. The electrical signal that is generated by the reading of magnetic impulses on the surface of the drive is scanned and samples of that signal are taken at precisely timed intervals. This is the "partial response" half of the equation. The controller then calculates the most likely sequence of bits that would occur as a result of those samples. That is the "maximum likelihood."

Doesn't sound very accurate, does it? The fact is, bit errors from this method are only one in every several trillion bits read. And because PRML permits up to thirty-five percent more storage capacity per platter (or *areal density*, as it's called) without changing the formulation of the medium, it is a logical choice for high-capacity drives.

Extended PRML (EPRML) works in exactly the same manner. However, improvements in the algorithms used and in the circuitry employed allow for faster write operations as well as faster reads. In addition it substantially increases areal density over that of PRML. This has been the method used for the last couple of generations of hard drives.

FILE SYSTEMS

Now that I've discussed the basics of how information is stored on a magnetic disk, it is time to take a look at how the computer manages how it's stored. The writing of data is complex enough, but before the drive can read that data back later on down the road, there needs to be some way of locating that information. This is the function of the file system.

The *file system* is a direct function of the operating system. As such, the OS a user chooses affects many different functions of the computer system. Many of the functions impacted are under the control of the file system. For example, these days, most people take it for granted that they can name a file My Business Proposal.doc and every computer of every user who will access that document can read it. Most people don't even realize that prior to 1995, most operating systems would have returned a message along the lines of "invalid file name" if a user attempted to use such a name.

> **BUZZ WORDS**
>
> **Areal density:** The total amount of storage capacity for a specific unit of area on the surface of the drive platter.
>
> **File system:** The mechanism used by a hard drive to map the specific sectors used by any given file.

OS VERSUS FS

Most operating systems these days support multiple file systems. A problem that is occasionally encountered is that a file system supported by one OS may or may not be supported by another OS. Over a network, this isn't a problem. But it is something that must be considered if you are attempting to configure a computer to dual-boot. Dual-booting consists of installing two or more different operating systems and allowing the user to select which OS to use when he or she starts the machine.

For the most part, a discussion of file systems is more appropriate in a book on operating systems. I consider this to be an area of understanding that is critical to the hardware technician, though, and therefore am including it in this book. The file systems I will discuss in depth will be the File Allocation Table (FAT) system and New Technology File System (NTFS). Another file system not frequently seen today is High Performance File System (HPFS). Even though not as common, it is worth taking a brief look. Your CD-ROM drive uses its own file system known as Compact Disk File System (CDFS), which I will take a closer look at in Chapter Seventeen, Multimedia. Users of Linux and Unix make use of the Unix File System, which is completely incompatible with any of the FAT-based systems.

FAT

File Allocation Table, or FAT as I'll call it from here, was the original file system used by the first IBM-compatible PCs. It works by creating a database of entries that the operating system uses to find data on the hard drive. In fact, two different copies of that database are maintained. If you read some of the articles out of the popular press, you might think that there are only two versions of FAT: FAT16 and FAT32. You would, of course, be wrong. The first version of FAT was FAT12. The numbers represented in these different versions of FAT indicate how many bits are allocated to the binary number that identified individual clusters. In other words, FAT12 uses a 12-bit number, FAT16 makes use of a 16-bit number, and not surprisingly, FAT32 allows for a 32-bit number. Obviously, the more bits used to create the number, the more numbers the file system can generate. It also dictates cluster sizes and the maximum size of volume that was possible using a particular system. **Table 13.3** lists the various versions of FAT and how they differed.

FAT12 FAT12 has lived a long and healthy life as a file system. It continues to be used on floppy disks and on very small partitions. Both FAT16 and FAT32 have no trouble reading and writing to FAT12 partitions.

FAT16 FAT16, for the longest time, was the file system of choice for nearly every computer in use. It allowed for partitions of up to 2GB, which at the time was considered to be unthinkably large. Four different primary partitions could be maintained on a single physical drive, allowing the user to create multiple logical drives or to install more than one OS on a single machine. If you were to open the FAT with a disk-editing tool (and I highly recommend you **not** do this unless you are either extremely capable, extremely careful not to edit anything, or have a strong desire to reformat your hard drive), you would see a list of every cluster on your

Table 13.3 Comparison of FAT Systems

File System	Size of FAT Entry	Range of Cluster Sizes	Max Clusters	Max Volume Size
FAT12	12 bits	.5K to 4K	4,086	16,736,256 bytes
FAT16	16 bits	2K to 32K	65,526	2,147,123,200 bytes
FAT32	28 bits[1]	4KB to 32KB	268,435,456	~2 terabytes[2]

The differences among the versions of FAT are clear.

[1] While the actual entry for FAT32 is 32 bits, 4 bits are reserved for OS use and not used for generating cluster numbers.
[2] Roughly 2 terabytes is the theoretical limit to volume size in FAT32. However, limitations in the file allocation tables prevent drives from reaching this size under current technology.

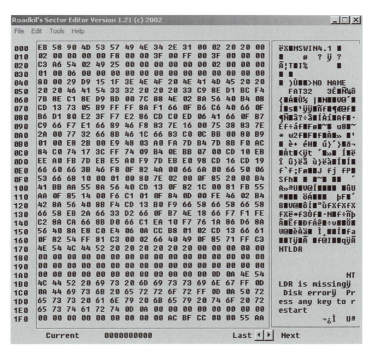

Figure 13.6 A disk editor is a tool that allows an experienced user to modify the contents of a drive, including areas normally not accessible by the user.

hard drive, like the one shown in **Figure 13.6**. Of course, it wouldn't look much like a list to you, since it would consist of a bunch of binary code all run together. But each entry would contain certain information that allows the OS to find every cluster that hold data for that file. This information includes the following:

- A designation whether the cluster is in use or not
- A point to the next cluster that contains data owned by that particular file
- A marker preventing it from being used if it has been marked bad

FAT16 is limited to a total of 512 entries in the root directory. This is due to a physical limitation of FAT16. The root directory has to start in the first sector immediately following the file allocation tables. Therefore, in order to make certain that the drive is efficiently used, the concept of directories was brought into play. As far as FAT is concerned, a directory is just another file. To allow the OS to distinguish between files and directories, FAT places a special marker in each directory. Directory entries contain information that directs the OS to the files or subdirectories that reside within it.

- 11 bytes identifying the name of the file or directory
- 8 bits defining the attributes of the file or directory
- 24 bits identifying the time the file was created
- 16 bits identifying the date the file was created
- 16 bits showing the last date on which the file was accessed
- 16 bits showing the time the file was last modified
- 16 bits showing the date the file was last modified
- 16 bits indicating the first cluster number occupied by the entry
- 32 bits indicating the size of the entry

I pointed out earlier that the hard drive's most basic element of storage is the sector. I also told you that hard drives no longer read single sectors, but rather file allocation units (FAUs) or clusters. FAT16 is not terribly efficient in its use of clusters. The larger the partition, the greater the number of sectors required to make a cluster. This is, of course, true of all file systems. It is simply more noticeable with FAT16.

The *cluster* is the smallest element into which the hard drive can actually store a file. As you can see in Table 13.4, the smallest cluster used by FAT16 is 2K. What that means is that no matter how small a file might be, it will occupy a minimum of 2K of hard drive space. An example of this is the Windows icon. Those little pictures you see floating on your desktop are frequently less than 800 bytes. However, since they are individual files, each one of them eats up an entire 2K cluster. And the larger the partition, the more sectors, and therefore the more hard drive space you will need for individual files.

Table 13.4 details the cluster sizes used by FAT16 with the different partition sizes it supports.

As you can see, when you start to get up into those larger partitions (as far as FAT16 is concerned, anyway), those clusters start to get really big. Let me give you an example of how this can impact your system.

BUZZ WORDS

Cluster: The minimum number of sectors a specific file system can recognize as a single data unit. Another term for file allocation unit (FAU).

Table 13.4   FAT16 File Allocation Unit Size by Partition Size

Partition Size	FAT Type	Cluster Size
16MB to 128MB	12-bit	4 Sectors (Appx. 2K)
128MB to 256MB	16-bit	8 Sectors (Appx. 4K)
256K to 512K	16-bit	16 Sectors (Appx. 8K)
512K to 1GB	16-bit	32 Sectors (Appx. 16K)
1GB to 2GB	16-bit	64 Sectors (Appx. 32K)

Partition sizes and cluster sizes for FAT16

There is a CD I've seen in some of the discount bins that has 10,000 different Windows icons. As I mentioned before, a Windows icon is a very small file, as little as 800 bytes. Now what would happen if you had a 2GB hard drive partitioned to FAT16? As you see in Table 13.4, that 2GB partition is going to use clusters of 64 sectors, or 32K. That means that each and every one of those icons is going to take up 32K of space when you copy it to your hard drive, because each of them constitutes an individual file. One file equals one cluster. That's the rule.

Now if you look at the description of the files without knowing how FAT works, here is what you might think. There are 10,000 files of 800 bytes each. 10,000 × 800 = 8,000,000. Therefore, it's only going to require 8MB of hard drive space to store all of those files, right? As you can guess, it's not going to work that way. Since each cluster is 32K, it doesn't matter how small the file is. It needs its own cluster. Copying 10,000 icon files to the hard drive will require approximately 320MB of space.

FAT16 is also limited in the way it handles file names. It uses what is called the 8.3 file naming convention. This means that the file name can have eight characters, followed by a three-character extension. The extension is frequently used by applications to identify what kind of file it is. For example, a file with a .doc extension is a document file. Word processing programs know they can open this kind of file. Files that end in .txt are ASCII text files (usually). Programmers might create their own extensions for the particular data file created by their program. Microsoft's Excel uses an .xls extension. The file name itself can be anything you want it to be, as long as it is only eight characters long.

FAT32   The master boot record (MBR) that I will discuss in detail later in this chapter was expanded from a single sector to two sectors in FAT32. This allows for extended BIOS information to be stored in this section.

FAT32 supports long file names (LFN) as well. Instead of being limited to eight-character file names, the file name (including extension) can be up to 254 characters long. LFN will be discussed in detail in the next section.

As with FAT16, FAT32 uses different sized clusters as partition sizes increased. However, the 32-bit structure of the file system allows for much larger partitions to be created

Table 13.5 FAT32 File Allocation Unit Size by Partition Size

Partition Size	FAT Type	Cluster Size
<512MB-8GB	8 sectors	4K
8-16GB	16 sectors	8K
16-32GB	32 sectors	16K
32-2048GB	64 sectors	32K

FAT32 makes far more efficient use of hard drive space than previous file systems.

with each level of cluster. **Table 13.5** shows the effect of partition size on cluster size when using FAT32.

As you can see, FAT32 makes much more efficient use of hard drive space than does FAT16. If you want to store those 10,000 icons using FAT32, and your partition is 8GB or smaller, you will only eat up about 40MB of space.

NTFS

Users of Microsoft's Windows NT 4.0 or 2000 operating systems have the option of using the New Technology File System (NTFS). This is one of the more powerful file systems available today. There are some compatibility issues that you should be aware of. A FAT32 system cannot read NTFS files stored in the same system. Likewise, NTFS version 4.0 can't read FAT32 files. Version 5.0 can. As of this writing, there is an installable file system for Linux users that supports read-only capabilities for NTFS, but by the time you're reading this, that has probably been improved.

NTFS isn't simply a list of entries. It acts as a relational database of information and can provide far more than simply the location at which the data is stored. It allows for incredibly large volumes. It also allows for security to be imposed on specific files. This allows the operating system and those with permissions to administer the OS to allow or disallow access to files to specific users on an individual basis. In addition, it can generate a message log indicating successes and failures of accessing those files.

One unique talent possessed by NTFS is the ability to compress and decompress individual files on the fly (**Figure 13.7**). Compression allows the file to occupy far less hard drive space in storage than when in use. With some earlier compression techniques, there was always a danger of data corruption. Fortunately, with NTFS, compression and decompression don't carry that risk.

As far back as MS-DOS, computers had the ability to compress the contents of a hard drive and then have the OS decompress the files as they were used. This, however, was an all-or-none undertaking. You either compressed the whole drive, or nothing at all.

With NTFS, you can compress individual files or directories on an as-needed basis. Files that are only infrequently used can be compressed for storage. Some types of files, especially graphics and audio files, are well suited for compression. A typical graphics file can be squeezed down to a fraction of its original size.

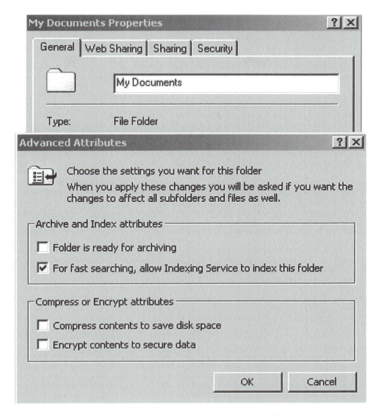

Figure 13.7   NTFS allows the user to individually compress or encrypt files on the fly.

NTFS is also capable of using much smaller cluster sizes than FAT systems. Small NTFS partitions can read individual sectors. Yet, like FAT32, NTFS is capable of very large partitions and long file names. **Table 13.6** shows relative partition information for NTFS.

The versions of NTFS used with NT 4.0 and Windows 2000 are not the same. Windows 2000 uses a newer version. NTFS version 5.0 adds a few new bells and whistles that version 4 didn't support. It can handle the same functions as version 4, including individual file and folder security settings and compression. But in addition, it can also allow an administrator to set drive usage limits for individual users.

The newer version of NTFS also supports the Encryptable File System (EFS). The user is able to take files and render them unreadable to anyone who doesn't possess the decryption key. In order the make sure that hostile departing employees don't encrypt the entire system before they move over to your competitors, Microsoft requires that there be an assigned EFS Recovery Agent delegated, or the process does not work. An EFS Recovery Agent has the necessary permissions to import and export encryption keys, so that the data can be recovered even if the employee is unable or unwilling to do it for you.

Table 13.6   NTFS File Allocation Unit Size by Partition Size

Partition Size	Number of Sectors/Cluster	Cluster Size
0–260MB	1 sector	512 bytes
261MB–8GB	8 sectors	4K
8–16GB	16 sectors	8K
16–32GB	32 sectors	16K
32–2048GB	64 sectors	32K

NTFS is very similar to FAT32 in terms of disk space usage, except for the fact that very small partitions can recognize a single sector as an FAU.

This new NTFS also has something called the Distributed File System (DFS) built into it. This actually isn't new to NTFS 5.0. It was available to NTFS 4.0 as an installable file system add-on. With 5.0, however, it's integrated into the file system. DFS allows an administrator to build up a collection of links to various resources, wherever they might happen to reside on the network, and locate them all in a singular server. Users can then browse to those links without having to know the location of the actual files. DFS finds the files for them.

HPFS

IBM and Microsoft actually worked together to design the High Performance File System for the OS/2 operating system. At the time this file system was released, the two companies were working together to co-develop an operating system that could compete with the Macintosh graphical interface. They were looking for a file system that was a little more user-friendly than FAT16, and might provide a little more horsepower.

It was the first of the PC-compatible file systems to support long file names. It also allowed for non-case-sensitive file names. If you named a file My Novel.doc, it would actually find your file even if you looked for my NoveL.doc. This was an improvement over HPFS's primary competitor, the Unix File System, which is case sensitive. It was pretty much everything that NTFS would eventually become (not surprising, since Microsoft co-developed it), but had a few minor issues.

It was incompatible with FAT. Installed onto a dual-boot system with OS/2, an MS-DOS or Windows system could not read the files from the HPFS. HPFS could read FAT, but not the other way around. A bigger problem with versions of MS-DOS prior to 4.01 was that MS-DOS couldn't see even FAT drives that existed downstream from an HPFS drive. For example, if you installed DOS onto drive C, and then OS/2 onto drive D using HPFS, drives E, F, and later couldn't be seen by MS-DOS, no matter what file system they used.

With MS-DOS 4.01 and later, you could see the FAT drives, but there was an additional problem. Since DOS couldn't see the HPFS drive, it effectively didn't exist. Therefore, in the system described above, under HPFS, drive C was MS-DOS, drive D was OS/2, and drives E, F, and later were whatever they happened to be. That same machine, booted to MS-DOS saw drive C, ignored the HPFS drive, and made the next drive it could see drive D. If drive E happened to be HPFS, then the next drive MS-DOS could see would be drive D. To HPFS, that same drive would be drive F. This played havoc on organization.

How did this affect your floppy drives? Not much, actually. By default, HPFS doesn't support removable media. Nobody has ever really considered the floppy disk drive to be a high performance device. Therefore only FAT12 is used with floppy drives. All other file systems can read it.

THE UNIX FILE SYSTEM

If you are reading this book specifically for the purpose of preparing for the A+ Core Exam, it is unlikely that you will get any questions relating to this file system. Still, there are a lot of computers out there in the real world that make use of the Unix operating system, and unless you know the basics of the file system used you're going to flounder like a duck on an oil slick.

The Unix File System (UFS) uses a tree structure for sorting directories, subdirectories, and individual files. In fact, I think it's safe to say that other OSs emulated Unix in this manner. With Unix, the root directory is represented by a single /. Beneath the root are several subdirectories. The most common subdirectories seen on a Unix system are as follows:

- ■ */bin:* Commands and directories needed by the user
- ■ */dev:* Files used to represent specific devices, either installed on the system or remotely connected
- ■ */etc:* Commands and utilities used for system administration
- ■ */lib:* Libraries used by various programs or programming languages
- ■ */tmp:* Temporary files
- ■ */usr:* Subdivided into subdirectories; includes the games that ship with Unix and the home directory for each user created on the system
- ■ */Kernel File:* Home of the Unix operating system files

UFS breaks the hard drive down into *blocks.* Depending on the version of Unix being used, blocks will consist of one, two, or four sectors. Data is stored in the blocks.

The file system can be broken down into four distinct components: the boot block, the Super block, the i-node list, and the data blocks. The boot block contains the information needed to initialize the operating system from a cold start. The Super block defines the state of the file system. This would include such information as how many files are already stored, how much available space remains on the device, and permissions associated with the device. The i-node list, usually simply referred to as the i-list, keeps track

BUZZ WORDS ————

Block: The number of sectors on a hard drive that UFS uses as the smallest recognizable data unit.

of the locations of individual files stored on the device. And, as you might imagine, the data blocks are where the data is actually stored.

By default Unix is a network operating system. As such, it must support the ability to service multiple users at once. One of the methods it uses to accomplish this is to assign users their own home directories in the /usr directory. When a user logs onto the system, he or she is automatically directed to the home directory. Unix uses a different method of accessing files than the file systems I discussed earlier in the chapter. Instead of a file system table that maps out specific FAUs on the hard drive, Unix provides a unique file system for each user. The OS opens a separate instance of a root file system for each new user who logs on.

BUZZ WORDS ————————

Pointer: A line of code used by UFS to map a cluster used by a specific file.

The i-list keeps track of the file systems that are mounted at any given time. The i-list is nothing more than a fixed memory location that contains a list of entries for each file system mounted. For each file system an i-node is generated. It is the i-node that contains the information used by UFS to locate files on the physical storage device. Each i-node can contain up to ten pointers. A *pointer* is a line of code that maps to a specific block. Each i-node can also contain one indirect pointer, one double-indirect pointer, and one triple-indirect pointer. An indirect pointer maps points to a cluster of pointers.

The ten pointers of an i-node can basically define a 5KB file. For a file larger than 5KB, an indirect pointer maps to a storage block that stores a table of additional block pointers. If an earlier version of Unix is installed, a block points to a single sector of 512 bytes. A pointer uses 4 bytes. Therefore, a table could contain 128 pointers. A 1024-byte block could contain 256 pointers and a 2048-byte block could contain 512. For the purposes of this discussion, I will stick to the 512-byte block. An indirect pointer adds 128 pointers per block, which would allow the system to manage a 64KB file.

Once file size exceeds 64KB a double-indirect pointer will be employed. A double-indirect pointer maintains a table of locations to up to 128 indirect pointers. Since an indirect pointer can map up to 64KB of storage space, a double-indirect pointer would map up to 128×64KB, or 8MB.

For files larger than 8MB, the system needs to make use of the services of the triple-indirect pointer. The triple-indirect pointer maps to 128 double-indirect pointers. This allows the UFS to support files up to a gigabyte in size.

As I mentioned earlier, the more recent versions of Unix make use of 2KB blocks. This means each block can contain up to 512 pointers. As a result, UFS can theoretically support up to 64GB files. However, a field contained in the i-node that defines file size is only 4 bytes long. This imposes a 4GB limitation on file size.

Other information stored in each i-node includes the following:

- *File owner ID:* A number generated by the OS that is used by the security file to identify the specific user on the system who created the file.
- *Group ID:* This identifies a group of users that can be granted specific levels of access by the owner.

■ *File type:* Files can be listed as any one of several file types. Among these are:

  ■ Regular file: a conventional data file

  ■ D file (directory file): a file that contains file names and their associated i-node numbers

  ■ L file (symbolic link file): a file that contains the path information needed to access a file

  ■ C file (character special file): a file that is intended to be accessed one character at a time. The file associated to your keyboard would be an example of a character file.

  ■ B file (block special file): a file that is accessed a block at a time. The file associated to your monitor is an example of a block special file.

  ■ P file (pipe file): A file associated to a device that streams data into a system, such as a modem or network card. This type of file is usually required by any device that needs to buffer data.

■ *File access permissions:* There are three sets of permissions. User access is automatically granted to the person that owns the file. This is generally the creator, unless someone with administrative privileges has taken ownership. Group access is restricted access granted to any member of a specified group. Other access consists of whatever level of access has been granted to anyone not recognized by user or group access lists. Permissions come in three types as well. Read access allows a user to inspect the data stored in the file, but that user can make no changes or delete the file. Write access allows the user to make changes to the file. Execute access allows the user to run any executable code contained within the file.

An i-node can also keep track of various access times, including the following:

■ *File access time:* This indicates when the file data last opened by the system. Events that will change this value include the following:

  ■ Displaying the contents of the file

  ■ Copying the file to a new location or file system

  ■ Editing the file

  These events will **not** change this value:

  ■ Moving the file to another directory in the current file system

  ■ Using redirection to append data to an existing file

■ *File modification time:* This indicates when data contained within the file was last changed. Events that will affect this value include the following:

  ■ Creating the file initializes the value.

  ■ Editing a file and saving it will update this value.

  ■ Overwriting the file with new data will update this value.

  ■ Appending data to an existing file will update this value.

- *I-node modification time:* This value shows when information in the i-node was last changed. Events that alter this value include the following:
  - Creating additional hard links to the file
  - Changes in file size

THE MASTER BOOT RECORD

In Chapter Six, Motherboards, BIOS, and the Chipset, I discussed in some detail the process of POST. I noted that the bootstrap loader locates and runs the Master Boot Record (MBR). The exact content of the MBR varies among operating systems, but the functionality remains the same. For the purposes of this discussion, I will use the FAT16 MBR used by MS-DOS.

In DOS, the MBR consisted of a single sector that held all of the information I will discuss throughout the rest of this section. This sector is located at Cylinder 0, Head 0, Sector 1 of the hard drive. In FAT16, that was the only place the MBR could be located. On the outset, this may seem to contradict what I said earlier about the hard drive reading clusters rather than sectors. Keep in mind, however, that this early in the boot process the file system has yet to be defined. In fact, it is this MBR that defines the file system. System BIOS reads sectors. Therefore, programmers had to fit all that information onto a single sector. One of the advances of different 32-bit file systems was that they could extend the MBR to two sectors, rather than just one.

The information stored on the MBR (see **Table 13.7**) tells the system several things. It defines the file system to be used. This is a string of executable code that once run, remains resident in memory. This code tells the computer which file system you chose when you first prepared your hard drive. This code is added to the MBR during the FDISK process in MS-DOS and Windows or by similar third-party utilities.

Table 13.7 Contents of the MBR

Process	Size of Process	Location on Drive
Boot Code (Defines file system and boots computer)	446 bytes	000h
First Partition Table	16 bytes	1BEh
Second Partition Table	16 bytes	1CEh
Third Partition Table	16 bytes	1DEh
Fourth Partition Table	16 bytes	1EEh
Executable Marker	2 bytes	1FEh

The MBR contains several specific pieces of information that the system requires in order to boot.

Next come the partition tables. If desired, a user can subdivide the available space on a disk into multiple logical sections called *partitions*. To the user, each partition appears as a separate hard disk, or *logical drive*.

Partition tables contain 16-byte blocks of data for each partition that exists on the hard drive. 16 bytes doesn't sound like a lot, but as you can see in **Table 13.8**, it manages to do a lot. A FAT16-formatted drive could contain up to four partition entries. The first would be the primary partition for that drive while the subsequent partitions will be extended partitions. There could be additional logical drive entries because each of the extended partitions contains an entry similar to the MBR called the volume boot record (VBR). The VBR is not limited to one sector and therefore can define as many logical drives as the user chooses to configure.

Following the partition tables is a marker that indicates the location of the first lines of executable code for the operating system. This is the *executable marker*, and it is only a 2-byte entry in MS-DOS.

BUZZ WORDS

Partition: Logical sections on a hard disk that divide the overall disk space into multiple logical drives.

Logical drive: A section of disk space isolated from the rest of the same physical disk so that it appears to the user as a separate disk drive.

Executable marker: A pointer in the MBR that directs the boot sequence to the first line of code for the primary kernel file of the OS installed.

Table 13.8 Contents of a Partition Table (First Primary Partition)

Process	Size of Process	Location on Drive
Partition State (active/inactive)	1 byte	00h
Begin Partition (which head)	1 byte	01h
Begin Partition (cylinder/sector)	2 bytes	02h
Partition Type	1 byte	04h
End Partition (which head)	1 byte	05h
End Partition (cylinder/sector)	2 bytes	06h
Sectors between MBR and Partition	4 bytes	08h
Number of Sectors in Partition	4 bytes	0Ch

Relative location of data for 2nd, 3rd, and 4th partitions is offset by 16 bytes from these positions.

The reason boot sector viruses are so dangerous is that, as you can see from this table, changing just a single bit of data can make it impossible for the hard disk controller to accurately locate a partition.

FILE ALLOCATION TABLES

Once the file system has been loaded, the drive will now be read in clusters rather than individual sectors. The FAT occupies the sectors of the hard drive directly following the MBR. FAT16 generated two different copies of the tables, while FAT32 generates four. The purpose of the FAT is to identify the locations of all clusters that contain data for a specific file. Every single cluster on the drive is assigned a FAT entry, whether it initially contains data or not.

Each FAT entry will consist of a 16-bit entry (hence the name FAT16) that defines the usage of that particular cluster. That entry will have certain information telling the system whether or not there is data in the cluster, if the cluster has been marked bad, and if another cluster elsewhere also holds data relevant to that file. If so, the directory table will point the direction to the next cluster for that file. **Table 13.9** details the possible entries that would describe a cluster.

The directory tables and the file allocation tables are not the same thing. The *directory table* maintains a list of file names and all of the information associated with those files that lets the operating system know how to deal with them. Each file name takes up eight bits, the extension another three bits. *Directory attribute* information is stored in a single bit and will include such information as whether the file is hidden, or read only, whether it has been archived or not, and whether it constitutes a system file or not. A subdirectory is treated as if it is a file by the directory tables, except that it is assigned a directory attribute.

In addition to attribute information, the directory tables store information that tells the system the time and date that the file was created, what cluster to go to, and finally, the overall size of the file. This last bit of information sends the disk controller back to FAT to look up

BUZZ WORDS

Directory table: A database of all file names on a hard drive and the partitions with which they are associated. Other information pertaining to file system security is also contained here.

Directory attribute: A single bit that identifies an entry in the directory table as being a subdirectory rather than a file.

Table 13.9 Defining Clusters

FAT Entry (range)	Definition
0000h	Cluster is empty.
0002h-FFEFh	Cluster is used; points to next cluster in file.
FFF0h-FFF6h	Cluster is reserved.
FFF7h	Cluster is marked "bad."
FFF8h-FFFFh	Cluster is used and is the last cluster in file. This is the End of File Marker.

The entries in the FAT have specific functions.

the next cluster in that file, if the End of File (EOF) marker has not been reached. The original FAT16 file system provided for a 32-bit entry for each file or directory, yet only made use of 22 bytes. The layout of a typical directory entry is detailed in **Table 13.10**.

When manufacturers made the move to FAT32, they opened up the possibility of those long file names I discussed earlier. The file allocation tables not only have to deal with much longer file names, but also create an 8.3 file name compatible with older applications. With FAT32, those 8.3 entries were redesigned to make use of all 32 bits available to the entry. This allowed the directory table to provide additional information, including far more refined time and date information, as well as the ability to tell when the file was last accessed and not simply when it was created.

Table 13.10   FAT16 Directory Table Entries

Table Entry Value	Size of Entry
File Name	8 bytes
File Extension	3 bytes
File Attribute	1 byte
Time	2 bytes
Date	2 bytes
Cluster Location	2 bytes
File Size	4 bytes

A listing of the functions in a file table entry for FAT16

CHAPTER SUMMARY

This chapter introduced you to the technology behind hard drives. As with most of the chapters of this book, I provided far more detail than is required simply to pass the A+ Exam. I discussed how hard drives are made and covered some of the key components of the hard drive. I also introduced you to some of the different file systems that have been used, past and present.

As hard drives evolve, so must file systems, system BIOS, and the operating systems. As you will see in the next chapter, hard drives haven't always been the humongous high-speed devices you enjoy today.

BRAIN DRAIN

1. Describe how CHS defines the capacity of a hard drive.

2. List as many critical components of a hard drive as you can think of and describe their function.

3. Describe how data is stored to a hard disk and then subsequently read back.

4. Describe the MBR of FAT16.

5. In as much detail as you can, define how the FAT works.

THE 64K$ QUESTIONS

1. The physical surface on which data is stored on a hard drive is known as a _____.

   a. Spindle

b. Cylinder

c. Disk

d. Platter

2. Int13h limits the maximum capacity that a computer can recognize to approximately _____.

a. 512MB

b. 2GB

c. 8GB

d. 137GB

3. Modern hard drives use a _____ to move the actuator arms.

a. Voice coil

b. Servo motor

c. Stepper motor

d. Resistive coil

4. The speed at which data can be moved from the surface of the medium to the hard drive's buffers is a direct function of _____.

a. Access time

b. Latency

c. The size of the buffer

d. Rotational speed

5. Of the following encoding systems, which is most likely to be used on a hard drive purchased today?

a. EPRML

b. PRML

c. MFM

d. RLL

6. What is the size of the MBR used by FAT16?

a. 256 bytes

b. 512 bytes

c. 1024 bytes

d. There is no limit.

7. As a systems administrator, you want to enforce as much security in your organization as you possibly can. Therefore, you have decided that all computers will run an OS that uses the _____ file system.

a. FAT16

b. FAT32

c. NTFS

d. HPFS

8. File Allocation Tables are generated by _____.

a. FDISK

b. FORMAT

c. A low-level format that occurs at the factory

d. The OS when it is installed

9. What part of the MBR is created and added during the OS installation?

a. File system

b. Partition tables

c. Boot ID

d. OS pointer

10. A partition created by FAT16 is limited to _____.

a. 512MB

b. 2GB

c. 4GB

d. 137GB

TRICKY TERMINOLOGY

Areal density: The total amount of storage capacity for a specific unit of area on the surface of the drive platter.

Average access time: The amount of time required by a disk drive to lock on to the first sector that contains data requested by the controller.

Average seek time: The amount of time it takes to locate and lock on to the first track that contains data requested by the controller.

Bit cell: The collection of magnetized particles that comprise a single bit on magnetic media.

Block: The number of sectors on a hard drive that UFS uses as the smallest recognizable data unit.

Burst mode: The speed at which data moves from the R/W heads to a drive's buffer memory. Also known as internal host transfer rate.

Cluster: The minimum number of sectors a specific file system can recognize as a single data unit. Another term for file allocation unit.

Cylinder: A virtual structure created by the tracks that line up vertically on the surface of each of the platters.

Data encoding mechanism: The method used by a device to convert digital information into an electronic format recognizable by the target device.

Directory attribute: A single bit that identifies an entry in the directory table as being a subdirectory rather than a file.

Directory table: A database of all file names on a hard drive and the partitions with which they are associated. Other information pertaining to file system security is also contained here.

Drive translation: A technique by which an address space beyond what Int13h can read is converted into something that it can understand.

Executable marker: A pointer in the MBR that directs the boot sequence to the first line of code for the primary kernel file of the OS installed.

External host rate: How fast data moves from a drive's controller to RAM.

File system: The mechanism used by a hard drive to map the specific sectors used by any given file.

Floating height: The distance above a hard drive's platter that the R/W heads hover as the platter spins beneath.

Flux reversal: A transition of magnet charge from a positive to a negative state, or vice versa.

Head crash: A disastrous event caused by the R/W head in a drive coming into physical contact with the platter while it is spinning.

Head parking: A process of positioning R/W heads in a hard drive in a place where contact with the platter will do no harm.

Int13h extensions: Additional instructions added to the BIOS that intercept hard disk I/O operations and provide the drive translation required by hard disks larger than 8GB.

Internal host rate: The speed at which data moves from the R/W heads to a drive's buffer memory. Also known as burst mode.

Landing zone: An area on the hard disk's platter where the R/W heads can be safely parked.

Latency: The amount of time that elapses between the instant the R/W heads lock onto the first track that contains information requested by the controller, and then lock onto the first sector.

Logical drive: A section of disk space isolated from the rest of the same physical disk so that it appears to the user as a separate disk drive.

Partition: Logical sections on a hard disk that divide the overall disk space into multiple logical drives.

Platter: One of two or more physical disk structures installed in a typical hard drive.

Pointer: A line of code used by UFS to map a cluster used by a specific file.

Thin-film metal: A metalized magnetic medium applied by evaporating metal and allowing it to "condense" back onto the surface being coated.

Transition cell: The minimum number of particles that can be affected by a single magnetic flux.

Vapor deposition: The process of applying a metal coating by the process of evaporation.

Voice coil: An extremely fast and highly accurate motor that works by applying an electrical current to a tightly wrapped coil of wires surrounding, but not touching, a permanently magnetized cylinder. When current is applied to the coil, the cylinder rotates. Negative voltage rotates the cylinder one direction, positive the other. The amount of voltage determines how far the cylinder moves.

Zone bit recording: A technology that allows the sectors on the outer tracks of a hard disk to be the same physical size as those toward the center. This allows for far more sectors per track on the outer tracks.

Acronym Alert

CHS: Cylinders, Heads, Sectors-per-track. The parameters of hard drive configuration that define total capacity of the drive as well as specific locations on the drive.

DFS: Distributed File System. A subset of NTFS that allows users to browse to remote resources on a network without requiring the user to know the specific path information.

DTR: Data Transfer Rate. How fast information moves from one device to another.

EFS: Encryptable File System. A subset of NTFS that allows individual files to be scrambled on an as-needed basis and subsequently unscrambled only by a user with appropriate permissions.

ENDEC: Encoder/Decoder

EPRML: Extended PRML. A data encoding mechanism used by most hard disk drives currently being manufactured.

FAT: File Allocation Table

FAU: File Allocation Unit. The smallest usable amount of drive space in sectors used by a file system for a single file, regardless of how small that file may be.

HPFS: High Performance File System

IOPS: I/O Operations Per Second. The maximum number of times a device can receive and then execute either a request for data or a request to write data to the device, assuming the smallest block of data the device utilizes.

LFN: Long File Names

MFM: Modified Frequency Modulation. One of the early data encoding mechanisms used by hard disk drives.

NTFS: New Technology File System

PRML: Partial Response/Maximum Likelihood. A data encoding mechanism used by more recent hard disk drives.

R/W: Read/Write

RLL: Run Length Limited. One of the early data encoding mechanisms used by hard disk drives.

UFS: Unix File System

VBR: Volume Boot Record

CHAPTER 14

HARD DISK INTERFACING AND DISK MANAGEMENT

By now, you should have a pretty good understanding of how data is stored on the hard drive and how the computer system goes about locating that data. Getting data from the drive to memory is the next thing that I will discuss. This is done across the hard drive interface. There have been a fair number of different interfaces used over the years, and even now there are several to choose from. When people discuss the differences between IDE drives and SCSI drives, they're not talking about the kind of hard drive they have, but rather the interface across which data is moved. This chapter will cover the various interfaces that have existed over the years.

File maintenance and disk management are things that don't just take care of themselves. There's a lot going on in a hard drive, and failure to properly care for your drive can carry a severe penalty in overall system performance. The second half of this chapter will deal with those issues.

A+ CORE HARDWARE EXAM OBJECTIVES

Exam objectives covered in this chapter include the following:

1.1 Identify the names, purpose, and characteristics of system modules. Recognize these modules by sight or definition.

1.2 Identify basic procedures for adding and removing field-replaceable modules for desktop systems. Given a replacement scenario, choose the appropriate sequences.

1.5 Identify the names, purposes, and performance characteristics of standardized/common peripheral ports, associated cabling, and their connectors. Recognize ports, cabling, and connectors by sight.

1.6 Identify proper procedures for installing and configuring common IDE devices. Choose the appropriate installation or configuration sequences in given scenarios. Recognize the associated cables.

1.9 Identify procedures to optimize PC operations in specific situations. Predict the effects of specific procedures under given scenarios.

1.10 Determine the issues that must be considered when upgrading a PC. In a given scenario, determine when and how to upgrade system components.

2.1 Recognize common problems associated with each module and their symptoms, and identify steps to isolate and troubleshoot the problems. Given a problem situation, interpret the symptoms and infer the most likely cause.

Hard Drive Interfaces

In Chapter Thirteen I described how much impact hard disk I/O operations have on overall system performance. As you may have noticed, it is rather significant. How fast the interface can move data from the drive to RAM is the next bottleneck to be considered. In an application that makes use of lots and lots of little tiny files, I/O operations per second (IOPS) will be the performance-limiting factor. Conversely, an application that consistently reads and writes large files will be more greatly impacted by the speed of the interface. Large chunks of data that are contiguously stored will require but a single I/O operation before data begins to be transferred. It is the interface that will limit the speed of that transfer.

> ## Buzz Words
>
> **Command overhead:** The number of instructions that must be executed in order to carry out a specific request, combined with the speed at which the device can carry out those instructions.

Many factors influence overall performance of the hard drive interface. One of these is the system bus on which it resides. It should not come as a surprise that an interface on an 8MHz bus is going to be slower than one that sits on a 33MHz bus. Another aspect of the interface that affects performance is the hard drive's *command overhead*. All I/O operations begin when a command is issued by the chipset. The controller accepts this command and executes it. Executed commands will result in a variety of actions occurring, including moving the actuator arm to a specific position, or initiating the transfer of data to or from the surface of the platter to cache or the transfer of data to or from the cache to RAM. As interfaces evolved, their command structure became more sophisticated. As command cycles become shorter, it takes fewer commands to perform the same operation, and the process by which commands are moved through the system becomes more efficient.

What hard drive interface you choose directly impacts both the number of devices you can hang off the chain and the type of devices that are supported. For example, some of the early interfaces I will discuss could only handle hard disk drives and two connected devices. Later developments provide support for practically any device you can dream of. And it's theoretically possible to hang over a hundred devices onto some of the newer interfaces.

ST-506 AND ST-412

As I mentioned in Chapter Thirteen, Hard Disk Drive Structure and Geometry, modified frequency modulation (MFM) can be considered to be both a data translation method and an interface.

This is because the MFM required a special adapter and cables that were unique to an MFM drive. Technically speaking, the interface is usually referenced by the two drives that made use of this method. Among the first hard drives manufactured for use in personal computers was the ST-506. Al Shugart released this drive back in 1980. It was a 5MB drive that required a separate controller card and two separate cables. IBM wanted something a little larger than 5MB and went with the ST-412, which was a 10MB version.

File data was carried across a 20-conductor ribbon cable, and a 34-conductor cable handled control data, including timing signals, commands, and so forth. Unlike modern drives, which house a lot of controller circuitry on the drive itself, these older drives relied exclusively upon the controller card.

> ### BUZZ WORDS
>
> **Interleave ratio:** The number of sectors that must pass beneath the R/W heads between the reading of one sector and the time the heads will be ready to read the next sector. For example, on a 3:1 ratio, the heads will read or write one sector, two sectors will pass by completely ignored, then the next sector will be written. The unused sectors will be filled in during the next two rotations of the platter.

In order to make sure that the timing of drives was accurate, it was essential that the drive be properly configured. People complain about the work that goes into prepping a drive these days. Yet compared to what you used to have to go through, today's technology is a piece of cake.

Drives had to be not only manually configured for the number of cylinders, heads, and sectors per track, they also had to be set up with the proper interleave ratio. A modern hard drive finds the first sector that holds the data the controller seeks and starts streaming it across the interface. Sectors are read sequentially, one after the other. The older controllers used with the ST-506 and ST-412 weren't fast enough to keep up with that kind of data stream, however. They would miss the next sector every time.

Therefore, sectors were not written and/or read back sequentially. The interleave ratio reordered the way sectors were written to the track. These older drives only managed to squeeze seventeen sectors onto any given track. In a perfect world, when the controller could keep up with the spinning of the head, the sectors on track one would be numbered 1, 2, 3, . . . 17. That track would be read sequentially, and then the next track would begin. Since that wasn't possible, the drive and controller you purchased would tell you what *interleave ratio* to set. Really fast controllers might be able to handle a 1:2 interleave. In this case, the tracks would be numbered 1, 10, 2, 11, 3, 12, and so forth to the end of the drive. A 1:3 ratio would be numbered 1, 12, 7, 2, 13, 8, 3, 14, 9, 4, 15, 10, 5, 16, 11, 6, and finally 17.

Of course, it wasn't the users' responsibility to set up the sector number. They simply had to know the correct interleave. An improperly configured drive was a corrupted drive.

One reason you can't really call this an MFM interface is that some of the later drives that used exactly the same interface made use of the run length limited (RLL) data encryption. Yet the controllers and the cable remained the same.

> **EXAM NOTE:** While these older interfaces may not seem relevant in today's context, CompTIA's A+ Core exam considers the history of the different components to be important. Make sure you know them.

ESDI

The next step in the evolution of the hard drive was the Enhanced Small Device Interface. This interface was the result of a cooperative effort among several manufacturers, led by Maxtor Corporation. ESDI drives were more complex devices than the ST-506 and ST-412s, in that some of the controller circuitry was housed directly on the drive. This assured better data integrity on the transfer cycle.

ESDI did enjoy a decent throughput. It had a theoretical top bandwidth of about 24Mb/s. Unfortunately, the interface didn't live long enough to see if manufacturers would ever be able to achieve these speeds. In terms of ease of installation and overall user-friendliness, it wasn't any better that the drives it was supposed to replace. Also, it had only been around for a very short while before the next standard hit the streets and pretty much blew ESDI off the pavement.

IDE

That next standard was Integrated Drive Electronics (IDE). IDE moved all of the controller circuitry onto the drive itself, leaving only an interface port on the computer. Early IDE-enabled computers had I/O cards that installed into a free ISA slot, but the port would eventually migrate onto the motherboard, where it remains to this day. Even though the port may be housed on an expansion card, it is important that you understand that the 40-pin plug on the card was nothing more than a port. The controller is on the drive.

Initially, IDE drives hooked up by way of a 40-pin ribbon cable. Beginning with ATA-4, which I will be discussing shortly, the number of conductors was increased to eighty, while the number of pins on the port remained forty. **Figure 14.1** and **Table 14.1** show the pinouts of the 40-pin IDE port.

IDE has got to be one of the most confusing terms in the industry, and that is primarily because it is such a generic term. There have been a myriad of different IDE standards, and more than a fair share of nonstandards. Still newer standards are on the horizon. To make matters worse, not everybody uses the same term to mean the same thing. Here are some of the different terms you hear that are associated with IDE:

- *ATAPI*: ATA Packet Interface
- *ATA*: Advanced Technology Attachment
- *EIDE*: Enhanced IDE; Western Digital's version of ATA-2
- *Ultra-ATA*: ATA device that is capable of using direct memory access
- *Ultra-DMA*: A form of direct memory access controlled by the device rather than the motherboard; often (incorrectly) used interchangeably with Ultra-ATA

ATAPI

Before I get into a detailed discussion of the different IDE modes the industry has seen over the years, it would be a good idea to have some understanding of the concept of the Advanced

Table 14.1 Pinouts of the 40-pin IDE port

Pin	Description	Pin	Description
1	Reset	21	DRQ 3
2	Ground	22	Ground
3	Data Bit 7	23	-IOW
4	Data Bit 8	24	Ground
5	Data Bit 6	25	-IOR
6	Data Bit 9	26	Ground
7	Data Bit 5	27	I/O channel ready
8	Data Bit 10	28	SPSYNC: Cable select
9	Data Bit 4	29	-DACK 3
10	Data Bit 11	30	Ground
11	Data Bit 3	31	RQ 14
12	Data Bit 12	32	-IOCS 16
13	Data Bit 2	33	Address Bit 1
14	Data Bit 13	34	-PDIAG
15	Data Bit 1	35	Address Bit 0
16	Data Bit 14	36	Address Bit 2
17	Data Bit 0	37	-CS1FX
18	Data Bit 15	38	-CS3FX
19	Ground	39	-DA/SP
20	Cable key (pin missing)	40	Ground

IDE connector pinout chart

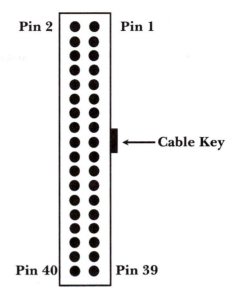

Figure 14.1 Pinouts for IDE connector

Technology Attachment Packet Interface (ATAPI). In the next chapter, I'm going to be discussing the Small Computer Systems Interface (SCSI) in great detail. But for now, one characteristic of SCSI I want to introduce is the fact that it has a command set that supports different kinds of devices on the same interface. Therefore, a single SCSI host adapter can control a hard drive, a CD-ROM drive, and a tape drive. This, combined with some advanced features that I will discuss in the next chapter, made SCSI the preferable interface for "serious" computer users.

ATAPI takes some of the features of SCSI and incorporates them into the IDE interface. As a result, it supports multiple devices. It also allows for devices other than hard drives to become bootable devices.

Devices that make use of ATAPI move data in a completely different way than the earlier IDE devices. Instead of moving information across the bus a bit at a time, the information is combined into packets and moved from device to device in little packages of data. This is where the name is derived. Starting with ATA-4, all ATA modes incorporated ATAPI.

> **EXAM NOTE:** Disk capacity limitations imposed by the different versions of IDE are something that show up on the A+ Exam on a regular basis.

ATA

The Advanced Technology Attachment (ATA) was the first incarnation of IDE to appear. The debut of the interface supported only hard drives, allowed for but a single port per computer, and each port could only have two drives on it. To differentiate between drives, jumpers on the drive set them to either master or slave status. Only a master drive was bootable.

Data transfer could occur in one of three programmable input/output (PIO) modes: PIO-0, PIO-1, and PIO-2. This technique requires the CPU to get into the middle of things by executing commands that shuffle the data to or from RAM and the drive. The end result is that instead of spending its time processing instructions and data, the CPU is tied up playing go fetch. Another limitation of this data transfer method is that the time overhead involved in putting data in the cache, reading each byte into the CPU, sending it out to the cache again, and then routing, it limited the maximum throughput that was possible.

Later versions of ATA would support PIO-3 and PIO-4 as well. Each mode had a specific *cycle rate*, or amount of time it took to complete a cycle. In this case, I am referring to the clock cycles of the hard drive controller rather than that of the FSB. The controller's speed is dictated by the speed of the bus onto which it is installed. How is this different? An IDE controller installed in a standard PCI slot is going to be running at 33MHz. The system board onto which it is installed may have a 133MHz FSB.

A single cycle is both the rising edge and the falling edge of a single tick of the bus clock. I examined the sine-wave effect in Chapter Nine, Searching Your Memory. This cycle rate, in effect, dictates maximum data transfer rate. Unfortunately, hard drives can't keep up with the overall system clock, and therefore, the device must set its own pace. The different PIO modes worked on different clock cycles, as is illustrated in **Table 14.2**. For purposes of comparison, I have included FSB speeds of 100 and 133MHz.

You'll notice that the fastest of the PIO modes indicates a cycle rate of 120ns. If you're working with a computer with a 100MHz front-side bus (slow by today's standards), then a single cycle of the drive controller eats up twelve cycles of the front-side bus. On a 133MHz bus, that's sixteen clock cycles that go by simply waiting for the hard drive controller to run just one of its own cycles. And remember, your CPU is operating at speeds several times that of the FSB.

The ATA standards did define a data transfer method known as direct memory access (DMA). DMA had been around for a long time, and was nothing new. Floppy disk drives and sound cards both made use of DMA long before hard drives. With DMA, the CPU sets up the initial transfer of a given file, but once the transfer is set up, the data

> **BUZZ WORDS**
>
> **Cycle rate:** The amount of time it takes for a specific device under the control of a timing mechanism to complete one "tick" of that timer.

Table 14.2 Comparisons of PIO Modes

PIO Mode	Defining Standard	Cycle Rate	Theoretical Transfer Rate	Cycles/sec for		
				33MHz Bus	100MHz Bus	133MHz Bus
PIO-0	ATA	600ns	3.3Mb/s	~20	60	80
PIO-1	ATA	383ns	5.2Mb/s	~12.5	~38	51
PIO-2	ATA	240ns	8.3Mb/s	8	24	32
PIO-3	ATA-2	180ns	11.1Mb/s	6	18	24
PIO-4	ATA-2	120ns	16.7Mb/s	4	12	16

Each generation of PIO got increasingly faster, but it never caught up to ATA.

Table 14.3 Comparisons of ATA-1 DMA Modes

Mode	Standard	Cycle Rate	Theoretical Transfer Rate	Cycles/sec for		
				33MHz Bus	100MHz Bus	133MHz Bus
Mode 0	AT	960ns	2.1Mb/s	~32	96	128
Mode 1	AT	480	4.2MB/s	~16	48	64
Mode 2	AT	240	8.3MB/s	~8	24	32

ATA-1 was only marginally faster than PIO, but it was somewhat more efficient.

can move directly from the hard drive's controller to RAM, without having to make a pit stop at the CPU. The CPU goes back to work processing instructions and data, and the overall transfer of data is much faster.

Under original ATA standards, the only DMA modes supported were single-word DMA. The ATA interface was a 16-bit interface and therefore, on each transfer, it could move two bytes of data, or a word. Three modes of DMA were defined, as illustrated in **Table 14.3**.

In one respect, designers of the original ATA interface kind of shot themselves in the foot. Under the original Int13h CHS parameters that I discussed in Chapter Thirteen, the addressing scheme called for 1024 cylinders, 256 heads, and a maximum of 63 sectors per track. If you do your math, you see that $1024 \times 256 \times 63$ equals 16,515,072. That is the maximum number of sectors that Int13h can recognize. Multiply that number by 512, which is the number of bytes in a sector, and you see that under Int13h is capable of seeing hard drives of up to 8,455,716,864 bytes, or 8GB.

ATA addressing standards call for 65,536 cylinders, 16 heads, and 256 sectors per track. Now, theoretically, this allows for drives up to 137,438,953,472 bytes, or 137GB. Unfortunately, in the

Table 14.4 ATA and Int13h

Standard	Cylinders	Heads	Sectors/Track	Maximum Address Space
Int13h	1024	256	63	~8GB
ATA	65,536	16	256	~137GB
Combined	1024	16	63	504MB

The first implementation of ATA actually resulted in a dramatic decrease in the maximum capacity of hard disks.

initial release, the effect this had on the system was that, for each of those parameters, the system would use the lower of either standard (see **Table 14.4**).

ATA-2

As computer bus speeds were increasing, the need for a more efficient means of moving data was becoming critical. This is where Multiword Direct Memory Access (MDMA) comes into the picture. With the release of ATA-2 in 1994, forcing the CPU to negotiate the transfer of data became unnecessary. Of course, everybody wanted to own the technology, so before ANSI finally stepped in with some defined standards, there was a bit of confusion as to what ATA-2 really was. Western Digital had its Enhanced IDE (EIDE), which still shows up in many publications as being a "standard." Seagate had Fast-ATA. Both of these were improvements on the original AT standards, but were never accepted in their entirety as true standards. Both of these technologies did possess features in common and contributed to what would eventually become the ATA-2 standards. I'll take a brief look at both of these after the official ATA-2 standards are clearly defined. There were some distinct improvements introduced by ATA-2, which include the following:

- *PIO Modes 3 and 4*: The initial PIO modes supported by ATA were rather limited in their speed. As I mentioned earlier, Mode 2 topped out at 8.3Mb/s throughput. Mode 3 bumped this up to 11.1Mb/s, while Mode 4 achieved 16.7Mb/s. One thing I think I should point out here is that these are theoretical maximums. In the real world, no drive ever truly achieved these speeds.

- *Multiword DMA*: DMA did prove to be a nice enhancement for data transfer, but moving information across the bus a single word at a time was a bit cumbersome and inefficient. Under multiword DMA, once the data transfer is set up, information is sent out in bursts. One word follows the other in rapid sequence, and there is no need to set up separate transfers for each word. These days, multiword DMA is accepted as the norm, and, in fact, there are no current interfaces that even support single-word DMA.

- *Logical block addressing*: Prior to ATA-2, all drives used the standard CHS parameters that I discussed early in this chapter. This meant that there was a limitation of 528MB

(504MB in binary calculation) of address space visible to the hard drive. This was a limitation of the Int13h BIOS call trying to interface with the original ATA standards. A few companies had experimented with different extensions to Int13h that would allow for larger drives, including Extended CHS (ECHS). This still shows up in the BIOS settings of many computers as Large Mode. Logical block addressing (LBA) numbers each sector on the drive with its own unique number. This doesn't permit drives that use this method to address CHS parameters beyond the limitations described above. What it does is translate addresses down into something that fits CHS's comfortable little world. It does this through a process called LBA assist translation. This is a mathematical algorithm that takes actual cylinder numbers and translates them into expressions CHS can use. Theoretically, there is no limit to the size of hard drive LBA can address. However, ATA modes 2-5 are still limited to the 137GB ceiling dictated by their address space.

■ *Block transfer*: In the same way that multiword DMA allows for more data to move across the bus on any given cycle, block transfer allows multiple commands to be moved from the CPU to the controller on a single interrupt. Prior to the introduction of this technology, every transfer of data and every command moved across the bus required the drive's controller circuitry to generate an interrupt to let the CPU know it was ready for activity. Moving one command across an interrupt meant that, until that command was executed and the results moved across the bus (requiring an additional interrupt for the data transfer), no other commands could be moved.

When a hard drive uses *block mode*, it allows one interrupt to move several commands. This not only improves drive performance, but overall system performance as well. The drive can hold several commands in cache, executing them without needing to stop what the CPU is doing to ask for the next command. The CPU is no different than people in that respect. The more you interrupt it the slower it works.

■ *Identify drive command*: Have you ever wondered how your system was able to automatically recognize your hard drive without you having to go in and configure anything? As much as it might seem like magic, it's really a result of the identify drive command (IDC). This is a simple command to which the hard drive can respond by spewing out information concerning the number of cylinders, heads, and sectors per track. System BIOS can use this to automatically configure the drive, and the OS can use it for file system management. You also see a lot of hard drive utilities on the market these days. Many of the functions of these applications would not be possible without the identify drive command.

I mentioned earlier in this section that there were some proprietary technologies used by certain manufacturers that occasionally get confused with ATA-2. These were EIDE and Fast ATA.

> **BUZZ WORDS** ─────────
>
> **Block transfer:** The movement of multiple commands over an interface on a single interrupt cycle.
>
> **Block mode:** The data transfer setting that allows multiple commands to be moved over an interface in a single interrupt cycle.

■ **EXAM NOTE:** Be able to differentiate between the UDMA modes and the ATA modes.

EIDE was merely an incorporation of some new technology onto the original ATA interface. It was never a standard. Western Digital had come up with a better mousetrap, and didn't want to wait around for the notoriously slow hand of the standards committees to approve its work. So it simply released product using that technology. It incorporated most of what would later become the ATA-2 standards. Among the new features, EIDE supported ATAPI.

Another improvement of EIDE over ATA was that it defined the use of two different IDE ports on a single machine: a primary port and a secondary port. This allowed for up to four different IDE devices to be installed on a machine. Interestingly enough, there was nothing about the original ATA standards that kept manufacturers from putting an additional channel onto a system board or I/O card. However, since there were no specific standards defined for how to go about doing this, it was rarely if ever done.

Fast ATA was Seagate's version of EIDE. Like Western Digital, Seagate had developed a better interface and was unwilling to wait out the standards committees, especially since WD was entering the market with its EIDE. Fortunately, for the most part, neither term, EIDE or Fast–ATA, is much in use any more.

ATA-3

This particular set of standards was really no more than a fine-tuning of ATA-2. The only real improvements over ATA-2 were the addition of SMART drive technology and the ability to password-protect IDE devices.

Self Monitoring Analysis and Reporting Technology (SMART) was a method by which a hard drive could self-administer a few simple tests and try to predict if it was about to fail. SMART kept track of several factors in its efforts to predict the future. Among the information monitored was the following:

- *Remapped sectors*: If the drive is constantly being forced to move data from one location to another because of bad sectors, this is a sign of impending disaster.
- *ECC error counts*: SMART drives use error correction code to detect and correct data errors on the fly. SMART can monitor error correction code (ECC) usage and if it seems to be called upon with increasing frequency, this is assumed to be a sign of a failing drive.
- *Head flying height*: The drive's R/W heads are supposed to float on a cushion of air a certain distance above the spinning platter. If this height is slowly diminishing, this is a bad thing. You've got a head crash coming your way.
- *Temperature*: Is the drive suddenly starting to run hotter? A motor bearing failure is imminent.
- *Spin-up time*: If the drive is taking longer to reach the correct rotational velocity every time it spins up, the motor is starting to fail.
- *Data throughput*: If the speed at which data can be moved from the drive to RAM is starting to diminish, this means something is going wrong. SMART has no way of knowing what the problem is, only that there is one.

SMART requires two components in order to work properly. First off, you obviously need a drive that supports it. Second, you need some sort of monitoring software. The drive doesn't perform these tricks by itself. Drives that support it usually ship with a utility that you can load to do this monitoring. If you didn't know why that floppy disk shipped with your new drive and you simply threw it away, most third-party hardware diagnostics programs, such as Norton Utilities, provide some form of SMART monitoring.

■ **EXAM NOTE:** Know what SMART technology is and how it works.

The security features introduced in ATA-3 allow the user to go into BIOS and set password protection on devices. A computer on a network can have a separate hard drive for sensitive data that, in order to be accessed, requires that the user input a specific password.

ATA-4

The release of ATA-4 in 1998 opened the way for much faster hard drives on the IDE interface. It was the first of the versions to fully incorporate ATAPI. ATA-4 was developed by Quantum and then freely licensed to the industry. There were several improvements introduced in this release:

- Ultra-DMA (UDMA) modes
- Cyclical redundancy checking (CRC)
- Command queuing
- Command overlapping
- An advanced command set, with obsolete commands cleaned up

UDMA differs from legacy DMA in several respects. The older ATA-2 and ATA-3 hard drives that made use of DMA used a method called *third-party DMA*. What this means is that a controlling device separate from that controlling the drive itself was in charge of DMA transfers. In the case of IDE hard drives, that third party was the DMA controller chip on the motherboard. A key issue here is that those chips are limited to the speed of the older ISA bus. UDMA allows the device controller to directly handle data transfer through a process called bus mastering. Under bus mastering, the device takes charge of the bus on which it and its companion device reside, and data moves directly from one device to another. The DMA controller chip is not involved, and transfers occur at the speed of whatever bus the system is using. These days, that would be the PCI bus, although in the past, both MCA and VLB were used (see Chapter Ten, Examining the Expansion Bus).

Later modes of UDMA also sped up data transfer through a process called *double-transition clocking*. As I discussed in Chapter Nine, every clock

> **BUZZ WORDS**
>
> **Third-party DMA:** Direct memory access that is managed by a device other than the two devices utilizing DMA to exchange data.
>
> **Double-transition clocking:** The movement of two transfers of data on a single clock cycle.

cycle has two stages, a rising end and a falling end. Conventional DMA could only propagate a transfer of data on the rising end of the cycle. Double-transition clocking permits the device to transmit or receive on both the rising end and the falling end of each clock cycle. This has the same effect as doubling the clock speed, without the side effect of having to worry about timing issues imposed by other devices that may be using that same clock signal for its timing.

UDMA has survived the last several years, but in that time it has undergone several developmental stages. To date, there have been six modes of UDMA. Each mode has provided for faster data transfers as well as adding new features. The following is a list of UDMA modes that have been developed. Note, however, that the list contains modes that are native to ATA-5 and 6 as well as ATA-4. I simply felt it better to keep the list together.

- *Mode 0*: This could almost be considered the "experimental" mode. This release did not provide for double-transition clocking and didn't operate at a faster clock speed than PIO modes. Most operating systems of the day didn't support UDMA modes, nor did most BIOS routines. Therefore, on many machines, it caused more problems than people were willing to endure for an almost insignificant gain in performance.
- *Mode 1*: Aside from a slightly faster clock cycle, there were no improvements over Mode 0.
- *Mode 2*: Here is the introduction of double-transition clocking. Data transfer is noticeably faster. By now BIOS manufacturers have caught on to the fact that UDMA is the direction the industry is moving, and support for it is almost universal. Windows 95 now provides support for it, and IDE hard drives are becoming almost respectable.
- *Mode 3*: This mode was released with ATA-5. It simply increased the clock cycle of Mode 2. The only other improvement was that it provided support for ATAPI-5.
- *Mode 4*: This mode was released with ATA-5. More frequently known as UDMA-66, this interface requires the use of an 80-conductor cable, otherwise it drops back into Mode 3 operation. A key improvement to this mode, aside from speed, is the introduction of cyclical redundancy check (CRC) error correction.
- *Mode 5*: UDMA-100
- *Mode 6*: UDMA-133. Available memory space was also increased to 64 bits.

CRC is a form of error correction that treats an entire packet of data as if it were one long binary number. It performs a mathematical calculation on that number and stores the results in a data field at the end of the packet. On the receiving end, that calculation is performed again on just the data set. If the value of the new calculation matches that in the trailer, the data is assumed to be good. If there is any discrepancy, the packet is discarded and sent again.

Since ATAPI sends data across the bus in packets, CRC can basically treat those ones and zeros that make up the data in the packet as a large binary number and then perform a mathematical calculation on that number. The results of this calculation are made a part of the packet in the CRC trailer. Before that data is stripped out of the packet and reassembled into a file, the same calculation is performed. If the same results are achieved, the data is accepted. If not, the packet is rejected and a request is sent out to the transmitting device to resend that packet. CRC substantially reduces the likelihood of data being corrupted as it is sent over the bus.

Command queuing is a concept that was borrowed from SCSI. Using PIO mode, commands sent to an IDE device had to be completely executed and the operation initiated by that command had to be completed before the next command could be sent to the controller. This wasn't exactly the most efficient way of doing things, but at the time, technology hadn't provided for a better way. Under *command queuing*, the device can store commands in a cache. Several commands can be ready to go as soon as the drive is ready to execute them. *Command overlapping* provides a method of letting the drive have more than one command be in the pipeline at a time. This is very similar to the pipelining function I discussed in Chapter Seven, Understanding CPUs. The controller can be executing one command while the drive is performing the operation requested by the previous command. Meanwhile the I/O bus can be transferring the data generated by the command before that one. These concepts will be discussed in more detail in Chapter Fifteen, The Many Faces of SCSI.

> **BUZZ WORDS**
>
> **Command queuing:** Allows a device to store a series of commands in a buffer area, assuring that as one command is completed another one is rolled up to the gate and ready to go.
>
> **Command overlapping:** The ability of a device to start processing a command even before the command issued prior to it has completed its cycle.

ATA-5

ATA-5 is really nothing more than a tweak for ATA-4. When ATA modes 3 and 4 were introduced, speeds increased to 44.4 and 66.7Mb/s, respectively. An 80-conductor cable is required for the device to be able to approach these speeds. ATA-5 further bumps speed to 100Mb/s. There was a little tweaking of the command set. A few new commands were added; some obsolete ones were removed. For the most part, however, it is merely a faster ATA-4.

ATA-6

If you recall from the earlier discussion about the ATA interface, it had an address bus of 32 bits, only 28 bits of which were used for actual addressing. This imposes a limitation of 137GB as the largest drive it can support. We have now reached that limitation. ATA-6 standards define a 64-bit address bus and bump the speed to 133Mb/s. The address space handling sectors was increased from eight to sixteen. This allows for drives in excess of several hundred terabytes.

A new command set provides enhanced support for streaming audio-video data, something that until now has been almost the exclusive domain of SCSI drives. Several other changes improved timing control and overall data throughput.

SERIAL ATA

All of the IDA technologies that I've discussed so far have been varying forms of Parallel ATA (PATA). The latest standards to emerge in 2002 defined Serial ATA (SATA). SATA offers a number of improvements in areas of speed and ease of configuration. The initial specification,

SATA 1.0, came out of the gates at 150Mb/s throughput. While on paper that only represents a 14 percent improvement over ATA-6, the improvement is actually greater than it appears. If you recall, I've mentioned several times in this and other chapters that theoretical throughputs are rarely, if ever, achieved. SATA comes closer to achieving its maximum data transfer than other technology discussed so far.

Easier configuration comes about because only one device can be installed on each SATA channel. Since there is only one device per channel, there is no longer the confusion of managing master/slave relationships (more on that later). The reduced size of the cable means that there is far less "cable clutter" inside the enclosure. Airflow is improved, and accessing other devices inside the system is greatly facilitated.

So how is having one device per channel an advantage over the ATA modes that supported two devices per channel? The answer to that is several-fold. For one thing, two devices don't compete on the same cable for bandwidth.

Next, consider the interface. PATA used a 40-pin connector on the motherboard that was 2.3″ × .4″ in size. SATA uses a 7-conductor cable. Two connectors for these cables fit into an area that is .6″ × .4″. In other words, a controller card or motherboard that uses SATA can fit the same number of devices. While the initial offering of SATA controller cards offered only two ports for devices, there are now more advanced devices that support up to sixteen ports with onboard RAID architecture. I'll be discussing RAID in Chapter Fifteen, The Many Faces of SCSI.

SATA uses a high-speed differential signal using Gigabit technology. What this means is that for each data cable, there is a matching cable that carries an exact inverse of the data signal (see **Figure 14.2**). If the two signals were blended together, in theory, they would cancel each other out, resulting in zero voltage. As electrical signals travel over wire, they pick up noise. The farther they travel, the more noise they pick up. Noise shows up as voltage fluctuations. A device using *differential signaling* compares the matched pair of signals. Any voltage differences between the two are filtered out. This contrasts with *single-ended signaling*, in which the active signal wire is coupled with a ground. As a result, cable lengths can be longer.

A conventional 40-conductor IDE cable is limited to approximately 18″ in length. Any longer, and data corruption becomes a serious risk. SATA cables can be up to 1 meter in length, or nearly twice that of standard IDE.

Power consumption is also reduced. Standard 1″ IDE hard disks operate at 5V. SATA devices require a peak operating voltage of a mere 500mv.

SATA also borrows some technology that has been around for a while for SCSI users. One of these is tagged command queuing. Earlier in the chapter, I discussed how command queuing could line up commands in a row in the controller's buffer rather than being forced to feed the controller one command at a time. Tagged command queuing allows the controller to re-sort those commands into a different order if doing so will provide more efficient operation.

BUZZ WORDS —————

Differential signaling: A method by which a single data wire on a parallel cable is matched up by a wire carrying the inverse of the signal being carried by the data wire.

Single-ended signaling: A method by which a single data wire on a parallel cable is matched up by a ground wire.

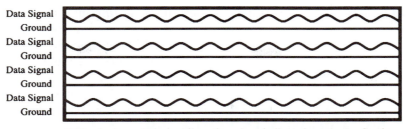

With single-ended signaling, there is a dedicated conductor for the signal, coupled to a ground.

With differential signaling, there is a dedicated conductor for the signal, coupled to an inverse of that signal. When the two signals are measured together, the result should be 0. Any difference is assumed to be noise, and is filtered out.

Figure 14.2   A conceptual diagram of differential signaling

SATA-II became available to users in 2004. The primary difference is in bandwidth. SATA-II handles a full 300Mb/s. SATA-III, scheduled for a 2007 rollout, bumps that up to 600Mb/s. We can only hope that the rest of hard drive technology is able to keep pace with interface technology.

SCSI

Since the SCSI interface provides support for many devices other than hard drives and it is such a complex subject on its own, it is covered separately in its own chapter. It will be discussed in much greater detail in the Chapter Fifteen, The Many Faces of SCSI. In order to provide a complete discussion of hard drive interfaces, however, it is important to provide a simplified overview of SCSI.

Even the earlier releases of SCSI supported up to seven devices, plus the host adapter itself, on a single chain controlled by a single IRQ. In addition, SCSI supported more than just hard drives, so you could have a tape drive, a CD-ROM, and two or three hard drives hanging off the same cable.

From the start, SCSI provided support for functions that IDE wouldn't make available for several years. These included command queuing, command overlapping, and bus mastering.

Overall, SCSI is now, and has always been, a faster and more efficient interface. The thing that has always kept IDE alive and well has been the added expense and configuration difficulties imposed by SCSI. This will all be discussed in greater detail in the next chapter. Toward the end of Chapter Fifteen, I will take a look at the differences and similarities and consider when one interface or the other might be desirable.

THE NONSTANDARD INTERFACES

Most of the options I've discussed so far have described the interfaces for internally mounted hard disk drives for desktop computers or servers. However, sometimes it is convenient, or even essential, to make use of an externally mounted hard drive. Some other options for connecting a hard drive to a computer include the following:

- Parallel port
- Universal Serial Bus
- Personal Computer Memory Card International Association (PCMCIA)

All of these interfaces have special niches that they occupy and need to be addressed. With parallel port and USB devices, the drive itself uses one of the technologies previously discussed, usually IDE. The enclosure is equipped with the interface that will be used to interconnect with the computer and a logic board that will act as a translator. PCMCIA makes use of its own interface.

PARALLEL PORT HARD DRIVES

People frequently think of the parallel port as being the exclusive domain of printers. Yet as I pointed out in Chapter Twelve, Working With Removable Disks, it is used for a number of other devices. Hard drive manufacturers have long made use of the parallel interface for designing external hard drives. Relying on a parallel port has one advantage over either IDE or SCSI, and that is its portability. Not all computers have an external SCSI port. But have you ever seen a computer without a parallel port?

It is, of course, very slow compared to anything else you might use. Data throughput is limited to a maximum of 1.2Mb/s. Nobody will ever confuse it with a high-performance device.

The parallel port is rapidly losing ground to USB for an external interface, however. You will see why in the next section.

USB

In Chapter Ten, I discussed the features of USB. By default, it is Plug 'n Play. It loads and unloads drivers on the fly and automatically recognizes when a device has been added. You can add the drive while the computer is up and running, and it will automatically be recognized and introduced to the machine. And you won't have to unplug your printer to make room for the drive.

Even for people who need a permanently connected external drive, USB is a better choice than the parallel port. While stacking devices on the parallel port is definitely possible, it isn't all that desirable. An already slow interface suffers even more. Since USB 1.0 only supports a maximum throughput of 12Mb/s, which is a much faster interface than the parallel port, it's still no speed demon. That still only works out to about 1.5MB/s. USB 2.0 is the better choice (and by the time this book is in print, will probably be the only choice) with a throughput of 480Mb/s.

The USB enclosure of most of the drives being shipped these days also have a USB hub built in. This allows you to daisy chain additional devices off the back of the drive. You may recall from Chapter Ten that a USB chain can have up to 127 devices installed.

PCMCIA

While PCMCIA is technically the name of the association that developed the standard, it is also used as the name of the bus that the standard defines. PCMCIA devices are the small card-sized devices used in notebook computers. The bus offers reasonably good speed, combined with a very small interface. Hard disks on this interface are only 2.5″ across and only about a quarter of an inch high. As far as performance goes, they can be every bit as fast as conventional IDE drives.

The nice thing about PCMCIA drives is that they are easily removed from the host computer and added to a different machine. Several manufacturers make devices that install into an external drive bay in your home computer and allow you to insert the PCMCIA drive from your notebook. While not the easiest method of maintaining files, it assures you of having the data you need on whatever computer you need it on.

NOTEBOOK IDE

Internal hard disks for notebook computers these days are generally IDE drives. They differ physically in a couple of respects, however. The overall width is consistent at 2.5″. However, over the years, they have been released in heights of 9.5mm, 12.7mm, and 19mm. Putting a thinner drive in a larger bay is no problem as long as the drive is secured in some fashion. If the notebook was designed as a friction enclosure (pressure from the two sides and the top and the bottom), this is not a good idea. There is a risk of the drive bouncing around. Most if not all modern designs make use of the 9.5mm, and that's about all that's shipping today.

The cable is also different in a notebook. Instead of being a 40-conductor cable, it uses 44 conductors. There is no separate power plug for these drives, so power is supplied through the same cable as the data. The ends of the cable are extremely small and use spring clips to hold them in place. This prevents them from being dislodged as the computer is carried from place to place.

HARD DISK PREPARATION

Hard disk drives don't arrive at your doorstep from the factory ready to read and write data. A certain amount of preparation is involved. First off, you have to get the drive installed into your machine. Depending on what kind of drive you've selected the procedures for that will vary slightly. Once it is installed, you have to introduce the drive to the file system you intend to use. Most Microsoft operating systems use a utility called FDISK to perform that function. Finally, once the drive has been installed and prepared for a file system, it needs to be formatted to the particular operating system you have chosen to use. In the next few pages, I will take a detailed look at installing and configuring your hard drive.

INSTALLING A HARD DRIVE

Overall, this is actually a fairly easy task. Before you begin, you will want to make sure you have an available drive bay in which to seat the drive. You don't just want it hanging from the cables in the middle of the case. Second, you need to make sure you can get power to the drive. If you've used up all your Molex plugs from the power supply, you can get a Y-connector from any electronics supply house. You can see an example of one of these in **Figure 14.3**. Basically, these inexpensive little devices turn one Molex into two. However, before you do that, you might want to examine your system and the devices you have already installed carefully. If the system has a small power supply, say around 65 watts, and you start stacking too many devices onto it, you could cause a premature failure. Many power supplies, on the other hand, are perfectly capable of powering far more devices than they have plugs for, so this is usually a pretty safe solution.

The kind of computer case you're using will dictate how the drive physically mounts. Most cases these days have drive bays that can be removed from the case. This makes the process of mounting the drive a whole lot easier. While the drive is still outside of the case, the process of connecting cables is a much easier job.

While the drive is still outside of the case is also the time to be setting any jumpers there may be. PATA IDE devices need to be either a master or a slave. If you're installing an SATA device, this is not an issue.

If the drive is to be your primary boot device, it is best (and in many cases necessary) to make it the master device on the primary port. There is a jumper on the back of the drive that performs this function. Just put the shunt over the correct pair of pins and you're good to go.

SCSI devices may or may not have either jumpers or switches for setting the device ID. It is becoming more and more common for this function to be handled by the firmware of the host adapter card. I'll be addressing that in more detail next chapter.

One little detail that needs to be examined is directly related to the master/slave relationships on IDE devices. There is another setting on most drives that is labeled cable select (CS). If both drives are set for CS, the drive's position

Figure 14.3 If you run out of Molex plugs to supply power to devices in your system, perhaps a Y-connector is in order. Be cautious of using too many. You don't want to risk overstressing your power supply.

on the cable determines whether it is master or slave. This is done by having conductor number 28 disconnected from the end connector. Manufactures do this either by clipping a short length of the wire from somewhere between the middle and end connector, or by simply not connecting the twenty-eighth wire to the end connector. The first type is easy to recognize. There's a hole in the cable. The latter is not. The original idea was that this would make configuring IDE drives much easier. You put the slave drive in the middle of the cable and the master at the end.

> **EXAM NOTE:** Master/slave relationships of IDE devices can be presented in a number of ways. If you're lucky, you'll just get a multiple choice question of definitions. More likely, you'll get a scenario in which a drive isn't working and you have to explain why.

Unfortunately, it didn't. If either drive is not set to CS, it won't be recognized by the system if its jumper is set opposite of its position on the cable. For example, if a drive is set to be a slave, you cannot force your system to recognize it if you place it on the end connector. If all you have is a CS cable and you need the device on the end to be a master, then you're only solution is to manually solder a jumper between the thirty-ninth conductor on the cable over to the twenty-eighth. If conductor 28 was simply never connected at the factory, all this work will do you no good. You're better off spending a few bucks on a standard IDE cable. And along those lines, by default, all 80-conductor cables are CS.

Once the jumpers are set, the ribbon cable properly installed (and don't forget to make sure the pink or red wire is linked to pin number 1), and the power cable hooked up, you are ready to mount the cage back into the case and prepare the drive. I wouldn't recommend sealing up the case, however, until you know the system is booting properly. It's easy to forget to set a jumper or to inadvertently knock loose another cable while poking around inside the system.

FDISK

While operating systems written by companies other than Microsoft use their own utilities to prepare a hard drive for formatting, FDISK is far and away the most common utility used. FDISK is the utility that writes that master boot record that I discussed in Chapter Thirteen. It assigns the file system to be used and creates the partition tables, based on selections you make while running the utility. In this section, I will look at the utility and how to effectively use it.

To start with, you should never run FDISK from the drive that you're actually working with. With newer OSs, that isn't possible, so it's a moot point. However, some older versions do not employ any fail-safe mechanisms to prevent you from doing this. As a standard operating procedure, I recommend preparing a boot diskette with both the FDISK.EXE and FORMAT.COM files copied on to it. It is particularly useful for users of the WIN95 or earlier operating systems to add CD-ROM support to that diskette as well. Detailed instructions on preparing this diskette can be found in Chapter Seventeen, Multimedia.

> **EXAM NOTE:** Be able to describe in detail what FDISK and FORMAT do, and how they affect the system.

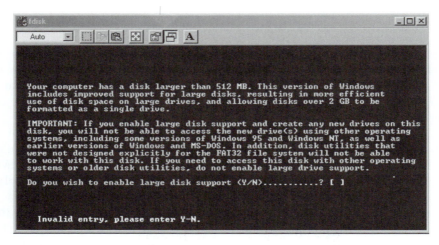

Figure 14.4 The opening screen of FDISK. And if you press the wrong key, such as the hot-key for your screen capture software, this is the message you'll get.

Figure 14.5 The FDISK Options screen. If you only have one physical hard drive installed, option 5 will not appear.

When you boot to that disk, you'll be at a DOS screen with an A:\ prompt. Type fdisk at the command prompt and you'll be presented with a screen that looks like the one in **Figure 14.4**. What this is telling you is that the version of FDISK you're running supports both FAT16 and FAT32. If you answer Yes (Y) to the question at the bottom, you are enabling FAT32. Answering No (N) puts you in FAT16.

This brings you to the FDISK Options screen shown in **Figure 14.5**. In this particular illustration, you are presented with five options. This is because the computer I'm using to create

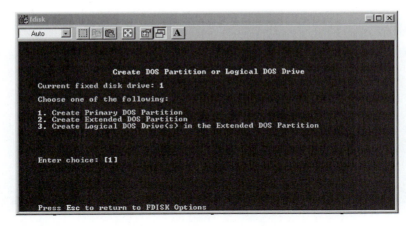

Figure 14.6   Creating partitions or Logical DOS Drives

the illustrations has more than one physical disk installed. If you run this utility on a machine with only one physical disk, option 5, Change current fixed disk drive, will not appear.

How you work with this first screen is entirely dependent upon whether this is a brand-new machine you're configuring for the first time or if it is an older computer that you are servicing. If you are working with a drive that already has an operating system installed and you're trying to blow it away, you will be better off if you work backward through the menu and then work forward. For the purposes of this discussion, however, I'll take the screens in order.

OPTION 1, CREATE DOS PARTITION OR LOGICAL DOS DRIVE

This option brings up the screen shown in **Figure 14.6**

If you select 1. Create Primary DOS Partition, then you are creating the partition that will begin on the physical sectors immediately following the file allocation tables. 2. Create Extended DOS Partition is where you further subdivide your drive into smaller pieces. Note that you cannot create an extended partition if no primary partition has been created. There is a specific order in which things must be done.

3. Create Logical DOS Drive(s) in the Extended DOS Partition allows you to further subdivide the extended partitions into even smaller chunks. Since the MBR only supports four partitions, these logical DOS drives are defined in the Volume Boot Record (VBR) contained within the extended partitions themselves. Every extended partition requires that at least one logical DOS drive be created.

OPTION 2, SET ACTIVE PARTITION

The second option shown in the FDISK Options screen is 2. Set active partition. If you have created a single large partition, this will be done automatically for you. If not, you will get the screen shown in **Figure 14.7**. The message you see in the illustration indicates that an active partition has already been set. This will not be the case on a newly installed drive. Users with

Figure 14.7   Setting the active partition

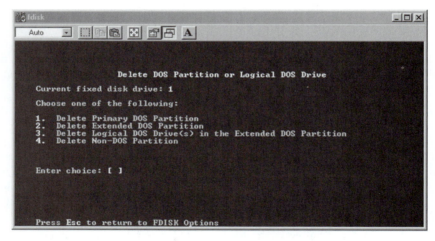

Figure 14.8   Deleting partitions

drives configured with more than one unformatted partition will be shown a list of all partitions on the drive. You select the one you want marked active by typing in its number.

OPTION 3, DELETE PARTITION OR LOGICAL DOS DRIVE

Selecting 3. Delete partition or Logical DOS Drive brings up the screen shown in **Figure 14.8**. The options are as follows:

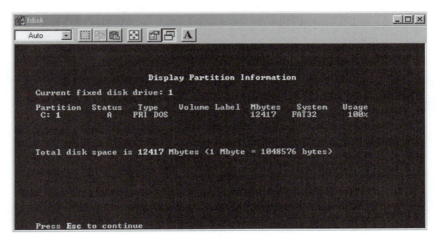

Figure 14.9 Viewing partitions

■ *Delete Primary DOS Partition.* You cannot do this if there is an existing extended DOS partition. That's one of the reasons why on an existing machine you view the partitions first. That way you know there are extended partitions that need to be deleted.

■ *Delete Extended DOS Partition.* You can't do this while there are logical DOS drives defined. Therefore, it is necessary to delete all logical DOS drives before you can delete the partition. That is the purpose of the next option.

■ *Delete Logical DOS Drive(s) in the Extended DOS Partition.* It does exactly what it describes. Once you've done this, you can proceed to option 2.

■ *Delete Non-DOS Partition.* This is the other reason you view partition information before you begin. Drives partitioned with NTFS, HPFS, or the Unix File System will not be seen by FAT. They'll only appear as non-DOS partitions.

OPTION 4, DISPLAY PARTITION INFORMATION

Back on the FDISK Options screen, option 4 brings up a screen that lists all DOS partitions, primary and extended, and all non-DOS partitions (**Figure 14.9**). In this particular image, there is only a single primary partition. You can't manipulate anything from this screen; you can simply view it. But on that machine that you're servicing for somebody else, knowing how the drive was originally prepared can save you several steps later on.

OPTION 5, CHANGE CURRENT FIXED DRIVE

Option 5 (**Figure 14.10**) allows you to redirect the actions of FDISK from your primary drive to any of the others installed on a system. This option has also caused more disasters than any other I've described. After installing a second physical hard disk into a computer, when you run

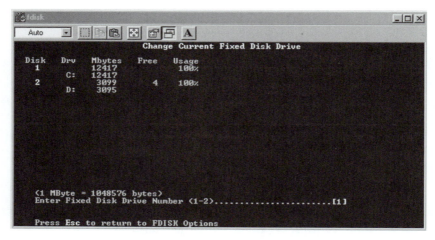

Figure 14.10   Changing physical drives in FDISK

FDISK it is essential that you switch over to the new drive before configuring partitions. You will be warned that a primary partition already exists if you try to create one on your existing drive. Unfortunately, it's all too easy for the beginner to simply go ahead and delete the primary partition after they read that message.

FORMATTING DRIVES

Now that you've got your partitions prepared and a file system selected, you are ready to format the drive for use. FDISK created the MBR, now the FORMAT command is going to prepare your file allocation tables for use. The format command is the utility that groups sectors into clusters, based on the file system and partition size selected. When you format a drive for the first time, it can seem to take forever. The bigger the drive, the longer it takes.

Interestingly, it only takes a few seconds to generate the file allocation tables. Effectively, that's all the drive really needs to have done before it's ready to be used. However, you don't want to be copying crucial and highly sensitive data, such as your saved games from *Redneck Rampage,* to a bad sector. Therefore, on an initial format, as the format command is creating the FAT, it is also scanning the hard drive, looking for bad or suspicious spots on the surface of the drive. It maps those sections as being bad sectors. Here's where a technology called *spare sectoring* comes into play. Virtually every hard drive manufactured, even under today's modern methods, has a certain number of sectors that can't be used to store data. Yet how often do you ever format a drive and have it tell you that it found a bunch of bad sectors?

BUZZ WORDS

Spare sectoring: A technique hard drive manufacturers use in which extra tracks of recordable space are included with each drive that ships. As bad sectors are discovered on the drive, new sectors are made available from this space to replace the bad ones.

Spare sectoring assumes that there will be bad sectors. However, it's bad PR to ship a drive that, fresh out of the box, starts spewing out a report of bad sectors when it's formatted. Every drive coming off the assembly line has a few extra tracks, over and above the rated capacity of the drive. At the factory, the drive undergoes a preliminary test, and defective sectors are already mapped and additional sectors made available from the spare tracks. To be on the safe side, the format routine is looking to see if the initial process missed any.

Once a drive has been formatted for the first time, it is possible to bypass the quality control stage. Typing in the FORMAT command with the /q trigger simply rewrites the file allocation tables without doing a surface scan.

HARD DISK MAINTENANCE

Okay, now it's been a while. For the last several months you've been using your hard drive daily and have given it a heavy workout. Several gigabytes worth of data have been added, deleted, edited, massaged, and manipulated. And all of a sudden your drive is becoming slower than death. What can you do about it? Several third-party software vendors offer basic utilities that help deal with this problem, as well as with the possibility that your drive may be developing bad sectors. Microsoft includes basic versions of these utilities in its product. These utilities are ScanDisk and Disk Defragmenter, usually called Defrag. ScanDisk can scour your hard drive for errors such as bad sectors, lost clusters, and invalid files. Defrag takes files that have been scattered all over your hard drive and puts them back together all in one place.

EXAM NOTE: While the A+ Exam is supposedly vendor-neutral, the only disk maintenance tools you're likely to be asked about are ScanDisk and Defrag. Even if you're a Linux user, make sure you understand how these utilities work.

SCANDISK

ScanDisk is a utility that first appeared in Windows 95 and has been with Windows users since (**Figure 14.11**). When ScanDisk is run on a drive, there are two options. A standard check simply checks your files and folders for errors such as invalid names and/or date stamps. A thorough scan finds much more. A thorough scan scans the surface of the hard disk looking for bad sectors. It can also find other errors such as lost file fragments, cross-linked files, duplicate file names, and errors that occur when Windows converts a long file name to MS-DOS's more primitive naming conventions.

Two of these errors are worth taking a closer look at. These are the lost file fragments and cross-linked files. Many third-party utilities will refer to the lost file fragments as *lost clusters*.

Lost file fragments generally occur when there has been an unexpected system shutdown. If the OS suddenly crashes or if the user turns the machine off without going through the standard shutdown procedures, temporary files are left open, data that has been copied to virtual memory has not been saved, and open files are not properly closed. All of these can result in the FAT finding file allocation units (FAUs) on the hard drive that are occupied, but have no reference in FAT to a specific file. These unclaimed clusters are the ones that are being reported. When ScanDisk finds

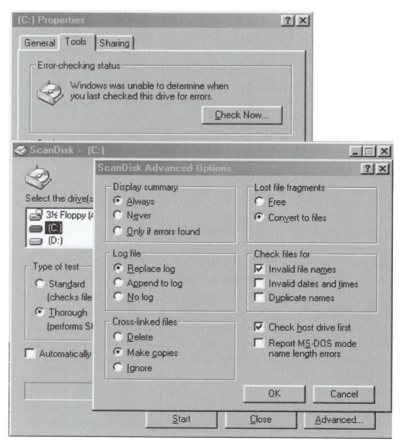

Figure 14.11   ScanDisk is a Microsoft utility that should be run on a regular basis. The Advanced Options allow the user to select a number of different errors to look for.

them, by default, they are converted to files in the system root directory with names of file0000.chk, file0001.chk, and so on. In most cases, these were temporary files the system still had open at the time of the shutdown. They have little or no impact on the permanent copy of that file still written to the hard drive. Still, from time to time, they are user data that was never written to file. In many cases, the data is corrupted, but if you can recognize what it is and where it goes, sometimes you can recover it. The vast majority of the time, your best bet is to delete the .chk files and free up the space.

BUZZ WORDS

Lost cluster: See Lost file fragment.

Lost file fragment: An FAU on the hard drive that contains data, but that has lost the pointers that identify the file to which it belongs.

Cross-linked file: An FAU that is claimed by two or more different files, and is therefore available to none.

Cross-linked files can be a more serious issue. You may recall when I discussed the formatting of hard drives, I pointed out that every single FAU on the hard drive is mapped, whether it is in use or not. When a file uses the FAU, the entry for that file in FAT marks that FAU as occupied and claims it. If two or more files mark the same FAU as being a part of that file, there is a problem. None of the files that claim those sectors can access the data on them. This situation can be caused by unexpected shutdowns, failure of a device controller, a glitch that occurred in the application that created the file, or any number of other things.

The way ScanDisk "fixes" these files is to compare the creation date in the file entry. The file with the most recent date gets the cluster. Most of the time this will be correct. That doesn't, however, mean that the other file didn't, at some time or the other, have data that occupied that file.

Other problems ScanDisk can find are invalid dates and invalid file names. No OS allows the user to create an invalid file name. But data corruption can cause it to happen. If the OS thinks that an invalid character exists, it will mark the file name as invalid. Invalid dates occur when the date of the file is later than the date the system reports as being current, or an invalid date format. ScanDisk fixes either of these problems.

DISK DEFRAGMENTER

When files are first copied to the hard drive, the controller attempts to find enough contiguous space for the entire file to fit. On a new drive, that's no problem. As time goes on and the drive fills, more files have been added to the FAUs following the end of any given file, the drive is fuller than it used to be, and there aren't as many really large spaces in which to fit data. When you open a file and edit it, and then subsequently save it back to disk, that file will be stored on the same FAUs it originally occupied. If that file can no longer fit into contiguous space, the controller will simply take the overflow and store it someplace else on the drive. The file now exists in two separate places on the drive. The more often a file is opened, edited, and resaved, the more different places it occupies.

The converse happens as files are deleted. That space becomes available. As the drive fills, contiguous space may become a premium. So new files get copied to wherever the controller can find space.

I pointed out in Chapter Thirteen when discussing I/O operations that a contiguous file only requires one I/O operation to set up the data transfer, and then the data can move to memory in bursts. If the file has been fragmented, each fragment requires a new I/O operation, from setup to breakdown.

Another performance hit caused by a heavily fragmented drive comes as a result of the way Windows maintains its swap file. The swap file needs to be contiguous. You may have 2GB of free space, but if only 200MB of it is contiguous, then Windows effectively has a 200MB swap file. This is too small for optimum performance and can degrade overall system speed noticeably. Defrag (**Figure 14.12**) can put the files on your system back together again, and put all free space toward the end of the drive, where it belongs. Files are accessed much more quickly, and Windows can make a larger swap file.

Whenever possible, users should run Defrag in Safe Mode. This is because open files cannot be defragmented. In Safe Mode, critical system devices will obviously be running, but unused

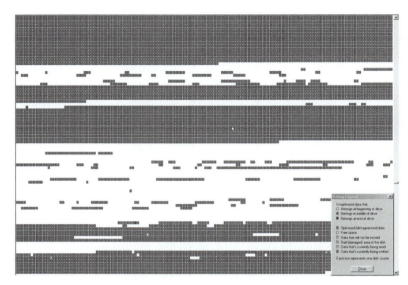

Figure 14.12 As with ScanDisk, Windows users should run Disk Defragmenter on a regular basis.

drivers, such as for a scanner, digital camera, printer, NIC, sound card, and so on, won't load, so those files can be relocated.

Linux and Unix users don't really have a need to defrag their drives. The file system used by these two OSs have code built in that relocates files to contiguous space when they outgrow their old living quarters.

TROUBLESHOOTING HARD DRIVES

Much of what will appear in this section is simply a reiteration of things I've said before. It's simply collected into one place for ease of use. There is also some additional material that you might find useful, however, so don't just automatically assume I'm just trying to make the book fatter.

Problems with hard drives will fall under one of two categories. They either don't work at all, or they seem to work when you start the machine, but they're acting up in some way, shape, or form. I'll cover both bases.

> **EXAM NOTE:** Hard disk troubleshooting is one of the more prominent troubleshooting subjects on the entire exam. Rather than point out everything you are likely to encounter, suffice it to say that the next few pages are very important.

WHEN THE DRIVE ISN'T SEEN

If the drive isn't being seen at all by the system, nine times out of ten, it's a configuration issue. You boot the machine and all you have is drive A. You might know this is happening right off the bat if you get error messages like "No Fixed Disk Present," "Hard Disk Controller Failure," or any one of several numeric error messages in the 17** range, including 1701, 1780, 1781, 1790, and 1791. Other error messages that point to this include "Hard Disk Configuration Error," "Hard Disk 0 Failure," or "Invalid Drive Specification."

Ask this question: Was this drive just installed, or has it been in place for a while? If you just installed it, check the following:

- Is the power connector (Molex) hooked up? Drives have a tendency to not work as well when there is no electricity coming to them.

- Check the Molex to make sure there's current coming through it. This is where having a multimeter comes in handy.

- Did you use a Y-cable to get power to the drive? If so, try hooking it up directly to one of the cables coming straight out of the power supply. The Y-connector might be bad.

- Is the ribbon cable connected? Even if there's power going to the drive, the BIOS finds the drive on POST by sending signals down the cable. No cable, no signals. No signals, no drive.

- Is the ribbon cable connected to the proper port on the motherboard or I/O card? On older machines, it was necessary for the boot drive to be on the primary port, or it wouldn't be recognized.

- Check the jumpers for master/slave if it is an IDE drive. If the settings are right, check and see if you have a CS cable. Those can drive you nuts, too. A notch clipped out of the twenty-eighth conductor tells you it is CS, but not seeing a notch doesn't necessarily tell you it isn't. To be on the safe side, put the slave drive in the middle connector and the master on the end.

- Check device ID numbers on SCSI drives. Two devices can't share the same ID unless they're part of an array. I'll cover that in more detail in the next chapter.

- Check your CMOS settings. On many machines, it's possible to disable the IDE ports. Maybe the IDE port got disabled somehow. If the CMOS thinks there isn't a drive there, nothing else matters. The drive isn't there. On most machines, the default is "AUTO," so this shouldn't be an issue. But people do play with CMOS settings, even though they should know better.

- Is the drive any good? Hey, face it! Sometimes, you just get a bad drive. Make it the only device on the primary IDE port, set it to master, put it in the middle connector, make sure it's got power, and fire it up. Still not there? You might have a bad drive, but you also might have a bad port. Try a drive you know works.

WHEN THE DRIVE IS THERE, MORE OR LESS

While booting the machine, the POST routine usually displays its progress. On some brands of computer, these messages are concealed by the manufacturer's logo. You need to disable this screen if possible. The POST messages can contain information that helps with troubleshooting certain problems. Press the Esc key as soon as the promo screen appears, and you should see the POST messages. Usually. One of the messages displayed is a listing of IDE devices found.

If you can't clear that screen, or are a little late on the uptake, you should also get a message telling you what key to push to enter the CMOS Setup program. These are discussed in detail in Chapter Six, Motherboards, BIOS, and the Chipset. Many BIOS products have an IDE Autodetect utility that will tell you if it's finding a drive or not. Run that.

If the machine makes it all the way through the POST routine and then fails, there are several things to look at:

- Is the hard drive recognized by the BIOS, but not the operating system? Check the following:

  - Are the installation parameters set correctly?

  - Does your BIOS support the type of drive you're using? This is mostly a problem on older machines.

  - Are you using the correct translation mode? If the CMOS somehow got accidentally moved from LBA to Large or Normal, the OS is going to choke.

  - Did somebody accidentally FDISK or format the drive? Fix the problem, then take the machine away from the user!

- Did you get an error message saying "I/O error reading Drive C:"? This could be a bad thing. Many viruses attack the boot sector, and this is the message you're likely to get. Most reliable antivirus programs, such as McAffee or Norton AntiVirus, provide a bootable diskette that starts machines that are so affected. Maybe you'll get lucky and that can fix the problem. Then again, maybe you won't. If you prepared the drive using one of Microsoft's versions of FDISK, use that same version and try the command fdisk/mbr. That can sometimes repair a corrupted master boot record. That same error message can result from a damaged boot sector. If this is the case, the drive is dead. It might be possible to salvage the data from the drive.

- You get the message "No Operating System Found." If this happens, take that boot diskette you made earlier and boot to the A:\ prompt. Now log onto the C: drive by typing C:\ and pressing the <Enter> key. If you get a C:\ prompt, type CD WINDOWS or CD DOS depending on what you're using for an OS. Does your prompt change to C:\WINDOWS? If it does, it's unlikely you have a bad drive, but rather a corrupted installation of your OS. Before you get rash and FDISK the drive and start over, try reinstalling the OS over the previous installation. That way you don't blow away all of your other directories. Most of your data can be salvaged, although you will probably have to reinstall most, if not all of your applications.

- Your machine boots okay, but Windows always has to start a ScanDisk. This could be a sign of impending drive failure. Is ScanDisk finding a lot of bad sectors? If so, back up your data and replace the drive now, while you still have your data intact.

- "Invalid Command Interpreter," "No Boot Device Available," or "Missing Operating System" usually indicates that the MBR has become corrupted. Try the FDISK /MBR (which only occasionally works) or use one of several third-party utilities that are available for restoring MBRs.

■ "General Failure Reading Drive C:" can occur either on bootup or long after the system boots, while you're running an application. This indicates bad sectors on the drive. Run ScanDisk. Boot to a floppy and run it from there, if necessary.

Since hard drives have become so incredibly cheap (relatively speaking), it is becoming easier for an IT administrator to take a hard drive exhibiting any of the above symptoms, especially a drive that announces bad sectors, and circular file it, replacing it with a new drive. In a mission-critical installation, it is probably not a bad idea to replace the drive, but you might want to try something before you are too quick to throw away what might be a perfectly good drive.

Sometimes, the operating system has a hard time reading a particular cluster, so it relocates the cluster and marks it bad. That is a safety net programmed into the OS to protect your data. The cluster might not necessarily be bad, however. There may have simply been a temporary problem. Shutting down a system while the OS is still running can do that.

So before you discard the drive, FDISK it, format it, and put it to use in a less critical installation. It might continue to work for years.

THE DRIVE DOES NOT FORMAT TO CAPACITY

A problem that is gradually working its way out of modern installations occurs when a larger hard drive is installed, and then only formats to a fraction of its capacity. Years ago, it was possible to have your drive format to 508MB, regardless of how large it was. This was because the BIOS and/or chipset on the motherboard only supported the first generation of IDE devices. If it was just the BIOS that was the issue, the problem could be solved by installing an I/O card equipped with ATA-3 or later IDE, as long as it was equipped with supplemental BIOS. If the chipset was the limitation, the only solution was a new motherboard.

Next came the 8GB limitation. If the BIOS and/or chipset did not support the Int13h extensions that I discussed, then a 40GB drive might be easily identified by the system, but would only format to a maximum of 8GB. The problem and solution here was the same as described in the previous paragraph.

The problem most recently seen is a 32GB limitation. Once again, this may be a BIOS limitation. If the BIOS version is prior to 1998, this is most likely the problem. Once again, an adapter card with supplemental BIOS may fix the problem as long as it's not inherent in the chipset. If your BIOS version is after 1999, it's most likely an OS-related issue. Windows 2000 and XP will only allow FAT32 partitions of 32GB. If you require a larger partition using those operating systems, you need to use NTFS.

CHAPTER SUMMARY

That concludes my discussion of hard drives. Chapter Thirteen dealt with the construction of hard disks and drive geometry, and in this chapter I discussed the various interfaces that have existed along the way, hard disk preparation and maintenance, and some troubleshooting issues.

The key points for exam candidates to take away from this chapter are the interfaces up to and including ATA-4. Also spend some extra time on disk preparation and maintenance and troubleshooting.

BRAIN DRAIN

1. List as many hard disk interfaces as you can think of.

2. You have installed a new 80GB hard drive in your computer and everything seems to be working fine, except it only formats to 32GB. What is the cause of this problem and what is a possible solution?

3. Discuss as many improvements in the second generation of IDE compared to the first generation as you can think of.

4. Describe in detail the preparation of a hard disk once it has been installed, assuming a FAT32 file system.

5. Based on the discussion generated by Question 4, describe what is happening to the hard disk on each step along the way.

THE 64K$ QUESTIONS

1. The ST-506 hard disk drive offered a maximum capacity of _____ MB.
   a. 2
   b. 5
   c. 10
   d. 20

2. The first release of the ST-506 used the _____ encoding scheme.
   a. RLL
   b. DRML
   c. MFM
   d. ESDI

3. Which of the following was not a feature of the first generation of IDE?
   a. It only supported drives up to 528MB.
   b. Only one IDE channel was allowed per system.
   c. It supported devices other than hard drives.
   d. Two devices could be put on each channel.

4. The maximum capacity limitation for ATA-5 devices is _____.
   a. 528MB
   b. 8GB
   c. 32GB
   d. 137GB

5. Most hard drives in use today use _____ addressing.
   a. ECHS
   b. Large
   c. CHS
   d. LBA

6. Notebook IDE devices use a _____ -pin cable.
   a. 32
   b. 40
   c. 44
   d. 50

7. The Microsoft utility that re-creates the MBR is _____.
   a. FORMAT
   b. SCANDISK
   c. RESTORE
   d. FDISK

8. Serial ATA devices operate on a maximum peak voltage of _____.

    a. 2.2V

    b. 5V

    c. 500mv

    d. 12V

9. A CS cable differs from a standard IDE cable in that _____.

    a. It has eighty conductors

    b. It automatically configures the drive for master/slave settings

    c. Conductor 39 is swapped with conductor 28

    d. The twenty-eighth conductor has been clipped between the center connector and the one on the end

10. Why does the /q trigger on the FORMAT command not work the first time you format a disk.

    a. Who are you kidding? It does!

    b. The sectors have not yet been mapped out.

    c. Format tests each FAU before registering its entry in AT.

    d. The File Allocation Tables have not yet been written.

TRICKY TERMINOLOGY

Block mode: The data transfer setting that allows multiple commands to be moved over an interface on a single interrupt cycle.

Block transfer: The movement of multiple commands over an interface on a single interrupt cycle.

Command overhead: The number of instructions that must be executed in order to carry out a specific request, combined with the speed at which the device can carry out those instructions.

Command overlapping: The ability of a device to start processing a command even before the command issued prior to it has completed its cycle.

Command queuing: Allows a device to store a series of commands in a buffer area, assuring that as one command is completed another one is rolled up to the gate and ready to go.

Cross-linked file: An FAU that is claimed by two or more different files, and is therefore available to none.

Cycle rate: The amount of time it takes for a specific device under the control of a timing mechanism to complete one "tick" of that timer.

Differential signaling: A method by which a single data wire on a parallel cable is matched up by a wire carrying the inverse of the signal being carried by the data wire.

Double-transition clocking: The movement of two transfers of data on a single clock cycle.

Interleave ratio: The number of sectors that must pass beneath the R/W heads between the reading of one sector and the time the heads will be ready to read the next sector. For example, on a 3:1 ratio, the heads will read or write one sector, two sectors will pass by completely ignored, then the next sector will be written. The unused sectors will be filled in during the next two rotations of the platter.

Lost cluster: See Lost file fragment.

Lost file fragment: An FAU on the hard drive that contains data, but that has lost the pointers that identify the file to which it belongs.

Single-ended signaling: A method by which a single data wire on a parallel cable is matched up by a ground wire.

Spare sectoring: A technique hard drive manufacturers use in which extra tracks of recordable space are included with each drive that ships. As bad sectors are discovered on the drive, new sectors are made available from this space to replace the bad ones.

Third-party DMA: Direct memory access that is managed by a device other than the two devices utilizing DMA to exchange data.

ACRONYM ALERT

ATA: Advanced Technology Attachment

ATAPI: Advanced Technology Application Programming Interface

ECHS: Extended CHS

EIDE: Enhanced IDE

ESDI: Enhanced Small Device Interface. An earlier hard disk drive interface that preceded IDE.

PATA: Parallel ATA

PIO: Programmed Input/Output. A transfer of data in which each byte of data must be negotiated and managed by the CPU.

SATA: Serial ATA

SMART: Self Monitoring Analysis and Reporting Technology. Commands built into a hard disk interface that allows the drive to do some rather extensive self-diagnostics.

CHAPTER 15

THE MANY FACES
OF SCSI

The Small Computer Systems Interface (SCSI), pronounced *skuzzy*, was another brainchild of Al Shugart and was initially released as Shugart Associated System Interface (SASI). It evolved from something called the OEM Bus, which had been developed by IBM to interconnect peripherals to the 360 mainframe computer. The idea is that multiple unrelated devices can interface together in a single chain.

The American National Standards Institute (ANSI) released the first set of standards in 1986 as ANSI X3.131-1986. ANSI defined an interface that would accept a number of peripheral devices on a single chain, using a parallel bus. SCSI-1, as it's now called, supported a total of eight devices, including the host adapter. Each device would carry a unique ID number to prevent conflicts. Unfortunately, very few technical specifications were provided and many of the commands included were considered optional. As a result many different devices and adapters appeared on the market that were incompatible with one another. The later release of SCSI-II alleviated much of the confusion, and eventually SCSI-III would define a cross-platform interface.

A+ CORE HARDWARE EXAM OBJECTIVES

Interconnecting SCSI devices has long been a topic that intimidates novice hardware technicians. It shouldn't. This chapter will lead you through the ins and outs of SCSI. If you're taking the CompTIA Exam, it will also cover the following objectives.

1.5 Identify the names, purposes, and performance characteristics of standardized/common peripheral ports, associated cabling, and their connectors. Recognize ports, cabling, and connectors by sight.

1.7 Identify proper procedures for installing and configuring common SCSI devices. Choose the appropriate installation or configuration sequences in given scenarios. Recognize the associated cables.

2.1 Recognize common problems associated with each module and their symptoms, and identify steps to isolate and troubleshoot the problems. Given a problem situation, interpret the symptoms and infer the most likely cause.

HOW SCSI WORKS

The core of the SCSI chain is the *host controller*. This can either be a card that plugs into the expansion bus, or it can be built right onto the motherboard in many cases. The host controller is the device that is assigned the IRQ and I/O.

A single SCSI chain consists of the host controller and all the devices connected to it. This would include both internal and external devices. Many controllers provide an external connection that allows the user to hook up devices like scanners, external SCSI hard drives, and CD-ROMs. Any given controller will be capable of controlling a set number of devices. SCSI-I and II support eight devices, including the controller. SCSI-III supports sixteen devices, including the controller. All internal devices, external devices, and the controller itself count toward this number. However, many adapters are equipped with two or more channels, allowing a separate SCSI chain for each channel.

> ## BUZZ WORDS
>
> **Host controller:** The adapter installed on a system or embedded in the motherboard that manages SCSI devices.
>
> **Device ID:** A unique number assigned to each device on a SCSI chain, including the host adapter, that identifies it to other devices on the chain.

Devices on the chain are subsequently assigned *device ID* numbers. Every device on the chain, including the host controller itself, must have a unique ID. The IDs need not go in order, and you can skip numbers in the sequence. Typically, the host adapter is assigned ID #7.

The reason for this is that ID numbers are assigned a priority. The highest priorities are assigned the highest numbers, therefore, with SCSI-I and SCSI-II, ID7 carried the highest priority. In order to maintain compatibility, SCSI-III devices place the order of priority, from highest to lowest, 7 through 0, followed by 14 through 8.

No two devices can share an ID number. To do so will result in one of two things. If the devices are designed to support logical unit numbers (LUN), and each device is assigned a different LUN, then all of those devices will be seen by the controller as a single device. If no LUNs are assigned, then the first device with that ID is recognized and subsequent devices with the same ID are ignored.

Internally, SCSI devices hook up on the same cable. If you have three devices, you need a cable with four connections: one for the host controller, one each for the three devices. It doesn't matter what order they are installed in the system. Device IDs will determine the order in which the system "sees" them. Externally, they hook up a little differently. The back of each external SCSI device has an input port and an output port. A cable goes from the external SCSI port to the device. Another cable goes from that device to the next one, and so on until you reach the end.

Any device that is on the end of the SCSI chain must be *terminated*. Any electrical signal that reaches the end of a wire will simply turn around and come back home unless there is something on the end of the cable to prevent this from happening. This is referred to as echo in computer networks and SCSI chains. Nearly all SCSI devices have been equipped with a termination circuit. This is generally done with resistors, although how those resistors are used varies with the equipment. Sometimes you need to physically plug them into the device; other times they are hardwired into the device and engaged by a switch. With some host adapters, termination can be accomplished through the software, and some older devices have a termination device that must be plugged in. Refer to your manual for the proper procedure for any device you're working with. You can also purchase SCSI cables with terminating resistors installed at one end.

> **BUZZ WORDS**
>
> **Terminate:** To create a dead end for electrical signals traveling down a wire so that they do not echo back the other direction.

Parallel SCSI has a serious problem with attenuation and noise. This problem is exacerbated as speeds increase, and is substantially greater with older devices. In Chapter Fourteen, Hard Disk Interfacing and Disk Management, I discussed the differences between single-ended (SE) and differential signaling. Early SCSI was single-ended. Each of the bits in the 8-bit signal travels over a pair of wires. One of these wire pairs carried the actual signal, while its partner acted as a ground. On the better cables, these wires were twisted together to reduce cross talk. One of these cables could effectively carry a signal about 6 meters, or 20 feet. Standard ribbon cables were even less than that. As speeds increase, and as the number of devices on the chain increase, this distance is shortened even more. **Table 15.1** compares cable lengths to SCSI standards.

Differential SCSI (now called HVD, for high-voltage differential) was developed to offset this limitation. Differential SCSI uses two wires per bit of information transmitted. This is referred to as a balanced signal, and is the same differential signaling discussed in Chapter Fourteen. It allows for up to 25-meter runs of SCSI devices.

However, that inverse signal wire takes the place of the ground on single-ended devices. As a result, single-ended and differential devices are not compatible on the same SCSI chain. Differential devices can fry any SE devices on the same chain. Also, a different controller is required to handle the signal differences. You can use differential devices in the same system as single-ended devices by adding a separate SCSI controller and creating an isolated differential chain. While differential SCSI was primarily a mainframe peripheral, there were a number of differential controllers and devices produced for the PC market.

Table 15.1 Cable Distance Limitations with Single-Ended SCSI

SCSI Level	No. of Devices	Distance
SCSI-I/II, 5MHz	1	6M
SCSI-I/II, 10MHz	3	3M
SCSI-I/II, 10MHz	>3	1.5M

Single-ended SCSI was severely limited in terms of cable length. The more devices on the chain, the worse it got.

Low-voltage differential (LVD) appeared in 1998. As the name implies, LVD devices operate on a much lower voltage than standard differential devices. They can also sense the presence of single-ended devices on the chain and automatically switch to single-ended operation themselves. If no other SCSI device is detected, or if all the other devices are also LVD devices, the device will operate as LVD. These devices can operate on up to 12 meters of cable. SCSI-III standards dictate that all devices must be LVD. Therefore, it's safe to assume that a device marked SCSI-III is LVD, and that if the device is HVD it is SCSI-II. As with SE devices, LVD and HVD cannot exist on the same chain without adapters in place.

> **NOTE:** One other way to get around the issue of SE and HVD on the same chain was to add an SE-HVD converter to the chain, instead of using a controller and an isolated chain. The problem there was that a new controller would only set you back $100 to $150. A converter can run upwards of $300 and effectively reduces the length of the HVD chain.

Aside from the voltage differences of the wires carrying the signals, differential SCSI was no different than standard SCSI in all other respects. All of the rules concerning termination and device IDs hold fast.

USING SCSI EXPANDERS

Even with LVD devices in place, there are times when more distance is needed. A device known as a *SCSI expander* allows this to be done. The expander takes the SCSI bus and splits it into up to three different segments. Each segment can support a run of cable equal to that of the bus that it's on. Therefore, if you have a bus of all LVD devices, three segments of 12 meters are possible. Also, if you are not adding any devices to the middle segment, a longer cable than would otherwise be acceptable can be used.

Expanders work by taking the signal, cleaning up the noise that has been picked up along the way, amplifying it back to its original signal strength, and then sending it along its way. The device and the process are completely invisible to the host adapter. In fact, it is not even considered a device, and therefore requires no device ID. **Table 15.2** shows how much extra distance one can achieve on a SCSI chain using expanders.

Another thing that makes the SCSI expander a very versatile device is that you can mix early SCSI modes with some of the more advanced modes. You can get devices that move a parallel interface across copper wire to a serial fiber-optics interface. There are even devices that move an HVD signal across to an SE interface.

Use of SCSI expanders, on its simplest level, allows someone to stretch a SCSI chain a little farther than he or she would otherwise be able to. This allows external devices to be installed at a greater distance from the host adapter. **Figure 15.1** shows how this might be done.

BUZZ WORDS

SCSI expander: A device that allows a technician to effectively increase the length of a SCSI chain without the risk of data corruption.

Table 15.2 Distance Extensions Using SCSI Expanders

Bus Type	Standard	Fast	Ultra	Ultra2
Single-Ended SCSI				
No Expander	6M	3M	1.5M	N/A
1 Expander	12M	6M	3M	N/A
2 Expanders (populated)	18M	9M	4.5M	N/A
2 Expanders (point to point)	24M	12M	6M	N/A
Low-Voltage Differential				
No Expander	12M	12M	12M	12M
1 Expander	Not Used	Not Used	Not Used	24M
2 Expanders (populated)	Not Used	Not Used	Not Used	36M
2 Expanders (point to point)	Not Used	Not Used	Not Used	48M
High-Voltage Differential				
No Expander	25M	25M	25M	N/A
1 Expander	50M	50M	50M	N/A
2 Expanders (populated)	75M	75M	75M	N/A
2 Expanders (point to point)	100M	100M	100M	N/A

Adding expanders can greatly extend the range of a single SCSI chain.

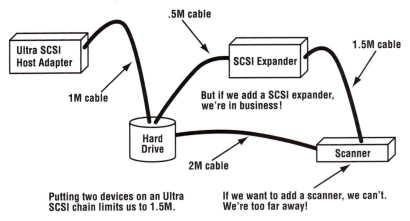

Figure 15.1 Extending the length of a SCSI chain using a SCSI expander

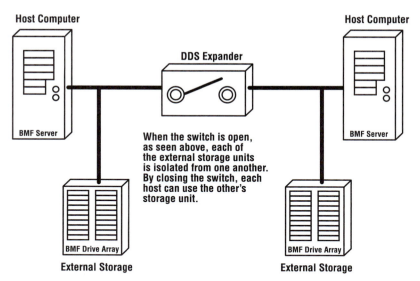

Figure 15.2 Storage systems can be shared among systems when a domain divider switch is used.

Another use of this device involves using it as a *domain divider switch*. For example, if you have two separate computers, each with its own array of hard drives in an external storage bank, it is possible to share those devices between the two host computers. By placing a SCSI expander between the two banks of drives, each computer has access to either array

Buzz Words

Domain divider switch: A device that allows external SCSI devices to be shared by multiple host computers.

when the switch is closed. If for any reason you need to isolate them, you open the switch and they are separated. A diagram of this in **Figure 15.2** shows you how it works.

Techniques of Spanning Disks

While not the exclusive realm of SCSI, one key reason for wanting to use SCSI on a high-end system or network server is to facilitate the use of either RAID arrays or to create a single volume set from several drives. While those two concepts may at first sound redundant they really are not. I'm going to start with volume sets for a simple and very scientific reason. It doesn't take as long to discuss and it provides the foundation for later discussions.

Volume Sets

While it's true that hard drives are getting bigger every day, every once in a while you run into a situation where you just have too much data to fit onto a single hard drive. Yet for some

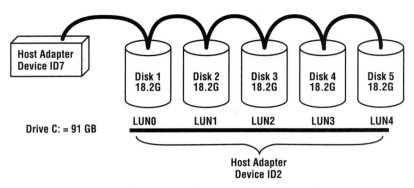

Figure 15.3 Putting five separate hard drives into a single volume set allows you to store much larger chunks of data than single hard drives allow.

reason, it is essential that this data be maintained as a single set. An example of this would be trying to fit a 240GB database onto a single drive. Even if you could find a drive that large, there is still one very good reason you would want to span it across multiple drives. If you have several hundred people accessing that data on a regular basis, a single drive will not be up to the task. A *volume set* takes multiple drives and combines them together to appear to the system and the user as a single drive.

BUZZ WORDS

Volume set: A storage array of very large capacity created by combining multiple drives of smaller capacity.

Earlier in the chapter, I mentioned that if LUNs were used, two devices could be assigned the same ID and the controller would see those two devices as being one. A volume set is an example of where you would do this. Three 72GB hard drives given the same device ID but different LUNs will appear to the controller as a single 216GB drive. These drives become a single volume set.

When you set up a volume set, you are usually doing so with a small collection of hard drives that you are installing into the computer. In this situation, you would decide how many of your drives belong in the set and assign that set a device ID. On a unit level, each of the individual drives would receive its own LUN. From that point on, however many drives you assigned to that set are now all seen as a single drive by the operating system. **Figure 15.3** shows five 18.2GB hard disk drives configured as a single 91GB drive.

RAID ARRAYS

RAID is an acronym for Redundant Array of Independent Disks. RAID allows you to configure several disks to appear as one, similar to a volume set. Unlike a volume set, however, you can build in a certain degree of fault tolerance using RAID. Fault tolerance is a safety cushion that allows a system to keep running in the event of a single (or in some cases, even multiple) component failure.

There are several different levels of RAID, which provide varying degrees of fault tolerance from none to extremely high. I'm not going to discuss all levels of RAID here simply because some levels are proprietary to specific manufacturers and others just aren't used any more. Also, there are single RAID layers and nested RAID layers. Nested layers are when you combine two different single layers. Doing this generally requires more complex hardware, specialized software, or possibly both.

The levels I will discuss here include RAID levels 0, 1, 5, 10, and 50. These are the ones you might actually use some day. Levels 0, 1, and 5 are considered single layers, while 10 and 50 are the two nested layers I'll cover.

SINGLE RAID LEVELS

RAID can be fairly simple, or it can be pretty complex. On the most basic level are the single RAID layers. These are pretty simple and straightforward. Those layers include the following:

- *RAID 0*: Disk striping without parity
- *RAID 1*: Disk mirroring or Disk duplexing
- *RAID 2*: Disk striping with error correction code
- *RAID 3*: Disk bit striping with parity on a dedicated disk
- *RAID 4*: Disk block striping with parity on a dedicated disk
- *RAID 5*: Disk block striping with parity distributed across all disks
- *RAID 6*: Disk block striping with two parity sets distributed across all disks
- *RAID 7*: Proprietary

The difference between disk bit striping and disk block striping is simple. In disk bit striping, the data is striped across the disk in 512-bit sectors. This is the smallest increment that the disk can read. In block striping, there is a user-configurable "chunk" of data that goes onto each disk, dividing the file across disks. Data blocks generally are configured as 2K, 4K, 8K, or 16K blocks. For optimum performance, you want your data block to be the same size as your FAU (see Chapter Thirteen, Hard Disk Drive Structure and Geometry).

RAID 0 RAID 0 is the one level of RAID that provides for no fault tolerance. It is simple disk striping without parity. This is one of the RAID levels that is supported by Windows NT 4.0 and Windows 2000 out of the box, as well as several versions of NetWare, Unix, and Linux. RAID 0 (shown in **Figure 15.4**) requires a minimum of two hard drives and can support up to as many drives as you can fit onto your controllers.

When you use RAID 0, you are taking your data and dividing it across multiple drives in stripes. Then, when your hard drive goes back looking for the data again, it can read it back off the drives, reading all the drives simultaneously. The advantage lies in the fact that I/O performance is greatly increased. The amount of performance increase is proportionate to the number of drives in the array. The more drives, the faster your computer will be. You also get to use all the space on all the drives for data storage.

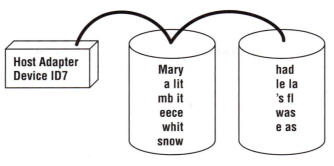

Disk striping without parity

Figure 15.4   RAID 0, disk striping without parity

Of course, the downside to all this is that there is no fault tolerance. If one drive dies, then all your data is gone unless you have developed an appropriate disaster recovery plan. Everything that I said about I/O operations increasing proportionately to the number of drives in your system also holds true to a hard drive specification called mean time before failure (MTBF). This basically is an average number of hours a particular model of drive will last before it dies. If you have five drives, each with an MTBF of 100,000 hours, you have a system MTBF of 20,000 hours.

> **BUZZ WORDS**
>
> **Disk mirroring:** The duplication of data on two different hard drives hanging off of the same controller.
>
> **Disk duplexing:** The duplication of data on two different hard drives hanging off of different controllers.

RAID 1 RAID 1 comes in two forms. There is *disk mirroring* and *disk duplexing*. They differ in only one minor respect. Both require two disks, and both make a duplicate volume. For every byte of data written to one disk, that identical byte is written to the second. This provides a reasonable level of fault tolerance. If one of the drives fails, the other will automatically take over.

The difference between mirroring and duplexing is in the number of controllers used (see **Figure 15.5**). On a mirrored system, there is a single controller for both disks. The argument against this technique is that your system is dead in the water in the event of a controller failure. Disk duplexing, on the other hand, puts each disk on a separate controller. If either a controller or a disk fails, its clone can take over. Logic dictates that this is the superior method, because it is unlikely that you would lose either both controllers, both hard drives, or one controller plus the opposite hard drive at the same time. Therefore your data is safer. Either way, performance suffers noticeably on write operations, but can actually be enhanced on read operations. Your actual storage capacity is cut in half, however.

RAID 5 RAID 5 is probably the most common form of RAID that you'll encounter on servers today. RAID 5 is disk striping with parity. RAID 5 requires a minimum of three hard drives. The maximum number of drives you can use depends on whether you are using a hardware

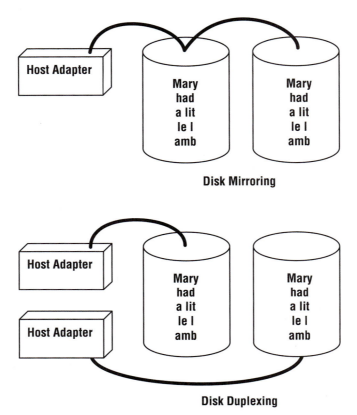

Figure 15.5 Disk mirroring needs only a single controller, while disk duplexing puts each hard drive on a separate controller.

controller or the software RAID included in NT or Novell. Software RAID can make use of up to thirty-two drives. Your hardware will dictate its own limitations.

RAID 5 (**Figure 15.6**) resembles RAID 0 in that it spreads the data across the drives equally. It adds fault tolerance because for each block of data copied to the array, it generates a mathematical image of that data called a *parity block*. The parity information is also distributed evenly across the drives. If a single drive fails, the system continues as if nothing had happened. The parity information is used to rebuild all data in its entirety.

The more drives you put into your system, the more efficiently your system will run. Not only does it have the same effect as more hard drives in a RAID 0 setup as far as performance is concerned, but there is the issue of storage as well. Using a larger number of drives will result in a larger percentage of total available drive space actually being used for data.

BUZZ WORDS

Parity block: A data set that represents a mathematical image of data stored elsewhere in a RAID array.

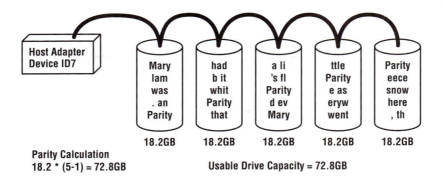

Figure 15.6 RAID 5 provides a high degree of fault tolerance but at the expense of storage capacity.

In order to store the parity information, your system will need space to hold that data. The partitions created on each drive will be no larger than the largest partition that can be created on your smallest drive. Therefore, if you're trying to create a RAID 5 using one 9.1GB and two 18.2GB drives, all three drives will be configured with 9.1GB partitions sewn into the array. You can use the following formula to figure out how much space you'll end up with on your final volume.

(Capacity of Smallest Drive) / (Total Number of Drives in System − 1)

Here's an example. You're going to build a RAID 5 array using five 18.2GB drives plus one 9.1GB drive. How much space will you have? The smallest drive is 9.1GB, and you have six drives. So the first value in the equation is 9.1. You will need the equivalent of one of those six drives for the parity information, leaving five for data. $9.1 \times 5 = 45.5$. Our final volume will be 45.5GB.

Now, what would happen if you took that 9.1GB drive out of the array and only used the five 18.2GB drives? Right away, overall system drive capacity jumps to 72.8GB. $18.2 \times (5 − 1)$ = 72.8GB. You actually lose capacity by including that 9.1GB drive in the array.

NESTED RAID ARRAYS

People being what they are, it doesn't matter how good you make something, there will always be somebody who thinks that it needs to be better. Nested RAID is a perfect example of that. The techniques for nesting RAID all involve large numbers of disk drives and either proprietary controllers or specialized software. Some require both. However, extremely high levels of fault tolerance can be achieved with these techniques.

RAID 0+1 and RAID 10 Trying to understand the difference between these two techniques is understandably confusing. Still, there is actually a difference between a true RAID 10 implementation and simply combining RAID 0 with RAID 1. You now know what RAIDs 0 and 1 can do. You get great performance with RAID 0 but no fault tolerance. You get fault tolerance with RAID 1, but the performance is slower than using a single hard drive. But what if you could have a combination?

A combined RAID 0/1 is a software-based solution, requiring some form of third-party volume manager. RAID 0 can conceivably be placed across a large number of disks, whereas a mirror requires that you use two. RAID 0/1 is a technique of mirroring a disk stripe set without parity. The RAID 0 portion of your system can be any number of drives that your controllers support. However many you use, that number must be exactly duplicated in the mirror. In other words, it would be possible to create a stripe across five disks, greatly enhancing I/O performance. Then, in order to make the system fault tolerant, that stripe set is duplicated to five more disks. While it is possible to set up this configuration on a single controller, it actually makes more sense to place each RAID 0 on its own controller, as seen in **Figure 15.7**. In the event that any single disk fails, that entire side of the mirror is broken and the system is dependent on the other side until the defective disk is replaced.

RAID 10 is stranger yet. RAID 10 requires a minimum of four hard disk drives. Two of these drives will be mirrored. The other pair will be striped in a RAID 0 array for performance. It requires specialized hardware and software support, which adds to the cost of implementation. The advantage is that the machine benefits from a performance standpoint as well as enjoying a certain degree of fault tolerance. The disadvantage to this scheme is that the cost is somewhat high for the limited protection it offers.

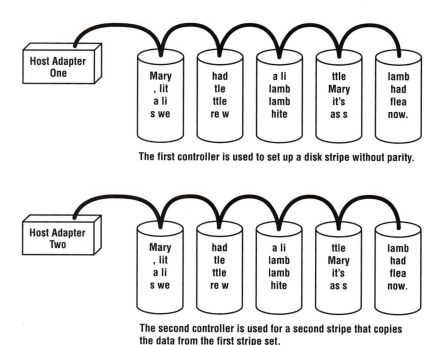

Figure 15.7 RAID 1/0 is a mirror of a stripe set without parity.

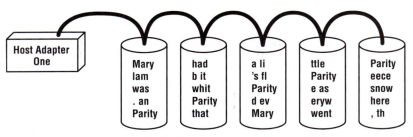

On the first adapter we configure a RAID 5 array.

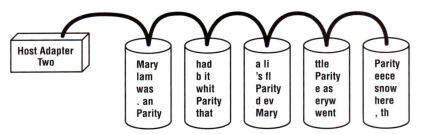

A second RAID 5 array precisely duplicates the first array.

Figure 15.8   You could have more fault tolerance than a RAID 50 array provides. You could have an identical backup server with another RAID 50 array!

RAID 50   This is the most expensive technique to implement of all the ones I will discuss; yet it is by far the most fault tolerant. First, you configure the first RAID 5 array, using anywhere from three to thirty-two disks. Then, on a separate controller, an identical collection of disks duplicates that array. Take a look at **Figure 15.8** and see how it's done. Due to the expense involved, this strategy would only be employed on critical systems. However, security of data is up there with the highest that can be obtained. For the system to fail completely, you would have to have four drives fail simultaneously. Failure of one drive in either array would not bring it down. Parity would simply rebuild the array. Failure of two drives in the same array would cause the second array to kick in. Even if two drives in one array fail, failure of a drive in the second array won't kill the computer. Parity rebuilds that array. Therefore, for total failure, two drives in each array would have to go down at the same time. I think it's safe to assume that if all that happens at once, you've probably got a bigger problem on your hands than a few hard drives.

THE EVOLUTION OF SCSI

Since Al Shugart first introduced his brainchild, SCSI technology has undergone two major evolutionary changes. SCSI-I and II were methods of parallel communication. SCSI-III introduced us to serial SCSI. The different technologies called SCSI have gone from a mere 5MB/s to speeds in excess of a gigabyte per second.

SCSI

The initial SCSI specifications defined an 8-bit, 5MHz bus. Since data could only be moved once per clock cycle, that provided for a 5Mbs throughput. These standards also called for every request for data made by the host adapter to be acknowledged by the target device. This assured accuracy of data transfer. SCSI-I defined only single-ended signaling. As an 8-bit parallel bus, it could never exceed 8MHz in speed.

One major problem that nearly prevented SCSI from ever getting off the ground was a lack of defined standards. Shugart Industries had provided a nice set of ideas with no instructions on how to implement them. There were no defined command sets. Manufacturers would pick and choose from the features and commands suited to the product they were designing and implement only those commands. Then they would ship the device with a controller card specific to their device. Of course, that meant that the card that controlled a hard drive didn't work with a CD-ROM, which in turn didn't work with a scanner, which in turn didn't work with the hard drive.

Another source of frustration for early SCSI users was the diversity of different connectors used. There were DB-25 and DB-50 connectors. The DB-25 appeared in two different sizes. External devices hooked up by way of a 50-pin low-density Centronics connector. This connection looked very similar the one on your printer.

SCSI-I did not provide for any error correction. One of the optional parameters of the original specification allowed for use of bus parity for error detection. Parity, however, does nothing to correct errors. It simply shuts down the system to prevent data corruption. Therefore, it was rarely used.

SCSI-II

The lack of uniform standards prompted the industry to another joint summit. A group calling itself The X3T9 Group met and hammered out the preliminary specifications for SCSI-II (X3.131-1990). One significant change in the SCSI-II standards was that the group defined a total of eighteen commands, called the Common Command Set (CCS), that must be supported by any SCSI-II device. CCS assured that any SCSI-II controller would work with any SCSI-II device.

X3T9 also defined some new bus specifications in the SCSI-II document. To address issues of speed, 16- and 32-bit busses, along with a 10MHz bus speed, were defined. The 10MHz bus was labeled *Fast SCSI*. The 16-bit versions became generically known as *Wide SCSI* (5MHz), and Fast/Wide SCSI (10MHz). In addition, 32-bit *Ultrawide* standards were written. **Table 15.3** shows the differences between these different bus specifications.

SCSI-II also introduced the concepts of command queuing and tagged command queuing that I described in Chapter Fourteen. Another technology introduced that has found its way to other devices on the system since then is that of *scatter-gather data*

> **BUZZ WORDS** ——————
>
> **Fast SCSI:** SCSI over a 10MHz bus.
>
> **Wide SCSI:** SCSI over a 16-bit bus.
>
> **Ultrawide SCSI:** SCSI over a 32-bit bus.
>
> **Scatter-gather data transfer:** The ability of a device to execute a command on one set of data and output the results to multiple devices.

Table 15.3 Comparison of the SCSI-II Standards

SCSI Type	5MHz	10MHz
SCSI-I 8-bit	5MB/s	N/A
SCSI-II 8-bit	5MB/s	10MB/s (Fast SCSI)
SCSI-II 16-bit	10MB/s (Wide SCSI)	20MB/s (Fast/Wide SCSI)
SCSI-II 32-bit	20MB/s (Wide SCSI)	40MB/s (Fast/Wide SCSI)

By today's standards, SCSI-II devices are slow. In their heyday, they were the fastest hard drives available.

transfer. This technology allows a device to execute a command on one set of data and output the results to multiple devices and/or addresses on the system.

SCSI-III

With the release of SCSI-III ANSI broke away from describing the bus in a single document. Instead, its approach involves a collection of documents, each of which describes a different aspect of SCSI-III. Different documents have been created to define protocols, commands, and interfaces. One of these papers defined what is now known as the SCSI Architectural Model (SAM) that covers the physical and electrical aspects of SCSI, including signal characteristics and physical terminations.

The thing that makes SCSI-III such an open standard is that, since it has been defined in a collection of papers instead of a single set of standards, work can be done independently on each layer of the suite. This has allowed for newer and faster technologies to emerge at a much faster rate. Published standards related to SCSI-III include the following:

- SCSI-III Primary Commands (SPC)
    - SCSI-III Primary Commands
    Commands common to all SCSI-III Devices
    - SCSI-III Block Commands
    Commands related to block-oriented devices, such as disk drives
    - SCSI-III Stream Commands
    Data-streaming commands for devices such as tape drives
    - SCSI-III Graphics Commands
    General input/output device commands for devices such as printers and scanners
    - SCSI-III Medium Changer Commands
    For devices such as CD-ROM carousels
    - SCSI-III Controller Commands
    Commands specific to the host adapter, to include hardware RAID controllers

- SCSI-III Protocols
  - SCSI-III Interlocked Protocol (SIP)
  - SCSI-III Fiber Channel Protocol (FCP)
  - SCSI-III Serial Bus Protocol
  - SCSI-III Serial Storage Protocol (SSP)
  - SCSI-III Interconnects
  - SCSI-III Parallel Interface (SPI)
  - Fiber Channel Physical and Signaling Interface (FC-PH)
  - IEEE-1394 High Performance Serial Bus (FireWire)
  - Serial Storage Architecture Bus (SSA)

The result of this division of labor is that new technologies can be developed much more quickly. If a company develops a new protocol, it won't have to wait for an entire new standard to be developed around it before the protocol can be implemented. Protocols can be developed independently of command sets and interfaces. Since this process became a reality, there has been a burst of new technologies released for high-end PCs.

The most significant changes that both computer technicians and end users have to deal with involve connections, so I think that's the best place to start.

SCSI-III INTERCONNECTS

From the start, SCSI has always been a parallel interface that depended exclusively on copper wires to carry the signals. Emerging technologies and speed limitations imposed by parallel communications has caused the industry to look beyond parallel communication over copper wire for the future of SCSI. SCSI interfaces are now being released that use fiber optics instead of wire and a serial data transfer instead of parallel. Therefore, separate sets of standards were developed for different ways of moving data. The modular approach to writing standards means that as new technologies emerge, products based on those technologies appear faster.

SPI Just because new ways of dealing with SCSI have emerged doesn't mean that the old ways are dead. The copper-based parallel interface is still alive and well. The SCSI-III Parallel Interface (SPI) defines the standards manufacturers use to make devices that sit on this interface. Currently, a lot of hard drives are still manufactured that use parallel data transfer. Also, it is still a favorite technology for external devices, such as scanners (although it is starting to lose ground to FireWire, which I will discuss later in this section). The different SPI standards are compared in **Table 15.4**.

Rounding off the list of improvements afforded by SPI is its approach to handling errors that may occur. Previous versions of SCSI were able to use parity in order to check for errors, but could do nothing to correct them. The SCSI-III standards defined a method of using cyclical redundancy checking (CRC) to detect errors and fix them on the fly. Since data is being moved across the bus in chunks, CRC treats the zeros and ones that make up the data as if they represented a very large binary number. It performs a rather complex mathematical algorithm

Table 15.4 Comparison of SCSI-III SPI Modes

SPI Level	SCSI Type	Narrow Mode	Wide Mode
SPI-1	Ultra-SCSI/Fast20	20Mb/s	40Mb/s
SPI-2	Ultra2-SCSI/Fast40	40Mb/s	80Mb/s
SPI-3	Ultra3 (or Ultra160)	N/A	160Mb/s
SPI-4	Ultra320	N/A	320Mb/s
SPI-5	Ultra640		640Mb/s

on each burst of data and includes the results of that calculation as part of the data packet. On the receiving end, the reverse of that calculation is performed. If the results are consistent, the data is accepted. If not, the controller will request that the data be resent.

> **BUZZ WORDS**
>
> **Domain validation:** A process by which a SCSI host adapter sends out a series of commands to each device on the chain and calculates each device's maximum data transfer rate.

There's another feature that has become part of the SCSI-III architecture that should be noted. A process called *domain validation* occurs on boot up. The host adapter sends a series of I/O commands to each device on the chain, testing its throughput capabilities. At this time, a maximum data transfer rate is negotiated between the device and the controller, and that is the rate that will be used from there on out.

SCSI-III introduced the technology of double-transition clocking (DTC) that I discussed in Chapter Fourteen, Hard Disk Interfacing and Disk Management. Previous parallel connections allowed for data to be transferred only on the rising edge of each clock cycle. DTC uses both the rising edge and the falling edge to effectively double throughput. Ultra 160 SCSI can deliver burst modes of 160 megabytes per second.

Ultra640 SCSI is the latest current standard, as of this writing, and was defined under the SP-5 standards released in October of 2002. It is really nothing more than an improvement on SPI-4, or Ultra320. Ultra320 requires that the device be low-voltage differential. It also isolates the host adapter from the interconductor interference by putting it on a separate 80MHz clock that controls data transfer. This clock controls all request (REQ) and acknowledgment (ACK) commands as well as a signal known as the P1 Gating signal. A change unique to SPI-5 is that data is moved in packets instead of a byte at a time.

FC-PH FC-PH (Fiber Channel Physical and Signaling Interface) is one of the three serial interfaces that were introduced with the SCSI-III standards. A serious problem facing the parallel interface is that as speeds get faster it gets increasingly difficult to synchronize the signals. Preventing data corruption becomes a problem.

Serial data, on the other hand, can be moved at incredibly high speeds. So what might be presumably lost in stepping back from the 8-bit bandwidth of parallel communications to moving data a bit at a time, as serial does, is more than made up for when the speed of the transmission is fifty to sixty times faster.

In addition to the significant boost in the speed limit, the serial bus is immune to attenuation and noise. Serial communications over fiber optics eliminates both factors. Therefore, much longer cable runs are possible. Even with copper-based transfer methods, such as FireWire (discussed in Chapter Ten, Examining the Expansion Bus), potential cable lengths are much longer. And because they contain far fewer strands per cable, the medium is much more manageable. More and more devices are moving to one of the different serial media as time moves on.

Of course, to move data in a serial fashion requires that data be packaged differently. The hardware needs to be able to interpret what constitutes the beginning and the end of a transmission, and then be able to assemble a mass of raw digital information back into usable form. In addition, in order to remain compatible with other SCSI-III devices, it needs to be able to accomplish that using the command set defined by SCSI-III standards. It accomplishes both goals by breaking data into packets and sending it across the medium. This is a concept that will become increasingly familiar to you, as this is how data is transferred over modems and across networks as well.

The most common implementation of this interface currently in use is Fiber Channel Arbitrated Loop (FC-AL). The name of this interface can be slightly deceiving. While the specifications were written with the intent of fiber optics, actual implementations use electronic (copper-base) media as well as optical. Media choices include twin-axial cable, coaxial cable, fiber optics, and an FC-AL backplane. Fiber optics promises to be an extremely high-speed bus. The specifications actually define throughput of 1.0625GHz, which would translate out to slightly over a billion bits per second if maximum efficiency could be extracted. Throughput could approach 135MB/s. On the table for consideration and review are proposals that would include 2.12GHz and 4.24GHz standards as well.

Current implementations support 100MB/s per second per loop on mass storage devices with standards already proposed for 200 and 400MB/s loops. FC-AL supports a number of different types of devices ranging from mass storage to network to multimedia. A single loop can support up to 126 devices with up to 30 meters between each device. Termination is not an issue with FC-AL, either. Therefore, it is a whole lot easier to configure an FC-AL loop than an SPI chain. Many manufacturers of high-end servers are already employing FC-AL RAID adapters in their premium lines.

The preferred method for installing FC-AL hard drives is to design the enclosure with a specialized backplane. The drives then fit directly to the backplane. This eliminates the confusion of having a lot of cables inside the box. In addition, FC-AL backplanes are equipped with a circuit called the Port Bypass Circuit (PBC). The PBC automatically detects any drive that has been removed from the loop and instantly re-creates the loop around the vacated connector.

FC-AL does not use device IDs in the conventional manner. Embedded in the device's circuitry is an IEEE Fiber Channel Address (IFCA). Every device manufactured is assigned a unique IFCA that is used by no other device in the world. When the device is plugged into the cable or backplane, the controller uses that ID to enter it into the loop. The user does not have to worry about setting any jumpers or switches. No special software needs to be run. The new device is simply there. This makes installing FC-AL devices the proverbial piece of cake.

One aspect of FC-AL that hard drives specifically benefit from is the fact that it has a greatly reduced processing overhead for commands. Devices hooked up to a traditional parallel SCSI chain can only transmit commands at their asynchronous bus speed. What this means is that, while these devices may be on a bus theoretically capable of 160Mbs (20MB) burst speeds, commands are limited to around 2Mbs. Installing multiple drives as a non-striped single volume can have a negative impact on performance in many cases because of this.

> **BUZZ WORDS** ———————
>
> **Hot-pluggable:** Another term for hot-swappable. A hot-pluggable device can be added to or removed from its bus without the necessity of bringing the computer down.

Conversely, FC-AL transmits at full loop speed, or 100Mbs. This, coupled with high-speed cache ram on the controller for command queuing and controller-operated tagged command queuing, can increase throughput of small file transfer by as much as 200 to 600 percent!

Therefore, while the 160 megabytes per second of Ultra 160 appears on the outset to be faster than that of FC-AL, this is a classic case of looks being deceiving. FC-AL can be dual-ported for a total bandwidth of 200 megabytes per second. And even if this wasn't the case, its lower command overhead alone makes it a much faster interface.

IEEE-1394 (FireWire)   FireWire was discussed in detail in Chapter Ten. The reader should, however, note that IEEE-1394, or FireWire, is actually one of the serial SCSI interfaces.

SSA   Serial Storage Architecture (SSA) is a set of standards optimized specifically for mass storage devices and associated devices such as hardware RAID controllers. SSA does have a slower throughput than any of the other serial standards. The standard allows for bidirectional data transfer of 20Mbs in each direction, although a few high-end devices claim 80Mbs sustained throughput. SSA allows for up to 128 devices to be installed in a single loop. This allows for the construction of huge mass storage devices containing a large number of individual drives.

The physical connectors for an SSA device are quite a bit smaller than the standard SCSI interface. With hard drives and other internal storage devices becoming smaller with each generation, this is an important feature. Also, the cabling standards of SSA call for *hot-pluggable* devices. This means that an SSA device can be pulled from the system and replaced on the fly without the added expense of hot-swappable drive bays.

Because the interface does allow for full-duplex operation, several devices can be active on the bus simultaneously. Read/write operations are much faster, as data from one request can be streaming in at the same time as other requests are being generated.

SSA seems to be rapidly losing ground to FC-AL, however. One of the primary supporters, Conner, was purchased by Seagate, which was a strong supporter of FC-AL. And even IBM, the company that originally developed SSA, is shipping FC-AL product, but not SSA.

Of course, with all the different types of serial interfaces I've discussed, don't feel embarrassed if this seems a little confusing. On the outset, it might seem like the industry should just make it simple, stick to the fastest interface, and drop all the rest. However each of the standards has advantages over the other in specific implementations. **Table 15.5** outlines some of the different standards and how they get used.

Table 15.5 Comparison of Serial SCSI Standards

Serial Standard	Speed	No. of Devices	Max. Bus Length	Common Use
SSA	+/–80Mbs	128	25M	Mass storage arrays
FireWire	+/–400Mbs	63	72M	High-speed external devices
FC-AL	+/–1.06Gbs	126	10KM (theoretical)	A high-speed internal interface

While the three different serial SCSI standards exhibit varying performance, each one shines in a different set of implementations.

UNDERSTANDING ASPI

The Advanced SCSI Programmer Interface (ASPI) really doesn't do much in terms of making your system perform any faster. What it does do is make sure that each of your devices does what it's supposed to do properly and efficiently, without tying up immense amounts of memory using very large and complex drivers for each device. Still, to a certain extent, ASPI does have an impact on performance.

Initially, SCSI drivers and devices were extremely common causes of system lock-up and intermittent application failures. There were numerous reasons for this. For one, SCSI controllers often maintain onboard cache memory. Like any other memory in the computer, SCSI cache must be addressed by the address bus through the MCC (nowadays, part of the chipset). Also, a good many SCSI adapters use their own onboard BIOS chip that communicates with the system through a mini-driver. Many times, conflicting commands generated between the system BIOS and the SCSI BIOS or conflicts between device drivers loaded into upper memory would cause random and intermittent crashes. To solve this, a new standard for SCSI device drivers and command interpretation was developed.

ASPI functions in two layers. The ASPI-Manager is a set of files in the operating system that handles communication between the OS and the host adapter. These files reside within the Hardware Abstraction Layer (HAL) of the various Windows operating systems. The second layer is a device mini-driver for the specific component. This driver communicates with ASPI-Manager to link the specific device to the host adapter. This permits a uniform method by which all SCSI devices function. An advantage that shouldn't be overlooked is the fact that device manufacturers have a much simpler task of interfacing their device with the operating system. Lowering the costs of production effectively lowers the cost of the device.

INSTALLING SCSI DEVICES

Installing serial SCSI is so automatic it requires no discussion. As with USB, installation and configuration is fully Plug 'n Play. Installing parallel SCSI devices is only slightly more complicated than any other peripheral in your machine. Following a few simple rules will make installing even older devices simple. Failing to follow them can make you want an aspirin. There are three things you have to deal with in working with SCSI: the host adapter, the cable, and the device itself. Let's take a look at them one at a time.

HOST ADAPTERS

Host adapters come from many different companies and in many different forms. Things to consider are the level of SCSI you want the adapter to support, the level of support you want it to provide, and the bus on which it will reside. All of these contribute to whether or not the device does what you want it to or not. It is also possible to purchase motherboards with onboard SCSI host adapters.

SCSI adapters are available in both ISA and PCI buses. In the realm of PCI, many companies are providing cards for the 66MHz 64-bit PCI bus. This would be the adapter of choice if your requirements are the ultimate in performance. If you're planning on taking advantage of the performance gains offered by Ultra 160 or FC-AL, and your system has an appropriate slot, this is the way to go.

Any computer, however, will benefit by choosing a 32-bit PCI host adapter over an ISA adapter. An 8MHz bus is somewhat of a bottleneck for a 20MHz adapter, as you might imagine. Since the goal of SCSI is to push the limits of system performance, ISA should only be used if it is the only alternative. PCI will provide substantially better performance. The PCI bus also will make it a whole lot easier to install and configure the card.

Also, consider the devices you intend to install. Separate adapters are needed for HVD and SE devices (although, admittedly, HVD devices are becoming rare). This is a nonissue if your system will be equipped with SCSI-III devices. Some SCSI adapters also provide hardware RAID control. If the goal is to build a high-end server, hardware RAID can greatly enhance performance.

Once you've selected the host adapter, it's time to put it in the system. Plug 'n Play has made this pretty easy with most of the major brands. On older systems using an ISA adapter, PnP might not be an option. Non-PnP devices will need to be configured for an IRQ and an I/O address. On some cards (the majority of them, these days), this is done in software. Some, on the other hand, are configured by way of DIP switches or jumpers. In this case, you'll need to know in advance what one of your available IRQs is. If you know you must manually configure the card, then prior to bringing the system down for the installation, identify what resources are available. In Windows, this can be done in Device Manager. That covers about 80 percent of the systems in use today.

THE COMPONENTS OF A SCSI CARD

If you look at most SCSI adapters, you see that there is a BIOS chip on them. For simple SE SCSI signaling, it is possible to include into the BIOS of the system the total command set required. Supporting any of the protocols that require balanced signaling or make use of advanced SCSI functions requires a little more help than that. The BIOS chip on the adapter provides the full command set for that specific card. In the old days, computers didn't recognize a SCSI hard drive as a bootable device. There is information in the host adapter BIOS that allows the machine to boot to SCSI. This BIOS information is shadowed to memory on boot and supplements BIOS information provided by the computer.

SCSI host adapters usually include as part of the BIOS a configuration utility that can be initialized on system boot. This program also provides some decent diagnostics utilities that can come in very handy with a SCSI device that doesn't want to install. It will identify any device IDs it finds on the chain, helping to locate conflicts. From here, a SCSI hard drive can be low-level formatted.

Like motherboards, SCSI host adapters are equipped with chipsets that control their functions. This chipset will determine the host adapter's capabilities and performance levels, so picking a brand that uses a decent chipset is important. The manufacturers of host adapters frequently make chipsets as well. For example, Adaptec makes its own chipsets. Some brands get their chipsets from third-party manufacturers and what you're getting can turn into a guessing game. When it comes to SCSI adapters, it's really a good idea to stick with manufacturers you know and trust.

There will also be a small amount of memory built into each host adapter. This is the memory that is used for command queuing. Most adapters also include a certain amount of cache memory. Some adapters allow you to add more memory for additional cache. These adapters will have empty SIMM or DIMM sockets on board for this purpose.

As far as users are concerned, the most significant component on the card is the place where they plug the cable. Some cards provide only a single interconnect for the standard they support. Others support multiple interfaces. For example, a SCSI III adapter might be equipped with both a 50-pin SCSI II interconnect and a 68-pin or 80-pin connector for the SCSI III devices. While both can be used, you should keep in mind that unless the card specifically states that it is a dual-channel card, all devices on that adapter card, regardless of the port they're connected to, are part of the same chain, and therefore cannot have duplicated IDs anywhere on the device.

SCSI CONNECTORS AND CABLES, PAST AND PRESENT

As I've mentioned before, there have been a number of SCSI connectors used throughout the years. Different devices might have different connectors, so it's important to pay attention to what you've got. There are adapters to go from one type to the other, but you'll never have one when you need it.

The most common cables you'll run into are the A cable and the P cable. The A is for 8-bit SCSI signals, and comes in two different varieties: 50-pin shielded and 50-pin unshielded. The unshielded cable will be a ribbon cable similar to the one you used with your IDE hard drive. It is commonly used for internal devices. Shielded cables are used for external devices and are round, somewhat thick cables with the individual wires clustered in layers. **Figure 15.9** shows the pinouts for a 50-pin A cable.

16-bit signals are carried over a P cable and connector. This is a 68-pin interface. One notable difference is that with the P connector, even- and odd-numbered wires are not on opposite sides of the connector, as they are with the A-connector. Side A of the interface carries

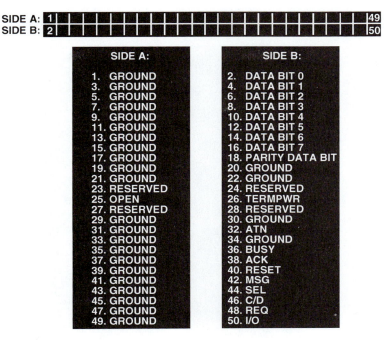

Figure 15.9   Pinouts for 50-pin A connector

wires 1 through 34, while Side B carries 35 through 68. The pinouts for this connector are illustrated in **Figure 15.10**.

There are also some proprietary SCSI connectors that you might occasionally run into. Two notable examples are the 60-pin IBM connector used on certain PS/2 models of its line. There were also 25-pin connectors used on both Macintosh computers and some PCs. Since this book does not target proprietary standards, I mention them only in passing to make you aware of their existence. In the modern world of computers it is unlikely that you will run into them.

SCSI DEVICES

Installing an actual device onto a SCSI chain works just like any other interface. The one thing that can cause a small amount of initial confusion occurs when all you've ever worked with are IDE devices. SCSI drives can look very similar to IDE at a casual glance. However, if you look closer, you'll find that they're quite different.

The socket where you plug the cable has a lot more pins for one thing. Admittedly, unless you happen to have one of each in your hand, a 50-pin SCSI socket doesn't look that much different from a 40-pin IDE. An IDE device, however, will have the jumpers for setting master/slave relationships. A SCSI drive either has no jumpers, if it is a software-configurable device, or a lot more than just three if you have to set the device ID by jumpers.

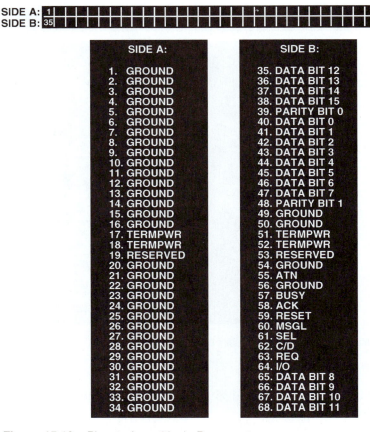

Figure 15.10 Pinouts for a 68-pin P connector

SETTING UP THE SCSI CHAIN

With today's lineup of Plug 'n Play host adapters, terminated cables and auto-configuring devices, this section is almost unnecessary. However, not everything you're going to see is modern. So it is a good idea to be familiar with the concepts for those times you're doing work on an older Pentium-based server with SCSI II devices. One of the very first sections of this chapter mentioned that two essential factors of setting up SCSI are termination and device IDs. Both are crucial, or the chain won't work properly, if at all.

TERMINATION

An electrical anomaly that all circuits have to deal with is reaching the end of the wire. Where does the signal go after that? It might be easy to imagine that it simply stops at the end of the wire, and then disappears. Unfortunately (or fortunately, depending on which viewpoint you want to take) the universe doesn't operate that way. The signal I keep discussing is created by the movement of electrons along a piece of wire. When those electrons reach the end of the wire, they can't just jump out into air. There has to be something there to accept them, otherwise they will simply turn around and go back the other way, which can be a problem for the next signal that was sent. The two collide and the SCSI chain goes down.

To stop this, you simply place a resistor in the chain at the last device you install. The resistor absorbs those electrons and the signal stops. This terminating resistor must be in place at both ends of the chain. On the host adapter, there is a resistor built in. Most adapters these days are auto-terminating. If there is no device hooked up to the external port, the terminator is activated. Plugging a device onto that port acts to disconnect the terminating resistor.

It's on the other end of the chain that you need to be careful. There are terminators that can be installed onto the cable itself. Also, SCSI devices are equipped with their own terminating circuits. How these are employed vary from device to device. On some internal drives, it consists of a jumper. There is a shunt that goes over the jumper to engage termination; it is removed to disable it. Most external devices use a simple switch.

One mistake that almost everyone who works with older SCSI devices makes eventually is to add a device onto the chain without removing the termination from the device that had previously been on the end. The new device, as a result, is farther downstream than the terminating resistor and is simply not recognized. Before you spend several fruitless minutes trying to troubleshoot the device, check termination. That's most likely your problem. This is SCSI's equivalent of getting the master/slave configuration wrong. If you find that termination is set correctly and the new device still can't be recognized, then your problem may be because of a duplicate device ID on the chain.

DEVICE IDS

The final SCSI concept that I need to discuss is that of device IDs. I mentioned earlier that each device on the chain has to have a unique device ID. This is how the host adapter keeps track of what is transferring data. The exception to this rule is when you're putting multiple devices into an array, such as the volume sets or RAID arrays that I talked about a few pages back. In this case, the array owns the device ID and each device is given its own LUN.

That seems pretty straightforward, but just how do you go about doing it? On newer devices, it's about as simple as anything you'll ever do in this industry. Most devices that ship these days have their device IDs and/or LUNs set by software. When you run the SCSI setup utilities of a host adapter, device IDs are doled out. If the adapter is one that supports RAID arrays from within the hardware itself, you will be given the opportunity to identify those devices that you wish to be part of the array. The adapter will then configure LUNs for those drives.

Older drives aren't always so easy. The majority of drives were built with a set of jumper switches on the back of the drive, and setting the device ID is done through those jumpers. Different manufacturers had different settings to achieve specific IDs. So it's a good idea to have the manual available when setting up your drive. If none is available, you can take the trial-and-error approach, or you can be more scientific about it.

Table 15.6 SCSI Settings: MSB to the Right

Device ID	SW1	SW2	SW3
0	Off	Off	Off
1	On	Off	Off
2	Off	On	Off
3	On	On	Off
4	Off	Off	On
5	On	Off	On
6	Off	On	On
7	On	On	On

This table shows switch settings for a device whose most significant bit is located on the right.

Table 15.7 SCSI Settings: MSB to the Left

Device ID	SW1	SW2	SW3
0	Off	Off	Off
1	Off	Off	On
2	Off	On	Off
3	Off	On	On
4	On	Off	Off
5	On	Off	On
6	On	On	Off
7	On	On	On

This table shows switch settings for a device whose most significant bit is located on the left.

With three switches, you have a total of eight different combinations in which they can be set. It's simple mathematics; you have two positions in which a switch can be set, and three switches. Two raised to the power of three gives you a total of eight. That should sound like a familiar number to you if you've already made it this far into the book (and I know I have). All you're doing when you set those switches is setting the binary pattern for the number of the device ID you're choosing. There are two different methods that these drives can be figured. Some manufacturers put the most significant bit (MSB) to the right, others to the left. **Table 15.6** and **Table 15.7** identify switch positions for these settings.

There were also some brands of hard drive that had a bank of pins over which you placed shunts. These are easier to figure out. There are eight banks of two pins each. They represent the ID numbers 0 through 7. Counting from zero up, put the shunt over the pair that represents the number you want to use.

The beauty of some of the newer standards, such as FireWire and FC-AL, is that they require neither device IDs nor termination. They are Plug 'n Play all the way through. Installing a device onto either of these busses is easier than programming your microwave. The downside for the technician is that people no longer have to pay a technician a hundred bucks an hour to come in and set up their hardware.

COMPARING IDE AND SCSI

Which of the two different interconnects to use in your hard drive subsystem can be a critical decision for certain types of computers. The overall performance of a computer is largely dependant upon the hard drives. After reading this chapter, you should have come to the realization that SCSI is definitely the faster interface, especially with some of the newer incarnations of SCSI.

There is no denying that is the truth. Yet UDMA-66 and UDMA-100 drives continue to dominate the marketplace. Why is that?

Cost is a big reason. Right now IDE hard drives are dirt-cheap. Immense amounts of storage can be purchased for small amounts of jingle. And these drives are pretty darned good in terms of performance as well. The same size drive on the SCSI interface will cost more than double that of an IDE, and you have to purchase an additional host adapter card as well.

In that case, why do people continue to buy SCSI? Because of the advanced capabilities of SCSI and the fact that it remains moderately faster than IDE, SCSI still has a loyal following. And for hot-swapping devices in RAID arrays, there is no equal.

THE ADVANTAGES OF SCSI

With SCSI, you can have up to fourteen devices on a chain, and if necessary, you can add another host adapter and double that. For computers with huge storage requirements, such as a server with a secure RAID 5 array, this is key. Overall speed is superior to IDE, as I've already pointed out, but the ways it goes about being faster come into play as well.

On a server where many different users will be asking for files at the same time, SCSI's tagged command queuing is a distinct advantage. Multiple requests for I/O operations are handled much more quickly and efficiently. And the data from those requests gets moved on and off the bus at a much faster rate. Set up a striped set, as I discussed earlier, and the benefits are even greater.

People who regularly work with large files that need to be transferred quickly will also appreciate the SCSI interface. Anybody who's ever done any computerized video editing appreciates that fact. A streaming video file needs to move from the drive to RAM and then to the graphics adapter much more quickly than any word processing document would need to move through a system. Poor data throughput will result in a jittery image and most likely a grainy effect as well.

SCSI is also not as limited to platform as other interfaces. SCSI works on PCs, MACs, and other systems with equal ease. An administrator who has to use multiple platforms can make life easier if all computers are on SCSI. That way a few spare drives can be kept in stock without worrying about which computer they may eventually be used on.

Therefore, a good place to consider SCSI usage would include the following:

- Network servers
- Graphics workstations
- Digital audio-video workstations
- Mixed platform environments
- Any system on which large numbers of devices need to be installed

Obviously, any time excellent performance is the key issue, and cost is not a consideration, you should go with SCSI. However, there are times when users simply won't appreciate the advantages of SCSI. That's when you should consider...

THE ADVANTAGES OF IDE

First and foremost, the biggest advantage of IDE is cost. Anytime you can pick up 40GB of storage space for just about a day's pay, that's a real advantage. It wasn't that long ago that I wanted a 1.2GB drive so bad it hurt. But it was going to set me back two weeks worth of pay. It was really hard to justify that kind of expense. SCSI has dropped quite a bit in price as well, but a 32GB Ultra 160 plus the controller can still make you say "Ouch!"

Performance isn't all that bad, either. The newer ATA-5 drives can move some data across the bus. These drives won't handle the multiple hits that drives on a server can expect, but for a single user on a single machine, that's not an issue. Even large files open quickly with a 7,200rpm UDA-100 drive. The machine I'm using for this book has a 20.4GB drive with those specifications and a 40MB Photoshop image opens in a couple of seconds.

For the novice, IDE can be a lot easier to configure as well. Even though SCSI has gone a long way in this respect, it can still require a little knowledge on the part of the person setting up the system. IDE isn't completely without issues, but on the whole, it is a lot easier for the beginner than SCSI.

SUMMARY OF COMPARISONS

If you're building a server, a high-end graphics workstation, or audio-video editing workstations, by all means go with SCSI. You'll need the performance. But for most single-user computing applications, there is no reason in the world to avoid IDE. Any time you're putting a system together for home use, or a number of systems to sit on corporate desktops or in a school environment, go with IDE. **Table 15.8** compares and contrasts some of the differences between the two interfaces in order to help you better understand them.

Table 15.8　Comparing IDE and SCSI

Comparison Factor	SCSI	IDE
Number of devices supported	High	Low
Type of devices supported	High	Moderate
Device availability	Fair	Excellent
Device cost	High	Moderate
Overall performance	High in most cases	High in single user, single application environments. Low in multiuser environments or with applications requiring extremely high throughput.
Ease of configuration	Moderate to low	High
Cross-platform usage	Good	Poor

By comparing the most significant factors side-by-side, it is easier to decide if a system should use SCSI or IDE devices.

I think it becomes pretty clear from all of this that SCSI and IDE shouldn't be considered competing interfaces, but rather complementary options. Each has a special set of circumstances in which it shines. Until such time as an interface such as FireWire becomes as inexpensive as IDE, I don't think you'll be attending IDE's funeral any time soon.

CHAPTER SUMMARY

For years, understanding the concepts of SCSI has been a major roadblock to novice technicians. Hopefully after reading this chapter, you realize just how difficult it isn't. There are some issues on older SCSI devices that need to be taken into consideration, such as manually setting ID numbers and properly terminating the chain. But for the most part, on modern devices, even these procedures have become automated.

For the exam, understand the concepts of device IDs, LUNs, and termination. But also know the evolution of SCSI. CompTIA likes to make sure you know the differences between Fast SCSI and Wide SCSI. Also understand the different signaling methods discussed in this chapter.

BRAIN DRAIN

1. You've just installed an older SCSI card you pulled from another machine. It was working fine in the other machine, but now the only device the system recognizes is the hard drive. The tape drive and CD-ROM are ignored. What are some of the things that may have caused this?

2. Discuss the differences between single-ended and differential SCSI. Include in your discussion advantages and disadvantages, and discuss how LVD has addressed some of these issues.

3. What was the one thing lacking from the very first release of SCSI specifications that caused so much confusion? What was one of the problems caused and why did this omission cause the problem?

4. You want to configure three hard drives on a chain to be seen by the system as a single larger volume. How can you go about doing this?

5. Discuss why termination of a SCSI chain is necessary. What happens if you don't terminate the chain properly and why is it this happens?

THE 64K$ QUESTIONS

1. How many devices could a SCSI-I chain support?
   a. 5
   b. 7
   c. 8
   d. 14

2. What device ID does the host controller typically occupy?
   a. 0
   b. 1
   c. 7
   d. 14

3. What are two methods of terminating a SCSI chain?
   a. Placing a null device on the last connector of the cable.

b. Installing a resistor into a specially designed socket.

c. Clipping the twenty-eighth wire of the last device.

d. Setting a jumper on the last device on the chain.

4. If you want three devices on the chain to be seen as a single device on the system you would set each device to the same _____.

a. Device ID

b. Device Unit Number

c. Channel

d. Logical Unit Number

5. How many devices can be supported by a parallel SCSI-III chain?

a. 5

b. 7

c. 8

d. 14

e. None of the above

6. A high-voltage differential chain consisting of the controller and a single device can be as much as _____ meters long.

a. 1.5

b. 6

c. 12

d. 25

7. High-voltage differential devices cannot be on the same chain as a single-ended device.

a. True

b. False

8. What are two methods of combining multiple disk drives into a single larger volume without any loss of available storage capacity?

a. RAID 5

b. Volume set

c. RAID 10

d. RAID 0

9. Which of the following is an example of serial SCSI?

a. Ultra 640

b. SPI-5

c. FireWire

d. USB

10. A two-layered device driver scheme incorporated by SCSI is called _____.

a. HAL

b. ASCI

c. PLM

d. ASPI

TRICKY TERMINOLOGY

Device ID: A unique number assigned to each device on a SCSI chain, including the host adapter, that identifies it to other devices on the chain.

Disk duplexing: The duplication of data on two different hard drives hanging off of different controllers.

Disk mirroring: The duplication of data on two different hard drives hanging off of the same controller.

Domain divider switch: A device that allows external SCSI devices to be shared by multiple host computers.

Domain validation: A process by which a SCSI host adapter sends out a series of commands to each device on the chain and calculates each device's maximum data transfer rate.

Fast SCSI: SCSI over a 10MHz bus.

Host controller: The adapter installed on a system or embedded in the motherboard that manages SCSI devices.

Hot-pluggable: Another term for hot-swappable. A hot-pluggable device can be added or removed to its bus without the necessity of bringing the computer down.

Parity block: A data set that represents a mathematical image of data stored elsewhere in a RAID array.

Scatter-gather data transfer: The ability of a device to execute a command on one set of data and output the results to multiple devices.

SCSI expander: A device that allows a technician to effectively increase the length of a SCSI chain without the risk of data corruption.

Terminate: To create a dead end for electrical signals traveling down a wire so that they do not echo back the other direction.

Ultra wide SCSI: SCSI over a 32-bit bus.

Volume set: A storage array of very large capacity created by combining multiple drives of smaller capacity.

Wide SCSI: SCSI over a 16-bit bus.

ACRONYM ALERT

ACK: Acknowledgment

ASPI: Advanced SCSI Programmer Interface. A two-tiered device driver scheme employed by SCSI.

CCS: Common Command Set. Eighteen specific commands that must be included for every device that carries the SCSI-II label.

FC-AL: Fiber Channel Arbitrated Loop

FCP: Fiber Channel Protocol

FC-PH: Fiber Channel Physical and Signaling Interface

HAL: Hardware Abstraction Layer. A layer of the operating system that intercepts all calls to the hardware to prevent the applications from actually accessing the hardware.

HVD: High-Voltage Differential

IFCA: IEEE Fiber Channel Address. A unique address assigned to all FC-AL devices at the factory that allows them to be automatically configured onto the FC-AL loop.

LUN: Logical Unit Number. A setting on SCSI devices that allows multiple devices to be seen by the controller as a single device.

LVD: Low-Voltage Differential

MTBF: Mean Time Before Failure. An average of the number of hours a particular model of device is expected to operate before it dies.

PBC: Port Bypass Circuit. A circuit that manages an FC-AL loop and automatically detects when a device has been removed.

REQ: Request

SE: Single-Ended

SIP: SCSI Interlocked Protocol

SPC: SCSI Primary Commands

SPI: SCSI Parallel Interface

SSA: Serial Storage Architecture

SSP: Serial Storage Protocol

CHAPTER 16

YOUR COMPUTER AND GRAPHICS

I commented earlier in the book that people don't buy a computer because they want something that computes. They buy a computer because they want a word processor or a $2000 deck of cards or an in-house video arcade. Any one of these functions requires that the user have a nice pretty display for all those fancy pictures or a crisp, clear screen for displaying the austere prose they are composing.

That image doesn't just magically appear on the screen. In this chapter, I'll show you a little more about how it really gets there. I'll take you on a tour of different monitor types, and I'll show you what makes a $300 adapter better than a $50 one. I'll also explain why, for some people, that more expensive video card might not be the better choice. Also, even though this is not a book that is intended to instruct you on matters of software, when it comes to video, it is rather important that you understand certain issues dealing with operating systems, graphic file formats, and user applications specific to computer graphics. So, with that in mind, let's dive into the hardware end.

A+ CORE HARDWARE EXAM OBJECTIVES

For those of you studying for the exam, objectives covered will include the following:

1.1 Identify the names, purpose, and characteristics of system modules. Recognize these modules by sight or definition.

1.2 Identify basic procedures for adding and removing field-replaceable modules for desktop systems. Given a replacement scenario, choose the appropriate sequences.

1.5 Identify the names, purposes, and performance characteristics of standardized/common peripheral ports, associated cabling, and their connectors. Recognize ports, cabling, and connectors by sight.

1.8 Identify proper procedures for installing and configuring common peripheral devices. Choose the appropriate installation or configuration sequences in given scenarios.

1.10 Determine the issues that must be considered when upgrading a PC. In a given scenario, determine when and how to upgrade system components.

2.1 Recognize common problems associated with each module and their symptoms, and identify steps to isolate and troubleshoot the problems. Given a problem situation, interpret the symptoms and infer the most likely cause.

4.2 Identify the types of RAM (Random Access Memory), form factors, and operational characteristics. Determine banking and speed requirements under given scenarios.

COMPUTER MONITORS

While this may sound like a gross oversimplification, there are only two types of monitors in general use by the PC-using public these days. The most common is the cathode-ray tube (CRT). These are relatively inexpensive and frequently are bundled with a computer when you purchase a complete system. Moving in on the CRT's space (both literally and figuratively) is the flat panel display. Flat panels are elegant little creatures that take up a fraction of the desktop space required for a standard CRT and still manage to deliver an image that is arguably superior to that of the CRT. The method by which each type delivers an image to the screen is different; therefore, the different types of monitor require separate discussions.

This chapter is devoted to the various forms of Video Graphics Array (VGA) standards that have evolved over the years. Toward the end of the chapter, I will include a short section on the Enhanced Graphics Adapter (EGA) and the Color Graphics Adapter (CGA) as historical references. If you see any of these displays today, it'll either be at a flea market on in a museum somewhere.

CATHODE-RAY TUBE MONITORS

So far, it's safe to say that the cathode-ray tube (CRT) is by far the most popular monitor in use today. The primary reason for its popularity is price. Over the years, the quality has improved dramatically as well. **Figure 16.1** illustrates a 19″ CRT monitor in use.

The design of a CRT is virtually identical to that of a television. As such, it has many similarities. However, since it's dealing with information coming in from a computer rather than over the air or cable, there are some key differences as well.

The CRT monitor consists of several different components that make it work. First off is the CRT itself. It's what makes the picture. Toward the back of the tube is a grouping of three electron guns. In control of the entire operation is a bank of electronics. Finally, since the monitor requires more power than anything else in a typical computer system, there is a rather large power supply.

THE CRT

The CRT is one of the last remaining vacuum tubes to be used on a regular basis in modern electronic technology. It consists of a large glass tube from which all the air has been evacuated.

The front of the tube is the flat surface visible to the user, while toward the rear, it stretches out into a long point (see **Figure 16.2**).

The inner surface of the front panel is coated with a compound consisting primarily of phosphorous. This is essentially the same substance that fireflies use to produce their remarkable display. Toward the back of the tube are mounted three electron guns. *Electron guns* are electrical components called cathodes. These are negatively charged devices that, when heated, emit a barrage of electrons. The stream of electrons is directed toward the front panel of the monitor, exciting the phosphorous and making it glow. The graphics adapter controls the rate at which the electron guns fire. I'll get to that in a bit.

In order to make sure that the electrons don't overlap each other, causing the

Figure 16.1 The venerable CRT is still the most popular monitor on the market today.

colors of the image to bleed into one another, a *shadow mask* is placed against the back surface of the front panel, over the phosphorous layer. Frequently, you will hear manufacturers talk about the Invar mask that they use in their product. This isn't a type of mask as much as it is the kind of metal from which the mask is made. Invar is a metal that can handle extremely high temperatures without having its shape distorted. Since the steady barrage of electrons hitting the mask does result in the mask getting hot, this is a characteristic that is prized by manufacturers.

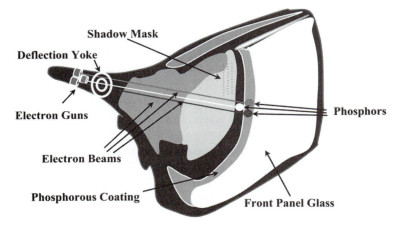

Figure 16.2 The anatomy of a standard CRT makes it an extremely complex apparatus.

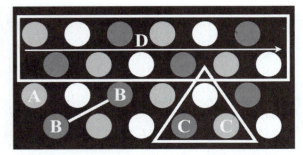

A: Phosphor   B: Dot Pitch

C: Triad   D: Raster Line

Figure 16.3 The picture on your monitor is made up of several million little dots of phosphorous that glow when struck by electrons.

BUZZ WORDS

Electron gun: A cathode that, when heated, emits a stream of electrons.

Shadow mask: A thin metal sheet perforated with tiny holes that outline the individual phosphors in a CRT monitor.

Phosphor: A single dot of color created when the phosphorous layer of a CRT is excited by electrons.

Triad: The three separate phosphors, each of a separate primary color, that when combined form the separate hues of color perceived by the user.

Dot pitch: The distance separating two like-colored phosphors that are adjacent to one another.

This mask allows only specifically defined areas of phosphorous to be exposed to the electron beams. There are different layers of phosphorous, each compounded with a different substance to make it glow in a different color. The phosphorous compound is known as a *phosphor*. Each phosphor will always be exposed by the same electron beam and will always glow in one of the three primary colors: red, green, or blue. **Figure 16.3** illustrates this concept, as well as some of those to follow. The intensity at which the electrons strike the phosphor determines how brightly that phosphor glows. In order to produce the myriad of colors that you perceive on your computer screen, it takes three of those phosphors, one of each primary color, working together to produce a hue. These three phosphors working together form a *triad*.

Once struck by the electrons, however, that phosphor doesn't glow very long. A few hundredths of a second is all it's good for until it fades away. Therefore, the electron gun has to keep redrawing the screen over and over again to keep a stable image. How frequently it redraws the screen is the monitor's refresh rate. Refresh rates are measured in hertz and range from a low end of around 48Hz to as high as 200Hz on some brands. Maximum refresh rate is directly linked to the monitor's selected resolution. The maximum refresh rate advertised by a manufacturer can rarely be used in conjunction with the maximum resolution advertised. To get higher resolutions, a lower refresh rate must usually be used.

An advertised specification of computer monitors is the *dot pitch*. While dot pitch and resolution are directly related, they are not the same thing. Back in Figure 16.3 I illustrated the individual phosphors that make up the image. Dot pitch is the distance between two adjacent like-colored phosphors. This will be measured in some fraction of a millimeter. Dot pitch limits the absolute maximum resolution that a particular monitor can display.

The graphics adapter, and how the user has set it up, dictates actual display resolution. This is defined by how many pixels it takes to fill a line that moves across the screen, along with how many of these lines, called *raster lines*, it takes to produce the entire screen from top to bottom. Note that there is a big difference between pixels and phosphors or even triads. Or not, depending on the resolution you've selected.

A *pixel* is an individual colored dot that consists of several phosphors. A computer image is built up from thousands or millions of these pixels. Let's take a look at a typical color monitor and put some of these terms to use. I'll use a 19″ monitor capable of 1600×1200 resolution, with a maximum refresh rate of 200Hz as an example. If you set that monitor at its maximum resolution of 1600×1200, then each pixel consists of a single triad. Lower resolutions simply absorb more phosphors per pixel.

> ### BUZZ WORDS
>
> **Raster line:** A single row of pixels that make a horizontal line across an image.
>
> **Pixel:** The collection of phosphors that collectively generate a single dot of color in a monitor's image.
>
> **Bezel:** The plastic frame that masks off the unusable part of a monitor's image.

Now, consider the size. The advertised size of the display is a diagonal measurement from one corner of the tube to the opposite corner, for example, from upper right to lower left. On a CRT, unfortunately, maximum size does not equate to usable size. As the image progresses toward the outer perimeters of the tube, sharpness and contrast drop off dramatically. The *bezel*, or the plastic frame that makes up the front of your monitor's external case, masks off a portion of the tube so you won't see the fuzzy, murky part. What's left is the viewable area. The 19″ monitor I'm using has a viewable area of 18″.

The maximum resolution of 1600×1200 comes from the fact that there are a total of 1600 triads that make up each line going from left to right. These are the raster lines I mentioned. From top to bottom, there are 1200 of these lines. As the monitor creates the image you see, the electron guns scan from left to right, drawing a single line. The time it takes for the guns to finish one line and then return to start the next line is known as the horizontal refresh rate (HFR). Since there are a lot of lines to draw, HFR is usually a fairly high number. In fact, it is this number that limits the maximum vertical refresh rate (VFR) that a monitor can produce.

VFR is the number of times per second an entire screen can be drawn. VFR has a direct impact on the quality of image. It also can have a dramatic impact on the comfort level of the user. Way back in the day, when color monitors were first becoming the rage, many people who sat in front of a computer for hours on end complained that their computers gave them headaches. Many people insisted that the CRT was emitting some form of radiation that was harmful to human health.

Millions of dollars were spent researching this problem, and this was the conclusion. Yes, computer monitors do emit varying levels of low-level radiation. This isn't the same kind of radiation caused by nuclear bombs or power plants, but rather more akin to the radiation emitted by your radio station. There was no evidence whatsoever that this radiation had any impact on human health.

They did find, however, that VFR was directly responsible for the headaches people experienced. Most offices are illuminated by fluorescent lights. These lights are powered by a device called a ballast and flicker at a rate of sixty times per second, or 60Hz. This is a high enough frequency that most people don't even notice it. It also happens to be the refresh rate for standard VGA. Therefore, people were being bombarded by ambient light flickering at sixty times per second, while sitting in front of a computer screen doing the same thing. Enough hours of that would result in a headache. The solution was simple. You simply redesign VGA standards so that a higher VFR is used. 72Hz is a good starting point and higher is better, although there is some argument that 120Hz is not a good thing because it supposedly sets up another synchronization with the 60Hz cycle of the fluorescents.

> **BUZZ WORDS**
>
> **Deflection yoke:** A circular array of powerful magnets that act to deflect a beam of electrons from its natural path.
>
> **Cathode:** A negatively charged device that emits a stream of electrons when heated.
>
> **Convergence:** The accuracy with which multiple beams of electrons or light can focus on the same point.

CONTROLLING THE ELECTRON BEAMS

Since the image is actually created by the electron beams, it only stands to reason that controlling the electrons is key to controlling the image. There are actually several components within the monitor that contribute to this task. There are, first off, the electron guns that initially emit the electrons. The electrons are distributed across the rear surface of the front panel by a circular array of magnets called a *deflection yoke*. The shadow mask makes sure phosphors don't overlap. If you look back, Figure 16.2 illustrates the key components to a CRT monitor.

CAUTION: When discussing the internal components of a computer system, I suggested you peek inside and follow along as you read. Even though I am discussing some of the internal components of a computer monitor, I highly recommend that you not go inside of a monitor unless you have been properly trained. There are capacitors inside of monitors and television sets that can hold a lethal charge for weeks, or even months, after the unit has been unplugged. Accidentally coming in contact with a charged circuit inside the monitor could easily be the last mistake you ever make!

Electron Guns Color monitors have three of these devices, one for each of the primary colors. The gun consists of a cathode, some form of heat source, and a method by which the electrons can be focused. As I mentioned earlier, a *cathode* is a negatively charged device that, when heated, emits a stream of electrons. This is the purpose of the heating device. The higher the temperature, the more electrons that spew out of the cathode. The three electron guns are arranged in a triangular pattern toward the back of the tube. The three guns work in synchronization with one another and fire their beams simultaneously, all focused on precisely the same point. How well those three beams focus on the same point is a factor known as *convergence*. The better convergence is controlled, the sharper the image will appear.

The electron guns are devices that maintain a fixed position. This is, of course, not very conducive to 19″ screens, because unless there is a way of scattering those electrons across the entire surface of the monitor, our image will consist of one tiny little circle so small an electron microscope would have trouble finding it. Since manufacturers can't move the electron guns, they move the electron beams.

The Deflection Yoke Also occasionally called the deflection plates or the deflection coil, this device consists of an array of electromagnets distributed around the circumference of the tube. These magnets create a strong magnetic field that the beam of electrons must pass through on its way to the front panel. By varying the strength of the field generated by specific magnets, the beam of electrons can be deflected in a very precise pattern. This rapid changing of magnetic fields causes the horizontal and vertical movement I discussed earlier.

Since the electrons are spewing out of the electron guns continuously, and since the magnetic fields are merely moving the beam, there needs to be some way of sorting out the blue dots from the red dots from the green dots. In order to do that the designers put a "template" between the layers of phosphorous and the electron guns.

The Shadow Mask The shadow mask is what separates the individual phosphors. It is also what determines dot pitch. The shadow mask is an extremely thin sheet of metal perforated with millions of tiny little holes. Since this metal is going to be subjected to a constant barrage of electrons, it's going to get very hot, as I mentioned earlier. That is why it needs to be manufactured with a metal that can handle the stress without changing the size and shape of the holes.

One of the things that happens when any substance gets hot is that it expands. The shadow mask can't be doing that. Otherwise, the individual phosphors would change size as the mask heated up. This would result in image distortion. Invar is a type of metal that resists this distortion better than most other materials. Therefore, it is frequently used on high-quality monitors.

The Monitor Cable The signals that control how all of the above devices do their job actually come from the display adapter installed in the computer. In order to get that signal from the computer to the monitor, you use a cable. Standard VGA cables use the 15-pin connector you've grown to know and love. Each conductor in the cable has a specific job to do, as is illustrated in **Figure 16.4**. One of the easiest troubleshooting jobs you'll ever get is when somebody complains that the color on his or her monitor has suddenly changed radically. Each of the three primary colors moves down a specific wire. If the pin connecting that wire to the display adapter gets broken or bent, it will no longer transmit its signal and the image the user sees will be composed of only the remaining two colors. It isn't a pleasant sight.

LCD MONITOR

A technology that is seeing increasing popularity is the LCD monitor. The display gets its name from the fact that the pixels are formed from a liquid crystal display (LCD) instead of glowing phosphorous. As you might imagine, the technology is somewhat different. There are some distinct advantages to LCD displays over the more conventional CRTs. The one most

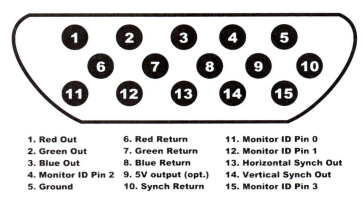

1. Red Out	6. Red Return	11. Monitor ID Pin 0
2. Green Out	7. Green Return	12. Monitor ID Pin 1
3. Blue Out	8. Blue Return	13. Horizontal Synch Out
4. Monitor ID Pin 2	9. 5V output (opt.)	14. Vertical Synch Out
5. Ground	10. Synch Return	15. Monitor ID Pin 3

Figure 16.4   A standard 15-pin VGA connector

immediately noticeable is how much of your desktop you get back when you migrate from a CRT to an LCD. The LCD takes up a whole lot less space.

Another distinct advantage they have is in the amount of power they consume. A typical CRT can pull between 120 and 200 watts of electricity from the wall, even more for some of the bigger displays. An LCD requires between 30 and 50 watts. For the individual user, that may not amount to much. A corporation, on the other hand, that has hundreds or thousands of computers in use can see significant savings on its electrical bill if it makes the move.

A difference between CRTs and LCDs that might take a little longer for some people to appreciate is the fact that, because there are no electron guns at work here, image refresh is handled in a completely different manner. The result of this is a much more solid image with virtually no measurable flicker.

LCDs come in three different packages. On the most basic level, that of your handheld games, PDAs, and such, a common-plane display is used. Notebook computers of the past used either a passive matrix or an active matrix design. The differences among the three are significant.

COMMON-PLANE LCDS

As I mentioned, this is the display commonly used in handheld games, advanced calculators, and pocket computers. You also see them on watches, panel displays for household appliances, and on the dashboards of automobiles. These displays offer a very limited number of colors and can create graphic images that are composed of certain predefined shapes. Almost any shape is possible, but creating a graphic from scratch is inordinately slow.

Common-plane displays can be either backlit or reflective. This means that the manufacturer can either project light through the display from a source behind the crystals, or it can simply require the user to make use of available light to see the image.

PASSIVE MATRIX DISPLAYS

The passive matrix display is a complex and cumbersome display. It starts with two glass panels, or substrates. A *substrate* is simply a solid surface of some sort, over which an active material can be applied. The substrates work together to form a grid consisting of rows and columns. These panels receive a coating that contains a conductive material that is transparent to the naked eye. On one of the panels, the coating is laid out in rows; on the other, it is laid out in columns.

> **BUZZ WORDS** ——————
>
> **Substrate:** The supportive material over which an active substance can be applied.

The liquid crystal material is added between the substrates, and a thin coating of polarizing material is applied to the outer surface of the panel. Each of the rows and columns of conductive material is connected to an integrated circuit (IC). The graphics controller sends a signal down a particular row and column. Where two signals intersect, the material is activated.

The technology works well enough for very simple applications, but is too slow to be of any use in streaming video. For example, I used to own an older notebook computer that used a passive matrix display. As I moved the mouse cursor along the screen, I could see a little trail of pointers following the cursor itself, and I didn't have mouse trailers enabled. My new notebook uses an active matrix display.

ACTIVE MATRIX DISPLAYS

Another way you'll see these displays described is TFT displays. This comes from the fact that the active matrix makes use of thin film transistors (TFT) in order to generate the image. The term is slightly misleading, because the TFT actually consists of a transistor coupled to a capacitor. TFTs are arranged in rows and columns, each of which is under the control of an IC.

To make a specific pixel glow, the IC activates a particular row. Then a charge is sent down the column where the pixel is supposed to reside. Since all of the other rows on the display are turned off, there is only one pixel on that particular column that can be made active. Its capacitor is charged and as long as the charge lasts, the pixel will glow. As with CRT monitors, there is a separate element for each primary color. The millions of colors available are derived by having the elements glow in varying intensity.

GRAPHICS ADAPTERS

The second part of the graphics subsystem is the graphics adapter. This is the device that generates the signals that created the images I discussed in earlier sections of this chapter. It is the job of the graphics adapter to convert a series of zeros and ones into all those pretty pictures you see on the tube in front of you.

Graphics adapters can appear as either independent devices that you install into a computer, or they can be onboard devices that are a part of the motherboard, as I pointed out in Chapter Six, Motherboards, BIOS, and the Chipset. However the device is packaged, the way it functions is going to be the same.

The user's perception of how well a system performs can be a direct function of the graphics adapter. It doesn't matter how quickly the CPU, RAM, and hard drives are doing their jobs. If you have a seriously slow video card, then the results of all that processing is taking its own sweet time getting to you and, as far as you're concerned, you have a slow computer!

In this section, I'll take a closer look at how video cards do their job and what differentiates a really good card from a mediocre one. I'll even discuss reasons why even a mediocre adapter might be able to provide more horsepower than many people will ever need. Finally, I'll examine some compatibility issues specific to video cards.

> **BUZZ WORDS** ────────
>
> **Co-processed:** Any adapter or device that is equipped with a microprocessor that offloads some of the work of the PC's CPU.

THE MECHANICS OF GRAPHICS ADAPTERS

Today's video cards are *co-processed* adapters. A microprocessor on board the video card relieves the computer's CPU of the task of processing graphics. In addition, VGA cards all ship with a fairly substantial amount of memory installed on the card itself. These days it is fairly difficult to find any product on the market with anything less than about 8MB of RAM installed. Later in this chapter, I'll be taking a look at what that memory is used for.

Modern graphics adapters feature a chipset and a video BIOS. As with motherboards, these two collections of commands dictate what functions the card can perform. Graphics functions have gotten far too complex and change too rapidly to be included as a subset of system BIOS and/or chipsets.

THE VIDEO CHIPSET

The chipset is a collection of integrated circuits in which all the instructions specific to a particular card are housed. Therefore, if two different brands of graphics adapter both have the same chipset, it can be safely assumed that they will share most, if not all, features and will have nearly identical specifications. By embedding a video chipset onto a motherboard, and programming the system BIOS accordingly, it is relatively easy to include video as an onboard function.

As with the system, the video chipset will determine basic hardware functions. If a video chipset does not support 3D functions, you do not have a 3D video card. (See later in this chapter for how graphics adapters simulate 3D effects and a discussion of different 3D algorithms used.) The type and amount of memory supported by a specific adapter is a direct function of the chipset.

VIDEO BIOS

The video BIOS performs exactly the same function as the system BIOS, except that it is specific to the graphics adapter. As with system BIOS, it consists of a set of instructions permanently encoded onto a ROM chip. On some video cards, this ROM chip is removable, allowing users to upgrade their BIOS if necessary. On most modern cards, it can be flashed with new instructions using an executable program.

The video BIOS has two important services that it provides. First and foremost is that, while the system is booting and prior to video drivers being installed onto the system, it provides rudimentary video support so that you can read the messages your system spits out while it is spinning up. Without this most basic function, you wouldn't be able to read the error messages that might be generated.

> **NOTE:** The instructions on a video BIOS are generally specific to a chipset. The chipset isn't going to be changed during the life of the card; therefore, be cautious about burning new instructions to video BIOS. About the only time this should be necessary would be when the manufacturer has discovered a flaw in the original programming. In some cases, it might be necessary to flash new BIOS in order to accommodate a newly released operating system, but for the most part, this is rarely necessary. Unless you have a real issue that can only be addressed by a new BIOS, don't experiment with video BIOS!

The second function that video BIOS provides is to act as a translator between the instructions and data handed off between the graphics adapter and the system board. As I mentioned earlier, it isn't possible to include BIOS instructions for every graphics adapter ever made on the system BIOS. Therefore, manufacturers provide their own instruction sets that are written to interact with the system BIOS.

VIDEO MEMORY

When computers first became available, everything was monochrome. All these fancy color monitors hadn't been invented yet. All there was to display on the screen was plain text. There were no elaborate graphics to contend with. As a result, there was very little memory required to produce screen shots, and the processor had no problems whatsoever putting information up on the screen. IBM allocated the first 128K of upper memory to video usage. That was all designers figured users would ever need.

These days, the GUI of our operating systems and the full-motion graphics of games makes video one of the biggest bottlenecks on the computer. One component of graphics adapters that has more impact on performance than anything else is the kind of memory installed on the card. Not the amount of memory, mind you, but rather the type. There have been several forms of memory used in video cards over the years. The most commonly used were VRAM, WRAM, and SGRAM. VRAM is the faster of the three because it is dual-ported and can be receiving data from an outside source and outputting data to either the video processor or the I/O stage on the same clock cycle. WRAM is a form of VRAM tuned exclusively to Microsoft's Windows functions. SGRAM works in a manner very similar to that used by the computer as main system memory, but its designers have fine-tuned the read/write operations specifically around graphics functions.

One additional technology is a type of memory called Multibank DRAM (MDRAM). As the name indicates, grouping larger numbers of smaller banks of memory is how the module is designed. Typically 32KB banks are used. Since each bank can be read to or written from independently, and I/O operations can occur across multiple banks simultaneously, data retrieval is much faster. However, it is a much more expensive alternative and, while it's been around for a while, hasn't been greeted by the industry with much enthusiasm.

Table 16.1 Memory used in Graphics Adapters

Type	Description	Relative Speed	Relative Cost	Relative Usage
FPM	Fast Page Mode	Very slow	N/A	Obsolete
SDRAM	Extended Data Out	Slow	Cheap	Obsolete
SGRAM	Synchronized Graphics RAM	Moderate	Cheap	Midrange and OEM
WRAM	Windows RAM	Fast	N/A	Obsolete
VRAM	Video RAM	Fast	Fairly expensive	Upper range; becoming obsolete
DDRAM	Double Data RAM	Extremely fast	Moderate	High-end cards
MDRAM	Multibank DRAM	Extremely fast	Extremely expensive	Rarely used

Types of video memory and their relative usage

Note: It is not unheard of for some high-end video cards to make use of two different types of memory on one card. Fast memory will be used for functions related to video processing, while a slower type, typically EDO, might be used for storing texture maps.

Many other types of memory have been embraced, and types that you might normally associate with conventional memory are used in graphics adapters today. These include FPM, EDO, SDRAM, and DDRAM. (See Chapter Nine for detailed discussions on how each of these types of memory works.)

So which of these types is the best memory to use, and why can't the manufacturers just pick a technology and stick with it? The answer to both is in the end user. What is the machine going to be used for? It would be senseless to always use an expensive high-end technology on every device you run off your assembly line. For many users, that would be prohibitively expensive. Also, the applications that will be run on the computer will determine your needs. Someone running word processing applications and spreadsheets all day won't need anything all that fancy. It is primarily the gaming world that drives the high-end market. **Table 16.1** groups the types of memory used by video cards in the order of their speed and relative price.

The main reason you need memory on a video card is that it acts as the *frame buffer*. Every time the monitor draws a screen (which, if your refresh rate is 80Hz, will be 80 times per second), the video card needs to be able to throw enough pixels up on the screen to create the image. Video memory acts as a place to assemble the next screen while the current screen is being drawn. The amount of memory you need on your graphics adapter is related to both the color depth and resolution you've selected. A simple formula is

BUZZ WORDS

Frame buffer: Dedicated memory used by a graphics adapter to build the next image frame to be displayed in the time that the current image frame is on the screen.

Horizontal resolution × Vertical resolution × Color depth (in bits) / (8 × 1,048,576)

Let's do an example. How many megabytes do I need for my 1600×1200 monitor set for 24-bit color?

$$1600 \times 1200 \times 24 = 46,080,000$$

This is how many bits are required to generate a single screen. Now, to break that down into megabytes, complete the equation. There are 8 bits to a byte and 1,048,576 bytes to a megabyte, therefore

$$8 \times 1,048,576 = 8,388,608$$

To finalize the answer, simply divide the results of the first equation by the results of the second.

$$46,080,000 / 8,388,608 = 5.4931640625$$

Therefore, in order to create each frame that a video card must produce at that color depth and resolution, I need 5.5MB of RAM just to act as a frame buffer. The first commercially available video card that would suit these needs would be equipped with 8MB of RAM.

Now, if life were only that simple, no one would ever need anything more than 8MB installed on video cards. However, several of the functions that I will discuss later in the chapter also require dedicated memory, and those will impact on the total requirements.

THE RAMDAC

Key to the video subsystem is a chip called the random access memory, digital analog converter (RAMDAC). This is the microprocessor that processes the video signals. To do its job it has to be able to perform a few key tasks. One of the main ones is to take the digital information produced by the video card and convert it into an analog signal. While virtually all of today's graphics adapters feature a RAMDAC, this hasn't always been the case. Early ISA and some PCI video cards relied on the CPU of the computer to handle all video processing. As you might imagine, there was a tremendous performance hit that resulted from using cards of this nature.

Refresh rate, resolution, and the speed of video reproduction is all directly limited by the speed of the RAMDAC. Your screen has a lot of pixels that it has to reproduce. The higher the resolution setting, the more pixels there are that are being generated. Higher refresh rates mean that they have to be reproduced more times per second. That's a lot of data that's being processed by the RAMDAC. **Table 16.2** lists some common resolution and refresh rates and shows just how much data is being reproduced per second.

While the numbers shown in Table 16.2 represent millions of pixels per second, they also provide a good measure of the speed of the RAMDAC a card would need in order to use those settings. As the table footnote indicates, since the entire screen is not actually being used by the image, you would need to apply a conversion factor of some sort to calculate the actual number of pixels being reproduced. Once you've done that, you know how fast of a RAMDAC you will need. For example, if I figure my monitor is using approximately 80 percent of the total CRT,

Table 16.2   Resolution and Refresh Rate Data Generation

Resolution	43.5Hz (87 interlaced)	60Hz	72Hz	80Hz	85Hz	90Hz	100Hz
800x600	20.1	28.8	34.6	38.4	40.8	43.2	48
1024x768	34.2	47.2	56.6	62.9	70.8	93.4	78.6
1280x1024	57	78.6	94.4	104.9	111.4	118	131.1
1600x1200	83.5	115.2	138.2	153.6	163.2	172.8	192

Data throughput is a direct function of resolution and refresh rate.

Numbers in each cell represent millions of pixels per second that are being reproduced. The amount of data being transmitted is dependent on the color depth selected.

Values represent only pixels in visible area of screen. To accurately calculate exact values, one would need to know the exact percentage of screen not being used by image. A good rule of thumb is to multiply these values by a factor of 1.2 to 1.35 to generate actual data throughput.

if I set it at 1600×1200 with a 100Hz refresh rate, I'm going to need a RAMDAC slightly faster than 240MHz. My card actually has a 250MHz RAMDAC, so I'm all set.

COLOR DEPTH AND RESOLUTION

> **BUZZ WORDS**
>
> **Color depth:** The number of individual hues that can be generated by a given display setting.

Technically speaking, controlling the color depth and resolution of a monitor is a combined function of the display adapter and monitor in unison. The monitor has to support the resolution you've selected on your graphics adapter, and your adapter has to be able to generate signals usable by the monitor. For that to happen, certain characteristics of the monitor will determine your capabilities.

Any individual phosphor is capable of glowing on only a single color. Yet the world around us is a bit more varied than that—on the outside, anyway. In reality, the colors of nature aren't that much different than digitized color. Three primary colors make up every one of the colors humans can perceive. The myriad of hues we see all around us are created by mixing these three colors. The intensity of any one color in relation to the other two determines the color we perceive.

The colors that come out of a computer monitor are derived in exactly the same manner. There are three phosphors per triad, and the three of them work together to create a hue. How many bits of data are used to generate colors is known as the bit depth. *Color depth* is the number of colors offered by a particular bit depth. If you look at the standard Windows settings for color depth, you'll see 256 Colors, High Color (16-bit), True Color (24-bit), and True Color (32-bit). You can find these settings in the Display Properties dialog box shown in **Figure 16.5**.

The original 256-color VGA was based on three separate 6-bit digital/analog converters, one for each of the primary colors. That is a total of 18 bits of data for the triad. As a result, you

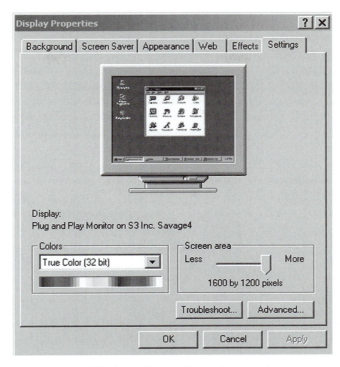

Figure 16.5   Windows Display Properties panel

had a total palette of 2^{18}, or 262,144 colors that could be generated. The VGA standard allowed users to select a total of 256 colors from that overall collection of colors that they could use at any one time. This became the working palette.

High Color, as described above, provides up to 16 bits of data for each triad. There are two ways a card manufacturer can allocate those bits of data. This is a function of the driver that ships with the card. One method is to evenly allocate five bits for each of the primary colors and drop the sixteenth bit. This allows for a display of 32,768 colors. The other, more commonly used, method is to allocate 5 bits each for red and blue, plus 6 bits for green. This provides the 65,536 colors promised by Windows.

True Color (24-bit) allows for the maximum number of colors displayed by any of today's graphics adapters. Each phosphor of the triad is allotted 8 bits to determine its intensity. As I pointed out in my discussion of binary, an 8-bit block of data provides for up to 256 combinations. By having three different primary colors working in synch, that allows for 256^3 colors. That is a total of 16,777,216 colors.

True Color (32-bit) is 24-bit true color with an added 8-bit alpha channel. The *alpha channel* allows programmers to add effects other than raw

BUZZ WORDS

Alpha channel: Eight bits used by 32-bit True Color to apply effects such as translucency and fogging.

color to the digital video. These extra 8 bits of data are used for generating the effect of translucency, or how well you can see through the color, to the overall image. It does not, however, increase the number of colors available.

Other terms you see thrown about a lot include SVGA, XGA, and UVGA. SVGA stands for Super VGA, and generally refers to resolution settings of 800x600 and up. Less frequently seen is the Extended Graphics Array (XGA). This was a favorite term of IBM for its 1024x768 setting available on certain onboard PS/2 computers. Ultra VGA (UVGA) refers to a resolution of 1280×1024. These particular options have been pretty much universally accepted by the industry as part of the SVGA set.

To the beginner, making the move to higher resolutions can have a disconcerting affect. Something about human psychology makes people want to have everything be the same, even after they change it! Changing resolution settings on a monitor does make the overall image sharper. It also expands the desktop so that you see more of your work. Someone accustomed to an 800×600 setting could expect to see something along the lines of the screen capture shown in **Figure 16.6**.

Making the move to 1280×1024, as shown in **Figure 16.7**, makes for an image with much lower granularity and overall sharpness. It also allows for more of the page to be seen at once. However, the letters are really tiny. You're squeezing more onto the monitor, but the monitor isn't getting any bigger. Since it can't get bigger, information displayed on it has to get smaller.

All is not lost, however. Windows users can go into the Display Properties, click on the appearance tab and bring up a screen like the one in **Figure 16.8**. The Item field shown in this image only displays one of many different elements you can manually resize, customizing the display to your liking.

Figure 16.6   A Windows Desktop set at 800×600

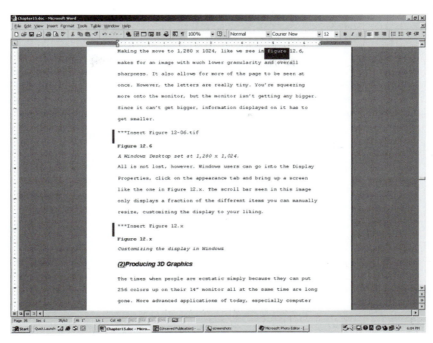

Figure 16.7   A Windows Desktop set at 1280×1024.

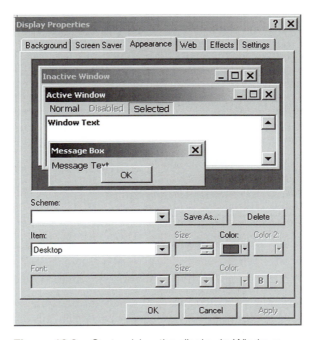

Figure 16.8   Customizing the display in Windows

PRODUCING 3D GRAPHICS

The times when people were ecstatic simply because they could put 256 colors up on their 14″ monitor all at the same time are long gone. More advanced applications of today, especially computer games and graphics applications, require a much greater semblance of realism and finer degrees of color management. To achieve that degree of realism, programmers are trying to make their images look as three-dimensional as possible. As 3D technology has developed, different techniques have been used to produce this effect. Some of these techniques involve hardware and driver technology while others fall under the category of Application Programming Interfaces (API). An API is a library of programming functions that can be applied as a unit.

HARDWARE AND DRIVER 3D

Some of the tricks your computer needs to be able to perform must occur on the hardware level. Some of these happen on the chip level, while the device driver handles others. For the purposes of this discussion, I can pretty much bundle those together. However, it should be noted that while I will be discussing APIs separately, it is a function of the chipset that determines whether or not a particular API is supported, because it is the API that will be calling on the functions I'll be discussing here.

Hardware Triangle Setup   On the most basic level, the graphics that appear on your screen consist of a collection of triangles and polygons. 3D effects are generated by constantly repositioning these fundamental shapes. In order to do this, a tremendous amount of mathematical work has to be done in order to calculate new angles and vectors. This can seriously drag down the performance of your computer if your CPU has to do all the work.

Many video cards provide an onboard 3D graphics processor, which offloads these functions from the CPU to itself. This dramatically improves the performance of both the computer and the video subsystem.

Double Buffering   One of the biggest obstacles of moving animation is the jittery effect that slower video cards create. This is a result of the frame buffer being called upon to supply an image before it is completely assembled. Since the digital world can't wait, the buffer sends through what it has.

Double buffering sets up two completely separate frame buffers for image generation. While one buffer is spitting out its contents to the RAMDAC, the other has already starting compiling the next frame. That frame will be complete by the time the RAMDAC comes back for it, and the other buffer will already be at work on the next frame. The result is very smooth animation.

This doesn't require any additional video processing overhead to speak of, but it does require a

BUZZ WORDS

Double buffering: The use of two separate buffers, so that as a frame is displayed on the monitor, another frame is the queue, ready for display, while yet a third is being assembled by the graphics adapter.

memory address space double that of what you need for simple frame buffering. This is the first of several reasons why today's video cards ship with such huge amounts of memory.

Texture Mapping   One of the most basic methods of creating realism is to apply texture to the objects on the computer screen. To see why this is important, simply go to your clothes closet. A brown leather jacket doesn't look at all similar to a brown silk skirt, even if the shade of brown is identical. If you hold them up side by side, you might see that the colors match perfectly, but the surface is completely different. The leather jacket has a slightly rough, almost pebbled surface, while the silk skirt has that sensuous, soft, and slinky look and feeling. The skirt also gives off a slight shimmer if the light is just right.

Another example would be a brick house with a stone façade. Even if the stone and brick are the same color, you don't have any trouble telling them apart. They have different textures. Programmers use texture to make things look more real. Therefore, an image on your screen consists of two parts. First, there are the geometric shapes that make up the image. On a most basic level, images consist of a complex collection of triangles, circles, and polygons. Over the geometric pattern, colors and textures are applied.

The process of *texture mapping* creates the textures as separate bitmaps and stores them in memory. These bitmaps consist of very small images, ranging from 32×32 pixels up to 256×256 pixels. A term you might see used for these bitmaps is *texels*. As a new screen is drawn, the texture won't have to be redrawn for each new screen. The bitmaps can simply be poured over the corresponding patterns.

Keeping these textures resident on the video card is essential for maximizing performance. Therefore, texture mapping is reason number two for having extra memory. The more memory you have available on your card, the more of these texels you can store.

> **BUZZ WORDS**
>
> **Texture mapping:** A process by which predrawn textures are stored in memory and applied to an image as needed.
>
> **Texel:** A small clip that serves as the sample of a texture used in texture mapping.

Bump Mapping   Closely related to texture mapping is bump mapping. And it isn't any more complicated than the name makes it sound. A key aspect of texture is the collection of tiny (or not so tiny) bumps scattered across any given surface. The stone surface I talked about doesn't have an evenly spaced collection of texels, the way your computer is going to reproduce it. There will be randomly spaced bumps scattered across the surface.

Bump mapping placed raised surfaces here and there across the surface of the texture map and can even generate the illusion of tiny little shadows made by the bump. This adds an even greater sense of realism. It also requires additional memory. Reason number three.

Anti-aliasing   One of the problems inherent with a separate bitmap for textures becomes apparent as soon as the image starts to move. To keep a sense of perspective, as the character in your game moves closer to an object, that object needs to get bigger. Conversely, as she moves farther away, it needs to get smaller. If the object gets smaller, but the texture bitmaps stay the same size, there's going to be a problem, isn't there?

As you approach an object, you have to add more detail if you want a realistic affect. Otherwise, the screen starts filling in the extra space with randomly generated pixels. Moving away from the object isn't any better. If you're starting with a 256 × 256 texel and start moving away, the only way to make it look smaller is to start stripping away pixels. As a result, the textures started to show either a granulated or interlaced effect. The latter problem is solved by anti-aliasing.

Anti-aliasing samples the image size for each frame and recalculates texture maps. The recalculated bitmap provides a much more accurate rendition than the one originally stored in memory. This does not specifically require adding more memory, but the technique does place an additional burden on the RAMDAC. Therefore, a faster RAMDAC than would be estimated by the simple resolution and refresh rate calculation will be in order. Hmmm. Maybe my 250MHz RAMDAC isn't fast enough after all!

> **BUZZ WORDS**
>
> **Anti-aliasing:** A process through which textures in an image are redrawn to more accurately reflect perceived distance.
>
> **Fogging:** A technique of implying distance in an image by making objects that are farther away less distinct.
>
> **Depth queuing:** A mathematical algorithm that recalculates the hue and intensity of colors in respect to increasing distances.

MIP Mapping The problems caused by moving the character closer to an object can be solved through a technique called MIP mapping. The acronym comes from a Latin phrase, *multium in parvo*, which means "many in one." Programmers who use this technique create multiple versions of the same bitmap.

They produce a bitmap that represents a texture for the largest object they intend to represent. This is stored as one bitmap. Then this bitmap is scaled down in size by increments of 50 percent, 25 percent, and so forth. A mathematical algorithm selects the appropriate version of the bitmap, based on distance to the object. This technique not only represents reason number four for having more memory, it's also an argument for a faster RAMDAC.

Fogging and Depth Queuing In the real world, as you move farther away from an object, atmospheric haze starts to make details of the object less distinct. It becomes softer and the colors start to shift toward blue. Graphics cards reproduce this affect through various forms of *fogging* techniques.

Properly applied, as objects or characters become closer to your point of view, they will become more and more distinct. Details will appear that you hadn't noticed before and colors will become more saturated. Fogging intensity can be increased or decreased, based on the affect the programmer is trying to achieve.

Fogging can be used in conjunction with another technique called *depth queuing*. This process takes the color shift I was just talking about and uses a mathematical algorithm that generates an exponential curve that is used to calculate both the hue and intensity of the color.

Dithering One of the problems of earlier computer games was that a character's face or costume was all one color and then abruptly ended. The leaves in the trees and where the mountains touched the sky were the same way. That is what make them look like the cartoons you watched when you were a kid.

BUZZ WORDS

Dithering: A process of blending colors of adjacent areas in an image to make the appearance more natural.

In nature, we like to see colors run together. *Dithering* is a technique that simulates that effect. From a limited palette of colors, blending two existing colors creates a completely new color. By dithering transition lines between colors a more natural appearance can be created.

Another use for dithering is the ability to work with a 256-color palette and generate more colors than are provided by that palette. Conversely, you can take a 16K color image and drop it down to 256 colors without generating overly harsh cutoffs. This allows programmers to worry less about the kind of video their end users will have available and spend more time creating useful programs.

Filtering Techniques By now, you're starting to get the idea that a lot is going on in order to create the image on your screen. Because objects are constantly moving around and changing positions, they also need to change their appearance. One of the problems that must be addressed is not just in changes to the color hues based on distance, but deciding just what the new color needs to be. There are four filtering techniques that are commonly used to generate colors in 3D graphics engines.

- *Point-sampled filtering:* The most basic method of generating a new pixel is point sampling. This technique simply copies the color of the adjacent pixel to the position of the new pixel. All video cards are capable of this method, but it is the least desirable of the filtering methods. It results in a very "blocky" appearance to the image. For some images, however, this is not a major issue, and because it is the fastest of the methods, it is the one that will be used.

- *Bilinear filtering:* This technique goes a long way in eliminating the blocky appearance of point filtering. It does so because it samples the four adjacent pixels, the ones to the right, to the left, above it, and below it, and then interpolates a new value based on what it sees. This is a much smoother filtering method and allows for a more realistic color pattern to emerge when an image needs to be resized. The downside to this is that this is a memory intensive technique. It greatly increases the amount of memory you need to have available for texture mapping. Add this to the list of reasons you need a 32MB video card.

- *Trilinear filtering:* This basically applies bilinear filtering to a moving object. The information from two separate MIP maps (see MIP mapping) is extracted and bilinear filtering applied to each map. This literally doubles the amount of memory required, over and above that needed for bilinear filtering. Therefore, this is usually an option that can be turned on and off in the driver settings of video cards that support the technique. Now let's start looking for a 64MB card!

■ *Anistropic filtering*: Of course, characters and objects in a moving image don't always move at 90- or 180-degree angles to everything around them. When you come in from all sides of an object, or if an object needs to be rotated at an odd angle, you need to be able to calculate pixels based on new angles as well. Otherwise, angled and curved lines will take on a "stair-stepped" appearance that most people find quite unattractive. This effect is quite apparent in early computer games. Anistropic filtering takes multiple samples from multiple MIP maps and interpolates values to smooth out these lines and angles. This technique provides the best moving images so far available, but requires some pretty intense overhead on the part of your video card and system overall. If you've got the video card that supports it and the horsepower in your system to support the video card, then by all means give it a try. The worst-case scenario is that the graphics slow down to a crawl and you hate it. That's why it's an option that can be turned on and off on video cards that support the feature.

3D APIs

These days, everything is modular. It's all built up from preassembled blocks. You have modular homes, modular stereo systems, and modular exercise equipment. Programmers have modular programming languages. One of these modules is the API. The API can also function as part of the hardware abstraction layer (HAL) for the operating system. When a video card manufacturer includes support for a particular API, it does so by incorporating that support into the chipset of the video card. As long as the appropriate version of the API is installed into the operating system, that video card will now support all of the functions the particular API supports. The more APIs a card supports, the more choices a user has.

OpenGL   OpenGL is an API that was originally developed by Silicon Graphics. The idea was to produce a 3D graphics API that could be used across multiple platforms. Therefore, a graphics adapter that supported OpenGL could be designed to work on PCs, Macs, or Silicon Graphics workstations. The interface is completely independent of operating system.

OpenGL can be implemented with either an installable client driver or a mini client driver. An installable client driver provides all of the support that the current version of OpenGL as released by Silicon Graphics offers. Not all applications require this much horsepower. Games, for example, might only make use of a small collection of the functions supported by OpenGL. That's where a mini client driver comes into play. This is a stripped-down version of the driver that provides only the level of support required by the application. The functions supported by OpenGL include the following:

■ Modeling

■ Directional lighting

■ Smooth shading

■ Color transformation

■ Texture mapping

■ Alpha blending

- Fogging
- Motion blur

The various ways in which these functions are implemented are beyond the scope of this book, but a white paper can be downloaded from Silicon Graphics' Web site at www.sgi.com.

DirectX   DirectX is actually a collection of different APIs that support both audio and video functions that was developed by Microsoft. One of the key limiting factors to multimedia in a Windows environment has been the separation of applications from the system's hardware by the HAL. While the HAL provides for a more stable computing environment, it has proved to be a hindrance to multimedia performance. DirectX provides a much thinner layer between the hardware and the applications that use it. While some of the components of DirectX are specific to audio reproduction, others are specific to video. The ones that deal with video are listed here:

- *DirectDraw*: This function of DirectX is responsible for accelerating the generation of two-dimensional images. Applications that require no 3D modeling can make use of this API for smoother 2D animations and faster screen draws in more conventional applications, such as word processors and spreadsheets.
- *Direct3D*: Here, Microsoft has provided an API that simulates direct access to hardware. 3D acceleration can be handled on a software level, providing enhanced 3D animations. A computer that is not blessed with a dedicated accelerator card can benefit from the affects of acceleration as long as the software being run, as well as the graphics adapter, both support the API.
- *DirectPlay*: Some games are best played over the Internet. Internet connections, however, are not exactly conducive to fast video response. DirectPlay is an API that provides enhanced response for games played in this fashion.
- *DirectShow*: Of course, in order to really enjoy the overall experience of a multimedia presentation, both the graphics and the sound are involved. DirectShow is an API that allows for a smooth blending of audio and video information.

Glide   This API was developed by 3dfx for its line of high-end video cards. Originally developed for its Voodoo2 and Banshee chipsets, it had previously been considered a proprietary API. However, in 2001, 3dfx released the API to the public for open-source development. It differs from the more common APIs discussed above in two respects. It uses on-chip lookup tables for textures. While this technique isn't currently enjoying much support from the gaming industry, now that the API has been open-sourced, that may change. The second major difference is that it supports higher frame rates than are currently supported by either OpenGL or DirectX.

VIDEO CARD BUS CONSIDERATIONS

With any add-on device the I/O bus on which it resides has a serious impact on the performance of that device. In Chapter Ten, Examining the Expansion Bus, I discussed the significant differences that exist among the different technologies. One of the things I also pointed out was that graphics performance was a driving element in the development of faster busses. With graphics adapters, however, you have to take two different busses into consideration. They work on both an internal and an external bus.

THE EXTERNAL VIDEO BUS

The external graphics bus is the interface between the graphics adapter and the motherboard. Add-on graphics adapters are installed onto the expansion bus and are therefore going to be subject to the limitations of whatever choices are available on a particular computer. This is information I covered in detail in Chapter Ten and therefore, I will only briefly recap the essentials in this chapter. In the early days of computing, an OS such as MS-DOS placed no heavy burden on the graphics subsystem at all. The advent of the GUI changed all that. As Windows 3.x began to gain popularity the public began to demand faster and faster graphics. For purposes of clarity, I'm going to repeat in this chapter a table I used in Chapter Ten to compare the different evolutionary stages of the expansion bus. This information can be seen in **Table 16.3**.

For maximum performance, you're going to want to make use of the fastest bus your system has available. In most cases, this will be AGP, but which version of AGP your computer can handle will be determined by its particular chipset.

THE INTERNAL VIDEO BUS

Here the situation becomes a little more convoluted. While the external bus may be limited to 32-bit or, if you're lucky, 64-bit architecture, inside, the graphics adapter might be steaming along on a completely different stream. The chipset of the video card might produce 32-bit, 64-bit, 96-bit, or 128-bit data paths internally.

However, don't automatically assume that a 128-bit video card is going to be faster than a 64-bit card. Other factors that I discussed earlier have just as strong of an impact on performance. Overall performance takes into account the following factors:

- Chipset features and performance
- Type of memory installed on adapter
- Speed of RAMDAC
- Bit width
- How much process is offloaded to system processor
- Type of interface (PCI or AGP)
- Quality of device driver

Each of these factors contributes to performance. However, all else being equal, if the character in your game is trying to escape a burning building, a chipset operating with a 128-bit data path will kick ash.

Table 16.3   The Evolution of the Expansion Bus

BUS	Year Released	Bus Width	Maximum Speed	Address Space	Available Memory	Bandwidth	CPU Release
PC1	1981	8-bit	4.77MHz	8-bit	1MB	7.9MB/s	8088
ISA	1984	16-bit	8MHz	20-bit	16MB	15.9MB/s	80286
MCA	1987	32-bit	10MHz	20-bit	16MB	~38.6MB/s	80386
EISA	1988	32-bit	8MHz	32-bit	4GB	31.8MB/s	80386
PC Card	1990	16-bit	8MHz	24-bit	64MB	~15.8MB/s	80386
VLB	1991	32-bit	33MHz	32-bit	4GB	127.2MB/s	80486
PCI 1.0	1992	32-bit	33MHz	32-bit	4GB	127.2MB/s	80486
PCI 2.1	1995	32- or 64-bit	66MHz	32-bit	4GB	~510MB/s	Pentium
AGP 1.0	1996	32-bit	66MHz	32-bit	4GB	254MB/s	Pentium
AGP 2.0	1998	32-bit	66MHz	32-bit	4GB	~533MB/s	Pentium
PCI-X 1.0	2000	64-bit	133MHz	64-bit	N/A	~1.2GB/s	Pentium II
PCI-X 2.0	2002	64-bit	<533MHz	64-bit	N/A	~4.3GB/s	Pentium IV

Each new release of a PCI bus is not only faster, but can also have increased bit width and more efficient transfer of data in each clock cycle.

Another thing to consider is that two different manufacturers might design their video cards completely differently and still be able to call them 128-bit cards. A "true" 128-bit card will have a 128-bit chipset and graphics engine as well as a 128-bit path from chipset to video memory. Another less expensive card might call itself 128-bit but have a 64-bit engine. Only the path from chipset to memory is 128 bits wide. The latter implementation would have only a negligible effect on performance. The reason they design it this way is that advertising an inexpensive 128-bit card can have a substantial impact on sales.

A DISCUSSION OF OBSOLETE DISPLAY MODES

I promised in the introduction of this chapter that I would provide some information on earlier display modes as a historical reference. This is important to the exam candidate because CompTIA rightfully insists that a properly trained technician knows the history of the industry and not just current events.

In the earliest days of computing everybody worked on monochrome displays that were one of two types. The least expensive, and therefore most common, examples displayed cyan type over a very dark green background. For the writer or desktop publisher, a "deluxe" paper white monitor was available. These placed dark type over a bright background.

In 1981, IBM introduced the first color displays in the form of the Color Graphics Adapter (CGA). CGA monitors offered an amazing 320×200 resolution and the user could enjoy four whole colors! A proprietary implementation of CGA was introduced by Tandy Corporation that provided 640×480 resolution and up to sixteen colors, but it was a classic case of too little, too late. VGA had already established a strong foothold.

The Enhanced Graphics Adapter (EGA) was another development of IBM that was released in 1984. EGA was capable of sixteen colors at a resolution of 640×350. While this was a great improvement over CGA, sitting in front of one of these monitors for eight hours a day was no treat.

CGA and EGA both used the computer's system memory for drawing screens. At those resolutions and color depths, only a small amount of memory was required. I mentioned earlier that in the old days, the first 128K of high memory located directly above the 640K of conventional memory was dedicated to video. In fact, that 128K block was subdivided into two separate 64K address spaces. One of these spaces was dedicated to CGA and the other to EGA.

When IBM released VGA in 1987 the 640×480 resolution was just enough of an improvement to make text less painful to read. The real improvement was realized in how many colors could be displayed. While there were still only sixteen colors possible at the maximum resolution, if the user was willing to sacrifice resolution in exchange for more colors, at 320×200, up to 256 colors could be displayed at once.

CHAPTER SUMMARY

Now that you have a better understanding of the graphics subsystem of a computer, you should be able to make more informed decisions about how to equip computers, based on their intended use. It's interesting how graphics cards receive so much attention, especially in the gaming market, when monitors don't. Both work together to create the image the user sees.

Certification candidates should take special note of issues such as resolution, color depth, and basic memory requirements. A great deal of emphasis is placed on display settings and what they mean. If I seemed to spend a lot of time discussing video memory, it's because it is such an important component. But it is no more important than the quality of the chipset and the speed of the RAMDAC.

BRAIN DRAIN

1. Describe in as much detail as possible how an image is generated on a typical CRT monitor.

2. You have just purchased a new 21″ monitor that can provide an 1880×1400 display and you want to use 32-bit True Color. Assuming you need no texturizing or other advanced features, what is the minimum memory your graphics card will require?

3. Why are TFT displays considered better than passive matrix displays?

4. What are three critical components for a graphics card and what are their functions?

5. What are the factors that contribute to the overall speed of a graphics card?

THE 64K$ QUESTIONS

1. In a CRT monitor, the phosphors are separated from one another by _____.
   a. The electron guns
   b. A shadow mask
   c. The deflection yoke
   d. A RAMDAC

2. In a CRT, the beams of electrons are redirected across the screen by _____.
   a. The electron guns
   b. A shadow mask
   c. The deflection yoke
   d. A RAMDAC

3. Smoother animation is made possible by a technique called _____.
   a. Texture mapping
   b. Anti-aliasing
   c. Frame buffering
   d. Dithering

4. Diagonal lines are made smoother and less jagged by employing _____.
   a. Texture mapping
   b. Anti-aliasing
   c. Frame buffering
   d. Dithering

5. If a programmer wants her colors to appear more natural with smoother blending, she will take advantage of a technique called _____.
   a. Texture mapping
   b. Anti-aliasing
   c. Frame buffering
   d. Dithering

6. The best way to speed up a video card is to add more memory.
   a. True
   b. False

7. The LCD display most likely used on a PDA is a _____.
   a. Common plane

b. Diagonal crystal

c. Passive matrix

d. TFT

8. If you were to purchase a high-end video card today, it would most likely be equipped with _____ memory.

a. VRAM

b. WRAM

c. MDRAM

d. DDRAM

9. Programmers can add extra effects to graphics without changing the actual color by using _____.

a. Anti-aliasing

b. A frame buffer

c. The alpha channel

d. Dithering

10. Which of the following is not an example of a graphics API?

a. DirectX

b. Glide

c. Cg

d. OpenGL

TRICKY TERMINOLOGY

Alpha channel: Eight bits used by 32-bit True Color to apply effects such as translucency and fogging.

Anti-aliasing: A process through which textures in an image are redrawn to more accurately reflect perceived distance.

Bezel: The plastic frame that masks off the unusable part of a monitor's image.

Cathode: A negatively charged device that emits a stream of electrons when heated.

Color depth: The number of individual hues that can be generated by a given display setting.

Convergence: The accuracy with which multiple beams of electrons or light can focus on the same point.

Co-processed: Any adapter or device that is equipped with a microprocessor that offloads some of the work of the PC's CPU.

Deflection yoke: A circular array of powerful magnets that act to deflect a beam of electrons from its natural path.

Depth queuing: A mathematical algorithm that recalculates the hue and intensity of colors in respect to increasing distances.

Dithering: A process of blending the colors of adjacent areas in an image to make the appearance more natural.

Dot pitch: The distance separating two like-colored phosphors that are adjacent to one another.

Double buffering: The use of two separate buffers, so that as a frame is displayed on the monitor, another frame is in the queue, ready for display, while yet a third is being assembled by the graphics adapter.

Electron gun: A cathode that, when heated, emits a stream of electrons from the positive pole.

Fogging: A technique of implying distance in an image by making objects that are farther away less distinct.

Frame buffer: Dedicated memory used by a graphics adapter to build the next image frame to be displayed in the time that the current image frame is on the screen.

Phosphor: A single dot of color created when the phosphorous layer of a CRT is excited by electrons.

Pixel: The collection of phosphors that collectively generate a single dot of color in a monitor's image.

Raster line: A single row of pixels that make a horizontal line across an image.

Shadow mask: A thin metal sheet perforated with tiny holes that outlines the individual phosphors in a CRT monitor.

Substrate: The supportive material over which an active substance can be applied.

Texel: A small clip that serves as the sample of a texture used in texture mapping.

Texture mapping: A process by which predrawn textures are stored in memory and applied to an image as needed.

Triad: The three separate phosphors, each of a separate primary color, that when combined form the separate hues of color perceived by the user.

Acronym Alert

API: Application Programming Interface

CRT: Cathode-Ray Tube. A video display that uses a device called a cathode to fire a beam (or ray) of electrons towards a phosphorus-coated surface.

HAL: Hardware Abstraction Layer

HR: Horizontal Refresh. The speed at which a monitor can draw individual raster lines.

LCD: Liquid Crystal Display. An imaging device that consists of transistors suspended in a liquid emulsion.

MDRAM: Multibank DRAM. A form of memory that can be accessed in blocks, rather than sequentially.

MIP: *Multium in Parvo*. Latin for "many in one." It is a technique by which several samples of the same texture are created in different sizes.

TFT: Thin Film Transistor. An LCD that utilizes microscopically thin layers of transistors laid out in a grid pattern in a liquid crystal emulsion.

UVGA: Ultra VGA. High resolution VGA.

VR: Vertical Refresh. The number of times per second a monitor regenerates the image on the screen.

XGA: Extended Graphics Array. A proprietary display created by IBM.

 View the Video

A video clip on Video Cards, Monitors, and Sound Cards is available on the accompanying CD.

CHAPTER 17

MULTIMEDIA: COMPUTERIZED HOME ENTERTAINMENT

In the early days of computing, the entire concept of streaming video coupled with high-quality sound coming from a computer was not even a designer's fantasy. Keep in mind that in those days, the best audio systems derived the maximum sound quality from a turntable dragging a diamond needle across a vinyl platter. Computers had a 1″ speaker through which a single beep could be played. As programmers learned fancier tricks, they could vary the frequency of that beep to the point that rudimentary tunes could be played.

Tandy Corporation took that a step further with Tandy Sound. A more advanced sound chip on the TL2000 series of computers allowed for some relatively sophisticated audio, including music and sound effects combined. About the only thing that kept this from really taking off was the nearly simultaneous release of the Ad Lib brand of sound card. The Ad Lib allowed the user to hook up higher-quality external speakers and even get stereo.

Multimedia, these days, has taken on near-theater-like qualities. 5.1 Digital Audio, MPEG II, and the 3-D graphics enhancements I introduced in Chapter Sixteen, Your Computer and Graphics, now allow *Terminator IV* to play in a window on your monitor while you're working on your spreadsheets. Today's computer games combine animation with actual video clips of live actors. (And frighteningly enough, this is still being done with a constant stream of zeros and ones.)

In this chapter, I will introduce you to two different elements of multimedia. Because the majority of these applications are now housed on some variation of optical medium, I have chosen to include the various members of the CD family in this chapter and show you how music is stored on a CD. Then, I'll discuss sound cards and their role in the overall process.

A+ CORE HARDWARE EXAM OBJECTIVES

Some exam objectives that will be covered include the following:

1.1   Identify the names, purpose, and characteristics of system modules. Recognize these modules by sight or definition.

1.2 Identify basic procedures for adding and removing field-replaceable modules for desktop systems. Given a replacement scenario, choose the appropriate sequences.

1.4 Identify typical IRQs, DMAs, and I/O addresses, and procedures for altering these settings when installing and configuring devices. Choose the appropriate installation or configuration steps in a given scenario.

1.6 Identify proper procedures for installing and configuring common IDE devices. Choose the appropriate installation or configuration sequences in given scenarios. Recognize the associated cables.

2.1 Recognize common problems associated with each module and their symptoms, and identify steps to isolate and troubleshoot the problems. Given a problem situation, interpret the symptoms and infer the most likely cause.

The Components of Multimedia

Three pieces needed to complete the multimedia puzzle are decent storage media, good sound reproduction, and a way to create cinematic quality graphics. Since I discussed the reproduction of graphics in Chapter Sixteen, I need not rehash that here. But one thing you need to keep in mind is that all those audio clips and graphics files require some CPU horsepower in addition to as much available memory as you can provide. Since they also take up a lot of space, some sort of portable storage mechanism is in order. For these files, the floppy disk just isn't going to cut it.

The CD-ROM

The CD-ROM has almost universally been accepted as storage medium of choice for multimedia (see **Figure 17.1**). While it started out as an acronym for Compact Disc/Read Only Memory, CD-ROM is one of the few acronyms that has made the successful migration to the status of a "real word." CD-ROMs have made a few evolutionary advances in the years since they were first released. For one thing, they continually get faster.

Manufacturers have a unique method of measuring speed. When shopping for a CD-ROM drive, you find a range of speeds starting these days at about 32x and moving upward to 56x. Just what do those numbers mean? The first CD-ROM released had a maximum data throughput of 150KB/s. That's incredibly slow, by today's standards. When the first bump from 150 to 300KB/s was released, the marketing hype was "Two times the speed of regular CD-ROMs." Advertising slicks labeled them as "2x" CD-ROMs and the convention has stuck. **Table 17.1** compares the speeds of CD drives over the years.

> **Exam Note:** Make sure you know the throughput of the initial release of the CD-ROM and how that relates to the speed factors the industry uses to rate CD-ROM speed.

Figure 17.1   The CD family has grown a lot since that first 150KB/s device. This machine is equipped with a 16X DVD/40X CD-ROM as well as a 52X CD-RW.

Table 17.1   Conventional CD-ROM Specifications Past, Present, and Future

Speed	Classification	Actual Bits per Second	Transfer Rate (KB/s)
1x	Single speed	153,600	150
2x	Double speed	307,200	300
4x	Quad	614,400	600
6x	Six speed	921,600	900
8x	Eight speed	1,228,800	1200
12x	Twelve speed	1,536,000	1500
16x	Sixteen speed	1,843,200	1800
24x	Twenty-four speed	2,457,600	2400
32x	Thirty-two speed	3,686,400	3600
40x	Forty speed	4,915,200	4800
48x	Forty-eight speed	7,372,800	7200
56x	Fifty-six speed	8,601,600	8400
72x*	Seventy-two speed	11,590,200	10,800

Each generation of CD drive has a speed based on a multiple of the original CD-ROM drive.

*Don't try finding a 72x drive at this point in time. For a short while, a proprietary technology known as TrueX provided this speed. TrueX has been subsequently abandoned. It is included here for informational purposes.

Until the release of DVD (I'll get into that), the one thing that didn't change with time was the amount of data stored on the disc. To understand that, let's take a look at how the data is stored. The first thing that is important is that CDs are not magnetic media like your hard drive, floppy disks, or Zip disks. They're an optical medium. Information is extracted from a disc by a laser beam.

HOW THE CD WORKS

A standard CD is a disc 120mm in diameter and consisting of three layers. The back layer (where the label is traditionally printed) is made of polycarbonate, a fairly durable plastic. However, that is an extremely thin layer of about .002mm. If you're worried about scratches on your CD (and you should be), worry most about the label side. Do not use standard felt-tip markers to write on this side, as many of those inks contain a solvent. Over time, they can actually eat into the plastic and damage the data on recordable CDs. Use only labels designed for CDs or specially designed felt markers for writing on that surface.

BUZZ WORDS

Pit: A tiny hole embedded in the recording layer of optical media that prevents the laser from reflecting back into the photoelectric sensor.

Land: All of the reflective surface of the recording layer in optical media that has not been burned or punched into a pit.

Optical stylus: A mechanism consisting of a laser-emitting diode coupled to a beam splitter.

EXAM NOTE: While this section admittedly gets more involved in how data is written to and read back from the surface of the CD-ROM than CompTIA requires, it's still good information to know. What CompTIA does expect is that you be able to describe the purpose of split beams and the function of pits and lands.

Onto that back surface of a conventional CD a .002mm layer of aluminum is deposited. The metal coating acts as a mirror onto which billions of little tiny *pits*, one-sixth of a micron wide, have been stamped. These pits vary in length from slightly under a micron to about three microns and are only one-sixth of a micron deep (see **Figure 17.2**). These pits are put onto the disc in a concentric spiral moving from the center of the disc to the outside. The area of disc surface outside of the pits is known as the *lands*. Data is grouped in sectors, similar to the way hard disks manage data, except that the sector size is 2KB (on data CDs) rather than 512 bytes. Track density on CDs is much higher than that of hard drives as well. CD manufacturers squeeze in excess of 16,000 tracks into every inch of the CD. That's roughly 400 times the density of magnetic media.

When your CD player reads the data off the disc, it shines an infrared laser, 780 nanometers wide, past a prism that splits the beam into three separate beams. This laser/beam-splitter combination is known as the *optical stylus*. On the first-generation CD-ROMs and most current audio CD players, the disc spins under the beam at 200 to 500rpm, the speed increasing as the laser reaches the outside edge of the disc. Higher throughput for data CDs requires that the disc spin faster. Rotation speeds have exceeded 11,000rpm on several models.

Light reflecting from pits is polarized 180 degrees from the light reflected from the lands. The difference in intensity between lands and pits results in a flickering beam of light that is

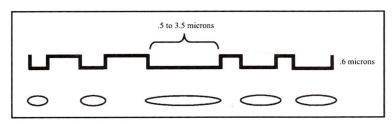

The top diagram represents a cross-section of a CD track, with its pits and lands. Beneath is a representation of the pits seen from above.

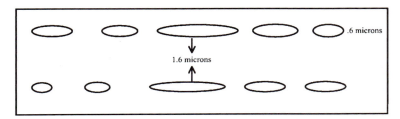

All pits are uniformly .6 microns wide and .6 microns deep, but they vary in length. All tracks are separated by 1.6 microns of land.

Figure 17.2   The pits etched into a CD are microscopically small, yet are all that is needed to store large amounts of data onto a relatively small surface.

picked up by a very sensitive photoelectric cell. This cell converts the beam into a pulsating electronic signal, which is translated by the controller into a series of zeros and ones.

As you might imagine, keeping a laser beam that tiny accurately focused on a stream of microscopic holes in plastic is a formidable task. It wouldn't be quite as difficult if disc surfaces were always mathematically flat, and spindle holes were punched into the absolute center of the CD so that as it rotated there would be no positional deviation of the tracks. Manufacturing CDs to such perfect standards would most likely drive their price out of the range of most users. Therefore, some fail-safe measures have to be taken.

A common approach to this problem is the technique of beam splitting. The CD reader doesn't focus the beam directly onto the disc itself. Instead, it is focused on a diffraction grid, which divides the original laser beam into three different light sources. The beam splitter is designed in such a way that the three outbound beams are passed through to the medium. The reflected light coming back from the CD is bounced ninety degrees to the photoreceptor diode, where the signals are interpreted.

Of the three beams directed at the CD, the center one is supposed to remain focused on the track containing the data. The two outside beams focus on the land surface on either side of the track (**Figure 17.3**). Since there are no pits in this area, the reflections that bounce back from either of these two beams should always be constant. Any flickering of these reflected beams generates electrical signals that cause the servomotor that positions the laser to adjust its focus accordingly.

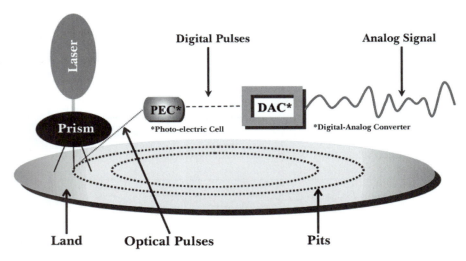

Figure 17.3 Diagram of a beam splitter in action

STORING DATA ON CDs

In order for a CD reader to accurately interpret what the CD burner created, there are standard file formats. Digital audio discs require very little in the way of error correction, and the original compact disc/digital audio (CD-DA) format is still used for audio CDs. Executable programs and critical data require error-free translations. For this, the International Organization for Standardization (ISO) wrote a series of standards for the CD data format called ISO 9660. This is the file format currently used in the manufacture of CD software. It allows approximately 650MB to be stored on a single compact disc.

AUDIO CD RECORDING

As I mentioned, audio CDs have completely different requirements than those used for storing digital data. Error correction is not as much of an issue. Accurately reproducing musical pitch is the requirement. To do so, the musical waveform being recorded is sampled many thousands of times per second. How many times per second a sample is extracted is the sample rate. The industry standard for CD-quality sound is 44,100 times per second. Sample rates for the sound track on computer games can vary. The conversion of analog waveforms into a digital file format is known as Pulse Code Modulation (PCM).

The sample taken is a 16-bit chunk of data called a *chop*. 147 chops can be stored in each 2352-byte sector. Typically, audio files end with a .wav extension. A standard WAV file is made of a sequential series of chops. If you recall your binary, you will be able to calculate that a 16-bit sample is

> **BUZZ WORDS** ⎯⎯⎯⎯⎯⎯
>
> **Chop:** A 16-bit piece of data generated when music is sampled once during the digital recording procedure.

capable of generating 65,536 levels of sound. In order to record a stereo signal, two separate audio channels are simultaneously recorded onto individual tracks. Reading 44,100 16-bit samples simultaneously across two tracks yields an effective data transfer rate of 176,400 bytes per second. On playback, the digital signal passes through a circuit called the Digital-Analog Converter (DAC). This conversion is called Signal Quantisation.

Standards for audio CD recording are published and updated regularly in a publication known as the Red Book. This set of standards defines standard methods for manufacturing CDs, the specifications for PCM, how to manufacture and calibrate the optical stylus, and many other technical standards. As new or updated standards emerge, this book is updated.

DATA CD-ROM

The structure of a CD-ROM drive designed to read data differs very little from what I described for audio CD players. How data is stored is significantly different, though. Data CDs make use of the Compact Disc File System (CDFS). Whereas the audio CD creates a large file of 16-bit chops, typical computer data isn't so evenly structured. As a result, the file format used by data CDs uses a file system similar to that of other media. It differs in the size of sectors from magnetic media. While a hard drive contains 512-byte sectors, a CD-ROM uses those 2352-byte sectors I mentioned earlier. The CD/DA file system uses the entire sector to store data. CDFS can store 2000 bytes into each sector and reserves the remaining bytes for file system overhead.

While losing a byte of Beethoven now and then isn't critical, losing a byte of WINWORD.EXE can keep the program from running. Therefore, Error Detection Code (EDC) is incorporated into the data CDFS file structure. EDC works in conjunction with traditional ECC to assure that data integrity is maintained. Another 304 bytes, known as *synchronization bits*, assures that data is delivered in the correct order. Altogether, this results in a data CD being able to store only 650MB, as opposed to the 680MB of the audio CD. Data transfer, due to the additional overhead of EDC, was 150KB/s on the first generation of CD-ROMs. This is the root transfer that became the basis for the speed multipliers I discussed earlier in the chapter. One of the ways manufacturers have achieved higher throughput has been by increasing the rotational velocity of the disc.

> **EXAM NOTE:** Know why synchronization bits are necessary for data CDs but not for musical CDs. Also be aware that this is why data CDs format to a different capacity than music CDs.

Another key difference is reflected in how the different discs need to be able to access data. An audio disc is frequently played from beginning to end. Even if only selected tracks are being played there are very few files (relatively speaking) on an audio CD. Random access of data is rarely an issue, and even when it is, speed of that access isn't that critical. A data CD, conversely, can have tens of thousands of files. The reader needs to be able to access any one of these files

BUZZ WORDS

Synchronization bits: Data included on each sector of a data CD that assures that the information will be processed in the correct sequence.

as quickly as possible when requested by the system. How the drive moves the laser head across the disc directly affects how quickly data can be extracted from the drive. Different methods for reading the data from the surface of the disc have emerged over the years.

CLV The first CD-ROM drives for computers were identical to those used in the audio industry. Manufacturers employed a technology called constant linear velocity (CLV) to read data from the disc. Unlike early hard drives, where every track across the drive has the same number of sectors, the number of sectors per track increases from the center of the CD to the edge. CLV drives use a mechanism called a servo to constantly adjust the rpm of the disc rotation in order to make sure that data throughput remains constant.

On audio CDs and the first-generation data CDs, this velocity changed from 210 rpm to 539 rpm. Audio CD players still use this method and spin the disc at these speeds. The method by which data throughput was increased on early generation CD-ROM drives was to increase the maximum rotational velocity of the disc. 4x drives would spin faster than 2x, 8x spun faster than 4x, and so on up the line.

The problem with this technique was that in order to randomly access data, the head not only has to locate the appropriate track, but it also has to adjust to the correct rotational speed for that track. This led to rather poor access times for data. Drives of this era were afflicted with access times of 400ms and some exceeded 500ms. As you might imagine, this did not exactly enhance the effect of trying to play an interactive game directly from a CD. Pioneer was the first company to abandon this approach in 1986 when it released its 10x CD-ROM drive.

CAV These drives developed by Pioneer incorporated a new technology called constant angular velocity (CAV). This approach keeps rotational speed constant and requires that the controller adapt to different speeds of data throughput as the heads move from center to edge. Now, when data needs to be accessed randomly, the laser head can find the track it needs and doesn't have to wait for the disc to settle into its new speed. Most drives currently manufactured actually employ both CAV and CLV modes. They use CAV to read data toward the middle of the disc and switch to CLV to read data from the perimeter.

The inclusion of digital signal processors (DSP) offloads much of the work of the DACs to these chips and provides much faster data transfers. A DSP is a microprocessor whose only reason for existence is to scan a nondigital signal and convert it to a digital stream of data.

Since CAV drives don't actually have a fixed data throughput, where do the manufacturers arrive at their published speeds? In some cases, the published speed ratings frequently represent only the inside track. Most reputable manufacturers actually publish the speed of their drives as a dual-speed rating; for example, you might be looking at a 24/48x CD-ROM drive. These numbers represent the speed obtained at both the outside track and the innermost track. In other words, your fancy new 56x CD-ROM only works at that speed when it's reading the inside track, then gets slower from there.

DATA TRANSFER AND THE REAL WORLD

As I have already pointed out, data throughput was increased primarily by way of increasing rotational speed of the disc. The question that needs to be asked is when do users realize the benefit of these gains? A blind answer to this question would be that faster is always better. The fact of the matter is that high transfer rates are rarely utilized in the majority of applications that CDs are put to.

As I said earlier, digital audio requires a mere 178KB/s to maintain CD-quality sound. Recorded video files (in compressed format) will not benefit from anything greater than about 300KB/s. Therefore, higher speeds really only strut their stuff if you're installing an application from the CD. For example, many of the office suites shipped by software companies these days fill from four to as many as eight CDs! Installing one of these applications from a 2x CD is not high on my list of pleasures. In order to provide a rough comparison, I did a very unscientific little experiment. I happened to have an old 4x CD-ROM lying around. I installed it on the same IDE port as a 48x CD-ROM. I then proceeded to install Office 2000 Small Business Edition. This application resides on two CDs for a complete installation. (The things I do for my readers!)

From the 4x drive the installation took an hour and forty-eight minutes. I then uninstalled the application, made sure the registry was cleaned of any entries generated by the first installation, and then repeated the installation from the 48x. I was finished in seventeen minutes. Based on raw speed measurements alone, the installation should have been eight times faster. If you do the math, you'll see that the actual improvement I realized was in the range of 6.35x.

Several factors can account for the discrepancy. Command overhead on the controllers is one of these (See Chapter Thirteen, Hard Disk Drive Structure and Geometry, for a discussion of command overhead). The 48x drive would have also benefited greatly had the system I used for the experiment allowed me to use the UDMA mode supported by that drive. But the presence of the older PIO drive on the same channel forced the newer drive into PIO mode as well. Another factor that undoubtedly affected the different times was how much time I sat in a daze while the setup routine waited for me to either input data it was requesting or to click the Next button. (I told you it was a very unscientific experiment!)

Games that are played directly from the CD benefit very little from this extra speed, however. In time, you can expect the best computer games to ship in DVD format in order to be able to take advantage of MPEG-II technology that I'll be discussing later in this chapter.

THE CD INTERFACE

Modern CD-ROM drives will ship as either SCSI or ATAPI devices. In terms of performance, neither standard currently can claim an advantage over the other. Data throughput is still lower than the slowest of the available interfaces. However, it is still possible, even in this enlightened day and age, to stumble across computers that use one of the proprietary interfaces of yesteryear. At one time, the user had to choose among Sony, Mitsumi (or Panasonic, which is the same thing), and IDE. Eventually everybody gave way to IDE.

It can be pretty hard to tell the difference between the IDE and the early proprietary drives. The connectors looked identical. Unfortunately, the pins on those connectors didn't perform identical functions, and your CD-ROM drive would not work if plugged into the wrong connector. It didn't do any harm; it just didn't work. Differentiating SCSI from IDE can prove difficult if you look too quickly. The connectors look the same. However, SCSI will have fifty pins, while IDE only has forty. Also, the IDE device has to have a way of determining whether its role is master or slave on the port. On the back of the IDE drive will be three or four jumpers that perform that function. The manufacturers are pretty good about labeling these jumpers on the drive itself, so figuring it out shouldn't be too tough.

People sometimes get a little confused about SCSI versus ATAPI when it comes to CD-ROMs. As far as the interface goes, I pointed out when discussing the SCSI interface that in most cases, SCSI is the faster of the two. That's no different with CD-ROM drives than it is with any other devices. However, before rushing out and converting everything you own, including the CD-ROM, to SCSI, there are a few things you should consider.

The SCSI interface is a shared bandwidth. Any device on the chain is competing for space on that bandwidth. Raw performance of CD-ROM drives, at this point in technology anyway, doesn't even begin to approach the bandwidth available across the ATAPI interface. Therefore, even if you're using the fastest CD-ROM drives available, they won't become any more of a bottleneck than they already are if put them on the IDE interface. In fact, if the CD-ROM and the hard drives are both being hit constantly, such as in a server environment that accesses data from CDs a lot, then having the CD-ROM on the SCSI chain can actually hinder the performance of the hard drives and other father SCSI devices.

EXTERNAL CD-ROMS

External CD-ROM drives have always enjoyed a certain degree of popularity. You can add one to the system without having to open the case. Fighting with master/slave relationships is not an issue, and the drive can be moved from one machine to another. As a result, external devices are as popular today as they were a few years ago. Putting them onto the machine has been accomplished basically in one of several ways: external SCSI (including FireWire), parallel port operation, and, more recently, USB. Hooking up a SCSI CD-ROM drive differs in no way from hooking up any other SCSI device, which is covered in Chapter Fifteen, The Many Faces of SCSI.

Putting the drive on the parallel port is simple. It hooks up the same way as any printer. Operating systems that support PnP will automatically detect the new drive and load the appropriate drivers. To make the drive work properly, however, you must make sure that your BIOS is set to use the IEEE-1284 ECP/EPP mode. While the older bidirectional modes will work, performance will be really, really bad. ECP supports up to 1200KB/s throughput, as opposed to the 530KB/s that bidirectional can handle. (I'll be discussing these different modes in greater detail in Chapter Eighteen, Printing Technologies.)

Even with ECP enabled, parallel CD-ROM drives do not approach a decent internal drive in performance levels. They can also create compatibility issues with other parallel devices. Even though the CD-ROM drive is equipped with a pass-through parallel port for attaching a printer, some older printers don't coexist peacefully on the same port as another device.

USB or FireWire are far more desirable interfaces for external drives of any nature. USB provides throughput of up to 12Mb/s and is fully Plug 'n Play. USB is not afflicted with the compatibility issues of the parallel port and is also hot-pluggable. FireWire shares all of the above and has a much faster 400Mb/s throughput. That means when you're done using the drive on one machine and want to use it on another, you just pop it off the port and off you go. There is no need to shut down either machine.

Of course, for this to work, your machine must be able to accept USB or FireWire devices. As I discussed in the chapter on the expansion bus, both of these technologies require BIOS that supports them, along with the physical interface.

THE LOADING MECHANISM

Most CD-ROM drives currently manufactured utilize a tray-loading mechanism for inserting the CD. However, this isn't true for all drives. Loading mechanisms that have been used, past and present, fall into one of three types. They will be a tray, a caddy, or a slot. There are advantages and disadvantages to each. Each has it own little quirks, so understanding the differences can be important.

The tray is far and away the most common mechanism seen today. Its advantages are that it is the simplest to manufacture, and therefore the least expensive. On the other hand, the disc gets a lot of handling and, if loaded incorrectly into the tray, may get damaged.

The caddy gets a lot of use with multi disc changers, but has appeared in the past on a few single-disc drives. With the caddy, the disc must be inserted in a carrier (the caddy), which is inserted into the drive. Discs get the most protection in this manner. For the user, on the other hand, changing between discs is much more inconvenient.

The slot has become popular with some manufacturers, and many customers like them as well. With a slot-loading drive, the user simply inserts the disc into the slot and a loading mechanism draws the disc into the drive and seats it properly. When the user pushes the eject mechanism, the disc is pushed back out. Unfortunately, this approach puts the maximum amount of wear on the disc.

INSTALLING CD-ROM DRIVES

Installing a CD-ROM drive into a computer couldn't be easier. The drive itself simply slides into any available externally accessible $5^1/_4''$ drive bay. It's generally a good idea to attach the cables before you attach the screws. In many enclosures, these bays back up to the power supply. The cables can be pretty difficult to access once the drive is in position. Another tip is to determine in advance which is the #1 connector so you get the IDE cable on right. Plug one of the Molex power connectors in and then make sure the audio cable is in place. Feed the wires down through the case the way you want them and then slide the drive back into place. It's probably not a good idea to tighten the screws down until you know the system is up and running.

Usually, if you can't get your new CD drive to work, it's because you have it on the same port as your hard drive and there's a master/slave conflict. The rules for CD-ROM drives are the same as the rules I discussed in Chapter Fourteen.

One short note on port/drive relationships: computers these days have two IDE ports, as I've already discussed. Theoretically, there's no reason the CD drive can't be either the master drive on the secondary port or the slave on the primary port. The only time this might come into play is when it comes time to add other ATAPI devices. Some CD-RWs won't operate as a slave. The only way to get the drive to work is if the CD-RW is the master device on the port. With Windows

98 (or earlier) operating systems, the primary system hard drive must be the master device on the primary port in order to boot. With many older systems, this is the case regardless of the OS in use. These situations limit the CD-RW to being installed on the secondary port. If you're having trouble getting a CD-RW to install correctly, check to see if this is your problem.

DEVICE DRIVERS

Any contemporary operating system will generally have support for CD-ROM drives built in. For example, Microsoft Windows detects the existence of a CD drive and loads the appropriate device drivers, virtual drivers, and DLLs automatically. Linux does the same. However, you might discover that, when you restart your computer to the command prompt, your CD-ROM drive disappears. For the drive to work from the command prompt, the appropriate drivers must be loaded on boot from the config.sys file, and a crucial program called MSCDEX must load from the autoexec.bat file. Most manufacturers make this a pretty simple task by including a floppy disk with an installation program for creating the necessary entries. Of course, that's usually the disk your client threw away because he or she didn't think it was necessary.

Since this will probably happen to you at least once in the course of your career, it's a good idea to be prepared. While it is true that CD-ROM manufacturers have never standardized on a universal DOS driver, CD-ROM drives operate over a very simplified command set. Because of this, a CD-ROM driver for one drive will usually work pretty well for another.

Generally, DOS drivers end in a .sys extension. For example, Toshiba drives ship with a file called toshiba.sys included on their installation disks. Mark the location of this file, and edit your config.sys file to include a line to load the driver, just as shown in **Figure 17.4**. In order to identify the device created as being a drive, a /D: parameter must be included. The line for a typical config.sys file would look something like Figure 17.4.

Figure 17.4 Standard config.sys command to load CD-ROM device driver

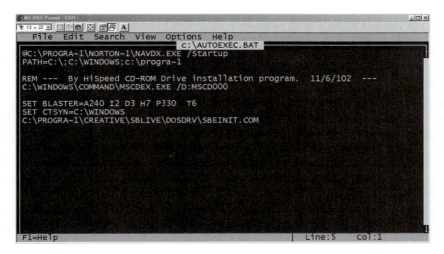

Figure 17.5 Standard autoexec.bat line to load mscdex.exe

In the autoexec.bat file, a related line must also be added, loading the MSCDEX program and identifying the driver and device it will control. The proper syntax for this line can be seen in **Figure 17.5**. The critical aspect of this line is that the /D: parameter must be identical to that in the line loaded by config.sys. If you do not do this, then when the autoexec.bat file loads, it won't find any devices under the control of the device driver.

A side note is that the device identification is not really critical. As long as the device ID in both autoexec.bat and config.sys are identical, you can use whatever you want. I could have written in the config.sys

```
DEVICE=C:\TOS\TOSHIBA.SYS  /D:RABBIT
```

as long as the line in autoexec.bat read

```
C:\WINDOWS\MSCDEX  /D:RABBIT
```

I would then have a CD-ROM drive loaded with the device name of Rabbit, under the control of toshiba.sys. My system would hop right along.

What is critical is that the files toshiba.sys and mscdex.exe really exist, and that they are where you say they are. If you want to make a bootable floppy disk with CD-ROM support, you can simply run the SYS command on the floppy, as such SYS A: This copies critical system files to the floppy disk. Then copy the files toshiba.sys (or whatever your brand requires) and mscdex.exe to the floppy. Create a file called config.sys in your text editor and add the line

```
DEVICE=TOSHIBA.SYS   /D:MSCD001
```

Then create one called autoexec.bat and add

```
MSCDEX   /D:MSCD001
```

THE DESCENDANTS OF CD-ROM

The CD-ROM drive has lived a long and fulfilling life, but it may be coming to an end. Recordable CD (CDR), Rewritable CD (CD-RW), Digital Video Disc (DVD), and the Recordable DVD (DVD-R) drives threaten its existence more and more each day with declining prices and increasing performance. Most manufacturers offer combo drives that incorporate features of all of the above. Currently installed in my system is a CD/DVD along with a CD/CDR/CD-RW. And lately, I've been getting an acquisitive itch for one of those drives that incorporate DVD-R/-RW, DVD+RW/+R, and even run CDR/CD-RW discs.

CDR AND CD-RW

CD-ROMs were wonderful devices and enthusiastically embraced by the industry. By about 1997 it had reached the point that a computer without a CD-ROM drive was a special order item. It had become standard equipment. Long before that was the case, users were already clamoring for a device that would let them make their own CDs. Philips answered that demand in 1993 with the CDR. Naturally, consumers in general were unhappy that they could not overwrite the contents of a disc with an updated version. Therefore, CD-RW became the next must-have toy.

THE CDR

CDR drives allow the end users to create their own compact discs. Conventional CDs use an aluminum base on which the pits are stamped. Considering that the melting point of aluminum is 1220 degrees, it's a pretty sure bet that you're not going to make CDs by melting pits in aluminum.

Therefore, a special medium had to be developed to make this work. The standard CD would obviously not be something the average person was going to make on his or her home computer. Therefore, a new disc emerged that made use of dyes in the recording layer that were easily melted by a low-power laser beam. A spiral track on the CDR blank is imprinted onto the blank at the factory at the time of manufacture. This is known as the *pregroove*, and it is the target area for the pits that will be eventually burned by the CDR drive. The dye is poured over the grooved base in a very thin layer. To simulate the reflectance of the aluminum layer of standard CDs a microscopically thin layer of metal is placed over the dye. If you look at **Figure 17.6**, you'll see a simplified illustration of how this is done.

CDR drives are equipped with a dual-powered laser. The lowest power is similar to that of a conventional CD. However, when the user wants to record data to a CDR, the write power of the laser is sufficiently powerful to burn a hole in the dye layer. The burned area becomes opaque, effectively duplicating the function of a pit in the read process.

The first dye used in CDRs was *cyanine dye*. More recent discs make use of *pthalocyanine dye*. Pthalocyanine is better than cyanine in two respects. First of all, it lasts longer. Cyanine dye is not archival, in that it has a life expectancy of twenty years or less. Certain light frequencies, including UV and other frequencies found in normal sunlight, can degrade the dye. Leaving the

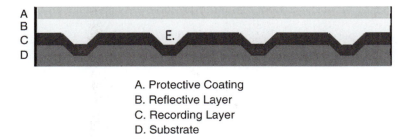

A. Protective Coating
B. Reflective Layer
C. Recording Layer
D. Substrate
E. Pregroove

Figure 17.6 Layers of CDRs differ from that of CDs in several respects. The most significant difference is that the data is burned into a layer of dye.

CDR that contained the overheads for a critical presentation on the dashboard of your car in the middle of July could result in unemployment. Pthalocyanine is not nearly as susceptible to photo-sensitivity and can be expected to last in excess of a century.

Another benefit of pthalocyanine is that a much higher degree of accuracy can be achieved when burning the pits, which in turn allows for higher speeds. When cyanine-based CDR media is used at high speeds, the pits are not nearly as deep and can be poorly defined, rendering the disc unreadable to many conventional CD-ROM players, especially those of an earlier vintage.

The metal layer is usually silver or gold. It is pretty easy to tell which has been used by the color of the disc. Gold is considered preferable to silver simply because it is far more resistant to corrosion. Either works equally well as a reflectance material, and due to cost considerations nearly all media currently manufactured use silver.

For CDRs to work, a different method of formatting had to be developed. ISO 9660 did not provide for addition of data after the initial master was made. To make the CDR attractive to the average user, data would need to be added in increments. Most people don't have 650MB they want to submit to disc in one session. Manufacturers put the standards for *multisession* CD burning into a group of specifications known as the Orange Book. Companies that make CD mastering software have incorporated these features into their product, making it a simple matter for users to leave a CD open for future data to be added. Part of this procedure involves writing a Table of Contents (TOC) for each CDR, which can then be updated when new files are added. The TOC performs a similar function to that of the file allocation table on your hard drive.

BUZZ WORDS

Cyanine dye: A bluish-colored dye that was used in the recording layer of early generations of CDR media.

Pthalocyanine dye: A more stable dye used in recent generations of CDR that is less sensitive to UV light and lasts for up to a 100 years.

Pregroove: A spiral track engraved on CDR and CD-RW media at the factory that acts as a target for the recording laser.

Multisession: The ability to record data onto a CDR or CD-RW in several stages without closing out the TOC.

The CD-RW

CDRs became very popular, very fast. Still, there was something missing. If you're working on a large project that takes a long time to complete, say this book, for example, the data changes on a constant basis. CDRs allowed for archiving data, but not modifying it. The CD-RW solved this problem.

In place of dyes on which to record data, the CD-RW blank has a layer of a rather exotic material made out of silver, antimony, tellurium, and indium. This compound reacts to different intensities of heat in different ways. Like all metals, it has a melting point. Unlike most metals, however, this compound also has a crystallization point. Melting point occurs at a moderately low temperature. Intense heat crystallizes it.

Therefore, in order to do its job, the CD-RW drive has a laser beam capable of three different intensities. The lowest is for reading back data. This is known as *read power*. *Erase power* is the next setting, because it actually requires less power to melt the material than it does to crystallize it. *Write power* is the setting that generates sufficient heat to crystallize the material. When data is written to the medium, the laser burns a crystalline pit.

> ### Buzz Words
>
> **Read power:** The lowest power setting for the optical stylus of a CD-RW, which it uses to read data from the surface.
>
> **Write power:** The highest power setting for the optical stylus of a CD-RW, which it uses to record data onto the surface.
>
> **Erase power:** A medium power setting for the optical stylus of a CD-RW, which it uses to melt the crystals generated by the previous recording session back into the uncrystallized recording layer.
>
> **Phase change layer:** The recording layer of a CD-RW disk.
>
> **Dielectric layer:** A transparent layer of material above and below the recording layer of a CD-RW that dissipates the heat built up in the CD during the recording process.

The CD-RW has a layer of this material called the *phase change layer*. This layer is located between two other layers of material that dissipate excess heat during the write process. These are the *dielectric layers*. The remainder of the disc is similar to the CDR.

The Orange Book had allowed for multisession recording, but it hadn't provided for rewriting the Table of Contents to allow for changes in the location of data on the disc. This was added with the release of the Orange Book III.

DVD

Digital Video Discs (also known as Digital Versatile Discs, depending on who you want to listen to) are actually a different technology all together. The disc looks the same; it's the same size, refracts light into pretty colors, and all that. But there, the resemblance ends.

DVD didn't get off to the most auspicious of starts. There was a rather bitter battle over control of the technology among several different companies, each with its own idea of how it should be done. The end result was five different file formats. See **Table 17.2** for an overview.

A major technological difference is that DVD can be pressed in layers, and both sides of the disc can contain data. Combine that with a file format that fits more information onto a

Table 17.2   DVD File Formats

Format	Description
DVD-ROM	High-capacity data storage
DVD Video	Use for full-length motion pictures
DVD Audio	Audio-only content
DVD-R	Recordable DVD
DVD-RAM	Rewritable DVD

DVD actually needs to support five different file formats.

Table 17.3   DVD Formats

Format	Description	Capacity
DVD 5	Single sided, single layer	4.7GB
DVD 8	Single sided, double layer	8.5GB
DVD 10	Double sided, single layer	9.4GB
DVD 18	Double sided, double layer	17GB

DVD capacities vary with the number of layers embedded.

single layer, and you have a disc that can store several gigabytes of data. This is done by creating the first layer on one side, coating it with a microscopically thin, transparent gold layer, and then pressing the second layer. If you do that to the second side you can have four layers of data. Multilayer discs are easily discernible from regular ones by their gold color. Discs are made as shown in **Table 17.3**.

The way capacity was increased so dramatically was managed on several levels. To start with, the lands created during the creation of masters were reduced in width from 1.6 microns to about .75 microns. By itself, this change allowed for double the number of tracks. The relative lengths of the pits were also cut by half. Now manufacturers can fit twice the number of pits onto four times as many tracks.

DVD 8 and DVD 18 further increase storage by allowing for two separate data storage layers on the medium. A microscopically thin layer of semireflecting material separates these layers. When the optical stylus needs to read the lower layer, it simply changes its focus to that layer. The bottom layer can't hold quite as much data as the top. Therefore, capacity isn't quite doubled.

It's interesting to note that double-sided discs are actually two separate discs bonded together by adhesive. The fact is, all DVDs are two layers. The layers actually required by a single-sided DVD are only half as thick as a standard CD. Manufacturers were concerned about the durability and stability of such thin material and bonded a layer of polycarbonate plastic to the back of the disc to make it the same thickness as a CD. By bonding two DVD discs, back-to-back, you get the double-sided variety.

As you might imagine, new file formats had to be developed to support this medium. As I mentioned earlier, the race to develop DVD resulted in five different formats. The call to arms led the Optical Storage Technology Association (OSTA) to develop the Universal Disc Format (UDF). This format merges video, audio, and data, allowing a file to support any of the three, or to mix any two or even all three into a single file. UDF also permits any type of optical disc to access any of these types of file, even if made by another medium.

Most DVD drives double as CD-ROM drives. In other words, they'll read either format. Manufacturers do this by mounting two separate optical styli on a swivel mount. Once the drive has detected the type of medium that has been inserted, the proper head moves into place and the fun begins. However, to take advantage of the motion picture capabilities of DVD, you need to have a video card capable of MPEG II standards. (See Chapter Sixteen, Your Computer and Graphics.)

SOUND CARDS

Until the early 1980s, the only sound you could get out of your computer was that which came from the built-in speaker. Unless, of course, you had one of several different models of Tandy computer made by Radio Shack. Tandy developed onboard 3-voice sound and 16-color CGA graphics. (If you recall from Chapter Sixteen, CGA was only four colors!) Then a company out of Canada released a PC expansion card called the Ad Lib that provided FM quality sound through a pair of external speakers. It offered a total of *eleven* voices.

Confused about what is meant by "voices" in a sound card? Basically, a *voice* is a collection of sampled frequencies that simulate the sound of a particular instrument. In the real world, sound occurs in waves. These waves are measured in cycles per second, or hertz. The more cycles per second, the higher the perceived pitch. In order to convert sound to a digital computer file, the sound is sampled thousands of times per second. CD-quality sound (audio quality equal to that of a Compact Audio Disc) is generally sampled 44,000 times per second. FM quality, or that of a decent radio broadcast, is considered to be around 11,000 samples per second.

If two instruments play the same note, say a guitar and a trumpet, even though the pitch may be the same, the two instruments still sound dramatically different. This is because, along with the base frequency, which is what determines pitch, there is a very complex collection of additional sound frequencies that the instrument produces that are generated along with the root frequency of the note. The *root frequency* is the single frequency that makes a C sharp a C sharp, regardless of the instrument playing that note.

> ## BUZZ WORDS
>
> **Voice:** A collection of preprogrammed harmonics that are used to simulate the sound made by a particular instrument.
>
> **Root frequency:** The single frequency of any given musical note that makes that note sound the way it does, regardless of what instrument plays it.

The additional frequencies generated by specific instruments are called harmonics and subharmonics. *Harmonics* are frequencies of sound that are higher than the root frequency of the note being played. *Subharmonics* are frequencies lower than root.

The harmonics of a stringed instrument differ greatly from those of a brass instrument, which differ greatly from those of a woodwind. It's the harmonics that make them sound different. By preprogramming a sound card to play a root frequency, along with a predetermined set of harmonics, that sound card can simulate the sound of a guitar or a trumpet or a saxophone. The magic of the sound card is that it takes this wide range of harmonics and re-creates it using only the zeros and ones that your computer can understand. The more preprogrammed sets of harmonics a sound card has, the more voices it is said to have. A basic sound card these days has a minimum of sixty-four voices, and it can reach into the thousands if you have a lot of money to spend (**Figure 17.7**).

However, before you get too carried away, keep in mind that, just as your eye can't determine even a tiny fraction of the colors your video card can synthesize, neither can your ear distinguish between more than a few hundred voices. The frequency range that a finely tuned human ear can consciously detect is about 20Hz to 20,000Hz. The older a person gets, the narrower this range becomes. In addition, musical instruments are capable of a very narrow range of root frequencies. For example, the root frequencies on a grand piano range from 27.5Hz on the very lowest note to 4186Hz on the highest. Harmonics, on the other hand, have been measured to extend far beyond the capabilities of human hearing.

The original file format for sound was the WAV file (it is still the most commonly used). If you've ever opened up the actual files on an audio CD to see what they look like, you'll see that they are basically just WAV files. Very big WAV files. A five-minute song can run upwards of 80MB in size. That's what makes the

> **BUZZ WORDS**
>
> **Harmonics:** Sound frequencies above the root frequency that are generated by an instrument or voice when a certain note is generated.
>
> **Subharmonics:** Sound frequencies below the root frequency that are generated by an instrument or voice when a certain note is generated.

Figure 17.7 Modern sound cards are capable of reproducing sounds that make first- and second-generation audio CD players sound positively primitive.

CD-ROM format so essential to multimedia. These files may be big, but they don't change. A CD can hold about seventy minutes of music in .wav format.

These days, other file formats are becoming increasingly popular for computerized music files. MP3s fill the Internet, and many emerging artists offer free samples of their work for the cost of a simple download. Be careful, however, that you are actually downloading the file with the artist's consent. Any other use would be an infringement of copyright.

An MP3 (which stands for MPEG Layer III, not MPEG Version III) of that same five-minute song will only be four or five megabytes. The music is still nothing more than a collection of zeros and ones. MP3 is simply an advanced compression algorithm. The sound card takes these data files and converts them from digital format to an analog waveform that can be amplified and sent to speakers.

How the Sound Card Works

The typical sound card takes the functions of a CD player and adds them to your computer system. If you look carefully at a sound card, you see that it's covered with different chips. The back has plugs unlike any other in your system. There will be either three or four eighth-inch mini-plugs for microphone, speaker out, and line in. Many cards also provide for line-out functions. The large 15-pin female connector can actually serve two purposes. It can be used to hook up a joystick or to hook up musical instrument device interface (MIDI) devices.

The speaker-out plug is fairly self-explanatory. It's where you plug the speakers into your sound card. Line in and Line out are for hooking up external audio devices, such as a tape player. Line in brings the signal of the device into the sound card, while line out sends the output of the sound card to the external device. The microphone connector allows the user to hook up a microphone to the sound card, and, with many applications, provide voice overlays to other types of files, including presentations, Web sites, and anything else where a little human explanation might not hurt.

These plugs will pass their signals to, or receive their signals from, one of two chips. The analog-digital converter (ADC) is the chip that processes incoming analog signals. This device samples the signal anywhere from 8000 to 48,000 times every second and takes that mini-slice of sound and converts it to a 16-bit chop, exactly as the CD player described earlier in the chapter handles sound waves. Sound leaving the computer passes through the digital-analog converter (DAC), which is pretty much identical to the ones used in CD players.

There is an amazing amount of mathematics involved in handling these conversions, and on most good sound cards a DSP identical to the one I described when discussing audio CD players handles this task. To further enhance the sound card's capabilities, wave table synthesis maintains common voices, including most musical instruments and human voice samples on a ROM chip. Whenever a violin is played, the ROM already has a sample of that instrument and all the harmonics that make that instrument sound unique precalculated. The DSP, in effect, has less work to do.

Sounds that are not stored in ROM can be either generated by an application or piece of hardware or can be encapsulated into a file. Usually when you're playing the latest version of

Kill the Alien Slime, the sounds unique to the game are stored in files, although many manufacturers keep them on the CD and require that the user play them directly from there.

INSTALLING AND TROUBLESHOOTING SOUND CARDS

With the possible exception of network cards, there is no device anywhere that has greater potential for problems. Nor is there any device easier to install when things work the way they should. Most of the problems you encounter can be traced right back to the "good old days" when sound card manufacturers all had to make their products SoundBlaster-compatible in order to be marketable.

IRQ CONFLICTS

IRQ conflicts are a primary source of trouble. Plug 'n Play was supposed to eliminate these hassles. A good PnP BIOS coupled with a PnP sound card and you never have conflicts, right? If only life were so easy! It's the history of the sound card that became its biggest headache. While Ad Lib may have invented the sound card, it was Creative Labs that made it popular. It did so by making its product so easy to install that the average user could easily do it with little technical background. Creative Labs did this by creating a software installation method that automatically created all the lines in the users' autoexec.bat and config.sys files for them. What Creative Labs realized was that LPT2 was rarely used in most computers. Therefore, that particular combination of IRQ and I/O address was available for the sound card on most installations. This installation routine worked on 95 percent of the IBM-compatible DOS-based computers in existence at the time. The five percent that gave people headaches were those that had second parallel ports installed.

Naturally, there were options for those computers on which LPT2 was actually in use. Installation was far less automatic, however. In any case, there were several generations of the Creative Labs SoundBlaster line of sound cards that defaulted to IRQ5. Subsequent crops of sound cards that followed had to be SoundBlaster-compatible in order to be marketable. One of the things that required was the use of IRQ5, IO 0220, and DMA1. In essence, Creative Labs succeeded in taking a reserved IRQ and essentially claiming it as its own. The majority of resource conflicts you'll encounter are when legacy sound cannot install onto IRQ5.

Worse yet, many sound cards will frequently try to claim two IRQs. The one currently installed on the machine I'm using right now has IRQ10 as a base IRQ and IRQ5 for Creative SB16 emulation. If a sound card doesn't want to install smoothly, check to see what resources it's trying to use. When possible, use the techniques described in the section on the PCI bus to resolve the issues. Sometimes, you'll have no choice but to manually reallocate resources. Windows users can do this in the Properties screen for any given device in Device Manager. Be careful in doing this, however. As you recall, manual resource allocation takes those resources out of the hands of Plug 'n Play. This can compound issues later on when it comes time to install the next device.

DMA CONFLICTS

Conflicts across DMA channels are far more rare than IRQ conflicts. They do, however, occur. Usually, it is because the user just reconfigured a parallel port to use ECP (extended capabilities port) mode. ECP requires that the parallel port be assigned a DMA channel. The problem is that when you are in the BIOS Setup program of the CMOS reconfiguring devices, the rest of the system hasn't booted yet. Therefore, whatever DMA channel your sound card is using appears to be available to the parallel port. This usually isn't a problem, but if the parallel port decides to grab the one you happened to have chosen for your sound card, a conflict will develop.

It's an easy fix. Simply find out what you configured your sound card to use and go back to the CMOS and change the ECP configuration to a different DMA. Problem solved.

CHAPTER SUMMARY

When discussing multimedia, there are a number of different components that are involved in the overall equation. No one would call it multi-anything if there weren't

This chapter covered primarily optical storage mechanisms and sound reproduction. However, there were a number of discussions in previous chapters that could have been just as easily included in this chapter. In Chapter Eleven, Input Devices, I discussed various tactile feedback game controllers. Of special note was the tactile feedback computer chair my wife is supposed to get me for our anniversary.

In Chapter Sixteen, Your Computer and Graphics, I discussed several different video functions that would be completely unnecessary without multimedia applications. Among these were the various 3D effects and specialized memory designed specifically for streaming media files.

And if you think all the way back to Chapter Seven, Understanding CPUs, you will recall that there were discussions of embedded instruction sets specific to multimedia functions. Among these were MMX, Streaming SIMD, and 3D-Now!

So as you see, true multimedia applications do more to stress a computer system than any other function, with the possible exception of certain specialized server operations. Improving on multimedia performance requires an understanding of the complete system.

BRAIN DRAIN

1. Discuss in as much detail as possible how data is written to a conventional CD and subsequently read back. Include in your discussion as many components of the CD-ROM drive as you can recall.

2. Discuss some different ways in which the CDR drives and media differ from the drives and media that are considered CD-RW.

3. Describe how it is possible to have a double-sided, double-layered DVD.

4. Why are harmonics important in recorded music? How do modern sound cards deal with harmonics in a way that reduces processing overhead for both the CPU and the sound card?

5. In as much detail as you can muster, describe how each component of a computer system contributes to the overall multimedia process. Don't

confine your thinking to just this chapter, but consider what you've learned from previous chapters as well.

THE 64K$ QUESTIONS

1. The first CD-ROMs designed for use on a computer provided data throughput of _____.
   a. 1.2Mb/s
   b. 150Kb/s
   c. 512Kb/s
   d. 20Mb/s
   e. None of the above.

2. A 2x CD-ROM provides data throughput of _____.
   a. 1.2Mb/s
   b. 250Kb/s
   c. 512Kb/s
   d. 20Mb/s
   e. None of the above

3. The recording layer on a CDR consists of _____.
   a. Pthalocyanine dye
   b. Aluminum
   c. Gold
   d. An alloy of four different metals

4. Which of the following drives requires a laser beam that can operate at three different power levels?
   a. CD
   b. CDR
   c. CD-RW
   d. DVD

5. Which of the following media separates two separate recording layers with a microscopically thin layer of gold?
   a. CD
   b. CDR

   c. CD-RW
   d. DVD

6. It is the root frequency of a note played by a piano that makes it sound different than when that same note is played on a guitar.
   a. True
   b. False

7. The 15-pin connector on the back of a sound card is used for what device? Choose all that apply.
   a. Joystick
   b. 5.1 Surround Sound speaker setups
   c. Multimedia devices
   d. MIDI devices

8. Which chip can directly sample an electronic current and extract digital information from that current?
   a. DAC
   b. PROM
   c. RISC
   d. DSP

9. The conversion of an analog waveform into a digital signal is known as _____.
   a. Pulse Code Manipulation
   b. Frequency Spectrum Sampling
   c. Pulse Code Modulation
   d. Digital Encapsulation

10. A voice on a sound card is _____.
    a. A prepackaged sound byte
    b. A frequently used chop
    c. A preencoded selection of harmonics unique to a specific instrument
    d. The chip that modifies sound files as they come in from an application

TRICKY TERMINOLOGY

Caddy: On a CD-ROM (or similar) drive, it is a form of loading mechanism that consists of a plastic CD holder that encases the CD while it is in the drive.

Chop: A 16-bit piece of data generated when music is sampled once during the digital recording procedure.

Cyanine dye: A bluish-colored dye that was used in the recording layer of early generations of CDR media.

Dielectric layer: A transparent layer of material above and below the recording layer of a CD-RW that dissipates the heat built up in the CD during the recording process.

Erase power: A medium power setting for the optical stylus of a CD-RW, which it uses to melt the crystals generated by the previous recording session back into the uncrystallized recording layer.

Harmonics: Sound frequencies above the root frequency that are generated by an instrument or voice when a certain note is generated.

Land: All of the reflective surface of the recording layer in optical media that has not been burned or punched into a pit.

Multisession: The ability to record data onto a CDR or CD-RW in several stages, without closing out the TOC.

Optical stylus: A mechanism consisting of a laser-emitting diode coupled to a beam splitter.

Phase change layer: The recording layer of a CD-RW.

Pit: A tiny hole embedded in the recording layer of optical media that prevents the laser from reflecting back into the photoelectric sensor.

Pregroove: A spiral track engraved on CDR and CD-RW media at the factory that acts as a target for the recording laser.

Pthalocyanine dye: A more stable dye used in recent generations of CDR that is less sensitive to UV light than cyanine dye and lasts for up to a 100 years.

Read power: The lowest power setting for the optical stylus of a CD-RW, which it uses to read data from the surface.

Root frequency: The single frequency of any given musical note that makes that note sound the way it does, regardless of what instrument plays it.

Slot: On a CD-ROM (or similar) drive, it is a form of loading mechanism that engages a CD when it is inserted into the opening and draws the disc into the drive.

Subharmonics: Sound frequencies below the root frequency that are generated by an instrument or voice when a certain note is played.

Synchronization bits: Data included on each sector of a data CD that assures that the information will be processed in the correct sequence.

Tray: On a CD-ROM (or similar) drive, it is a form of loading mechanism that consists of a platform that ejects when the user pushes a button, and retracts with the CD in place.

Voice: A collection of preprogrammed harmonics that are used to simulate the sound made by a particular instrument.

Write power: The highest power setting for the optical stylus of a CD-RW, which it uses to record data onto the surface.

ACRONYM ALERT

ADC: Analog-to-Digital Converter

CAV: Constant Angular Velocity. A data reading mechanism used by optical drives that allows the rotational velocity of the disc to remain constant, forcing the controller to interpret the data at faster speeds as the optical stylus moves from the center to the edge.

CDAD: Compact Disc, Audio Disc. The file system used by CD-ROMs to store music.

CDFS: Compact Disc File System. The file system used by CD-ROMs to store computer data.

CDR: Recordable CD

CD-ROM: Compact Disc-Read Only Memory

CD-RW: Rewriteable CD

CLV: Constant Linear Velocity. A data reading mechanism used by optical drives in which the rotational velocity of the disc must slow down as the disc is tracked from center to edge, thus assuring that the relative number of tracks per millisecond that passes beneath the optical stylus always remains the same.

DAC: Digital-to-Analog Converter

DSP: Digital Signal Processor. A microprocessor that can sample an electronic current and convert it into a digital signal.

DVD: Digital Video Disc, or Digital Versatile Disc

DVD-R: Recordable DVD

DVD-RW: Rewriteable DVD

EDC: Error Detection Code. Code embedded in a file system that enables the system to detect that an error in the transmission of that data has occurred, and where possible alerts the system to take corrective action.

ISO: International Organization for Standards. One of several groups that oversees the development and ratification of standards in the computer industry, as well as many other industries.

MIDI: Musical Instrument Device Interface

PCM: Pulse Code Modulation. The process of converting electrical current into a digital signal.

 VIEW THE VIDEO

A video clip on CD-ROM and DVD Drives is available on the accompanying CD.

CHAPTER 18

PRINTING TECHNOLOGIES: GETTING IT ALL ON PAPER

The previous chapters have all dealt with the various technologies of the computer. I've discussed how the computer processes data and how it stores data. I've talked about various ways users can interact with the computer and how all sorts of pretty pictures are made by a series of ones and zeros. Now I will tackle the various ways data can be moved from a digital file stored on a magnetic or optical disk surface to the surface of a piece of paper.

These days, there is a tremendous variety of printers on the market, ranging from incredibly inexpensive machines to devices that make my mortgage seem paltry. Across the board, capabilities vary, but you can break them down into two categories to start the decision making process. There are printers that print color and printers that don't.

In terms of technologies, there are six that I'll be discussing in this chapter. I'll start with the impact printers, then move on to inkjets. Because monochrome laser printers receive the most attention on the exam, these devices will get a bit more detailed coverage. This is where many books stop. You picked this book over all the rest, so you also get a discussion on color laser printers and thermal and phase-change inkjet printers (sometimes called dye sublimation printers).

A+ CORE HARDWARE EXAM OBJECTIVES

Exam objectives that will be covered in this chapter include the following:

1.5 Identify the names, purposes, and performance characteristics of standardized/common peripheral ports, associated cabling, and their connectors. Recognize ports, cabling, and connectors by sight.

1.8 Identify proper procedures for installing and configuring common peripheral devices. Choose the appropriate installation or configuration sequences in given scenarios.

2.1 Recognize common problems associated with each module and their symptoms, and identify steps to isolate and troubleshoot the problems. Given a problem situation, interpret the symptoms and infer the most likely cause.

3.1 Identify the various types of preventive maintenance measures, products, and procedures and when and how to use them.

3.2 Identify various safety measures and procedures, and when/how to use them.

4.4 Identify the purpose of CMOS (Complementary Metal-Oxide Semiconductor) memory, what it contains, and how and when to change its parameters. Given a scenario involving CMOS, choose the appropriate course of action.

5.1 Identify printer technologies, interfaces, and options/upgrades.

5.2 Recognize common printer problems and techniques used to resolve them.

IMPACT PRINTERS

Impact printers can be safely broken down into three categories. Among the first printers to come out was the line printer. These were ungainly devices that hung off of the old mainframe computers. However, don't call the line printer old-fashioned. It's a technology that refuses to die, and they are still around today. A similar technology that is also still with us is the dot matrix printer. Finally, I'll take a look at daisy wheel printers and see why they had a short but lucrative life span.

LINE PRINTERS AND DOT MATRIX PRINTERS

The technology behind these two types of printer is so similar that it will be easier simply to discuss them together. The primary difference between the two lies in how they handle an image. Early line printers, or line matrix printers, as they're often called, printed just a single line at a time. As such, they could only reproduce standard ASCII characters and were incapable of generating graphics beyond simple boxes and borders created with these characters. In 1996, Tally Corporation introduced a technology called Page Segment Architecture that divided the page into zones before sending the data to the printer. This allowed the devices to create more complex graphics. Dot matrix printers compile the entire page before sending it to the printer, so very complex graphics are possible, including rudimentary color on printers equipped with four-color ribbons and the appropriate device driver.

The driving technology behind producing the printed output is fundamentally the same, however. Therefore, for the remainder of this section, when I refer to a dot matrix printer, you should automatically think of both. The way they transfer an image to a sheet of paper is to thrust steel pins against a ribbon saturated in ink. The impact of the pin against the ribbon forces the ink onto the paper where it was struck.

Everywhere the pin strikes the ribbon a single dot is formed. By collecting enough dots into a familiar pattern, you can make it look like letters, numbers, punctuation marks, or even a crude facsimile of your spouse's favorite pet. Sounds simple enough, but there's a lot that has to go on in order to make the dots appear on paper in the right order to reproduce the image

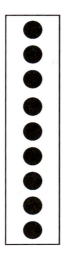

Figure 18.1 Alignment of pins on a 9-pin printer

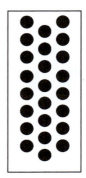

Figure 18.2 Alignment of pins on a 24-pin printer

you see on screen onto paper. This starts with the *print head*. On the dot matrix printers, there were a few choices in this respect. The most basic printers had a simple 9-pin print head. The nine pins were aligned vertically, as you see in **Figure 18.1**.

In order to achieve higher resolution, manufacturers developed the 24-pin printer. The idea was the same, except that by having a greater number of pins, which were made of a finer wire, a document could be printed that exhibited much finer resolution and detail. The print head squeezed twenty-four wires onto a single print head by arranging them into three rows of eight pins, as you can see in **Figure 18.2**. 24-pin printers were a bit slower, but that was a sacrifice people were willing to make in order to produce "letter-quality" documents.

These weren't the only options offered. Some manufacturers also came out with 18-pin and 48-pin printers. These really never caught on all that well. The 9-pin and 24-pin printer is still alive and well, thanks to the fact that many people still need to be able to print out multipart forms. The impact printer is able to do this.

THE DOT MATRIX PRINTING PROCESS

The key to printing a readable document is getting all those pins to hit the paper at just the right moment in time. Also, the pin has to hit the ribbon with enough impact to force ink onto the paper.

The way the print head is manufactured, the pins are seated into sleeves, linked to strong springs. The natural position of the spring is such that the pin would be in contact with the

BUZZ WORDS ─────────

Print head: The mechanism on any impact or inkjet printer that is responsible for depositing the pigment onto the paper.

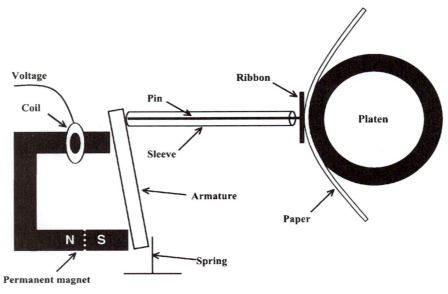

Figure 18.3 A diagram of a dot matrix print head

paper at all times, were a very strong magnet not holding it back. An electrical coil is wrapped around one pole of the magnet that forms an electromagnet. When current is applied to the electromagnet, it neutralizes the energy from the fixed magnet. The spring releases, and the pin

Buzz Words —————

Platen: The hard cylinder that supports the paper on impact printers.

pops back to its natural position. The dot is pressed into the paper and the electromagnet is turned back off. The fixed magnet pulls the pin back away. **Figure 18.3** is a rough diagram of the process that takes place.

Therefore, the printing process consists of sending electrical signals down wires attached to the magnets. Every time a dot is needed, the electromagnet is turned on for a very brief instant. The real trick here is timing. The print head needs to move across the paper at exactly the right speed, and the paper transport mechanism needs to be able to advance the paper at precisely the right time and precisely the right distance.

The paper feed mechanism isn't all that complicated. The core component is a stepper motor. The paper is fed through a geared assembly that has little teeth that move the paper. This assembly is coupled to a platen. The *platen* is the hard rubber-encased cylinder against which the paper rests. Gears on either end of the platen core engage with a stepper motor that advances or feeds the paper. The stepper motor is user adjustable so that whoever is using the printer can have it advance the paper in different increments to approximate single-spacing and double-spacing. Most also provide for space-and-a-half, and some provide even more options.

If you've seen paper designed for dot matrix printers, you already know that there are holes running along each side of the paper. These are needed because the paper transport method used by dot matrix printers is a *tractor feed*. The teeth on the paper feed assembly fit into these holes. There is a geared belt that keeps the print head moving in synch with the motor. All of this is under the control of commands sent by the printer driver.

DOT MATRIX MAINTENANCE

Since dot matrix printers are almost purely mechanical devices, they require significantly more care and feeding than most other components in a system. Unfortunately, they're all too often the devices that get the least attention. As a result, many dot matrix printers don't enjoy nearly as long a life span as they should be able to expect. That they last as long as they do is a tribute to the manufacturers!

First and foremost, these printers need regular cleaning. The condition of both the platen and the print heads directly impacts print quality. If too much dried ink and print fiber gets jammed into the print head, the pins might not be ejected by the springs. This would result in sketchy print quality. A dirty or damaged platen can be just as harmful. Never let somebody send a print job onto a dot matrix printer when there's no paper installed. Pay attention to the warning the printer issues saying it's out of paper. On dot matrix printers, if you send a print job despite the warning, the print head will stream along, sending the print job to the platen, polluting it with ink and perhaps even punching holes into the hard rubber. If there are holes in the platen, the pins will punch through the paper, putting holes in your page. If there is ink on it, the back of your page will be covered with stray marks.

Both the print head and the platen need to be in proper alignment as well. If they're not, individual characters will shade from light to dark. **Figure 18.4** illustrates what can happen if the print head itself is out of alignment. The illustration illustrates a vertical alignment problem, but print heads can be offset either vertically or horizontally.

If the platen itself goes out of alignment the entire line will be affected. It will go from light to dark from the beginning of the line to the end, or vice versa. **Figure 18.5** shows you what I mean.

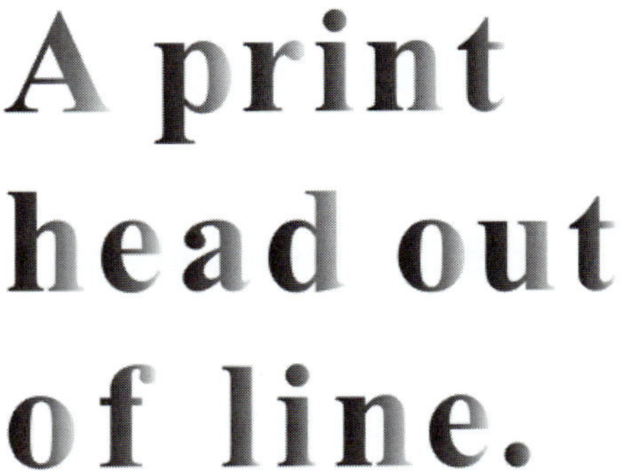

> ### BUZZ WORDS
>
> **Tractor feed:** A paper transport mechanism that uses a set of gears on a printer to advance the paper by engaging in perforations along each side of the paper.

Figure 18.4   A print head out of alignment affects individual letters.

Figure 18.5   A platen out of alignment throws the whole line out of whack!

As far as realigning either the head or the platen, how that is done or even whether or not it can be done is dependent on the make and model of your printer. Most print heads can be aligned. With many models, aligning the platen is a factory service job. If you can get your hands on a service manual for your model, it should give you instruction on how to perform these tasks.

Figure 18.6   The only way to change fonts on an old daisy wheel was to change the type wheel.

DAISY WHEEL PRINTERS

Daisy wheel printers were one of the most simplified of the printer designs that were sold. They did produce very high output quality, but were abysmally slow and extremely noisy. The letters themselves were molded onto a disk made of a springy material, usually steel or plastic. Each character was on a separate tab. In a way, it made the whole thing look like a high-tech flower (See **Figure 18.6**). This disk spun at high speed. In order to produce a particular character, a piston hammered that particular tab against a ribbon and onto the paper. The technology behind this goes all the way back to Johannes Guttenberg, except Mr. Guttenberg didn't have the benefit of electricity to speed up the process. Printers such as these are referred to as fully formed character printers. As you might imagine, these were text printers. Generating complex graphics was far beyond their capability.

Two types of ribbons were available for the venerable daisy wheel. You could get the standard inked-cloth ribbon. A printer equipped with one of these produced quality akin to a decent typewriter. ("Typewriter?" you ask, "What's a typewriter?") Another ribbon consisted of a coating of ink on a Mylar ribbon. Print quality from these ribbons exceeded that of many typesetters. Because of this quality difference, despite the array of disadvantages, the daisy wheel printer was an incredibly popular device for anyone who required top-quality output but couldn't afford the two grand that a laser printer cost at the time.

INKJET TECHNOLOGIES

Inkjet printers fall under one of three categories. There are thermal, piezoelectric, and phase-change printers. In spite of the diverse sounding nature of their names, they actually work in a very similar manner. Ink flows into a tiny little tube and some force of nature ejects it onto the paper at exactly the right moment. It's the force of nature chosen by the manufacturer that makes the technologies different. Oddly enough, the methods that inkjet printers use to select when and where to place ink is very similar to dot matrix printers. Instead of magnets and pins, they have tubes of ink and the force of nature.

The paper transport mechanism on inkjet printers is very similar to that of the laser printer that will be discussed later in the chapter. Because the exam tests on laser printers in this regard, but not inkjets, I have chosen to defer the discussion of this topic to the section on laser printers.

THERMAL INKJETS

BUZZ WORDS ———————

Thermal inkjet printer: A printer that ejects ink onto a page of paper by heating the fluid.

Bubblejet printer: Another term for a thermal printer.

As you might imagine from the description, the force of nature used by *thermal inkjet printers* is heat. Heat brings ink up to the boiling point, and forces it through a very small nozzle and onto the paper. In order to assure that the ink can be brought to boiling at precisely the right instant, a thermal inkjet printer keeps the reservoir of ink at a temperature just under the critical point. At the instant a droplet of ink is needed, a heating circuit applies a sudden burst of heat. Poof! Out comes a bubble of ink. This is one of the reasons this type of printer is sometimes called a *bubblejet*. **Figure 18.7** is a conceptual diagram of how the thermal print head works.

While Canon discovered the technology back in 1977, it wasn't until 1984 that HP came to market with its Thinkjet. This first-generation product was capable of 96 dots per inch (DPI) and could pump out 150 characters per minute. This doesn't sound like much by today's standards, but keep this in mind. A dot matrix printer, at best, could manage 72dpi. The dot matrix might have been a little faster, but the inkjet beat it by a long shot in terms of print quality.

A key issue with thermal inkjets is that heating the nozzle constantly shortens its life. HP gets around that problem by making the print head part of the ink cartridge. When you change the ink cartridge, you're automatically changing the print head as well.

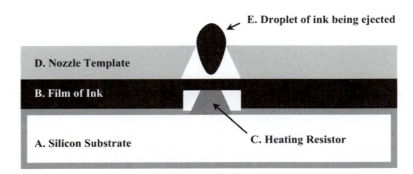

Figure 18.7 Conceptual diagram of a thermal inkjet head in action. A piezoelectric head would look very similar to this one, except that the entire nozzle of the print head is a piezoelectric device. A microscopic filament toward the back vibrates and the tube contracts.

PIEZOELECTRIC INKJETS

Have you ever decorated a birthday cake? If so, you might have used one of those devices that squeezes frosting onto the cake through a nozzle, so you can put pretty shapes on the top. As strange as it may seem, this is how the piezoelectric inkjet printer does its thing.

The nozzles are made from a *piezoelectric crystal* (PEC). A PEC has the unique characteristic that when given a shot of electricity, it changes shape. PECs squeeze inward. A combination of gravity and surface tension keeps a droplet of ink in place inside the nozzle. When the printer needs to eject it onto the paper, it zaps the nozzle with a charge of electricity. The nozzle squeezes inward and the ink is forced out onto the paper.

Proponents of piezoelectric inkjets claim that this method forms a cleaner image than does the thermal inkjet. Their reasoning is that when the bubble produced by a thermal inkjet printer strikes the page, it is going to burst, producing a halo effect. The piezoelectric printer is putting a solid droplet of ink onto the page, they claim, and that won't happen. I'm not getting involved in that argument. All I know is that I've used both Hewlett Packard and Epson inkjet printers. HP uses thermal technology and Epson uses piezoelectric. I have never been dissatisfied with either one. Long live competition!

> ### BUZZ WORDS
>
> **Piezoelectric crystal:** A substance that changes shape when exposed to electricity.
>
> **Phase-change printer:** A printer that liquefies solid inks before applying them to paper.
>
> **Cold fusing:** A process used by some phase change printers that uses pressure rollers to press the ink into the paper.

PHASE-CHANGE INKJETS

Phase-change inkjet printers use a radically different technology than either of the above. The phase-change inkjet starts with a stick of solid ink. The print head melts the ink and holds the melted ink in a specially designed reservoir. When the print head is called upon to apply ink to the paper, it uses a mechanical mechanism to eject the ink. The ink then hardens almost immediately.

These printers have an amazing capability of producing a more photo-realistic image for one simple reason. Ink applied by either thermal inkjets or piezoelectric inkjets is going to adhere to the paper in an extremely thin layer. Phase-change printers result in a much thicker coating. So thick, in fact, that Tekronix, one of the leading manufacturers of this kind of printer, uses a final process called *cold fusing*. That is where the paper is run through a pressure roller to flatten the droplets of hardened ink.

This has two different but complimentary side effects. The surface of the image takes on a more photographic nature. This is because conventional photographic prints are produced on a gelatin surface that is much thicker than a layer of ink. It gives the image a greater feeling of depth. The thicker coating of the phase-change printer more closely simulates that surface.

The second thing that provides a subtle improvement is that the pressure of the fusing roller creates a blending effect between adjacent droplets of ink. There is less pixelization of the image.

A NOTE ON RECYCLING INK CARTRIDGES

There is a thriving business that has developed around the ecologically sound principle of recycling ink and toner cartridges. There is also a bit of controversy over the idea. Since you are unlikely to get an unbiased discussion from either the printer manufacturers (who want to sell you their new cartridges) or the recyclers (who want you to buy their product), I thought I'd throw in my two cents' worth.

The cost savings of refilling your own ink cartridges or purchasing remanufactured toner cartridges are substantial. However, along with those savings come some inherent tradeoffs. With ink cartridges, in order to make the process work, the ink must have the same drying time as the manufacturer's original ink, and it must exhibit the same mixing characteristics. Inkjets use cyan, magenta, yellow, and black inks (CMYK). In the printing industry, these are known as subtractive colors. This is as opposed to the additive colors of red, green, and blue used by monitors. A chemical anomaly that liquid pigments possess is that different formulas do not necessarily produce the same hue when two of the subtractive colors are mixed. Another factor relating to color quality is that the inks used in the remanufacturing process are, by necessity, thinner than the original inks. As a result of the above factors, the print quality delivered by remanufactured ink cartridges can range from fairly decent (but not as good as the original) to abysmal.

Manufacturers claim that the use of these remanufactured cartridges shortens the life of the printer. While I have located no detailed research along these lines, I can see how this is theoretically possible. The inkjet process centers around the ink, and since the ink used in the remanufacturing process is thinner, this would have an impact on the rest of the printing mechanism. And since the seals must be punctured in order to insert the inks into the cartridge, if the seals are not properly restored, the cartridge can burst, spewing ink into the printer. This is rare, but I have seen the results of this happening, and it isn't pretty.

There are fewer risks involved in the use of remanufactured toner cartridges, and with one notable exception, these risks all center around print quality and not the life of the printer. As laser printers have evolved over the years, they have become capable of increasingly fine resolution. In order to produce that finer resolution, the particles used in the manufacture of the toner must be correspondingly smaller. Many remanufacturers take the "one size fits all" approach to toner refills. As a result, your fancy new 1200dpi laser printer may not be able to perform to that level. This will show up in the reproduction of graphics. Other issues affecting print quality involve the proper replacement of different components in the cartridge. A damaged imaging drum that isn't properly replaced will result in print defects on the page.

The one risk of recycled toner cartridges that can affect the life of the printer is in how well the remanufacturer refitted the seals. As with the inkjet cartridges, if a seal in a toner cartridge bursts, the effects can be disastrous.

However, the risks involved are low-percentage risks. Disaster is extremely rare, so it's like the reverse of playing the lottery. If lower print quality is not an issue, recycling toner and ink cartridges can save money and is friendly on the environment. But before you make the jump to recycled products on a newer printer, check and see if there is any fine print in the warranty concerning their use.

OPTICAL PRINTERS

There are two different forms of optical printer that dominate the market today. The lion's share goes to the laser printer that everyone knows and loves. Another competing technology that has only a small portion of market share is the LED printer. For the most part, these printers differ only in the light source they use for generating images, and therefore will be considered as one. Therefore, for the rest of the chapter, unless I say otherwise, when I refer to a laser printer, you can apply whatever it is I'm saying to an LED printer as well.

Laser printers involve a combination of mechanics, optics, and electronics that so closely borders on magic as to make Merlin shiver. Yet at the heart, it's all relatively simple. First of all, I'll give you a look at the key components that make the process of laser printing do what it does. Then I'll follow a sheet of paper through a print job.

COMPONENTS OF THE LASER PRINTER

As you read this next section, it might help to refer to **Figure 18.8** to see the relationship of the parts to one another. The parts that a typical laser printer uses to generate the image include a photosensitive drum, the laser itself, the formatter, a special roller known as the charging roller (in the old days, an array of wires called the transfer corona was used for this), a developing roller, a transfer roller, and finally a fusing roller. A key ingredient, of course, is the toner itself.

The photosensitive drum consists of a roller made of milled aluminum. Onto the surface of the aluminum, a coating of a special organic compound is applied. This compound has the unique nature of electrical photosensitivity. Unlike photographic film or paper that has a mixtures of substances that change color when exposed to light, the photosensitive drum changes electrical charge. The drum can hold very high charges of electricity, but when exposed to light, that charge will dissipate. A conductor at the core of the drum carries away that dissipated charge.

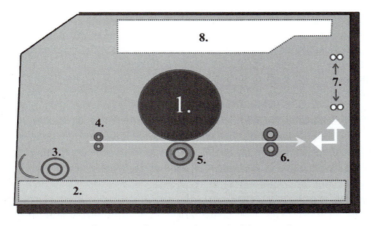

1. Photosensitive drum
2. Paper tray
3. Pickup roller
4. Registration roller
5. Transfer roller
6. Fuser assembly
7. Output rollers
8. Output bin

Figure 18.8   Cutaway diagram of a typical laser printer

The light source that a printer uses to dissipate charge in selected areas on the photosensitive drum is a laser-emitting diode. The diameter of this laser beam directly affects the resolution of the printer. For higher resolutions, smaller beams are required. The laser flashes on and off at a high rate of speed exposing "dots" onto the surface of the photosensitive drum. This is where the LED printer differs from the laser, in that it does not use a laser beam.

The image is assembled in the printer by a device called the formatter. You'll also see this referred to as the raster image processor. This is the logic of the system. In many respects it is much like the motherboard of a computer. A laser printer needs to have enough RAM to hold an entire image, and it needs a processor to assemble all the zeros and ones that comprise the print job into an order that will create the final image. On a monochrome printer, a one causes the laser to fire while a zero does not.

In order to start the print job the photosensitive drum has to have a uniform charge across the entire surface. Otherwise, there might be irregularities in the image. It is the task of the charging roller to apply this charge. The developing roller brings an even layer of freshly charged toner from the toner cartridge and makes it available to the surface of an electrically charged sheet of paper.

In order to attract the toner from the developing roller to the paper, the paper needs to have a charge opposite of that of the toner adhered to the photosensitive drum. The transfer roller applies a positive charge to paper as it is fed through the printer. In older printers a wire called the transfer corona did this job.

Once the toner has been applied to the paper, there needs to be a way to make it stick. The fusing roller heats the paper, along with its coating of toner, to the melting point of certain materials within the toner. Toner used by laser printers is a finely powdered mixture of three main ingredients. First and foremost is the powder that gives it color. On monochrome printers, this is predominately carbon. Carbon, however, is not very conducive to either taking an electrical charge or melting at any temperature to which paper could be exposed. To allow the mixture to take a charge a small amount of iron oxide is added. To make it melt at a lower temperature a powdered plastic is used.

A couple of ancillary parts important to the overall process are the erase lamp, the static discharge unit, and the cleaning blade. The erase lamp is used to eliminate any residual charge from the last print job, allowing the photosensitive drum to start from a clean charge. The cleaning blade scrapes away any residual toner left on the drum. The static discharge unit is responsible for draining away the charge from the paper before it gets sucked up around the photosensitive drum. Now that you have a good idea of the parts that are used by the printer, take a look at the printing process.

THE LASER PRINTING PROCESS

The whole process of creating a laser image can be broken down into six steps. Each of these is going to make use of one of the components I described in the previous section. As you go through the next few paragraphs, you will follow a typical print job from start to finish. The first thing that's going to happen is that the computer is going to send the print job to the printer driver, which in turn converts the data to the format supported by whatever printing language you've selected. (Printer languages will be discussed later in the chapter.) When this happens, the printer starts heating up the fuser assembly. While the next two steps are being performed, the formatter will be assembling the image.

CLEANING

By the time you get to the end of this, you'll see that you are looking at an endless cycle. But for the sake of discussion, I have to assume that the process starts somewhere. The first thing you have to do is remove any vestiges of the previous print job. Therefore, the first stage of the image formation process consists of preparing the photosensitive drum to accept a new image. This involves both physical and electrical cleaning. Before a new image is formed on the drum, leftover toner from the previous image must be removed. In order to get rid of all the electrical charge left over by the last job, the erase lamp gives the drum a strong dose of light. A rubber cleaning blade scrapes toner off the drum into a debris cavity.

CONDITIONING

Now that the mess from the last job is cleaned up, it's time to prepare the photosensitive drum for the next one. First off, it must be conditioned. The charging roller, or on some older printers, the primary corona, applies a very strong negative charge. How much of a charge depends entirely upon the make and model of printer, but typically this charge can be in the range of −800 to −1200V. Now the printer has a blank sheet of "electronic paper."

WRITING

By now, the formatter has finished processing the image. It will send the data from that image as a series of on/off pulses to the laser assembly. The beam turns on and off very rapidly. Everywhere that the beam exposes the photosensitive drum, a fairly large portion of the charge on the drum's surface is bled away. A wire in the center of the imaging drum carries the dispersed charge to ground. Once this job has been completed, you'll have a surface that consists of a −800 to −1200V sheet of virtual paper sprinkled with −200 to −400V dots that make up the letters and graphics.

DEVELOPING

Meanwhile, a small amount of toner is moved from the storage reservoir of the toner cartridge to a smaller charging reservoir. The toner in the charging reservoir receives a charge of approximately −600V. Notice that so far, everything has been given a negative charge. However, if you go back to Chapter Four, Basic Electricity and the Power Supply, you will recall that voltage is simply the difference in charge between two objects. Therefore, while all of these different charges may be negative relative to ground, relative to one another, these surfaces will contain positive charges as well as negative charges. A positively charged object will try to attract objects that are negatively charged relative to itself. The toner will be attracted to the exposed areas of the drum because, relative to the toner, these dots represent a positive differential. The more strongly charged unexposed areas are going to repel the toner.

TRANSFER

At this point in time, were you to stop the print process and look inside the toner cartridge, you would see perfectly shaped letters and images on the photosensitive drum, although they would appear in reverse. While the above steps were going on, the sheet of paper that this toner is intended for has been passing under the transfer roller (or transfer corona on older printers). The transfer roller applies a strong positive charge to the paper. The negatively charged toner particles adhering to the imaging drum are attracted to the paper. As the paper moves through the transport mechanism, the static discharge unit drains away the positive charge. This unit consists of a row of metal teeth that carry a strong negative charge. This separates the photo-sensitive drum and paper. Were the static discharge unit to fail, the paper, along with the accompanying image, would be magnetically sealed to the imaging drum.

THE FUSING ROLLER

You now have a perfectly formed image on the paper. However, at this point in time the only thing keeping that toner on the page is the love the toner and paper feel for one another, with the help of inertia, gravity, and some slight residual electrical charge. If you want the image to stay, you're going to need to do something to fix it there permanently. That is the job of the fusing roller. The paper rolls between the fusing roller and a pressure roller. The fusing roller heats the paper and toner up to the melting point of the plastic in the toner and the pressure roller squeezes it onto the paper. You now have a final print job. Congratulations.

MOVING PAPER

A part of the process that was not described in the previous sections involves how the paper gets from the paper tray (usually located at the base of the printer) to all the places it needs to be, when it needs to be there. That is the responsibility of the paper transport mechanism. The following discussion is going to be based on Hewlett Packard's line of printers. While different brands may have variations on the process here and there, for the most part, it will be pretty much the same.

The process of paper transport starts when a pickup roller rotates around and snatches the top sheet of paper from the stack loaded in the paper tray. The paper tray itself is a fairly complex component. It needs to be able to keep the top sheet in the stack properly aligned in order for the pickup roller to find anything to grab. In order to prevent more than one sheet of paper from being fed into the mechanism, a separation roller (or separation pad on some models) keeps two sheets from sticking together.

The paper moves into the registration rollers. At this point in time, a mechanism called the DC controller causes the paper to pause momentarily while it makes sure the leading edge of the paper proper lines up with the image written to the photosensitive drum. You can easily hear this part of the process while it is taking place. Once proper alignment is achieved, the paper can move on.

The paper then moves between the photosensitive drum and the transfer roller. From here, the paper moves into the fuser assembly. As I discussed earlier, this assembly consists of a fusing roller heated to the melting point of the toner and a pressure roller. As the paper exits the fuser assembly, the leading edge activates the exit photo sensor. This notifies the DC controller that the paper is leaving the fuser assembly, and when the trailing edge passes the sensor, the DC controller is notified that Elvis has left the building. On a printer that only does single-sided printing, the paper moves from the fuser assembly and into the exit rollers, which move the printed page into the output bin.

Printers capable of duplex printing still have more work to do before they allow the paper to move into the exit rollers. Duplex printing is where the printer can print onto both sides of the page. In order to do that, the printer has to be able to get the paper turned over and sent through the printing process a second time.

With duplex printing, instead of moving from the fuser assembly into the exit rollers, a deflection pawl directs the paper into the duplex feed rollers. The duplex feed rollers carry the paper into the switchback station, where the leading edge of the paper activates the switchback photo sensor. When the trailing edge passes the sensor, the DC controller knows the paper is fully loaded into the switchback station, and the reverse side is ready for printing. The trailing edge of the paper now becomes the leading edge. It is moved back into the registration rollers, where the image and paper are properly aligned and the reverse side goes through the printing process. This time, however, as the page exits the fuser assembly, the deflection pawls are retracted and the paper is allowed to move into the exit rollers. Out comes your page, printed on both sides.

COLOR LASER PRINTING

The theoretical concepts of color lasers are really no different that those of monochrome printers. The complexity of the process is somewhat greater, but the technology is the same. Instead of having a single toner cartridge with an associated transfer roller, the color laser has four cartridges. For standard text printing, there is the conventional black toner cartridge, and for full-color printing, there is a cartridge for each of the subtractive colors: magenta, cyan, and yellow.

A full-color image has a portion of itself printed by each of these four cartridges onto an intermediate transfer surface. This usually consists of a belt assembly. When the image has been assembled in its entirety, the intermediate transfer belt moves the image to the paper and then the fuser does its thing. **Figure 18.9** is a conceptual diagram of the process at work, and not a diagram of the actual mechanism.

MAINTAINING AND TROUBLESHOOTING LASER PRINTERS

The beauty of laser printers is that they actually vary very little from one brand to another. Since I'm trained on Hewlett Packard's line of LaserJet printers, I'll be using them as an example throughout this section, but there isn't anything I'll say here that doesn't directly apply to other brands as well.

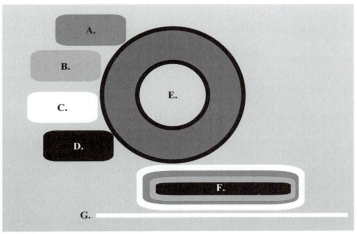

A. Magenta Toner   E. Imaging Drum
B. Cyan Toner   F. Intermediate Transfer Surface
C. Yellow Toner   G. Paper
D. Black Toner

Figure 18.9   A conceptual overview of the laser color printing process

Printer errors will generally fall under one of four categories:

■ Communication errors

■ Processing errors

■ Paper transport errors

■ Imaging errors

Communication errors occur when the computer can't find the printer. Obviously, the first thing to check is the cable itself. If the printer is hooked up directly through the parallel port, this is generally no problem. A networked printer has its own issues related to networking that do not fall within the scope of this book. Assuming that the cable is properly installed and is not defective, and that the printer is hooked up to the parallel port, your next step is to bypass the driver. You can do this by opening a command prompt and copying an ASCII text file directly to LPT1. As an example, you could open Notepad, type out a few characters, and save the file as C:\document\test.txt. Now, at the command prompt, type copy c:\document\test.txt LPT1 and see if the printer fires up and spits out the document. If it does, you have physical connectivity to the printer. The problem is in the configuration. Reinstall the drivers, and use the correct ones this time.

Processing errors occur when the data gets to the printer, but nothing but gobbledygook comes out. Frequently this is simply a corrupted printer driver, and can be fixed easily by reinstalling the drivers. On laser printers, there are two other things that can cause this. One is bad memory. As I mentioned earlier, the laser printer relies on RAM in much the same way as a computer. The second thing is a chip failure on the formatter board. The latter is relatively rare, in that when formatter boards fail, they usually fail completely. Other processing errors include insufficient memory to process a given job, or in the case of older printers, the data might be coming in so fast the printer can't keep up. Most laser printers are able to generate an error message to the front panel. The service manual for the printer will interpret the error messages that are delivered.

Paper transport errors can come in the form of paper jams or the paper not being picked up out of the delivery tray. This is the result of worn rollers. On laser printers, the rollers that receive the most wear and tear are generally user-replaceable. Paper rollers are a lot like good snow tires. To properly work, they need some decent tread. If your rollers are smooth, they won't generate the friction they need to move paper. Another cause of paper jams is simply using a medium that is not supported by the printer. Stock that is either too light or too heavy can result in jams when the rollers are perfectly good. If you have checked the rollers and know them to be good, compared the stock in use to the manufacturer's specifications and found it acceptable, but you are still getting a jam in the input area of the printer, you might have either a bad paper tray or a defective paper sensor. The paper tray needs to be properly adjusted for the type of paper installed. Putting 8.5″ × 11″ paper in a legal-sized tray can cause jams. The sensors on the trays indicate what kind of paper is installed in multiformat trays. If the sensor reports the wrong size, paper jams will result.

Imaging errors can be defined in many ways. Unwanted marks on the page, smearing, a totally black page, or a skewed image are all examples of imaging errors. Defects that repeat themselves at regular intervals down the page are generally the result of a roller gone bad or defects on the imaging drum. Transfer rollers, developing rollers, and the rollers in the fusing assembly can all leave marks on the page if they're damaged. Most printer service manuals have a repetitive defect guide to help you troubleshoot what roller is causing what defect. If you don't have a manual at your disposal, start with the easy ones. Pull the toner cartridge, and in dim light open the shutter and rotate the imaging drum around. If there is a defect on the drum that matches that on the page, you've solved the problem. Change out the toner cartridge. Nothing there? Try the same thing on the fuser assembly. Turn the printer off and wait for it to cool down before pulling a fuser assembly. Those things get hot!

There are literally hundreds of other issues related to laser printers. Enough to fill a book by itself. Any certified (or certifiable) technicians out there could point at any one of these issues and say, "Yeah, but it could also be this, this, this, or this!" What I have provided here are some of the most common problems and the most common solutions. For more detailed information on printers, there are a number of good books that have been written. Also, each of the major manufacturers provides technical training on their products at very reasonable cost.

PRINTER LANGUAGES

All those dots don't just magically appear. They are created as a result of zeros and ones being converted into pulses of laser light, electrical signals that release the charge of an electromagnet, or the signal that ejects the ink. All printers, whether they're impact, inkjet, or optical, require a fixed set of instructions that tell them when to put a dot onto paper. In the case of color printers, it also has to inform the printer which color of ink to eject. Printer languages provide those instructions. Three commonly used languages include HP's Printer Control Language (PCL), Adobe's Postscript, and the Microsoft Windows Graphical Device Interface (GDI). Each of these languages works in a slightly different manner and different versions of each have appeared over the years.

ASCII

In Chapter One, PC Basics, I provided a detailed explanation of the American Standard Code for Information Interchange, (ASCII), and there are tables of both printable and nonprintable characters in Appendix G. It's easy to overlook ASCII as being a printer language simply because it is frequently considered to be simply a character set. However, the early line printers depended on ASCII to provide the common commands that controlled the printer as well. It should be noted that, while ASCII is considered to be old technology, it is still alive and well. In fact, as you will see a little later in this chapter, continued support of ASCII is a requirement for maintaining IEEE 1284 standards.

PCL

HP developed the original PCL as a language by which dot matrix printers could be controlled. By the time the first laser printers appeared, the language was already in its third generation. PCL versions one and two first appeared back in the 1980s. PCL3 was the first of the versions to provide support to laser printers. The original HP LaserJet, released in 1984, used this language.

As a language, PCL is considered to be an escape code language. In other words, the ASCII escape character precedes specific commands. These commands are embedded in the document. An example of this would be in how PCL would print a specific word on a specific position on the page. ESC *p75x150Yprinter would start at the printable edge of the page and count off 75 units. It would then drop down 150 units and print the word "printer."

When the Laserjet Plus was released in 1985, PCL was modified to allow fonts and graphics to be generated as bitmaps. While these bitmaps provided relatively primitive output by today's standards, they handled simple word processing, along with simple graphics tasks, such as box drawing, relatively well. Later versions improved upon the ability to generate and output graphical information, and current generations are capable of near photographic output.

PCL5 added another embedded language called the Hewlett Packard Graphics Language (HPGL) to PCL. This provided for the ability to use outline fonts instead of bitmap fonts. Outline fonts are much more easily scaled to different sizes. It also supplies support for vector graphics. Vector graphics allows for the mathematical calculation of dot position. A printer that can do that can produce virtually any form or shape you might imagine.

The most recent implementation of PCL is (not surprisingly) PCL6. This language incorporates a new modular architecture that can be easily modified for future HP printers. The benefits to the user include a faster return to the application after sending a job to the printer.

The language uses a more efficient data stream. This allows for faster printing of complex graphics and can substantially reduce network traffic generated by network print jobs.

POSTSCRIPT

Apple Computer Corporation's Laserwriter first implemented Adobe's Postscript on its Macintosh. It came out at a time when PCL was still limited to crude bitmap drawings of the overall image. The fact that Postscript supported outline fonts and vector graphics gave the Laserwriter a huge advantage in terms of print quality. Many people, myself included, credit the incorporation of Postscript into its printers for the massive acceptance of Macintosh computers as the platform of choice for graphic artists.

Postscript, however, is platform independent. As a language, it can be incorporated into virtually any printer design. The original release of Postscript, Postscript Level One, was very processor intensive and required much more memory to be installed into the printer. For someone to whom output quality was of primary importance, this was an acceptable sacrifice.

Postscript Level Two was the next step. It did everything Level One could do, along with several major enhancements. These included the ability to add a Postscript driver to the display. This allows the image on the monitor to more closely resemble the final output. It also provided support for image typesetters. Users of Postscript could transport their files, regardless of platform, to the typesetter and have the final product precisely duplicate the document they originally created.

Postscript Level Three made further improvements. It allows for up to 4096 levels of gray in monochrome printing. When printing color, different levels of transparency can be applied to any given hue. In addition, the blending of adjacent colors is considered to be more natural.

WINDOWS GDI

One thing of which many Windows users are no doubt unaware is that there is a significant difference between a "printer" and a "print device." The key to understanding Windows is that it never allows hardware to directly interact with applications. That is all done through the Hardware Abstraction Layer (HAL) that I've mentioned several times throughout this book. To Windows, the printer is the collection of files the OS uses to communicate with the print device. The print device is the actual machine that spits out the final page.

Part of the Windows GDI is the inclusion of its own printer language. Since that language is embedded into the OS, it allows printer manufacturers to write simplified device drivers. Applications developers have a single interface to which they can write their code as well. Like Postscript, the language is independent of the printer hardware. Unlike Postscript, it is specific to the Windows platform. As such, the GDI language is considered to be host-based.

A key issue to consider here is whether or not the printer supports any languages other than GDI. A printer that supports only GDI can only be used in the Windows environment. The language is compatible with neither PDL nor Postscript. Also, GDI requires that your computer build and process the images. This places a fairly large burden on the CPU and memory.

Therefore, it is essential that you take into consideration the performance hit such a printer will impose on your system as well as the overall speed of the printing process. If you have a slow computer, print jobs will take longer to send to the printer. And while that is happening, trying to run any other application will be greatly hampered by the overhead imposed by the GDI language. Most users will find trying to use their computer for another application while a large print job is being processed is impractical.

On the plus side, GDI offers a much richer set of features than the more conventional languages. N-plus printing allows smaller versions of multiple pages to be printed onto a single sheet of paper. People who want the ability to do duplex printing without the necessarily high cost of a duplex printer can take advantage of manual duplexing.

The advantage that appeals to most people, however, is the inherently lower cost of GDI printers. Since they offload most of the work to the computer, a slow processor and small amounts of RAM (used for buffering) are all that the printer needs. As a result, a plethora of inexpensive yet highly functional printers are now available on the market.

IEEE 1284

If you've gotten this far through the book, by now you've realized that the Institute of Electrical and Electronic Engineers (IEEE) plays a key role in keeping the industry as near to "standard" as it can possibly be. IEEE 1284 was ratified as a standard in March of 1994 and defines several aspects of the printing process. Among these, any device bearing the IEEE 1284 standard must support five different printer modes, as follows:

- *Compatibility mode*: A unidirectional signal that is used to send data to the printer. This is also known as Centronix mode. Very slow, at approximately 150KB/s.
- *Nibble mode*: Sends the 8-bit byte of data to the printer in two cycles, each of which carries four bits, or a nibble of data. This method requires software support and more overhead on the part of the host computer. Even slower than compatibility mode, ranging from 50KB to 65KB/s.
- *Byte mode*: Like nibble mode, it provides bidirectional communication between the printer and the computer. Unlike nibble mode, it sends eight bits on each cycle. Speeds in byte mode are comparable to those of compatibility mode.
- *Enhanced parallel port (EPP)*: Because it provides for different types of signals to be transferred on any given clock cycle, EPP provides for faster and more efficient communication between peripherals. EPP allows continuous data transfer of around 500KB/s with burst rates of up to 2MB/s.
- *Extended compatibility port (ECP)*: Provides for both data and command cycles, therefore supporting more advanced devices, including scanners, storage devices, and such. Data throughput is similar to that of EPP. However, since DMA is used, there is less delay imposed on the application.

CONFIGURING PARALLEL PORTS

Pay special attention to the latter settings, EPP and ECP. In the CMOS of your computer, usually in the Integrated Peripherals section, is a place where you can configure your parallel port. Many versions of BIOS ship with bidirectional or byte mode enabled. For maximum performance, nearly every user will benefit by reconfiguring the parallel port to EPP. If you wish to control more than one device from your parallel port, ECP is the better choice. ECP can actually set up virtual channels for each device.

Note, however, that ECP requires a DMA channel. Since you are configuring the parallel port directly from the CMOS, any sound cards or other devices that may be using DMA will not yet be initialized. Therefore, there is a possibility that ECP will grab a DMA channel that another device is configured to use. This will only cause problems if both devices are active at the same time. For example, if ECP and the sound card are both on DMA3, and you like to play music while you work, the first time you attempt to print a document while playing Pachelbel, your computer is going to lock up like a tomb. The fix is easy. Simply reboot the machine, go into CMOS, and select a different DMA channel for ECP.

In addition to defining the minimum printing modes supported, IEEE 1284 devices also must follow certain other standards as well. For one thing, there are certain restrictions to any defined methods by which the printing mode that is to be used is negotiated. A byte of data is sent from the peripheral to indicate the mode for which it is configured, and the computer moves into that mode. **Table 18.1** shows the bytes sent during the negotiation for each mode.

Other aspects of parallel printing under the auspices of IEEE include the structure of the connectors used. There are some specific parameters that must be met before "IEEE 1284" can be stamped on the cable or device. These include, but are not limited to, the following:

- All signals move across a twisted pair and must provide for a signal and ground return.
- The cable will have a minimum of 85 percent optical braid coverage over foil.
- Signal and ground returns must have an unbalanced impedance of 62 ohms (+/- 6 ohms) over the frequency band of 4 to 16 MHz.
- Crosstalk between wires can be no greater than 10 percent.
- Cable shielding must be connected to the connector back shell using a 360-degree concentric method. Pigtail connections are not acceptable.
- Compliant cable assemblies shall be marked with "IEEE Std. 1284-1994 Compliant."

The connectors defined include the standard 25-pin connector described in Chapter Three. In order to maintain IEEE-1284 compliance, cables used to connect peripherals other than printers must be wired with a standard Type A cable. These cables can be male-to-male or male-to-female.

Table 18.1   Bit Values Used for Determining Printing Mode

Bit	Description	Valid Bit Values
8	Request extensibility link (REL)	1000 0000
7	Request EPP mode	0100 0000
6	Request ECP mode with REL	0011 0000
5	Request ECP mode without REL	0001 0000
4	Reserved	0000 1000
3	Request device ID	Nibble mode—0000 0100; Byte mode—0000 0101; ECP mode without REL—0001 0100; ECP mode with REL—0011 0100
2	Reserved	0000 0010
1	Byte mode	0000 0001
none	Nibble mode	0000 0000

Printers don't automatically know what printing mode an application has chosen. Information contained in the print job identifies the mode.

Most printers will require a cable that goes from the 25-pin male to a connector that in the past has been called the Centronix port. The IEEE description for the connector is the Type C connector.

The final parameters defined by IEEE had to do with the way in which printer drivers and interfaces were defined. These include voltage levels of specific signals, output signal impedance, and other electrical signals that are generated on a driver level. Manufacturers are expected to follow these standards when designing their product.

While this may seem to be a little on the dictatorial side on the part of IEEE, the end result is that if you buy a device stated to be IEEE 1284 compliant and an IEEE 1284 compliant cable, you know your new toy is going to work. There are many devices on the market today that will not work unless the cable is IEEE 1284.

CHAPTER SUMMARY

This chapter provided only the briefest overview of how printers work. A more detailed discussion would require an entire book in and of itself. The key details to remember from this chapter are primarily in the overall construction of a printer. Modern printers are modular devices and just knowing what makes them tick puts you halfway toward learning how to fix them.

BRAIN DRAIN

1. Describe in as much detail as possible the differences between how a line printer and a dot matrix printer compile images.

2. How does the print head of an impact printer deliver a single dot to the printed page?

3. What are the key differences between thermal inkjet printers and piezoelectric inkjet printers?

4. From beginning to end, describe in detail the monochrome laser printing process.

5. List as many different things as you can that define an IEEE 1284 compliant device and/or cable.

THE $64K QUESTIONS

1. Two different forms of impact printer include (pick two) _____.
   a. LED
   b. Thermal
   c. Dot matrix
   d. Daisy wheel

2. Bubblejet printers use piezoelectric print heads.
   a. True
   b. False

3. During the laser printing process, the paper is charged by _____.
   a. The primary corona
   b. The charging roller
   c. The developing roller
   d. The transfer roller

4. The imaging drum typically receives a _____ charge during the conditioning cycle.
   a. 200 to 400V
   b. −800 to −1200V
   c. −400 to −600V
   d. 400 to 600V

5. What component prevents the paper from adhering to the print drum after the toner is transferred?
   a. The separation pad
   b. The transfer roller
   c. The static discharge unit
   d. The fuser input assembly

6. Color laser printers apply the image from each toner cartridge _____.
   a. Directly to the paper
   b. To the imaging drum
   c. To an intermediate transfer belt
   d. To a film surface

7. If you wished to hang a scanner, an external CD-ROM, and a printer all off the same parallel port, which mode would be most suitable?
   a. Compatibility mode
   b. Nibble mode
   c. EPP
   d. ECP

8. There are _____ conductors on a standard parallel cable.
   a. 18
   b. 25
   c. 32
   d. 40

9. A printer capable of duplex printing does what?

    a. It prints on both sides of the page.

    b. It prints both color and black-and-white images.

    c. It can print thumbnails of several pages on a single sheet of paper.

    d. It can collate multiple print jobs into separate output bins.

10. A deflection pawl is unique to _____.

    a. Line printers

    b. Daisy wheel printers

    c. Color laser printers

    d. Duplex printers

TRICKY TERMINOLOGY

Bubblejet printer: Another term for a thermal printer.

Byte mode: Like nibble mode, it provides bidirectional communication between the printer and the computer. Unlike nibble mode, it sends eight bits on each cycle. Speeds of byte mode are comparable to those of compatibility mode.

Cold fusing: A process used by some phase-change printers that uses pressure rollers to press the ink into the paper.

Compatibility mode: A unidirectional signal that is used to send data to the printer. This is also known as Centronix mode. Very slow, at approximately 150KB/s.

Nibble mode: Sends the 8-bit byte of data to the printer in two cycles, each of which carries four bits, or a nibble of data. This method requires software support and more overhead on the part of the host computer. Even slower than compatibility mode, ranging from 50KB to 65KB/s.

Phase-change printer: A printer that liquefies solid inks before applying them to paper.

Piezoelectric crystal: A substance that changes shape when exposed to electricity.

Platen: The hard cylinder that supports the paper on impact printers.

Print head: The mechanism on any impact or inkjet printer that is responsible for depositing the pigment onto the paper.

Thermal printer: A printer that ejects ink onto a page of paper by heating the fluid.

Tractor feed: A paper transport mechanism that uses a set of gears on a printer to advance the paper by engaging in perforations along each side of the paper.

ACRONYM ALERT

DPI: Dots Per Inch

ECP: Extended Compatibility Port. A parallel mode that provides for both data and command cycles, therefore supporting more advanced devices, including scanners, storage devices, and such. Data throughput is similar to that of EPP. However, since DMA is used, there is less delay imposed on the application.

EPP: Enhanced Parallel Port. Because it provides for different types of signals to be transferred on any given clock cycle, EPP provides for faster and more efficient communication between peripherals. EPP allows continuous data transfer of around 500KB/s with burst rates of up to 2MB/s.

GDI: Graphical Device Interface. A subset of Microsoft's Windows operating systems that manages imaging devices such as printers, scanners, and graphics cards. Printers that use this interface as their printer language are referred to as GDI printers.

HAL: Hardware Abstraction Layer. A subset of Microsoft's Windows operating systems that provides a virtual barrier between the computer's hardware and the applications and upper-level OS functions.

HPGL: Hewlett Packard Graphics Language. A printer language developed by HP to add complex graphics to the printer's toolset.

PCL: Printer Control Language. Hewlett Packard's printer language, originally developed for dot matrix printers and later adopted for use with laser printers.

 VIEW THE VIDEO

A video clip on Laser Printing Imaging is available on the accompanying CD.

CHAPTER 19

PORTABLE COMPUTING

All too often when a hardware technician first makes the move from fixing desktop systems to fixing his or her first laptop, it is hard not to feel a bit intimidated. After all, this is a laptop and not a regular computer! Laptops are *different*!

Well, I hate to be the one to break the news to you, but laptop computers really aren't that much different than their larger counterparts. They're just tinier is all. In fact, a vast majority of the technology that goes into the manufacture of portable computers has already been discussed in previous chapters.

Therefore, I'm going to start this chapter by reviewing material already covered that relates to portable computing before I dive into new material.

A+ CORE HARDWARE EXAM OBJECTIVES

Along the way, candidates for the A+ exam are going to see several objectives:

1.3 Identify basic procedures for adding and removing field-replaceable modules for portable systems. Given a replacement scenario, choose the appropriate sequences.

1.10 Determine the issues that must be considered when upgrading a PC. In a given scenario, determine when and how to upgrade system components.

2.1 Recognize common problems associated with each module and their symptoms, and identify steps to isolate and troubleshoot the problems. Given a problem situation, interpret the symptoms and infer the most likely cause.

4.2 Identify the types of RAM (Random Access Memory), form factors, and operational characteristics. Determine banking and speed requirements under given scenarios.

4.3 Identify the most popular types of motherboards, their components, and their architecture. (Bus structures)

If this list seems to induce a strong sense of déjà vu, that's probably because you've seen these same objectives over and over again. Here, I'm going to be concentrating on how these objectives relate to portable computing.

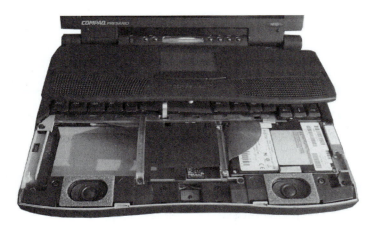

Figure 19.1 Pulling the palmrest off of this notebook shows just how small the components really are. The sound system, trackpad, and hard disk all fit underneath where your hands rest.

A LITTLE REVIEW

Laptop computers, as I said earlier, are nothing more than desktops with a hormone deficiency in most respects. They follow the same computer model that I introduced in Chapter One, PC Basics. Where they differ is in how the individual components are packaged. **Figure 19.1** shows just how many things fit under something as simple as the palmrest. Everything must be smaller, and where possible, designed to consume less power. When each individual component is designed to consume less power, then the overall system consumes less power. That means the battery lasts longer. And the one aspect in which laptops differ the most from desktops is in the fact that they frequently don't have the luxury of that little umbilical cord that attaches them to a power outlet in the wall.

With that in mind, I would like to spend the next few pages going over the basic components required by a computer system and discussing how they are designed differently for laptops. Where relevant, I'll also discuss commonly used methods of assembling laptops so that you will have a head start in figuring out how to take one apart.

CPUs

In the early days of computing, up into the release of the first generation of Pentium by Intel, CPUs were almost universally designed to be 5V devices. As a result, early laptop computers (behemoths by today's standards) could only run for short periods of time between battery charges.

Intel first addressed this issue with the 80386SLC. This was a processor designed with portable computing in mind that operated on 3.3V. Since then, most CPU manufacturers have maintained separate lines of CPUs for desktops and notebooks. The CPU capabilities are similar, if not identical, but CPUs designed for portable computing are designed to consume less power.

Another difference that stands out is in how the CPU is mounted to the motherboard. Many designs featured a CPU that was soldered onto the main system board. In fact, some early models used a gold-plated tape to actually tape the processors into their sockets. That kind of put a crimp in the upgrading process. Most current designs allow the CPU to be swapped out, but you might have to get used to a different type of socket. Instead of the ZIF socket common to most desktops, many laptops incorporate Very Low Insertion Force (VLIF) sockets.

If you're looking for the release handle on one of these sockets, you can stop searching. In its place is a small screw. Turning the screw one way releases the CPU, while turning in the other direction locks it in place.

MEMORY

In Chapter Nine, Searching Your Memory, I discussed a memory package called the SO-DIMM (small outline dual inline memory module, in case your memory has failed you). Laptop manufacturers are by far the largest consumer of this particular memory package.

Generally, laptops will feature one of two designs. The first of these designs makes use of motherboards on which a base amount of memory is integrated right onto the motherboard. Then, for purposes of upgrades, one or two SO-DIMM sockets are provided. The second method is to simply put SO-DIMM sockets on the motherboard and ship the unit with one socket populated.

Upgrading or replacing memory on notebooks isn't any more difficult than it is on desktop systems. You just have to know where to look for the sockets. On some models, such as the one in **Figure 19.2**, you flip the laptop over and on the base of the unit is a small door held shut by a single screw. Remove the screw, pop the door open with a small flat-bladed screwdriver, and there are the sockets.

Other manufacturers weren't so friendly. On some models, the memory sockets are located underneath the keyboard. In order to replace or upgrade the memory, you must remove the keyboard. I'll discuss how you go about that a bit later in the chapter.

HARD DRIVES

The vast majority of laptops released today incorporate standard IDE drives in a 2.5″ form factor. As you can see in **Figure 19.3**, these drives

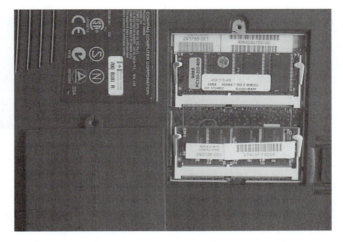

Figure 19.2   One of two common places to put the memory on laptops is beneath a door on the base of the computer. The other place is under the keyboard.

are much thinner that their 3.5″ counterparts and consume far less power. The cable is typically a 2″ 44-conductor cable, rather the 40 conductors used on desktop drives. The extra four conductors provide power to the drive. One conductor provides power to the motor, another provides power to the logic, and then there is a ground for each of them.

Changing out a hard drive in a notebook requires a bit more dexterity than does a desktop computer. In most cases, it is necessary to remove the keyboard, and in a few isolated models, the palmrest must come off as well.

Most laptop computers also offer the benefit of allowing the user to install hard drives in a PCMCIA slot (see Chapter Ten, Examining the Expansion Bus). These generally fit into a Type II slot and can be installed and removed as needed.

VIDEO DISPLAYS

The one thing you won't see on a laptop computer is a CRT display. Wouldn't that be fun to carry around? Some of the very first "portable" computers were equipped with CRT monitors and weighed nearly twenty pounds. Not exactly unnoticeable weight to be carrying around, but for the professional in the field who needed a computer, it was a way to go.

Today's laptops all come equipped with one of the LCD displays I discussed in Chapter Sixteen, Your Computer and Graphics. **Figure 19.4** shows an example of an LCD display. While many earlier

Figure 19.3 The only real difference between hard drives used by laptops and those used in PCs is the size. And that's quite a difference.

Figure 19.4 Even a venerable old classic like Windows 98 looks pretty decent on today's laptop displays.

models of laptops sported passive matrix displays, these days even the cheapest models give the user the benefits of active matrix. These are of the TFT variety discussed in Chapter Sixteen, Your Computer and Graphics.

Because of the rough usage laptops are subjected to, their displays are all too frequently damaged or broken. While it's not an inexpensive part to replace, on a perfectly usable computer, it might be a less expensive option to replace a damaged LCD panel than to go out and buy a new computer. And on most models, it isn't all that complicated a repair.

With some models, the screen must be replaced separately and is a rather complex process that involves removing and disassembling the display. How you do this varies greatly from model to model. On most units shipping today, the display is an integrated component consisting of the display, the bezel, and the circuitry involved. A hinged bracket assembly usually holds this assembly in place. Two screws on the back of the computer (or on the bottom on some models) hold the display in place and the bracket slides backward away from the laptop. There are a few models that have additional screws on the bottom of the laptop that must be removed before the bracket can come out. But most have just those two screws.

The tricky part is not damaging the ribbon cable that interconnects the display to the motherboard. The terminals used are a bit different than the ones you get used to in desktop designs. They're actually a smaller implementation of the Sub-D assembly. The end of the cable slides into a slot on the motherboard. The slot is equipped with two tabs that lock the cable into place when pressed down.

Finally, there will be two other wires that need to be disconnected. These are the high-voltage wires and generally coexist in a single plug-in terminal that makes removal and replacement an easy task.

REMOVABLE DISK DRIVES

The two most commonly seen removable media used by laptop computers are the floppy diskette and the CD-ROM. The key limitation to many laptop designs is the distinct lack of space for installing lots and lots of drives. Early on, one solution to this problem was to make the floppy and the CD interchangeable.

Here is another area in which PCMCIA shows its forte. Disk drives can be designed into PCMCIA Type III devices and then subsequently inserted and removed on the fly, as needed. Also, many manufacturers of laptops include a module bay that is used to swap out various devices, including floppy drives, CD/DVD drives, and even an extra battery if necessary.

DEVICES UNIQUE TO PORTABLE COMPUTING

Now that the review is out of the way, it's time to move on to some items you'll only see used in conjunction with laptop computers. Among these are the types of batteries used, AC adapter/chargers, PC cards, pointing devices unique to portables, and the docking station. Another device that deserves mention is a little toy called the port replicator. While it's true that most if not all of these devices see a certain degree of use outside the arena of portable computers, since it is with portables that they get the most exposure, this is where I've chosen to discuss them.

BATTERIES AND CHARGER/ADAPTERS

One of the key issues that had to be resolved when the first portable computers were developed was how to keep a constant and reliable supply of electricity available. A 250-mile extension cord didn't seem to be the answer, so batteries became the power source of choice. Some early models used standard alkaline batteries like you buy at the grocery store. When they were dead you put in some new ones and threw the old ones out.

This was neither cost-effective nor ecologically sensible. But rechargeable batteries of that era, like the one in **Figure 19.5**, were not very efficient for the purpose of laptop computers. The earliest of these batteries used an alloy of nickel and cadmium to generate and store current. These were called NiCad

Figure 19.5 The battery is sole reason you can take your laptop on the road. Show it some respect.

batteries and had a couple of rather serious inherent problems. The first of these was efficiency. It could take three hours of charging to give the batteries enough oomph to power a typical notebook computer of that time for half an hour. Second, NiCads exhibited a phenomenon called *battery memory*. Unless they were frequently discharged completely before recharging, they would "remember" how much of a charge they took in the last few recharging cycles and the amount of charge became its total capacity. The battery lost its ability to take a full charge.

> **EXAM NOTE:** Of all questions relating to portable computing, questions regarding the different types of batteries are the most common. Know your battery types.

NiCads were eventually replaced by Nickel Metal Hydride (Ni-MH) batteries. They really weren't a significant improvement over NiCads, but they helped a bit. While they still suffered from battery memory, it wasn't anywhere near as severe as it had been with NiCads. The recharge-to-usage ratio was a lot friendlier as well, giving slightly more usage time than it required to fully charge them. The most serious downside to Ni-MHs was that if overcharged, they could be permanently damaged.

Still, there was a lot of room for improvement. Today's notebooks all ship with Lithium-Ion (Li-Ion) batteries. Li-Ions don't suffer from battery memory, you can plug them in for hours, or even days at a time and they won't overcharge, and it only takes about an hour of charging to get three to five hours of use.

The AC adapter/charger that ships with a particular unit will be specific to that computer/battery combination. Just because the connector tip of another adapter seems to fit your computer is not an indication that it will work properly. You could even destroy a notebook computer by using the wrong AC adapter/charger. If you examine the terminal that plugs into the computer, you see a small pin in the center, while the outside resembles a

BUZZ WORDS —————

Battery memory: A phenomenon exhibited by rechargeable batteries where the pattern of recent charge cycles affects the maximum charge the battery will accept.

barrel. The pin is considered the tip. On adapters that output DC voltage, the adapter may be tip-positive or it may be tip-negative. What this means is that the tip is carrying either the positive or the negative current. Needless to say, they're not interchangeable.

Output voltages of different adapters also vary. A quick perusal of one online source of replacement AC adapters for notebooks turned up a range between 9V and 20V.

Figure 19.6   Putting this PCMCIA NIC on the keyboard gives a good idea of just how small a PC card really is.

PC CARDS

The *PC card* (**Figure 19.6**) is basically another way of describing devices designed for the PCMCIA slots. While the PCMCIA bus was discussed in detail in Chapter Ten, I have chosen to reserve a discussion of the cards themselves for this chapter.

For the most part, PC cards are truly PnP. In general, they require no intervention on the part of the user as far as installation and configuration of a device, other than providing the driver disk when needed during the first installation of a new device.

As was mentioned in Chapter Ten, PCMCIA slots are either Type I (3.3mm), Type II (5mm), or Type III (10.5mm). Type I and II slots are generally used for accessory cards such as NICS or modems. Type III slots see more use when designing drives.

One thing unique to PC cards is the typical structure of the device drivers used. PC cards use a two-tiered device driver. The first level is the *socket driver*. The socket driver notifies the computer when the device has been either inserted or removed and provides I/O operations. The second level is the *card service*. The card service interprets the command set for a particular device. As a result of this multitiered approach, PC cards can be added and removed on the fly as needed. However, before you simply start yanking devices out of your notebook, you might want to check with the manufacturer's instructions in this respect. There are some model-specific recommendations in this regard.

EXAM NOTE: A good understanding of PC card drivers is useful even if you're not taking the exam. If you are planning to take the exam, it's essential. That's another popular subject.

BUZZ WORDS

PC card: Any auxiliary device designed to be plugged into a PCMCIA slot.

Socket driver: The portion of a PC card driver that is responsible for I/O services and insertion/removal notification.

Card services: The portion of a PC card driver that interprets the command set for a specific device.

POINTING DEVICES USED ON PORTABLES

The three most common pointing devices used on laptops are the trackpad, the trackpoint, and the trackball (discussed in Chapter Eleven, Input Devices). The trackball is rarely used on modern computers and has already been discussed, so in this section I'll concentrate on the trackpad and the trackpoint.

Trackpads (**Figure 19.7**) work by sensing the electrostatic energy generated by the user's finger. An array of transistors tracks the movement of the finger as it moves across the surface and relays vector information to the device driver. The driver converts this information into the data needed to display the mouse cursor in the proper position on the screen.

Because of this, the sensitivity of a trackpad is directly proportional to the amount of electrostatic energy emitted by the person using the computer. For example, if you have long fingernails, and try to operate the trackpad with the tip of a nail, in most cases, it won't work. A technician who has just finished servicing a laptop and is still wearing an antistatic wristband is often surprised to find that the trackpad either responds poorly, or not at all.

In general, the trackpad is part of the palmrest. A small ribbon cable that uses an LIF connector similar to the one used by the display connects to the motherboard. With some models, the trackpad can be replaced, if necessary, separately from the palmrest. With other models, it is necessary to replace the entire palmrest.

A *trackpoint* uses technology similar to trackballs, except that it is a scaled-down version, usually embedded in the keyboard. It is very small, operated by the tip of a single finger, and sports a textured rubber surface. These characteristics earned it the nickname eraser-point. The signals generated by the trackpoint are sent through the ribbon cable interconnected the keyboard to the motherboard. Should a trackpoint fail, it will be necessary to replace the entire motherboard.

Since many people dislike both trackpads and trackpoints, most manufacturers provide some way of hooking up a standard mouse or trackball to their models of laptop. This can consist of either a USB or a PS2 port. While this does add one more accessory to be carting around in the carrying case, many people find that minor inconvenience far less annoying than the inconvenience of fighting with one of these other devices.

BUZZ WORDS

Trackpoint: A small pointing device used on laptop computers, similar to a trackball, but much smaller.

Trackpad: A pointing device used on laptop computers that makes use of an electrostatically sensitive surface. The user runs a finger across the surface and the trackpad tracks the movement of the electrostatic charge.

Figure 19.7   The trackpad is one of the more commonly used pointing devices on notebook computers.

DOCKING STATIONS

More people are deciding that owning and maintaining two separate computer systems is more trouble than it's worth. (I don't know why! I have half a dozen!) Today's laptop designs are every bit as powerful as their desktop counterparts. The only drawback is that you can't install as many toys.

The *docking station* eliminates even that argument. The docking station is a device to which a portable computer is attached that allows full-sized components to be installed. A portable computer designed for docking station use will have an interface called a docking connector on the back of the computer.

Docking stations provide all the standard I/O connectors of a desktop computer and also allow additional drives and/or PCI cards to be installed that are not part of the original laptop's configuration. I went to Dell Computer Corporation's Web site and examined the specifications for one of its docking stations. It offers the following:

- Standard I/O ports installed include serial, parallel, video, two PS/2, four USB, VGA, DVI, S-Video, and audio ports
- One half-height standard PCI slot and one internal media bay with battery charging support
- RJ-45 and RJ-11 jacks for network and modem hookups
- Cable lock security with latch

This is not intended as a promotion for Dell's products, it is just an example of the array of options available. All notebook manufacturers offer similar options for their line of portable products.

One issue involved with using docking stations is the fact that the device list that the operating system must support changes between portable and docked configurations. This isn't really a problem, but each change does require that the OS detect and install drivers for the appropriate devices. This slows the boot process. The Windows user can get around this by creating a separate hardware profile for each configuration. In Device Manager, there is a tab called Hardware Profiles that allows you to copy the existing profile. You then highlight the devices unique to the docking station and for each of these devices select the option "Disable in This Profile." Save that profile as Portable and rename the original as Docked. The next time you boot the computer, you will be asked which profile you wish.

PORT REPLICATORS

A *port replicator* is actually nothing more than a scaled-down docking station. In fact, with most models, the replicator attaches to the docking connector. A port replicator provides all the I/O ports of the docking station, but lacks additional PCI slots and/or drive bays. For many

> **BUZZ WORDS**
>
> **Docking station:** A device to which a laptop computer can be attached that provides additional hardware support, including I/O ports, PCI slots, and drive bays.

portables that lack integrated network support, it is usually possible to get a port replicator with a built-in NIC. As with docking stations, it is possible for the user to create separate profiles for each configuration to speed up the boot process.

> **EXAM NOTE:** Another pair of devices that see their share of coverage on the A+ exam are the docking station and the port replicator. Know the differences between the two and the issues that arise when using either one.

BUZZ WORDS

Port Replicator: A device to which a laptop computer can be attached that provides additional I/O services to the computer.

THE PDA

The personal digital assistant (PDA), like the one illustrated in **Figure 19.8**, is a device that is currently enjoying tremendous popularity. While not a full-blown computer system by most people's standards, the PDA can take many day-to-day applications and put them in a shirt pocket. These applications include schedules, expense records, small database applications, and literally hundreds of others. Some models can interconnect to a cellular modem and allow for full Internet or networking capability while on the road.

Data is usually input with a stylus. The PDA makes use of the touchscreen technology I discussed in Chapter Eleven. The user opens the appropriate application and taps the surface of the display with the stylus. Text is usually entered in one of two ways. Some incorporate little teeny keyboards. The keys are depressed either with the tip of a fingernail or with the stylus if the user possesses sufficient coordination. Touch typing is not much of an option. Other models bring up a display of a typical keyboard layout and the user taps the desired character with the stylus.

An emerging technology that has become incredibly popular is handwriting recognition. A popular implementation of this technology is called Graffiti. The user scrawls the message onto the space provided and the PDA converts it to text format. The problem that I see with that technology is that nothing exists that can recognize my handwriting. Not even my wife.

PDAs generally have their own specific and unique operating system. Currently the two most popular are the Palm OS, used by Palms, most Sony models of PDA, and many others, and Windows CE, used by many of the HP models as well as others.

Figure 19.8   I often take short trips without a notebook computer. But I don't leave home without my PDA!

Whichever way the user chooses to go, the PDA will offer some method by which he or she can interconnect the PDA to a standard PC and migrate data back and forth. Most PDAs also feature a slot into which external accessories can be connected. These accessories include memory cards, cellular modem hookups, and many others. As a technician, you probably won't see too many PDAs; they aren't really serviceable. When they die, generally the only option is to buy a new one.

CHAPTER SUMMARY

As you can see from this chapter, working with portable computers need not be intimidating. They're just smaller versions of the desktops you're already familiar with. The few differences that do exist are not technically challenging and are easy enough to understand and remember. The one thing that nobody tells you before you start servicing laptops is that your hands can't be more than an inch or so wide, but your fingers must be fourteen inches long with at least five sets of knuckles.

BRAIN DRAIN

1. How many different components can you think of that are designed differently for laptops than they are for desktops?

2. Explain the purpose of having a 44-conductor IDE cable in a laptop computer.

3. Describe the three main forms of battery used by laptops over the years and how they differ.

4. Describe how a docking station differs from a port replicator.

5. You own a laptop computer and a docking station. Nearly every time you boot your machine it goes through the Plug 'n Play process. Why is this and how can you stop this from happening?

THE 64K$ QUESTIONS

1. The memory package typically used by notebook computers is the _____.
   a. SDRAM
   b. SO-DIMM
   c. DIMM
   d. RDRAM

2. Modern laptop computers typically use _____ displays.
   a. Passive matrix
   b. CRT
   c. TFT
   d. NRF

3. However, many older laptops were equipped with _____ displays.
   a. Passive matrix
   b. CRT
   c. TFT
   d. NRF

4. An optional hard drive available for laptop computers fits into a _____ PCMCIA slot.
   a. Type I
   b. Type II
   c. Type III
   d. Either Type II or Type III

5. Two characteristics that might prevent two different AC adapters

from being interchangeable are _____ and _____. (Pick two.)

a. The AC outlet

b. The type of connector used to interconnect the adapter to the laptop

c. Input voltage

d. Output voltage

6. A type of battery used in laptops that exhibits no battery memory whatsoever is a _____ battery.

a. NiCad

b. Ni-MH

c. Li-Ion

d. Alkaline

7. Which layer of a PC card driver notifies the computer when a device has been removed or inserted?

a. Card service

b. SCSI services

c. ASPI

d. Socket services

8. Which layer of a PC card driver handles the interpretation of the device's command set?

a. Card service

b. SCSI services

c. ASPI

d. Socket services

9. What pointing device is most sensitive to the person's individual electrostatic charge?

a. The trackball

b. The mouse

c. The trackpoint

d. The trackpad

10. Two major differences between a port replicator and a docking station are _____ and _____.

a. PCI card support

b. External SVGA support

c. Additional PS2 connectors

d. Support for additional drives

TRICKY TERMINOLOGY

Battery memory: A phenomenon exhibited by rechargeable batteries where the pattern of recent charge cycles affects the maximum charge the battery will accept.

Card services: The portion of a PC card driver that interprets the command set for a specific device.

Docking station: A device to which a laptop computer can be attached that provides additional hardware support, including I/O ports, PCI slots, and drive bays.

PC card: Any auxiliary device designed to be plugged into a PCMCIA slot.

Port replicator: A device to which a laptop computer can be attached that provides additional I/O services to the computer.

Socket driver: The portion of a PC card driver that is responsible for I/O services and insertion/removal notification.

Trackpad: A pointing device used on laptop computers that makes use of an electrostatically sensitive surface. The user runs a finger across the surface and the trackpad tracks the movement of the electrostatic charge.

Trackpoint: A small pointing device used on laptop computers, similar to a trackball, but much smaller.

ACRONYM ALERT

PDA: Personal Digital Assistant. Any one of several computing devices designed for maximum portability.

NiCad: Nickel Cadmium. A type of rechargeable battery.

Ni-MH: Nickel Metal Hydride. A type of rechargeable battery.

Li-Ion: Lithium Ion. A type of rechargeable battery.

CHAPTER 20

TELECOMMUNICATIONS

These days people take the Internet for granted. In fact, while I haven't taken any formal surveys, based on the service work I've done, I would guess that well over half the PCs owned by individuals are used more as Internet appliances than they are as work tools. Corporate culture has learned to rely on electronic communications as well. People want to get on the Internet, and companies want all their offices to talk to one another. So one of the questions that was raised in the early days of computing was, "How can we get computers on different sides of the country to talk to one another?"

The government had been connecting computers over secure telephone lines for several years by the time Dennis Hayes invented the first PC modem in 1977. In 1978 they began to ship in quantity. From that day forth, the world as we knew it changed. It wasn't too long after that before there were electronic bulletin boards, and then electronic mail. Now the Internet owns everything, or so it seems. How many times have you purchased an item that carried a rebate, and found that you had to process it online? My friends, we've only seen the beginning!

A+ CORE HARDWARE EXAM OBJECTIVES

In this chapter, I'm going to address several different technologies used by computers in order to remotely communicate. In doing so, the following A+ objectives will be covered:

1.2 Identify basic procedures for adding and removing field-replaceable modules for desktop systems. Given a replacement scenario, choose the appropriate sequences.

1.4 Identify typical IRQs, DMAs, and I/O addresses and procedures for altering these settings when installing and configuring devices. Choose the appropriate installation or configuration steps in a given scenario.

1.5 Identify the names, purposes, and performance characteristics of standardized/common peripheral ports, associated cabling, and their connectors. Recognize ports, cabling, and connectors by sight.

1.8   Identify proper procedures for installing and configuring common peripheral devices. Choose the appropriate installation or configuration sequences in given scenarios.

2.1   Recognize common problems associated with each module and their symptoms, and identify steps to isolate and troubleshoot the problems. Given a problem situation, interpret the symptoms and infer the most likely cause.

MODEMS

The term *modem* (**Figure 20.1**) is derived from its original name of modulator/demodulator. It is a device that takes digital data in binary form and sends it over a telephone wire as electrical signals. In order to accomplish this, a modem has two tricks to perform. First of all, it has to be able to convert data from digital form to analog waveforms. Second, since the modem is moving data over the line using serial communications, the data needs to be converted from parallel to serial. A device called the Universal Asynchronous Receiver Transmitter (UART) handles the serial/parallel conversions. A DAC, very much like the one I introduced in Chapter Seventeen, Multimedia, is responsible for digital/analog and analog/digital conversions.

As a device, the computer treats the modem pretty much like any other I/O device. In the early days, because modems are serial devices, they were assigned a COM port. Therefore, a preset IRQ and I/O allocation was standard for most modems. Over the years that has changed, and it isn't uncommon to see modems grabbing resources not common to the standard COM port settings.

In all other respects, it's a typical I/O device. But it's one that has to convert data from serial format to parallel and from digital to analog. Let's say you're chatting with a friend over the Internet. You type a letter and the keyboard turns the action into a series of zeros and ones that are processed and sent to the modem. The UART breaks the bytes down into bits and the DAC converts the bits into the frequencies outlined above. **Figure 20.2** shows the waveforms of two modems working in duplex mode.

Figure 20.1   Today's modems transfer data at rates that approach 200x that of the one Dennis Hayes gave to the public back in 1978. And people still are not happy.

CONVERTING DATA TO ELECTRICAL SIGNALS

Early modems worked by using a frequency-shifting key. Using this technique, the modem that initiates communication became

BUZZ WORDS

Modem: Modulator/demodulator. A device that converts parallel digital signals into serial analog signals for transmission over a wire.

the *originate modem*. The modem that answers the call was called, oddly enough, the *answer modem*. The two modems operated across separate frequency ranges. The originate modems sent zeros at 1070Hz and ones at 1270Hz. The answer modem used 2.025Hz and 2225Hz, respectively.

Because frequencies between the two modems were different, it was possible to design modems that could transmit and receive at the same time. This is known as *full duplex* operation. Any device that can only send or receive at any given time is *half duplex*. There have been in the past some specialized devices that were designed to send data only or to receive data only. They could not do both. This type of communication is known as *simplex*. **Figure 20.3** represents signals transferring back and forth between two modems using duplex operation.

Unfortunately, this method wasn't very conducive to high-speed communications. Something a

BUZZ WORDS ————————

Originate modem: The device that initiates a call.

Answer modem: The device that is being called.

Full duplex: A communications method by which a device can be transmitting and receiving at the same time.

Half duplex: A communications method by which a device can either transmit or receive, but not both at the same time.

Simplex: A communications method by which a device can either transmit or receive but cannot do both.

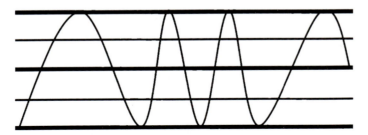

Figure 20.2   Frequency shifting in modem transmissions results in waveforms that look something like this.

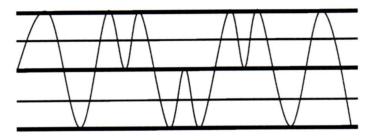

Figure 20.3   Phase-shifting modulation keeps the frequencies the same but changes the time of the phases to encode data.

little more sophisticated was needed. From frequency-shift keying, modems moved into phase-shift keying. As you saw in Figure 20.2, the electrical signal in a typical frequency-shifting scheme transmits a signal over a nice clean sine wave. Each wave cycle has two phases. One of those phases is the time in which the signal represents positive voltage. This is known as the rising end of the signal. The other phase is when the signal dips down into the negative range. Under phase-shift keying, the frequency of the signal doesn't change. The modem alters the waveforms in order to manipulate the phases.

The phases can be a full phase, a three-quarter phase, a half-phase, or a one-quarter phase. Each of the phases possible on the positive end of the frequency range represents four bits, and as you might imagine, the other four bits come from the negative spectrum.

Quadrature amplitude modulation (QAM) is a 24-carat term that simply describes a hybrid of frequency shift and phase-shift keying. Because phase and frequency can both be modified, more data can be crammed into a single wave cycle.

The UART

The other job the modem has is to get the data from the native parallel format used by the computer into serial form so it can go out over the wire. On the receiving end, it has to do the opposite. That is the function of the universal asynchronous receiver transmitter. That's a bit of a mouthful for just about anybody, so it is simply called a UART (pronounced you-art).

Every serial device needs a dedicated UART in order to do its job. Later in the chapter, when I discuss ISDN and DSL, you can rest assured that a UART is handling serial/parallel conversions. Your computer generally comes with two serial ports, although in recent models, there has been a propensity to ship systems with only a single serial port. On the earliest PCs, the UART was a chip soldered onto the motherboard. The first IBM PC used an 8250 chip for each serial port. This chip had no buffering capability and therefore was painfully slow. Also, it had enough bugs in the design to populate the Amazon River basin and was quickly replaced by the 8250A. Which wasn't a whole lot better, by the way. **Table 20.1** lists the UARTs commonly used by serial modems or other telecommunications devices.

UARTs are very common chips and are used on a wide variety of serial devices. It would be a misrepresentation to let you think that only the few that I discussed when talking about modems are all that ever existed. A quick search of the Internet turned up over 300 different models of UART by a number of different manufacturers.

Most current modems ship with 16550A UARTs. It isn't uncommon for system boards and supplemental I/O cards to have 16750, 16850, or even 16950 chips installed. The device will dictate the type of UART required.

Transmitting Data Over the Wire

Which brings me to the difference between bits per second (bps) and baud rate. In the days of frequency-shift keying, transmission speeds were limited to the frequency of the signal traveling across the telephone wire. The telephone companies, for some reason, were resistant to changing the way they sent voice across the wire just so users could have faster modems. The frequency

Table 20.1   UART Comparison Chart

UART	Buffer	Throughput	Comments
8250	None	19.2Kbps	Very buggy and short-lived
8250A	None	19.2Kbps	Fixed some of the bugs, but not all; slightly faster than the 8250
8250B	None	19.2Kbps	Finally got the 8250 series to work just in time for the 16450 to come out
16450	None	38.4Kbps	16-bit UART; buggy and still no buffer
16550	16 bytes	115.2Kbps	Problems with chip
16550A	16 bytes	115.2Kbps	Fixed bugs from the 16550; still commonly used today
16650	32 bytes	460.8Kbps	Programmable flow control and high speed throughput
16750	64 bytes send/56 bytes receive	921.6Kbps	Developed by Texas Instruments
16850	128 bytes	1.5Mbps	Has onboard infrared serial decoder
16950	128 bytes	3Mbps	Found on high-end multiport serial devices

The speed of the UART directly dictates the maximum speed of a serial device.

they chose was ~3400Hz. That is referred to as the *baud rate*. That's the actual frequency of the carrier signal going over the wire.

For several years, baud rate and bps were, for all intents and purposes, the same thing, because frequency-shift keying could only send one signal per wave cycle. The old 300bps modems were simply not making use of the full frequency spectrum available on the telephone line. When manufacturers made the move from 300 baud to 1200 baud, they started using half of the bandwidth available, and at 2400bps, while they weren't using the full bandwidth of the telephone line, they were going as fast as they could go using the binary values by which data is measured. At that point in time frequency-shift modulation was no longer an option if they wanted faster speeds.

That's where phase shift and QAM come into play. They both allow for more than one bit of data to be transmitted on a single wave cycle. This means that it is no longer accurate to refer to your modem as 56,000 baud. It isn't. It is still only 2400 baud, but it is theoretically capable

BUZZ WORDS

Baud rate: The electronic frequency over which data is transmitted.

Bit rate: The speed at which data travels over the wire, usually expressed in bits per second (bps) or kilobits per second (Kbps). Don't confuse this with bytes per second, and don't confuse it with baud rate.

Transmission rate: The number of bits per second that is being transmitted.

of transmitting 56,000 bits per second. In practical use, modems can't reach the theoretical maximum. But I'll get into that a little later.

This makes it sound like your data is moving over the telephone wire as individual bits. In reality, modems work a lot like network cards. Data is broken up into pieces and sent across the wire. What kind of pieces get sent depends entirely upon the communications session that is established between two modems. The two types of session are asynchronous and synchronous transmission.

ASYNCHRONOUS TRANSMISSION

Asynchronous mode is sometimes referred to as a connectionless communication. This doesn't mean you don't have some form of connection established between the two hosts. Obviously, that is not the case, or you wouldn't be able to communicate. It simply means that the originate modem throws its data onto the wire and assumes it will reach its intended destination.

In asynchronous mode, each byte of data is sent, one byte at a time. It is packaged into an "envelope" that consists of the data tucked in between a start bit and a stop bit. Accompanying each byte of data are another two bits that keep the clock cycles of the sending and receiving modems synchronized.

A key disadvantage to asynchronous transmission is that there are no error correction mechanisms in place to assure the integrity of the data. Parity (see Chapter Nine, Searching Your Memory) can be used to detect an error, but nothing can be done to correct it.

The reason it continues to exist as a transmission method is that some forms of communication work best in this manner. If you're just chatting with a friend over the Internet or browsing, it works fine. On the other hand, if you download a service pack for your NOS, you probably want to be sure that your data is arriving intact. For this type of communication you are much better off using. . .

SYNCHRONOUS TRANSMISSION

That service pack might be 30MB long, and it's going to take a long time to move it across the telephone wires to get it from one computer to the other. You can rest assured that quite a large number of blocks of data will be lost along the way. You need a way of determining when that happens and also a way of fixing the problem.

Synchronous transmission sends data across the wire in *message blocks*. A file is broken down into smaller chunks and sent out over the wire. On the receiving end, those piece are reassembled into the correct order. Each message block consists of several portions, as shown in **Figure 20.4**.

Direction of Data Travel

Figure 20.4   A synchronous message block is broken down into several key sections.

SYN: *Synchronization character.* This makes sure all the bytes in the frame stick together as they move across the wire and then get reassembled in the right order at the other end. If no data is being transmitted, SYN blocks can be transmitted to keep the session alive.

SOH: *Start of Header.* A header is not always used, but is an important part of most protocols.

HEADER: Placed into message block by protocol and can include information such as the sending computer's IP address, the intended recipient's IP address, and so forth.

STX: *Start of Text.* Pretty self-explanatory. It tells you that the next series of bits is the data being sent.

TEXT: The data

ETX: *End of Text.* Okay, I'm done sending text in this block. The next bytes are more control information.

BCC: *The Block Check Character.* Includes error detection and correction data, which may include parity (rarely used these days), checksum (on its way out), or cyclical redundancy check (the most common method in use today).

EOT: *End of Transmission.* I hope I don't have to explain that one.

BUZZ WORDS

Message block: A piece of data being transmitted by a modem that represents a portion of the overall data being sent.

All of this additional information is used by the system to make sure data gets where it's going and gets there intact. Two key sections that I will take a closer look at are the SYN and BCC blocks.

The primary purpose of the SYN block is synchronization of the session. It carries information that allows the two modems to keep the session alive. A key issue in telecommunications is packet loss. You spend all that money on a nice fast modem and then discover you're leaving behind 20 to 30 percent of the data you send, only to have to resend it. Packet loss kills bandwidth. For every message block that gets corrupted in transit, the intended recipient must send a NACK. While this makes sure the data is resent, it adds even more congestion to the session.

The BCC blocks carry information that allow for error detection and correction. Over the years there have been three major error correction mechanisms used, but only two remain commonplace in synchronous communication. An older method, still used by asynchronous communication, is parity checking. The two methods commonly used in synchronous sessions are checksum and cyclical redundancy check (CRC).

Parity Checking I discussed parity checking in Chapter Nine, Searching Your Memory. Unlike RAM, however, which uses only odd parity, modems can be set to use either even parity or odd parity. If odd parity is selected, the number of ones in a byte are counted. If there is an even number of ones, the parity bit is set to one, making it an odd number. If there is already an odd number of ones, the parity bit is set to zero. In either case, with odd parity, at the receiving end

Odd Parity

Data Bits = Even number of Ones
A One is added to the Parity Bit
We now have an Odd Number

Data Bits = Odd number of Ones
A Zero is added to the Parity Bit
We still have an Odd Number

Figure 20.5 Parity checking at work

there should always be an odd number (see **Figure 20.5**). With even parity, there should always be an even number of ones.

Unlike the parity checking mechanism used by early RAM, errors detected by modems do not shut the computer down. They result in a NACK packet being returned to the originating computer, requesting that the corrupted packet be resent.

The problem inherent with parity checking across telephone lines is that noisy lines have a tendency to cause a lot of distortion. It is quite possible for a message block to drop a one here and gain a one somewhere else. The parity checks out fine, but you've got two corrupted bits and not just one. In asynchronous transmissions, where only a byte at a time is going across the wire, parity can still be an effective error checking mechanism.

Checksum and CRC Checksum and CRC are error checking and correction schemas that work well with large blocks of data. Under *checksum*, the number of ones in the message block is simply added up. The result is stored in the BCC and off goes the data. On the receiving end, your computer adds up the ones and if the answer it gets matches what is stored in the BCC, all is considered to be well. The packet is accepted and an ACK is sent out.

BUZZ WORDS

Checksum: An error detection/correction mechanism that works by counting the number of ones present in the payload and storing that value in the BCC block of the packet.

Of course, if along the line the message block picked up two ones someplace and lost two ones someplace else, then the checksum results are "accurate" and a corrupt packet is accepted. This is not good. Another possibility is that the data in the checksum itself might become corrupted and report perfectly good packets as being bad. At least in the latter case, the worst that happens is that the packet is unnecessarily resent.

CRC performs a complex mathematical equation on the block. It treats the entire message block as if it were a single very large binary number. A rather complex mathematical equation is performed on the number the message block represents and the results of that equation are stored in the BCC. On the receiving end, the process is repeated. If the results match, the packet is accepted. The mathematical possibilities of any bits being shifted and still yielding the same CRC are rather minute. In fact, you could consider them to fall somewhere between slim and nonexistent.

SOH AND THE HEADER

Another key issue is that the protocol of the Internet is TCP/IP. In order to move data across the wire, TCP/IP encapsulates the message block into a TCP/IP packet. TCP/IP packets have their own header and trailer information that is required in order to get data from one place to another.

The SOH block indicates that the following bits of data are going to be a header of some sort (not specifically TCP/IP, but across the Internet it will usually be). A little earlier I was talking about the futility of having a high-speed connection if too many of your packets were being lost. One feature designed into TCP/IP is the ability to detect packet loss. The two primary reasons for packet loss are congestion and poor line conditions. In either case, it's better to slow the transmission down than to lose too many packets. Lower transmission rates where the data is accurately sent are much more efficient than having to fill a high-speed wire with the same messages over and over again.

SOME MODEM TERMINOLOGY

Modem aficionados have their own collection of buzz words that set them apart from normal people. Unless you know some of the terms they use, figuring out what the guy on the other line is trying to tell you can be pretty challenging. While the following list of terms is by no means all encompassing, it should give you a pretty decent start.

- *Bell 103*: 300 bps U.S. standard
- *Bell 212A*: 1200 bps U.S. standard
- *Compression*: The process of reducing information in data storage or transmission by the elimination of redundant elements. Various compression protocols have evolved over the years. Most current modems use V.90bis as the data compression method of choice.
- *Firmware*: Similar to the computer's BIOS, this is built-in software stored on a ROM chip that controls the operation of a dedicated, microprocessor-based device.

- *Flash ROM*: A type of memory used for firmware in modems and other digital devices. Unlike conventional ROM (read-only memory), flash ROM can be erased and reprogrammed, making it possible to update a product's firmware without replacing memory chips.

- *International Telecommunications Union (ITU)*: The agency in charge of overseeing telecommunications sponsored by United Nations. The ITU is charged with establishing and coordinating standards for electronic communications worldwide.

- *ISDN*: Integrated Services Digital Network; an all-digital replacement for analog telephone service. ISDN provides two 64 kbps channels, which can be combined or used independently for both voice and data.

- *K56flex*: A protocol, jointly developed by Lucent Technologies and Rockwell International Corp., to achieve 56 kbps modem transmissions over ordinary phone lines. K56flex requires that the host device (at an ISP or online service) be connected to a minimum of an ISDN or preferably a T1 line. K56flex allows downloads at up to 53.3 kbps, uploads are limited to the normal V.34 speed of 33.6 kbps. See x2.

- *MNP*: Microcom Networking Protocol (Proprietary)

- *T1*: A digital phone line that provides up to twenty-four channels of data at 64 kbps. A fractional T1 is one or several of those channels connected to form a singular link. T1 lines can carry data or digital telephone signals and are commonly used for high-speed WAN connections between offices.

- *V.32*: 9600bps, 4800bps

- *V.32bis*: 14.4kbps, 12kbps, 9600bps, 7200bps, 4800bps

- *V.32terbo*: Pseudo-standard extending V.32bis to 16.8 and 19.2kbps. Never really took off.

- *V.34*: An ITU standard for data transmission at up to 33.6 kbps. V.34 is the successor to several earlier ITU standards, and modems using this standard are designed to be backwardly compatible with older, slower modems.

- *V.42*: MNP 4 and Link Access Protocol/Modems (LAP/M) modem-to-modem error correction

- *V.42bis*: LAP/M and 4-to-1 data compression

- *x2*: A technology developed by U.S. Robotics for achieving modem transmissions at close to 56 kbps over ordinary phone lines. In most respects, it is similar to K56flex.

The AT Command Set

In the good old days, modems were operated in the same manner as your computer. You had to issue specific commands to perform a specific function. Since these commands were used only for modems, they were not DOS commands. You had to be running some form of terminal emulation software. These days, you double-click your favorite Web browser and the software does all that for you. However, it is still a good idea to know your way around a modem, should you ever find yourself in the position of having to manually communicate with another device or needing to troubleshoot a modem. The standard modem command set is called the AT Command Set and is modeled after the original Hayes Command Set. There are the basic command set and the extended set. **Table 20.2** lists the Basic AT Command Set, along with descriptions of what each one does.

The Extended Command Set provides for far more control of modem functions and performance. Using these will require fairly substantial knowledge of modem registers and other aspects that are beyond the scope of this book.

Table 20.2 The Basic AT Command Set

Command	Function
AT	Attention (precedes all commands except A/ and +++)
A/	Repeat previous command (does not require a <CR>)
A	Takes the modem off hook while inactive; otherwise, the modem will try to answer all incoming calls
B0	Select CCITT V.22 (1200 bps)
B1	Select Bell 212A (1200 bps)
B2	Select CCITT V23 — Originate modem will transmit data at 75 bps and receive data at 1200 bps; answer modem will transmit data at 1200 bps and receive data at 75 bps; the command N0 (disable auto mode) must be selected
D	Takes the modem off-hook and waits for a dial tone, allowing the modem to dial out (see X command for exceptions)
Dmn	ATDmn will dial a phone number where "m" is a modifier: L, W, ,, ;, @, or S; "n" represents a number dialed by the user
L	Dial last number
W	Wait for dial tone; if you have selected X0 or X1 (disable dial tone detection), then you can use this modifier to override that setting
,	Pause during dial; the amount of time the modem waits is determined in register S8
;	Return to command mode after dialing; it does not wait for carrier or hang up
@	Wait for 5 seconds of silence (used for systems that do not provide a dial tone)
!	Hook flash; forces the modem to go on-hook for a half second; used in PBX systems and for certain voice features such as call waiting
S=(0-9)	Dials a stored number; up to ten numbers can be stored, and the addresses are from 0 to 9; to store a number into one of these addresses, use the "&Z" command

(Continued)

Table 20.2   The Basic AT Command Set *(Continued)*

Command	Function
E0	Turns Echo off; commands issued to the modem are not displayed on the screen
E1	Turns Echo on; commands issued to the modem are displayed on the screen
H0	Hang up modem
H1	Bring modem on-line
I0	Return numeric product code
I1	Return hardware variation code
I2	Report internal code
I3	Report software revision number
I4	Report product feature listing
L0	Speaker volume off
L1	Speaker volume low
M0	Speaker always off
M1	Speaker on until carrier detected, then turns speaker off
M2	Speaker always on
M3	Speaker on during answering only
N0	Disable automode; this will fix the speed at which the modem connects to the speed specified in register S37
N1	Enable automode; the modem will negotiate the highest available line speed and ignore any ATBn command
O0	Return to data mode
O1	Retrain the modem; line conditions may change after the original connection; retraining the modem will force a renegotiation of speed based on the current line conditions
P	Some older telephone systems still support only pulse dialing, this forces the modem to dial in pulse mode
Q0	Enable response to DTE
Q1	Disable response to DTE; the modem does not respond to the terminal; issuing a command will not produce a response (unless the command is something like ATZ, which will restore this setting to default)
Sn	Set default S-register; any subsequent = or ? commands will modify the default S register
Sn=m	Set register n to value m
Sn?	Return the value of register n
T	Touch-tone dialing; the default on nearly all modems
V0	Result codes will be sent in numeric form (stored in a file called the result code table)

(Continued)

Table 20.2 The Basic AT Command Set *(Continued)*

Command	Function
V1	Result codes will be sent in work form (see the result code table)
W0	Report DTE speed only; Error Correction or Data Compression methods in use will not be reported
W1	Report DCE speed; Error Correction/Data Compression protocol and DTE speed will be reported
W2	Report DCE speed only
X0	Send OK, CONNECT, RING, NO CARRIER, ERROR, and NO ANSWER; busy and dial tone detection are disabled
X1	Send X0 messages and CONNECT speed
X2	Send X1 messages and NO DIAL TONE
X3	Send X2 messages and BUSY and RING BACK; dial tone detection is disabled
X4	Send all responses
Y0	Prevents disconnections caused by long spaces
Y1	Forces a disconnect after a long space; with error correction, hang up after sending 1.6-second long space; without error correction, hang up after 4-second long space
Z0	Reset modem to profile 0
Z1	Reset modem to profile 1
+++	Escape sequence; transfers the modem from data mode to command mode; must be preceded by at least 1 second of no characters and followed by one second of no characters; O0 (ATO0 or ATO) returns the modem to data mode
=n	Sets the value of the default S register

The AT Command Set is starting to go the way of the platypus. Still, there are enough modems running around that having a reference of the commonly used commands might be useful.

INITIALIZATION STRINGS

When a modem first initiates contact with another modem, there are certain parameters that must be set simply in order to initialize communications. In order to accomplish this, the modem is programmed with the *initialization string*. This tells the modem on the other end precisely what the originate modem is capable of doing in terms of compression and speed. Modems ship with a default string that works most of the time. Sometimes fine-tuning the string will do wonders for modem performance. How you go about doing this is determined by the operating system you're running.

BUZZ WORDS

Initialization string: A series of AT commands that are issued by the originate modem during the connection process.

Windows 95/98

1. Double-click My Computer, then double-click Dial-Up Networking. (If a Dial-Up Networking folder is not present in My Computer, try this: From the Start button, choose Programs, and then Accessories. There you will see Dial-Up Networking.)
2. Right-click your connection icon and choose Properties.
3. Click the Configure button.
4. Click the Connection tab.
5. Click the Advanced button.
6. Enter the init string in the Extra Settings field.
7. Click OK to save changes.

Windows NT 4.0\2000

1. Click the Start Menu, then click Settings, and then select Control Panel.
2. Double-click the icon labeled Modems.
3. Select the modem you wish to configure and click the Properties button
4. On the window that pops up, select the Connection tab.
5. Click the button that says Advanced.
6. Type the initialization string in the Extra Settings box.
7. Click OK repeatedly until you are at back the Control Panel window.

Some of the problems that can be solved by editing the initialization string include dropped connections, poor connect speeds, and many others. Each brand of modem will have initialization strings specific to that modem, and therefore, you will need to be able to access the documentation for your particular model. If you've thrown away or lost the documentation that shipped with your modem you can usually retrieve that information off of the technical support area of the manufacturer's Web page. Also, specific ISPs might suggest initialization strings different from the default.

INSTALLING AND TROUBLESHOOTING MODEMS

All that said and done, just what is going to be involved when you go to install a modem and what kinds of problems can you expect on down the road? The answers are, "That depends," and "More than you care to think about." But I'm willing to bet you're looking for a little more detail than that. So I'll start with installing a modem.

INSTALLING MODEMS

First off, there is a fairly wide variety of modems available to choose from, ranging from incredibly inexpensive to outrageously expensive. A better way to break them down would be into external modems and internal modems. Which way you go is an entirely personal decision, but having some insight into the differences will make that decision easier to make intelligently. In many respects, the decision you make here will affect you later on down the road when you're trying to troubleshoot problems that will inevitably arise.

- *Internal modems*: These install into an available expansion slot inside the computer. While ISA modems are becoming increasingly hard to find, they do still exist. PCI modems will fall into two different categories. There are software dependent, or soft, modems, and then there are real modems. I'll talk about the pros and cons of software-dependent modems at great length a little later on.

- *External modems*: While the most commonly available external modems are those that install onto a serial port, there is an increasing number of USB modems becoming available. Serial modems can be the easiest to troubleshoot because of the function lights that are easily seen on the front panel of the device. USB modems are generally more limited in the number of function lights, if any, that are available.

Installation of external modems is usually pretty straightforward. There isn't really a whole lot that can go wrong. You simply have to make sure that you have an available serial port, or USB port in the case of USB modems, and the correct cable. Once the system detects the new device, it is simply a matter of installing the software drivers.

Two things that can cause an external modem installed on a serial port to not be detected are IRQ conflicts and/or a disabled serial port. With Plug 'n Play, IRQ conflicts are pretty rare these days, but they can still occur. An external modem is going to want one of the standard COM ports. Whether it is COM1, COM2, COM3, or COM4 usually doesn't matter, as long as one of them is available. Plug 'n Play will usually detect other devices that occupy COM ports and give the modem one that isn't occupied.

If, for some reason, Plug 'n Play isn't working, it could be because of one of two things. Either the serial port is disabled, or another device in the system is occupying the same base I/O address as the modem. External modems hook up to an existing serial port; therefore, IRQ conflicts are incredibly rare.

I/O conflicts are equally rare, but there is one notable case where this can become an issue. Some motherboards are shipping with tertiary and quaternary IDE ports on board. By default, they are disabled. However, should you choose to activate these ports, they need I/O base addresses the same way everything else does. The base address for a tertiary IDE port happens to overlap with COM3. Therefore, installing an external modem set to COM3 on a system with a tertiary IDE enabled is going to cause a conflict. And it's one that can be difficult to diagnose.

The more likely cause for a serial modem failing to be recognized is that the serial port to which it is attached has been disabled. If you were previously using a soft modem that was installed at the factory, there is a very strong possibility that, in order to get the soft modem to work, one of your serial ports was disabled. Murphy's Law dictates that the disabled port will be the port you're trying to use. Go into the CMOS settings and enable the port and all should be well.

Internal modems have their own set of problems. Once again, for the most part, Plug 'n Play minimizes these problems. However, you can occasionally bump into IRQ problems with internal modems. If you're installing a PCI soft modem, the issue I discussed in the previous

Table 20.3 Modem Light Functions

Marking	Meaning	Modem function
PWR	Power On	Lights when power is applied to the modem
MR	Modem Ready	Lights when the modem self-check has satisfactorily completed
TR (DTR)	Terminal Ready	Lights when Data Terminal Ready (DTR) signal from the PC is present
SD (TD)	Send (Transmit) Data	Lights while modem is transmitting data to a remote modem
RD	Receive Data	Lights while modem is receiving data from a remote modem
OH	Off Hook	Lets you know the modem is off hook
HS	High Speed	Lights when connected to high-speed link
AA	Auto Answer	Indicates that modem is set to accept calls
CD	Carrier Detect	Lights when remote carrier has been detected
RS	Request to Send	Lights when an RTS signal is being generated
CS	Clear to Send	Lights when a CTS signal is being generated

The lights on an external modem aren't just for show. They indicate whether or not certain functions are working.

paragraph applies to you in reverse. It is possible that the reason you can't get the system to see your new modem is that the serial port is claiming the IRQ. Serial and parallel ports grab their resources during POST, long before PCI devices get their shot. The only way to get the soft modem to work is to disable the serial port. This can be a bummer if you have something attached to that port.

TROUBLESHOOTING MODEMS

One of the beauties of external modems is that collection of pretty lights on the front. You should know, however, that those lights weren't put there just for show. They have some very important functionality. While not all external modems have the same collection of lights, the ones most commonly seen are outlined in **Table 20.3**.

Having all those lights out in plain sight makes the work of troubleshooting modem problems a lot easier. Internal modems don't give you benefit of any visible lights, but the problems you face will be the same. I've put together a list of some of the more commonly seen problems modem users experience and possible solutions.

- *Windows doesn't see the modem*: Check for IRQ conflicts. Does it show up in Device Manager at all? If so, is there either a yellow exclamation point or a red X? A yellow exclamation point tells you it sees the modem but the device is not working. This is usually a driver issue. A red X means you told Windows there is a modem installed, but Windows disagrees.

- *Windows sees the modem, but it won't dial*: Won't even go there. Way too many things cause that, but you can tell if it's the modem's fault. Open a Hyperterminal session (Start, Programs, Accessories, Communications, Hyperterminal), and at the prompt, type the command AT. If the echoed response is "OK," then the modem itself is working. Next you follow the procedures in the previously described symptom.

- *You get a "No Dial Tone" message*: Is the phone line hooked up to the modem? If it is an external modem, is it actually plugged in and turned on? If both answers are yes, check and see if you have dial tone on a voice phone. You may be having a service outage. If so, did you pay your bill?

- *My 56K modem only connects at 28.8K*: Don't be surprised to hear that you're not alone. In some localities, the quality of the phone lines is too poor to maintain any speeds higher than that. If you know the phone lines are not the issue, check and see if your settings are correct. If the COM port settings are set to 28.8Kbps, that's all you're ever going to get, regardless of what modem you use or line quality.

- *My Connection Status tells me I'm hooked up at 49.2K but I'm only downloading at 4.3K*: That's not a problem. For one thing, the 4.3K represents bytes per second, while the 49.2 is bits per second. Therefore, that 4.3K translate out to 35,225 bits per second. Since your modem is also sending out ACK and SYN messages all the time, 4.3K is actually a good rate.

- *I'm having problems with downloads*: This could include corrupted files or files that won't open (basically the same thing). Usually caused by a data overrun. The remote computer is sending data faster than your modem is able to process it. This usually means your flow control is set incorrectly. In the Advanced Settings you will see settings for Xon/Xoff as well as RTS/CTS. If you have a fast modem, you don't want to be using Xon/Xoff. Make sure you and the other computer are in agreement on which setting you're supposed to be using.

- *My connection is constantly being dropped for no apparent reason*: Most frequently this is a result of poor line quality. Keep in mind that line quality is not a constant thing. Electrical signals that are perfectly good on a nice sunny day pick up a lot of noise during a thunderstorm. However, if the line is not to blame, it could be that the modem is causing a timeout generated by a DTR signal not arriving in time. On most modems, adding a parameter to the initialization string can rectify this. Check with your manufacturer for the correct string.

- *My modem keeps getting slower the longer I remain connected*: This is a result of the retraining I discussed earlier. Either line conditions or congestion is preventing high-speed connection and the two modems keep renegotiating slower speeds.

- *I click on a site that contains data for a project I'm doing at work and I get football scores instead*: This is a problem?

SOFT MODEMS

Throughout this chapter I've made references to soft modems and real modems. Another term you might see thrown about is Winmodem. Please note that Winmodem is a registered trademark of 3Com/USRobotics, and should not be used interchangeably. The term soft modem is derived from the fact that the device is dependent on the OS to function. These modems typically hand off many of the functions that I've discussed in this chapter onto the computer itself.

Soft modems will fall into two categories: those with onboard digital signal processors (DSP) that provide both UART and DAC functions, and those that make the computer do everything. If a modem has its own DSP, it will perform the functions of both signal processing and that of the UART. This modem will be relatively easy to install and offer little or no performance degradation.

Conversely, the modem that lacks a DSP will make the computer's CPU handle all data processing. It will require one of the UARTs resident on the motherboard in order to function. And every time it is in use, other programs will suffer because the modem is using a substantial amount of CPU time for its own purposes.

A real modem has an onboard controller, its own UART, and its own DSP to handle all those functions. They are much easier to install and to troubleshoot than soft modems. That is not to say, however, that there is not a time and a place to use soft modems. They are inexpensive, for one thing. This can become a big issue for a lot of people.

Also, if the primary reason for the computer's existence is to hook the household up to the Internet, then it is less likely that large numbers of applications are going to be running in the background. For someone like me, however, who routinely has two or three Internet connections active at once, a word processor, a desktop publisher, a photo-editing program, and a drawing program all running at once, soft modems can become an issue. They key here is to know what your computer is intended to do and buy appropriately.

ISDN

For some people, the speed of a modem is simply too slow. Yet some of the faster technologies that I will discuss in the next section are simply too expensive. If you happen to fall into that category, you might want to see if any providers in your area provide for an Integrated Services Digital Network (ISDN). This is a service that, on its most basic level, provides noticeably faster throughput in both directions.

Unlike a telephone line, an ISDN signal stays digital from beginning to end. The only conversion necessary is to move from parallel to serial and back again. As with modems, this is done through a UART.

Basic Rate ISDN (BRI) provides the user with two 64K channels for carrying data (although some service providers drop that to 56K due to the type of switches they use). These are the *B-channels*.

> **BUZZ WORDS**
>
> **B-channel:** A carrier channel used by ISDN for transmitting user data at 64Kbps. Multiple B-channels can be combined for higher transmission rates.

These carry nothing but user information. This can include digital data, digitized voice communications, and so forth. A third channel, the *D-channel*, is a 16K connection that carries the transmission control signals.

Primary Rate ISDN (PRI) provides even higher speeds. Up to twenty-three channels can be combined to provide the user with up to 1536K of throughput. In Europe, ISDN services can provide for up to thirty channels for 1920K. Another difference between BRI and PRI is that with PRI, you get a 64K D-channel as well.

For those who need speeds in between the high and low bandwidths of BRI and PRI, the International Telegraph and Telephone Consultation Committee (CCITT) defined the H-channels. These channels (listed in **Table 20.4**) provide speeds from 384K up to 1920K.

How you interconnect your system to the ISDN line will be determined by where you live. In the U.S., the signal is going to enter the

BUZZ WORDS ───────────────

D-channel: A 16Kbps or 64Kbps channel used by ISDN for control data, including synchronization, ACKs and NACKs and other non-user data.

Table 20.4   Summary of ISDN Services

ISDN Service	Structure	Maximum Speed
H0	6B, 1D	384K
H10	23B, 1D	1472K
H11	24B, 1D	1536K
H12	30B, 1D	1920K

The H channels define intermediate ISDN speeds.

Note: H11 and H12 service is available in Europe

building by way of a U interface. The U interface only supports a single device, and that device is going to be the Network Termination-1 (NT1). All the NT1 really does is convert the incoming 2-wire circuit to a 4-wire S/T interface. The S/T interface provides access to more than one device. It is possible to get S/T interfaces that support up to seven different devices. It is also possible that your provider might install equipment that has the NT1 and S/T interface designed into the device, making it impossible to add other devices.

The signal must also pass through a Network Termination-2 (NT2) interface. It's unlikely that you'll have to deal with that interface directly because it is built into the ISDN equipment, and not a separate device. From here, the circuit can now be interconnected with the user's equipment. It sounds pretty complicated, but since much of this can be integrated into the equipment supplied by your provider, it need not be intimidating. **Figure 20.6** shows a block diagram of a complete ISDN circuit.

This equipment will fall under one of two categories. Devices that are designed around ISDN are Terminal Equipment-1 (TE1) devices. Those devices that were originally designed to interface with conventional telephone lines are designated Terminal Equipment-2 (TE2). In order to interconnect TE2 devices, you're going to need a terminal adapter (TA). A TA brings the ISDN into your building and provides either RJ-45 ports or a standard serial port for interconnecting to your computer. An ISDN modem is a prime example of a TA.

By using a channel aggregation protocol, the two incoming channels can be combined into a single 128K connection. The two protocols most commonly used are Bonding (Bandwidth on Demand) and Multilink-PPP. The latter is the more recently introduced protocol and is supposedly superior in its error handling capabilities.

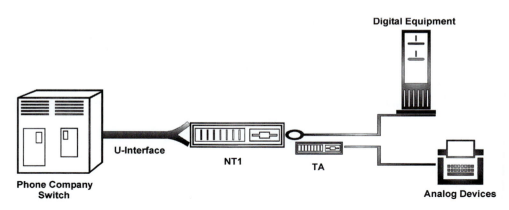

Figure 20.6 The makings of ISDN

It isn't necessary to combine the two channels if your requirements are not purely data transmission. The signals can be separated, allowing voice over one and data over the other.

CAUTION: While the TA provides an RJ-45 connection, you must pay attention to the type of TA installed. Plugging an analog device into a digital circuit will kill that device. If a TA is designed for analog circuits, it will have a port labeled either A/B or POTS (an acronym for plain old telephone service). Along those same lines (figuratively speaking), it is essential that, in an office environment, you know if a digital telephone system is in place. If you plug the analog modem in your laptop into a digital line, you'll be shopping for a new modem that afternoon. The one you plugged into a digital line will be fried.

Throughout this book, I've made mention of specific programming interfaces for different types of hardware. The Common ISDN Advanced Programming Interface (CAPI) is the one used by Windows to interface with ISDN. CAPI intercepts programming calls made directly to the ISDN and directs them to the correct port. This is how multiple applications can access the device.

DSL

An increasing number of people are finding that Digital Subscriber Lines (DSL) are the answer to their bandwidth needs. The beauty of DSL is that it comes in over your regular telephone wires. Therefore, you don't have a bunch of people coming into your building, ripping and tearing. And since it comes in on a different frequency than standard telephone service, you can make a phone call while your DSL connection is active, without having to pay for a second telephone line.

DSL has a lot of advantages over standard telephone service or ISDN. Then again, there are some disadvantages as well. I'll look at both, starting with the advantages.

- *Speed*: A DSL line, depending on your provider and the distance you are from its central office, can provide up to 1.5Mbps.
- *Cost*: In order to approach that speed with ISDN, you would need a PRI with the maximum number of available channels. This would cost substantially more than typical DSL rates.
- *Convenience*: No new lines need to be run into your building. Existing telephone lines work fine.
- *Multifunction access*: The DSL connection and the telephone lines can be simultaneously active.
- *One-stop shopping*: In most cases, your provider comes in with all the hardware you'll need to make the connection.

But as I mentioned, DSL is not without its shortcomings. It isn't for everyone, and quite frankly, at this point in time, it isn't available to everyone. Some of the disadvantages include:

- *Availability*: Currently, DSL is only being offered in higher-population centers.
- *Location*: You have to be within a certain distance from the main office or the company can't hook you up. Under ideal circumstances the maximum distance from the switching station is 18,000 feet.
- *Consistency*: The farther you get from the main office, the slower your connection gets. You might get 1.5Mbps at work, but less than 400K at home.
- *Disparity between incoming and outgoing signals*: The connection from your ISP to you is four to six times faster than the connection from you to them.

The concept behind DSL is that the wires used by your telephone are severely under-utilized. The copper wires are perfectly capable of carrying signals of several gigahertz, yet the telephone line is lazing along at 3.4K. DSL takes advantage of the rest of that bandwidth. It is technically possible to provide bandwidth in excess of 8Mbps over a DSL link (although current FCC regulations limit service to 1.5Mbps).

However, as I mentioned earlier, there are some distance limitations involved. The maximum distance that a signal can be run is around 18,000 feet, or slightly more than three miles. As that distance increases, throughput drops.

Even if you live with 18,000 feet of the main office, you might find that you can't get DSL service. There are several factors that can knock you out of the loop:

- *Distances can be deceiving*: The main office may be less than 18,000 feet away as the crow flies. But the wires may loop up and down several blocks, back and forth, before they reach your location. Therefore, there might be more than 18,000 feet of cable separating you from it.

■ *Fiber-optic cables*: DSL signals can't do the digital-to-analog, analog-to-digital conversions needed to send the signal over fiber-optic cables. Therefore, a fiber-optic circuit is a glass wall that blocks the signal.

■ *Bridge taps*: These are circuits that are inserted into the line that route service to other customers. They add to the total length of the circuit and can force you to logically be more that 18,000 feet away.

■ *Loading coils*: These are small devices that clean up and regenerate the analog signal that carries voice over the telephone wire. DSL is incompatible with loading coils. They are like a brick wall that blocks the signal.

There are two devices that make DSL work. One of these, the DSL transceiver, is installed on the subscriber's end. Sometimes you'll see this device referred to as the DSL modem, but that is an inaccurate term. In that the data that passes over DSL is purely digital, no modulation or demodulation is necessary. This device will accept the incoming signal and send it out to either an RJ-45 port or a USB port. Many times, you will find devices that combine the functions of either a hub, switch, or router with the transceiver, making it a multifunction device.

On the service provider's end, a device called a DSL Access Multiplexer (DSLAM) is installed to combine the incoming signals from all the customers into a single huge connection to the Internet. The DSLAM will provide other services, such as dynamic IP assignment and routing functions.

One of the things that you'll see about cable modems in the next section is that, under that technology, as you add users to the loop, performance drops. The DSLAM prevents this from happening. As long as the total bandwidth used by users currently active does not exceed the ISP's connection to the Internet backbone, all will be well.

CABLE MODEMS

Another increasingly popular connection to the Internet merges your cable TV services with your Internet service. To understand how cable modems do their thing, it is probably a good idea if you understand how basic cable television service works.

In the good old days, you were lucky if you had two channels that your TV could pick up, unless you lived in or near a big city. Then you might be able to get four or five. Because standard network television is freely available to the public, it has to be supported through the commercials that you've all grown to know and love. Also, content is carefully monitored.

The alternative that was offered involved piping in as many signals as possible into a central location and sending them out over wires to those who were willing to help pay for the service. This became known as cable TV. With cable, it became possible to combine hundreds of different channels over a broadband connection. It also became possible to pick and choose what signals a service provider sent out to a specific household, and subscription services became possible.

It was a logical move from providing television service to providing Internet access. After all, you've already got the infrastructure laid out. A coaxial cable can carry bandwidth approaching nearly a gigahertz, and each TV channel only occupies 6MHz. Even with 150 channels, there's plenty of bandwidth still available on the wire. So why not use it for Internet access? The biggest obstacle was getting the FCC to approve it. Once FCC approval was obtained, the way was cleared for any cable TV provider to add Internet access as an option.

The device that makes it possible is the cable modem. And in this case, it really is a modem. The cable modem is broken down into the following components:

- *The tuner*: This makes sure that the Internet stays the Internet and that the History Channel stays the History Channel.

- *The modulator/demodulator*: This performs the same function as your analog modem.

- *A Media Access Control (MAC) interface*: This provides access to the wire for your computer. (See Chapter Thirty-Two, The Hardware of the Network, for more information on this subject.)

- *A microprocessor*: Prevents the process of converting a cable signal to a computer signal from overloading the computer's CPU.

- *A network interface*: Provides access to the signal by your computer. Typically, this is a standard RJ-45 connector.

When I was discussing DSL services, I talked about the function of the DSLAM. On a cable network, a device called the Cable Modem Termination System (CMTS) handles that function. It is the CMTS that bundles all of the customers' Internet connections and pipes them to the backbone. The service provider uses standard DHCP services (see Chapter Thirty-Two, The Hardware of the Network) to hand out IP addresses.

The CMTS takes a single 6MHz channel and uses it to pipe Internet services to customers. This provides bandwidth that can approach 40Mbps. Up to 1000 customers can be bundled into a single channel. The more people on the channel, the less bandwidth there is available for each user.

This also opens up a potential security issue. Since all the users on a channel are sharing bandwidth, it is pretty much the same thing as putting them all on the same network. Let's assume for a moment that you're one of the growing number of people out there that have several computers in their home and have decided to network them. In order to make your network functional, you needed to share out files and directories that needed to be accessed by the machines on your network. So you've shared out the My Documents directory on computer A. Now you can go to computer B or computer C and double-click Entire Network and see those folders.

And so can your neighbors if they happen to be online at the same time as you. Therefore, it is imperative that you install some form of firewall to protect your computer from intrusion by others. A *firewall* is a logical barrier that allows people on

BUZZ WORDS

Firewall: A hardware or software barrier that allows access to external networks for users inside the firewall, but denies access from the outside.

your side to get out to the outside world, but keeps the outside world from getting in. You can create a firewall in one of two ways. Some companies, like Bay Networks, manufacture cable modem routers that have a hardware firewall built in. This is the method that will provide the fastest performance, and quite frankly, the devices aren't that expensive. It is the method I most strongly recommend.

If your security needs aren't that stringent, there are software firewalls that can be installed on your local machines that do the same job. However, because they are software based, they are using memory and CPU resources that could be put to better use elsewhere. My experience with software firewalls is that, while they can be every bit as effective as a hardware firewall, the commercial versions can cost every bit as much as an inexpensive hardware device, and the hardware device won't result in a degradation of performance.

HIGH-SPEED WAN CONNECTIONS

The aforementioned technologies pretty much cover the range available to household communications. Business-to-business connections can be substantially more complicated and are the subject of several different books all by themselves. I thought it would be useful to include a list of options along with some of the speeds you can expect. While no means an all-inclusive list, **Table 20.5** covers the vast majority of telecommunications links in use today.

CHAPTER SUMMARY

In this chapter I have provided a brief overview of the ways different computers can link together remotely. You can clearly see that this technology has come a long way from the days of 300bps modems to the present situation of DSL links in every home (well, a lot of homes, anyway).

Still, this is only scratching surface of this technology. Some companies are predicting that before this decade is out, the vast majority of computers across the world will have a capacity for communication over high-speed wireless links at speeds we can only dream of now. It's going to be fun to watch.

Table 20.5   Overview of High-Speed Telecommunications Links

Technology	Appx. Speed	Description
ISDN-BRI	128.0K	BRI (Basic Rate Interface) 2x64K B-channels, 1x64K D-channel
Euro-ISDN	144.0K	128K usable. Allows full transparent internetworking between all European countries
B-ISDN	1.500M	Broadband Integrated Services Digital Network
G.lite	1.500M	18,000 feet Asymmetric Digital Subscriber Line, sends at 512K, receives at 1.5M
IDSL	1.500M	18,000 ft, DSL over ISDN, sends 64K-1.5M, receives 1.5-9M
Cable Modem	1.500M	Sends at 10M, receives at 56M (on a good day, with a tailwind)
DS1	1.544M	Digital Signal Level 1, 24 Channels (1xT1)
HDSL	1.544M	12,000 ft, High bit-rate DSL, sends at 2.048M, receives at 1.544M
SDSL	1.544M	12,000 ft, Symmetric DSL, sends at 2.048M, receives at 1.544M
T1	1.544M	Digital Trunk Line 1, 24 Channels (1xT1)
ISDN-PRI	1.544M	Primary Rate Interface 23x64K B-channels, 1x64K D-channel on T1, 23B+D
Euro-ISDN/PRI	2.048M	Primary Rate Interface 30x64K B-channels, 1x64K D-channel on E1, 30B+D
16C952	3.000M	Dual-channel version of the 16950 UART
DS1c	3.152M	Digital Signal Level 1c, 48 Channels (2xT1)
T1c	3.152M	Digital Trunk Line 1c, 48 Channels (2xT1)
UMTS	3.500M	Universal Mobile Telephone System
DS2	6.312M	Digital Signal Level 2, 96 Channels (4xT1)
T2	6.312M	Digital Trunk Line 2,96 Channels (4xT1)
ADSL	8.000M	Asymmetric DSL, sends at 1.500M, receives at 8.000M
E2	8.448M	120 Channels, Europe & Japan
CAIS bus	10.000M	Common Airborne Instrumentation System
RS-485	10.000M	4000ft, Balanced line interface, 2-wire, half-duplex, differential.
RS-530	10.000M	30km, Fiber-optic point-to-point
Wireless LAN	11.000M	Limited Range Wireless Ethernet
DS3	44.736M	Digital Signal Level 3, 672 Channels (28xT1)
T3	44.736M	Digital Trunk Line 3, 672 Channels (28xT1)
V-ADSL	51.000M	51.00M at 1000 feet, drops to 25.600Mbps from 3000-4000 feet

(Continued)

Table 20.5 Overview of High-Speed Telecommunications Links

Technology	Appx. Speed	Description
STS-1	51.840M	Synchronous Transport Signal, Level 1
OC1	51.840M	Optical Carrier 1, fiber-optic networks
VDSL	52.000M	Very high speed DSL, upstream data = 1.5-2.3M, downstream data = 13-52M
DS3c	89.472M	Digital Signal Level 3c, 1344 Channels (56xT1)
T3c	89.472M	Digital Trunk Line 3c, 1344 Channels (56xT1)
DS3d	135.000M	Digital Signal Level 3d, (87xT1)
T3d	135.000M	Digital Trunk Line 3d, (87xT1)
OC3c	155.520M	Optical Carrier 3, fiber-optic internet backbone
DS4	274.176M	Digital Signal Level 4, 4032 Channels (168xT1)
T4	274.176M	Digital Trunk Line 4, 4032 Channels (168xT1)
STM-3	466.560M	Synchronous Transport Module, Level 3
STS-9	466.560M	Synchronous Transport Signal, Level 9
OC9	466.560M	Optical Carrier 9, fiber-optic networks
ATM	622.000M	Asynchronous Transfer Mode
STM-4	622.080M	Synchronous Transport Module, Level 4
STS-12	622.080M	Synchronous Transport Signal, Level 12
OC12c	622.080M	Optical Carrier 12
OC18	933.120M	Optical Carrier 18
WidebandATM	1.000G	Gigabit Ethernet over fiber-optic cable.
OC24	1.244G	Optical Carrier 24
OC36	1.866G	Optical Carrier 36
SONET	2.488G	Synchronous Optical Network
STM-16	2,488G	Synchronous Transport Module, Level 16
STS-48	2,488G	Synchronous Transport Signal, Level 48
OC48c	2.488G	Optical Carrier 48
OC96	4.976G	Optical Carrier 96
FLAG	5.300G	Fiber-optic Link Around the Globe, 27,300km linking Great Britain and Japan.
OC192c	9.953G	Optical Carrier 192, fiber-optic networks
OC256	13.271G	Optical Carrier 256, fiber-optic networks
OC768	39.813G	Optical Carrier 768, fiber-optic networks
OC3072	159.252G	Optical Carrier 3072, fiber-optic networks

The variety of different broadband communications options used around the world is actually staggering.

BRAIN DRAIN

1. Describe in detail two main tricks a modem must perform to transmit data over a telephone wire.

2. In your own words explain why, if a modem is connected at 53.2K, data is only moving at 4.2K.

3. Describe in detail how asynchronous communication works and where it might be used.

4. Describe in detail how synchronous communication works and where it might be used.

5. What are some limitations of DSL?

THE 64K$ QUESTIONS

1. What device on a modem is responsible for serial/parallel conversions?
   a. The UART
   b. The DAC
   c. The RAMDAC
   d. The RJ-11

2. What device on a modem is responsible for digital/analog conversions?
   a. The UART
   b. The DAC
   c. The RAMDAC
   d. The RJ-11

3. A device that can only transmit data, but not receive it, is working in _____ mode.
   a. Duplex
   b. Condominium
   c. Simplex
   d. Half duplex

4. A V.92 modem is capable of 53,200 baud.
   a. True
   b. False

5. When transferring large files, most modems manufactured today use _____ as their error correction method.
   a. Parity
   b. Checksum
   c. CRC
   d. NACK

6. You just finished installing a Plug 'n Play soft modem and the computer doesn't even see it during POST. What is the most likely cause of the problem?
   a. An IRQ conflict
   b. An I/O address conflict
   c. A COM port is not available
   d. A UART is not available

7. Basic Rate ISDN provides _____.
   a. Two 64K B-channels and one 64K D-channel
   b. Twenty-three 64K B-channels and one 64K D-channel
   c. Two 64K B-channels and one 16K D-channel
   d. Two 64K B-channels and two 16K D-channels

8. A key reason DSL has not achieved greater market penetration than it has is because _____.
   a. It costs too much
   b. It is too difficult to configure
   c. It is too severely regulated
   d. The subscriber has to be within 18,000 feet of the central office

9. Cable modem users should ALWAYS install a _____.
   a. Tuner
   b. Firewall
   c. HSDL
   d. Security password

10. Which of the following services is purely digital, end to end?
   a. POTS
   b. ISDN
   c. Cable
   d. DSL

TRICKY TERMINOLOGY

Answer modem: The device that is being called.

B-channel: A carrier channel used by ISDN for transmitting user data at 64Kbps. Multiple B-channels can be combined for higher transmission rates.

Baud rate: The electronic frequency over which data is transmitted.

Bit rate: The speed at which data travels over the wire, usually expressed in bits per second (bps) or kilobits per second (Kbps). Don't confuse this with bytes per second, and don't confuse it with baud rate.

Checksum: An error detection/correction mechanism that works by counting the number of ones present in the payload and storing that value in the BCC block of the packet.

D-channel: A 16Kbps or 64Kbps channel used by ISDN for control data, including synchronization, ACKs and NACKs and other nonuser data.

Duplex: A communications method by which a device can be transmitting and receiving at the same time.

Firewall: A hardware or software barrier that allows access to external networks for users inside the firewall, but denies access from the outside.

Half duplex: A communications method by which a device can either transmit or receive, but not both at the same time.

Initialization string: A series of AT commands that are issued by the originate modem during the connection process.

Message block: A piece of data being transmitted by a modem that represents a portion of the overall data being sent.

Modem: Modulator/demodulator. A device that converts parallel digital signals into serial analog signals for transmission over a wire.

Originate modem: The device that initiates a call.

Simplex: A communications method by which a device can either transmit or receive but cannot do both.

Transmission rate: The number of bits per second that is being transmitted.

ACRONYM ALERT

BCC: The Block Check Character. Includes error detection and correction data, which may include parity (rarely used these days), checksum (on its way out), or cyclical redundancy check (the most common method in use today).

BRI: Basic Rate ISDN. Two 64K B-channels and one 16K D-channel.

CMTS: Cable Modem Termination System. A device on the ISP's end that combines all incoming cable modem signals into a single channel for transmission over the Internet backbone.

DSL: Digital Subscriber Line. A broadband high-speed data connection that moves over standard telephone cable.

DSLAM: DSL Access Multiplexer. A device on the ISP's end that combines all incoming DSL signals into a single channel for transmission over the Internet backbone.

DSP: Digital Signal Processor. A chip that performs multiple processing functions on a signal. For example, the DSP on a modem combines the functions of a UART and a DAC.

EOT: End of Transmission. I hope I don't have to explain that one.

ETX: End of Text. Okay, I'm done sending text in this block. The next bytes are more control information.

ISDN: Integrated Services Digital Network. A telecommunications technology that provides high-speed data transfer over standard telephone lines.

PRI: Primary Rate ISDN. Twenty-three 64K B-channels and one 64K D-channel.

QAM: Quadrature Amplitude Modulation. A method of encoding data sent over a modem using a combination of frequency-shifting and phase shift-keying.

SOH: Start of Header. A header is not always used, but is an important part of most protocols.

STX: Start of Text. Pretty self-explanatory. It tells you that the next series of bits is the data being sent.

SYN: Synchronization character. This makes sure all the bytes in the frame stick together as they move across the wire and then get reassembled in the right order at the other end. If no data is being transmitted, SYN blocks can be transmitted to keep the session alive.

PART 2

A+ GUIDE TO PC OPERATING SYSTEMS

INTRODUCTION

A+ OPERATING SYSTEM TECHNOLOGIES

CompTIA's A+ certification program is an extensive testing program designed to demonstrate the examinees' proficiency working with personal computers. In order to achieve full certification, the examinee must pass two exams. The first is the A+ Core Hardware examination. Material for this exam was covered in Part 1.

Part 2 of this book prepares the candidate for the Operating System Technologies examination. This exam measures essential operating system competencies for an entry-level IT professional or PC service technician. This is not intended to be a "paper certification." It is assumed that candidates who attempt the exam go in with the equivalent knowledge of at least 500 hours of hands-on experience in the lab or field.

While the vast majority of CompTIA's certification programs are vendor neutral, this is one exam where it makes an exception. Operating systems covered on the exam include Microsoft products, including Windows versions 95, 98, 98SE, Me, 2000, and XP. Non-Microsoft operating systems are not covered.

The Operating System Technologies exam has been broken down into four different categories CompTIA calls domains. These domains are not given equal treatment or exposure on the exam. **Table I.1** itemizes the four domains and their relative predominance on the exam.

Each domain is subsequently broken down into a series of objectives. These objectives represent areas of knowledge for which CompTIA assumes the entry-level technician should be able to demonstrate adequate knowledge. The rest of this introduction, which lists more specifically the content that will be covered in each domain, has been extracted from the information available on CompTIA's Web site at www.comptia.org. I have added to the list chapters where you will find information addressing each objective.

Table I.1 OS Technologies Exam Domains

Domain	Percent of Examination
1.0 Operating System Fundamentals	28%
2.0 Installation, Configuration, and Upgrading	31%
3.0 Diagnosing and Troubleshooting	25%
4.0 Networks	16%
Total	**100%**

CompTIA A+ Operating System Objectives

DOMAIN 1: OPERATING SYSTEM FUNDAMENTALS

1.1 IDENTIFY THE MAJOR DESKTOP COMPONENTS AND INTERFACES AND THEIR FUNCTIONS. DIFFERENTIATE THE CHARACTERISTICS OF WINDOWS 9X/ME, WINDOWS NT 4.0 WORKSTATION, WINDOWS 2000 PROFESSIONAL, AND WINDOWS XP.

Content may include the following:

- Contrasts between Windows 9x/Me, Windows NT 4.0 Workstation, Windows 2000 Professional, and Windows XP (Chapter 23, Chapter 24, Chapter 25, Chapter 26, Chapter 27, Chapter 28, Chapter 29, and Chapter 30)
- Major operating system components (Chapter 2, Chapter 21, Chapter 25, Chapter 27, Chapter 29, and Chapter 30)
  - Registry (Chapter 24)
  - Virtual memory (Chapter 22, Chapter 24, Chapter 27, and Chapter 30)
  - File system (Chapter 2, Chapter 24, Chapter 25, and Chapter 30)
- Major operating system interfaces (Chapter 2, Chapter 21, Chapter 22, Chapter 23, Chapter 25, Chapter 27, and Chapter 30)
  - Windows Explorer (Chapter 23)
  - My Computer (Chapter 23 and Chapter 29)
  - Control Panel (Chapter 23 and Chapter 29)
  - Computer Management Console (Chapter 31)
  - Accessories/System tools (Chapter 23, Chapter 24, Chapter 28, and Chapter 30)
  - Command line (Chapter 22)
  - Network Neighborhood/My Network Places (Chapter 24 and Chapter 29)
  - Task Bar/Systray (Chapter 24)

- Start Menu (Chapter 24, Chapter 28, and Chapter 30)
- Device Manager (Chapter 24, Chapter 28, and Chapter 30)

1.2 Identify the names, locations, purposes, and contents of major system files.

Content may include the following:

- Windows 9x specific files (Chapter 23)
    - IO.SYS (Chapter 23)
    - MSDOS.SYS (Chapter 23)
    - AUTOEXEC.BAT (Chapter 23)
    - COMMAND.COM (Chapter 23)
    - CONFIG.SYS (Chapter 23)
    - HIMEM.SYS (Chapter 23)
    - EMM386.exe (Chapter 23)
    - WIN.COM (Chapter 23)
    - SYSTEM.INI (Chapter 23)
    - WIN.INI (Chapter 23)
    - Registry data files (Chapter 23)
        SYSTEM.DAT (Chapter 23)
        USER.DAT (Chapter 23)
- Windows NT specific files (Chapter 25 and Chapter 26)
    - BOOT.INI (Chapter 25 and Chapter 26)
    - NTLDR (Chapter 25 and Chapter 26)
    - NTDETECT.COM (Chapter 25 and Chapter 26)
    - NTBOOTDD.SYS (Chapter 25 and Chapter 26)
    - NTUSER.DAT (Chapter 25 and Chapter 26)
    - Registry data files (Chapter 23 and Chapter 25)

1.3 Demonstrate the ability to use command-line functions and utilities to manage the operating system, including the proper syntax and switches.

Command line functions and utilities include:

- Command/CMD (Chapter 23 and Chapter 25)
- DIR (Chapter 21)
- ATTRIB (Chapter 21)
- VER (Chapter 21)
- MEM (Chapter 21)

- SCANDISK (Chapter 23)
- DEFRAG (Chapter 23)
- EDIT (Chapter 21)
- XCOPY (Chapter 21)
- COPY (Chapter 21)
- FORMAT (Chapter 21)
- FDISK (Chapter 21)
- SETVER (Chapter 21)
- SCANREG (Chapter 24)
- MD/CD/RD (Chapter 21)
- DELETE/RENAME (Chapter 21)
- DELTREE (Chapter 21)
- TYPE (Chapter 21)
- ECHO (Chapter 21)
- SET (Chapter 21)
- PING (Chapter 33)

1.4 IDENTIFY BASIC CONCEPTS AND PROCEDURES FOR CREATING, VIEWING, AND MANAGING DISKS, DIRECTORIES, AND FILES. THIS INCLUDES PROCEDURES FOR CHANGING FILE ATTRIBUTES AND THE RAMIFICATIONS OF THOSE CHANGES (FOR EXAMPLE, SECURITY ISSUES).

Content may include the following:

- Disks
  - Partitions (Chapter 2, Chapter 27, and Chapter 30)
    Active Partition (Chapter 2)
    Primary Partition (Chapter 2)
    Extended Partition (Chapter 2)
    Logical Partition (Chapter 2 and Chapter 30)
  - Files systems
    FAT16 (Chapter 2)
    FAT32 (Chapter 2)
    NTFS4 (Chapter 2 and Chapter 25)
    NTFS5.x (Chapter 2 and Chapter 30)
- Directory structures (root directory, subdirectories, etc.) (Chapter 2)
  - Create folders (Chapter 24, Lab Manual)

- Navigate the directory structure (Chapter 2 and Chapter 24, Lab Manual)
- Maximum depth (Chapter 2)

■ Files (Chapter 2)

- Creating files (Chapter 2 and Chapter 24, Lab Manual)
- File naming conventions (Most common extensions, 8.3, maximum length) (Chapter 2)
- File attributes (Read Only, Hidden, System, and Archive attributes) (Chapter 2)
- File compression (Chapter 2, Chapter 24, and Chapter 28)
- File encryption (Chapter 28 and Chapter 30)
- File permissions (Chapter 25)
- File types (text vs. binary file) (Chapter 2)

1.5 Identify the major operating system utilities, their purpose, location, and available switches.

Content may include the following:

■ Disk management tools

DEFRAG.EXE (Chapter 24 and Lab Manual)
FDISK.EXE (Chapter 2, Lab Manual)
Backup/Restore Utilities (MSbackup, NTBackup, etc.) (Chapter 24, Chapter 25, Chapter 28, and Chapter 30)
ScanDisk (Chapter 24, Lab Manual)
CHKDSK (Chapter 21 and Chapter 24, Lab Manual)
Disk Cleanup (Chapter 24, Lab Manual)
Format (Chapter 2, Lab Manual)

■ System management tools

Device Manager (Chapter 24 and Chapter 30, Lab Manual)
System Monitor (Chapter 24)
Computer Manager (Chapter 28)
MSCONFIG.EXE (Chapter 24, Lab Manual)
REGEDIT.EXE (View information/Backup registry) (Chapter 23)
REGEDT32.EXE (Chapter 23, Lab Manual)
SYSEDIT.EXE (Chapter 23, Lab Manual)
SCANREG (Chapter 21, Lab Manual)
COMMAND/CMD (Chapter 21 and Chapter 23, Lab Manual)
Event Viewer (Chapter 27, Lab Manual)
Task Manager (Chapter 24, Lab Manual)

■ File management tools

ATTRIB.EXE (Chapter 21)
EXTRACT.EXE (Lab Manual)
EDIT.COM (Chapter 21)

Windows Explorer (Chapter 24, Chapter 25, Chapter 28, and Chapter 30)

DOMAIN 2: INSTALLATION, CONFIGURATION, AND UPGRADING

2.1 IDENTIFY THE PROCEDURES FOR INSTALLING WINDOWS 9x/Me, WINDOWS NT 4.0 WORKSTATION, WINDOWS 2000 PROFESSIONAL, AND WINDOWS XP AND BRINGING THE OPERATING SYSTEM TO A BASIC OPERATIONAL LEVEL.

Content may include the following:

- Verify hardware compatibility and minimum requirements (Chapter 23, Chapter 25, Chapter 27, and Chapter 30)

- Determine OS installation options (Chapter 25, Chapter 28, and Chapter 30)
  - Installation type (typical, custom, other) (Chapter 25, Lab Manual)
  - Network configuration (Chapter 25, Chapter 28, and Chapter 30, Lab Manual)
  - File system type (Chapter 2, Chapter 28, and Chapter 30)
  - Dual boot support (Chapter 25, Lab Manual)

- Disk preparation order (conceptual disk preparation) (Chapter 25 and Chapter 28, Lab Manual)
  - Start the installation (Chapter 24, Chapter 25, and Chapter 28, Lab Manual)
  - Partition (Chapter 2, Chapter 21, Chapter 24, and Chapter 28, Lab Manual)
  - Format drive (Chapter 2, Chapter 21, Chapter 24, and Chapter 28, Lab Manual)

- Run appropriate setup utility (Chapter 21, Chapter 24, Chapter 28, and Chapter 30, Lab Manual)
  - Setup (Chapter 2, Chapter 21, Chapter 24, and Chapter 28, Lab Manual)
  - Winnt (Chapter 25)

- Installation methods (Chapter 24, Chapter 25, and Chapter 28, Lab Manual)
  - Bootable CD (Chapter 24 and Chapter 28, Lab Manual)
  - Boot floppy (Chapter 24 and Chapter 25, Lab Manual)
  - Network installation (Chapter 25 and Chapter 30)
  - Drive imaging (Lab Manual)

- Device driver configuration (Chapter 2, Chapter 21, Chapter 23, Chapter 24, Chapter 25, Chapter 28, and Chapter 30, Lab Manual)
  - Load default drivers (Chapter 24 and Chapter 28)
  - Find updated drivers (Lab Manual)
- Restore user data files (if applicable) (Chapter 23 and Chapter 24, Lab Manual)
- Identify common symptoms and problems (Chapter 21, Chapter 22, Chapter 23, Chapter 24, Chapter 25, Chapter 26, Chapter 27, Chapter 28, Chapter 29, and Chapter 30, Lab Manual)

2.2 Identify steps to perform an operating system upgrade from Windows 9.x/Me, Windows NT 4.0 Workstation, Windows 2000 Professional, and Windows XP. Given an upgrade scenario, choose the appropriate next steps.

Content may include the following:

- Upgrade paths available (Chapter 23, Chapter 24, Chapter 26, Chapter 28, and Chapter 30)
- Determine correct upgrade startup utility (e.g. WINNT32 vs. WINNT) (Chapter 26 and Chapter 28)
- Verify hardware compatibility and minimum requirements (Chapter 23, Chapter 25, Chapter 27, and Chapter 30)
- Verify application compatibility (Chapter 25)
- Apply OS service packs, patches, and updates (Chapter 25, Chapter 26, and Chapter 28)
- Install additional Windows components (Chapter 30, Lab Manual)

2.3 Identify the basic system boot sequences and boot methods, including the steps to create an emergency boot disk with utilities installed for Windows 9x/Me, Windows NT 4.0 Workstation, Windows 2000 Professional, and Windows XP.

Content may include the following:

- Boot sequence (Chapter 21, Chapter 24, and Chapter 26)
  - Files required to boot (Chapter 21, Chapter 24, and Chapter 26)
  - Boot steps (9x, NT-based) (Chapter 21, Chapter 24, and Chapter 26)

- Alternative boot methods (Chapter 23, Lab Manual)
  - Using a startup disk (Chapter 21, Chapter 23, and Chapter 26, Lab Manual)
  - Safe/VGA-only mode (Chapter 24 and Chapter 28, Lab Manual)
  - Last Known Good configuration (Chapter 27, Chapter 28, and Chapter 30, Lab Manual)
  - Command Prompt mode (Chapter 21 and Chapter 24)
  - Booting to a system restore point (Chapter 23 and Chapter 30, Lab Manual)
  - Recovery console (Chapter 28)
  - BOOT.INI switches (Lab Manual)
  - Dual boot (Chapter 25, Lab Manual)
- Creating emergency disks with OS utilities (Chapter 24 and Chapter 27, Lab Manual)
- Creating emergency repair disk (ERD) (Chapter 25 and Chapter 28, Lab Manual)

2.4 IDENTIFY PROCEDURES FOR INSTALLING/ADDING A DEVICE, INCLUDING LOADING, ADDING, AND CONFIGURING DEVICE DRIVERS AND REQUIRED SOFTWARE.

Content may include the following:

- Device driver installation (Chapter 24 and Chapter 28, Lab Manual)
  - Plug 'n Play (PNP) and non-PNP devices (Chapter 23)
  - Install and configure device drivers (Chapter 24 and Chapter 28, Lab Manual)
  - Install different device drivers (Lab Manual)
  - Manually install a device driver (Lab Manual)
  - Search the Internet for updated device drivers (Chapter 29)
  - Using unsigned drivers (driver signing) (Chapter 29)
- Install additional Windows components (Chapter 23 and Chapter 30)
- Determine whether permissions are adequate for performing the task (Chapter 26, Lab Manual)

2.5 IDENTIFY PROCEDURES NECESSARY TO OPTIMIZE THE OPERATING SYSTEM AND MAJOR OPERATING SYSTEM SUBSYSTEMS.

Content may include the following:

- Virtual memory management (Chapter 2, Chapter 22, and Chapter 26)
- Disk defragmentation (Chapter 21 and Chapter 24, Lab Manual)
- Files and buffers (Chapter 21)
- Caches (Chapter 26, Chapter 28, and Chapter 33)
- Temporary file management (Chapter 21, Chapter 22, Chapter 24, Chapter 25, and Chapter 30)

DOMAIN 3: DIAGNOSING AND TROUBLESHOOTING

3.1 RECOGNIZE AND INTERPRET THE MEANING OF COMMON ERROR CODES AND STARTUP MESSAGES FROM THE BOOT SEQUENCE, AND IDENTIFY STEPS TO CORRECT THE PROBLEMS.

Content may include the following:

- Common error messages and codes
  - Boot failure and errors (Chapter 23, Chapter 27, Chapter 29, and Chapter 35)
    Invalid boot disk (Lab Manual)
    Inaccessible boot device (Chapter 28, Lab Manual)
    Missing NTLDR (Chapter 28, Lab Manual)
    Bad or missing Command interpreter (Lab Manual)
  - Startup messages
    Error in CONFIG.SYS line XX (Chapter 21, Lab Manual)
    HIMEM.SYS not loaded (Lab Manual)
    Missing or corrupt HIMEM.SYS (Lab Manual)
    Device/Service has failed to start (Chapter 27, Lab Manual)
  - A device referenced in SYSTEM.INI, WIN.INI, Registry is not found (Lab Manual)
  - Event Viewer – Event log is full (Chapter 27, Lab Manual)
  - Failure to start GUI (Chapter 23, Lab Manual)
  - Windows Protection Error (Chapter 23, Lab Manual)
  - User-modified settings cause improper operation at startup (Lab Manual)
  - Registry corruption (Chapter 21, Chapter 22, Chapter 23, Chapter 27, Chapter 28, and Chapter 30)
- Using the correct utilities (Chapter 24, Chapter 25, Chapter 27, Chapter 28, Chapter 29, and Chapter 30, Lab Manual)
  - Dr. Watson (Chapter 23 and Chapter 27, Lab Manual)
  - Boot disk (Chapter 21, Chapter 23, and Chapter 26, Lab Manual)
  - Event Viewer (Chapter 27, Lab Manual)

3.2 RECOGNIZE WHEN TO USE COMMON DIAGNOSTIC UTILITIES AND TOOLS. GIVEN A DIAGNOSTIC SCENARIO INVOLVING ONE OF THESE UTILITIES OR TOOLS, SELECT THE APPROPRIATE STEPS NEEDED TO RESOLVE THE PROBLEM.

Utilities and tools may include the following:

- Startup disks (Chapter 21, Chapter 23, and 26, Lab Manual)
  - Required files for a boot disk (Chapter 21, Chapter 23, and Chapter 26, Lab Manual)
  - Boot disk with CD-ROM support (Chapter 21, Lab Manual)
- Startup modes (Chapter 23, Chapter 24, and Chapter 28, Lab Manual)

- Safe mode (Chapter 23, Chapter 24, and Chapter 28, Lab Manual)
- Safe Mode with command prompt (Chapter 23, Chapter 24, and Chapter 28, Lab Manual)
- Safe mode with networking (Chapter 23, Chapter 24, and Chapter 28, Lab Manual)
- Step-by-step/Single step mode (Chapter 23, Chapter 24, and Chapter 28, Lab Manual)
- Automatic skip driver (ASD.exe) (Chapter 28)

- Diagnostic tools, utilities, and resources (Chapter 24, Chapter 26, Chapter 27, Chapter 28, and Chapter 30, Lab Manual)

  - User/installation manuals (Chapter 31, Lab Manual)
  - Internet/web resources (Lab Manual)
  - Training materials (Lab Manual)
  - Task Manager (Chapter 23, Lab Manual)
  - Dr. Watson (Chapter 28, Lab Manual)
  - Boot disk (Chapter 21, Chapter 23, Chapter 28, and Chapter 30, Lab Manual)
  - Event Viewer (Chapter 28, Lab Manual)
  - Device Manager (Chapter 23, Lab Manual)
  - WinMSD (Lab Manual)
  - MSD (Chapter 21, Lab Manual)
  - Recovery CD (Chapter 25 and Chapter 28)
  - CONFIGSAFE (Chapter 23)

- Eliciting problem symptoms from customers (Chapter 35)

- Having customer reproduce error as part of the diagnostic process (Chapter 35)

- Identifying recent changes to the computer environment from the user (Chapter 24, Lab Manual)

3.3 RECOGNIZE COMMON OPERATIONAL AND USABILITY PROBLEMS AND DETERMINE HOW TO RESOLVE THEM.

Content may include the following:

- Troubleshooting Windows-specific printing problems
  - Print spool is stalled (Lab Manual)
  - Incorrect/incompatible driver for print (Lab Manual)
  - Incorrect parameter (Lab Manual)
- Other common problems
  - General Protection Faults (Chapter 23, Lab Manual)
  - Bluescreen errors (BSOD) (Chapter 28, Lab Manual)
  - Illegal operation (Chapter 15 and Chapter 27)
  - Invalid working directory (Chapter 2, Lab Manual)
  - System lock up (Chapter 2, Chapter 24, and Chapter 28, Lab Manual)

- Option (Sound card, modem, input device) or will not function (Chapter 23, Lab Manual)
- Application will not start or load (Lab Manual)
- Cannot log on to network (option—NIC not functioning) (Chapter 33)
- Applications don't install (Chapter 24 and Chapter 35)
- Network connection (Chapter 33, Lab Manual)

■ Viruses and virus types

- What they are (Chapter 35)
- TSR (Terminate Stay Resident) programs and virus (Chapter 21, Lab Manual)
- Sources (floppy, emails, etc.) (Chapter 34 and Chapter 35)
- How to determine presence (Lab Manual)

DOMAIN 4: NETWORKS

4.1 IDENTIFY THE NETWORKING CAPABILITIES OF WINDOWS. GIVEN CONFIGURATION PARAMETERS, CONFIGURE THE OPERATING SYSTEM TO CONNECT TO A NETWORK.

Content may include the following:

■ Configure protocols

- TCP/IP
  Gateway (Chapter 33, Lab Manual)
  Subnet mask (Chapter 33, Lab Manual)
  DNS (and domain suffix) (Chapter 33, Lab Manual)
  WINS (Chapter 33, Lab Manual)
  Static address assignment (Chapter 33, Lab Manual)
  Automatic address assignment (APIPA, DHCP) (Chapter 33, Lab Manual)
- IPX/SPX (NWLink) (Chapter 33)
- Appletalk (Chapter 33)
- NetBEUI/NetBIOS (Chapter 33, Lab Manual)

■ Configure Client options (Chapter 33, Lab Manual)

- Microsoft (Chapter 33)
- Novell (Chapter 33)

■ Verify the configuration (Chapter 33)

■ Understand the use of the following tools (Chapter 33)

- IPCONFIG.EXE (Chapter 33)
- WINIPCFG.EXE (Chapter 33)
- PING (Chapter 33)
- TRACERT.EXE (Chapter 33)
- NSLOOKUP.EXE (Chapter 33)

- Share resources (Understand the capabilities/limitations with each OS version) (Chapter 33)
- Setting permissions to shared resources (Chapter 33)
- Network type and network card (Chapter 33)

4.2 IDENTIFY THE BASIC INTERNET PROTOCOLS AND TERMINOLOGIES. IDENTIFY PROCEDURES FOR ESTABLISHING INTERNET CONNECTIVITY. IN A GIVEN SCENARIO, CONFIGURE THE OPERATING SYSTEM TO CONNECT TO AND USE INTERNET RESOURCES.

Content may include the following:

- Protocols and terminologies
  - ISP (Chapter 35)
  - TCP/IP (Chapter 33, Lab Manual)
  - E-mail (POP, SMTP, IMAP) (Chapter 33)
  - HTML (Chapter 35)
  - HTTP (Chapter 32)
  - HTTPS (Chapter 33)
  - SSL (Lab Manual)
  - Telnet (Lab Manual)
  - FTP (Chapter 33)
  - DNS (Chapter 33, Lab Manual)
- Connectivity technologies
  - Dial-up networking (Chapter 33 and Chapter 35)
  - DSL networking (Chapter 33)
  - ISDN networking (Chapter 33)
  - Cable (Chapter 33)
  - Satellite (Chapter 33)
  - Wireless (Chapter 33)
  - LAN (Chapter 33, Lab Manual)
- Installing and Configuring browsers (Lab Manual)
  - Enable/disable script support (Lab Manual)
  - Configure Proxy Settings (Chapter 33, Lab Manual)
  - Configure security settings (Lab Manual)
- Firewall protection under Windows XP (Lab Manual)

CHAPTER 21

MS-DOS AND THE COMMAND PROMPT

In Chapter Two of this book, I provided a general overview of the OS and how it interacts with the hardware in a system. It probably wouldn't hurt for you to go back and review that material once again before digging into Part Two of this book. From this point on I will be covering the general features of a variety of operating systems. Most of what will be covered is from Microsoft, but I will provide some functional basics of Unix and Linux as well. To kick off these discussions, I thought I would toss you feet first into the world of DOS.

First off, let me say that MS-DOS is no longer covered on CompTIA's A+ operating systems exam and hasn't been for a long time. A working knowledge of the command prompt is expected, however, and since the command prompt is a direct offshoot of the MS-DOS operating system, I feel very strongly that anyone who claims to be a working professional in the computer industry needs to have more than just a passing knowledge of the OS that started it all.

In this chapter, I will provide a brief history and overview of MS-DOS, followed by a discussion of some of the key commands still in use today by all of Microsoft's OSs anytime the command prompt is opened. And while the command prompt may not be a favorite place for the average computer user to spend much time, the working professional spends a good amount of time there. In addition to that, a vast amount of the technology used on the modern OS was derived directly from what you'll learn here. Get used to it, and get to know it well.

A+ OPERATING SYSTEM TECHNOLOGIES EXAM OBJECTIVES

There are two key CompTIA exam objectives covered in this section:

1.1 Identify the major desktop components and interfaces and their functions. Differentiate the characteristics of Windows 9x/Me, Windows NT 4.0 Workstation, Windows 2000 Professional, and Windows XP.

3.1 Recognize and interpret the meaning of common error codes and startup messages from the boot sequence, and identify steps to correct the problems.

A Brief History of MS-DOS

MS-DOS got its start in May, 1979 at the hands of a hardware company called the Seattle Computer Company. SCC was one of those companies that got off to an incredible start, and but for a few bad decisions might have been the pre-eminent company in the personal computer industry. Its first product had been a memory card for a personal computer known as the S100. IBM had not yet entered the fray with its version of a personal computer, and dozens of companies were competing for a market dominated primarily by Commodore, Timex, Osborne, and Kaypro. (Aren't those all name brands we constantly throw about these days?)

The release of a processor board based on Intel's 8086 microprocessor led SCC to develop an OS that would support the new product. The fact that it managed to throw together a workable OS in under three weeks lead to the whimsical name of QDOS, which was short for Quick and Dirty Operating System.

On a similar note, Microsoft had started an 8086 software-development program. It had developed a version of the BASIC programming language intended to run on the 8086. SCC and Microsoft decided to join forces and see what might happen. SCC provided Microsoft with some samples of its product, and the BASIC project was completed. In the last two weeks of May 1979 Seattle Computer Company displayed the complete package, including its computer running the OS along with Microsoft's 86-BASIC, in June 1979 at the New York National Computer Conference.

In 1980, SCC released a new version of the DOS that it called 86-DOS version 0.3. By this time, Microsoft had purchased nonexclusive rights to market 86-DOS. In July 1981 Microsoft bought all rights to DOS from Seattle Computer, and the name Microsoft Disk Operating System (MS-DOS) was adopted.

When IBM released the IBM PC, it was in need of an OS that would run on the 8088 microprocessor it had chosen to power its computer. IBM approached Microsoft, who almost immediately realized that only a slight reworking of the code was necessary. In 1981, Microsoft signed a licensing agreement with IBM to ship MS-DOS with its newly released IBM PC. Thus began the reign of one of the most powerful business entities ever known.

Some of the key features of MS-DOS actually read today like a litany of its limitations. However, to put it in perspective, it's only fair to remind you that in its day, the average personal computer (prior to the release of the IBM PC) had a 4.7MHz microprocessor and supported a maximum of 64 kilobytes of RAM. For those of you with 256MB installed, that's less than one twentieth of the amount of data you can store on a floppy disk.

There was no such thing as a hard disk drive (not for PCs anyway), the CD-ROM hadn't been invented, and what the heck was a scanner or a digital camera? In the summer of 1981, those who were affluent enough to afford the roughly $6000.00 that a fully equipped IBM PC cost were absolutely delighted that they were able to bring the power of an actual computer into their homes or offices.

The IBM PC with DOS 1.0 installed supported a single-sided 5.25″ floppy disk drive, up to 1MB of RAM (640K of which could be used for programs), and, if you were really rich, you could buy a monitor that actually displayed four colors!

FAT12 was the file system used (FAT16 would replace it on the subsequent release of the IBM PC-XT). There was no support for hard disks, since none had yet been invented for the PC. It used the 8.3 file naming convention discussed in Chapter Thirteen, and the closest thing to a graphical interface was a dark green background with a very coarse and grainy C:\ taunting the new user to figure out what to do next. MS-DOS would remain the only available choice of OSs for computer users for the next nine years, until the release of Windows 3.0, although it would go through several generations of development. In fact, DOS is still alive and relatively well today, being resurrected every time someone opens the command prompt in virtually any version of Windows. **Table 21.1** lists the various versions of MS-DOS over the years, along with a brief description of each version.

THE STRUCTURE OF MS-DOS

As with all operating systems, MS-DOS centers around a relatively small kernel and provides subroutines (usually called utilities) for the upper layers of its work. In MS-DOS, the three files that make up the kernel are IO.SYS, MSDOS.SYS, and COMMAND.COM. By necessity, these files have to be located in the root directory. Each of these files plays a key role and is worthy of a brief discussion.

IO.SYS

IO.SYS is a hidden, read-only file that, as its name implies, was responsible for managing the input/output functions of the OS. For you to understand its key role a basic review of computer hardware is in order.

In order for a computer system to boot, it requires the services of a collection of files and programs that must be run prior to booting the OS. These files are located on a Programmable Read-Only Memory (PROM) chip. Collectively, the files are known as the Basic Input Output Services (BIOS). Some of the files stored on the BIOS chip provide command support to the CPU for all the devices installed on the computer system. These files are called *interrupts*. This can get a bit confusing because the same word is used to describe the process by which a piece of hardware requests the attention of the CPU. An example of a BIOS interrupt is the command set that supports hard disk drives. It is called Int13h (the letter h indicates that the number 13 is a hexadecimal value and not a decimal value).

To explain what I mean by a BIOS interrupt, the CPU, even today, only hosts a limited number of native commands. All of the other devices on the system, including RAM, serial ports, parallel ports, and floppy (and other) drives, function by way of their own separate command set. Devices can't issue commands to the CPU, but they need to think they can. So when a device on the system needs to request the services of the CPU or to send data to the CPU, it will issue its commands to the interrupt. The interrupt will process those instructions and translate them into instructions the CPU can understand.

BUZZ WORDS

Interrupt: On a software level, it is a string of code that is called in order to perform a specific function. The BIOS uses software interrupts to manage hardware. On a hardware level, it is an electrical signal that notifies the CPU that a device needs to open communications (or vice versa).

Table 21.1   The Versions of DOS

Version	Date	Comments
1.0	1981	Renamed and slightly revised version of a program called QDOS, developed by Seattle Computer Company.
1.25	1982	Added support for double-sided floppy disks.
2.0	1983	First DOS version with support for hard disk drives and double-density 5.25" floppy disks with capacities of 360KB.
2.11	1983	Support for the Extended ASCII character set.
3.0	1984	Support for high-density (1.2MB) floppy disks; hard disk support increased to 32MB.
3.1	1984	Added network support.
3.3	1987	Added support for high-density 3.5" floppy disks, multiple partitions on hard disks, and for hard disks larger than 32MB.
4.0	1988	Provided support for partitions on hard disks up to 2GB, XMS support, and an optional graphical shell.
4.01	1989	A fix for the plethora of bugs that existed in version 4.0.
5.0	1991	Provided rudimentary support for expanded memory and allowed non-kernel portions of DOS to load in upper memory. It also allowed some device drivers and TSRs to run in the unused addresses of upper memory area between 640K and 1024K. Disk caching and support for 2.88MB floppy disks were also included. Included several utilities, including an a BASIC interpreter (a computer programming language popular at the time), a text editor, an undelete utility, and a hard-disk partition-table backup program.
5.0a	1992/3	A bug fix for 5.0.
6.0	1993	Mostly an increase in the number of utilities included. These included a disk-compression utility called DOUBLESPACE, a very rudimentary anti-virus program, and a disk defragmenter. It also finally included a MOVE command, MSBACKUP, and the ability to configure multiple boot configurations. Also included was a memory manager called MEMMAKER.
6.2	1993	SCANDISK, DISKCOPY, and SMARTDRIVE were added.
6.21	1993	DOUBLESPACE was removed in response to successful legal action from Stac Electronics. A voucher for an alternative disk compression program was included instead, and no compression application was present on the disks.
6.22	1994	Microsoft licensed a disk-compression package from VertiSoft Systems and called it DriveSpace.
7.0	1995	This version constitutes the command prompt of Windows 95. It provides support for long filenames when Windows is running.
7.1	1997	Released with Windows 95, Service Release 2; adds FAT32 support.

From its innocuous beginnings, MS-DOS eventually evolved into a relatively sophisticated operating system.

The OS needs to be able to do the same thing. So IO.SYS consists of a number of different subroutines that interface with the BIOS interrupts to provide hardware support for the OS. These are referred to as the *BIOS extensions*. IO.SYS is not the only source of BIOS extensions. Many devices require device drivers to be loaded in CONFIG.SYS that provide extensions, and some devices even have code programmed into their firmware that provide them.

A critical subroutine of IO.SYS is one called SYSINIT. This is the last routine that IO.SYS loads during the boot process and is the file that goes out looking for. . .

MSDOS.SYS

MSDOS.SYS is often mistakenly referred to as the DOS kernel. This file provides file system services and memory management to the applications running on the system. In addition, it takes the upper-level instructions issued by applications and breaks them down into the simpler commands understood by IO.SYS.

In the last paragraph, I said that this file was mistakenly credited as being the kernel. There are many who would object to that phrase. However, MSDOS.SYS and IO.SYS rely on each other for many of their functions. When an application makes a request for an I/O operation with any given device, it comes in the form of a logical request. It is MSDOS.SYS that must intercept and interpret that logical request and convert it into a physical command. It subsequently passes that command onto IO.SYS, which executes it.

Processor control is also a key function of MSDOS.SYS. Which files get processed in what order is under its control. It also controls what registers within the CPU are responsible for processing a thread of code. In the old days of the 8088, this wasn't much of a challenge. There were only two sets of registers: one for data and one for instructions. As processors evolved and became more sophisticated, this responsibility became more critical.

COMMAND.COM

COMMAND.COM was the DOS command interpreter. It was a busy little file. On the OS side of the equation, it was responsible for managing both the resident commands and the transient commands. Don't let those terms throw you. They're not as complex as they sound.

The *resident commands* are commands built into COMMAND.COM's structure and can be executed without the aid of any external files. *Transient commands* are those that are run from an external executable. An example of a resident command is DIR. Search as you might, you won't find a DIR.COM, DIR.EXE, or DIR.BAT anywhere on your hard drive. Yet, when you type DIR at the C:\ prompt, your monitor spews out a listing of every file and/or subdirectory contained within. That's because DIR is a function of COMMAND.COM.

BUZZ WORDS

BIOS extension: A string of code that interfaces the operating system to the BIOS interrupts.

SYSINIT: A subroutine of IO.SYS that seeks out and runs MSDOS.SYS during the MS-DOS boot process.

Resident command: In an OS, it is any command that is an integral part of the command interpreter and does not require an external executable program.

Transient command: A command that is issued and run from an external source.

On the other hand, the FORMAT command is a transient command. There is a file called FORMAT.COM in the DOS directory. If you delete that file from the hard drive and type **FORMAT**, you will get a message that says "Bad command or file name." It is not a direct function of COMMAND.COM.

THE DOS BOOT PROCESS

Before I can effectively discuss how DOS boots, I must first take yet another excursion into the world of hardware. I'm going to describe the boot process in two steps. The first of these is to describe how your computer makes its way from a cold off position to the point where it can load the OS. After that, I'll describe the process DOS uses to load itself. If it will help you to understand the process better, consider these steps to be the hardware boot and the software boot (even though, in reality, it's all software).

THE HARDWARE BOOT

Earlier in the chapter, I mentioned that the system BIOS was critical in all system operations. Nowhere is that more evident than in system startup. Without the BIOS, the system couldn't start at all.

As I said before, the BIOS contains a number of different files that manage the devices on the system. In addition, there are three critical executable programs stored in BIOS. These are Power On Self Test (POST), Setup, and Bootstrap Loader.

Setup is a program that allows the user to adjust certain configuration settings related to the BIOS. That is more relevant to the hardware end of your training, and for a detailed discussion of Setup, I'll refer you to your favorite hardware book. POST and Bootstrap Loader are both part of the boot process and, therefore, need to be discussed before I move on.

POST is the first program your computer runs when it is first turned on. When you push the ON button, power is applied to the CPU, and the default command that is executed is for the CPU to go out to a specific address and run whatever program it finds there. That address is listed in hexadecimal as F000.FFF0h. This address is precisely 16 bytes below the uppermost address in conventional memory. Stored here is an instruction that jumps the system to the actual address of the BIOS chip. The program that the CPU finds and runs from there is POST.

POST actually accomplishes two functions. The first thing it does is to poll every device on the system to make sure it is up and running and functioning properly. If not, BIOS will generate an error message in one of two ways. If there is reason to suspect that the video subsystem has not successfully initialized, error messages are issued as beep codes. If video is available, error messages will appear on your display.

After the system devices have all initialized, BIOS will run the Plug 'n Play (PnP) scans. A *recognition scan* checks each expansion slot, USB connection, and serial and parallel port, as well as

---

Buzz Words

Recognition scan: A BIOS routine that polls each device installed on a computer system to see whether that device is Plug 'n Play, and if so, what resources it currently claims.

any other available connection, looking for any new PnP devices. The *allocation scan* assigns resources to any new device it discovers. Once again, a more detailed discussion of this process can be found in a hardware book.

When POST has finished the PnP scans, it hands the boot process over to the Bootstrap Loader. Bootstrap Loader checks all devices that have been identified in the BIOS as being bootable, looking for a master boot record (MBR). The MBR contains executable code that introduces the file system, defines how the disk has been partitioned, and includes a pointer to the first lines of executable code for the OS. Next comes the software portion of the boot process.

BUZZ WORDS

Allocation scan: A BIOS routine that reassigns resources to Plug 'n Play devices installed on a computer system.

THE SOFTWARE BOOT

After the BIOS has completed its job and the code located in the MBR has been run, it hands control of the boot process over to the OS. The OS pointer in MBR locates the first file to be run. In the case of MS-DOS, this file is IO.SYS. In the days of DOS, this was a more primitive process. In order for MBR to find it, IO.SYS had to be the first file on the disk, following the file allocation tables.

IO.SYS loads itself into memory and will remain RAM-resident as long as the system is running. As I mentioned earlier, it contains the BIOS extensions for the system devices and provides the hardware support for the OS. It also runs a small program called SYSINIT, which locates and loads the next file in the boot sequence.

This file is MSDOS.SYS and must be the second file on the drive. MSDOS.SYS will go out looking for a file called CONFIG.SYS. CONFIG.SYS is actually an optional file and not required by the boot process. However, when present, CONFIG.SYS provides certain startup parameters, such as how many files can be opened at once, additional device drivers that may be required, and others. Later in this chapter will be a detailed discussion of CONFIG.SYS.

Finally, COMMAND.COM loads. COMMAND.COM will load another optional file called AUTOEXEC.BAT. AUTOEXEC.BAT loads any terminate and stay resident (TSR) programs required by the system. As its name implies, a TSR is a program that gets run, but when it's finished, stays loaded in memory just in case it's needed again. Once COMMAND.COM has been loaded, you get the screen shown in **Figure 21.1**.

Informative, isn't it? Now just dive right in and get to work.

Figure 21.1   The MS-DOS command prompt

MS-DOS AND MEMORY

We've grown so spoiled by modern OSs that even us old-timers sometimes forget exactly how limited DOS was in its use of memory. In its original incarnation, DOS could not read anything beyond 1MB of physical RAM. It wasn't until Version 5.0 that support for memory beyond 1MB became available. And even then there was an inherent limitation within the OS that would forever prevent it from being able to address memory beyond 64MB. Memory can be divided into three different types: conventional memory, expanded memory, and extended memory.

Conventional memory consists of the first megabyte of RAM. This is all that the original versions of DOS prior to 5.0 could address. Everything that DOS and the applications running on top of it required had to be loaded into this space. That included the system BIOS, device drivers, and, in those days before the invention of VGA, video memory, as well as the applications themselves. When the first prototypes of the IBM PC were originally being studied, the engineers decided to divide this 1MB of RAM into two areas: one area of 640K and one of 384K.

Applications had to share the lower 640K with key DOS files and some of the BIOS functions, including the interrupt pointers. The upper 384K, often called *upper memory*, was divided up into three 128K sections. The first 128K was used for video, the next 128K was where the BIOS copied itself, and the final block was where the supplemental BIOS of devices other than the motherboard could be copied. **Figure 21.2** shows a detailed map of conventional memory.

> ## BUZZ WORDS
>
> **Conventional memory:** The first megabyte of RAM, divided into 640K for running programs and 384K reserved for system use.
>
> **Upper memory:** The 384K of conventional memory located above the 640K usable by applications.
>
> **High memory:** The first 64K above the 1MB of conventional RAM, used as a paging window to Expanded memory.
>
> **Extended memory:** All memory installed on a system above the 1MB of conventional memory.
>
> **Expanded memory:** Memory beyond conventional memory that is under the direct management of a paging frame and a expanded memory manager.
>
> **Page frame:** 64KB of high memory that is used for moving data down from addresses above 1MB into the 640K used by DOS programs.

Expanded memory was defined in the Expanded Memory Specification (EMS) and was DOS's first foray into using memory beyond 1MB. This was accomplished by creating a *page frame* of 64KB in the first 64K of RAM beyond 1MB, also known as *high memory*. This provided a window through which all of the information stored above 1MB could be accessed. For this to work an expanded memory manager (EMM) had to be installed and running on the system. The first and most popular of these was a product by Quarterdeck called QEMM386, which started the ball rolling. Microsoft would eventually come on board with the file EMM386.EXE.

Expanded memory needed be "protected" by the CPU. Data beyond 1MB needed to be sorted out according to what application was using it. And data from one application could never encounter data from another. This presupposed that you had a CPU that was capable of providing that protection, known as protected mode. The first Intel processor to provide protected mode was the 80286.

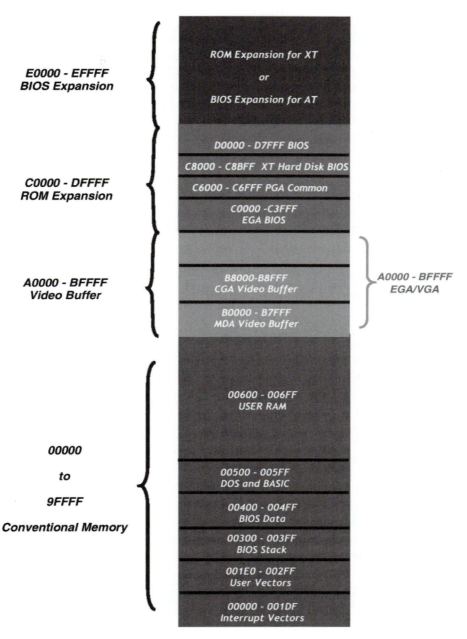

Figure 21.2   The DOS memory map

Data from expanded memory would be copied to the page frame and subsequently moved down into the lower 640K where the application could access it. The biggest limitation of this scheme was that an executable program could not run in expanded memory. It did, however, allow for significantly larger data files to be created and managed.

Extended memory was defined in the Extended Memory Specification (XMS). You would think XMS must take expanded memory to the next level. In reality, it's probably the other way around. Extended memory was simply any memory beyond 1MB. DOS needs help to get there and uses an EMM manager to provide that help. XMS provided a method by which DOS could read an additional 64K beyond the 640K originally provided for running apps. Under XMS, executable code can be loaded into the 64K of high memory. That ubiquitous Gate A20 that you frequently see as an optional setting in BIOS is the secret to using high memory.

Modern OSs were designed with extended memory in mind. XMS support was inherent in the code, and OSs actually load themselves above 1MB, so the issue of how to address beyond 1MB never arises. You'll see how these OSs use extended memory when I discuss it in the appropriate chapters.

NAVIGATING IN DOS

The file structure used in DOS is no more and no less complicated than what is used in the more modern OSs of today. It's identical. The key difference is that with DOS users don't have that pretty little Explorer window in which to view files, and they can't just grab onto files with the mouse cursor and drag them where they want. It's all command-line driven.

That means users have to understand the path. The path is nothing more than a verbal road map to the location of a file. Disk drives are divided into directories, subdirectories, and files. To find a file, DOS needs to know the correct order of the drive, directory, and each subdirectory, in order, leading down the file.

DOS drives are lettered from A to Z. However, by default, unless a line is added to CONFIG.SYS telling it otherwise, DOS will only recognize through Drive F. Drives can be either physical or logical drives. A physical drive is just what it sounds like. A floppy disk or a hard disk installed into the system is a physical drive. Drives A: and B: are reserved for floppy disk drives. The first hard drive in the system is Drive C:.

However, a hard disk can be divided into two or more partitions, and each partition is seen by the OS as a separate logical drive or *volume*. So if your hard disk is divided into three partitions, you would have drives C:, D:, and E:. Where it gets confusing is when you have two physical disks installed and each disk is divided into multiple partitions. In that case, the first physical disk is Drive C:, and the second physical disk is Drive D:. From that point all the partitions on the first physical drive will be lettered, followed by those on the second physical drive. Since this concept is probably confusing as all get-out, take a look at **Figure 21.3**. That should clarify it a bit.

BUZZ WORDS

Volume: A single managed unit of storage on a computer system. This can be a single hard disk, if that disk has been formatted to only one partition, or it can be an individual partition on a disk.

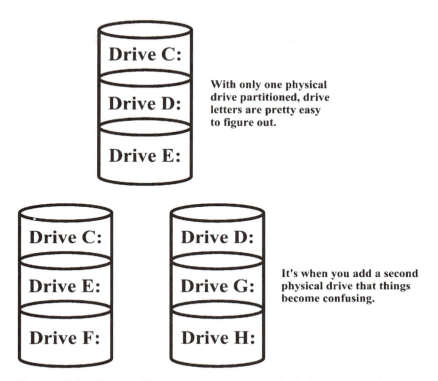

Figure 21.3 New partitions on a drive become logical drives or volumes. When two or more physical disks are installed, figuring out which physical disk holds a particular logical drive gets confusing.

The most basic and fundamental directory is the *root directory*. This would be the entire partition on which all the files and directories are stored, and it is represented by a back-slash (\) in DOS. Generally, whenever the default prompt is used, the back-slash is preceded by the letter of the drive in which the partition resides. For example, the root

BUZZ WORDS

Root directory: The volume description into which all other directories and files will be stored.

directory of the first partition on the first physical drive would be seen as C:\. In MS-DOS, since the file system used was FAT16, there could only be 512 total entries to the root directory. As soon as you attempt to enter the 513th entry, you will get a message that says DISK FULL. If you had a 2GB partition and tried to copy 513 1KB files, that would only be 512KB of data, but if all those files were being dumped into the root directory, that would still be the message you get.

Therefore, it becomes essential to store files in directories. You can store as many files as you want in the directories, as long as there is sufficient space on the disk. Not only does this prevent the root directory from becoming overloaded, but it also makes your files easier to find. Any directory that is added directly to the root directory is called a primary directory. DOS installs

Figure 21.4 Okay, so the last entry isn't a valid directory structure. What's wrong with a little humor here and there?

itself into a directory called DOS. Beneath the DOS directory, it is possible to create additional subdirectories. Subdirectories can be added to subdirectories as far deep as you wish (or need) to go up to the limitation of twenty-one nested directories. Files can be added anywhere along the line. Once again, the path is the road map from the root directory to the file, listing each directory and subdirectory along the line. **Figure 21.4** shows the path in action.

WORKING WITH THE COMMAND PROMPT

Okay, here comes the juicy part. You get to start working with the actual commands. And just in case you've been reading along in this chapter wondering whether I was ever going to get around to anything relevant, this is it. The command prompt is still alive and well and uses the same basic command structure today is it did in 1985. Certainly there has been some fine-tuning, but for the most part, the command prompt is a classic illustration of the old saying, "the more things change, the more they stay the same."

In WIN9x, the command prompt is reached in one of two ways. The first way is to click Start→Programs→MS-DOS Prompt. I find it easier to click Start→Run, and type **command** into the command line. In WIN2K and WINXP, the Start Menu shortcut is located in Start→Programs→Accessories→Command Prompt. With XP, unless you've been there recently, you'll have to click All Programs to get to Accessories. In either of the latter two OSs, the command prompt can also be reached with Start→Run and typing **cmd** into the command line.

Commands aren't as simple as they initially appear. For every command, there is a set of *switches* that allow that command to perform certain advanced functions. A switch, also called a *trigger*, consists of a letter preceded by a forward-slash. In Windows 2000 and later, the forward-slash has been replaced by the hyphen. The simplest switch, one that is common to all commands, is **/?**. While exploring the basic commands discussed in the following sections, you can always use this trigger to get a listing of every possible switch, along with a brief description of what that trigger accomplishes.

BUZZ WORDS

Switch: In reference to an OS, it is an additional parameter added to the end of a command that defines advanced functions for that command to perform. The switch turns a specific function on or off.

Trigger: Another name for a switch.

One thing I'd like to point out is that I am not covering every command available. I have selected those that are most commonly used and described them as completely as I can. I used a computer running Windows 98 to create the screenshots used in the following sections. The descriptions are accurate, in spite of any difference in OS.

BROWSING COMMANDS

Some of the basic hard disk management functions a user faces are to make new directories on a disk as needed, and then be able navigate between directories. If a directory is no longer needed, there must be a way of getting rid of it as well. When a directory has been found, it's nice to be able to see what is in that directory without leaving the command prompt behind.

MD is short for Make Directory. Another command that works in the same way is MKDIR, but why type five letters when you can get away with two? The syntax is **MD {drive}{path}**. From the C:\ prompt, typing **MD TEST** will create the primary directory C:\TEST. If the TEST directory already exists and you type **MD TEST\TEXT**, a subdirectory of the C:\TEST directory called TEXT will be created.

After a while there are lots and lots of directories and subdirectories on a drive. The CD and CHDIR commands allow the user to navigate between the different directories on the drive. **CD** followed by a space and then a directory name assumes the directory name typed is a primary directory. If a primary directory of the name typed doesn't exist, you will get a message that says "Invalid Directory." It doesn't matter whether that was a valid name for a subdirectory or not. If you know the exact path to a subdirectory buried deep on your hard drive, you can type, for example, **CD\TEST\TEXT\CHAPTERS**. You will be moved directly to that directory.

Now, assuming you're using a default DOS configuration, your prompt should look like C:\TEST\TEXT\CHAPTERS> with a blinking line following it. If you type **CD..** at that prompt, you will be taken back one level to C:\TEST\TEXT. If you type **CD** at any level, you are taken back to the root directory.

RD or RMDIR allows you to eliminate the specified directory. However, for this command to work, the directory must be completely empty. There can be no files and/or subdirectories remaining, or you will get a message that says, "Invalid path, no directory, or directory not empty," and you will not be allowed to continue. If you wish to blow away a directory, all of its subdirectories, and the files within in one fell swoop, then you must use the DELTREE command described in the next section.

DEL, ERASE, AND DELTREE

If you need to delete commands from the command prompt, two commands useful for this purpose are DEL and DELTREE. DEL (or DELETE) and ERASE eliminate a single file and are pretty much the same command with different names. The correct syntax is **DEL {d:}{path}filename {/P}**. The /p trigger tells the system to prompt you before actually deleting the file. An example of this command in action would be **del c:\myfiles\novel.doc /p**. It will ask me if I'm sure, and if I type **Y** for yes, my great American novel will be erased, something my wife insists should have happened long ago.

DELTREE can be a bit more dangerous. It eliminates an entire directory, along with all the directories and files that reside beneath it. As with DEL or ERASE, the /p switch prompts the user to confirm that he or she actually wishes to perform this operation. Typing **deltree c:\myfiles** at the command prompt will eliminate the MYFILES directory, any subdirectories beneath it, such as the C:\MYFILES\NOVELS directory, the C:\MYFILES\COMPUTER directory, the C\MYFILES\PHOTOS directory, and all the other directories and every file that resides in those directories. Now what happens since I didn't use the /p switch? It still asks me if I'm sure I want to continue.

ATTRIB

A file may possess various attributes, including Hidden (H), Read-Only (R), System (S), and Archive (A). Many times these attributes are set by the OS or a program. However, there needs to be some way by which the user can edit the attributes if required. The ATTRIB command does that. The proper syntax for this command is: ATTRIB {+R +A +S +H} (DRIVE){PATH}{FILENAME} to assign the attributes to a file. It is not necessary to include each attribute in the command. To clear the attribute bits on any given file, replace the plus sign (+) with the minus sign (-). An example of this command at work:

```
ATTRIB +H +R C:\MYFILES\NOVEL.DOC
```

This command will make the file named NOVEL.DOC, stored in the C:\MYFILES directory, a hidden, read-only file. Now my wife can't take it on herself to delete it for me.

MEM

This is a command that has lost much of its allure over the years. It's easier to obtain this information from other places in the OS. However, typing **MEM** at the command prompt will tell you how much memory is installed on the system. It also tells you how much conventional and extended memory you have and how much has been used.

SCANDISK AND CHKDSK

ScanDisk is a command line utility that checks for a number of different file system errors. It also can do a surface scan of the hard disk looking for surface errors or damaged sectors. In Windows, ScanDisk can also be run in graphical mode. From Windows Explorer, right-click the disk you wish to check and select <u>P</u>roperties from the pop-up menu. Click the Tools tab and in the Error-checking status section, click <u>C</u>heck Now.

ScanDisk is the more modern implementation of an earlier Microsoft utility called CHKDSK. CHKDSK was able to report disk size and usage, and it could report certain errors such as cross-linked files, but it could do nothing about them.

DEFRAG

DEFRAG is the Microsoft Disk Defragmenter. As files are opened and closed repeatedly over the life of the computer, they sometimes get scattered in small pieces over the hard disk. How this happens is covered in detail in *The A+ Guide to PC Hardware Maintenance and Repair.* For now, suffice it to say that scattering files like this can have severely negative impact on system performance. Typing **DEFRAG** at the command line will start a utility that puts as many files back into contiguous form as possible. Files that are open by the system can't be defragged, however.

DIR

The directory function was the fundamental method for locating files and directories in DOS. These days, Microsoft users rely on Windows Explorer, but I still find that if I haven't got a clue where a file I'm looking for is located, the command prompt is still the way to go. This simple command, used correctly with its associated switches, puts a lot of power at the fingertips of the user. The various options are as follows:

DIR {drive} {Path} (filename): allows the user to narrow the directory listings down to increasingly granular levels.

/p: Pause. When a full screen of listings appears, they will stop until the user presses the space bar.

/w: Wide. Displays five columns worth of listings but eliminates file and directory attributes. Can be used in conjunction with /p for directories with large numbers of entries. See **Figure 21.5**.

/a: Attributes. Displays the file or directory attributes after each listing.

/o: Order. Sorts the displayed listing into the order desired. In order to select the sort criteria, add after the letter O the letter N for name, S for size (smallest first), G for group, E for extension, D for creation date, or A for last access date.

/s: Search. Displays all files in the resident directory or those beneath it that fulfill the other search requirements used in the command.

/b: Bare. Displays no information other than file or directory name.

/l: Lowercase. Uses all lowercase. It must have been useful to somebody at some time or the other.

/v: Verbose. Displays all attributes of the file including size, time and date created, date last accessed, and file attributes.

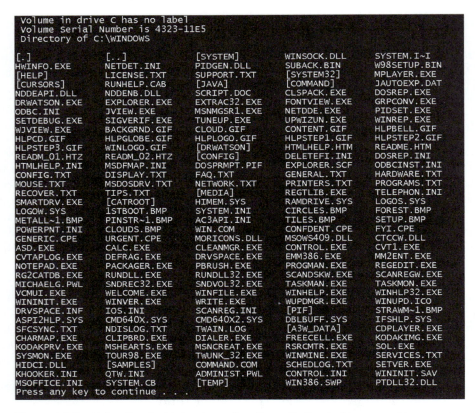

```
Volume in drive C has no label
Volume Serial Number is 4323-11E5
Directory of C:\WINDOWS

[.]             [..]            [SYSTEM]        WINSOCK.DLL     SYSTEM.I~I
HWINFO.EXE      NETDET.INI      PIDGEN.DLL      SUBACK.BIN      W98SETUP.BIN
[HELP]          LICENSE.TXT     SUPPORT.TXT     [SYSTEM32]      MPLAYER.EXE
[CURSORS]       RUNHELP.CAB     [JAVA]          [COMMAND]       JAUTOEXP.DAT
NDDEAPI.DLL     NDDENB.DLL      SCRIPT.DOC      CLSPACK.EXE     DOSREP.EXE
DRWATSON.EXE    EXPLORER.EXE    EXTRAC32.EXE    FONTVIEW.EXE    GRPCONV.EXE
ODBC.INI        JVIEW.EXE       MSNMGSR1.EXE    NETDDE.EXE      PIDSET.EXE
SETDEBUG.EXE    SIGVERIF.EXE    TUNEUP.EXE      UPWIZUN.EXE     WINREP.EXE
WJVIEW.EXE      BACKGRND.GIF    CLOUD.GIF       CONTENT.GIF     HLPBELL.GIF
HLPCD.GIF       HLPGLOBE.GIF    HLPLOGO.GIF     HLPSTEP1.GIF    HLPSTEP2.GIF
HLPSTEP3.GIF    WINLOGO.GIF     [DRWATSON]      HTMLHELP.HTM    README.HTM
READM_01.HTZ    READM_02.HTZ    [CONFIG]        DELETEFI.INI    DOSREP.INI
HTMLHELP.INI    MSDFMAP.INI     DOSPRMPT.PIF    EXPLORER.SCF    ODBCINST.INI
CONFIG.TXT      DISPLAY.TXT     FAQ.TXT         GENERAL.TXT     HARDWARE.TXT
MOUSE.TXT       MSDOSDRV.TXT    NETWORK.TXT     PRINTERS.TXT    PROGRAMS.TXT
RECOVER.TXT     TIPS.TXT        [MEDIA]         REGTLIB.EXE     TELEPHON.INI
SMARTDRV.EXE    [CATROOT]       HIMEM.SYS       RAMDRIVE.SYS    LOGOS.SYS
LOGOW.SYS       1STBOOT.BMP     SYSTEM.INI      CIRCLES.BMP     FOREST.BMP
METALL~1.BMP    PINSTR~1.BMP    AC3API.INI      TILES.BMP       SETUP.BMP
POWERPNT.INI    CLOUDS.BMP      WIN.COM         CONFDENT.CPE    FYI.CPE
GENERIC.CPE     URGENT.CPE      MORICONS.DLL    MSOWS409.DLL    CTCCW.DLL
ASD.EXE         CALC.EXE        CLEANMGR.EXE    CONTROL.EXE     CVT1.EXE
CVTAPLOG.EXE    DEFRAG.EXE      DRVSPACE.EXE    EMM386.EXE      MM2ENT.EXE
NOTEPAD.EXE     PACKAGER.EXE    PBRUSH.EXE      PROGMAN.EXE     REGEDIT.EXE
RG2CATDB.EXE    RUNDLL.EXE      RUNDLL32.EXE    SCANDSKW.EXE    SCANREGW.EXE
MICHAELG.PWL    SNDREC32.EXE    SNDVOL32.EXE    TASKMAN.EXE     TASKMON.EXE
VCMUI.EXE       WELCOME.EXE     WINFILE.EXE     WINHELP.EXE     WINHLP32.EXE
WININIT.EXE     WINVER.EXE      WRITE.EXE       WUPDMGR.EXE     WINUPD.ICO
DRVSPACE.INF    IOS.INI         SCANREG.INI     [PIF]           STRAWM~1.BMP
ASPI2HLP.SYS    CMD640X.SYS     CMD640X2.SYS    DBLBUFF.SYS     IFSHLP.SYS
SFCSYNC.TXT     NDISLOG.TXT     TWAIN.LOG       [A3W_DATA]      CDPLAYER.EXE
CHARMAP.EXE     CLIPBRD.EXE     DIALER.EXE      FREECELL.EXE    KODAKIMG.EXE
KODAKPRV.EXE    MSHEARTS.EXE    MSNCREAT.EXE    RSRCMTR.EXE     SOL.EXE
SYSMON.EXE      TOUR98.EXE      TWUNK_32.EXE    WINMINE.EXE     SERVICES.TXT
HIDCI.DLL       [SAMPLES]       COMMAND.COM     SCHEDLOG.TXT    SETVER.EXE
KHOOKER.INI     QTW.INI         ADMINIST.PWL    CONTROL.INI     WININIT.SAV
MSOFFICE.INI    SYSTEM.CB       [TEMP]          WIN386.SWP      PTDLL32.DLL
Press any key to continue . . .
```

Figure 21.5   Using the /w trigger in conjunction with the /p trigger enables you to display a lot of files on the screen at one time.

Switches can be used together to provide the greatest versatility. Also the asterisk character can be used as a wild card. What's a wild card? Simply put, the asterisk instructs the command to replace that character with any other character or collection of characters it finds in its place. For example the command DIR *.DOC will display a listing of every file in the resident directory that ends in a DOC extension. Not sure what directory a file is in, but you know it was a letter to Bill, so the filename starts with Bill and ends in DOC? Start at the C:\ prompt in the root directory and type **dir bill*.doc /s**. The DIR command will search every directory and subdirectory of your hard drive and display each result along with the directory in which it was found. Too many results? Add the /p switch and the screen will pause each time it fills up and wait for you to press the space bar to continue (**Figure 21.6**).

COPY, DISKCOPY, AND XCOPY

Once in a while it becomes necessary to create a copy of data you've created. There are two commands that perform this function and each one is slightly different. The COPY command takes a file and copies it from one location to another. Files can be copied between different drives and/or different directories. The syntax is **COPY {trigger} {source path}(source**

```
Directory of C:\My Documents

CHAPTE~1 DOC        75,776  08-29-03   9:30a Chapter19.doc
NEWRES~1 DOC        41,472  08-17-03  11:14a New Resume.doc
CHAPTE~2 DOC       163,840  08-31-03   6:31p Chapter19_1.doc
SEPTEM~1 DOC        21,504  09-25-03   8:19p September 25 letter to parents.doc
LABONE~1 DOC        72,704  09-26-03   3:03p Lab ONe.doc
         5 file(s)         375,296 bytes

Directory of C:\Program Files\Creative\EAX Demo

README   DOC       970,752  09-21-98   1:00a readme.doc
         1 file(s)         970,752 bytes

Directory of C:\Program Files\Infogrames Interactive\Civilization III

CIV30-~1 DOC        46,080  09-18-01   7:28p CIV 3 O-D I G.DOC
         1 file(s)          46,080 bytes

Directory of C:\Program Files\Microsoft Office\Templates\Business Planner Templa
tes

SAMPLE~1 DOC       633,344  03-10-99  10:37p Sample Business Plan.doc
SAMPLE~2 DOC        72,192  03-10-99  10:37p Sample Outline.doc
SAMPLE~3 DOC        35,328  03-10-99  10:37p Sample Marketing Strategy Document.d
oc
SAMPLE~4 DOC        37,376  03-10-99  10:37p Sample Marketing Materials Document.
doc
         4 file(s)         778,240 bytes

Directory of C:\Program Files\Microsoft Office\Templates\Business Planner for UK
 and AUS Templates

EXAMPL~1 DOC       475,136  03-10-99  10:35p Example Business Plan.doc
SAMPLE~1 DOC        65,024  03-10-99  10:37p Sample Plan Outline.doc
         2 file(s)         540,160 bytes

Directory of C:\WINDOWS

SCRIPT   DOC        38,400  04-23-99  10:22p SCRIPT.DOC
Press any key to continue . . .
```

Figure 21.6 Using wild cards and multiple switches is possible with virtually every command.

filename) {destination path}(destination filename). Paths and filenames need not be identical. For example the command `copy a:\files\letter.doc c:\myfiles\letter2.doc` takes the file named letter.doc located in the FILES directory on Drive A:, moves it over to the MYFILES directory of Drive C:, and renames it to LETTER2.DOC. Triggers include the following:

- **/a:** Indicates an ASCII file
- **/b:** Indicates a binary file
- **/v:** Verifies that files are written correctly
- **/y:** Prevents the system from prompting you before overwriting an existing file of the same name.
- **/-y:** Forces the system to prompt you before overwriting an existing file of the same name.

Entire directories can be copied using wildcards. An example of this would the following: `copy a:\win98\*.* c:\temp` will copy all files located in the WIN98 directory on the floppy disk in Drive A: to the TEMP directory on Drive C:.

DISKCOPY makes a duplicate of an entire disk. The correct format is **DISKCOPY {drive} {drive}**. The drives must be identical, so you cannot use DISKCOPY to move the contents of a floppy disk to a Zip drive. You can, however, copy from one floppy to another using the same drive. If you type **diskcopy a: a:** at the command prompt, all the contents of Drive A: will be copied to RAM, you will be prompted to insert the target diskette, and then the information will be copied from RAM back to Drive A:. There are three triggers for the DISKCOPY command:

/1: Copies only side one of the source disk.

/v: Verifies the integrity of the data on the target disk by comparing it to the source.

/m: Forces the process to make multiple passes between source and target diskettes using only RAM to store data.

The XCOPY command is good for copying entire directory trees. With this command, if you type **xcopy c:\myfiles a:** then the directory MYFILES, along with any subdirectory beneath it and all files contained within, gets copied. There are a lot of XCOPY triggers:

/a: Copies any file on which the archive attribute has been set but does not change the attribute.

/m: Copies any file on which the archive attribute has been set and changes the attribute.

/d:{date}: Copies only files that were created or changed after the specified date.

/p: Prompts the user before creating any new files.

/s: Copies only directories and subdirectories that actually contain entries.

/e: Copies directories and subdirectories even if they are empty.

/w: Prompts the user to press a key before copying a file.

/c: Continues copying even in the event of an error.

/i: If a destination does not exist, and more than one file exists in the target, the source is assumed to be a directory.

/q: Quiet. Does not echo file names while copying them.

/f: Full. Displays full source and destination file information while copying.

/h: Copies system and hidden files.

/r: Overwrites Read-Only files.

/t: Copies directory structure from source to destination but does not copy files.

/u: Update. Replaces files of the same name that exist in the destination.

/k: Copies attributes. If this switch is not used, Read-Only attributes will be removed.

/y: Overwrites existing files of the same name without prompting the user.

/-y: Does not overwrite existing files of the same name without prompting the user.

FORMAT

This command prepares a new hard disk or diskette to store files. It is the FORMAT command that creates the initial file allocation tables for any given disk. These tables are subsequently modified as data is added and/or removed. If the command is used with no triggers at all, the entire contents of the disk will be formatted using the default file system of the OS. As the disk is formatted, each FAU will be tested for integrity. Bad sectors will be marked as such and will not be made available for the OS to use when storing files. The syntax is **FORMAT {drive}**. The FORMAT command has a fairly large number of triggers.

- **/v:{label}**: Specifies a volume label (up to thirteen characters) that will be used to identify the disk (or partition) once the format is completed.
- **/q**: Quick format. Does not perform surface scan looking for bad sectors, but simply rewrites the FAT.
- **/F:{size}**: Specifies what size of disk is being formatted. For example if an old 720K 3.5″ floppy disk drive was all that you had in an older machine, a 1.44MB diskette could be formatted to that capacity by typing **format a: /F:720** at the command prompt.
- **/b**: Reserves enough space on the disk for future use by system files.
- **/s**: Copies the system files to the correct location on the disk after the format procedure is complete.
- **/t:{tracks}**: Specifies the number of tracks to be formatted on each side of the disk.
- **/c**: Tests clusters that are currently marked as bad.

SCANREG

A utility that exists in WIN98 that is very useful is SCANREG. This particular utility can be run from Windows or from the command prompt. However, there is one trick it can do from the command prompt that it can't do in graphical mode. Its basic function is to scan the registry for errors. Unfortunately, no matter how badly the registry might be corrupted, it never seems to find any errors.

The one trick it does well from the command prompt is to restore the system using an old copy of the registry. By selecting the option to View Backups, a user can select the last copy of the registry that started successfully and restart the system using those files.

MOVE

The move command is very similar to the copy command, except that once the selected file is copied to the target location, it is deleted from the original location. For example, the command **move c:\myfiles\novels\novel.doc c:\document\novels\novel.doc** will copy the file NOVEL.DOC from the c:\myfiles\novels directory to the c:\document\novels directory and then erase it from the c:\myfiles\novels directory.

SETVER

This is a command that isn't required as much any more, but does still come in handy once in a while. In the early days of DOS, many DOS programs would only run on certain versions (or later) of MS-DOS. So in order to ensure that the version of DOS currently running on the machine was suitable, the program would do a version check. Unfortunately, many programs were not programmed well enough to understand the concept of "or later." A program would require DOS 5.0 and the system would have 6.22. There would be no problem running that program on the system, but since the version reported was not identical to the version required, the program refused to run. SETVER looks at the version required by the program and, as long as the version running on the system is equal or later, reports that it is whatever the program wants it to be. So if that program that needed DOS 5.0 starts to install on a 6.22 box with the SETVER command in the AUTOEXEC.BAT file, the program checks the DOS version and SETVER reports back, "How convenient! I just happen to be DOS 5.0."

SYS

The SYS command transfers the key system (or kernel) files to the correct location on any formatted disk or diskette. The correct syntax is **SYS {drive}**. In DOS, if I may be so bold as to repeat myself yet again, these files are IO.SYS, MSDOS.SYS, and COMMAND.COM.

TYPE

This convenient little command allows the user to view the contents of any given file without the necessity of opening an editor of some sort. This is really only useful on text files, however, many of the different files used by DOS, including CONFIG.SYS, AUTOEXEC.BAT, any other batch file, and most .INI files are nothing more than text files. The syntax for the command is **TYPE {path}{filename}**.

VER

It's rather difficult to get too verbose describing this command. It reports what version of the OS is running, whether is be DOS or Windows.

EDIT

The EDIT command brings up the venerable old DOS editor. This is a pure ASCII text editor that completely lacks anything resembling basic formatting functions. However, for editing configuration files on the fly from the command prompt, there is nothing better.

CREATING CONFIG.SYS AND AUTOEXEC.BAT FILES

Brief mention of the CONFIG.SYS and AUTOEXEC.BAT files was made earlier in the chapter when discussing the boot process, and I threatened that I would cover them in more detail later on. It's time to carry out that threat. These files are optional startup files that are user-configurable and continue to be relevant even in today's modern OSs (although to an increasingly lesser degree).

As I said before, CONFIG.SYS is where certain user-configurable parameters relevant to the OS can be added. It can be compared to the BIOS Setup program, except the OS uses it during boot up. AUTOEXEC.BAT consists of a collection of executable commands that the user wants to run each time the system boots.

In both of these files, a key concept to remember is that each line in either of these files is run in the order in which it is placed within the file. This may seem like a no-brainer, but certain commands are dependent on another command. If loaded in the wrong order, the dependent command cannot run. I'll show you an example of this in just a bit.

Another thing to remember is that it is possible for a command in AUTOEXEC.BAT to be dependent on something loaded by CONFIG.SYS. If a file or parameter that was supposed to be loaded by CONFIG.SYS is either incorrect or not present, then that entry in AUTOEXEC.BAT will fail. I'll give you an example of that as well.

CONFIG.SYS

It is upon this venerable old file that the task of loading device drivers and custom system parameters falls. The device drivers loaded here would be basically any device not directly supported by the system BIOS. And there are a number of system parameters. There are also certain commands relative to configuration that must be run from CONFIG.SYS.

EMM386.EXE is one command that is run from CONFIG.SYS. If you think about it for a minute, it will make sense. For the system to be able to address expanded or extended memory, it must be configured to do so. And configuration is the purpose behind CONFIG.SYS (in case you were wondering where it got its name).

Device drivers are also loaded using one of two commands. DEVICE loads the driver into conventional memory. DEVICEHIGH loads the driver into upper memory as long as an expanded memory manager is loaded beforehand. This is an example of making sure that the lines in the file are arranged in the correct order. For example, the following CONFIG.SYS won't do what you want it to do because of the order.

```
DEVICEHIGH=C:\MOUSE\MOUSE.SYS
DEVICEHIGH=C:\CDROM\CDROM.SYS  /D:0001
C:\DOS\EMM386.EXE
```

The reason is that I've attempted to load the drivers into upper memory without the benefit of an expanded memory manager. The drivers will load; they'll just load into conventional memory.

Another thing that you may have noticed about the preceding example is that the entire path to the file must be listed. If not, CONFIG.SYS can't find the file to load it, and the device that requires that driver fails completely.

There are a few other commands that you can put into CONFIG.SYS that allow you to customize your configuration a bit. The following sections describe them.

FILES

DOS manages open files by way of something called a file handle. A separate file handle is required for each file that is opened. By default, DOS only loads eight file handles, which means that only eight files can be open at any given instant. Unfortunately, most programs needed to keep far more than eight files going at a time. By adding a line that reads **FILES=32** to CONFIG.SYS, you are creating thirty-two file handles. You can specify any number from eight to 255. The one thing to keep in mind is that for every file handle you open you are grabbing a certain amount of conventional memory. This amount varies with the number of file handles you create, as you can see in **Table 21.2**, so you don't want to be putting a value of 255 in every CONFIG.SYS you ever write. You'll be eating up 15K of valuable memory.

Table 21.2   Conventional Memory Used by the FILES= Statement

Files Value	Bytes Consumed
8 (Default)	192
10	496
15	608
20	896
25	1200
30	1488
35	1776
40	2080
45	2368
50	2672
55	2960
60	3260
65	3552
70	3856
75	4144

Increasing the number of files open in CONFIG.SYS consumes additional conventional memory.

BUFFERS

Whenever DOS is asked to perform an I/O operation, it needs a space to store the data it is moving. Some devices, such as disk drives, supported a form of buffering called read-ahead. Using read-ahead buffering, when the OS requests a sector of data, the device delivers that sector plus the next few sectors in the data stream. The more read-ahead buffers configured, the more additional sectors that are read. By default, DOS establishes the number of buffers on the basis of how much conventional memory is available. If there is 512KB of conventional memory, then fifteen buffers are created. No read-ahead buffers are created. The correct syntax is **BUFFERS={#CONVENTIONAL BUFFERS}, {#READ-AHEAD BUFFERS}**. To configure a system to use thirty conventional buffers plus an additional four read-ahead buffers, the following line should be added to CONFIG.SYS:

    BUFFERS=30,4

As with the FILES command, a little caution is in order. Each buffer configured requires 532 bytes. More buffers means less available memory.

STACKS

Computer programs, including the OS, need a place where data can be temporarily stored until it is needed—or in many cases, needed again. DOS provides a collection of memory addresses just for this purpose. Data is stored in stacks and then retrieved on a first in, last out (FILO) basis. The proper syntax for configuring a STACKS command is **STACKS={#STACKS}, {SIZESTACKS}**. The acceptable range for the number of stacks is between eight and sixty-four, while the size of each stack can range from 32 bytes to 512 bytes. To configure a system to use nine stacks of 256 bytes, you would use the following line:

    STACKS=9,256

Although this may appear to mean that you're configuring 9256 stacks, it does not. However, each of those stacks is more conventional memory you're eating up.

LASTDRIVE

When computers were first unleashed on the unsuspecting public, a fully loaded computer might have two floppy disk drives and, if the user was exceptionally affluent, a hard disk drive. CD-ROMs, DVDs, and Zip drives hadn't even crossed the minds of the most delusional of designers. Therefore, assigning drive letters beyond Drive F: was considered overkill. These were the same engineers that told us that one megabyte of RAM was more than anyone would ever need.

   With multiple large hard disks divided into several partitions each, coupled with a CD-ROM and a DVD, we move into a different world. We need more drive letters. Add the following line to CONFIG.SYS:

    LASTDRIVE=Z

Most of us will be all right now.

AUTOEXEC.BAT

There are certain programs that every computer needs to have running in the background in order to operate properly. For example, many mouse drivers run as executable programs in the background. For a CD-ROM to work, the program MSCDEX.EXE must be running at all times. These are the TSRs I described earlier in this chapter.

Imagine if every time you started your computer, you had to go through and start each and every one of these programs manually? Users would have to have sticky notes taped to their monitors reminding them of what they had to do to start their computers each morning!

Fortunately, that's not the way it works. AUTOEXEC.BAT is a batch file that runs each and every time the computer starts and launches all of these programs. Even today, if you still have older DOS programs that you're running, it may be necessary to create an AUTOEXEC.BAT, so the concept hasn't been totally beaten to death yet. There are a few commonly inserted DOS commands that routinely appear in this file, and those are the ones that I'll cover in this section. Keep in mind that virtually any program that you want to automatically launch every time a DOS-based computer starts can be added to AUTOEXEC.BAT. If the only thing you use the computer for is one program that only runs in DOS, add the command that runs that program as the last line and the computer will boot right to that program. Before I dive into the commands, I'd like to point out just a couple of things regarding the creation and execution of this file.

AUTOEXEC.BAT CONCEPTS

As with CONFIG.SYS, the lines that you add to AUTOEXEC.BAT will be executed in the order in which they appear in the file. Therefore, if one program needs to be running in order for another one to start, make sure you have them in the right order. Also, as I'll point out in a few moments, you can have lines of text appear as the computer boots, prompting the user for some action or the other or simply telling the user what's going on.

Sometimes while fine-tuning an AUTOEXEC.BAT file, you want to disable a particular line, but you don't want to eliminate it completely. If you add the command REM in front of that line, it treats the line as a remark rather than a command and does not run any executables contained in the line.

Batch files don't need to be a simple listing of existing commands. An experienced user can program very complex AUTOEXEC.BAT files using some of the batch file programming commands listed in the next section. Also, a batch file can call on another batch file, run that file, and then complete its own cycle. Let's take a look at some advanced batch file programming.

BATCH FILE PROGRAMMING

Creating a customized batch file will usually require knowledge and use of the batch file programming commands included in DOS. The following is a list of DOS commands and how they can be used.

@: Any text following the @ symbol will not be echoed on the screen. For example, the command @ECHO OFF prevents future commands in the batch file from being displayed on the screen as they are being processed, but in addition, the @ sign prevents the ECHO OFF command from being displayed.

:{SECTION}: By adding a colon in front of any word such as SECTION, the lines following the command up to the next similar entry form a category, also known as a label. This allows you to use the GOTO command to skip to certain sections of a batch file.

CALL: This brings up and runs another batch file within a batch file. When the batch file that is called is completed, the remainder of the original batch file is completed. If the batch file called cannot be found, an error message will be displayed.

CHOICE: Prompts the user to input a selection, based on predefined choices.

CLS: Clears the screen.

ECHO: Displays any text following the command on the screen. ECHO OFF stops commands from the batch file from being displayed as they're processed; ECHO ON causes them to be displayed. If you have not typed **@ECHO OFF** prior to using the ECHO command to display text on the screen, a command such as **ECHO You may now remove the floppy disk** will display "ECHO You may now remove the floppy disk" and "You may now remove the floppy disk." The command ECHO. (including the period) creates an empty line.

GOTO {LABEL}: Allows the batch file to redirect processing to a specific section. An example of GOTO would be to **GOTO END**.

IF: Checks for a certain condition. If that condition exists the batch file will perform the function included in the IF statement.

PAUSE: Stops processing of the batch file and prompts users to press any key when they're ready to continue.

REM: Allows you to place comments into the batch file without executing that line when the batch file is run.

%1: The percent followed by a numeric value, beginning with one, allows the insertion of a variable within the batch file. For example, if you write a batch file called greeting.bat and include the line **echo Good day, %1**, typing the command **greeting Master Graves** will output the text Good day, Master Graves.

The majority of DOS AUTOEXE.BAT files don't require anything as fancy as customized programming and generally include just a few DOS commands. Here are some of the more commonly used commands.

SET: Allows the user to specify an environment variable and then assign a value to that variable. Syntax is **SET {VARIABLE}={VALUE}**. An example: **SET TEMP=C:\FILES\TEMP** tells DOS that all temporary files will be stored in the C:\FILES\TEMP directory. That directory must exist in advance, however. MS-DOS will not automatically create it.

PATH: Loads a predefined listing of directories that COMMAND.COM should search any time a command is issued, looking for the executable code needed to execute the command. Syntax is **PATH {DRIVE:}{DIRECTORY;}{DIRECTORY;} {DIRECTORY;}** **{DIRECTORY;}**. An example: **PATH C:\;DOS; WINDOWS;CDROM; MYFILES**. In this example, if a command is issued, COMMAND.COM first looks in the root directory. If it doesn't find the code it needs there, it then looks in C:\DOS, C:\Windows, C:\CDROM, and finally C:\MYFILES. If it still hasn't found what it needs, the user gets the "Bad command or filename" message.

PROMPT: Defines how the command prompt will appear to the user. Includes a number of parameters for configuring the prompt. These parameters must be preceded by the $ symbol and include the following:

$Q	the equal sign (=)
$T	current time
$D	current date
$P	current drive and path
$V	OS version
$N	current drive
$G	greater-than sign (>)
$L	less-than sign (<)
$B	the pipe symbol (|)
$E	Backspace

The syntax is **PROMPT ${VARIABLE}${VARIABLE}**. An example: **PROMPT PGTD$B** will yield a prompt that looks like

```
C:\DOS> 10:30:45SAT 11-15-2004|
```

LOADHIGH: Instructs the program following the command to load into the upper memory area between 640K and 1MB. Syntax is **LOADHIGH {DRIVE}{PATH}{FILENAME}**. An example: the command **LOADHIGH C:\MOUSE\MOUSE.COM** will go the C:\MOUSE directory and run the MOUSE.COM program in upper memory.

SETVER: Allows COMMAND.COM to report to an application any DOS version request by the application, as long as it is equal to or later than the version actually running. Syntax is **SETVER {DRIVE}{PATH} filename x.xx**, where the drive and path specify the location of SETVER.EXE, filename indicates the program that requires the services of SETVER, and x.xx is replaced with the DOS version required by the application. An example: **SETVER C:\DOS WP51.COM 3.3** tells SETVER that SETVER.EXE is located in the DOS directory and if the user runs WP51.COM, this file needs to be told that DOS 3.3 is installed on the system.

MSCDEX: This is the DOS command that provides CD-ROM support and must be loaded on any machine with a CD-ROM drive installed. Syntax is **{DRIVE}{PATH}MSCDEX.EXE /D:XXXX**, where D specifies the device name and

XXXX is replaced with the name desired. The same variable /D:XXXX must be included as a switch in CONFIG.SYS in the line that loads the CD-ROM device driver.

CHAPTER SUMMARY

After you've read this chapter and tried some of the commands a few times, you should be starting to feel a little more comfortable dancing around in the command prompt. Never again will a black screen with that C:\ challenging you to figure out what to do next bother you in the least.

BRAIN DRAIN

1. Review the various versions of MS-DOS and come up with the following answers:

   a. What was the first version of DOS that supported 1.44MB floppy diskettes?

   b. What version supported the first hard drive?

   c. What year did MS-DOS provide the first support for memory beyond 1MB?

2. Describe the hardware boot process in detail.

3. Now describe the software boot process in detail, specifically using MS-DOS as the OS being booted.

4. Define the function and purpose of CONFIG.SYS and discuss some of the commands that might be used in that file.

5. Define the function and purpose of AUTOEXEC.BAT and discuss some of the commands that might be used in that file.

THE 64K$ QUESTIONS

1. What is the file loaded on the ROM BIOS chip that locates the MBR and turns the boot process over to the OS?

   a. POST

   b. IO.SYS

   c. Setup

   d. Bootstrap Loader

2. What is the first file called during the OS boot process in MS-DOS?

   a. COMMAND.COM

   b. SETUP.EXE

   c. IO.SYS

   d. MSDOS.SYS

3. Which DOS file is credited with being the kernel?

   a. COMMAND.COM

   b. SETUP.EXE

   c. IO.SYS

   d. MSDOS.SYS

4. Which DOS file hosts the internal instruction set supported by MS-DOS?

   a. COMMAND.COM

   b. SETUP.EXE

   c. IO.SYS

   d. MSDOS.SYS

5. How much conventional memory was available to a program running in MS-DOS?

   a. <640K

   b. 640K

   c. 728K

   d. 1MB

6. What was the area of memory above 640K and below extended memory called?

   a. Expanded memory

   b. DOS memory

   c. High memory

   d. Phantom memory

7. The function of DOS that provides a roadmap that leads to a specific file on a drive is known as the _____.

   a. Prompt

   b. Path

   c. VFAT

   d. File handle

8. If you wish to add a new device to a system running DOS, how do you introduce the device driver to the OS?

   a. You put it in CONFIG.SYS.

   b. You add it to the AUTOEXEC.BAT file.

   c. It runs as an application.

   d. The drivers load from a chip on the device.

9. A variable applied to a specific command that instructs that command to perform in a particular manner is known as a _____.

   a. Switch

   b. Pipe

   c. Hash

   d. Trigger

10. DOS was able to handle an unlimited number of nested directories.

    a. True

    b. False

11. If you wanted to erase an entire directory, along with all of its subdirectories and all the files contained within, which command would you use?

    a. DELETE /ALL

    b. DEL -A

    c. ERASE *.*

    d. DELTREE

12. DOS only provided for eight files to be open at once by default.

    a. TRUE

    b. FALSE

13. Which of the following is the correct syntax for a STACKS command?

    a. STACKS,9,256

    b. STACKS={9},{256}

    c. STACKS=9x256

    d. STACKS=9,256

14. How does adding /Q to the end of the format command made it perform its job quicker?

    a. It doubles the rotational speed of the disk.

    b. It bypasses the surface scan of the disk.

    c. It uses the existing FAT.

    d. It doesn't.

15. You've added a new device to your system. Which of the following must you do in order to make the device work properly under DOS?

    a. Run SETUP.

    b. Add a DEVICE= statement to AUTOEXEC.BAT to load the driver file.

    c. Add a DEVICE= statement to CONFIG.SYS to load the driver file.

    d. Nothing. It will load itself.

16. The TYPE command would display nothing at all if used on a binary file.

    a. True

    b. False

17. By default, DOS will keep _____ file handles active at once.

    a. 4

    b. 8

    c. 16

    d. Unlimited

18. Why wouldn't you use WordPerfect to edit a CONFIG.SYS file?

    a. Formatting codes could corrupt the file.

    b. WordPerfect can't recognized the file type used by CONFIG.SYS.

    c. WordPerfect would save the file using the wrong extension.

    d. You could if you wanted to.

19. Which of the following prompts is the result of PROMPT PG?

    a. C:

    b. C:\09:28PM

    c. C:\DOS

    d. C

20. What is the largest stack that can be managed by DOS?

    a. 32 bytes

    b. 128 bytes

    c. 256 bytes

    d. 512 bytes

TRICKY TERMINOLOGY

Allocation scan: A BIOS routine that reassigns resources to Plug 'n Play devices installed on a computer system.

BIOS extension: A string of code that interfaces the operating system to the BIOS interrupts.

Conventional memory: The first megabyte of RAM, divided into 640K for running programs and 384K reserved for system use.

Expanded memory: Memory beyond conventional memory that is under the direct management of a paging frame and a expanded memory manager.

Extended memory: All memory installed on a system above the 1MB of conventional memory.

High memory: The first 64K of memory beyond the 1MB of conventional memory, usually used as a paging file for access into extended memory.

Interrupt: On a software level, it is a string of code that is called in order to perform a specific function. The BIOS uses software interrupts to manage hardware. On a hardware level, it is an electrical signal that notifies the CPU that a device needs to open communications (or vice versa).

Page frame: 64KB of high memory that is used for moving data down from addresses above 1MB into the 640K used by DOS programs.

Recognition scan: A BIOS routine that polls each device installed on a computer system to see whether that device is Plug 'n Play, and if so, what resources it currently claims.

Resident command: In an OS, it is any command that is an integral part of the command interpreter and does not require an external executable program.

Root directory: The volume description, in which all other directories and files will be stored.

Switch: In reference to an OS, it is an additional parameter added to the end of a command that defines advanced functions for that command to perform. The switch turns a specific function on or off.

SYSINIT: A subroutine of IO.SYS that seeks out and runs MSDOS.SYS during the MS-DOS boot process.

Transient command: A command that is issued and run from an external source.

Trigger: Another name for a switch.

Volume: A single managed unit of storage on a computer system. This can be a single hard disk, if that disk has been formatted to only one partition, or it can be an individual partition on a disk.

Wild card: A character that instructs a command to replace that character with any other character or collection of characters it finds in its place.

ACRONYM ALERT

QDOS: Quick and Dirty Operating System

MS-DOS: Microsoft Disk Operating System

PROM: Programmable Read-Only Memory. A chip that contains permanently embedded code.

BIOS: Basic Input Output Services. The instruction set on a computer system that provides the startup code along with a number of routines that provide command support for the hardware installed on the system.

PnP: Plug 'n Play. An Intel/Microsoft technology that allows the computer system and OS to automatically detect and configure certain settings for PnP compatible hardware.

MBR: Master Boot Record. Information contained on the first one or two sectors of a hard disk that contain code that initializes the file system, defines disks and partitions, and provides a pointer to the OS.

TSR: Terminate and Stay Resident. Any program that is launched, performs a task, but then remains in memory in case its services are required again.

FILO: First In, Last Out.

 VIEW THE VIDEO

A video clip on Command Prompt Procedures is available on the accompanying CD.

CHAPTER 22

THE EVOLUTION OF WINDOWS AND WINDOWS BASICS

As the world moved on, so did the nature of operating systems. In the early 1980s there was a flurry of activity as a number of different companies competed furiously to create and dominate a market for a graphical operating system. Several different software companies, including Microsoft, developed applications with a graphical interface. But very few were rushing to the market with a true-blue OS.

Xerox Corporation had been producing a very high-end (for its day, anyway) computer called the Alto with a graphical interface since the early 1970s. However, since these machines boasted a starting price of $32,000 and up for a single machine, there is a justifiable argument that these machines didn't really qualify as personal computers. Apple Computer was the first to step up to the plate with a true personal computer that sported a GUI in 1983 with the LISA, short for *Logical Integrated Software Architecture*. (The story goes that the name really was in honor of Steve Jobs' secretary.) At $10K, it's hard to call this one a personal computer, too. Judging by the number that sold, I'd have to say that the public agreed with me in that respect. However, it paved the way for the tremendously successful Macintosh computer (named for Steve's favorite apple).

The majority of this chapter will concentrate on the various versions of Windows starting with 3.0, going through 3.11WFW. However, because I think you might find it interesting, I'm going to provide a little of the history leading up to the release of Windows 3.0.

A+ OPERATING SYSTEM TECHNOLOGIES EXAM OBJECTIVES

In spite of the fact that CompTIA announces that it does not cover Windows 3.x on the exam, much of the Windows technology that is covered was introduced in this version. Therefore, there is some very important exam material covered in this chapter:

1.1   Identify the major desktop components and interfaces and their functions. Differentiate the characteristics of Windows 9x/Me, Windows NT 4.0 Workstation, Windows 2000 Professional, and Windows XP.

2.4   Identify procedures for installing/adding a device, including loading, adding, and configuring device drivers and required software.

The History of Windows

In 1982, a company called VisiCorp demonstrated a product they called VisiOn. It was a graphical user interface for MS-DOS that allowed point and click functionality. The product was full of bugs, ran only VisiCorp software, and was never a commercial success. Its real claim to fame was that present for the demonstration was a fellow by the name of Bill Gates. He was so impressed by the concept that he flew several top-level executives from Microsoft out to the Computer Dealer Expo (COMDEX) to see the demonstration. From that point on, it became a race to see who could reach the market first. Xerox, VisiCorp, Microsoft, IBM, and Tandy Corporation were just a few of the competitors trying to be the first to release a true graphical OS. And how many from that list are still writing OS applications?

The first commercial product to be released by Microsoft was Windows 1.0 (**Figure 22.1**). The idea behind this release was to provide bitmap displays supporting a menu-driven mouse-based environment. To call Windows 1.0 an operating system is a bit like comparing a bottle rocket to a spacecraft. In truth, it was nothing more than a DOS shell that provided mouse

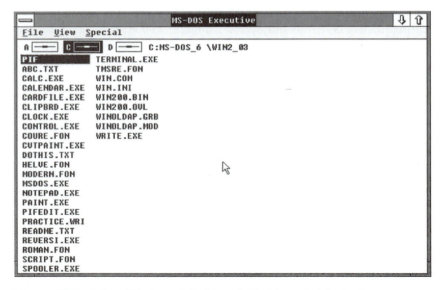

Figure 22.1   When Windows 1.0 shipped, it's biggest claim to fame was a graphical file manager.

support. It also shipped with a few rudimentary applications. These included a calendar, a notepad, a calculator, a clock, and a telecommunications program. A full install required just a hair under a megabyte of space, and the product shipped on five 360K 5.25″ floppy disks.

With the release of the 80286, Microsoft had the technology of higher-speed processors that supported protected mode to work with. While Windows 2.0 didn't take full advantage of protected mode, it did provide support for expanded memory and took advantage of computers with more than 1MB installed. This was the first OS to support a technology called *Dynamic Data Exchange* (DDE). Data could be moved between applications. Another addition was MS-DOS Executive, which provided a graphical method for browsing and launching files from a point and click environment.

Windows 2.03 was the first product to support the protected mode capabilities of the 80386. It also took advantage of extended memory. In essence, it was the predecessor to the version that would eventually make Microsoft a giant. The consumer had a choice of either 360K floppies or 720K 3.5″ floppies. A full install required 1.41MB.

WINDOWS 3.X VERSIONS

Windows first established itself as a mainstream desktop environment with the release of Windows 3.0 in 1990. Unlike version 2.03, which could take advantage of only some of the more advanced features of the 80386 microprocessor, Windows 3.0 took full advantage of this CPU.

It wasn't its computing power that appealed to the masses, however. It was the 16-color display that made the 4-color displays of the competition pale in comparison (**Figure 22.2**). It didn't hurt that Microsoft also showed their usual business savvy by releasing a Software Development Kit (SDK) that made programming applications for Windows 3.0 easier. The result was a plethora of new applications designed specifically for this new environment.

Some technological improvements that provided added horsepower to the 3.x products in general were hidden beneath the hood, but without them, Windows 3.x would not have enjoyed quite the success it did. One that was noticeable was the fact that MS-DOS Executive was replaced with a more powerful program called Program Manager (PM). PM was the predecessor of the Windows Explorer we all know and love today. Some of the hidden improvements included the following:

- Full support for virtual memory (swap files)
- A *Virtual Machine Manager* that supported virtual real mode operation for multiple programs in separate windows (more on that later)
- The ability to take control of the hardware from MS-DOS
- The ability to run programs in extended memory
- Cooperative multitasking

A key concept to keep in the back of your mind throughout the remainder of this chapter is that, in truth, none of the Windows 3.x products were true operating systems. They required

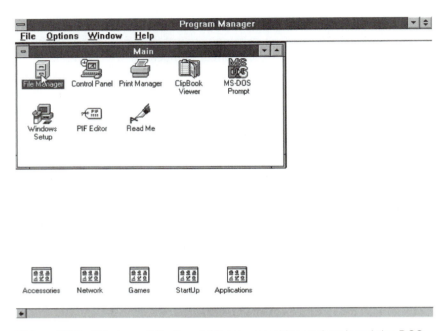

Figure 22.2 Windows 3.0 offered 16-color graphics and replaced the DOS Executive with Program Manager.

MS-DOS to be present in order to boot the system, and they still relied on the MS-DOS kernel. Therefore, the structure of Windows 3.x needs to be examined.

WINDOWS 3.X STRUCTURE

In Chapter Two, An Introduction to Operating Systems, I pointed out that every OS has at its very core a collection of critical files around which the rest of the system is built. With MS-DOS, those files were IO.SYS, MSDOS.SYS, and COMMAND.COM. There are six critical files in the Windows 3.x foundation. **Table 22.1** lists those files and their functions.

Notice that WIN.COM isn't listed there? Although this file is essential for loading Windows, once loaded, this file steps aside and lets the core files take over. Which brings me to the boot process of Windows 3.x.

WINDOWS 3.X BOOT PROCESS

As I pointed out earlier, a computer system doesn't directly boot Windows 3.x. DOS must be running for any of these Windows products to function properly. Therefore, the first part of the boot process is identical to that of MS-DOS. Refer to Chapter Twenty-One, MS-DOS and the Command Prompt, for a detailed description.

Table 22.1   Windows 3.x Core Files

File Name	File Description
IO.SYS (loads with DOS)	A hidden read-only file located in the root directory of the active primary partition. Interfaces with system BIOS for hardware interaction.
MSDOS.SYS (loads with DOS)	A hidden read-only file located in the root directory of the active primary partition. Acts as the OS kernel.
COMMAND.COM (loads with DOS)	Read-only (but not hidden) file located in the root directory of the active primary partition. Manages the internal and external command structure for the OS.
KRNL386.EXE (loads with Windows)	Takes over control of I/O requests from IO.SYS. Handles memory management and CPU control.
USER.EXE (loads with Windows)	Creates and maintains windows on the screen for running programs. USER.EXE also handles requests regarding the icons and other components of the user interface. USER.EXE directs input to the appropriate application from the keyboard, mouse, and other input sources.
GDI.EXE (loads with Windows)	The graphics device interface, which executes graphics operations that create images on the system display and directs graphical output to other devices such as printers.

These six files are essential for Windows 3.x operation.

After DOS is loaded, the user enters **WIN.COM** at the command prompt. Since most dealers who configured Windows 3.x computers for their customers added WIN.COM as the final line to AUTOEXEC.BAT, this command was entered automatically, and to most users, it appeared that Windows loaded directly.

WIN.COM runs a quick check of processor functions to make sure that the processor supports protected mode and that all the basic processor subcomponents are available. It then starts the graphical interface of Windows, which is apparent to the user because of the pretty little Windows banner that appears on the screen (**Figure 22.3**).

At this point, WIN.COM passes control of the boot process over to a file called WIN386.EXE and steps aside. WIN386.EXE first switches the CPU over to protected mode, unless the user has inserted a switch in the WIN.COM command that instructs it not to do so. Next KRNL386.EXE is loaded.

When the kernel has successfully loaded, WIN386.EXE reads a file called SYSTEM.INI. This file controls and initializes all the resources for the computer. It contains system hardware settings and associated information. In addition, it maintains a list of drivers for each piece of hardware installed. It also contains information about each and every application installed on that system.

As soon as SYSTEM.INI has done its job, WIN386.EXE goes out looking for GDI.EXE and USER.EXE. Once these files are loaded, the full GUI is in place and operational. Next WIN386.EXE locates and loads PROGMAN.EXE, which loads the Windows Desktop. In doing so, it reads a file called WIN.INI. Another text file called PROGMAN.INI defines the desktop environment. Once PROGMAN.INI has loaded, Windows is ready for the user to start playing Minesweeper.

MULTITASKING IN WINDOWS 3.X

Windows 3.0 was the first Microsoft application to support true multitasking. Several previous third-party applications had provided task-switching capabilities, but there is a huge difference between task switching and multitasking. With *task switching* there are not two different programs running at once. While one program is running, it has full and complete control of the system. When the user switches over to another program, the first program must be closed.

Figure 22.3 The Windows 3.x banner (3.11 for Workgroups in this illustration) indicates that WIN.COM has successfully started the GUI of Windows.

So if the program was closed, how is it that users can get back to that program when they're ready to use it once again? Certain information, such as user data and what program threads were running at the time the program was exited, get stored to temporary files. When it is time to return to that application, those files are reopened, and users continue where they left off.

There are two problems associated with this approach. First off, the time involved in closing one program and opening another is noticeable enough to be annoying. Second, this does not permit data to be moved seamlessly from one application to another.

Multitasking keeps multiple programs open on the system at once. The CPU simply runs a series of instructions for one program and then switches over to another program and runs a few instructions for that one. Windows 3.0 and its siblings all use cooperative multitasking.

Cooperative multitasking places the responsibility for relinquishing control of the CPU and other resources onto the application running at the time. Programmers were required to place break points into their code that suspended the program so that another program could take over for a few clock cycles, until one of its break points was reached.

BUZZ WORDS

Task switching: The ability of an OS to close a program, run another, and then return to the same point in the program previously closed.

Multitasking: The ability of an OS to simultaneously run more than one program at once.

Cooperative multitasking: The ability of an OS to simultaneously run more than one program, placing responsibility on the application for relinquishing control of the system.

The problem with this approach is that if a routine needs to run from beginning to end (which most did) other applications running on the system appear to freeze up until the system is released by the application in control.

Still, multitasking did lead the way to Dynamic Data Exchange and Object Link Embedding (OLE), two features that turned Windows into a household name. DDE allows users to move data back and forth between applications. OLE allows an object such as an embedded table to be automatically updated if the source of that data changes, even if that source is another app.

WINDOWS MODES

The Windows 3.x versions were all designed to be able to run on anything from a 286-based PC and up. As such, there had to be some way in which the features specific to 386 and higher microprocessors could be switched off. To accomplish this, Microsoft designed Windows 3.x to run in three different modes. These modes were real mode, standard mode, and 386 enhanced mode. Which mode you selected dictated how much functionality your system had.

REAL MODE

As I've pointed out repeatedly, the early versions of Windows started out as nothing more than a point and click shell for MS-DOS. Versions prior to 3.0 had no memory management functions and couldn't even dream of multitasking. But then again, neither could any of the CPUs these versions were designed to run on. *Real mode* basically defines the behavior of an original MS-DOS program. It is capable of running only in the lower 640K of conventional RAM. No more than one application could be running on the computer at any given time. The presence of any data or command from another application would result in something called a non-maskable interrupt (NMI). An NMI occurs when something on the system has occurred which requires the CPU's immediate and instantaneous attention. If the CPU has a command loaded that knows what to do about the situation, the CPU fixes the problem and the system moves on along as if nothing ever happened. If the CPU *doesn't* know how to deal with the situation, it shuts off completely. An NMI generated by software always falls into the latter category.

So, to briefly summarize real mode: any program running in real mode must run in the lower 640K, it must be the only software running on the machine, it cannot share memory addresses with any other application, and it must have full control of the CPU. In the dark ages of computing, users with 8088 processors in their computers had no alternative to running in real mode. Machines with 80286 processors could run in protected mode, but in order to make use of virtual memory and run in enhanced mode, an 80386 processor or later was required.

BUZZ WORDS ————————

Real mode: An operational mode for either a CPU or an OS in which only one application can be present on the system at a time and only 1MB of RAM can be addressed by that application.

STANDARD MODE

Standard mode took advantage of the protected mode functions of a 286 (or higher) processor. This allowed Windows to address up to 16MB of RAM, and it also allowed multiple applications that were designed for protected mode to run simultaneously (well, sort of, anyway). As you might imagine, this ability caused problems with programs that ran in MS-DOS's real mode. Also, DOS programs could only run full screen. They could not run in a window.

So if two programs are going to run at the same time on a Windows 3.0 machine, and one of those programs happens to be an MS-DOS program, then Windows has to make sure that the DOS program thinks that it is the only ticket holder in the theater. For that to happen, the user needs to be able to run in . . .

BUZZ WORDS

Standard mode: An operational mode specific to Windows in which the OS could access expanded memory beyond 1MB and could task switch among multiple applications.

Enhanced mode: An operational mode specific to Windows that took advantage of advanced functions available in the 80386 microprocessor, including the ability to use virtual memory and to function in virtual real mode.

---

386 ENHANCED MODE

As its name implies, 386 enhanced mode takes full advantage of the advanced functions of the 386 microprocessor. This mode supports extended memory addresses up to 4GB. It also adds support for virtual memory, and a Virtual Machine Manager (VMM) that runs in 386 enhanced mode allows multiple MS-DOS programs to run simultaneously. I'll be describing how this function works a little later in this chapter. In order to run in 386 enhanced mode, Windows has to have a minimum of 2MB of RAM available.

A key feature of enhanced mode operation is that programs can actually run in addresses beyond conventional memory. No longer is the programmer restricted to making a program run in a mere 640K of RAM. An expanded memory manager brought over from DOS and modified for use in Windows made this possible. The file is EMM386.EXE. Unless this file successfully loads, running in enhanced mode is not possible. Also, the user can enjoy the ability to run a word processor and a spreadsheet at the same time. OLE and DDE substantially reduce the amount of work a user has to do in order to complete a given task.

WINDOWS ARCHITECTURE

As I've said, technically speaking, Windows 3.x is not an operating system in the true sense. However, once loaded, it takes over the role of OS from DOS. As such, it becomes responsible for managing the core OS functions. Yet at the same time, it is also responsible for making sure that DOS is able to function when and where needed. The architecture of Windows was designed around those premises.

WINDOWS MEMORY MANAGEMENT

Windows may rely on DOS in order to start, but once loaded, it takes over the system completely, including the critical functions of memory management. Windows is capable of performing several tricks in order to more efficiently utilize the memory that is available and to assure that programs receive the amount and the type of memory they require. Among these techniques are the following:

- BIOS shadowing
- Expanded memory (discussed in Chapter Twenty-One)
- Upper memory blocks
- Memory mapping
- Virtual memory

BIOS SHADOWING

While shadowing is not exclusively the domain of Windows, it is a technique that Windows always used. Since the system relies heavily on the BIOS interrupts I discussed in Chapter Two, calls are constantly being made to the BIOS chip. However, compared to RAM, the PROM chip used to store BIOS is unacceptably slow.

Windows takes the core hardware interrupts of BIOS and copies them to the middle 128K block of upper memory. This process of copying code to a secondary location is called shadowing. It differs from a direct copying function, because once the code is copied to the new location, the original addresses of the interrupts are disabled, and the new addresses in upper memory are used instead. On older machines the technique could improve the performance of hardware I/O operations a substantial margin.

UPPER MEMORY BLOCKS

The meticulously laid out map of upper memory that was used for DOS didn't make quite as much sense by the time Windows 3.0 was released. VGA was rapidly replacing EGA and CGA, so that region of memory wasn't used to the same extent. The top 128K had always been available for device drivers, but management of that space was notoriously inefficient in DOS. And since Windows managed memory more efficiently, it made more sense to use that space in other ways.

In Chapter Twenty-One, I discussed how EMM386.EXE provided access to memory addresses beyond 1MB. Another function of this program is to manage the upper and high memory areas. It divides upper memory into blocks called upper memory blocks (UMB). These blocks are created based on the amount of space required by the program intended to occupy them. The programs generally loaded into upper memory are things like device drivers and are generally quite small.

Typically UMBs are created in 8KB increments and cannot be larger than 64KB. A program running in UMB must be contiguous. If a 16KB program wants to run in upper memory and there are two noncontiguous 8KB blocks available, then that program cannot load.

The Windows version of EMM386.EXE does a much more efficient job of looking at the programs it wants to load in upper memory and then creating the UMBs needed. As a result more programs get loaded in upper memory.

MEMORY MAPPING

Windows 3.x had a couple of issues it had to deal with when managing the memory space above 1MB. For one thing, due to compatibility issues with DOS programs, it had to be able to support expanded memory. The page frame was a strictly defined 64KB address space through which everything moved from extended memory down into conventional memory and back. Programs running exclusively in extended memory obviously didn't need the page frame. They needed to be able to map everything to spaces above 2MB.

Windows got around potential memory conflicts by using a virtual address space of 4GB for every application opened. Since no system of the time had that much space available, there was a little bit of trickery involved here. The 4GB assigned is "pretend" space, but is mapped out with addresses the same as is physical memory. The physical memory is mapped out on a hardware level by the chipset's memory control circuit and on a software level by EMM386.EXE. EMM386.EXE can translate these virtual addresses into the real physical addresses occupied by the application or its data and use virtual memory to store any excess.

VIRTUAL MEMORY

Virtual memory is a method by which a chunk of hard drive space can be reserved for use by the OS and treated as if it is physical RAM. In the days when Windows 3.0 was first released a well-loaded computer consisted of a 127MB hard disk, 8MB of RAM, and a 386 microprocessor. While 8MB seemed like an immense amount of memory at the time, for a user running four or five apps at the same time, keeping DOS and Windows alive in the background, it wasn't enough.

So the *Virtual Memory Manager* (VMM) creates a hidden file on the hard disk called 386SPART.PAR. This is the file commonly known as the swap file (see **Figure 22.4**). When code or data is required by an actively running application, and there isn't enough physical RAM in which to store it, inactive code or data is moved from RAM to the swap file. When the application or data that had been banished to the swap file is once again needed, something else moves out of RAM to make room for it.

Of course, all of this data movement requires large numbers of hard disk I/O operations. These seriously impact system performance. Therefore, the more physical RAM the user has installed, the less the swap file is used. Increasing memory had (as it does today) much more impact on system performance than upgrading to a faster processor.

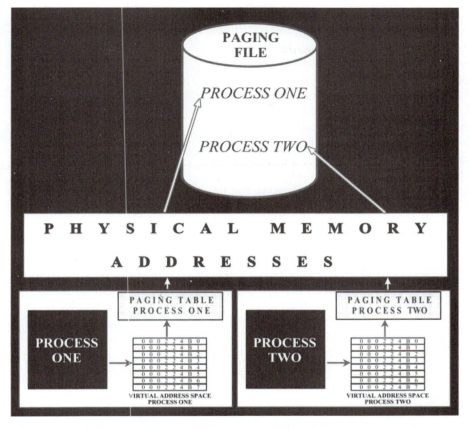

Figure 22.4   Virtual memory basically treats a portion of the hard disk as if it is physical RAM.

PROCESSOR CONTROL IN WINDOWS 3.X

When Windows is started in 386 enhanced mode, it is assumed that multitasking is going to be required. And sometimes that multitasking is going to involve older DOS applications that have to run in real mode. It will *always* require that the application share CPU time with core OS files.

One of the features of the 80386 microprocessor that made this all possible was the fact that Intel designers incorporated into the processor design four separate *privilege levels*. A privilege level basically determines the priority that any given line of code has over another line of code, assuming both want to run at the same time. These privilege levels are called *processor rings*. Processor rings are ordered on the basis of their current privilege level (CPL) and range from CPL-0 to CPL-3. A line of code running in Ring 0 (or CPL-0) has priority over Ring 1, which has priority over Ring 2, which has priority over Ring 3. Get the idea?

By having certain functions run in certain rings, the possibility that a renegade string of code from a poorly designed application might bring the entire system down is minimized. Windows specifications call for core system functions, such as the Virtual Machine Manager and the kernel, to run in Ring 0, where they enjoy maximum protection. In Windows 3.0, code running in real mode, such as DOS programs and BIOS code, run in Ring 3, and all other applications run in Ring 1. Starting with Windows 3.1 and in all subsequent 3.x releases, all the code running in Ring 1 is moved over to run in Ring 3. So essentially, Rings 1 and 2 are left under the control of the processor.

Microsoft products to this day continue to utilize this architecture. However, a slightly different vocabulary is used. Processes running in Ring 0 are said to be running in *supervisory mode*. These are the processes that require the most protection and the highest processor priority. All other processes, which would be running in Ring 3, are running in *user mode*.

> ## BUZZ WORDS
>
> **Privilege level:** A level of protection and priority that certain lines of code running within an OS have over other lines of code.
>
> **Processor ring:** Another term for privilege level.
>
> **Supervisory mode:** A process by which an OS runs code at the highest possible privilege level.
>
> **User mode:** A process by which an OS runs code at a lower privilege level.
>
> **Virtual machine:** An environment set up in system memory that emulates all functions of a working computer, providing the illusion that a program is the only code running on a computer system.

VIRTUAL MACHINES

To understand how an OS manages to juggle several different applications running at once along with their associated data, you must understand the concept of *virtual machines*. Like anything else virtual, a virtual machine doesn't really exist. But the things that require its services, such as applications, think that it does. Don't confuse a virtual machine with virtual memory. They're not the same. However, a virtual machine is capable of addressing virtual memory, so in that sense, they're virtually related.

A virtual machine is emulated in memory. The program running in that virtual machine is allotted its own share of CPU time and is under the impression that it owns the CPU. It just can't figure out why there are times in which the CPU seems to have gone to sleep. It doesn't know about the other programs that think *they're* the only ones the CPU will deign to address.

The OS intervenes on behalf of each virtual program for every service it requires. It has to. The virtual machine has absolutely no access to any code running in Ring 0. So if the program issues a hardware interrupt, it issues it to the VMM.

What happens if two different applications attempt to run at the same instant? That depends entirely on the CPU. Some of the more modern CPUs have multiple pipelines and can process more than one thread of code at the same time. On one of these processors, both apps will run concurrently. On earlier CPUs without this capability, the VMM intercepts both calls and based on priority, determines which one runs first.

VIRTUAL DEVICE DRIVERS

It only makes sense that if you're going to have a virtual machine, then you're going to have to use virtual device drivers (VDD). In the old days of DOS, the device driver basically acted as an extension to the BIOS and, in essence, any application running in DOS could directly access the hardware. However, in the days of DOS, two programs could never run at the same time, and therefore, there was no possibility that a device would receive two hardware calls at the same time. Such an event would result in one of those NMIs I discussed earlier.

In order to maintain backward compatibility with DOS programs, Windows 3.x requires that AUTOEXEC.BAT and CONFIG.SYS files contain any relevant information for a device and load DOS drivers. However, in order to make sure the system remains stable while multitasking, when any program (including a DOS program) is loaded into a virtual machine, it is assigned a VDD. The VDD intercepts any hardware calls, and the VMM issues calls directly to the hardware. In Windows 3.x these driver files end in a .386 extension.

DYNAMICALLY LINKED LIBRARIES

A concept Windows 3.0 borrowed from the world of UNIX was that of the Dynamically Linked Library (DLL). These are also called dynamic link libraries. Since many programs might require exactly the same subroutines or code as another at any given time, rather than write this code into each and every application that runs under Windows, that code is stored in a *library*. The library serves as a repository for this information. When an application requires the services of a particular DLL, it issues a call for a subroutine, and the OS intercepts that call and loads the appropriate DLL in its place. The app neither knows nor cares that what it originally requested wasn't exactly what it got. Its needs were fulfilled either way.

There are a couple of advantages to using DLLs. For one thing, DLLs can be changed to accommodate new programs and/or services that may be developed. For example, a company might write a DLL to provide a direct link to the virtual driver for a its brand of digital cameras. When that DLL was first conceived, there were only a handful of models of that camera available. As the manufacturer comes out with more advanced models, it takes the DLL, adds the new subroutines, and replaces the older file with the newer one when users install the device drivers for their new toys.

A second advantage of a DLL is that it only gets loaded into RAM when and if it is needed. When the driver call for that camera is made, the DLL is dynamically loaded into RAM (bet you wondered where that part of the name came from), runs, and is unloaded when its task is completed. This prevents resource requirements for an OS from being any greater than they already are.

> **BUZZ WORDS**
>
> **Library:** In programming, a collection of subroutines that are required by several or all applications running on a computer. By storing this code in a single file, it does not need to be duplicated many times over.

Chapter Summary

In the past several pages you have been introduced to a number of the concepts that would go on to make Windows what it is today. Although it is totally unnecessary for a technician these days to understand how Windows 3.1 is installed and how to run the OS, an understanding of its basic architecture goes a long way in understanding some of the concepts that will be introduced later in this book.

Brain Drain

1. Several times in this chapter, it was pointed out that Windows 3.x products were not true OSs. Explain why this is so.

2. It was also pointed out that Windows 3.x takes over the role of OS once it is loaded. Discuss several ways how it does that.

3. Discuss the concept of the virtual machine. Why is it that several virtual machines can be running on a single computer at any given time?

4. What is a DLL, and why is it so important to the Windows environment?

5. How do virtual device drivers differ from a "real" device driver?

The 64K$ Questions

1. Steve Jobs named the LISA after _____.

   a. His wife
   b. His daughter
   c. His mother
   d. His secretary

2. What is one key reason why most people today won't load Windows 1.0 onto their computer just to see what it could do?

   a. It only runs under DOS, and DOS won't run on today's machines.
   b. The presence of memory over 1MB causes WIN.COM to fail.
   c. It had no VGA drivers, and most of us today don't have an old EGA video card and monitor lying around.
   d. It would corrupt their current OSs.

3. Which of the following features of the 80386 microprocessor did Windows 3.x exclusively take advantage of when running in 386 enhanced mode?

   a. Protected mode
   b. The 32-bit address bus
   c. Virtual real mode
   d. Virtual memory

4. DOS has already been loaded on the system and the user types in the command **WIN**. What is the first file to be loaded by WIN.COM?

   a. WIN386.EXE
   b. KRNL386.EXE
   c. USER.EXE
   d. GDI.EXE

5. Windows 3.x versions all use _____ in order to give the user the sense that multiple programs are running at the same time.

a. Pre-emptive multitasking

b. Cooperative multitasking

c. Task switching

d. Preoperative multitasking

6. The core OS files in Windows 3.x all run in _____.

a. Ring 0

b. Ring 1

c. Ring 2

d. Ring 3

7. Applications in Windows 3.x all run in _____.

a. Ring 0

b. Ring 1

c. Ring 2

d. Ring 3

8. Which operational mode of Windows requires an 80386 (or higher) processor in order to function?

a. Real mode

b. Standard mode

c. Enhanced mode

d. Virtual mode

9. Which operational mode of Windows takes advantage of memory beyond 1MB but cannot address virtual memory?

a. Real mode

b. Standard mode

c. Enhanced mode

d. Virtual mode

10. Which Windows feature allows the user to put an Excel table into a Word document that will automatically update in Word every time the user changes the source data in Excel?

a. OLE

b. DDX

c. OSI

d. DDE

11. Which operational mode of Windows did legacy DOS applications run in?

a. Real mode

b. Standard mode

c. Enhanced mode

d. Virtual mode

12. Which of the following functions in Windows ensured that DOS programs never knew that other applications were running on the system?

a. The legacy DLL

b. The VMM

c. WIN.COM

d. EMM386.EXE

13. Which of the following Windows functions allowed memory beyond 1MB to be utilized?

a. The legacy DLL

b. The VMM

c. WIN.COM

d. EMM386.EXE

14. A file that provides a unified set of instructions to a number of different applications is known as an _____.

a. DLL

b. VXD

c. API

d. INI

15. Which Windows feature allows the user to move data seamlessly from one application to another on the fly?

a. OLE

b. DDX

c. OSI

d. DDE

16. The reason several DOS applications can be run at the same time in Windows 3.x is that _____.
    a. Windows drops back to task switching when DOS programs are involved
    b. Cooperative multitasking prevents each DOS app from seeing one another
    c. Each app runs in a separate virtual machine
    d. They can't.

17. What is the default size of a typical UMB?
    a. 8K
    b. 12K
    c. 16K
    d. 32K

18. Where was information stored in virtual memory located in Windows 3.x?
    a. A hidden partition created when Windows was first installed
    b. A file called VMM.DLL
    c. A file called 386SPART.PAR
    d. A file called SYSMEM.VMM

19. What was the typical extension for a virtual device driver in Windows 3.x?
    a. .VXD
    b. .DLL
    c. .VDD
    d. .386

20. A process running in Ring 0 is said to be running in _____.
    a. User mode
    b. Supervisory mode
    c. Restricted mode
    d. Access mode

TRICKY TERMINOLOGY

Cooperative multitasking: The ability of an OS to simultaneously run more than one program, placing responsibility on the application for relinquishing control of the system.

Enhanced mode: An operational mode specific to Windows that took advantage of advanced functions available in the 80386 microprocessor, including the ability to use virtual memory and to function in virtual real mode.

Library: In programming, a collection of subroutines that are required by several or all applications running on a computer. By storing this code in a single file, it does not need to be duplicated many times over.

Multitasking: The ability of an OS to simultaneously run more than one program at once.

Privilege level: A level of protection and priority that certain lines of code running within an OS have over other lines of code.

Processor ring: Another term for privilege level.

Real mode: An operational mode for either a CPU or an OS in which only one application can be present on the system at once and only 1MB of RAM can be addressed by that application.

Standard mode: An operational mode specific to Windows in which the OS could access expanded memory beyond 1MB and could task switch multiple applications.

Supervisory mode: A process by which an OS runs code at the highest possible privilege level.

Task switching: The ability of an OS to close a program, run another, and then return to the same point in the program previously closed.

User mode: A process by which an OS runs code at a lower privilege level.

Virtual machine: An environment set up in system memory that emulates all functions of a working computer, providing the illusion that a program is the only code running on a computer system.

ACRONYM ALERT

COMDEX: Computer Dealer Exposition. An annual trade show for businesses in the computer industry.

CPL: Current Privilege Level. The level of priority at which code is running on machines. It is the method by which processor rings are defined.

DDE: Dynamic Data Exchange. A technology for exchanging data between two autonomous programs running on a single computer.

DLL: Dynamically Linked Library. A file that contains a collection of subroutines that can be called on the fly by any application running on the system that requires the services it provides and then can be flushed from memory when its task is finished.

NMI: Non-Maskable Interrupt. Any software or hardware induced interrupt that requires instantaneous attention from the CPU.

OLE: Object Linking and Embedding. A technology that allows an object to be created in one application, imported into a second application; should the properties of the object ever change in the first, it is automatically updated in the second.

PM: Program Manager. A file and application management utility provided in Windows 3.x products.

SDK: Software Development Kit. A collection of utilities and programs provided by an OS manufacturer that makes the development of applications to run on its OS much easier.

UMB: Upper Memory Block. A segment of memory created by an extended memory manager in the address range between 640K and 1MB of conventional memory.

VDD: Virtual Device Driver. A piece of software running within an OS that emulates a hardware device driver.

VMM: Virtual Machine Manager and Virtual Memory Manager. The first is a piece of software running within an OS that creates, maintains, and breaks down in memory an environment that emulates an actual computer. The second is a piece of software running within an OS that creates and manages the swap file on a hard drive.

CHAPTER 23

INTRODUCING WIN9x

The Windows versions from 3.0 to 3.11WFW provided a useful and formidable entry into the GUI for Microsoft. Unfortunately, they lacked the punch and the stability offered by some of its competitors: most notably the Apple Macintosh. As the 80386 gave way to the 80486 there was no driving need to change OS technology. The 486 was little more than a 386 on steroids.

However, when the Pentium was released in 1993, it offered several features not supported by Windows 3.x. The most notable of these features was the presences of multiple processing pipelines. The CPU could process several lines of code at the same time, but Windows could not. At about the same time, Intel threw another wrench into the works. That wrench was called Plug 'n Play.

Microsoft's original intent had been to release a 32-bit multi-threading OS in 1992. Delays in development and production haunted the product practically from its inception, but once Windows 95 (WIN95) was released in the summer of 1995, it was an unmitigated commercial success. It sold more than a million copies in the first day and essentially put an end to competition in the OS world for nearly a decade.

This chapter will cover the various versions of WIN9x. The more advanced users among you will know these versions as the 4.xx.xxxx versions. The number four indicated that they were in reality Windows Version 4. The two digits following the 4 indicated sub-versions, and the final three or four digits were revision numbers.

For the most part, the core remains essentially the same. There are, however, some differences between versions that should be pointed out.

A+ OPERATING SYSTEM TECHNOLOGIES EXAM OBJECTIVES

In this chapter, I will cover the following CompTIA exam objectives:

1.1 Identify the major desktop components and interfaces and their functions. Differentiate the characteristics of Windows 9x/Me, Windows NT 4.0 Workstation, Windows 2000 Professional, and Windows XP.

2.1 Identify the procedures for installing Windows 9x/Me, Windows NT 4.0 Workstation, Windows 2000 Professional, and Windows XP, and bringing the software to a basic operational level.

2.2   Identify steps to perform an operating system upgrade from Windows 9x/Me, Windows NT 4.0 Workstation, Windows 2000 Professional, and Windows XP. Given an upgrade scenario, choose the appropriate next steps.

HARDWARE REQUIREMENTS AND NEW FEATURES OF WIN95

Contrary to popular belief, WIN95 was not the first Microsoft OS to feature a GUI. Windows NT 3.1 earned that honor in 1993. However, that OS was designed for high-end workstations and network environments and didn't get a lot of public exposure. Its lifespan was relatively short, it is rarely, if ever, seen today, and it isn't covered on any certification exams. Therefore, I won't be covering NT 3.1 in this book.

WIN95 was the first graphical OS to capture the public's fancy. Previous versions of Windows had required MS-DOS to be properly configured and running on the computer before they could load. WIN95 stands on its own. It is a 32-bit OS as well and, therefore, could take full advantage of emerging processors.

MINIMUM HARDWARE REQUIREMENTS FOR INSTALLATION

Microsoft's intent had originally been for WIN95 to run on any machine that had been capable of running WIN3.x in 386 enhanced mode. In this respect, it fell a little short. The requirements were a bit more stringent. Still, by today's standards the requirements were quite modest. In order to run WIN95 a computer needs the following at the minimum:

- 20MHz 386DX microprocessor
- 4MB of RAM
- 1.44MB floppy diskette drive
- 85MB free hard disk space (for local installation)
- VGA graphics

EXAM NOTE: For virtually all of the Microsoft OSs, CompTIA expects you to know the minimum hardware requirements for installation. Know them all. You never know which OS it will hit you with.

Just having hardware that meets the minimum specifications is no guarantee that a computer will successfully run WIN95. The hardware also has to support virtual device drivers exclusively. As a result, Microsoft would only support the product if a customer's computer consisted entirely of hardware that was included in its Hardware Compatibility List (HCL).

NEW FEATURES

For the user whose computer satisfied all the requirements, a plethora of new features were available. Some of these new features focused on OS stability, while others focused on the user experience. All of them collectively were really little more than a brief glimpse of what was to come.

PLUG 'N PLAY

Plug 'n Play (PnP) was a new standard incorporated into WIN95 that (in theory, at least) allows a user to install a new piece of hardware and have the OS automatically configure the device. The first versions of PnP worked pretty well as long as the user was using:

- A device that was fully PnP compliant
- A computer with a PnP-compliant BIOS
- A PnP-compliant OS

Anyone who ever fought with a device installation when even one of these three critical elements was missing understands fully why, in its early stages, PnP developed the nickname Plug 'n Pray. When it did work, it was a blessing. A device was automatically recognized by the BIOS during POST and assigned an IRQ. Windows automatically detected the new device once it was loaded and launched a device installation wizard that led the user through the process of driver installation.

> **EXAM NOTE:** It is very likely that you might get a question relating to the three essential elements required for PnP to be 100% functional. Even though many consider this to be a hardware issue, you can expect to see it on the OS exam as well.

In the early stages of PnP there were three types of devices that could be auto-configured by PnP:

- PnP-compliant ISA devices
- PCI devices
- PCMCIA devices

All PCI and PCMCIA devices were designed to be PnP compliant by default. ISA devices were not PnP compliant by nature, and the capabilities had to be incorporated into the device.

FAT32

Previous Microsoft desktop offerings had supported only the FAT16 file system. Windows NT 3.1 had introduced the NTFS file system, but as I mentioned earlier, that OS didn't see much use on the desktop environment. FAT32 appeared in Service Release 2 (SR2) of WIN95 and offers all of the advantages of that file system. For a more detailed discussion, refer back to Chapter Two, An Introduction to Operating Systems.

PRE-EMPTIVE MULTITASKING

Instead of using the cooperative multitasking used by WIN3.x, WIN95 uses *pre-emptive multitasking*. No longer are the applications in charge of when, where, and how they give up control of the system. A *task scheduler* runs as an integral part of the OS and makes sure each and every application running on the system has an equal chance at system resources.

BUZZ WORDS

Pre-emptive multitasking: A way to manage multiple applications on a computer system that puts the responsibility for releasing system resources onto the OS.

Task scheduler: A system file that determines how long a particular application can retain control of system resources.

> **EXAM NOTE:** Be able to distinguish between cooperative multitasking and pre-emptive multitasking. It's a popular exam topic.

INTEGRATED 32-BIT TCP/IP

WIN95 is the first OS in which TCP/IP was included as a default networking protocol. Windows 3.11WFW provided support only for Microsoft's native NetBEUI protocol and its own version of IPX/SPX in order to allow it to work on Novell networks. For 3.11 to run on a TCP/IP network, the protocol had to be installed separately.

INTEGRATED MULTIMEDIA CAPABILITIES

Microsoft incorporated into WIN95 several new features specific to the enjoyment of multimedia applications. For one thing, CD-ROM support and the CDFS file system were part of the default installation. A new video playback engine called Video for Windows was also part of the OS.

WIN9x STRUCTURE

In nearly every respect, WIN95 was a dramatic departure from the 3.x products. One of the more glaring differences is that it is a true OS and not simply an application running on top of DOS. Second, it was the first consumer-level 32-bit OS from Microsoft to hit the market. In order to maintain backward compatibility with WIN3.x and MS-DOS, certain key elements from each were carried over.

KERNEL FILES

If you recall from Chapter Three, The Evolution of Windows and Windows Basics, Windows 3.x relied on the three core files of MS-DOS, IO.SYS, MSDOS.SYS, and COMMAND.COM, to

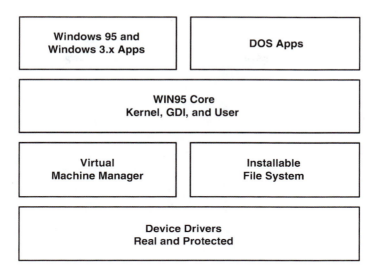

Windows 95 and Windows 3.x Apps	DOS Apps

| WIN95 Core Kernel, GDI, and User | |

| Virtual Machine Manager | Installable File System |

| Device Drivers Real and Protected | |

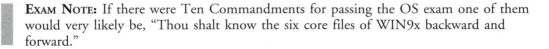

Figure 23.1   WIN95 Architecture

be fully loaded and operational before Windows could be run. And then Windows ran as a separate application. The three core files of WIN3.x were KRNL385.EXE, GDI.EDE, and USER.EXE.

For the purposes of backward compatibility, Windows retains all of these files. These files continue to make up the core of WIN9x (**Figure 23.1**). However, their significance and, in one case, even the structure differs greatly. First consider the core files retained from MS-DOS.

EXAM NOTE: If there were Ten Commandments for passing the OS exam one of them would very likely be, "Thou shalt know the six core files of WIN9x backward and forward."

IO.SYS

In WIN95, IO.SYS has been retooled and actually performs the functions for which IO.SYS and MSDOS.SYS had been responsible in the days of DOS. All of the information required to start the computer following a successful POST is contained in this one file. Now, if you recall from Chapter Twenty-One, MS-DOS and the Command Prompt, IO.SYS had been responsible for calling up CONFIG.SYS, and MSDOS.SYS loaded AUTOEXEC.BAT.

WIN95 requires neither CONFIG.SYS nor AUTOEXEC.BAT in order to boot. They're both present for that elusive goal of backward compatibility. WIN95 extracts its system information from a structure called the registry, which I'll be covering in detail later in this chapter.

MSDOS.SYS

If MSDOS.SYS has been combined with IO.SYS, then why is there still a file by that name? Once again, it's for backward compatibility. Microsoft had no illusions that people who had spent the last several years accumulating expensive software for their Windows 3.1 computers were going to upgrade to WIN95 if they knew they would have to shell out several hundred (or even several thousand) dollars for all new software.

In WIN95, MSDOS.SYS exists as an ASCII text file with a structure very similar to one of the INI files used by WIN3.x. **Figure 23.2** shows the default MSDOS.SYS open in a DOS editor. As you can see from the text in the illustration, this file must be a minimum of 1024 bytes long. According to Microsoft, a file smaller than this size is likely to be seen by many antivirus applications as being infected and will be quarantined. The array of Xs following that final statement is there for a reason as well. As long as the file size of 1024 bytes remains consistent, there are a number of statements that can be added to MSDOS.SYS that will fine-tune or modify the performance of windows. **Table 23.1** lists some of those statements and the effect each has on the system.

Making any changes to MSDOS.SYS does require that the attributes of Hidden, Read-only, and System be reset to 0. You cannot do this from Windows Explorer or even from a command prompt once Windows has booted to the GUI. In order to change the attributes on this file, you must boot into DOS mode and make the changes from there.

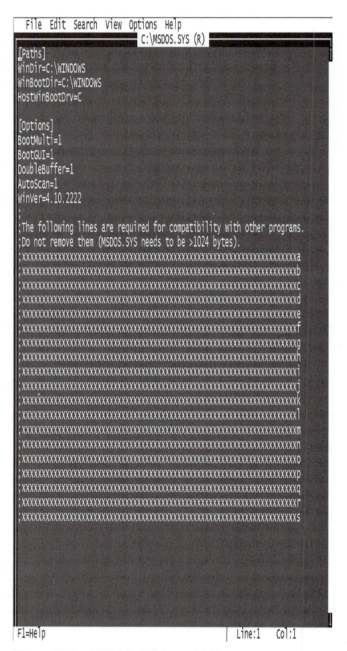

Figure 23.2 MSDOS.SYS is an ASCII text file in WIN9x.

COMMAND.COM

COMMAND.COM retains the same role in WIN9x as it did in MS-DOS. It is the command interpreter for DOS. WIN9x carries with it a version of DOS called DOS 7.0. This version is

Table 23.1   Custom Entries for WIN9x MSDOS.SYS

Entry	Description
Autoscan=	Disable \I "BYPASS" ScanDisk check after system lockup (OSR 2.x + Win98/Me ONLY)
BootDelay=0/1	Skip 2 seconds boot delay (In Win98/Me defaults to 0)
BootGUI=0/1	Boot to MS-DOS mode
BootKeys=0/1	Enable/Disable Startup Menu keys
BootMenu=0/1	Display WIN9x Startup Menu
BootMenuDefault=0/1	Select Normal boot option (loads WIN9x)
BootMenuDelay=0/60	Boot delay (in seconds)
BootMulti=0/1	Enable/Disable Dual-Boot
BootWin=0/1	Enable/Disable WIN9x as OS
DblSpace=0/1	Enable/Disable DoubleSpace
DisableLog=0/1	Enable/Disable BOOTLOG.TXT creation
DoubleBuffer=0/1	Enable/Disable Double Buffer
DrvSpace=0/1	Enable/Disable DriveSpace
HostWinBootDrv=	Set Host WIN9x OS Boot Drive
LoadTop=0/1	Enable/Disable loading of COMMAND.COM in upper memory
Logo=0/1	Display/Not Display Windows Logo during boot
Network=0/1	Enable/Disable boot with Network/TCP/IP support
SystemReg=0/1	Enable/Disable System Registry scan
WinBootDir=	Set WIN9x OS Boot Directory
WinDir=	Set WIN9x OS Directory
WinVer=4.xx.xxxx	Windows 98/Me version check (Win98/Me ONLY)

Entries containing 0/1: 0 disables the function and 1 enables it.

actually a bit scaled down from Version 6.2 and does not support all of the same commands. Still, it provides all of the requisite services of the command prompt.

COMMAND.COM is used only when a command prompt is opened. In GUI mode, WIN.COM acts as the command interpreter. Since WIN9x supports multiple MS-DOS windows being open at once, it is possible for several different instances for COMMAND.COM to be open at the same time.

INI FILES

Also described in Chapter Twenty-Two were several different .INI files. Two key files were SYSTEM.INI and WIN.INI. WIN9x retains these files for backward compatibility with programs designed for WIN3.x. They have exactly the same structure and perform the same functions.

THE WIN9X KERNEL

After you get into the WIN9x kernel, things start to change a bit. Microsoft touted WIN95 as being a 32-bit OS. Windows broke a long-standing tradition in one respect in order to provide this 32-bit support. It stopped supporting older CPUs. If you didn't have a 386DX (or faster) microprocessor, WIN9x didn't run. Calling WIN95 a 32-bit OS was sort of true. However, if I want to be a little more accurate, it really should be called a 16-bit OS with a 32-bit overlay.

BUZZ WORDS —————————

Thunking: A Microsoft process of translating 16-bit commands and data into a 32-bit format, and vice versa.

EXAM NOTE: Be able to define the process of thunking. Whether you like it or not, it's a real word.

By this, I mean that the OS was built on the basis of older 16-bit technology. Other files were sewn into the OS to provide 32-bit functionality without losing the OS's ability to run 16-bit software. In order to accomplish this, Microsoft developed a technique it called thunking. *Thunking* is merely the translation of 32-bit commands into 16-bit format and vice versa. For every 16-bit kernel file, there is a 32-bit file (see **Figure 23.3**). The files involved are KERNEL32.DLL, KRNL386.EXE, USER.DLL, USER.EXE, GDI.DLL, and GDI.EXE. The DLLs are all 32-bit components, while the EXE files are 16-bit.

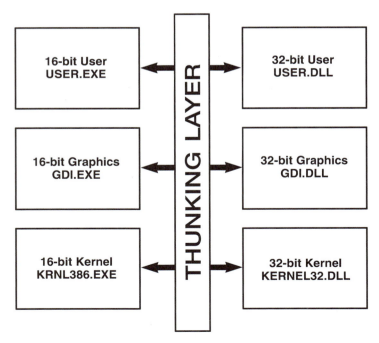

Figure 23.3 Thunking at work.

If a 16-bit application or device is communicating with a 32-bit process, it first communicates with the 16-bit entity, which translates the request and passes it on to the 32-bit version.

Two other features incorporated into the WIN9x architecture were a beefed-up Virtual Machine Manager (VMM) and an Installable File System (IFS). While the VMM provides a similar functionality to the one used in WIN3.x, since it now has the responsibility of sorting out 32-bit applications from 16-bit Windows applications and older DOS apps, Microsoft made it a bit more sophisticated. IFS allows file systems not native to the OS be added. This would include the file system used by various CD formats and the Network File System (NFS) used by networking clients.

> **Buzz Words** ————————
>
> **System virtual machine:** An environment in Windows that emulates a complete computer system and houses all of the critical processes and functions of the OS.

The WIN95 Virtual Machine Manager

In Chapter Twenty-Two, when I was discussing the various modes in which Windows could run, I pointed out that the three basic modes were real, standard, and 386 enhanced modes. WIN95 also included the pre-emptive multitasking I discussed earlier in the chapter. So now, when multiple applications are running on the system, VMM has to keep track of which are 16-bit and which are 32-bit; it has to manage real and protected mode operations running at the same time, and now it has to assure that applications that employ cooperative multitasking don't interfere with those that use pre-emptive multitasking.

As with WIN3.x, the WIN95 VMM accomplishes this by running apps in separate virtual machines. A couple of key things to remember are these: VMM runs in Ring 0, while the machines it creates and manages all run in Ring 3. When WIN95 first boots, it creates its first virtual machine for itself. System services and kernel files all run in this *system virtual machine*. Any WIN95 apps that are started will open a separate VM that runs inside of the system VM.

WIN3.x apps will all run within the same VM. If a WIN3.x application is started, a single VM will be created in which all 3.x apps will subsequently load. This allows the WIN3.x apps to make use of the cooperative multitasking they require. However, it also has the negative effect that, if any WIN3.x app crashes, they all do. And in doing so, they will most likely take all 16-bit support down along with them. **Figure 23.4** illustrates the concept behind the WIN95 Virtual Machine structure.

Each DOS application runs in a separate virtual machine that resides outside of the system machine. DOS VMs occupy no more than 1MB of RAM, divided into 640K of conventional memory and 384K of upper memory, and run in real mode. They can also be configured to use expanded memory, if so desired. For every DOS app on the system, a program information file (PIF) will be created. When users edit the properties of a DOS application, they are editing the PIF. Use of expanded memory is one of the options available (see **Figure 23.5**). Obviously, for this to work, protected mode must be enabled. But the executable cannot run outside of its 1MB shell.

WIN95 can open as many of these real mode virtual machines as the user sees fit, but only one can ever be active at a time. Within each machine a separate instance of IO.SYS, MSDOS.SYS,

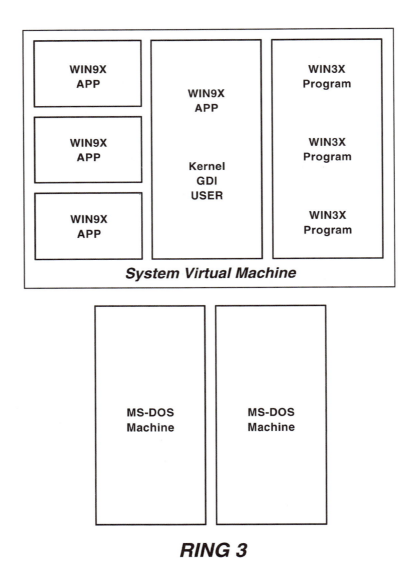

Figure 23.4 The WIN95 Virtual Machine Manager at work.

and COMMAND.COM will run. A separate copy of each DOS device driver required by the system will also be running within each DOS virtual machine. And when one of these apps is active, no other application will attempt to access the CPU.

INSTALLABLE FILE SYSTEM

A critical component of WIN95 is the installable file system (IFS). Under MS-DOS and Windows 3.1, applications and system components that needed to handle file I/O requests had

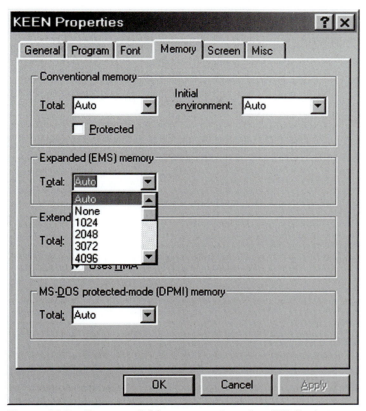

Figure 23.5   For every DOS program, there is a PIF file that describes how that program runs.

to make a direct call to the BIOS in order to fulfill those requests. The file system drivers of WIN95 exist as virtual device drivers running in Ring 0, instead of as real-mode MS-DOS drivers. Not only does this allow file system drivers to run in 32-bit protected-mode, it beefs up WIN9x networking capabilities.

EXAM NOTE: Make sure that you're aware that a key function of IFS is to load the network redirectors.

For any OS to join a network a piece of software called a *client* must be installed and running. An integral part of the client is the *redirector*. So what is a redirector? On a non-networked system, any time your computer goes out looking for any system resource, it knows it will find it locally. On

BUZZ WORDS

Client: A piece of software running from within an OS that allows the device to connect to a network.

Redirector: An OS function (usually running within a client) that intercepts hardware and software calls that are intended for remote devices and points them in the right direction.

a network, the user might be requesting the services of a piece of hardware on the other side of the building, or even the other side of the world, for that matter. The redirector examines a request and determines whether that request can be fulfilled locally. If not, it redirects that request to the appropriate destination. Hence the name.

IFS also supports a 32-bit virtual file allocation table (VFAT) driver, the 32-bit CD-ROM file system (CDFS) driver, and integrated 32-bit network redirectors for Windows NT and NetWare servers. With an IFS, third-party vendors can add specialized file systems under the IFS Manager. Applications and system components are now accessing the hard disk file system through VFAT, instead of making a direct hardware call (which is prohibited in WIN9x and later Microsoft OSs).

THE WINDOWS REGISTRY

In all previous versions of Windows, certain system settings and parameters were all incorporated into the .INI files. During the boot process these files were read and as a result, device drivers and parameters were loaded. .INI files were also responsible for mapping the locations of critical system files and where applications loaded on the system could be located.

BUZZ WORDS

Registry: In Windows, it is a relational database that contains all system and application settings and/or parameters.

This was a functional method, but it was resource intensive and provided additional overhead on the system that WIN9x could not afford. As a result, all of this responsibility was migrated over to the registry. The *registry* acts as a relational database of every setting, parameter, device driver, or file location the system requires for full functionality.

The registry consists of a series of six primary registry keys. A key consists of a specific category of setting relevant to a specific area of Windows functionality. Any number of subkeys can exist beneath the primary keys. All of this information is initialized when Windows is first installed and is constantly being updated every time a new piece of hardware or software is installed and every time a user makes a change to the system configuration. It is all stored in two primary files: USER.DAT and SYSTEM.DAT. In WIN95, a backup of each of these files existed, but carried .DAO extensions. Windows 98 increased the number of backup files from one to three.

REGISTRY ORGANIZATION

There are six primary keys in the registry. These are HKEY_CLASSES_ROOT, HKEY_CURRENT_USER, HKEY_LOCAL_MACHINE, HKEY_USERS, HKEY_CURRENT_CONFIG, and HKEY_DYN_DATA. Each of these primary keys holds specific information critical to the system. Oddly enough, one of these keys does not get stored in the .DAT files I just mentioned. I'll get to that in a minute.

Beneath the primary key are subkeys. These are frequently referred to as hives. Each hive contains sections specific to the properties of a particular function within the OS. For example, later on, when I discuss the primary key called HKEY_LOCAL_MACHINE, I mention that this key holds information specific to hardware and software. One of the subkeys is called Software. Beneath this folder are additional folders for each and every brand of software installed on the system, as well as folders for software Microsoft thinks you are likely to install later. The folder specific to Microsoft (or any other brand) would be called a hive file.

> **BUZZ WORDS** ————
>
> **Profile:** Various settings and preferences specific to particular user or piece of hardware on a system.

EXAM NOTE: You need to know all six primary keys of the Windows Registry.

HKEY_CLASSES_ROOT

HKEY_CLASSES_ROOT provides the information that OLE requires in order to work. It also stores the mappings used by different programs when the user takes advantage of the drag-and-drop functionality offered by Windows. Other information, including how different applications deal with different file types based on their extensions, is stored in this key.

HKEY_CURRENT_USER

HKEY_CURRENT_USER contains information specific to the preferences of the user logged onto the machine. WIN95 is capable of storing the settings for each person who creates an account on a machine. The various settings, preferences, desktop configuration, and applications groups for a specific individual make up that user's *profile*.

HKEY_LOCAL_MACHINE

HKEY_LOCAL_MACHINE stores information specific to the hardware and software running on the machine. For most technicians, this key is where the majority of registry changes you'll ever make will take place.

HKEY_USERS

HKEY_USERS is where the information for all users that have a profile on a specific machine will be stored. If two or more users have created profiles on a machine, this key will be different from that of HKEY_CURRENT_USER. Each profile will point to a specific set of subkeys. When a user logs on, this subkey will form HKEY_CURRENT_USER. If there is only one profile, there will be little or no difference between the two keys.

HKEY_CURRENT_CONFIG

HKEY_CURRENT_CONFIG loads a specific hardware profile. As Windows supports multiple user profiles, it also supports more than one hardware configuration on a single machine.

For example, you might have a computer with two video cards. When you are running your photo editor, you keep your image on one monitor and the software menus on another. But when you're only using your word processor, you have no use for the second monitor. By creating a separate profile in which the second video card is disabled, when Windows is booting you have the option of selecting the hardware configuration of your choice.

HKEY_DYN_DATA

HKEY_DYN_DATA is the one key that is not permanently stored on a hard drive. It is configured on the fly as the system boots, based on what user has logged onto the system and what specific hardware profile has been selected. It stays RAM-resident until Windows is shut down.

THE REGISTRY EDITOR

For the most part, the registry is best left alone. Most configuration changes can be made in the OS within different applets or fields that I'll discuss in Chapter Twenty-Four. However, once in a while, it is necessary for a technician to manually edit entries in the registry. This is done through a command-line utility called REGEDIT. Later versions of Windows also included REGEDT32. REGEDIT was included in the first version of WIN95 as a 16-bit registry editor and has been included in every version of Windows released since that date. As its name implies, REGEDT32 is a 32-bit editor. REGEDIT is somewhat limited:

- You can't set security on registry values.
- Not all entries can be edited. Entries whose value types are marked REG_EXPAND_SZ or REG_MULTI_SZ contain binary data. Attempting to edit them will render them useless.
- Individual keys cannot be saved or restored as hive files.

REGEDT32 allows for securing registry keys and editing binary entries (although I recommend that you avoid this practice unless directed by help desk professionals!). It does not, however, allow the user to import or export .REG files. These are files that contain precoded registry entries, and are often provided by help desk personnel to fix specific problems.

In some instances, this can be a tricky and potentially hazardous adventure. There are some settings in the registry that consist of hexadecimal notation that points to specific OS functions or identifies specific hardware and/or application calls. Changing a single character can make an application or piece of hardware act up or possibly not work at all. It is conceivable that some changes could even cause your system to refuse to boot.

That's why it's a good idea to back up the registry before you play around in it. The Registry Editor allows you to back up and restore certain parts of the registry or even the entire registry. And it is where you make all the changes that might cause you to have to restore it.

Some entries are benign enough. For example, if you installed a particular piece of software and then decided you didn't like it all that much after all, chances are pretty good you're going to uninstall it. Unfortunately, uninstalling software does not back out all the changes to the

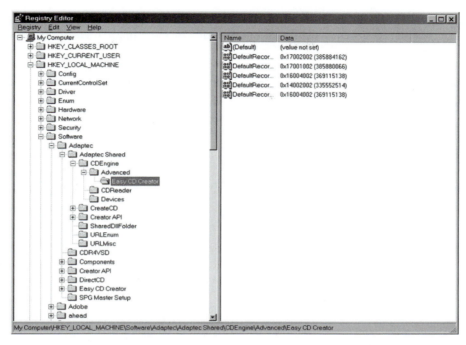

Figure 23.6 The registry maintains information on every piece of software you've ever installed, including software that no longer exists on your system.

registry that installing the program initiated to begin with. As you can see in **Figure 23.6**, under HKEY_LOCAL_MACHINE>Software, every application you've ever installed creates a folder with its settings. If the application is no longer installed, it's pretty safe to delete that folder.

CONFIGSAFE

Registry corruption is such a common issue in Windows that third-party manufacturers have made a killing by providing failsafe software to protect the end user. One of the most popular of these that is worth mentioning is a product called ConfigSafe by a company called Imagine-Lan.

ConfigSafe tracks changes to a system's configuration over time. In the event of a system failure, or should the system suddenly start experiencing repeated system crashes, the software allows users or technicians to quickly restore a problem system to a working configuration.

ConfigSafe currently offers versions that support Windows 95/98/Me and Windows NT/2000/XP operating systems. ConfigSafe works by taking a *snapshot* of a system's configuration. This can be done at any specific point by the user, and the

BUZZ WORDS

Snapshot: In reference to an OS, it is a small binary file that contains information useful in replicating the organization and structure of an application or configuration.

program will automatically do so whenever there is a configuration change. The snapshot stores information about the system's configuration at that exact point in time. Some examples of information tracked are as follows:

- Configuration files (WIN.INI, SYSTEM.INI, AUTOEXEC.BAT, CONFIG.SYS)
- System changes (memory, processor, Windows version)
- Drives (hard drives, CD-ROMs, network connections)
- Directories
- Windows registry
- System assets (for example, the Windows desktop)

Should the end user or a technician discover that some change to the system has rendered it unstable, he or she can "go back in time" to one of the snapshots taken when the system was working properly and restore those versions of the system files. The system will now work properly. As I will discuss in Chapter Thirty, Introducing XP, XP has incorporated a similar feature called System Restore into the OS, so that a third-party utility is no longer needed.

WIN9X VERSIONS

Starting with its initial release on August 4, 1995, and all the way through to the release of Windows 2000 (oddly enough, in the year 2000), Windows enjoyed a five-year reign as the most popular OS in the world. Several different versions appeared over those five years, and many of them continue to exist on machines to this day. Therefore it is important for the technician to be able to navigate all of them.

WIN95 SR2

Most of the features of the initial release of WIN95 were discussed in detail in earlier sections of this chapter. Therefore, it isn't necessary to go over it all again. So I'll begin my discussion of the various versions with WIN95-SR2.

FAT32 had originally been intended to be a part of WIN95 in its initial release. However, problems integrating the file system into the OS were threatening to delay a release that had already been put off several times over the previous eighteen months. Therefore, the decision was made to release WIN95 without this important feature. Therefore, FAT32 support first appeared in SR-2.

SR-2 also featured the first release of a new graphics API by Microsoft called DirectX. DirectX consists of a collection of various routines that allow different multimedia components, such as the video card, CD-ROM, and sound card, to share common command sets and to seamlessly communicate with one another.

Another feature that was provided for SR-2, but that was only available as a download from Microsoft at first, was USB support. In 1996, Microsoft released WIN95 OSR2.5, which included USB on the CD. What a lot of users didn't realize was that this feature was required in order to get AGP video cards to function as well.

WINDOWS 98

As with the remainder of the WIN9x products, WIN98 was not really a technical improvement over WIN95, but rather an improvement that sported added features. The basic core of the product didn't change much. Most of the new features benefited the users whose computers were high-priced home video arcades rather than business tools. As such, the thrust of Microsoft's marketing campaign was targeted at the home user rather than the corporate environment.

WIN98 upped the ante in terms of installation requirements as well. Its added features put a little more strain on hardware and as a result, Microsoft was a little less liberal in stating minimum requirements. WIN98's published requirements included the following:

- 66MHz 80486DX microprocessor
- 16MB of RAM
- 140MB free hard disk space (minimum install)
- 1.44MB 3.5" floppy diskette drive
- VGA monitor

WIN98 was the first OS to recognize the impact of the Internet on the average home user, and it sewed a new version of Internet Explorer so tightly into the OS that uninstalling it could render the system unstable (although independent programmers would release a bevy of shareware products on the market that claimed to perform this feat). Microsoft also added support to some newly emerging technologies and dramatically increased PnP capabilities by expanding the database of built-in device drivers. For the most part, however, WIN98 was little more than a collection of utilities bundled with WIN95 and given a pretty new face.

One of these utilities was an improved backup/recovery program that Microsoft licenses from Seagate (**Figure 23.7**). While it did not support scheduled unattended backups, it did provide support for a variety of different backup devices. There was also a file system converter that was capable of a one-time FAT16 to FAT32 conversion. Just don't change your mind once the conversion is completed. The process isn't reversible.

For those times when PnP didn't work, and the user couldn't get a piece of hardware to work, there was the System Troubleshooter. While this utility did very little to actually solve a problem for the user, it did lead users through a systematic approach to figuring out what went wrong and gave tips on how they might fix problems.

A System File Checker could monitor critical system files and if any change in version number or file size was detected, automatically restore the file to its original version. Unfortunately, if the utility detected a change that was the result of a piece of software that was intentionally installed, the results were occasionally (although rarely) undesirable.

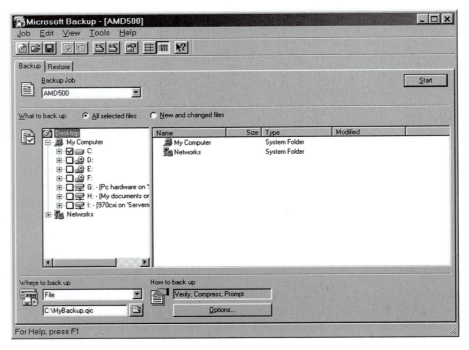

Figure 23.7   The Windows 98 backup utility provided an easier way for users to recover from a hard drive failure.

Dr. Watson was a utility that monitored system errors and generated a text log. The first thing the utility did on its first execution was to create a snapshot of the system. This snapshot consisted of a complete list of drivers running on the system. In the advanced view (**Figure 23.8**), the user could view a complete listing of virtually everything going on within the system at the time the snapshot was made. It worked by intercepting software interrupts. If the system failed abruptly, the last entry in the log would be the guilty culprit.

WINDOWS 98SE

Was Windows 98SE really a new version? Or was it more of a bug fix for Windows 98? Fortunately, as a writer, that's not up to me to decide. Its greatest claim to fame was really that it was more stable than its predecessor. There were a few new features added.

For one thing, a product that Microsoft had previously sold separately, Windows 98 Plus, was incorporated into the package. This allowed the user to select from a large variety of themes and to pick from a number of different pretty pictures for their desktop wallpaper.

The version of Internet Explorer was upgraded to 5.0, and DirectX 6.1 was added during the installation. In an attempt to fend off the image Microsoft had created for itself that Windows 98 could not be taken seriously as an OS for the working environment, it included a piece of software

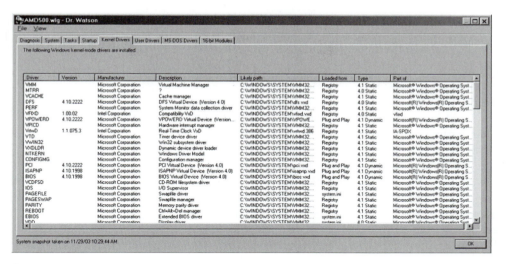

Figure 23.8   Dr. Watson was Windows 98's resident troubleshooter.

called NetMeeting. This allowed teleconferencing over the Internet using both audio and video data streams. While this first version was admittedly primitive by today's standards, it did lead the way to the more sophisticated conferencing features taken for granted today.

The new version of DirectX may have been the most under-rated improvement of all the WIN98SE features. In addition to allowing the OS to take advantage of the latest and greatest toys on the market (mostly targeted at gamers), it also provided the first user-level offering for Internet Connection Sharing (ICS). Microsoft took a look at the increasing numbers of households in the US and abroad that boasted multiple computers and offered this audience a way to get two or more computers on the Internet at the same time.

WINDOWS ME

Windows Millenium, or WINMe as it was more commonly known, turned out to be quite a controversial product. In many respects, it was Microsoft's way of moving the consumer out of the world of backward compatibility. It incorporated some of the technology that was present in the already-released Windows 2000, abandoned some of the features that supported legacy programs, but still maintained a comfortably familiar look and feel. In some respects, this caused more problems than it provided solutions.

One of the key architectural changes was that this version of the OS no longer supported real mode. If you wanted to run an older DOS program on Me, you were on your own. And while it gave the impression of being a faster OS because of how much faster it booted, when running 32-bit apps it was measurably slower than WIN98.

It was the first Microsoft product to implement Universal Plug 'n Play. By the time Me was released, Microsoft had released development of PnP to the UPNP Forum. One of the first things this body did was to make some minor modifications to PnP in order to allow the technology to be incorporated into other brands of OS such as Linux. Some of the older versions of PnP devices and BIOS versions performed unpredictably in the UPNP environment. If anything, these devices could be more troublesome to install than an older legacy device with no PnP capabilities whatsoever.

BUZZ WORDS

Cabinet file: A compressed file that holds a large number of smaller files that can be uncompressed and installed as needed.

But WINMe is not without its plus side. System File Protection (SFP) prevents a poorly written application from deleting or overwriting critical system files. The *cabinet (CAB) files* used by the OS during installation were stored locally on the hard drive by default. CAB files are single compressed files that store a large number of smaller files. Should a critical file be altered in any way, SFP would regenerate that file on the fly.

System Restore is another new feature in Me that has saved many an adventurous experimenter. Suppose a user purchases a new toy and the install goes awry. This utility allows the user to step back in time, so to speak, to a system configuration prior to the installation that worked properly and then try the installation again. And fail again.

SUMMARY OF WIN9X VERSIONS

If the WIN9x versions proved nothing else, they proved the old adage that "the more things change, the more they stay the same." Until WINMe came around, there were no real structural changes at all. So to summarize the changes made in Windows between the years 1995 and 2000, I have put together **Table 23.2**. I hope you find it useful.

Table 23.2 History of WIN9x Releases

Version	Release Date	Improvements	Version Number
WIN95	August 1995		4.00.950
WIN95 SP1	February 1996	Bug fix for WIN95	4.00.950A
WIN95 OSR2	August 1996	FAT32	4.00.950B
WIN95 OSR2.1	April 1997	USB as download	4.00.950B + USB
WIN95 OSR2.5	November 1997	IE4 and incorporated USB	4.00.950C
Windows 98	June 1998	DVD, DirectX	4.10.1998
Windows 98 SE	May 1999	IE5, ICS, DirectX 6.1, NetMeeting	4.10.2222A
Windows Me	September 2000	UPNP, SFP, System Restore	4.90.3000

The WIN9x series went through a number of changes from its inception to the final death knell.

CHAPTER SUMMARY

So, if you were looking for a tour of WIN95 and all of its features, you were probably pretty disappointed in this chapter. What I covered here is the core technology behind the WIN9x series and a brief review of the evolution of Windows 4.xx.

The 4.xx versions of Windows provided some very important technological breakthroughs over the 3.xx versions of yesteryear. A couple of key points to this chapter are how Windows now handles multitasking and its usage of memory.

BRAIN DRAIN

1. Discuss the differences between cooperative multitasking and pre-emptive multitasking.

2. What is a key reason for placing all WIN3.x apps into a common virtual machine?

3. Draw a rough diagram of how the WIN9x Virtual Machine Manager handles different applications, including legacy DOS apps, WIN3.x, and WIN9x apps.

4. Why was Plug 'n Play so problematic with certain devices in its early years?

5. Discuss how WINMe was responsible for a number of gray hairs in the heads of technicians worldwide.

THE 64K$ QUESTIONS

1. WIN95 was originally intended for release in the year _____.

    a. 1995
    b. 1994
    c. 1993
    d. 1992

2. Even if a consumer's hardware met the minimum requirements for WIN95, Microsoft still wouldn't provide support if _____.

    a. The computer was made prior to 1995
    b. Any of the hardware was not listed on the HCL
    c. The computer didn't have a 32-bit bus
    d. Any of the hardware was listed on their UCL

3. WIN95 required, at the minimum, _____.

    a. A 16MHz 386SX processor
    b. A 20MHz 386SX processor
    c. A 16MHz 386DX processor
    d. A 20MHz 386DX processor

4. WIN95 required, at the minimum, _____.

    a. 2MB of RAM
    b. 4MB of RAM
    c. 8MB of RAM
    d. 16MB of RAM

5. WIN95 required, at the minimum, _____.

    a. 16-color CGA
    b. EGA
    c. VGA
    d. SVGA

6. WIN95 required, at the minimum, _____ (for a full installation).
   a. 85MB free hard disk space
   b. 120MB free hard disk space
   c. 240MB free hard disk space
   d. 540MB free hard disk space

7. Which of the following was not a requirement for full PnP functionality?
   a. A PnP BIOS
   b. A PnP device driver
   c. A PnP device
   d. A PnP OS

8. Pre-emptive multitasking adds the services of _____.
   a. A virtual machine manager
   b. A task scheduler
   c. An event scheduler
   d. A process timer

9. Which protocol was incorporated into WIN95 for the first time in Microsoft's history?
   a. NetBEUI
   b. IPX/SPX
   c. Banyan Vines
   d. TCP/IP

10. Which of the following files became a text file in WIN95?
    a. MSDOS.SYS
    b. COMMAND.COM
    c. IO.SYS
    d. WIN.INI

11. WIN95 did not incorporate any version of MS-DOS into its structure.
    a. True
    b. False

12. The 32-bit graphics drivers were managed by _____.
    a. USER.DLL
    b. GDI.EXE
    c. GDI.DLL
    d. KERNEL32.DLL

13. A 16-bit mouse driver would interface with _____.
    a. USER.DLL
    b. GDI.EXE
    c. GDI.DLL
    d. KERNEL32.DLL

14. Opening a new DOS window was the responsibility of _____.
    a. KRNL386.EXE
    b. KERNEL32.DLL
    c. The Virtual Memory Manager
    d. The Virtual Machine Manager

15. Multiple networking clients on a single computer were made possible by the addition of _____.
    a. The Virtual Memory Manager
    b. The Virtual Machine Manager
    c. The Installable File System
    d. The Network Device Interface

16. What version of WIN9x was the first to provide support for FAT32?
    a. Windows 95
    b. Windows 95 SR2
    c. Windows 98
    d. Windows 98SE
    e. None of the above

17. What version of WIN9x was the first to provide support for USB?
    a. Windows 95
    b. Windows 95 SR2

c. Windows 98

d. Windows 98SE

e. None of the above

18. What version of WIN9x was the first to provide support for DVD?

a. Windows 95

b. Windows 95 SR2

c. Windows 98

d. Windows 98SE

e. None of the above

19. What version of WIN9x was the first to provide support for DirectX?

a. Windows 95

b. Windows 95 SR2

c. Windows 98

d. Windows 98SE

e. None of the above

20. What version of WIN9x dropped support for real mode operation?

a. Windows 95

b. Windows 95 SR2

c. Windows 98

d. Windows 98SE

e. None of the above

TRICKY TERMINOLOGY

Cabinet file: A compressed file that holds a large number of smaller files that can be uncompressed and installed as needed.

Client: A piece of software running from within an OS that allows the device to connect to a network.

Pre-emptive multitasking: A way to manage multiple applications on a computer system that puts the responsibility for releasing system resources onto the OS.

Profile: Various settings and preferences specific to a particular user or piece of hardware on a system.

Redirector: An OS function (usually running within a client) that intercepts hardware and software calls that are intended for remote devices and points them in the right direction.

Registry: In Windows, it is a relational database that contains all system and application settings and/or parameters.

Snapshot: In reference to an OS, it is a small binary file that contains information useful in replicating the organization and structure of an application or configuration.

System Virtual Machine: An environment in Windows that emulates a complete computer system and houses all of the critical processes and functions of the OS.

Task scheduler: A system file that determines how long a particular application can retain control of system resources.

Thunking: A Microsoft process of translating 16-bit commands and data into a 32-bit format, and vice versa.

ACRONYM ALERT

CAB: Cabinet. A compressed file that houses a number of smaller files that can be independently extracted as needed.

CDFS: CD-ROM File System

HCL: Hardware Compatibility List. A list of devices that have been approved by an OS manufacturer for use with a specific product.

ICS: Internet Connection Sharing. A service that allows multiple computers to simultaneously use a single hookup to the Internet.

IFS: Installable File System. A feature in WIN9x and later OSs that allows network redirectors and third-party file systems to be installed as needed.

PIF: Program Information File. A small descriptor file that tells Windows how a specific DOS application is going to behave.

SFP: System File Protection. A Windows utility that prevents critical OS files from being deleted or overwritten, and if they are, can replace them on the fly.

UPNP: Universal Plug 'n Play. Revised PnP standards that are constantly monitored and updated by the UPNP Forum.

VFAT: Virtual File Allocation Table. A software driver that emulates the file allocation tables stored on a hard disk and prevents applications from making direct calls to the hardware.

 VIEW THE VIDEO

A video clip on System Boot Sequences is available on the accompanying CD.

CHAPTER 24

MANAGING WINDOWS 9X

In the previous chapter, I discussed the structure and architecture of the WIN9x products. Here I will go through the installation and configuration of WIN95, and, where relevant, discuss how these procedures may differ for other WIN9x products. After that, there will be a brief discussion of the WIN9x user interface and a more detailed discussion of WIN9x use and management.

In previous chapters, most of the discussion has revolved around OSs that are no longer in use. That is no longer the case. While the WIN9x products are long discontinued, they proved to be a viable enough product that, as of this writing, there are an estimated 20,000,000 computers still running one or the other of these venerable old systems.

A+ OPERATING SYSTEM TECHNOLOGIES EXAM OBJECTIVES

There is also a lot of coverage on the CompTIA exam concerning these products. Among the topics you might see from this chapter are the following:

1.1   Identify the major desktop components and interfaces and their functions. Differentiate the characteristics of Windows 9x/Me, Windows NT 4.0 Workstation, Windows 2000 Professional, and Windows XP.

1.2   Identify the names, locations, purposes, and contents of major system files.

2.1   Identify the procedures for installing Windows 9x/Me, Windows NT 4.0 Workstation, Windows 2000 Professional, and Windows XP and bringing the operating system to a basic operational level.

2.2   Identify steps to perform an operating system upgrade from Windows 9x/Me, Windows NT 4.0 Workstation, Windows 2000 Professional, and Windows XP. Given an upgrade scenario, choose the appropriate next steps.

2.3   Identify the basic system boot sequences and boot methods, including the steps to create an emergency boot disk with utilities installed for Windows 9x/Me, Windows NT 4.0 Workstation, Windows 2000 Professional, and Windows XP.

2.4   Identify procedures for installing/adding a device, including loading, adding, and configuring device drivers and required software.

3.1   Recognize and interpret the meaning of common error codes and startup messages from the boot sequence, and identify steps to correct the problems.

3.2   Recognize when to use common diagnostic utilities and tools. Given a diagnostic scenario involving one of these utilities or tools, select the appropriate steps needed to resolve the problem.

BUZZ WORDS ――――――――

Clean install: The fresh installation of an OS over a newly partitioned and formatted hard disk.

Upgrade: The replacement of an older OS with a newer, migrating as many settings and applications as possible.

INSTALLING WINDOWS 95

When WIN95 was first released, there were two different approaches commonly used in installing the product. Since there were a plethora of people who owned computers with WIN3.x already installed, the *upgrade* path was popular with them. However, for users to expect the most reliability and stability out of their systems, Microsoft suggested a *clean install*. Even though it is unlikely that you'll ever encounter a situation in which you'll be upgrading a WIN3.x system to WIN9x, I'm going to provide a brief discussion of the procedures. I'll start with the clean install.

PERFORMING A CLEAN INSTALL

The first thing you ever want to do when performing any clean install is make sure you have a clean hard drive or partition onto which the OS can be installed. If a previous installation of Windows existed, then you want to repartition that disk prior to performing a clean install. Don't just format the disk. For most Microsoft OSs, the partitioning utility of choice will be FDISK.

After you have FDISKed the hard disk and formatted it, you are ready to perform your installation. WIN95 distributions did not ship on bootable CDs; therefore, it is essential to boot to the WIN95 Startup Diskette enclosed in the product. Place the CD-ROM into the drive and from the command prompt, type `D:\Setup` (where D: represents the correct drive letter for your CD drive). The rest is a matter of following the yellow brick road. If you are using the lab manual designed to accompany this book, you'll be doing an installation of Windows 98.

PERFORMING AN UPGRADE

Performing an upgrade of Windows 3.x or MS-DOS to WIN95 is a bit different than a clean install in a couple of respects. The upgrade migrates all configurations, personal preferences, and

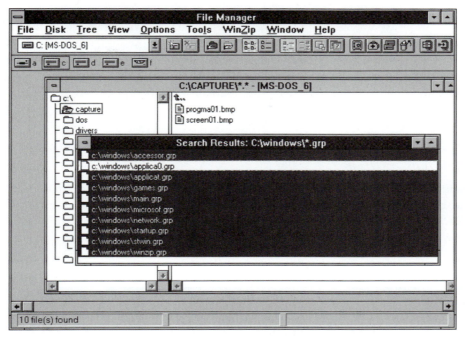

Figure 24.1 In WIN3.x, group files contained information about installed applications that was useful in migrating those apps into a WIN95 install.

applications that were installed under the old OS, making the new installation as close to what the user is accustomed to as possible.

From a DOS installation, the Setup program derives the majority of the information it requires for this migration from CONFIG.SYS and AUTOEXEC.BAT. In an upgrade from WIN3.x, it also scours files such as SYSTEM.INI and WIN.INI and migrates desktop settings and applications. It also uses a WIN3.x utility called Program Manager (PM) for locating applications. PM maintained a series of descriptor files called group files. There were files with a .GRP extension (**Figure 24.1**) that defined the groups in which the applications were installed. Setup uses these to migrate path information and program configuration.

Certain device settings could be migrated as well. Printers could be migrated, and some devices designed for Windows such as modems and sound cards were occasionally migrated successfully. For the most part, however, nonprinter devices were best installed separately after the Windows 95 installation was completed.

The biggest problem with the WIN95 upgrade was that it also migrated any problems that existed. Also, if a program or device was incompatible with the 32-bit drivers of Windows, there were occasionally problems uninstalling the offending resource and reinstalling it under WIN95. Some hardware devices simply weren't compatible with WIN9x and couldn't be used at all. The remainder of this section will deal with a clean install and will only point out issues specific to an upgrade where relevant.

COMPLETING AN INSTALLATION

Aside from those rather important differences, the process of installing WIN95 was the same regardless of which option was chosen by the user. A big difference for WIN3.x users upgrading from the WIN95 Upgrade CD was that they did not start from the command prompt. There were a few additional steps involved in the upgrade while Setup located and migrated pre-existing settings, but the primary stages of installation remained the same. DOS users and those performing a clean install would generally have to start from the command prompt.

COMMAND LINE SWITCHES

Command line switches allowed the user to select certain installation options before Setup began to do its thing. These switches are applied just like the switches used in MS-DOS. **Table 24.1** lists the various switches and the effects they had on installation.

Table 24.1 Windows 95 Setup Switches

Switch	Function
/?	Provides descriptions for these switches in case you don't have this book at your fingertips.
/c	Instructs Setup not to load the SmartDrive disk caching utility.
/d	Prevents Setup from using earlier versions of Windows in the initial phases of installation.
/id	Prevents Setup from performing a test to see whether the minimal amount of free hard disk space is present.
/in	Prevents Setup from running the Network Setup Module.
/iq	Prevents Setup from performing a ScanDisk quick-check when running Setup from DOS.
/is	Prevents Setup from performing a ScanDisk quick-check when running Setup from Windows.
/iw	Prevents Setup from running the End User License Agreement.
/t:[dir]	Where DIR specifies a designated directory, this switch instructs Setup where to store temporary files during installation.
[batchfile.bat]	Where the actual name of the batch file is used, it runs the specified batch file containing specific setup instructions.
/NOSTART	Instructs setup to load a minimal set of files and then exit without installing Windows.

The Windows Setup switches allow the user to modify the way Setup runs in a specific fashion.

WINDOWS 95 SETUP PHASES

There are four separate phases to the installation of WIN95. The first three involve preparing your computer for the WIN9x GUI. The final phase occurs after a reboot, when the user is in graphical mode. These phases are:

- Startup
- Information gathering
- File copy
- Final system configuration

Startup and Information Gathering If Setup is run from a command prompt, the first thing it will do is search your computer for previous installations of any version of Windows. If one is found, you will be given a suggestion to start Windows and run Setup from there. If no Windows installation is found, Setup installs a base configuration of WIN3.1 files and moves on to perform a series of basic system checks (**Figure 24.2**).

These checks are designed to confirm that the system onto which you're attempting to install WIN95 has the minimum requirements. Should it find a problem, such as insufficient

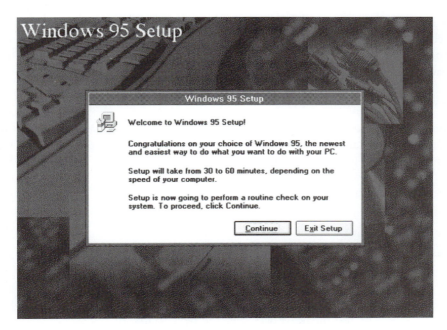

Figure 24.2 The first thing WIN95 does is make sure you have enough computer to run it. The sign of things to come!

drive space or insufficient memory, Setup will issue an error message indicating what type of problem it found.

Next Setup checks for an XMS manager such as EMM386.EXE. If one is not present, Setup installs it. Setup also looks for a disk caching utility such as SmartDrive. Once again, if not present, one will be installed.

Now, Setup scans CONFIG.SYS and AUTOEXEC.BAT, looking to see what TSRs are running on the system. In the event that it detects any programs that could potentially cause a conflict (and this would include incompatible drivers), Setup will issue a warning message. During this phase, it is also checking both files for device information on installed hardware so that it can load any necessary drivers.

File Copy This is the part of the process where most users go out for a cup of coffee and a donut. On older computers, this process can take quite some time. At the very end of the file copy stage, the user will see a series of Setup prompts. The information provided in these fields will be used in the creation of the registry later on.

Final System Configuration It's too late to turn back now. If you were running WIN3.x or DOS before, your OS has been permanently changed. The MBR on the hard drive is rewritten to point to WIN95. Also the registry is fully configured and written to the hard drive. On the next boot, your system will initialize from the registry for the first time and perform a PnP scan for hardware.

Once the hardware setup phase has been completed, which may or may not require yet another reboot, you will be offered the opportunity to take a tour of Windows. In the lower left-hand corner of that window is a check box; leave that box checked if you want to see this window each time Windows starts.

WINDOWS 98 SETUP PHASES

WIN98 and WINMe users will see some extra stages during their installation. First off, these versions separate the startup preparation from the information-gathering phase. Also, since WIN98 is Plug 'n Play, it adds a hardware detection phase. Here is the order of WIN98 Setup:

- Preparing to run Windows 98 Setup
- Collecting information about your computer
- Copying Windows 98 files to your computer
- Restarting your computer
- Setting up hardware

Even the phases that look like they should be identical to WIN95 Setup phases have some differences. So don't be too quick to pass over the next couple of pages.

Preparing to Run Windows 98 Setup What happens here depends on whether you're upgrading from WIN95 or running Setup from a command prompt. If Setup is run from

WIN95, a directory called WININST0.400 is created. Two files, called PRECOPY1.CAB and PRECOPY2.CAB, are copied into this directory. These files contain setup and information files that Setup will extract and use later in the installation process.

If you're installing Windows from a command prompt (and this would include installation from a Startup diskette), then there is no previous installation of Windows. Since Setup is going to be looking for certain files, it copies a file called MINI.CAB. This file is a compressed bare-minimum installation of Windows that Setup can use.

Collecting Information About Your Computer   This phase also has a bit of variation, depending on whether Setup is being run from DOS or Windows. From DOS, users will be prompted to read and agree to Microsoft's licensing agreement. Next they will be asked what directory they would like WIN98 installed into. The default C:\WINDOWS will already be filled out, but it is possible for users to install Windows into any directory they chose. They must then supply a directory for temporary files. Once again, the one Setup suggests should be used unless there are qualifying reasons (such as a previous OS that you wish to preserve) for not doing so. The last part of this phase is to prepare an Emergency Startup Diskette.

Those running Setup from Windows 95 will first see the license agreement. Then ScanDisk will run a check on the system to ensure that all is well. ScanReg scans the WIN95 registry and prepares the WIN98 registry. Then the user is prompted to prepare an Emergency Startup Diskette.

Copying Windows 98 Files to Your Computer   This phase isn't really that much different that the WIN95 file copy phase. It uses the information it found in the prior phases to determine what files need to be copied, and, until it's finished, the user can return his or her attention to the playoffs.

Restarting Your Computer   This *sounds* like a simple enough phase, right? A bar starts ticking off fifteen seconds, after which your computer will restart automatically. If you're in too much of a hurry to wait fifteen seconds, you can press the spacebar and the system will reboot immediately.

It's what is happening *during* reboot that matters, though. Setup takes any information it was able to extract from CONFIG.SYS, AUTOEXEC.BAT, and any .INI files from previous OS installations and integrates them into the WIN98 registry. If any device drivers are found that Setup knows to be incompatible with WIN98, Setup edits these entries to be preceded by a REM (remark). This prevents them from being loaded during this and any subsequent reboots of the system.

Setting Up Hardware and Finalizing Settings   During this phase, Setup utilizes the PnP abilities of WIN98 to automatically detect any PnP hardware installed on the system, copy the appropriate files, and make any necessary entries to the Windows registry. During an upgrade, information from .INI files and/or the WIN95 registry is used to collect information about non-PnP devices. Any settings it finds in these locations are retained. On a clean install, non-PnP devices will have to be installed separately after installation is completed.

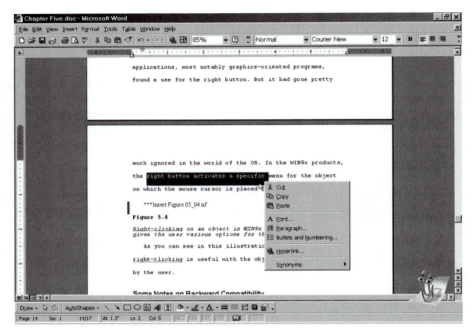

Figure 24.3 Right-clicking an object in WIN9x brings up a menu that gives the user various options for the selected object.

WIN9X AND THE MOUSE

All of Microsoft's previous versions of Windows provided mouse support. WIN95 was the first Microsoft OS to take this ingenious little device and move it from a role of a convenient toy to a powerful tool. Having finally realized that the mouse was equipped with two buttons (sometimes three), Microsoft finally provided a role for the right mouse button.

The left button (the one generally manipulated by the index finger on right-handed people) has always been used for selecting objects and launching applications. Some applications, most notably graphics-oriented programs, found a use for the right button. But it had gone pretty much ignored in the world of the OS. In the WIN9x products, the right button activates a specific menu for the object on which the mouse cursor is placed (see **Figure 24.3**).

As you can see in this illustration, the process of right-clicking is useful with the objects and data created by the user. Another term to be familiar with is double-clicking. Many actions require that the left mouse button be clicked twice in succession. This is the infamous double-click.

MAKING YOUR WAY AROUND WINDOWS

For the rest of this chapter, I'm going to be going over the various elements of WIN9x as they affect the user. From here on, unless otherwise specified, I'll be using WIN98 as the subject of

SOME NOTES ON BACKWARD COMPATIBILITY

Several times in the course of this book, I've mentioned things that were done or features that were retained from previous OSs in order to maintain backward compatibility with older systems. In the first couple of decades of the personal computer, Microsoft and Intel had a tacit agreement that new advances in computing would not render existing systems and/or software totally obsolete. They realized the backlash that would occur if users had to replace an entire computer system just to use an OS or program or had to replace thousands of dollars worth of software just because they had upgraded to a new computer and OS.

With that objective in mind, each advance in CPUs and each advance in OS was designed with some method integrated into it that allowed older technology to coexist with the new. For Microsoft, achieving this goal with WIN9x was a daunting task. In Chapter Twenty-Three, I discussed how the VMM was redesigned with this goal in mind. I also discussed the changes made to MSDOS.SYS.

A key point to be made here is that WIN9x does not use AUTOEXEC.BAT and CONFIG.SYS, nor any of the .INI files previously found in WIN3.x products for its own purposes. These files are all retained to make DOS and WIN3.x programs run on the WIN9x platform. Therefore, when running programs designed for WIN9x on WIN9x, nothing you do to any of the previously mentioned files will have any impact whatsoever.

On the other hand, if you choose to run an older DOS program on WIN9x after having completed a clean install, you might find it more of a challenge than you might have expected. A clean install of WIN9x does not load any devices drivers into either CONFIG.SYS or AUTOEXEC.BAT. When your DOS program tries to run, it's going to be looking to those files for its driver information the majority of the time. Devices such as a CD-ROM drive or a sound card will need to have DOS drivers installed and the appropriate lines added to these files.

my discussion. It is far more likely that you, as a technician, will be running into that particular version than any other. The various aspects of Windows I'll be discussing include the following:

- The desktop
- Menus
- Control Panel
- Windows Explorer
- Hot keys
- Help

The information I give you in this chapter is rather important even if you feel you'll never spend any time with WIN98. The basic design of this OS formed the template that Microsoft has continued to follow in subsequent versions. In later chapters, as I discuss more recent OS releases by Microsoft, I'll be pointing out new features and differences. I'm going to be assuming you already know the information provided in this chapter.

BUZZ WORDS

Icon: A small picture linked to an application shortcut.

THE DESKTOP

The Windows desktop (**Figure 24.4**) provides the launch pad where everything else you ever do in Windows begins. The various aspects of the desktop have come to be things now taken for granted, and, therefore, people probably don't really know as much about them as they should. As a technician, you need to know your way around the system extremely well. After all, it's really quite embarrassing to be on a customer's site, poking around in their computer, mumbling, "Now where did they put Device Mangler in *this* version?"

The Desktop consists of several different components, each with a specific task. The main desktop screen is only one of these components. There are also the Start menu, the taskbar, and the toolbar.

THE DESKTOP REGION

The largest area of the desktop is devoted to the main desktop region. This area is where the pretty little pictures that represent your programs are stored. These pictures are called *icons*. In

Figure 24.4 The Windows Desktop acts as the launch pad for everything else you do in Windows. Know it well!

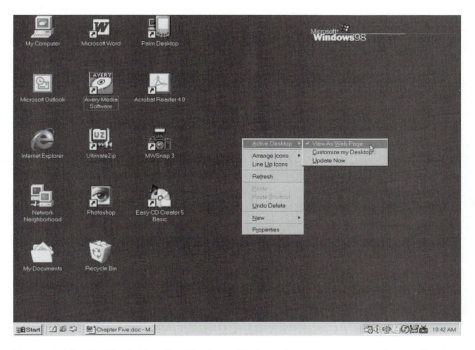

Figure 24.5   Right-clicking the Windows Desktop brings up a menu for configuring the desktop options.

WIN95, double-clicking an icon launches the program. In WIN98 and later, the user can configure an *Active Desktop.* If an Active Desktop is configured, users can configure their desktops to act as if they are Web pages. In this case, a single click on an icon launches the program (**Figure 24.5**).

Right-clicking the desktop and selecting Properties opens the Display Properties dialog box. From here, you can configure a wide variety of options affecting the look of your desktop and applications. You can also get to this dialog box from the Control Panel, and I will cover all the options it offers fully when I address all the applets you can access through Control Panel.

> ### BUZZ WORDS
>
> **Active Desktop:** A method of configuring the Windows desktop to behave as if it is a Web page, allowing single-click activation of icons and other Web-like features.

THE START MENU

The Start Menu (**Figure 24.6**) is more than just a place for launching programs that don't have an icon. Here is also where you go to shut down your computer. If you're on a network, or have set up multiple user profiles, an option for logging off as one user and logging on as another is also available.

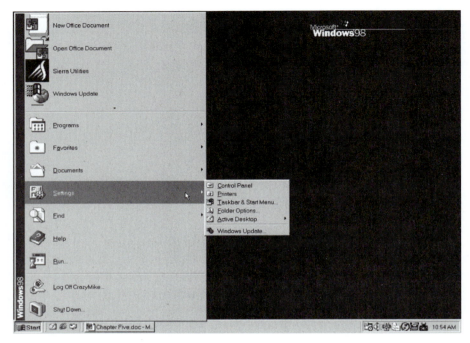

Figure 24.6   The Windows Start Menu

Clicking Run in the Start Menu opens a command line interface that allows users to type in a command the same way they would if they were at the command prompt. Unlike the command prompt, the Run option also allows users to use Windows Explorer to browse their computers looking for the application or command they wish to launch.

Help opens the Windows Help. Since I'll be covering that in more detail in a later section, I'll pass on discussing it for now.

The Find option is where users can go to browse for files or folders. They can also browse the network looking for another computer, or they can search for resources on the Internet with this tool. The Find → People option opens users' address books and allows them to search for information about the individuals stored there. An option that appears if you have Microsoft Outlook installed is Find → Using Microsoft Outlook. Using this option, you can look for files, folders, computers, people, or your car keys.

The Settings option on the Start Menu is an important one for technicians. Here is where you can find shortcuts to Control Panel, the Printers menu, and a place to configure your Taskbar to your liking, as well as another way of getting to the Folder Options that I discussed earlier. On WIN98 and later, you can also configure your Active Desktop from here or link directly to Microsoft's Updates Web site (assuming you have an active Internet connection.)

Documents basically has only one default shortcut, and that is to the My Documents folder on your hard drive. However, it also maintains a list of recently opened documents. So if you've been working on Chapter Twenty-Four of your OS book for several days, instead of opening your word processor and going through the rigmarole of browsing to the document through the menus and Windows Explorer, you can just click the document. The correct program will automatically open, and that document will load.

The Favorites option is a direct link to Internet Explorer's Favorites menu. If you click any of the items listed under this option, WIN98 will automatically launch whatever version of IE you have running on your machine and browse to that Web site.

Programs is where shortcuts to all of the programs installed on your system can be found. Even if an icon has not been created on the desktop for a particular application, the installation program will generally place a shortcut here. You can also create shortcuts for your desktop from this component. Right-click the application and select Create Shortcut. A second entry for that application, with its name followed by the number two in parentheses (2), will appear. Drag and drop that entry over to the desktop. An icon will magically appear.

Above the Programs entry there is a separator bar, and above that bar are shortcuts to common tasks. These tasks include creating a new document, yet another shortcut to Windows Update, and just about any other thing that some program you installed chose to add. For example, in my Start menu, I have a shortcut to Sierra Utilities. This is because I installed a game from Sierra Entertainment, Inc. I didn't particularly care for it, so I uninstalled it. (Okay, I'll admit it. It was too hard, and I couldn't figure out how to win!!!) Uninstalling the game, however, did not uninstall the Sierra Utilities entry, and I've been too lazy to do it since then.

THE TASKBAR

Starting with WIN95, and in every version since, Microsoft OSs have sported a taskbar that, by default, appears at the bottom of the screen. For every application you open, a button for that app appears in the taskbar. In **Figure 24.7**, I've opened several different applications.

When you right-click the taskbar, the menu that appears gives you several options. You can manage the toolbars (discussed in the next section); you can choose to either cascade your windows (as shown in **Figure 24.8**) or tile them (as shown in **Figure 24.9**). Note that the menu items from Photoshop didn't cascade or tile along with the program.

Another useful function found here is the ability to minimize all windows. This takes you straight back to an uncluttered desktop without the hassle of having to minimize each window one at a time.

On the left side of the task bar are usually several shortcuts to frequently used applications, such as Internet Explorer and Outlook. Other applications you install may choose to insert an icon here. If you don't want it there, right-click it and select Cut. The middle section of the

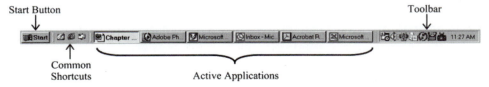

Figure 24.7   Clicking one of the buttons on the taskbar takes you straight to that application.

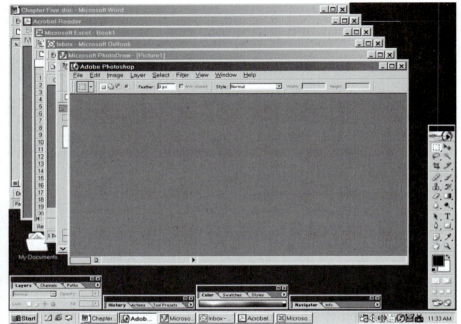

Figure 24.8
Cascading your applications makes the various windows appear like a hand of cards spread out.

Figure 24.9
Tiling your applications places them all in nice even little squares distributed across your desktop.

taskbar is where the shortcut buttons for applications active on your system will appear. And to the left is the Toolbar.

THE TOOLBAR

On the lower right-hand corner of your screen is a small section of the Taskbar known as the Toolbar. Here is where the user can open and manage some of the TSRs of Windows. One of the useful functions here is Time/Date. These are the programs that automatically launch every time you start Windows. It's also a source of some of your biggest headaches.

It seems that every application you ever install assumes that the only reason you purchased a computer was to run that particular program. Therefore, it adds itself to your Startup folder. This is a folder where Windows places shortcuts to these apps that automatically launch.

Each one of these TSRs takes up memory and swap file space. And each one adds several more seconds to the amount of time it takes Windows to load. A good housekeeping task is to occasionally weed out the Startup items you don't need, keeping only those that are useful to you. WIN98 and WINMe have a useful utility called MSCONFIG (which I'll be discussing in a few pages) that allows you to manage this and several other Windows functions.

MENUS

One of the key features of Windows that made it a successful OS was the fact that Microsoft insisted that all applications written for the WIN9x (and later) platform maintain a degree of consistency in organization and appearance. This common functionality is known as the Common User Interface (CUI). Under the CUI, this includes how the menus used in applications look and feel.

Each Windows application features a base menu bar at the top of the screen. Although there are certain differences allowed among applications based on the specific functions of those applications, for the most part, the base menu bar of any given application will share most of the same options, and those options will all appear in the same order on the menu. **Figure 24.10** illustrates the base menu bar for Microsoft Word compared to that of Adobe Photoshop.

Another toolbar that can be specific to the application is the base icon toolbar. This consists of a secondary toolbar (usually located directly beneath the base menu bar) that consists primarily of icons. To get a description of the function of any given icon, the user rests the cursor over that icon, and a description will appear (**Figure 24.11**). Various other toolbars and menu bars are permitted and frequently seen, but they must follow the same conventions described previously.

File Edit View Insert Format Tools Table Window Help

The base menu of Microsoft Word

File Edit Image Layer Select Filter View Window Help

The base menu of Photoshop

Figure 24.10   The base menu bar for Microsoft Word compared to that of Photoshop

Figure 24.11 The base icon toolbar

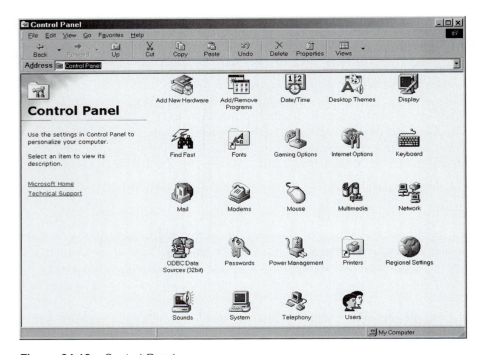

Figure 24.12 Control Panel

CONTROL PANEL

For the technician, Control Panel (**Figure 24.12**) is one of the key places to get to know well. This is where the various settings in Windows can be found in one tidy location. Here you find a collection of applets for managing and configuring virtually every part of your machine.

The next several pages are going to deal with the primary applets of Control Panel. I'm not going to attempt to go through all of them for three reasons. First of all, not all of them are critical to a technician. Second, there are applets that are added by applications and devices that the user installs onto the system. And finally, since I plan on discussing Control Panel only once in this book, and this feature varies slightly among versions of the OS, I figure it's easier to point out differences as I go.

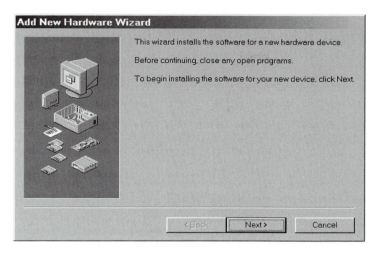

Figure 24.13 The Add New Hardware Wizard

ADD NEW HARDWARE

In Windows 2000 and XP this applet is known as Add/Remove Hardware. Normally, when PnP is working properly, when a new device is added to the system, Windows picks it up on the next boot and starts the Add New Hardware Wizard (**Figure 24.13**). At this point, Windows either locates the drivers it needs in the INF directory, or it prompts the user to insert the disk containing the drivers. If for any reason Windows fails to detect a new device, or should the user not install the drivers at that time, the Add New Hardware Wizard can always be started from this applet. It leads you through the procedures of detecting and installing new hardware.

ADD/REMOVE PROGRAMS

One of the advantages of Windows is that it recognizes and makes use of Autorun applications on a CD. Autorun applications are the little snippets of code that cause a program to automatically launch simply by inserting the CD. This makes it very easy to install applications these days. It will probably grieve you to no end to learn that this is the least desirable way to install an application. Add/Remove Programs (**Figure 24.14** and **Figure 24.15**) should be used for installing programs as well as removing them.

When you use this applet to install programs, it generates an uninstall script. The uninstall script is a small file that maintains a log of every new directory that was created on the hard drive and what files were installed into those directories. It also logs what common files were overwritten with newer versions, and it records any changes that were made to the registry during the installation of that program.

Later on, when you realize just how bad that program really is, Windows does a better job of removing all traces of that application when you uninstall it. Although it is true that some

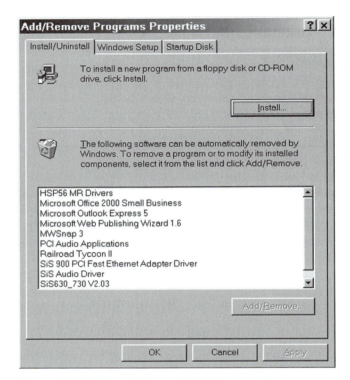

Figure 24.14   The Windows 98 Add/Remove Programs applet

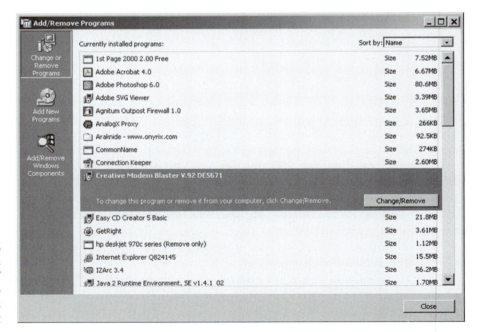

Figure 24.15
The Windows
2000 Add/
Remove
Programs
applet

of the new installer utilities used by software companies now provide this function, not all do. Windows 2000 and XP use a beefier version of the Windows Installer that generates these scripts whether you use Add/Remove Programs at the install or not.

Removing a program is a simple matter of opening the applet, highlighting the program you wish to blow away, and clicking the Add/Remove button (the Change/Remove button in Windows 2000 and XP). The applet asks you whether you're really sure you want to do this, and when you click OK, it's bye-bye program. That's happened to just about every game I've bought lately. Isn't *anyone* out there writing a decent computer game any more?

THE DATE/TIME APPLET

Hopefully, the Date/Time function (**Figure 24.16**) won't require a lengthy technical discussion. This is where you adjust your Windows clock and calendar settings. One other setting you can adjust here is whether or not you want your computer to automatically adjust for Daylight Savings time. If you live in one of the states that do not recognize Daylight Savings time, then you'll find it very annoying to have your clock changed twice a year. Right-clicking the time display in your toolbar and selecting Properties can also access this function.

THE DISPLAY APPLET

Should you wish to adjust the resolution or color depth on your monitor, the Display applet (**Figure 24.17**) is where you'll want to go. The Display applet is one of those applications that

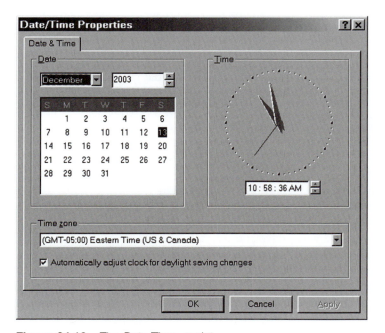

Figure 24.16   The Date/Time applet

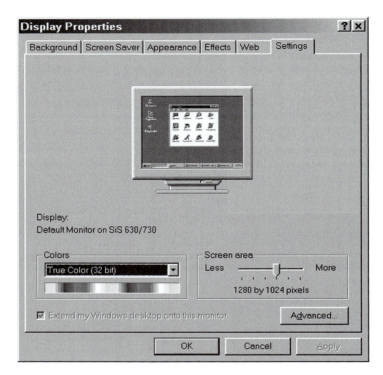

Figure 24.17 The Display applet might vary in appearance and available options from one machine to another, depending on the graphics adapter that is installed.

can vary in appearance and options, depending on what graphics adapter you have installed on your system. Some graphics adapters can be adjusted for advanced properties such as gamma (image density), moiré (a circular distortion that can occur), and other properties. Therefore, it is possible that when you open Display on your system, you may get a somewhat different screen than you see in the illustration.

The system I used to make these illustrations has a pretty fundamental display adapter installed and offers only the basic options. These are Background, Screen Saver, Appearance, Effects, Web, and Settings. Background is where you pick which pretty picture you wish to be part of your desktop. You can make your own background if you wish. Just browse to an image on your hard drive that you prefer and select it.

Screen savers are programs that blank the screen and then run animated little images across the screen in random patterns. This is necessary on cathode-ray tube (CRT) monitors to prevent a phenomenon called *burn-in*. Burn-in occurs when the same screen is left open on the monitor for an extended

BUZZ WORDS

Burn-in: The tendency for a CRT monitor to permanently etch an image onto the inner surface of the tube if the image stays on the screen for too long a period.

period, and the phosphorous layer on the inside surface of the CRT is permanently etched with that image. This is not so much of a factor with LCD monitors.

The Appearance tab allows you to adjust virtually every aspect of the Windows desktop. This includes the size and font used for menus, icons, and buttons as well as the different sizes and colors of borders and bars. It's a great place for users to play around without hurting anything.

You can create an active desktop by clicking the Web tab. With an active desktop, icons are activated with a single click, and the overall effect is that of the desktop being like a Web page. In fact, by selecting a URL from the Internet, the desktop becomes that Web page. This is useful for companies that make computers accessible to the public. Having their Web page as the desktop background is great promotion.

In the Settings tab, you can adjust things like color depth and monitor resolution. If the computer is equipped either with two graphics cards, or with a dual-output graphics card, dual-monitor displays can also be set up here. The Advanced tab will bring up settings specific to the graphics adapter as well as some system settings common to all adapters. These include adjustments such as the smoothing of screen fonts, what size screen fonts the user wishes to use, and whether or not a restart of the machine is necessary to apply display changes.

FONTS

The term "font" is one of those words that get misused a lot. Many people mistake the typeface for the font. The *typeface* is the basic shape of the letters and numbers that appear on the page. For example, Times New Roman is a typeface. The *font*, technically speaking, is a particular size and style of that typeface. 12-point italic Times New Roman is a font.

> **BUZZ WORDS** ——————
>
> **Typeface:** The basic shape that letters and numbers of a particular character set will assume.
>
> **Font:** The size and characteristic (such as bold or italic) of a particular typeface.

One of the best features of any GUI OS is the ability to use different typefaces in documents and to be able to see what that document is going to look like on the screen before it is printed. If a user is involved in desktop publishing, it is likely that he or she makes use of a number of different typefaces. The Fonts applet (**Figure 24.18**) is where different typefaces can be installed or removed. As you can see in this illustration, it is also where you can view that typeface to see what it looks like. This preview page can be printed up as a sample page if desired.

INTERNET OPTIONS

I guess there's no doubt that a large reason for the popularity of PCs can be attributed to the popularity of the Internet. Internet Options (**Figure 24.19**) is where you go to configure an Internet connection and then make it behave the way you want it to.

This applet consists of six different tabs. The General tab is the one to appear on top by default. Here you can select the URLs that your browser will load when it first starts. It's also where you manage the temporary files that build up on a computer over time. In order to allow frequently used pages to load faster, the files for that page are downloaded and stored locally on

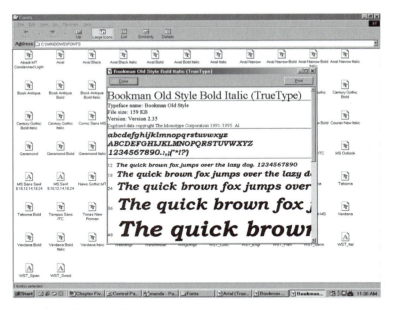

Figure 24.18 The Fonts applet

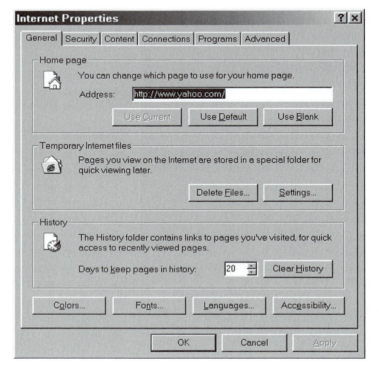

Figure 24.19 Internet Options

the user's hard disk. The Delete Files button does just what it says it's going to. When you click it, the folder that holds all those files is emptied. The Settings button allows you to dictate the maximum amount of hard drive space that these files will be allowed to occupy and, if you choose, select a different folder where those files will be stored.

The History section allows you to figure out how many days worth of temporary files will be stored before the older ones are overwritten. This is also how your Web browser keeps that pull-down list in the address bar up to date. Clearing the history doesn't delete the files, but it will empty out the pull-down menus.

The other buttons along the bottom of this tab allow you to configure what colors and fonts you like on your browser and what language you want to display. The Accessibility button allows you to configure the display for people with poor eyesight.

The Security tab is where you can configure what types of material you want to allow users on this system to access. Microsoft is fully aware that downloading applications, screensavers, macros, and so on is a likely way to pick up viruses and other malignant software. Here is where you can control what actions a user can take when browsing the Internet.

The Privacy tab lets you configure how your system handles cookies. Cookies are small files that some Web administrators place on your system that allow them to track your activity while on their site. Unfortunately not all cookies limit their activity to the host site that dumped them on your system. Some cookies track you wherever you go. Here you can block all cookies, have the system prompt you yea or nay when a cookie is on its way, or let them all come aboard.

The Content tab lets you configure the type of material that can be viewed. If the Content Advisor is enabled, you can filter sites based on language, nudity, sexual content, or violence. This can be a particularly good feature for families with children. On the other hand, one of my children was assigned to write a paper on the Ku Klux Klan but was unable to use school computers because all sites that even mentioned the group were blocked. A little care is in order here.

The Connections tab is where the methods by which the system accesses the Internet are configured. This includes dialup connections and proxy settings.

The Programs tab lets you configure which program is the default program to run and/or edit certain types of files. You can tell Windows what program edits HTML files, what your email client happens to be, what program handles your calendar and contacts, where your newsgroup reader is located, and how virtual meetings are handled.

Last is the Advanced tab. Here is where you find all the other settings that didn't fit nicely into a particular category. There are more than fifty different configuration settings in this tab. To cover them all in detail is somewhat beyond the scope of this book.

KEYBOARD

The Keyboard applet (**Figure 24.20**) is one of the simpler applets in Control Panel. Here you can configure how fast keys should repeat characters when held down and how fast the cursor within a document page blinks. On the Language tab, you can pick what language you prefer.

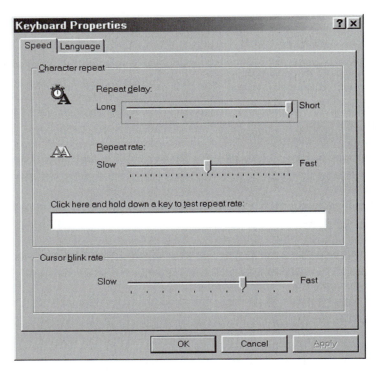

Figure 24.20 The Keyboard applet

MAIL

Configuring an email account in Windows needn't be all that hard. Oddly enough, it's done in the Mail applet shown in **Figure 24.21**. The one thing that might make it little more challenging is that you need some information from your Internet service provider concerning its systems. Most ISPs are willing to provide that information, but you bump into a few that won't go that extra step. In the latter case, you need to rely on them for assistance. That assistance usually arrives in the form of a disk.

The window in Figure 24.21 doesn't look like much. There's no place for configuring an address or anything. Clicking the Add button runs you through a wizard for setting up your new account. For an existing account, you highlight the account you wish to reconfigure and click Properties. That will bring up the screen shown in **Figure 24.22**, where the various settings are configured. Some information that you will need from your ISP is the server names for their incoming and outgoing mail servers. For many ISPs one server performs the same function. A server name commonly looks something like *mail.ISPname.net*.

MODEMS

As DSL and cable modems become increasingly popular, the Modem applet (**Figure 24.23**) is seeing less of a workout. Still, for people who live out in the boonies, modems are all too often

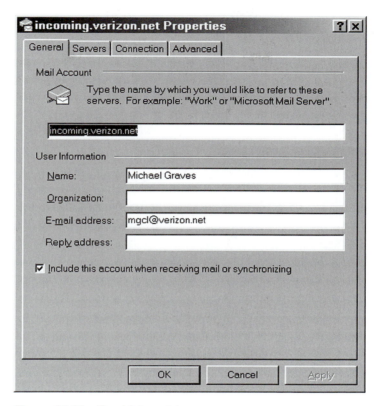

Figure 24.21   The Mail applet

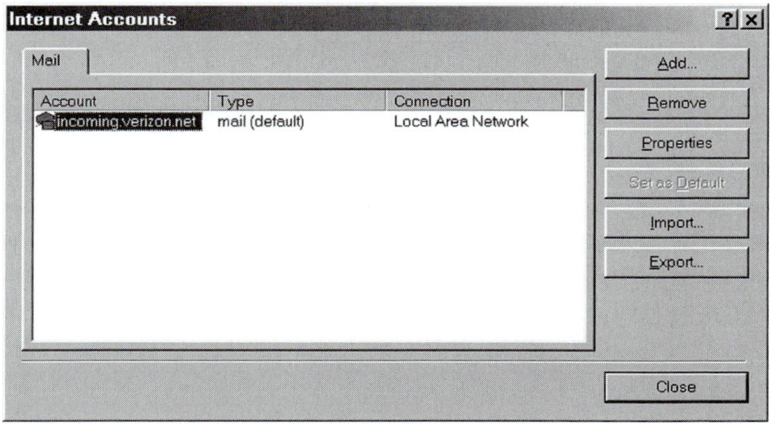

Figure 24.22   Configuring a mail account

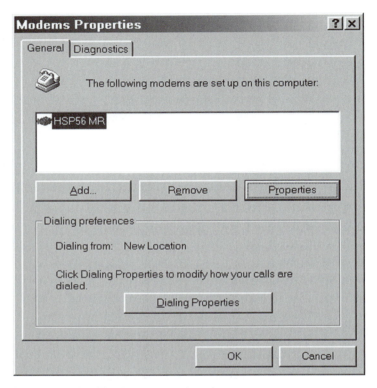

Figure 24.23   The Modem applet

the only choice for connecting to the outside world. So a good technician needs to be able to configure them.

Clicking the A̲dd button starts the Add/Remove Hardware wizard, which detects the modem and prompts you for the CD if it can't find the drivers. As surprising as this may sound, the R̲emove button is the one you click should you wish to uninstall a modem. The P̲roperties button allows you to configure settings such as maximum speed, how loud the modem speaker squawks, the size of the transmit and receive buffers used during a session, whether or not to use parity, and how many data bits to use. In general, the default settings are best left alone unless a particular server requires different settings. In that case, the provider will let you know.

MOUSE

One rarely thinks of the lowly little mouse as requiring any special attention. However, you'd be amazed at the number of settings that can be changed on this device. In the Mouse applet (**Figure 24.24**), you can adjust the speed required for the double-click of your mouse and whether it is a device for a right-handed or a left-handed user. Different options for pointers and the infamous hourglass can be selected, and mouse speed can be adjusted.

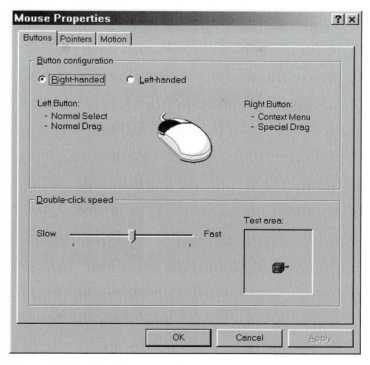

Figure 24.24 The Mouse applet

MULTIMEDIA

Multimedia (**Figure 24.25**) is another of those applets with a fairly sizeable number of options available. Here is where you can select which device performs which functions. The advanced properties vary with the device, but as an example, for a particular sound card you might be able to select whether a single pair of speakers is installed or whether the system is equipped with a full-blown 5.1 surround-sound system. The Video tab simply allows you to select whether video clips are shown full screen or in a window. The MIDI (an acronym for *musical instrument device interface*) tab provides the different options for voice selection. Unless there is a driving reason for changing it, the default is usually best left in place here. The CD Music tab is where you tell Windows which CD drive to use for playing music, should more than one drive be installed. The Devices tab lists each multimedia device installed on the system and allows you to configure the appropriate properties.

THE NETWORK APPLET

The Network applet (**Figure 24.26**) is another busy place for the professional technician. This is where you will configure and troubleshoot network hardware, clients, and protocols. And because network issues constitute a large percentage of problems in the corporate or institutional

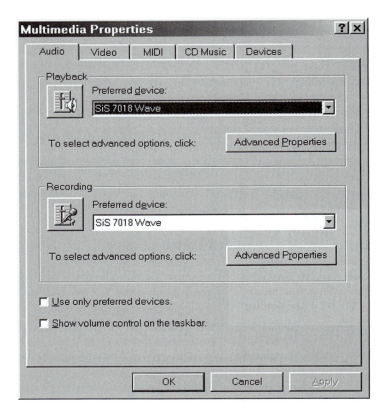

Figure 24.25 Multimedia

environment, it's a good idea to be comfortable with this applet. This applet is accessed by right clicking Network Neighborhood on the desktop (My Network Places in Windows 2000 and XP) and selecting Properties. A detailed discussion of everything that goes on in here is far beyond the scope of this book. For that, refer to *The Complete Guide to Networking and Network+*, by this same author. A brief tour is in order here, and there will be a more detailed description later in this book.

The Configuration tab is where you would add a NIC, a networking client, or a new protocol. Obviously, you do this by clicking the Add button. If you highlight an existing resource, the Remove and Properties buttons will become active. The function of the Remove button is self-evident. The Properties button is where the specific resource can be configured.

The Identification tab is where you configure the network name for the computer and identify what particular workgroup the computer will join. Windows 2000 and XP machines do not have the Identification tab in the Network Properties. With those two OSs, identification is a System property.

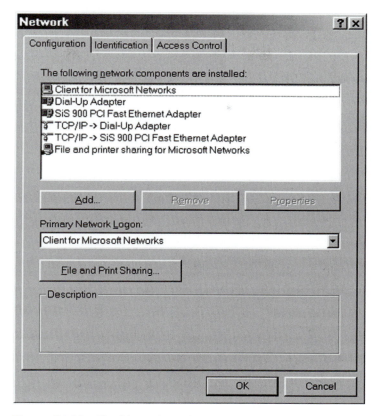

Figure 24.26 The Network applet

Access Control is where you define whether or not security on files will be Share Level or User Level security. With Share Level security, the user places permissions on the file or folder, and those permissions and any passwords the user assigns determine who may or may not access that resource. User Level security checks a User ID and password against a security database stored on a server and allocates permissions based on the individual users' privileges.

POWER MANAGEMENT

In this day and age of ecological awareness, users need to be conscious of the amount of energy they consume. By properly configuring the Power Management applet (**Figure 24.27**), at least their computer will do its part.

In this applet you can select specific time intervals for how long a specific device remains idle before reverting to sleep mode. In sleep mode, only the minimal amount of power is applied to the system to protect the data. Unnecessary devices are powered down. Intervals range from Always On (in which the system never powers down) to as short as one minute.

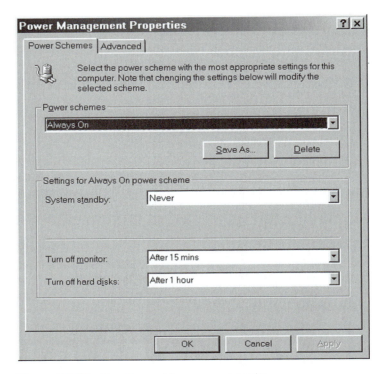

Figure 24.27 The Power Management applet

PRINTERS

As you can see in **Figure 24.28**, clicking Printers doesn't open an applet, but rather a folder. The Add Printer icon launches a wizard that allows you to install a new local printer or to browse to an existing printer on the network and install that printer locally.

When a printer is installed, you can click the printer's icon with the left mouse button to manage the print queue for that particular printer. This is where you can delete pending print jobs or assign priorities to print jobs. You can also right-click the icon and select Properties to configure the printer. Different printers offer different configuration options, depending on their capabilities.

SOUNDS

The Sounds applet (**Figure 24.29**) is where you go to change what sound is played for any given event in Windows. (Or if you're like me, it's where you go to turn the pesky things *off*!) If you selected the various Windows themes as you were installing Windows, then you have the option of selecting those from the different sound themes here as well.

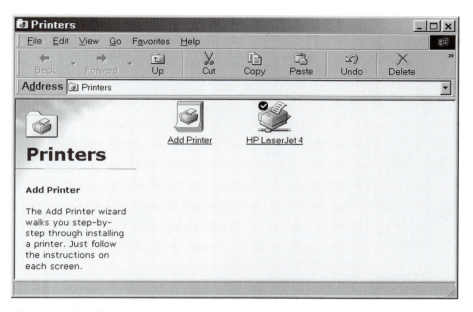

Figure 24.28   The Printers folder

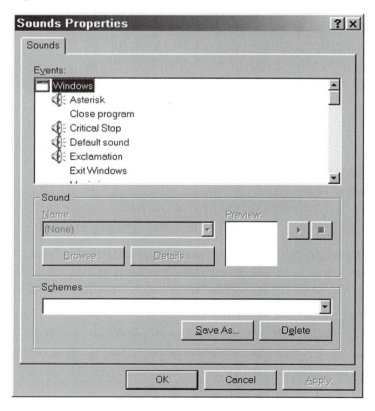

Figure 24.29
The Sounds applet

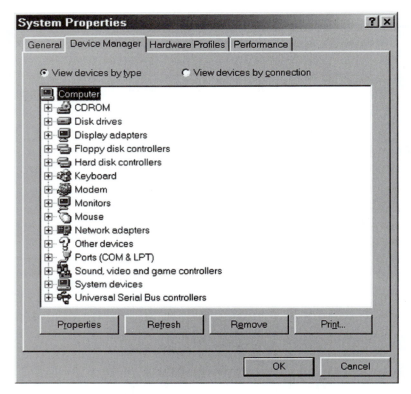

Figure 24.30   The System applet

SYSTEM

The System applet (**Figure 24.30**) is by far the most frequently visited Control Panel app for any technician. The General tab provides basic information about the computer system, including the version of OS running, how much RAM is installed, and what kind of CPU powers the system. It also provides the serial number for the specific OS installation.

Device Manager provides configuration settings for the different pieces of hardware installed on the system. If you elected to purchase the lab manual that accompanies this text, you will have the pleasure of spending quite a bit of time poking around in this section.

Because Windows allows more than one hardware configuration to exist on a single computer, there needs to be a way of deciding which hardware configuration you want to use at any given time. The Hardware Profiles tab allows this.

The Performance tab allows you to adjust certain settings critical to system performance. These include making adjustments to file systems used by the various storage devices installed on the system, setting hardware acceleration for your graphics adapter, and managing the swap file.

WINDOWS EXPLORER

One of the key features of Windows that all too often gets taken for granted is Windows Explorer. Explorer is a GUI shell that places all file and directory management functions into a single application that is intuitive and easy to manage.

To fully take advantage of the power Explorer offers, it is necessary to understand the seven important elements of the Explorer application. **Figure 24.31** points out the location of each of these elements:

- The folders (or navigation) pane
- The details (or contents) pane
- The title bar
- The menu bar
- The toolbar
- The address bar
- The status bar

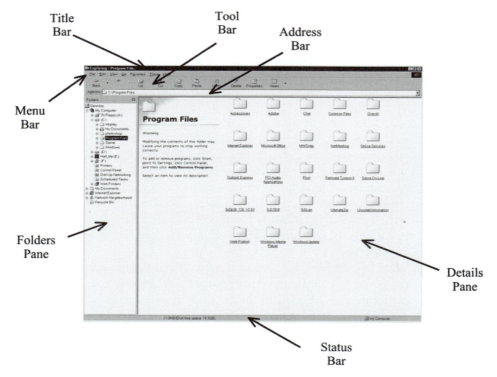

Figure 24.31   The essential elements of Windows Explorer

The title bar basically just displays what folder is currently opened or highlighted. It doesn't, however, show the full path. The menu bar is identical to the menu bars I discussed earlier in the chapter, as is the toolbar.

The address bar is something different for Explorer. Not only can this be used to type a path and/or file name, it can also be used to locate Internet sites or other machines on the network. In the absence of a full-fledged browser, it makes an acceptable substitute. The status bar provides such information as the size of the file currently highlighted and how much free space remains on the selected disk.

The two features of Explorer I want to spend the most time discussing are the folders, or navigation, pane and the details pane. These are the most heavily used features of Explorer. After that, I will cover a few of the more commonly used menu items.

The Folders Pane

The folders pane is the tool that allows the user to locate specific resources, both on the local computer as well as across the network. These resources are displayed starting with the desktop and then expanding into wider and more diverse resources. They are organized into a tree structure similar to that of the file systems I discussed earlier in the book. This shouldn't come as too much of a surprise, since what you're basically viewing is the file system for every device available to the system.

The basic resources offered for browsing are My Computer, My Documents, Internet Explorer, Network Neighborhood, and the Recycle Bin. In front of each of these resources (except for Recycle Bin) is a checkbox, usually containing a plus sign (+). The plus sign indicates that there are one or more subdirectories beneath that entry that can also be viewed. If you click the plus, the folder opens, and the plus becomes a minus. Clicking the minus closes the folder.

If you click the checkbox next to My Computer, it opens a folder for each drive on your computer, including floppy disk drives, hard disk drives, CD and DVD drives, and any removable media drives you own. It also presents folders for Printers, a shortcut to Control Panel, one for Dial-up Networking, and one for Scheduled Tasks. If you have an active Internet connection, there will also be an icon for Web folders.

My Documents is nothing more than a shortcut to the My Documents folder on your hard drive. Ditto with Internet Explorer. Network Neighborhood (My Network Places in WIN2K and WINXP) will appear only on systems equipped with NICs, and it will appear whether there is an active network connection or not.

Recycle Bin is where all the files that you delete go. When you delete a file in Windows, the data doesn't really go anywhere. Its directory attributes are merely changed to reflect that the file is now a member of the Recycle Bin folder. Only if you decide to erase the file from Recycle Bin is that file permanently erased.

Another task that be accomplished from the folders pane include moving entire directories from one location to another. As you can see in **Figure 24.32**, right-clicking a folder brings up a pop-up menu. From this menu you can open the folder, which brings the contents of that folder, including all subdirectories and files, into a separate window. You can also explore that folder, which opens the folder in the details pane on the right-hand side of the screen. The Find option

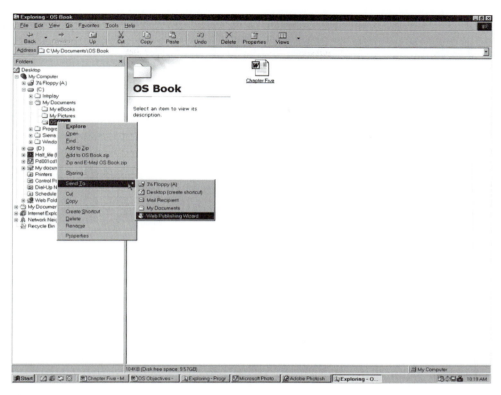

Figure 24.32 Working with the folders pane

opens Explorer's search engine and allows you to look for specific files or directories within the folder. From there, that search can be expanded to include the entire system, if desired.

On a networked computer on which File and Print Sharing has been enabled (more on that in Chapter Thirty-Three, Operating Systems and Networking), a user with appropriate rights can also share that directory for others on the network to use. The Cut and Copy commands need to be used with discretion, because they affect the entire directory that has been selected, including all files and subdirectories contained within. Cut deletes the directory from its current location. After you have selected a new location, a new command, Paste, will appear the next time you right-click a new location. This moves the directory from the previous folder to the new location, and it no longer exists in the first location. Copy allows you to make an identical copy of a folder while retaining the original copy in its previous location.

If you have browsed to a network location, another item that will appear on this menu is the Map Network Drive command. This is useful on networks where data is stored on servers. You can browse to a folder that contains data frequently used, and by mapping that folder as a network drive, it looks, feels, smells, and tastes just like a local hard disk to both the user and the computer. That folder is now directly accessible from the File menu of all Windows applications as a drive letter.

The <u>D</u>elete command moves the folder and all its contents to the Recycle Bin. First you'll be asked whether you're really sure you want to make such a drastic move. Then you will be prompted again for any executable or system files before the folder is deleted. Selecting the Yes to All button stops those prompts.

The Rena<u>m</u>e command is pretty self-explanatory. However, there can be unexpected side effects of renaming a folder. If it is a system folder, such as the Windows directory, you'll first be prompted that renaming it can stop the system from functioning properly, and Windows won't let you do it. If you rename a shared folder, not only will it no longer be shared, but should you elect to share it out once again under the new name, all permissions will have to be reconfigured. Those out there who have mapped this folder as a network drive will not be happy.

The <u>P</u>roperties command can be an interesting tool when used properly. It has two tabs: the General tab and the Sharing Tab. The General tab tells you how many files and subdirectories exist within that folder. It also tells you how many bytes of data reside within that folder as well as how much disk space is being occupied by that data. If there is a huge discrepancy between these two numbers, it can mean one of two things. It's time to convert from FAT16 to FAT32, if you haven't already, or you may have a problem with your file system, and it's time to run ScanDisk.

Also on this tab you can see the folder's attributes. On WIN98 and later there is also an option for Enable <u>t</u>humbnail view. If this option is selected, when a file is selected from the Contents Pane, a small image of that file will appear. (Note that the latter feature is not installed by default in a Typical installation and must be either selected optionally during installation, or installed later before it is available.)

THE CONTENTS PANE

The contents pane is where you go to see details and manage more specific resources on a computer. Here individual files can be copied, moved, renamed, created, or erased. Right-clicking a specific file or subdirectory will bring up a menu identical to the one I just discussed in the previous section. Rather than repeat the last few pages, I'll just move on to the differences.

Right-clicking a part of the contents pane other than over an icon will bring up a menu specific to the functions of this pane. As with all other Windows menus, an arrow pointing to the right indicates submenus that can be opened. **Figure 24.33** shows the <u>N</u>ew option selected.

The <u>V</u>iew option allows you to select how you want files and folders to be displayed on the screen. As Web Page enables a single click of the mouse to open a file or folder. The graphic in the upper left corner and the description of the folder also disappears. The Thumbnails option puts the icon for each file or folder into a separate bitmap. If it is a registered graphics file, a small reproduction of the image appears within the box. Other file types will simply show the icon of the program that has been configured to open that type of file in the folder options (which I'll discuss in a few paragraphs.)

The Large Icons and S<u>m</u>all Icons options are fairly self-explanatory. They determine how big the pretty picture that represents the file will appear in the contents pane. The two options that are interesting are <u>L</u>ist and <u>D</u>etails. <u>L</u>ist simply places the files in rows, with a small icon

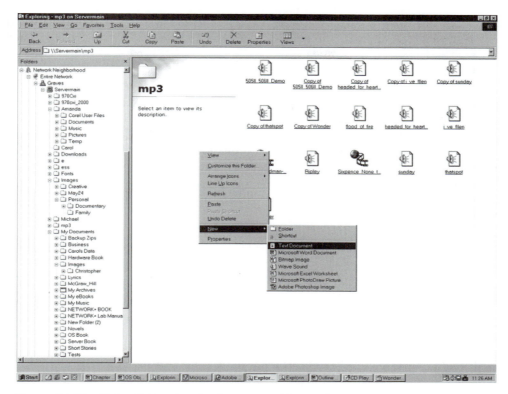

Figure 24.33 Right-clicking the details pane enables a whole new set of options for the user

to indicate file type. Details arranges files and folders in the directory by name, size, type, and the date on which it was last modified.

If you are using the Detail view, at the top of each column is a button labeling the column. If you click the button for Size, then all the files are sorted in size, from smallest to largest. Click the Size button a second time, and now they're sorted from largest to smallest. Click the Type button, and files are sorted by their extension. The Modified button sorts by date last modified. Clicking once on this button sorts by most recent; clicking a second time sorts by least recent.

The Customize this Folder option allows you to configure a specific folder to been seen as a Web page. Or you can choose a background image to appear behind the files and folders list.

The third command in the pop-up menu allows you to arrange the icons in the pane by a specific order. Files can be arranged by Name, Type, Size, or Date regardless of the view mode selected. This is identical to the function I discussed when viewing the folder in the Details mode. The Line Up Icons command simply tidies up the screen, without resorting icons.

Next, you have a Refresh command. Now what good would that be when viewing files on a hard drive? Are they likely to change while you watch? If you're looking at a remote location, such as a file server, they very well might. And if you're waiting for someone to post a file for you, simply having Explorer open won't help. You'll need to refresh the screen periodically to see when that file finally appears. You can accomplish the same thing by pressing the F5 button on your keyboard.

The Cut and Paste commands are identical to the ones I discussed in the section on the folders pane. An interesting item that comes next is the New command. What you see listed on this option can depend entirely on what applications you have installed on your system. By default, you can create new folders within a folder, new shortcuts, and new text documents. If you've installed a word processor such as Microsoft Word, then the option to create a new Word document becomes available. Many other applications add options to this menu as well. When you select New and then Word Document, Explorer launches Microsoft Word and allows you to start working from there.

Properties opens the same screen that you saw in the folders pane when you right-clicked a particular folder and selected Properties.

THE EXPLORER MENU

For the most part, the items found in the main menu of Windows Explorer are identical to items discussed in previous sections of the chapter. To show you where the items can be found, I've created a montage in **Figure 24.34** showing each of the menu items opened simultaneously. (Remember! I'm a trained professional. Don't try this stunt at home!)

A couple of items I want to discuss in greater detail are Folder Options (found under both the Tools menu item and the View menu item in WIN98) and the Go menu. Both of these applets offer you some added power that often goes unused.

FOLDER OPTIONS

Although I've already discussed the contents of the three tabs in the Folders Options dialog box in a previous section, I want to take a more detailed look at the View tab and the File Types tab. There are a couple of things you can do in here that can be done nowhere else.

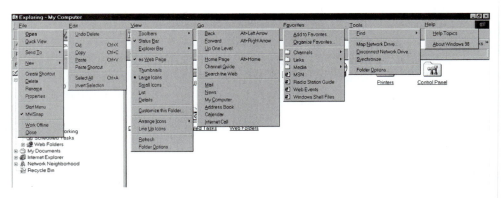

Figure 24.34   Windows Explorer with all the menus open at once

In the View tab there are two sets of advanced settings. One is for Files and Folders, and the other, Visual Settings, allows you to adjust certain settings relevant to Explorer's appearance. At this point, I'm only interested in the Files and Folders section.

Earlier in this section, I mentioned how the title bar only shows the name of the folder you are in. One of the options you can select is to show the entire path. This is an option I prefer to have selected on a Windows machine I'm using, except when I'm making illustrations that show Windows default settings.

Notice that there are three different options for viewing hidden and/or system files. One of the options hides only files whose attributes are set for Hidden, and the other hides those with the attributes of Hidden and System. The last option displays all files. If you need to copy all the files in a directory from one location to another, and elect to use Windows Explorer for this task rather than doing it from a command prompt, then you need to adjust this setting to show all files. When you select all the files in the details pane, files that are not displayed are not selected and, therefore, not copied.

By default, Windows is configured to not show extensions for commonly used file types. This means that in Explorer, Novel.doc only appears as Novel, with the icon of your word processor above or next to it. Checking this box forces Windows to show all file extensions. The other settings in this section are fairly self-explanatory and are of little use to the technician.

In the File Types tab, the user can change how the extension of a file affects that file's behavior. In the details box of this window, you see the extension for the file type that has been selected in the Registered files types list along with its content type. Content type basically indicates whether the file is a document, an application, image file, or whatever. This is generally not something you want to change. Where it says Opens with, you see what program (if any) will automatically launch if you double-click that file in Explorer (or single-click if you are in Web mode).

You can change these settings (except for the extension itself, of course) by clicking the Edit button. You can also change the icon that is displayed in Explorer if you so desire. In the Edit File Type window, there is another Edit button. Clicking this allows you to change what program runs a particular file type. You can change what actions Windows performs when you double-click an icon by clicking the Add button.

HOT KEYS

Windows has been designed to be a point-and-click environment in order to make it easier to use. In a way, this is Microsoft's way of acknowledging that the majority of people who use computers have no intention or desire to learn *how* to use them beyond the minimal level they require.

However, excessive use of a mouse has two negative effects. One of these is repetitive stress injury. This is a physical ailment that many people develop from repeating the same motions over and over again. The second negative effect isn't quite as serious, but is still something to consider. And that is the fact that reaching for the mouse, navigating the cursor to the place where it needs to be, and then performing whatever function is needed can often be much slower than simply pressing a couple of keys.

Windows is programmed with a large number of predefined key sequences that, when pressed, accomplish some function that might require searching through several levels of menu items to find if using the mouse. These are called hot keys. Some of the Windows hot keys involve only a single keystroke. However, most involve some combination of the <Ctrl> or the <Alt> keys along with one or more other keys on the keyboard. For example, when I want to type in *italics*, I don't use my mouse to click the italics button in the tools menu. That would seriously impact on my blazing typing speed (126 mistakes per minute, thank you very much!). I press <Ctrl>+I to get the same effect. Appendix E contains a table listing the most commonly used hot keys.

MSCONFIG

Earlier in the chapter, I mentioned a utility present in WIN9x that would allow the user to manage the TSRs that started automatically. That utility is MSCONFIG (**Figure 24.35**), and it does a lot more than just that. There are several tabs in this section, but for most technicians, only two are truly relevant in most situations.

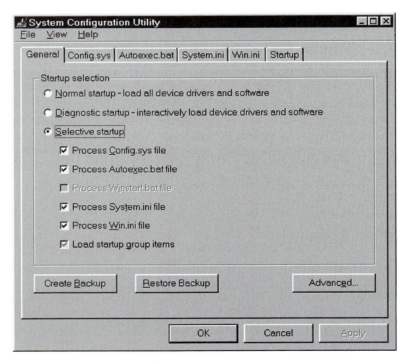

Figure 24.35 The MSCONFIG utility is an easy way to edit the startup parameters and other aspects of your system.

The General tab is the first to appear when you launch the application by clicking Start →
Run and typing **MSCONFIG**. Here you can select between a normal startup, a diagnostic startup,
or a selective startup. Obviously, a normal startup is the default, and, unless there is a good
reason, it is the one that you should retain. A diagnostic startup does come in handy when you
have a system that starts fine in Safe Mode but won't start normally. While the procedure can
be time-consuming, using the diagnostic startup enables you to selectively load drivers. By
leaving drivers out, one at a time, on successive reboots, it is possible to locate the offending
device and decide what to do about it. Selective startup allows you to tell Windows which file
to load and which ones not to load during startup. This can be useful if you have an old DOS
program that you run regularly.

Create Backup and Restore Backup are for creating or restoring backups of the configuration file that's created by MSCONFIG. There is an Advanced button that takes you to a
number of settings that in most cases should be left alone. These are mostly settings relating to
hardware and are best covered in a hardware book.

The four tabs for CONFIG.SYS, AUTOEXEC.BAT, SYSTEM.INI, and WIN.INI allow
you to view and edit these specific files. This is usually unnecessary, since WIN9x applications
do not make use of these files. They exist for backward compatibility with older DOS and
WIN3.x programs.

Finally, the Startup tab is where you go to enable or disable the applets that start automatically
every time Windows loads. Although not 100 percent complete, there is a table in Appendix E
that shows some of the items commonly located in the Startup menu along with descriptions.

WINDOWS HELP

Microsoft has incorporated a help function of some form since the earlier incarnations of
MS-DOS. In DOS, it consisted of typing the command you wanted help with followed by
/?. Doing that listed the possible triggers for that command. With WIN3.x, the help function
became more of a formatted text document. These days, Windows help (**Figure 24.36**) is a full-
blown application. It is a relational database of topics that cover a vast majority of the common
problems people face.

Topics are hyperlinked between one another where relevant so navigation between topics
is much easier. By hyperlinked, I mean that clicking a hyperlinked topic automatically redirects
you to another page with more or related information on the topic. In addition, Windows help
can hyperlink you to a number of different troubleshooters. Hardware troubleshooters help
diagnose problems with misbehaving devices, and the Network Troubleshooter can help you
figure out why you can't log on to the domain.

Windows help is also context-sensitive. That means if you are in a particular function or
application and press the F1 key, a window will appear with tips relevant to what you were doing
when you pressed the key. If you wish more general help, you can get there by clicking
Start → Help. If it is the first time you've used help, you might have to wait a couple of seconds
while the application indexes the topics for the first time. After that, you're off and running.

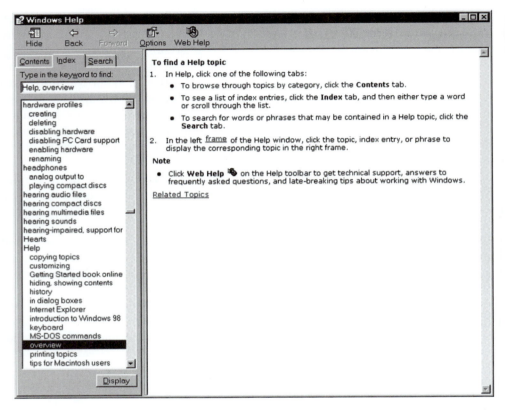

Figure 24.36 The Windows Help function provides literally volumes of information that is context sensitive.

CHAPTER SUMMARY

Okay, I'll admit. This was a long chapter. However, since it prepares you for much of what is to come, that simply means that you've gotten the basics out of the way. For the rest of the book I can concentrate on specifics.

By the time you've finished this chapter, you'll have a pretty good idea of how to get around Windows. The nice thing about later versions is that, for the most part, they stick to a very similar format and structure. Making a move from an older OS to a newer version isn't quite as painful as it might be. However, Microsoft does like to slip in a few changes here and there, so there will still be much to discuss in the chapters to come.

Installing the OS was the first thing I covered. This is one area that does change somewhat with future versions, so I'll be looking at those differences. An understanding of the Windows Desktop is critical, but fortunately, it also comes easily. There are also a good number of questions on the CompTIA exam relevant to the desktop, so don't slack off on the subject just because you think you know it. And *really* make sure you understand Control Panel.

One of the topics I covered in this book that I rarely see covered in other books is that of hot keys. This is a sad omission because someone who truly understands hot keys and knows them well is far more productive than the user who is chained to a mouse.

BRAIN DRAIN

1. Discuss the differences between a clean install and an upgrade. While you're at it, discuss the pros and cons of each type of installation.

2. What are the different setup phases for Windows 95 and what is happening to your computer at each phase?

3. Now discuss the different setup phases for Windows 98 and how they differ from Windows 95.

4. Discuss how an understanding of the Taskbar can help you determine why a computer takes its own sweet time every time it boots up.

5. How did Microsoft take the mouse from a cute little toy to a powerful tool with the release of Windows 95?

THE 64K$ QUESTIONS

1. During an upgrade, Windows 95 could extract information about programs installed to WIN3.x by opening and reading the _____.
   a. Registry
   b. SETUP.INI file
   c. Group files
   d. CONFIG.SYS and AUTOEXEC.BAT

2. You want to run the Windows Setup program from a command prompt and want it to skip the network configuration portion of Setup. What command would you type?

   a. `SETUP /NONET`
   b. `SETUP /IN`
   c. `SETUP /N`
   d. `SETUP /IS`

3. Which of the following is not a setup phase for WIN95?
   a. Startup and information gathering
   b. File copy
   c. Final system configuration
   d. Hardware setup

4. What is the first thing the WIN95 Setup program does after it is launched?
   a. Perform a system check
   b. Install the Setup Wizard
   c. Prompt the user for the License Key
   d. FDISK the hard drive

5. How does Windows setup remove AUTOEXEC.BAT or CONFIG.SYS lines that may cause problems during an upgrade?
   a. It deletes them completely.
   b. It places a REM statement in front of the offending command.
   c. It places a NO statement in front of the offending command.
   d. It doesn't.

6. The right button on the mouse can do what in WIN9x?
   a. Highlight an entire line with a single click.
   b. Move to the next active window.

c. Bring up context-sensitive help.

d. Bring up a menu specific to the object clicked upon.

7. In order to bring up Display Properties, the user can _____.

a. Right-click the Desktop and click Properties

b. Open My Computer and click Display Properties

c. Click Start → Control Panel → System → Display Properties

d. Click Start → Settings → Control Panel → Display Properties

8. A user's desktop that is setup for single-click activation of a menu item has been configured to be _____.

a. A Web page

b. An interactive desktop

c. An active desktop

d. You can't do that.

9. Control Panel can be accessed from which two of the following places?

a. My Computer

b. An active desktop

c. The taskbar

d. The Start menu

10. How would you create an icon on the desktop for a program that appears in your Start menu, but not on the desktop?

a. Dragging and dropping the Menu item over to the desktop.

b. From the Application's menu, clicking Tools → Create Shortcut.

c. Right-clicking the Desktop, selecting Create New Shortcut, and typing in the application's name.

d. Clicking Start → Programs, right-clicking the Application's name, and selecting Create Shortcut. When a new item appears on the menu with the application's name followed by (2), drag and drop it over to the desktop.

11. You've just installed a new sound card and it places a handy little applet somewhere on your computer that allows you to adjust volume without constantly reaching up to the speakers. Where is the icon for that program most likely to be placed?

a. On the Start menu

b. On the Desktop

c. On the Taskbar

d. On the Toolbar

12. You've installed about a hundred different things that all assume that you want them to automatically start every time you run Windows. What handy little applet did Microsoft include with WIN98 that allows you to easily reconfigure startup options?

a. SCANREG

b. MSCONFIG

c. START.BAT

d. SYSCONFIG

13. Windows applications are consistent among themselves because of a feature built into Windows called the

_____.

a. GUI

b. CUI

c. UID

d. IRD

14. How does using Add/Remove Programs (in WIN95) to install software differ from simply allowing

a CD's autorun feature to install it automatically?

a. It forces all programs to be installed into the Program Files directory.

b. It creates an Uninstall script.

c. It allows greater user control of what files are installed.

d. It doesn't.

15. Which Control Panel applet allows the user to turn off Daylight Savings Time?

a. System

b. Regional Settings

c. Users

d. Time/Date

16. Which of the following can't you browse to from Windows Explorer?

a. A networked printer

b. A Novell server

c. An Internet location

d. You can browse to any of those.

17. What are two methods of mapping a folder on the network server to your local machine so that it appears as though it were a local drive?

a. In the folders pane of Windows Explorer, right-click the remote resource and select Map Network Drive.

b. In the contents pane of Windows Explorer, right-click the remote resource and select Map Network Drive.

c. Add the location to the Favorites menu.

d. Click Tools → Map Network Drive.

18. Which of the following keys is not used in a key combination for a keyboard shortcut?

a. <Alt>

b. <Enter>

c. <Shift>

d. <Ctrl>

19. Which of the following shortcuts selects all text in an open document?

a. <Alt>+A

b. <Alt>+S

c. <Ctrl>+A

d. <Ctrl>+S

20. <Ctrl>+<Alt>+<Delete> _____ on a WIN9x computer.

a. Opens the Task Manager

b. Opens a Close Program window

c. Resets the computer

d. Is used when you first log onto the computer

TRICKY TERMINOLOGY

Active Desktop: A method of configuring the Windows desktop to behave as if it is a Web page, allowing single-click activation of icons and other Web-like features.

Burn-in: The tendency for a CRT monitor to permanently etch an image onto the inner surface of the tube if the image stays on the screen for too long a period.

Clean install: The fresh installation of an OS over a newly partitioned and formatted hard disk.

Font: The size and characteristics (such as bold or italic) of a particular typeface.

Icon: A small picture linked to an application shortcut.

Typeface: The basic shape that letters and numbers of a particular character set will assume.

Upgrade: The replacement of an older OS with a newer, migrating as many settings and applications as possible.

ACRONYM ALERT

PM: Program Manager. An applet in WIN3.x that acted as a DOS shell for file and program management functions.

CUI: Common User Interface. A feature of many OSs that dictates how certain functions related to user interaction with the programs are handled, ensuring that all applications have a similar look, feel, and function.

MIDI: Musical Instrument Device Interface. A connector for hooking up computerized musical instruments to a computer system.

 ## VIEW THE VIDEO

A video clip on Windows 9X System Files and a video clip on Safe Mode are available on the accompanying CD.

CHAPTER 25

THE WORLD OF NT

As I pointed out in the previous two chapters concerning the WIN9x products, one of Microsoft's main concerns had been that of maintaining backward compatibility with previous products. As such, the WIN9x products (except for WINMe) were hybrid OSs, consisting of a 16-bit component plus a 32-bit component. To further enhance their ability to run DOS applications, these products shipped with DOS 7.0.

With the release of Windows NT 3.51, this all changed. Although NT did have a command prompt, it did not support any version of DOS. It was a purely a 32-bit OS with only rudimentary support for 16-bit code. Microsoft's goal here was to provide a faster OS that exhibited greater stability. Windows NT (WINNT) was the first in a growing line of products that have pursued that goal.

A+ OPERATING SYSTEM TECHNOLOGIES EXAM OBJECTIVES

CompTIA exam objectives covered in this chapter include the following:

1.1 Identify the major desktop components and interfaces and their functions. Differentiate the characteristics of Windows 9x/Me, Windows NT 4.0 Workstation, Windows 2000 Professional, and Windows XP.

1.2 Identify the names, locations, purposes, and contents of major system files.

1.4 Identify basic concepts and procedures for creating, viewing, and managing disks, directories, and files. This includes procedures for changing file attributes and the ramifications of those changes (for example, security issues).

2.1 Identify the procedures for installing Windows 9x/Me, Windows NT 4.0 Workstation, Windows 2000 Professional, and Windows XP and bring the operating system to a basic operational level.

2.2 Identify steps to perform an operating system upgrade from Windows 9x/Me, Windows NT 4.0 Workstation, Windows 2000 Professional, and Windows XP. Given an upgrade scenario, choose the appropriate next steps.

2.3 Identify the basic system boot sequences and boot methods, including the steps to create an emergency boot disk with utilities installed for Windows 9x/Me, Windows NT 4.0 Workstation, Windows 2000 Professional, and Windows XP.

2.4 Identify procedures for installing/adding a device, including loading, adding, and configuring device drivers and required software.

3.1 Recognize and interpret the meaning of common error codes and startup messages from the boot sequence, and identify steps to correct the problems.

3.2 Recognize when to use common diagnostic utilities and tools. Given a diagnostic scenario involving one of these utilities or tools, select the appropriate steps needed to resolve the problem.

3.3 Recognize common operational and usability problems and determine how to resolve them.

THE HISTORY OF NT

While there would not be an official release of a product with NT in the name until 1993, Microsoft began work on the concept of a 32-bit OS in 1988. A gentleman by the name of David Cutler, Sr., moved over to Microsoft from Digital Equipment Corporation (DEC), bringing to Microsoft a profound knowledge of OS architecture. Most notably, Cutler had been involved with the development of DEC's Virtual Memory System (VMS).

By 1991, Microsoft had developed a version of NT that it considered stable enough to demonstrate at the Microsoft Windows Developers Conference. Designated NT 3.0, it was never deemed stable enough for a public release, but it still possessed most of the features that were to become the NT core.

What happened to versions 1.0 and 2.0? They never existed. Microsoft doesn't explain the reasoning behind their version numbering system, but here are the two most popular explanations:

1. They wanted the version numbers to coincide with Windows 3.0 and 3.1 desktop OSs.
2. Because the similarities between NT and VMS were so strong, the version number was selected to coincide with the current version of VMS.

Fortunately for me, it isn't up to me to decide. Fortunately for you, it isn't something that's covered on the exam. I simply thought it interesting enough to mention.

In July of 1993, Microsoft released the first version of NT designed for public consumption, Windows NT 3.1. There were two separate releases of this OS. NT 3.1 was an OS designed for high-end desktops, and NT 3.1 Advanced Server was Microsoft's first foray into a true network operating system (NOS).

NT 3.1 could never be mistaken for a bastion of stability in any respect. It had a number of issues that prevented it from really taking off as an enterprise-level product. Still, for Microsoft, this OS broke new ground in several respects.

- It was a true 32-bit OS.

- It was the first OS to implement pre-emptive multitasking.

- The NTFS file system provided much greater local security.

- Domain Server security provided network level security that had previously not existed on any Microsoft product.

- File and Print services provided network-wide access to files and printers distributed across the network.

- It supported multiprocessor systems.

- Virtual memory support was an embedded function of the OS.

- It was the first Microsoft OS to have versions designed to run on non-Intel microprocessors.

On a more familiar note, one of the biggest claims to fame for NT was that it became the foundation over which future Microsoft products would be developed. It was the first to abandon 16-bit code as part of the architecture, although it did continue to provide support for running 16-bit applications. More notably, it was the first OS to separate the hardware interface from the applications interface. Applications could no longer make direct calls to the hardware.

EXAM NOTE: It is a key point that NT was Microsoft's first true 32-bit OS. WIN9x was touted as being a 32-bit architecture, but in reality it was a hybrid OS, running both 16-bit and 32-bit code.

Microsoft continued to work out the kinks in the NT code, and a year later, in September of 1994, NT 3.5 was released. This version proved to be much more stable. More notably 3.5 also introduced internetworking capabilities that allow Microsoft networks to mingle with Novell and UNIX networks. NT 3.5 was followed up in July of 1995 with NT 3.51.

More than just a bug fix, NT 3.51 introduced some new capabilities to NT. Features were added to make the OS more accessible to people with hearing or sight impairments. Support for the BackOffice product line made it easier to manage network applications and licensing. A desktop version of the OS, NT 3.51 Workstation, was designed to accommodate applications written for the newly released WIN95. It also provided hardware support for the new Personal Computer Memory Card International Association (PCMCIA) devices.

Still, even with all these improvements, the IT industry wasn't exactly moving toward NT in droves. If anything, there was exactly the opposite direction of movement. In 1996, Microsoft successfully reversed that trend with the release of NT 4.0. With many of the features that made WIN95 so popular, along with a massive improvement in stability, NT 4.0 became the mainstay for servers and high-end workstations for the next four years and contributed greatly to Microsoft's ascending dominance in the OS industry. The remainder of this chapter will deal exclusively with NT 4.0, as all other versions are considered obsolete.

NT'S TENUOUS RELATIONSHIP WITH VMS

VMS is an OS that isn't covered in the A+ exam, but nonetheless, it deserves an acknowledgment here. It is frequently credited as being the most stable OS ever written. (At one point in time, there was a computer system running VMS that had run non-stop for twelve years without a reboot.) Because of its stability, the OS still sees a lot of use in computing environments where the system can never go down.

Since Cutler was so heavily involved in the VMS project at DEC (and since he brought a big chunk of his programming team with him from DEC to Microsoft), it should come as no surprise that similarities between the two OSs abound. There are many characteristics of the two OSs that are virtually identical in both form and function:

- A process scheduler that imposes thirty-two priority levels
- A process called boosting that prevents a process from hogging the CPU
- Symmetric multiprocessing support
- Memory mapping imposed on files
- Demand-paged virtual memory for physical memory management
- Device drivers built in a layered model
- I/O commands issued asynchronously in a packet-based structure
- All resources, including files, devices, and users represented as objects managed by an Object Manager
- A tighter security subsystem that links to the Object Manager to control user access based on access control lists (ACL)
- Hardware diagnostics—in VMS the utility is called Monitor, in NT it's called Performance Monitor.
- A hard disk backup utility

VMS, on the other hand, isn't exactly what one would call user-friendly. Cutler and his team approached this issue, as well as the native file system of VMS, which would have been completely unfamiliar to users already immersed in the Microsoft world. To ensure that NT would be a friendlier environment to existing Windows users, Microsoft embedded the WIN32 API and the NTFS file system. The result was a more stable OS with a familiar look and feel.

SYMMETRIC MULTIPROCESSING

NT 4.0 incorporated most of the features of previous versions of NT, but in many cases it took these features to a higher lever. Earlier in the chapter I provided a bulleted list of the ways that NT is similar to VMS. One feature that deserves a closer look is that of *symmetric multiprocessing* (SMP).

This .44 caliber term basically means that the OS is capable of utilizing the services of more than one microprocessor. When a system can do this, it runs faster and responds to user requests

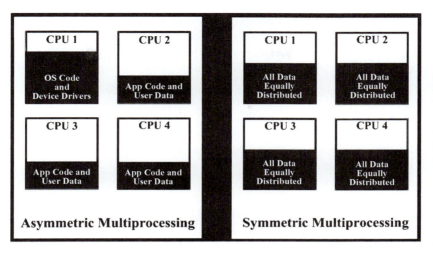

Figure 25.1   With ASMP, the OS code and device drives all run on one CPU while application code and user data is evenly distributed among the remaining processors. With SMP, all data is distributed equally.

more quickly. However, different OSs over the years have made use of two different forms of multiprocessing. Those two forms are asymmetric and symmetric multiprocessing (**Figure 25.1**).

Asymmetric multiprocessing (ASMP) operating systems typically utilize the primary microprocessor (Processor 1) for the execution of operating system code. The other processors in the system run application code or process user data. Typically, an ASMP-configured machine has more than one processor, but the processors do not necessarily have access to the same memory addresses, or even the same amount of memory for that matter.

> **EXAM NOTE:** Be prepared to be able to identify the differences between symmetric and asymmetric multiprocessing.

BUZZ WORDS ————————

Asymmetric multiprocessing: A method by which an operating system makes use of more than one processor, loading OS code onto one processor and application code and user data onto all others.

Symmetric multiprocessing: A method by which an operating system makes use of more than one processor, distributing all code equally across all available processors.

The vast majority of operating systems that support multiprocessing make use of SMP. This includes all versions of Windows NT. SMP allows the operating system code, application code, or user data to run on any free processor. Most hardware configurations share all available memory between all available processors.

In Chapter Two, I discussed the difference between threads of code and processes. NT 4.0 makes use of multiple threads within a single process wherever possible. As a result, different threads from the same process can be running on different CPUs at the same time.

SMP is a much more efficient utilization of multiple processors because operating system code has a tendency to hog the processor. Allowing the operating system to run on only one processor frequently results in that one processor becoming overloaded, while the others are sitting back twiddling their virtual thumbs.

All versions of NT 4.0 can take advantage of multiprocessor systems. However, the different versions have different limitations in the number of processors they can address. This will be discussed in the next section.

NT 4.0 VERSIONS: HARDWARE REQUIREMENTS AND OS FEATURES

Microsoft shipped several different versions of NT 4.0 over the life of the product line. Each version offered different capabilities, and each one exhibited its own unique system requirements for successful installation and operation. These are the different versions I'll discuss in this chapter:

- NT 4.0 Workstation
- NT 4.0 Server
- NT 4.0 Server, Enterprise Edition
- NT 4.0 Terminal Server

It should be noted that there were also a number of different service packs that were issued over the life of the product. Installation of a service pack impacted the minimum hardware requirements in some cases. Later in the chapter, as I discuss service packs, I'll point out some exceptions.

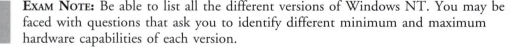

EXAM NOTE: Be able to list all the different versions of Windows NT. You may be faced with questions that ask you to identify different minimum and maximum hardware capabilities of each version.

NT 4.0 WORKSTATION

NT 4.0 Workstation (NTWS) was the OS of choice for many high-end workstations during its era. Although it could only address two processors, it was still one of the few over-the-counter OSs that supported SMP.

Another interesting addition to NTWS was Remote Access Service (RAS). The user could configure a NTWS machine to accept an incoming connection from a remote computer. While NTWS was limited to only one RAS connection at a time, this was still an improvement over previous OSs. And as with all other versions of NT 4.0, NTWS could be installed on computers

Table 25.1 Minimum and Maximum Hardware Requirements, NTWS

Device	Minimum	Maximum
Processor	Single 486-DX33	Two >486-DX33
Hard Disk (CISC/RISC)	110MB/148MB	16EB
Memory (CISC/RISC)	12MB/16MB	4GB
Graphics	VGA	VGA
Pointer	Mouse or trackball	Mouse or trackball

Minimum and maximum hardware requirements for NTWS 4.0. Note that the minimum requirements differ between a CISC installation and a RISC installation.

powered by Intel (and compatible), DEC Alpha, Motorola Power PC, or Silicon Graphics (and compatible) MIPS processors. **Table 25.1** lists the system requirements for NTWS.

NT SERVER 4.0

NT Server was designed to be a full-blown NOS, providing a scalable architecture that would allow networks to enjoy virtually unlimited growth. With NT 4.0 Server, Microsoft bet the bank on a domain model of networking. Under this model, all users, servers, workstations, and other devices that were under the administrative control of a single collection of security data became the domain. This information was stored on one computer called the primary domain controller (PDC). The PDC provided security control and logon authentication services for every user and device on the domain. Other computers, called backup domain controllers (BDC), can maintain copies of this database, but only the PDC maintains an original. This information is stored in the Security Account Manager (SAM). However, SAM is part of the registry, and there is a built-in limitation to the maximum size to which the registry can grow.

SAM AND THE REGISTRY

By default, NT sets the maximum registry size to 25 percent of the paged pool. The paged pool consists of all data currently stored in RAM that can be written to the hard disk in order to free up physical RAM. The maximum size of the paged pool in NT 4.0 is 128MB; therefore, the default maximum size of the registry is 32MB.

If the administrator requires a larger registry, it is simply a matter of changing one of the entries in the registry. This can be done by editing the registry, but it's safer and easier to use Control Panel. In the System Applet, under Performance, registry size can be configured either in megabytes or as a maximum percentage (up to 80 percent of the paged pool). The minimum size that be configured is 4MB. Since the paged pool is limited to 128MB, then the maximum size is 102.4MB.

Table 25.2 Minimum and Maximum Hardware Requirements, NT Server

Device	Minimum	Maximum/ NT Server	Maximum/ Enterprise	Maximum Terminal Server
Processor	Single 486-DX33	Two >No max. speed	Eight >No max. speed	Four >No max. speed
Hard Disk (CISC/RISC)	125MB/160MB	16EB	16EB	16EB
Memory (CISC/RISC)	16MB/16MB	4GB	8GB	4GB
Graphics	VGA	VGA	VGA	VGA
Pointer	Mouse or trackball	Mouse or trackball	Mouse or trackball	Mouse or trackball

Minimum and maximum hardware requirements for NT 4.0 Server versions.

Hardware requirements for the server versions vary in maximum capabilities. However, minimum requirements are consistent. **Table 25.2** lists minimum and maximum requirements for the different server versions.

NT SECURITY

Increased security was a key issue for Microsoft during the developmental phase of NT 4.0. This security tightening began at the logon screen and worked its way down into the basic architecture of the OS.

LOGON SECURITY

Previous versions of the software had users logging on from a prompt that was little more than an elegantly designed DOS screen. As a result users and network administrators could easily find themselves victims of a malicious piece of software called a Trojan Horse. A *Trojan horse* is a piece of software that mimics the look and function of another piece of software familiar to users, but in reality it is performing a completely different function all together.

One of these Trojan horses particularly embarrassing to Microsoft was a program that was designed to look, feel, taste, and smell just like the logon screen for Windows NT. When users typed in their user IDs and passwords, nothing appeared to happen. All too frequently, this resulted in a

> **BUZZ WORDS**
>
> **Trojan horse:** A malicious program designed to mimic another commonly recognized program, but that is, in fact, performing some other action in the background without the knowledge or consent of the user.

frustrated user calling the network administrator down to fix the problem. And what was the first thing this person would do? Type in his or her user ID and password, of course! But the program wasn't doing nothing. It was doing something. It collected all those user IDs and passwords into a file that the attacker could come and collect at leisure.

> **EXAM NOTE:** My discussion of OS security and the logon process is probably a bit more detailed than really required for the CompTIA exam. However, it's basic OS information with which any IT professional should be comfortable. One key point that is brought up on the exam a lot is the logon security added to protect against Trojan horses. File system security is also covered.

With the release of NT 4.0, logging onto the system is mandatory. To do so, the user must press <Ctrl>+<Alt>+<Delete> to begin. On older DOS-based computers and those with DOS programs, this key sequence resets the computer. With NT it brings up the logon screen. This is the door that locks out the Trojan horses, because as DOS-based programs, the key sequence will give them away.

PERMISSIONS AND PRIVILEGES

The basis for internal security on an NT network is grounded in the concept of permissions and privileges. This is one of those situations where two words mean the same thing, only different. *Permissions* apply to various resources on the network and whether or not a specific user has access to a specific resource, and if so, just how much control that user can have over the resource. *Privileges* dictate what actions or functions a user can perform on his or her own system or on the network in general.

PERMISSIONS

Permissions have been around the OS world for a long time and tend to vary slightly from one OS to the next. The Microsoft world is divided into two different forms of permissions. There are share level and user level security.

Share Level Security *Share level permissions* are attributes that are assigned directly to a specific resource on the network. For any given resource, there will be a specific password that will allow access. Access comes in one of four different forms.

Read permission allows you to access and view the object, but not to modify it in any way. You cannot edit, delete, or rename the object. If changes are made to a file with Read permission, that file cannot be saved under the same name.

BUZZ WORDS

Permissions: The degrees of access a particular user has been granted to a specific resource on the network.

Privileges: The rights a particular user has been granted to perform specific functions or tasks on a system or the network in general.

Share level security: A method of protecting resources on the network that involves applying the security attributes, such as password protection, to the object itself. As such, each secured object on the system may have a unique password.

Full Control permission allows you to do what you will with the file. You can edit, delete, or rename the file. You can even change the permissions on it, should you so desire.

No Access permission should be fairly self-explanatory. A file with No Access assigned to it cannot be opened at all.

Depends on Password gives you specific permissions based on what password you supply. There will be one password for Full Control and another for Read.

A problem inherent with share level security is that for every resource, there is a password. If 200 users have all created 10 files, each with a different password, then if you want to be able to access all 2,000 files, you need to know 2,000 passwords. That's handy, isn't it?

Buzz Words

User level security: A method of securing resources on a system or network that involves assigning the security attributes to an account provided to the user. After the user has logged on, access to resources is provided based on the permissions assigned to the account.

Credentials: Information provided by the user, including but not restricted to the user ID and password, that grants that user access to a system or network.

User Level Security   That's why network OSs all employ *user level security*. With user level security, the user is assigned a user ID and password. These are the user's *credentials*. When the user logs on, he or she types in the credentials, and from that point forward, the permissions granted to that user control access to any given resource on the network. As a result, user level security makes heavy use of file system security.

With file system security, file and folder level permissions are used. But unlike share level security, access is controlled by a centralized security database. This is the SAM I discussed earlier. File system security is much more granular than share level. Any given permission on a resource can be specifically denied to a given user or group. There are also a number of other different permissions that can be assigned:

- *Read*: Similar to the Read permission in share level security.

- *Write*: The user can edit the file but cannot delete it or rename it.

- *List Contents*: A user with this permission can view a directory listing of a given folder but cannot access the individual files.

- *Read and Execute*: Applications can be secured as well as data files. If the administrator denies this permission to a user or group, then that application cannot be run.

- *Modify*: A Modify permission allows the user to open, edit, rename, or even delete the file. This is not, however, the same as full permission.

- *Full Control*: Full Control grants the user all the abilities granted by Modify permission. In addition, the user with Full Control can change permissions on a resource and take ownership of a resource. In essence, Full Control is putting the security of that file into the users' hands. By default, the original creator of a file has Full Control, as does anyone with administrative privileges on the network. More on privileges later.

The more astute reader may notice that there is no mention of a No Access permission in the preceding list. No Access would be the permissions level one might expect to see that blocks a user from even knowing a file or directory even exists. The administrator can accomplish No Access simply by denying Full Control.

PRIVILEGES

There is, however, more to network security than simply accessing data. There is a lot of administration that needs to be done and a lot of administrative functions that the administrator doesn't want just anybody doing. For example you don't want just anyone to have the right to go in and change other peoples' passwords. You don't want just anyone to have the right to shut down the server.

Privileges are administrative rights allowed by the system. These can either be assigned directly to a user on an individual basis, or they can be assigned by adding a user to one of NT's built-in groups. Most administrators prefer the latter approach. Built-in groups in NT vary slightly between NT Workstation and the versions of NT Server. **Table 25.3** lists the built-in groups for all versions along with the privileges that go with those groups.

SAM AND THE LOCAL SECURITY AUTHORITY

Earlier in the chapter, I discussed how account information was stored in the SAM. Here, I will talk about how SAM is used to keep the network secure, with a little help from another piece of NT architecture called the Local Security Authority (LSA).

I'll start with how a user's account is actually managed by SAM. When the network administrator first creates an account for a new user, that user is assigned a user ID and (usually) a password. Most users think that it is this user ID and password that is their key to the network. As far as they're concerned, it is. But SAM could care less about that. It's looking at a number called the Security Identifier (SID) that is generated by the system when the account is created. As long as that account remains on the system, that SID follows the user wherever he/she goes.

When the user first logs onto the system (after having pressed <Ctrl>+<Alt>+<Delete>, of course), a process called WinLogon passes the user ID and password that are entered to LSA. LSA compares the information provided by the user to that which is stored in SAM. If the data is correct, the user is allowed onto the system. If not, that user is rejected. Across a network, LSA will transmit this information to either a PDC or a BDC.

When a user is successfully logged on, LSA will generate a security access token that validates the user's session on the network. That token is the key to network resources. If the user logs off and then back on, a new token will be generated. The token includes the following:

■ The user's SID
■ The SID for any user groups to which the user has been assigned
■ The list of permissions and privileges assigned to that user

Table 25.3 NT Built-in Groups

Local Group Name	Default Members	Who Can Modify?	Inherent Privileges	Available on Domain Controller (DC) or Workstation (WS)
Account Operators	None	Administrators, Account Operators, Server Operators	Create, delete, modify user accounts and groups. Cannot modify the Administrators or Server Operator groups	DC
Administrators	Domain Administrators, Administrators	Administrators	Create, delete, or manage user accounts and groups. Manage resource shares. Grant resource permissions. Install programs, OS patches, and device drivers.	WS, DC
Backup Operators	None	Administrators	Backup and restore servers and workstations. Logon locally. Shut down the server.	WS, DC
Guests	Guest	Administrators, Account Operators	None defined.	WS, DC
Power Users	None	Administrators, Account Operators	Install programs, OS patches, and device drivers. Manage local printers.	WS
Print Operators	None	Administrators	Share and remove sharing printers. Manage printers. Logon locally. Shut down servers.	DC
Replicator	None	Administrators, Account Operators, Server Operators	Used with the Directory Replication Service.	WS, DC
Server Operators	None	Administrators	Share and remove sharing resources. Format the server disks. Logon locally. Backup and restore servers. Shut down servers. Lock and unlock servers. Install programs, OS patches, and device drivers.	DC
Users	Domain Users	Administrators, Account Operators	None defined.	WS, DC

The built-in groups in NT are a convenient way of managing user privileges.

Now that the token has been generated, WinLogon opens a new session of EXPLORER.EXE. The access token assigned to the user is attached to this process, and from that point forward, everything the user attempts to do must be validated by the token.

THE SECURITY DESCRIPTOR

Users aren't the only targets of system security. NT security treats every single resource on the system,

> ### BUZZ WORDS
>
> **Security descriptor:** A token attached to a resource that defines security attributes assigned to that resource.
>
> **Object:** In reference to an OS, an object is any resource, user account, or group account present on the system or network.

including the users, as *objects*. All of these objects are defined by a specific security descriptor. The *security descriptor* is a token that defines the security attributes of a specific object. In many cases, by default, this security is minimal unless the administrator chooses to increase it. The security descriptor comprises four components.

The first two are the individual SID and the group SID discussed in the previous section. Another component called the discretionary Access Control List (ACL) identifies what users and groups are allowed to access a particular object. The system maintains its own ACL, conveniently named the System ACL, that oversees all security descriptors. The System ACL is used by the system for internal security audits when defined by the administrator and is what allows an administrator to set and enforce security policies over the entire network.

Now let's go back to those discretionary ACLs for a moment. As I mentioned, it is the discretionary ACL that defines what users and groups are allowed to access a specific object. I called it a list, but what is it a list of? The ACL consists of a series of Access Control Entities (ACE). Each of these entities either grants or denies access to the object for a specific user or group. It does this on the basis of the permissions granted to that user.

ACCESS VALIDATION

The process of access validation is what makes all of the preceding work the way it does. When the user attempts to access an object for the first time, an NT function called the Security Reference Monitor (SRM) examines the user's access token and compares it to the object's ACL. Each ACE in the ACL is read in the order it is listed. No Access entries are all listed first. This reduces system overhead for processing requests that won't be honored anyway. Once any ACEs in the ACL specific to the user's token indicate that the user should be allowed access, SRM opens the object to the user. Is it just me, or are there too many acronyms in this industry?

NT DOMAIN MODELS

As a result of these registry limitations, there is an inherent limitation to the number of user accounts that can be stored on a single machine. If the network begins to get too large for a single PDC to manage, the administrator has several options available. These options appear as the different domain models available to NT. Microsoft defines four different domain models:

- The Single Domain
- The Single Master Domain
- The Multiple Master Domain
- The Complete Trust

But before I get into a heavy discussion of NT's domain models, perhaps it would be a good

Buzz Words ———————

Workgroup: A collection of devices on the network that share common resources and responsibilities.

Domain: A collection of all resources and users that fall under the control of a single administrative unit. In the case of Windows NT, the administrative unit would be the PDC.

idea to define the concept of a domain. Earlier Microsoft OSs, starting with Windows for Workgroups 3.11, included rudimentary built-in networking support. These OSs depended upon the concept of the workgroup for network management and communication. Simply put, a *workgroup* is a collection of devices on the network that share common resources and (usually) common responsibilities. This concept was fine for small networks but was virtually unusable for enterprise level networking.

The *domain* allows for much greater expansion and tighter control of the network. The domain consists of all users and resources that are under the oversight of a single administrative unit. Since large numbers of smaller networks can be combined into a single large network and still be under the control of a single PDC, domains can become quite large.

THE SINGLE DOMAIN

Under the Single domain (**Figure 25.2**), there is only one PDC that controls the entire network. All changes to the network infrastructure must be recorded on the PDC. This is where the master copy of SAM is stored. Additional BDCs may be used for balancing the load of logon requests for networks with large numbers of users. However, BDCs only maintain copies of SAM. These copies are updated from the PDC periodically in a process called synchronization, where the PDC checks with all BDCs on the network. If SAM has changed since the last synchronization, a new copy will be sent.

THE SINGLE MASTER DOMAIN

With the Single Master domain, there is still only a single PDC that houses the SAM that manages user accounts. However, there are one or more additional domains called Resource domains that maintain the security for some aspect of the network other than users. An example of a Resource domain would be as follows (and as illustrated in **Figure 25.3**). An organization might have a very large managed database with extremely critical security requirements. Access requirements for this database vary greatly from user to user. The network administrator has a

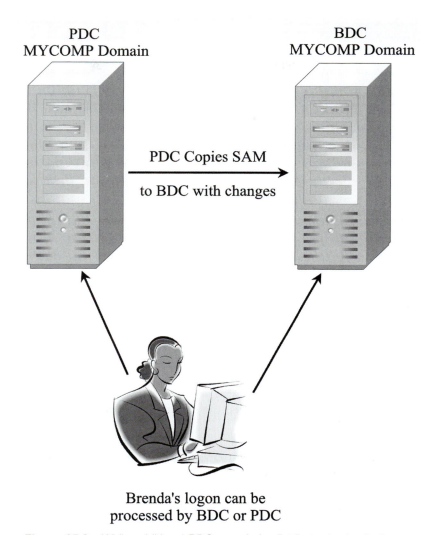

PDC
MYCOMP Domain

BDC
MYCOMP Domain

PDC Copies SAM

to BDC with changes

Brenda's logon can be
processed by BDC or PDC

Figure 25.2   While additional BDCs can help distribute the load of
logon authentication across a large network, there is only one PDC that
manages the master SAM.

reputation for being the best there is at overall network design, management, and maintenance. Unfortunately, what he knows about database management can be engraved on the sharp edge of a razor blade—with room left over for the Gettysburg Address.

Fortunately, the company also has an expert database administrator. She's the best there is at what she does, but neither knows, nor cares, what goes on in the overall workings of the network. The Single Master domain model provides the perfect solution. Two domains are

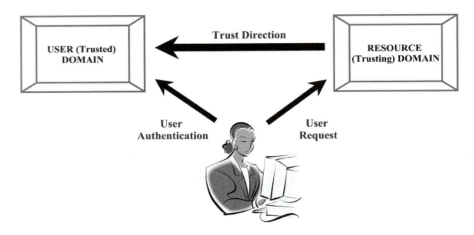

User logs onto User Domain. When she requires access to the resources on the Resource Domain, the Resource Domain will perform a non-interactive authentication with the User Domain. Once approved, the user has access to whatever resources the administrator of the Resource Domain has permitted.

Figure 25.3 With a single master domain, there is still only one PDC handling logon authentication, but this PDC represents an independent domain. Network resources are secured on separate domains.

created. The network manager assumes control of the user domain while the database administrator takes over the resource domain. Then the two administrators establish a trust between their separate domains.

A trust is a link between two domains over which user authentication is performed on one domain, but the permissions and privileges associated with that user's accounts are honored on another domain. In a trust relationship, there is a trusting domain and a trusted domain. The trusting domain is the domain that allows user authentication to occur over there on somebody else's domain. It trusts the authentication to be accurate. The trusted domain is the domain that maintains the SAM for the user account that is being verified.

Trusts are only one-way. There is no such thing as a two-way trust in the Windows domain structure. For a two-way trust to exist, a separate trust must be established in each direction on an NT network. For that to occur, the administrators of each domain must be actively involved, or one or the other of the administrators must know the user name and ID of the other.

Another thing about trusts in an NT 4.0 network is that trusts are nontransitive. This means that if I set up a trust between Domain A and Domain B, and then another trust between Domain B and Domain C, a trust between Domain A and Domain C will not be created by default. If I want that trust to exist, I will have to create it separately.

Under the Single Master domain model, there can be as many Resource domains as the organization requires, but as I've already pointed out, there will be only one Master domain that is managing authentication. Setting up multiple Resource domains allows for a tighter reign on security.

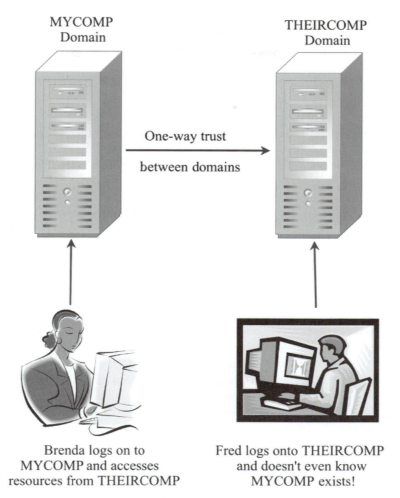

Figure 25.4   Larger organizations may benefit from the load balancing and added security of a Multiple Master domain.

THE MULTIPLE MASTER DOMAIN

Some organizations reach the point where a Single Master domain isn't sufficient. This can occur when the number of user accounts and groups exceeds that which a single PDC can manage. And it can also happen when security issues dictate that different groups of users be separated from other users on the network. This is where the Multiple Master domain (**Figure 25.4**) comes into play.

With the Multiple Master domain, two or more PDCs are configured, each managing a different domain. Each of these domains is handling user authentication. However, unless trusts are established between the different domains, they can't see one another on the network.

For example, a company might have an office set up in Baton Rouge and another set up in Atlanta. The network in each office is managed by its own domain. The Baton Rouge office is BRCOMP and the Atlanta office is ATLCOMP. When a user logs on in Atlanta, if there is no trust established between Atlanta and Baton Rouge, then that user isn't even aware that the BRCOMP domain even exists.

This structure gives the administrators a bit of leeway in how they want to handle user access. For instance, if there is a pressing demand for the BRCOMP users to be able to access resources in the ATLCOMP domain, but not the reverse, then the administrators of the two domains might want to establish a single trust in which ATLCOMP domain trusts the BRCOMP domain, but not vice versa. ATLCOMP shares out the resources required by BRCOMP and then assigns permissions as it sees fit.

As with the Single Master domain, Resource domains can also be established to manage specific resources on the network. These are handled in exactly the same manner as I discussed in the section on the Single Master domain. As a result, a very complex network might have five Master domains and a dozen different resource domains, or even substantially more. Networks are practically limitless in terms of scalability.

THE COMPLETE TRUST

The most complex of the NT domain models is the Complete Trust (**Figure 25.5**). In this scenario, a number of different Master and Resource domains are created, and every domain on the network trusts every other domain on the network in both directions. This model requires a literal maze of trust relationships and a massive amount of administration in terms of individual user and/or group access requirements between the domains.

Generally, this approach is not the most favorable, and where it exists, it usually exists by accident. An example would be a network that just seemed to keep growing. As each new domain was added, the administrators simply decided it was easier to simply establish trusts in each direction between their own domain and the new one. This prevents the administrators from having to make too many complex decisions, but it does lead to an overly complex and cumbersome network that is full of security holes.

INSTALLING NT 4.0

As with previous Microsoft OS versions, there are two ways to install NT as the only OS on the system. The best and safest method is the clean install. However, as with other Windows versions, there is also the option for an upgrade. All of the possible problems that exist with upgrades are also apparent in an NT upgrade.

A third option with NT is to create a dual-boot system. This option allows the user to boot the system either to NT or to another OS installed onto another partition on the hard disk. I will discuss dual-boot systems toward the end of this chapter.

Regardless of the installation method you chose, there will be four separate phases to the NT installation process:

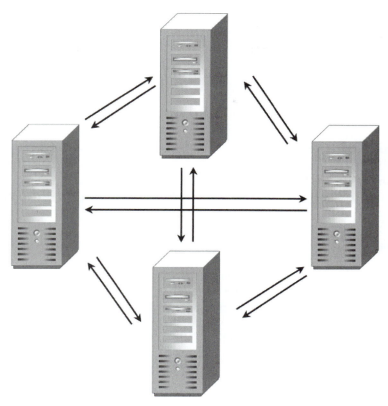

Figure 25.5   The complete trust is not considered to be an ideal structure for a network.

CREATING THE BOOT DISKETTES FOR NT 4.0

Many older machines won't boot to the CD, so it is essential for those users to have access to the installation disks. Even if you can successfully boot to a CD, it is a very good idea to keep a set of these diskettes on hand at all times. In recovery mode, the CD drive is quite often not readable.

To create the three boot diskettes for NT, have three blank formatted 1.44MB floppy diskettes available and label them "NT Installation Disk One," "NT Installation Disk Two," and "NT Installation Disk Three." Insert the CD into the drive of any working DOS or Windows machine. Open a command prompt and browse to the i386 directory on the CD-ROM. From the command prompt, type **WINNT /OX**. (The command is not case-sensitive). Read the prompts carefully. You'll note that the process creates disk three first, then disk two, and finally the boot diskette.

- The initial phase
- The text phase
- The GUI phase
- Finalizing the installation

THE INITIAL PHASE

The initial phase begins in one of two ways. If this is a clean installation onto a new hard drive then the installation file that will be used is WINNT.EXE. For the installation to succeed, the hard disk must already be prepared with a DOS partition to hold temporary files. This is a 16-bit file, and it only recognizes FAT16 for this installation partition. Therefore, if the FDISK utility from a WIN9x boot diskette was used to prepare the hard disk, and Large Disk Support was selected, then WINNT.EXE will not be able to recognize the disk.

If the computer can boot to a CD-ROM drive, then the installation procedure is as simple as inserting the NT 4.0 CD into the drive and booting the computer. If for any reason the system cannot boot to a CD, then the user will have to use the installation diskettes. This is a set of three diskettes that shipped with the product. If the diskettes have been lost or damaged, do not despair. They can be recreated on any DOS or Windows-based machine. See the sidebar for instructions.

After the system has booted, WINNT.EXE will create a temporary directory called win_nt.~ls. This is where all the files required for installation will stored for the remainder of the process. Once installation has been completed, WINNT.EXE deletes that directory and all the files it holds. Once in a while, if for any reason an installation is aborted and subsequently resumed at a later time, this temporary directory remains on the hard drive. When installation is complete, if that directory is still there, it is safe to remove it.

THE TEXT PHASE

After all the files are copied, you are prompted to remove any floppy diskettes from the drive and the system reboots. Now the installation enters the text phase. A program called NTDETECT.EXE scans the system for any installed hardware and generates a list of drivers that will be installed. (Note that NT 4.0 is not a PnP OS.) You will be prompted to press F5 if there are any hardware devices that are not internally supported by NT, such as SCSI adapters, which require installation of third-party drivers. This notifies WINNT.EXE that during the driver installation, it should prompt you to insert the floppy diskette with those drivers. Note that WINNT.EXE will not read drivers from a CD-ROM during installation.

If the system onto which you are installing NT is a multiprocessor machine, it is likely that you will be prompted to enter a disk supplied by the motherboard or system manufacturer. SMP machines require an updated version of a file called HAL.DLL. If this is not installed during the initial installation, it can be added later. But until that time, the system will be making use of only one CPU.

In a server installation, this is also the phase in which you are asked to enter the type of licensing you wish to use. The two options are Per Server and Per Seat. With Per Server licensing, the administrator fills in the number of Client Access Licenses (CAL) that have been purchased. Only that number of users can access the server at one time. This is useful for organizations that use shift workers. For example if there are three shifts of 100 users, but each user has a dedicated computer assigned, there might be 300 computers, but only 100 users will ever be logged on at any one time. Per seat requires a CAL for each workstation on the system.

Finally, during this phase you are asked to select the partition on which you want NT installed. WINNT.EXE also asks whether you prefer to use FAT or NTFS. Note that this is FAT16, and if this file system is selected, the subsequent limitations of that system are selected as well. NT does not support FAT32. After the partition and file system have been selected, a quick scan of the disk is performed and the system reboots once again. If the NTFS file system was selected, during this reboot a utility called CONVERT.EXE converts the hard disk partition's file system from FAT to NTFS. This might take a few minutes.

THE GUI PHASE

When the reboot is completed, the NT installation enters the GUI phase. Now you have access to all those pretty little boxes with the Next and Back buttons. The mouse has suddenly come alive, and everything is now point and click. During this phase you will be prompted to enter a computer name and password for the administrator account. Other wizards automatically open that run through the installation of any modems and set up networking.

At one point you are asked whether the computer should obtain its address automatically from a DHCP server. DHCP stands for the Dynamic Host Configuration Protocol, which is a protocol that automatically hands out IP addresses (and other information) for networks using the TCP/IP protocol. If this is an NT 4.0 Workstation installation and you know for sure that there is a DHCP server on the network, you might want to select this option. If this is a server installation, a static IP address should always be assigned. For more information on configuring TCP/IP, refer to *The Compete Guide to Networking and Network+*, by this same author.

Toward the end of the GUI phase, you will be asked whether you wish to create an Emergency Repair Diskette (ERD). The ERD is useful for repairing an NT installation gone bad and will be required if you wish to perform one of those dual-boot installations to which I alluded earlier in the chapter. The cautious type selects Yes for this option and inserts a blank, formatted 1.44MB floppy diskette into the drive.

I don't. I wait until the installation is completed and all third-party device drivers are successfully installed, and then I create the ERD manually. I'll have instructions on how to do this later in the chapter. But take note that the ERD should be updated any time system configuration changes or after the addition of new accounts. The ERD is definitely not a one-size-fits-all type of disk.

After the GUI phase is completed, the system reboots yet again. This time it boots to a working NT machine. However, for the vast majority of users, this isn't the end of the installation process.

Finalizing the Installation

This is a phase that doesn't seem to appear an a lot of the books I've seen. However, before the system can be used, there is generally a bit more work to do. Any third-party device drivers that weren't detected by NTDETECT.EXE must be installed before the device will work properly.

Typically the graphics card will have to be installed separately. Until this happens the system will only be capable of 640×480 resolution at sixteen colors. This is because NT does not maintain a substantial collection of drivers for video adapters and simply installs standard VGA.

Many network cards need to be installed separately. You'll know if yours is one of those, because during the GUI phase you weren't asked to set up networking. Therefore, if your NIC didn't install, you'll have to do it manually. There will be a discussion of installing device drivers in NT in Chapter Twenty-Six, Windows NT Architecture. When this process has been completed and you have a fully configured NT system, it is now time to create (or update) the ERD.

Creating or Updating the ERD

I cannot emphasize the importance of having an updated ERD for Windows NT. Just installing an NT system is work enough. All of the configuration and creation of user accounts adds to that burden. The less work you have to redo should you have to rebuild the system, the happier you'll be.

The ERD contains all the configuration data for the system, along with a list of user and group accounts that have been added. Proper use of this disk allows the administrator, in many cases, to repair a corrupted system without losing everything.

ERDs are managed through a utility called RDISK. There is no icon for this utility, and it doesn't have an entry in the Start menu (although if you desire, you can create either one). To run RDISK for the first time, you must open a command prompt (or click Start → Run) and type **RDISK** in the command prompt.

A little window will open with two buttons. One says Update Repair Info and the other says Create Repair Disk. If you select the first option, you will need to have your existing ERD in hand. It won't create a new one from scratch. That is the purpose of the second option.

The Dual-boot System

Once in a while, it becomes necessary to have access to more than one OS at any given time, but there is only one computer on which an OS can be installed. For example, you may be perfectly comfortable with your existing OS, but it becomes necessary for some reason to introduce a new one. A dual-boot system gives you access to the OS you're comfortable with until such time as you have mastered the new one.

If you wish to create a dual-boot system running NT 4.0 as one of the OSs, then there is a specific order in which you must do things. And there are a couple of things to be considered. You have to prep your hard drive, and the order in which you install the OSs is important.

If you are planning to dual-boot your system, you might want to consider this when preparing your hard drive. Although it isn't absolutely necessary to have NT on a different partition if both it and your other OS are using FAT16, I would still strongly advise it. Putting each OS on a separate partition is absolutely necessary if NT is going to be on an NTFS partition. In fact, I would strongly recommend a dedicated disk drive.

With NT you need to complete the NT installation first and make sure that it's properly configured. All device drivers should be installed, and configurations adjustments such as display settings should be to your satisfaction. Now either update the ERD or create a new one.

Reboot the machine to the installation disk of the second OS and perform that installation. When that is completed, you'll be aghast to realize that all your hard work installing NT was to no avail. The new OS wiped it out!

Don't panic. Simply start the NT installation either from the CD or by booting to the boot floppies. However, this time, instead of selecting a fresh installation, tell WINNT.EXE (or WINNT32.EXE if you're running from another Windows application) that you want to repair an existing installation. That will be the second option on the checklist. Have your ERD ready and follow the prompts as they appear. When your machine reboots after completion, during the boot process you will be presented with a menu giving you thirty seconds to pick which OS to load. If you don't make a selection, NT 4.0 will load by default.

When making a dual-boot system, decide in advance whether or not you're going to need to be able to access files created by one OS when running the other. Not all file systems work well together, as I've already pointed out. If you're setting up a dual boot between NT 4.0 and WIN9x, it can be particularly problematic. Choosing NTFS as the file system for NT will prevent the WIN9x installation from even seeing that the NT partition is present on the system. Likewise, selecting FAT32 for WIN9x will prevent NT from seeing the WIN9x partition. The only mutually accessible file system between the two OSs is FAT16.

PROFILES IN NT

NT is designed to be an OS that supports a multitude of users. This is true whether it's NT Workstation or one of the server versions. In order to ensure that each user has his or her own unique operating environment, NT makes use of separate profiles for each user. A profile is simply an overview of individual user settings and preferences.

As discussed in Chapter Twenty-Three, the registry contains two different root keys to define users. HKEY_CURRENT_USER defines the user that is currently logged on, while HKEY_USERS contains the information for every user that has an account on the system. To create individual user profiles, NT also stores this information in the %SystemRoot%\PROFILES folder in a file called NTUSER.DAT.

Profiles can be treated in one of two different ways. A more permissive administrator will allow each user to create a unique profile that reflects individual work habits and personality. This might include the ability to install personalized screen savers, desktop backgrounds, and programs. Conversely, an administrator might think this practice is too risky and may prefer to enforce a standard profile. This is something that NT allows as well.

CHAPTER SUMMARY

Microsoft's first implementation of a true 32-bit OS launched the company's ascendancy to the position it now holds as the largest manufacturer of operating systems in the world. The server versions of Windows represented its first line of NOS that genuinely addressed the needs of an enterprise.

In this chapter I introduced some of the key features of the different versions of the OS. I spent a great deal of time on the security implementations Microsoft added and defined its different domain models. This is all information that will serve you in good stead in later chapters, as these are features that will be compared and contrasted in discussions of later Microsoft operating systems.

BRAIN DRAIN

1. Discuss the differences between symmetric and asymmetric multiprocessing. Why is one more efficient than the other?

2. How is a BDC different than a PDC? And why might a larger network need several BDCs?

3. Discuss some of the security enhancements Microsoft incorporated into NT.

4. How are privileges and permissions different from one another? Discuss some examples of each.

5. List the different domain models supported by NT and describe the differences.

THE 64K$ QUESTIONS

1. The first version of an NT product was demonstrated in _____.
   a. 1984
   b. 1991
   c. 1993
   d. 1994

2. The first version of NT to be released was NT 3.5. There never was a version 3.0.
   a. True
   b. False

3. The NT feature that provided security on a file or folder level was called _____.
   a. File and Print Services
   b. Domain Server Security
   c. SMP support
   d. NTFS

4. A system that runs OS code on one processor and application code and user data on a second processor is an example of _____ multiprocessing.
   a. Asymmetric
   b. Symmetric
   c. Hierarchical
   d. Demand Priority

5. NT 4.0 Server, Enterprise Edition can support up to _____ processors.
   a. 2
   b. 4

c.   8

d.   16

6.   NT 4.0 Workstation requires a minimum of _____ RAM in order to run on a RISC machine.

a.   8MB

b.   12MB

c.   16MB

d.   32MB

7.   NT 4.0 Server requires a minimum of _____ RAM in order to run on a RISC machine.

a.   8MB

b.   12MB

c.   16MB

d.   32MB

8.   In order to install NT 4.0 Workstation, you need a minimum of _____ free hard disk space.

a.   85MB

b.   110MB

c.   125MB

d.   150MB

9.   In an NT domain, the machine that maintains a copy of the security database that is updated periodically is called a _____.

a.   Primary Domain Controller

b.   Backup Domain Controller

c.   Security Accounts Manager

d.   Domain Controller

10. A piece of software that looks like a friendly game of Pac Woman but that is actually harvesting emails from your system while you play would be called a _____.

a.   Virus

b.   Worm

c.   Back door

d.   Trojan horse

11. In order to get to the logon screen in Windows NT 4.0 (any version) you must first _____.

a.   Type in a unique security authenticator

b.   Provide your user credentials

c.   Press <Ctrl>+<Alt>+<Delete>

d.   Press <Shift>+<F5>

12. As a user, you have been granted the ability to add new users to the network. From an OS standpoint you have been given _____.

a.   A new permission

b.   A promotion

c.   A new privilege

d.   More work to do for the same pay

13. You have created a new file on the system and assigned one password on the file that allows the users who access it full control and another password that only lets them read the file. This is an example of _____.

a.   Workgroup security

b.   File and folder security

c.   Share level security

d.   User level security

14. When the administrator first creates a new account on an NT system, NT assigns a unique _____ to that account.

a.   SID

b.   SAM

c.   SLC

d.   SAC

15. In order to tighten up security on your network, your administrator has divided the network into two separate domains. One of these domains is where all the users log on, and the other hosts the company's database servers. This is an example of _____ .

    a. The Single domain

    b. The Single Master domain

    c. The Multiple Master domain

    d. The Complete Trust

16. NT 4.0 trusts are said to be _____.

    a. Transitional

    b. Transitory

    c. Nontransitional

    d. Nontransitory

17. In order to install NT onto a machine, it is best to start with a freshly prepared hard disk on which no partitions have been defined. This allows NT to prepare the drives using its own utility.

    a. True

    b. False

18. NTDETECT runs during the _____ phase of the installation.

    a. Initial

    b. Text

    c. GUI

    d. Finalizing installation

19. The licensing mode is selected during the _____ phase of the installation.

    a. Initial

    b. Text

    c. GUI

    d. Finalizing installation

20. Before attempting to create a dual-boot system between NT 4.0 and another OS, you must first make sure you have a fresh _____.

    a. ERD

    b. Partition

    c. Formatted diskette

    d. Cup of coffee

TRICKY TERMINOLOGY

Asymmetric multiprocessing: A method by which an operating system makes use of more than one processor, loading OS code onto one processor and application code and user data onto all others.

Credentials: Information provided by the user, including but not restricted to the User ID and password, that grants that user access to a system or network.

Domain: A collection of all resources and users that fall under the control of a single administrative unit. In the case of Windows NT, the administrative unit would be the PDC.

Object: In reference to an OS, an object is any resource, user account, or group account present on the system or network.

Permissions: The degrees of access a particular user has been granted to a specific resource on the network.

Privileges: The rights a particular user has been granted to perform specific functions or tasks on a system or the network in general.

Security descriptor: A token attached to a resource that defines security attributes assigned to that resource.

Share level security: A method of protecting resources on the network that involves applying the security attributes, such as password protection, to the object itself. As such, each secured object on the system may have a unique password.

Symmetric multiprocessing: A method by which an operating system makes use of more than one processor, distributing all code equally across all available processors.

Trojan horse: A malicious program designed to mimic another commonly recognized program that is, in fact, performing some other action in the background without the knowledge or consent of the user.

User level security: A method of securing resources on a system or network that involves assigning the security attributes to an account provided to the user. Once the user has logged on, access to resources is provided based on the permissions assigned to the account.

Workgroup: A collection of devices on the network that share common resources and responsibilities.

ACRONYM ALERT

ACE: Access Control Entity. An individual entry of the ACL defining a specific object and its security attributes.

ACL: Access Control List. A data token attached to the descriptor of a specific object on the network that defines what users and/or groups are allowed to access that object and what degree of access they are allowed.

ASMP: Asymmetric Multiprocessing. The ability of an OS to use more than one processor, where the OS code runs on one processor and all other application code and user data is distributed across the remaining processors.

BDC: Backup Domain Controller. Any server on an NT domain that houses a copy of the security database that is periodically updated by the PDC.

CAL: Client Access License. A license granting one user permission to access a system or network.

DEC: Digital Equipment Corporation

ERD: Emergency Repair Diskette. A floppy diskette that holds system configuration and account information for a machine running NT (or later) operating systems.

LSA: Local Security Authority. An NT service that manages the logon process and all subsequent access to system or network resources.

NTWS: NT Workstation

PCMCIA: Personal Computer Memory Card International Association

PDC: Primary Domain Controller. The server in an NT domain that houses the master security database.

RAS: Remote Access Services. An NT service that allows a direct dial-up connection from a remote computer to access the host system.

SAM: Security Account Manager. An encrypted file stored within the registry of NT that hold the security attributes for all user and group accounts.

SID: Security Identifier. A unique number generated and assigned to an object on the system or network that allows LSA to manage the security for that object.

SMP: Symmetric Multiprocessing. The ability of an OS to run OS or application code equally distributed across all available CPUs.

SRM: Security Reference Monitor. An NT service that compares a user's access token to the ACL and either allows or denies access to a specific resource accordingly.

VMS: Virtual Memory System. An OS written by DEC.

CHAPTER 26

WINDOWS NT ARCHITECTURE

As you might imagine, since the NT operating systems were composed entirely of 32-bit code, some changes to the OS architecture had to be made. It wasn't entirely the 32-bit code that forced certain architectural changes either. Changes to security functions that I discussed in Chapter Twenty-Five, The World of NT, as well as to the way the OS interfaced with the hardware, required changes as well. Even the overall boot process is different between NT and the WIN9x versions. This chapter will discuss some of the internal technology that makes NT what it is. A lot of what is covered in this chapter relates to later chapters in this book pertaining to the Windows 2000 versions and Windows XP as well, so don't be too quick to pass this information over.

A+ OPERATING SYSTEM TECHNOLOGIES EXAM OBJECTIVES

The CompTIA exam objectives covered in this chapter include the following:

1.1 Identify the major desktop components and interfaces and their functions. Differentiate the characteristics of Windows 9x/Me, Windows NT 4.0 Workstation, Windows 2000 Professional, and Windows XP.

1.4 Identify basic concepts and procedures for creating, viewing, and managing disks, directories, and files. This includes procedures for changing file attributes and the ramifications of those changes (for example, security issues).

2.1 Identify the procedures for installing Windows 9x/Me, Windows NT 4.0 Workstation, Windows 2000 Professional, and Windows XP and for bringing the operating system to a basic operational level.

2.2 Identify steps to perform an operating system upgrade from Windows 9x/Me, Windows NT 4.0 Workstation, Windows 2000 Professional, and Windows XP. Given an upgrade scenario, choose the appropriate next steps.

2.3 Identify the basic system boot sequences and boot methods, including the steps to create an emergency boot disk with utilities installed for Windows 9x/Me, Windows NT 4.0 Workstation, Windows 2000 Professional, and Windows XP.

2.4 Identify procedures for installing/adding a device, including loading, adding, and configuring device drivers and required software.

3.1 Recognize and interpret the meaning of common error codes and startup messages from the boot sequence, and identify steps to correct the problems.

3.2 Recognize when to use common diagnostic utilities and tools.

THE NT BOOT PROCESS

In NT, getting a computer up and running from the off position to being ready for user input is a far more complicated process than it is for WIN9x systems. There are actually two separate steps involved. The first step is the boot process, in which the computer is raised from the dead and a basic OS is loaded. The second step is called the load process. This is where the system initializes, allows the user to log on, and loads any programs that are configured to automatically run.

THE BOOT PROCESS

For the NT boot process to be successful, a number of files need to be present on the root directory of the hard drive. These files are placed there during the installation process, and therefore, it's a good idea to leave them there. The following is a list of these files, followed by a brief description.

- *BOOT.INI*: This file provides the full path to the NT core files. It also generates the menu at startup that allows the user to select which OS to launch. In a system that is purely NT, the choices are NT 4.0 and NT 4.0 VGA Mode. In the event that the system is set up for multi-boot, these options will be included in the menu, and the paths to the core files for the alternate OS will also be provided. BOOT.INI attributes are read-only and system.

- *NTLDR*: This is the OS loader. After an OS has been selected, NTLDR launches the requisite file. In a multi-boot environment, many other OSs cannot launch without the services of this file. Its attributes are hidden, system, and read-only.

- *BOOTSECT.DOS*: Present on multi-boot systems. The boot sector of the hard drive as it existed prior to the installation of NT is copied to this file. When the earlier OS is selected for boot, BOOTSECT.DOS plays the role of the master boot record for that OS. Its attributes are hidden and system.

- *NTDETECT.COM*: This utility examines the system's hardware and builds the list of device drivers that NT will need to load. This information is passed on to NTLDR. Its attributes are hidden, read-only, and system.

- *NTBOOTDD.SYS*: This file is only present on systems that boot from a SCSI device on which the SCSI BIOS has been disabled. It acts as a device driver for the boot device. There are no specific attributes required for this file.

In addition to the files located in the root directory, two other files are called on by NTLDR:

- *NTOSKERNEL.EXE*: This is NT's base kernel file. It manages I/O and file system functions and is located in the WINNT\SYSTEM32 directory.
- *SYSTEM*: This file directs the loading of device drivers and OS services during the boot process and manages those drivers and services while the system is running. It is located in the WINNT\SYSTEM32\CONFIG directory.

The actual boot process in NT as a bit more complex than the process I described in Chapter Twenty-Three for WIN9x. The first step is the system POST. After that has been completed, the file that the MBR goes out looking for is NTLDR. One of the key services this file offers is to act as a rudimentary file system manager. It is capable of reading FAT12, FAT16, CDFS, and NTFS. NTLDR initializes the proper file systems and then goes out looking for BOOT.INI. After it finds it, it loads that file and displays the boot menu for the user. After the user has made his or her selection, one of two things will happen.

EXAM NOTE: As in previous discussions of operating systems, it is very likely you will be tested on the boot process of NT. Know the files that are required and the order in which they're run.

Should the user select an alternative OS, NTLDR runs BOOTSECT.DOS. NTLDR will then pass control of the boot process over to BOOTSECT.DOS and exit. From that point the boot process of the selected OS will continue. For the users that select NT, NTLDR will load and run NTDETECT.COM. This file checks all the hardware, and this is where the user sees a bit of system activity. Keyboard lights flash, and if there is a printer or tape drive installed, these devices will most likely blink or perhaps even make noise. The floppy disk light will flash as well. When NTDETECT is done, it passes the information it gathered on to NTLDR, which generates the hardware hive in the registry.

The last part of this process is for NTLDR to initialize NTOSKERNEL.EXE and hand off the hardware information it collected to that file. NTOSKERNEL.EXE is now in control of the machine, and NTLDR exits. Technically speaking, that is the end of the boot process. The system still isn't in a position for the user to take over and start working, though. Next comes the load process.

A TOUR OF **BOOT.INI**

As I mentioned earlier, the BOOT.INI file is critical for the correct loading of NT. So just what is that file? If you were to open the file for viewing, it would look something like **Figure 26.1.**

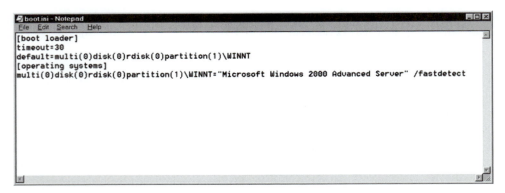

Figure 26.1 BOOT.INI determines both the parameters of the boot process and provides NTLDR with the correct ARC paths to all OSs loaded on the system.

This file isn't quite as intimidating as it first appears. Something you need to understand is that BOOT.INI uses the ARC file naming convention and ordinal counting. And that clarified everything didn't it?

ARC is an acronym for Advanced RISC Computing and is the file system used by operating systems such as UNIX and Linux. I'll describe that over the next few paragraphs. Ordinal counting simply means you start counting at zero instead of one. So the first drive in the system is Drive 0 and the second one is Drive 1. Makes sense.

Now let's translate the lines of BOOT.INI. The lines enclosed in brackets—**[boot loader]** and **[operating systems]**—are simply headers for separate sections of the file. All lines following **[boot loader]** define boot process parameters, and all lines following **[operating systems]** lay out the ARC path to each OS installed on the system. In the example shown in the figure, there is only one OS installed. In a moment, I'll show how another line can be added that defines a second OS on the system.

timeout=30 defines how long the user will have to select an OS during the boot process. Thirty seconds is the default. This means that the boot menu that appears will count down 30 seconds before the default OS loads. You can use the up and down arrows on the keyboard to select an OS and press <Enter> at any time to start the OS of your choice. That can be a bit annoying to someone with only a single OS loaded. Hmmm, which one do I want to load? I can't decide! **timeout=0** eliminates the 30-second countdown.

> **EXAM NOTE:** You are very likely to be asked to break apart an ARC path on the OS exam. Understand what each section of the path points to and that the OS can never reside on partition(0).

default=multi(0)rdisk(0)disk(0)partition(1)\WINNT is the line that defines the ARC path to the default OS. An ARC path is divided into five parts. **multi(0)** indicates that the first, or primary, hard disk controller is the host for the boot drive. If the OS is installed on a drive located on a secondary controller, this portion would read **multi(1)**. Computers equipped with SCSI controllers will read **SCSI(0)** or **SCSI(1)** instead of multi.

Rdisk(0) indicates the node number that the disk occupies on the defined controller. For example, the illustrated BOOT.INI file indicates that it is the primary drive on the first controller. IDE controllers are true multi-disk controllers, and that number will always read 0. If it was the second drive on a SCSI chain, that section would read **rdisk(1)**. The third drive on a SCSI chain would be **rdisk(2)** and so on and so forth.

Disk(0) tells you which disk at a particular node address houses the system files. Since IDE controllers might host two different drives at the same node address, **disk(0)** indicates it is the master drive on that port. **Disk(1)** would indicate a slave drive. SCSI drives only support one drive per node and, therefore, will always read **disk(0)**.

Partition(1) states that the system files are located on the first partition of the drive that was defined in previous sections. ("Now, wait a minute," the astute reader thinks. "I thought in ordinal counting the first partition would be **partition(0)**!") Microsoft operating systems define **partition(0)** as being the hard disk in its entirety, including all partitions and unpartitioned space such as the MBR and the file system tables. Therefore, the first usable partition is **partition(1)**. WINNT defines the directory on that partition that houses the system files.

Now under the **[operating systems]** portion of BOOT.INI, you see two things. First of all, each OS installed will have its ARC path defined. A user with WIN98 installed on the first partition of the slave of the primary IDE port would have a line that reads **multi(0)rdisk(0)disk(1)partition(1)\WINDOWS="Windows 98"** listed in that section as well. The second thing defined in this section is what name will be given the OS in the boot menu. That is the text enclosed in the quotes. If I type **Old Operating System** between the quotes, then during the boot process, I will have the choice of **Windows NT 4.0** or **Old Operating System** to choose from.

THE NT LOAD PROCESS

There are four phases to the load process:

- Kernel Load
- Kernel Initialization
- Services Load
- Subsystem Start

The Kernel Load phase initializes the HAL and effectively tucks all the system hardware away and out of sight of any applications running on the system. The file SYSTEM.DAT (which is the part of the registry that controls system functions) is loaded and scanned for a list of drivers and services that must be started.

Kernel Initialization is that part of the boot process that displays little more than a blue screen. The list of drivers and services generated during the Kernel Load phase is initialized, and the files for the drivers are located and loaded. The CurrentControlSet section of the registry is generated and loaded as well.

The Services Load Phase takes over and, as the name implies, takes the list of system services and locates and runs the files associated with those services. Note, however, that these services are not actually launched at this time. Not all services are necessarily required in order for the system to run. A file called SMSS.EXE is loaded and executed. This is the Windows Session Manager. It prepares a list of all programs listed in the Startup menu and prepares the system to launch those applications. They won't actually be launched, however, until the user has successfully logged on.

Finally, the Subsystem Start phase loads LSASS.EXE. This is the Local Security Authority (LSA) that I discussed in the previous chapter. This brings up the dialogue box that instructs the user to press <Ctrl>+<Alt>+<Delete> in order to log on. Another file loaded during the Subsystem Start phase is SCREG.EXE. This is the Windows Service Controller. It scans the registry looking for all the services that are set to load automatically and launches those services.

The final part of the boot process is the user logon. This is where the user presses <Ctrl>+<Alt>+<Delete> and enters his or her credentials. LSA compares these credentials to the entry for that user in SAM. If the information matches, the user logon is accepted. If not, a message is generated notifying the user that the user ID and/or password entered was not recognized by the system. After a user has been authenticated, the desktop loads, and the programs that are part of the Startup menu are finally launched. The system is ready to go.

NT ARCHITECTURE

One of the key factors that made NT such a success was the fact that it was so much more stable than previous Microsoft OSs. People liked the point-and-click ease of the WIN9x versions. But they weren't exactly ecstatic about having to restart their computers three and four times a day because of system crashes and application errors. For many organizations, the occasionally erratic behavior of the WIN9x versions was totally unacceptable. NT was the better choice.

Key changes made to the NT architecture were responsible for this increased stability. To begin with, NT is basically divided into two separate parts—Kernel Mode and User Mode. *Kernel Mode* is responsible for managing system functions, while *User Mode* manages the logon process, security, and application functions. An overview of NT's architecture is provided in **Figure 26.2.**

KERNEL MODE

One of the primary reasons NT is more stable than previous products released by Microsoft is that the hardware is completely isolated from the applications. The WIN9x versions had taken steps in this direction, but NT made the process complete. Applications cannot directly communicate with hardware. Plain and simple.

BUZZ WORDS

Kernel Mode: An operational mode for an OS that manages system functions.

User Mode: An operational mode for an OS that manages applications and security functions.

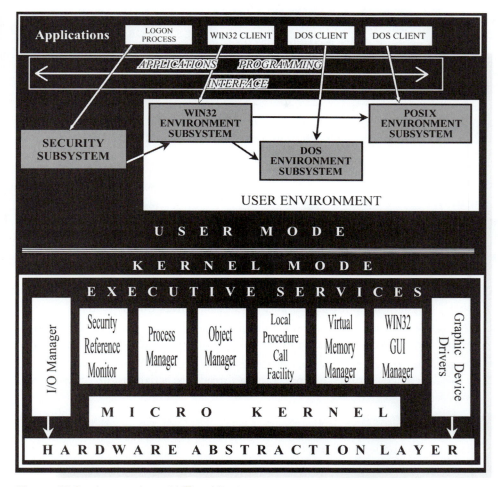

Figure 26.2   An overview of NT architecture

Kernel Mode can be broken down into three basic components. Each of these components brings user data and commands progressively closer to the point of being able to interface with the hardware. These three components are listed here:

- Executive Services
- Micro Kernel
- Hardware Abstraction Layer

If you recall from Chapter Twenty-Two, The Evolution of Windows and Windows Basics, I included a lengthy dissertation on the different processor rings. NT has clearly defined how processor rings are used. All Kernel Mode processes run in Ring 0.

EXECUTIVE SERVICES

Executive Services does not derive its name from the fact that it wears a suit and tie and commutes from the suburbs to work every day. This is the layer of the OS that is responsible for executing commands. Every device driver, service, or application is under the control of Executive Services. But other critical services are at its command as well. The various services managed by Executive Services include the following:

BUZZ WORDS

Executive Services: The layer of the operating system responsible for running commands.

- *Hardware device drivers*: Generate the commands that will eventually be sent to the hardware.

- *The Security Reference Monitor*: Tracks user activity and allows access to only those resources for which the user has the appropriate permissions.

- *The Virtual Memory Manager*: Controls the paging file created by NT for temporary storage of data not required in physical RAM at the moment.

- *The Object Manager*: Provides resource management support needed by virtually every other subsystem for both logical and physical resources on the system.

- *The I/O Manager*: Controls input/output requests from applications running on the system and, conversely, manages data being returned by the devices on the system.

- *Process Manager*: Controls which processes (refer back to Chapter Two for a discussion of the differences between a process and a thread) are active on the system at any given time.

- *Local Procedure Call Facility*: Provides a communications platform for applications to local resources. This would include interaction with other applications and interaction between the applications and the OS.

- *Configuration Manager*: Manages the system registry and directs calls and functions to the I/O Manager in order to prevent resource conflicts.

- *Cache Manager*: Manages NT's file system cache. By mapping specific memory to specific functions, NT is able to manage existing cache memory more efficiently and utilize system memory as cache memory where needed.

EXAM NOTE: Although it isn't necessary to know every single one of the Executive Services, it is necessary to be able to identify what the Executive Services do.

THE MICRO KERNEL

The Micro Kernel acts as the central core for the entire operating system. It controls the functions of the Executive Services layer, dictating what service will be called when. It also directly manages all I/O functions between the applications and HAL.

THE HARDWARE ABSTRACTION LAYER

This is the layer that actually isolates applications from the physical devices on the system. When a device driver makes a system call to a particular piece of hardware, it actually sends that command to a program called an Application Programming Interface (API). The API is a piece of software that collects commands generated by applications and translates them from the upper-level programming languages used by applications to the machine-level languages used by hardware.

APIs take it a step further. Since a number of different devices might use a similar command set, HAL uses the APIs to treat all devices of a particular type as if they were the same device. For example, the Advanced Technology API (ATAPI) provides hardware support for a vast majority of devices that make use of the IDE interface. This includes devices such as hard disks, CD-ROMS, CD-RWs, and the list goes on and on. (For more detailed information on APIs and IDE, see *The A+ Guide to PC Hardware Maintenance and Repair,* by this same author.)

After HAL has translated the commands from the application, it can then issue the simpler commands directly to the device. On the flip side, data and/or commands coming from the hardware must be processed by HAL and translated to the upper-level languages understood by the applications.

A key function of HAL that is often overlooked is this: While modern OS have absolutely no problem whatsoever running multiple applications on the system, the devices themselves can only communicate with a single application at a time. Therefore, in a multitasking system, it is the responsibility of HAL to monitor the traffic of multiple applications back and forth between the individual pieces of hardware.

USER MODE

NT architecture is based on a layered model. The Kernel Mode processes that I just discussed can be considered the bottom layer of the cake. The next layer up would be the User Mode processes. These are the NT services that intercept requests from the applications or from user input and transfer them over to the Kernel Mode processes that I just discussed.

User Mode processes are considered to be non-privileged, and as such, run in processor Ring 3. To better understand User Mode, just remember that it is broken down into two basic types of services. These are user environment services and security services.

The user environment services define what types of applications can run on the computer. Technically speaking, it isn't actually the user environment that is being defined, but rather an environment in which the user's applications can run. NT has been written to support the following OS environments:

- MS-DOS
- 16-bit Windows
- 32-bit Windows
- POSIX
- OS/2

If you're wondering about POSIX and OS/2, don't be too paranoid about running into these types of applications any time soon. POSIX is an acronym for Portable Operating System Interface (and no, I don't know where the X came from). It is a platform designed to make applications written for different forms of UNIX OS versions, as well as certain other OSs, compatible with one another. As a result, with POSIX support enabled, an NT user could run UNIX applications. OS/2 was an OS designed by IBM to run on personal computers.

> **EXAM NOTE:** A common subject for NT-related exam questions relates to the OS environment. Know which OS environments are supported by NT. Also make sure you remember what POSIX stands for.

The security component of User Mode starts with the <Ctrl>+<Alt>+<Delete> logon function. From that point on, the security component maintains a constant link with SRM. Once the user's credentials have been verified and accepted, the authentication token that I discussed in the previous chapter is generated. This token identifies the correct user profile to load from the registry, ensuring that the user sees the same desktop every day. From that point forward, SRM uses that token to verify user permissions and/or privileges for every action the user attempts on the system or network.

MANAGING PHYSICAL RESOURCES IN NT

In this section, I am going to discuss how NT manages the physical resources of the computer system. This will include the processor(s), memory, and hard disks. Much of the technology that NT uses was derivative of WIN9x, but in most cases it has been modified or refined for NT's advanced architecture. Therefore, if some of this seems familiar, start digging for the differences.

PROCESSOR CONTROL

In previous chapters, I've discussed how various Microsoft versions take advantage of processor rings to enhance stability. There is more to processor management than processor rings. NT exacerbated the complexity of managing processors by introducing SMP. Now it's quite possible that the machine is going to have more than one CPU to keep track of. To further emphasize the complexity of this responsibility, consider that the processor(s) are not only managing application and user data; they are also playing conductor to the orchestra of hardware devices that make up the system.

On a hardware level, distribution of interrupt requests across multiple CPUs was made possible by rebuilding the I/O subsystem of the OS from the ground up. A central engineering feature of this subsystem is SMP support. NT manages this by maintaining two separate versions of HAL.

When NT 4.0 is installed on a single-processor system, the basic version of HAL is installed. This version consists of an interrupt handler that targets a single CPU and the main file that supports the HAL, which is a file appropriately named HAL.DLL. If NT is installed on a multiprocessor system, a different version is installed. The file for this version of HAL is HALMPS.DLL. Along with these two primary files are a number of different driver files that are substituted as well.

The end result is that upgrading a machine from single-processor support to SMP support isn't quite as simple as copying a couple of new files onto the system. Therefore, for most people, an upgrade requires reinstalling the OS. Microsoft did provide a utility with NT to assist the user in performing this upgrade. This utility is UPTOMP.EXE. Unfortunately, this file was provided only in the resource kit and not on the original CD.

A feature added to NT that ensured that application and user data got their fair share of CPU time was the NT Scheduler. As with the I/O Manager, NT Scheduler was designed from the ground up with SMP support as part of its basic structure. Whether you have one processor or sixteen, the process of running applications or processing data is going to be the same.

NT was designed to function with pre-emptive multitasking. As such, it is up to the OS to determine how much time a particular string of code will be allowed to tie up the CPU. NT is designed to be a multi-user as well as a multiprocessor environment. However, it's also designed to be a *real time OS*. This means that it needs to be able to perform specific threads of code at a specific time. An example of real time processing would be the systems at an automated factory.

Here is an example of real time processing at work. Here in Vermont there is a company that produces engraved metal furniture. Their product line includes tables that feature incredibly detailed illustrations and designs etched onto the surfaces. These designs are all computer rendered. The application that controls the etching process must be able to manipulate the equipment in extremely precise movements; otherwise the etching will be flawed. This, too, is a function of the NT Scheduler.

This is where being able to set priorities on specific threads of code becomes essential. The NT Scheduler assigns each thread that is called a priority between 1 and 31. Higher numbers represent higher priorities. Therefore, a thread with a priority of 16 will be run before a thread with a priority of 12. Priority 0 is reserved for the System Idle function, which will cause this thread to run only when no other thread is present on the system. Priorities 16 through 31 are reserved for real time functions. Priorities can be assigned either by the OS (for system generated threads) or by the application (as in the example related previously).

When the thread receives its allotted CPU time, it will be given specific time slots to run. These time slots are very short, and vary between Workstation and Server versions. Threads on NT Server versions are typically 120ms in duration, while the threads on NT Workstation can run in 20ms, 40ms, or 60ms increments. Multiple threads running on a system will still appear to run seamlessly because the time slots occur so frequently that they appear to the user to be continuous.

The problem Microsoft engineers foresaw with this technique was this: If a particular thread has a very low priority, and there are a number of high-priority threads running on the system, the low-priority thread may never have the opportunity to run. A process called *priority boosting* prevents this from happening. Periodically a service running in NT called the Balance Set

BUZZ WORDS

Real time OS: An OS designed to be able to perform specific functions at the precise time at which those functions are needed.

Priority boosting: A process by which the privilege level of a thread of code is promoted to a higher level in order to enhance its chances at the CPU.

Manager scans the system looking for CPU-starved threads. When it finds one, it doubles the priority number of the starved thread. If the next time the Balance Set Manager runs, that thread still hasn't had a shot at the CPU, it will be boosted again. This process repeats until the thread is finally run.

Another method by which a thread can receive a boost is from an event-induced boost. An example of this would be a process that was waiting for user input from the keyboard or mouse. Rather than shut the entire system down for the whole time the user is out getting coffee and donuts, these threads start out with a very low priority. When the user performs the action the thread has been waiting for, the thread's priority is bumped. For keyboard and mouse events, it amounts to a six-point boost in priority.

MEMORY MANAGEMENT

One of the biggest advances in NT was the way it managed memory. Unlike previous Microsoft OS versions that depended on an age-old separation of memory between conventional and extended memory, NT uses a flat memory model. By this, I mean that once NT is up and running, each application that is launched is assigned a specific address space and that application runs within that space. That address space will appear to the applications to be 4GB per application, with 2GB being allocated to the application processes, and 2GB allotted to system processes needed to support the application. This is true whether you have 64MB installed or 4GB installed. How does it do this? It's simple. NT lies to the applications.

> **NOTE:** Starting with Service Pack Three, it became possible for the user to configure the virtual address space of NT a little differently. 2GB was far more space than was needed for an OS that only took up 300MB in its entirety. After SP3 was released, it became possible to allocate 1GB to OS functions and 3GB to applications. For the most part, that amounted to fixing a problem that didn't exist. Every paper I've ever read on the subject came to the conclusion that making this change had little or no effect on the stability or the performance of the OS.

This vast space assigned by NT is known as the *memory pool* and consists of physical memory and virtual memory. As with WIN9x, virtual memory is hard drive space that has been reserved as a place to move items in physical memory when they're not being used in order to make space in physical memory for items that are needed immediately. In WIN9x, the term for this hard drive space is the swap file. In NT, Microsoft engineers got fancier. It's now called the paging file.

> **EXAM NOTE:** Make sure you can identify the key points for virtual memory management in NT. Make special note of the memory pool and the 4GB virtual address space.

All memory functions in NT are under control of the Virtual Memory Manager (VMM). The

BUZZ WORDS

Memory pool: The total address space available to an OS and the applications running on top of it.

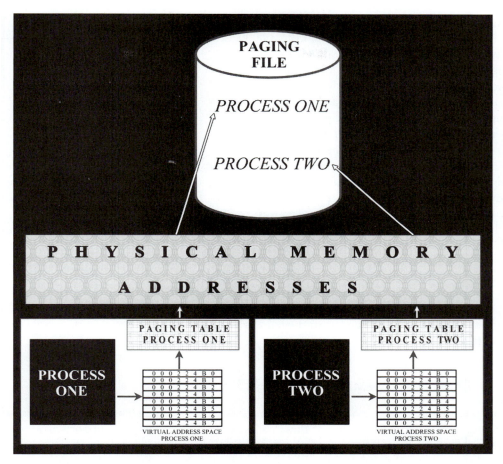

Figure 26.3   Windows has some pretty nifty tricks for convincing an application that it has 2GB of free memory on a computer that doesn't.

functions of NT's VMM are identical to those of the WIN9x VMM that I discussed in Chapter Twenty-Three, but the structure of the file is different. In NT there is only a single 32-bit memory manager. In the following discussion of how Windows manages memory, it might help if you occasionally refer to **Figure 26.3**.

VMM maps all available physical addresses, both physical RAM and paging file space. The applications are given a range of virtual addresses that they will use. Now, if you're following this correctly, you've already seen the minor glitch in this scheme. There are obviously more virtual addresses assigned than there can possibly be physical addresses on the system.

So, when a process is given an address range that starts at byte number 2,000,000,000, this is provided to the system as a binary address of 1110111001101011001010000000000. VMM locates a contiguous physical address large enough to store the code for that process and records the physical address. Let's say for example, that this actual physical address starts at byte number 120,540,000.

VMM records the binary equivalent of this address, which would be 11100101111010010101101100000. For every call to the virtual address, VMM translates this call to the actual address in which the data is stored.

Buzz Words ─────────────

Page fault: A noncritical error state that occurs when the OS looks for data in the paging file and fails to locate it.

If there is no contiguous space in RAM large enough for this process, then some process that is not currently being used will be moved from RAM to the paging file, and the RAM it previously occupied will be cleared for the new process. If there are more applications, with their associated processes, running on the system than there is physical RAM and paging file combined, then data from the paging file is simply dumped to make room for the new applications. The data to be dumped is determined by how recently it has been accessed. The data least recently used is what goes.

Now what happens to the application that might have needed the data that was dumped? VMM is still telling that application that the data is there. And if that application becomes active once again and requires that data, it will issue a call to the virtual address. VMM translates the virtual address to the physical address and sees that that address no longer holds data associated with the application making the request. VMM will then issue a *page fault*. All this means is that the paging file didn't have the data it was looking for, and it doesn't have a clue where it is. The system will issue a new I/O request to the hard drive to look for the data, and the whole process will start all over.

Hard Disk Management Under NT

In previous chapters I have already discussed some of the major technical issues faced when managing hard disks in NT. One of these issues is the file systems NT supports, and another is the fact that NT need not be loaded onto the root drive in order to run. From the outset, this makes it appear that managing disks in NT becomes more difficult. It needn't be all that challenging as long as you keep some basic concepts in the back of your mind when administering disks.

First off, when installing NT, it is not possible to create an NTFS partition on the fly. Therefore, for the initial installation of NT to succeed, there needs to be a FAT16 partition present. If the NTFS file system has been chosen, that FAT16 partition will be converted to NTFS during the installation process. If FAT was chosen and the user later chooses to convert the drive to NTFS, it is possible to do a one-time conversion of the drive from FAT to NTFS using the Convert utility. It is not possible to convert an NTFS drive to FAT16. FAT32 is not supported.

FAT16 partitions created by NT are somewhat different than those created by earlier OSs. If you recall the discussion of file systems from Chapter Two, An Introduction to Operating Systems, you'll remember that the largest partition supported by FAT16 is 2GB. This is due to the fact that the largest cluster readable by DOS and earlier Windows versions was 64 hard disk sectors, or 32KB. NT supports 64KB clusters, and, therefore, a FAT16 partition can be as large as 4GB.

After the OS is installed, a large hard disk can then have the remainder of its available space formatted as a single NTFS partition. For example, if you are installing NT onto an 80GB hard disk, you would have to create one smaller FAT16 partition for the installation of NT and leave the remainder of the drive unallocated. A utility called Disk Administrator can then be used to configured the remaining drive space.

Now what about this Disk Administrator? Just what is it, and how does it work? In a nutshell, it's a utility that allows the user to add and remove and/or format partitions on the fly without having to reboot the system.

The first time you run Disk Administrator (**Figure 26.4**), it asks for your permission to configure your system. At this point it adds a signature to the disk. This signature consists of four bytes of data that are added to the first physical sector on the hard disk. The signature identifies a specific volume on the drive and follows the physical disk wherever it goes, even if it is moved to a different hard disk controller on the same system. For Disk Administrator to perform any of its advanced magic, you need to allow this signature. Conversely, if your alternate OS on a dual-boot system includes UNIX, VMS, or Linux, you need to refuse this permission. The signature will corrupt the partition tables for these OSs.

There are two partitions that cannot be deleted or formatted in Disk Administrator. These are the root partition and the system partition. The root partition is the partition with all of the key files necessary for NT to boot. These files were listed earlier in the chapter. The system partition is the directory into which NT was installed.

In the majority of installations these partitions are one and the same, but not always. For example, in a dual-boot system, you might have WIN98 installed on the first partition and NT installed onto the second. Under these circumstances, neither of these partitions can be deleted or formatted by Disk Administrator because the root files exist on the WIN98 partition and the system files on the NT partition.

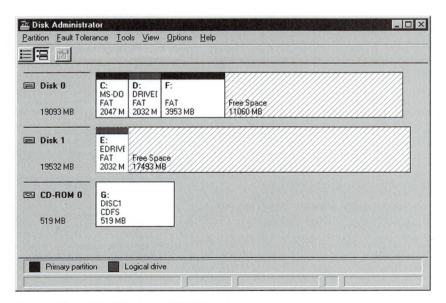

Figure 26.4   The Windows NT Disk Administrator

Nonallocated space on hard drives can be managed any way the user sees fit. New partitions can be added and formatted in either FAT16 or NTFS, and logical DOS drives can be incorporated into these partitions.

> **CAUTION:** If you are one of those people (like me) who likes to experiment with different operating systems and are always changing OSs, there is one thing you should know about Disk Administrator. When you add logical DOS drives to an NTFS partition, you will render the partition unreadable by Microsoft's FDISK utility. FDISK will see that a non-DOS partition exists, but when you attempt to delete it, FDISK reports that the logical DOS drives must be deleted first. However, since FDISK can't read NTFS, it can't delete the logical drives. In order to recover the hard disk, you need to start the installation of NT (or any later version of Microsoft OS) and delete all partitions through Disk Manager. Another option is to use a third-party utility, such as PowerQuest's Partition Magic.

As additional disks are added to the system, Disk Administrator will prompt the user to sign these disks as well. Once the disks have been signed, there are a number of different tricks that become possible for the user. Its best trick is the ability to manage *volume sets*. Although there are different types of volume sets, they all amount to the same. Multiple partitions or physical disks are combined to create what appears to the system as a single disk drive. The most commonly seen volume sets are spanned volumes, striped volumes, and mirrored volumes.

A *spanned volume* occurs when a user creates a logical single drive that incorporates unallocated space for more than one physical disk. For example, if you have three different hard disks installed in a computer and each disk has some free space on it, Disk Administrator will allow you to merge the free space into a single logical drive (see **Figure 26.5**).

A *striped volume* is similar to a spanned volume in that one logical drive is distributed across multiple physical disks. The striped volume differs in the fact that data is broken up into small chunks (called stripes) and distributed equally across all the drives in the set. Striped sets can be used either to enhance hard disk performance on a system or to add a degree of fault tolerance to the system. The *mirrored volume* exists when two different drives house exactly the same data. As new data is added to one drive, it is automatically copied to all other drives in the mirrored volume.

Striped sets and mirrored sets are different ways of incorporating a Redundant Array of Independent Disks (RAID) set into the system. These

---

BUZZ WORDS

Volume set: A single logical disk drive that is created when multiple partitions or physical disks are combined.

Spanned volume: A larger logical drive that is created by combining space located on two different partitions or disks.

Striped volume: A logical drive that is created by storing data in chunks that are distributed among multiple physical drives.

Mirrored volume: A single logical drive that is made of two disks, both of which contain identical data.

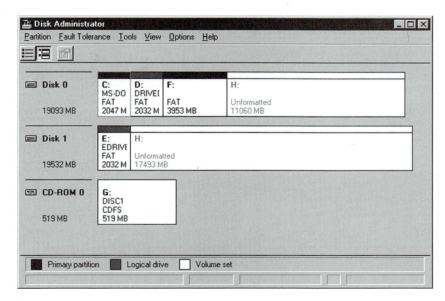

Figure 26.5   A spanned volume is a single logical disk that physically exists on two separate drives.

are generally referred to as RAID arrays, but as you can see from the acronym, a Redundant Array of Independent Disks Array is somewhat redundant.

WINDOWS NT AND RAID

Having said all that about volume sets, striped sets, and mirrored sets, I want to take a look at the different disk structures that are supported internally by NT, as well as a few versions that required external software and/or hardware support in order to function. Over the next few pages, I'm going to be discussing several different versions of RAID. Of these, only RAID levels 0, 1, and 5 are supported internally. The levels that exist, or that have existed over the years, are outlined in **Table 26.1**.

> **EXAM NOTE:** It is unlikely that you'll be asked to identify anything other than RAID Levels 0, 1 and 5 on the exam. Still, the other RAID levels have been known to rear their heads from time to time.

RAID 0

Of all the levels listed in Table 26.1, only three are actually in common use. RAID 0 provides no fault tolerance. It simply stripes the data across multiple drives, as shown in **Figure 26.6**.

Table 26.1 Levels of RAID

Level	Technique Used	Description	Tolerance
0	Disk striping without parity	Data is striped across multiple disks in blocks with no parity information stored.	None
1	Mirroring or Duplexing	Data is copied directly to a second hard drive.	Good
2	Disk striping with error correction code	Data is spread across multiple disks on a bit level with error correction rather than parity used. Now defunct.	Very High
3	Byte-level striping with dedicated parity disk	Data is striped across multiple disks in bytes, with a single disk being used to store the parity information.	Good
4	Block striping with dedicated parity disk	Data is striped across multiple disks in blocks of data, with a single disk being used to store the parity information.	Good
5	Block striping with distributed parity	Data is striped across multiple disks in blocks of data, with parity being equally distributed among all disks.	Good
6	Block striping with dual distributed data	Data is striped across multiple disks in blocks of data, with two sets of parity blocks being equally distributed among all disks.	Very Good
7	Proprietary. Not used in the open market.		
0/1	Combines RAID 0 with RAID 1	A stripe set w/o parity is duplexed onto an identical set on a different controller.	Good
50	Combines RAID 1 with RAID 5	Two RAID 5 arrays are mirrored.	Extremely High

RAID 0, 1, and 5 are the only RAID levels in common use.

Figure 26.6 Although RAID 0 provides no fault tolerance whatsoever, it is still used in cases where improved disk performance is a must.

Figure 26.7   Disk mirroring simply duplicates the data on two separate disk drives.

Its key reason for existing is that it provides for extremely good drive performance. For machines designed exclusively for doling out data to large numbers of users, or one on which large files need to be opened quickly, this might be a viable choice. Just make sure you have a suitable backup strategy in place.

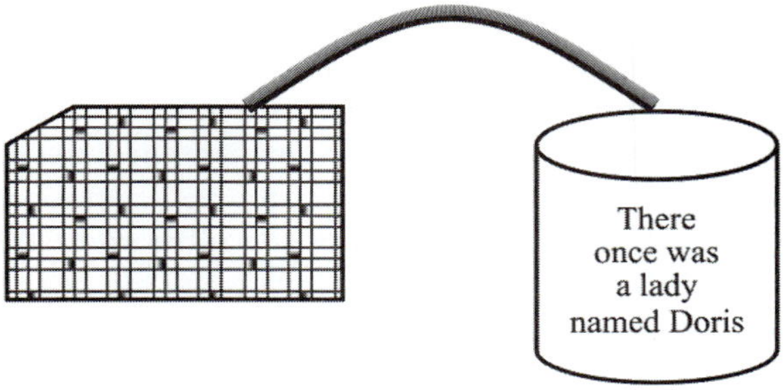

RAID 1

RAID 1 does provide a degree of fault tolerance in that the data is duplicated on two different drives. This duplication covers everything from the MBR to the last byte of data on the drive. With RAID 1 implemented, every bit of data written to Disk One is also written to Disk Two. If either disk fails, the other disk is available, and the system does not go down.

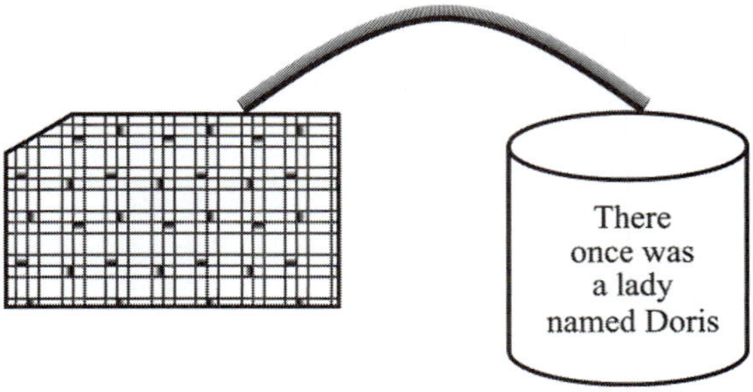

RAID 1 can be implemented two ways. *Disk mirroring* involves putting two separate drives on the same controller. The other implementation of RAID 1 is *disk duplexing*. This is identical to disk mirroring in every respect, except that each disk is on its own separate controller. The thought here is that should the controller be the cause of failure, both drives would go down. By putting each drive on its own controller, failure of a single controller will not bring the system down. **Figure 26.7** and **Figure 26.8** illustrate the difference between mirroring and duplexing.

Figure 26.8   Disk duplexing is the same as mirroring, only each disk is on a separate controller.

BUZZ WORDS

Disk mirroring: Exactly duplicating the data on a system on two different drives hanging off of a single controller.

Disk duplexing: Exactly duplicating the data on a system on two different drives, each hanging off of a separate controller.

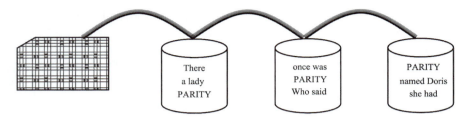

Figure 26.9 A RAID 5 implementation. As with RAID 0, in actual practice all data blocks would be the same size.

RAID 5

The RAID level most commonly used by network administrators is RAID 5, which requires a minimum of three hard disks. The maximum number of drives you can use depends on whether you are using a hardware controller or the software RAID included in NT or Novell. Software raid can make use of up to thirty-two drives. Your hardware will dictate its own limitations.

> **BUZZ WORDS** ─────────
>
> **Parity block:** A mathematical image of data that can be used to reconstruct that data in the event it is lost.

RAID 5 resembles RAID 0 in that it spreads the data across the drives equally. It adds fault tolerance because for each block of data copied to the array, it generates a mathematical image of that data called a *parity block*. The parity information is also distributed evenly across the drives. If a single drive fails, the system continues as if nothing had happened. The parity information is used to rebuild all data in its entirety. As soon as the dead drive has been replaced, the array can be rebuilt. It should be noted, however, that while the faulty drive is still in place you have no fault tolerance. **Figure 26.9** shows you how RAID 5 works.

RAID 0/1

The RAID levels I've been discussing so far have all been what are called single RAID levels. In order to provide maximum security for your data, it is also possible to configure nested RAID levels. These are when you combine two different RAID levels onto a single machine. The most commonly used nested raid level is RAID 0/1.

In this implementation, you create a RAID 0 array of however many disks you require in order to provide for disk performance. Then, in order to implement some level of fault tolerance, you duplex the RAID 0 array on a separate controller. In the event that one disk fails, that entire side of the mirror is broken, and the system is dependent on the other side until the defective disk is replaced. See **Figure 26.10**.

RAID 50

RAID 50 is another combination of multiple RAID levels. Two separate RAID 5 arrays are implemented, using anywhere from three to thirty-two disks. Then, a separate, identical collection of disks duplexes that array. **Figure 26.11** illustrates how this works. As you might imagine,

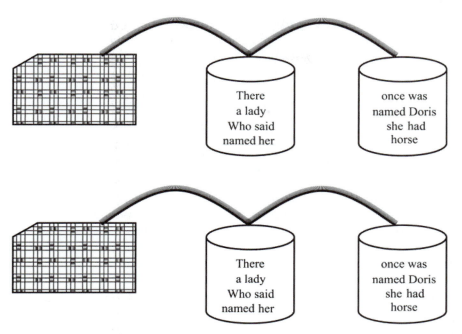

Figure 26.10   A RAID 0/1 implementation gives you the best of RAID 0 and RAID 1.

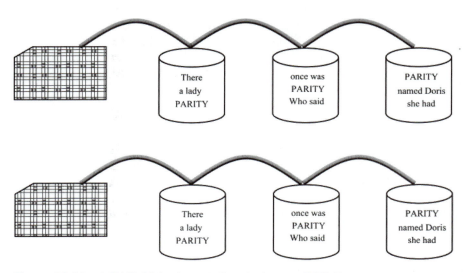

Figure 26.11   A RAID 50 implementation duplexes a RAID 5 array.

implementing this configuration can be a more costly approach. However, your data is about as secure as it can get. In order for the data to be completely unavailable, a total of four different drives would have to fail at the same time. Failure of one drive in either array wouldn't generate so much as a flutter in the system. Should two drives in the same array fail simultaneously, the second array will automatically take over. To have a disaster resulting in total system failure, two drives in each array would have to go down at the same time. If this happens, you can only hope you have a good tape backup as well as a new server. You're going to need both.

MANAGING DEVICES IN NT

The key to understanding device management in NT (or any other OS, for that matter) is that no matter how complicated the OS seems be to, the devices all have the same requirements. To refresh your memory, on a hardware level, the devices will all require an assigned IRQ and I/O address. Some devices will require, in addition, a DMA channel and a range of system memory addresses. If you need review on these principles, refer back to Chapter Two.

It's how these resources are managed that vary from OS to OS. NT, from outward appearances, seems to be identical to the WIN9x OS versions that were discussed in previous chapters. However, there are some key differences.

First of all, NT is not PnP-compliant. NTDETECT provides functionality that is similar to PnP, but it is severely limited in the types of devices it can detect. There are a great many devices that are not properly detected by NTDETECT. For these devices, it is essential to be able to manually install device drivers.

EXAM NOTE: Pay special attention to the fact that NT is *not* a PnP OS. Not knowing that might trip you up on a couple of questions.

Two NT utilities that make this job a bit easier are Add New Hardware and Windows NT Diagnostics. Add New Hardware differs very little from the utility of the same name that I discussed in Chapter Twenty-Four, Managing Windows 9x. NT Diagnostics can come in handy when attempting to resolve a resource conflict for a new device that won't come in handy.

NT Diagnostics can be accessed in one of two ways. Click Start→Programs→Administrative Tools Common→NT Diagnostics, or click Start→Run and type `winmsd` into the command line. Either approach will get you the screen illustrated in **Figure 26.12**. The various tabs seen at the top of this applet are briefly described in **Table 26.2**.

As far as device management is concerned, the information you'll be most concerned with is contained in the Resources tab. This is where you see what is already used in the system. That way you can identify possible resource conflicts.

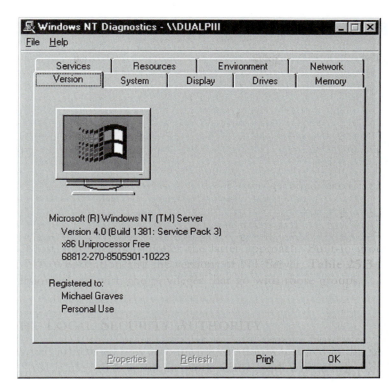

Figure 26.12
NT 4.0 ships with its own diagnostics utility.

Table 26.2   Contents of NT Diagnostics Utility

Tab	Information Contained
Version	OS version, latest service pack, serial number, and to whom registered
System	Number and type of processors and BIOS version
Display	Display adapter settings, type of adapter, installed memory on adapter, the chipset, and driver files
Drives	Information about all physical and mapped network drives on system
Memory	The amount of physical memory installed, size and location of paging file, how much data is stored in memory (File Cache), how much data is stored in the paging file (Commit Charge), and how much RAM is used by system processes
Services	A list of all services installed on the system and whether they are running or stopped
Resources	Information about IRQ, I/O address, and DMA settings
Environment	Identifies file for a command prompt, various processor information, path to system files, path to library files, and path to root directory
Network	User access level, whether computer is on a workgroup or a domain, version, number of logged on users (locally), and User IDs for those users

NT 4.0 ships with a basic diagnostics utility that contains valuable information about the system.

CHAPTER SUMMARY

The information found in this chapter is going to provide the foundation for much of what you will see in later chapters. Subsequent versions of Microsoft OSs, including Windows 2000 and XP, rely very heavily on the underlying technology of NT.

There are several key points to remember from this chapter. First and foremost is understanding the boot process. This information is critical to troubleshooting NT, and it also makes a frequent appearance on the exam. Another critical area covered is that of virtual memory.

RAID levels are also heavily covered on the exam, but more importantly, any technician who doesn't know about RAID isn't really a technician at all. At the minimum, you need a solid understanding of RAID levels 0, 1, and 5.

Device management in NT makes up a large part of many technicians' jobs. And I know what you're thinking. When will I ever see NT actually deployed? The answer is, you never know. As of this writing, Microsoft estimated that there were still approximately 10 million desktops with NT 4.0 Workstation installed. And hundreds of thousands of organizations have resisted the commercial clamor for them to upgrade their existing NT 4.0 servers.

BRAIN DRAIN

1. Discuss several ways that the NT boot process differs from that of WIN9x.

2. What is the NT load process? Discuss it in detail.

3. What are the two operating modes of NT? Discuss them in as much detail as you can muster.

4. What does Microsoft mean when it discusses the OS environment? How does NT maximize the options for the OS environment?

5. Discuss memory management in NT and how the concept of virtual memory is critical to the OS.

THE 64K$ QUESTIONS

1. Which of the following files is not a part of the NT boot process?
   a. WIN.COM
   b. BOOT.INI
   c. NTLDR
   d. NTDETECT

2. If you have created a multi-boot system, which of the following files will contain the information needed in order to boot the other OS?
   a. NTBOOTDD.SYS
   b. NTDETECT
   c. BOOTSECT.DOS
   d. BOOT.INI

3. What file system is not supported by NT?
   a. FAT12
   b. FAT16
   c. NTFS
   d. FAT32

4. The file path system used by NT in the BOOT.INI file is _____.
   a. ARC
   b. ANC

    c. FAT

    d. HPFS

5. Which of the following is not a phase of the NT load process?

    a. Kernel Load

    b. Subsystems Start

    c. Services Load

    d. File System Initialization

6. User Logon is initiated _____.

    a. By logon screen that prompts for User ID and password.

    b. By screen that prompts the user to press <Ctrl>+<Alt>+<Delete>

    c. Prior to NT booting

    d. User Logon is only initiated if configured to do so by the Administrator.

7. Kernel Mode services run at processor _____.

    a. Ring 0

    b. Ring 1

    c. Ring 2

    d. Ring 3

8. User Mode services run at processor _____.

    a. Ring 0

    b. Ring 1

    c. Ring 2

    d. Ring 3

9. The Executive Services run at _____.

    a. Ring 0

    b. Ring 1

    c. Ring 2

    d. Ring 3

10. An API runs as a service of the _____.

    a. I/O Manager

    b. Executive Services

    c. HAL

    d. Configuration Manager

11. UNIX applications running in the NT environment are known as _____ apps.

    a. POSIX

    b. UNIXServe

    c. UNINT

    d. POSIT

12. The service running in NT that prevents a renegade application from hogging processor time is called the _____.

    a. Task Scheduler

    b. Task Manager

    c. NT Scheduler

    d. Thread Scheduler

13. Threads of code that are time sensitive can be assured of getting first crack at the processor because they will be given a priority _____.

    a. Of 1

    b. Of 31

    c. Between 0 and 15

    d. Between 16 and 31

14. A process that has not been allowed access to the CPU for an extended period of time is given an increased priority through a process of _____.

    a. Thread promotion

    b. Priority boosting

    c. Priority override

    d. It isn't given any increased chance.

15. On a system with 128MB of installed RAM, an application in NT will be assigned an address space equal to _____.

    a. The amount of free RAM divided by the number of concurrently running applications

    b. The amount of free RAM divided by the number of concurrently running applications plus an equal division of free paging file space

    c. 16MB

    d. 2GB

16. Two hard disks configured to maintain identical copies of one another are a form of _____.

    a. RAID 0

    b. RAID 1

    c. RAID 5

    d. RAID 0/1

17. If a computer has been configured to divide all data equally between two or more hard drives, with no allowance for data recovery, this computer has been configured for _____.

    a. RAID 0

    b. RAID 1

    c. RAID 5

    d. RAID 0/1

18. A computer with five hard disks on which data is equally divided between all drives, with parity information that can be used for data recovery also divided across all drives, has been configured for _____.

    a. RAID 0

    b. RAID 1

    c. RAID 5

    d. RAID 0/1

19. If you want to see what IRQs are being used by your system under NT, you would use _____.

    a. Device Manager

    b. Configuration Manager

    c. Resource Manager

    d. NT Diagnostics

20. NT 4.0 is an example of a true PnP OS.

    a. True

    b. False

TRICKY TERMINOLOGY

Disk duplexing: Exactly duplicating the data on a system on two different drives, each hanging off of a separate controller.

Disk mirroring: Exactly duplicating the data on a system on two different drives hanging off of a single controller.

Executive Services: The layer of the operating system responsible for running commands.

Kernel Mode: An operational mode for an OS that manages system functions.

Memory pool: The total address space available to an OS and the applications running on top of it.

Mirrored volume: A single logical drive that is made of two disks, both of which contain identical data.

Page fault: A noncritical error state that occurs when the OS looks for data in the paging file and fails to locate it.

Parity block: A mathematical image of data that can be used to reconstruct that data in the event it is lost.

Priority boosting: A process by which the privilege level of a thread of code is promoted to a higher level in order to enhance its chances at the CPU.

Real time OS: An OS designed to be able to perform specific functions at the precise time at which those functions are needed.

Spanned volume: A larger logical drive that is created by combining space located on two different partitions or disks.

Striped volume: A logical drive that is created by storing data in chunks that are distributed among multiple physical drives.

User mode: An operational mode for an OS that manages applications and security functions.

Volume set: A single logical disk drive that is created when multiple partitions or physical disks are combined.

ACRONYM ALERT

API: Application Programming Interface. A set of uniform commands common to a group of devices of the same type.

ARC: Advanced RISC Computing

ATAPI: Advanced Technology Application Programming Interface. The API that controls IDE devices.

LSA: Local Security Authority. A Microsoft service that authenticates users' rights.

POSIX: Portable Operating System Interface

RAID: Redundant Array of Independent Disks

VMM: Virtual Memory Manager. A service of an OS that maps hard drive space out and presents it as being available physical memory.

CHAPTER 27

ADMINISTRATIVE TOOLS IN NT

With the release of NT, users found themselves with several new tools to help keep their systems running at their best and to help figure out problems that might exist. Among these are Dr. Watson, the Event Viewer, Performance Monitor, and Network Monitor. These four items are the most commonly used of the Administrative Tools in NT. Even when these fail, NT has a built-in tool for helping the troubleshooting process. To most users, this last tool is affectionately known simply as the "blue screen of death." Most people, when faced with the blue screen, moan loudly and shut the machine off. But it can actually provide some useful information, if you know how to read it. The final thing I'll tackle in this chapter will be a brief overview of the rest of the set of administrative tools NT provides.

A+ OPERATING SYSTEM TECHNOLOGIES EXAM OBJECTIVES

CompTIA exam objectives covered in this chapter include the following:

2.3 Identify the basic system boot sequences and boot methods, including the steps to create an emergency boot disk with utilities installed for Windows 9x/Me, Windows NT 4.0 Workstation, Windows 2000 Professional, and Windows XP.

3.1 Recognize and interpret the meaning of common error codes and startup messages from the boot sequence, and identify steps to correct the problems.

DR. WATSON

Everyone has experienced system crashes before, and had applications crash. In previous versions of Windows, you basically just had to live with it and move on. NT provided a tool for diagnosing the cause of application crashes. This tool is called Dr. Watson. Dr. Watson automatically launches itself whenever an application stops responding to the system. It then generates a log file called drwtsn32.log that holds information specific to the condition of the system at the time of the crash. I should point out that Dr. Watson exists in Windows 98 as well. However, it's deeply integrated into the system in NT.

Dr. Watson can also create something called a *crash dump file*. The crash dump file is a byte for byte copy of the entire contents of system memory that is written to the hard disk. To the average user, this file is all but meaningless. But in the event of a disastrous system crash on a mission critical system, this file can be retrieved and sent to Microsoft for analysis. (There is a significant fee for this service.)

> **BUZZ WORDS**
>
> **Crash dump file:** A direct copy of the entire contents of system RAM copied to a file on the hard disk.

EXAM NOTE: Understand what a crash dump is and what it can be used for. But don't bother trying to understand how to read one unless you're an accomplished programmer.

There are a number of ways you can tweak Dr. Watson to work for you instead of for itself. The following few pages will take you on a tour of this often-ignored utility.

CONFIGURING DR. WATSON

Configuring Dr. Watson first requires starting the utility. In order to start Dr. Watson, click Start→Run and into the command line, type `drwtsn32`. You can do the same thing from a command prompt if you prefer. Either way will result in a window similar to **Figure 27.1**.

As you can see, there are several options. The first is the Log File Path. This is the directory in which the log file will be stored. In the illustration the path selected is called *%windir%*. This refers to the system directory. If you perform a typical installation, allowing Setup to use all of the default paths, then this directory will be C:\WINNT. If you chose to install to a different drive or direction, you'll need to know what that path was. Many administrators change this directory to C:\. That way, in the event of a system crash, it's easier to find the file.

The next entry is Crash Dump. This indicates the directory and filename where the crash dump will be stored in the event of a total system crash. The default directory is *%windir%\user.dmp*.

Below this, you see two number boxes. One is for Number of Instructions and the other for Number of Errors to Save. The default for both is 10. The Number of Instructions entry allows the user to configure how many program threads that were executed prior to the error state will be recorded. Number of Errors to Save actually doesn't refer to Dr. Watson's log file, but rather to Event Viewer. In addition to creating the log, Dr. Watson will write errors to another utility called Event Viewer (discussed later in this chapter.)

Beneath the instructions and errors options are six other options that are selected simply by checking the boxes. These options include the following:

- *Dump Symbol Table*: Records each application module running at the time of the crash, along with every program thread and the memory address at which that thread was running.

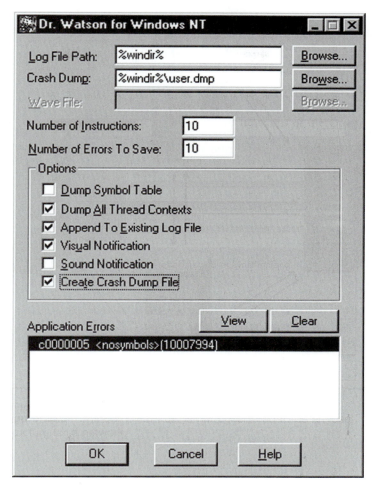

Figure 27.1 The Dr. Watson utility is a good tool for troubleshooting the probable cause of application errors.

- *Dump All Thread Contexts*: By default only the offending thread is recorded. By clicking this box, all threads running at the time of the failure will be recorded.
- *Append To Existing Log File*: When this box is checked, information is added at the bottom of a constantly growing file. If unchecked, the new log file will overwrite the old one.
- *Visual Notification*: If checked, when a failure occurs, a popup box will appear for five seconds, notifying the user of the event. If the OK is not clicked, the box will automatically disappear.

- *Sound Notification*: When an event occurs, Windows will play a sound file through the speakers.
- *Create Crash Dump File*: If unchecked, the crash dump file discussed earlier in this section will not be created.

At the bottom of the window is a text box labeled Application Errors. Any errors recorded in Dr. Watson's log will be listed here. Above the text box are two buttons. Clicking View allows the user to open Dr. Watson's log in a separate window and browse the entire file. Clicking Clear will erase the log file and start a new one.

A TOUR OF DR. WATSON'S LOG FILE

The log file that Dr. Watson generates can contain a plethora of useful information, if you know how to read it. To the beginner's eyes, it simply causes headaches. In this section, I'll provide the information that might prevent those headaches.

The log file is broken down into several sections, and each section contains specific information. **Figure 27.2** shows the opening two sections of the file. It always starts out with Microsoft's copyright information. You would never want to forget about that. Next will be the line that reads **Application exception occurred**. As if you didn't already know. The file then identifies the application that generated the error (although not always in a fashion that the user can understand), the time and date at which the error occurred, and the type of error

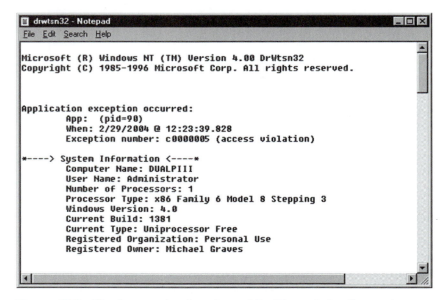

Figure 27.2 The first couple of sections of Dr. Watson's log file are the most informative to the average technician.

Figure 27.3 The Dr. Watson log lists all threads that were running at the time of the program fault.

that occurred. Following the opening sequence is some basic information about the system configuration.

After the system information section, the log file provides a list of all open threads at the time of the event (**Figure 27.3**). The number on the left side of the column is the Task Identifier and on the right is the name of the process running. This list is for information purposes only and does not indicate that these threads were at fault.

Now comes a list of all the program modules that were running on the system at the time of the error and the range of memory addresses that these modules occupied. (Note that in **Figure 27.4**, the list of modules contains only debug files, because the system from which this log file was obtained had no program errors.)

The State Dump section (**Figure 27.5**) is where Dr. Watson finally starts to dig into the problem. This section is divided into four columns. The first is the address of the instruction; the second is the machine code (in hexadecimal), while the last two are programming code. The only thing that matters to you as a technician is the line that says FAULT in front of it. That is the instruction that crashed the system. Microsoft's TechNet Web site contains a database of different fault codes and what they mean. Therefore, you can use this information on its Web site to troubleshoot the problems.

Following the State Dump are three other sections. These are the Stack Back Trace, the Raw Stack Dump, and the Symbol Table. These are useful only to programmers and will not be discussed here.

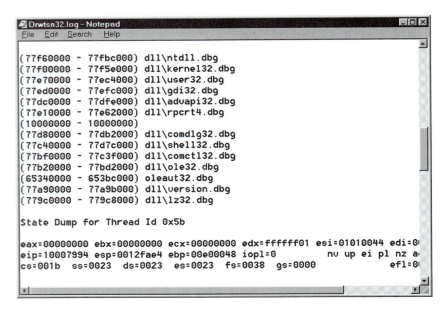

Figure 27.4 The Dr. Watson log now lists all program modules running on the system.

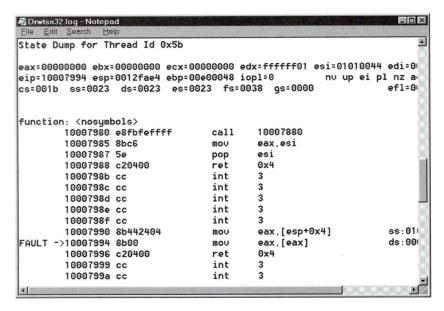

Figure 27.5 It is in the State Dump that you finally see what crashed the program.

THE EVENT VIEWER

One of the better troubleshooting tools provided by WINNT is one called Event Viewer. Event Viewer collects information on different activities that are generated by either hardware or software action. These events range from benign to critical, and Event Viewer frequently can provide information that helps the administrator diagnose what led up to the event.

Event Viewer reports three degrees of severity in its logs, as illustrated in **Table 27.1**.

Table 27.1   Event Viewer Severity Classifications

Symbol	Severity	Description
	Information	Information describes the successful operation of an application, driver, or service.
	Error	A significant problem, such as loss of data or loss of functionality.
	Warning	An event that is not necessarily significant, but may indicate a possible future problem.

There are three ways to get to Event Viewer. The first is to click Start→Programs→ Administrative Tools→Event Viewer, and another is to click Start→Run and type **eventvwr** into the command line. The third way is to type that same command at the command prompt. However you get there, the result will be similar to the screen shown in **Figure 27.6**.

The NT Event Viewer maintains three separate event logs. These are the Application Log, the System Log, and the Security Log. I've already mentioned that the Application Log is where Dr. Watson stores the event notifications that it generates when an application error occurs. The security log is only used if the system administrator has enabled a function called auditing. Auditing is a method by which a user's activities on the system can be tracked. A large number of events, including logon attempts, attempts to access system resources, and literally hundreds of others, can be tracked in NT. It is the Security Log that hosts the event notifications that are generated by auditing.

> **EXAM NOTE:** Make *sure* you know all three of the logs maintained by the NT 4.0 Event Viewer, as well as the type of information that is stored in each log.

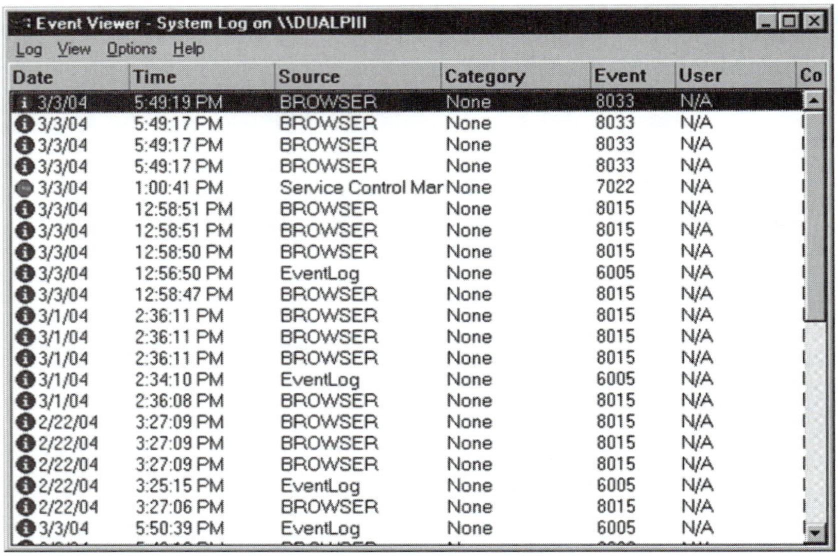

Figure 27.6 The Windows NT Event Viewer

The log that is used most frequently is the System Log. Here is where situations relating to system and network performance can be analyzed. When an error is generated, an event message similar to the one shown in **Figure 27.7** will be generated. Within this message is frequently good information relating to what caused the error.

TROUBLESHOOTING THE NOS THROUGH EVENTS

When you're first getting started with this network administration thing, it can appear to be overwhelming at first. You'll soon get over that. You'll find that all providers of network operating systems provide a substantial amount of support for their products. In Windows NT, 2000, and XP, the Event Viewer provides information on what caused a failure. If this doesn't help, you can take it a step further and make use of Microsoft's TechNet services on the Web page (currently at www.microsoft.com/technet/). A search of key words from the message is very likely to bring up several articles related to your problem. Novell offers very similar services, and Linux help can be obtained from Red Hat, Mandrake, and numerous other Linux vendors.

Another good resource for Microsoft users is the Windows 2000 or Windows XP Resource Guide. Again, Novell provides similar references for its NOS. In this kit you will find reams of information. Nearly every error message generated by the NOS is explained, and most causes of service or driver failure can be found in this guide. These are not inexpensive books, but compared to the cost of your NOS and/or the cost of the administrator's time, the resource guide is an essential tool for any administrator.

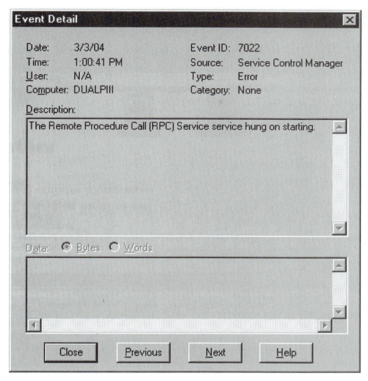

Figure 27.7   An error notification in the NT Event Viewer System Log

PERFORMANCE MONITOR

Performance Monitor is an application that ships with Microsoft server products that can monitor a huge number of system variables. Variables are broken down into groups called *system objects*. Within these objects are the *counters* themselves. The actual number of items that can be monitored is vast and to attempt to cover them all would require a complete volume in and of itself. However, a few items are of sufficient value to the network engineer to justify a brief discussion.

While Performance Monitor is not necessarily limited to monitoring hardware statistics, it is very useful in that respect. It can measure certain statistics concerning your processor, your memory, and the network interface. **Figure 27.8** is a graphic of Performance Monitor keeping track of system resources while I processed an image.

BUZZ WORDS

System object: On a system in general, it is any hardware or software entity to which specific properties can be assigned. In Performance Monitor, it is a category of events that can be monitored.

Object counter: In Performance Monitor, it is the specific property or variable for which data is being collected.

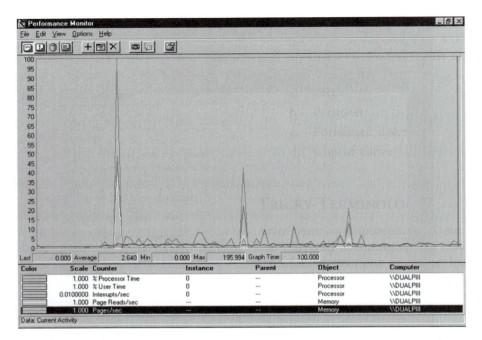

Figure 27.8 Performance Monitor allows you to collect data on the amount of strain specific aspects of your system's software or OS are experiencing.

Performance Monitor can be used in this way to generate a report that can let you know whether it is time to increase the amount of memory installed in a server, whether a second processor is in order, or whether your bandwidth is insufficient for your needs. To do this there are several key functions to watch.

EXAM NOTE: It isn't really necessary to know all of the different objects that can be studied by Performance Monitor. All you really need to know for the exam is the function of the tool and how it can be used to isolate problems. The rest of the information contained in this section is for the real-world user.

There are two system objects with very similar names that are not very similar in what they do. One is process, and the other is processor. Process keeps tab of the different processes from different applications running on the server, while Processor watches certain performance variables of the CPU. Both are useful to monitor if you think that your CPU might be a bottleneck.

Under Process, one of the key counters to watch is % Processor Time. This is the percentage of elapsed time that all of the threads of a specific process used the processor to execute instructions (the basic unit of execution in a computer). A thread is the object that executes instructions, and a process is a virtual object that is created when a program is run. If this value continually runs much higher than 60 percent, you should get a noticeable increase in performance if you add a second processor. On that note, if you already have multiple processors, it is possible to get values beyond 100 percent. Maximum percentage totals would be 100 percent times the number of processors installed in the system.

Another counter that can indicate the need for an additional processor is found in the Processor object. Unfortunately for beginners, the counter has the same name as the one I just discussed: % Processor Time. The difference here is that under the Process object, the variable describes the amount of processor time used by specific processes. Under the Processor object, it describes the amount of processor time used by *all* non-idle processes on the machine. (Each processor has an Idle thread that consumes cycles when it has no other threads to run.)

Under the Memory object, there are two key counters to watch. One is Pages/sec. Pages/sec is the number of pages read from (a *page read*) or written to (a *page write*) disk to resolve hard page faults. A hard page fault occurs when the CPU requires code or data that is not resident in physical memory and was not found in the page file. This indicates that, somewhere along the line, the processor expected to need that data, but there was insufficient memory to store it in RAM or the paging file. Any time this happens, the CPU experiences extensive and unnecessary delays.

> ## BUZZ WORDS
>
> **Page read/write:** When physical RAM in a system becomes full, data will be temporarily stored in a file called the paging file. A Page Read is a read operation from this file, while a Page Write is when data is moved from RAM to the paging file.
>
> **Page fault:** A non-critical error state that occurs when the OS looks for data in the paging file and fails to locate it.
>
> **Hard fault:** A situation in which data sought by the CPU was neither in memory nor in the paging file. As a result a new hard disk search must be initiated.
>
> **Soft fault:** The data requested by the CPU is in memory, but not part of the current working set of data. As a result, a new memory search must be initiated.

The second counter to watch is Page Faults/sec. This is somewhat like pages per second, but lets you know how many times the system hit the paging file looking for data that wasn't there. There are two types of page faults. A *soft fault* is where the data was actually present in memory, but not part of the working set. They generally don't affect the system too badly. A *hard fault* requires a search and retrieval by the hard drive and is an even more significant delay than a simple page read. Excessive Pages/sec and Page Faults/sec are indications that you need to install more RAM in your system.

The Network Interface Object can let you know how heavily the interface to the server is being hit. Two counters to monitor are Bandwidth and Output Queue Length. Bandwidth suggests how much of your available bandwidth is being used. Output Queue Length shows how many packets are resident in the buffer. You want this to be zero. One is acceptable, but two or more means you have a problem and need to locate the source of the bottleneck.

As I said earlier, there are literally hundreds of different counters in Performance Monitor. A good network engineer will make a more detailed study of this handy little application and put it to use.

NETWORK MONITOR

Most of Microsoft's OSs, since the days of Windows 9x, have shipped with a utility called Network Monitor (**Figure 27.9**). Network Monitor is a diagnostics tool that monitors traffic on the LAN and collects information by capturing packets and analyzing the headers and, in some cases, the contents of the packets.

Basic information displayed includes the following:

- The source address of the frame
- The destination address of the frame
- The protocols used in sending the frame
- The payload

The interesting thing is that Network Monitor is not installed by default. In order to use this service, it must first be installed. To do this, open Control Panel, click the Network applet, and then click the Services tab. Now click Add and select Network Monitor Tools and Agent. Make sure the NT CD is in the drive. After the files have been copied, you'll be prompted to restart your computer. Upon completion of the reboot cycle, Network Monitor will appear in the Administrative Tools (Common) menu.

EXAM NOTE: A question that frequently appears on the exam in various forms is one that checks to make sure you are aware that Network Monitor does not appear in a default installation. Keep that in the back of your mind.

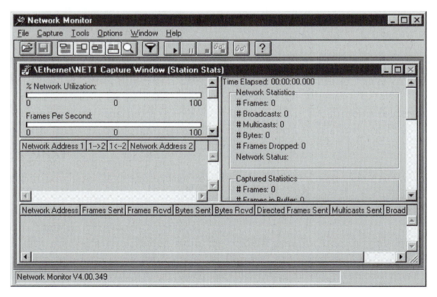

Figure 27.9 Network Monitor captures frames off of the network and provides the tools by which an engineer can analyze the frame.

In order for Network Monitor to work, the NICs installed in the computers need to work in *promiscuous mode.* This term is a colorful way of describing a mode of operation in which a network interface card (NIC) will accept all packets that arrive, regardless of intended destination.

Although Network Monitor will capture all packets passing through the NIC in a default configuration, it can be configured to filter packets on a large number of criteria. These criteria include addresses, protocols, NetBIOS names, and the list goes on.

Unfortunately, the version of Network Monitor that comes with Windows OSs is much like some of the evaluation software that can be downloaded off the Internet. Many of the functions displayed are disabled, working only on the version that ships with Microsoft's Systems Management Server (SMS).

BUZZ WORDS

Promiscuous mode: An operating mode for any network interface in which all incoming packets will be accepted, even if they are not intended for that specific interface.

Stop code: A number assigned to a particular catastrophic event, along with certain parameters that further define the event.

INSIDE THE BLUE SCREEN OF DEATH

When NT does crash and burn, it at least has the decency to leave behind one final message lingering on your screen. This is the infamous blue screen of death (BSOD) shown in **Figure 27.10**. Most people, upon being faced with a BSOD, either start panicking or begin lamenting their now lost data. Before you shut the machine down, you might want to take a look at the information presented on that screen.

There are five sections of the BSOD. The first section indicates precisely what failed. It simply doesn't tell you in English. The first line on the screen begins with ***** STOP**, followed by a rather long number. After this number are some additional numbers in parentheses, and finally a description strung together by underscores. In truth, this is the only section that contains information useful to the hardware technician or network engineer.

The second section identifies the CPU, and in the third section you get a list of all drivers that were running on the system at the time of the crash. The fourth section is a copy of each byte of data that was housed in the system stacks at the time of the crash. The stacks are areas of system memory reserved for the CPU to temporarily hold data until it needs it again. The last section simply tells you to try again, and, if necessary, to start in debug mode. Unless you are a seasoned programmer with experience writing code for operating systems, these last three sections will be about as useful to you as an ejection seat in a helicopter. So let's go back to that first section.

The number following ***** STOP** (in the illustration, the number shown is **0x00000019**) is a *stop code.* The only part of that number you really need is the 0x and any characters that follow the string of 0s. These characters are hexadecimal and, therefore, may contain the numbers 0–9 or the letters A–F. The stop code in the illustration would be referred to as Stop 0x19. A number of 0x0000000A would be Stop 0xA. You can look up stop codes on Microsoft's Web site.

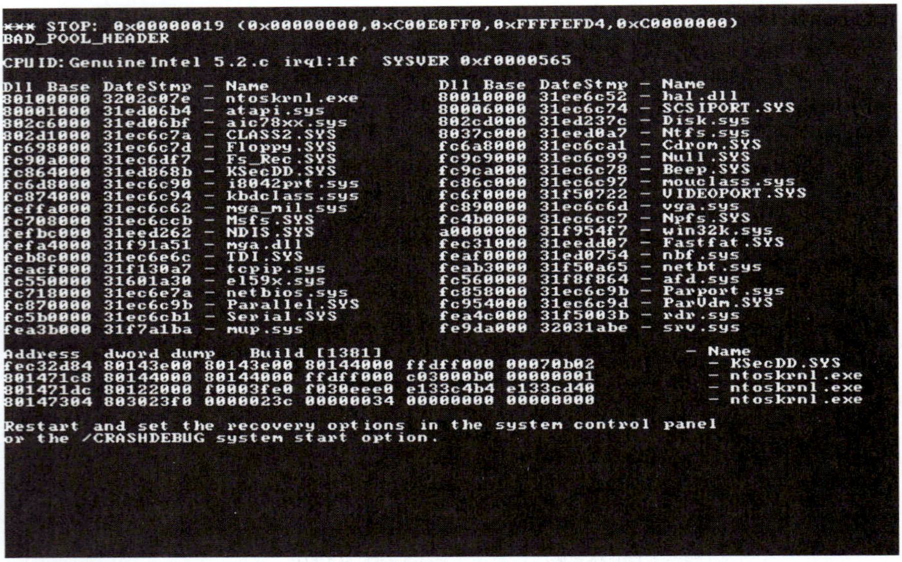

Figure 27.10 The blue screen of death contains information relating to the event that caused your system to crash.

The numbers in the parentheses are the stop code parameters. These parameters are also listed in hexadecimal and indicate, in order:

- The memory address of the error
- The IRQ level that was active
- The type of access that was being attempted (i.e., read or write)
- The address of the function that requested the function listed in the first parameter

There are several hundred stop codes listed on Microsoft's TechNet Web site. Fortunately, about 99 percent of all BSODs are the result of a few errors. **Table 27.2** lists the most commonly seen stop codes, their explanations, and possible fixes when they appear.

The parameters are rarely useful to the average technician in terms of troubleshooting. They are useful when searching TechNet for information. Some stop codes exhibit different parameters, depending on the failure, and by searching the knowledge base using the specific parameters, you get more specific help.

THE OTHER ADMINISTRATIVE TOOLS

One thing that differentiates NT from "lesser" operating systems is the array of tools that are provided to assist the user or administrator in the process of system and/or network administration. As you might expect, the collection of tools that ships with NT Workstation is not quite

Table 27.2 Blue Screen Stop Codes and their Meanings

Stop Code	Description	Explanation
0x19	BAD_POOL_HEADER	Frequently appears as a one-time failure, and the machine boots fine afterward. Can be the result of a failed remote procedure call, a corrupted driver, or an invalid application instruction. If it occurs repeatedly, try Last Known Good. If this fails, it's time for the backup/restore procedure.
0x1E	KMODE_EXCEPTION_NOT_HANDLED	A device driver has attempted an illegal CPU function. Either that or an application issued an instruction that could not be decompiled by NT. Unfortunately, you'll probably never know which. The error may or may not repeat itself.
0x35	NO_MORE_IRP_STACK_LOCATIONS	Either someone has attempted to access a shared resource on this computer for the first time and the remote procedure call failed, or you've just installed a new virus scanner. If it is the first situation, rebooting the machine will resolve the issue, and you'll probably never see it again. If it's the latter, you may need to check with the software vendor for a patch.
0x51	REGISTRY_ERROR	Oh, oh!! The registry is corrupted. If you're lucky, during the boot process, you can press F8 and select "Last Known Good." As long as there hasn't been a reboot that got as far as the logon screen since the last known good, this will restore that copy of the registry. If there has been, then I hope you have a backup.
0x77	KERNEL_STACK_INPAGE_ERROR	Information requested from the paging file could not be read. This can be the result of the data simply being corrupted, or it can be the result of a bad sector on the drive. Worst-case scenario is your controller is failing. Reboot the machine. If it is a bad sector, NT will mark it bad, and life will move on. If it's a bad controller, you may or may not get it again.
0x7B	INACCESSIBLE_BOOT_DEVICE	BOOT.INI is pointing to a partition that does not exist. If a new drive has just been installed, this simply means that drive letters changed. Edit BOOT.INI to point to the correct drive letter. Unfortunately, it can also mean a failed drive.
0x7F	UNEXPECTED_KERNEL_MODE	See 0x1E
0x80	NMI_HARDWARE_FAILURE	The CPU was just issued a nonmaskable interrupt that it couldn't handle. It's virtually always related to bad memory. A failed parity or ECC memory module will cause this; mixing parity with non-parity or ECC and non-ECC in the same system will also cause it. Replace the offending memory with good memory and reboot.
0xA	IRQL_NOT_LESS_OR_EQUAL	A device driver has attempted an illegal memory access function. Reinstall the device driver.

Most blue screens result from one of these stop codes.

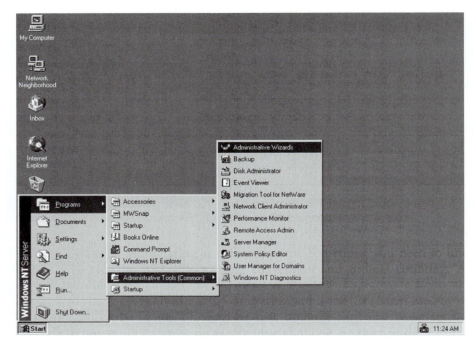

Figure 27.11   The NT Administrative Tools menu

as robust as that which NT Server sports. So in the following few pages, I'm going to list the tools that ship with Server. As I go, I'll point out the ones that do not ship with Workstation. I would also like to point out that because this is not intended to be a instructional manual on NT, I'm only going to give an overview of each tool and not spend a great deal of time on how to use each one.

To get to the Administrative Tools in NT, click Start→Programs→Administrative Tools (Common). The list of available tools appears in a menu, as shown in **Figure 27.11**. The list of tools in NT 4.0 includes the following:

- Administrative Wizards (Server only)

- Backup (Workstation and Server)

- Disk Administrator (Workstation and Server)

- Event Viewer (Workstation and Server)

- Migration Tool for Netware (Server only)

- Network Client Administrator (Server only)

- Network Monitor (Workstation and Server, but must be installed separately before it is available)

- Performance Monitor (Workstation and Server)

- Remote Access Admin (Workstation and Server)
- Server Manager (Server only by default; can be added to Workstation for remote server administration)
- System Policy Editor (Server only)
- User Manager for Domains (simply User Manager on Workstation)
- Windows NT Diagnostics (Workstation and Server)

As the list indicates, the available tools vary between the Server versions of NT and NT Workstation. In a couple of cases, a tool can be added to Workstation.

Some of the Administrative Tools were discussed previously and will not be rehashed here. This includes Backup. The backup tool in NT 4.0 is virtually identical to the one in WIN98. That was discussed in Chapter Twenty-Three, Introducing WIN9x. Disk Administrator and NT Diagnostics were discussed in Chapter Twenty-Six, Windows NT Architecture. Performance Monitor, Network Monitor, and Event Viewer were all discussed earlier in this chapter.

ADMINISTRATIVE WIZARDS

The Administrative Wizards applet (**Figure 27.12**) is a method by which eight of the most common administrative tasks can be accomplished by a user with little or no training. You select a task, and the Wizard provides step-by-step instructions for accomplishing that task. Naturally, you must have the appropriate privileges assigned, or the Wizard will bump you out.

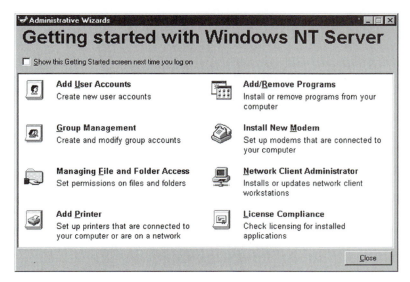

Figure 27.12   The NT Administrative Wizards applet allows even an untrained user to perform certain otherwise complex tasks.

Note that for each of these tasks there is an appropriate Administrative tool for accomplishing that same task. In most cases the Administrative Tool is going to offer some more advanced options not available in the Wizards.

CAUTION: If you are administering an NT 4.0 Small Business Server network and plan on using the Wizards on a regular basis, you should be cautious of using the Administrative Tool with Wizards you want to use. A small glitch in the software exists. If you ever use the Administrative Tool for a specific task, for some reason the Wizard will frequently (although not always) become disabled.

MIGRATION TOOL FOR NETWARE

At the time NT 4.0 was released, a company called Novell had an iron grip on the network server market. One of the goals Microsoft set for NT was to take some of this market share away from Novell. They were aware that very few network administrators were willing to rebuild a network from scratch simply so they could have the pleasure of using a Microsoft product. Microsoft needed a way of importing key network settings and resources from a NetWare server over to a Microsoft NT server.

The Migration Tool for NetWare was Microsoft's answer. This tool imports user accounts along with their associated permissions and privileges, security settings on various files and other resources, and all path information. The tool even had a facility for doing a test migration prior to attempting the real thing. During the test, any errors were detected and recorded in a log. This allowed the administrator to find these errors and fix them before performing the final migration.

NETWORK CLIENT ADMINISTRATOR

For a computer to become a member of any given network, the appropriate client software must be installed. The client software acts as the user interface between the workstation and the network server, and it also acts as a redirector. The redirector is a piece of software that looks at user requests and determines whether those requests can be fulfilled on the local machine or whether they require the services of some remote resource. If it is the latter, the client will issue a remote procedure call to the remote device.

Client software is specific to the OS running on the host computer and to the NOS running on the server. For example, if you have a Novell server and a WIN98 machine, the WIN98 machine would have to have the Microsoft Client for Novell NetWare installed. For an NT network, the Client for Microsoft Networks would be required.

The Network Client Administrator allows the administrator to create a bootable floppy diskette. This diskette then can be used to accomplish several tasks. It can install client software, ensuring that all hosts on the network have identical configurations. It can also be used to remotely install WIN9x OSs onto a host computer from a network location. And it can be used to install the Administrative Tools I've been discussing onto a WIN9x machine. Doing this would allow the administrator to remotely administer the network from a WIN9x workstation.

REMOTE ACCESS ADMIN

A feature of NT 4.0 that was popular with administrators was its ability to allow a user to log onto the network from a remote location. For example, if you were unable to make it in to work one day, you could log onto the network over a modem and work from home. For this to happen, two things need to be configured. The server has to have Remote Access Services (RAS) installed and configured, and the user's account has to be configured to allow access from outside the network. Remote Access Admin is the utility that allows easy configuration of RAS and user accounts.

SERVER MANAGER

Server Manager is where the administrator goes to administer NT domains and computers. One of the tasks that can be accomplished here is promoting a BDC to a PDC. In the event that the PDC goes down, or needs to be taken down for service, one of the BDCs can take its place. The administrator can also synchronize the PDC to all BDCS. By this, I mean that the SAM can be force-fed to the BDCs without waiting for the usual cycle. Server Manager is also where computers are added or removed from the domain (although a computer can also be added to the domain remotely). And certain other tasks, such as viewing connected users and in-use shares and resources, configuring administrative alerts, managing services and shares, and sending pop-up messages to connected users, can be accomplished here.

SYSTEM POLICY EDITOR

System Policy Editor is a utility that allows the administrator to create, edit, and manage policies that control the actions of individual users or computers, or that affect the entire network. A policy is a defined set of rules that control, restrict, and configure user desktop settings, profiles, and system configurations. System Policy Editor creates a file that overrules the local registry with new settings, so be cautious when you use it. For example, instead of editing default user and computer policies, create policies for specific users, computers, or groups on which you want to impose policies. If you get carried away with your policy, you can wind up prohibiting everyone, including administrators, from doing anything on a particular computer. This would include being able to override the policy you just created.

USER MANAGER FOR DOMAINS

User Manager for Domains is where the administrator goes to create and manage individual user accounts as well as group accounts. Throughout this book, I have pointed out that certain OSs allow the administrator to define permissions and privileges for any given user. This is where these tasks are performed in NT. The administrator can configure certain options as well. These options would include group membership of individual accounts, profile settings, and a predefined home directory for each user. It can also include logon script pointers, access scheduling, workstation privileges, and RAS restrictions.

Exam Note: Of all the Administrative Tools available in NT, the one that seems to get the most exposure on the Exam is User Manager. Understand its functions.

You can also control system policies regarding accounts, user rights, and audits. The account system policy sets parameters for user passwords and account lockouts for failed logon attempts. The user rights system policy sets rights for each group or user, such as accessing computers over the network, changing the system time and device driver controls, adding new software, and even shutting down the system. Another feature available from this tool is auditing. The administrator can select from a rather extensive list of events that he or she wants to watch. The events can be monitored for successful attempts, unsuccessful attempts, or both. Any time an audited event is detected by the server, an entry is added to the Security Log in Event Viewer.

Chapter Summary

Although this may be one of the shorter chapters in this book, it is nonetheless a very important one. Most of the tools discussed in this chapter carry over into subsequent versions of Microsoft OSs with little or no change. Therefore, as the book progresses, I will only be pointing out new additions or changes that occur.

This is also a chapter that holds a lot of information that shows up on the CompTIA exams. Even though NT is no longer "officially" considered an exam objective, there is still a great deal of coverage on the Administrative Tools. From the standpoint of practical applications, since there is still a large number of computers out there in the world that use NT 4.0, you need to be prepared when you run into one.

Brain Drain

1. What are some of the different actions that are taken by Dr. Watson when there is an application error on the system? How are they useful to the user?

2. Discuss how Event Viewer can be used as a troubleshooting tool.

3. You suspect that CPU performance has become a serious bottleneck in the system. How can you use Performance Monitor to back up your suspicions?

4. There is a computer on the network that is broadcasting thousands of random packets onto the network each second. How can you use Network Monitor to determine which computer on the network is responsible?

5. Discuss as many of the Administrative tools as you can think of. Point out how they are useful to the system administrator.

The 64K$ Questions

1. A crash dump is _____.

   a. A critical system error that results in a blue screen

   b. A sudden loss of all information from RAM, resulting in a system crash

c. A byte-by-byte copy of all information stored in RAM to the hard drive that occurs after a fatal system error

d. A place where they haul all the cars after a Demolition Derby

2. The entry *%windir%* _____.

a. Refers to the location of the NT Boot files

b. Refers to the location of the NT System Files

c. Always points to the WINNT directory

d. Always points to the root directory

3. When a fatal system error does occur, NT will copy all the information in RAM to a file. By default that file is stored in the _____ directory.

a. Root

b. WINNT

c. %windir%

d. WINNT/SYSTEM32

4. Which of the following is not a log maintained by the NT 4.0 Event Viewer?

a. Application

b. System

c. Security

d. Services

5. The individual variables that can be watched by Performance Monitor are called _____.

a. Threads

b. Object counters

c. System objects

d. Objects

6. A variable that Performance Monitor can study to keep track of memory performance is Pages/sec. This variable measures _____.

a. How many times the CPU requests data that does not exist in RAM

b. How many times the CPU requests data that does not exist in the paging file

c. How often the Virtual Memory Manager writes data to the paging file

d. How often the Virtual Memory Manager reads or writes data to the paging file

7. Page faults/sec is a variable that measures _____.

a. How many times the CPU requests data that does not exist in RAM

b. How many times the CPU requests data that does not exist in the paging file

c. How often the Virtual Memory Manager writes data to the paging file

d. How often the Virtual Memory Manager reads or writes data to the paging file

8. In order to function properly, Network Monitor requires that the system be equipped with a NIC that _____.

a. Features a boot PROM

b. Works in promiscuous mode

c. Supports full-duplex operation

d. Sits in a PCI slot

9. Network Monitor automatically loads when you install NT for the first time.

a. True

b. False

10. The blue screen of death is divided into _____ different sections.
    a. Three
    b. Four
    c. Five
    d. Six

11. Of these sections, _____ of them might be useful to the average technician.
    a. One
    b. Two
    c. Three
    d. Four
    e. Five
    f. Six

12. The code presented on the blue screen that specifically identifies the event that crashed the system is known as the _____.
    a. Stop code
    b. Crash dump
    c. Event identifier
    d. Event parameter

13. Which of the following Administrative tools will be found in NT Server, but not on NT Workstation?
    a. User Manager
    b. Network Client Administrator
    c. Disk Administrator
    d. Remote Access Admin

14. A redirector is a piece of software that is a function of the _____.
    a. Network client
    b. NOS
    c. Network-aware application
    d. Network protocol

15. RAS is a service that exists on Server versions of NT only.
    a. True
    b. False

16. In order to promote a BDC to PDC, the administrator would go to
    _____.
    a. Administrative Wizards
    b. System Policy Administrator
    c. Remote Access Admin
    d. Server Manager

17. Which two of the following tasks can be accomplished from the boot diskette created by Network Client Administrator?
    a. Restore the registry.
    b. Install an OS onto a workstation remotely.
    c. Install a client onto a workstation remotely.
    d. Rebuild the SAM.

18. Which of the following tools allows the Administrator to send a message across the network to a specific user?
    a. Administrative Wizards
    b. System Policy Administrator
    c. Remote Access Admin
    d. Server Manager

19. The Policy Editor is where the administrator would go in order to enable auditing.
    a. True
    b. False

20. Two ways to add a new user to the network in NT 4.0 Server are _____ and _____.
    a. Type **useradmin** from the command prompt

    b.   Run the Administrative Wizards

    c.   Go to Server Manager

    d.   Go to User Manager for Domains

TRICKY TERMINOLOGY

Crash dump: A direct copy of the entire contents of system RAM copied to a file on the hard disk.

Hard fault: A situation in which data sought by the CPU was neither in memory nor in the paging file. As a result, a new hard disk search must be initiated.

Object counter: In Performance Monitor, it is the specific property or variable for which data is being collected.

Page fault: A non-critical error state that occurs when the OS looks for data in the paging file and fails to locate it.

Page read/write: When physical RAM in a system becomes full, data will be temporarily stored in a file called the paging file. A Page Read is a read operation from this file, while a Page Write is when data is moved from RAM to the paging file.

Promiscuous mode: An operating mode for any network interface in which all incoming packets will be accepted, even if they are not intended for that specific interface.

Soft fault: The data requested by the CPU is in memory, but not part of the current working set of data. As a result, a new memory search must be initiated.

Stop code: A number assigned to a particular catastrophic event, along with certain parameters that further define the event.

System object: On a system in general, it is any hardware or software entity to which specific properties can be assigned. In Performance Monitor, it is a category of events that can be monitored.

ACRONYM ALERT

BSOD: Blue Screen of Death. The last message NT (and later Microsoft OSs) manages to choke out in its dying breath.

NIC: Network Interface Card

RAS: Remote Access Services. A service that allows clients to log onto the network from locations physically isolated from the network.

CHAPTER 28

AN INTRODUCTION TO WINDOWS 2000

Up until now, this book has served primarily as a history of operating systems. Starting with Windows 2000 (WIN2K) I am going to start treating these discussions as current events rather than history. There are vast numbers of machines in the world on which WIN2K serves as the OS. In fact, I have seen several instances where large organizations migrated to Windows XP, which is a more recent OS, and then reverted back to WIN2K because they felt it was more suitable for their operation.

WIN2K and NT share a lot of common ground. That is to be expected since WIN2K is based entirely on the NT kernel. However, there are a number of significant differences, both in internal architecture and in the user interface that need to be discussed. In this chapter, I'll go over the differences and similarities. In addition, I'll cover some different installation methods for WIN2K and compare the boot process to that of NT. Finally, I will go over some methods of troubleshooting the boot process.

A+ OPERATING SYSTEM TECHNOLOGIES EXAM OBJECTIVES

CompTIA objectives covered in this chapter include the following:

1.1 Identify the major desktop components and interfaces and their functions. Differentiate the characteristics of Windows 9x/Me, Windows NT 4.0 Workstation, Windows 2000 Professional, and Windows XP.

1.2 Identify the names, locations, purposes, and contents of major system files.

1.3 Demonstrate the ability to use command-line functions and utilities to manage the operating system, including the proper syntax and switches.

2.3 Identify the basic system boot sequences and boot methods, including the steps to create an emergency boot disk with utilities installed for Windows 9x/Me, Windows NT 4.0 Workstation, Windows 2000 Professional, and Windows XP.

2.4 Identify procedures for installing/adding a device, including loading, adding, and configuring device drivers and required software.

3.1 Recognize and interpret the meaning of common error codes and startup messages from the boot sequence, and identify steps to correct the problems.

THE WIN2K VERSIONS

In many respects, WIN2K is really nothing more than a hybrid of NT and WIN98. It takes the 32-bit infrastructure of NT along with its core architecture and then adds the PnP and multimedia capabilities of WIN98. For the most part, the interface is that of WIN98, although the seasoned WIN98 user is going to discover that some familiar utilities have changed, at least one notable one has disappeared, and several have been moved to different places.

WIN2K, like WINNT, ships in several different versions. **Table 28.1** lists those different versions and identifies their different memory and CPU requirements, their maximum capabilities, and their hard disk requirements. Over the next few pages, I'll give an overview of each of the versions.

WIN2K PROFESSIONAL

This is the OS that was intended for stand-alone computers or hosts on a network. This is the version of WIN2K you would want to install for running basic applications. For users migrating from WIN98, there are pros and cons. Anyone who has affection for older DOS or 16-bit Windows applications won't like it. At best, it's difficult to get these apps to run. In many cases, it's all but impossible for anyone but the most advanced user.

Table 28.1 A Comparison of the WIN2K Versions

Version	RAM (min/rec/max)	CPU (min/# supported)	HDD Requirements
Professional	64MB/4GB	P166/2	650MB for installation/ 2GB min recommended
Server	128MB/256MB/4GB	P166/4	1GB
Advanced Server	128MB/256MB/8GB	P166/8	1GB
Datacenter[1]	256MB/512MB/64GB	PIII Xeon/16 (32 via OEM)	2GB

[1] Datacenter information is included for comparison only. This OS is **not** available unbundled from a configured server.

The four different versions of WIN2K

On the other hand, many of the features added to WIN2K enhance productivity and increase security. Therefore, in the working environment, as long as updated productivity software is used, it is often the better choice. There were a large number of new features added to WIN2K to make this true. I've listed the most significant new features here, along with a brief description of what they are.

- *Automated Proxy*: Automatically locates a proxy server and configures Internet Explorer 5.01 (or later) to connect to the Internet through that server.

- *Driver Certification*: Informs the user as to whether or not a device driver has been tested and certified by Microsoft and gives the user the option of continuing or not.

- *Encrypting File System (EFS)*: Allows individual files and/or folders to be encrypted so that only the owner of the files can view them.

- *Group Policy*: Allows administrators to define the computing environment, including such aspects as security, user rights, desktop settings, applications, and resources, either locally or across the network. Group Policy works in conjunction with the Active Directory service and requires a Windows 2000 Server to be on the network.

- *Hibernate*: Copies the entire contents of RAM to a file on the hard drive, retains the paging file intact, and then shuts the system completely down. When the system is reactivated, hibernate mode is able to restore all programs and settings exactly the way they were before the system shut down.

- *Hot Docking*: Allows a user to dock or undock a notebook computer without changing hardware configuration or rebooting.

- *IEEE 1394*: Provides FireWire support.

- *IP Security Support (IPSec)*: Provides encryption of data over TCP/IP.

- *IrDA Support*: Provides secure, wireless communications between devices using the infrared communication.

- *Kerberos Support*: Provides industry-standard and high-strength authentication with fast, single logon multi-platform networks consisting of different operating systems such as UNIX, the most recent versions of NetWare, and Windows.

- *Microsoft Installer*: Works alongside the Windows Installer Service. Installation and removal of software is managed by the OS, minimizing the risk of user error and possible corruption of the registry.

- *Microsoft Management Console (MMC)*: Provides a centralized and consistent environment for management tools.

- *Multilingual User Interface (MUI)*: Allows the user interface to be presented in any one of several languages.

- *Offline Files and Folders*: Mirrors documents stored on a remote machine to the local machine and allows the user to disconnect from the network.

- *Offline Viewing*: Makes entire Web pages with graphics available for viewing offline. The user can view Web pages on the system when there is no network or Internet connection.

- *Personalized Menus*: Adapts the Start menu to show only the applications most recently used.

- *Plug 'n Play*: PnP was described in detail in Chapter Twenty-Three, Introducing WIN9x.

- *Preview Windows for Multimedia*: Allows the user to preview a snapshot of a multimedia file in Windows Explorer before opening the file.

- *Recovery Console*: A command-line console that allows the user to start and stop services, format drives, and read and write data on a local drive. Other administrative services are provided as well.

- *Reduced Reboot Requirements*: Eliminates many situations that required a system reboot in previous OSs. Many software installations also will not require reboots.

- *Remote Installation Services (RIS)*: Permits an operating system to be installed over the network. RIS also allows administrators to dictate standard settings in accordance with organizational requirements. RIS requires a Windows 2000 Server to be present on the network, but it does not need to be installed on each client computer.

- *Scalable Memory and Processor Support*: Supports up to 4GB of RAM and up to two symmetric multiprocessors.

- *Setup Manager*: Provides a graphical wizard that guides administrators through the process of creating installation scripts.

- *Smart Card Support*: Integrates smart card capabilities into the operating system.

- *Synchronization Manager*: Allows the user to compare and update offline files and folders with those on the network.

- *System Preparation Tool*: Helps administrators clone computer configurations, systems, and applications, resulting in simpler, faster, and more cost-effective deployment.

- *Troubleshooting Wizards*: Leads the user through some basic troubleshooting processes in order to isolate a problem.

- *Universal Serial Bus (USB) Support*: Lets the system interface with USB devices.

- *Windows File Protection*: Protects core system files from being overwritten by application installs. Should a file be overwritten, Windows File Protection can automatically replace that file with the correct version.

- *Windows NT Security Model*: See Chapter Twenty-Five, The World of NT, for a description of the NT security model.

- *Disk Defragmentation*: This old friend from WIN9x had disappeared from NT. However, fragmentation can have more impact on servers than it does workstations. Defrag can be done on the fly while users continue to access the network.

- *Safe Mode Boot*: Another old friend from WIN9x that returns in W2K. Booting in Safe Mode allows users to troubleshoot the system during startup by changing the default settings or removing a newly installed driver that is causing a problem.

- *Backup and Recovery*: A more advanced backup utility than was present in WIN9x, this utility allows unattended backups.

WIN2K SERVER AND ADVANCED SERVER

These two products were Microsoft's mainstays in the NOS market for three years. Even the release of XP Server did nothing to slow their sales. It wasn't until the release of Windows 2003 server products that IT professionals' attention began to turn elsewhere.

The enhanced security offered by the WIN2K products was adequate reason for many organizations to make the move from NT. For many others, just the idea of having a Plug 'n Play server was attractive.

W2K Server is the basic server product offered in this line and is more than adequate for even large networks. It offers all of the advantages of NT 4.0 and then adds features such as the Encrypted File System (EFS), Kerberos and IPSec security, and much more. W2K Advanced Server goes even further. With Advanced Server multiple servers can be combined into a single "super server" using clustering services. Servers with as many as eight CPUs and up to 8GB of RAM are possible. The features are so many and varied that it's best if I simply provide a list of features, followed by short descriptions of each one. The server products include all of the features listed in W2K Workstation, as well as the following advanced features:

- *4GB Memory Support (8GB for Advanced Server)*: Larger amounts of memory serve to improve performance of applications and NOS functions.

- *4-way Symmetric Multiprocessor Support*: Scale up by utilizing the latest 4-way SMP servers for more processing power. Windows 2000 Advanced Server delivers support for up to 8-way SMP servers.

- *Active Directory Integration*: Active Directory incorporates the underlying security infrastructure into an encrypted relational database that serves as the focal point for network security.

- *Active Server Pages (ASP) Programming Environment*: A scripting language that allows a server to run interactive Web-based applications.

- *Application Certification & DLL Protection*: Applications certified to run on Windows 2000 Server are tested by Microsoft to ensure high quality and reliability. Protects DLLs installed by applications from conflicts that can cause application failure.

- *Automatic Restart*: Administrators can configure services throughout the operating system to restart automatically if they fail.

- *Centralized Desktop Management*: Manage users' desktop resources by applying policies based on the business needs and location of users. IntelliMirror management technologies install and maintain software, apply correct computer and user settings, and ensure that users' data is always available.

- *Cluster Administrator (Advanced Server)*: Run Cluster Administrator from any Windows NT or Windows 2000 system to remotely control multiple clusters from a single location.

- *Cluster Service (Advanced Server)*: 2-node Cluster Service can be configured to maintain a backup server to keep the network running in the event of hardware or software failure, or failure of critical applications, including databases, knowledge management, and file and print services.

■ *Component Object Model + (COM+)*: A collection of integrated services and features that makes it easier for developers to create and use software components in any language, using any tool. COM+ includes Transaction Services and Message Queuing Services for reliable distributed applications.

■ *Delegated Administration*: Active Directory allows administrators to assign selected administrative privileges to appropriate individuals in order to distribute the management and improve administration efficiency.

■ *Directory Synchronization Tools*: These tools make it easier for the administrator to maintain and synchronize data between Active Directory and Microsoft Exchange or Novell servers running Network Directory Services (NDS).

■ *Directory-Enabled Applications*: Developers can use a number of standard interfaces to write applications that utilize information stored in the Active Directory service about users, other applications, and devices. All Active Directory functions are available through the Lightweight Directory Access Protocol (LDAP), the Active Directory Service Interface (ADSI), and the Messaging Applications Programming Interface (MAPI) for extending and integrating with other applications, directories, and devices.

■ *Disk Quotas*: Administrators can set limits on the amount of disk space usage each user and/or volume can consume and then strictly enforce those limits.

■ *Distributed File System (DFS)*: Build a single, hierarchical view of multiple file servers and file server shares on a network. DFS makes the entire network look like a really big hard disk to the average user.

■ *Dynamic System Configuration*: Add new volumes, extend existing volumes, break or add a mirror, or repair a RAID 5 array while the server is online, without impacting the end-user.

■ *Hierarchical Storage Management*: This service automatically migrates data that hasn't been accessed for a while to alternative storage locations, maximizing disk space for the most heavily accessed data on the disk.

■ *High Throughput and Bandwidth Utilization*: Increased bandwidth support combined with decreased overhead increases overall network performance.

■ *IIS Application Protection*: Application protection keeps Web applications running separately from the Web server itself, preventing an application from crashing the Web server.

■ *IIS CPU Throttling*: Prevents a single application and/or Web site from dominating available CPU process time.

■ *Integrated Directory Services*: Microsoft's implementation of LDAT, Active Directory is a scalable, standard-compliant directory service that makes Windows 2000 easier to manage, more secure, and more interoperable with existing investments.

■ *Internet Information Services 5.0 (IIS)*: Integrated Web services enable users to easily host and manage multiple Web sites on a single server. Web-based business applications and file and print services can be extended over the Internet.

- *Internet Printing*: Print jobs can be transmitted over the Internet to a URL.

- *Kernel-Mode Write Protection*: Helps prevent errant code from interfering with system operations.

- *Kill Process Tree*: Stop all processes related to an errant process or application without rebooting the system.

- *Multi-Master Replication*: Unlike NT 4.0 where there was only a single master copy of SAM, Active Directory uses multi-master replication to ensure high scalability and availability in distributed network configurations. There are no longer specific PDCs and BDCs. All authentication servers maintain master copies and then synchronize with other authentication servers on the network.

- *Multimedia Delivery Platform*: With integrated Windows Media Services, administrators can distribute high-quality digital media content across the Internet and intranets. This includes the simultaneous delivery of live and on-demand content to a large number of users.

- *Network Load Balancing (NLB) (Advanced Server)*: Multiple servers can be configured to share the burden in high-traffic areas of the network.

- *PKI Group Policy Management*: Centrally manage domain-wide PKI policies. Specify which Certificate Authorities a client will trust, distribute new root certificates, adjust IPSec policy, or determine whether a user will be required to use smart cards to log on to a particular system.

- *Public Key Infrastructure (PKI)*: The Certificate Server is a critical part of a public key infrastructure that allows customers to issue their own x.509 certificates to their users for PKI functionality such as certificate-based authentication, IPSec, secure email, and so on. Integration with Active Directory simplifies user enrollment.

- *Remote Management with Terminal Services*: Allows Terminal Services to be safely used for remote administration purposes. Up to two concurrent sessions are supported.

- *Routing and Remote Access Service*: Connects remote workers, telecommuters, and branch offices to the corporate network through dial-up, leased line, and Internet links.

- *Security Configuration Toolset (SCTS)*: A management console that allows the administrator to use Group Policy to set and periodically update security configurations of computers on the network.

- *Terminal Services*: Windows-based applications run on the server rather than from the workstation. This maximizes performance in low-bandwidth networks

- *Virtual Private Networking (VPN)*: A full-featured gateway that encrypts communications to securely connect remote users and satellite offices over the Internet. Now with an updated PPTP support and advanced security with Layer 2 Tunneling Protocol.

- *Web Folders*: Web Folders provide the utilitarian comfort of an Explorer-like interface to the Web using Web Document Authoring and Versioning (WebDAV). This service enables the user to extend drag and drop capabilities to Web publishing.

- *Windows DNA 2000*: Windows Distributed InterNet Applications Architecture (Windows DNA 2000) is an application development model for the Windows platform.

With this architecture, programmers can build secure, highly scalable cross-platform applications.

- *Windows Management Instrumentation*: A uniform model through which management data from any source can be managed in a standard way. Windows Management Instrumentation (WMI) provides this for software such as applications, while WMI extensions for the Windows Driver Model (WDM) provide this for hardware or hardware device drivers. WMI in Windows 2000 enables management of even more functions.

- *Windows NT 4.0 Domain Migration Tools*: Allows the administrator to migrate an NT 4.0 domain to W2K with a minimum of effort.

- *Windows Script Host (WSH)*: A command line utility that allows the administrator to manage scripts.

- *XML Parser*: Support for the Extended Markup Language. This is the latest in interactive Web page scripting languages.

W2K DATACENTER

Microsoft Windows 2000 Datacenter Server is designed for enterprises that demand the highest levels of availability and scalability. An organization that is running extremely large mission-critical databases or is involved in the processing of a large volume of real-time transactions might consider this product.

Windows 2000 Datacenter Server is the most powerful and functional server operating system ever offered by Microsoft. In fact, it's so powerful, you're not even allowed to buy it! Not by itself, anyway. This NOS comes bundled with preconfigured servers provided by a select number of vendors that have been approved by Microsoft. It supports SMP servers of up to thirty-two CPUs and up to 32GB of physical memory. The latter is accomplished through a technology Microsoft calls Physical Address Extension (PAE). It provides both 4-node clustering and load balancing services as standard features.

Because W2K Datacenter is such a specialized NOS, the only thing you really need to know about it for the CompTIA exam is that it exists, how many processors it supports, and how much RAM it supports. The advanced features of this NOS are beyond the scope of this book.

INSTALLATION METHODS FOR W2K

As with previous versions of Windows, WIN2K can be installed as either an upgrade to an existing Windows operating system or as a clean install. And once again, unless there are overwhelming reasons for performing an upgrade, I'm going to once again strongly recommend the clean install.

Regardless of which installation you select, there are three options available for installing WIN2K:

- Setup boot disks
- CD-ROM
- Network installation

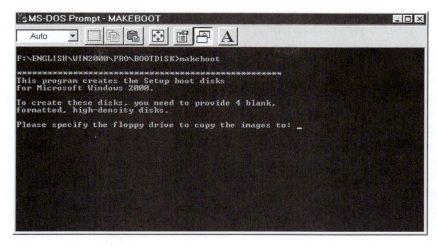

Figure 28.1   The MAKEBOOT utility is located in the BOOTDISK directory of the WIN2K Installation CD.

SETUP FLOPPIES AND CD-ROM INSTALLATION

The setup boot disk installation method requires the use of four setup floppy disks. As with NT, these disks can be made from the WIN2K installation CD on any machine running a Microsoft operating system. The command for creating those disks is different for WIN2K, however. You can create the WIN2K installation floppies in one of two ways. The files required for creating these disks are located in the bootdisk directory of the WIN2K installation CD. The command is MAKEBOOT.BAT. You can either browse to this file in Windows Explorer and double-click, or you can click Start→Run and type **D:\bootdisk\makeboot** (where D represents the actual drive letter of your CD-ROM drive). You'll get a screen like the one in **Figure 28.1**. You will need four blank formatted floppy diskettes available to complete the process. If there is data on a disk, MAKEBOOT will reject it.

The setup boot disk method of installation will be required if the computer on which the operating system is to be installed does not support the bootable CD-ROM format. If your system supports booting from a CD (which they all have done for several years now), the easier method is to boot from the CD-ROM and let Setup take it from there. Many machines that are capable of doing this simply haven't been configured to do so. Therefore, if your machine is not booting to the WIN2K installation CD, before going to the trouble to make the floppies check your CMOS settings to ensure that your computer is configured to boot from CD.

NETWORK INSTALLATION

One of the newest features of WIN2K, in both the Server and Workstation versions, is that the installation files can be located on a remote server, and a large number of computers can be configured at the same time over the network. The remote location on which the installation files will be stored is called a *distribution server.* The client computers wishing to install the WIN2K OS will need to be able to boot to an appropriate network client. This can be done in one of two ways.

BUZZ WORDS

Distribution server: A centralized storage location for the installation files of operating systems or applications.

The easiest way is if you're performing an upgrade on machines with an existing Microsoft OS installed. Simply boot the machine, log on to the network, and browse to the distribution server. Double-click WINNT32.EXE and let the fun begin. For machines requiring a clean install, the process is a bit more complicated.

For a clean install to a fresh system over the network, you must have a network card that is PXE-compliant. This means that the NIC supports the BootP protocol. BootP is a protocol that allows a computer to boot from files stored on a remote device. If it was made in the last several years, it most likely does. Next, you must create a boot disk that loads a NIC driver and a basic network client that can then connect to the distribution server. How this is done varies slightly among manufacturers, but many make it easy. For example, on its support site, 3Com provides a utility called MBADISK.EXE that creates the floppy for you. When you run this utility, as it creates the disk it asks you to configure what protocol to use. (I'll be discussing network protocols in more detail in Chapter Thirty-Three, Operating Systems and Networking.) The default protocol is the Preboot Execution Environment (PXE) protocol. This is a newer implementation of the BootP I mentioned earlier. Either of these protocols works by sending a broadcast out over the network, looking for a distribution server. This server then provides the essential information for booting the network client.

At this point, most professional administrators rely on scripts that they create in order to make the process work smoothly. However, scripting an unattended installation is beyond the scope of a book on basic operating systems. For more information on how to do this, refer to a good reference on your specific NOS.

After the network client machine has been booted to the distribution server, the installation can be performed in a manner similar to that of the floppy diskette or CD-ROM installation. You do need to remember to remove the network boot diskette from the drive before the first system reboot, unless you want to start all over again.

THE WINDOWS 2000 UPGRADE

There are situations where an upgrade is the best way to go, assuming that it's possible. The different versions of WIN2K have different requirements in terms of what previous OSs can be upgraded. If you are installing a WIN2K Professional OS, you can upgrade from the following:

- Windows 95 (any release)
- Windows 98 (any release)
- NT 3.51 Workstation
- NT 4.0 Workstation

You may *not* upgrade to WIN2K Professional from these OSs:

- MS-DOS (any version)
- WIN3.x (any version)
- WINMe

If you are upgrading a network operating system the requirements are slightly different. You *may* upgrade to WIN2K Server or Advanced Server from the following NOS versions:

- NT Server 3.51
- NT Server 4.0
- NT Server 4.0 Enterprise Edition
- NT Server 4.0 Terminal Server Edition

You may *not* upgrade from these:

- MS-DOS (any version)
- WIN3.x (any version)
- WIN9x (any version)
- NT Workstation (any version)
- NT Server 3.51 for Citrix
- Microsoft BackOffice Small Business Server (any version)

> **BUZZ WORDS** ─────────
>
> **Report phase:** A part of the WIN2K installation procedure that seeks out and logs programs and device drivers that are likely to cause problems.

There is no upgrade path for Datacenter. But since that is available only on preconfigured servers, that should come as no surprise.

When performing an upgrade, an additional phase is added to the installation procedure. This is called the *report phase*. During this phase, WINNT.EXE (or WINNT32.EXE) will scan the system registry and all .INI files looking for installed components, software, and device drivers. Any inconsistencies that it finds at this time, such as programs that are known to not run on WIN2K or incompatible device drivers, are reported to the user. It also generates an installation script based on the information it finds.

After the user has prompted the setup program to continue, it will keep track of all registry settings, user profiles, user accounts and associated security settings, and path locations. All of this will be migrated into the new installation.

THE WIN2K BOOT PROCESS

If you were to watch two machines, one running WINNT and the other WIN2K, booting side by side, it would be very easy to think that the boot process between the two OSs was identical. In terms of the files that are required during the boot process, there are no differences. But the boot process is somewhat different in the steps that it takes to load different files. The boot process can essentially be broken down into two steps. The first step is the hardware boot, and the following things happen:

- During the hardware boot, POST checks all hardware devices on the system, including memory, video, and all communications ports.
- PnP scans for any new hardware that has been installed since the last POST.
- Bootstrap Loader searches for a viable master boot record.

Once the MBR has been located, the hardware boot phase has come to an end. The rest of the process involves loading all the necessary software to make the system work well enough to initiate the Kernel Load. In step two these things happen:

- The MBR locates and reads BOOT.INI.
- If WIN2K is selected, NTLDR is located and loaded.
- If an earlier OS is selected, BOOTSECT.DOS is located and loaded.

Since I'm not interested in earlier OSs at this point in time, I'll assume WIN2K has been selected and take the process from there. As with NT, WIN2K locates and loads NTLDR, and the Kernel and Executive Systems begin to initialize. This can be broken down into three phases, the Kernel Load, the Kernel Initialization, and the Services Load.

KERNEL LOAD

This brings you to Step Three, Kernel Load. The first thing that NTLDR does is to locate and load NTOSKRNL.EXE, followed by HAL.DLL. If the user has more than one hardware profile configured, a menu will appear prompting the user to select which profile to load. NTLDR reads the system registry key into memory and selects the hardware configuration and control set that will be used based on the profile selected by the user. NTLDR scans the registry looking for any device drivers that have a start value of 0x0 and loads them.

> **NOTE:** By adding the switch /SOS to BOOT.INI, the user can see the drivers listed on the screen as they are loaded. This can be useful in troubleshooting if, for any reason, Windows doesn't want to load. It's easy to see what driver is trying to load when the system hangs.

KERNEL INITIALIZATION

After NTOSKRNL.EXE has been initialized, a copy of the current control set is made and transferred into memory as the Clone control set. The information collected by NTDETECT.COM during step two is used to create the HARDWARE key in the registry. The device drivers loaded in step two are initialized, and NTOSKRNL.EXE will now scan the registry looking for device drivers that have a start value of 0x1.

SERVICES LOAD

This step begins when NTOSKRNL.EXE loads the Session Manager (SMSS.EXE). SMSS.EXE reads a section of the registry with the heading of BootExecute and runs the programs listed in that section. Next, a file called WINLOGON.EXE is located and loaded. This launches LSASS.EXE. The familiar window that prompts the user to press <Ctrl>+<Alt>+<Delete> to log on appears. You'd think that the Services Load procedure is finished at this point. But you'd be wrong. The Service Controller (SCREG.EXE) now scans the registry for services with a start value of 0x2, and loads them. When these files are loaded and running, this phase has ended.

> ### BUZZ WORDS
>
> **Control set:** A collection of registry settings that defines the system configuration for Windows during the boot process.

LOGON

Finally, the user gets to make use of that logon prompt. Here is where the user types in his or her credentials and is either allowed onto the system or not. LSASS.EXE compares the information typed into these fields with information stored in SAM.

In WIN2K, the boot is not logged as successful until there has been an attempt at a logon. Note that it does not have to be a successful logon, merely an attempt. As far as the boot process is concerned, whether or not LSASS.EXE authenticates the user or not, once the credentials have been typed in and either accepted or rejected, it's considered a successful logon. After a successful logon is registered, the Clone control set that was created in the Kernal Initialization phase is copied to a new control set. A *control set* is a collection of registry settings that define system configuration information such as what device drivers to load and any parameters that have been set for those drivers. The next time the system boots, it becomes available as an advanced boot option in the later half of Step 2. **Figure 28.2** shows the control sets in the Windows registry.

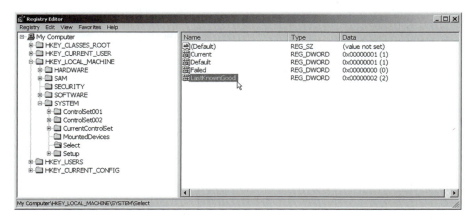

Figure 28.2 Windows 2000 (and up) maintains multiple control sets. A line in the registry (highlighted) identifies which control set contains Last Known Good information.

ABOUT CONTROL SETS

The Windows registry maintains all the information relating to the service configuration of the OS, such as drivers, customized driver settings, and so forth in a hive in the registry called a control set. Control sets are stored in HKEY_LOCAL_MACHINE>SYSTEM. There are usually three control sets (although there can be more) stored. These control sets are identified with the names ControlSet001, ControlSet002, and CurrentControlSet. The CurrentControlSet contains the parameters that are necessary for the system to boot up correctly.

ControlSet001 is created when the system is first configured. Later on down the road, if any changes are made to the system configuration, a copy of the original control set is made into the registry and called ControlSet002. A new set with the changes is called ControlSet001. Under HKEY_LOCAL_MACHINE>SYSTEM>SELECT is a registry key labeled LastKnownGood. This entry identifies which control set to load in the event that the user selects Last Known Good as an advanced boot option.

Advanced Boot Options

During Step 2 of the boot process, a message appears at the bottom of the screen telling the user that in order to view the Advanced Boot Options, he or she should press F8. F8 brings up a menu that allows the user to boot WIN2K in a number of different modes. These options are listed, along with brief descriptions, in **Table 28.2**.

Changes to the User Interface

Primarily, WIN2K was designed to add a WIN98 desktop to a WINNT environment. All of the user functionality, including right-button mouse functions, menu structures, and icons migrated from the older OS to the newer. There were a few changes that must be noted. Some of the things I'll be looking at in this section include the Start menu, Administrative Tools, and Control Panel. I'll also take a look at some utilities that have been either added or modified greatly in WIN2K and some changes that have been made to common file locations, such as My Documents and the Desktop.

Start Menu

The Start menu saw a lot of changes in the transition from WIN9x/NT to WIN2K. WIN2K borrowed the concept of personalized menus from WINMe. Certain items that were originally not part of the Start menu were added. In addition, there are more ways in which the Start menu can be customized (see **Figure 28.3**). By clicking Start→Settings→Task Bar & Start Menu, and then selecting the Advanced tab, a number of different options can be configured:

- *Display Administrative Tools*: Includes the Administrative Tools as menu items.

- *Display Favorites*: Web sites bookmarked in IE Explorer's Favorites menu are displayed.

- *Display Logoff*: An option to log off as user is included.

- *Expand Control Panel*: Generates a sub-menu in the Control Panel option that includes a shortcut to each applet within the control panel.

- *Expand My Documents*: Shows most recently opened documents.

- *Expand Network and Dialup Connections*: Generates a sub-menu that includes a shortcut to each configured network interface or dialup connection on the system.

Table 28.2   Windows 2000 Advanced Boot Options

Start Menu Option	Description
Safe Mode	Loads the minimum device drivers and system services needed to start the system. Does not load programs located in the Startup program group.
Safe Mode with Networking	Similar to standard Safe Mode; however, essential services and drivers needed to get the system on the network are loaded.
Safe Mode with Command Prompt	Similar to standard Safe Mode, but boots the machine to a command prompt rather than the GUI shell.
Enable Boot Logging	Creates a log file, NTBTLOG.TXT in the %SystemRoot% folder, during normal startup, which logs the name and the load status of all drivers as they are loaded into memory.
Enable VGA Mode	Bypasses advanced video drivers and loads only basic VGA. In the event of a corrupted or incorrect video driver, this allows the system to be booted and the situation corrected.
Last Known Good Configuration	Reverts to the last successfully started system configuration. (Discussed in the previous section.)
Directory Services Restore Mode	This option only appears on Windows 2000 domain controllers. Displays system information such as the number of processors, amount of main memory, Service Pack status, and build number during startup.
Debugging Mode	Starts Windows 2000 in kernel debug mode, which allows a debugger to break into the kernel for troubleshooting and system analysis.
Boot Normally	Starts Windows 2000, loading all normal startup files and registry values.

If WIN2K won't boot normally, the Advanced Boot Options offer a number of different ways in which it might be loaded.

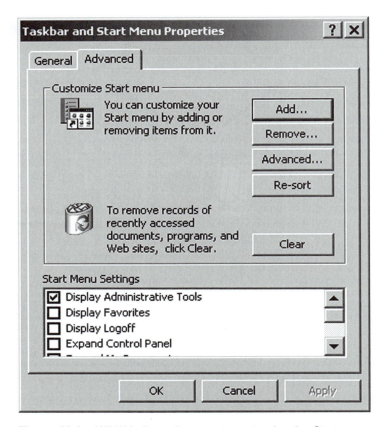

Figure 28.3 WIN2K allows the user to customize the Start menu in a number of different ways.

- *Expand Printers*: Generates a sub-menu that includes a shortcut to each installed printer on the system.
- *Scroll Programs Menu*: Determines whether the Programs section of the Start menu will be displayed in multiple columns or provide a scrolling action when there are too many items to display in a single column on the screen.

ADMIN TOOLS

Most of the changes made to Admin Tools (**Figure 28.4**) are additions of new elements. Many of these new items are the result of changes in the WIN2K architecture, such as the inclusion of Active Directory. Some of the changes involve renaming familiar faces from NT. Admin Tools changes present in WIN2K include the following:

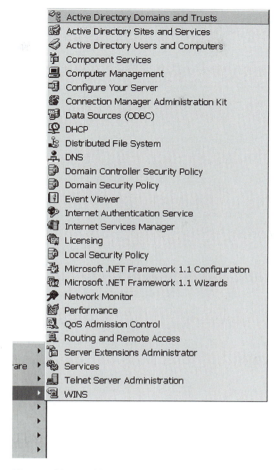

Figure 28.4   WIN2K sports a new collection of Admin Tools to aid the administrator.

- *Active Directory Domains and Trusts*: Replaces Server Manager and adds several new features.
- *Active Directory Sites and Services*: Administers the virtual network topology, including various locations, installed authentication servers, and replication services.
- *Active Directory Users and Computers*: Replaces Account Manager for Domains in NT.
- *Component Services*: Provides a model for building applications that makes use of blocks of existing code, rather than assembling programs one line at a time.

- *Computer Management*: Assembles the applets used for monitoring or administering local system resources, including Event Viewer, Performance Monitor, Disk Manager, and others.
- *Domain Controller Security Policy*: Manage Security Policies of the network domain specifically managed by the local server.
- *Domain Security Policy*: Allows local domain administration, including user rights and audit policies.
- *Local Security Policy*: Administers security on the local machine.

CONTROL PANEL

There are really only two drastic changes to the Control Panel. One of them is that Administrative Tools can now be accessed from Control Panel in WIN2K Professional. (Although one of the Start menu options is to include these tools in the Start menu as well.)

A second change is in the structure of the System Applet. In previous Microsoft OS versions, certain network settings such as computer identification and domain membership were included in the Network applet. WIN2K migrates these two functions over to the System applet. A Hardware tab collects several different tools from previous OSs and puts them under one roof. In the Hardware tab of the System applet, the user will find a shortcut to the Add/Remove Hardware Wizard, a Driver Signing applet, a shortcut to Device Manager, and a wizard for managing hardware profiles.

WIN2K UTILITIES

The first thing I'm going to do in this section is revisit an old friend from WIN9x: the Backup utility. In the WIN2K Backup utility, the user gets all of the same functionality of the WIN9x version, and then some. The most prominent difference is that this utility now supports scheduled unattended backups of system and user data (**Figure 28.5**). Users can now schedule nightly backups, weekly backups, and one-time backups to occur at a time that is convenient. As long as they make sure that a usable tape is in the drive, the backup will occur. Users can also specify whether to perform a full, incremental, differential, or daily backup.

Another nifty little tool included by Microsoft is the Microsoft Management Console (MMC). Even though you may not have been aware of it at the time, as I was discussing certain Admin Tools, I was discussing applets generated by MMC. Microsoft provided users with the ability to create their own custom Admin Tools through MMC (**Figure 28.6**). Each one of the tools available, either through the Start menu or through Control Panel, is available as a *snap-in.* The user opens MMC, elects to create a new console and adds whatever snap-ins he or she desires. Once that console has been saved under a unique name, it will appear in the collection of Admin Tools.

BUZZ WORDS

Snap-in: An applet that can be added to customized consoles in Microsoft Management Console.

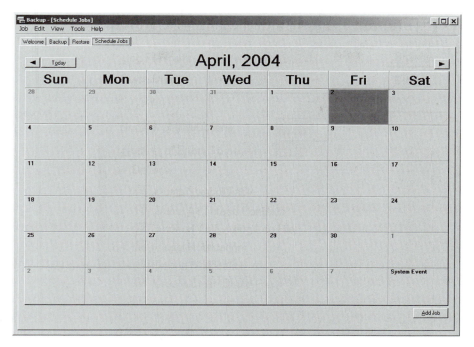

Figure 28.5
The WIN2K Backup utility adds the ability to schedule unattended backups to its arsenal.

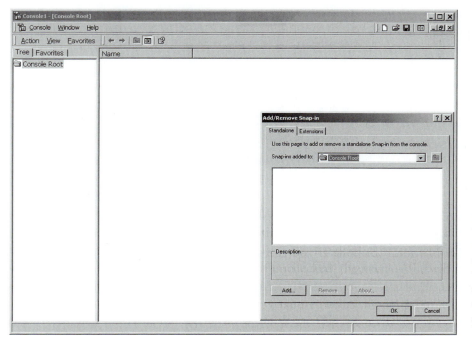

Figure 28.6
The Microsoft Management Console allows the user to create customized Administrative Tools.

TROUBLESHOOTING THE WIN2K BOOT PROCESS

Because the boot process of WIN2K is so complex, when things go wrong, it can sometimes be difficult to figure out what went wrong. Fortunately WIN2K provides a number of different tools for troubleshooting this process. One of these is the BSOD, which I discussed in Chapter Twenty-Seven. There are no notable differences between the blue screen of WIN2K and that of NT. Some other tools that are available include Last Known Good, Safe Mode, the System File Checker, the Recovery Console, and the Emergency Repair Diskette. Each one of these tools offers a different way into the system in the event of failure.

LAST KNOWN GOOD

This is a failsafe method that allows the user to boot the machine in the event that, during the previous session, a new device driver is installed that renders the computer unbootable, or an existing driver is somehow corrupted. By pressing F8 during Step 2, a menu of advanced boot options appears (**Figure 28.7**).

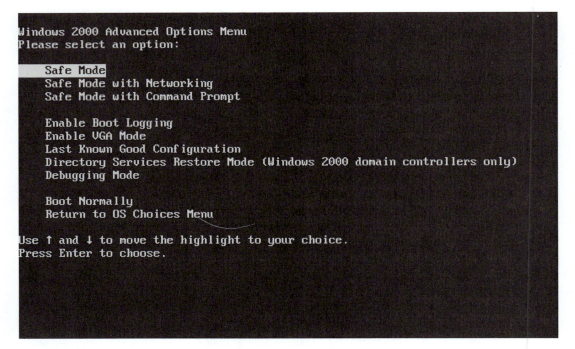

Figure 28.7   Press F8 during the boot process to bring up the Advanced Boot Options. Last Known Good forces the system to boot to the last configuration that successfully booted to a logon prompt.

Selecting this option forces the system to load the registry settings loaded in the Control Set identified by the registry as being the Last Known Good. This is in contrast with a normal boot, which loads device information collected by NTDETECT.COM. Since the LastKnownGood control set was created before the user installed the bad driver, your system makes no attempt to load the offending driver. The system starts normally.

SAFE MODE

Safe Mode is a boot option that had been a part of WIN9x, which was dropped in WINNT. When Last Known Good fails, usually because the problem wasn't detected until a successful attempt at a user logon, then Safe Mode becomes your new best friend. As mentioned in Table 28.2, Safe Mode loads only a minimal set of drivers. For example, unless you choose Safe Mode with Networking, device drivers for the NIC and all networking protocols and services are not loaded. Advanced graphics drivers are not loaded, but rather WIN2K loads using the standard VGA driver. Sound card drivers, drivers for CD-RWs, tape drives, Zip drives, and such do not load.

The one time that Safe Mode may not work is when the system employs a third-party disk drive controller not supported internally by WIN2K, which requires an advanced driver. This can result in the BSOD informing you that a valid boot device was not found.

If Windows 2000 boots successfully in Safe Mode, the problem is generally a corrupted device driver or a hardware conflict. Once you're booted into Safe Mode, you can open the Event Viewer and search the System log for any critical errors. If this fails, it's time for some trial and error. Open the Device Manager and disable every device that requires a third-party driver. Reboot the machine in Normal mode.

If the machine boots properly, enable one of the devices that you disabled and reboot. Repeat this process, enabling one device at a time, until you find the device that's causing the problem.

COMPUTER MANAGER

The Computer Manager is a management console that provides access to a great number of local system functions. This applet can be accessed by clicking Start→Administrative Tools→Computer Management. This will bring up the screen shown in **Figure 28.8**.

From this console, anyone with administrative privileges can work with system tools and all storage devices on the system, as well as manage all running services and applications. Everything that is accomplished in here is discussed in more detail in other sections of this chapter. However, this is a centralized point from which it all can be launched.

THE SYSTEM FILE CHECKER

If checking the devices doesn't cure the problem, you can try to use the System File Checker (SFC) to test the integrity of your critical system files. SFC is a command-line utility that checks the version of all files and ensures that the files are the correct size (to eliminate the possibility of file corruption.) **Figure 28.9** shows the different triggers available for SFC.

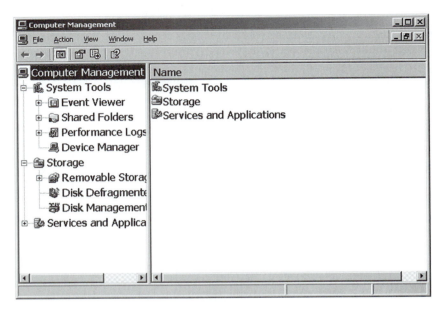

Figure 28.8 The Windows 2000 Computer Manager

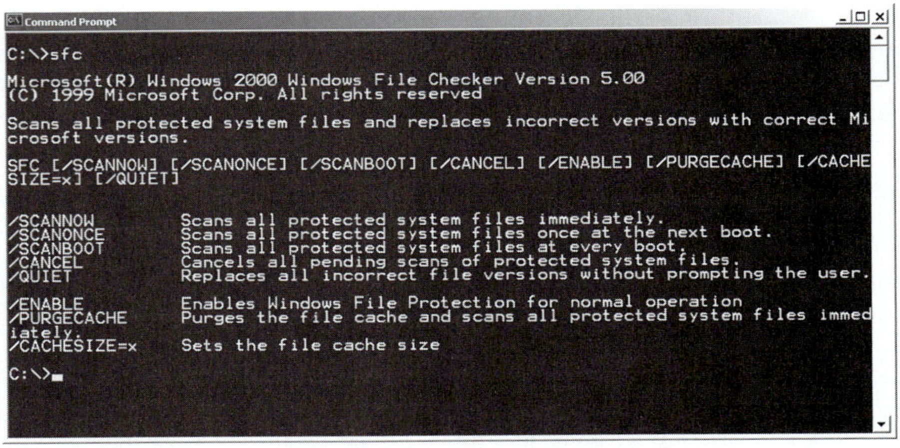

Figure 28.9 There are a number of different options for running SFC.

To run SFC, go to a command prompt and enter the command **SFC /SCANNOW**. This performs a real-time check of the files. If the utility finds any anomalies, it will replace the offending file with a new copy (this may require having a copy of all installed Service Packs as well as the WIN2K installation CD). In addition to real-time files comparison, SFC offers a few other options that can be engaged with command-line switches. **Table 28.3** lists the switches, along with a brief description of what each switch does.

Table 28.3 Options for Running System File Checker

Trigger	Description
/scannow	Scans all protected system files and replaces incorrect versions or corrupted files with official Microsoft versions. This command scans the DLLCache folder and replaces any offending files with the most recent versions. This requires access to the Windows installation source files and also the installed Service Pack files. You will be prompted for the location of these files during the scan operation.
/scanonce	Scans all protected system files once at the next boot. Requires access to the Windows installation source files along with any Service Packs.
/scanboot	Scans all protected system files each time the system is started. This requires local access to the Windows installation source files.
/cancel	Cancels all pending scans of system files.
/enable	Enables Windows File Protection (WFP) during normal operation.
/purgecache	Purges the file cache and scans all of the protected system files immediately. This command requires access to the Windows installation source files. This command is required after you run the /cachesize=x command.
/cachesize=x	Sets the file cache size in megabytes. This command requires a reboot followed by a /purgecache command to adjust the size of the on-disk cache.

There are a number of command-line triggers useful when running SFC.

RECOVERY CONSOLE

The Recovery Console is a tool that is a bit more advanced than the average technician will use. It's more of a tool for the systems administrator. As such, it is beyond the scope of this book to attempt a complete discussion here. Briefly, the Recovery Console is a utility that allows access to the entire system from a command prompt. The Recovery Console can be used in place of SFC for replacing corrupted or incorrect versions of files when the system won't boot to Windows. The utility can also be used to repair logical damage to the hard disk. However, Recovery Console is one of those options that do not get installed by default. Before it becomes available to the user it must have been previously installed. The only other way to access it is through the Windows 2000 installation routine. After Recovery Console has been loaded and is up and running, there are a number of command-prompt utilities that weren't available before:

chkdsk /f: Allows the user to correct most common hard-disk problems. This includes file system errors and moving data from bad sectors to good ones.

Fixmbr: A utility that attempts to repair the master boot record.

Fixboot: A utility that will attempt to repair the hard disk's boot sector.

Fdisk: A disk partitioning utility designed specifically for the different FAT file systems. It does not enable creating NTFS partitions, but it can remove them.

Format: A utility for performing a high-level format onto a disk drive.

Emergency Repair Disk

In Chapter Twenty-Five, The World of NT, I introduced the concept of the ERD. I mentioned that this diskette could be created during the installation procedure, but that it was better to wait until the system was fully configured. This diskette contains a backup copy of the BOOT.INI file along with several critical registry keys. However, every time changes are made to system configuration or user accounts, the ERD must be updated, or it is useless.

In order to make use of the ERD, the user boots the system either to the WIN2K installation CD or to the installation floppies. There will come a point at which Setup asks whether you want to set up Windows 2000 or repair an existing installation. Select the repair option and have the ERD ready. As the repair process begins, the user is asked whether the system should perform a fast repair or a manual repair.

A fast repair automatically updates some key system files, the registry, the boot sector, and the startup environment. Unless you're a very astute user and know exactly what went wrong with the system, this is the appropriate choice.

If you are that astute user, a manual repair allows you to specify what changes to make. This prevents you from having to overwrite anything you don't have to. These options include the following:

- *Inspect registry files*: Choosing this option displays a screen that lists the registry hives. Users can choose the hives they wish to load. Under Inspect registry files, there is also the option to restore user accounts.

- *Restore user accounts*: The Setup program transfers the Security and SAM files from the Emergency Repair Disk to the registry. At this point, the files become registry hives. Since this is a nonreversible procedure, users will be required to confirm that they want to proceed.

- *Inspect startup environment*: This option checks the NT system's boot files. If it finds a problem with any of these files, the corrupted files will be replaced with one from the NT Setup disk.

- *Verify Windows NT system files*: This procedure runs an error-checking algorithm called checksum against each of the installation files. If checksum does not get back the expected value from any given file, or if a file cannot be located, NT replaces it with a file from the installation disks or CD-ROM.

- *Inspect boot sector*: If the user selects this option, the MBR will be examined for errors. Critical boot files, including NTLDR, BOOT.INI, and NTDETECT.EXE, are re-created.

Chapter Summary

After reading this chapter, you should be able to see the differences and the similarities between WIN2K and WINNT. WIN2K was just the next step along the evolutionary chain of Microsoft OSs. I discussed some of the changes that occurred in WIN2K as they involve the boot process, as well as some changes to the user interface.

Some of the more useful changes are in the methods by which WIN2K is, in a way, self-healing. Proper use of the tools provided by the OS can keep a system running longer and more stably without a constant need to rebuild the system from scratch every six months.

BRAIN DRAIN

1. Describe the ways the four WIN2K versions differ. Include in your discussion such details as min/max memory support and how many CPUs each one will support.

2. Describe the process of creating boot diskettes for WIN2K. What are two major differences between that process and the process WINNT uses?

3. What is the function of Last Known Good? Explain why the user logon process is important concerning whether Last Known Good will work or not.

4. List some changes that were made in the user interface between WIN9x, WINNT, and WIN2K.

5. How does Safe Mode differ from Safe Mode with Networking Support?

THE 64K$ QUESTIONS

1. Windows 2000 Professional requires a minimum of _____ RAM in order to work.
   a. 32MB
   b. 64MB
   c. 128MB
   d. 256MB

2. Windows 2000 Professional supports up to _____ RAM.
   a. 2GB
   b. 4GB
   c. 8GB
   d. 32GB

3. Windows 2000 Server requires a minimum of _____ RAM in order to work.
   a. 32MB
   b. 64MB
   c. 128MB
   d. 256MB

4. Windows 2000 Server supports up to _____ RAM.
   a. 2GB
   b. 4GB
   c. 8GB
   d. 64GB

5. Windows 2000 Datacenter requires a minimum of _____ RAM in order to work.
   a. 32MB
   b. 64MB
   c. 128MB
   d. 256MB

6. Windows 2000 Datacenter supports up to _____ RAM.
   a. 2GB
   b. 4GB
   c. 8GB
   d. 64GB

7. Only the Server versions of WIN2K support EFS.
   a. True
   b. False

8. The WIN2K Service that identifies corrupted system files and replaces them with good copies is _____.
   a. Windows File Protection
   b. Windows Security Model

    c. File Synchronization Manager

    d. Recovery Console

9. WIN2K Advanced Server supports up to _____ processors.

    a. 2

    b. 4

    c. 8

    d. 32

10. WIN2K Datacenter supports up to _____ processors.

    a. 2

    b. 4

    c. 8

    d. 32

11. The WIN2K floppy disk setup procedure involves _____ diskettes.

    a. 3

    b. 4

    c. 5

    d. There is no option for installing from floppies.

12. WIN2K boot disks can be created by _____.

    a. Running the MAKEBOOT utility from a command prompt

    b. Clicking the Add/Remove Programs icon in Control Panel and selecting the Add/Remove Windows Components tab

    c. Typing **WINNT /OX** at a command prompt.

    d. WIN2K won't boot from floppy diskettes.

13. Which of the following two items are required in order to install WIN2K from a remote network location?

    a. A distribution server

    b. A PXE-compliant boot diskette

    c. A copy of Microsoft's MSDN Network Installation CD

    d. It can't be done.

14. Which of the following does not support an upgrade path to WIN2K Professional?

    a. Windows 95 (any release)

    b. Windows 98 (any release)

    c. WFW 3.11

    d. NT 4.0 Workstation

15. Which of the following does not support an upgrade path to WIN2K Server?

    a. NT Server 3.51

    b. NT Server 4.0

    c. NT Server 4.0 Enterprise Edition

    d. NT Server 4.0 Terminal Server Edition

16. From which Microsoft products can an administrator upgrade his or her servers to WIN2K Datacenter?

    a. NT Server 3.51

    b. NT Server 4.0

    c. NT Server 4.0 Enterprise Edition

    d. Datacenter does not provide an upgrade path.

17. At what point does the WIN2K boot process write final information to the LastKnownGood section of the registry?

    a. Immediately prior to displaying the BSOD

    b. Immediately prior to displaying the user logon screen

    c. The instant the user hits enter after providing his/her credentials

    d. As soon as LSASS attempts to verify the user's credentials

18. A user can create personalized Admin Tools in WIN2K using the _____ utility.

    a. Microsoft Management Console
    b. Customize Taskbar
    c. Control Panel→Create New
    d. This can't be done.

19. You've just attempted to boot the system using Safe Mode, and you get a BSOD informing you that a valid boot partition could not be found by the system. This most likely means that _____.

    a. The hard disk MBR is corrupted
    b. The controller has failed
    c. BOOT.INI can't be read
    d. The system uses a third-party hard disk controller not supported internally by WIN2K

20. You have just completed repairing a WIN2K installation using the ERD. Only now, two new users you added last week no longer have accounts on the system. What went wrong?

    a. The new user accounts were not registered in Active Directory.
    b. You did. You didn't update the ERD after adding the accounts.
    c. Nothing. User accounts are not a function of ERD.
    d. You forgot to select the "Include Active Directory Information" when starting the recovery process.

TRICKY TERMINOLOGY

Control set: A collection of registry settings that defines the system configuration for Windows during the boot process.

Distribution server: A centralized storage location for the installation files of operating systems or applications.

Report phase: A part of the WIN2K installation procedure that seeks out and logs programs and device drivers that are likely to cause problems.

Snap-in: An applet that can be added to customized consoles in Microsoft Management Console.

ACRONYM ALERT

ADSI: Active Directory Service Interface

EFS: Encrypting File System

IIS: Internet Information Services

IPSEC: Internet Protocol Security

LDAP: Lightweight Directory Access Protocol

MAPI: Messaging Applications Programming Interface

MMC: Microsoft Management Console

NLB: Network Load Balancing

PAE: Physical Address Extension

PKI: Public Key Infrastructure

PXE: Preboot Execution Environment

RIS: Remote Installation Services

SCTS: Security Configuration Tool Set

SFC: System File Checker

VPN: Virtual Private Network

WDM: Windows Driver Model

WMI: Windows Management Instrumentation

WSH: Windows Script Host

VIEW THE VIDEO

A video clip on NFTS 4 vs. NFTS 5 and a video clip on Windows 2000 and XP System Files are available on the accompanying CD.

CHAPTER 29

WIN2K SYSTEM ADMINISTRATION

Managing systems becomes a bit easier in WIN2K because of the introduction of Active Directory. As I said in Chapter Twenty-Eight, An Introduction to Windows 2000, Active Directory is the Microsoft implementation of the Lightweight Directory Access Protocol (LDAP). Much of this chapter is going to involve an examination of Active Directory.

In the second half of the chapter, I'll take a look at device installation and hard disk management in WIN2K. The evolution of NTFS to Version 5 added some very interesting features and opened up new possibilities for the system administrator in terms of both security and resource management.

A+ OPERATING SYSTEM TECHNOLOGIES EXAM OBJECTIVES

CompTIA objectives covered in this chapter include the following:

1.1 Identify the major desktop components and interfaces and their functions. Differentiate the characteristics of Windows 9x/Me, Windows NT 4.0 Workstation, Windows 2000 Professional, and Windows XP.

1.2 Identify the names, locations, purposes, and contents of major system files.

1.4 Identify basic concepts and procedures for creating, viewing, and managing disks, directories, and files. This includes procedures for changing file attributes and the ramifications of those changes (for example, security issues).

2.4 Identify procedures for installing/adding a device, including loading, adding, and configuring device drivers and required software.

AN OVERVIEW OF ACTIVE DIRECTORY

In the days when most computer systems were stand-alone devices, there was no need for anything as sophisticated as directory services. All necessary resources could be found locally.

Today's world has increasingly become a networked world, and the networks become more complex each day. For the average user, finding resources on the network could be a real challenge, were it not for the assistance of directory services. Active Directory provides these services to the Microsoft environment.

JUST WHAT IS ACTIVE DIRECTORY?

With Active Directory, information about network-based resources, including applications, files, printers, and even other people on the network, can be accessed from a unified interface. Active Directory also ensures that there is a consistent method for naming, accessing, and managing these resources.

In a way, you could compare Active Directory to the telephone book, only it's easier to browse and, in a sense, it's interactive. Through Active Directory, the user can browse network resources as easily as one finds a file or printer on a local computer using the My Computer applet.

All of this information is stored in a relational database that can be accessed through a variety of different applications. Other devices on the network can also use this information to enforce permissions and privileges, and it can be used by applications such as Microsoft's System Management Server. Active Directory makes it easier for an administrator to manage the network's infrastructure as well.

ACTIVE DIRECTORY STRUCTURE

Active Directory treats each resource on the network as though it was an *object*. This includes printers, workstations, servers, files, directories, and even the users. As insensitive as it may sound, to Microsoft the person using the computer is no more than an object. In order to facilitate management of these objects, they are put into *containers*. So if you want a comparison that might be more familiar, if you were examining just the file system on a computer, individual files would be considered objects, and the folders in which those files are stored would be containers.

These containers are organized into a hierarchical format. Containers can contain other containers; they can contain objects; or they can contain both, in the same way that a folder can have either subfolders or files. **Figure 29.1** illustrates how Active Directory might organize a very small network.

As detailed as this seems, it gets even better. The individual objects can be assigned a large number of different attributes. For example, a user object can be described by the user's full name, a variety of different numbers, including a Social Security number, various telephone numbers, or an ID number. Security settings can be applied, or a home address can be added. And then all of this information is collected into an encrypted relational

BUZZ WORDS

Object: In reference to the OS, an object is any single resource on the system and/or network, including files, users, or devices.

Container: A collection of objects on the system or network that have been gathered together into a single administrative unit.

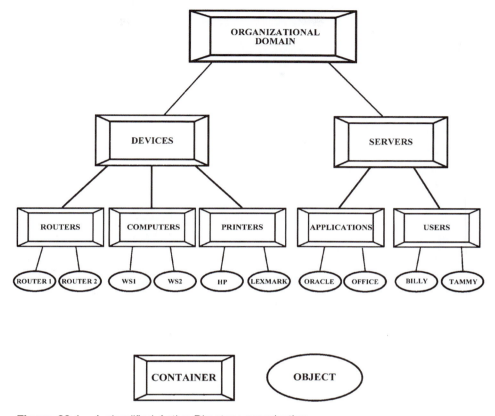

Figure 29.1   A simplified Active Directory organization

database and managed by the administrator as needed. **Figure 29.2** shows just a fraction of the different attributes that can be collected within a single user account.

MANAGING ACTIVE DIRECTORY

In Chapter Twenty-Eight I described how someone could make use of Microsoft Management Console to create customized Admin Tools. Microsoft also uses MMC to facilitate the administration of Active Directory. The administrator can perform specific functions with the ease of a point and click interface using three predefined consoles:

- Active Directory Users and Computers
- Active Directory Sites and Services
- Active Directory Domains and Trusts

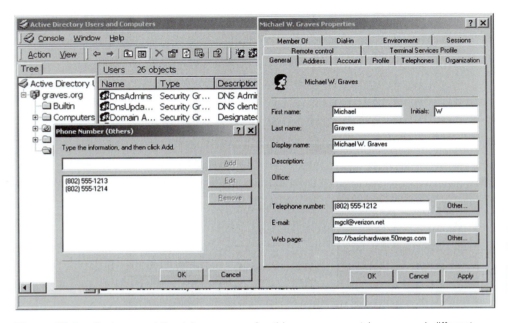

Figure 29.2 Each one of the tabs you see for this user account has several different fields that contain information. The user's entire profile is stored in Active Directory as part of the object.

There are others as well. However, a complete description of all of Active Directory's capabilities is far beyond the scope of this book.

ACTIVE DIRECTORY USERS AND COMPUTERS

WIN2K was designed to be a multi-user environment. This is true of both the Server versions as well as WIN2K Professional. An additional requirement for the server versions is to be able to manage the different computers on the network. This is the function of Active Directory Users and Computers (**Figure 29.3**). Through this console, the administrator can add new users and manage existing accounts. Also, as new computers are added to the network, this console can be used to administer computer accounts.

ACTIVE DIRECTORY SITES AND SERVICES

The server versions of WIN2K are capable of managing a number of different physical networks as well as logical subnets. And unlike WINNT, there are no longer primary and backup domain controllers. If a server has been designated as a domain controller, then it is active. It can service logon and subsequent authentication requests, and it can act as a repository for new information added by administrators. Active Directory Sites and Services (**Figure 29.4**) ensures that managing the different servers does not become an overly complex procedure.

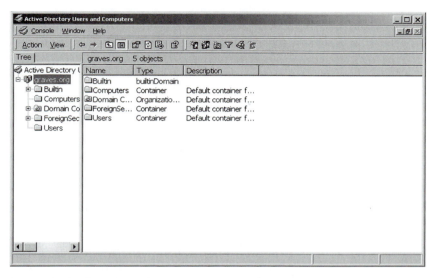

Figure 29.3   The Active Directory Users and Computers console

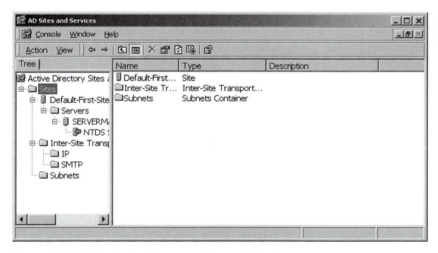

Figure 29.4   The Active Directory Sites and Services console

WIN2K designates the local network as well-connected computers. In a well-connected network, or local area network (LAN), authentication is easily managed by the local servers. However, on a wide area network (WAN) a number of different networks might be distributed around the entire globe. The Sites portion of this console allows the administrator to manage parts of the network that are not physically accessible.

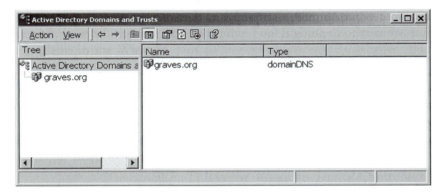

Figure 29.5   The Active Directory Domains and Trusts console

ACTIVE DIRECTORY DOMAINS AND TRUSTS

I've discussed in previous sections of this book how Microsoft networks can consist of several domains interconnected through trusts. If a network consists of more than one domain, the Active Directory Domains and Trusts console (**Figure 29.5**) allows an administrator with the appropriate permissions to create and manage trusts across the network. This would include the ability to manage other domains, if the correct permissions exist for the administrator.

When discussing WINNT, I pointed out that trusts in NT are non-transitive. To review, that means that if I establish a trust between Domain A and Domain B, and then I establish another between Domain B and Domain C, a trust between Domain A and Domain C is **not** automatically created. Trusts in WIN2K are transitive. The trust between Domain A and Domain C **would** be created automatically.

DEVICE INSTALLATION IN WIN2K

Adding PnP to WIN2K's arsenal of tools was supposed to make adding new hardware foolproof and trouble-free. For the most part, it has done just that. It features an Add/Remove Hardware Wizard that automatically runs when new hardware is detected and supports hot-pluggable devices in both USB and FireWire. One new feature Microsoft added threw a small wrench into the works, but as long as you know how to deal with it, it won't cause major headaches. That little wrench is called driver signing. First, I'll discuss some minor differences in the Add/Remove Hardware Wizard, and then I'll take a quick look at driver signing.

ADD/REMOVE HARDWARE WIZARD

There are two changes that occurred in the transition of PnP and the Add/Remove Hardware Wizard from WIN9x to WIN2K (**Figure 29.6**) that make installing new hardware substantially easier. The most obvious (aside from the name change, that is) is that the driver database of

Figure 29.6 The Add/Remove Hardware wizard in Windows 2000

WIN2K is dramatically larger. Far more devices are automatically recognized and installed without the need for external driver sources than was ever possible in any of the WIN9x versions.

The second major change is in how PnP actually works. In the old WIN9x versions, PnP was based on a technology known as the Advanced Power Management Basic Input Output Services (APM BIOS). Industry veterans who were around when WIN95 was first released can tell you basically that this technology worked so well that PnP was more frequently called "plug and pray" than it was by its correct name. Some devices, notably network cards and graphics adapters, hardly ever installed correctly the first time and had to be force-fed.

WIN2K incorporates a more up-to-date technology known as the Advanced Configuration and Power Interface (ACPI). This is an industry standard initiative that defines the interface between the system board and the system BIOS. The result is a far more stable approach to PnP.

When a new device is installed in the system, WIN2K will automatically detect its presence. Devices that are installed internally, requiring the system to be shut down, will be detected on the next boot. Hot-pluggable devices, such as USB or FireWire, can be added on the fly, and the Add New Hardware Wizard will start automatically.

If the device is one of the many that are supported by the internal database of WIN2K drivers, the user won't even have to supply a driver disk. This database is located in a hidden directory called INF. If WIN2K cannot find an appropriate driver in the INF directory, it will then prompt the user to insert a disk.

Unlike previous versions of Windows OS, WIN2K adds a new trick. Drivers can be obtained over the Internet through the Windows Update functionality. If this option is selected, the wizard will first check the disk drives or preselected locations. Assuming the driver is not found in one of these locations, Windows will automatically connect to the Internet and log on to Microsoft's Windows Update site to search for drivers.

BUZZ WORDS

Digital signature: An encrypted piece of data added to a file to guarantee its authenticity.

DRIVER SIGNING

In Chapter Twenty-Eight, when I was listing off all of the new features added to WIN2K, support for digital signatures was one of these new features. A *digital signature* is an encrypted piece of data that is added to a file to ensure that the file is the correct file. In the case of driver signing, the signature does not actually become a part of the file. This data is included in a catalogue (CAT) file, and this CAT file is subsequently referenced in the INF file that is generated.

In order for a device driver to receive a digital signature, the company that writes the driver must submit the software to Microsoft. Microsoft engineers will then submit this driver to very thorough testing in their Windows Hardware Quality Lab (WHQL). After the driver has passed these tests, it will receive the digital signature and be an official digitally signed driver. Any updates or revisions to this file cannot carry the digital signature until Microsoft has subjected the revised files to the same testing procedures.

There are three different security settings that can be assigned for installing new hardware, based on these digital signatures:

- *Ignore*: Any driver can be installed, whether it carries a digital signature or not.
- *Warn*: If a driver does not carry a digital signature, the user will be notified that this is the case and will be presented with the option of halting the installation or continuing.
- *Block*: If a driver does not carry a digital signature, it cannot be installed without changing this setting.

To adjust these settings, click Start→Setting→Control Panel and then double-click the System icon. Under the Hardware tab, click the Driver Signing button. It should look something like the illustration in **Figure 29.7**.

By default, the intermediate setting of Warn is selected. I would advise that unless you have overpowering reasons for doing so, you not change this. Many companies elect not to submit their driver files to Microsoft for testing. They have this strange notion that they know as much about writing drivers for their hardware as Microsoft and elect not to pay the associated fees. Not being signed by Microsoft is not an automatic indication that the driver either will not work or will somehow corrupt the system.

DISK MANAGEMENT IN WIN2K

The inclusion of NTFS, Version 5 in WIN2K added a number of different options for disk management that were never available in previous versions of Windows operating systems. There were actually dozens of changes made, but there are five that I intend to discuss here:

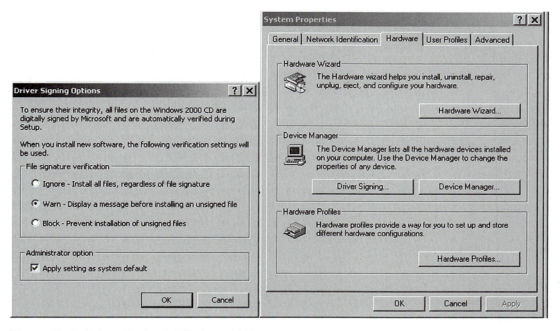

Figure 29.7   *Driver Signing in Windows 2000*

- EFS
- Selective file compression
- Disk quotas
- Selective file/folder compression
- Volume junction points

THE ENCRYPTING FILE SYSTEM

The Encrypting File System (EFS) allows a user to protect sensitive data in files by scrambling them in such a way that nobody else can read them. It depends on public and private key encryption and a technology called the CryptoAPI. Unlike encryption methods that work on top of the file system, EFS is an integral part of the file system. This makes EFS easier to manage and transparent to the file owner and to any applications that require access to the data.

   In order to enable EFS, the user right-clicks the file or folder that is to be encrypted in Windows Explorer and selects Properties. On the General tab, there is a button labeled Advanced. When the user clicks this button, he or she will get a screen similar to the one in **Figure 29.8**. Click the checkbox next to the phrase "Encrypt contents to secure data."

   When a user enables EFS, the OS generates a private key. The private key consists of a data set associated with the user's account that determines precisely how data will be scrambled and

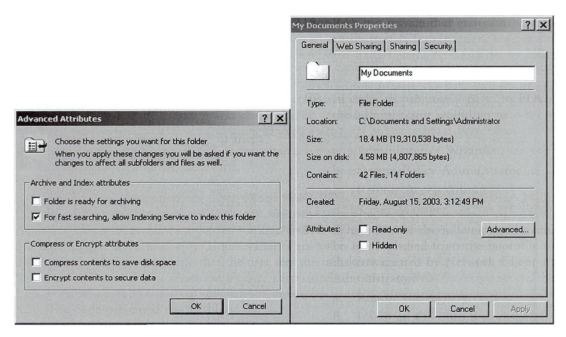

Figure 29.8   EFS is one of the Advanced file properties of a file stored on a partition formatted to NTFS.

how to put that scrambled data back into its correct form when needed. The user can be selective about the files or folders that need to be encrypted. It is not an all-or-nothing option.

For each file that is encrypted, Windows assigns a randomly generated encryption key that becomes part of that file's attributes. When the user goes to open the file, the user's private key calls up the file's encryption key. The file's encryption key will only respond to the user's private key or to a public key generated by an authorized recovery agent. A recovery agent is any user account that has been given the privilege of being a recovery agent. Having the file's encryption key respond to a recovery agent is the fail-safe that allows the user to recover data in the event that the private key is lost, or in the event that a rogue employee encrypts all the data on a machine before an unexpected departure.

So how can a recovery key get lost if it's nothing more than a piece of data stored on the system? There are two ways this can happen. If the OS is reinstalled, the key will be lost, and if the user account is deleted and recreated, the key will be lost.

Since the private key is associated with the user's account, it is possible for multiple users on the same system to protect their data. When users log on, their accounts cannot open the encrypted files of other users.

Encryption and decryption are done on the fly, without any need for user intervention. The only cost for this added security is a very slight performance hit. Opening and closing files can take longer, but on a fast system, the difference is rarely noticeable.

FILE COMPRESSION

File compression has been a part of Microsoft OSs since the days of MS-DOS. Prior to the release of NTFS5, however, it's always been an all-or-none type of thing. You either compressed the entire hard drive, or you didn't. Also, file compression techniques took a substantial toll on system performance.

With NTFS5, individual files and folders can be compressed on the fly. If a user has a very large directory of graphics or music files taking up a big chunk of hard disk real estate, compressing that folder can free up a drive space that can be used for other functions.

As with EFS, file or folder compression is one of the advanced properties. Refer back to Figure 29.8. You will see another checkbox labeled "Compress contents to save disk space." By checking this option, the contents of the file or folder will be compressed for storage but can be uncompressed and used as needed. Unless your system is exceedingly slow, the performance penalty is so minimal as to be almost unnoticeable.

DISK QUOTAS

One of the features most enthusiastically embraced by network administrators is disk quotas. On a busy network, disk storage has always been at a premium. No matter how many disk drives you install, or how big those drives are, they always manage to fill up. There are users collecting high-resolution graphics and never deleting them when no longer needed. Other users think the server is their own private jukebox and fill it up with music files. When Internet access is available on every desktop in the enterprise, users can quickly consume vast amounts of storage space with downloaded graphics, MP3s, and other downloaded files. Usually, it's only a few people causing problems, but that doesn't prevent the problem from becoming severe.

Disk quotas allow the administrator to limit the amount of storage space an individual can use. Disk quotas can be enforced on a per-user, per-partition, or per-volume basis. It doesn't work on a folder level. What this means is that the administrator can configure individual partitions or even spanned volumes independently of one another. If quotas are applied on a partition level, each partition can be configured differently even if those partitions are part of the same physical hard disk.

As a user approaches his or her allocated limit of storage space, WIN2K will warn that user that the end is near. If the administrator chooses to configure it this way, users will not be allowed to exceed their assigned storage. If each user is allowed 400MB of space, that user won't be allowed to use 401MB just because one file is going to take him or her over the limit. In order to copy that file, some disk space must be cleared up. Disk quotas don't take compression into consideration either. The system uses a file's uncompressed size when calculating user's storage consumption. This little fact has resulted in a great number of irate users. Also, file ownership is what the system uses to track disk use. If one user creates a file and another user adds to it, charges against the storage limits are applied to the creator of the file, and not the one who changed it.

Disk quotas are a function of a NTFS hard disk's properties. In order to enable disk quotas, right-click the drive letter for the selection partition or disk and select Properties. Click the

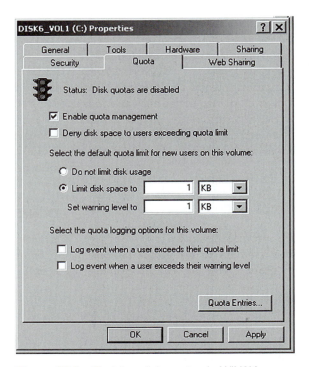

Figure 29.9   Enabling disk quotas in WIN2K

Quota tab, and you'll get the screen shown in **Figure 29.9**. Click the box labeled "Enable quota management." For strict enforcement of the quotas, also check the box labeled "Deny disk space to users exceeding quota limit." If you enable quotas, but choose not to check the latter box, an administrator can track disk usage by individual users without limiting user storage capabilities. This can be useful for a couple of reasons.

Primarily it's useful for determining who the disk hogs are. Perhaps you can convince them to limit usage without enforcing a company-wide policy. It can also be used to determine whether it's time to enforce disk quotas. There is also a commercial use for this function. If your company charges for storage, this is a method of monitoring how much storage space a particular user is consuming, and subsequently how much to charge that user for the service.

If an administrator chooses to enforce storage limitations, there are some options to configure. First, the storage limitations need to be established. How much storage space do your users need in order to properly do their jobs? The default setting applies the same quota to each user on the system who uses that volume for storage. I'll get to setting individual user quotas in a minute.

The next thing to configure is the warning limit. This is the amount of storage consumption that will trigger an alert to users that they are approaching their limit. If you want to get really

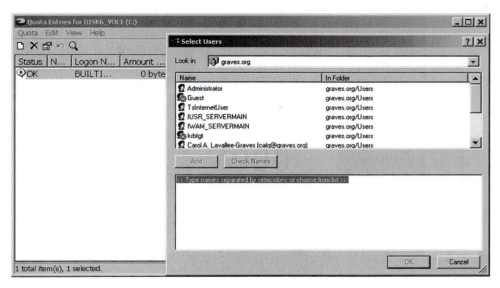

Figure 29.10   Setting disk quotas for individual users

annoying, you can do one of two things. Either set the warning limit to 1MB so that warnings start getting issued every time users save a new file to the partition. Or set it 1MB beneath the actual limit so that they get warned and cut off at the same time. On the other hand, if you want to be fair, set it at a value somewhere around 75 percent of allocated space so that there is time for users to do some house cleaning before they run out of space.

Not all users necessarily have the same storage requirements, though. Your graphics designer or in-house digital photographer is going to require a whole lot more space than a part-time receptionist. This is where individual quotas come in handy. In order to assign individual quotas, click the button labeled "Quota Entries." On the screen that follows, click Quota, and then New Quota Entry. This will bring up the screen in **Figure 29.10**. Now you can browse the individual users on the system or network and do one of two things.

By clicking the button marked "Do not limit disk usage," that user is excused from disk quota limitations on that particular volume. The other option is to set a disk quota specific to that user, along with an appropriate warning level. This setting will override general disk quota settings.

VOLUME JUNCTION POINTS

Volume Junction Points are a rarely used feature of NTFS5. But when this feature is needed, it is one that is greatly appreciated. All previous Microsoft OSs have been limited in the number of physical disks that can be installed on the system by the number of letters in the alphabet.

Since A and B are typically reserved for floppy disk drives, that allowed only twenty-four drive letters for hard disks, CD-ROM drives, CD burners, Zip drives, and so on and so forth.

For the vast majority of users, twenty-four drive letters was more than enough. For huge network storage systems containing seventy-two CD-ROM drives or seventy-two hard disks, it could be a bit of a problem. To accommodate these devices, another OS, such as UNIX, had to be selected.

Volume Junction Points (or Volume Mount Points, as they're also called) allows the user to get around the alphabet limitation. Drives no longer need to be Drive C: or Drive D:. They can now be Drive Oracle or Drive WINNT. Also, they can be physical or logical drives. So network mapped drives can be expanded beyond the alphabet as well.

The way it works is that a folder is created on the root partition with the name of the drive. The only thing contained in this folder is a pointer to the physical location of the drive or partition. There are three utilities provided by Microsoft for creating and managing junction points:

- *LINKD.EXE*: Grafts the target folder into an NTFS folder, displays the target of the junction point, and can be used to delete targets that were originally created by LINKD.EXE.

- *MOUNTVOL.EXE*: Mounts the root folder of the local volume and displays targets of junction points used to mount other volumes. It also lists all local volumes that are available for use by the system and can be used to delete volumes that were created by MOUNTVOL.EXE.

- *DELRP.EXE*: Deletes junction points.

THE WIN2K DISK MANAGEMENT CONSOLE

In WINNT, managing the disks and partitions in the system is the function of the Disk Administrator. In WIN2K these responsibilities have been absorbed into the Computer Management MMC under the Storage folder. **Figure 29.11** shows the MMC opened to Disk Management. With Disk Management, you can create volumes, format volumes with file systems, initialize disks, and create fault-tolerant disk systems. Under WIN2K disk administration, there are a few new tricks the administrator can perform, including the following:

- Create Dynamic Disks
- Manage local drives, or even remote network drives
- Mount drives

Since these are new concepts to WIN2K, they deserve a closer look. I'm going to start with Dynamic Disks, because the Dynamic Disk is what makes a lot of WIN2K's disk management functions possible.

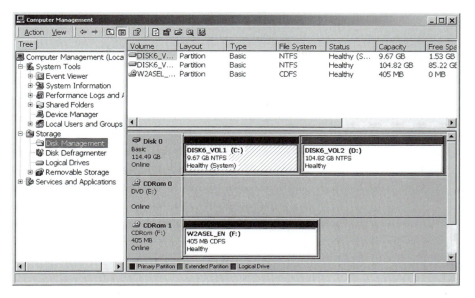

Figure 29.11   The Disk Management MMC

DYNAMIC DISKS

Under WIN2K there are two basic types of physical disk: basic and dynamic. A *basic disk* is any physical disk in the system that can be recognized, but that has not been converted to a dynamic disk. Basic disks adhere to the partition-oriented scheme of file structure typical to previous Microsoft operating systems. When Windows 2000 is first installed, the default configuration for all disks is that of a basic disk.

Only basic disks are capable of the following functions:

- Creation or deletion of primary and/or extended partitions
- Creation or deletion of logical drives
- Formatting a partition
- Deletion of volume sets, stripe sets, mirror sets, and stripe sets with parity
- Breaking a mirror from a mirror set

Microsoft provides a wizard for upgrading a basic disk to a dynamic disk. A *dynamic disk* is one that is organized into volumes rather than partitions. Once created, a dynamic disk cannot

BUZZ WORDS

Basic disk: A disk that has been configured to conform to the legacy partition-oriented approach to file systems.

Dynamic disk: A disk that has been configured for a file system based on volumes rather than partitions.

be accessed directly by legacy OSs such as MS-DOS or WIN9x. They are, however, available over the network. Basic and dynamic disks can be used simultaneously on the same computer system, but you cannot mix disk types in a volume set that utilizes multiple physical disks.

Once a disk has been converted over to a dynamic disk, the following functions become available that are possible only on dynamic disks:

- Create and delete simple or spanned volumes, stripe sets, and mirrored or RAID 5 volumes
- Extend volumes
- Break a mirrored volume
- Split a volume into two volumes
- Repair mirrored or RAID 5 volumes
- Reactivate a missing or offline disk
- Revert to a basic disk

Some functions can be performed whether the disk is basic or dynamic:

- View disk properties
- View volume and partition properties
- Manage drive letter assignments for disk volumes or partitions, including CD-ROM devices
- Manage file and folder sharing and establish security for a volume or partition
- Upgrade to a dynamic disk

It should be noted that it is not possible to use dynamic disks on a portable computer. There are also a couple of other limitations that dynamic disks impose. For example, WIN2K cannot be installed onto a existing dynamic volume that was created from unallocated space. The setup program requires information that is supplied by the partition tables. Since unallocated space contains no partition tables, Setup will crash and burn.

REMOTE ADMINISTRATION

With Windows 2000 it becomes possible for the administrator to manage disks that are connected to remote computers. For this to happen the person attempting to manage the volume must have administrative privileges on the remote computer. In addition, the host and the remote computer must either be members of the same domain or a trust must have been established between the domains. To do this, however, you need to make a couple of minor changes to Disk Management. This is another place where MMC comes in handy.

Start MMC (click Start→Run and then type **MMC**). This opens the Microsoft Management console that I discussed earlier in the chapter. On the console menu, select Add/Remove Snap-in. In the window that appears will be a button labeled Add. Scroll down until you see

Disk Management and click Add. The default choice is to manage the local system only. Click Another Computer and either browse to the computer you want to manage, or type in the UNC name for that computer if you already know it. Click Finish, and you now have a console for managing that computer.

CHAPTER SUMMARY

As you can see, WIN2K provides the user and/or administrator with a whole new collection of tools for managing the computing environment. This chapter only touched on some of the major issues.

A key concept introduced in this chapter was NTFS5. Without this new file system, the majority of the other subjects discussed can't exist. Another major topic was Active Directory. Before attempting the exam, make sure you understand the material presented here. Also, the tools described in this chapter are essential for the exam and are useful in real life.

BRAIN DRAIN

1. Which of the topics discussed in this chapter aren't possible without the introduction of NTFS5?

2. Define Active Directory. On what industry standard protocol does Active Directory depend for its services?

3. Describe three MMC consoles that assist the administrator in managing Active Directory components.

4. Discuss Driver Signing and why this tool can protect unwary users.

5. What are some of the major differences between basic and dynamic disks?

THE 64K$ QUESTIONS

1. Which of the following is Active Directory not capable of managing?
   a. Users
   b. Remote Domains
   c. Other Domain Controllers
   d. System Accounts
   e. It manages all of the above.

2. A specific user on the network would be considered by Active Directory to be a(n) _____.
   a. Account
   b. Object
   c. Container
   d. Branch

3. Active Directory is an implementation of the _____ protocol.
   a. DAP
   b. ADS
   c. NetBEUI
   d. LDAP

4. Which of the following is not a predefined MMC console for managing Active Directory?
   a. Active Directory Accounts and Security
   b. Active Directory Users and Computers

c. Active Directory Sites and Services

d. Active Directory Domains and Trusts

5. Information about a remote server would be found in _____.

a. Active Directory Accounts and Security

b. Active Directory Users and Computers

c. Active Directory Sites and Services

d. Active Directory Domains and Trusts

6. WIN2K trusts are considered to be _____.

a. Non-transitive

b. Transparent

c. Bi-directional

d. Transitive

7. New hardware can be configured in the _____ wizard.

a. Add New Hardware

b. Plug 'n Play console

c. Add/Remove Hardware

d. Device Manager

8. The technology that is used by the version of PnP incorporated into WIN2K is called _____.

a. APM BIOS

b. PNPBIOS

c. ACPI

d. Active Scan

9. When a digital signature is added to a device driver, that information is stored in the _____ file.

a. INF

b. VXD

c. DRV

d. CAT

10. Selective encoding and subsequent on-the-fly decoding of data on a WIN2K FAT32 drive is made possible by _____.

a. NTFS 4.51

b. ASPICrypt Technology

c. EFS

d. It isn't possible.

11. Decoding of files encrypted by a disgruntled employee is made possible by way of the _____.

a. EFS Recovery Agent

b. The administrator's Private Key

c. Use of any administrator account

d. It's not possible.

12. Selective File Compression can be accomplished by anyone with _____.

a. Administrative privileges

b. Server Manager privileges

c. Any user can apply compression to any file he or she owns.

d. Any user can apply compression to any file he or she can access.

13. If disk quotas have been enabled on a server, the user can double his or her storage capacity by using compression.

a. True

b. False

14. If Disk Quotas have been enabled, the administrator must enforce a maximum disk allocation and a warning level.

a. True

b. False

15. In WIN2K, there is a limit of
_____ disk volumes on a system.

    a. 16

    b. 24

    c. 256

    d. There is no limit.

16. You have a disk quota set for
500MB for all users on a system. A
new user comes aboard who requires
2GB of storage space. In order to
give this person the needed space
you must _____.

    a. Change the global allocation to
2GB

    b. Assign the new user Server
Manager privileges

    c. Click Quota Entries in the Quota
Manager and highlight the new
user, assigning the extra space

    d. Place that user's account onto a
different volume

17. Which of the following cannot be
done on a dynamic disk?

    a. Create extended volumes

    b. Create junction points

    c. Create partitions

    d. You can do anything on a
dynamic disk.

18. If you want to _____, you must
have a basic disk.

    a. Create a junction point

    b. Create an active partition

    c. Span two volumes

    d. Create a RAID 5 array

19. Managing disks in WIN2K is done
in the _____ console.

    a. Disk Management

    b. Disk Administrator

    c. System Applet

    d. System Management

20. Once you've opened the appropriate
utility for managing disks in WIN2K,
you can manage the disks on a
remote device.

    a. True

    b. False

TRICKY TERMINOLOGY

Basic disk: A disk that has been configured
to conform to the legacy partition-
oriented approach to file systems.

Container: A collection of objects on the
system or network that have been
gathered together into a single administrative unit.

Digital signature: An encrypted piece of
data added to a file to guarantee its
authenticity.

Dynamic disk: A disk that has been
configured for a file system based on
volumes rather than partitions.

Object: In reference to the OS, an object is
any single resource on the system and/
or network, including files, users, or
devices.

ACRONYM ALERT

ACPI: Advanced Configuration and Power
Interface. An upgrade to the PnP
functionality of Windows.

APM BIOS: Advanced Power Management
Basic Input Output Services

CAT: Catalog File. A compressed file in
Windows that contains driver signing
information.

EFS: Encrypting File System. A functionality of the NTFS 5 file system that allows individual files or directories to be encrypted on the fly.

LAN: Local Area Network

LDAP: Lightweight Directory Access Protocol. A protocol that allows network resources to be browsed in a manner similar to local disk drives.

WAN: Wide Area Network

WHQL: Windows Hardware Quality Lab. A division of Microsoft that tests hardware and driver functionality in the Windows OS. There are some who might say this is an oxymoron.

 VIEW THE VIDEO

A video clip on Replacing Windows 9X with Windows 2000 is available on the accompanying CD.

CHAPTER 30

INTRODUCING XP

Windows XP was released in October of 2001 as a result of Microsoft's resolve to move desktop computers into a truly 32-bit world. There was a great deal of brouhaha surrounding this release. Microsoft even posted a large and very detailed page on its Web site outlining dozens of "new features" in XP.

In truth, XP is a slightly improved version of WIN2K with a few added features and a facelift. The vast majority of the new features listed on Microsoft's site had already existed in WIN2K. There were a number of features that were tweaked a bit, but the majority were familiar friends who'd had cosmetic surgery. There are, however, a few brand new features in XP worth discussing. And since there was a major change in the interface, I'll spend some time on that as well.

A+ OPERATING SYSTEM TECHNOLOGIES EXAM OBJECTIVES

CompTIA objectives covered in this chapter include the following:

1.1 Identify the major desktop components and interfaces and their functions. Differentiate the characteristics of Windows 9x/Me, Windows NT 4.0 Workstation, Windows 2000 Professional, and Windows XP.

2.3 Identify the basic system boot sequences and boot methods, including the steps to create an emergency boot disk with utilities installed for Windows 9x/Me, Windows NT 4.0 Workstation, Windows 2000 Professional, and Windows XP.

2.4 Identify procedures for installing/adding a device, including loading, adding, and configuring device drivers and required software.

THE WINDOWS XP VERSIONS

Initially XP was released in three versions, with an intent that a server version would follow. However, Microsoft's .NET technology superceded XP and, until the release of Windows 2003 Server, was the only alternative to WIN2K server versions for an NOS in the Microsoft world.

A little later, two modified versions of XP were released. To summarize, the five versions of XP are listed here:

- XP Home Edition
- XP Professional Edition
- XP Tablet PC Edition
- XP Media Center Edition
- XP 64-bit Edition

XP HOME EDITION

As its name implies, this is the OS Microsoft targets as the single stand-alone PC that gets used mostly for games and a few productivity applications. Although it can be networked, it cannot be made to join a domain. Therefore, it is not suitable for the corporate environment. A small peer-to-peer network is possible.

Think of XP Home Edition as a replacement for WIN9x users. XP Home does not support SMP. If installed onto a system with multiple processors, the extra processors will not be recognized or used.

XP PROFESSIONAL EDITION

For users who took advantage of the features of WINNT Workstation or WIN2K Professional, and for computers that exist in a network domain, XP Professional is the appropriate choice. XP Professional also integrates a number of additional security measures not present in Home Edition, including the following:

- *EFS*: Discussed in Chapter Twenty-Nine, WIN2K System Administration.
- *Remote Desktop*: Allows a computer to be used from anywhere on the network.
- *Offline File and Folder Synchronization*: Files that are normally stored on the network can be downloaded and subsequently used offline. Changes can then be synchronized with the network version. Offline folders can be encrypted for security.
- *Windows Management Instrumentation*: Allows remote monitoring and management of networked systems.
- *Dual Processor Support*
- *Active Directory Support*: Allows the computer to be joined to a domain.

Minimum requirements for XP Home and Professional are listed in **Table 30.1**.

EXAM NOTE: Note that with XP, it is possible to be asked for both absolute minimum hardware requirements as well as minimum recommended requirements. Make sure that you know both.

Table 30.1 Minimum Requirements for Installing XP Home or Professional Edition

Resource	Min.	Recommended
CPU	300MHz PII	500MHz PIII
RAM	128MB	256MB+
Disk Space	1.5GB	N/A
Video	800x600 SVGA	N/A
Other Media	CD-ROM or compatible device	

Remember, the minimum requirements are not the same as the recommended requirements.

XP TABLET PC EDITION

Microsoft was quick to recognize the popularity of the new tablet PCs. These are devices that combine many of the features of a laptop computer with the features most desirable in a hand-held device. Instead of using a physical keyboard, a user inputs information either through an optional detachable keyboard, or simply by jotting it directly on the screen. The OS uses handwriting recognition technology to convert the user's scribbles into data the tablet PC can use.

Most Microsoft Office applications can be run on this OS, with a few minor caveats. For one, as of this writing, Word and Outlook don't support handwriting recognition technology. And if you choose to send your handwritten messages by email, they can be sent only as GIF image files. This might cause issues for users who block email messages containing attachments from unfamiliar sources.

XP 64-BIT EDITION

Obviously a major difference found in this version is the fact that it supports 64-bit microprocessors. However, the advantages reach farther than that. The 64-bit address spaces allow it to address up to 16GB of physical RAM and up to 8 *terabytes* of virtual RAM. This allows applications to work with incredibly large data sets without excessive paging calls slowing the system. In terms of user operability, the OS is similar to XP Professional Edition.

AN OVERVIEW OF XP FEATURES

As I mentioned in the introduction to this chapter, many of the so-called new features of XP are actually features of WIN2K that received a facelift before being migrated over. For the most part, XP has the same basic engine as WIN2K and offers the same features. There are a few brand new embellishments as well. First, I'll examine some of the migrated features, and then I'll go over some new additions.

> **EXAM NOTE:** Be able to distinguish between features that are new to XP and those that were brought over from other OSs. Also make sure that you know from which OS a migrated feature originated.

MIGRATED FEATURES

Many of the features of WIN2K were inserted into XP with absolutely no changes made. Microsoft figured those features worked well enough. Some features were redesigned for better functionality. Among the changed features are the following:

- Encrypting File System (EFS)
- System Restore
- Network Installation
- Dynamic Update
- Group Policy Management

EFS

Although EFS isn't new to XP, it provides a major improvement over WIN2K's rendition. In XP, EFS has been enabled with multiuser support.

WIN2K users could encrypt their files, but once encrypted those files could not be accessed by other users. This was not very conducive to group efforts. If a file had to be accessed by several users, the security of encryption was not an option that could be employed. With XP Professional, a file can be encrypted and accessed by a group of users.

SYSTEM RESTORE

Technically speaking, WIN2K did not have a System Restore utility. This is something borrowed from WINMe. With WIN2K, if a new driver or application is installed that prevents the system from working properly, the only options are to use Last Known Good or the ERD.

With System Restore, if a system running XP fails to boot normally, or is functioning erratically, the user can "go back in time" to a system configuration that existed before the offending changes were made. It does so by using *restore points*. A restore point is a copy of critical system files and registry entries that were in use before a system change occurred. When a restore point is created, copies of critical system files are made and stored in a hidden directory. The restore point points to that directory, and when called upon, uses those files to copy over the files that aren't working correctly in the target directory.

System Restore automatically creates a restore point every twenty-four hours, if this feature is enabled. It also allows the user to manually establish a restore point. You can store up to three weeks worth of past restore points. The number of restore

---

BUZZ WORDS

Restore point: A copy of system files and registry entries that were in place at the time a major system change was introduced.

points you can save depends on how much disk space you allocate to restore points. This can be up to 12 percent of available disk space.

NETWORK INSTALLATION

Network installation has been an option in Microsoft OSs for the past several versions. XP improves on this by enhancing the security of the process. Using a utility called SysPrep, the administrator can install the OS on a number of machines simultaneously over the network using an image file. This image file can include configuration settings and applications as well as the basic installation of the OS. This can be used in conjunction with Dynamic Update to make rollouts of multiple machines faster and more efficient.

DYNAMIC UPDATE

In Chapter Twenty-Nine, I discussed how Windows Update could keep the system more secure by ensuring that the most recent service packs and file versions were installed on the computer. Dynamic Update takes this process to the next level. With Dynamic Update, the system automatically logs onto Microsoft's Updates page as soon as the OS is installed and immediately downloads new files and service packs. It can then be left running in the background. On a scheduled basis, it will check with Microsoft, and if there are new files, these files will be downloaded. Of course, this is only done with the user's permission. Dynamic Update can be disabled at any time, and any downloads can be refused or aborted if already in progress.

GROUP POLICY MANAGEMENT

To review, the ability to administer group policies was introduced in WINNT. Group policies allow the administrator to establish a predefined set of rules and to enforce those rules for everyone who uses the system. Group policies can also be used across the network.

XP improves on this feature in two ways. First off, there are more than a hundred new policies the administrator can enforce. So if you think your network administrator was hard-core before, wait until he or she gets a hold of this! The other new feature that has been welcomed by the IT industry with enthusiasm is a feature called Resultant Set of Policy (RSoP).

RSoP is a feature that lets the administrator create a new policy and try it out on a small group of guinea pigs before enforcing on every system. This way the ramifications of a new policy can be examined before an overly restrictive policy plays havoc on the network. After the policy has been fully tested and approved, it can then be globally applied.

COMPLETELY NEW FEATURES IN XP

Although XP is primarily WIN2K with a coat of whitewash, it is not without some completely new features. Some of these enhance performance; some enhance stability. Among the totally new features that I will discuss are the following:

- Side-by-side DLL support
- Integrated CDR/CD-RW write capabilities

- Remote Desktop
- ClearType
- Network Location Awareness
- Device Driver Rollback
- Product Activation

SIDE-BY-SIDE DLL SUPPORT

With all previous versions of Windows, there could be only a single instance of any given system file. Critical files, such as DLLs, often make a difference as to whether a program runs properly or crashes. Old DLLs were overwritten by newer versions. Older programs that used a particular DLL had no choice but to use the newer version. The vast majority of the time this wasn't a problem. Side-by-side DLL support allows Windows to keep both versions on the system and run them simultaneously.

INTEGRATED CDR/CD-RW WRITE CAPABILITIES

In order to get a CDR or CD-RW to work on older versions of Windows, a third-party application needed to be installed. With XP, the device becomes another removable media device. Files can be added to the device in a simple drag and drop operation. For more sophisticated CD production, a third-party utility might still be eminently more usable by a large number of users.

REMOTE DESKTOP

In the past, there has been a fairly strong market for programs that allowed a user on the go to connect up to his or her home or office computer and run it from a laptop or other remote computer. After all, users are more familiar with their own setup than they are a computer they've never seen. Remote Desktop is a feature that makes use of the Remote Desktop Protocol (RDP) to allow this to happen. Once logged on, the local computer displays the desktop and allows browsing of all the resources stored on the remote computer.

CLEARTYPE

Almost anyone who looks at an XP desktop for the first time remarks on how much sharper and cleaner the display looks. It's almost like buying a new monitor. ClearType is a technology that allows the graphics adapter to display screens that triple the horizontal resolution of text. This doesn't work with graphical images, and it is software driven.

> **EXAM NOTE:** It would be a very good idea to know the functionality of both ClearType technology and Network Location Awareness (NLA).

NETWORK LOCATION AWARENESS

Network Location Awareness is a feature built into Microsoft that allows a computer to be a member of several different networks, and yet always know what to do, regardless of which network it is on at the moment. Different situations that would result in a multinetworked computer could include a portable system that moves from office to office. Or it could be a home- or office-based computer that maintains simultaneous connections between two different networks. For example, a home-networked computer that has a VPN established with the corporate offices over dialup would be a member of two different networks at the same time.

NLA can automatically detect logical network interface conditions and properly associate them with the physical attributes of the system. Logical information would come in two forms. Logical Network Identity, as the name implies, identifies which network the system is trying to join. In descending order, NLA uses the network's domain name, static information read from the registry, or finally the subnet of the network. The other form of logical network information is the Logical Network Interface. Each physical interface, including NICs and modems, and each logical interface, such as a RAS connection, is assigned an AdapterName value. The IP Helper API is a piece of software located in Windows that automatically configures each logical interface, binding the configuration to the AdapterName.

DEVICE DRIVER ROLLBACK

Have you ever downloaded a new driver for your computer, installed it, and then had the entire system go down in flames because the driver didn't work right? This can happen from a corrupted download or simply because the wrong driver was downloaded by accident and was not compatible with the device or the OS. Of course, this doesn't always result in system failure. More often than not, you simply can't get the device to work no matter how hard you try.

Device Driver Rollback copies all files related to a specific driver to another location. If the new driver turns out to be a disaster, it is a simple matter of reinstalling the older driver until it can be determined what the problem with the new driver is.

PRODUCT ACTIVATION

Product activation is a feature that really doesn't help the user all that much. It's present simply so that the same OS cannot be installed on more than one computer. This prevents software piracy from occurring on such a regular basis. With product activation, there are two processes involved in proving ownership of a license to run the OS. During installation, the user will be prompted to enter a product key. This is a long series of letters and numbers that is virtually impossible to type without mistake. When the product key is properly inserted, the OS installs.

> **BUZZ WORDS**
>
> **Product activation:** A newer technology that requires the end user to physically activate the product through a database managed by the product's manufacturer. This prevents the product from being installed on multiple machines.

Product activation is a separate process and is usually run concurrently with product registration. To the beginner, it may appear that these two processes are one and the same, but they are not. Product activation is mandatory and must be done within thirty days of installation, or the OS will stop functioning (except for the activation feature). Product activation collects no personal information to be transmitted to Microsoft's site. During installation a unique number called the Installation ID is generated. When users activate their software, the Installation ID and the product key are transmitted to Microsoft. This information is stored in a database. An attempt to install the OS using the same product key will fail.

Product registration is *not* required. Product registration will register you in Microsoft's database of users. However, to get the limited product support Microsoft offers, it should be done. You will also automatically be notified whenever new product updates are available.

WINDOWS XP INSTALLATION AND BOOT PROCESS

For almost every part of the XP installation process and boot sequence I can say, "See WIN2K." The differences are very few. But there are differences. Much of the reason for these differences is Microsoft's new product activation feature, which is something that cannot be turned off.

INSTALLATION DIFFERENCES

Installing XP looks, feels, and smells no different than installing WIN2K. You will go through the same basic steps. If using the upgrade version, you will still have the option of doing an upgrade or a clean install. As with WIN2K, unless there is an overpowering reason for performing an upgrade, the clean install is the way to go. If you choose to perform a clean install from an upgrade CD, make sure you have a CD for a qualifying OS at hand. During setup from the upgrade, there is a point where it will check for a specific file on the CD and compare its attributes and file size to some predefined values.

One major difference becomes evident when the installation is completed. If there is an Internet connection present and available, Setup automatically prompts you to connect to the Microsoft Activation server and activate your software. You will have the option of doing this by telephone, but the Internet activation is faster and simpler.

THE XP BOOT PROCESS

The XP boot process is virtually identical to WIN2K up to the point where NTLDR loads. As with WIN2K, the boot process is broken into stages. The XP stages are

- Initial Boot Loader
- Operating System Selection
- Hardware Detection
- Configuration Selection

INITIAL BOOT LOADER

During this stage, NTLDR switches the CPU from real mode to protected mode. From this point, memory will be read in 32-bit format. Also, the paging services are started, and the Windows Paging file is loaded. Based on the file system that was detected when the MBR was read, the correct file system drivers are loaded at this point. Then NTLDR moves into the next stage.

OPERATING SYSTEM SELECTION

Assuming that XP is the only OS loaded on this system, this is a very short phase. In the event of a multiboot system, it can become a bit more complex. NTLDR locates and loads the BOOT.INI file. The operating system options are displayed on the screen with the default OS highlighted for the number of seconds defined in the **TIMEOUT=** line of BOOT.INI. When a selection has been made, either automatically by the OS or manually by the user, the steps taken by NTLDR are identical to the WIN2K process. One difference in XP is that, if BOOT.INI cannot be located, NTLDR will attempt to load XP from the first partition of the first physical disk defined in the BIOS. If XP was installed onto that partition, then XP can load without the services of BOOT.INI.

It is also during this phase that NTLDR provides the <F8> option for loading the Advanced Boot options. These are identical to the Advanced Boot options of WIN2K and will not be discussed again here.

HARDWARE DETECTION

This is another phase that is identical to WIN2K. NTLDR locates and loads the file NTDETECT.COM. NTDETECT.COM scans the system for any hardware installed on the system and generates a list. NTDETECT.COM loads this list into memory, and NTLDR will later use it to generate the HKEY_LOCAL_MACHINE\HARDWARE hive of the registry.

CONFIGURATION SELECTION

This is another stage that is incredibly short if only a single hardware profile has been configured onto the system. If multiple profiles are configured, then the user will be shown a list of available profiles and have thirty seconds to make a selection before the default profile is loaded.

THE XP LOAD PROCESS

Now that the computer system is ready, the OS can complete the process of initialization. The first step of the load process is kernel load. The user can tell when kernel load had begun. This is when the screen clears and the progression of white markers starts marching across the bottom of the screen. While this is happening, NTLDR is finding and loading HAL.DLL. This loads the hardware abstraction layer that provides the barrier between the OS or applications running on the OS and the physical hardware. Next NTLDR loads the boot device drivers and relinquishes control of the load process to NTOSKRNL.EXE.

Next comes kernel initialization. Kernel initialization can be broken down into two sub-phases. During the first sub-phase, physical interrupts are completely disabled. After this, the second sub-phase begins to load the Executive services in this order:

- Object Manager
- Executive
- Microkernel
- Security Reference Monitor
- Memory Manager
- Cache Manager
- LPCS
- I/O Manager
- Process Manager

The I/O Manager can now assume the responsibility of locating and loading the various device drivers and all the files associated with those drivers. Should any driver fail to properly initialize, the OS will do one of two things. If the CPU can recover from the failure, it will reboot the system and attempt to load using Last Known Good. If it cannot, the adored BSOD will appear, and the user will be forced to manually reboot.

Next the Session Manager subsystem loads. This is the part of the XP kernel that allows the multiuser environment that has made XP so popular. It is *not* here, however that user logon occurs. The next file to load is WIN32K.SYS. This is the XP graphics subsystem. Any services that have been configured either by the user or by the system to be AUTO-START services will now load as well.

Now WINLOGON.EXE loads as an XP system service. The first thing WINLOGON.EXE does is locate and load LSASS.EXE. Here is where XP Pro and XP Home differ. With Pro, the network logon screen will appear. If Home Edition is installed, the pretty little screen with icons for the various users will be displayed. With Pro, the user types in his or her credentials and LSASS.EXE compares them to the information stored in SAM. This security is not enforced in Home Edition. Users have the option of securing their accounts with passwords or not. If password security is not selected, simply clicking the icon will load the user profile.

When the logon has been deemed successful by WINLOGON.EXE, Last Known Good information is written to the registry. Users are logged into their profiles, and the XP Load process is completed.

THE XP INTERFACE

Superficially, XP has undergone what appears to be a complete transformation. To the experienced Windows user, it can be a little intimidating at first. The Start button and taskbar don't look the same. When you open the Start menu for the first time, it's almost like entering a whole new world. Power users and technicians are presented with a completely different approach to the Control Panel.

If you really don't want to learn a whole new interface, don't panic. It's possible to select options that present the older WIN2K menus. Of course, rehashing old stuff doesn't make for a good book, so in this section, I'm going to take the updated Start menu and Control Panel apart and show you how they've changed in XP.

The Start Menu

The Start menu (**Figure 30.1**) in XP was redesigned from the ground up in a manner intended to make it easier to reach the most recently accessed programs without having to sift through rarely used applications. This is similar to the personalized menus in WIN2K, but takes a more sophisticated approach. In addition, commonly accessed system functions, such as the Control Panel and My Computer, have been more conspicuously placed.

> **Exam Note:** As far as XP is concerned, the majority of exam questions are likely to center on the Start menu and Control Panel. Read the following sections carefully.

The XP Start menu is divided into two sections. The programs list can be found on the left side. The programs list has actually been divided into three sections. The first section (located at the top) is called the *pinned list*. The pinned list is similar to the Favorites list in other

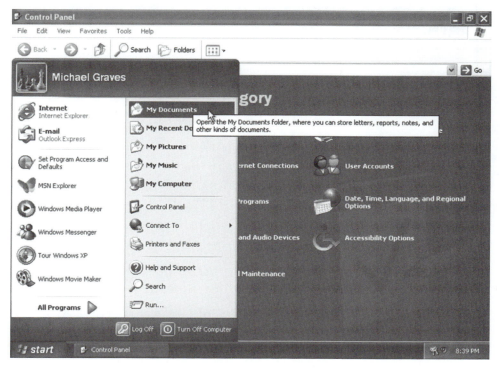

Figure 30.1   The XP Start menu in all its glory

Windows OSs and applications such as Internet Explorer. A user can place shortcuts to applications that are used day in and day out in this section. Default shortcuts that appear in the pinned list include the user's Web browser of choice and email client.

Any program can be added to the pinned list. Simply right-click the item in any Explorer window. In the popup menu that appears (**Figure 30.2**), click Pin to Start Menu. Another way an item can be added is by dragging and dropping it to the Start button or the Start menu. If a user no longer wants an item to be a part of the pinned list, it can be removed from this list by right-clicking it and clicking Unpin from Start Menu or Remove from This List. If a user is not happy with the order in which the items appear on this list, he or she can rearrange them simply by dragging and dropping items to the preferred position.

Beneath the pinned list is the Most Frequently Used (MFU) list. There is a separator line that divides the two sections. Windows keeps track of how often programs are used and displays the ones used most frequently on top, while programs that are rarely used appear on the bottom. A program that is no longer wanted on the list can be removed by right-clicking the shortcut and then clicking Remove from This List. One thing that might irk a meticulously organized user is the fact that items in this list cannot be manually arranged.

> **BUZZ WORDS**
>
> **Pinned list:** A list of shortcuts to applications that are used on a regular basis.

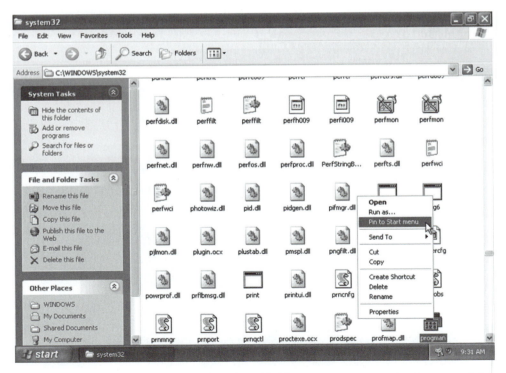

Figure 30.2 Adding a program to the pinned list is as easy as a couple of mouse clicks.

Beneath the MFU list is another horizontal line, and beneath that line is the All Programs option. Clicking that option will open a list of all applications installed on the system.

The section of the Start menu on the right-hand side provides links to user folders, such as My Documents, My Pictures, and My Music, and to frequently accessed system areas such as My Computer, Search, and Control Panel.

The Start menu that appears is specific to the profile that is selected at startup. If a user chooses to configure his or her menu differently, that is easily done. By right-clicking the Start button or by right-clicking any empty area within the Start menu, a user can make changes to the way the Start menu appears. This includes selecting the "Classic" Windows menu. This choice will make the start menu look and feel like the WIN2K menu. A user's changes will be evident only when that user is logged on. They will not affect other users on the system.

THE CONTROL PANEL

For the vast majority of users, the change in XP that gave them the most pause was Control Panel (**Figure 30.3**). Microsoft's approach to system management was so drastically changed

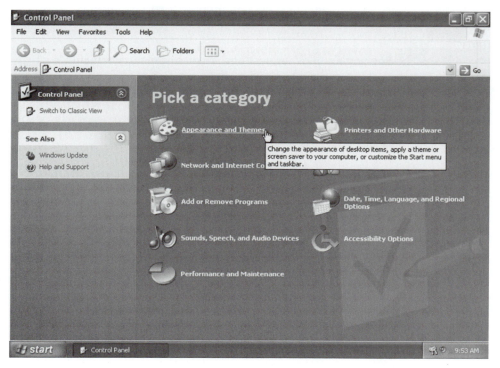

Figure 30.3 The XP Control Panel has been subdivided into several sections for better organization.

that even veteran technicians found themselves lost at first. However, once people got used to the new approach, most began to appreciate the change. The new Control Panel divides the different applets into specific categories, rather than piling them all into a single screen, arranged in alphabetical order. The categories include the following:

- Appearance and Themes
- Network and Internet Connections
- Add or Remove Programs
- Sounds, Speech, and Audio Devices
- Performance and Maintenance
- Printers and Other Hardware
- User Accounts
- Date, Time, Language, and Regional Options
- Accessibility Options

In each section, the user will be presented with shortcuts to specific tasks and shortcuts to Control Panel applets. This is handy because the user need not navigate through a number of different folders and/or menu items to get to a commonly used task such as adjusting screen resolution.

EXAM NOTE: The key to the following sections is not so much to remember where all the shortcuts to the tasks are as it is to learn the shortcuts to Control Panel applets. Make sure you know where each Control Panel applet can be found in the various sections. CompTIA is more interested in the applets.

APPEARANCE AND THEMES

Appearance and Themes (**Figure 30.4**) is the collection of utilities that allows the user to configure how the desktop and applications appear to the eye. Features like colors, fonts, background pictures, and so forth are selected here. There are four tasks that can be performed here:

- *Change the computer's theme*: This option allows the user to choose between a variety of different preconfigured themes. A theme basically consists of colors and fonts that have been selected to work well together, as well as a default screen saver and background picture.
- *Change the desktop background*: This brings up a large selection of different choices of desktop patterns or photographs. Users can also select from custom designed bitmaps of their own choosing.

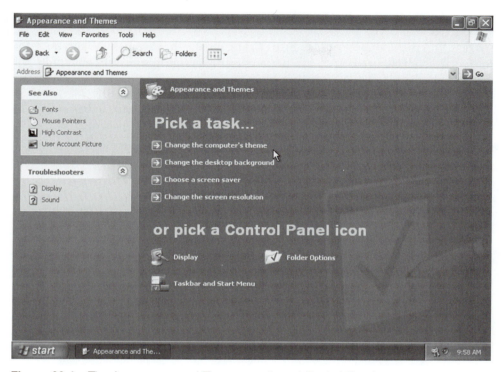

Figure 30.4   The Appearance and Themes section of Control Panel

■ *Choose a screen saver*: When a screen saver is selected, after a predesignated amount of time the image displayed on the screen when the user last left it is blanked out and the selected screensaver image appears on the screen in its place, randomly moving from position to position. The prevents a phenomenon called monitor burn-in.

■ *Change the screen resolution*: At the risk of sounding overly technical, this is where the user goes to change the dots per inch that the graphics adapter will use to create the images on the screen.

There are three Control Panel applets that have shortcuts in this section. Since these work exactly the same way they did in WIN2K and were described in detail in earlier chapters, they will not be described again here.

■ Display

■ Task Bar and Start Menu

■ Folder Options

NETWORK AND INTERNET CONNECTIONS

Network and Internet Connections (**Figure 30.5**) contains the various configurations for both local network connections as well as Internet configurations. The different tasks that are available include the following:

■ *Set up or change your Internet connection*: A new Internet account can be configured here, or changes in the configuration of an existing account can be made.

■ *Create a connection to the network at your workplace:* This is a more user-friendly way of telling users that they will be creating a virtual private network (VPN). A VPN is a secure connection to a remote LAN over the Internet.

■ *Set up or change your home or small office network:* LAN settings are adjusted here.

There are also two Control Panel applets located in this section:

■ Internet Options
■ Network Connections

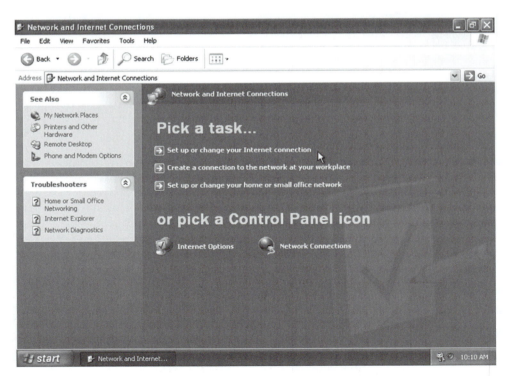

Figure 30.5 Network and Internet Connections

ADD/REMOVE PROGRAMS

The Add/Remove Programs (**Figure 30.6**) function of XP really isn't all that much different than in WIN2K. The real difference is that Microsoft brought all the functions out front where the user can see them. There are four functions available here.

- *Change or Remove Programs*: Any time the user wants to uninstall a program, Add/ Remove Change or Remove is the correct procedure. It is very rare that any changes can be made to a program once installed.

- *Add New Programs*: Allows the user to install new applications from CD or floppy disk, over the network, or from a Microsoft Update over the Internet.

- *Add/Remove Windows Components*: During a typical installation, there is a large number of features available to the user that do not get installed by default. Other features may have been added that are not useful. This utility allows the user to take out unused features and add those that were not originally installed. The original installation CD will be required for adding features.

- *Set Program Access and Defaults*: This is where users can select their preferences for the default program to open different file types and to select default email clients and Web browsers.

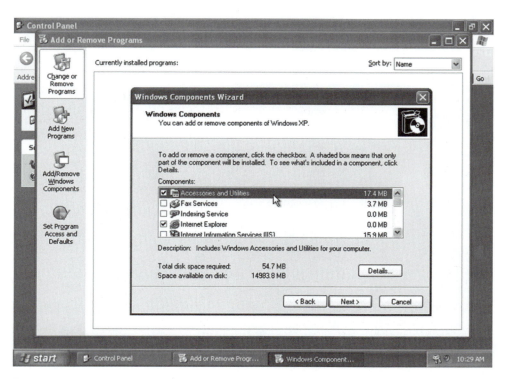

Figure 30.6   Add or Remove Programs

SOUNDS, SPEECH, AND AUDIO DEVICES

Windows XP is designed to be a multimedia OS. As such, it can be configured to play sounds to alert the user to specific events. It can also talk to you! Of course, for that to happen, the computer's hardware has to support these functions and be properly configured. The Sounds, Speech, and Audio Devices screen (**Figure 30.7**) is where the user makes all that happen.

There are three tasks and two Control Panel applets accessible from this section. The tasks, which are all self-explanatory, include the following:

- Adjust the system volume
- Change the sound scheme
- Change the speaker settings

The Control Panel applets are

- *Sounds and Audio Devices*: Hardware configuration and driver options for the audio portion of multimedia
- *Speech*: Allows the user to select the voice that will issue from the computer and how quickly the voice will speak if the Text to Speech function is enabled and selected.

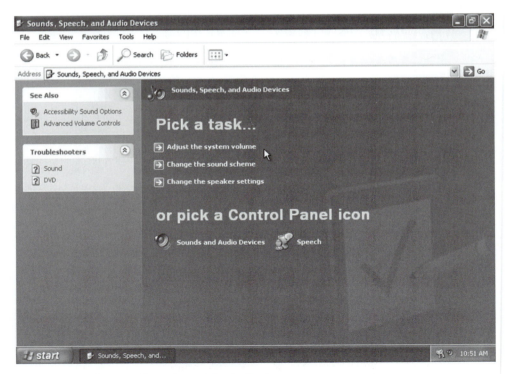

Figure 30.7 Sounds, Speech, and Audio Devices

PERFORMANCE AND MAINTENANCE

The Performance and Maintenance section (**Figure 30.8**) is one of the busiest of Control Panel's sublevels. In this grouping there are five different tasks and four different Control Panel applets available. The tasks include the following:

■ *See basic information about your computer*: This function simply lists the configuration of the system. No changes can be made.

■ *Adjust visual effects*: Here, the user can adjust a large number of different settings such as fading menus, animated windows, shadows, and various other items that make Windows more or less pretty.

■ *Free up space on your hard disk*: This is a maintenance utility that looks for duplicate files, temporary files, temporary Internet files, and files in the Recycle Bin that can be safely deleted.

■ *Back up your data*: This is a shortcut to the Windows Backup utility. This is very similar to the utility described in Chapter Twenty-Nine, WIN2K System Administration.

■ *Rearrange items on your hard drive to make programs run faster:* This is a shortcut to the Defrag utility.

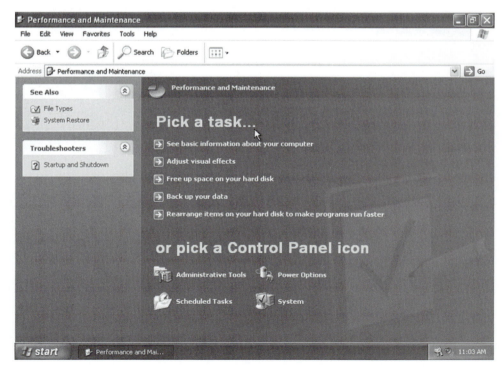

Figure 30.8   The Performance and Maintenance window

There are four Control Panel applets located here:

- Administrative Tools
- Scheduled Tasks
- Power Options
- System

PRINTERS AND OTHER HARDWARE

The place to configure graphical devices, such as printers, fax devices, digital cameras, and scanners, as well as other input devices, including the mouse, modem, and keyboard, is the Printers and Other Hardware section (**Figure 30.9**). There are two tasks and six Control Panel applets available from this screen.

The tasks include the following:

- *View installed printers or fax printers*: Allows the user to check the status and/or properties of a specific device already installed on the system.
- *Add a printer*: Allows the user to install a new device.

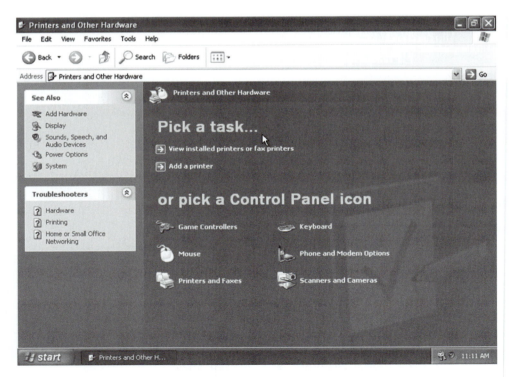

Figure 30.9 Printers and Other Hardware

The Control Panel applets found here include:

- Game Controllers
- Mouse
- Printers and Faxes
- Keyboard
- Phone and Modem Options
- Scanners and Cameras

USER ACCOUNTS

If a new user needs to be added to the system, an old user removed, or the security settings of an account changed, the User Accounts window (**Figure 30.10**) is the place to be. This is one Control Panel section that does not have a shortcut to a specific Control Panel applet. There are three basic tasks that have shortcuts here:

- *Change an account*: Personal information about users can be edited, and security settings can be modified to existing accounts. There are shortcuts at the bottom of the screen to go directly to existing user accounts. You must be logged on to an account with full administrative features to use this function.

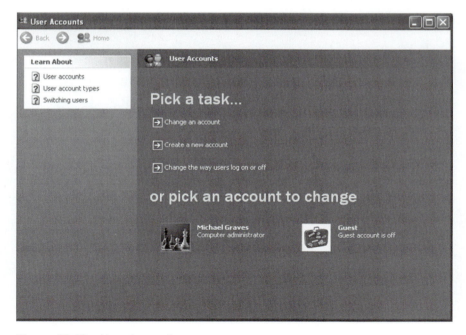

Figure 30.10 User Accounts

■ *Create a new account*: Self-explanatory, I hope.

■ *Change the way users log on or off*: The basic Welcome screen of XP Home edition can be used in place of the network logon screen if security is not an issue. Fast User Switching allows one user to log off and another to log on without closing programs.

DATE, TIME, LANGUAGE, AND REGIONAL OPTIONS

Most of these adjustments should be self-explanatory, although the regional options might not be familiar to all. The Date, Time, Language, and Regional Options screen (**Figure 30.11**) allows users to adjust the real time clock and calendar however they see fit. Languages other than the English language are available as well. The regional options allows users to select the symbols used for currency, and set other configurations, such as how the time and date are displayed, based on local custom. There are three tasks that can be accessed from here:

■ Change the date and time

■ Change the format of numbers, dates, and times

■ Add other languages

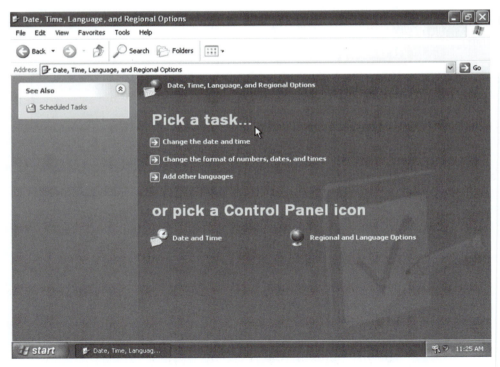

Figure 30.11   Date, Time, Language, and Regional Options

There are two Control Panel applets that can be accessed:

- Date and Time
- Regional and Language Options

ACCESSIBILITY OPTIONS

The final category in the Control Panel collection is the area where Accessibility Options are adjusted (**Figure 30.12**). Windows XP enables people with impaired hearing to replace the sound effects with visual effects. Likewise, people with eyesight problems can use audible menus and enhanced contrast screens. There are two tasks available here:

- Adjust the contrast for text and colors on your screen
- Configure Windows to work for your vision, hearing, and mobility needs

The one Control Panel applet located here is Accessibility Options.

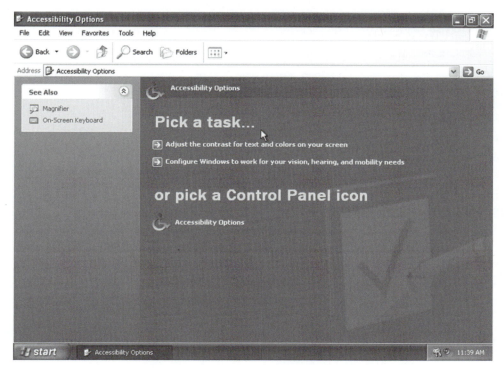

Figure 30.12 Accessibility Options

CHAPTER SUMMARY

Although XP is touted as the latest and greatest of Microsoft's desktop OSs, in reality, it's nothing more than an old engine mounted into a fancy new body. A few tweaks here and there give it a bit more speed and stability. A few new toys make it more attractive to the users. But under the pretty new skin, it's not that much different from WIN2K.

Important differences to remember, though, are the subdivision of the Control Panel and the Layout of the Start menu. In addition, remember that XP now offers drag-and-drop functionality for CD-RWs.

BRAIN DRAIN

1. List the various versions of Windows XP that are available, and discuss how they differ from one another.

2. What are some features that migrated over to XP from Windows 2000 but that offer enhanced functionality in XP?

3. List some features that are brand new to XP. Discuss how they improve the product.

4. Discuss the new layout of the Start menu and how it can improve usability of the OS.

5. How is Control Panel different between XP and WIN2K?

THE 64K$ QUESTIONS

1. Two of the limitations of Home Edition are that _____.
   a. It only supports one CPU
   b. It doesn't offer EFS
   c. It only supports five users per system
   d. It cannot join a domain

2. The only networking capability offered by XP Home is Internet connectivity.
   a. True
   b. False

3. XP Home requires a minimum of _____ RAM in order to run.
   a. 64MB
   b. 128MB
   c. 256MB
   d. None of the above

4. XP Professional requires a minimum of _____ RAM in order to run.
   a. 64MB
   b. 128MB
   c. 256MB
   d. None of the above

5. The absolute minimum CPU required by either Home or Professional is a _____.
   a. 266MHz PII
   b. 300MHz PII
   c. 300MHz PIII
   d. 500MHz PIII

6. XP Professional supports a maximum of _____ CPUs on a system.
   a. 1
   b. 2
   c. 4
   d. 8

7. The feature that was added to EFS that makes it different between XP and WIN2K is _____.

   a. The administrator can decrypt files

   b. A public key that will open the files is deposited in a hidden read-only directory

   c. Files can be encrypted for use by entire groups instead of only individuals

   d. There is no difference.

8. System Restore is a function that migrated over to XP from _____.

   a. WIN98SE

   b. WINMe

   c. WIN2K SP3

   d. It's a new feature.

9. Which of the following is not a new feature to XP?

   a. Group Policy Management

   b. Side-by-side DLL support

   c. ClearType

   d. Device Driver Rollback

10. You must register XP within thirty days, or it will lose functionality.

    a. True

    b. False

11. You can take over control of another user's system to help with a problem because of a protocol known as _____.

    a. Remote Systems Management Protocol

    b. Systems Management Services Protocol

    c. Remote Desktop Protocol

    d. Long Distance Management Protocol

12. ClearType works by _____.

    a. Improving the vertical resolution of text

    b. Improving the horizontal resolution of text

    c. Improving both the horizontal and vertical resolution of text

    d. Redefining the screen font used by text

13. XP offers two methods of recovering from an improperly installed device driver. What are these two methods?

    a. Auto-recovery

    b. Driver Signing

    c. Device Driver Rollback

    d. System Restore

14. The following information is transmitted to Microsoft when you activate XP.

    a. Name, address, and email address

    b. CPU serial number

    c. The file allocation tables on your hard drive

    d. The Installation ID

15. The Start menu in XP is divided into _____ sections.

    a. 1

    b. 2

    c. 3

    d. 4

16. The one section of the XP Start menu that cannot be edited by the user is _____.

    a. The pinned list

    b. The MFU

    c. All Programs

    d. The user can modify all sections of the Start menu

17. If you need to check the settings of your sound card's device driver, you would find them in the _____ section of Control Panel. (Choose all that apply.)

    a. Sounds, Speech, and Audio Devices

    b. Performance and Maintenance

    c. Printers and Other Hardware

    d. Accessibility Options

18. A digital camera can be managed from the _____ section of Control Panel.

    a. Sounds, Speech, and Audio Devices

    b. Performance and Maintenance

    c. Printers and Other Hardware

    d. Accessibility Options

19. Which of the following is not an adjustment a user can make in Accessibility Options?

    a. Screen contrast

    b. Speech options

    c. Text size

    d. Mouse cursor trails

20. Into how many different sections has Control Panel been divided in XP?

    a. 6

    b. 7

    c. 8

    d. 9

TRICKY TERMINOLOGY

Pinned list: A list of shortcuts to applications that are used on a regular basis.

Product activation: A newer technology that requires the end user to physically activate the product through a database managed by the product's manufacturer. This prevents the product from being installed on multiple machines.

Restore point: A copy of system files and registry entries that were in place at the time a major system change was introduced.

ACRONYM ALERT

MFU: Most Frequently Used. The portion of the XP Start menu that displays applications that have been opened over a predefined period of time, in the order which they were opened. Apps are displayed from most recently used to least recently.

NLA: Network Location Awareness. A feature in XP that automatically configures a computer system to the network or subnet to which the device is attached.

RDP: Remote Desktop Protocol. A protocol that allows remote administration of another computer over the network.

RSoP: Resultant Set of Policy. A feature in XP that allows the administrator to test the results of a new policy on a select group of guinea pigs before inflicting it on the entire network.

 VIEW THE VIDEO

A video clip on Windows 9X, NT4, ME, 2000, and XP is available on the accompanying CD.

CHAPTER 31

INTRODUCING LINUX

Up until this point, you were probably thinking that this book was going to be exclusively about Microsoft operating systems. Admittedly the book is weighted heavily toward Microsoft. There are two reasons for this, and neither of them relate to quality, whether it be the quality of Microsoft products or the quality of competing products.

The biggest reason in my own mind for writing the book in this fashion is that it is intended to be a training guide to the CompTIA A+ Certification exam. And although CompTIA is vendor neutral in practically every other exam it administers, the most recent versions of the OS exam exclusively target Microsoft products.

The second reason is that the vast majority of computer systems the technician will see are powered by Microsoft products. The bundling agreements computer manufacturers have with Microsoft only serve to increase this percentage.

However, in this chapter, I'm going to point out another very viable option that's available. I won't be going into quite the detail in this chapter as I did in previous chapters, because you won't be tested on any of the material in this chapter. Therefore, if your class is targeted exclusively for the A+ Exam, you can safely skip this chapter. This chapter can be considered optional reading. In addition, note that there will be no exercises or questions at the end of this chapter.

A HISTORY AND OVERVIEW OF LINUX

Linux is an operating system that, in a way, stumbled clumsily into glory. What started out as a college student's hobby has gradually evolved into one of the few industry standard OSs that competes openly and directly with Microsoft while still operating on the same hardware platform. Although the Macintosh system competes with Microsoft, it requires completely different hardware to run.

THE HISTORY OF LINUX

Many articles and books openly state that Linux is an offshoot of another operating system called UNIX. In so much as many of the technical features, including how it handles hardware interrupts, how addressing is accomplished in the applications, and so on, are similar, this is true. However, to state that Linux was derived from UNIX suggests that much of the same code was used. That is entirely untrue.

The UNIX OS first began development in Bell Labs back in 1971. Throughout the 1970s, UNIX code was provided to a number of different organizations. Many of these organizations reworked the OS to their own specifications, and as a result, before the decade of the 1980s began, there were a number of different varieties of UNIX.

The concept of open source development is credited to a man by the name of Richard Stallman. In 1985, he published an article entitled "The GNU Manifesto." The acronym was actually a tongue-in-cheek name that meant "GNU is Not UNIX." Since part of the acronym when spelled out is the acronym itself, it technically cannot exist. In this manifesto, Mr. Stallman presented the idea that software as fundamental as an operating system should belong to the public and not a large self-serving corporation. He proposed that open source software be developed that carried an anticopyright. By this, he meant that no single individual or organization would be allowed to place a copyright on open source software.

In 1987, Professor Andrew Tannenbaum developed an OS that he intended to be freely distributed. It was nearly a direct clone of UNIX that he called Minix. A college student by the name of Linus Torvalds got interested in Minix and decided to create his own version. This version was released in 1991 as Linux 0.01 and carried with it an official GNU Public License. He called his license copyleft, another term originated with tongue firmly in cheek. As he said, it is the opposite of a copyright, in that nobody gets to own it. Everybody owns it. He issued a public appeal for top-level programmers to lend a hand in making Linux a sufficiently viable product to compete with the big wigs like Microsoft and UNIX.

The response was far greater than he could have possibly imagined. By 1994, more than a hundred thousand programmers had contributed code. And as it turned out, Torvalds' free software proved to be a commercial success as well. Since Linux, in its earlier incarnations, was anything *but* user friendly, a number of companies sprang up that made available assembled distributions. As I shall point out in the next section, the Linux OS can be a bit complex to install. A distribution contains not only the OS kernel files, but a large collection of device drivers, user interfaces, and applications to go along with the OS. Current companies that provide Linux distributions include the following, in alphabetical order:

- Debian
- Gentoo
- Inspire
- Knoppix
- Lycoris
- Mandrake
- Red Hat (Fedora)
- Slackware
- SuSE
- Xandros

Although there may be others, these were the distributions I could find at the time of this writing. If I've left anybody out, it was unintentional, and I apologize.

AN OVERVIEW OF LINUX

One of the first things a Microsoft veteran needs to learn when trying to migrate to Linux is that it isn't Microsoft. Many things are done differently, and how some things are done is version specific. So for the next few pages, I'm going to go over some of the key issues in dealing with Linux. Some of the things I'll discuss include distribution packages, version numbering, the Linux File System, and installing packages.

DISTRIBUTION PACKAGES

As I indicated earlier in the chapter, Linux is designed to be a free OS. Yet, if you walk into any software store and most office supply stores, you see boxes advertising Linux ranging from twenty bucks on up. How is this free?

The idea of the distribution package is actually quite simple. Linux is not as easy to install and configure from scratch as is a more commercially recognizable product such as Windows. Various companies make their money by assembling packages that include the OS kernel along with a huge collection of installation packages. An installation package is an installable program that performs some specific functions. Device drivers and applications all ship as installation packages.

Different vendors have taken different approaches to developing their installation packages. For example, Red Hat favors the Red Hat Package Management (RPM) technology. Under Red Hat, an RPM is nearly as easy to install as any application that installs under Windows. Tarballs are favored by many other vendors. A tarball is a single compressed file that contains the installation package with its file system hierarchy intact. A decompression program, such as GZIP, is used to decompress the package. Tarballs can be a bit more intimidating for the beginner in that they are generally installed from a command prompt.

When you select a Linux distribution package, you are not paying for the software. Every single file (except help files and product documentation) can be obtained for free over the Internet. What you are purchasing is a collection of files and utilities that have been extensively tested and are known to work together. You are purchasing extended documentation, and in many cases, you are purchasing support from the vendor. If you are technically astute and have no need for documentation or support, there is no need to pay for a distribution package.

VERSION NUMBERING IN LINUX

This part of understanding Linux is enough to drive even the seasoned veteran over the edge. This is primarily because one distribution vendor's version has no relationship whatsoever with the version numbers used by other vendors. Therefore, it is not possible to take the version number from a Red Hat distribution and make a direct comparison to a Debian distribution. Some assumptions can be made, however.

The Linux kernel version will remain constant, regardless of the distribution or vendor. For example, as of this writing, Mandrake Linux has a version 9.0 out. It uses the Linux kernel version 2.4.19. Therefore, it is safe to assume that any other distribution by another vendor that uses that same kernel will offer the same capabilities. The various vendors, conversely, may include completely different collections of installation packages.

A kernel version will consist of three numbers, separated by dots. The first two numbers indicate the version of that file. The third number indicates the most recent OS patch updates. In the previous example, 2.4 is the version of the kernel, and 19 indicates that it is the nineteenth applied patch. A key thing to remember is that the second number will tell you whether the version you are running is a stable version or a developmental version. All stable versions carry an even number in the second position, while a version still under development will have an odd number. No distribution package sold over the counter should ever have an odd number in the second position.

THE LINUX FILE SYSTEM

For someone whose familiarity with OSs has exclusively been Microsoft products, the Linux file system can be very difficult to understand. In fact, this subject is of such great importance that I have a dedicated section to the file system later in this chapter. I wanted to include a brief note in this section, however, that the differences are so great that if you create a dual-boot system, Linux files and Microsoft files will not even be visible to the other OS.

The Linux file system is derived (like the majority of other Linux technology) from UNIX. As such, the method by which data is stored and the path naming conventions are different from Windows. Linux uses ARC conventions (which were discussed in Chapter Twenty-Six, Windows NT Architecture). Although Microsoft products are able to use ARC paths, ARC is not the default method used by Microsoft.

Unlike FAT or NTFS, the hard disks in the computer are not assigned drive letters. They are given names. The first drive in the system is a, the second b, and so on and so forth. But that letter is not the entirety of the drive name. A SCSI drive is sd, and an IDE drive is hd. So the first physical SCSI hard disk is sda. A second SCSI drive would be sdb. And that's still not all. Linux is going to divide the drive into multiple partitions with each partition getting a number, starting with 1. So the first partition in the primary SCSI drive is sda1; the second partition is sda2. Get the idea? **Figure 31.1** is an attempt to illustrate this concept.

Also, file names are case-sensitive. NOVEL.doc is not the same filename as novel.doc. Early Linux versions supported file names of up to 128 characters, including the three-character extension. More recent versions allow for file names up to 256 characters. As I said, there will be a more detailed discussion of the file system later in this chapter.

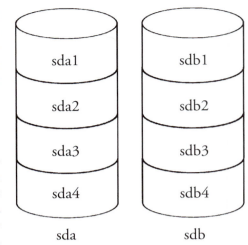

Figure 31.1 Linux divides the drive into multiple partitions. The first partition in the primary SCSI drive is sda1, the second partition is sda2.

LINUX DESKTOP OR LINUX SERVER?

As Linux has emerged over the years, it has become increasingly clear that, at its core, Linux has the potential to be a very powerful server application. Since it supports very large address spaces and multiple CPUs, many consider it to be the perfect platform for a Web Server.

Conversely, those very same features make it an ideal platform for building a powerful desktop. Today's business and graphics applications are requiring vastly increased CPU horsepower and eat up memory in megabytes. The fact that Linux has historically managed memory more efficiently than Microsoft OSs has always made it popular, but a lack of applications has turned many potential users away. These days a plethora of very powerful applications and suites are available for the Linux user. That excuse is no longer viable.

LINUX ON THE DESKTOP

In the past two or three years, Linux has made some remarkable gains on both Microsoft and Apple in terms of the number of desktop computers equipped with its OS. Although public awareness undoubtedly has a great deal of responsibility for this increase in market share, simple usability accounts for even more. Linux has made some remarkable gains in both the friendliness of the desktop environment and in terms of the number of applications available to the end user.

THE LINUX DESKTOP ENVIRONMENT

In its early years, Linux was a purely command-line interface. That was the key limitation that prevented it from becoming a mainstream OS. With this in mind, Linux developers starting pursuing a graphical point-and-click environment that would make former Windows users feel more at home. Two desktop environments for Linux have taken center stage: KDE and GNOME. Both of these options provide the user with a desktop environment, file manager, a set of applications ranging from simple games to integrated Web browsers to full-fledged office productivity suites, a number of administration tools, and a set of libraries and tools that help programmers develop applications for the respective platform.

Although it's true that neither of these desktop environments offer the polish and glitter of XP, what they lack in looks they make up for in stability. A Linux desktop doesn't think twice about running twenty-four hours a day, seven days a week without requiring a restart. Application protection at the CPU level assures the end user that even if a Linux app does crash and burn, the system can remain running and stable.

AVAILABILITY OF APPLICATIONS

In answer to early complaints that Linux lacked an array of user applications, a number of developers stepped up to the table. Sun developed a suite called Star Office (current version as of this writing is 6.0). While not free, this suite still costs only a fraction of Microsoft Office. It offers a word processor, a spreadsheet program, a presentation graphics application, and a database application. All applications offer file filters so that files created by Star Office can be shared with Microsoft Office users.

Perhaps more appealing is an offering by OpenOffice.ORG. It offers all the same functionality of Star Office as well as a powerful drawing program. On top of that, it's free! In addition, OpenOffice.ORG has versions of its product that will run on Windows and the Mac OS platforms. (Much of this book has been prepared in OpenOffice applications. Just don't tell my editors. They think I'm using "the real thing.")

Digital photographers have long eschewed Linux for its lack of any professional level photo-editing software. Justification for this complaint came to an abrupt end with the release of The GIMP. GIMP doesn't mean it's disabled. The acronym stands for Gnu Image Manipulation Program. Its features and interface compare favorably to that really popular and powerful commercial program I'm supposed to be using to create the images in this book.

One of the biggest fears the habitual Windows user has about Linux is that it is too difficult to learn. This is a holdover from the old days when Linux *was* too difficult for the average user to pick up. Both KDE and GNOME insist that their Linux release offers an easy migration path for Windows users. In truth, neither one is identical to Windows in either look or feel. However, either one can be configured to offer a similar computing environment to that of Windows.

THE LINUX SERVER

The same Linux that makes such an inviting desktop environment is an equally inviting server application, with a few slight modifications and a different collection of installation packages. As with the desktop systems, anything you need to configure a fully functional enterprise server can be downloaded for free over the Internet. On the other hand, the reasonable cost of a tested installation package certainly has its allure. All of the Linux distributors mentioned earlier in the chapter offer installation packages for Linux servers.

The beauty of Linux is that a core OS can be had that runs on Intel, Power PC, or even mainframe computers. Linux users were able to take advantage of 64-bit microprocessors long before the "big boys" had anything similar to offer. Recent extensions developed by SuSE, in conjunction with Siemans AG, allow for Linux to address up to 4GB of RAM on Intel-based machines.

As a result, a Linux box is more than capable of handling the requirements of an enterprise level mail server or file server. It has long been a favorite environment for Web servers. And recent extensions that support clustering have now made it attractive to administrators responsible for large databases that see heavy traffic as well.

THE LINUX FILE SYSTEM

If you are reading this book specifically for the purpose of preparing for the A+ Core Exam, it is unlikely that you will get any questions relating to this file system. Still, there are a lot of computers out there in the real world that make use of the Linux operating system, and unless you know the basics of the file system you're going to flounder like a duck on an oil slick.

The Linux File System is virtually identical to that of the UNIX File System (UFS). It uses a tree structure in which all directories stem out from the Root, and subdirectories can stem out from other directories. If this sounds similar to the structure used by Microsoft OSs, it should. In fact, I think it's safe to say that other OSs emulated UNIX in this manner.

There are differences in how to interpret the Linux directory tree. The root directory is represented by a single /. Beneath the root are several subdirectories. The most common subdirectories seen on a Linux system are as follows:

- */bin:* Commands and directories needed by the user
- */dev:* Files used to represent specific devices, either installed on the system or remotely connected
- */etc:* Commands and utilities used for system administration
- */lib:* Libraries used by various programs or programming languages
- */tmp:* Temporary files
- */usr:* Subdivided into subdirectories; these include the games that ship with the OS and the home directory for each user created on the system
- */Kernel File:* Home of the operating system files

UFS breaks the hard drive down into *blocks*. Depending on the version being used, blocks will consist of one, two, or four sectors. Data is stored in the blocks.

The file system can be broken down into four distinct components, the boot block, the super block, the i-node list, and the data blocks. The boot block contains the information needed to initialize the operating system from a cold start. The super block defines the state of the file system. This would include such information as how many files are already stored, how much available space remains on the device, and permissions associated with the device. The i-node list, usually simply referred to as the i-list, keeps track of the locations of individual files stored on the device. And, as you might imagine, the data blocks are where the data is actually stored.

By default Linux is a network operating system. As such, it must support the ability to service multiple users at once. One of the methods it uses to accomplish this is to assign users their own home directory in the /usr directory. When users log on to the system, they are automatically directed to their home directory. Linux uses a different method of accessing files than the file systems I discussed earlier in the book. Instead of a file system table that maps out specific FAUs on the hard drive, Linux provides a unique file system for each user. Another file system is opened called the root file system.

The i-list keeps track of the file systems that are mounted at any given time. The i-list is nothing more than a fixed memory location that contains a list of entries for each file system mounted. For each file system, an i-node is generated. It is the i-node that contains the information used by UFS to locate files on the physical storage device. Each i-node can contain up to ten pointers. A *pointer* is a line of code that maps to a specific block. Each i-node can also contain one indirect pointer, one double-indirect pointer, and one triple-indirect pointer. An indirect pointer maps points to a cluster of pointers.

Buzz Words

Block: The number of sectors on a hard drive that UFS uses as the smallest recognizable data unit.

Pointer: A line of code used by UFS to map a cluster used by a specific file.

The ten pointers of an i-node can basically define a 5KB file. For a file larger than 5KB, an indirect pointer maps to a storage block that stores a table of additional block pointers. If an earlier version of Linux is installed, a block points to a single sector of 512 bytes. A pointer uses 4 bytes. Therefore, a table could contain 128 pointers. A 1024-byte block could contain 256 pointers, and a 2048-byte block could contain 512. For the purposes of this discussion, I will stick to the 512-byte block. An indirect pointer adds 128 pointers per block, which would allow the system to manage a 64KB file.

After file size exceeds 64KB, a double-indirect pointer will be employed. A double-indirect pointer maintains a table of locations to up to 128 indirect pointers. Since an indirect pointer can map up to 64KB of storage space, a double-indirect pointer would map up to $128 \times 64KB$, or 8MB.

For files larger than 8MB, the system needs to make use of the services of the triple-indirect pointer. The triple-indirect pointer maps to 128 double-indirect pointers. This allows the UFS to support files up to a gigabyte in size.

As I mentioned earlier, the more recent versions of Linux make use of 2KB blocks. This means each block can contain up to 512 pointers. As a result, UFS can theoretically support up to 64GB files. However, a field contained in the i-node that defines file size is only 4 bytes long. This imposes a 4GB limitation on file size.

Other information stored in each i-node includes the following:

- *File Owner ID*: A number generated by the OS that is used by the security file to identify the specific user on the system who created the file.
- *Group ID*: This identifies a group of users that can be granted specific levels of access by the owner.
- *File type*: Files can be listed as any one of several file types:
  - *Regular file*: A conventional data file.
  - *D file (Directory file)*: A file that contains file names and their associated i-node numbers.
  - *L file (Symbolic link file)*: A file that contains the path information needed to access a file.
  - *C file (Character special file)*: A file that is intended to be accessed one character at a time. The file associated to your keyboard would be an example of a character file.
  - *B file (Block special file)*: A file that is accessed a block at a time. The file associated to your monitor is an example of a block special file.
  - *P file (Pipe file)*: A file associated to a device that streams data into a system, such as a modem or network card. This type of file is usually required by any device that needs to buffer data.
- *File access permissions*: There are three kinds of access, and three types of permissions:
  - *User access* is automatically granted to the person who owns the file. This is generally the creator, unless someone with administrative privileges has taken ownership.
  - *Group access* is restricted access granted to any member of a specified group.

- *Other access* consists of whatever level of access has been granted to anyone not recognized by user or group access lists.
- *Read access* allows a user to inspect the data stored in the file, but that user can make no changes or delete the file.
- *Write access* allows the user to make changes the file.
- *Execute access* allows the user to run any executable code contained within the file.

An i-node can also keep track of various access times:

- *File access time*: This indicates when the file data last opened by the system. Events that will change this value include:
  - Displaying the contents of the file
  - Copying the file to a new location or file system
  - Editing the file
- Events that will not change this value include:
  - Moving the file to another directory in the current file system
  - Using redirection to append data to an existing file
- *File modification time*: This indicates when data contained within the file was last changed. Events that will affect this value include the following:
  - Creating the file initializes the value
  - Editing a file and saving it will update this value
  - Overwriting the file with new data will update this value
  - Appending data to an existing file will update this value
- *I-node modification time*: This value shows when information in the i-node was last changed. Events that alter this value include:
  - Creating additional hard links to the file
  - Changes in file size

THE FUTURE OF LINUX

Will all these good things going for it, one would think that Linux would be the wave of the future. You can get it free if you want. Even if you need lots of handholding and personal attention along with a foolproof installation package, it's still a quarter of the price of commercial OSs. Every day seems to see more and more powerful commercial and personal applications emerge onto the marketplace that are either free or so darned cheap they may as well be free. So why is Linux showing up on fewer than 15 percent of desktops worldwide?

Much of this has to do with perception and awareness. Most individuals purchase their PCs at the local electronics store or over the Internet, and they come bundled with Windows.

Therefore, people perceive Windows as being free. Few people are aware that the OEM version of XP added between sixty and a hundred bucks to the cost of their PC, depending on which version of XP is installed on the machine and what kind of deal the manufacturer was able to cut with Microsoft.

Many corporations and institutions use Windows for the very same reason. It came bundled with the 1500 PCs they bought from Gateway or Dell or Compaq or whomever. Even those who do have the option of purchasing computers without a bundled OS feel that the lack of support available for Linux makes it a second-rate choice. Others feel that employee productivity would suffer if the workers came from Microsoft home environments to a Linux workplace. And they're probably right.

Still, signs on the horizon suggest that times may be changing. IBM, HP, Dell, and many other PC manufacturers are starting to include Linux bundles as an option with their computers. IBM has been particularly aggressive in their push toward Linux. So much so that in 2003, Santa Cruz Operations (SCO) sued IBM for a billion dollars.

It claims that IBM shared trade secrets relating to the UNIX OS with the freeware community in an effort to accelerate the already rapid growth of Linux. In its suit, SCO also claims that in migrating its systems over to Linux, IBM is severely undercutting SCO's ability to do business. Naturally, IBM denies the allegations and contends that SCO is simply attempting to retard the growth of Linux, and at the same time collecting a large chunk of cash to help bail it out of severe financial difficulties.

Whoever comes out on top in this battle may, to some extent, control the destiny of Linux in the corporate market. If it turns out that IBM is right and that there is no foundation for SCO's complaint, then Linux has a bright future. Conversely, if the computer giant winds up shelling out a cool billion dollars in damages, many other computer manufacturers are going to be wary of risking a similar lawsuit. The possibility exists that some companies already bundling Linux with their systems may curtail the practice or stop all together. We can only wait and see.

CHAPTER SUMMARY

Hopefully, this chapter made it clear that Microsoft isn't the only kid on the block. It's merely the biggest one with the most clout. Linux is a very stable OS with a lot of strong features. Each year sees more applications emerge for the business community and creative individuals alike.

I would like to think that reading this chapter at least gave you the urge to try Linux. If this is true, then I highly recommend that you log onto www.linux.org and begin your study. It might open up a whole new way of living for you.

CHAPTER 32

THE HARDWARE OF THE NETWORK

Once you have a number of computers in a business, or as is increasingly common, within the family, it becomes a very appealing thought to be able to access the files on one computer while you're working on another. In the business environment, this isn't just a luxury; it can be critically important. Oddly enough, as complicated as it may appear on the outset, setting up a small network doesn't have to be an overwhelming ordeal. In fact, it can even be fun! There are a few things that will make the job go much easier if you know them up front, rather than learning them along the way. That's what this chapter is all about. Also, while I won't be examining network infrastructure in any great detail (that could entail an entire series of books, and not simply a single chapter in one book), I will be taking a look at some of the hardware used in more advanced networks.

Along these lines, I will also be covering the different ways a network can be laid out. On the simplest level, two computers could be hooked up with a serial cable connecting them and that would constitute a network. On a much wider scale, the Internet itself comprises a very large worldwide network. This chapter will feature a brief discussion of some of the more commonly implemented local area topologies, both past and present.

Since this is a book on hardware, I won't be getting into a detailed discussion of protocols. However, I would be remiss in not providing an introduction to the most commonly used protocols and where you might see them in use. Also, they get some exposure on the exam.

A+ CORE HARDWARE EXAM OBJECTIVES

Exam objectives that will be covered in this chapter include the following:

1.2 Identify basic procedures for adding and removing field-replaceable modules for desktop systems. Given a replacement scenario, choose the appropriate sequences. (NIC)

1.5 Identify the names, purposes, and performance characteristics of standardized/common peripheral ports, associated cabling, and their connectors. Recognize ports, cabling, and connectors by sight.

1.8   Identify proper procedures for installing and configuring common peripheral devices. Choose the appropriate installation or configuration sequences in given scenarios.

6.1   Identify the common types of network cables, their characteristics and connectors.

6.2   Identify basic networking concepts including how a network works.

6.3   Identify common technologies available for establishing Internet connectivity and their characteristics.

WHY BUILD A NETWORK?

The first question an individual needs to ask before taking on the project of networking a home or business is simply, "Why am I doing this?" For the aspiring computer professional, the answer could be as simple as wanting the practice before taking the job for a paying customer. For a business, a little deeper analysis might be in order. For a business or individual with multiple computers, any one of the following reasons might offer sufficient justification to take on the challenge of building a network:

- *Sharing files*: Keeping multiple copies of the same file is neither efficient nor convenient. Security can also become an issue. With a network, management of resources becomes easier.

- *Sharing peripherals*: Devices that get relatively infrequent use can be installed in a convenient location and shared out to those who require their services.

- *Communications*: Email, intra-office communications, and even global communication are made substantially easier when those in contact with one another have a mutually accessible network link.

- *Managing resources*: While this may sound like a rehash of the first two listings, it isn't really. A well-designed network allows resources, such as the user accounts, to be managed by a single administrative entity.

- *Security*: A properly administered network can be rather precisely controlled in respect to who has access to what information or resources, or who has access to whom.

- *Software management*: Rolling out new software is dramatically easier if it is done over the network. In addition, managing all of those licenses is easier if all software is maintained in a single location, along with records of what licenses were used where.

PEER TO PEER, OR CLIENT/SERVER

On the most basic level, a network is achieved as soon as you get two computers to talk to one another. As networks grow and become more complex, a certain degree of organization becomes necessary. There have evolved two basic types of network: the peer to peer and the client/server.

PEER TO PEER

Peer-to-peer (P2P) networks are the easiest, and by far the least expensive networks to set up. However, they can turn into an administration nightmare. By definition, a peer is an equal. Therefore, your P2P network is a collection of equals. Every computer on the network performs both the roles of client machine and of server.

A couple of key definitions are in order here. A client is not the end user. The end user is referred to as the user. A client is any device or software that requires the services of another device or piece of software in order to perform a function. A server is any device or software that doles out services to those that need them.

On a P2P network, since every computer is acting in both roles, both security and resource administration become serious issues. Whoever happens to be logged on to a computer at any given time is the administrator. Therefore, he or she can set permissions on files, create passwords, share or unshare resources, and so on and so forth.

As a result, P2P networks are really unsuitable for larger networks. They're basically good for very small networks, where not a lot of information gets shared among users and security is not an issue. Somebody creating a home network so she can hook her computer up to her roommate's computer can easily get by with this level of network. Even smaller offices can survive on P2P as long as there is some organized methodology for managing information.

CLIENT/SERVER

Once security and data integrity become more important than ease of implementation, the client/server network becomes more attractive. In this design, the network has one or more computers that become dedicated servers, running a specialized network operating system (NOS). One person or a group of people will be assigned the responsibility of managing the network. Depending on the NOS selected, this person might be called the administrator, the supervisor, or even the superuser. Throughout this chapter I'll be using the term administrator.

People who need to have access to the network will be assigned a user account with a user ID and (usually) a password that they use to confirm their identities when they log onto the network. These are the user's *credentials*. The NOS uses the combination of user ID and password to determine what a person may or may not do while logged on. These are the user's *permissions*.

The administrator can centrally control all the resources on the network, which might include files, peripherals, and access to external communications. The beauty of this setup is two-fold. First off, each user only needs to know one password to access everything on the network to which he or she has been given permission. Second, a single individual or group of individuals controls all security. This allows for a much higher degree of both organization and security.

> **BUZZ WORDS**
>
> **Credentials:** On a network, these consist of the user ID and password that provide network access for the user.
>
> **Permissions:** Resource access or actions that a particular user is allowed.

THE HARDWARE OF NETWORKING

BUZZ WORDS

Tranceiver: Any device that is designed to be able to either transmit or receive data.

I said earlier that, on the most basic level, two computers could be hooked together over a serial cable. And that is true. The most basic need of computer networking is that the devices that are to communicate over the network be equipped with some form of transceiver and the media over which they will communicate.

A *transceiver* is any device which can both transmit and receive a signal, hence the name. Media can consist of wire, light beams, or radio waves, or any combination thereof. As a network grows in size and complexity, other devices become either necessary or desirable in order to help manage the network. These include hubs, repeaters, switches, bridges, routers, and brouters. Don't worry if some of these terms are unfamiliar to you. Each will be discussed in further detail in this chapter.

NETWORKING TRANSCEIVERS

In order to communicate on the network a device must be able to transmit and receive data. To do this, it must be equipped with a transceiver. The most basic transceiver is the network interface card (NIC). A modem is also a valid networking transceiver. However, modems will be discussed in more detail in Chapter Twenty, Telecommunications.

More specialized transceivers also exist. A print server is a small device that sits alongside a printer and connects it directly to the network. This way users access it the same way they would any computer on the network without causing some unfortunate user the inconvenience of having the office printer hanging off of his or her computer.

NETWORK INTERFACE CARDS

The NIC stands alone as the most commonly used networking transceiver in use today (**Figure 32.1**). When choosing a NIC, there are a couple of things to take into consideration:

- *Bus type*: NICs typically come on a PCI card. Some high-end cards are available on a 64-bit, 66MHz PCI 2.01 compliant bus. This will be the fastest, but make sure your computer supports the standard. Usually, it's only the high-end servers that do. If absolutely necessary, it is still possible to get a NIC on an ISA card.
- *Network interface type*: The older 10Mb cards were available with the RJ-45 connector and/or a BNC connector for coaxial cable. 10/100 cards will come with only the RJ-45. There are also cards for the various wireless media that will be discussed later in this chapter, as well as those for fiber-optic cabling.
- *Networking standard*: Typically, this will be some form of Ethernet. Some older networks are still on 10Mb/s Ethernet. Most, however, are running 100Mb/s, and a

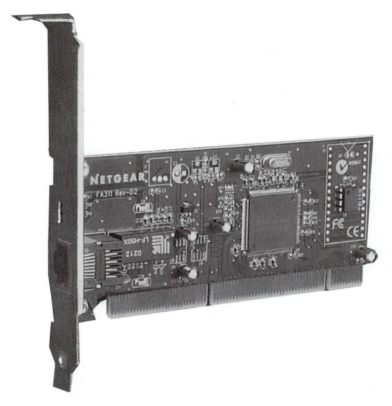

Figure 32.1   The NIC is the basic transceiver that gets data on and off the network for the vast majority of computers.

growing number of organizations have migrated to Gigabit Ethernet (1000Mb/s). While Ethernet dominates the market, it is still, as of this writing, possible to get cards that support token ring, even though the standard is all but dead.

On the back of the NIC, in addition to the interface for the medium, there will generally be two lights. One is a link light and the other is the activity light. The link light tells you that you have connectivity between the host and the rest of the network and should glow constantly. The activity light will flicker when data is being transmitted.

It isn't at all uncommon to see the NIC installed onto the motherboard itself. It may also show up as a combo card, sharing the same circuit board with another peripheral. There are some interesting variations in this respect. Hewlett Packard has included on some of its systems a combination of a SCSI adapter and NIC on one card. It's not at all uncommon for manufacturers of PCMCIA cards to ship a modem/NIC combo. There are even a few of these types of cards available that can be installed into a PCI slot.

INSTALLING AND TROUBLESHOOTING NICS

NIC installation, in the past, has rightfully earned a reputation as being one of the more challenging tasks. Thankfully, Plug 'n Play has started to make this a thing of the past. Still, when things go wrong, these devices can quickly make a day turn sour.

When a NIC fails to be recognized by the system after a fresh installation, chances are extremely good that you are experiencing an IRQ conflict (see Chapter Ten, Examining the Expansion Bus). If the device is PnP, it may mean that none of the IRQs that it has been programmed to accept is available. If you recall from Chapter Ten, sometimes simply swapping positions with another device on the PCI bus will solve the problem. If not, you may have to go into the CMOS and reserve one of the IRQs the NIC will use. This is very likely to cause the conflicting device to stop being recognized on the next boot, but at least you know which device needs reconfiguring.

On some older NICs, it is also possible that it is not an IRQ conflict, but rather an I/O address conflict. A good memory mapping utility can help you resolve what device is trying to use what addresses in memory. Most operating systems have ways in which you can manually reconfigure devices to use another I/O address. In Windows, you would go into Device Manager, select the afflicted device, and click the Properties button. On the window that pops up (shown in **Figure 32.2**), click the Resources tab and deselect the Use automatic settings checkbox. Select another option, if possible. If there are no other options available for that

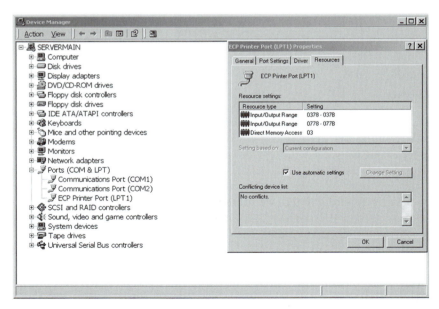

Figure 32.2   Most operating systems have a way by which many devices can be configured to use a different I/O address or IRQ than the one handed out by the BIOS.

device, try the same procedure on the other conflicting device. If neither device can be reconfigured,
it may be necessary to replace one or the other of
the devices.

NETWORKING MEDIA

Once the signal has been generated by the computer and is ready to be transmitted to the intended
recipient, the data is going to need a path over
which it can travel. This path is known as the
media. In terms of media, there are two forms.
Bounded media is any transmission method that

> **BUZZ WORDS** ——————
>
> **Media:** The substance or energy wave
> over which a data signal is transmitted.
>
> **Bounded media:** Any medium that
> physically connects a device to the
> network by way of a tangible cable.
>
> **Unbounded media:** Any medium
> that connects the device to the
> network using energy forms that
> travel through air and/or space.

physically links the two devices. It doesn't matter what the material is made of. All that matters
is that it be a tangible medium. Something you can touch.

    Unbounded media is anything that travels across space (or the airwaves) to get where it's
going. This can include radio waves, light waves, microwaves, or any other method that
technology may have invented in the meantime. It is the electronic equivalent of telepathy.

BOUNDED MEDIA

The majority of networks that are in existence today consist of some form of bounded media.
They are hooked up by way of copper wire or fiber-optic cables. While copper currently enjoys
the advantage, fiber optics is gradually moving in on its turf. Fiber optics has the advantage of
being able to carry light waves, and light waves are more easily modulated for high-speed
connections.

    Local area networks are almost exclusively the domain of twisted-pair cabling. However,
there are still a large number of older networks out there that make use of coaxial cable. Each
type of media has its own unique set of advantages and disadvantages.

TWISTED PAIR

Twisted-pair cable is available in two different physical packages, as well as several different
categories. Physically, there is unshielded twisted pair (UTP) and shielded twisted pair (STP).
UTP is the most commonly used and shows up on the majority of networks. Shielded twisted
pair has the advantage of being more resistant to outside influences exerted by electromagnetic
interference and radio frequency interference. However, its higher cost frequently keeps it from
being used in most installations.

    Twisted-pair cabling consists of four pairs of 22- to 24-gauge strands of wire. Each pair is
twisted together across the length of the cable. Oddly enough, this is where it gets its name. The
insulation around each of the strands consists of different colors; some are solid, some are
striped. See **Table 32.1** for the color combinations.

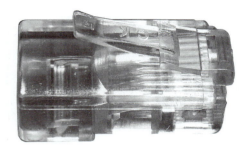

Figure 32.3 The RJ-45 connector is easily confused with a telephone jack by the beginner.

Table 32.1 Twisted-Pair Cabling Color Codes

Pair	Color Combinations
Pair 1	Orange-white/orange striped
Pair 2	Green-white/green striped
Pair 3	Blue-white/blue striped
Pair 4	Brown-white/brown striped

Twisted-pair cabling consists of eight strands of wire separated into four pairs.

Patch cables are generally terminated with connectors knows as RJ-45 connectors (like the one shown in **Figure 32.3**). They look very similar to the ends of your telephone wires, only larger. The telephone line uses an RJ-11 connector, which only has four connectors at the most. (Many telephone cables only make use of two of

BUZZ WORDS

Crossover cable: A network patch cord that routes the transmit signal from one device to the receive terminals on the other device.

them.) The Electronic Industry Association (EIA) and the Telecommunications Industry Association (TIA) worked together to ratify color-coding standards to assure that uniform wiring was used from installation from installation. There were two different standards adopted for twisted-pair wiring, EIA/TIA 568A and 568B. The most commonly used method follows the color-coding standard in 568B. Both standards are explained in **Table 32.2**.

Table 32.2 Wiring Pinouts for EIA/TIA 568A and 568B Twisted-Pair Cabling

Pin No.	Signal Carried	568A	568B
1	Transmit (+)	White/green	White/orange
2	Transmit (−)	Green	Orange
3	Receive (+)	White/orange	White/green
4	Not used	Blue	Blue
5	Not used	White/blue	White/blue
6	Receive (−)	Orange	Green
7	Not used	White/brown	White/brown
8	Not used	Brown	Brown

Note that the two standards differ only in the colors used for the wire that actually transmits signals.

Table 32.3 Wiring Diagram for Crossover Cable

Pin no. End 1	Sending Device	Color Coding	Pin no. End 2	Receiving Device
1	Transmit (+)	White/orange	3	Receive (+)
2	Transmit (–)	Orange	6	Receive (–)
3	Receive (+)	White/green	1	Transmit (+)
4	Not used	Blue	4	Not used
5	Not used	White/blue	5	Not used
6	Receive (–)	Green	2	Transmit (–)
7	Not used	White/brown	7	Not used
8	Not used	Brown	8	Not used

Crossover cables work by reversing the transmit and receive data signal carriers.

An accessory that comes in extremely handy for the computer technician is the *crossover cable*. A crossover cable is connected in such a way that the transmit+ and transmit- signals from one end of the cable are routed to the receive+ and receive- on the opposite end. This cable allows two devices to be directly hooked together without the need for a hub. Should you need to connect two computers, or should you wish to hook your notebook computer up to a router in order to be able to configure it, the crossover cable will be necessary. Crossover cables are most frequently based on 568B standards and are wired in the manner described in **Table 32.3**.

Twisted-pair cable is designated by its category. In each case but one, the cables are structurally the same, but each category is capable of handling different signal speeds. Category Five (Cat5) is the most commonly used, although a newer implementation, Cat5e, is quickly passing it by.

Increased signal speed can be achieved by increasing the number of twists per inch placed onto each twisted pair. Increasing the number of twists acts to reduce crosstalk between cables. Crosstalk occurs anytime you lay two runs of cable side-by-side. A portion of the signal carried by each strand will leak over to the other strand. This affects both the accuracy and the speed of data transmissions. If you can reduce crosstalk, you can increase data throughput. **Table 32.4** compares the most common twisted-pair cable types.

COAXIAL CABLING

An older style of cabling used in networks that is still seen frequently enough to merit discussion is coaxial cable. If you've ever hooked up a VCR to your television, you've used a form of *coaxial* cable, or coax. However, be aware that the coax used in video applications and that used in computer networks are not the same. Coaxial cable gets its name from the fact that the data

BUZZ WORDS

Coaxial: A cable over which the signal and ground both follow the same axis.

Table 32.4 Twisted-Pair Categories

Category	Max. Frequency	Usage
1	Voice only, no data	Telephone or modem
2	4MHz	Localtalk/ISDN
3	16MHz	Ethernet
4	20MHz	Token ring
5	100MHz	Fast Ethernet
5e	100MHz	Gigabit Ethernet/ATM to 622MB/sec
6*	250MHz	Gigabit Ethernet/ATM to 2.4GB/sec
7*	600MHz	Not typically used in U.S.

Twisted-pair cabling is available in many different incarnations. Be sure you use the correct wire for the job.

*Not yet officially ratified as of this writing.

signal travels along the same axis as the ground. As is shown in **Figure 32.4**, coax consists of a center core, an inside insulator, a mesh shielding (or ground), and an outside insulator.

The form of coax most commonly used in networking is RG-58U. This is a 50-ohm cable that meets all standards for Ethernet. It is frequently referred to as *thinnet*. It is capable of carrying an Ethernet signal for a distance of 185 meters without help. RG-59 is what you use in television installations and is a 75-ohm cable. They are not interchangeable.

Another coaxial cable used in networks is RG-8, or *thicknet*. RG-8 can be a bit difficult to manage, but because it can carry a signal for up to 500 meters, it was the medium of choice for any connection that had to run a longer distance. None of the coaxial cable types was able to keep up with contemporary twisted-pair categories. **Table 32.5** compares different coax types to different twisted-pair types.

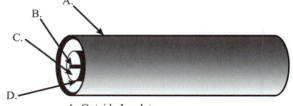

A. Outside Insulator
B. Center Core Conductor
C. Inside Insulator
D. Mesh Shielding

Figure 32.4 Cross-section of a coaxial cable

BUZZ WORDS

Thinnet: A name commonly given to RG-58U coaxial cable.

Thicknet: A name commonly given to RG-8 coaxial cable.

The connector that RG-58U cable hooks up to is not called a coaxial connector, however. It is a BNC connector. A typical coaxial connector is either a push-on or screw-on type of assembly. **Figure 32.5** shows the push-on type. The BNC connector is a bayonet assembly.

BUZZ WORDS

Vampire clamp: A device consisting of two halves that screw together. One half is fitted with sharp teeth that bite through the insulation of RG-8 cable.

Table 32.5   An Overview of Copper Media

Cable Type	Bandwidth	Max. Segment Length
RG-58	10Mb/s	180M
RG-8	10Mb/s	500M
CAT3	10Mb/s	100M
CAT5	100Mb/s	100M
CAT5e	1000Mb/s	100M
CAT6*	1000Mb/s	100M

A knowledge of maximum bandwidth and maximum segment length is essential both for the exam and for work in the field.

*CAT6 has not been ratified as of this writing and the specifications are subject to change.

Many books and articles define BNC as an acronym for British Naval Connector, or Bayonet Nut Connector. Technically speaking, although both definitions have become accepted, neither is correct. It's actually an acronym for Bayonet Neil-Conselman, in respect to the engineers who developed the connector.

RG-8 is connected to the network by way of a device called a *vampire clamp*. The rather macabre name of this device comes from the fact that it consists of two halves that are drawn together around the cable by tightening some screws. Sharp teeth sink in through the insulation and make contact with the conductor. On the outside of the clamp, a 15-pin D-shell connector, called an AUI connector (AUI is an acronym for attachment unit interface) hooks up to the patch cable.

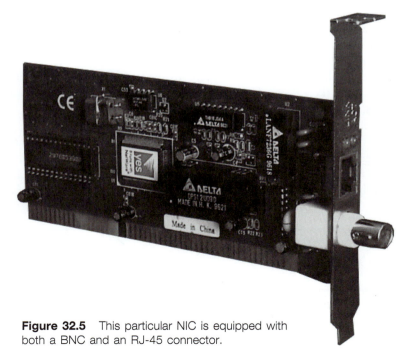

Figure 32.5   This particular NIC is equipped with both a BNC and an RJ-45 connector.

Depending on whether your network is going to be based on a bus topology or a star topology (both of which will be discussed later in this chapter), you may or may not need a couple of other little devices. A bus network basically consists of all the computers hooked up in a line. In order to do that, a T-connector, similar to the one shown in **Figure 32.6**, is fitted to the BNC on the back of the network card. You simply run cables from one T to the next.

At the end of the chain, you need to do something to stop the signal. As I've mentioned before, when an electrical current reaches the end of the wire, it doesn't simply stop dead in its tracks. If there isn't something there to absorb it, it will simply turn around and go back the way it came. This, of course, stops the network dead in its tracks. Therefore, you need to put a terminating resistor on each end of the bus to absorb the signal.

Figure 32.6   T-connectors link computers together in a chain. The cable coming in from one computer goes on one side of the T, the cable going to the next computer down the line hooks up to the other side.

FIBER-OPTIC CABLE

When you move into the high-tech world of fiber optics, you start learning a whole new vocabulary. You don't have a network card, you have an optical transmitter and an optical receiver, collectively referred to as the optical transceiver. The cable is different as well, in that light can only travel in one direction. Therefore, for a

BUZZ WORDS ————

Single-mode fiber: A fiber-optic strand that moves only a single signal through the core.

Multimode fiber: A fiber-optic strand that moves multiple signals through the core.

device to be capable of full duplex operation, there must be an incoming fiber and an outbound fiber that carry signals in their respective directions. Fiber optics is available in single-mode and multimode designs.

Single-mode fiber is a single strand of optical glass encased in a reflective tube and surrounded by a very tough PVC coating. The glass strand is typically between 8 and 10 microns in diameter and carries a single signal in one direction.

Multimode fiber (**Figure 32.7**) is also a single strand, but is typically 50 to 100 microns in diameter and is designed to have several different signals traveling over the fiber. Using different

Figure 32.7   Multimode fiber sends multiple signals down the fiber, using different light frequencies and bouncing each beam at a different angle.

light frequencies for each channel and then bouncing the signal along the fiber at varying angles enables this to happen.

Fiber-optic cable can be packaged in two different ways as well. Tight-buffered cabling bundles a single strand of fiber optic into the cable. This is frequently used for LANs and inter-device connections. However, large numbers of signals can be collected together in a single run by using loose-tube cabling. This consists of several strands of optical glass in a single cable. **Figure 32.8** shows a loose-tube and a tight-buffered cable side-by-side. Either one can be used for single-mode or multimode fiber. Loose-tube cable is generally used as a backbone between larger data centers.

Fiber optics carries several advantages over conventional copper cabling. For one thing, much faster throughput is possible. It's already being used to carry data in the range of several gigabits per second, and that is just beginning to tap its potential. Fiber optics can also carry a signal for much greater distances than copper before attenuation begins to degrade the signal.

Because it is not an electrical signal, it is immune to most of the forms of electrical interference that hamper copper-based digital systems. Neither RFI nor EMI has any effect on

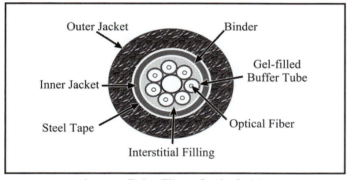

Loose-Tube Fiber-Optic Cable

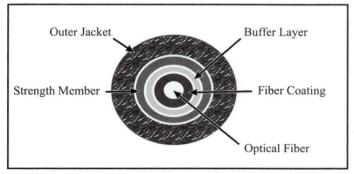

Tight Buffered Cable

Figure 32.8 Tight buffered cable runs a single optical strand, or in the case of duplex fiber, a pair of strands. Loose-tube cable carries many strands.

it. It could care less if you lay it directly along a high-voltage power line. The photons moving along the fiber optics will not be affected. Since it isn't made of metal, but rather glass, it does not corrode. As a result, it is not affected by the elements.

Fiber optics is also the best medium to use in an installation requiring a high degree of security. It is virtually impossible to tap into the medium without bringing the network down. People have a tendency to notice an event of this nature, and the disruption alerts them to the fact that something is going on.

If there is any downside to the use of fiber optics at all, it is in the higher cost of both the medium and the devices needed by the medium to move data. It is also somewhat more difficult to install. This results in a high cost for the initial installation.

UNBOUNDED MEDIA

A detailed discussion of the ins and outs of wireless telecommunications is quite beyond the boundaries of this book. Therefore, I will limit this section to a brief overview of the different forms of wireless networking that are available and when you might want to use which one. The different wireless technologies I will discuss will fall into three categories of signal transmission. There is radio, optical, and microwave transmission. Each has its advantages and disadvantages. Optical transmission is the most commonly used around the home and office, so I'll start there.

OPTICAL NETWORKING

Depending on what you're trying to accomplish, you might find yourself exploring one of two different network technologies that employ light waves traveling through air as a method of transmitting signals. One uses infrared light waves, while the other takes advantage of a laser beam.

INFRARED NETWORKING

If you've ever used a remote control to change the channel on your TV set, you've employed the technology used by infrared networks. Infrared networks can be one of four different types:

- *Line-of-sight networks*: Each device needs to have a direct and unobstructed path over which the beam can travel.
- *Reflective networks*: A transmission redirector is located in a spot common to all devices on the network. It, in turn, sends the signal to the appropriate location.
- *Scatter infrared network*: The signal bounces off of reflective surfaces and therefore can go around corners.
- *Broadband optical telepoint*: By far the fastest of infrared technologies, this method supports multimedia and streaming video. Unlike other methods of infrared wireless technology, multiple signals can be carried at once, each in a separate channel.

In all cases, zeros and ones are encoded into a unique series of light pulses. This series of pulses is picked up by the receiving devices and decoded back into digital form.

Networking Over Laser

One of the key disadvantages of infrared is speed. Or lack thereof, I should say. Also, distances between devices are seriously limited using infrared technology. While a laser connection can prove to be a little more difficult and expensive to install at the outset, it can provide very fast transmission rates over much greater distances between stations. Despite its initial outlay, laser technology can provide a much more efficient and cost-effective means for interconnecting offices, compared to high-speed dedicated lines leased from a telecommunications provider, assuming a line of sight can be maintained.

The technology involved in converting and transmitting data by way of optical means is very similar to that used by fiber optics. The key difference is that you don't have a contained medium over which data is sent.

The most common conventional laser systems provide speeds of either 155Mb/s or 622Mb/s. Distances of up to 4km are supported, although this can be affected by a number of factors. Inclement weather (such as a dust storm), atmospheric conditions (pollution), and physical obstructions (a flock of pigeons flying through the beam) all can affect your signal. Another thing that affects distance is the speed of the signal being transmitted. A 622Mb/s ATM transmission would be limited to about half the transmission distance of a 155Mb/s signal.

Some technologies, such as LightPointe Teledata Communications' Lightstation Multilink Series, use multiple beams to minimize the distance-limiting factors listed above. Therefore, if a bird should interrupt one beam, another beam will pick up the slack. In either case, most networking protocols have error correction mechanisms that will cause the offending or lost packets to be resent.

The laser interconnect is protocol-transparent. This means that, whatever networking protocols you might be using, the signal can be sent and received. Therefore, a 10BaseT network can move over the beam just as easily as a 622Mb/s ATM. If you're new to networking and don't know what 10BaseT and ATM are, they are discussed in more detail in Chapter Twenty, Telecommunications.

Networking Over the Radio

For most people, the only exposure to radio transmissions is listening to Q99 acid rock as they navigate the freeway on the way to work. Even that is going away, as everyone adds twelve-disc CD changers to their SUVs. Still, radio frequencies are alive and well, even in the high-tech world of computer networking.

Radio waves fall into three categories: shortwave, very high frequency (VHF), and ultra-high frequency (UHF). In the U.S., these frequencies fall under the jurisdiction of the Federal Communications Commission (FCC). If you want to use radio waves, you must first be licensed to operate your equipment, and then you need to be assigned your frequency.

There are some frequencies that do not fall under the watchful eye of the FCC. These are the public bands. The public bands are in the range from 902 to 928MHz and from 5.72 to 5.85GHz.

However, since anyone can use these, two factors impact on their usefulness. First of all, you are severely limited in the amount of power you use to broadcast. This is intended to reduce geographical overlap of the signals. Second, you do not have exclusive control of the frequency and if somebody else jumps in, that signal gets mixed with yours. If you are simply exchanging pleasantries with the trucker on I-89 about the smokies on the prowl, that's no big deal. However, when that signal is your precious data, you don't want it getting corrupted by unwanted signals, and just as importantly, you don't want just anybody picking it out of the air.

Networking over radio is generally done with either single-frequency or spread-spectrum. Single-frequency transmission is just what it sounds like. You are assigned a single frequency and that is what you use to transmit your data. When you use spread-spectrum, you are assigned several frequencies and you "hop" from one to the other. This provides for a greater degree of security.

SINGLE-FREQUENCY TRANSMISSIONS

As I stated in the last paragraph, the concept is simple. You have one frequency. Your data is converted from digital to analog radio waves and transmitted over the air. Installation of a single-frequency radio network will be one of two types:

- *Low power, single frequency (LPSF)*: You are permitted an extremely limited broadcast power. As a result, you have an operating range of between 20 and 25 meters between devices. Speeds (depending on choice of equipment) range from as low as 1Mb/s to a maximum of about 10Mb/s. These networks are useful for small offices where it is impractical to run wiring for any reason.

- *High power, single frequency (HPSF)*: This technology is useful for setting up low-speed wide area network (WAN) links where conventional bounded media are not an option. The broadcast equipment is permitted to operate at a higher power, allowing for line-of-sight telecommunications. In some cases, a controlled atmospheric bounce can extend the range of the network beyond the horizon. Speed limitations are similar to that of LPSF.

Whichever single-frequency model you choose, both are going to share some limitations. While virtually impervious to conditions such as smoke, smog, or birds, anything that generates electromagnetic interference (EMI) can degrade or interrupt the signal. A lightening strike, a radio transmitter, and almost any other electric thing you can think of may inadvertently generate signals that overlap yours. The signals are also easily picked out of the air and intercepted. Therefore security can become a very real issue.

SPREAD-SPECTRUM RADIO

Spread-spectrum transmission addresses the issue of security. Because the broadcast signal is continually bouncing from one frequency to another, it is far more difficult to intercept the data. This, of course, is not without its drawbacks. In order to make sure the transmitting station and the intended recipient get all the data that was sent, and receive it intact, some form of synchronization has to take place. Two different methods are used:

- *Direct-sequence transmission* is the faster of the two methods. A predefined sequence of radio frequencies is employed, and both sending and receiving devices jump from one to the other in that sequence, using a predefined timing sequence as well. This is the less secure of the two methods. While it will keep out the casual eavesdropper, a dedicated hacker will have no problem cracking either the frequencies in use, the hop sequence, or the timing sequence.

- *Frequency hopping* uses a far more complicated timing scheme for switching from frequency to frequency. Also, there can be no alternating patterns in the hop sequence. This makes it far more difficult to hack, since both the timing and the sequence change. This is a far more secure method of sending data; however, it comes at the cost of speed.

NETWORKING OVER MICROWAVES

No, we haven't come up with a scheme forcing everybody in the world to interconnect their microwave ovens. However, the same technology that bakes your potato or heats up your frozen burrito can also be used to send data. And it can send that data across extremely long distances. The key here is that microwave transmission requires that the sender and the receiver have a direct line-of-sight communications link. And unlike radio, you can't bounce the signal off the atmosphere.

Microwave networking comes in two flavors, terrestrial microwave and satellite microwave. As the names suggest, terrestrial microwave is ground-based, while satellite microwave bounces the signal off of a satellite orbiting in space.

- *Terrestrial microwave*: This is the technology that results in all those parabolic antennae that sit on top of the roof of all those federal agencies, such as NSA or the CIA. They are also used on the corporate level as a replacement for bounded WAN media. Microwave transmission requires direct line of sight, so the height of the antenna directly affects distance of transmission.

- *Satellite microwave*: You've all seen those spy movies where the good guy rolls out of his or her inflatable raft and sets up the little tiny antenna that looks like an umbrella. He or she points it at the sky and in mere moments is in contact with headquarters. This is the director's sorry attempt to accurately represent satellite microwave technology at work. All you need in order to set up a satellite link is to have the appropriate frequency assigned to you and the right equipment. Since there are multiple satellites in orbit that are capable of bouncing your signal, there are precious few (if any) places on the surface of the planet that you won't be able to receive the signal. The distances involved will generate something called a propagation delay. This is the amount of time that elapses from the time you send your signal out, have it travel 50,000 miles to the nearest satellite, bounce off and travel 50,000 miles to your intended recipient, get the reply, and follow the same path back. This results in delays of up to several seconds. Also, unlike in those movies I mentioned, the lock on the satellite must be accurate. You can't really just point the cute little antenna at the sky and automatically find a signal.

Whichever method you choose, you're going to spend a pretty good chunk of change on the hardware you need, an assigned frequency, and the licensed operators you need to keep the system up and running. This is not "basic" networking technology, and your average network engineer is going to give you a very blank, or possibly horrified, look if you ask him or her to troubleshoot a downed link.

OTHER NETWORKING HARDWARE

Throughout this discussion, I have mentioned that networks can grow almost infinitely if the right equipment is used. When discussing the different media types, I pointed out the distance limitations of each type. Yet, if those limitations were etched in stone, with no way of extending these boundaries, the Internet would not exist. Corporations would not be interconnected across continents. The following is a brief overview of some other networking components you might bump into from time to time.

REPEATERS

One of the more basic devices is the repeater. Since copper-based media has relatively short maximum runs, there needed to be a way of extending that distance. A *repeater* is a device that intercepts the signal, filters out any noise that has been picked up along the way, and then amplifies the signal back to its original strength. There is a bit of a limitation to the number of repeaters that can be used on a network, however. The 5-4-3 rule states that there can be up to five network segments interconnected, using four repeaters or active hubs (see the next section), as long as only three of those segments actually have devices installed. Still, they're good when you need to run twisted-pair cable beyond the 100 meters for which it is capable.

HUBS

Hubs are devices that interconnect several other devices on a star network. They generally consist of a rectangular box with several RJ-45 sockets (or BNC on some older models). **Figure 32.9** is an example of a small office/home office (SOHO) hub that can interconnect four computers on a network.

Hubs can be either passive or active. The passive hub is the most basic hub available. It simply takes a signal coming in from any one of its ports and broadcasts that signal out all ports, including the one from whence it came. An active hub doubles as a repeater. Therefore, before rebroadcasting a signal, it cleans it up and amplifies it back to original strength.

BUZZ WORDS

Repeater: A device that cleans up, amplifies, and retransmits a signal, effectively increasing the distance data can travel over any given medium.

Hub: A device that interconnects multiple hosts on a star network over a single segment.

While this may superficially seem to be a minor difference, it can have a great impact on the maximum physical dimensions of a network. With a passive RJ-45 hub, two devices can only have 100 meters of wire separating them. Therefore, if one device is 75 meters from the hub and the other device is 50 meters from the hub, the total distance exceeds the capabilities of the medium. They won't see each other. With an active hub, each device can be up to 100 meters from the hub and still communicate.

Figure 32.9   A four-port hub

SWITCHES

Superficially, *switches* don't look that much different than hubs. From an engineering standpoint, they're quite different. As I said earlier, a hub simply rebroadcasts any signal it receives out through all ports. It can't pick and choose. Also, a hub is shared bandwidth. If I have twenty-four devices

> **BUZZ WORDS**
>
> **Switch:** A device that breaks a larger network down into smaller segments, isolating each segment into its own collision domain.

hooked up to a 24-port 100Mb/s hub, those twenty-four devices are competing for the same 100Mb of bandwidth. On a 100Mb switch, each port represents a separate 100Mb segment. Also, the switch maintains a database of all host addresses that exist downstream of any given port. When the switch receives a signal from one port, it scans its database, locates the correct port for the intended host, and transmits that signal only through that port. Devices on the other ports don't have to deal with transmissions not intended for them.

As a result, network congestion can be significantly decreased when switches are used in place of hubs whenever possible. A relatively large network can be created using switches as well. On a 24-port switch, each port can host a 24-port hub. You now have up to 576 devices on the network, but only twenty-four of them will be competing for bandwidth on any given segment. Each port would represent a separate collision domain. A collision domain is simply a segment of the network on which it is possible for the devices on that segment to interfere with one another.

If you tried that same trick using a hub in place of the switch, you would have all 576 devices competing for the same bandwidth, and the entire network is a single collision domain. The lack of overall bandwidth and the frequency of collisions will result in an unbearably slow network. Replacing the central hub with a switch will greatly improve performance.

BRIDGES

Bridges are devices that interconnect two or more unlike networks. The networks may differ in topology or in platform. For example, if your network still has a couple of token ring segments in use, a bridge will be necessary to interconnect the token ring segments to the Ethernet network. Also, a bridge might be in order if a Macintosh network is trying to interconnect with a PC network.

A bridge can be a dedicated piece of hardware or it can be a piece of software running on a server. In order to reduce the performance hit that a software-based implementation will incur, it is best to use a hardware solution whenever possible.

Routers

Routers are used to interconnect two or more completely different networks to one another. As with switches and hubs, routers will have several different interconnects. Unlike switches and hubs, these interconnects are likely to be of different types. RJ-45 jacks will be required for the internal LAN, but different connections may be required in order to interconnect with telecommunications equipment and/or other routers in the network.

> **Buzz Words**
>
> **Bridge:** A device that interconnects two networks or segments of a network with different topologies or different platforms together.
>
> **Router:** A device that interconnects two autonomous networks into a single larger network.
>
> **Default gateway:** The route through which all packets that contain addresses that the transmitting device cannot resolve will be sent.
>
> **Topology:** The method through which a network is physically wired.

Each port can be configured to a different network address. Internally, the router maintains a list of all network addresses that exist downstream of each port. This list is known as the routing tables. When the router receives a packet, it examines the header for the network address and then compares that address to its tables. If it finds the address listed, it simply forwards the packet through the appropriate port. If not, it forwards the packet through the port that the administrator has configured to be the default gateway. The *default gateway* is the path to the next router downstream. It then becomes the responsibility of the next router to figure out what to do with that packet.

When discussing switches, I pointed out that each port on a switch was an independent collision domain. With routers, each port becomes an independent broadcast domain. Devices on a network are constantly sending out broadcasts to all devices on the network for many different reasons. The larger the network becomes, the more congestion is caused by these broadcasts. Routers (unless configured to do so by the administrator) do not forward broadcasts. Therefore, a very large network can be subnetted into several smaller networks using routers. The broadcasts generated by any given subnet will not interfere with the other subnets.

Network Topologies

Networks themselves vary widely in how they are laid out, both logically and physically. The way a network is physically wired is its *topology*. No matter how complex the physical layout may look, it is actually going to fall under one of four categories. There are bus networks, ring

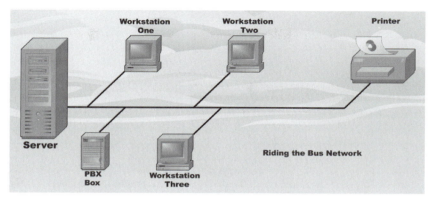

Figure 32.10   Layout of a typical bus network

networks, star networks, and mesh networks. This is the way they would be defined in that perfect world I keep fantasizing about. In the real world, you're going to find that many networks are mixtures of topologies. These are called hybrid networks.

BUS NETWORKS

These are the simplest networks to set up and the simplest to bring down. They're also among the simplest to understand. In the bus network, each computer is connected in a chain, just like that string of Christmas tree lights you had when you were a kid. The network cable runs from one computer or device to the next until you get to the last computer (see **Figure 32.10**).

This is a topology that is falling from favor for a couple of reasons. First off, in order to implement this network, you need to use coaxial cable. As I pointed out earlier in this chapter, this will limit you to 10Mb/s on your transmission speeds. Also, this network resembles that string of lights in more ways than just the symbolic. Remember how the whole string went out whenever one bulb died? That's what happens when one computer goes off the network. If Bob kicks his network cable off the back of his computer, the whole network goes down. Now nobody can print to the printer and nobody can share files. The computers themselves are working fine as stand-alones; you simply no longer have a network.

One of the things you have to keep in mind is that both ends of the network have to be terminated. Lose the termination, and you lose the network. Therefore, in Figure 32.10, the network adapters in the server and the printer will need terminating resistors plugged into the outbound ports of their T-connectors. On all other devices, both ends of the T-connections have cables hooked up.

Bus networks were reasonably efficient for small networks. Whether you were working with a peer-to-peer network or a client-server network was of no consequence. However, the larger the network becomes, the more cumbersome it is to manage. With one hundred people on a network, you have two hundred feet potentially kicking out connectors.

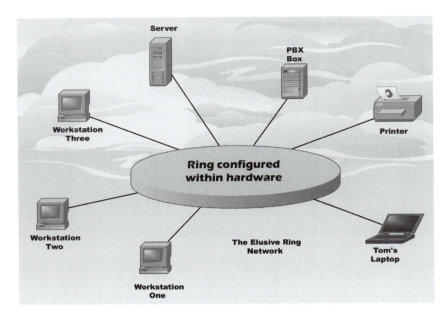

Figure 32.11   Logical diagram of the typical ring network

RING NETWORKS

For a while, it looked like the ring topology was on its way out as well. The most widely supported networking standard that made use of it was token ring, and token ring was going the way of the dinosaur. However, a newer technology, the fiber distributed data interface (FDDI), also makes use of the ring topology. (These different technologies will be discussed in detail later in the chapter.) Therefore, new life has been pumped into the topology.

The concept of the ring network is more logical than it is physical. **Table 32.11** illustrates the physical implementation of a ring network. However, in the real world, the ring is incorporated into the hardware. Physically, the network more strongly resembles the star network that I will be discussing next.

Were the computers laid out in a physical ring, it would be just like a bus network. Bringing one computer off-line would bring down the network. However, in actual implementation, devices called multistation access units (MAUs) interconnect the devices. They look, feel, smell, and taste just like a typical hub in most respects. A cable runs from the computer to the MAU, just like it would to a hub. Internally, however, they are wired in a ring. The circuitry of an MAU can detect when a computer goes off-line and redirect the signal around the port that went down. Also, MAUs have two additional ports on the back, a ring in and a ring out. These aren't for hooking up telephones. They are the input and output connectors for interconnecting MAUs. They allow the network to be expanded without losing the logic of the ring.

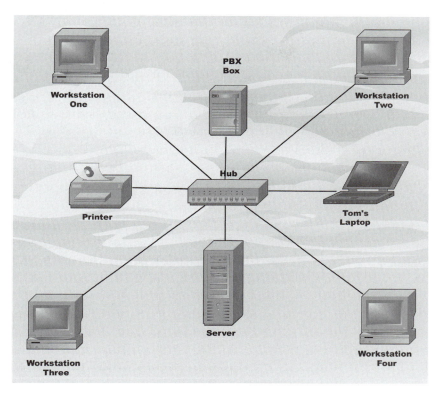

Figure 32.12   Layout of a typical star network

STAR NETWORKS

Star networks are by far the most commonly implemented topology in today's networking environment. On the simplest level, as shown in **Figure 32.12**, a star can consist of a single hub interconnecting devices. The beauty of the topology is that by using additional devices, such as routers and switches, networks can be as large and complex as necessity dictates.

Most administrators favor star networks because, regardless of geographic location of workstations and devices, the servers, hubs, routers, and so on can be centrally located. This greatly eases the administrative burden of larger networks. Troubleshooting is made easier as well. One of the easiest ways to tell if a workstation is physically connected when it is having trouble seeing the network is to check for "blinky lights." If both the NIC in the computer and the interface light at the hub are showing a link light, you have connectivity.

Star networks do require a more complex cabling scheme. Each workstation or other networked device needs to be wired to either a hub or switch. Hubs, switches, routers, and other devices all need to be interconnected. And somehow, you're expected to keep track of it all. A good topology map is a network administrator's best friend.

THE MESH NETWORK

The mesh network is one in which every single device in the network is directly linked by a dedicated circuit to every other device on the network. As you might imagine, the cabling infrastructure in a network of this nature would be extremely complex and confusing. Fortunately, it's really only used in a couple of places. The internal wiring of a router is basically a mesh network in a box. Also, there are certain network operating systems that allow the administrator to configure multiple servers to work together as though they were a single machine. This is known as a server cluster. Server clusters are frequently interconnected in a mesh.

THE OSI LAYERS AND IEEE

Networks are very complex and complicated mazes of computers, wires, and software. If every manufacturer was left to its own devices and allowed to make its own rules, there would be chaos. Fortunately, that is not the case. Two different organizations work hard to maintain standards that you can count on the manufacturers to follow. The International Organization for Standardization (ISO) came up with the Open Systems Interconnect (OSI) specifications. The Institute of Electrical and Electronic Engineers (IEEE) developed the 802 Standards Committees. These two organizations concentrate on different sets of standards that make the networking world a much nicer place to work.

THE OSI LAYERS

When you're looking at a network from a distance, especially a very complicated one such as the Internet, one thing stands out. It doesn't much matter what kind of computer you have, you still have access to the network. And all those files are there for you to use. One of the reasons this is possible is that data doesn't go across the wire as files. It is broken down and sent across as a stream of individual bits. In order to make sure the data gets put back together the right way, those bits are assembled into various packages that can be disassembled at one computer and reassembled at the next. ISO provided us with a set of standards that allows different platforms to break data down and put it back together in similar fashion. This is known as the OSI model. The OSI model is broken down into seven layers, as follows:

- *The Application Layer*: This layer provides a uniform interface for the applications running on a computer system to gain access to the network.
- *The Presentation Layer*: Here, the computers decide on what format they will use to transfer data. File formats such as JPEG, MP3, TIF, and others are managed at this layer. File compression is managed at this level as well.
- *The Session Layer*: Here is where the two computers set up and maintain a virtual connection while data is being exchanged.
- *The Transport Layer*: In this layer, data is broken down into smaller chunks called segments. In order to make sure the data goes from host to host without corruption,

error-checking mechanisms are put into place. Another mechanism, called flow control, makes sure that both devices are sending and/or receiving data at a speed that is acceptable.

■ *The Network Layer*: If you want to send somebody a letter, you need to know his or her address. Computers are the same way. The network layer handles addressing functions and makes sure a good route between hosts is maintained. It takes the segments made by the Transport Layer and packages them into frames.

■ *The Data Link Layer*: You want to make sure that when you break data into a series of pieces, the pieces get put back together in the right order. You also want to make sure that every single piece got there. This is the job of the Data Link Layer. The Data Link Layer has been subdivided into the Logic Link Control (LLC) Layer and the Media Access Control (MAC) Layer.

■ *The Physical Layer*: Of course, you don't send data over wires. You send electrical signals, or perhaps bursts of light. The Physical Layer takes the information and turns it into the signals that move across the wire.

The key to understanding the OSI layers is that they control neither how the hardware is manufactured, nor how software is written. Rather, they set specific rules as to how either one will communicate across a network.

THE IEEE 802 STANDARDS

In February of 1980, a group of engineers from several different areas of the industry got together to define networking standards. Because it was month two of year eighty, the standards that evolved from that conference have become known as the 802 standards. It should be noted that the numbers relate to the number of the committee assigned to research and implement standards under their jurisdiction. Each topology will fall under one of the following 802.x standards, as do certain key issues common to all topologies.

802.1   *AN/MAN Bridging and Management*: Covers different internetworking standards as well as the Spanning Tree Algorithm.

802.2   *Logic Link Control*: As its name suggests, this committee oversees the standards used by the LLC sublayer of the Data Link Layer. (Inactive)

802.3   *CSMA/CD Access Method*: Sometimes simply called Ethernet. This committee keeps up with the different advances in Ethernet technology.

802.4   *Token Passing Bus Access Method*: A bus network that used a token passing method of media access. (Inactive)

802.5   *Token Ring Access Method*: A ring network that uses a token passing method of media access. (Inactive)

802.6   *DQDB Access Method*: Distributed Queue Dual Bus access to media. (Disbanded)

802.7   *Broadband LAN*: A technology for building LANs using broadband technology instead of baseband technology. (Disbanded)

802.8   *The Fiber Optics Technical Advisory Group*: Oversees development of fiber optics solutions. (Disbanded)

802.9   *Isosynchronous LANs*: Frequently referred to as Integrated Voice/Data communications. (Inactive)

802.10   *Integrated Services*: Also known as Security. Administers development of methods by which access to the network and the transmission of data can be made secure. (Inactive)

802.11   *Wireless Networking*: Defines various methods of moving data without wires.

802.12   *Demand Priority Access*: Allows access to network media based on message priority. (Inactive)

802.14   *Standard Protocol for Cable TV-based Broadband Communications* (Disbanded)

802.15   *Working Group for Personal Area Networks*: Very short-range wireless networks.

802.16   *Broadband Wireless Access Standards*

802.17   *Resilient Packet Ring Working Group*: Uses fiber-optic ring networks and packet data transmission.

802.18   *Radio Regulatory Technical Advisory Group*

802.19   *Coexistence Technical Advisory Group*

802.20   *Mobile Broadband Wireless Access Working Group*

NAVIGATING THE HARDWARE PROTOCOLS

Once you enter the wild world of networking, you start getting a lot of strange names and acronyms thrown at you. Among these are things called protocols. A protocol is simply the collection of instructions that provide two devices a common method of talking to one another. One way you might look at this is what you might encounter if you were to take an international vacation. Once you got to Tibet, if you didn't understand the language, you couldn't communicate. But just as importantly, if you didn't understand their customs, you could find yourself in serious trouble, and fast!

Computers have the same problem. A Macintosh can't talk to a PC without a little help. Not only do the different platforms use a different language, but they also do things differently. Protocols act as your computer's translator. Protocols are employed on both a hardware level and a software level. Some of the various hardware protocols that I will discuss in this section include Ethernet, token ring, and FDDI. There are many others, but these are the most common, and this is a book on computer hardware and operating systems, not networking.

ETHERNET

Ethernet started out in 1972 at Xerox Corporation when David Boggs and Robert Metcalfe worked out a method by which multiple devices could send signals across the same wire without interfering with each other. Xerox called on the expertise of Digital Equipment Corporation and Intel to help it in developing something that could be looked at as industry standard. They were fairly successful. In fact, you can still find references to the old DIX network (short for Digital, Intel, Xerox) in modern literature.

Ethernet, as we know it, looks a little different than it did back then. IEEE expanded on the DIX specifications and came up with the 802.3 standards of Carrier Sense, Multiple Access/ Collision Detection (CSMA/CD). It provided specifications for moving data across both twisted-pair cable and coaxial cable and also defined the terminators still used today. Later revisions of Ethernet include Fast Ethernet, which is a 100Mb/s system, and Gigabit Ethernet, a 1000Mb/ s standard. But the key to Ethernet is CSMA/CD. Understanding just what that is will be easier if I break the phrase down into its components.

- *Carrier sense*: The computer gains access to the wire by listening for a moment of silence. It's the same thing you do when you're trying to merge onto a busy highway from the on-ramp. You wait for an empty spot and jump in.
- *Multiple access*: The freeway I'm talking about is designed for a lot of cars to travel on it, but only one can be in the lane at a time. Fortunately, they travel at the speed of light, just like that red convertible that cut me off this morning.
- *Collision detection*: If that red convertible jumps into the lane ahead of you just as you're moving in, you're going to have a collision. A collision on a network isn't quite so messy, however. The data is simply discarded. The offending computers send out a backoff algorithm, telling both computers to wait a randomly generated amount of time before sending again. That way, they will not collide with each other again. They'll probably collide with another computer, but at least they won't be exchanging phone numbers with each other again.

There are several Ethernet standards to choose from, ranging from 10Mb/s to the newer Gigabit Ethernet. The standards go by some rather arcane names, but once you understand the structure of the name, are actually pretty easy to understand (see **Figure 32.13**).

Here are some of the more commonly seen Ethernet types:

10BaseT   10Mb/s, Baseband, Twisted pair
10Base2   10Mb/s, Baseband, Thinnet (2 = 200 meters, which is rounded up from the actual 185 meters RG-58 cable will support)

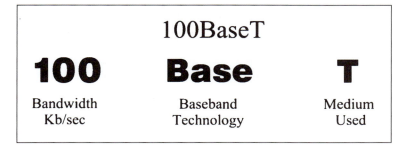

Figure 32.13 Understanding Ethernet standards doesn't have to be that hard.

10Base5	10Mb/s, Baseband, Thicknet (5 = 500 meters)
100BaseT	100Mb/s, Baseband, Twisted pair
100BaseTX	100Mb/s, Baseband, Twisted pair using two data-grade pairs
100BaseFL	100Mb/s, Baseband, Fiber-optic cable
1000BaseT	1Gb/s, Baseband, Twisted pair

> **BUZZ WORDS**
>
> **Beaconing:** A process that occurs on a token ring network in which each station on the network sends a signal to its upstream neighbor and its downstream neighbor asking if it has seen the token lately.

Anyone planning to set up a home network or a SOHO network is going to be looking at Ethernet as the basis for that network. The equipment is the most reasonably priced and most widely supported of all the hardware protocols. Any of the major office-supply chains and/or consumer electronics chains carries two or more lines of each of the main components you'll need for setting up a network. Read on, and once I make my way through the technical folderol, I'll explain how to set up a small Ethernet star network, using Windows 98 and Windows 2000-based machines.

TOKEN RING

Token ring had its day in the sun, but for the most part, it is becoming a forgotten standard. As a networking standard, token ring started out as a brainchild of IBM back in the early 1970s. While there are some minor differences that are not even worth discussing, the IEEE 802.5 standard and IBM's token ring is pretty much the same thing.

While the ideology of the token ring network is based on the concept of a ring network, actual implementation is achieved in a physical star. In place of a hub, an MAU (described earlier) is used, which is wired internally to achieve a ring topology.

On a token ring network, the first computer to come on during the day becomes the token generator. In the event that a token is lost or discarded, it is up to the token generator to figure out that this has happened, and then generate a new token. The way it figures out that a problem has occurred is through a process called *beaconing*.

When a computer has gone an inordinately long time without its chance at the token, it sends a broadcast signal down the wire. This is the beacon. It is basically a message saying "Who is hogging the token!!??" In reply, each computer on the network, in turn, replies, "not me," "not me," "not me," until all of a sudden, there's a computer that doesn't respond. This usually means that either some user has turned off the machine without properly shutting it down or that the system simply crashed. The MAU will bypass the offending port, the token generator will generate a new token and send it down the wire, and all will be well again.

FDDI

Fiber distributed data interface takes up where token ring left off. Like token ring, it uses a token-passing deterministic approach to media access. FDDI, however, uses a dual-ring topology. A primary ring sends data in one direction, while a secondary ring provides for an alternate path in the event of a failure in the first ring. It was designed to use fiber optics as the transmission medium, which is where it gets its name. There are, however, implementations of FDDI that use copper cable as well. The latter is known as the copper distributed data interface (CDDI).

Stations on an FDDI network can be either dual-attached or single-attached stations. A dual-attached station is connected to both rings, while a single-attached station is connected only to the primary ring.

Dual-attached stations will be connected to the network via at least one A port, where they attach to the primary ring, and one B port, where they attach to the secondary ring. They may or may not also have one or more M ports installed. The M port is the port that a single-station unit uses to attach to the network. These hook up only to the primary ring.

When using fiber optics as a medium, very large networks over great distances are possible. There is a maximum distance of 2km (nearly a mile) that is permissible between stations. While current implementations of FDDI are 100Mb/s, the potential is there for much higher speeds.

NETWORKING PROTOCOLS

In order to get data to move from application to application and from one platform to another over the network, it is also necessary that the software have its own protocol. Software makes use of one of many different networking protocols. However, since this is simply an overview, I will cover only the ones commonly seen. Those will include NetBEUI, IPX/SPX, and TCP/IP.

NETBEUI

The term stands for NetBIOS Extended User Interface. Of course, understanding that presupposes that you already know that NetBIOS stands for Network Basic Input Output System. But then, you already knew that, didn't you?

NetBEUI is by far the easiest protocol to implement and to administer. It requires no specialized setup by the end user other than making sure that every computer on the network has its own unique computer name, and that each of the computers that are supposed to talk to each other are all on the same workgroup. You can do this in Windows 9x by going to the Control Panel, double-clicking Network, and clicking Identification. You'll get a screen like the one shown in **Figure 32.14**. In Windows 2000, you get here by going to the System applet in Control Panel. The screen looks slightly different, but not enough to create confusion. All else being correctly set up, your computer is now on the network.

One of the biggest limitations of NetBEUI is that it is not a routable protocol. When a NetBEUI packet hits a router it's like hitting a brick wall. It goes no further. Therefore, as an internetworking protocol, it's useless. It can only be used on networks that are limited to single physical locations.

IPX/SPX

The Internet Packet Exchange/Sequenced Packet Exchange (IPX/SPX) was for several years the default protocol for Novel's NetWare. Like NetBEUI, it is very easy to install and configure.

Since it makes use of the actual hardware address of your network card for addressing, there are no special configurations required. The only thing you really have to watch for is if you have multiple adapters on a single machine. Then, the internal address needs to be unique for each adapter. Microsoft users will find an IPX compatible protocol in the form of NWLink.

As I mentioned before, every network card in the world has (or is supposed to have, anyway) a hardware address that is unique to it and only it. This is a 48-bit address. 24 bits are used as the manufacturer's ID and will be the same for everything that manufacturer puts out. (I would be remiss in my duties were I not to mention that some of the larger manufacturers, such as 3Com, have multiple manufacturer ID numbers.) The other 24 bits are used for a unique serial number for that particular card.

IPX makes use of a 32-bit network address and adds the 48-bit hardware address to make a computer's overall

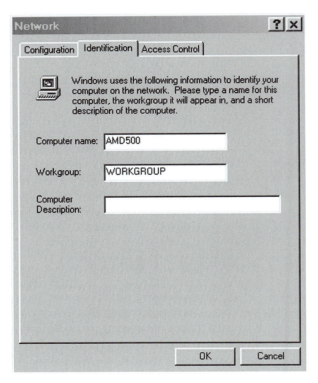

Figure 32.14 Setting the Identification and Workgroup in Windows

address. This 80-bit address becomes the computer's official identification on the network. Because there is not a great deal of address/name resolution required, IPX has very little memory and CPU overhead. Therefore, it's a fast protocol. It's also fully routable.

TCP/IP

The Transmission Control Protocol/Internet Protocol (TCP/IP) is the protocol of choice for the Internet. There are a good many reasons for this. The biggest reason of all is that it provides a hierarchical scheme for addressing that allows for very large networks with a minimal number of hop points to get to a given host on the network.

TCP/IP uses a logical address known as the IP address rather than a physical one. This logical address consists of a 32-bit address that is broken down into four octets (an octet being the eight bits that make up that particular byte). These octets appear to the end user in decimal form, as shown **Figure 32.15**. The address is divided into two sections. One part of the IP address is the network address and the other half is the host address. When data is transmitted from one computer to the other, TCP/IP breaks the information down into packets before sending it across the wire. Each packet contains the sending computer's IP address as well as the intended recipient's address.

Figure 32.15   This is what a 32-bit TCP/IP address looks like. It's a series of binary numbers that represent groupings of zeros and ones.

Another component of the TCP/IP configuration is called the *subnet mask*. For every IP address, there must be an associated subnet mask, which basically tells the system what part of the IP address is the network address and what part is the host address. The part of the subnet mask represented by the number 255 covers the network address.

There are five different classes of TCP/IP address, but networks use only three of them. The other two types of address are for specialized purposes. The three types commonly used are Class A, Class B, and Class C addresses.

> **BUZZ WORDS**
>
> **Subnet mask:** A configuration setting within TCP/IP that identifies to the system what part of an IP address is the network address and what part is the host address.

- *Class A addresses*: In a Class A address, only the first octet is used for a network address. The remaining three octets are used for host addresses, and the default subnet mask is 255.0.0.0. The range of addresses starting with 10.*.*.* are reserved for private addressing and cannot be exposed to public traffic.

- *Class B addresses*: Class B addresses use the first two octets for the network address and the last two for a host address. The default subnet mask is 255.255.0.0. All addresses between 172.16.0.0 and 172.31.255.255 are set aside for private use.

- *Class C addresses*: The first three octets identify the network and the last octet identifies host addresses. The default subnet mask is 255.255.255.0 The range of addresses reserved for private use is 192.168.0.0 to 192.168.255.255.

This is only the briefest overview of TCP/IP. As a subject, the protocol has been the subject of many books, some of them quite huge. In my view, the best of these books is Craig Zacker's *TCP/IP Administration*.

CHAPTER SUMMARY

While this may have seemed like a long and complex chapter, in truth, I merely exposed you to the proverbial tip of the iceberg when it comes to networking. Still, I thought it would be a good idea if you had at least a basic introduction to the protocols of networking as well.

Protocols are divided into hardware protocols and networking protocols. Don't be fooled into thinking I covered all of them in this chapter. That would require a textbook in and of itself. I introduced you to the most commonly used protocols, both in the area of hardware and networking. If you're interested in a more complete discussion, refer to my book *The Complete Guide to Networking and Network+*, also from Thomson/Delmar Learning.

BRAIN DRAIN

1. Should you desire to set up a small network in your home, what would be the bare necessities you would need to get up and running?

2. Describe the difference between bounded and unbounded media and give examples of each.

3. In detail, discuss the difference between a collision domain and a broadcast domain.

4. Define the term beaconing and describe the process in detail.

5. Discuss the differences between hardware protocols and networking protocols.

THE 64K$ QUESTIONS

1. The maximum distance twisted-pair cable can be run without assistance is _____.
   a. 100 feet
   b. 100 meters
   c. 185 meters
   d. 500 meters

2. The maximum distance coaxial cable can be run without assistance is _____.
   a. 100 feet
   b. 100 meters
   c. 185 meters
   d. 500 meters

3. The proper device for interconnecting a token ring network segment to an Ethernet segment is a _____.
   a. Repeater
   b. MAU
   c. Switch
   d. Bridge

4. A(n) _____ doubles as a repeater.
   a. Passive hub
   b. Switch
   c. Router
   d. Active hub

5. In order to interconnect two autonomous networks into a single larger network, you would need a _____.
   a. Passive hub
   b. Switch
   c. Router
   d. Active hub

6. The term CSMA/CD stands for _____.
   a. Collision sensing media access/Carrier detection
   b. Carrier secured multiple access/Collision detection
   c. Carrier sense multiple access/Collision detection
   d. Common sensing media access/Collision detection

7. Two hardware protocols that make use of a ring topology are _____ and _____. (Pick two.)

   a. CSMA/CD

   b. Ethernet

   c. FDDI

   d. Token ring

8. Bus networks typically made use of STP cabling.

   a. True

   b. False

9. The protocol of choice for the Internet is _____.

   a. NetBEUI

   b. IPX/SPX

   c. TCP/IP

   d. FDDI

10. 192.168.0.110 is an example of a _____ address.

   a. Class A

   b. Class B

   c. Class C

   d. Class D

TRICKY TERMINOLOGY

Beaconing: A process that occurs on a token ring network in which each station on the network sends a signal to its upstream neighbor and its downstream neighbor asking if it has seen the token lately.

Bounded media: Any medium that physically connects a device to the network by way of a tangible cable.

Bridge: A device that interconnects two networks or segments of a network of different topologies or different platforms together.

Client: Any device or software that requires the services of another device or piece of software in order to perform its function.

Coaxial: A cable over which the signal and ground both follow the same axis.

Credentials: On a network, these consist of the user ID and password that provides network access for the user.

Crossover cable: A network patch cord that routes the transmit signal from one device to the receive terminals on the other device.

Default gateway: The route through which all packets that contain addresses that the transmitting device cannot resolve will be sent.

Hub: A device that interconnects multiple hosts on a star network over a single segment.

Media: The substance or energy wave over which a data signal is transmitted.

Multimode fiber: A fiber-optic strand that moves multiple signals through the core.

Permissions: Resource access or actions for which a particular user is allowed.

Repeater: A device that cleans up, amplifies, and retransmits a signal, effectively increasing the distance data can travel over any given medium.

Router: A device that interconnects two autonomous networks into a single larger network.

Server: Any device or software that provides services to other devices or pieces of software that need them.

Single-mode fiber: A fiber optics strand that moves only a single signal through the core.

Subnet Mask: A configuration setting within TCP/IP that identifies to the system what part of an IP address is the network address and what part is the host address.

Switch: A device that breaks a larger network down into smaller segments, isolating each segment into its own collision domain.

Thicknet: A name commonly given to RG-8 coaxial cable.

Thinnet: A name commonly given to RG-58U coaxial cable.

Topology: The method through which a network is physically wired.

Transceiver: Any device that is designed to be able to transmit and receive data.

Unbounded media: Any medium that connects the device to the network using energy forms that travel through air and/or space.

Vampire clamp: A device consisting of two halves that screw together. One half is fitted with sharp teeth that bite through the insulation of RG-8 cable.

ACRONYM ALERT

AUI: Attachment Unit Interface

CDDI: Copper Distributed Data Interface

CSMA/CD: Carrier Sense, Multiple Access/Collision Detection

DIX: Digital, Intel, Xerox

EIA: Electronics Industry Association

FCC: Federal Communications Commission

FDDI: Fiber Distributed Data Interface

HPSF: High Power Single Frequency

IPX/SPX: Internetwork Packet Exchange/Sequenced Packet Exchange. An early Novell networking protocol.

ISO: International Standards Organization

LAN: Local Area Network

LLC: Logic Link Control

LPSF: Low Power Single Frequency

MAC: Media Access Control

MAU: Multistation Access Unit. A device similar to a hub that interconnects hosts on a token ring network.

NetBEUI: NetBIOS Extended User Interface. An early Microsoft networking protocol.

NIC: Network Interface Card

OSI: Open Standards Interconnect. A seven-layer model for developing networking standards.

P2P: Peer to Peer. A network on which all hosts are equals.

STP: Shielded Twisted Pair

TCP/IP: Transmission Control Protocol/Internet Protocol. The protocol of choice for the Internet.

TIA: Telecommunications Industry Association

UHF: Ultrahigh Frequency

UTP: Unshielded Twisted Pair

VHF: Very High Frequency

WAN: Wide Area Network

 VIEW THE VIDEO

A video clip on Introduction to Networks is available on the accompanying CD.

CHAPTER 33

OPERATING SYSTEMS AND NETWORKING

Although it is unlikely that any reasonable employer will ever ask a PC technician to take over the network engineer's job for any length of time, in this day and age it's essential that any person working in IT have some basic networking knowledge. Here I will take you through the steps of getting a computer to join either a workgroup or a domain, using WIN9x or WIN2K/XP. In the second half of the chapter, I'll go over a few basic troubleshooting techniques.

A+ OPERATING SYSTEM TECHNOLOGIES EXAM OBJECTIVES

CompTIA objectives covered in this chapter include the following:

4.1 Identify the networking capabilities of Windows. Given configuration parameters, configure the operating system to connect to a network.

4.2 Identify the basic Internet protocols and terminologies. Identify procedures for establishing Internet connectivity. In a given scenario, configure the operating system to connect to and use Internet resources.

WORKGROUPS AND DOMAINS

In the Windows environment, there are really only two models of network in use today. These are the workgroup model and the domain model. For the most part, the workgroup is used in smaller peer-to-peer (P2P) networks, and the domain is the model used by client/server networks.

By definition, a *workgroup* is any group of users and/or computers that share a common task over a network. The devices/users are set up in such a way that they are able to share files, exchange messages, and share peripheral devices. In the workgroup, each device and/or user is independently managed.

The *domain* is a bit more sophisticated. A domain consists of all users, devices, and other resources that are under the administrative control of a single entity. In the case of Microsoft networking, this control entity is the domain controller.

Although it is common to see the term workgroup used almost synonymously with the P2P network, this is not necessarily a correct assumption. It is true that the P2P network can only handle workgroup computing. However, it is possible (and relatively common) to configure workgroups within a domain.

NETWORKING IN WIN98

In today's world of the Internet, networking can mean different things to different people. To the network administrator, it means the LAN. The Internet is merely another resource to access, and to many administrators it poses a security risk. To the small office or home user, the Internet may be the only networking that is ever used. The basic definition of a network is two or more computers (or other devices) configured to communicate with one another. By that definition, a computer hooked up to the Internet is networked. Therefore, this section and the one that follows dealing with WIN2K/XP will be divided into two parts. The first will cover basic networking, and the second section will talk about Internet connectivity.

> **BUZZ WORDS**
>
> **Workgroup:** A collection of independently managed users and/or devices on a network that are configured to share files and devices.
>
> **Domain:** A collection of users, devices, and other resources that are under the control of a single management entity.
>
> **Network client:** A piece of software running on a computer that provides network access for the computer and all applications running on that computer.

CONFIGURING NETWORKING IN WIN9x

There are two ways to get to the Network Applet in WIN9x. You can click Start→Settings→Control Panel. When Control Panel opens, double-click the Network icon. The other way is to right-click the Network Neighborhood icon on the desktop and then select Properties. Either way will bring up a screen similar to the one shown in **Figure 33.1**. You'll notice that there are three different tabs available in the WIN98 screen shown here.

THE CONFIGURATION TAB

In this tab, there are four different configurations that can be managed. These configurations are the type of client that the computer will use, the network adapter, the protocol of choice, and the services that will be installed.

The Client In the OS, the *network client* is a piece of software that provides access to the network for the computer and all applications running on that computer. It is *not* the end user. The network client is not only specific to the OS running on the local computer, it is also specific to the NOS running on the server on a client/server network. Therefore, if a Novell server manages your network, then each workstation must be configured with a Novell client.

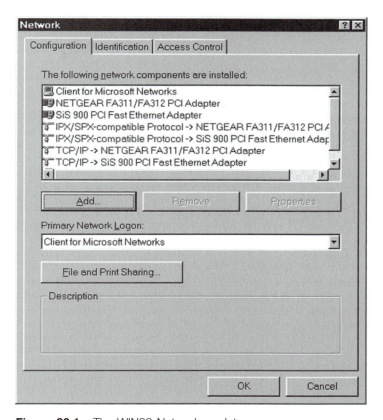

Figure 33.1   The WIN98 Network applet

If your network features both Novell and Windows servers, then in order to access all parts of the network, each workstation must be configured with a client for each NOS.

In the old days of 16-bit computing, this was sometimes a bit of a problem. Most OSs only allowed a single 16-bit client to exist on the computer at any given time. With 32-bit clients (which are about all that are ever used in modern networks), there is no issue with running multiple clients.

To select a client in WIN9x, click the Add button, double-click Client on the window that pops up, and then make your selection. WIN9x offers clients for Banyan Vines, Microsoft, and Novell networks. Banyan became obsolete in 1999, when the company changed its name to ePresence and announced that it would concentrate on Internet services from that point forward. All Banyan Vines products were discontinued.

In Microsoft, the user has the choice of Client for Microsoft Networks, Client for Novell Networks, and Microsoft Family Logon. There are two clients offered for Novell. One is the Novell NetWare Workstation Shell 3.x [NETX], and the other is the Novell NetWare Workstation Shell 4.0 and above [VLM].

Adapter Selecting this option will basically invoke an Add/Remove Hardware screen that prompts the user to select the proper network adapter. In the old days, when WIN9x was relatively inept at recognizing NICs, this function was needed with some frequency. The PnP version of WIN98 was significantly more efficient, and it was better to let PnP handle the installation process except in those cases where the card was simply not recognized.

One of the adapters listed under this tab is the MS Loopback Adapter. This is a virtual device that fools the computer into thinking there is a NIC installed when, in fact, there is none. Other virtual adapters available include the Microsoft Dial-up

> **BUZZ WORDS** ───────────
>
> **Protocol:** An application running on a computer that ensures that the computer will speak the same language and follow the same rules as the computers with which it communicates.
>
> **Service:** A networking function of the OS, such as file sharing, that can be turned on and off as needed.

adapter, which treats a modem as if it were a NIC. There is also the Microsoft PPP over ATM adapter. This allows the use of the Point to Point Protocol (PPP) across a network using Asynchronous Transfer Mode (ATM). PPP allows direct virtual connections to be made between hosts over the Internet. ATM is a high-speed serial connection protocol used in networking. For more information on these protocols and others, see *The Complete Guide to Networking and Network+*, by this same author.

Protocols A *protocol* is sort of like the language that a computer speaks. But it isn't just language that is involved. Just like when a person visits a foreign country, it's important to know the social rules that control that society it's necessary for two computers to follow the same rules. A basic truth is that for two different computer systems to talk to one another, both must be running identical protocols, and those protocols must be configured properly. Microsoft provides support for three different networking protocols. These are NetBIOS Extended User Interface (NetBEUI), Internetwork Packet Exchange/Sequenced Packed Exchange (IPX/SPX), and Transmission Control Protocol/Internet Protocol (TCP/IP).

Just configuring the machine to work with all protocols is not a shortcut to success. In fact, such a practice can cause serious performance issues, not only for the host computer, but across the network as well. When a computer is asked to take part in communications over the network, information is broken down into small chunks of data called packets. These packets vary in size based on the protocol being used. Your computer will try each protocol configured, in the order in which it was installed, until it finds a protocol that works. And it will do this for each communications session that is initiated. Pick a protocol and stick with it. Since this is the world of the Internet, chances are extremely good you will be picking TCP/IP. Later in this chapter, I will provide a detailed discussion for configuring and troubleshooting TCP/IP.

Services A network *service* is a specific function of the NOS that can be turned on or turned off at will. A basic host OS such as WIN98 is relatively limited in the services that are available. In fact, there are only three. These are File and Printer Sharing for Microsoft Networks, File and Printer Sharing for Novell Networks, and Service for Netware Directory Services.

Regardless of the type of NOS used by the network servers, if local files and printers on the host are to be shared, the appropriate File and Printer Sharing service must be installed. Otherwise sharing will not be an option. Obviously, for networks powered by Novell servers, you will pick the Novell version, and vice versa.

An additional service needed by Novell networks is the Services for NetWare Directory Services. This allows the local OS to interface with Novell's Directory Services (NDS). NDS is a function provided by Novell servers that allows a user to browse the entire network as if it were a part of the user's local machine.

THE IDENTIFICATION TAB

This very simple screen (**Figure 33.2**) seems to cause more network issues than anything so simple should be allowed to cause. There are only three fields here that contain information, and one of them is optional!

Two fields that must be filled out in order for the network to properly function are Computer name and Workgroup. On any given network, there may *not* be two computers or other devices

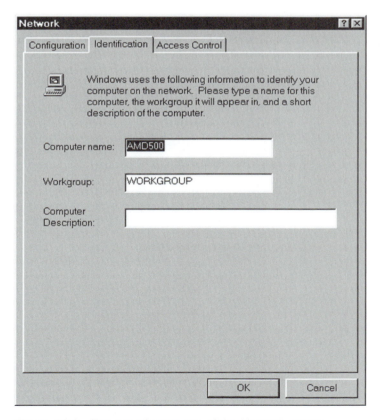

Figure 33.2   The Identification tab of the Network applet

that share the same name. If an administrator inadvertently gives two devices the same name, the first to log on will have no difficulty. The second device will not be able to log on, though.

For two devices on a workgroup to talk to one another, they must be members of the same workgroup. For example, in Figure 33.2, the computer is named AMD500 and the workgroup is simply named Workgroup. That's because Workgroup is the default name.

If I have two dozen computers on the same physical network, and half of them are assigned to the SALES workgroup while the other have are assigned to ADMIN, then all the SALES members can talk to one another. Likewise all the ADMIN computers will communicate. But SALES will not be able to communicate with ADMIN.

The third field is optional. This is the Computer Description field. Here the administrator can enter a brief line telling what that computer's function is, its location, or any other pertinent information.

THE ACCESS CONTROL TAB

The Access Control tab (**Figure 33.3**) defines how resources on the local system will be secured. The two options are share-level access control and user-level access control. Having discussed

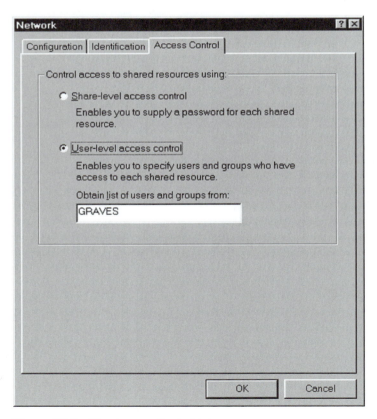

Figure 33.3 The Access Control tab

share-level versus user-level access control in Chapter Twenty-Five, I don't see any cause to go over that material again. Suffice it to say that this is where the selection is made.

SHARING RESOURCES IN WIN9x

There's no point in setting up a network if there's nothing on the network for users to share. For resources to be made available to the network, File and Print Sharing Services must be installed and configured, as I pointed out in the previous section. After this has been accomplished, sharing resources is actually a simple matter. The two most common devices to be shared are file locations and printers. Keep in mind, though, it also possible to share out a resource such as an external disk drive and/or CD-ROM drive (either internal or external).

SHARING DRIVES, FILES, AND FOLDERS

The easiest way to share out a file or folder in WIN9x is by way of Windows Explorer (**Figure 33.4**). Explorer can be accessed in one of two ways. The easiest way is to right-click the Start button and select Explore from the menu that appears. Some people find it annoying that using this method opens the Windows directory in Explorer and places them in the Start Menu folder. To avoid this inconvenience, simply click Start→Programs→Windows Explorer. You can easily

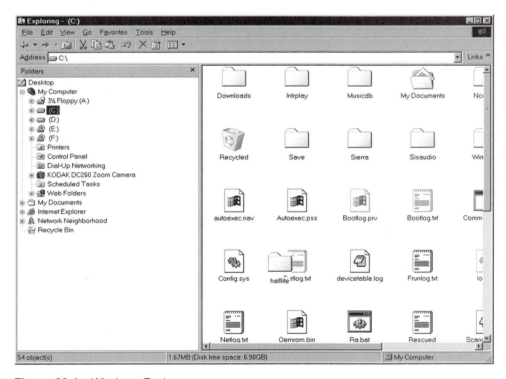

Figure 33.4   Windows Explorer

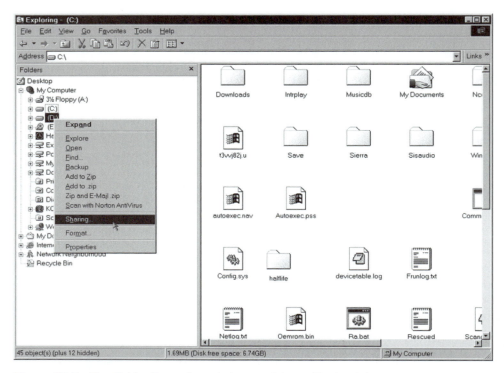

Figure 33.5 The Folder Properties window contains a Sharing tab.

create a shortcut to Explorer by right-clicking Windows Explorer in the Start menu and selecting Create Shortcut. Drag and drop the new Start Menu entry, now entitled Windows Explorer (2) to the desktop. Rename it if you so desire.

Once in Explorer, right-click the drive, file, or folder you want to share, as shown in **Figure 33.5**. This brings up the Folder Properties windows, with the Sharing tab opened. (Note that the Folder Properties windows will be named after the folder for which the properties are being viewed.)

When the Shared as button is clicked, the fields for Share Name, Comment, and Name appear (see **Figure 33.6**). By default, the share name will be the name of the folder (or device) as seen by Windows whenever possible. However, in WIN98, share names are limited to twelve characters. Therefore, long file or folder names will be truncated to that number. You can name the share anything you wish as long as you stick to names that are twelve characters or less, that is, if you have to worry about compatibility with WIN98 machines. This does not affect the name of the local file or folder, but merely how remote users see it. Therefore, in Figure 33.6, where I shared out the D drive, I chose to use a share name of SERVERD. On the local machine, this share will still be Drive D:, but when remote users browse to it over the network, they will see it as SERVERD.

In this window, you will also have the option of adding users and selecting their permissions. If share-level access has been selected, the options are limited. You can only select the

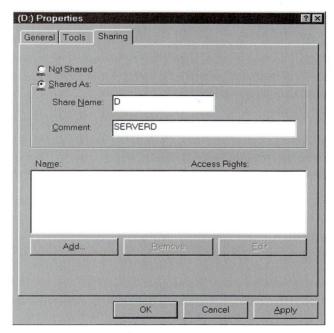

Figure 33.6   Sharing a folder in WIN98

option to use or not to use a password on the resource. If you choose to password-protect the folder, you will have the additional option of selecting whether or not to use separate passwords for full permissions and read-only permissions. With user-level security checked, you can open the list of users and groups from the domain controller and pick and choose from there.

SHARING PRINTERS IN WIN9X

Sharing printers is only slightly different than sharing folders in WIN9x. For one thing, if File and Printer Sharing is installed and configured to include printers at the time a printer is first installed, then the process is simple. The installation wizard asks whether you wish to share the printer. You select Yes and either accept the prompted share name or fill in a name of your choice (under twelve characters, once again).

If File and Printer Sharing is installed and configured after a printer has already been installed, it can be shared out over the network in a manner similar to what I discussed in Folder sharing. Open My Computer and double-click Printers. You can also get to the Printer applet through Start→Settings→Printers or Start→Settings→Control Panel, and double-clicking the Printers icon. There are a lot of ways to get to this one.

After you get there, right-click the printer you want to share. >From there, the process is identical to that of sharing a folder.

DIAL-UP NETWORKING IN WIN9x

As much as we'd like to imagine that the 56K modem is a thing of the past, the fact of the matter is, it's still alive and well. It's especially prevalent in rural areas where broadband has not yet reached. Therefore, setting up Dial-Up Networking (DUN) is still a task that every technician is likely to face at some time or the other.

The first thing you need to do is make sure the modem is properly installed and functioning. That's a hardware issue and details pertaining to hardware resources and device drivers are discussed in Chapter Twenty, Telecommunications. This discussion assumes the hardware end has already been taken care of.

In WIN9x versions, DUN is located in the My Computer folder on the desktop. Double-clicking the My Computer icon will bring up a window similar to the one shown in **Figure 33.7**. The number and variety of icons you seen in that window will vary based on the configuration of the computer. When you double-click the Dial-up Networking icon, it launches the Welcome to Dial-Up Networking wizard (**Figure 33.8**).

The first thing the wizard is going to do is ask you to name the connection and to select the device with which you want the connection to be made (**Figure 33.9**). On the outset, this may seem a bit superfluous. However, keep in mind that it is quite possible to install multiple modems in a computer system and that each modem can be dedicated to a specific function. These functions can include more than one DUN connection, with a dedicated modem for each connection and/or a modem dedicated to fax functionality. Naturally, for multiple modems to be of any benefit, each must have a dedicated telephone line.

In the next screen (**Figure 33.10**), there is a field for filling in the area code, along with a second field for the telephone number of the target connection. The third field on this screen is for the country or region from which you will be dialing. By default, the region that you

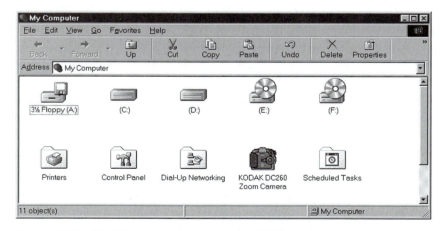

Figure 33.7 The My Computer window in WIN98

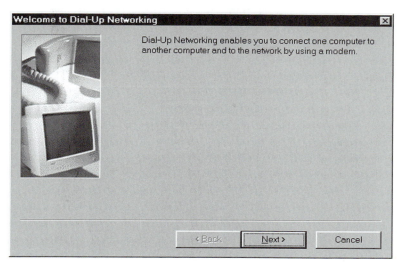

Figure 33.8   The Welcome to Dial-Up Networking wizard in WIN98

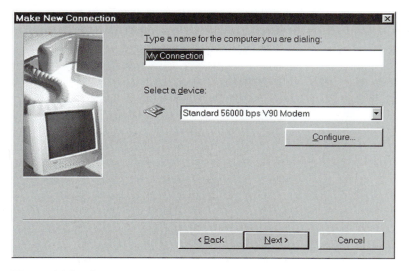

Figure 33.9   Step one is to name the connection and select a device for dialing out.

selected during the installation of Windows will appear in that field. It is something you can change if necessary.

That's the last thing you need to do. The next screen, entitled Make New Connection (**Figure 33.11**), is the final screen in this process. Click Finish, and DUN is configured.

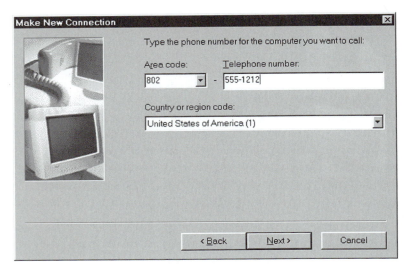

Figure 33.10   Configuring the target telephone number and country/region code

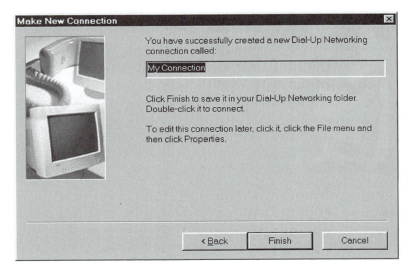

Figure 33.11   Finalizing your DUN connection

MANAGING INTERNET CONNECTIONS IN WIN9X

Since the entire reason for the existence of an extremely large percentage of personal computers in this world is to provide users with Internet access, it would be obvious that this is something with the technician should be familiar. In WIN9x, connecting to the Internet can be done in a variety of ways. The two most common are through a modem interface and through the LAN. Therefore, those are the two connections I'll discuss.

CONNECTING TO THE INTERNET BY MODEM

Once again, the following discussion assumes the modem is already configured and working in the target computer. If you have all the information you need, all you're doing is creating a new DUN connection, as discussed in the previous step. It's as simple as that. However, there is a second way to invoke the Wizard when the requested DUN is specifically for an Internet connection.

Open Control Panel by clicking Start→Settings→Control Panel and then double-click the Internet Options icon. The window that opens will have several tabs at the top. Click the Connections tab to open the window shown in **Figure 33.12**.

Click the Add button, and the DUN wizard will start. From there, it is just like the steps described in the previous section.

On a WIN98SE system, it is possible to share this Internet Connection with other computers on the network that are also using WIN98SE (or later). With Internet Connection Sharing (ICS), the computer directly connected to the Internet (called the Connection Sharing computer), doles

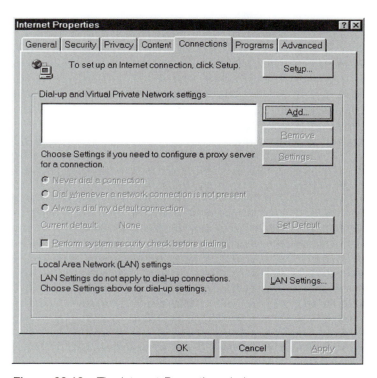

Figure 33.12 The Internet Properties window

out private IP addresses and name resolution services for the other computers on the home network. Then, the other computers on your network can access the Internet through the Connection Sharing computer using private IP addressing translation.

It stands to reason that, for this to work, each computer must be equipped with a NIC and a LAN configured and successfully running. The Connection Sharing computer can be hooked up to the Internet by way of Modem, Integrated Services Digital Network (ISDN), or Digital Subscriber Line (DSL). The latter two are high-speed connection options for the Internet.

ICS is not something that installs by default onto a WIN98 computer. It must be added unless the user performed a custom install at the time the OS was installed and configured. In order to add ICS, open Control Panel as before and click Add/Remove Programs. Click the Windows Setup tab, as shown in **Figure 33.13**, and scroll down to Internet Tools.

If you simply click the checkbox and proceed, you might be installing some components you neither need nor want. So before you continue, with Internet Tools highlighted, click the Details button. In **Figure 33.14**, I have deselected all but ICS. By default, if I had simply

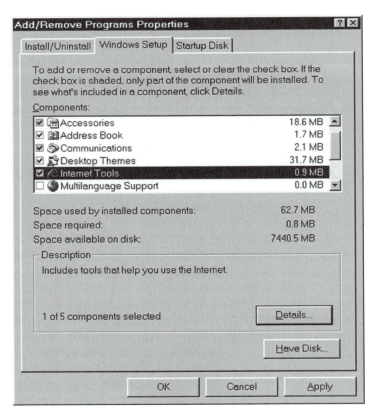

Figure 33.13 In order to install Internet Connection Sharing, you need to access the Add Windows Components wizard.

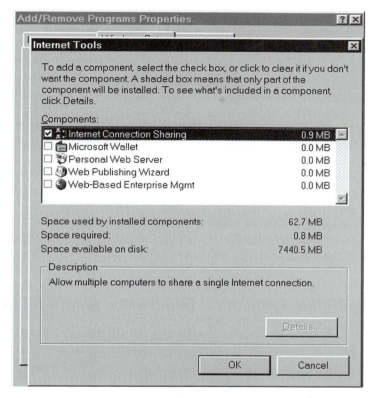

Figure 33.14   Before proceeding with the installation of Internet Tools, make sure you really need everything that will be installed.

checked the box next to Internet Tools in the previous screen, all of these would be checked and installed. Since I have no need for the rest of these tools, I chose not to install them.

Click OK, and you will be prompted to insert your WIN98 CD. Insert the CD and click next. The Add/Remove Programs Wizard will copy a bunch of files to your computer and make a few changes to the registry. Once this process has been completed, the Internet Connection Sharing wizard will launch itself. The user does not need to do anything to prompt it. Read all the information on this screen and make sure you have fulfilled all the requirements before proceeding. When you're sure, click <u>N</u>ext to move on to the next step. From that point, it's merely a matter of following the steps on the screen. Repeat the process on all client computers.

CONNECTING TO THE INTERNET BY LAN

Connection to the Internet over the LAN can either be much easier than setting up a DUN connection, or much more difficult, depending on the configuration of your network. If the computer with the primary Internet connection is a WIN98 computer with Internet Sharing enabled, you merely install Internet Connection Sharing on the other computers and run the wizard as described previously.

Another method is to install a third-party proxy application on the host computer. This turns the host into a *proxy server*. The proxy server acts as the portal to the Internet, and all the other computers on the network access the Internet through the proxy.

To configure a proxy server, open the Internet Connections applet in Control Panel and click Connections. Click LAN Settings to bring up the screen in **Figure 33.15**. Click the box under Proxy Server that is labeled Use a proxy server for your LAN. Click Advanced to bring up the screen in **Figure 33.16**. Type the IP address for the host computer in each of the Server fields. Check the instructions that come with your proxy server application for the appropriate ports to use. Many products use dedicated ports for various protocols. Click OK.

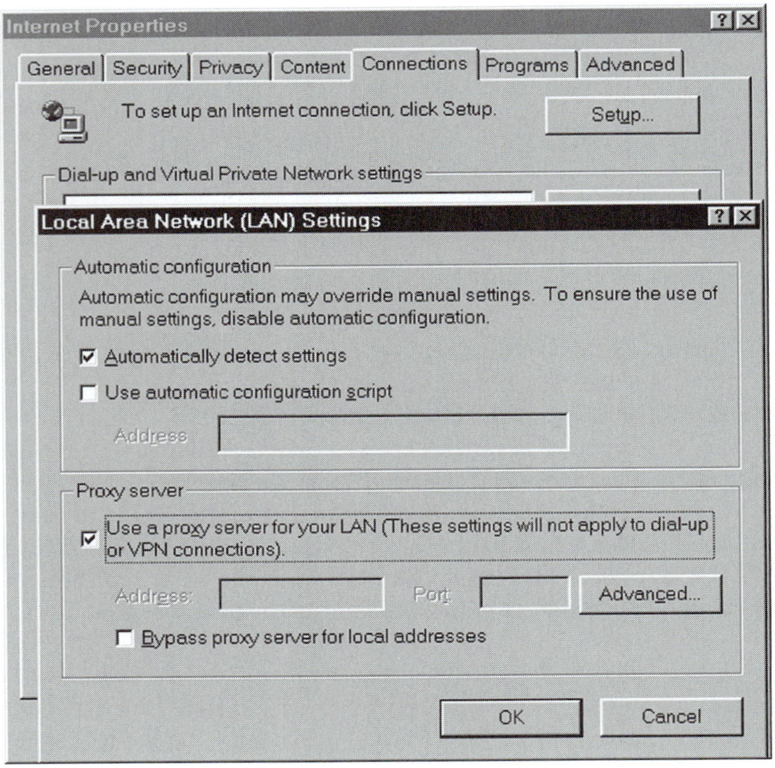

> ### BUZZ WORDS
>
> **Proxy server:** A machine on the network that has been configured to be the portal to the Internet, through which all other computers on the network gain access.

Figure 33.15   Configuring Internet LAN settings

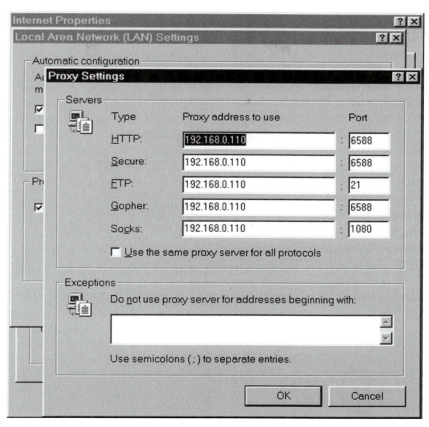

Figure 33.16   Configuring Proxy Server settings

NETWORKING IN WIN2K AND WINXP

There are really relatively few differences between WIN98 and the more recent versions of Windows in terms of networking. Most of these differences involve the location of applets and in some cases, the names of the applets. When you find where you're going, the procedures don't vary. The following list outlines various differences between the OS versions:

- *Browsing the network*: In WIN9x, the applet is called Network Neighborhood. In WIN2K and WINXP, it is My Network Places. Right-clicking the icon in any version will bring up a menu that includes an option for the Properties Screen.
- *Network identification*: In WIN9x, this is configured in the Network Properties applet, under the Identification tab. In WIN2K and WINXP, it is in the System applet under the Computer Name tab. This is also where the computer can be joined to a domain,

as long as the user knows the user ID and password for an account with administrative privileges on the domain.

■ *Internet sharing*: Installed by default on WIN2K and WINXP.

■ *Configuring a local area connection*: In WIN98, the Network applet shows all installed connections in a single screen. To bind or unbind protocols and services from an interface, the properties of that interface must be highlighted. In WIN2K and WINXP, each interface is listed as a separate entity and can be configured independently.

> **BUZZ WORDS** ———————
>
> **Octet:** A decimal alliteration of a single 8-bit string of data.

CONFIGURING TCP/IP

Since TCP/IP has become the preeminent networking protocol used by network professionals throughout the world over the last couple of years, it's imperative that technicians know how to configure a computer to use TCP/IP. To configure TCP/IP, open the Network applet in WIN98 or double click the Local Area Connections icon in WIN2K or WINXP. In WIN98, highlight TCP/IP→(selected interface) and click Properties. In WIN2K or XP, open the Local Area Connection you wish to configure and, under the General tab, click Properties. Highlight Internet Protocol (TCP/IP).

TCP/IP identifies computers by an IP address. An IP address consists of a 32-bit address listed in decimal format. An example of an IP address is 192.168.0.1. As you can see, the address consists of four numbers, called *octets,* divided by periods. They are called octets because each number represents an 8-bit value. While it is beyond the scope of this book to go into IP addresses in detail, a brief overview is in order.

The IP address can be broken down into two sections. The first section identifies what network the device is on, while the second identifies the device itself. This is true whether the IP address defines a computer, a printer, or a router interface. There are five different classes of IP address. An IP address class determines how many networks can exist and how many hosts can exist on each network. Network administrators can use only three classes of IP address: Class A, Class B, and Class C.

In a Class A address, only the first octet identifies the network. All other numbers in the address point to different hosts. The first number can be any number from 1 to 127. There can be only a few Class A networks, but each one has millions of hosts.

A Class B address uses the first two octets to identify the network and the last two to identify the hosts. The first number will always be from 128 to 191. There are nearly equal numbers of Class B networks and hosts that can occupy them. I say nearly, because limitations in the first octet lower the number of available network addresses.

Class C addresses use the first three octets to identify the network, but only the last octet identifies hosts. As you might imagine, there are lots and lots of class C networks, but each one is limited to a maximum of 255 hosts.

IP addresses can be configured one of two ways. If there is a server on the network configured with the Dynamic Host Configuration Protocol (DHCP) that can dole out addresses, the simplest way is to select <u>O</u>btain an IP address automatically. On boot up, the DHCP server will assign an IP address to the computer. If the administrator so desires, DHCP can also assign IP addresses to DNS servers, WINS servers, and default gateways. Don't worry at this moment what those are. I'll discuss them in a minute.

If there is no DHCP server on the network, or if the administrator simply has a reason for statically assigning IP addresses, then the box labeled <u>S</u>pecify an IP address must be checked. At a minimum, there are two items that must be configured. The first is the actual IP address. No two computers on the network can share the same IP address. If this happens by accident, the first computer to log on has no problems. The next one is denied access.

The second item that is required by all TCP/IP configurations is the subnet mask. Earlier in this section, I pointed out that all IP addresses consist of a network address and a host address. The subnet mask defines what part of the IP address identifies the network and what part identifies the host. Your network administrator can tell you what subnet mask to use. If you happen to be setting up a small home or office network, the default subnet masks should work just fine. Default subnet masks for each class of address are as follows:

- Class A address: 255.0.0.0
- Class B address: 255.255.0.0
- Class C address: 255.255.255.0

As you can see, default subnet masks consist of all 255 and 0 numbers. The number 255 identifies the network part of the address, and the 0 identifies the host address.

Three other items that are optionally configured in TCP/IP are the gateway, the WINS server, and the DNS server. Whether you configure these depends entirely on whether or not your network uses the services. These services are described in the next couple of sections.

GATEWAY (OR DEFAULT GATEWAY)

When a computer is asked to transmit a packet of data to a remote destination, it needs to know where to send that packet. If the OS examines a packet and sees an IP address in the header of that packet, it knows exactly where to send it, right?

Well, maybe it does and maybe it doesn't. If the address in the header is an address on the local network, there is no problem. If the user is trying to send information to a remote network, though, then the OS needs to know how to find the remote network. The gateway is the IP address of a port or interface that leads to the outside world. This can be a router or a computer that has access to another NIC or to a router.

When the OS examines a packet and finds an IP address it doesn't recognize, it simply transmits that packet to the device identified by the gateway. If there is no gateway, it discards that packet and pretends it never existed.

WINS SERVERS

Older Microsoft NOSs made use of a protocol called the Windows Internet Naming Service (WINS) to translate an IP address to a computer name. Newer NOSs maintain WINS support for backward compatibility. For WINS to work, there has to be one or more servers on the network configured to act as a WINS server. For a host to make use of the service, the IP address of the WINS server must be configured in the TCP/IP properties.

DNS SERVERS

These days, most OSs use a service called Domain Name Services (DNS) for resolving host names to IP addresses. As with WINS, for DNS to work, there must be a computer on the network configured to be a DNS server. If there is a gateway configured, the DNS server can be off the local network. For example, many network administrators, and most homes and small offices, take advantage of the fact that their internet service providers (ISPs) have a minimum of two DNS servers that are far more robust and have substantially more entries than any DNS server they could ever configure. To configure a DNS server, click the DNS tab and type one or more addresses.

TCP/IP UTILITIES

One of the beauties of using TCP/IP as your default protocol lies in the number of elegant little utilities that are part of the suite. These handy little programs provide an immense amount of troubleshooting capability without spending any extra money. In addition to the ones that are part of the suite, there are huge numbers of utilities available for download on the Web that are not officially part of the suite. It is a good idea to really know your way around the TCP/IP utilities. The ones I will be covering in this chapter include three of the most useful:

- Ping
- Route
- IPCONFIG and WINIPCFG

PING

The Packet InterNet Groper, usually just called *Ping*, is one of those utilities you must have a good understanding of. It works on the basis of the Internet Control Message Protocol (ICMP), which generates and delivers error messages when and where appropriate. Ping can tell you whether or not a particular host on the network is reachable. It works by sending out a series of ECHO packets. The intended host, upon receiving the packets, will return an ECHO REPLY. If the ECHO REPLY returns successfully, Ping will calculate the total time elapsed for the round trip. The information will be returned in a screen similar to the one in **Figure 33.17**.

> ### BUZZ WORDS
>
> **Ping:** Not only is Ping an acronym, it has been universally adopted as a term that can be either a noun or a verb. As a noun it represents the packets sent when pinging another host. As a verb, it represents the process of pinging another host.

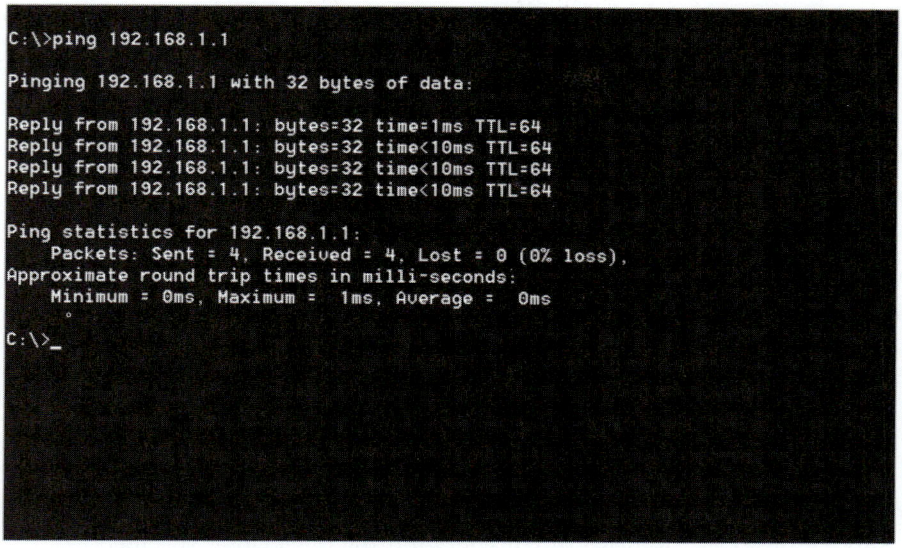

```
C:\>ping 192.168.1.1

Pinging 192.168.1.1 with 32 bytes of data:

Reply from 192.168.1.1: bytes=32 time=1ms TTL=64
Reply from 192.168.1.1: bytes=32 time<10ms TTL=64
Reply from 192.168.1.1: bytes=32 time<10ms TTL=64
Reply from 192.168.1.1: bytes=32 time<10ms TTL=64

Ping statistics for 192.168.1.1:
    Packets: Sent = 4, Received = 4, Lost = 0 (0% loss),
Approximate round trip times in milli-seconds:
    Minimum = 0ms, Maximum = 1ms, Average =  0ms

C:\>_
```

Figure 33.17   Ping provides a great deal of information.

ROUTE

The ROUTE command allows the user to add static entries to the local routing table, or it can be used to view the local routing table. These entries can include routes to networks or routes to hosts. They can also be introduced in numeric fashion or by name, if DNS is available.

When inputting a static entry using the ROUTE command, you would need to know the format of the routing tables used by the OS. By typing **route print** at the command prompt, the existing routing table will be displayed. When generating your own tables, type your entries accordingly.

BUZZ WORDS

Route: The path that data takes to move from point A to point B. It is also a TCP/IP utility that can be used to display the local router configuration on a TCP/IP-enabled device.

IPCONFIG: The TCP/IP utility that displays all TCP/IP configuration information for any given interface, or for all interfaces on a system.

IPCONFIG AND WINIPCFG

IPCONFIG is undoubtedly the most widely used of the TCP/IP utilities. This utility can return statistics on every connection configured to use TCP/IP. If a device is configured to use DHCP, a user can use IPCONFIG to release an IP address and subsequently renew it.

IPCONFIG displays information for all local TCP/IP connections, whether they be a NIC or a modem. As with the other utilities I've discussed, there are a number of triggers associated with IPCONFIG. IPCONFIG triggers vary a bit between Windows 98 and the subsequent Microsoft OSs. Therefore, I will list the triggers for both. Those for WIN98 are as follows:

/all Displays detailed report of all adapters on system.

/batch {filename} Writes a report to the file specified by filename.

/renew_all Renews the IP configuration for all adapters on the system.

/release_all Releases the IP configuration for all adapters on the system.

/renew N Renews the IP configuration for only the adapter specified in N.

/release N Releases the IP configuration for only the adapter specified in N.

The command line parameters for Windows 2000 are a bit different and there are more of them as well. They are as follows:

/all Shows complete configuration for all interfaces on system.

/release {adapter} Releases IP configuration for the adapter specified.

/renew {adapter} Renews IP configuration for the adapter specified.

/flushdns Dumps the contents of the current DNS Resolver cache.

/registerdns Refreshes all DHCP leases and reregisters DNS names.

/displaydns Displays contents of the DNS Resolver cache.

/showclassid Displays the DHCP classes allowed by the adapter.

/setclassid Modifies the DHCP class.

Windows 98 offers a graphical version of IPCONFIG that will display this information as well. This utility is called WINIPCFG. A user can access by clicking Start→Run, and typing **winipcfg** in the run field.

Chapter Summary

In this chapter, I introduced you to some of the basic concepts of networking, along with some OS-specific tips for configuring networking and accessing the network. This is a section of the exam that gets a fair amount of exposure, so it would be a good idea to make sure you're familiar with the material in this chapter.

Network configuration is a key aspect. Make sure that you are familiar with the different protocols and services. TCP/IP is the most commonly tested protocol on the exam, so be able to configure a computer using TCP/IP. Also know how to share devices and files.

BRAIN DRAIN

1. Define a workgroup and a domain. Discuss the differences between the two.

2. Precisely what is a network client (from a software standpoint) and why is it necessary?

3. Define what a protocol is, and describe its role in networking computers.

4. Describe the process of sharing a folder in WIN98.

5. Go through the process of configuring a computer to use TCP/IP on the network.

THE 64K$ QUESTIONS

1. A collection of independently managed computers and/or devices on a network would be called a _____.
   a. Workgroup
   b. Domain
   c. Subnet
   d. Segment

2. A collection of devices on a network that are all under the control of a single administrative unit is best defined as a _____.
   a. Workgroup
   b. Domain
   c. Subnet
   d. Segment

3. The icon for browsing the network in WIN9x is called _____.
   a. My Computer
   b. My Network Places
   c. Network Neighborhood
   d. Network

4. The icon for browsing the network in WINXP is called _____.
   a. My Computer
   b. My Network Places
   c. Network Neighborhood
   d. Network

5. Which of the following protocols is the one most commonly used on the Internet?
   a. NetBEUI
   b. IPX/SPX
   c. Banyan Vines
   d. TCP/IP

6. Which of the following protocols was developed by Novell for its NOS?
   a. NetBEUI
   b. IPX/SPX
   c. Banyan Vines
   d. TCP/IP

7. Which of the following protocols was developed by Microsoft for its NOS?
   a. NetBEUI
   b. IPX/SPX
   c. Banyan Vines
   d. TCP/IP

8. File and Printer Sharing in Microsoft networking is considered a _____.
   a. Logical Adapter
   b. Service
   c. Protocol
   d. Topology

9. If a small network has several users, and each user is capable of setting up his or her own shares and assigning individual passwords for each share, what kind of security is that network using?
   a. Kerberos

b. IPSec

c. Share level

d. User level

10. If the users on a network use a single user ID and password to access all resources, what type of security is in place?

   a. Kerberos

   b. IPSec

   c. Share level

   d. User level

11. Shares on a Windows network are created in _____.

   a. Internet Explorer

   b. Windows Explorer

   c. Network Neighborhood

   d. The Network applet

12. If a computer is equipped with a 56K modem, which service must be configured in order to access the Internet?

   a. RAS

   b. VPN

   c. DUN

   d. DSL

13. Internet Connection Sharing is installed by default on WIN98 computers.

   a. True

   b. False

14. A computer that acts as a portal to the Internet, through which all other computers on the network gain Internet access, is called a(n) _____.

   a. ISP

   b. Proxy server

c. Host computer

d. DUNS server

15. Which of the two following items must be configured on every computer running TCP/IP?

   a. IP address

   b. DNS server address

   c. Subnet mask

   d. WINS server address

16. Your computer has just received a packet that contains an unfamiliar target IP address in the header. If you have a _____ properly configured, the packet can be forwarded.

   a. DNS server

   b. WINS server

   c. Gateway

   d. ARP server

17. A single number in an IP address, divided by periods, is called _____.

   a. The network address

   b. The primordial

   c. An octet

   d. The target ID

18. A Class A address uses _____ to identify the host address.

   a. The first octet

   b. The last octet

   c. The first three octets

   d. The last three octets

19. A Class A address uses _____ to identify the network address.

   a. The first octet

   b. The last octet

   c. The first three octets

   d. The last three octets

20. What is the name of the graphical utility used to view IP configuration settings in WIN98?

   a. Ping
   b. IPCONFIG
   c. MSCONFIG
   d. WINIPCFG

TRICKY TERMINOLOGY

Domain: A collection of users, devices, and other resources that are under the control of a single management entity.

IPCONFIG: The TCP/IP utility that displays all TCP/IP configuration information for any given interface, or for all interfaces on a system.

Network client: A piece of software running on a computer that provides network access for the computer and all applications running on that computer.

Octet: A decimal alliteration of a single 8-bit string of data.

Ping: Not only is Ping an acronym, it has been universally adopted as a term that can be either a noun or a verb. As a noun it represents the packets sent when pinging another host. As a verb, it represents the process of pinging another host.

Protocol: An application running on a computer that ensures that the computer will speak the same language and follow the same rules as the computers with which it communicates.

Proxy server: A machine on the network that has been configured to be the portal to the Internet, through which all other computers on the network gain access.

Route: The path that data takes to move from point A to point B. It is also a TCP/IP utility that can be used to display the local router configuration on a TCP/IP enabled device.

Service: A networking function of the OS, such as file sharing, that can be turned on and off as needed.

Share-level access: A level of security in Windows that allows users to create their own shares and set their own passwords.

User-level access: A level of security in Windows that provides users with all permitted access to network resources using a single user ID and password.

Workgroup: A collection of independently managed users and/or devices on a network that are configured to share files and devices.

ACRONYM ALERT

ATM: Asynchronous Transfer Mode

DHCP: Dynamic Host Configuration Protocol. A protocol that assigns IP addresses to client computers on the fly.

DNS: Domain Name Services. A service that resolves host name to IP address on the Internet.

DSL: Digital Subscriber Line

DUN: Dial-Up Networking. A method of connecting to a network over a modem.

ICS: Internet Connection Sharing. A service that allows multiple computers to share a single Internet access line.

IPX/SPX: Internetwork Packet Exchange/Sequenced Packed Exchange. A Novell networking protocol.

ISDN: Integrated Services Digital Network

NetBEUI: NetBIOS Extended User Interface. A Microsoft networking protocol.

PPP: Point-to-Point Protocol

TCP/IP: Transmission Control Protocol/ Internet Protocol. The networking protocol of the Internet.

WINS: Windows Internet Naming Service. A service that resolves host name to IP address on the local network.

 VIEW THE VIDEO

A video clip on Windows and Networking is available on the accompanying CD.

CHAPTER 34

NAVIGATING THE INTERNET

Even though this is basically a book about computer hardware, it certainly wouldn't be complete without a rundown on the Internet. Everybody uses it. In fact, everybody these days pretty much takes it for granted. It's one of those things that is just there and always was, right? However, calling the Internet just another network is like calling the space shuttle just another airplane. And as difficult as it may be to believe, the Internet hasn't always been around. Although some of us old-timers might find it difficult to believe just how long it *has* been in place.

A+ OPERATING SYSTEM TECHNOLOGIES EXAM OBJECTIVES

CompTIA exam objectives covered in this chapter include the following:

4.2   Identify the basic Internet protocols and terminologies. Identify procedures for establishing Internet connectivity. In a given scenario, configure the operating system to connect to and use Internet resources.

THE HISTORY OF THE INTERNET

Although this may come as a disappointment to some, it is my grievous duty to report that Al Gore did not actually invent the Internet. The Internet is one of those multiheaded entities that came about as the result of the work of thousands of individuals developing protocols and hardware that would allow different systems running on different platforms to communicate. However, if you want to give any one specific individual credit for the concept, let's give it to Joseph Carl Robnett Licklider of MIT.

In 1962, he wrote a paper entitled "On-Line Man Computer Communication." In this paper, he described what he called the Galactic Network. This galactic network was composed of a worldwide conglomeration of computer systems interconnected in order to share and distribute information. Sound familiar? As the head of the Computer Research Program for the

Defense Advanced Research Projects Agency (DARPA), he was given the opportunity to put form to some of his concepts, although the work would eventually be completed by his successor, Lawrence Roberts.

Another MIT alumnus, Leonard Kleinrock, had written a paper entitled "Information Flow in Large Communication Nets," which described how information could be broken down into packets for communication over a wire. Roberts brought Kleinrock on board, and in 1965 they had their first success. They interconnected MIT's TX-2 mainframe to a Q-32 in California. To illustrate what a remarkable achievement this was for the time, the TX-2 was a computer system built by academics that used a 38-bit word and had no operating system as they are known today. Instead, programmers had to compile their own programs or data. The Q-32 was a machine custom built for the military by IBM and used a 48-bit word. The two systems made their first connection over a telephone line.

The following year, Roberts presented his plan for interconnecting a number of different computer systems scattered across the country into an integrated network. In 1969, there were a total of four computers linked together in the network now known as ARPANET. ARPANET became global in 1973 when The University College of London was successfully added to the network.

Two things happened in 1974 that provided momentum for the Internet to become the medium it is today. First and foremost was the publication of "A Protocol for Packet Network Intercommunication," by Vincent Cerf and Robert Kahn. It was in this paper that the Transmission Control Protocol was defined. The other significant event of that year was the release of the first commercial implementation of a packet-based data service. Bolt, Berenek, and Newman gave us Telenet.

Other global networks quickly began to emerge. In 1980 the Computer Science Network (CSNET) and the Because It's Time Network (BITNET) arrived. The year 1982 saw the European UNIX Network (EUNET). A major step toward interlinking all of these networks occurred in 1983 when a gateway between CSNET and ARPANET was created.

EXAM NOTE: One of the occasional exam questions you might see deals with the history of the Internet. Know about ARPANET in particular.

In order to keep track of who was who in this ever-growing collection of entities, the Domain Name System (DNS) was ratified in 1984. This provided a more user-friendly way for humans to locate computers over the wire. DNS provided each entity with a host name and created the domains that identified the type of organization. At first, there were only six primary domains: education (edu), commercial (com), government (gov), military (mil), organization (org), and network (net). That has been expanded over the years.

From there, it was only a matter of time. In 1987, there were approximately 10,000 hosts on the Internet. Two years later, the number exceeded 100,000. But for most of us, the pivotal year was 1991. This was the year that the European Organization for Nuclear Research (CERN) unveiled the World Wide Web. One of their researchers, a man named Tim Berner-Lee developed a method of linking documents to one another electronically called Hypertext Markup Language (HTML).

I give you the Internet. But I didn't invent it.

FOUNDATIONS OF THE INTERNET

In the early days of development, it was apparent that the Internet was going to be a collection of internetworked networks rather than one of individual computers. A few key issues had to be resolved early on before serious development could begin. For one thing, if you wanted an organization to become a part of this global movement, you had to earn its trust. Therefore, it was decided that each network would stand alone. The process of internetworking would not require that any modifications to network structure or administration be implemented. Second, on an operational level, there would be no control of the network permitted by outside sources.

Multiple networks would be linked together by routers or gateways. These devices would not retain data after a transmission was completed. Routers had to be platform-independent.

Another key issue, after the World Wide Web was implemented, dealt with how to get individual users onto the network. The following section explains the different intermediate levels that occur from the end-user's machine up to the actual source of data being accessed by that user. The concept is illustrated in **Figure 34.1**. These intermediate levels include the following:

- User's PC
- User's datacom
- The local loop carrier
- The ISP point of presence (POP)
- User services
- ISP backbone
- Online content
- Origin of content

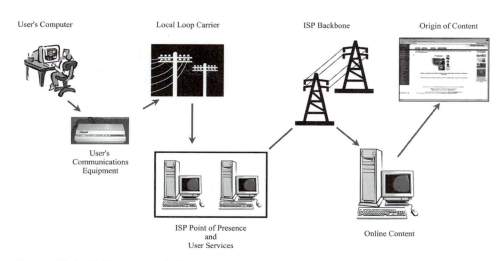

Figure 34.1 While your web browser makes it seem easy, getting online is actually a pretty complicated process.

THE USER'S PC

Of these different links, the user's PC should be the one that requires the least explanation (**Figure 34.2**). However, it should be noted that there are different hardware requirements for different applications. If you're involved in any activity requiring sound, it might be nice if you have the appropriate equipment installed. A sound card, speakers, and very likely a microphone are in order. Applications such as tele-conferencing will require this sort of setup. If you work with streaming video, an appropriate graphics adapter is in order. Obviously, you will also need some form of software interface. Most people use Web browsers such as Internet Explorer or Netscape Navigator. Other software packages that are useful include some form of FTP client, an email client, and perhaps a Telnet client.

Figure 34.2 Internet connections start with the user logging onto the Internet.

THE USER'S DATACOM

More simply put, the *datacom* is the communications equipment that allows the user's PC to hook up to another PC over a communications link of some sort (**Figure 34.3**). In the old days this was a simpler matter. Everyone used modems. These days the choices include the following:

BUZZ WORDS

Datacom: A term coined to describe any equipment used in data communications.

- Public Switched Telephone Network (PSTN) — Dial-up networking with a modem. ~53.3K

- Integrated Services Digital Network (ISDN) — Sometimes called digital modem. ~128K

- Digital Subscriber Line (DSL) — High-speed broadband. ~384K – 6MB

- Cable Modem — Internet over cable television services. Speed varies

- Satellite Internet — Broadband Wireless Internet. ~400K

Figure 34.3 The user's telecommunications equipment makes the connection.

Which choice you make impacts your speed of service, as you might imagine. However, be aware that not all services are available in all areas.

THE LOCAL LOOP CARRIER

Somebody has to maintain the circuits that carry the signal between you and your service provider (**Figure 34.4**). Depending on your choice of datacom, these options include your local telephone company, cable television company, or an independent contractor. Your selection here not only impacts performance, but security as well. Some carriers are less secure than others. For example, if you use a cable modem, when you log on you become part of a local segment for the company. Any files you have shared on your computer can be browsed by others on the same segment simply by visiting Network Neighborhood. A good firewall is in order here if you have any sensitive data at all.

Other carriers, such as satellites, can be impacted by external conditions. These would include elements such as the weather, solar flares, or other conditions beyond your control. If a constant connection is critical to your organization, you should consider this before investing in the equipment needed.

BUZZ WORDS

Local loop carrier: A communications service provider. It provides the electronic link between geographically separated devices.

Figure 34.4 Your local communications services provider connects you to your ISP.

THE ISP POINT OF PRESENCE (POP)

People can't just hook themselves up to the Internet arbitrarily. They need some sort of service that provides an access point to the Internet. This provides the control necessary to prevent the presence of identical IP addresses on the Net, as well as providing a certain degree (although it's a very limited one) of security. Your Internet Service Provider (ISP) provides this function. Larger ISPs will have more than one POP. For every metropolitan area they serve, in order to provide local dial-up services, they will provide a separate POP. This POP controls your connection type and speed as well as providing user logon and authentication services.

> **EXAM NOTE:** The role of the ISP is particularly important. Some things to know about your ISP include the services they provide, such as the HyperText Transfer Protocol (HTTP), the Simple Mail Transfer Protocol (SMTP), and the Post Office Protocol (POP), as well as the fact that they host DNS servers.

The ISP also provides certain supplementary services, such as POP and SMTP services. These are the protocols for sending and receiving email. They act as your DNS server, greatly expediting your search for locations on the Internet. They also control the presence of IP addresses on the Web.

The ISP does this because when it first established its services, it obtained a block of IP addresses from an administrative organization assigned to administer IP addresses. In the old days, this was InterNIC, or the Internet's Network Information Center. It used to be the sole administrator of IP addresses and domain names. These days, it only does domain names. IP addresses are allocated by The Internet Corporation for Assigned Names and Numbers (ICANN). Any given ISP has a certain number of addresses it can hand out and no more. In order for the ISP to efficiently manage its pool of addresses, they are usually handed out by the DHCP protocol. However, dedicated links require static IP addresses. Therefore, you must use the IP address assigned to you by your ISP.

EXAM NOTE: Know who it is that assigns IP addresses and who it is that assigns domain names.

THE USER SERVICES

User services can be administered either on a local level or through your ISP. They might also be provided by a third party. Most end users depend on their ISPs for the majority of their services, but not always. These services include the following:

- Domain name services
- Email hosting services
- Web hosting
- FTP services
- Newsgroup services
- Bulletin board services

Many of these services can be quite resource intensive and require dedicated servers in order to be implemented. Therefore, many companies and organizations depend on an ISP for these services. However, in a larger organization, Internet traffic can be minimized if the services are administered locally.

THE ISP BACKBONE

ISPs are not islands alone. Many of the larger companies, such as AT&T, Sprint, PSINet, and others, maintain their own infrastructure and lease it out to smaller ISPs. The signals are routed over high-speed broadband fiber circuits maintained by the major telecommunications corporations. These would include AT&T, Sprint, MCI, and others. The different providers link their services together over banks of routers and switches.

Most major metropolitan areas have one or more Network Access Points (NAP). These provide the entry point to a large capacity circuit. This is one of those fiber circuits mentioned previously. ISPs lease fiber optics connections to link each of their POPs together. However, if that is as far as anyone went, the customers of one company would have communications with all other customers of that company if they so desired, but not with other ISPs of the world. Therefore, the various ISPs set up gateways between their networks through these NAPs.

From there, data moves over large capacity circuits to its destination NAP. Large capacity circuits range everywhere from T1 lines operating at 1.544Mb/s over the smaller connections to an OC-48 line capable of moving 2.488 gigabits of data every second. Each of the major communications carriers maintains its own backbone infrastructure. Through various international arrangements, these corporations have agreed to communicate with one another, allowing the unobstructed passage of the data moving over the lines.

> **BUZZ WORDS**
>
> **Online content:** The overall availability of resources across an intranet or the Internet.
>
> **Origin of content:** A specific resource available to users of an intranet or the Internet.

ONLINE CONTENT

The material you're searching for generally resides on a Web server. Web servers are particularly potent computers running an NOS specifically designed for maintaining multiple incoming virtual connections. These operating systems include Apache, UNIX, Microsoft's Datacenter, and several others.

Web servers are likely to host hundreds or even thousands of sites on a single machine—or to be more accurate, a single cluster of machines. It is unlikely that any business seriously involved in Web hosting would entrust its future to a single box. Web sites are identified by their domain name. Any site created and published out to the Internet must be properly registered with one of the various agencies. When your computer wants to finds a specific Web site, it will make use of DNS to find it. When a specific site has been found, you will have access to any data for which you have the appropriate permissions.

ORIGIN OF CONTENT

This is the part of the chain that is providing much of the legal battleground for the Internet. The material that is actually made available for consumption constitutes *origin of content* (**Figure 34.5**). This consists of pretty much every form of medium that can be stored digitally. Hundreds of thousands of books, movies, images, musical recordings, and so on have been converted to digital format and made available to the public.

A huge stir of controversy has erupted over several issues relating to this. For one thing, how should children be protected from viewing unsuitable material? Or for that matter, is some information suitable for public distribution at all? Do we really want detailed instructions on how to make your own nuclear warhead generally available to the public? Fortunately, this book does not have to confront these issues head on.

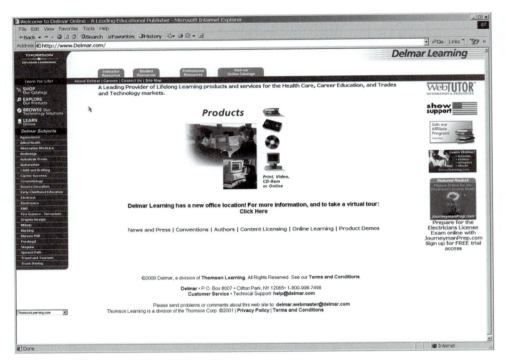

Figure 34.5 A single Web page created by an individual or organization makes up the origin of content, which is the final data you receive.

Know your copyright laws well. The laws that protect written materials are just as valid over the Internet as they are in the public library. Just because you have the technology and the resources to copy and publish another person's creations doesn't mean you have the right.

ADMINISTERING THE INTERNET

As of 2002, a crude estimate of the Internet population was approximately a half billion people per day (**Figure 34.6**). At that time, there were a little more than 170 million Web sites competing for their attention. In order to prevent this from being total chaos, someone needs to be responsible for keeping track of things like IP addresses, domain names, security, and enforcement.

This is far too much for a single agency to keep track of. Therefore, several agencies are assigned different tasks. Domain naming and the distribution of IP addresses on a global level fall under the jurisdiction of the Internet Assigned Numbers Authority (IANA). To make things run a little more smoothly, this organization has delegated much of its responsibility to regional groups. IP addresses are managed regionally by the American Registry for Internet Numbers (ARIN), the Asia-Pacific Network Information Center (APNIC), and Réseaux IP Européens

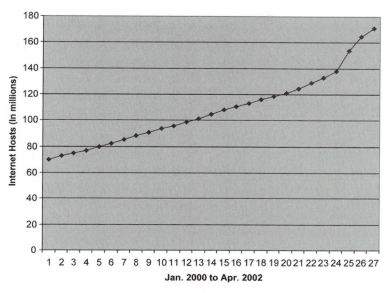

Figure 34.6   Internet growth from Jan. 2000 to Apr. 2002

(RIPE-NCC). Agencies that handle domain naming include InterNIC, RIPE-NCC, and Asia-Pacific NIC.

Even so, should you require an IP address, you would not approach any of these organizations directly. The proper procedure is to approach your ISP and make your request. It will contact an intermediate agency, known as an upstream register, in order to fill your request.

Operational control of the Internet falls under the watchful eye of the Internet Engineering Planning Group (IEPG). The American organization charged with this responsibility is the North American Network Operators Group (NANOG). It is an evolutionary offshoot of the National Science Foundation Network (NSFNET). This organization oversees the development of new Internet segments, maintains acceptable use policies, and, until it was retired in 1996, maintained the NSFNET backbone. The European entity that manages this is called EOF, and in the Asian-Pacific region, it is AP-NG.

The rash of critical viruses that erupted in 2001 brought to the spotlight another group that has been around for years. This is the Forum of Incident Response and Security Teams (FIRST). FIRST oversees a group of Computer Emergency Response Teams (CERT) in eight countries and a large number of ISPs that monitors the Internet and respond to these types of incidents. In an outbreak such as the Nimbda virus, these organizations respond quickly in an attempt to isolate the virus and stop its propagation. And then they work on finding its origin.

In addition to these organizations, there are literally hundreds of others focused on more granular issues. There are groups that oversee the development of protocols, and other groups that come up with the names for those protocols. There are legal organizations calling the shots and lobbying for or against various and sundry laws governing the Internet. There are organizations overseeing the dispersal and movement of email, newsgroups, and World Wide Web pages. It goes on and on. One organization that does a wonderful job of overseeing a large number of these groups is the Internet Society (ISOC). To get a good overview of its responsibilities and ongoing projects, visit its Web site at www.isoc.org.

CHAPTER SUMMARY

By now, I'm sure you realize that the Internet is an extremely complex entity. In some respects, it has taken on a life of its own, perpetually growing and occupying more virtual space. In this chapter, I examined a bit of the infrastructure of the Internet. Key features covered in this chapter are some of the administrative procedures involved in acquiring and maintaining an Internet presence, as well as how the millions of interconnected devices around the world make the concept of the Internet a reality.

NOTE: Since this chapter covers a topic not heavily addressed by the exam, I am intentionally including fewer practice questions.

BRAIN DRAIN

1. List the intermediate levels across which information traveling between two machines communicating over the Internet must travel.

2. Describe in as much detail as you can the structure of an ISP backbone.

3. Discuss the differences between origin of content and online content.

4. List as many organizations as you can that are involved in administering, policing, and protecting the Internet.

THE 64K$ QUESTIONS

1. Who invented the Internet?
   a. Al Gore
   b. JCR Licklider
   c. ISOC
   d. Nobody. It just grew.

2. Which of the following was the first network to span a nation?
   a. CSNET
   b. ARPANET
   c. NFSNET
   d. BITNET

3. The intermediate level that moves user data from the modem to the ISP is called _____.
   a. The user's datacom
   b. The ISP's POP
   c. User services
   d. The local loop carrier

4. The distribution of IP addresses is handled by _____.
   a. InterNIC
   b. ISOC
   c. ICAN
   d. IANA

5. The page you view when browsing the Internet is an example of _____.

    a. Online content

    b. Origin of content

    c. User services

    d. Host services

TRICKY TERMINOLOGY

Datacom: A term coined to describe any equipment used in data communications.

Local loop carrier: A communications service provider. It provides the electronic link between geographically separated devices.

Online content: The overall availability of resources across an intranet or the Internet.

ACRONYM ALERT

FIRST: Forum of Incident Response and Security Teams. An organization charged with maintaining the security of the Internet.

IANA: The Internet Assigned Numbers Authority. The organization that currently hands out IP address to those that need them.

ICANN: The Internet Corporation for Assigned Names and Numbers. One of several organizations involved in the administration of the Internet.

IEPG: The Internet Engineering and Planning Group. An organization involved in overseeing the operational control of the Internet.

InterNIC: Internet's Network Information Center. One of several organizations involved in the administration of the Internet.

ISOC: The Internet Society. The organization that oversees all the other organizations involved in managing the Internet.

ISP: Internet Service Provider. The end user's gateway to the Internet.

NAP: Network Access Point. The entry point to one of the several large capacity circuits that transport data across the Internet.

POP: Point of Presence. The physical connection supplied by an ISP that provides access to the Internet.

CHAPTER 35

BASIC TROUBLESHOOTING PROCEDURES

Now that you know everything there is to know about how computer hardware and operating systems work (or at least have glimpsed beneath the tip of the iceberg), fixing one of these babies should be a piece of cake, right? Oh, if it were only that simple. Throughout this book, I have discussed troubleshooting tips unique to specific pieces of hardware. In this chapter, I'm going to look at troubleshooting techniques, tools, and procedures in general.

One thing I would like to point out is that troubleshooting is as much art as it is science. Some people have a talent for it and others don't. Still, even those with only a rudimentary talent for troubleshooting can succeed if they learn to use a well-thought-out procedure. But I'll warn you right now: while a mathematical model for troubleshooting allows you to solve many problems, a little creative thinking is what separates the wanna-bes from the pros.

A+ CORE HARDWARE EXAM OBJECTIVES

As far as the A+ Core exam is concerned, this chapter really covers just two objectives:

2.1 Recognize common problems associated with each module and their symptoms, and identify steps to isolate and troubleshoot the problems. Given a problem situation, interpret the symptoms and infer the most likely cause.

2.2 Identify basic troubleshooting procedures and tools, and how to elicit problem symptoms from customers. Justify asking particular questions in a given scenario.

THE CompTIA TROUBLESHOOTING METHOD

Scour the books on computer hardware and networking and you'll find as many variations on this theme as there are books. Since some of the people who wrote these books are like me and actually worked on computers before they sat down to write a book, they provide some pretty good approaches. They all boil down to basically the same approach, once you strip away the veneer. Here are the steps, in order:

- Identify the problem
- Re-create the problem
- Isolate the cause of the problem
- Decide on a possible solution
- Test your idea
- Fix the computer
- Follow up

EXAM NOTE: The following pages outline the CompTIA approach to troubleshooting. The exam is rather insistent that you be able to describe the procedure in detail.

IDENTIFY THE PROBLEM

The customers walk in, slam their systems down on the counter, and say in a disgusted voice, "This thing doesn't work!" They seem to think they have just given you all the information you'll ever need to fix the problem. Some people think that hardware technicians have this magic wand hidden in back, and as soon as the door closes behind them, we pull it out, wave it a few times, and the computer is miraculously fixed. I hate to disillusion you, but the magic wand only has so many uses in it, so I only bring it out in dire emergencies.

A few leading questions will usually help you target the real problem. Several of the books I read when I was in training all suggested that first question you should ask a client is, "What changed since the last time it worked?" It took a couple of years for me to figure out that this was a useless question. The answer was always, "Nothing." This evidences the difference between an open-ended question and a closed-ended question. A *closed-ended question*, such as the one above, elicits a response that ends the conversation right there.

You need to be more specific. If the computer still works, but is exhibiting problems, a good question might be, "What were you doing at the moment the problem first appeared?" This represents an *open-ended question*. The answer provided by the user has a strong potential of leading to other questions. And it may even lead to a solution.

If a specific device, such as a sound card or a modem, is exhibiting peculiarities, you might ask if any new software has been installed, or if another device was installed on the system. Once in a while, you get lucky and the customer is able to be specific about the problem. That's always a nice head start.

> **BUZZ WORDS**
>
> **Open-ended question:** A question that will provide further insight into the discussion as a result of the answer provided.
>
> **Closed-ended question:** A question that leads to an answer that provides no further insight or leads to an abrupt dead end to the discussion.

RE-CREATE THE PROBLEM

The next thing you want to do is make the problem happen for you. If you are able to replicate the error or device failure, there might be an error message associated with the problem that you can use to point you in the right direction. Many messages will provide the memory address at which the error occurred and if you can find out what was running at that address, it might give you some ideas. For example, device drivers frequently load to the same memory address each time. Therefore, if the error repeats itself over and over and the address is always the same, it might be a device driver that is generating the error. It could also mean that the RAM stick is bad as well.

In any case, in order to successfully analyze a problem, you need to be able to re-create it. If the problem won't raise its ugly head for you, then the problem might not be with the computer. User errors are not so easily fixed by technicians. However a good technician can gently point out the errors and show the user how to correct them.

ISOLATE THE CAUSE OF THE PROBLEM

There is where the troubleshooting session frequently turns into a turkey-shooting session. If the address of the error points to a specific device, you have a head start. If not, you might find yourself resorting to one of the several hardware and software diagnostic tools that I'll discuss later in the chapter. The last thing you want to do is to arbitrarily start replacing parts, hoping you'll eventually get lucky. For one thing, that's not a very cost-effective approach, and for another, you run the risk of damaging good parts.

But what if all your diagnostic tools unearth nothing? You've successfully re-created the problem on the computer and now you and your colleagues are standing around scratching your heads and saying, "Never seen anything like that before!" And in this industry, the longer you work at your job, the more likely it is that will happen to you.

That's when it's time to find somebody who has seen the problem before. A good start is online technical support if you are working on a name-brand computer. Most manufacturers maintain an extensive knowledge base. If it's a known problem, they'll be familiar with it.

Even if the computer is a white-box clone made by the Mom and Pop operation that went out of business last year, all hope is not lost. Mom and Pop had to have bought the parts they used somewhere, and those parts came from a manufacturer. Once you've isolated the component that is giving you a hard time, see if you can find anything on the Internet that relates to the problem you're having. Later in this chapter, I will be going through each component, one at a time, and providing some of the more commonly seen issues and possible solutions.

DECIDE ON A POSSIBLE SOLUTION

Now that you think you know what's causing the problem, you probably already have a possible solution in mind. This is your *hypothesis*. Think about that solution carefully before you implement it. For

BUZZ WORDS

Hypothesis: Any theory that can be tested to be proven either true or false.

example, if your solution involves formatting the customer's hard drive, you might want to make sure there are backups of any critical data. If backups don't exist, you might want to think about possible ways of getting that data off before you destroy it permanently.

Also keep in mind that some symptoms are generated by multiple components. Memory errors can be caused by the memory itself, a faulty chipset, or even a bad power supply. Therefore, you need to be thorough in your analysis before you jump into the next step.

TEST YOUR IDEA

You think it's a bad CPU, but you're not 100 percent certain. If you have another computer lying around that uses a CPU your sick computer will support, you might try installing a known good CPU in the system. One of the things I do is to keep a collection of "known-goods." These are parts that I can use to test a sick computer. I have several CPUs, at least one example of each of the most commonly used memory sticks, and a couple of motherboards. I keep both an AT and an ATX power supply just for testing purposes.

One thing you probably want to avoid doing is simply ordering in new parts randomly. Distributors are justifiably reluctant to take back opened computer components. They have no way of knowing what precautions you may or may not have taken to protect those components from ESD while they were in your possession. By testing your idea first, you eliminate a lot of unnecessary hassles.

FIX THE COMPUTER

Once you're comfortable that your hypothesis is correct and that it fixes the problem, go ahead and implement your solution. Install new parts that the customer can keep and then test the solution. Run the customer's applications for a while. Do your best to replicate the original problem, but keep watching for new problems while you're doing that. It is not at all uncommon for a new problem to appear once the original problem has been fixed. Whatever you do, don't just fire the machine up and say, "This, my friend, is why they pay me the big bucks!" and hand it off to the user. That's a good way of having it come flying back in your face.

FOLLOW UP

You also need to provide customers with proof that you've fixed their problem. And by this, I don't simply mean an invoice that lists what you did and how much it's going to cost them. When they pick up their system, show them it's fixed. Let them poke around on it and try to re-create the original problem themselves. Once they're satisfied the problem has gone away, then you can give them the invoice and watch their eyes glaze over.

Doing this accomplishes two things. First off, you demonstrate to the customer that your solution has worked. That greatly eases the pain of seeing the bill. Second, in the event that the problem recurs, you will be able to point out the fact that it was working when it left. While this admittedly does provide for a very good method of covering your own bases (in the industry, that's called the CYA solution; don't ask why), it also might be providing some insight into what might be going on over on the customer's side. Is there an environmental issue causing the problem? I once had a computer system that kept coming back with bad power supplies. I finally got on my horse and rode over to the customer's site. I tested the outlet and found that it required immediate attention. You're not supposed to get 140V out of those things!

Just because the computer is now working perfectly doesn't mean your job is done. One of the things they teach you in the military is that no job is complete until the paperwork is done. That holds true of computer repair as well. You need to document exactly what you did. There are some pretty nifty help-desk software solutions that allow you to create a searchable database of problems and their solutions. The larger that database becomes, the more frequently you can simply turn to it for solutions.

TROUBLESHOOTING TOOLS

An auto mechanic wouldn't even consider trying to drop a transmission if he or she didn't have the right set of tools. As unbelievable as it may sound, there are problems that can't be fixed with a 16-ounce ball peen hammer. While a vast number of computer problems can be fixed with a keen wit and a Phillips screwdriver, sometimes you need a little extra help. The computer industry is blessed with a large number of troubleshooting aids that come in very handy. Some are pieces of hardware that perform certain functions, while others are software-based solutions. Somebody who wants to fix computers for a living should assemble a collection of necessities.

HARDWARE-BASED TROUBLESHOOTING TOOLS

There are certain tools you can't live without. Every technician needs a good set of screwdrivers, a pair of needle-nosed pliers, a 16-ounce ball peen hammer, and some duct tape. You may think I'm kidding about the hammer, but I'm not. Maybe I'm exaggerating about needing 16 ounces, but you'll find out what I'm talking about the next time you try to install a double-height drive into a pair of 5.25″ bays. That little shelf they put in to keep the drives properly seated really gets in the way. The duct tape is useful for taking specific items such as drive rails or drive bay covers and securing them to the inside of the case where they will be easy to find the next time you need them.

But then, these aren't really troubleshooting tools are they? Troubleshooting tools are the ones that help you solve problems. And there are some good ones on the market.

THE POST CARD

Unfortunately, this is not the one you send to your mother-in-law when you go on vacation. These are a bit expensive for that. The *POST card* I'm talking about is used to diagnose problems that occur during the boot process that prevent the computer from starting properly. It mounts into an empty expansion slot and while the computer is booting

BUZZ WORDS

POST card: A device that follows each step of the POST procedure and reports the results. Should the POST fail, the last successful process will be indicated in an encoded display.

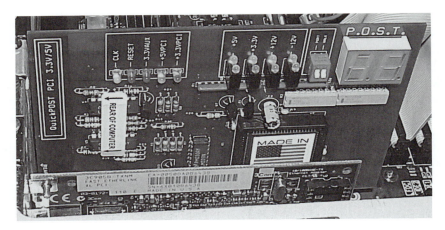

Figure 35.1 This POST card, by Ultra-X, is one of the most formidable tools you can have in your arsenal. It identifies problems that occur during the POST process.

(or trying to, anyway), it's zipping off light patterns on an LED readout so fast that you can't possibly read them. Don't worry about that. The ones you can't read are the ones you don't care about. They represent components that passed.

At the point that the boot process fails, the readout will display a pattern of lights that represents a specific component. The POST card ships with a booklet that itemizes all of those error messages. All you have to do is look up the number displayed, and it tells you what part of the POST process failed. JDR Microdevices in San Jose, California, offers four different options. It has standard POST cards in both PCI and ISA form. But it also has ISA and PCI versions that test the BIOS as well as the POST process.

A more advanced version of this card is available from Ultra-X, Inc. in Santa Clara, California. It can go beyond the POST test (which it does rather extensively) and continue to test RAM, drive operation including CD-ROM drives, and much more. The Professional Kit includes an impressive array of diagnostics software utilities, a collection of loopback plugs, and the PCI card. This is the card illustrated in **Figure 35.1**. A rather interesting option, offered by PCWiz out of Clearwater, Florida, offers a single card that has an ISA connector on one edge and a PCI connector on other.

THE MULTIMETER

Sometimes simply testing for power or continuity can tell you a lot about what's going on. A simple and inexpensive tool for that is a multimeter. I recommend that you spend a few extra bucks on this and get a digital version. They're easier to work with.

The multimeter will tell you if you have proper power coming out of the connectors coming from your power supply. You can use them to test a wire for continuity. They're also useful for testing those ceramic fuses that don't let you see the wire.

LOOPBACK ADAPTER

Testing a port can sometimes be a matter of having that port talk to itself. By doing this, you are verifying the functionality of the port itself and taking external variables, such as device drivers or cables, out of the equation. In order to do that, you'll need a specialized plug called a *loopback adapter* that wraps the signal back to the computer rather than sending it out to a device. This takes the device out of the loop and tells you whether or not it is the port that is bad rather than a device or cable. Loopback adapters are available for either serial ports or parallel ports (**Figure 35.2**).

There are also software variations on the loopback test. Most modems ship with a disk that has their diagnostics software. This will usually include some form of loopback test. In Microsoft products, a loopback adapter is available as an option when installing network cards.

LOGIC PROBES

The problem with a data signal is that it only lasts for a few nanoseconds. Most of us have a bit of difficulty in seeing an event that only lasts that long. Therefore, in order to detect the presence of one of these signals, you need a logic probe. A logic probe locks onto a signal and the display holds what it finds. These are good for testing a totally dead system to see if anything at all is happening on the board.

MEMORY TESTERS

In Chapter Nine, Searching Your Memory, I pointed out that sometimes it is very difficult to identify memory simply by looking at it. It is also very difficult to test memory. Even computer systems that have built-in diagnostics programs tell you that there is a problem, but they don't tell you where the problem resides. It's all fine and good if you only have one stick of memory installed. But a lot of trial and error is going to be involved any time you have more than one module installed.

Specialized devices designed just to test memory are a valuable addition to your collection of troubleshooting tools, if you can afford one. The problem is that they tend to be pretty

BUZZ WORDS

Loopback adapter: A piece of hardware that routes an output signal directly back to the computer, giving the impression that a device is present.

Figure 35.2 Loopback adapters help you diagnose problems with the serial and parallel ports on a machine.

expensive. And RAM is getting to be where it isn't. However, if you can justify the expense, a memory tester is able to identify memory by type, speed, and density. However, they can also do more specialized tricks. Some of the better ones can detect and locate broken solder joints, bad cells on DRAM chips, and more. Cool toys, if you can afford one.

THE ADVANCED CABLE TESTER

This is actually more of a networking tool than it is a hardware technician's tool. It can, however, come in handy. An advanced cable tester can test for continuity, do a signal test on each conductor along the cable, and even detect a break in the cable. Some of them not only detect the break, but also tell you how far down the cable from the tester that the break occurs. This greatly enhances your ability to fix the problem.

The cable tester may or may not come with a remote unit. If it doesn't, there will be two sockets for plugging the cable into. These can be of limited use when testing an installed cable. One with a remote unit provides a second smaller unit that can be plugged onto the cable at the user's end. Then, from the hub or patch panel, you can perform your tests.

SOFTWARE TROUBLESHOOTING ESSENTIALS

There are also some excellent software applications on the market that assist in the task of troubleshooting. These range from individual task-specific utilities to entire suites of programs that perform a myriad of tricks for the hardware technician. While I would like to emphasize that, throughout this book, it has never been my intention to promote or disparage any particular product, this happens to be one of those areas in which there really is no choice but to shine the spotlight on specific products. However, I should point out that the inclusion of a particular product in this chapter does not represent an endorsement. Conversely my failure to mention a competing product most likely means simply that I am not familiar with the product. I'm not a testing lab.

THE HARDWARE MANUFACTURERS' UTILITIES

One of the first places you might turn for help should be the company that made the computer. And that doesn't always mean calling its tech support line and seeing who can keep you on hold the longest. Many of the tier one manufacturers ship their systems with a CD that contains a plethora of diagnostics utilities specific to that machine. Among these are Compaq, Dell, Hewlett Packard, and IBM.

Many of IBM and Compaq's machines ship with a diagnostics program that can be initialized during the boot sequence that will perform an exhaustive test on every component in the system if you ask it to. It can also do simpler tasks, such as run a diagnostics on the hard drive. On the server end, some of these diagnostics are so sophisticated they not only detect faulty memory, they tell you specifically the slot in which the memory is installed.

Even if a specific machine doesn't ship with a diagnostics utility on board, it is likely that there is one available. Check the manufacturer's support site. I have found that a number of different manufacturers offer model-specific troubleshooting utilities. Some of these are specific to certain machines while others are more generic. Dell even provides an excellent "Ask Dudley" troubleshooting guide that leads you through most of the common problems. You will find that most of the manufacturers offer something similar to that. These manufacturers don't just offer these services out of the goodness of their hearts. They have millions of machines out there in the world, and eventually all of them need support. If everybody had to depend on telephone support, there wouldn't be enough people in the world to staff the support lines.

TASK-SPECIFIC UTILITIES

Earlier in the chapter, I mentioned that some symptoms might be induced by more than one component. One of the options I offered at the time was basically a trial-and-error method of replacing suspected parts with known good parts. While, personally, I don't think there's any substitute for testing with the real thing, I have been known to be guilty of taking shortcuts. Certain utilities exist that perform tests on just one component. The reason I don't put all my faith in them is because they are not a 100 percent accurate. However, I find them very useful in telling me which component to swap out first. Some of these are shareware, and you have the opportunity to try them for a while before you shell out your bucks. The following is a short list of some of the ones I've tested and think you might find useful. There are about a gazillion others.

- *Burnin Test*: Shareware, requires registration for continued use. If you build your own systems, a program of this nature is a necessity. Once a system is built, this program will perform stress tests on each component for a preset period of time.
- *CPUCheck*: Shareware, requires registration for continued use. Identifies the CPU and detects internal and external bus speeds.
- *CTBios*: Freeware. Identifies the manufacturer of your motherboard.
- *CTPCI*: Freeware. Identifies and reports all PCI devices installed in your system.
- *DocMemory*: Freeware. Detects bad memory and tells you which stick is defective.
- *FindIRQ*: Freeware provided by *PC Magazine*. No charge to download. Tests to see which IRQs are in use and returns a report on available IRQs.
- *Look RS232 Pro*: Shareware, requires registration for continued use. Tests each line on the serial cable to make sure it's doing what it's supposed to be doing.
- *Modem Doctor*: Shareware, requires registration for continued use. Does loopback testing, detects and reports conflicts, and helps you fine-tune your initialization string. Excellent tool to have.
- *RST*: Commercial program from Ultra-X. Short for the RAM Stress Test, this program works from a bootable floppy diskette and is completely independent of the operating system. It can detect the precise DRAM chip on which a failure occurred, allowing the tech to isolate the problem on a very granular level.
- *WhatChanged*: Commercial Program, costs $29.95. Finds changes in the Windows Registry. When the customer tells you nothing changed, you can clear your throat meaningfully and say, "Uh-huh."

UTILITY SUITES

Here's where I take a risk of offending some company or the other by leaving it out, but as before, my list is not all-inclusive. It only lists those with which I'm familiar enough to be able to accurately describe them.

Many companies have put together complete suites of utilities that can diagnose pretty much every component in your system. Some of the more basic ones do fairly simple tests and only report which component is faulty. They don't go so far as to identify a specific problem. Still, this is better than nothing. Others perform exhaustive diagnostics and probably tell you far more than you need to know.

- *BCM Diagnostics*: Shareware. Similar to Norton Utilities, except that it is hardware-specific. Runs diagnostics on processor, RAM, graphics adapter, modem, sound card, and attached drives. Doesn't do much for motherboard issues, however.

- *Checkit Professional by Smith-Micro*: Commercial program. Does extensive tests on all hardware components and identifies specific problems. Includes a DOS-based boot diskette that provides for troubleshooting when Windows won't boot. Extremely detailed and extremely powerful.

- *Dr. Hardware*: Commercial program. Doesn't actually perform diagnostics, but is an inexpensive way to do a total inventory of a system and generate a list of all hardware installed on a system.

- *Norton Utilities*: Commercial program. Provides simpler diagnostics as well as options for fine-tuning a system. Tends to be more OS-oriented with only a few simpler hardware diagnostics.

- *QuickTech Pro by Ultra-X*: Commercial program. An even more potent analysis program than Checkit Professional, in my opinion. This is the armored tank of all the programs that I've used. This even ships with a FAT editor and an IDE low-level format as part of the package. I'm still trying to find a problem that it can't diagnose. Tests can be run in either quick mode or detailed mode. In detailed mode, you get over sixty-five pages of information about your system.

TROUBLESHOOTING ROADMAPS

Most of the components in a computer system have been around for so long that that are some pretty straightforward approaches to troubleshooting problems with them. In the following sections, I will take a look at some common approaches to finding out what's wrong so you can fix it.

BOOT FAILURE OR POST-BOOT PROBLEMS

When the system won't even boot, your problems are exacerbated by the fact that you can't run most of the diagnostics utilities. That's when you want one of those POST cards I described earlier. Lacking one of those, try the following:

- *Are you plugged in?* Computers don't run without juice. Make sure there are no loose connections.

- *Are you plugged into a surge suppressor?* (I certainly hope so.) Make sure it is plugged in and turned on. And while this may sound like a no-brainer, check to make sure it isn't plugged into itself. Twice (not just once, but twice), I've gone on site to a "dead" computer and found the power strip looped back to itself.

- *Are you getting power from the power supply?* Use your multimeter to check voltage on one of the free Molex connectors. If there is no current, you most likely have a bad power supply.

- *Do you get any display at all?* Obviously POST messages won't show if you don't and you'll be counting on beep codes.

- *Does it beep?* Even a successful POST will send out a single beep through the PC speaker, indicating that the speaker works. No video combined with no beeps is a good sign that the problem exists on the motherboard. If you're getting more than one beep, check Appendix F: BIOS Beep Codes and Error Messages.

You've tried all of the above and still have no idea what's going on. Now it's time to strip the system down to just the motherboard and processor connected to the power supply and front panel connectors. In this state, there should be resounding beep codes generated. If not, either the motherboard and/or processor is bad. (Sorry I can't be more specific as to which it is.) If you do get a beep, add each component one at a time. Start with memory. If there is more than one RAM stick installed, add them each, one at a time. If, when RAM is added, the machine goes back to being a doorstop, you've found the problem. Next add expansion cards, one at a time. And finally hook up the drives, one at a time.

Sometimes the problem appears after a successful POST. The computer thinks it's working; you simply disagree. The following list itemizes some of the more common post-boot malfunctions that can occur.

- *Disk boot failure*: You may get a message telling you to "Insert system disk and press any key to continue." This means that Int19h failed to find a useable MBR and could not boot the system. This could mean a hard drive failure or a corrupted OS. In either case, use a boot diskette to boot the system and see if you can access the hard drive from there.

- *Diskette drive failure*: During POST, the CMOS reported a floppy diskette drive as being present, but one is not being detected. Check cables first. If the cable is properly seated and intact, replace the drive.

- *Diskette drive mismatch*: Your CMOS is reporting one type of drive, but POST is finding another. Check the CMOS settings. This is especially true if you recently replaced the system board battery.

- *FDD controller error*: This isn't necessarily a hardware problem. If you're booting to a defective diskette you will also get this message.

- *Fixed disk controller failure*: This error is generated when POST sends a query to the hard drive controller and the drive either fails to respond or responds improperly. If it is a

SCSI drive, the problem could exist on either the controller or the drive. If it is an IDE drive, the controller is on the drive.

■ *Fixed disk failure*: One of the drives on the system is not working properly. This message will also be generated from a corrupted MBR, so an FDISK and format frequently fixes this problem. There is, of course, the issue of what to do about all that data before you perform these steps.

■ *Fixed disk read faiurel*: Found the hard drive, all right. But now it can't read the MBR. See above.

■ *Floppy disk controller faiurel*: See Diskette controller failure.

■ *Floppy disk failure*: See Diskette drive failure.

■ *Gate A20 failure*: While Gate A20 is actually the twenty-first line off the address bus, and therefore the gateway to high memory, this error is most often reported because of a bad keyboard.

■ *Hard drive (or HDD) controller failure*: See Fixed disk controller failure.

■ *Invalid configuration information, please run setup*: That's pretty self-explanatory. During POST, the BIOS detected something that did not agree with the configuration settings in CMOS. For example, if you just installed new memory, it is common for this message to be displayed on the first boot following the install. On some models, new IDE devices have the same effect.

■ *Invalid media type*: This is usually the message displayed directly after an FDISK, but prior to a format. It finds the hard drive, but finds no MBR whatsoever.

■ *Invalid partition table*: You don't want to see this message. It means the information stored in the partition tables of the MBR does not correspond with the geometry of the hard drive. So now it can't read the hard drive. One time you might see this message without it meaning disaster is if you recently ran a third-party disk portioning utility and inadvertently set more than one partition as being active. A utility called Partition Doctor may get you out of this mess.

■ *Keyboard not found, press any key to continue*: And who thought up that message, I wonder. If it didn't find a keyboard, what the heck good is it going to do to press a key? I say that in jest, but in many computers, it's the case. However, on some systems, you can reseat the keyboard connector, press a key, and the boot process will continue.

■ *Keyboard locked – unlock*: This is another one of those nicely worded errors that doesn't mean what it says. It's really referring to a key lock on the system case that needs to be unlocked before you're allowed to use the system.

■ *Memory failure at xxxx xxxxx*: During POST, when the system memory test was run, the R/W operation wrote one set of data to RAM but got back something different when trying to read it back.

■ *Memory test fail*: See Memory failure at xxxx xxxxx.

■ *Missing operating system*: The system booted just fine, but never found an operating system. If you know the OS is installed, and it is the MBR that is corrupted, you might be able to get away with running a SYS command on the drive. Or it might mean that key files in the OS are corrupted. You will need to reinstall the OS in that case.

■ *No boot device found, press F1 to retry*: Int19h failed to find a device with a suitable MBR. Check your CMOS settings to see if the boot order has been changed. Otherwise check to see if your drive has failed.

There are many, many others from the different BIOS manufacturers. These are the key ones that you're likely to see on most systems. There might be slight wording variations, but they'll amount to the same thing.

TROUBLESHOOTING RAM

I covered memory troubleshooting in detail in Chapter Nine, Searching Your Memory. But a few brief pointers might be in order. Check the following list to see if your problem appears here.

■ *My computer is not reporting the correct amount of memory*: What OS are you running? DOS can't see past 64MB by itself. You can have 2GB of RAM installed and DOS will only report 64MB. On an older system, make sure the larger RAM sticks are in the lower banks. Some early BIOS routines would not recognize larger memory that was detected after a smaller stick was initialized. Do you have onboard video? If so, your system is most likely grabbing some of your system RAM to use as video memory.

■ *I just installed new memory and now my system doesn't work!*: Don't panic. This is a common problem. Most likely, you simply installed the wrong type of memory. EDO and SDRAM don't get along, nothing but FPM gets along with FPM, and so forth and so forth. Chapter Eight goes into this in great detail. If there is not a memory type mismatch, perhaps the new stick is simply defective. On newer systems, this will usually result in a successful boot, and the new memory will simply be ignored. On some systems, however, especially earlier ones, defective RAM will cause the whole system to go down in flames (figuratively speaking) when you try to boot it.

■ *I'm getting a memory mismatch error on boot*: If you just installed memory, it is common to have to run the setup utility in order to introduce the new RAM to the CMOS. Let it do its thing. If the message repeats itself over and over again, even after you've run the setup utility, there's a pretty good chance one of the RAM sticks is defective. Use one of the diagnostic utilities I discussed earlier.

■ *My system boots fine, but I get intermittent memory errors while I'm working*: Have fun. This could be defective memory, a corrupted system file, a corrupted device driver, or even a flaky power supply. Start with simplest to fix first. Run one of the diagnostics utilities I keep harping on and see if you have bad RAM. If not, start documenting the memory addresses reported by the error messages and use the memory map supplied by your OS to find out what's running at that address. If it's a device driver, try reinstalling the driver. If that doesn't work, if possible, pull the device from the system and see if the error persists. If it goes away, you've found the problem. If the RAM checks good, and all devices test out good, start thinking seriously about replacing your power supply.

- *My system says I'm out of memory and I've got lots of memory*: These messages don't always refer to physical memory. In fact, most often they refer to your swap file. Check your virtual memory settings. Maybe they need to be increased. In Windows, it's usually best to just let Windows manage its own. You also might need to run Defrag. Even if there's lots of free memory, the swap file needs a large contiguous space.

- *I added more memory and my system actually slowed down*: This is a chipset-related issue, and I'm willing to bet you've got an Intel 430FX, VX, or TX chipset. The reason for this is that a minor design issue (It's not a flaw. Intel never has flaws.) only allows data from the lower 64MB to be stored to cache. Anything stored in addresses above 64MB must be retrieved in multiple independent I/O operations. As I pointed out in Chapter Nine, this can add large numbers of clock cycles to each I/O operation.

TROUBLESHOOTING HARD DRIVES

Hard drive failures occur in a wide range of situations. Sometimes it's not found, sometimes it's the wrong size, and sometimes it's just too slow! In any case, hard drives have resulted in more gray hairs on my head than just about anything else, except of course, for my children. So let me try to break down some of the simpler problems and see which ones can be fixed.

- *I'm getting a general failure of the hard drive*: Sometimes this is a failure of the drive and other times it's a failure of the MBR. If it's an IDE drive, it's easy to tell. As you're booting the machine, enter the CMOS Setup utility. Most BIOS manufacturers provide a hard disk detection utility of some sort. If the utility can't find the drive, it is not being electrically detected. This could be as simple as a faulty or loose cable. Were you just working inside the machine? If either the ribbon cable or the Molex got knocked loose, you'll get this failure. If your CMOS detects your drive, the problem is most likely the MBR.

- *My CMOS found the drive, but it still won't boot*: Did you just now install the drive? Don't forget that drives don't work all by themselves right out of the box. You need to partition and format the drive before an MBR is generated. It won't work until you do that. If it is a drive that has been in the system for a while, you may have either a corrupted MBR or a file in the OS. Try booting the machine to a bootable floppy and accessing the drive that way. If that works, you may have picked up a boot sector virus or perhaps the drive has simply failed. Get your hands on a good antivirus software, such as Norton Antivirus or McAfee, and see if it finds anything.

- *I ran an antivirus program and it 1) found nothing and the system still won't boot or 2) it found a virus and claimed it fixed it, but the system still won't boot*: Now you're looking seriously at a corrupted MBR. In the old days of DOS, you would simply boot to a DOS boot diskette and run FDISK /MBR, which would regenerate a new MBR. This doesn't work on new systems and newer OSs. A good disk partitioning utility like Partition Magic might be able to bail you out. Most likely, you're going to wind up retrieving what data you can salvage from the drive and starting over from scratch.

- *I just installed a new 40GB drive on my computer and it tells me it's only 8GB*: This is a BIOS and/or chipset issue. If the system won't recognize past 8GB, it's only operating in Int13h mode. It recognizes none of the drive translation mechanisms you've grown to know and love (see Chapter Thirteen, Hard Disk Drive Structure and Geometry). It may be that a BIOS upgrade and a supplemental I/O controller will solve your problem. If you do not have a flashable BIOS, then a new motherboard is probably in order. Just as well. It probably means you're using an outdated CPU and RAM as well.

- *I just installed a new 80GB hard drive and it only formats to 32GB:* See above. It is a more recent BIOS limitation with the same solution.

- *I just installed a new hard drive and my computer doesn't see it at all*: If the drive you just installed was an IDE drive, check your jumpers. If it's the only drive on the cable, it needs to be set to Master. Some drives also have a setting for Single, and in this situation, that would work as well. If it is the second drive on the cable, one of the drives has to be Master and the other one needs to be Slave. Most drives also have a setting called Cable Select. For this setting to properly work, you need a cable-select cable. The position on the cable determines master/slave relationship. If a drive is jumpered to be a master and is placed on the slave position, it won't be seen.

- *My hard drive is making funny noises*: Without going into a lengthy explanation of everything that could be going wrong, it all boils down to the same thing. You're about to need a new drive. Back everything up and see what your local electronics store has on sale. The one exception to this is a light tapping sound that is common to all drives. They will periodically perform a thermal recalibration, especially shortly after bootup. A slight tapping sound is commonly heard while the drive is performing this task.

- *Every time I boot to a floppy, my 20.4GB hard drive is only seen as 504MB and I can't access it*: The most likely cause for this is that, at the time the hard disk was installed and configured, either you or the person that installed it used something called dynamic overlay software. This is a disk that ships from the manufacturer that provides for some proprietary drive translation mechanism that isn't loaded when you boot from a floppy. Nothing is intercepting the hard drive calls for Int13h and you can find out why that is a problem in Chapter Fourteen, Hard Disk Interfacing and Disk Management.

- *My machine keeps running ScanDisk on bootup and finding new bad sectors each time*: Several things can lead to this, and not all of them lead to the conclusion that your drive is failing. An IDE cable longer than 18″ can cause bits of data to be corrupted, which, when accessed, will show up as bad sectors, even though it's the data that's bad and not the drive. Another thing that can lead to this is that some BIOS manufacturers provide for manual control of the drive translation method used by your drive. If this is set too fast, data corruption will occur. See above. Then there is always the possibility that the disk itself is starting to fail. Far too many people assume it is because of surface damage, but this is unlikely. Hard drives are sealed devices, so dust and dirt can't get in. If your drive head impacted with the surface, you wouldn't be getting drive errors. You would have a dead drive. It can be caused by one of the chips on the drive controller getting zapped by ESD. The computer may be located too close to some device or object emitting high amounts of magnetic energy (such as a loudspeaker designed for home stereo systems or a poorly shielded monitor).

■ *My computer says, "Error Reading Sector 0" and freezes up on bootup*: One of two things has most likely happened. A primary cause for this error is that you have picked up a boot sector virus and it has not only wiped out the master boot record, it has rendered it unreadable. Many of these can be detected and cleaned by an antivirus program that can be loaded from a bootable floppy. The other problem is that you truly do have a bad sector on that spot. In either case, before you attempt any repair, try to boot from a floppy and see if you can access the drive. Just because the hard drive won't boot doesn't mean you can't still get the data off the drive. If possible, copy all critical files to another location. Norton Disk Doctor or one of the other utilities might be able to repair the sector (but probably not). If it can't, FDISK the hard drive and reformat. If FDISK returns the same error message, go see what your local electronics store has on sale.

■ *I'm getting a message that says "Not ready reading drive D:" on my second drive*: Most likely, this is a software issue and not a hardware issue. You may have recently installed a new toy on your system that forced a re-enumeration of the drive-lettering scheme. Your second drive changed letters, but your software doesn't know that. So it's trying to access what is now your CD-ROM drive, which has nothing in it. If you check and Drive D: truly is your second hard drive, that indicates a problem with the volume boot record. See "Error Reading Sector 0" in the previous point for possible remedies.

■ *I'm getting a "Runtime Error" reading when I try to perform an FDISK on my drive*: Don't tell me. Let me guess. You have a Western Digital hard drive. This results from the FDISK program being unable to read Track 0. Western Digital has a possible solution to this problem on its Web site at www.westerndigital.com called Data Lifeguard Tools. One of the options is to run a pseudo low-level format. (As we all know, pseudo means fake. You don't perform low-level formats on IDE drives, so even if your CMOS offers that option, don't use it.) Under the *diagnostics* menu, select "Write Zeros." When it's done, restart your machine and attempt FDISK again. When this fails, Western Digital recommends you contact its technical support. But what it really means is, it's time to see what the electronics store has on sale.

TROUBLESHOOTING MOTHERBOARD-RELATED ISSUES

Problems with your motherboard can sometimes be more challenging to diagnose, simply because they can appear to be so random. In fact, it would be a great idea if somebody put together a book just on that subject. In this section, I will touch on some of the basics and try to cover the more commonly seen problems relating to motherboard and component-level products on the motherboard.

■ *My machine fails to boot and returns a bunch of beeps. What do they mean?*: This was covered in Boot Failure or POST problems earlier. See Appendix F: BIOS Beep Codes and Error Messages.

- *I'm trying to boot my machine, but it tells me about an "Invalid Checksum" and hangs*: Your CMOS settings went south for the winter on you. Perhaps the battery went dead or maybe you took a voltage hit and are lucky your system isn't totally fried. Either way, you can usually run the BIOS Setup program from boot and reset the configuration to Factory Defaults. This will get the system up and running and you can tweak the settings either now or later.

- *Okay, wise guy. I went to try that, but my computer won't tell me what buttons to push to get into the CMOS Setup. What now?*: I can only say, "Been there, done that." Sometimes the brand-name computers don't provide an opening screen telling you where to go. If they've got a flash screen advertising a product you've already bought, try hitting the ESC key. That will usually clear the flash screen and you'll see POST messages. This might possibly tell you how to enter setup. If that doesn't work, try the following key sequences:

  - Del If it is an Award or an AMI BIOS this will probably work.
  - F1 Many of the "custom" Phoenix BIOS programs run from this.
  - F2 In recent years, Phoenix moved to this key. F1 was getting too easy to remember. Dell also uses this key sequence.
  - F10 This the key used by most Compaq products.
  - Alt + Esc Some proprietary BIOS chips used this.
  - Ctrl + Alt + Esc See above.
  - Insert Another proprietary alternative used by some manufacturers.
  - Ctrl + Alt + S Yet another proprietary alternative.

- *None of these work*: Yeah, well, that's why manufacturers have technical support. Give them a call, or better yet, check their Web sites. That's usually faster.

- *Oh, no! I made some changes to the settings to my CMOS and now my system won't boot*: Let that be a lesson to you. Don't ever change more than one parameter at a time. Wait till you see what effect that has before you make other changes. In this case, simply reset the system back to factory defaults and start over from scratch.

- *Every time I boot my machine it tells me that it's "Updating the ESCD" even though I didn't add any new devices*: The ESCD is your extended system configuration data, and on Plug 'n Play machines it tells the BIOS how to configure the devices. If you have an OS that is Plug 'n Play, such as Windows 95 or later, it might disagree with your BIOS on how to configure the settings. In most cases, it can do this without any problems and the BIOS accepts and remembers the changes. In some cases, however, the ESCD isn't permanently changed, but the device configuration was. So it resets the device on boot up. Windows sees this and says, "Hey, I'm the boss around here," and once again resets the configuration. And on and on it goes, a never-ending cycle. It isn't hurting anything, so you can simply ignore it. On the other hand, if it is annoying you to no end, you might see if your manufacturer supplies a BIOS upgrade to your computer. On some early Pentium machines (and just about anything made prior to that), that will involve replacing the BIOS chip. If your BIOS is flashable, you can burn the new code to your BIOS chip.

■ *Thanks for the tip buddy! I just flashed my BIOS and now my system is an oversized doorstop!*: One of two things happened here. You either chose, or were supplied, the wrong version of BIOS for your particular motherboard, or you downloaded the software from the Internet and got a corrupt download. If your computer is relatively recent, it will include a feature called boot block. When it encounters corrupted BIOS, it automatically checks the floppy for a new version to flash. Yet one more reason not to retire your floppy diskette drive! Get a correct or clean version, pop it in the floppy drive, and restart. You're back up and running. If your machine does not support boot block, then pray that you have a removable BIOS chip. Better yet, only purchase motherboards that do feature removable BIOS. You can order in a new chip from the manufacturer. (That'll be fifty bucks please. Will this be MasterCard or Visa?) If the BIOS is soldered on, why don't you see what is new in the world of CPUs while you're shopping for your new motherboard? And by the way—it wasn't my fault. I only told you what to do. I didn't download the flash for you!

■ *Somebody entered a password on one of the computers in our office and now nobody can access the system*: It's hard to get good help these days, isn't it? All is not lost. Many motherboards have a jumper for disconnecting the onboard battery from the CMOS chip. After a couple of minutes, put the jumper back on. Your BIOS settings will be back to factory defaults and you're good to go. If you can't find a jumper that does this, or aren't sure which one, just pull the battery out. Don't get any fingerprints on the battery, though. That will substantially shorten the life of the battery.

I've intentionally made this a short list, because a vast majority of chipset-related problems aren't easily detected as being a motherboard issue. It is the device under control of the chipset that exhibits the symptoms and not the motherboard. Some of the more common ones will be listed in the appropriate sections.

Diagnosing Processor-Related Failures

First off, if it is an outright processor-related failure, then the machine is doing nothing. You might hear the power supply spin up, but that's about it. Therefore, if your "blue screen of death" is telling you that the tragedy occurred in processor registers x and y, that really isn't indicating a processor failure. It is simply reporting at what register addresses the error occurred. That tells you the processor is doing its job, right up to the very end, and not that it's failing. However, ESD or a voltage surge could possibly damage a processor to the point that it is flaky but not outright dead. I would have to say, however, that this would be a pretty rare occurrence. Watch for the following, however.

■ *I turn the machine on and nothing happens. No video, no beeps, not a darn thing. Is that my processor?*: Maybe. Probably not. Did you have cause to reinstall the processor for any reason, or is this a system you have just finished building? If so, it's possible the processor is defective, but more likely it is simply seated incorrectly. If you are using a socketed processor, check to see if it is correctly oriented. Always remember some advice I gave you earlier in the book. Read the manual! Check for bent pins. If you find one, you might be lucky enough to be able to straighten it without snapping it off (I hate it when that happens). Many times, however, this same symptom is generated by bad or incorrect memory, a hard drive improperly configured, or one of several other possible causes that are not processor related.

■ *I get five short beeps when the machine starts to boot, and then that's all she wrote*: You have an AMI BIOS and it's telling you the processor failed. Buy a new one.

■ *I'm getting two short beeps followed by two long beeps when the machine starts to boot, and then that's all she wrote*: You have a Phoenix BIOS. See above.

■ *My machine boots fine, but after a few minutes the screen goes blank/blue screens*: See if the processor's cooling fan bit the bullet. If the CPU overheats, this will happen. If this happens too frequently, or if the machine fails to shut down, permanent damage can occur. I was once standing next to a Pentium 66 when the cooling fan died. That processor literally exploded! Customer wanted to know if I could fix it.

■ *I've got a* CPU *that is supposed to be a 600MHz, but it only shows up as 450MHz after the machine starts*: Check your motherboard for manual jumper settings or the CMOS for BIOS-controlled settings. The CPU will run at whatever speed you tell it to. Consistently running a processor faster than the speed for which it was designed can result in overheating and data corruption. Overclockers beware!

Sorry if this section seems short, but as I said, most processors are all or none. They either work or they don't. And most problems that the processor gets blamed for really aren't its fault. So let's just move on to the next section.

FIXING FLOPPIES

This is another subject that was pretty thoroughly covered in its respective chapter (Chapter Twelve, Working With Removable Disks). To keep everything consistent, I'll recap here.

■ *My computer reports "Floppy Drive Not Found. Press F1 to continue"*: Generally this is a result of a cable that has come loose, either the power connector or the ribbon cable. This is a common occurrence on new computers that were shipped by a commercial carrier service. If you were recently poking around in the machine, you may have knocked the cable loose. Check both the drive and the motherboard connection. Either one can come loose. If the cables are all intact, it's possible you do have a bad drive. I keep a known-good floppy drive around just for testing purposes. And no, you can't have it. Get your own.

■ *I'm not getting any error messages, but my floppy isn't detected*: Check the CMOS settings. On some machines "None" is the factory default. If you just replaced the battery, or if it just failed, the CMOS will revert to factory defaults. If the CMOS says you don't have a floppy, then by golly, you don't have a floppy. If there is a floppy disk enabled in this setting, dig a little deeper in the CMOS settings. There might be a security setting that disables the floppy controller in order to prevent unauthorized use. You might want to check with your boss before changing that one.

- *My system doesn't detect the floppy and the drive light stays on all the time*: This one's easy. Your ribbon cable is reversed on one side or the other. Swap it around and all will be well.

- *I've got a 1.44MB drive but it thinks it's only 720K*: Check your CMOS settings. On an older machine, this might be the factory default. If you recently changed the battery, or if your battery just died, this will be a symptom.

- *I can't boot from my floppy drive, but once the machine is up and running, it's always available and ready to use*: Check the boot order in your CMOS. If the floppy drive isn't selected as a potential boot device then this is normal. On some versions of BIOS, it is not uncommon for the machine to not recognize the floppy if it is set last in the order. Move it up a notch in the pecking order and it will most likely boot.

- *I'm trying to format a floppy diskette and it keeps telling me it found a bad Track 0. These are brand-new diskettes*: This is a problem that should have gone away by now. In the days of 720K drives, it was common to get this message when trying to format a high-density diskette.

- *I'm getting "I/O Error Reading Drive A:" messages more and more often lately*: This is most likely a problem with the diskettes themselves. How and where do you store them? Underneath the monitor is not a good place. EMI or proximity to magnets can cause the tracks to get corrupted on the diskettes. While ScanDisk can most likely restore the data, I highly recommend that you copy the diskettes over to new ones and throw the old ones away.

- *Data Error Reading Drive A: (or B:)*: See above

- *Sector Not Found Drive A: (or B:)*: See one step above above.

- *Not Ready Reading Drive A: (or B:)*: Duh! Put a diskette in, for gosh sakes! If there is a diskette in, try formatting it. If there is a diskette in the drive that supposedly already had data on it, you can rephrase that as, "a diskette that used to have data on it." Run a thorough ScanDisk on it and see if you can fix the problem. If ScanDisk asks if you want to format the diskette, that's a sure sign the FAT was corrupted. Bye-bye, data.

- *Invalid Drive Specification*: Either you're like me and type 128 mistakes per minute and there really is no Drive W: on the system, or the system didn't recognize the floppy during the boot process and you just didn't notice. It is not uncommon for CMOS settings to have a setting that says "Halt ON:" and give several options for errors that it will ignore. Floppy drive errors are one of those, and some manufacturers, in their infinite wisdom, chose to make this setting the factory default.

- *I got a diskette stuck in my floppy and I can't get it out! What will I do?*: Call me. I'll get it out for $50.00 plus travel and lodging expenses. Or you can do it yourself pretty easily. What happened is that the metal door on the diskette is jammed in the drive mechanism. Shut the machine down and unplug. Take something long and skinny, a butter knife usually works pretty well, and gently pry it out. But, while it's in there, you might want to copy its contents to a temporary directory on your hard drive so you can make a new copy.

■ *The metal door on the diskette is bent/deformed/missing and I have to have the data stored on it*: The metal door is there to protect the medium. It isn't required for the drive to read the data off the diskette. Pop the door off, copy the data to a temporary directory on your hard drive, and make a new copy. An unfortunate side affect to this problem is frequent I/O or Data Error messages once the drive is seated. Refer to those sections for those problems.

■ *I've got a lot of really tiny files that I want to store to a floppy diskette, but I get the diskette about halfway full and my system tells me the diskette is all the way full*: The solution is to not copy the files to the root directory. Diskettes use FAT12 as a file system, and as such, it uses 2 sectors per cluster. Therefore, it is technically possible to fit a hair over 1400 files onto the diskette, if they're all under 1K. However, the root directory is limited to 224 total entries. This includes file names and directory names. Entries in directories don't count, just the root directory. So by having a couple of directories, you can copy as many files as you can fit on the diskette.

■ *I just ran a directory of a diskette and didn't find what I wanted. After I inserted a new diskette and tried to read the directory, I got the same list of files*: When you run a directory on the diskette, the contents of the directory are stored in cache RAM. That way, if you need to read the directory a second time, the drive doesn't have to hit the file allocation tables again, it just reads back the contents from cache. The thirty-fourth conductor on your floppy cable is the drive change indicator. It sends a signal from the drive itself to the controller, telling the system that you have changed the diskette in the drive. That clears the cache and forces a new read. If the thirty-fourth conductor is crimped or broken, the signal doesn't arrive at the controller. The solution is to replace the cable. In the meantime, you can force the cache to clear by reading a different drive and then going back to the A: drive.

TROUBLESHOOTING GRAPHICS ADAPTERS

If you're having trouble with a video card, chances are extremely good that you're having a driver-related issue or are having an argument with your OS (you'll never win, by the way). If the graphics card is letting you see the screen, it is most likely doing its job. There are some little quirks here and there that are related to the video card. Some can be easily fixed, and others can be easily fixed by replacing the video card.

■ *The system goes through the whole boot process (or seems to) without ever once giving me a screen, but I don't get any beeps*: Check your cable. It helps to have the monitor hooked up to the computer.

■ *I get a long series of short beeps (usually eight) and the boot process stops*: You have an AMI BIOS and a video card failure. Try a new one. If you have an Award BIOS, this could mean bad memory instead.

- *I get one long beep and two short beeps and the boot process stops*: You have an Award BIOS and see above.

- *The computer boots fine, but all I can ever get is standard VGA*: This is a driver issue. Reload the drivers and try again. And this time try loading the correct drivers.

- *The computer boots fine until Windows starts to load and then the screen goes blank*: See above.

- *Windows loads fine, and I can select all the settings I want, but I keep getting sparkly little crystals all over the place, or black specks everywhere*: This is usually caused by bad video memory. If your card has replaceable memory, swap it out. Since video cards these days usually have it soldered on, it's a good excuse to get that new 256MB X-Force Accelerator Card you've been begging your significant other for.

- *My picture is a lovely shade of puke green/fuchsia/magenta/olive drab/cyan/whatever*: Check the pins on the monitor cable. One of them is probably bent. And then stop blaming the video card. It has nothing to do with it.

That's pretty much it for troubleshooting video. Almost everything else video related is a software or driver issue.

Troubleshooting Keyboards

Keyboard problems are, amazingly enough, fairly simple to diagnose. And they're usually easy to fix as well. A broken keyboard is simply replaced. The devices are way too cheap to justify spending a lot of time trying to repair them. There aren't that many issues to deal with, so let me get them out of the way.

- *I'm getting the message "Keyboard Not Found. Press Any Key to Continue"*: Check where you have it plugged in. The PS2 mouse and the PS2 keyboard connectors look, feel, smell, and taste alike. It's easy to get them reversed. Swap the cables and try again. Sometimes, it's simply a matter of reseating the cable. Keyboard cables are usually two inches shorter than you need them to be (even if they're ten feet long).

- *No matter what I do, I can't get the system to recognize my keyboard and I know it's good. I tried it on another machine*: You have two possibilities here, one of which you won't like. If you recently set up your machine to use the USB ports, you may have inadvertently told it to look for a USB keyboard. Whoops. Try again. If that's not the case, you may have a keyboard controller chip failure. And since that's part of the chipset these days, it's time to go shopping for a new motherboard.

- *My husband/wife spilled coffee onto the keyboard. I, of course, didn't do it because I never bring beverages near my computer. (Honey, could you refill my cup please? I'm busy working on my book.)*: This might be an exception to my "disposable" theory. Or it might not be, depending on how successful you are. Unplug the keyboard from the computer and shake out as much of the liquid as you can. Rinse it thoroughly in distilled water. Don't use tap water, as that can leave residues that cause problems. Then rinse it in alcohol.

Let it dry for several hours before you try to use it again, or you stand the risk of frying the keyboard when you turn the computer on. It'll either work or it won't. Which means you'll either be shopping for a new keyboard or you won't.

- *The keys are sticking*: Clean the keyboard.
- *When I turn my computer on, I get a Keyboard Failure message and the thing keeps on beeping*: One of the keys is stuck. Either that, or your cat is sitting on the space bar. See above.

I told you it was short.

TROUBLESHOOTING OPTICAL DRIVES

For the most part, unwell CD-ROM drives exhibit symptoms similar to those of hard drives, except that they generally will not prevent your computer from booting properly. Unlike the hard drive, a CD-ROM is totally dependent on software drivers to work right, so a majority of the problems you face are either configuration or software issues. There are a few things, however, that can drive you nuts. Since CD-ROMs, CD-RWs, and DVDs all exhibit the same hardware issues, in the following section just consider CD-ROM to mean any of the above. If the issue is unique to a type of optical drive, then it's more likely to be a software or driver issue.

- *I just installed a new CD-ROM and my system doesn't recognize it*: Check your jumpers first. They're just like hard drives in that they need to be either master or slave. Everything I talked about in the section on hard drives holds true here as well.
- *I just installed a new CD-ROM and my system doesn't recognize it. I've checked all the jumper settings and they're correct, and I've even checked to see if I have a cable-select cable. I still can't make it work*: Check and see if the IDE port onto which you are trying to install it has been disabled. Some CMOS setup programs allow for the disabling of ports for security reasons or simply in order to reclaim the IRQ.
- *I just installed a new CD-RW and my system doesn't recognize it. I've checked all the jumper settings and they're correct, and I've even checked to see if I have a cable-select cable. I still can't make it work*: Some CD-RWs only work if they're the Master drive on the port. Since most systems require the bootable drive to be on the primary port, the solution is to move the CD-RW to the secondary port and let it be the master of its domain.
- *My CD-ROM works fine in Windows, but when I restart in DOS mode, it disappears*: Like I said, CD-ROM drives are totally dependent on software drivers. Windows loads its own drivers from the registry. When you boot in DOS mode, you need an autoexec.bat and config.sys file, just like in the old days.
- *My CD-ROM drive letter keeps changing*: That probably means that you're also using some form of removable medium that hooks up either to the parallel port or a USB port. When that drive is present, it reassigns drive letters.
- *My CD-ROM won't read CDRs or CD-RWs*: This is usually only a problem with older drives, but there are a couple of things that can cause this problem. One is that the older

CD-ROM isn't capable of reading a multisession table of contents (see Chapter Seventeen, Multimedia: Computerized Home Entertainment). You need a drive that is "multisession compliant" to read the newer media. The second thing that could be causing the problem lies in the mechanism itself. Early models of CD-ROM expect a certain contrast between the pits and lands. They simply can't extract the data off the disc if the contrast is too subtle.

- *I'm getting an inordinately high number of I/O errors on discs that other computers have no problem with*: Try running one of those cleaning discs made specifically for CD players. If the lens on the optical stylus gets dirty, this will happen. If this doesn't work, check your CMOS settings for the drive and make sure it is correct. Many CD drives only work in PIO mode. If the drive is on the same cable as your UDMA hard drive, it may be forcing the CD-ROM into UDMA mode. Next, check the IDE cable. It shouldn't be longer than 18″, but many manufacturers cheat this length and ship 24″ cables. While this usually doesn't cause major problems, it can. Finally, if bus mastering has been set up on your machine, make sure you have a CD-ROM drive that is bus mastering capable. Pretty much any newer CD-ROM drive should be able to handle it, but if you brought an older drive into service for any reason, this can become an issue.

- *My kid (dog, husband, wife, best friend, but never me) scratched up one of my most critical CDs and now my drive won't read it*: The best solution is to replace the disc. If this isn't possible, try smearing a little toothpaste onto the surface of the disk. Take a moistened soft cloth and, in a circular motion, buff the scratched surface. Never do this on the label side! Once you've done this, rinse the disk and dry it with a soft cloth. This doesn't always work, but it has saved many a disc that my kid (dog, husband, wife, best friend, but never me) scratched for me.

FIGURING OUT THE I/O PORTS

Many of the devices you use with your computer aren't internal. They hang off of one of the externally accessible ports. Most of the time, that makes it much easier to add and remove devices, because you don't have to take the computer apart in order to access the device. Once in a while, though, you get something that just doesn't want to cooperate. How are you supposed to tell if it's the device that's flaky or the port you're trying to use? That's what I'll look at in this section.

- *No matter what I plug onto my serial device, I can't make it work*: With serial devices, one of the first things you should do is make sure the port is enabled in your CMOS. Many systems these days ship with soft modems installed (see Chapter Twenty, Telecommunications). With most of these, in order to get them to work one of the serial ports had to be disabled. My law of shifting reality specifically states that this will be the port you're trying to use, whichever one that happens to be. If you get into the CMOS and find that both of the serial ports are assigned COM ports, you might want to check the port itself. That's where one of those loopback connectors that I discussed earlier in the chapter comes in real handy. If the port tests good and is enabled in the CMOS, you've pretty much narrowed it down to the device configuration. Check and see if its settings agree with those in your CMOS. If the port is set to COM1 and the device to COM2, they won't communicate. That's like having the postman knock on the front door and you answering the back door. You won't get your mail.

- *I'm still using a serial mouse. Every time I use any programs that access the modem, my system freezes*: That's an easy one. They're both on the same COM port. The mouse is usually easier to change over than the modem (but not always), so try a different COM port. I'll bet the problem goes away.

- *I had a parallel Zip drive and a printer hooked up together and they worked fine. But then I added a scanner and now it takes forever to print anything and I can type a letter faster than I can copy it from the Zip. What happened?*: There are several parallel modes. If you want to use your parallel port for more than just a printer, you need to be using ECP mode. For more information on this, refer to Chapter Eighteen, Printing Technologies.

- *I bought a new printer, and for the life of me, I can't make it work*: As with the above problem, the parallel mode selected in your CMOS may be the culprit. Many new printers require that either EPP or ECP mode be selected in order to function properly. On the very minimum, they're going to need bidirectional mode. If you have Centronics, ASCII, or Compatibility Mode selected, they just won't work. Also check the type of cable you're using. With many printers, if it isn't IEEE 1284 compliant, forget about it.

- *I just set my parallel port to ECP like you told me to, and now my sound card doesn't work. Who made you the computer guru?*: My boss, so live with it. What happened there is that ECP requires a DMA channel. It decided to take the same one your sound card uses, and since the parallel port grabs the DMA channel before the sound card gets a chance, guess which one wins. Put one or the other on a different DMA channel. That's one resource where there's plenty to go around.

- *Since I've got two printers, I thought it would be a good idea to add a second parallel port. But I can't make it work*: That's probably because you need to configure LPT2 for the second port. By default, LPT2 is looking for IRQ5. If you've got a sound card, there's a pretty good chance it grabs IRQ5 also. See if you can reconfigure the sound card to another IRQ.

- *I've got USB ports on the back of my machine, but they don't work*: Check your CMOS. This is another one of those things that can be disabled in order to get the IRQ back. I've seen quite a few systems shipped with the USB option disabled by default.

TROUBLESHOOTING POWER SUPPLIES

I saved this section for last because it's the most fun. What makes troubleshooting power supplies such a challenge is that they rarely die a fast, clean, respectable death. They always do it the hard way. And when that happens, the errors they cause can get interpreted as almost anything but a power supply. So let me see if I can make some sense of this.

- *I push the power button on my machine and nothing happens. No lights, no fan—nothing:* First off, check and see if you're plugged in. Hopefully, you're on a surge suppressor, so see if it's plugged in and turned on. Sometimes the switch on the surge suppressor gets inadvertently switched to the off position. Now look around you. Are the lights on? Is there power coming into the house? You wouldn't be the first person in the world to simply be unaware that there was a power outage, and you certainly won't be the last. If there is power coming into the house, check the outlet for voltage. Maybe a circuit breaker kicked out. If all of these tests come out positive, pull the power supply and check to see if the fuse popped. Most power supplies these days do not have externally accessible fuses, so that will require popping the cover. Be careful of those capacitors. They can hold a charge for quite some time and if you touch a charged capacitor it can cause a nasty surprise. If the fuse is good and you still can't get power, then sorry, my friend. It's time for a new power supply. Fortunately, they're not that expensive. And in a way, that makes you one of the lucky ones. Your power supply died abruptly and was pretty easy to diagnose.

- *You would not believe what my computer sounds like when I turn it on. It scares my neighbors off!:* That's probably the fan in the power supply. When the bearing starts to go out, it will develop weird sounds ranging from that of a crying baby to a screeching banshee. I had one that sounded like far off in the woods, a woman with the most beautiful voice was singing with the wind. I didn't want to change that one, it sounded so nice. But I figured the data on the computer deserves respect, too.

- *I'm getting power to the computer, but the fan stopped making noise:* Check and see if there's air blowing out of the back of the power supply. If not, replace the power supply. Before you do that, however, you might want to peek inside the power supply. Some of those fans are the same type they sell at electronics stores for about five bucks and simply plug right in. That would be a cheap and easy fix if the power supply is otherwise good.

- *When I turn my machine on, it doesn't start up right away and hangs in the middle of the boot process. Yet when I try it a second time, it starts up just fine:* The capacitors in your power supply are beginning to lose their ability to take a charge. They're not powering up in time to provide power to all the devices on your PC. There is supposed to be a power good signal that the power supply delivers when it's up to speed, but failing capacitors tend to fool that circuit. I suggest you replace your power supply ASAP.

- *I'll be working along in on my computer and all of the sudden, it'll just reboot itself:* That sucks, doesn't it? There are actually a couple of things that can cause this. The power supply is the most likely culprit. It's delivering rated voltage for 99.9999999999999% of the time and for that tiny fraction of a second that it doesn't, your RAM and CPU lose everything that used to be in them. That causes a reboot.

- *More and more lately, I seem to be getting blue screens of death. I've been monitoring the memory addresses reported by the messages and they're random. I can't find a single address or program that seems to be causing the problem:* See above. Except instead of a reboot, you're getting a blue screen. I'm not sure which is worse. They have about the same effect on your data and they're both equally irritating.

■ *None of my power management functions works right. How come?*: 1) Power management is not properly configured in the CMOS, 2) power management is not properly configured in the OS, or 3) you have one of those AT/ATX combo boards that were so popular for a while. They're actually an AT-style board that happens to be designed along the lines of an ATX board, so they have all the peripherals on board. There were also hybrid cases so that you could use either style of board. So on the outside, it looks like an ATX, but in reality it's an AT power supply. And AT power supplies don't support power management.

CHAPTER SUMMARY

Well, that's about it for troubleshooting and that's about it for this book. Hopefully, reading this book was as good for you as writing it was for me. I'd hate to think I was the only one in the world having this much fun. One thing I should point out, as if you didn't already know this, is that this is a rapidly changing industry. Some technology that was state of the art when I began writing was already passé by the time I finished. So I polished the manuscript up a bit before sending it along to press. And by the time it hits the bookshelves, something else will have become obsolete.

There's nothing we can do about the industry except try to keep up. So don't ever stop reading and learning new things. And watch for future revisions of this book that take up changes in the industry. Hope to see you then.

BRAIN DRAIN

1. Discuss the differences between open-ended questions and closed-ended questions. Make up a list of open-ended questions that you might ask a client who is having computer problems.

2. Why is it so necessary to re-create the problem before attempting to fix it? Why can't you just take the customer's word?

3. How many different places can you think of that might provide documentation and/or troubleshooting help for a problem you can't diagnose?

4. Why are memory errors so hard to diagnose?

5. Why is a slowly failing power supply such a problem?

THE $64K QUESTIONS

1. Which of the following issues is addressed by re-creating a problem before trying to fix it?
   a. Hard disk errors
   b. Memory errors
   c. Motherboard errors
   d. User errors

2. Which of the following is an example of a software-based troubleshooting tool? (Select all that apply.)
   a. A RAMDISK
   b. A POST Card
   c. A memory mapper
   d. A partition manager

3. Of the following list, which one will test a serial port without having

either the device or the cable affect the test?

a. A loopback adapter

b. A partition manager

c. A multimeter

d. A POST Card

4. You think that the hard drive might actually still be good, but you want to test it. Which might be of use?

a. A partition manager

b. FDISK

c. Disk Doctor

d. All of the above

5. Boot failure problems are rarely the result of _____ failure.

a. CPU

b. Motherboard

c. Software

d. Hard disk

6. Memory errors can actually be generated because of a failing _____.

a. CPU

b. Hard disk

c. Power supply

d. Floppy disk drive

7. The twenty-eighth wire on a floppy disk cable is the _____ wire.

a. Power

b. Drive change indicator

c. Master/slave indicator

d. Null

8. You have a machine with 256MB of RAM installed, but once it is booted it only recognized 64MB. Why is this?

a. You are running OS2.

b. This is known as a Gate 20 failure.

c. The memory is bad.

d. You are running MS-DOS.

9. What two drive size limitations appear as a result of older BIOS?

a. 2.5GB

b. 8GB

c. 32GB

d. 128GB

10. What is a common cause of intermittently changing drive letters on a system?

a. A failing disk drive

b. A bad cable

c. A failing controller

d. An external removable disk that is not always present on the system.

Tricky Terminology

Closed-ended question: A question that leads to an answer that provides no further insight or leads to an abrupt dead end to the discussion.

Hypothesis: Any theory that can be tested to be proven either true or false.

POST card: A device that follows each step of the POST procedure and reports the results. Should the POST fail, the last successful process will be indicated in an encoded display.

Loopback adapter: A piece of hardware that routes an output signal directly back to the computer, giving the impression that a device is present.

Open-ended question: A question that will provide further insight into the discussion as a result of the answer provided.

Acronym Alert

Sorry. No new ones in this chapter.

ANSWERS TO CHAPTER EXERCISES

CHAPTER 1

BRAIN DRAIN

1. List and explain each of the basic functions that define a computer.

   Answers should include the terms *calculate, copy,* and *compare.* They should also show an awareness that the basic CPU functions limit calculation abilities to addition, subtraction, multiplication, and division of whole numbers.

3. You have a hexadecimal address of 02FE:CCC0. Convert that address to binary.

   10111111101100110011000000 is the correct answer.

5. Describe the five primary system busses and their functions.

   CPU Bus: Direct communication with the chipset and cache.

   Address Bus: Maintains, tracks and locates addresses of each individual device in the system.

   Local Bus: A direct path between the CPU and RAM or the CPU and L2 cache.

   The I/O Bus: The path that data uses to move from device to device as either input or output.

   The Power Bus: The wires that supply raw electricity to the various components on the motherboard.

THE 64K$ QUESTIONS

1. Which of the following is *not* a basic function of a computer?

   a. Provide user data for input

3. A byte that consists of the bits 0 1 1 1 0 0 1 0 has a decimal value of:

   b. 114

5. Which character set included control codes as part of the basic set?

   a. ASCII

7. Which of the primary system busses provides direct communications between the CPU and the chipset?

   a. The CPU Bus

9. Which of the primary system busses is responsible for locating data in the system?

   d. The Address Bus

Chapter 2

Brain Drain

1. List the five primary functions of the OS as they relate to the hardware and applications on the system.

   The File System, Processor Control, Memory Control, Device Control and Security.

3. What are some of the responsibilities of the OS in terms of controlling the microprocessor?

   In multi-tasking environments it manages which application can have The processor at any given time. It controls what priority level any given thread has in terms of protection and processing order.

5. Describe how HAL fools the applications into thinking they're talking to the hardware, while all the while it is actually blocking direct access.

   Virtual device drivers intercept hardware calls, interprets them and passes them on to the physical device drivers.

The 64K$ Questions

1. Which of the following is not a function of the OS?

   b. BIOS control

3. What was the largest partition allowed by FAT16?

   c. 2GB

5. A part of the hard disk treated as if it were physical memory is called _____.

   d. All of the above

7. Which of the following is not an example of an OS?

    a. MS Word

9. Windows uses a(n) _____ to prevent the applications from directly accessing the hardware.

    d. .vxd

CHAPTER 3

BRAIN DRAIN

1. List as many onboard components as you can that will be found on both AT-style and ATX-style motherboards.

    Typically, an AT-style motherboard will have only a large DIN connector for the keyboard. Some AT motherboards did feature serial and parallel ports as well, but they were the exception and not the rule.

3. Put together a list of as many expansion devices as you can think of that would require a slot on the expansion bus.

    Answers will vary here, but the list would include:

    SCSI adapters, modems, sound cards, video cards, specialized I/O controllers (including device controllers, USB, and Firewire), video capture cards, and add/on IDE controllers.

5. This task should be accomplished with a partner. Place a fully assembled computer on the table in front of you. Without looking at the back and using the sense of touch only, reach around to the back of the computer and identify as many connectors as you can.

    Sorry. I'm not your partner.

THE 64K$ QUESTIONS

1. A key precautionary measure to take before working inside a computer system is to:

    d. Protect the CPU from EMI. Generally, there is little danger of electrical shock to the technician working inside of a computer, unless taking the power supply apart.

3. On an AT-style power supply the correct orientation of the P8 and P9 connectors was:

    a. Black wires to the inside, colored wires to the outside.

5. A DIMM socket is equipped with _____ pin connectors.

    b. 168 and d. 184 are both correct. SDRAM uses the 168-pin design, while DDR uses the 184-pin.

7. A 40-pin ribbon cable connector is the hookup for _____.

    d. The IDE port.

9. A 25-pin male connector with two rows of female pins is _____.

    c. A parallel port or d. An external SCSI port.

CHAPTER 4

BRAIN DRAIN

1. Discuss the three primary measurements of electricity covered in this chapter and how they relate to one another.

    Voltage is the differential charge between two surfaces. Amperage is the number of electrons per second that flows from one surface to the other over a conductor. Resistance is the tendency for the conductor to prevent some of the electrons from passing. Together, the three of them dictate how many watts of electricity are produced, which is the measurement of how much work that current can do.

3. Discuss why those three components would be needed by a motherboard.

    Capacitors act to clean up current and eliminate fluctuations, resistors are used to "slow down" current for devices that need less juice, and coils eliminate any residual AC current as well as filter out low-frequency signals.

5. Talk about why a power supply can be such a problem to troubleshoot when it fails slowly.

    Many of the symptoms of a failing power supply mimic the symptoms of other devices, such as memory or hard drives. For example, if a power supply is too slow in achieving full output, a hard disk might try to initialize before there is sufficient current to power it. Extreme drop in voltage can flush CPU registers and memory even when the fluctuation didn't last long enough to cause a complete system shutdown. This can look like an application failure.

THE 64K$ QUESTIONS

1. Which of the following devices is used to reduce the amount of amperage on a circuit?

    c. A resistor

3. Which of the following devices would be measured in microfarads?

    a. A capacitor

5. What device will keep an individual computer running for a few minutes after a total power failure?

    d. An uninterrupted power supply

7. Power is provided to the motherboard from an AT power supply by way of
   _____.

   c. A pair of 6-pin connectors

9. Which of the following could be signs of a failing power supply?

   d. All of the above

CHAPTER 5

BRAIN DRAIN

1. Discuss why the computer enclosure might be the first decision a designer makes when putting together a new model of computer.

   A couple of things make this a critical decision to make first. For one, where is the system to be located? A full-tower design doesn't fit very well on a classroom desktop. Conversely, a micro desktop might not be the best thing to put on the floor. Also, consider how many devices the system must eventually support. That micro desktop won't go very far if you need a CD-RW, a DVD, a backup tape drive, and an internal Zip drive.

3. What are the pros and cons of using aluminum versus steel in designing a computer case?

   Aluminum is much lighter and it dissipates heat faster. But it's more expensive and more difficult to mill, making it a far more expensive choice. An advantage of steel over aluminum is that it blocks EMI much better than does aluminum.

5. List as many individual components that make up the enclosure as you can think of.

   The frame, the case cover, the drive bays, the front and back panels, and the wiring harness are all parts of the enclosure.

THE 64K$ QUESTIONS

1. Which of the following is a low-profile form factor?

   c. LBX

3. An advantage of aluminum over steel in enclosure construction is _____. (Choose all that apply.)

   a. Light-weight and d. It dissipates heat better.

5. Failing to replace the backplane filler after removing an expansion card is not a good idea, because _____.

   d. All of the above.

7. Hot-swappable drives are designed to fit into a _____ bay.

   a. 5¹/₄″ half-height

9. Which of the following is not likely to be a part of a typical wiring harness found in an enclosure?

   b. RLL. RLL is an old hard disk encoding method that will be discussed later in the book.

Chapter 6

Brain Drain

1. Discuss as many differences between at AT-style motherboard and an ATX-style motherboard as you can think of.

   First and foremost, the basic components of the motherboard, relative to the backplane, are rotated 90 degrees to that of the AT board. ATX boards generally feature far more integrated peripherals soldered onto the board than did AT. Also, ATX motherboards, by default, are designed to support advanced power management. An offshoot of this is that on/off functions are controlled by the motherboard and not the power supply.

3. Give an overview of the functions of the system BIOS.

   The BIOS contains the POST program, which brings the system from a cold start, checks all system components to make sure they're working properly and then performs Plug 'n Play scans. It contains a Setup program that runs from the BIOS chip, which allows the user to input parameters that BIOS will use in later boots. Finally, it contains the Bootstrap Loader, which goes out and finds the master boot record and turns the boot process over to the OS.

5. Discuss why there needs to be a separate expansion bus.

   Designers can't expect to build every computer they ever plan to sell with every device that's ever been invented for personal computing. For one thing, that would make computers prohibitively expensive for most people, and for another, different people have different needs. Also, we need a bus with a consistent speed for add-on peripherals. It wouldn't do to have to redesign a network card every time a faster CPU came out.

The 64K$ Questions

1. A typical motherboard consists of _____ layers of substrate.

   c. Four

3.   How many IDE controllers typically reside on an ATX-style motherboard?

   d.   Zero. The motherboard typically has two ports, each of which supports two drives. The controller, however, is on the device itself.

5.   POST is a function of _____.

   c.   The BIOS

7.   CMOS stands for _____.

   c.   Complimentary Metal-Oxide Semiconductor

9.   The Plug 'n Play Recognition Scan is a part of _____.

   b.   POST

CHAPTER 7

BRAIN DRAIN

1.   Describe how a semiconductor works and explain why it is such a useful material in making CPUs.

   A semiconductor is a substance that either allows a current to pass, or blocks it completely, based on whether or not the current reaches or exceeds a certain threshold voltage. This unique characteristic allows designers to create a "switch" based on whether or not that voltage is reached.

3.   Explain why the 8088 CPU was only capable of recognizing 1MB of memory.

   The 8088 possessed a 20-bit address bus. As such, its total memory map could be 2^{20} bits wide. That value is 1,048,576, or 1MB.

5.   Describe in as much detail as you can how the system moves data into the CPU after you press a certain key on your keyboard.

   When a key is first pressed, it prompts a chip on the keyboard to do three things. First it issues an interrupt request to the CPU, notifying the CPU that there is data on the way. Next it generates a make code that indicates the key has been pressed. And when the key is released, it generates a break code. The make and break code are combined to generate the actual data that will be sent to RAM. The keyboard controller chip will then move that data to a buffer in memory where it will stay until the CPU orders the prefetch to go retrieve it.

THE 64K$ QUESTIONS

1.   The binary language is an offshoot of the work of _____.

   a.   George Boole

3. The address bus of the 8088 was _____ bits wide.

    c. 20

5. In the example used in Question 4, what technology would allow the CPU to actually *process* those lines of code before the user made a selection, discarding any data generated by the wrong subroutine?

    d. Speculative execution

7. It is not possible for a CPU to have more than one FPU.

    b. False

9. The following is a collection of very useful circuits that appears on all modern CPU, but was not a part of the original 8088.

    d. L2 cache

CHAPTER 8

BRAIN DRAIN

1. Briefly describe the processor generations and how they differ in speed and bus width.

   Processor generations generally are defined by a key change in architectural design. Generation One processors consist of the 8088 and its clones. Generation Two included the 286s, Three the 386s, and so on. Pentiums are easier to differentiate because they are Pentium II, III, and IV. It's not so easy with aftermarket designs. With the exception of the move from the 386 to the 486, each generation doubled the external data bus until the release of the Pentium. It has since stabilized at 64 bits. The internal data bus stabilized at 32 bits. While clock speeds have gotten faster with each generation, there is no real formula you can use to correlate the advances to a specific generation.

3. Discuss why raw processor speed has far less impact on system performance than other factors, such as the amount of L1 cache or the amount of system memory installed.

   With the average application run by the average user, the CPU actually spends more time waiting for data that it does processing it. So by increasing the clock speed of the CPU by 200 percent, you are in effect increasing its idle time by 200 percent. If you speed up delivery of data to the CPU by that same margin, you increase performance by a substantially greater margin.

5. The fifth-generation CPUs showed a rather remarkable diversity of characteristics. Discuss some of the Generation 5 CPUs and how they differed.

   The basic 3.3V Pentium was really nothing more than an improvement on the original design. The MMX follows quickly on its bootheels, adding multimedia extensions. AMD offerings, such as the K6-2 added an instruction set for 3D graphics rendering.

THE 64K$ QUESTIONS

1. Which of the following saw no change in the migration from the 8086 to the 80286?
   d. The ALU

3. Which CPU was the first to support protected mode?
   c. The 80286

5. The 80286 microprocessor has a _____-bit address bus.
   c. 24

7. The address bus of the 80486 was twice that of the 80386.
   b. False

9. The AMD series of 80386 CPU suffered several compatibility issues when using Microsoft operating systems.
   b. False

CHAPTER 9

BRAIN DRAIN

1. In as much detail as you can recall, describe a typical memory I/O operation from beginning to end.

   Starting with the CPU, the control unit issues a request for data to the prefetch. First, the prefetch searches all cache locations. When it doesn't find it there, it turns the search over to the chipset, where the memory control circuit confirms that the data the CPU has requested does indeed reside in memory and that the first bit resides at this specific address. That address represents the X-Y coordinates of a spreadsheet-like grid. First, the row access strobe locates the correct row in which the data reside and subsequently turns the search over to the column access strobe, which finds the correct column. Once the address has been located, data can be moved in bursts until the next cycle must be completed. Depending on the type of memory this may be anywhere from two to four cycles.

3. What were some key differences that made SDRAM so much faster than EDO?

   SDRAM moves some of the MCC circuitry over to the memory module, in essence making it part of the chipset. As a result, data can be accessed on each and every cycle of the CPU's front-side bus.

5. Describe how ECC differs from parity and what makes it a superior error checking mechanism.

> Parity was simply an error checking mechanism. It counted the number of 1s in a byte. If there was an even number of 1s, it set the parity bit to 1 to assure that there was an odd number. If there was as odd number of 1s parity was set to 0 to keep the number odd. On the receiving end all 1s were counted. If there was an even number in the byte, including the parity bit, then a nonmaskable interrupt was generated and the computer locked up. ECC performs a mathematical calculation on the bits in the data being sent. The same calculation is performed on the receiving end. If the numbers in the ECC field match, the data is accepted. A single-bit error can be detected and corrected. An error of two or more bits will result in a nonmaskable interrupt and the computer will lock up.

THE 64K$ QUESTIONS

1. Memory I/O operations are controlled by _____.
   c. The MCC

3. A SIMM differs from a DIMM in its design in that _____.
   b. The terminating tabs on either side of the base of a DIMM can be assigned a separate function.

5. A typical DRAM cell consists of a transistor paired with _____.
   d. A microscopic capacitor.

7. Once the MCC has determined that the data being sought actually resides in RAM and resolves the address, the next thing to happen is a _____.
   a. Prerefresh

9. DDRAM is so named because it _____.
   c. Moves two bits of data for each clock cycle.

CHAPTER 10

BRAIN DRAIN

1. Discuss how IRQs, I/O addresses, and DMA channels are critical to configuring a device on the expansion bus, and list some of the problems you might encounter.

> IRQs are like the doorbell for the CPU. When any given device wants to send data to the CPU or the CPU wants to send data to that device, either the device

or the CPU will send an electrical signal down the IRQ line, alerting it to be ready for incoming data. Since neither device responds on the very same clock cycle they need to know where they're sending that data when the CPU is ready. The I/O address is a buffer area where data can be stored. The base I/O identifies the device, while any given devices can have a number of buffer addresses. DMA channels are direct circuits from the device to memory. A device configured to use DMA can dump data directly to memory once the I/O operation has been negotiated by the CPU.

3. What is the purpose of an I/O address?

An I/O address is like any other address. It's how you find a specific house, or in this case device. Only in the case of an I/O address, it is actually a virtual address rather than a physical one. It is where the data either generated or required by a device will be found when either the CPU or the device goes looking for that data.

5. List the different expansion busses used by computer systems over the years in the order that they appeared.

The PC Bus, ISA, MCA, EISA and VLB (about the same time), PCI, PCMCIA, AGP and PCI-X.

THE 64K$ QUESTIONS

1. An I/O Address is _____.
    d. A specific memory location that the CPU uses to locate data from a specific device.

3. An IRQ is _____.
    a. An electrical channel that notifies the CPU (or allows the CPU to notify a device) that there is data ready to be moved.

5. Which of the following busses were backwardly compatible with ISA? (Choose all that apply.)
    b. VLB and c. EISA

7. At what speed does an AGP 8x video card run?
    c. 133Mhz

9. When two devices on two different busses that operate at completely different speeds need to communicate, the process that allows this is _____.
    d. Flow control

CHAPTER 11

BRAIN DRAIN

1. Briefly describe how pressing on the W key on a keyboard generates data and moves it to the CPU for processing.

> When you first press the key, the keyboard's controller chip generates an interrupt to notify the CPU that there is data coming its way. It then issues a make code to indicate when the key was first pressed, and when the key is released, it issues a break code. The combination of the make and break code generates the data that will be sent to memory. The keyboard controller circuitry in the chipset will translate that data into what will be sent to the CPU.

3. Describe how a mouse does its job.

> The mouse ball turns rollers attached to a perforated wheel. A light beam shines through the perforations, creating a flickering beam. A photosensitive receptor converts that beam to electrical impulses that the mouse driver uses to interpret relative position of the mouse cursor.

5. Describe a method by which computerization will assure that the person bagging your order does not give you onion rings instead of fries.

> Computerize the production line rather than use humans.

THE 64K$ QUESTIONS

1. When you press down on a key, data is generated by two signals. These are the _____ and the _____. (Select two.)
   b. Break and d. Make

3. The type of mouse that uses a perforated wheel that spins in front of an LED is called a _____ mouse.
   d. Optomechanical. You might see it described as a mechanical mouse in a lot of literature. But technically, that is not correct.

5. A CCD is a _____.
   d. Charge Coupled Device

7. The file format frequently used by video editors is _____.
   d. MJPEG

9. Which of the following is not a form of touchscreen monitor?
   b. Resistive interpolative

CHAPTER 12

BRAIN DRAIN

1. List as many forms of removable media as you can.

    Lists will vary, but should include at the minimum: floppy diskettes, super-floppies, Zip drives, and Jaz drives. Syquest cartridges could be included as well. There have been others in the past. CD-ROMs and removable hard disks are technically not considered removable media, even though they are.

3. If you have an application that consists of 245MB worth of files and you want to run it from removable media, what options would be best?

    A Syquest would be best, because it is faster. But a 750MB Zip or a Jazz drive would work quite nicely as well.

5. Discuss as many differences as you can between DAT and DLT tape drives.

    DAT drives use helical-scan read/write mechanisms, while, as the name implies, DLTs use a linear read/write mechanism. The tape differs as well. DAT is a metal oxide tape, while DLT is metal film. DAT can store larger amounts of data per square inch of medium and can read and write data to the tape more quickly. DAT is much less expensive.

THE 64K$ QUESTIONS

1. 5.25″ floppy disk drives were available in _____ and _____ sizes. (Choose two)
    a. 360KB and c. 1.2MB

3. Double density floppies featured _____ sectors per track.
    d. 40

5. How many bytes are there per sector on a floppy disk?
    c. 512

7. The "click of death" is a failure that appears on _____.
    a. Zip drives

9. Two tape drives that use linear recording technology are_____ and _____.
    a. QIC and c. DLT

CHAPTER 13

BRAIN DRAIN

1. Describe how CHS defines the capacity of a hard drive.

    CHS stands for cylinders, heads, and sectors-per-track. There are 512 bytes per sector. A hard drive can only have so many platter surfaces. This will determine the number of heads. Each surface will have so many tracks. Multiplying the number of cylinders times the number of heads times the number of tracks per sector times 512 is the total capacity of the drive.

3. Describe how data is stored to a hard disk and then subsequently read back.

    The hard disk controller converts incoming digital data into pulses of electricity, which charge a magnet on the write head. The write head uses magnetic fluxes to apply charges to the platter surface. On playback, these fluxes are read by the write head. A magnetized data unit indicates a 1, lack of magnetization indicates a 0. Since the platter is spinning by the R/W heads at very high rates of speed, a very accurate timing mechanism assures that the heads remain synchronized with each other.

5. In as much detail as you can, define how the FAT works.

    The hard drive is divided into file allocation units, which consist of 2 to 64 sectors, depending on the file system used and the size of the partition. For each FAU, there is an entry in FAT. This entry will have fields for file name, whether the FAU is available for use or not, if it is the last FAU of the file contained, and a pointer to the next FAU of that file, if it is not. More advanced file systems, such as NTFS use a database system, rather than file tables and can include much more information in each entry.

THE 64K$ QUESTIONS

1. The physical surface on which data is stored on a hard drive is known as a _____.
    d. Platter

3. Modern hard drives use a _____ to move the actuator arms.
    a. Voice coil

5. Of the following encoding systems, which is most likely to be used on a hard drive purchased today?
    a. EPRML

7. As a systems administrator, you want to enforce as much security in your organization as you possibly can. Therefore you have decided that all computers will run an OS that uses the _____ file system.
    c. NTFS

9. What part of the MBR is created and added during the OS installation?

   d. OS pointer

CHAPTER 14

BRAIN DRAIN

1. List as many hard disk interfaces as you can think of.

> At the very minimum, the list should include IDE, Serial ATA, and SCSI. Older interfaces include ST506/412, MFM, and ESDI.

3. Discuss as many improvements of the second generation of IDE compared to the first generation as you can think of.

> First generation IDE only supports hard drives and one IDE port per computer. Each port supported two devices, so first-generation IDE basically supported two hard disks. The second generation introduced ATa. We now have two ports of two channels each for a total of four devices and a number of different types of devices are supported.

5. Based on the discussion generated by Question 4, describe what is happening to the hard disk on each step along the way.

> The partitioning of the hard drive prepares the MBR, including the file system executable and the partition tables. The formatting procedure scans the surface of the hard disk for defects and writes out the first set of file allocation tables. The installation of the OS adds the OS point to the MBR.

THE 64K$ QUESTIONS

1. The ST-506 hard disk drive offered a maximum capacity of _____ MB.

   b. 5

3. Which of the following was *not* a feature of the first generation of IDE?

   c. It supported devices other than hard drives.

5. Most hard drives in use today use _____ addressing.

   d. LBA

7. The Microsoft utility that re-creates the MBR is _____.

   a. FORMAT

9. A CS cable differs from a standard IDE cable in that _____.

   d. The twenty-eighth conductor has been clipped between the center connector and the one on the end.

CHAPTER 15

BRAIN DRAIN

1. You've just installed an older SCSI card you pulled from another machine. It was working fine in the other machine, but now the only device the system recognizes is the hard drive. The tape drive and CD-ROM are ignored. What are some of the things that may have caused this?

> For one thing, it might be a really old first-generation SCSI card that was designed specifically for hard drives. Other factors to look at are termination (including the host adapter) and the device IDs of the devices installed.

3. What was the one thing lacking from the very first release of SCSI specifications that caused so much confusion. What was one of the problems caused and why did this omission cause the problem?

> There was no predefined command set. As a result, controller cards designed for one device wouldn't work with other devices. This was because manufacturers were only interested in supporting the device they were selling.

5. Discuss why termination of a SCSI chain is necessary. What happens if you don't terminate the chain properly and why is it this happens?

> When an electrical signal travels down a wire, it doesn't simply stop or fly out into space when it reaches the end. Unless there is something there to absorb that current and dissipate it, it will turn around and travel down the wire in the opposite direction. It is not possible to encode data under these conditions. A terminating resistor coverts the current to heat and dissipates it into the air.

THE 64K$ QUESTIONS

1. How many devices could a SCSI-I chain support?
    c. 8. But that number includes the host controller, which is considered to be a device on the chain. So only 7 additional devices can be hung off the controller.

3. What are two methods of terminating a SCSI chain?
    b. Installing a resistor into a specially designed socket. And d. Setting a jumper on the last device on the chain. In the case of d, it is still a resistor. It's simply a resistor that is already in place.

5. How many devices can be supported by a parallel SCSI-III chain?
    e. None of the above. SPI supports fifteen devices, including the host adapter.

7. High-voltage differential devices cannot be on the same chain as a single-ended device.

    b. False. They can be installed on the same chain as long as a SCSI Expander was installed between the two devices. However, this was actually a more expensive alternative than simply installing a separate host adapter for each chain.

9. Which of the following is an example of Serial SCSI?

    c. FireWire

CHAPTER 16

BRAIN DRAIN

1. Describe in as much detail as possible how an image is generated on a typical CRT monitor.

    The graphics adapter sends out a burst of signals to each of three electron guns. The graphics adapter controls the strength of the stream of electrons generated by each gun. A deflection yoke sends the electrons across the back of the CRT, where a phosphorous coating has been applied. The stream of electrons causes the coating to emit a glow.

3. Why are TFT displays considered better than passive matrix displays?

    Speed. Plain and simple. Modern TFTs are also brighter and can be viewed from wider angles, but this is due more to improvements in design.

5. What are the factors that contribute to the overall speed of a graphics card?

    The speed of the RAMDAC, the type and speed of the memory used and the bus (AGP 2x, 4x, 8x or PCI-X).

THE 64K$ QUESTIONS

1. In a CRT Monitor, the phosphors are separated from one another by _____.

    b. A shadow mask

3. Smoother animation is made possible by a technique called _____.

    c. Frame buffering

5. If a programmer wants her colors to appear more natural with smoother blending, she will take advantage of a technique called _____.

    d. Dithering

7. The LCD most likely used on a PDA is a _____.

    a. Common Plane

9. Programmers can add extra effects to graphics without changing the actual color by using _____.

    c. The alpha channel

CHAPTER 17

BRAIN DRAIN

1. Discuss in as much detail as possible how data is written to a conventional CD and subsequently read back. Include in your discussion as many components of the CD-ROM drive as you can recall.

    Data is applied to a thin aluminum surface by punching holes called pits into a spiral track. The optical stylus shines a laser beam into the track. Where there are no pits the beam is reflected back into a photoelectric cell that converts the light to electrical current. Where there are no pits, no light is reflected back. This results in a pulsating electrical current which is converted to digital data.

3. Describe how it is possible to have a double-sided, double-layered DVD.

    A double-sided disc actually consists of two DVDs bonded together back-to-back. Each of these discs consists of two layers of recorded medium, separated by a microscopically thin layer of gold. When the read laser is focused on one layer, it ignores the other, and vice versa.

5. In as much detail as you can muster, describe how each component of a computer system contributes to the overall multimedia process. Don't confine your thinking to just this chapter, but consider what you've learned from previous chapters as well.

    CPU speed is important because a decision has to be made as to what data sets are going to be sent to what devices. The amount of RAM is also important because the fewer trips to the hard drive we have to make the faster overall performance is going to be. As far as the video card is concerned, both speed and overall capabilities come into play. Speed dictates how fast frames can be processed and sent to the monitor, while other capabilities dictate image quality. And when an application is being run directly from the CD-ROM, then the speed of that device is a critical factor.

The 64K$ Questions

1. The first CD-ROMs designed for use on a computer provided data throughput of _____.

    b. 150KB/s

3. The recording layer on a CDR consists of _____.

    a. Pthalocyanine dye

5. Which of the following media separates two separate recording layers with a microscopically thin layer of gold.

    d. DVD

7. The 15-pin connector on the back of a sound card is used for what device? Choose all that apply.

    a. Joystick and d. MIDI devices

9. The conversion of an analog wave form into a digital signal is known as _____.

    Pulse Code Modulation

Chapter 18

Brain Drain

1. Describe in as much detail as possible the differences between how a line printer and a dot matrix printer compile images.

    Older line printers generated only a single line of type at a time and delivered it to the printer. Later generations divided the page into zones, but either way, generating graphics was a process that ranged from impossible to primitive. Dot matrix printers treated the page as a single graphic and outputted the entire page at once. In this way, images could be created. Line printers are extremely fast and suitable for form generation, while dot matrix printers will be needed any time pictures must be drawn.

3. What are the key differences between thermal inkjet printers and piezoelectric inkjet printers?

    Both types begin with very tiny tubes that fill with ink. The thermal printer has a mechanism that keeps the ink in the print head heated to just below its boiling point. When a drop of ink is needed, a heating coil applies just enough heat to pass the boiling point and a bubble of ink pops out. The piezoelectric printer uses a crystal instead. An electrical charge causes the crystal to vibrate, forcing a drop of ink onto the page.

5. List as many different things as you can that define an IEEE-1284-compliant device and/or cable.

   It must support compatibility mode, nibble mode, byte mode, EPP, and ECP modes.

THE $64K QUESTIONS

1. Two different forms of impact printer include (pick two) _____.
   c. Dot matrix and d. Daisy wheel

3. During the laser printing process, the paper is charged by _____.
   d. The transfer roller

5. What component prevents the paper from adhering to the print drum after the toner is transferred?
   a. The separation pad

7. If you wished to hang a scanner, an external CD-ROM, and a printer all off the same parallel port, which mode would be most suitable?
   d. ECP

9. A printer capable of duplex printing does what?
   a. It prints on both sides of the page.

CHAPTER 19

BRAIN DRAIN

1. How many different components can you think of that are designed differently for laptops than they are desktops?

   At a minimum the list should include the keyboard, pointing device, hard drive, memory, and all removable drives. The display is debatable because LCD displays are becoming more popular for desktop machines these days.

3. Describe the three main forms of battery used by laptops over the years and how they differ.

   NiCad batteries were the earliest. They suffered greatly from battery memory and had a very poor ration of charging time to operating time. Ni-MH batteries greatly improved on the charge ratio, but still suffered from battery memory. Today's Li-Ion batteries don't suffer from battery memory at all and have very favorable charge ratios.

5. You own a laptop computer and a docking station. Nearly every time you boot your machine it goes through the Plug 'n Play process. Why is this and how can you stop this from happening?

    The docking station has a completely different device configuration than the bare laptop. So the OS needs to reconfigure each time the machine boots. By configuring a different hardware profile for each configuration, during the boot process you will be prompted to select which way you want the OS to boot.

THE 64K$ QUESTIONS

1. The memory package typically used by notebook computers is the _____.
    b. SO-DIMM

3. However, many older laptops were equipped with _____ displays.
    a. Passive matrix

5. Two characteristics that might prevent two different AC adapters from being interchangeable are _____ and _____. (Pick two.)
    b. The type of connector used to interconnect the adapter to the laptop, and d. Output voltage

7. Which layer of a PC card driver notifies the computer when a device has been removed or inserted?
    d. Socket Services

9. What pointing device is most sensitive to the person's individual electrostatic charge?
    a. The trackpad

CHAPTER 20

BRAIN DRAIN

1. Describe in detail two main tricks a modem must perform to transmit data over a telephone wire.

    First, it must convert parallel data into serial format for transmission over the wire. Then it must take digital data and turn it into an analog electrical signal. On the receiving end, it must reverse both processes.

3. Describe in detail how asynchronous communication works and where it might be used.

    With asynchronous communications, the transmitting device simply throws data onto the wire and assumes it will get there. There is no error correction possible, although error detection in the form of parity is sometimes used. It is used for broadcasts, browsing the network, and transmissions of single packets of data.

5. What are some limitations of DSL?

The user must be within 18,000 feet of the telecom's central office, and the signal can't pass over fiber, past bridge taps, or cross loading coils.

THE 64K$ QUESTIONS

1. What device on a modem is responsible for serial/parallel conversions?
    a. The UART

3. A device that can only transmit data, but not receive, it is working in _____ mode.
    c. Simplex

5. When transferring large files, most modems manufactured today use _____ as their error correction method.
    c. CRC

7. Basic Rate ISDN provides _____.
    c. 2 64K B channels and 1 16K D channel

9. Cable modem users should ALWAYS install a _____.
    b. Firewall

CHAPTER 21

BRAIN DRAIN

1. Review the various versions of MS-DOS and come up with the following answers:
    a. What was the first version of DOS that supported 1.44MB floppy diskettes?
        Answer: DOS 3.3
    b. What version supported the first hard drive?
        Answer: DOS 2.0
    c. What year did MS-DOS provide the first support for memory beyond 1MB?
        Answer: DOS 5.0

3. Now describe the software boot process in detail, specifically using MS-DOS as the OS being booted.

As the MBR is being read, a pointer directs the boot process to the first line of code. In MS-DOS, the first thing to run is IO.SYS. IO.SYS locates and loads (but does not run) lines in CONFIG.SYS. It then locates and runs MSDOS.SYS. MSDOS.SYS executes the commands in CONFIG.SYS, and then loads AUTOEXEC.BAT. It then locates and runs COMMAND.COM. COMMAND.COM runs AUTOEXEC.BAT, and the system is running.

5. Define the function and purpose of AUTOEXEC.BAT and discuss some of the commands that might be used in that file.

AUTOEXEC.BAT runs commands and loads programs that are designed to stay RAM resident while the system is running. This can include any executable file on the system. Internal commands include PATH, PROMPT, SET, CLS, and others.

THE 64K$ QUESTIONS

1. What is the file loaded on the ROM BIOS chip that locates the MBR and turns the boot process over to the OS?
   d. Bootstrap Loader

3. Which DOS file is credited with being the kernel?
   d. MSDOS.SYS

5. How much conventional memory was available to a program running in MS-DOS?
   a. <640K (Don't forget that certain device drivers and core OS files had to be loaded into conventional memory.)

7. The function of DOS that provides a roadmap that leads to a specific file on a drive is known as the _____.
   b. Path

9. A variable applied to a specific command that instructs that command to perform in a particular manner is known as a _____.
   d. Trigger

11. If you wanted to erase an entire directory, along with all of its subdirectories and all the files contained within, which command would you use?
    d. DELTREE

13. Which of the following is the correct syntax for a STACKS command?
    d. STACKS=9,256

15. You've added a new device to your system. Which of the following must you do in order to make the device work properly under DOS?
    c. Add a DEVICE= statement to CONFIG.SYS to load the driver file.

17. By default, DOS will keep _____ file handles active at once.
    b. 8

19. Which of the following prompts is the result of PROMPT PG?
    c. C:\DOS>

CHAPTER 22

BRAIN DRAIN

1. Several times in this chapter, it was pointed out that Windows 3.x products were not true OSs. Explain why this is so.

   WIN3.x cannot load itself without MS-DOS being present.

3. Discuss the concept of the virtual machine. Why is it that several virtual machines can be running on a single computer at any given time?

   The virtual machine assures the application running within that it is the only application running on the system. It keeps other applications from stepping on its memory addresses and from accessing the CPU while it is present.

5. How do virtual device drivers differ from a "real" device driver?

   A virtual device is a collection of software files that intercepts hardware calls. The virtual device is what actually communicates with the hardware.

THE 64K$ QUESTIONS

1. Steve Jobs named the LISA after _____.
   d. His secretary.

3. Which of the following features of the 80386 microprocessor did Windows 3.x exclusively take advantage of when running in 386 Enhanced mode?
   c. Virtual real mode

5. Windows 3.x versions all use _____ in order to give the user the sense that multiple programs are running at the same time.
   b. Cooperative multitasking

7. Applications in Windows 3.x all run in _____.
   c. Ring 3

9. Which operational mode of Windows took advantage of memory beyond 1MB, but could not address virtual memory?
   b. Standard mode

11. Which operational mode of Windows did legacy DOS applications run in?

    a. Real mode

13. Which of the following Windows functions allowed memory beyond 1MB to be utilized?

    a. EMM386.EXE

15. Which Windows feature allows the user to move data seamlessly from one application to another on the fly?

    d. DDE

17. What is the default size of a typical UMB?

    a. 8K

19. What was the typical extension for a virtual device driver in Windows 3.x?

    c. VDD

CHAPTER 23

BRAIN DRAIN

1. Discuss the differences between cooperative multitasking and pre-emptive multitasking.

    Cooperative multitasking allows the application to dictate whether or not to give up system resources, while pre-emptive multitasking gives that control to the OS. In cooperative multitasking, a renegade app can make the system appear to be hung.

3. Draw a rough diagram of how the WIN9x Virtual Machine Manager handles difference applications, including legacy DOS apps, WIN3.x apps, and WIN9x apps.

    Diagrams will vary somewhat, but all should have each WIN9x app in its own VM with unlimited resources, each DOS app in its own VM with 1MB of RAM allocated, and all WIN3.x apps in a single machine.

5. Discuss how WINMe was responsible for a number of gray hairs in the heads of technicians worldwide.

    While it had the look and feel of WIN98, it was actually a 32-bit app. It provided only limited support for 16-bit drivers and apps.

THE 64K$ QUESTIONS

1. WIN95 was originally intended for release in the year _____.

    d. 1992

3. WIN95 required, at the minimum _____.
   d. A 20MHz 386DX processor

5. WIN95 required, at the minimum _____.
   c. VGA

7. Which of the following was not a requirement for full PnP functionality?
   b. A PnP device driver

9. Which protocol was incorporated into WIN95 for the first time in Microsoft's history?
   d. TCP/IP

11. WIN95 did not incorporate any version of MS-DOS into its structure.
    b. False

13. A 16-bit mouse driver would interface with _____.
    c. GDI.DLL

15. Multiple networking clients on a single computer were made possible by the addition of _____.
    c. The Installable File System

17. What version of WIN9x was the first to provide support for USB?
    b.   WIN95 SR2

19. What version of WIN9x was the first to provide support for DirectX?
    d. Windows 98SE

CHAPTER 24

BRAIN DRAIN

1. Discuss the differences between a clean install and an upgrade. While you're at it, discuss the pros and cons of each type of installation.

   > A clean install involves partitioning and formatting the hard drive from scratch and installing a brand new OS. The upgrade takes an existing OS and migrates all the old settings into the new OS. This is good in that the user gets a familiar look and feel. It's bad in that any flaws in the old installation show up in the new one.

3. Now discuss the different setup phases for Windows 98 and how they differ from Windows 95.

   > *Phase 1*: Preparing to Run Windows 98 Setup. Some preliminary files are copied to temporary hidden directories. On an upgrade, these files are PRECOPY1.CAB and PRECOPY2.CAb. On a clean install, it is simply MINI.CAB.

Phase 2: Collecting Information About Your Computer. The user reads the license agreement and selects a directory into which Windows will be installed. The user is given the opportunity to create a startup diskette.

Phase 3: Copying Windows 98 Files to Your Computer. This phase copies the Windows 98 files to your computer.

Phase 4: Restarting Your Computer. During this first restart, Setup collects the information it extracted from CONFIG.SYS and AUTOEXEC.BAT and integrates those settings into the registry. Devices known to cause issues are REM'ed out.

Phase 5: Setting up Hardware and Finalizing Settings. PnP does its thing, device drivers are installed, and any networking settings that were selected are burned into the registry. You now have a WIN98 computer. Congratulations, I think.

5. How did Microsoft take the mouse from a cute little toy to a powerful tool with the release of Windows 95?

Popup menus were added that can be brought up with the click of the right mouse button. This makes it significantly easier to navigate Windows.

THE 64K$ QUESTIONS

1. During an upgrade, Windows 95 could extract information about programs installed over WIN3.x by opening and reading the _____.
   c. Group files

3. Which of the following is not a setup phase for WIN95?
   d. Hardware setup

5. How does Windows Setup remove AUTOEXEC.BAT or CONFIG.SYS lines that may cause problems during an upgrade?
   b. It places a REM statement in front of the offending command.

7. In order to bring up Display Properties, the user can _____.
   a. Right-click the Desktop and click Properties or d. Click Start→Settings→Control Panel→Display Properties

9. Control Panel can be accessed from which two of the following places?
   a. My Computer
   OR
   d. The Start menu

11. You've just installed a new sound card, and it places a handy little applet somewhere on your computer that allows you to adjust volume without constantly reaching up to the speakers. Where is the icon for that program most likely to be placed?
    d. On the Toolbar

13. Windows applications are consistent amongst themselves because of a feature built into Windows called the _____.

   b. CUI

15. Which Control Panel applet allows the user to turn off Daylight Savings Time?

   d. Time/Date

17. What are two methods of mapping a folder on the network server to your local machine to appear as though it were a local drive?

   a. In the folders pane, right-click the remote resource and select Map Network Drive and d. Click Tools→Map Network Drive

19. Which of the following shortcuts selects all text in an open document?

   c. <Ctrl>+A

CHAPTER 25

BRAIN DRAIN

1. Discuss the differences between symmetric and asymmetric multiprocessing. Why is one more efficient than the other?

With asymmetric multiprocessing, one processor handles OS and system, while the other processor crunches data and applications files. With symmetric multiprocessing, all processors are sharing tasks equally. With asymmetric, one processor might be running full tilt while the other is virtually idle.

3. Discuss some of the security enhancements Microsoft incorporated into NT.

Resources can be individually secured, with different users having different levels of access, or no access at all. Also, the ability to perform certain tasks on the machine and/or network can be managed.

5. List the different domain models supported by NT and describe the differences.

Single Domain: One PDC controls all accounts. Multiple BDCs can assist with logon authentication.

Single Master Domain: One PDC controls all user accounts, but other resource domains may control non-user objects on the network, such as a large database.

Multiple Master Domain: Several single domains have been collected into a large network. Trusts determine how much access each domain has with the others.

Compete Trust: It's a multiple master domain in which every domain trusts every other domain explicitly.

THE 64K$ QUESTIONS

1. The first version of an NT product was demonstrated in _____.
   b. 1991

3. The NT feature that provided security on a file or folder level was called _____.
   d. NTFS

5. NT 4.0 Server, Enterprise Edition can support up to _____ processors.
   c. 8MB

7. NT 4.0 Server requires a minimum of _____ RAM in order to run on a RISC machine.
   c. 16MB

9. In an NT domain the machine that maintains a copy of the security database that is updated periodically is called a _____.
   b. Backup Domain Controller

11. In order to get to the logon screen in Windows NT 4.0 (any version), you must first _____.
   c. Press <Ctrl>+<Alt>+<Delete>

13. You have created a new file on the system and assigned one password on the file that allows the users who access it full control, and another password that only lets them read the file. This is an example of _____.
   c. Share level security

15. In order to tighten up security on your network, your administrator has divided the network into two separate domains. One of these domains is where all the users log on and the other hosts the company's database servers. This is an example of _____ .
   b. The Single Master Domain

17. In order to install NT onto a machine, it is best to start with a freshly prepared hard disk on which no partitions have been defined. This allows NT to prepare the drives using its own utility.
   b. False

19. The licensing mode is selecting during the phase of the installation.
   b. Text

CHAPTER 26

BRAIN DRAIN

1. Discuss several ways that the NT boot process differs from that WIN9x.

   First of all, the MBR doesn't point to the first line of OS code. It points to a Boot Loader file that allows the user to select what OS will be run. Also, unless a file called NTLDR is located on the root partition, NT won't boot. Toward the end of the boot process, before the user can log on, he or she must press <Ctrl>+<Alt>+<Delete> to bring up the logon screen.

3. What are the two operating modes of NT? Discuss them in as much detail as you can muster.

   Kernel mode and user mode. Kernel mode is where the OS kernel files and executive services all run. These all run in privileged mode. The user mode processes are the OS processes that intercept requests from the user or applications. These run in nonprivileged mode.

5. Discuss memory management in NT and how the concept of virtual memory is critical to the OS.

   Since there is only so much physical memory available to NT, the OS makes use of physical hard drive space as virtual memory. When a thread becomes inactive for a period of time, it will be moved over to virtual memory to make space for a process that needs to be moved to physical memory. Once that process is needed again, the procedure is reversed.

THE 64K$ QUESTIONS

1. Which of the following files is not a part of the NT boot process?
   a. WIN.COM

3. What file system is not supported by NT?
   d. FAT32

5. Which of the following is not a phase of the NT load process?
   d. File System Initialization

7. Kernel Mode services run at processor _____.
   a. Ring 0

9. The Executive Services run at _____.
   a. Ring 0

11. Unix applications running in the NT environment are known as _____ apps.

    a. POSIX

13. Threads of code that are time sensitive can be assured of getting first crack at the processor because they will be given a priority _____.

    d. Between 16 and 31

15. On a system with 128MB of installed RAM, an application in NT will be assigned an address space equal to _____.

    d. 2GB

17. If a computer has been configured to divide all data equally between two or more hard drives, with no allowance for data recovery, this computer has been configured for _____.

    a. RAID 0

19. If you want to see what IRQs are being used by your system under NT, you would use _____.

    d. NT Diagnostics

CHAPTER 27

BRAIN DRAIN

1. What are some of the different actions that are taken by Dr. Watson when there is an application error on the system? How are they useful to the user?

    It generates a log file in which it stores information specific to the crash. Next it will create a crash dump file, which consists of all the information that was stored in RAM at the time of the failure. The end user might find the log file useful in determining what failed and when. The crash dump is useful only to Microsoft programmers and their accountants.

3. You suspect that CPU performance has become a serious bottleneck in the system. How can you use Performance Monitor to back up your suspicions?

    By logging the percentage of time the CPU is being utilized by both system processes and user processes, the administrator can not only see how often the CPU is maxed out, but at what times of the day saturation occurs.

5. Discuss as many of the Administrative tools as you can think of. Point out how they are useful to the system administrator.

    At a minimum, the student should mention User Manager (for creating and maintaining user accounts), Disk Administrator (for managing mass storage), Event Viewer (for troubleshooting system errors), Network Monitor (for monitoring network traffic), and Remote Access Admin (for creating and managing network access over a modem).

THE 64K$ QUESTIONS

1. A crash dump is _____.
   c. A byte-by-byte copy of all information stored in RAM to the hard drive that occurs after a fatal system error

3. When a fatal system error does occur, NT will copy all the information in RAM to a file. By default that file is stored in the _____ directory.
   c. %windir%

5. The individual variables that can be watched by Performance Monitor are called _____.
   d. Objects

7. Page faults/sec is a variable that measures _____.
   a. How many times the CPU requests data that does not exist in RAM

9. Network Monitor automatically loads when you install NT for the first time.
   b. False

11. Of these sections, _____ of them might be useful to the average technician.
    b. Two

13. Which of the following Administrative tools will be found in NT Server, but not on NT Workstation?
    b. Network Client Administrator

15. RAS is a service that exists on Server versions of NT only.
    b. False

17. Which two of the following tasks can be accomplished from the boot diskette created by Network Client Administrator?
    b. Install an OS onto a workstation remotely and c. Install a client onto a workstation remotely

19. The Policy Editor is where the administrator would go in order to enable auditing.
    b. False

CHAPTER 28

BRAIN DRAIN

1. Describe the ways the four WIN2K versions differ. Include in your discussion such details as min/max memory support and how many CPUs each one will support.

Version	RAM (min/rec/max)	CPU (min/# supported)	HDD Requirements
Professional	64MB/4GB	P166/2	650MB for installation/2GB minimum recommended
Server	128MB/256MB/4GB	P166/4	1GB
Advanced Server	128MB/256MB/8GB	P166/8	1GB
Datacenter	256MB/512MB/64GB	PIII Xeon/16 (32 via OEM)	2GB

3. What is the function of Last Known Good? Explain why the user logon process is important concerning whether Last Known Good will work or not.

The Last Known Good points to the registry entries that were valid the last time the system successfully booted as far as the user logon. If the failure occurred after user logon was complete, Last Known Good is useless.

5. How does Safe Mode differ from Safe Mode with Networking Support?

Safe Mode with Networking Support loads the device drivers for the NIC and all network configuration settings.

THE 64K$ QUESTIONS

1. Windows 2000 Professional requires a minimum of _____ RAM in order to work.
   b. 64MB

3. Windows 2000 Server requires a minimum of _____ RAM in order to work.
   c. 128MB

5. Windows 2000 Datacenter requires a minimum of _____ RAM in order to work.
   d. 256MB

7. Only the Server versions of WIN2K support EFS.
   b. False

9. WIN2K Advanced Server supports up to _____ processors.

   c. 8

11. The WIN2K floppy disk setup procedure involves _____ diskettes.

    b. 4

13. Which of the following two items are required in order to install WIN2K from a remote network location?

    a. A distribution server and b. a PXE-compliant boot diskette

15. Which of the following does NOT support an upgrade path to WIN2K Server?

    a. NT Server 3.51

17. At what point does the WIN2K boot process write final information to the Last Known Good section of the registry?

    c. The instant the user hits enter after providing his/her credentials.

19. You've just attempted to boot the system using Safe Mode, and you get a BSOD informing you that a valid boot partition could not be found by the system. This most likely means that _____.

    d. The system uses a third-party hard disk controller not supported internally by WIN2K

CHAPTER 29

BRAIN DRAIN

1. Which of the topics discussed in this chapter aren't possible without the introduction of NTFS5?

   EFS and disk quotas

3. Describe three MMC consoles that assist the administrator in managing Active Directory components.

   Active Directory Sites and Services: Allows the administrator to control the services that are running and to manage the network topology.

   Active Directory Users and Computers: Allows the administrator to create and manage accounts for devices, individual users, and groups on the network.

   Active Directory Domains and Trusts: This is where administrators manage local and remote domains and create or break down the trusts between domains.

5. What are some of the major differences between basic and dynamic disks?

   A dynamic disk can be used to create disk arrays, it can host pointers to remote disks, and it can support drives beyond the letter Z.

THE 64K$ QUESTIONS

1. Which of the following is Active Directory not capable of managing?
   e. It manages all of the above.

3. Active Directory is an implementation of the _____ protocol.
   d. LDAP

5. Information about a remote server would be found in _____.
   c. Active Directory Sites and Services

7. New hardware can be configured in the _____ wizard.
   a. Add/Remove New Hardware

9. When a digital signature is added to a device driver, that information is stored in the _____ file.
   d. CAT

11. Decoding of files encrypted by a disgruntled employee is made possible by way of the _____.
    a. EFS Recovery Agent

13. If disk quotas have been enabled on a server, the user can double his or her storage capacity by using compression.
    b. False

15. In WIN2K, there is a limit to _____ disk volumes on a system.
    d. There is no limit

17. Which of the following cannot be done on a dynamic disk?
    c. Create partitions

19. Managing disks in WIN2K is done in the _____ console.
    b. Disk Administrator

CHAPTER 30

BRAIN DRAIN

1. List the various versions of Windows XP that are available, and discuss how they differ from one another.

   Home: Can only handle peer-to-peer networks and doesn't support multiprocessing
   Professional: Can join a domain and supports dual-processor machines.

Tablet PC: Scaled down version that only has I/O functions for this type of hardware

64-bit Edition: Coded to take advantage of 64-bit microprocessors.

3. List some features that are brand new to XP. Discuss how they improve the product.

Side-by-side DLL Support: Allows older versions of a Dynamic Link Library coexist with a new one without being overwritten.

Integrated CDR-CD/RW operation: Allows drag and drop capabilities for these devices without requiring a third-party applicationl

Remote Desktop: Allows a user to take control of an XP machine from across the country.

ClearType: Makes for a prettier display Network Location Awareness: An appropriately enabled machine can reconfigure itself if moved to another segment on the network.

Device Driver Rollback: When you install the inevitable driver that crashes your machine, you can turn back time to the one that still worked.

Product Activation: The Piracy Police can keep track of what machines a product is installed on

5. How is Control Panel different between XP and WIN2K?

The differences are primarily cosmetic. Applications and shortcuts have been collected into "logical" groupings.

THE 64K$ QUESTIONS

1. Two of the limitations of Home Edition are that _____.
    a. It only supports one CPU and d. It cannot join a domain
3. XP Home requires a minimum of _____ RAM in order to run.
    b. 128MB
5. The absolute minimum CPU required by either Home or Professional is a _____.
    b. 300MHz PII
7. The feature that was added to EFS that makes it different between XP and WIN2K is _____.
    c. Files can be encrypted for use by entire groups instead of only individuals
9. Which of the following is not a new feature to XP?
    a. Group Policy Management

11. You can take over control of another user's system and help with a problem because of a protocol known as _____.

    c. Remote Desktop Protocol

13. XP offers two methods of recovering from an improperly installed device driver. What are these two methods?

    c. Device Driver Rollback and d. System Restore

15. The Start menu in XP is divided into _____ sections.

    b. 2

17. If you need to check the settings of your sound card's device driver, you would find them in the _____ section of Control Panel. (Choose all that apply.)

    a. Sounds, Speech, and Audio Devices

19. Which of the following is not an adjustment a user can make in Accessibility Options?

    d. Mouse cursor trails

CHAPTER 31

There are no exercises in Chapter Thirty-One.

CHAPTER 32

BRAIN DRAIN

1. Should you desire to set up a small network in your home, what would be the bare necessities you would need to get up and running?

    Transceivers on each networked device, an OS installed that supports networking, properly configured networking protocols, and a properly configured client.

3. In detail, discuss the difference between a collision domain and a broadcast domain.

    A collision domain is all wiring segments over which any two packets might encounter one another without being blocked by a router or bridge. A broadcast domain is all devices that are configured in such a way as to receive broadcast messages from one another.

5. Discuss the differences between hardware protocols and networking protocols.

    Hardware protocols dictate how data will be encoded and sent out over the medium. This would include protocols such as Ethernet, Token Ring or FDDI. Networking protocols are the ones that set the rules for two applications or

THE 64K$ QUESTIONS

1. The maximum distance twisted-pair cable can be run without assistance is _____.
    b. 100 meters

3. The proper device for interconnecting a token ring network segment to an Ethernet segment is a _____.
    d. Bridge

5. In order to interconnect two autonomous networks into a singler larger network, you would need a _____.
    c. Router

7. Two hardware protocols that make use of a ring topology are _____ and _____. (Pick two.)
    c. FDDI and d. Token Ring

9. The protocol of choice for the Internet is
    c. TCP/IP

CHAPTER 33

BRAIN DRAIN

1. Define a workgroup and a domain. Discuss the differences between the two.

    A workgroup is any group of devices configured into a communications link that can communicate among each other and that perform similar functions. A domain is all devices and objects within a single administrative umbrella.

3. Define what a protocol is, and describe its role in networking computers.

    A protocol is a piece of software running on a system that acts as a translator so that it speaks the same language as the other devices on the network, and also acts as an ambassador so that all devices follow the same rules of behavior.

5. Go through the process of configuring a computer to use TCP/IP on the network.

    Start the Network Properties applet, highlight TCP/IP and select Properties. If you want to use DHCP, then select the box that allows it to automatically be assigned a configuration, and that's it. To statically configure TCP/IP, you must type in a compatible IP address, and a correct subnet mask.

THE 64K$ QUESTIONS

1. A collection of independently managed computers and/or devices on a network would be called a _____.
   a. Workgroup

3. The icon for browsing the network in WIN9x is called _____.
   c. Network Neighborhood

5. Which of the following protocols is the one most commonly used on the Internet?
   d. TCP/IP

7. Which of the following protocols was developed by Microsoft for its NOS?
   a. NetBEUI

9. If a small network has several users, and each user is capable of setting up his or her own shares and assigning individual passwords for each share, what kind of security is that network using?
   c. Share level

11. Shares on a Windows network are created in _____.
    b. Windows Explorer

13. Internet Connection Sharing is installed by default on WIN98 computers.
    b. False

15. Which of the two following items must be configured on every computer running TCP/IP?
    a. IP address and c. Subnet mask

17. A single number in an IP address, divided by periods, is called _____.
    c. An octet

19. A Class A address uses _____ to identify the network address.
    a. The first octet

CHAPTER 34

BRAIN DRAIN

1. List the intermediate levels across which information traveling between two machines communicating over the Internet must travel.

   User's PC   User services
   User's datacom   ISP backbone
   The local loop carrier   Online content
   The ISP point of presence   Origin of content

3. Discuss the differences between origin of content and online content.

   Online content refers to the overall availability of information on a network or across the Internet. Origin of content is a specific URL or Web page.

THE 64K$ QUESTIONS

1. Who invented the Internet?

   Hopefully, you didn't take this question seriously. If you answered at all, b. Licklidder is the most appropriate choice, unless you happen to be a member of DNC.

3. The intermediate level that moves user data from the modem to the ISP is called _____.

   d. The local loop carrier

5. The page you view when browsing the Internet is an example of _____.

   b. Origin of content

CHAPTER 35

BRAIN DRAIN

1. Discuss the differences between open-ended questions and closed-ended questions. Make up a list of open-ended questions that you might ask a client who is having computer problems.

   An open-ended question will result in a reply that leads to the possibility of further questioning. A closed-ended question results in an answer that goes nowhere. Make up your own darned list.

3. How many different places can you think of that might provide documentation and/ or troubleshooting help for a problem you can't diagnose?

    A hard-copy manual; the CD of the OS driver or application causing the problem; and Web-based options, including the manufacturer's support site as well as independent sites such as http://basichardware.50megs.com.

5. Why is a slowly failing power supply such a problem?

    Because it can mimic the symptoms of just about every other device on the system, yet still power the computer.

THE $64K QUESTIONS

1. Which of the following issues is addressed by re-creating a problem before trying to fix it?

    d. User errors

3. Of the following list, which one will test a serial port without having either the device or the cable affect the test?

    a. A loopback adapter

5. Boot failure problems are rarely the result of _____ failure.

    c. Software. A corrupted OS can prevent a system from getting past POST. But the system itself has booted to the point of locating the hard disk. An argument could be made that a corrupted boot sector is a software problem. But I'm not getting involved in that argument. It's purely semantic.

7. The twenty-eighth wire on a floppy disk cable is the _____ wire.

    c. Master/slave indicator

9. What two drive size limitations appear as a result of older BIOS?

    b. 8GB and c. 32GB

GLOSSARY

8.3 naming convention: A file-naming scheme used by earlier file systems that permitted file names of up to eight characters, plus an extension of up to three characters.

Active Desktop: A method of configuring the Windows desktop to behave as if it is a Web page, allowing single-click activation of icons and other Web-like features.

Active partition: A primary partition on a hard disk drive that has been identified in the MBR as being the bootable partition.

Address bus: A bank of wires running throughout the system and into the CPU that specifies specific locations. The total addressable space is calculated as 2x, where x represents the total number of wires in the bus.

Allocation scan: A BIOS routine that reassigns resources to Plug 'n Play devices installed on a computer system.

Alpha channel: Eight bits used by 32-bit True Color to apply effects such as translucency and fogging.

Alternating current: An electrical current that reverses the direction of current flow many times each second.

Answer modem: The device that is being called.

Anti-aliasing: A process through which textures in an image are redrawn to more accurately reflect perceived distance.

Areal density: The total amount of storage capacity for a specific unit of area on the surface of the drive platter.

Arithmetic logic unit: A subcomponent of a microprocessor responsible for executing simple mathematical calculations, such as add, subtract, multiply, and divide. It cannot perform floating point calculations.

Asymmetric multiprocessing: A method by which an operating system makes use of more than one processor, loading OS code onto one processor and application code and user data onto all others.

Asynchronous communication: A form of serial communication that transmits data a byte at a time over a single conductor.

Asynchronous timing: A device on a bus can deliver its data at any speed it sees fit to a reserved area of memory called a buffer. Data is then fed to the CPU at a rate optimal to the CPU.

Attribute: A property assigned to a file or directory on the system that defines certain characteristics of that file.

Average access time: The amount of time required by a disk drive to lock on to the first sector that contains data requested by the controller.

Average seek time: The amount of time it takes to locate and lock on to the first track that contains data requested by the controller.

Back-side bus: A portion of the EDB. It is the path that data takes as it moves from cache loaded on the CPU's die into the CPU's registers.

Basic disk: A disk that has been configured to conform to the legacy partition-oriented approach to file systems.

Battery memory: A phenomenon exhibited by rechargeable batteries where the pattern of recent charge cycles affects the maximum charge the battery will accept.

Baud rate: The electronic frequency over which data is transmitted.

B-channel: A carrier channel used by ISDN for transmitting user data at 64KB/s. Multiple B-channels can be combined for higher transmission rates.

Beaconing: A process that occurs on a token ring network in which each station on the network sends a signal to its upstream neighbor and its downstream neighbor asking if it has seen the token lately.

Benchmarking: A method of measuring the base performance of a device or system before any load is placed on it.

Bezel: The plastic frame that masks off the unusable part of a monitor's image.

Binary: A Base2 counting system that consists of the two characters 0 and 1.

BIOS extension: A string of code that interfaces the operating system to the BIOS interrupts.

Bit cell: The collection of magnetized particles that comprise a single bit on magnetic media.

Bit rate: The speed at which data travels over the wire, usually expressed in bits per second (bps) or kilobits per second (KB/s). Don't confuse this with bytes per second, and don't confuse it with baud rate.

Bit: A single zero or one, resulting in a single transition between off and on.

Blackout: A complete loss of power to an entire area.

Block mode: The data transfer setting that allows multiple commands to be moved over an interface on a single interrupt cycle.

Block transfer: The movement of multiple commands over an interface on a single interrupt cycle.

Block: The number of sectors on a hard drive that UFS uses as the smallest recognizable data unit.

Boot block: A feature present on most modern system boards that allows the system to boot to a minimal configuration, including floppy drive support, in the event that the BIOS is corrupted or destroyed by a virus.

Bootstrap loader: A program that resides on the BIOS chip that is responsible for locating and initializing the Master Boot Record.

Bounded media: Any medium that physically connects a device to the network by way of a tangible cable.

Branch prediction: The ability of certain CPUs to be able to predict a situation where either one of two separate subroutines may be run, depending on the results of processing code not yet completed. A CPU capable of branch prediction will load a few lines of code from each subroutine.

Break code: A signal generated by a keyswitch when the key is released.

Bridge: A specialized circuit that moves data between two disparate devices or busses in a such a manner that both devices become compatible.

Brownout: A drop in voltages that lasts a noticeable period of time.

Bubblejet printer: Another term for a thermal printer.

Burn-in: The tendency for a CRT monitor to permanently etch an image onto the inner surface of the tube if the image stays on the screen for too long a period.

Burst mode: The speed at which data moves from the R/W heads to a drive's buffer memory. Also known as internal host transfer rate.

Bus mastering: A technology that allows two compatible devices to exchange data directly without requiring arbitration or processing of that data by the CPU.

Byte: Any combination of eight zeros or ones.

Byte mode: Like nibble mode, it provides bidirectional communication between the printer and the computer. Unlike nibble mode, it sends eight bits on each cycle. Speeds of byte mode are comparable to those of compatibility mode.

Cabinet file: A compressed file that holds a large number of smaller files that can be uncompressed and installed as needed.

Caddy: On a CD-ROM (or similar) drive, it is a form of loading mechanism that consists of a plastic CD holder that encases the CD while it is in the drive.

Capacitor: An electrical component that stores electrical current and provides it to the circuit as needed.

Capacity: The total number of bits a memory chip holds.

Card services: The portion of a PC card driver that interprets the command set for a specific device.

CAS latency: The delay that occurs between RAS and CAS. Also known as RAS/CAS delay.

Cascade: A process by which multiple circuits are linked together in such a way that they appear to the system as a single device.

Cathode: A negatively charged device that emits a stream of electrons when heated.

Central arbitration point: A circuit that offloads the responsibility for refereeing and processing the transfer of data between two bus-mastering devices.

Channel: A dedicated path for data to take that prevents other data from competing for time on the bus.

Character set: The code used to generate printable symbols that human users can understand.

Checksum: An error detection/correction mechanism that works by counting the number of ones present in the payload and storing that value in the BCC block of the packet.

Chipset: A matched set of two (three on some of the older systems) ICs that control critical system functions, including bus speeds, memory types and capacity, and the type of hardware supported by a motherboard.

Chop: A 16-bit piece of data generated when music is sampled once during the digital recording procedure.

Clean install: The fresh installation of an OS over a newly partitioned and formatted hard disk.

Client: Any device or software that requires the services of another device or piece of software in order to perform its function. Also, A piece of software running from within an OS that allows the device to connect to a network.

Clock cycle: A timing signal generated by an electrical current that synchronizes data movement throughout the system. As an electrical current, a clock cycle resembles a sine wave with a rising half of the signal and a falling half.

Closed-ended question: A question that leads to an answer that provides no further insight or leads to an abrupt dead end to the discussion.

Cluster: The minimum number of sectors a specific file system can recognize as a single data unit. Another term for file allocation unit.

CMOS setup: One of the programs loaded on the BIOS chip. This particular program allows user-defined parameters relating to BIOS settings to be configured.

Coaxial: A cable over which the signal and ground both follow the same axis.

Codec: A coined term derived from two other terms, coder and decoder. A codec is an IC that has been programmed to convert data from one form to another. An example of this would be a chip that takes analog signals and converts them to digital, and vice versa.

Coil: An electrical component consisting of tightly wound wire that is used to filter out AC current and low-frequency signals.

Cold fusing: A process used by some phase-change printers that uses pressure rollers to press the ink into the paper.

Color depth: The number of individual hues that can be generated by a given display setting.

COM port: A predefined combination of an IRQ and an I/O address configured for communications devices.

Command overhead: The number of instructions that must be executed in order to carry out a specific request, combined with the speed at which the device can carry out those instructions.

Command overlapping: The ability of a device to start processing a command even before the command issued prior to it has completed its cycle.

Command queuing: Allows a device to store a series of commands in a buffer area, assuring that as one command is completed another one is rolled up to the gate and ready to go.

Compatibility mode: A unidirectional signal that is used to send data to the printer. This is also known as Centronix mode. Very slow, at approximately 150KB/s.

Computer: Any device that can accept the input of user data, process that data according to a specific set of instructions, and then provide the results of that processing in the form of output to the end user.

Conductor: Any substance that encourages the flow of electricity. Also the man at the podium that waves a white stick in front of the musicians.

Container: A collection of objects on the system or network that have been gathered together into a single administrative unit.

Continuity module: A null memory module that fills the empty banks on a system using Rambus memory.

Control set: A collection of registry settings that defines the system configuration for Windows during the boot process.

Conventional memory: The first megabyte of RAM, divided into 640K for running programs and 384K reserved for system use.

Convergence: The accuracy with which multiple beams of electrons or light can focus on the same point.

Cool: A shift in the color of an image toward the blue side.

Cooperative multitasking: The ability of an OS to simultaneously run more than one program, placing responsibility on the application for relinquishing control of the system.

Co-processed: Any adapter or device that is equipped with a microprocessor that offloads some of the work of the PC's CPU.

Crash dump: A direct copy of the entire contents of system RAM copied to a file on the hard disk.

Credentials: Information provided by the user, including but not restricted to the User ID and password, that grants that user access to a system or network.

Cross-linked file: An FAU that is claimed by two or more different files, and is therefore available to none.

Crossover cable: A network patch cord that routes the transmit signal from one device to the receive terminals on the other device.

Current: The number of electrons that flow through a circuit in a fixed amount of time.

Cyanine dye: A bluish-colored dye that was used in the recording layer of early generations of CDR media.

Cycle rate: The amount of time it takes for a specific device under the control of a timing mechanism to complete one "tick" of that timer.

Cylinder: A virtual structure created by the tracks that line up vertically on the surface of each of the platters.

Data cache: A set of registers used for storing data loaded by the prefetch until such time as the CPU is ready to use it.

Data encoding mechanism: The method used by a device to convert digital information into an electronic format recognizable by the target device.

Data phase: The portion of an I/O operation that performs the actual transfer of data from device to device.

Datacom: A term coined to describe any equipment used in data communications.

D-channel: A 16KB/s or 64KB/s channel used by ISDN for control data, including synchronization, ACKs and NACKs and other non-user data.

Decimal: A Base10 counting system that consists of ten characters, 0 through 9.

Decode unit: The subcomponent of a microprocessor that takes complex instructions and breaks them down into a series of simpler instructions that the CPU is able to understand.

Default gateway: The route through which all packets that contain addresses that the transmitting device cannot resolve will be sent.

Deflection yoke: A circular array of powerful magnets that act to deflect a beam of electrons from its natural path.

Depth queuing: A mathematical algorithm that recalculates the hue and intensity of colors in respect to increasing distances.

Device driver: A piece of software running on the system that provides the command set for a specific piece of hardware.

Device ID: A unique number assigned to each device on a SCSI chain, including the host adapter, that identifies it to other devices on the chain.

Dielectric layer: A transparent layer of material above and below the recording layer of a CD-RW that dissipates the heat built up in the CD during the recording process.

Differential signaling: A method by which a single data wire on a parallel cable is matched up by a wire carrying the inverse of the signal being carried by the data wire.

Digital noise: Unwanted color artifacts introduced into a digitized image during capture and/or by imaging software during the processing of that image.

Digital signature: An encrypted piece of data added to a file to guarantee its authenticity.

Diode: An electrical component that freely permits the flow of electrons in one direction, but resists electron flow in the opposite direction.

Direct current: An electrical current that exhibits a steady directional flow from a source of relative positive voltage to a target of relative negative voltage.

Directory attribute: A single bit that identifies an entry in the directory table as being a subdirectory rather than a file.

Directory table: A database of all file names on a hard drive and the partitions with which they are associated. Other information pertaining to file system security is also contained here.

Directory: A container node of a file system that can contain other directories or files.

Disk duplexing: The duplication of data on two different hard drives hanging off of different controllers.

Disk editor: A piece of specialized software that allows a user to examine and alter the contents of a disk drive bit by bit. Disk editors even allow access to parts of the drive not normally accessible by the user, such as FAT.

Disk mirroring: The duplication of data on two different hard drives hanging off of the same controller.

Disk slack: The amount of disk storage that is wasted by null files and/or small files stored on the hard disk.

Diskette: A term typically applied to the 3.5″ floppy disk in order to distinguish it from the 5.25″ floppy disk.

Distribution server: A centralized storage location for the installation files of operating systems or applications.

Dithering: A process of blending the colors of adjacent areas in an image to make the appearance more natural.

Docking station: A device to which a laptop computer can be attached that provides additional hardware support, including I/O ports, PCI slots, and drive bays.

Domain divider switch: A device that allows external SCSI devices to be shared by multiple host computers.

Domain validation: A process by which a SCSI host adapter sends out a series of commands to each device on the chain and calculates each device's maximum data transfer rate.

Domain: A collection of all resources and users that fall under the control of a single administrative unit. In the case of Windows NT, the administrative unit would be the PDC.

Dot pitch: The distance separating two like-colored phosphors that are adjacent to one another.

Double buffering: The use of two separate buffers, so that as a frame is displayed on the monitor, another frame is in the queue, ready for display, while yet a third is being assembled by the graphics adapter.

Double-transition clocking: The movement of two transfers of data on a single clock cycle.

Drive bay: A metal frame within a computer enclosure (which may or may not be removable) that supports disk drives.

Drive rails: Devices that attach to the side of a disk drive that allow the user to install or subsequently remove it without needing any tools.

Drive translation: A technique by which an address space beyond what Int13h can read is converted into something that it can understand.

Duplex: A communications method by which a device can be transmitting and receiving at the same time.

Dynamic disk: A disk that has been configured for a file system based on volumes rather than partitions.

Edge triggered: Any response that elicited and/or is controlled by a direct electrical signal coming from a pin or wire on a device. The voltage is applied and the device depends on the interrupt controller to "remember" that it sent the signal.

Electron gun: A cathode that, when heated, emits a stream of electrons from the positive pole.

Ending delimiter: A single bit at the end of a byte of data being transmitted asynchronously that marks the end of a byte.

Enhanced I/O controller hub: The IC in the newer Intel chipsets that manages all function other than memory and AGP.

Enhanced mode: An operational mode specific to Windows that took advantage of advanced functions available in the 80386 microprocessor, including the ability to use virtual memory and to function in virtual real mode.

Erase power: A medium power setting for the optical stylus of a CD-RW, which it uses to melt the crystals generated by the previous recording session back into the uncrystallized recording layer.

Executable marker: A pointer in the MBR that directs the boot sequence to the first line of code for the primary kernel file of the OS installed.

Executive services: The layer of the operating system responsible for running commands.

Expanded memory: Memory beyond the first megabyte of RAM that can be used for storing data. Expanded memory could not be used for executing programs.

Expansion bus: A circuit on a motherboard that allows accessory devices to be added to the system. The expansion bus straddles several of the primary system busses.

Extended memory: Memory beyond the first megabyte of RAM that can be used for data storage and the execution of program code.

Extended partition: Also called a logical disk drive, this is a partition contained within a primary partition.

External data bus: The wires that move data from outside the CPU to the internal registers of the CPU.

External host rate: How fast data moves from a drive's controller to RAM.

Farad: The major measurement of a capacitor's ability to store energy.

Fast SCSI: SCSI over a 10MHz bus.

Fatal exception: Any event that stops the CPU completely. These can include programming errors, such as a request to divide any number by zero, or a hardware event that returns a non-maskable interrupt.

Faux parity: A null chip that fools a system into thinking parity memory was installed, when in fact, it was not.

File system: The mechanism used by a hard drive to map the specific sectors used by any given file.

File: A collection of data that is intended to stay together.

Firewall: A hardware or software barrier that allows access to external networks for users inside the firewall, but denies access from the outside.

FireWire: A high-speed serial SCSI connection originally developed by Apple Computer Corporation that is capable of 400Mb/s throughput.

Floating height: The distance above a hard drive's platter that the R/W heads hover as the platter spins beneath.

Floating point unit: A subcomponent of a microprocessor that is responsible for more complex mathematical calculations.

Flux reversal: A transition of magnet charge from a positive to a negative state, or vice versa.

Fogging: A technique of implying distance in an image by making objects that are farther away less distinct.

Font: The size and characteristics (such as bold or italic) of a particular typeface.

Form factor: A preconfigured size, orientation, and design layout for a particular component used in order to assure compatibility among manufacturers.

Frame buffer: Dedicated memory used by a graphics adapter to build the next image frame to be displayed in the time that the current image frame is on the screen.

Frame: The metal skeleton that provides the primary support for a computer enclosure.

Front-side bus: A portion of the EDB. It is the path that data takes from outside locations to make its way into the CPU.

Full-height bay: A term that describes a disk drive that is $3^1/2''$ from top to bottom.

Fuse: An electrical component that consists of a filament that vaporizes when more than a certain amount of current tries to pass.

Gauge: A measurement of the thickness of a substance such as sheet metal or wire. Larger numbers indicate smaller sizes.

Half duplex: A communications method by which a device can either transmit or receive, but not both at the same time.

Half-height bay: A term that describes a disk drive that is 1.62″ from top to bottom.

Hard fault: A situation in which data sought by the CPU was neither in memory nor in the paging file. As a result, a new hard disk search must be initiated.

Harmonics: Sound frequencies above the root frequency that are generated by an instrument or voice when a certain note is generated.

Head crash: A disastrous event caused by the R/W head in a drive coming into physical contact with the platter while it is spinning.

Head parking: A process of positioning R/W heads in a hard drive in a place where contact with the platter will do no harm.

Helical scan: A recording technology that places data in diagonal tracks along the tape, as opposed to a linear track that follows parallel to the tape edge.

Hexadecimal: A counting system that uses Base16 as it root. As such, this system requires a total of sixteen different characters to represent base values.

High memory: The first 64K of memory beyond the 1MB of conventional memory, usually used as a paging file for access into extended memory.

Host controller: The adapter installed on a system or embedded in the motherboard that manages SCSI devices.

Hot swap: The ability to replace or remove a device from a computer system without having to shut the system down.

Hot-pluggable: Another term for hot-swappable. A hot-pluggable device can be added or removed to its bus without the necessity of bringing the computer down.

Hub: A device that interconnects multiple hosts on a star network over a single segment.

Hyperthreading: The ability of certain CPUs to execute multiple lines of code at the same time.

Hypothesis: Any theory that can be tested to be proven either true or false.

I/O address: A location in memory that identifies where data from a specific device will be stored as it moves from either the application or the CPU to the device, and vice versa.

i386 instruction set: The basic CPU-level instructions embedded in the 80386 microprocessor. These instructions went on to become the core instructions for subsequent generations of Intel-compatible microprocessors.

Icon: A small picture linked to an application shortcut.

Index hole: A small opening in the covering of a floppy disk that allows the R/W heads to properly align to Track 0, Sector 1.

Initialization string: A series of AT commands that are issued by the originate modem during the connection process.

Initiator: The device in a bus-mastering chain that is to act as the source of the data being transferred.

Input: Any data that is intended and/or ready to be sent to the CPU for processing.

Instruction cache: A set of registers used for storing instruction code loaded by the prefetch until such time as the CPU is ready to use it.

Instruction pipelining: The ability of certain CPUs to be loading the next set of instructions or data at the same time they process the current set.

Insulator: Any substance that tends to resist the flow of electricity.

Int13h extensions: Additional instructions added to the BIOS that intercept hard disk I/O operations and provide the drive translation required by hard disks larger than 8GB.

Interleave ratio: The number of sectors that must pass beneath the R/W heads between the reading of one sector and the time the heads will be ready to read the next sector. For example, on a 3:1 ratio, the heads will read or write one sector, two sectors will pass by completely ignored, then the next sector will be written. The unused sectors will be filled in during the next two rotations of the platter.

Internal host rate: The speed at which data moves from the R/W heads to a drive's buffer memory. Also known as burst mode.

Interrupt: On a software level, it is a string of code that is called in order to perform a specific function. The BIOS uses software interrupts to manage hardware. On a hardware level, it is an electrical signal that notifies the CPU that a device needs to open communications (or vice versa).

Inverter: A device or circuit that converts DC current to AC current.

IPCONFIG: The TCP/IP utility that displays all TCP/IP configuration information for any given interface, or for all interfaces on a system.

Journaling: A process used by certain OSs and applications by which any changes made to the basic infrastructure or code are recorded in a log prior to being enforced.

Kernel mode: OS Functions dealing with security, I/O requests and executions, and the hardware interface.

Kernel: The microcode running on the system that provides the most fundamental OS services.

Key: A null space on an edge card connector or memory module that is used for properly aligning the device into its slot.

Key matrix: The specific geometric layout of the keyswitches on a keyboard.

Keycap travel: The actual distance a user must press a key on a keyboard in order to produce results.

Keycap: The plastic button the user presses down when typing on a keyboard.

Keyswitch: The electromechanical connection that informs the keyboard controller circuitry that a key has been pressed.

Land: All of the reflective surface of the recording layer in optical media that has not been burned or punched into a pit.

Landing zone: An area on the hard disk's platter where the R/W heads can be safely parked.

Latency: The delay that occurs from the time the CPU makes a request for data and the time that information can be accessed from the device holding the data. All devices, including memory and hard drives, exhibit latency.

Lazy writing: A disk-caching scheme that allows the OS to perform write operations to a disk at a time when the controller and disk aren't involved with read operations.

Level triggered: A response that is arbitrated by a control circuit and/or device driver that allows the same device to make use of one of several interrupt channels. The level-triggered interrupt raises the voltage on the appropriate wire and holds it until the expected response is received.

Library: In programming, a collection of subroutines that are required by several or all applications running on a computer. By storing this code in a single file, it does not need to be duplicated many times over.

Line conditioner: A device that is able to filter out transient noise, such as EMI, from the current.

Linewidth: The actual thickness of traces used within the CPU.

Load point: The physical location on a tape where data begins to be stored.

Local loop carrier: A communications service provider. It provides the electronic link between geographically separated devices.

Logic gate: Two or more transistors whose position will direct the positioning of the next bank of transistors downstream.

Logical drive: A section of disk space isolated from the rest of the same physical disk so that it appears to the user as a separate disk drive.

Logical partition: A pointer on a hard disk that identifies itself as a partition on the local drive, but in reality points to a partition on a remote disk.

Loopback adapter: A piece of hardware that routes an output signal directly back to the computer, giving the impression that a device is present.

Lost cluster: See Lost file fragment.

Lost file fragment: An FAU on the hard drive that contains data, but that has lost the pointers that identify the file to which it belongs.

LPT port: A predefined combination of an IRQ and an I/O address configured for line printers.

Make code: A signal generated by a key-switch when the key is first pressed down.

Media: The substance or energy wave over which a data signal is transmitted.

Megabyte: Depending on whether you are calculating a value in binary or decimal, a megabyte is either 1 million bytes (decimal) or 1,048,576 bytes (binary). A binary megabyte is used in virtually every circumstance except when calculating hard drive capacity. Hard drive manufacturers typically define capacity in decimal values.

Memory bank: The total number of memory modules required to assure that the bit width of available memory matches the bit width of the CPU in use.

Memory controller hub: The IC in the newer Intel chipsets that manages RAM and AGP bus.

Memory pool: The total address space available to an OS and the applications running on top of it.

Message block: A piece of data being transmitted by a modem that represents a portion of the overall data being sent.

Metafile: A related string of streaming data that contains the information that is used to implement the file system structure. Also, a metafile is a structured graphical file, also containing streaming data.

Microfarad: The minor measurement of a capacitor's ability to store energy.

Microkernel: a single file (or a very small set of files) that provides basic I/O functions and command interpretation.

Miniconnector: A smaller four-pin connector coming off a power supply that delivers current to devices such as floppy disk drives.

Mirrored volume: A single logical drive that is made of two disks, both of which contain identical data.

Modem: Modulator/demodulator. A device that converts parallel digital signals into serial analog signals for transmission over a wire.

Molex: The larger four-pin connector coming off a power supply that delivers current to devices such as CD-ROM drives or hard drives. Technically speaking, it is the name of the company that invented the plug.

Multimode fiber: A fiber-optic strand that moves multiple signals through the core.

Multisession: The ability to record data onto a CDR or CD-RW in several stages, without closing out the TOC.

Multitasking: The ability of an OS to simultaneously run more than one program at once.

Native capacity: How much data any given medium can store without benefit of compression. Various compression techniques allow data beyond native capacity to be recorded.

Native file encryption: A technology introduced into the NTFS file system that allows files and directories to be selectively scrambled for local storage.

Network client: A piece of software running on a computer that provides network access for the computer and all applications running on that computer.

Nibble: Any combination of four zeros or ones.

Nibble mode: Sends the 8-bit byte of data to the printer in two cycles, each of which carries four bits, or a nibble of data. This method requires software support and more overhead on the part of the host computer. Even slower than compatibility mode, ranging from 50KB to 65KB/s.

Node: Any one of several addressable types of allocated space on a hard disk that can contain the data that makes up a file.

Northbridge: The faster of the ICs in the chipset that is responsible for managing RAM, cache, and AGP functions.

Object counter: In Performance Monitor, it is the specific property or variable for which data is being collected.

Object: In reference to the OS, an object is any single resource on the system and/or network, including files, users, or devices.

Octet: A decimal alliteration of a single 8-bit string of data.

Online content: The overall availability of resources across an intranet or the Internet.

Open-ended question: A question that will provide further insight into the discussion as a result of the answer provided.

Operating system: A program running on a computer system that manages all of the services required by applications that are to run on the system and interfaces with the hardware.

Optical stylus: A mechanism consisting of a laser-emitting diode coupled to a beam splitter.

Optomechanical mouse: A mouse that uses perforated wheels passing in front of an LED to generate pulses of light that are used to track movement along the X and Y axis.

Originate modem: The device that initiates a call.

Output: Data that is being transmitted by one device to another once that data has been processed.

Overclocking: A technique of forcing a CPU or system bus to run faster than its rated speed in order to extract maximum performance.

Page: The amount of data that can be moved on a single memory read/write cycle; usually between 1 to 20KB.

Page fault: A noncritical error state that occurs when the OS looks for data in the paging file and fails to locate it.

Page frame: 64KB of high memory that is used for moving data down from addresses above 1MB into the 640K used by DOS programs.

Page read/write: When physical RAM in a system becomes full, data will be temporarily stored in a file called the paging file. A Page Read is a read operation from this file, while a Page Write is when data is moved from RAM to the paging file.

Paging file: A file on the hard disk that holds the information stored in virtual memory. Also called a swap file.

Parallel communications: The act of transferring an entire byte of data on a single cycle, using eight separate conductors.

Parity: An error checking mechanism that simply counted the number of 1s in a byte of data. A ninth bit is available on a parity chip for the parity bit. With odd-parity checking, if an even number of 1s is found in the byte, a 1 is placed in the parity bit to keep the number of 1s odd. With even parity, a 0 would be placed in that position to keep the number of 1s even.

Parity block: A data set that represents a mathematical image of data stored elsewhere in a RAID array.

Partition: Logical sections on a hard disk that divide the overall disk space into multiple logical drives.

PC card: Any auxiliary device designed to be plugged into a PCMCIA slot.

Permissions: The degrees of access a particular user has been granted to a specific resource on the network.

Phase change layer: The recording layer of a CD-RW.

Phase-change printer: A printer that liquefies solid inks before applying them to paper.

Phosphor: A single dot of color created when the phosphorous layer of a CRT is excited by electrons.

Piezoelectric crystal: A substance that changes shape when exposed to electricity.

Ping: Not only is Ping an acronym, it has been universally adopted as a term that can be either a noun or a verb. As a noun it represents the packets sent when pinging another host. As a verb, it represents the process of pinging another host.

Pinned list: A list of shortcuts to applications that are used on a regular basis.

Pit: A tiny hole embedded in the recording layer of optical media that prevents the laser from reflecting back into the photoelectric sensor.

Pixel: The collection of phosphors that collectively generate a single dot of color in a monitor's image.

Platen: The hard cylinder that supports the paper on impact printers.

Platter: One of two or more physical disk structures installed in a typical hard drive.

Plenum: An architectural term referring to the space between the ceiling of one floor in a building and the floor of the one above it.

Pointer: A line of code used by UFS to map a cluster used by a specific file.

Polarity: The characteristic of an electrical circuit to have one point of relative positive charge (or pole) and another point of relative negative charge (or pole).

Port replicator: A device to which a laptop computer can be attached that provides additional I/O services to the computer.

POST Card: A device that follows each step of the POST procedure and reports the results. Should the POST fail, the last successful process will be indicated in an encoded display.

P-rating: short for performance rating, this was a labeling method that, instead of designating a CPU by its clock speed, labeled it as the Intel CPU that it could be compared to, even though the actual clock speed and bus speed were both lower.

Pre-emptive multitasking: A way to manage multiple applications on a computer system that puts the responsibility for releasing system resources onto the OS.

Prefetch: The subcomponent of a microprocessor that is responsible for retrieving data and moving it into the CPU.

Pregroove: A spiral track engraved on CDR and CD-RW media at the factory that acts as a target for the recording laser.

Primary partition: Any one of four partitions on a hard disk drive that is defined in the MBR and can be converted into a bootable partition.

Print head: The mechanism on any impact or inkjet printer that is responsible for depositing the pigment onto the paper.

Priority boosting: A process by which the privilege level of a thread of code is promoted to a higher level in order to enhance its chances at the CPU.

Privilege level: A level of protection and priority that certain lines of code running within an OS have over other lines of code.

Privileges: The rights a particular user has been granted to perform specific functions or tasks on a system or the network in general.

Process: A single section of code from an application that must run from beginning to end.

Processing: Any manipulation of data that can occur between the time the data has been inputted into the computer and the time that is provided as output. Processing can consist of calculations performed on the data, replication of that data to alternative locations, and the comparison of one data set to another. Not all processing is done by the CPU.

Processor ring: Another term for privilege level.

Product activation: A newer technology that requires the end user to physically activate the product through a database managed by the product's manufacturer. This prevents the product from being installed on multiple machines.

Profile: Various settings and preferences specific to a particular user or piece of hardware on a system.

Promiscuous mode: An operating mode for any network interface in which all incoming packets will be accepted, even if they are not intended for that specific interface.

Protected mode: A function of a CPU that prevents two separate programs from seeing each other's code or from attempting to use overlapping memory addresses. Should either event occur, the CPU would lock up.

Protocol: An application running on a computer that ensures that the computer will speak the same language and follow the same rules as the computers with which it communicates.

Proxy server: A machine on the network that has been configured to be the portal to the Internet, through which all other computers on the network gain access.

Pthalocyanine dye: A more stable dye used in recent generations of CDR that is less sensitive to UV light than cyanine dye and lasts for up to a 100 years.

Quad-pumped: A technique of moving four bits of data over each wire on each clock cycle of the front-side bus.

RAS/CAS delay: The delay that occurs between RAS and CAS. Also known as CAS latency.

Raster line: A single row of pixels that make a horizontal line across an image.

Read power: The lowest power setting for the optical stylus of a CD-RW, which it uses to read data from the surface.

Real mode: An operational mode for either a CPU or an OS in which only one application can be present on the system at once and only 1MB of RAM can be addressed by that application.

Real time OS: An OS designed to be able to perform specific functions at the precise time at which those functions are needed.

Recognition scan: A BIOS routine that polls each device installed on a computer system to see whether that device is Plug 'n Play, and if so, what resources it currently claims.

Rectifier circuit: A specialized series of components that converts AC current to DC current.

Redirector: An OS function (usually running within a client) that intercepts hardware and software calls that are intended for remote devices and points them in the right direction.

Refresh: The process of recharging the capacitors that link to the transistors of each memory cell on a chip.

Refresh rate: The number of columns of memory cells per cycle that the MCC will recharge.

Register: A bank of transistors grouped together to perform a specific function.

Registry: In Windows, it is a relational database that contains all system and application settings and/or parameters.

Repeater: A device that cleans up, amplifies, and retransmits a signal, effectively increasing the distance data can travel over any given medium.

Report phase: A part of the WIN2K installation procedure that seeks out and logs programs and device drivers that are likely to cause problems.

Resident command: In an OS, it is any command that is an integral part of the command interpreter and does not require an external executable program.

Resistance: The tendency for a substance to block the flow of electrons.

Resistor: An electrical component that restricts the flow of current by a precisely measured amount.

Restore point: A copy of system files and registry entries that were in place at the time a major system change was introduced.

Riser: A specialized expansion card that supports other expansion devices such as PCI or ISA cards horizontally, parallel to the motherboard, in order to save space.

Root directory: The volume description, in which all other directories and files will be stored.

Root frequency: The single frequency of any given musical note that makes that note sound the way it does, regardless of what instrument plays it.

Route: The path that data takes to move from point A to point B. It is also a TCP/IP utility that can be used to display the local router configuration on a TCP/IP enabled device.

Router: A device that interconnects two autonomous networks into a single larger network.

Sag: A sudden transient decrease in voltage.

Scatter-gather data transfer: The ability of a device to execute a command on one set of data and output the results to multiple devices.

SCSI expander: A device that allows a technician to effectively increase the length of a SCSI chain without the risk of data corruption.

Sector: The smallest data storage unit recognized by a disk on a hard drive.

On magnetic media, the sector is consistently 512 bytes. It can vary for other types of optical media.

Security descriptor: A token attached to a resource that defines security attributes assigned to that resource.

Segment register cache: Separate cache locations maintained by Pentium II (and later) for keeping 16-bit code running separately from 32-bit code.

Semiconductor: A substance that exhibits the characteristics of both a conductor and a resistor, depending on the amount of voltage passing through.

Serial communications: The act of transferring data a single bit at a time over a single connection.

Server: Any device or software that provides services to other devices or pieces of software that need them.

Service: A networking function of the OS, such as file sharing, that can be turned on and off as needed.

Shadow mask: A thin metal sheet perforated with tiny holes that outlines the individual phosphors in a CRT monitor.

Share level security: A method of protecting resources on the network that involves applying the security attributes, such as password protection, to the object itself. As such, each secured object on the system may have a unique password.

Sideband addressing: The ability of a device to send and receive data in a single memory access.

Signal saturation: The maximum strength of a recording signal that a device can handle before the recording becomes unusable.

Simplex: A communications method by which a device can either transmit or receive but cannot do both.

Single-ended signaling: A method by which a single data wire on a parallel cable is matched up by a ground wire.

Single-mode fiber: A fiber optics strand that moves only a single signal through the core.

Slot: A mounting assembly designed to support edge card-mounted devices. Also, on a CD-ROM (or similar) drive, it is a form of loading mechanism that engages a CD when it is inserted into the opening and draws the disc into the drive.

Snap-in: An applet that can be added to customized consoles in Microsoft Management Console.

Snapshot: In reference to an OS, it is a small binary file that contains information useful in replicating the organization and structure of an application or configuration.

Socket: A mounting assembly designed to support pin-mounted devices.

Socket driver: The portion of a PC card driver that is responsible for I/O services and insertion/removal notification.

Soft fault: The data requested by the CPU is in memory, but not part of the current working set of data. As a result, a new memory search must be initiated.

Southbridge: The slower of the ICs that make up the chipset. The southbridge manages serial and parallel communications, USB, and most of the expansion slots.

Spanned volume: A larger logical drive that is created by combining space located on two different partitions or disks.

Spare sectoring: A technique hard drive manufacturers use in which extra tracks of recordable space are included with each drive that ships. As bad sectors are discovered on the drive, new sectors are made available from this space to replace the bad ones.

Speculative execution: When two different subroutines have been loaded by branch prediction, speculative execution will actually process the lines of each branch loaded.

Speed mismatch compatibility: A technology that allows two devices on the same bus to operate at different speeds and still successfully communicate with one another.

Spike: A sudden transient increase in voltage.

Standard mode: An operational mode specific to Windows in which the OS could access expanded memory beyond 1MB and could task switch multiple applications.

Standby power supply: A device that uses a generator to provide electrical current to a room or building in the event of a total power failure.

Starting delimiter: A single bit at the beginning of a data byte being transmitted asynchronously that marks the beginning of the byte.

Stepper motor: A motor that has been designed in such a way that, rather than rotating smoothly, it jumps from one position to another in precisely measured increments.

Stop code: A number assigned to a particular catastrophic event, along with certain parameters that further define the event.

Streaming SIMD: The ability of certain CPUs to execute an instruction only once, but apply that instruction to several sets of data.

Striped volume: A logical drive that is created by storing data in chunks that are distributed among multiple physical drives.

Subdirectory: Any directory that exists beneath another directory.

Subharmonics: Sound frequencies below the root frequency that are generated by an instrument or voice when a certain note is played.

Subnet mask: A configuration setting within TCP/IP that identifies to the system what part of an IP address is the network address and what part is the host address.

Substrate: The supportive material over which an active substance can be applied.

Supervisory mode: A process by which an OS runs code at the highest possible privilege level.

Surge suppressor: A device that is able to filter out voltage surges and prevent them from reaching the devices plugged into its outlets.

Swap file: A file on the hard disk that holds the information stored in virtual memory. Also called a paging file.

Switch: A device that breaks a larger network down into smaller segments, isolating each segment into its own collision domain. In reference to an OS, it is an additional parameter added to the end of a command that defines advanced functions for that command to perform. The switch turns a specific function on or off.

Symmetric multiprocessing: A method by which an operating system makes use of more than one processor, distributing all code equally across all available processors.

Synchronization bits: Data included on each sector of a data CD that assures that the information will be processed in the correct sequence.

Synchronous communication: A form of serial communication that transmits large amounts of data at once in packets.

Synchronous timing: Bus speeds are a submultiple of the CPU's clock speed, and data is delivered at a steady rate based on that speed.

SYSINIT: A subroutine of IO.SYS that seeks out and runs MSDOS.SYS during the MS-DOS boot process.

System call: A request for a service not directly provided by the application.

System object: On a system in general, it is any hardware or software entity to which specific properties can be assigned. In Performance Monitor, it is a category of events that can be monitored.

System virtual machine: An environment in Windows that emulates a complete computer system and houses all of the critical processes and functions of the OS.

Target: Any device that is to be the intended recipient of data.

Task scheduler: A system file that determines how long a particular application can retain control of system resources.

Task switching: The ability of an OS to close a program, run another, and then return to the same point in the program previously closed.

Terminate: To create a dead end for electrical signals traveling down a wire so that they do not echo back the other direction.

Texel: A small clip that serves as the sample of a texture used in texture mapping.

Texture mapping: A process by which pre-drawn textures are stored in memory and applied to an image as needed.

Thermal printer: A printer that ejects ink onto a page of paper by heating the fluid.

Thicknet: A name commonly given to RG-8 coaxial cable.

Thin-film metal: A metalized magnetic medium applied by evaporating metal and allowing it to "condense" back onto the surface being coated.

Thinnet: A name commonly given to RG-58U coaxial cable.

Third-party DMA: Direct memory access that is managed by a device other than the two devices utilizing DMA to exchange data.

Threshold voltage: The amount of electrical differential required to move a semiconductor from a state of resistance to a state of conductance.

Thunking: A Microsoft process of translating 16-bit commands and data into a 32-bit format, and vice versa.

Topology: The method through which a network is physically wired.

Trace: The fine copper path seen on printed circuit boards that acts as a conductor for a signal.

Track: A virtual circle of sectors on a magnetic drive that makes a complete ring around the disk surface.

Trackpad: A pointing device used on laptop computers that makes use of an electrostatically sensitive surface. The user runs a finger across the surface and the trackpad tracks the movement of the electrostatic charge.

Trackpoint: A small pointing device used on laptop computers, similar to a trackball, but much smaller.

Tractor feed: A paper transport mechanism that uses a set of gears on a printer to advance the paper by engaging in perforations along each side of the paper.

Tranceiver: Any device that is designed to be able to either transmit or receive data.

Transient command: A command that is issued and run from an external source.

Transistor: A microscopic on/off switch that uses the electrical characteristics of a semiconductor to reverse positions.

Transition cell: The minimum number of particles that can be affected by a single magnetic flux.

Transmission rate: The number of bits per second that is being transmitted.

Tray: On a CD-ROM (or similar) drive, it is a form of loading mechanism that consists of a platform that ejects when the user pushes a button, and retracts with the CD in place.

Triad: The three separate phosphors, each of a separate primary color, that when combined form the separate hues of color perceived by the user.

Trigger: Another name for a switch when referenced by an OS command.

Trojan horse: A malicious program designed to mimic another commonly recognized program that is, in fact, performing some other action in the background without the knowledge or consent of the user.

Tunnel erasure: A technique of erasing the magnetic charge from the edges of a recorded track on a magnetic disk.

Typeface: The basic shape that letters and numbers of a particular character set will assume.

Ultra wide SCSI: SCSI over a 32-bit bus.

Unbounded media: Any medium that connects the device to the network using energy forms that travel through air and/or space.

Uninterruptible power supply: A device that uses batteries to provide electrical current to another device in the event of a total power failure.

Upgrade: The replacement of an older OS with a newer, migrating as many settings and applications as possible.

USB device: Any component designed to be operated on the USB.

USB host: Any computer or other device equipped with USB-compatible BIOS, firmware, and controller.

USB hub: A device that manages the I/O for two or more USB device chains.

User-level access: A level of security in Windows that provides users with all permitted access to network resources using a single user ID and password.

User-level security: A method of securing resources on a system or network that involves assigning the security attributes to an account provided to the user. Once the user has logged on, access to resources is provided based on the permissions assigned to the account.

User mode: OS functions dealing with the user interface, logons, services needed to run applications, and network access.

Vampire clamp: A device consisting of two halves that screw together. One half is fitted with sharp teeth that bite through the insulation of RG-8 cable.

Vapor deposition: The process of applying a metal coating by the process of evaporation.

Virtual device driver: A set of files that intercepts hardware calls from applications in order to prevent direct access of hardware by the applications.

Virtual machine: An environment set up in system memory that emulates all functions of a working computer, providing the illusion that a program is the only code running on a computer system.

Virtual memory: A section of hard disk space that is set aside and used by the OS as though it were memory. Also called a swap file or a paging file.

Virtual real mode: A technique of creating separate address spaces and time slicing the CPU time so that legacy applications think they're the only programs running on the machine, even though there may be several running at once.

Voice: A collection of preprogrammed harmonics that are used to simulate the sound made by a particular instrument.

Voice coil: An extremely fast and highly accurate motor that works by applying an electrical current to a tightly wrapped coil of wires surrounding, but not touching, a permanently magnetized cylinder. When current is applied to the coil, the cylinder rotates. Negative voltage rotates the cylinder one direction, positive the other. The amount of voltage determines how far the cylinder moves.

Volatile: Unstable or changeable. Requires constant power in order to continue to exist.

Voltage: The difference in charge between two objects or surfaces. This is sometimes referred to as electrical pressure.

Volume: A single managed unit of storage on a computer system. This can be a single hard disk, if that disk has been formatted to only one partition, or it can be an individual partition on a disk.

Volume set: A single logical disk drive that is created when multiple partitions or physical disks are combined.

Warm: A shift in the color of an image toward the red side.

White balance: A measurement of how pure the reproduction of white is accomplished in an image.

Wide SCSI: SCSI over a 16-bit bus.

Wild card: A character that instructs a command to replace that character with any other character or collection of characters it finds in its place.

Word: The amount of data that can move across the CPU's external data bus in one clock cycle; usually between two and four bytes.

Workgroup: A collection of independently managed users and/or devices on a network that are configured to share files and devices.

Write power: The highest power setting for the optical stylus of a CD-RW, which it uses to record data onto the surface.

Write protect: A process or mechanism that prevents the data on a disk or other medium from being erased or overwritten.

Zone bit recording: A technology that allows the sectors on the outer tracks of a hard disk to be the same physical size as those toward the center. This allows for far more sectors per track on the outer tracks.

GLOSSARY OF ACRONYMS

AC: Alternating Current. Current that reverses direction many times in a second.

ACE: Access Control Entity. An individual entry of the ACL defining a specific object and its security attributes.

ACK: Acknowledgment

ACL: Access Control List. A data token attached to the descriptor of a specific object on the network that defines what users and/or groups are allowed to access that object and what degree of access they are allowed.

ACPI: Advanced Configuration and Power Interface. An upgrade to the PnP functionality of Windows.

ACR: Audio Communications Riser. A specialized card that takes the concept of the AMR and adds networking functionality as well.

ADC: Analog-to-Digital Converter

ADSI: Active Directory Service Interface

AFS: Automatic File Compression. A technology built into NTFS that allows files and directories to be compressed and uncompressed on the fly.

AGP: Advanced Graphics Port. A high-speed bus designed exclusively for graphics.

AIT: Advanced Intelligent Tape. A tape format that incorporates a linear recording mechanism in conjunction with a memory chip embedded in the tape cartridge to allow for advanced features.

ALDC: Adaptive Lossless Data Compression. An advanced data compression algorithm that allows a greater degree of compression without any loss of data.

ALU: Arithmetic Logic Unit. The subcomponent of a CPU that handles rudimentary mathematical functions.

AMR: Audio Modem Riser. A specialized card found on certain motherboards that supports either a modem, a sound card, or a device that combines both functions.

ANSI: American National Standards Institute. This term refers to an organization charged with establishing standards for several different industries, including the computer industry.

It also refers to an early character set developed by that organization.

API: Application Programming Interface. A collection of files used by Microsoft OSs that maintains and translates the basic command set required by all devices of a particular type.

APM BIOS: Advanced Power Management Basic Input Output Services

ARC: Advanced RISC Computing

ASCII: American Standard Code for Information Interchange. An early character set used by computers.

ASMP: Asymmetric Multiprocessing. The ability of an OS to use more than one processor, where the OS code runs on one processor and all other application code and user data is distributed across the remaining processors.

ASPI: Advanced SCSI Programmer Interface. A two-tiered device driver scheme employed by SCSI.

AT: Advanced Technology. A form factor promoted by IBM in the early days of personal computing.

ATA: Advanced Technology Attachment

ATAPI: Advanced Technology Application Programming Interface. The API that controls IDE devices.

ATM: Asynchronous Transfer Mode

ATX: Advanced Technology Extended. An improvement of the older AT form factor that provided greater accessibility to components and far more efficiency in the use of space.

AUI: Attachment Unit Interface. A 15-pin female connector used by some early network cards and sound cards.

BCC: Block Check Character. Includes error detection and correction data, which may include parity (rarely used these days), checksum (on its way out), or cyclical redundancy check (the most common method in use today).

BDC: Backup Domain Controller. Any server on an NT domain that houses a copy of the security database that is periodically updated by the PDC.

BIOS: Basic Input Output Services. The basic instruction set usually (but not always) loaded onto a Read Only Memory chip on a computer system that provides the startup code along with a number of routines that provide command support for the hardware installed on the system.

BNC: Bayonet Neil-Conselman. A barrel-shaped connector named after the two engineers involved in the design.

BRI: Basic Rate ISDN. Two 64K B-channels and one 16K D-channel.

BSB: Back-Side Bus. The portion of the EDB that moves data back and forth between onboard cache and the CPU.

BSOD: Blue Screen of Death. The last message NT (and later Microsoft OSs) manages to choke out in its dying breath.

CAB: Cabinet. A compressed file that houses a number of smaller files that can be independently extracted as needed.

CAL: Client Access License. A license granting one user permission to access a system or network.

CAS: Column Access Strobe. A circuit that is part of the MCC, responsible for locking onto the first column in a memory module in which the target data is located.

CAT: Catalog File. A compressed file in Windows that contains driver signing information.

CAV: Constant Angular Velocity. A data reading mechanism used by optical drives that allows the rotational velocity of the disc to remain constant, forcing the controller to interpret the data at faster speeds as the optical stylus moves from the center to the edge.

CCD: Charge Coupled Device. A sensor consisting of an array of cells that interpolates a physical image and converts it into a digital file.

CCS: Common Command Set. Eighteen specific commands that must be included for every device that carries the SCSI-II label.

CDAD: Compact Disc, Audio Disc. The file system used by CD-ROMs to store music.

CDDI: Copper Distributed Data Interface

CDFS: CD-ROM File System

CDFS: Compact Disc File System. The file system used by CD-ROMs to store computer data.

CDR: Recordable CD

CD-ROM: Compact Disc-Read Only Memory

CD-RW: Rewriteable CD

CHS: Cylinders, Heads, Sectors-per-track. The parameters of hard drive configuration that define total capacity of the drive as well as specific locations on the drive.

CLV: Constant Linear Velocity. A data reading mechanism used by optical drives in which the rotational velocity of the disc must slow down as the disc is tracked from center to edge, thus assuring that the relative number of tracks per millisecond that passes beneath the optical stylus always remains the same.

CMOS: Complimentary Metal-Oxide Semiconductor. The type of chip that houses the user-configurable parameters needed by BIOS.

CMTS: Cable Modem Termination System. A device on the ISP's end that combines all incoming cable modem signals into a single channel for transmission over the Internet backbone.

CNR: Communications Network Riser. A specialized card that takes the concept of the AMR and adds networking functionality as well.

COMDEX: Computer Dealer Exposition. An annual trade show for businesses in the computer industry.

CPL: Current Privilege Level. The level of priority at which code is running on machines. It is the method by which processor rings are defined.

CPU: Central Processing Unit. The primary microprocessor on a modern computer that is responsible for executing programs and processing user data.

CRT: Cathode-Ray Tube. A video display that uses a device called a cathode to fire a beam (or ray) of electrons towards a phosphorus-coated surface.

CSMA/CD: Carrier Sense, Multiple Access/Collision Detection

CUI: Common User Interface. A feature of many OSs that dictates how certain functions related to user interaction with the programs are handled, ensuring that all applications have a similar look, feel, and function.

DAC: Digital-to-Analog Converter. Also, Discretionary Access Control. A feature written into the NTFS file system that allows an administrator to apply security on a file or directory level.

DAT: Digital Audiotape. A tape format that uses an 8mm recording tape and a helical scan recording mechanism very similar to that used by digital audio recorders.

DC: Direct Current. A unidirectional current that flows from the positive side of the circuit to the negative side.

DDE: Dynamic Data Exchange. A technology for exchanging data between two autonomous programs running on a single computer.

DDR: Dual Data Rate. A form of memory that is capable of executing two transfers of data on each clock cycle.

DDRAM: Double Data-rate RAM. A form of memory that moves two bits of data for each clock cycle.

DDS: Digital Data Storage

DEC: Digital Equipment Corporation

DFS: Distributed File System. A subset of NTFS that allows users to browse to remote resources on a network without requiring the user to know the specific path information.

DHCP: Dynamic Host Configuration Protocol. A protocol that assigns IP addresses to client computers on the fly.

DIMM: Dual Inline Memory Module. A 168- or 184-pin memory module that allows the connection on either side of the base to perform disparate functions.

DIX: Digital, Intel, Xerox

DLL: Dynamic Link Library. A file that contains shared code that can be used by more than one application.

DLT: Digital Linear Tape. A tape format that records data in a straight line along the tape, parallel to the tape's edge.

DMA: Direct Memory Access. A technique by which a large amount of data is moved directly from an application or device to memory, without constant intervention from the CPU.

DNS: Domain Name Services. A service that resolves host name to IP address on the Internet.

DPI: Dots Per Inch

DRAM: Dynamic Random Access Memory

DSL: Digital Subscriber Line. A broadband high-speed data connection that moves over standard telephone cable.

DSLAM: DSL Access Multiplexer. A device on the ISP's end that combines all incoming DSL signals into a single channel for transmission over the Internet backbone.

DSP: Digital Signal Processor. A chip that performs multiple processing functions on a signal. For example, the DSP on a modem combines the functions of a UART and a DAC.

DUN: Dial-Up Networking. A method of connecting to a network over a modem.

DVD: Digital Video Disc, or Digital Versatile Disc

DVD-R: Recordable DVD

DVD-RW: Rewriteable DVD

Dword: Double Word

EBX: Embedded Board Expandable. One of several form factors whose objective was to keep the system as small as possible.

ECC: Error Correction Code. An error correction method that stored a mathematical image of data being moved on a nibble chip and could correct single-bit errors as they were detected.

ECHS: Extended CHS

ECI: Extended Capabilities ID. Information programmed onto a PCI card that defines any enhanced functions that device can perform beyond the basic functions defined by its device class.

ECP: Extended Compatibility Port. A parallel mode that provides for both data and command cycles, therefore supporting more advanced devices, including scanners, storage devices, and such. Data throughput is similar to that of EPP. However, since DMA is used, there is less delay imposed on the application.

EDB: External Data Bus. The path that data uses to move from the CPU to an outside circuit, or vice versa.

EDC: Error Detection Code. Code embedded in a file system that enables the system to detect that an error in the transmission of that data has occurred, and where possible alerts the system to take corrective action.

EDO: Extended Data Out. A form of memory that replaced FPM and that allowed the RAS/CAS operations for the next I/O operation to be performed at the same time as data from the previous operation is being moved out of the chip.

EEPROM: Electronically Erasable Programmable Read Only Memory. A more modern implementation of an IC that can be wiped clean and rewritten if necessary.

EFS: Encryptable File System. A subset of NTFS that allows individual files to be scrambled on an as-needed basis and subsequently unscrambled only by a user with appropriate permissions.

EIA: Electronics Industry Association

EIDE: Enhanced IDE

EISA: Enhanced ISA. A 32-bit 8.33MHz bus released by a coalition of manufacturers led by Compaq. VLB was designed to be backwardly compatible with ISA.

ENDEC: Encoder/Decoder

EOT: End of Transmission. I hope I don't have to explain that one.

EPP: Enhanced Parallel Port. Because it provides for different types of signals to be transferred on any given clock cycle, EPP provides for faster and more efficient communication between peripherals. EPP allows continuous data transfer of around 500KB/s with burst rates of up to 2MB/s.

EPRML: Extended PRML. A data encoding mechanism used by most hard disk drives currently being manufactured.

EPROM: Erasable Programmable Read Only Memory. An IC that can be wiped clean and rewritten if necessary.

ERD: Emergency Repair Diskette. A floppy diskette that holds system configuration and account information for a machine running NT (or later) operating systems.

ESDI: Enhanced Small Device Interface. An earlier hard disk drive interface that preceded IDE.

ESN: Electronic Serial Number. On Pentium III CPUs (and later) this is a number embedded by Intel at the factory that identifies that specific CPU.

EXT: End of Text. Okay, I'm done sending text in this block. The next bytes are more control information.

FAT: File Allocation Table. A file on a disk, hidden from the user, that identifies what file is using each sector on the disk. It is the disk's roadmap, if you will.

FAU: File Allocation Unit. The smallest usable amount of drive space in sectors used by a file system for a single file, regardless of how small that file may be.

FC-AL: Fiber Channel Arbitrated Loop

FCC: Federal Communications Commission

FCP: Fiber Channel Protocol

FC-PGA: Flip Chip Pin Grid Array. A CPU socket designed for easy CPU installation or replacement used in modern machines.

FC-PH: Fiber Channel Physical and Signaling Interface

FDDI: Fiber Distributed Data Interface

FILO: First In, Last Out

FIRST: Forum of Incident Response and Security Teams. An organization charged with maintaining the security of the Internet.

FPM: Fast Page Mode. An early form of memory that eliminated the RAS cycle from any read operation retrieving data from the same row as the previous operation.

FPU: Floating Point Unit. The subcomponent of the CPU that handles more advanced mathematical functions.

FSB: Front-Side Bus. The portion of the EDB that moves data in and out of the CPU from external locations.

GDI: Graphical Device Interface. A subset of Microsoft's Windows operating systems that manages imaging devices such as printers, scanners, and graphics cards. Printers that use this interface as their printer language are referred to as GDI printers.

GPF: General Protection Fault. A failure of an application (and possibly the CPU) that results from one program invading another program's address space.

GUI: Graphical User Interface. The pretty point-and-click interface common to OSs today.

HAL: Hardware Abstraction Layer. A subset of Microsoft's Windows operating systems that provides a virtual barrier between the computer's hardware and the applications and upper-level OS functions.

HCL: Hardware Compatibility List. A list of devices that have been approved by an OS manufacturer for use with a specific product.

HPFS: High Performance File System

HPGL: Hewlett Packard Graphics Language. A printer language developed by HP to add complex graphics to the printer's toolset.

HPSF: High Power Single Frequency

HR: Horizontal Refresh. The speed at which a monitor can draw individual raster lines.

HVD: High-Voltage Differential

Hz: Hertz. A measurement for frequency, or the number of times during any given timing cycle that the measured event occurs.

I/O: Input/Output. The process of sending or receiving data between devices.

IANA: The Internet Assigned Numbers Authority. The organization that currently hands out IP address to those that need them.

IC: Integrated Circuit. A single microchip onto which the code necessary to provide several different functions has been burned.

ICANN: The Internet Corporation for Assigned Names and Numbers. One of several organizations involved in the administration of the Internet.

iComp: Intel Comparative Microprocessor Index. A benchmarking method developed by Intel.

ICS: Internet Connection Sharing. A service that allows multiple computers to simultaneously use a single hookup to the Internet.

IDE: Integrated Drive Electronics. A method of managing hard drives and other devices that takes the controller circuitry off the motherboard or separate controller card and places it on the device itself.

IEPG: The Internet Engineering and Planning Group. An organization involved in overseeing the operational control of the Internet.

IFCA: IEEE Fiber Channel Address. A unique address assigned to all FC-AL devices at the factory that allows them to be automatically configured onto the FC-AL loop.

IFS: Installable File System. A feature in WIN9x and later OSs that allows network redirectors and third-party file systems to be installed as needed.

IIS: Internet Information Services

InterNIC: Internet's Network Information Center. One of several organizations involved in the administration of the Internet.

IOPS: I/O Operations Per Second. The maximum number of times a device can receive and then execute either a request for data or a request to write data to the device, assuming the smallest block of data the device utilizes.

IPS: Instructions Per Second. An early measurement of CPU performance that was based solely on how many times in one second the device could execute commands.

IPSEC: Internet Protocol Security

IPX/SPX: Internetwork Packet Exchange/ Sequenced Packet Exchange. A Novell networking protocol.

ISA: Industry Standards Architecture. An 8- or 16-bit expansion bus designed by IBM.

ISDN: Integrated Services Digital Network. A telecommunications technology that provides high-speed data transfer over standard telephone lines.

ISO: International Organization for Standardization. One of several groups that oversees the development and ratification of standards in the computer industry, as well as many other industries.

ISOC: The Internet Society. The organization that oversees all the other organizations involved in managing the Internet.

ISP: Internet Service Provider. The end user's gateway to the Internet.

JEDEC: Joint Electron Device Engineering Council. An organization that oversees standards for many of the electronic devices in use, including memory modules.

L1: Level 1. A small amount of extremely fast memory used to store data or instructions that the CPU expects it will need within a few clock cycles, or that it uses frequently.

L2: Level 2. A secondary level of slower cache memory. This is usually a larger amount of memory than the L1 and is the second place the CPU looks for needed instructions or data.

L3: Level 3. A third layer of cache supported only by a select few CPUs.

LAN: Local Area Network

LCD: Liquid Crystal Display. An imaging device that consists of transistors suspended in a liquid emulsion.

LDAP: Lightweight Directory Access Protocol. A protocol that allows network resources to be browsed in a manner similar to local disk drives.

LFN: Long File Names

Li-Ion: Lithium Ion. A type of rechargeable battery.

LLC: Logic Link Control

LPSF: Low Power Single Frequency

LPX: Low-Profile Extended. A form factor designed to take up a minimum of desktop real estate that puts the expansion slots onto a single riser card that supports the cards parallel to the motherboard. Most LPX designs were proprietary.

LSA: Local Security Authority. An NT service that manages the logon process and all subsequent access to system or network resources.

LUN: Logical Unit Number. A setting on SCSI devices that allows multiple devices to be seen by the controller as a single device.

LVD: Low-Voltage Differential

MAC: Media Access Control

MAPI: Messaging Applications Programming Interface

MAU: Multistation Access Unit. A device similar to a hub that interconnects hosts on a token ring network.

MB: Megabyte. In binary, this would be 1,048,576 bytes. In decimal, it would be 1 million bytes.

MBR: Master Boot Record. Information contained on the first one or two sectors of a hard disk that contain code that initializes the file system, defines disks and partitions, and provides a pointer to the OS.

MCA: Micro Channel Architecture. A proprietary 32-bit 12MHz bus released by IBM shortly after Intel's release of the 80386 CPU.

MCC: Memory Controller Chip or Memory Controller Circuit. The chip or circuitry on the chipset that manages memory mapping and refresh functions.

MDRAM: Multibank DRAM. A form of memory that can be accessed in blocks, rather than sequentially.

MFM: Modified Frequency Modulation. One of the early data encoding mechanisms used by hard disk drives.

MFU: Most Frequently Used. The portion of the XP Start menu that displays applications that have been opened over a predefined period of time, in the order which they were opened. Apps are displayed from most recently used to least recently.

MIC: Memory In Cartridge. The embedded memory chip of an AIT.

MIDI: Musical Instrument Device Interface. A connector for hooking up computerized musical instruments to a computer system.

MIP: *Multium in Parvo*. Latin for "many in one." It is a technique by which several samples of the same texture are created in different sizes.

MJPEG: Motion-picture Joint Photographic Experts Group. An organization that develops and maintains standards for digitizing images. Also a file format used for compressing and storing editable versions of motion pictures developed by that group.

MLP: Mid-Load Point. A tape drive technology that places the load point in the center of the tape. Also, Multiple Load Point. A tape drive technology that allows a single tape to be mounted from several different locations on the tape. They wanted to confuse you.

MMC: Microsoft Management Console

MMX: Multimedia Extensions. A set of instructions targeted specifically at multimedia.

MOV: Metal Oxide Varistor. An electrical component that can absorb abrupt spikes in current.

MPEG: Motion Picture Experts Group. An organization that developed a standard for compressing and storing digital video. Its format is not as editable as MJPEG.

MRH-S: SDRAM Memory Repeater Hub. A chip in newer Intel chipsets used to arbitrate memory requests between multiple banks of memory.

MS-DOS: Microsoft Disk Operating System

MTBF: Mean Time Before Failure. An average of the number of hours a particular model of device is expected to operate before it dies.

MTH: Memory Translator Hub. A chip in newer Intel chipsets that replaces the northbridge chip used by contemporary chipsets.

NAP: Network Access Point. The entry point to one of the several large capacity circuits that transport data across the Internet.

NetBEUI: NetBIOS Extended User Interface. An early Microsoft networking protocol.

NIC: Network Interface Card

NiCad: Nickel Cadmium. A type of rechargeable battery.

Ni-MH: Nickel Metal Hydride. A type of rechargeable battery.

NLA: Network Location Awareness. A feature in XP that automatically configures a computer system to the network or subnet to which the device is attached.

NLB: Network Load Balancing

NLX: New Low-profile Extended. One of several form factors whose objective was to keep the system as small as possible.

NMI: Non-Maskable Interrupt. Any software or hardware induced interrupt that requires instantaneous attention from the CPU.

NTFS: New Technology File System

NTWS: NT Workstation

OLE: Object Linking and Embedding. A technology that allows an object to be created in one application and imported into a second application; should the properties of the object ever change in the first, it is automatically updated in the second.

OS: Operating System

OSI: Open Standards Interconnect. A seven-layer model for developing networking standards.

P2P: Peer to Peer. A network on which all hosts are equals.

PAE: Physical Address Extension

PATA: Parallel ATA

PBC: Port Bypass Circuit. A circuit that manages an FC-AL loop and automatically detects when a device has been removed.

PCI: Peripheral Components Interconnect. A 32- or 64-bit expansion bus designed by Intel.

PCI-X: PCI Extended. A recently released 133MHz version of the PCI bus.

PCL: Printer Control Language. Hewlett Packard's printer language, originally developed for dot matrix printers and later adopted for use with laser printers.

PCM: Pulse Code Modulation. The process of converting electrical current into a digital signal.

PCMCIA: Personal Computer Memory Card International Association

PDA: Personal Digital Assistant. Any one of several computing devices designed for maximum portability.

PDC: Primary Domain Controller. The server in an NT domain that houses the master security database.

PGA: Pin Grid Array. A pin-mounted CPU on which the pins are arranged in perfectly symmetrical patterns of squares.

PIF: Program Information File. A small descriptor file that tells Windows how a specific DOS application is going to behave.

PIO: Programmed Input/Output. A transfer of data in which each byte of data must be negotiated and managed by the CPU.

PKI: Public Key Infrastructure

PM: Program Manager. An applet in Win3.x that acted as a DOS shell for file and program management functions.

PnP: Plug 'n Play. An Intel/Microsoft technology that allows the computer system and OS to automatically detect and configure certain settings for PnP compatible hardware.

POP: Point of Presence. The physical connection supplied by an ISP that provides access to the Internet.

POSIX: Portable Operating System Interface

POST: Power On, Self Test. A program run from the BIOS chip that initializes system hardware and handles the Plug 'n Play scans.

PPB: PCI to PCI Bridge. The circuitry that arbitrates data transfer between two different PCI busses on the same system.

PPP: Point-to-Point Protocol

PRI: Primary Rate ISDN. Twenty-three 64K B-channels and one 64K D-channel.

PRML: Partial Response/Maximum Likelihood. A data encoding mechanism used by more recent hard disk drives.

PROM: Programmable Read-Only Memory. A chip that contains permanently embedded code.

PXE: Preboot Execution Environment

QAM: Quadrature Amplitude Modulation. A method of encoding data sent over a modem using a combination of frequency shifting and phase shift keying.

QDOS: Quick and Dirty Operating System

QIC: Quarter Inch Cartridge. A tape format so named because of the size of the tape used (not the size of the cartridge).

R/W: Read/Write

RAID: Redundant Array of Independent Disks

RAM: Random Access Memory. A device used for short-term storage of data or instructions that are or will soon be required by the CPU in order for it to do its job.

RAS: Remote Access Services. An NT service that allows a direct dial-up connection from a remote computer to access the host system. Also, Row Access Strobe. A circuit that is part of the MCC responsible for locking onto the first row in a memory module in which the target data is located.

RDP: Remote Desktop Protocol. A protocol that allows remote administration of another computer over the network.

RDRAM: Rambus Dynamic Random Access Memory. A specialized form of memory manufactured by Rambus, Inc.

REQ: Request

RIS: Remote Installation Services

RLL: Run Length Limited. One of the early data encoding mechanisms used by hard disk drives.

ROM BIOS: Read Only Memory-Basic Input Output Services. A chip on the motherboard that contains all the necessary code for jumpstarting a computer from a dead off condition to the point where the OS can take over.

RSoP: Resultant Set of Policy. A feature in XP that allows the administrator to test the results of a new policy on a select group of guinea pigs before inflicting it on the entire network.

RTC: Real Time Clock. The chip that keeps actual time, as humans keep track of it, on the systems.

SAM: Security Account Manager. An encrypted file stored within the registry of NT that hold the security attributes for all user and group accounts.

SATA: Serial ATA

SCSI: Small Computer Systems Interface. An interface that allows several different types of device to hook up to the same controller circuit.

SCTS: Security Configuration Tool Set

SDK: Software Development Kit. A collection of utilities and programs provided by an OS manufacturer that makes the development of applications to run on its OS much easier.

SDRAM: Synchronous Dynamic Random Access Memory

SE: Single Ended

SECC: Single Edge Contact Cartridge. A type of CPU package that makes use of an edge card connector and mounts in a slot.

SFC: System File Checker

SFP: System File Protection. A Windows utility that prevents critical OS files from being deleted or overwritten, and if they are, can replace them on the fly.

SID: Security Identifier. A unique number generated and assigned to an object on the system or network that allows LSA to manage the security for that object.

SIMD: Single Instruction, Multiple Data. A process by which a CPU can execute an instruction once, but apply that instruction to several sets of data simultaneously.

SIMM: Single Inline Memory Module. A 30- or 72-pin memory module on which two opposing pins on the base perform the same function.

SIP: SCSI Interlocked Protocol

SIPP: Single Inline Pin Package. An earlier memory module that put eight or nine DRAM chips on a single IC and mounted into the system board by way of a single row of pins protruding from the base.

SLR: Scalable Linear Recording. A tape drive technology that uses linear recording technology and allows multiple channels of data to be stored across the width of the tape.

SMART: Self Monitoring Analysis and Reporting Technology. Commands built into a hard disk interface that allow the drive to do some rather extensive self-diagnostics.

SMP: Symmetric Multiprocessing. The ability of an OS to run OS or application code equally distributed across all available CPUs.

SO-DIMM: Small Outline Dual Inline Memory Module. A compact form of memory used primarily in notebook computers, but also seen in some video cards.

SOH: Start of Header. A header is not always used, but is an important part of most protocols.

SPC: SCSI Primary Commands

SPGA: Staggered Pin Grid Array. A pin-mounted CPU on which the pins are arranged in offsetting rows of pins that results in a pattern of diagonal rows.

SPI: SCSI Parallel Interface

SPS: Standby Power Supply. A device that uses a generator to continue to provide power to an entire room or building after a total loss of electricity.

SRAM: Static RAM. A form of very high-speed memory typically used for cache.

SRM: Security Reference Monitor. An NT service that compares a user's access token to the ACL and either allows or denies access to a specific resource accordingly.

SSA: Serial Storage Architecture

SSE: Streaming SIMD Extensions. The set of instructions that supports the execution of a single instruction on several sets of data at once.

SSP: Serial Storage Protocol

STP: Shielded Twisted Pair

STX: Start of Text: Pretty self-explanatory. It tells you that the next series of bits is the data being sent.

SYN: Synchronization character. This makes sure all the bytes in the frame stick together as they move across the wire and then get reassembled in the right order at the other end. If no data is being transmitted, SYN blocks can be transmitted to keep the session alive.

TCP/IP: Transmission Control Protocol/Internet Protocol. The networking protocol of the Internet.

TFT: Thin Film Transistor. An LCD that utilizes microscopically thin layers of transistors laid out in a grid pattern in a liquid crystal emulsion.

TIA: Telecommunications Industry Association

TIFF: Tagged Image File Format. An image file format used for storing digital images that does not result in any loss of quality.

TSR: Terminate and Stay Resident. Any program that is launched, performs a task, but then remains in memory in case its services are required again.

UFS: Unix File System

UHF: Ultrahigh Frequency

UMB: Upper Memory Block. A segment of memory created by an extended memory manager in the address range between 640K and 1MB of conventional memory.

UPNP: Universal Plug 'n Play. Revised PnP standards that are constantly monitored and updated by the UPNP Forum.

UPS: Uninterruptible Power Supply. A device that uses a bank of batteries to continue to provide current to the devices plugged in when there has been a total loss of electricity.

USB: Universal Serial Bus. A moderate-speed bus that allows 127 devices to share a single chain and a 12Mb/s bandwidth.

UTP: Unshielded Twisted Pair

UV: Ultraviolet. Wavelengths of light beyond the upper range of the visible light spectrum.

UVGA: Ultra VGA. High-resolution VGA.

VBR: Volume Boot Record

VC-SDRAM: Virtual Channel SDRAM. A newer form of memory that gives each operational application its own address space and path to move data back and forth, so that they don't compete for bandwidth.

VDD: Virtual Device Driver. A piece of software running within an OS that emulates a hardware device driver.

VESA: Video Electronics Standards Association. The organization charged with maintaining standards surrounding graphics adapters and monitors.

VFAT: Virtual File Allocation Table. A software driver that emulates the file allocation tables stored on a hard disk and prevents applications from making direct calls to the hardware.

VGA: Video Graphics Array. The most commonly used video display in use today.

VHF: Very High Frequency

VID-VRM: Voltage Identifier, Voltage Regulator Module. A device that automatically locks on to the correct voltage of the installed chip and configures the device accordingly.

VLB: VESA Local Bus. A 32-bit 33MHz bus designed by VESA to address issues surrounding the transfer of large amounts of graphics data. VLB was designed to be backwardly compatible with ISA.

VMM: Virtual Machine Manager and Virtual Memory Manager. The first is a piece of software running within an OS that creates, maintains, and breaks down in memory an environment that emulates an actual computer. The second is a piece of software running within an OS that creates and manages the swap file on a hard drive.

VMS: Virtual Memory System. An OS written by DEC.

VPN: Virtual Private Network

VR: Vertical Refresh. The number of times per second a monitor regenerates the image on the screen.

WAN: Wide Area Network

WDM: Windows Driver Model

WHQL: Windows Hardware Quality Lab. A division of Microsoft that tests hardware and driver functionality in the Windows OS. There are some who might say this is an oxymoron.

WINS: Windows Internet Naming Service. A service that resolves host name to IP address on the local network.

WMI: Windows Management Instrumentation

WORM: Write Once Read Many. A recording technology that write protects the contents of the medium in order to prevent that data from being erased or overwritten.

WSH: Windows Script Host

WTX: Workstation Technology Extended. One of several form factors whose objective was to keep the system as small as possible.

XGA: Extended Graphics Array. A proprietary display created by IBM.

COMMONLY USED FILE EXTENSIONS

First off, let me say that there is *no way* I intend to provide an exhaustive list of file extensions. Such a list would easily fill a book this size if I tried to describe not only every extension in use, but every way in which any given extension is used. The same collection of letters may represent half a dozen or more different file types.

What I've done here is put together a relatively comprehensive list that shows the extensions used by the majority of programming languages in use as well as those used by popular applications. There are many extensions I've missed. Some I left out simply because a program is now obsolete or is targeted to a very exclusive audience. There are no doubt others that are commonly used that I simply missed. I'm a human being. It happens. So if you have a file you're trying to identify, hopefully this list will be of help.

A List of File Extensions

Extension	Description
A02	OzWin CompuServe E-mail/Forum Access SYSOP File, Archive Section
A03	OzWin CompuServe E-mail/Forum Access SYSOP File, Archive Section
A04	OzWin CompuServe E-mail/Forum Access SYSOP File, Archive Section
A05	OzWin CompuServe E-mail/Forum Access SYSOP File, Archive Section
A06	OzWin CompuServe E-mail/Forum Access SYSOP File, Archive Section
A07	OzWin CompuServe E-mail/Forum Access SYSOP File, Archive Section
A08	OzWin CompuServe E-mail/Forum Access SYSOP File, Archive Section

Extension	Description
A09	OzWin CompuServe E-mail/Forum Access SYSOP File, Archive Section
A10	OzWin CompuServe E-mail/Forum Access SYSOP File
A11	AIM Graphic
A2A	APLASCII EISPACK
A31	Authorware Ver. 3.x Library
A3D	Amapi 3D Modeling (Eovia)
A3K	Yamaha A3000 Sampler File
A3L	Authorware Ver. 3.x Library
A3M	Unpackaged Authorware File
A41	Authorware Ver. 4.x Library
A4L	Authorware Ver. 4.x Library
A4M	Unpackaged Authorware MacIntosh File

(continued)

Extension	Description
A4P	Authorware File without Runtime
A4W	Unpackaged Authorware Windows File
A65	Macromedia Authorware v6.5
A6P	Authorware Application (Macromedia, Inc.)
A86	A86 Assembler Source Code
AA	Audio Book
AA	PROGNOSIS Automated Analyst Document File
AAA	Sybase SQLAnywhere Temp File
AAB	Authorware Binary (Macromedia)
AAC	MPEG-2 Advanced Audio Coding File
AAF	Advanced Authoring Format File
AAM	Authorware Shocked File (Map) (Macromedia)
AAO	America's Army Map
AAP	Apollo Advanced Playlist
AAPKG	ArchestrA IDE Package (Invensys)
AAS	Authorware Shocked Packet (Segment) (Macromedia)
AAS	Movie Clip; Autodesk Animation Setup; used by Compton's Reference Collection
AAS	Audible Words File (Audible, Inc.)
AAT	Arcinfo Line Data Attribute Data
AB	Applix Builder
AB$	AutoCAD Spooled Plot
AB3	PhotoImpact Album File
ABA	Palm Address Book File (Palm)
ABAP	ABAP Source Code (SAP AG)
ABC	ABC Programming Language and ACT! E-mail Address Book File
ABD	AmBiz Bonus Calculator Data File
ABI	AOL 6 Organizer
ABK	CorelDraw AutoBackup and HP-95LX Appointment Book File
ABM	HitPlayer Audio Album File
ABR	Photoshop Brush
ABU	ACT! E-mail Address Book File
ABW	AbiWord Document File
ABX	WordPerfect Address Book File
ABY	AOL
AC3	AC3 Audio File Format
ACA	Agent Character (Microsoft)
ACAD	AutoCAD Database
ACB	AOL Cab Launcher and Photoshop Color Book
ACD	Agent Character Definition (Microsoft)
ACF	Agent Character (Microsoft)
ACF	DB/TextWorks Database Access Control File and Photoshop Custom Filter

Extension	Description
ACG	Agent Preview and Age of Wonders Saved Game
ACGI	AppleSearch CGI Interface
ACL	Access Control List
ACM	Windows System File
ACO	Photoshop Color Swatch File
ACT	FoxPro Documenting Wizard Action Diagram and Photoshop Color Table
ACW	Accessibility Wizard Settings
AD2	Compressed Voice File
AD3	Compressed Voice File
ADA	Advanced Digital Audio Compressed Audio
ADB	ACT! Activity Data File
ADD	PageMaker
ADE	Access Project Extension
ADF	Adapter Description File and Admin Config File
ADI	AutoCAD Plotter File
ADM	After Dark Screen Saver Module
ADN	Access Blank Project Template
ADO	Photoshop Duotone Options
ADP	Access Project
ADP	AOLserver Dynamic Page and FaxWorks Modem Setup File
ADR	Address Book
ADS	ADS Applications File
ADT	AutoCAD Audit Report and ACT! Document Template
AG	Lotus Agenda Application
AG4	Access G4 File
AHP	AutoCAD Help
AHQ	AudioHQ Plug-in Module
AHS	Photoshop Halftone Screens
AHTM	HTML File
AHTML	HTML File
AI	Corel Trace Drawing
AIF	Audio Interchange File
AIFC	Audio Interchange File
AIFF	Audio Interchange File
AIM	Instant Messenger
AIML	Artificial Intelligence Markup Language
AIP	Illustrator Plug-in
AIR	Flight Simulator Aircraft Performance Info File
AJL	ARCserve Backup Journal File (Computer Associates)
AKF	Acrobat Key File
AL	Oracle File
ALBM	HP Photosmart Photo Printing Album
ALC	Norton Internet Security Ad Server File

(continued)

Extension	Description
ALF	LANDesk Client Manager Configuration File
ALL	WordPerfect Printer Info
ALM	Alpha Five Database Information File (Alpha Software)
ALR	VirusScan Alert File
ALT	WordPerfect Menu File
ALV	Photoshop Levels
ALX	ActiveX Layout File and Alpha V Library Index
AME	ACT! E-mail System Library
AMF	Advanced Module Format Music
AMP	Photoshop Arbitrary Map Settings
AMS	Photoshop Monitor Setup
ANI	Windows Animated Cursor
ANS	Word Text and Layout
AOB	DVD Audio File
AOL	AOL
AOM	Download Manager Online Manager Shortcut
AOT	Novell snAppShot Application Binary Object Template File
APC	Lotus Printer Driver Characters
APD	Lotus Printer Driver
APD	PageMaker Printer Description
APE	Winamp Plug-ins AVS File
APF	Acrobat Profile File and Lotus Printer Driver Fonts
API	Application Program Interface and Acrobat Plug-in
APM	Aldus Placeable Metafiles
APP	dBASE Application Object File
APR	ArcView Project File
APS	Visual C++ File
APX	C++ Appexpert Database
AQL	AOL Windows DLL
AR	Javasoft JRE 1.3 Library File
ARA	ATI Radeon Video Driver
ARG	AutoCAD Profile Export
ARI	Compressed Archive
ARJ	Compressed Archive
ARL	AOL Organizer
ARLOLD	AOL 6 Organizer
ARQ	Compressed Archive
ART	Used by a variety of different companies for graphics files
ARV	AutoRoute User Information
ARX	AutoCAD Runtime Extension and ARX Compressed Archive
ARX	ARX Compressed Archive
ARY	Compaq SmartStart Scripting Toolkit File

Extension	Description
AS	Macromedia Flash Action Script
AS4	AS/400 Client Access
ASA	Active Server Document
ASC	ASCII Text
ASD	Word Automatic Backup
ASF	Lotus Screen Font
ASHX	ASP.NET Web Handler File
ASI	Assembler Include
ASIC	ASIC Language Source Code
ASL	Photoshop Layer Style
ASO	Assembler Object
ASP	Active Server Page, Photoshop File Index, and Photoshop Separation Setup
ASPHTML	ASP HTML
ASPX	ASP.NET Source File
ASR	Photoshop Scratch Area
AST	Photoshop Separation Tables
ASV	Photoshop Selective Color
ASX	ActiveSite Extension (Jonathon Rossi)
AT	Rescue Disk file
ATF	Photoshop Transfer Function
ATN	Photoshop Action File
ATX	A ZIP-formatted Compressed Archive
ATX	Alphasoft Trueterm 2001 Dictionaries
AT_	Audio Utility Winatb Compressed File
AU	uLaw/AU Audio File
AU3	AutoIt Ver. 3 Script
AUD	Winamp Media File
AUT	Authentication File
AUTOCONF	UNIX File
AVA	Photoshop Variations File
AVB	Inoculan Anti-Virus Virus Infected File
AVC	Kaspersky Antivirus Toolkit File
AVD	DOS7 File and Avery Label Pro Data File
AVG	AVG Virus Information Database
AVI	Audio Video Interleave File
AVS	Animation
AVS	Winamp Advanced Visualization Studio
AVX	ArcView Extension File
AWD	Award BIOS
AWE	Acrobat Bookmark XML File
AWP	MS Fax Key Viewer
AWR	Ad-aware Reference File
AWW	Office Write Document
AWX	DirectX 8.1
AX	MPEG-4 DVD Filter
AXD	Actrix Technical 2000
AXE	Paradigm C++ Integrated Debugger File and AutoRoute Export File
AXG	AutoRoute Trip File
AXS	HTML; ActiveX Script

(continued)

Extension	Description
AXT	Photoshop Replace Color/Color Range
AZ	WinDVD File
AZM	CP/M Disk Fix File
B	BASIC Language Source
B!K	Flight Simulator Scenery File
B4S	Winamp 3+ Playlist
B5I	IsoBuster CD/DVD Image File
B5T	IsoBuster Description File for a CD-Image
B64	Base 64 MIME-encoded File
BA$	MS Compressed BAS Decompress with UNPACK.EXE
BAC	Backup
BACKUP	Ad-aware Reference File
BAD	Oracle bad File
BAG	AOL 6 Organizer
BAG	Instant Messenger
BAK	Backup
BAL	BAL Borland Programming Language Source
BAN	Creatacard Banner Project
BAR	dBASE Application Generator Horizontal Menu Object
BAS	BASIC Source Code
BAT	Batch File
BBM	Deluxe Paint Image File
BBS	Bulletin Board System Text
BCB3	BC3
BCC	C++ File/Makefile
BCD	Turbo Pascal DOS File
BCH	dBASE Application Generator Batch Process Object
BCK	Backup
BCM	Compaq Easy Access Keyboard Driver
BCO	Bitstream Fontware
BCP	C++ Makefile
BCS	Windows95 Browse Information
BCT	Business Card Designer Template
BCW	C++ Version 4.5 Environment Settings
BDB	Works Database File
BDE	Borland Database Engine
BDF	Backup To CD-RW Backup Definition File and UNIX Font File
BDX	JavaBib Index File
BEN	Syssoft Sandra File
BER	German Bericht Report File
BEX	Pretty Good Privacy (PGP) Binary Extracted Public Key
BEXPK	Pretty Good Privacy (PGP) Binary Extracted Public Key
BEZ	Bezier Surface File and Bitstream Fontware

Extension	Description
BFC	Windows 95 Briefcase File
BFF	AIX Backup File Format
BFM	UNIX Font Metrics File
BFX	BitFax Document
BG	Lotus Agenda File
BGI	Borland Graphic Interface
BGL	Babylon Glossary File
BGT	Quicken 2002 Internet Common File
BHF	pcAnywhere Host File
BHI	Partminer Lib file
BHL	Partminer Lib file
BHTML	BabuHTML Embedded Software File
BHX	BinHex Compressed File ASCII Archive
BI	Binary File
BIB	Bibliography
BIC	Civilization III Scenario
BIF	GroupWise Initialization File
BIG	Chinese Text
BIG5	Chinese Text
BIL	ArcView Image File
BIN	Binary File, CDR-Win CD Image File, Linux Executable and AVG Antivirus Update File
BIP	ArcView Image File
BIX	Civilization III Scenario
BK	Backup
BK!	Backup
BK$	Backup
BK1	Bach Preludes and Fugues MIDI akmi Source, Book 1
BK1	Backup
BK2	Backup
BK3	Backup
BK4	Backup
BK5	Backup
BK6	Backup
BK7	Backup
BK8	Backup
BK9	Backup
BKF	Windows XP Backup Utility
BKG	Background File
BKP	Backup
BKS	Works Spreadsheet Backup and Windows 2000 Scheduled Backup File
BLA	Black Color Separation
BLB	ACT! Database File
BLC	BIACORE Instruments and BIAlite Project
BLD	ACT!
BLF	Beast 2.02 Trojan File
BLG	Windows Binary Performance Log
BLK	WordPerfect Temporary File

(continued)

Extension	Description
BLL	VBS/European-A Worm
BLR	BIACORE Instruments and BIAlite Project
BLS	BIACORE Instruments and BIAlite Project
BLT	Wordperfect for DOS
BLZ	Serial Number File
BM	X Windows System Bitmap
BMF	Corel Flow Image File
BML	Alpha Five Image Library File
BMM	Tacmi Pixia Palette File
BMP	Windows Bitmap Graphics
BMP24	Bitmap Graphic
BMT	Ami Pro Button Image and Alpha Five Image Library File
BMX	Alpha Five Image Library File
BMZ	Compressed BMP File
BN	AdLib Instrument Bank
BND	Flight Simulator Panels File
BNK	AdLib Instrument Bank
BOE	Outlook Express Backup File
BOF	IBM Voice Type Language Task Enroll File
BOI	Botje Bot-file (TNHteam)
BOL	Booasm Compressed Archive Library
BOM	Bill of Materials File
BONK	BONK Lossless/Lossy Audio Compressor
BOO	Compressed Archive File
BOOK	FrameMaker Book
BORLAND	C Makefile
BOX	Notes (and others) Mailbox
BOZ	BZIP Over ZIP Compressed File Archive
BP	Binary Picture TIFF Bitmap
BPG	Borland Project Group
BPI	IBM Voice Type languages Newuser File
BPK	C++ Builder Package File
BPL	AutoCAD R2000 Batch Plot List and Winamp Playlist File
BPP	Clarion for Windows Backup Application
BPP	MUSICMATCH Burner Plus Project
BPR	C++ Builder 6 Project
BPS	Works Document
BPT	Corel Bitmap Master File
BPW	ArcView World File for BIP or BMP Images
BRI	Basic Rate Interface File
BRS	Corel Painter Brush File
BRU	Photoline4 Brushes File
BRX	Multimedia Browsing Index
BS2	Basic Stamp 2 Code File
BSA	BSARC Compressed Archive

Extension	Description
BSB	MapInfo Sea Chart
BSN	MIDI File
BSP	Various Game Maps
BSQ	ArcView Image File and Oracle Control File
BSV	BASIC Bsave Graphics
BSY	FTN Soft Busy Flag
BS_	Bookshelf Find Menu Shell Extension
BTOA	Binary-to-ASCII Format
BTR	Btrieve Database File
BTR	FrontPage Binary-Tree Index
BTX	DB/TextWorks Database Term and Word Indexes
BU	Pegasus Mail Temporary File
BUD	Quicken Backup
BUF	WinXL File
BUFR	Binary Universal Form for the Representation
BUFR	Meteorological Data
BUG	Bug (Problem) File
BUGS	Generally Bugs File
BUNDLE	iMovie 3 Plug-in Bundle
BUP	Backup DVD Info File
BUY	Movie Data File
BV1	WordPerfect Overflow File
BV2	WordPerfect Overflow File
BV3	WordPerfect Overflow File
BV4	WordPerfect Overflow File
BV5	WordPerfect Overflow File
BV6	WordPerfect Overflow File
BV7	WordPerfect Overflow File
BV8	WordPerfect Overflow File
BV9	WordPerfect Overflow File
BVC	IBM Voice Type Language Newuser File
BVH	Biovision Motion File
BVI	IBM Voice Type Language Newuser File
BVL	Micrografx Picture Publisher 8 Textures File
BVS	BVS Solitaire Collection
BW	Silicon Graphics Raw Black and White Bitmap
BW1	Byteworx FMEA_ FMEA Database
BWA	BlindWrite CD Image
BWB	Visual Baler Spreadsheet File
BWC	BeadWizard Color Palette
BWP	Book Writer Project
BWR	Kermit Beware Bug List
BWS	BlindWrite
BWT	BlindWrite CD Image File and CD Mage TOC File
BWZ	WinImage Batch Configuration File
BXP	BootXP File

(continued)

Extension	Description
BYU	Movie File
BZ	Bzip UNIX Compressed File
BZ1	WinTOTAL Automatic Backup
BZ2	Bzip 2 UNIX Compressed File
BZA	BZA Compressed Archive
BZF	Textures and Other Information
B~K	Backup
C	C/C++ Program File and Unix Compact File Archive
C#=	C#
C++	C++ Source Code
C—	Sphinx C— Source
C00	Ventura Print File
C2D	WinOnCD CD Image
C2I	Driver File
C2X	WinonCD File
C3D	Micrografx
C4	Joint Engineering Data Management (JEDMICS) DoD Engineering Data Format
C4D	Cinema 4D
C64	Commodore 64 Game ROM
C86	Computer Innovation C86 C Program
CA	Telnet Server Initial Cache Data File
CA0	Installer Packed and Split File
CA1	Delphi Install Disk11 File
CA2	Delphi Install Disk12 File
CA3	Delphi Install Disk9 File
CA4	Delphi Install Disk10 File
CA5	Delphi Install Disk11 File
CAB	Cabinet File
CAC	dBASE IV Executable File
CAD	Softdesk Drafix CAD File and QuickCAD Drawing
CAF	Southern Company Terrestrial Data Acq
CAG	Clip Gallery Catalog File
CAL	Cakewalk Application Language Script
CAL	Calendar File and SuperCalc Worksheet
CAP	Various Capture Files and Compressed Music Files
CAPS	Visimetrics Digital CCTV Recording
CAR	Card format file for various programs
CAS	Comma-delimited ASCII File
CAT	Catalog File
CAZ	Computer Associates Archive
CA_	Cakepro Compressed Audio File
CB	Brief Macro Source Code
CBD	System DLL Catroot File
CBF	Calendar Builder Saved Calendar
CBF	Infinity Game Engine Archive of Resources
CBH	ChessBase Chess Database File

Extension	Description
CBI	IBM Mainframe Column Binary Formatted File
CBK	System DLL Catroot File
CBL	COBOL Program
CBM	Fuzzy Bitmap and Xlib Compiled Bitmap
CBP	CD Box Labeler Pro
CBS	Computer Based Training
CBT	Computer Based Training
CBV	ChessBase Archive File
CBW	Cardbox Workspace
CBX	Rational XDE
CBZ	CDisplay ZIP Archived Comic Book File
CC	C++ Program File
CC5	Calendar Creator 5.x 6.x File
CCA	CC:Mail Archive File
CCAD	ClarisCAD data
CCB	Visual Basic Animated Button Configuration
CCC	WordPerfect Office Calendar File
CCD	Vector CAD Program File
CCE	Calendar Creator 2 Event File
CCH	Corel Chart
CCH	PhotoModeler
CCI	CCITT Group 3 and Group 4 Encoding
CCITT	CCITT Group 3 and Group 4 Encoding
CCJ	Crossword Compiler Compiled Crossword Applet
CCK	Corel Clipart Format
CCL	Intalk Communication Command Language
CCM	CC:Mail Mailbox
CCN	IMSI Multimedia Fusion Express File
CCO	CyberChat Data File
CCP	C Converter Profiles
CCR	Internet Chat Room Shortcut
CCRF	Calcomp Raster Bitmap
CCS	CCS-lib File
CCT	Macromedia Director Shockwave Cast
CCX	Corel Compressed Exchange File and CorelDraw File
CC_	Audio Utility Midimach Compressed File
CDA	CD Audio Track Shortcut
CDAT	Internet Security and Acceleration (ISA) Server Cache File
CDB	Clipboard File and Turbo C Database
CDBK	SPSS Database File
CDC	Nero Burning ROM CD Cover File and Claris Draw Document
CDF	ASCII Format Describing VRML Worlds and Comma Delimited Format
CDI	Phillips Compact Disk Interactive Format

(continued)

Extension	Description
CDL	CADKEY Advanced Design Language (CADL)
CDM	Compressed Music Format and Novell NetWare Disk Drivers
CDQ	CD Indexer
CDR	Corel Vector Graphic Drawing and generic sound file
CDT	Corel Draw Template
CDW	CADKEY Organized Dialog File
CDX	Active Server Document, FoxPro Index and Corel Draw Compressed Document
CE3	Calendar Creator 3.x 4.x Event List
CEL	Audition Loop File
CEM	Computer Graphics Metafile
CEO	Extension associated with Winevar Worm
CER	Internet Security Certificate File
CEV	LOUT Character Encoding File
CF	Sendmail Configuration File
CF1	Common File Format 1
CF2	Common File Format 2
CF4	Catfish File Manager Support File
CFB	Inmos Binary Configuration File
CFC	Cold Fusion File
CFD	CryptoForge Document (Ranquel Technologies)
CFE	CryptoForge Encrypted File (Ranquel Technologies)
CFF	Common File Format
CFG	Configuration File
CFL	Corel Flowchart File
CFM	Cold Fusion Template File and Corel FontMaster
CFO	Turbo C
CFR	IBM Configurator Report
CFT	Flow Chart; Corel Flow Template
CFW	ChemFinder Form
CFX	Creative DSP File
CG	Norton Crashguard File
CG3	Dungeons & Dragons Character File
CGA	CGA Resolution BMP Bitmap
CGM	Computer Graphics Metafile
CHA	Character Data
CHF	pcAnywhere Remote Control File
CHG	Quicken On-line Data File
CHH	C++ Header
CHI	Help File Index
CHJ	Help Composer Project
CHK	CHKDSK/SCANDISK Output and WordPerfect Temporary File
CHL	Configuration History Log
CHM	HTML Help Compiled Help File

Extension	Description
CHP	Ventura Publisher Chapter
CHQ	Help Combined Full-text Search File
CHR	Character or Font File
CHS	Corel WP Chart Style
CHT	Harvard Graphics Vector File
CHW	HTML Help General Index Funtionally comparable to .GID.
CHZ	ChArc Compressed File Archive
CIF	Chip Layout Information and Easy CD Creator Image File
CIK	Corel Graphics Ver. 10 Custom Dual Tone File
CIL	Clip Gallery Download Package
CIM	CompuApps Drive Backup Image
CIX	TCU Turbo C Utilities Database Index
CKB	C++ Keyboard Mapping File
CKD	CADKEY Design File
CKT	CADKEY Template File
CL	Generic LISP Source Code
CL3	Bruker Aspect NMR Data File
CL3	Easy CD Creator Layout File
CL4	Easy CD Creator Layout File
CL5	Easy CD Creator Layout File
CLA	Java Class File
CLASS	Java Class File
CLB	Corel Library
CLC	Corel Catalog
CLD	CA Clipper Debugger Configuration File
CLF	ListPro File
CLG	Disk Catalog Database
CLK	Corel R.A.V.E. Animation File
CLM	Micrografx Picture Publisher 7 Macro
CLN	Backup Configuration File
CLP	Windows Clipboard/Picture
CLS	Class Definitions for Various Programming Languages
CLW	Visual C++ Class Wizard File
CLX	Acrobat
CLY	Corel Graphics Ver.10 Custom Layouts File and ACT! Layout
CLY	ACT! Layout (Best Software CRM Division)
CMB	Xtree for Windows Button Bar
CMD	Command File for Windows NT, CPM and OS2 Plus dBASE II Program File
CMF	Corel Metafile
CMP	Address Document and JPEG Bitmap
CMR	MediaPlayer Movie
CMT	Corel Draw
CMU	CMU Window Manager Bitmap
CMV	Corel Move Animation
CMW	Custom Maintenance Wizard File

(continued)

Extension	Description
CMX	Presentation Exchange Image or Generic Patchfile
CMYK	Raw Cyan, Magenta, Yellow, and Black Samples
CNF	Configuration File
CNM	Windows Application Menu Options and Setup File
CNR	Pegasus Mail Mail Message in Systemwide Folder
CNS	Windows2000 Client Connection Manager Export File
CNT	Help File Contents
CNV	WordPerfect Temporary File
CNV	DB2 Conversion File
CNX	Rational XDE
CN_	Regeditx File
CO	Cult3D ActiveX Player Application
CO$	MS Compressed COM Decompress with UNPACK.EXE.
COB	COBOL Program File
COD	C Compiler Output and Character Set Code File
COL	HTML Help Collection File
COM	Command
CONSOLE	WinNT Console File
COV	Fax Cover Page
CPD	Corel PrintOffice File
CPE	Fax Cover Sheet
CPF	Complete Fax File
CPH	Corel PrintHouse Image
CPI	Windows or DOS International Code Page
CPL	Corel Color Palette and Windows Control Panel Extension
CPL	Windows Control Panel Extension
CPO	Corel Print House File
CPP	C++ Builder 6 and C++ Source Code File
CPR	Corel Presents Presentation
CPS	Color Postscript File, Antivirus Checksum, PC Tools Backup
CPT	Corel Photo-Paint Image and dBASE Encryted Memo
CPX	Control Panel Applet
CRC	JPEG Sheriff CRC Info File
CRD	Windows Cardfile
CRF	Database Cross-Reference File
CRP	Corel Presents Run-Time Presentation, dBASE Encrypted Database and dBASE Custom Report
CRS	WordPerfect 5.1 for Windows File Conversion Resource

Extension	Description
CRS	Dance With Intensity
CRT	Certificate File
CRV	Corel Graphics Ver. 10 Custom Gradients File
CSA	Comma Deliminated Text
CSB	Corel Photo-Paint Script
CSD	Bitstream Fontware
CSH	Photoshop Custom Shape
CSL	AOL Modem Script
CSM	C++ Symbol File or C++ Compiled Header
CSP	AudioZip Encoded Audio
CSQ	Foxpro Query
CSS	Hypertext Cascading Style Sheet
CST	Macromedia Director Cast File
CSV	Comma-Separated Variables
CSW	WordPerfect Setup Info File
CTB	AutoCAD Color-dependent Plot Style Table
CTC	PC Installer Control
CTD	Cardtable File
CTF	Calculator Text Format or Compressed TIFF File
CTL	Setup Information or User Control File
CTR	Counter file and Corel40 Trace File
CTS	ABC Programming Language Permanent Location Contents
CTT	MSN Messenger Saved Contact List
CTX	Chinese Character Input File and Compressed Text
CUR	Windows Cursor
CUS	AutoCAD Custom Dictionary
CV	Corel Versions Archive
CVA	Compaq Diagnostics
CVB	Borland BDE File
CVF	Compressed Volume File
CVP	WinFax Cover Page (Symantec)
CVS	Sound File
CVT	dBASE Converted Database Backup
CWK	Claris Works Data
CWL	ClarisWorks Library
CWS	Claris Works Template
CW_	Corel Graphics Ver. 10 Workspace
CXE	Common XML Envelope
CXT	Macromedia Director Protected Cast File
CXX	Visual C++ Source Code File
CYA	Cyan Color Separation
C~G	Windows 3.x System File
D	D Programming Language Source Code File

(continued)

Extension	Description
D00	AdLib Format File and Blaster Master Pro File
D11	Macro Mania Data File
D2V	DVD Ripper File
D30	Driver
D32	Lotus Visualisation File
D3D	Various 3D Graphics Files
D3T	Doom Texture
DA0	Windows Registry Backup
DA1	Registry Backup
DAC	Sound File
DAF	Download Accelerator
DAL	SpeedBit Download Accelerator Plus DAP List
DAN	ATI Radeon Video Driver
DAO	Windows Registry Backup
DAP	Access Data Access Page
DAS	Download Accelerator File List
DAT	Commonly Used Extension for Data Files
DAX	Daxaif Compressed Audio
DAY	Journal
DAZ	Poser 3D File
DB	Commonly used extension for database files
DB$	dBASE Temporary File
DB0	dBASE Initialization File
DB1	Adressmn
DB2	dBASE II
DB3	dBASE III File
DB4	dBASE 4 Data
DBA	Commonly Used Extension for Data Files
DBB	ANSYS Database Backup
DBC	Visual Foxpro Database Container
DBD	Oracle Record Type
DBE	Database Engine File
DBF	Commonly Used Extension for Database Files
DBG	Commonly Used Extension for Debug Files
DBI	Borland Database Explorer Information
DBK	dBASE Database Backup
DBL	Windows XP Product Activation File
DBM	Cold Fusion Template
DBO	dBASE IV Compiled Program File
DBP	Visual Studio .NET Database Project
DBQ	AutoCAD DB Query
DBR	DB/TextWorks Database
DBS	Commonly Used Extension for Database Files
DBT	Commonly used extension for database text or database template files
DBV	Abacus Law Ver. 10 Data

Extension	Description
DBW	DataBoss Database File
DBX	Database Index and Outlook Express E-mail Folder
DB_	CAD File
DC	DesignCAD CAD File
DC$	Ntgraph Visual C Wizard File
DC+	DataCAD Plus Drawing
DC2	DesignCAD CAD File
DC5	DataCAD Drawing File
DCA	Visual Basic X DateBook File
DCA	DCA Archiver Compressed Archive
DCD	FORTRAN Data File
DCD	INMOS Transputer Development System Occam Object Code
DCE	AutoCAD R2000 Dialog Error Log
DCF	Commonly Used Extension for Database Configuration Files and Disk Image Files
DCL	AutoCAD Dialog Control Language Description
DCM	Sound
DCP	Delphi Compiled Packages
DCR	Kodak Digital Camera Raw Image File
DCS	Color Separated EPS Format, Bitmap Graphic and Desktop Color Separation File
DCT	Dictionary
DCU	Delphi Compiled Unit
DCV	DriveCrypt Volume
DCW	Draft Choice for Windows
DCX	DesignCAD and PC Paintbrush File Extension
DDB	Commonly Used Extension for Database Files
DDD	Acrobat Distiller
DDE	Dynamic Data Exchange
DDF	Btrieve Data Dictionary File
DDI	Disk Doubler Image
DDL	SQL Data Definition Language File
DDM	Alpha Five Table Objects
DDP	Delphi 6 File
DDP	Inor DSoft Software File
DDR	FileMaker Pro Database Design Report
DDS	Photoshop Compressed Textures and DirectDraw Surface
DDV	Xbase Dbfast Example Ivadbsp File
DDW	CSPro File
DDX	Alpha Five Dictionary Index File
DEB	DOS Debug Script
DEC	DEC DX, WPS Plus Document and Decoded File
DEF	Definition File
DEL	Deleted Data List

(continued)

Extension	Description
DEM	Delphi Edit Mask
DEO	Creator Simulator Compiled Module
DEP	Visual Basic Setup Wizard Dependency
DEPLOY	DeployMaster Setup Script
DES	Description Text and Quickbooks Forms Template
DET	ACT! Saved E-mail File
DEV	Device Driver
DEX	Excel File
DEX	WinGlucofacts File
DEZ	DES Encrypted Zip File
DF	Data File
DFL	Signature Default Program Settings
DFM	C++ Builder 6 Form
DFN	Definition File
DFP	Digital Fusion Plug-in
DFS	AutoCAD Utility Defaults
DFT	WaveMaker File
DFX	AutoCAD 3D Vector Graphics and Micrografix Designer Effects
DGC	TurboTax
DGF	Acrobat
DGK	Delcam Powershape/Powermill
DGL	DynaGeo License File
DGM	Freelance Diagram
DGN	ArcView Design Drawing File
DGR	Fax Page
DHE	Visual Basic Dialog Box Help Editor Document
DHF	Help Maker File
DIC	Dictionary
DID	Acrobat Distiller
DIF	Data Interchange Format
DIL	Delphi File
DIM	AutoCAD Dimension File
DIR	Directory Indicator
DIS	Corel Draw Thesaurus
DIT	Windows2000 Active Directory Schema
DIVX	Movie Encoded with DivX-codec
DIZ	Description In Zip File
DKZ	Description In Zip File
DL	Masked .DLL File
DLD	Lotus File
DLE	Macromedia Designer 3D Translator File
DLF	Belkin Router Firmware Update
DLG	C++ Dialogue Script
DLI	Beast 2.02 Trojan File
DLK	INMOS Transputer Development System Occam Compiler Link Info
DLL	Dynamic Link Library
DLM	ASCII Delimited File, FileMake Pro Data File and Dynamic Link Module

Extension	Description
DLO	3ds max Plug-in
DLS	dataLive Database Engine File
DLV	CATIA Export File
DLW	DALiM LiTHO Line Work Bitmap
DLZ	Compressed Data File
DL_	Compressed DLL File
DM	Borland dBASE
DMA	Direct Memory Access Programming File
DMD	Corel Data Modeling Desktop
DME	Medical Manager DML System Data Merge
DMF	Windows Disk Map File
DML	Medical Manager DML System Script
DMP	Screen or Memory Dump
DMT	Delphi Menu Template
DMV	Acrobat Catalog and MPEG-1 File
DMY	Container File
DNC	Compressed Dictionary File
DOB	Visual Basic User Document Form File
DOC	Document File
DOCHTML	Word HTML Document
DOCMHTML	Word HTML Document
DOF	Delphi Option File
DOK	German or Dutch Text
DOL	D-PAS Portfolio Manager Flexible Benchmarking Analysis File
DON	Textur Editor File
DOS	DOS 7 System Files; Win 95 Boot up in DOS
DOT	Word Document Template
DOTHTML	Word HTML Document Template
DOV	Temporary File
DOX	MultiMate Document and General Extension for Text Documents
DP	Text
DPA	Archive
DPB	ProWORX Nxt Descriptor Pointer File
DPC	Delphi Package Collection File
DPD	ABC Programming Language Dyadic Predicate
DPF	Dynamic Process Format Database
DPJ	Delphi Project
DPK	Deleted Package, Windows Applications Manager
DPL	Delphi Package Library
DPMI	DOS Protected-Mode Interface Programming
DPO	Delphi Object Repository
DPP	Serif DrawPlus Drawing
DPQ	PCX Format
DPR	C++ /Delphi Default Project

(continued)

Extension	Description
DPS	DivX XP Skin
DPT	Desktop DNA Template and Publish It! Data File
DPT	Publish-It! Publication File
DPX	Animation
DQC	CP/M Disk Information File
DQY	Excel ODBC Query File
DR$	Modem Bitware Fax Disk2 File
DR9	Directory File
DRA	Dragon Naturally Speaking
DRC	Delphi Compiled Resource File
DRF	Photoline Drawing Filter
DRML	Protected Digital Content
DRS	BMP Bitmap
DRV	Device Driver
DRW	Commonly Used Extension for Drawing Programs
DRX	Photoshop Tutorial
DS	TWAIN Data Source
DSC	Description File
DSD	Document Structure Definition File
DSES	Diagnosis Session
DSF	Micrografx Designer
DSK	Commonly Used Extension for Disk Image Files
DSM	Delphi Symbol Module
DSN	ODBC Data Source
DSP	Developer Studio Project
DSQ	Corel QUERY File
DSR	Visual Basic Active Designer File and WordPerfect Driver
DSS	Digital Speech Standard File
DST	C++/Delphi Desktop Settings
DSW	C++ Desktop Settings and Visual Studio Workspace
DSX	Visual Basic Active Designer Binary File
DSY	PC Draft Symbol Library
DSZ	Win Help Related File
DT	DAT Backup
DTA	Data
DTC	Windows Applog Journal
DTE	Win Applog File
DTEA	Diagnosis Template Archive
DTF	Exchange Header File
DTG	Windows Applog File
DTH	Windows Applog File
DTI	Delphi or C++ Design Time Information and Windows Applog File
DTJ	Windows Applog File
DTL	Windows Applog File
DTP	Common Extension for Desktop Publishing Data Files

Extension	Description
DTQ	Database Tools Query
DTR	DTREG Project File
DTS	Digital Surround Audio File Format
DTX	E-Book File
DUN	Dial-Up Networking Export File
DUP	Duplicate Backup
DUT	Dutch Text File
DV	Digital Video File
DVB	AutoCAD VBA Source Code
DVC	Lotus 1-2-3 File
DVD	Animation
DVM	DVM Movie File Format
DVP	AutoCAD Device Parameter
DVR	Device Driver
DW2	DesignCAD Drawing File
DWG	AutoCAD Drawing Database
DWL	AutoCAD Drawing Database File Locking Information
DWS	AutoCAD Standarization
DWT	AutoCAD Template/Prototype and FrontPage Dynamic Web Template
DWV	WAV
DWZ	Compressed AutoCAD Drawing File
DX	Document Imaging File
DXB	AutoCAD Drawing Exchange Format
DXF	AutoCAD Drawing Interchange Format
DXP	Dynamic XML Page
DXR	Acrobat
DXX	AutoCAD Drawing Interchange Attribute File
DYN	Lotus 1-2-3 File
DZ	Dzip Compressed File
DZS	Character File
D~L	Creative DLL Copy
D~V	Windows 3.x System File
E2	Thinkdesign CAD Design
E2P	PonyProg Device File
E3	Thinkdesign CAD Design
E32	Inno Setup 1.3 File
E3D	Instant3D Project
E3D	Macromedia Extreme3D Object
E48	Emu48 HP48 Emulator File
E78	IBM 3270 Terminal Emulator Screen Layout Definition
E99	Steuer99 Daten File
EA3	Fifa 2001 Environment Data
EAC	EmEditor Auto Completion File
EAF	MicroEmacs Abbreviation File Format
EAR	Java Enterprise Application Packaging Unit
EAZ	Express Assist File
EBA	Mobile Phone Data Manager

(continued)

Extension	Description
EBF	Pocket PC Windows CE Form File
EBK	EARS Database Backup
EBK	eBook
EBO	Reader Ebook Format
EBP	Pocket PC Windows CE Project File
EBS	Windows XP Scanner File
EBX	Electronic Book Exchange
ECA	electroCAD File
ECF	Micrografx Media Manager
ECR	Ecrypt E-mail File
ECS	Encrypted Compressed GIS Software Geographic Shape File
ECW	Enhanced Compressed Wavelet
ECW	Ensoniq Waveset Format
ED	EasyDraw CAD File
EDA	Ensoniq ASR Disk Image
EDB	ACT! E-mail Data File and Exchange Server Property Store
EDD	FrameMaker Element Definition Document
EDE	Ensoniq EPS Disk Image
EDK	Ensoniq KT Disk Image
EDL	Edit Decision List
EDM	CAD Contouring Parameter Data File
EDM	Eclipse Data Module (Active Media)
EDML	Dreamweaver MX Extension File
EDN	Acrobat Document
EDQ	Ensoniq SQ1/SQ2/KS32 Disk Image
EDT	External Editor Definition
EDV	Ensoniq VFX-SD Disk Image
EDX	Editor Dictionary
EEB	WordPerfect Equation Editor Button Bar
EFA	Ensoniq ASR File
EFD	EARS Filter Definition
EFE	Ensoniq EPS File
EFK	Ensoniq KT File
EFP	Exchange Forms Designer Template
EFQ	Ensoniq SQ1/SQ2/KS32 File
EFS	Ensoniq SQ80 File
EFV	Ensoniq VFX-SD File
EGA	Enhanced Graphics Adapter Graphics Data
EGS	GIS Software Encrypted Grid Shape File
EID	IBM ViaVoice Vocabulary File
ELD	EARS Label Definition
ELF	Electronic Application Form File
ELG	EARS Log
ELH	Electronic Application Help File
ELI	ELI Compressed File Archive
ELL	ATI Radeon Video Driver
ELM	FrontPage Theme-Pack File
ELOG	McAffee Firewall Log

Extension	Description
ELT	Event List Text
EMAIL	Outlook Express Mail Message
EMB	ABT Extended Module
EMD	Micrografx System4 Media Manager File
EMF	Extended (Enhanced) Windows Metafile Format
EML	Outlook Express Electronic Mail
EMP	E-Music File Format
EMU	Emulation
EMX	MS-DOS Extender file
EMZ	Windows Compressed Enhanced Metafile
ENC	UUENCODE Encoded File
END	Corel Draw Arrow Definition
ENG	Dictionary and English Documentation
ENL	Endnote Library File
ENT	SGML Entities, Character Mapping
ENU	ATI Radeon Video Driver
ENV	Envelope or Environment
EPA	Award BIOS Logo
EPD	EARS Printer Definition
EPDF	Encapsulated Portable Document Format
EPI	Encapsulated PostScript Interchange Format
EPJ	Java-clients File
EPL	Encirq \PL Programming Language Source File
EPS	Encapsulated PostScript
EPS2	Level II Encapsulated PostScript
EPS3	Level III Encapsulated PostScript
EPSF	Encapsulated PostScript
EPSI	Encapsulated PostScript Interchange Format
EPSON	Epson Printer Graphics File
EPT	Encapsulated PostScript Interchange TIFF Preview
EQF	Winamp2/Winamp3 Equalizer Settings File
EQL	DART Pro 98 Fabric Equalization Presets
EQN	Equation
EQU	Assembly Language Equates
EQW	SPEFO Stellar Spectra Analysis File
ERM	Bitmap Graphic
ERR	Error Log
ERS	Earth Resource Mapping Satellite Image Header
ER_	Winhelp Compressed File
ES	EasySIGN Drawing Sheet
ESL	Visual FoxPro Distributable Support Library

(continued)

Extension	Description
ESO	FoxPro
ESP	Ventura File
ESPS	ESPS Audio File
ESR	4D Database Windows Procedure
EST	Streets & Trips 2001 Trip File
ET2	Electronic Tax Return Security File
ETF	Enriched Text File
ETH	HP Internet Advisor Capture File
ETL	Windows2000 Trace Log
EUC	Japanese
EUI	Ensoniq EPS Family Compacted Disk Image
EV2	Java File
EVP	Sound Envelope
EVT	Commonly used extension for event logs or event files
EWD	Express Publisher for Windows Document
EWL	Encarta Document
EX	Symantec Ghost Template File
EX$	MS Compressed EXE Decompress with UNPACK.EXE.
EX1	Renamed .EXE File
EXB	Flash Image File
EXC	Word Exclusion Dictionary
EXD	Control Information Cache
EXE	Executable File
EXO	System File
EXP	Viscal C++ Export File
EXR	OpenEXR Bitmap
EXT	E-mail Text Attachment
EXU	Euphoria File
EXW	Euphoria File
EX^	Norton Live Update File
EX_	Compressed EXE File
EZM	Text File
EZP	Edify Electronic Workforce Backup Utility
F	Compressed Archive File and FORTRAN Source Code
F01	Perfect Fax Document
F06	DOS 6-pixel Screen Font
F07	DOS 7-pixel Screen Font
F08	DOS 8-pixel Screen Font
F09	DOS 9-pixel Screen Font
F10	DOS 10-pixel Screen Font
F11	DOS 11-pixel Screen Font
F12	DOS 12-pixel Screen Font
F13	DOS 13-pixel Screen Font
F14	DOS 14-pixel Screen Font
F15	DOS 15-pixel Screen Font
F16	DOS 16-pixel Screen Font

Extension	Description
F2	Flash Bios File
F2F	File to File
F3	Flash Bios File
F32	Raw 32-bit IEEE Floating Point Values
F6	Fonts File
F64	Raw 64-bit IEEE Floating Point Values
F7	Fonts File
F77	FORTRAN 77 Program
F8	Fonts File
F90	FORTRAN Program
F96	Frecom FAX96 Document
FAD	Data File
FAQ	Frequently Asked Questions
FAQT	FAQTool XML Contents File
FAS	AutoCAD Fast-load Auto LISP
FAV	Outlook Bar Shortcuts
FAX	Fax File
FBM	Fuzzy Bitmap
FBN	ArcView Spatial Index File For Read-Only Datasets
FBS	File Burner Skin
FBX	3D Data Exchange Format
FC$	Basic Realizer Disk1 L File
FC2	Curious Labs Poser Face File
FCB	FAAST Builder File
FCD	FastCAD/EasyCAD Output and Virtual CD-ROM
FCF	HP-95LX Filer Configuration File
FCG	Mystic Photo Format
FCT	Foxpro Catalog
FCW	FastCAD File
FCX	Vax VMS Compressed File
FD	FORTRAN Declarations
FDB	FoxPro Database
FDC	Sniffer Capture File
FDE	Fade-It for AOL
FDF	Acrobat Portable Document Input Form and Format Definition File
FDL	Paradox
FDM	Floppy Disk Manager File
FEB	WordPerfect Figure Editor Button Bar
FEC	U.S. Federal Campaign Expense Submission File
FF	AGFA CompuGraphics Outline Font Description
FFA	Fast Find Status File
FFD	Flash Filer
FFE	DirectInput Force Feedback Effect
FFL	Fast Find Document List
FFP	Corel Graphics10 Custom File
FFT	DisplayWrite Document
FFX	Fast Find Index

(continued)

Extension	Description
FGX	Formula Graphics Project File
FGZ	Formula Graphics Standalone Presentation Archive
FH10	Freehand Ver. 10 File
FH11	FreehandMX Ver. 11 File
FH3	Freehand Ver. 3 Drawing
FH4	Freehand Ver. 4 Drawing
FH5	Freehand 5
FH6	Freehand 6
FH7	Freehand 7
FH8	Freehand 8
FH9	Freehand 9
FHC	Freehand
FHD	PCL Tool Form File
FHTML	HTML File
FI	Bitstream Intellifont
FIC	Windev Database System
FID	Bruker Aspect NMR Data File
FIDX	Fiasco Database Index
FIF	Font Information File
FIG	XFIG Graphic File
FIL	ACL For Windows Data, dBASE Files List Object and WordPerfect Overlay
FIN	ATI Radeon Video Driver
FIO	ULead Viewer Support File
FIP	FingerPost Information Processor File
FIT	Windows NT File Index Table
FIX	Generic Patch File
FIXED	DLL Backup Root File
FKY	Foxpro Macro
FL	Floating Format Sound
FLA	Flash Movie Authoring File and Free Lossless Audio Codec
FLASK	FlasKMPEG Language Definition File
FLC	Corel Show
FLD	VersaPro Folder Contents
FLE	Scanner Settings File
FLF	Corel Paradox Form and ASCII Editor Font File
FLF	ASCII Editor Font File
FLL	Foxpro Library
FLM	AutoCAD/Auto Shade Film and FoxPro Library
FLM	FoxPro Library
FLP	Corel Flow Project Flow Chart and Floppy Disk Image File
FLR	Live3D File
FLS	ArcView Windows Help Supporting File
FLT	Common extension for filter file
FLV	Flash Video File
FM	FileMaker Pro Spreadsheet

Extension	Description
FM1	Lotus 1-2-3 Release 2.x Spreadsheet File
FM2	Maestro Mama Demo File
FMB	Oracle Binary Form Source Code
FMD	Open Access File
FMK	FaxMaker File
FML	Oracle Mirror List
FMO	dBASE Ordered Format
FMP	AutoCAD Font Map and FileMaker Pro Document
FMS	Lotus 1-2-3 Impress Add-in
FMT	Commonly Used Extension for Format File
FMV	Frame Vector Metafile
FMX	Oracle Executable Form
FND	Explorer Saved Search
FNG	Font Navigator Group File
FNT	Font File
FO1	Turbo C Font
FO2	Turbo C Font
FOG	Fontographer Font
FOL	pfs:First Choice Database File
FOLDER	Mail Folder
FON	Font File
FOR	FORTRAN Source
FOT	Installed TrueType Font
FP	FileMaker Pro File
FP3	FileMaker Pro 3.0 File
FP5	FileMaker Pro Database
FP7	FileMaker Pro Ver. 7 Database Document
FPC	FoxPro Catalog File
FPHTML	FrontPage HTML Document
FPM	FoxPro Startup File
FPT	FileMaker Pro File Database Memo and FoxPro Memo Field
FPW	FoxPro Configuration
FPWEB	FrontPage Disk Based Web
FPX	Compiled FoxPro Program and FlashPix Bitmap
FQF	FlashFXP Queue File
FQY	FLAMES (FLARE) Command File
FR3	dBASE IV Renamed dBASEIII+ Form
FRA	FrameViewer File
FRE	Creative Digital Blaster Digital VCR File
FRF	FontMonger Font
FRG	dBASE IV Uncompiled Report
FRM	Commonly used extension for Form Files and dBASE IV Report File
FRO	dBASE IV Compiled Report
FRP	Fractal Explorer Palette

(continued)

Extension	Description
FRS	Corel Painter Pattern, Selection or Texture File
FRT	FoxPro Report File
FRX	FoxPro Report File
FRZ	FormFlow File
FS5	Flight Simulator Scenery File
FS6	Flight Simulator Panels File
FSG	IBM Voice Type Language Map File
FSI	FileSplit and Borland Paradox Form File
FSP	Floating Point Data Files
FSS	Iomega Backup File Selection Set
FST	dbFast Linkable Program
FSX	Lotus 1-2-3 Data
FT	Lotus Notes Full Text Index
FT5	FH5 File
FT7	Macromedia Freehand Drawing
FT8	Macromedia Freehand Drawing
FT9	Macromedia Freehand Drawing
FTB	Roots3 Index File
FTBL	PIPE-FLO Professional Fluid Data Table (Engineered Software)
FTC	FluxTime Clip (pCode Software)
FTG	Windows Help Full-text Search Group File
FTM	MicroGrafx Font
FTP	FTP Configuration Information
FTS	Borland BDE File
FW	Framework Database
FW2	Framework II File
FW3	Framework III File
FW4	Framework IV File
FWB	FileWrangler Data File Backup
FWEB	Fortran WEB
FWF	Xwave FWF File
FWI	PhotoSmart 850 Digital Camera Firmware Update
FWL	FileWrangler EXE Library
FWP	Worms Armageddon Fiddler Weapons Module
FWS	FileWrangler Data File for File Splitting Configuration
FX	WordPerfect Office Template File
FX2	WordPerfect Office Calendar File
FXD	FoxPro FoxDoc Support and WINFAX Sent Document
FXM	WinFax Fax
FXM	Fuxoft AY Music Chip Language
FXO	Fax Image Document
FXP	FoxPro Compiled Source
FXR	WinFax Received Document
FXS	WinFax Fax Transmit Graphic
FZF	FontZip Font Packer

Extension	Description
FZP	Fargo Primera Color Printer Dye Sub Support File
FZX	CP/M Fix File
G	Applause Data Chart and Paradox File
G4	Access
GAL	Commonly Used Extension for Image Galleries
GAM	Commonly used extension for saved game files
GAML	Generalized Analytical Markup Language
GANI	Graal Game Animation
GAP	Electrical Generation Analysis and Planification
GAS	Intelligence Tracking System Data File
GAU	Flight Simulator Gauge
GB$	BASIC VB Beispiel Kartei File
GBA	GrabIt Batch Files
GBF	InteGrade Pro Gradebook File
GBL	Visual Basic Global Definition
GBR	GIMP Brush File
GBT	Photoshop
GBX	Gerber File
GC	Sierra Print Artist Greeting Card
GCA	G Compression Archiver Compressed File
GCD	Generic CADD Drawing
GCF	WinXComp Grouped Compressed File
GCM	Group Mail CMessage Store File and GeoConcept Map File
GCP	Ground Control Point File
GCR	Visual EPR COSEUL.EXE Output
GD2	GDLib Image
GDB	ACT! Group Data File
GDB	Group Mail File
GDF	GEOS Dictionary
GDG	ReliaSoft RG
GDM	Bells, Whistles, and Sound Boards Module
GDR	SymbianOS Bitmap Font File
GDS	Chip Layout Information and Image File
GED	Micrografx Simply 3D Geometry
GEF	Graphics Exchange Format
GEM	Digital Research GEM Paint
GEN	dBASE Application Generator Compiled Template
GER	German Text/HTML Info File
GEX	GEcho Configuration File
GF	METAFONT Generic Font File
GFA	Bitmap Graphic
GFB	GIFBlast Compressed GIF Image
GFM	Computer Graphics Meta-file

(continued)

Extension	Description
GFW	ArcView World File for GIF Image and BASIC GFA File
GGP	GemCom Graphic Format
GHO	Symantec Ghost Disk Image File
GHS	Symantec Ghost Disk Image Span File
GID	Windows Help Index File
GIF	Graphic Interchange Format
GIFF	Graphic Interchange Format
GIG	Sound File
GKH	Ensoniq EPS Family Disk Image
GKS	Graphics Kernel System
GLD	Glide File
GLUT	OpenGL Glut-3.6 File
GLUT2	OpenGL Glut-3.6 File
GLUT3	OpenGL Glut-3.6 File
GLY	Word Glossary
GLY	ACT! Layout
GM	Autologic Bitmap
GM0	S.A.P.S.—Sharp Advanced Presentation Software Professional
GMB	GoldMine Business Contact Management Backup Data
GML	NetRemote XML-based Configuration File
GMM	Group Mail Message Log File
GMP	Group Mail List Information File
GMS	Corel Global Macro File
GMX	Group Mail Message File
GNT	Micro Focus Generated COBOL Code
GNX	Genigraphics Graphics Link Presentation
GO	CompuServe
GOBJ	Geoworks Object Code
GOC	Geoworks GOC Source Code
GOE	McIDAS System Satellite Image Data
GOES	McIDAS System Satellite Image Data
GOH	Geoworks GOC Header
GP4	CCITT Group 4 File
GPH	Lotus 1-2-3 Graph
GPI	Bitware Fax File
GPX	BASIS File
GQ	Epson Printer Page Description Language
GQA	BI/Query Data Model Admin Layer
GQL	BI/Query Data Model
GQU	BI/Query Data Model User Layer
GR	XGMML (eXtensible Graph Markup and Modeling Language) File
GR2	Windows 3.0 Screen Driver
GR3	Windows 3.0 Screen Grabber
GR4	Pathloss Network File Sharing File
GRA	OpenGL Object
GRADS	Metafile

Extension	Description
GRAY	Raw Gray Samples
GRB	MS-DOS Shell Monitor and Gridded Binary
GRD	Photoshop Gradient File
GREY	RAW RGB 24-bit Graphic
GRF	Graph Plus Drawing
GRIB	Gridded Binary
GRP	Windows Program Manager Group and ACT! Group Data File
GRY	RAW RGB 24-bit Graphic
GRZ	GRZip Compressed Archive
GSD	Professional Draw Vector Graphics
GSM	Raw GSM 6.10 Audio Stream
GTH	Domino.Doc
GTO	Quicken On-line File
GWI	Groupwise File
GZ	Gzip Compressed Archive and GIMP Image File
GZA	GZA Compressed Archive
GZIP	Gzip Compressed Archive
H	ADS Include File and Header
H++	C++ Header File
H—	Sphinx C—Header File
H16	VC98 Include 16-bit File
HA	Compressed Archive
HAM	Image File and Novell Netware Disk Drivers
HAZ	Flight Simulator Texture File
HC	Header File
HCL	Handwritten Claims Log
HCM	IBM HCM Configuration
HCR	Half-fold Card File
HCSP	Content Server Web Page
HCT	Symantec Anti-Virus Live Update File
HCX	Harvard Graphics Chart XL Chart
HDAT	Objective Analysis Package Data File
HDB	Nero and ACT! History File
HDF	Help Development Kit Help File and Hierarchical Data Format File
HDM	Handheld Markup Language File
HDML	Handheld Markup Language File
HDMP	WinXP Trouble Report
HDO	Helpdesk-One File
HDR	ArcInfo Binary and Commonly Used Extension for Header Files
HDS	Hierarchical Data System
HDW	Harvard Graphics Draw Vector Graphics
HDX	Help Index
HEP	Novell NetWare Help Librarian Data File
HER	Grafic GIF File
HEX	Hex Dump
HFI	HP Font Info

(continued)

Extension	Description
HFX	Harvard Graphics F/X File
HGL	HP Graphics Language (Plotter File)
HH	C++ Header
HHC	HTML Help Table of Contents
HHH	Power C Precompiled Header
HHK	HTML Help Index
HHL	Visual Basic File
HHP	HTML Help Project
HHS	HTML Help Samples
HHTML	Realmedia Adstream HTML File
HIF	Quicken On-line File
HIPS	Bitmap Graphic
HIR	Hidden Icon Resource
HIS	Commonly Used Extension for History Files
HIX	System SYSUTIL File
HK5	ACT! Database File
HKC	HTML-KIT Auto Complete Short-cuts
HL$	Compressed DOS Help File
HLB	VAX Help Library
HLF	BASIC QuickBAS QuickB01 File
HLM	Winhelp Vbhilfe File
HLN	Microstation Hidden Line File
HLP	Help File
HLX	Visual C++ Syntax Coloring Instructions
HLZ	Multi-Edit Packed Help File
HM	Windows Help Context IDs used by MAKEHM.EXE.
HM2	Help & Manual Help File Project
HM3	Help & Manual Help File Project (ver 3)
HMF	HOOPS Metafile
HMS	MS SMS Inventory File
HM~	Help&Manual Backup Help File Project
HNC	CNC Program File Heidenhain Dialog
HP	HP Graphics Language (Plotter)
HP$	NTgraph Visual C Wizzard File
HP-	HP Distribution Binary File
HP-UX	HP-UNIX File
HP8	HP NewWave Write ASCII Roman8 Character Set
HPF	PageMaker HP LaserJet Font
HPG	HP Graphics Language (Plotter)
HPGL	HP Graphics Language (Plotter)
HPH	Designer Graphics System2 File
HPJ	Help Project File
HPJ	Visual Basic Help Project
HPK	Compressed Archive
HPL	HP Graphics File
HPLJ	Hewlett-Packerd LaserJet Vector Image
HPP	C++ Program Header
HPPCL	Hewlett-Packard Printer Control Language Vector Image

Extension	Description
HPUX	HP-UNIX File
HPW	CompuServe Home Page Wizard
HP_	Winhelp Compressed File
HP~	V-help File
HQP	CP/M Disc Utility Information
HQX	Macintosh BinHex 4 Compressed Archive
HR2	Curious Labs Poser Hair File
HRH	C++ and Resources Common Header
HRU	HRU Bitmap
HSI	HSI JPEG Bitmap
HSK	Nimbus 7 SAMS Data File
HSS	Photoshop Hue/Saturation Information
HST	Commonly used extension for History Files
HT3	HTML File
HTA	Hypertext Application
HTC	HTML Component
HTF	HTF Sounding File and Virtual HyperText Font
HTI	Win Help Related File
HTM	Hypertext Markup Language
HTML	Hypertext Markup Language
HTMLS	Secure HTML File
HTR	HTML-like script
HTT	Microsoft Hypertext Template
HTX	Extended Hypertext Template
HTZ	HTML Editor Archive
HWL	Corel Shared Writing Tools 9.0 File
HX	THOR Database Cross-reference Hash File
HXC	Help 2 Project/Collection File
HXI	Help 2 Compiled Help File
HXK	Help TOC/Index File
HXK	Help 2 Keyword Index
HXM	Descent2 HAM File
HXM	Procomm Plus Alternate Protocol Selection Menu for All Users
HXS	Help 2 Compiled Help File
HXT	Help TOC/Index File
HXX	C++ Header
HX_	C Poet Compressed Disk1 File
HYC	WordPerfect Hyphenation File
HYD	WordPerfect for Windows Hyphenation Dictionary
HYP	Hypertext File and Hyphenation FIle
HZ	Chinese Text
H_	Winhelp Compressed File
H__	C++ Header Seldom used C++ Header (same as H++ and H)
I	C++ Preprocessor Intermediate File
I0	Winter Windows Scheduler File

(continued)

Extension	Description
I00	Winphone Phonebook
I16	Nokia Phone Logo File
I2S	Invision for mIRC Settings
IAF	Outlook Express, Outlook 97 and 2000 E-mail Account Settings
IBA	IBasic Source Code File and Type of Image File
IBD	Windows Installer File
IBF	Instant Backup
IBG	NASA PDS Graphic Format
IBK	Sound Blaster Instrument Bank
IBS	i2 iBase File
IC1	Imagic Bitmap Graphic
IC2	IMagic Bitmap Graphic
IC3	IMagic Bitmap Graphic
ICA	Citrix Independent Computer Architecture File
ICB	Image Capture Board
ICC	ICC Profile Format File
ICL	Icon Library File
ICM	Image Color Matching Profile File
ICMP	Internet Control Message Protocol
ICN	AT&T Graphic Format
ICO	Icon File
ICS	Outlook Calendar File
ICT	TIFF and ISO Image Related File
ICW	MS Internet Explorer Internet Connect Wizard
ID	Lotus Notes ID File and MS Data Map
IDAPI	Integrated Database Application Programming Interface
IDB	Delphi Pascal Object File
IDC	Internet Database Connector Document and SQL Connector File
IDD	MIDI Instrument Definition
IDE	C++ Project
IDF	Identification File and MIDI Instruments Definition File
IDIF	Netscape Saved Address Book
IDL	Visual C++ Interface Definition File
IDM	Ulead Photo Express Messages File
IDQ	Internet Data Query File and SQL Query
IDT	Identification File and Windows Installer File
IDW	IntelliDraw Vector Graphic
IDX	Index
IDY	Debug Information File and Index File
IE1-3	Internet Explorer 3 Address Book
IE3	Internet Explorer 3 File
IEE-695	IEEE 695 Information
IEF	Image File

Extension	Description
IFF	Bitmap Graphic and Simple Musical Score
IFO	Information File
IFS	IconForge Image EXE Library and Installable File System
IFX	Fax File
IGF	Vector Graphic
IGN	ICQ Igonre List
IGS	CAD Overlay
IHT	Intranet Connector Script File
IHTML	Inline HyperText Markup Language
II	GCC Preprocessed C++ Source Code
IIF	QuickBooks Import/Export Interchange File
III	Intel IPhone Compatible File
IKO	Windows Icon Resource
IL	Icon Library
ILM	Iomega Zip Drive Speed Configuration File
ILS	Internet Security And Acceleration Server Summary
ILSR	Iomega Reader
IMA	WinImage File
IMF	MIDI Music File
IMG	Commonly Used Extension for an Image File or for a Disk Image File
IMI	Turbo Pascal DOS File
IMJ	JFIF File with a Microsoft Windows BMP Header
IML	ACT! Internet Mail Message File
IMP	FileMaker Database Translation Filter and DVD File
IMS	Music File
IMV	Yahoo Instant Messenger IMVironment
IMZ	Compressed Floppy Image
IN	Input File
IN0	INI Backup
IN1	INI Backup
INA	DOS File
INC	Commonly Used Extension for Include Files
IND	dBASE IV and Windows Shared Database File
INDEX	Index File
INDIGO	Indigo Graphics Format
INF	Information File
INI	Initialization/Configuration File
INL	Visual C++ Inline Function File
INP	Oracle Source Code
INS	Instrument Music File and Internet Communication Settings
INST	Object Oriented Graphics Library

(continued)

Extension	Description
INT	Foxpro Code Page
INV	Windows Update file, Invoice File and Inventory File
INX	Foxpro Foxbase Index
IN_	Setup Information
IOCA	Image Object Content Architecture (IOCA) Graphics File
IP	Files serving the Internet Protocol
IPF	SMS Installer Script
IPJ	Inventor Project
IPK	internet Package Archive
IPL	Corel Pantone Spot Reference Palette
IPP	Help & Manual Proprietary Image
IPR	IntelliJ Project XML File
IPZ	ICQ Skin
IQ	IBM Query File
IQF	Integra 3.0 Query File
IQI	IBM Query
IQR	IBM Query
IQS	AmeriCalc Security File
IQT	IBM Query
IQU	AmeriCalc Update
IQY	Excel Web Query and Internet Inquiry File
IRC	IRCAM Format Sound
IRIS	Silicon Graphics RGB
IRS	WordPerfect Resource File
IRX	IBM Mainframe Rule File
ISH	Compressed Archive File
ISO	ISO-9660 CD Disc Image
ISP	IIS Internet Service Provider Settings
ISR	Uninstaller Text File
ISU	Easy CD Creator 4 Uninstall File
ITG	Intergraph Format
ITM	Item or Article or Zone
ITX	Texture File
IVI	MSDN InfoViewer 5.0 Topic
IVT	MSDN InfoViewer 5.0 Information Title
IW	IBM Updater File
IWA	IBM Writing Assistant Text
IWP	Wang Text File
IWR	i-write 2.0 File
IWR_BAK	i-write 2.0 Backup File
IX	FrameMaker Index File and WordPerfect Office Template File
IX2	WordPerfect Office Template File or WP Calendar File
IXA	Ulead Image File
IXC	Index+ for Windows Code Definition File
IXF	Index+ for Windows Form Definition File
IXL	DB/TextWorks Database Indexed List

Extension	Description
IXP	ISIPublisher Publication Information Export (Image Solutions, Inc.)
IXR	Index+ for Windows Report Definition File
IXS	ArcView Geocoding Index For Read-Write Shapefiles (ESRI)
IXT	ISIPublisher Publication Template (Image Solutions, Inc.)
IXX	C++ Include File
IZD	Intrexx Application Export Format
IZT	IZL Binary Token
IZX	Intermezzon Designer E-Learning Published File (Intermezzon Learning Systems AB)
I_I	Eru/erd File
J	JPEG / JFIF Image, Java Source Code and JAR Compressed File
J2K	JPEG-2000 JP2 File
JA	IBM Tools Updater File
JAD	Java Application Descriptor File
JAG	Jaguar Server File
JAM	E-mail
JAR	Java Archive
JAS	Paint Shop Pro Compressed Graphic
JASC	JAS Compressed Graphic
JAV	Java Source Code
JAVA	Java Source Code
JBF	Paint Shop Pro Browser Cache
JBR	Paint Shop Pro Brush
JBS	DesignArt
JBX	Project Scheduler File
JCF	JAWS for Windows Configuration File
JCL	Job Control Language IBM
JCM	Java Commerce Message Commerce Message
JCS	Flashget Script HTML Table
JED	JEDEC Programming Specification
JFF	JPEG Image
JFI	JPEG/JIFF Image
JFIF	JPEG/JIFF Image
JGD	Paint Shop Pro Gradient
JIF	JPEG/JIFF Image
JIS	Japanese Industrial Standard Text File
JJ	JavaCC File
JJC	Canvas Compressed Audio File
JLA	VisualPro BMP Image
JLS	JPEG-LS File
JMD	Paint Shop Pro Image Map Settings
JMF	Java Multimedia File
JMH	JPEG File Interchange Format
JMM	Digital Camera Video Clip

(continued)

Extension	Description
JMP	SAS JMP Discovery Chart-to-Statistics File
JNC	Communication Log File
JNG	JPEG Network Graphic Bitmap
JNK	Junk
JNLP	Java Web Start
JNT	Windows XP Tablet PC Edition Journal
JOB	Job File
JOR	SQL Server Journal File
JOY	Joystick Calibration File
JP2	JPEG-2000 JP2 File
JPC	JPEG-2000 Code Stream Bitmap and Japan Picture Format
JPE	JPEG/JIFF Image
JPEG	JPEG/JIFF Image
JPG	JPEG/JIFF Image
JPR	Oracle JDeveloper Model JProject
JPS	Stereo Image
JPX	JPEG-2000 JP2 File
JRC	Jrchive Compressed Archive
JS	JavaScript Source Code
JSD	Join-Split File
JSE	JScript Encoded Script File
JSF	Macromedia Fireworks Batch Script
JSL	Paint Shop Pro Shapes File
JSP	Java Server Page
JSP10	Java Server Page
JSV	Java Structure Viewer
JSV	VXML JavaServer Page
JSW	WML JavaServer Page
JTF	JPEG Tagged Interchange Format Image
JTIF	JPEG Tagged Interchange Format Image
JTK	Java ToolKit File
JTP	Windows XP Tablet PC Edition Journal
JW	Q & A Write for Windows 3.0
JWL	Easy CD Creator's CD Label
JXX	C++ Header File
JZZ	Jazz Spreadsheet
K	Desktop Color Separation Specification Black Layer
K01	Clarion DOS Database Key File
K02	Clarion DOS Database Key File
K03	Clarion DOS Database Key File
K04	Clarion DOS Database Key File
K05	Clarion DOS Database Key File
K06	Clarion DOS Database Key File
K07	Clarion DOS Database Key File
K08	Clarion DOS Database Key File
K09	Clarion DOS Database Key File
K1S	Wave Glib19 File

Extension	Description
K25	Kodak DC25 Digital Camera File
K3D	3DS Macro Language Description
K7	DCMO6 Emulator Tape Image
KAR	FOX+ 2.0
KB	C++ Keyboard Script
KBD	Keyboard Script File Layout
KBM	Reflection Keyboard Script File Layout
KBM	Scala Keyboard Mapping
KDC	Kodak Photo-Enhancer/Photogen File
KDK	Kodak Proprietary Decimated TIFF Format
KDO	Kudo Picture Browser
KE$	Modem Bitware Fax Disk2 File
KED	KEDIT Profile and Macro File
KEN	Player CDcheck Compressed File
KEP	Turbo Pascal DOS TP19 Compressed Kepler File
KEY	Keyboard Definition File
KFX	2D Graphic
KGB	Z80 Spectrum Emulator Snap/File Formats
KGP	Image
KIC	Kodak Image Compression File
KID	Tonline Bsw4 Install Mdmimp File
KIF	AutoCAD Key Index
KIZ	Kodak Digital Postcard File and UU Encoded File
KMA	Kodak Memory Album
KNN	Clarion for Windows Database Key
KNO	Personal Knowbase Data
KNW	Known Problems
KOD	Code
KOE	Turbo Pascal DOS File
KOR	Korean Text File
KPL	Kazaa Playlist
KPS	IBM KIPS Bitmap
KS	Works Sheet
KSH	UNIX Shell Script
KST	Olivetti Olitext Plus Script File
KTP	Clarion for Windows Temporary Key File
KTT	KeyText Data File
KVT	BASIC QuickBAS QuickB03 File
KW$	NTgraph Visual C Wizzard File
KWB	KeyWord Braille File
KWD	Keyword
KWF	Delphi Pascal Chart
KXS	Kexis Lossless Compressed Audio
KYB	Keyboard Layout
KYE	Kye Game Data
KYF	Visual-Voice Mouth Movement File
KYS	Photoshop CS Keyboard Shortcut
KZP	Kazoo3D or KazooStudio KazooPicture

(continued)

Extension	Description
L95	Library File
LAA	LucasArts AdLib Audio File Format
LAB	Mailing Labels
LAD	Daylon Leveller Animation Data
LAM	Netscape Media Player Streaming Audio Metafile
LAN	Novell NetWare LAN Drivers
LBA	Liberty BASIC File
LBG	dBASE IV Label Generator
LBI	Dreamweaver Library File
LBL	Label
LBO	dBASE IV Ordered Labels
LBR	Compressed Archive File
LBT	Foxpro Label Memo
LBX	Foxpro Label
LCF	Linker Control File
LCH	IBM Works for OS/2 Chart
LCK	Lock File
LCL	FTP Software Data
LCN	WordPerfect Dictionary File
LCS	ACT! History File
LD1	dBASE Overlay File
LDB	Access Lock File
LDF	SQL Server Transaction Log File
LDI	LDIF File
LDIF	LDAP Data Interchange Format
LDIF	LDIF File
LDL	Corel Paradox Delivered Library
LDR	Symantec Ghost Template File
LDS	Corel40 Programs Data File
LE$	BASIC VB
LES	Lesson File
LET	Letter
LEX	Lexicon (Dictionary) and Lexmark Printer Installation File
LE_	BASIC VB Compressed Disk1 File
LF	SoftwareKey License File
LFA	LifeForm File
LFD	LucasArts Games Resource
LFF	LucasFilm Format
LFL	LucasFilm Library
LFM	LifeForm File
LFP	LifeForm File
LFQ	LeechFTP Queue File
LG	Logo Procedure Definition
LGA	Windows Applog File
LGC	Windows Application Log
LGD	Windows Application Log
LGE	Windows Application Log
LGF	Windows Application Log
LGG	Windows Application Log
LGH	Windows Application Log

Extension	Description
LGI	Windows Application Log
LGJ	Windows Application Log
LGK	Windows Application Log
LGL	Windows Application Log
LGM	Windows Application Log
LGN	Windows Application Log
LGO	Windows Logo Driver
LGP	Windows Application Log
LGQ	Windows Application Log
LGR	Windows Application Log
LGS	Windows Application Log
LGZ	Windows Application Log
LHA	Compressed Archive File
LHZ	LHA Compressed Archive File
LI$	MS Compressed Library
LIA	P-CAD Schematic Library
LIB	Library File
LIC	License File
LID	WinDVD File
LIF	Compressed Archive File
LIM	Limit Compressed Archive
LIN	AutoCAD Linetype Definition
LIS	Compiler Listing File
LIT	Reader eBook File
LIVEREG	Symantec Norton Anti-Virus Update Session
LIVESUBSCRIBE	Symantec Norton Anti-Virus Update Catalog
LIVEUPDATE	Norton Anti-Virus Update Settings File (Symantec)
LJ	HP LaserJet Graphic Bitmap
LKO	Outlook Express Linked Object
LKS	WinAmp Links File
LLD	Links Language Data File
LM8	Picture File
LMA	Netscape Packetized Audio
LNG	Commonly used extension for Language Files
LNK	Windows Shortcut File
LNM	WordPerfect SGML Alias
LOC	Localisation String Resource Header File
LOD	Load File
LOG	Log File
LPK	License Package
LQT	Winamp File
LRF	C/C++ Linker Response File
LRG	Macromedia XRes Multi-resolution Bitmap
LRM	Encarta Class Server Learning Resource
LRP	IBM Works for OS/2 Report
LRS	Language Resource File
LS1	Winhelp Source File

(continued)

Extension	Description
LSF	Libronix DLS Resource
LSI	Corel Layout Specification Instance SGML
LSL	Corel Paradox Saved Library
LSL	Lotus Script Library
LSN	Works File
LST	List or Spooler File
LSZ	WinFax
LTM	Lotus Form
LTR	Letter
LTT	HP Library and Tape Tools Log File
LUN	DB-MAIN Project File
LVP	Lucent Voice Player
LWD	LotusWorks Text Document
LWP	Wordpro 96/97 Document (Lotus)
LYR	Song Lyric File
LZD	Binary Difference File
LZH	Compressed Archive File
LZO	Izop Compressed Archive
LZS	Compressed Archive File
LZS	LARC Compressed File Archive
LZX	Compressed File
M	Desktop Color Separation Specification Magenta Layer and Objective C Source
M12	S-BASIC File
M1A	MPEG-1 Audiostream
M1S	MPEG Media File
M1V	MPEG-1 Video File
M2A	MPEG-2 Audio
M2P	MPEG-2 Program Stream Format File
M2S	MPEG-2 Audio and Video
M2V	MPEG-2 Video Only File
M3A	MPEG Archive Enhanced .M3U Playlist File
M3D	Corel Motion 3D Animation
M3U	MP3 Playlist File
M3URL	MP3 Playlist File
M4	Meta4 Source Code
M4A	MPEG-4 Audio Layer
M68	Turbo Pascal DOS File
MA3	Harvard Graphics Macro
MAB	Mozilla Personal Address Book or Collected Address Book B
MAC	Macro and Access Shortcut
MAD	Access Module Shortcut
MAF	Access
MAG	Access Diagram Shortcut and Magenta Color Separation
MAI	MS Mail Message
MAILHOST	E-mail Server Preferences File
MAILVIEW	MSN Mail

Extension	Description
MAK	Visual Basic Ver. 3.0 Project and Visual C++ Project
MAKI	Winamp3 Compiled Script
MAN	Windows 2000 Mandatory User Profile
MAP	Color Palette and Common Extension Used for Map Files
MAPIMAIL	Outlook Express Mail File
MAPIMAIL	Sendto File
MAPISEND	MAPISEND File
MAPLET	Maplet Design File
MAQ	Access Query Shortcut
MAR	Access Report Shortcut and Bibliographic Data Format
MAS	Access Stored Procedures
MAT	Access Table Shortcut
MAV	Access View Shortcut
MAW	Access Data Access Page
MB	Paradox Memo Holder
MBD	Multimedia Builder MP3 Authoring File
MBF	Money Backup File
MBG	MS Mail Mailbag
MBK	dBASE IV Multiple Index Backup
MBS	Mailbag Assistant Script
MBX	Database Index and Mailbox Message File
MC6	C File/Makefile
MCC	Microsoft Network Shortcut
MCF	Master Command File and Media Container Format
MCI	Media Control Interface Command Set
MCL	Macro Command Language
MCM	Enable Macro
MCP	Master Compiler Profile
MCQ	McAfee Quarantined File
MCR	CuteFTP Script
MCX	Graphic File
MD5	MD5 Checksum File
MD8	CDrom Database File
MDA	Access Add-in
MDB	Access Application or Database
MDE	Office File
MDF	Menu Definition File and SQL Master Database File
MDHTML	Access HTML File
MDI	MIDI-sequention Sound and Office Document Imaging File
MDMP	Win XP Trouble Report
MDN	Access Blank Database Template
MDO	Internet Information Server Configuration Backup
MDP	Visual C++ MAK File and Visual J++ Project Workspace

(continued)

Extension	Description
MDS	Directx Mid2stream File
MDT	Access Add-in Data
MDW	Access Workgroup Information
MDX	Borland Database Engine Index
MDZ	Access Wizard Template
MEB	WordPerfect Macro Editor Bottom Overflow File
MED	WordPerfect Macro Editor Delete Save
MEM	FoxPro Memory Variable Save File
MEN	Menu
MEQ	WordPerfect Macro Editor Print Queue
MER	WordPerfect Macro Editor Resident Area and Data Interchange Format
MES	Message File
MET	Presentation Manager Meta File
MEU	DOS Shell Menus
MEX	WordPerfect Macro Editor Expound File
MF	MetaFont Text File
MFD	Adobe Multiple Master Font Metrics Directory File
MFF	MIDI File Format
MFM	DMP Music Format
MGC	Clipart Collection Catalog
MGF	Image File and Micrografx Font
MGR	MGR Bitmap
MGX	Micrografx Picture Publisher Clipart
MHG	Multimedia File
MHT	MHTML Document
MHTM	MHTML Document
MHTML	MHTML Document
MI	Miscellaneous
MIB	Management Information Base File
MIF	FrameMaker Interchange Format and MIDI Instrument File
MIP	Paint Shop Pro Multiple Image Print File
MIPSEL	Mips File
MIX	Multi-layer Picture File and Windows Sound Mix
ML	ML language Source Code File
MLB	FoxPro for Macintosh Library
MLI	AutoCAD Material-Library File
MLM	Novel Groupwise E-mail File
MLN	AutoCAD Multiline Definition
MMB	Oracle Forms Menu Binary Source Code
MMC	Media Catalog
MME	Multi-Purpose Internet Mail Extensions (MIME) File
MMF	Mail File
MML	Mail Meta Language
MMM	Multimedia Movie
MMP	MS Music Producer

Extension	Description
MMS	JPEG-6b File
MMW	Media Content
MMX	Oracle Forms Compiled Menu
MN1	Money Ver 1 Data File
MN2	Money Ver 2 Data File
MN3	Money Ver 3 Data File
MN4	Money Database
MN4	Money Ver 4 Data File
MN5	Money Ver 5 Data File
MN6	Money Ver 6 Data File
MN7	Money Ver 7 Data File
MN8	Money Ver 8 Data File
MN9	Money Ver 9 Data File
MNC	AutoCAD Compiled Menu
MND	AutoCAD Menu Program
MNF	Saved MSN Search
MNR	AutoCAD Compiled Menu
MNS	AutoCAD ASCII Menu
MNT	Foxpro Menu Memo
MNU	AutoCAD Menu Template or FoxPro Menu
MOD	Digital Music Sound Clip and Commonly Used Extension for a Modeling File
MOF	MSinfo
MOI	French Text File
MOM	CDrom Runtime Database File
MOO	QuickTime Movie Clip
MOOV	QuickTime Movie
MOS	System DOS 6.2 File
MOV	Movie File
MOZ	Netscape Temp File
MP+	MPEG Plus Audio File
MP1	MPEG Audio Stream, Layer I
MP2	MPEG Audio Stream, Layer II
MP2S	Max Payne 2 Saved Game (Rockstar Games)
MP2S	MPEG-2 Video
MP2V	MPEG Audio Stream, Layer II
MP3	MPEG Audio Stream, Layer III
MP3PRO	mp3PRO Enhanced MP3 File
MP4	MPEG-4 Video File
MPA	MPEG Audio Stream, Layer I, II, or III
MPD	Windows Mini-port Driver
MPE	MPEG Movie Clip
MPEG	MPEG Movie
MPG	MPEG Animation
MPG4	MPEG-4 Media File
MPGA	Mpeg-1 Layer3 Audio Stream
MPKG	Meta Package File
MPM	MPEG Movie
MPP	CAD Drawing File

(continued)

Extension	Description
MPR	FileMaker Spelling Dictionary
MPS	MPEG-1 Audio and Video File
MPT	Multipage TIFF Bitmap
MPV	MPEG-1 Video File
MPV2	MPEG Audio Stream, Layer II
MPX	Foxpro Compiler Menu
MRB	C++ Multiple Resolution Bitmap Graphic
MRC	Bibliographic Data Format
MRG	Merge File
MRI	MRI Scan
MRK	Markup File
MRS	WordPerfect Macro Resource File
MS	Checksum File for Anti-Virus
MSC	C Makefile and Microsoft Management Console Snap-in File
MSD	Microsoft Diagnostic Utility Report
MSF	Multiple Sequence File
MSG	Message File
MSI	Windows Installer File
MSM	Windows Installer Merge Module
MSN	Microsoft Network Document
MSO	FrontPage File
MSP	Windows Installer Patch
MSPX	XML-based Web Page
MSQ	MIDI File
MSR	OzWin CompuServe E-mail/Forum Access SYSOP File
MSS	Manuscript Text File
MST	Test Document
MSW	Word Text File
MSWMM	Windows Movie Maker Project
MTT	Messenger Saved Contact File
MTW	Minitab Data File
MTX	Adobe Atmosphere File and Marked Text Source File
MT_	Encore Compressed Audio File
MUD	ACT! Database File
MUI	Configuration Resource File
MUS	Music File
MVA	Setup Program Archive
MVB	Manual Storage Format and Multimedia Viewer File
MVD	MicroDVD DVD Movie
MVF	AutoCAD / AutoFlix Stop Frame File
MVI	AutoCAD Movie Command
MVP	MediaView Project
MVX	Mixer File
MWP	Lotus Wordpro 97 Smartmaster File
MX3	MP3 Encoded File
MXE	Quatro Pro Startup Macro
MXI	Macromedia Extension Information
MXP	Macromedia Extension Manager

Extension	Description
MXT	C Data
MYD	MySQL Database
MYDOCS	MyDocs Drop Target
MYI	MySQL Database Index
NA2	Netscape Communicator Address Book
NAB	Netscape Communicator or Novell Groupwise Address Book
NAI	WinINSTALL File
NAM	Office Name File
NAP	NAP Metafile Vector Image
NAPLPS	North American Presentation Layer Protocol Syntax = Vector image
NAS	NASTRAN File
NAV	Microsoft Network Component
NB	Mathematica Notebook
NCD	Norton Change Directory
NCF	Lotus Notes Internal Clipboard and NetWare Command File
NCH	Outlook Express Folder File
NCS	Netscape Conference Call File
NCT	Nero Cover Designer Template
NDB	ACT! Notes Data File
NDF	SQL Server Secondary Data File
NDL	Lotus Notes
NED	MSN Application Extension
NEF	Nikon Digital SLR Cameras Raw Graphic File Format
NET	Network Configuration
NEW	New Information
NEWS	News Bitmap Image
NFL	AutoCAD Multiline Filter List
NFO	System Info File
NG	Norton Guide Online Documentation
NHF	Nero HFS-CD Compilation
NHV	Nero Burning ROM HFS CD
NIB	Corel Graphics10 Photopoint File
NIF	Network Initialization File
NIP	Network Interface Plug-in
NK2	Outlook AutoComplete File
NL	Norton Desktop Icon Library
NLB	Oracle 7 Data
NLD	ATI Radeon Video Driver
NLU	Norton Live Update E-Mail Trigger File
NMD	Nero Burning ROM miniDVD
NOR	ATI Radeon Video Driver
NOT	Acrobat Spelling File and Notation File
NPI	dBASE Application Generator Source
NPM	Corel Graphics Ver 10 Draw Media Lines File
NPS	Lotus Agenda File
NPS	NeroMix
NR3	Nero MP3 CD-ROM Compilation

(continued)

Extension	Description
NR4	Nero Burning ROM
NRA	Nero Audio-CD Compilation
NRB	Nero CD-ROM Boot Compilation
NRC	Nero UDF/ISO CD-ROM Compilation
NRD	Nero DVD Compilation
NRE	Nero CD Extra Compilation
NRG	Nero CD-Image File and Norton Registration Entries
NRH	Nero Hybrid CD-ROM Compilation
NRI	Nero ISO CD-ROM Compilation
NRM	Nero Mixed-Mode-CD Compilation
NRS	Nero Burning ROM CD Boot
NRU	Nero UDF/ISO CD-ROM Compilation
NRV	Nero Video-CD Compilation
NRW	Nero WMA CD-ROM Compilation
NS2	Lotus Notes 2 Database
NS3	Lotus Notes Database
NS4	Lotus Notes Database
NS5	Lotus Notes Domino File
NSC	Windows Media Station File
NSD	Norton System Doctor Sensors Configuration
NSD	Nero Burning ROM Super Video CD
NSF	Lotus Notes Database
NSF	NES Sound File
NSG	Lotus Notes
NSH	Lotus Notes Database (Older Form)
NSV	Winamp3 Video Format File
NSX	Apollo Database Engine Index
NT	Windows NT Startup File
NTF	Notes Database Template
NTS	Norton Tutorial
NTX	Clipper Index
NU4	Norton Utilities DLL Root File
NU6	Norton Utilities System DLL File
NUM	DOS 7 File
NW3	Netware.3x File
NW4	Netware.4x File
NWS	Outlook Express News File
NZL	Corel Painter Nozzle File
O	Object File
O$$	Output File
OAB	Outlook Address Book
OAF	ETH Oberon Applet File
OB$	Compressed OBJ
OBD	Office Binder Template
OBJ	Object File
OBR	C++ Object Browser Data File
OBS	ObjectScript Script
OBT	Office Binder Template
OBV	ObjectScript Visual Interface
OBZ	Office Binder Wizard

Extension	Description
OCA	OLE Custom Control Library Information
OCF	Object Craft File
OCM	Netscape Communicator Aim File
OCP	Advanced Art Studio
OD1	Omnis5 Database File
OD2	Omnis5 Database File
OD3	Omnis5 Database File
OD4	Omnis5 Database File
OD5	Omnis5 Database File
OD6	Omnis5 Database File
OD7	Omnis5 Database File
OD8	Omnis5 Database File
OD9	Omnis5 Database File
ODB	ArcView Object Database ASCII File
ODC	Office Data Connection
ODE	Office Object Data Embedding File
ODIF	Open Document Interchange Format
ODL	Object Definition Language
ODL	Visual C++ Type Library Source
ODS	Outlook Express Mailbox
OEB	Outlook Express Backup Wizard
OEM	OEM Data Used During Device Install
OFC	Open Financial Connectivity File
OFD	ObjectView Form Defintion
OFM	PostScript Font Description File
OFT	Outlook Item Template
OGX	C++ Component Gallery Exported Classes and Resources
OHP	DOS 7 File
OLB	MS Project Object Library
OLD	Old Version
OLE	Object Linking and Embedding (OLE) Object
OLK	MS Mail Mailbag Lock
OLK	Outlook Address Book
OLN	Visual C++ Outline Examples
OLT	Visual C++ Outline Examples
OMO	Oracle Media Objects File
OND	Lotus Notes-related File
OP	Rescue Disk File
OPC	Office Upgrade Control File
OPS	Office Profile Settings File
OPX	OPL Extension DLL
OQY	Excel OLAP Query File
OR2	Lotus Organizer 2 File
OR3	Lotus Organizer 97 File
OR4	Lotus Organizer File
OR5	Lotus Organizer File
OR6	IBM Organizer Data File
ORA	Oracle 7 Configuration
ORC	MIDI File and Oracle Scripting File
ORF	Olympus Digital Camera Raw Image File

(continued)

Extension	Description
ORG	Lotus Organiser File
ORI	Original
ORIG	Gen Original File
OSF	Distribution Bin File
OSS	Office Saved Search
OST	Exchange or Outlook Offline File
OTF	Open Type Font Format
OTM	Outlook VBA Module
OUT	Outlines or Output File
OVL	Program File - Overlay
OVR	Program File - Overlay
OYZ	Lotus Approach Alternate dBASE Index
P	PASCAL Program File
P01	Toast CD Image
P01	Parity Volume Set
P02	Parity Volume Set
P03	Parity Volume Set
P04	Parity Volume Set
P05	Parity Volume Set
P06	Parity Volume Set
P07	Parity Volume Set
P08	Parity Volume Set
P09	Parity Volume Set
P1	MicroImages Print Driver File
P10	Certificate Request
P12	Personal Information Exchange File
P3E	PC-Doctor File
P3I	PC-Doctor File
P3P	Platform for Privacy Preferences
P56	Patch
P64	H.261 Encoded Video File
P65	PageMaker Version 6.5 File
PA3	Turbo Pascal DOS File
PA4	Turbo Pascal DOS File
PA5	Turbo Pascal DOS File
PAB	Personal Address Book (Microsoft)
PAC	Windows Applications Manager Added or Changed Package
PAD	Scanner Output
PAE	PowerArchiver 20002 Encrypted Archive
PAF	Ensoniq PARIS Audio Format and Personal Ancestral File
PAG	Visual Basic Property Page File
PAK	Compressed Archive File
PAL	Color Palette File, Personal Ancestral File and Compressed File Format
PAM	Tonline Ob4hbci Smartupdate File
PAN	CorelDraw Printer-Specific File
PAP	Corel Painter Pattern, Selection or Texture File
PAQ	HP System Recovery File

Extension	Description
PAR	Commonly Used Extension for Parameter Files and Windows 3.x Swap File
PAR2	Parity Archive Volume Set
PAS	C++, Pascal and Delphi Source Code File
PAT	Commonly used extension for both Pattern Files and Patch Files
PATCH	General Patch File
PATTERN	Photoline5 Defaults File
PAU	OzWin CompuServe E-mail/Forum Access Paused Message
PAV	Panda Antivirus File
PB	WinFax Pro Phone Book
PB1	First Publisher Document
PB2	STABCAL (Stability Calculation for Aqueous Systems) File
PBA	PowerBASIC Source Code
PBB	MS Mail Address Information File
PBD	Faxit Phone Book, PowerBuilder Dynamic Library and Graphic Format
PBF	Portable Bitmap Format File and PBook E-book Format
PBH	PowerBASIC Help File
PBI	AXIALIS image JPEG JFIF and PowerBASIC Include File
PBK	Phonebook
PBL	PowerBASIC and PowerBuilder Library File
PBM	UNIX Portable Bitmap Graphic
PBMV	Portable Bitmap File
PBN	Portable Bridge Notation
PBO	Profiler Binary Output
PBP	Perl Builder File
PBQ	Audio
PBR	PowerBuilder Resource File
PBS	PowerArchiver Backup Script
PBT	Profiler Binary Table
PBV	Paint Shop Pro Bevel Preset
PBX	Outlook Express Message Folder
PC	PC-specific Text File and Oracle Pro-C Source Code
PC2	AutoCAD R14 Plotter Configuration
PC3	AutoCAD R2000 Plotter Configuration
PC8	ASCII Text IBM-8
PCA	PCAnywhere Registry Backup
PCB	Broderbund Print Shop Business Card
PCB	Ivex Winboard Design File, PrintShop Business Card and PC Doctor File
PCC	PC Checkup System Information and PC Paintbrush Image File
PCD	Images CD Creator Corel Adaptec

(continued)

Extension	Description
PCDS	Photo-CD Image
PCE	Borland Package Collection Editor File, Mail Signature and PC Doctor FIle
PCF	Profiler Command File and Unix Font File
PCF	Cisco VPN Client Configuration
PCG	Photo CD Graphic File
PCH	C PreCompiled Header and Patch File
PCI	PC-Doctor File and Windows PCI Mini-port File
PCK	Package and Turbo Pascal Pick File
PCL	HP Printer Control Language
PCM	LaserJet Printer Cartridge Metric and Sound File
PCN	Paint Shop Pro Contour Preset
PCP	AutoCAD R13 and Prior Plotter Configuration, PC Paint Bitmap and Symantec Live Update Package
PCR	PCMark Benchmark File
PCT	Commonly Used Extensions for Various Graphics Files
PCW	PC Write Text File
PCX	PC Paintbrush Bitmap Graphic
PD	Paradox Table
PDA	Print Shop Bitmap Graphic
PDB	Photo Deluxe Image and Visual C++ Program Database File
PDBX	Insight II X-PLOR Coordinate File
PDD	PhotoDeluxe Image
PDF	Acrobat Portable Document Format and ArcView Preferences Definition File
PDG	PrintShop Deluxe File
PDL	C++ Project Description Language, Print Shop Project and Programmable Driver Language
PDM	Sybase Power Designer File
PDN	Plan de Negocio
PDO	Access Package Deployment Script
PDP	Broderbund Print Shop Deluxe File and Photoshop PDF Format
PDR	Port Driver
PDS	Print Shop Graphic and Source Code File
PDV	Paintbrush Printer Driver
PDW	Professional Draw Document
PDX	Acrobat Catalog Index and PageMaker Printer Description
PDZ	GZipped Brookhaven Protein Databank File
PD_	Visc15 Images Setup File
PE	Portable Executable File

Extension	Description
PEB	WordPerfect Program Editor Bottom Overflow File
PEBPRJ	PEBundle File
PED	WordPerfect Program Editor Delete Save
PEM	Audio Module and WordPerfect Program Editor Macro
PEP	TurboProject Project File
PEQ	WordPerfect Program Editor Print Queue File
PER	WordPerfect Program Editor Resident Area
PERL	Perl Source File
PES	WordPerfect Program Editor Work Space File
PET	WordPerfect Program Editor Top Overflow File
PEW	IAR Embedded Workbench
PEX	Proboard Executable Program
PF	Archive and Monitor or Printer Profile File
PFA	PostScript Font
PFB	PostScript Type 1 Font
PFC	First Choice Text File
PFE	Programmers File Editor
PFK	XTree Programmable Function Keys
PFR	Paint Shop Pro Frame
PFS	First Publisher ART File and PFS Data File
PFX	Personal Information Exchange File
PF_	Encore Compressed Audio File
PGA	IBM Professional Graphics Adapter Image
PGC	Compressed Portfolio Graphic
PGD	Pretty Good Privacy Virtual Disk File
PGE	Solitaire Peg Back
PGF	PGC Portfolio Graphics Compressed Bitmap
PGL	HP Plotter Language
PGM	Portable Graymap Graphic
PGN	Portable Game Notation
PGP	Program Parameter and Pretty Good Privacy
PGR	Pretty Good Privacy PGP Groups
PGS	Commonly used extension for a Page File
PGX	Visual Basic Binary Property Page File
PG_	Improve Compressed Audio File
PH	PERL Header
PHB	Arcsoft PhotoBase and TreeView File
PHD	PC Help Desk File
PHL	Database Configuration File

(continued)

Extension	Description
PHM	DN—Lync Phone Book
PHN	Commonly used extension for a Phonebook File
PHP	Picture It! Publishing Project File
PHT	Partial Hypertext File
PHTM	PHP Script
PHTML	web-iPerl Document
PH_	C Poet Compressed Disk1 File
PI	Extension Associated with W32.Sobig.D@mm Worm
PI$	MS Compressed PIF
PIC	Commonly used extension for a Picture file
PICIO	Pixar Picture
PICON	Personal Icon
PICS	PICT Drawing Sequence
PID	UNIX Process ID File
PIF	GDF Format Vector Image and Windows Program Information File
PIM	Personal Information Manager File
PIP	JPEG,JPG,JPE, JFIF,PJPEG Compressed Bitmap Picture
PIPL	Photoshop 5.0 SDK Samplecode Colorpicker File
PIX	Commonly used extension for Picture Files
PIXAR	Pixar Picture
PI_	Compressed PIC or PIF File
PJ	PaintJet PCL Bitmap
PJG	Photo Assistant Image
PJL	ProCite Term Lists and Journal Title Lists
PJP	JPEG Image
PJPEG	JPEG Image
PJT	Foxpro Project Memo
PJX	Foxpro Project Index
PJXL	PaintJet XL PCL Bitmap
PK	Audition Graphical Waveform
PKA	Compressed Archive File
PKB	Oracle Package Body
PKD	Turbo Pascal DOS Compressed Batch File
PKD	PowerKaraoke Project File (PAW)
PKG	Commonly Used Extension for Package Files
PKO	PublicKey Security Object
PKP	MS Development Common IDE Pakage Project File
PKPAK	Archive
PKR	Pretty Good Privacy Public Keyring
PKS	Oracle Package Specification

Extension	Description
PL	Harvard Graphics Palette and PERL Program File
PL3	Harvard Graphics Chart Palette
PLB	Commonly used extension for Library Files
PLC	Lotus Add-in
PLD	PhotoDeluxe PhotoLine Image Document
PLEX	Visual Perl File
PLF	InterVideo WinDVD Playlist File
PLH	Paint Shop Pro Light Preset
PLI	Oracle 7 Data Description
PLIST	Property List XML File
PLJ	PlayJ Music Format
PLK	ATI Radeon Video Driver
PLN	ArchiCAD Project and WordPerfect Spreadsheet File
PLOT	UNIX Plot Format
PLR	Player File
PLS	Commonly used extension for a Playlist File
PLT	AutoCAD Plot drawing, HP Graphics Language and Palette File
PLX	Executable Perl Script
PLY	Harvard Graphics Spotlight Presentation Screen
PLZ	Lotus Freelance Presentation
PM	Perl Module and PageMaker Document
PM3	PageMaker Version 3 Document
PM4	PageMaker Version 4 Document
PM5	PageMaker Version 5 Document
PM6	PageMaker Version 6 Document
PMA	Windows Performance Monitor File
PMB	Bitmap Image
PMC	Windows Performance Monitor File
PMD	PageMaker
PMF	ArcReader GIS Mapping
PMG	Paint Magic
PML	NT4 Performance Monitor Log File and PageMaker Library
PMO	Print Master Gold Text
PMP	AutoCAD R2000 Plotter Model Parameters
PMR	Windows Performance Monitor File
PMT	PageMaker Template
PMW	Windows Performance Monitor File
PN3	Harvard Graphics Printer Driver
PNF	Portable Network Graphics Frame Bitmap and Windows Precompiled Setup Information
PNG	Portable (Public) Network Graphic
PNL	Panel File

(continued)

Extension	Description
PNQ	ICQ Instant Message File
PNT	ARC Format Vector Point Data
POD	Text
POL	Windows Policy File
POP	dBASE Popup Menu
POR	Corel Painter Portfolio File
POT	PowerPoint Template
POTHTML	Powerpoint HTML Template
PP4	Picture Publisher
PP5	Picture Publisher
PPA	PowerPoint Add-in
PPB	WordPerfect Print Preview Button Bar
PPC	Roxio Easy CD Creator File
PPD	PostScript Printer Description
PPF	Paint Shop Pro Soft Plastic Preset File and Micrografx Picture Publisher File
PPG	PowerPoint Presentation
PPI	PowerPoint Graphics File
PPK	PPK Archive
PPL	Harvard Graphics Polaroid Palette Plus ColorKey Driver
PPP	Point to Point Protocol
PPS	PowerPoint Slideshow
PPT	PowerPoint Presentation
PPTHTML	Powerpoint HTML Document
PPW	Micrografx Picture Publisher Wizard
PPX	Serif PagePlus Publication
PPZ	PowerPoint Packaged Presentation
PQ	PageMaker Default Printer Style
PQB	PowerQuest Batch File
PQF	Corel Presentations File
PQG	Rescue ME/OS2/DOS File
PQI	PowerQuest Drive Imaging Software
PQW	Corel Presentations 9 Runtime
PQX	Power Quest Drive Image Index
PR2	dBASE IV Printer Driver
PR3	dBASE IV PostScript Printer Driver
PR4	Harvard Graphics Presentation
PRC	Corel Presentation
PRE	Freelance Presentation
PRF	Commonly Used Extension for Preference Files and Profile Files
PRG	Program File
PRH	Cold Fusion Studio 3.1 Project
PRJ	Project File
PRL	Perl Script
PRM	Parameter File
PRN	Commonly used extension for Printer Definition or Printer Driver Files
PRO	PROLOG Program File
PRP	InstantDB Database File
PRR	Perfect Resume Data

Extension	Description
PRS	Printer Resource File, dBASE Procedure and Harvard Graphics Presentation
PRT	Commonly used extension for Printer Information or Driver File and Presentations Template
PRV	Previous Version
PRX	Foxpro Compiler Program
PRZ	Freelance Graphics 97 File
PR_	Compressed Project File
PS	PostScript and Works File
PS1	PostScript File
PS2	Level II PostScript File
PS3	Level III PostScript File
PSA	Photoshop Album Photo Album File
PSB	Paint Shop Pro Sunburst Preset and Project Scheduler Configuration File
PSC	Paint Shop Pro Sculpture Preset
PSD	Photoshop Format
PSF	PostScript Support File and PhotoStudio Graphic
PSH	Lexmark Firmware Flash File
PSI	Psion A-law Audio (Psion PLC)
PSID	PostScript Image Data
PSM	Turbo Pascal Symbol Table
PSN	Post-it Software Notes
PSP	Paint Shop Pro Image
PSP	Project Scheduler Planning File
PSQ	Postscript Graphic
PSR	PowerSoft Report and Project Scheduler Resource File
PST	Commonly used extension for Preset Files and for Post Office Box Files
PSW	Windows Password File and Print Shop Deluxe Ver. 6 File
PT	Kodak Precision Color Management System
PT3	PageMaker Version 3 Document Template and Harvard Graphics Device Driver
PT4	PageMaker Version 4 Document Template
PT4	ProtoTRAK Design Control File (Southwestern Industries, Inc.)
PT5	PageMaker Version 5 Document Template
PT6	PageMaker Version 6 Document Template
PTB	Peachtree Complete Accounting Backup Data File
PTC	ABBYY Finereader 5.0 Pro
PTDB	Peachtree Accounting Database
PTE	Picture to EXE Project

(continued)

Extension	Description
PTE	Pop!site
PTI	IBM Configurator Configuration
PTN	CADKEY Pattern File
PTP	ACT! Modem Sync File
PTX	Paint Shop Pro Texture Preset
PUB	Pretty Good Privacy Public Key Ring
PUT	PUT Compressed File Archive
PVD	Install-It Script
PVG	Encarta World Atlas Pushpins
PVK	MS Development Common IDE Resources File
PVL	Instalit Library
PVR	PVR-CONV
PW	Professional Write Text File
PWA	Password Agent File
PWK	Password Keeper File
PWL	Windows Password List
PWP	Professional WritePlus Document
PWT	AutoCAD Publish-to-Web Template
PWZ	PowerPoint Wizard
PXI	Associated with a Trojan
PXN	Twain32 File
PXP	3D Studio Process File
PXR	Pixar Picture
PXW	Twain32 File
PY	Oracle Batch Procedure
PYC	Python Compiler Script
PYD	Python Dynamic Module
PYO	Python Optimized Code
PYW	Python Script
PZ	PNG Compressed File
PZA	MGI PhotoSuite II/III/4 Album File
PZC	GraphPad Prism Script
PZP	MGI PhotoSuite II/III/4 Project File
PZS	MGI PhotoSuite II/III/4 Slide Show File
Q	Win95 Fax Queue
Q00	Quicken 2000 File
Q01	Quicken 2001 File
Q1	Winamp Equalizer Settings
Q1A	QuickClean Restore Point
Q3D	Quickdraw 3D File
Q3O	Quick3D Model
Q4Q	Solar Cell Photoshop/Paint Shop Pro Plug-In
Q5Q	SuperBladePro Preset
Q5R	Melancholytron Photoshop/Paint Shop Pro Plug-In
Q7Q	India Ink Photoshop/Paint Shop Pro Plug-In
Q8R	Flood Photoshop/Paint Shop Pro Plug-In
Q98	Quicken 98 File

Extension	Description
Q99	Quicken 99 File
Q9Q	BladePro Graphic Plug-in File
Q9R	Glitterato Photoshop/Paint Shop Pro Plug-In
Q9S	Mr. Contrast Photoshop/Paint Shop Pro Plug-In
QAB	SYBYL Binary Field Files
QAD	PF QuickArt Document
QAG	Norton Desktop Quick Access Group
QAP	Omnis Quartz Application File
QAX	ExpressTracker Data File
QB	Tony Hawk's Pro Skater Script
QB1	Quicken File
QBA	QuickBooks Accountant's Copy File
QBB	QuickBooks Backup File
QBD	Keyboard Layout
QBE	Database Saved Query
QBF	QuickBASIC Font File
QBI	Quickbooks Crash Roll Back File
QBL	Business Lawyer Document
QBO	dBASE IV Ordered Query
QBS	Quick Basic Program File
QBW	QuickBooks Primary Data File
QBX	Intuit de Online File
QCC	QC-CALC File
QCH	Quicken for DOS ver 2 Data File
QCK	Quick Charts File and QuickCard File
QCS	CADQC Standard File
QCT	Memory-Map File
QD3	QuickDraw 3D Metafile
QD3D	QuickDraw 3D Metafile
QDB	Quicken Data File Backup
QDF	Quicken for Windows Data File
QDI	Quicken Data File
QDK	Quarterdeck QEMM File
QDP	MPQDraft Plug-in
QDT	QuarkXpress Dictionary File and Quicken Data File
QEF	Excel Query
QEL	Quicken Electronic Library File
QEM	Expense Report
QEP	IRMA Wordstation for Windows
QEX	Expensible Data File
QFC	Quick File Collection Archive
QFI	Quicken 2002 File
QFX	Quicken Transfer File
QIC	Backup Set
QIF	Quicken Interchange Format
QIX	Quicken for DOS ver 2 Data File
QL$	MS Compressed QLB
QLB	C and QuickBasic-DOS and Visual Basic Quick Library

(continued)

Extension	Description
QLC	PostScript Help File and Type Manager ATM Type 1 Font Script
QLP	QuickLink Printer Driver
QMD	Quicken for Windows ver 5,6 Data File
QME	Win3 Quicken Windows File
QMF	Lotus Approach Database Query
QML	Quicken for DOS ver 2 Data File
QMR	OzWin CompuServe E-mail/Forum Access Quickscan History
QMT	Quicken Memory List
QN2	QuickNote File
QNA	High ASCII Quake Name Maker
QNX	Quicken Indexes
QPB	Quicken Payroll File
QPD	Win3 Quicken Windows File
QPH	Quicken Price History File
QPI	Win3 Quicken File
QPR	FoxPro Relational Query
QPS	Quattro Pro Software Application File
QPW	Quattro Pro Project File
QPX	FoxPro Ordered Query
QR2	Delphi Database Quick Report File
QRD	BI/Query Query Result
QRS	WordPerfect Equation Editor
QRT	QRT Ray Tracing Graphic
QRY	Query
QSA	Encrypted QSA Specifications Database Export File
QSD	Quicken for Windows Data File
QSF	Micrografx QuickSilver Compressed Internet Live Graphic
QST	Ami Pro QuickStart Tutorial Image
QTC	QuickTime Ver 2.0+ Windows CODEC
QTE	Questionnaire Specification Language File
QTF	Qtracker Filter
QTI	QuickTime Image
QTIF	QuickTime Image
QTK	Apple Quicktake
QTL	QuickTime Movie
QTM	QuickTime Movie
QTP	QuickTime Preferences
QTPF	QuickTime PreFlight Text
QTPP	Qtracker Program Package
QTR	QuickTime Resource File
QTS	QuickTime System File
QTSK	Qtracker Skin
QTV	QuickTime Virtual Reality Movie
QTVR	QuickTime VR
QTW	QText File
QTX	Quicken Data File and QuickTime Ver 3/4 Windows CODEC

Extension	Description
QUE	Task Scheduler Queue Object
QUP	QuickTime Update Package
QW	Symantec Q&A Write Program File
QW5	Quicken 5 File
QW6	Quicken 6 File
QWB	Money Quotes WriteBack Import File
QWK	QWK Reader Message
QXB	QuarkXpress Books File
QXD	QuarkXpress Document
QXL	QuarkXpress Element Library
QXP	QuarkXpress Project
QXT	QuarkXpress Template File
R	Paradox File
R00	WinRAR Split Compressed Archive
R01	WinRAR Split Compressed Archive
R02	WinRAR Split Compressed Archive
R03	WinRAR Split Compressed Archive
R04	WinRAR Split Compressed Archive
R05	WinRAR Split Compressed Archive
R06	WinRAR Split Compressed Archive
R07	WinRAR Split Compressed Archive
R08	WinRAR Split Compressed Archive
R09	WinRAR Split Compressed Archive
R1M	RealOne Metadata Package
R3D	Realsoft 3D Image
R8	RAW Graphic File
R8L	LaserJet Landscape Font
R8P	Intellifont PCL 4 Bitmap Font File
R8P	LaserJet Portrait Font
RA	RealMedia Streaming Media
RA	Remote Access Data File
RAD	Reality AdLib Tracker 2-op FM Music
RAM	RealMedia Metafile
RAP	Rapidocs Document
RAR	WinRAR Compressed Archive
RAS	Commonly used extension for Raster File
RAT	Rating System File
RAW	RAW RGB 24-bit Graphic and Raw Signed PCM Data
RAX	RealMedia Streaming File
RB0	Anti-Virus Backup
RB1	Anti-Virus Backup and R:Base Data
RB2	Anti-Virus Backup and R:Base Data
RB3	Anti-Virus Backup and R:Base Data
RB4	Anti-Virus Backup and R:Base Data
RB5	Anti-Virus Backup
RB6	Anti-Virus Backup
RB7	Anti-Virus Backup
RB8	Anti-Virus Backup
RB9	Anti-Virus Backup
RBB	Top Secret Crypto Gold File

(continued)

Extension	Description
RBF	Oracle Backup File and R:Base Data
RBF	Rollback File
RBH	RoboHelp Configuration
RBN	Real Sound File
RBO	Sometimes associated with the Magistr.B Worm
RBPM	Portable Bitmap
RBS	Rollback Script
RBX	XStream Multimedia Simulation Format
RBZ	Rail Baron Player Saved Game
RC	C++ Resource Compiler Script File and Resource Script
RC2	Developer Studio Non-editable Resources
RCD	PC Anywhere Recorded Session File
RCG	Netscape Newsgroup File
RCV	Resource Compiler; Resource Script
RC_	Winhelp Compressed File
RD	Philips Raw Data
RD3	CorelDream 3D
RDA	Oracle Storage Area File
RDB	Oracle Database Root File and Netscape Communicator Aim File
RDF	Oracle Report Binary Source
RDI	Device-Independent Bitmap
RDL	Paradox
RDO	Oracle Redo Log File
RDP	Remote Desktop Connection
README	Documentation File
REC	ARCSERVE Archivation Protocol and Commonly Used Extension for Recorded Macros
REF	Reference
REG	Registration Data
REL	ACT! Alarm Data File and Norton Internet Security 2001 Log File
REM	Annotation and ACT! Database Maintenance File
REN	Renamed File
REP	Report File
REQ	Request
RES	Resource
REV	FrameMaker Document and Revised File
REX	Oracle Report Definition
REZ	Resource File
RF	FrameMaker Document
RFG	RFG Integrator System Database
RFM	Rich Music Format
RFR	Photoshop Frame Filter File
RG	Bitmap Graphic
RGB	RGB Bitmap

Extension	Description
RGE	R.A.G.E. Driver
RH	C++ Resource Header File
RI	Lotus 1-2-3 File
RIF	Raster Image File Format
RIP	Remote Imaging Protocol and Notes Error File
RJS	RealJukebox Skin
RL4	Bitmap Graphic
RL8	Bitmap Graphic
RLB	Harvard Graphics
RLC	Run Length RLC Bitmap
RLE	Run Length Encoded Bitmap
RLL	SQL Server Resource Library
RMF	Acrobat Rights Management Document
RMI	MIDI File
RMJ	RealJukebox Media
RMS	RealMedia Secure Media File
RND	Pretty Good Privacy (PGP) Random Seed (PGP Corporation)
RNX	RealPlayer File
ROB	Microsoft Art Gallery File
ROL	AdLib Visual Composer Music File
ROM	Read Only Memory Image
ROY	TrueType
RPBM	Portable Image
RPF	AutoCAD Raster-pattern Fill Definition
RPG	RPG Programming Language
RPGM	Portable Greyscale
RPL	Replica Text File and Reply Message
RPM	RealMedia Player Plug-in
RPS	Borland Translation Repository
RPT	Report
RPV	Real Player Visualization File
RPX	Oracle Visual Information Retrieval Raw Pixel Format File
RQY	Excel OLE DB Query File
RRF	Musicmatch Jukebox File
RSA	PKCS7 Signature, MD5 + RSA
RSC	Resource File
RSG	EPOC Compiled Resource Header
RSL	PageMaker File, Paradox 7 Report and PC Tools Resources Library
RSML	Real Player File
RSP	Commonly used extension for a Response File
RSS	Rich Site Summary File
RS_	ArcView Image File
RT	Rich Text
RTC	Rescue Me File
RTF	Rich Text Format File
RTH	ANSYS Results
RTK	Run Time Library

(continued)

Extension	Description
RTP	Patch File and TurboTax Update File
RTS	RealAudio RTSL Document
RTX	Rich Text Document
RT_	Winhelp Compressed File
RU	Javasoft JRE 1.3 Library File
RUJ	Oracle Recovery-Unit Journal
RUL	Rule Repository
RUN	PC Tools Script Tools Program
RUS	Russian Text
RV	RealVideo Clip
RVML	Rich Vector Markup Language
RVW	Review
RWG	Random Word Generator
RWP	IBM Configurator Report
RWS	C++ Resource Workshop Symbol File
RWX	Netscape Live 3D
RWZ	Outlook Rules Wizard File
RX	DOS 7 File
RXC	Easy CD Creator Drag to Disk File
RXD	Reflex Database
RXF	Recipe Exchange Format
RXH	Reflex Database Help File
RXN	MDL Rxn File
RXP	Easy CD & DVD Creator 6 Playlist
RXR	Reflex Database Report
RXS	Reflex Database Screen Driver and AudioCentral Roxio Markup Sound
S	Source Code
S$$	Temporary Sort File
S01	WordPerfect Distribution File
S02	WordPerfect Distribution File
S03	WordPerfect Distribution File
S11	Sealed MPEG-1 Video
S14	Sealed MPEG-4 Video
S16	Sigames File
S17	SubSeven Saved Settings File
S19	Motorola Assembly-Language Program ASCII-HEX Data File
S1A	Sealed Acrobat Document
S1E	Sealed Excel Worksheet
S1G	Sealed GIF Image
S1H	Sealed HTML Document
S1J	Sealed JPEG Image
S1M	Sealed MP3 Audio
S1N	Sealed PNG Graphic
S1P	Sealed PowerPoint Presentation
S1Q	Sealed QuickTime Movie
S1W	Sealed Word Document
S3D	Micrografx Simply 3D Project
S7P	SubSeven Trojan File
S??	RAR Compressed File
SAK	Software Administration Kit

Extension	Description
SAL	Database Program; SQL Application Language
SAM	Ami Pro Document and Office 97 File Converter
SAS	VMS SAS Source Code
SAT	Surprise! AdLib Tracker
SAV	Saved File
SBC	SBC Compressed Archive
SBI	Selfboot Inducer and Sound Blaster Instrument File
SBK	Creative Labs SB AWE 32
SBL	Softbridge Basic Language
SBP	Superbase DML Program
SC	Framework Screen Driver
SC$	Modem Bitware Fax Disk1 File
SC2	Schedule+ File
SC3	dBASE Screen Mask File
SCA	Norton Anti-Virus File
SCB	System Cleaner
SCF	Windows Explorer Command
SCH	Schedule+ File
SCI	System Configuration Information
SCM	ICQ Sound Compressed Sound Scheme
SCN	Compressed Screen Format
SCP	Dial-Up Networking Script
SCR	Screen Font or Screen Dump and Windows Screen Saver File
SCT	Foxpro Screen and Scripting Tools
SCT	Lotus Screen Capture Text
SCX	FoxPro Screen File
SD	Simple Diary
SD2	Base SAS Database
SDA	OpenOffice.org Drawing and Star Office Drawing
SDB	Simply Accounting File and Windows Compatibility Solution Database
SDC	OpenOffice.org Spreadsheet and StarOffice Spreadsheet
SDD	OpenOffice.org Presentation and StarOffice Presentation
SDF	Standard Data Format and Schedule Data File
SDG	Star Office Gallery
SDI	Borland Single Document Interface and Quickbooks Data
SDK	AutoSketch Drawing
SDL	Paradox Script
SDN	Shell Archive
SDO	Sealed Word Document
SDOC	Sealed Word File

(continued)

Extension	Description
SDP	Real Player File and StarOffice Picture File
SDS	OpenOffice.org Chart and StarOffice Chart
SDT	QuickBooks Data
SDW	OpenOffice.org Text and StarOffice Text
SE1	Flight Simulator Scenery File
SEA	StuffIT Expander Archive Format
SEB	Franklin eBookMan Format
SEC	MP3 Music File
SED	Sed/unix Doc File
SEL	Paint Shop Pro Selection File
SEM	Sealed E-mail and Alpha Five Set Object File
SEP	TIFF Bitmap Separation
SEQ	Commonly Used Extension for Sequence File
SERVER	Analog File
SES	Commonly Used Extension for Session File
SET	Configuration File and Backup File Set
SEX	Alpha Five Set Index
SE_	Cakepro Compressed Audio File
SF	Signature Instructions File
SF0	Windows Sytem File Check File
SF2	Creative Labs Soundfont 2.0 Bank File
SFB	HP Soft Font
SFC	Windows System File Check File
SFF	Scene File Format
SFI	Ventura Printer Font
SFL	LaserJet Landscape Font
SFO	CuteFTP Search File
SFP	LaserJet Portrait Font
SFS	OpenOffice.org Frame and StarOffice Frame
SFX	Self-extracting Archive
SFZ	SFzip SoundFont File Archive
SGF	StarWriter Document
SGI	Sealed GIF Image
SGIF	Sealed GIF File
SGL	OpenOffice.org Master Document and StarOffice Master Document
SGM	Standard Generalized Markup Language IETF Document
SGML	Standard Generalized Markup Language IETF Document
SGT	Signature Keyboard Macro
SH	UNIX/LINUX Shell Script
SHA	CorelDRAW Shader
SHB	Windows Shortcut into a Document
SHD	Print Spooler Shadow File
SHE	Windows 95 .ShellExt

Extension	Description
SHM	WordPerfect Shell Macro
SHP	Commonly Used Extension for a Shape File
SHT	S-HTML Document
SHTM	HTML File Containing Server Side Directives
SHTML	HTML File Containing Server Side Directives
SHTML3	SHTML File
SHW	Presentation SlideShow
SIC	Quicken 2002 Order File
SIF	Windows NT Setup Information File
SIG	Signature File
SIK	Backup
SIM	Simulation
SITX	StuffIt StuffIt X Archive
SJF	Split Files Shell Extension
SJP	Sealed JPEG Image
SJPG	Sealed JPEG File
SKF	AutoSketch
SKN	Commonly Used Extension for Skin Files
SLB	AutoCAD Slide Library
SLD	AutoCAD Slide
SLG	AutoCAD Status Log
SLL	Static Link Library
SLM	Visual FoxPro
SLN	Visual Studio .NET Solution
SLT	Selection
SMD	OpenOffice.org Mail and StarOffice Mail Document
SMF	OpenOffice.org Formula and StarOffice Formula
SMI	CC:Mail Smart Icon
SML	Simple Markup Language
SMP	Ad Lib Gold Sample
SMP3	Sealed MP3 File
SMPEG	Sealed MPEG Movie
SMPG	Sealed MPG Movie
SMT	QuickBooks
SMV	Streaming Mobile Video File
SN	Serial Number File
SNC	ACT! E-mail/Folder Synchronization File
SND	Commonly Used Extension for a Sound File
SNF	UNIX Font File
SNP	Commonly Used Extension for a Snapshop File
SNX	QuickBooks Data
SOB	Visual Basic
SOM	Paradox Sort Info
SPC	Multiplan Program

(continued)

Extension	Description
SPD	Postscript Mini-driver and Harvard Graphics Bitstream Typefaces
SPDF	Sealed PDF File
SPEC	General Specification File
SPF	Setup File
SPIFF	Still Picture Interchange File Format Bitmap
SPJ	Site Publisher Project File
SPK	Acorn Spark Compressed Archive
SPL	Compressed Archive File and Printer Spool File
SPM	WordPerfect
SPN	Sealed PNG Graphic
SPNG	Sealed PNG Graphic
SPP	Sealed PowerPoint Presentation
SPPT	Sealed PowerPoint File
SPR	Foxpro Generated Screen Program
SPS	Oracle Package Specification
SPT	Split File
SPX	Foxpro Compiler Screen Program
SQB	SyQuest Backup
SQC	Structured Query Language Common Code File
SQL	Structured Query Language Data
SQW	Archive
SQZ	Compressed Archive File
SR	Netscape File
SRB	Corel ClipArt ScrapBook
SRC	Sourcecode
SREC	ASCII Load File
SRP	QuickLink Script
SRQ	Unprocessed Microsoft Server Request
SRT	DVD Subtitle File
SRV	Help Maker File
SSC	HP Library and Tape Tools Script
SSF	Enable Spreadsheet File and Sound Set File
SSL	Paradox 5 File
SSW	Sealed Flash File
SSWF	Sealed Flash File
STA	Eudora File
STB	AutoCAD R2000 Plot Style Table
STC	OpenOffice.org Spreadsheet Template
STD	OpenOffice.org Drawing Template
STF	Setup Information
STG	SNMP Traffic Grapher Network Graphic
STI	OpenOffice.org Presentation Template
STL	C++ Standard Template Library
STM	SHTML File and Sound Set File
STML	Sealed HTML File
STML	SHTML File
STR	dBASE Structure List

Extension	Description
STS	C Project Status Info
STW	OpenOffice.org Text Document Template and Staroffice Writer Template
STY	Commonly used extension for Style Files
SUB	DIVX Subtitles
SUM	Summary
SUP	Startup Screen Bitmap and Supplemental Data
SUR	Surveyor Document
SVC	Simple Visual Compiler
SVF	Simple Vector Format
SVG	Scalable Vector Graphics File
SVGZ	Compressed Scalable Vector Graphics File
SWA	Shockwave Audio File
SWB	PageMaker or Photoshop Version 7 ColorSync Component
SWFS	Dreamweaver File
SWL	Macromedia Flash Format
SWP	Swap File
SWT	Macromedia Authoring Flash File
SXC	OpenOffice.org Spreadsheet and Staroffice Spreadsheet File
SXD	OpenOffice.org Draw File
SXG	OpenOffice.org Master Document
SXI	OpenOffice.org Presentation File
SXL	Sealed Excel Worksheet
SXLS	Sealed Excel File
SXM	OpenOffice.org Math File
SXM	Sealed XML Document
SXML	Sealed XML Document
SXW	OpenOffice.org Text Document and Staroffice Writer Document
SY3	Harvard Graphics Symbol File
SYM	Commonly Used Extension for Symbol Libraries and C++ Precompiled Headers
SYN	Synonym File
SYS	System Configuration and System Device Driver
SYW	Harvard Graphics Symbol Graphic
SY_	Compressed SYS File
T	Paradox Database File
T$	Modem Bitware Fax Disk5 File
T02	TaxCut 2002 Tax Return File
T03	TaxCut 2003 Tax Return File
T2	TrueType Font
T2W	NTgraph Turbo Pascal File
T3	Tarshare File
T32	Drive Image5 File
T3D	Fifa2000 Environment Data
T44	dBASE IV Temporary File

(continued)

Extension	Description
T65	PageMaker Template
T98	Kiplinger Tax Cut File
T99	Kiplinger Tax Cut File
T??	Ingres Table/Index File
T??	RAR Compressed File
TA0	TaxACT Tax Year 2000 Form
TA1	TaxACT Tax Year 2001 Form
TA2	TaxACT Tax Year 2002 Form
TA8	TaxACT Tax Year 1998 Form
TA9	TaxACT Tax Year 1999 Form
TAB	Commonly Used Extension for a Table File
TAH	Turbo Assembler Help File
TAI	INMOS Transputer Development System Occam Analyse Info
TAL	Typed Assembly Language File
TAP	Tape File
TAR	Tape Archive File
TAT	Text File
TAX	TurboTax Tax Return
TAZ	Compressed File
TB1	Turbo C Font
TB2	Turbo C Font
TBD	MSE File and Visual Studio File
TBH	Turbo Basic Help File
TBL	Commonly used extension for Table Files
TBR	Norton Desktop Custom Toolbar
TBR	SoftQuad XMetaL Toolbar/Menu Configuration
TBS	German Word Text Elements
TBX	Project Scheduler Table
TC	Borland Configuration File
TCC	Turbo C / GCC Include Std File
TCH	Borland Help File
TCT	TurboCAD Template
TCW	TurboCAD Drawing
TCX	TurboCAD Drawing as Text
TD	Turbo Debugger for DOS Configuration File
TD2	Turbo Debugger for Win32 Configuration File
TDB	ACT! Transaction Data File
TDF	Setup Program Data and Typeface Definition File
TDO	Compressed File
TDT	ASCII Data File in CSV Format
TEL	Telnet Host File
TEM	Turbo Editor Macro Language
TEMP	Temporary File
TER	CorelFlow Line Terminator
TET	Tetris Results

Extension	Description
TEX	Text File or Texture File
TEXT	ASCII Text
TFR	IBM Client Access File Transfer
TGT	Watcom C/C++ Individual Target
TH	Javasoft JRE 1.3 Library File
THEME	Plus! Theme File
THM	Thumbnail Bitmap Image
THML	Theological HTML
THN	Graphics Workshop for Windows Thumbnail
THS	WordPerfect Thesauraus
TIF	Tagged Image Format File
TIFF	Tagged Image Format File
TIM	TIFF Image (rev 6)
TLB	Commonly Used Extension for Type Library Files
TLD	Tag Library Descriptor
TLF	Short Message Service File
TM	HP Internet Advisor Capture File
TMD	Lotus TvMap Document
TMF	WordPerfect Tagged Font Metric File
TMO	Zortech C++ Global Optimizer Output File
TMP	Temporary File/Folder
TMPL	Website META Language Template
TNC	SuperJPG ThumbNail Cache File
TNEF	Transport Neutral Encapsulation Format File
TNF	Transport Neutral Encapsulation Format File
TNL	Thumbnail
TOC	Table of Contents
TOK	C++ 4.x External Token
TP	Turbo Pascal Configuration File
TP3	Harvard Graphics Template
TPA	Corel Graphics10 Custom File
TPH	Turbo Pascal Help File
TPL	Access Workflow Designer
TPL	Commonly Used Extension for Template Files
TPM	TextPad Macro
TPP	Turbo Pascal Protected Mode Unit
TPU	Turbo Pascal Compiled Unit
TPZ	Compressed File
TQL	Tree Query Language File and SQL Server Query Analyzer Header File
TR	Turbo Debugger Session-state Settings
TR1	Novell LANalyzer Capture File
TRC	Commonly Used Extension for Debug Files
TRE	PC Tools Directory Tree
TRG	Symantec LiveUpdate File

(continued)

Extension	Description
TRI	LiveUpdate Product Update List
TRM	Terminal Settings
TRN	PageMaker and SQL Server Transaction Backup
TRU	True BASIC Source Code
TRW	Turbo Debugger Session-state Settings
TSC	Win Help Related File
TSG	Enable File
TSN	MIDI File
TSP	Windows Telephony Service Provider
TSQ	ODBC Script
TST	WordPerfect Printer Test File
TTC	TrueType Compressed Font and TrueType Font Collection
TTF	TrueType Font
TTR	TrueType Font
TT_	Compressed TTF File
TURBOC3	Turbo C Make File
TUT	Tutorial
TUW	Office File
TV	Paradox Table View Settings
TVF	dBASE Table View Settings
TVL	TurboTax
TVR	Boot File
TVS	VectorMAX Streaming Video
TVT	RealPlayer
TVVI	InterVideo WInDVR
TWE	ThinkWave Educator Data File
TX8	DOS Text File
TXE	Enriched Text File
TXF	Compressed File
TXF	Tax Exchange Format
TXR	Corel Graphics Ver 10 Custom File
TXT	Text File
TX_	Compressed TXT File
TZ	Compressed File
TZB	Compressed File
TZT	CP/M Information File
U	Subsampled Raw YUV Bitmap
U8	Raw Unsigned 8-Bit Audio Data
U96	EasyZip Temporary File
UAP	User Agent Wireless Telephony Profile
UB	Raw Unsigned Byte
UBB	BASIC UBAS File
UBD	BASIC UBAS File
UC2	Compressed File
UCN	Compressed Archive
UCS	Universal Classification Standard Database File
UDB	Works File and Windows 2000 Uniqueness Database File

Extension	Description
UDF	Excel User Defined Function and Windows NT Uniqueness Database File
UDL	Data Link
UDW	Raw Unsigned Double-Word
UE2	Encrypted Archive
UEF	Unified Emulator Format
UFA	UFA Compressed File Archive
UHA	UHARC Compressed Archive
UHS	Universal Hint System File
UI	User Interface
UKS	Works File
ULS	Internet Location Service
UMB	MemMaker Backup Archive
UMI	CDDB Database and PC Music Library in PlayCenter
UND	A86 Assembler Undefined Symbols
UNF	Btreive Unformatted File
UNQ	Fax View File
UNT	AutoCAD Unit Definition
UNX	Text File
UPD	dBASE Update File and Universal Print Driver
UPF	Universal Picture Format Bitmap
UPG	Firmware Upgrade File
UPO	dBASE Compiled Update File
UPR	FileMaker User Spelling Dictionary
UPS	Works File
UPT	Connectivity Memory Model Update Timing Input File
URI	List of Uniform Resource Identifiers
URIS	List of Uniform Resource Identifiers
URL	Internet Location
URLS	GetRight URL List
USA	Office Header File
USL	LaserJet Landscape Font
USP	LaserJet Portrait Font and PageMaker Printer Font
USR	User Database
USTAR	POSIX tar Compressed Archive
UTL	QuickBooks Data
UU	Compressed Archive File
UUD	Uudecoded
UUE	Uuencoded
UW	Raw Unsigned Word
UWL	WordPerfect User Word List (Corel)
UX	UNIX File
UZE	Ultimate Zip Compresion Agent
V	Subsampled Raw YUV Bitmap
V$$	Cheyenne/Inoculan AntiVirus Temporary File
VAF	Visual Studio Common Tools Vanalyzer Project Item

(continued)

Extension	Description
VAL	dBASE Values and Paradox Validity Checks
VAM	Visual Studio Common Tools Vanalyzer Project Item
VAP	Annotated Speech Audio
VAR	Commonly used extension for Variables File
VB	VBScript File or Any VisualBasic Source
VBA	VBase File
VBB	VirtualBoss Backup File (VirtualBoss Development Co.)
VBD	ActiveX
VBD	Visual Basic 5 Active Document
VBF	Outlook Free/Busy File
VBG	Visual Basic Group Project
VBK	VisualCADD Backup File
VBL	User Control Licensing File
VBN	Norton Corporate Anti-Virus Quarantined File
VBO	Access Package Deployment References
VBP	Visual Basic Ver. 4.0-6.0 Project
VBPROJ	Visual Studio .NET Visual Basic Project
VBPROJ. USER	Visual Studio .NET File
VBR	Remote Automation Registration Files
VBS	MPEG Movie Clip and VBScript Script File
VBS	VBScript Script File
VBW	Visual Basic Project Workplace
VBX	Visual Basic Extension
VBZ	Wizard Launch File
VCA	Visual Clip Art
VCD	VisualCADD Drawing File
VCL	Borland Visual Component Library
VCM	Visual Component File
VCP	Visual C++ Wordspace Information
VCS	vCalendar File
VCT	FoxPro Class Library
VCW	Visual C++ Workbench Information File
VCWIN32	Visual C Make File
VCX	FoxPro Class Library or Spreadsheet File
VDA	CAD File
VDB	Norton AntiVirus Update File
VDB	PC-cillin Quarantined File
VDF	Commonly Used Extension for Anti-virus Definition Files
VDM	VDM Play
VDP	Visual Studio .NET Setup and Deployment Project

Extension	Description
VDPROJ	Visual Studio .NET Setup and Deployment Project
VDX	Vector Graphic File and Virtual Device Driver
VEM	Voice E-mail File
VER	TurboTax Installed Version Record
VEW	Lotus Approach or Novel Groupwise View File
VFA	FontLab Database File
VFB	Font Description File
VFD	Virtual Floppy Drive Image
VFF	DESR VFF Greyscale Bitmap Image
VFM	Ventura Publisher Font Metrics File
VFW	Video for Windows
VGA	VGA Screen Driver
VGR	Ventura Graphic
VHD	Virtual PC File
VHDL	VHDL Design File
VH~	V-help File
VID	Media Player Video
VIR	Virus Infected File
VKL	Virtual Edit
VL	Visual Labels File
VLB	Corel Ventura Library
VLM	Novell Virtual Loadable Module
VMB	Quicken 2002 Order File
VMC	Virtual Memory Configuration
VMDC	VMware Virtual Disk File
VMDK	VMware Virtual Disk File
VME	Virtual Matrix Encryption File
VMF	FaxWorks Audio File
VNC	Virtual Network Computing
VOC	Creative Labs Sound and Other Sound Files
VOR	OpenOffice.org Template
VP	Ventura Publisher File
VPF	Vector Product Format
VPS	Visual Pinball Script
VPT	Visual Pinball Table
VRB	Dictionary File
VRF	Oracle 7 Configuration File
VRM	Quattro Pro Overlay File
VRML	Virtual Reality Modeling Language
VRO	DVD Recorder File
VRS	WordPerfect Graphics Driver
VRT	Virtual World
VRW	VREAMScript Command Language ActiveX 3D
VS	Vivid Include File
VS2	Roland-Bass Transfer File
VSB	VSampler Soundbank
VSC	VirusScan Configuration

(continued)

Extension	Description
VSD	Visio Drawing
VSH	VirusShield Configuration File
VSK	Microsoft Development Common IDE File
VSL	Visio Library
VSM	VisSim Simulation Model
VSR	Access Branded Report Format
VSS	Visio Stencil
VST	Visio Template
VSW	Visio Workspace File
VSX	XML for Visio Stencil File
VTM	Cold Fusion Studio Query
VTS	VTune Performance Monitor Project File (Intel)
VTX	XML for Visio Template File
VUE	dBASE View File and Schedule+ Configuration File
VWR	PC Tools File Viewer
VWT	MGI VideoWave Video Wave Thumbnail
VXD	Virtual Device Driver
VXML	VoiceXML Source File
VXP	VTune Performance Monitor Pack and Go File (Intel)
VXS	Voice Xpress User Profile
VXX	IOsubsys Driver File
W$	Modem Bitware Fax Disk3 File
W20	Windows 2000 Related File
W31	Windows 3.1 Startup File
W32	Win32 File
W40	Win95 Backup File
W44	dBASE Temporary File
W51	WordPerfect Ver. 5.1 Document
W60	WordPerfect Ver. 6.0 Document
W61	WordPerfect Ver. 6.1 Document
W95	Windows95-related Data File
W98	Windows98-related Data File
WAB	Outlook Address Book
WAD	Programming Library
WAL	Winamp3 Skin Format
WAP	WAVPAC Filtered .WAV File Output
WAR	Java Web Archive
WAS	Procomm Plus Script Source Code File
WAT	IBM Voice Type Language Map File
WAV	Waveform Audio
WAVE	Waveform Audio
WAX	Windows Media Audio Redirector
WA_	Doko Compressed Install File
WA~	Outlook Address Book Temporary File
WB	Dictionary Project Data File
WB1	QuattroPro for Windows
WB2	QuattroPro for Windows
WB3	QuattroPro for Windows

Extension	Description
WBD	Works Database File
WBF	Windows Batch File
WBK	Word Backup and WordPerfect Workbook
WBMP	Wireless Bitmap File Format
WCD	WordPerfect Macro Token List
WCH	Corel Office PerfectScript
WCM	Corel Presentations and WordPerfect Macro
WCP	WordPerfect Product Information
WDB	Works Database
WDL	Windows XP Watchdog Log File
WDM	Visual Interdev98 Templates Web Project Items File
WEB	Corel Xara Web Document
WEBPNP	Support for Internet Printing
WED	Windows Editor File
WFM	dBASE Form Designer Form Object
WFN	Corel Symbols and Fonts
WFO	Delphi Runimage Delphi Demos Doc Formdll DB File
WFP	Turtle Beach WaveFront Program
WFS	Windows Installation Script
WFT	WaveFront 3D Object
WFW	Pci Smc File
WFX	WinFax Data File
WG1	Lotus 1-2-3 Worksheet
WG2	Lotus 1-2-3 Worksheet
WGL	Wingate License File
WHT	NetMeeting Old Whiteboard Document
WI	Wavelet Image and All Corel Products Compressed Image
WIF	Wavelet Image File and Window Intermediate File Template
WIL	WinImage File
WIN	FoxPro/dBASE Window File and Windows Backup File
WIP	Windows Installer Project
WIZ	Word Wizard File
WK!	Lotus Spreadsheet File
WK1	1-2-3 Spreadsheet File
WK3	Lotus Spreadsheet File
WK4	Lotus Spreadsheet File
WKB	Workbook and WordPerfect and WordPerfect for Windows Document
WKQ	Quattro Spreadsheet
WKS	Lotus or Works for Windows Spreadsheet File
WKZ	Compressed Spreadsheet
WLD	Acrobat Distiller
WLG	Dr. Watson Log
WLL	Word Add-in

(continued)

Extension	Description
WLZ	WinImage File
WM	Windows Media A/V File
WM$	BASIC VB
WM2D	Working Model Motion Simulation
WM5	Dyndlg2 File
WMA	Windows Media Audio File
WMC	WordPerfect Macro
WMD	Windows Media Download File
WMDB	Media Player Ver. 9+ Library
WME	Windows Media Encoder Session Profile
WMF	Windows Metafile
WML	Wireless Markup Language File
WMP	Windows Media Player File
WMR	Windows Media Recorder Media Stream
WMS	Windows Media Skin File
WMV	Windows Media File
WMX	Audio Playlist
WMZ	Windows Media Compressed Skin File
WNF	Outline Font
WOA	Windows Swap File
WOC	Windows OrgChart Organization
WP	WordPerfect Document
WP4	WordPerfect Ver. 4 Document
WP5	WordPerfect Ver. 5.0/5.1/5.2 Document
WP6	WordPerfect Ver. 6.0/6.1 Document
WPA	ACT! Word Processor Document
WPB	openCanvas Image
WPC	Word and Write File Converter
WPD	Windows Printer Driver and ACT! Word Processor Document
WPF	WordPerfect Text File
WPG	WordPerfect/Drawperfect Graphic
WPJ	Watcom C/C++ Project
WPK	Keyboard Information File and WordPerfect Macro
WPL	PFS WinWorks Spreadsheet
WPM	WordPerfect Macro
WPP	WordPerfect Color Palette
WPS	Works Text Document
WPT	WordPerfect Template
WPW	PerfectWorks Document and WordPerfect Document
WPX	Printer Information File
WQ	Spreadsheet
WQ!	Compressed Quattro Pro Spreadsheet
WQ1	Quattro Pro Spreadsheet
WQ2	Quattro Pro Spreadsheet
WR!	Compressed Lotus Spreadsheet
WRI	Write Document
WRK	Spreadsheet File
WRML	Plain Text VRML File

Extension	Description
WRS	WordPerfect Windows Printer Driver
WS	Windows Script File and WordStar Ver. 5.0/6.0 Document
WS1	WordStar for Windows Ver. 1 Document
WS2	WordStar for Windows Ver. 2 Document
WS3	WordStar for Windows Ver. 3 Document
WS4	WordStar for Windows Ver. 4 Document
WS4D	Web Server 4D Custom Web Page
WS5	WordStar for Windows Ver. 5 Document
WS6	WordStar for Windows Ver. 6 Document
WS7	WordStar for Windows Ver. 7 Document
WSA	Animation Shop Workspace
WSC	Windows Script Component
WSD	WordStar Ver. 2000 Document
WSDL	Web Services Description Language
WSF	Windows Script File
WSH	Windows Script Host Settings File
WSI	Wise Windows Installer Project
WSP	Paint Shop Pro Workspace and Visual C++, FORTRAN Workspace Info
WST	WordStar Text File
WSX	WinMX Protocol List
WSZ	WinAmp Skin Zip File
WS_	Visc15 Adressen Setup File
WT	WildTangent Branded .X 3D Model
WT2	WordExpress Document Template
WTA	WinTune DLL
WTC	Watertec Encrypted Database (Watertite Limited)
WTD	WinTune Document
WTH	WildTangent Says Hello
WTK	WinTalk URL Address
WTR	Winter Windows Scheduler File
WTS	WION Technology Setup (WION Technology)
WTX	ASCII Text
WVE	Component of a DIVX Movie Conversion
WVL	Wavelet Compressed Bitmap
WVX	Windows Media Redirector
WVZ	Brazilian Music Format
WWB	WordPerfect Button Bar
WWD	Works Wizard File
WWF	WWF Rant Pakk Sound File
WWK	WordPerfect Keyboard Layout
WWL	Word Add-in File

(continued)

Extension	Description
WWP	Works Wizard File
WWS	Works Wizard File
WZ	WinAmp Skin
WZS	MS Word Wizard
X	Direct3D Object
X01	Paradox Secondary Index
X02	Paradox Secondary Index
X03	Paradox Secondary Index
X04	Paradox Secondary Index
X05	Paradox Secondary Index
X06	Paradox Secondary Index
X07	Paradox Secondary Index
X08	Paradox Secondary Index
X09	Paradox Secondary Index
X10	X Window Dump Bitmap
X11	X Windows System Window Dump Bitmap
X13	Hooligans
X16	Macromedia Program Extension
X32	Macromedia Program Extension
X3D	Xara 3D Project File
X3F	Sigma Camera RAW Picture File (Sigma)
X4M	TeamLinks Mail File Data
X5	Rockwell Software Logix 5 File
X64	C64 Emulator Disk Image
XA	Extended Architecture File
XAB	Mail Address Book
XAD	eXotic AdLib Format
XAR	Corel Xara Drawing
XBF	Database File
XBL	Extensible Binding Language
XBM	X Bitmap Graphic
XB~	IC File
XC	X Server Constant Screen Image Bitmap
XCF	GIMP Image File
XDB	Norton AntiVirus Update File
XDF	Extended Disk Format Image
XDK	XML Development Kit Project
XDP	UNIX File
XDS	OpenGL Performer Script
XEX	KERMIT Control File
XFD	XML Form in XFDL Format
XFDF	Acrobat Forms Document
XFM	OmniForm XML Format
XFN	Ventura Printer Font
XFR	Ventura Publisher Bitmap Editor Font File
XFX	Fax File
XG0	Database Index; Paradox Secondary Index

Extension	Description
XG1	Database Index
XG1	Techno Toys XG-909 MIDI Drum Machine File
XG2	Database Index
XG3	Database Index
XG4	Database Index
XG5	Database Index
XGO	Paradox Database-related File
XHDML	XML Version of HDML File
XHT	Extensible HyperText Markup Language File
XHTM	Extensible HyperText Markup Language File
XHTML	Extensible HyperText Markup Language File
XHTML	Libxml HTML File
XIF	Xerox Image File
XJS	WinExplorer Java Script
XJT	Compressed GIMP Image with Properties of GIMP
XJTGZ	Compressed GIMP Image with Properties of GIMP
XJTZ2	Compressed GIMP Image with Properties of GIMP
XL	Excel Spreadsheet
XLA	Excel Add-in
XLB	Excel Worksheet
XLC	Excel Chart
XLD	Excel Dialog
XLK	Excel Backup
XLL	Excel Add-in
XLM	Excel Macro
XLR	Works
XLS	Excel or Works Worksheet
XLSHTML	Excel HTML Document
XLSMHTML	Excel Archived HTML Document
XLT	Excel Template
XLTHTML	Excel HTML Template
XLV	Excel VBA
XLW	Excel Workspace
XLXML	Excel XML Worksheet
XMI	Winamp Extended MIDI File
XML	Extensible Markup Language File
XMLBACKUP	EnABLE Backup File
XMP	Graphic File
XMS	AutoCAD External Message
XMX	AutoCAD External Message Compiled File
XNK	Exchange Shortcut
XNML	NML Language Language Extension
XP	System Utility File
XPL	Music File

(continued)

Extension	Description
XQT	SuperCalc Macro Sheet
XRF	Cross Reference
XSC	XML Schema
XSD	XML Schema
XSL	XML Stylesheet
XSLT	XSL Transform File
XSU	Fortran Libf77 File
XTD	XML Type Definition
XTP	XTree Data File
XUL	XML User Interface Language
XVP	Xview Package File
XVS	Xview Scene Package File
XWD	X Windows Dump
XWP	Xerox Writer Text File
XWS	Xara Webstyle File
XX	Xxencoded File
XXE	Xxencoded File
XXL	Archive
XXT	Extension DLL
Y	Desktop Color Separation Specification Yellow Layer
Y01	Paradox Secondary Index
Y02	Paradox Secondary Index
Y03	Paradox Secondary Index
Y04	Paradox Secondary Index
Y05	Paradox Secondary Index
Y06	Paradox Secondary Index
Y07	Paradox Secondary Index
Y08	Paradox Secondary Index
Y09	Paradox Secondary Index
YBK	Encarta Yearbook
YBS	YBS Compressed Archive
YC	YAC Compressed Archive
YEL	Yellow Color Separation
YENC	yEnc Encoded File
YG0	Paradox Secondary Index
YG1	Paradox Secondary Index
YG2	Paradox Secondary Index
YG3	Paradox Secondary Index
YG4	Paradox Secondary Index
YGM	YahooGroupManager Ver. 1.x Database
YGM2	YahooGroupManager Ver. 2.x Database
YGO	Paradox Database-related File
YIF	Graphic
YMG	Yahoo! Messenger File
YNC	yEnc Encoded File
YPL	Yahoo! Player Playlist
YPS	Yahoo! Messenger File
YPT	Cryptic File
YSP	Bitmap Graphic
YUV	Color Space Pixel Format
YUV3	CCIR 601 2:1:1 Bitmap

Extension	Description
YYC	Wave Sapphire Distribution File
YZ	YAC Compressed Archive File
YZ1	DeepFreezer Compressed Archive
Z	UNIX Compressed Archive File
Z0	ZoneAlarm Mailsafe Renamed .JS File
Z01	WinZip Split Compressed Archive
Z02	WinZip Split Compressed Archive
Z03	WinZip Split Compressed Archive
Z04	WinZip Split Compressed Archive
Z05	WinZip Split Compressed Archive
Z1	ZoneAlarm File
Z2	ZoneAlarm Mailsafe
Z3	ZoneAlarm Mailsafe
Z3D	Zmodeler Model File
Z4	ZoneAlarm Mailsafe
Z5	ZoneAlarm Mailsafe
Z6	ZoneAlarm Mailsafe
Z7	ZoneAlarm Mailsafe
Z8	ZoneAlarm Mailsafe
Z9	ZoneAlarm Mailsafe
ZABW	AbiWord Compressed Document
ZAP	FileWrangler Compressed File
ZBF	Z-Buffer Radiance File
ZBX	Disk Volume Identification
ZC	Zipkey Configuration File
ZDB	EPSQ Security Officer Submission
ZFD	ABC Programming Language Zeroadic Function
ZFS	C++ Assembly Source
ZH	Communicator Java Classes File
ZH_TW	Communicator Java Classes File
ZIP	Compressed Archive File
ZKA	Quicken6 File
ZL	Easy CD Creator Drag to Disk File
ZMK	Z-Up Maker Project File
ZMS	ECLIPSE Server Macro Script File
ZMV	ZSNES Movie File
ZOO	ZOO Compressed Archive File
ZPD	ABC Programming Language Zeroadic Function
ZPJ	ECLIPSE Server Project File
ZPK	Z-Firm Package
ZPL	ZIG File
ZPW	ZippedWeb Archive
ZS	ECLIPSE Server Script File
ZTE	E-Tabs Reader File
ZTL	ZBrush ZTool Native File
ZTM	ZTreeWin Macro
ZW	Chinese Text
ZWL	WinLabel Ver. 3.0 Label
ZZ	ZZip Compressed Archive
ZZE	ASCII Encoded File Archive

APPENDIX E

WINDOWS FUNCTIONS

Table E.1 Windows Hotkey Shortcuts

Shortcut	Action
\<Alt\>	Activates or deactivates the current window's menu bar.
\<Delete\>	Deletes selected Item(s).
Drag and Drop	Press and hold left mouse button. Slide selected object(s) over the icon that depicts the desired destination folder or device and then release.
\<End\>	Moves cursor to end of current line, except for Internet Explorer. In IE, moves to the bottom of the page.
\<Enter\>	Opens selected item or activates highlighted button.
\<Esc\>	Cancels current operation.
\<F1\>	Displays context-sensitive help for selected item.
\<F2\>	In IE, activates the Rename command.
\<F3\>	In IE, opens a file search.
\<F4\>	In IE, displays "My Computer" menu.
	In IE, displays "Address" history list.
\<F5\>	Refreshes the contents of the current window.
\<F6\>	Switches between active panes of current application.
\<Home\>	Moves cursor to beginning of line (except IE).
	In IE, moves to the top of the page.
Menu Button (🖹)	Duplicates the function of the right mouse button.
\<Print Screen\>	Copies the current screen to clipboard as bitmap image.
Space Bar	Toggles current check box or radio button.
\<Tab\>	Moves between fields and/or objects of current window.
Windows Button (🪟)	Open the Start menu.

(continued)

Table E.1 Windows Hot-key Shortcuts (*continued*)

Shortcut	Action
	<Ctrl> Shortcuts
<Ctrl>+A	Selects all items.
<Ctrl>+<Alt>+<Delete>	In Win98, opens Close Programs window.
	In Win2K or XP, opens Security window (allows you to lock workstation, log off, shutdown, change password, and start Task Manager).
<Ctrl>+<Backspace>	Deletes all text from the cursor to beginning of current word or punctuation mark.
<Ctrl>+C	Copies the selected item(s) to the Windows Clipboard.
<Ctrl>+Drag and Drop	Copies selected file(s) or directory(s) to target location.
<Ctrl>+<Esc>	Opens the Windows Start menu.
<Ctrl>+F	Opens a text search for current window.
<Ctrl>+<F4>	Closes active window.
<Ctrl>+G	Go to function. Allows user to move to a selected page in document.
<Ctrl>+H	In Office applications, opens a Search and Replace window.
	In IE, it opens a History bar.
<Ctrl>+<Home>	Goes to beginning of document.
<Ctrl>+<End>	Goes to end of document.
<Ctrl>+<Insert>	Copies selected item(s) to Windows Clipboard.
<Ctrl>+Left Arrow	Moves cursor to previous word in the document.
<Ctrl>+N	Opens a new file or window.
<Ctrl>+O	Starts the File→Open function.
<Ctrl>+P	Prints the contents of the current window.
<Ctrl>+Right Arrow	Moves cursor to the next word in the document.
<Ctrl>+S	Saves the current file to previous location on disk.
<Ctrl>+<Shift>+<Esc>	In WIN98, opens the Start menu. In WIN2K or XP, opens Task Manager.
<Ctrl>+V	Pastes the contents of Windows Clipboard to selected location.
<Ctrl>+X	Cuts the selected item(s) from its current location and copies it to the Windows Clipboard.
<Ctrl>+Y	Repeats the previous action.
<Ctrl>+Z	Reverses the previous action

(continued)

Table E.1 Windows Hotkey Shortcuts (*continued*)

Shortcut	Action
	<Alt> Shortcuts
<Alt>+<Backspace>	Reverses the previous action (similar to <Ctrl>+Z).
<Alt>+Double-click	In a document, selects entire document.
<Alt>+<Enter>	Repeats previous action.
<Alt>+<F4>	Closes the current window.
<Alt>+<Print Screen>	Copies current window to Windows Clipboard as bitmap image.
<Alt>+Space Bar	Open current Window's controls (Restore, Move, Size, Minimize, Maximize, Close).
<Alt>+<Tab>	Switches between active Applications (while holding Alt, press Tab or Shift+Tab to go to next or previous app; release Alt to restore the selected app).
	<Shift> shortcuts
<Shift>+<Alt>+<Tab>	Switches among running applications (while holding Alt, press Tab or Shift+Tab to go to next or previous app; release Alt to restore the selected app).
<Shift>+<Delete>	In Windows Explorer, deletes selected item(s) immediately and does *not* move them to the Recycle Bin.
	In other apps, cuts and moves selected items to Windows Clipboard.
<Shift>+Down	Selects all of current line. Repeating the function selects the next line.
<Shift>+Drag and Drop Selected File(s)	Moves file(s) to target folder except when target folder is Recycle Bin. When moving to Recycle Bin, it deletes the file(s) permanently.
<Shift>+<F1>+0	Displays Shortcut menu for current window (same as clicking right-mouse button).
<Shift>+<Insert>	Pastes the contents of Windows Clipboard to selected location.
<Shift>+Left	Removes the previous character from text selection.
<Shift>+<Print Screen>	Copies current window to Clipboard as bitmap image.
<Shift>+Right	Adds the current character to selected text.
<Shift>+<Tab>	Moves to previous field or control in current window.
<Shift>+Up	Removes previous line from selected text.

(continued)

Table E.1 Windows Hotkey Shortcuts (*concluded*)

Shortcut	Action
Windows Key Shortcuts	
⊞ +<Ctrl>+F	Allows user to search for a specific computer on the network.
⊞ +D	Minimizes (or restores when repeated) all open windows. (Does not work in WIN95.)
⊞ +E	Launches Windows Explorer, starting with My Computer
⊞ +F	Opens a Find Files window.
⊞ +<F1>	Launches Windows Help.
⊞ +L	Locks the computer when connected to a network domain or switches users on a computer not connected to a network domain (WINXP only).
⊞ +M	Minimizes current window.
⊞ +<Pause/Break>	Opens the Control Panel System Properties applet.
⊞ +G	Quick-switches between users (WINXP only).
⊞ +R	Opens a Run dialog box in the Start menu.
⊞ +<Shift>+M	Restores all minimized windows.
⊞ +<Tab>	Cycles through the buttons on the taskbar.
⊞ +U	Launches the Accessibility Utility Manager (WINXP only).
⊞ +V	Open voice settings (Narrator settings window must be open) (WIN2K/XP only).

Windows and Windows applications contain a large number of keyboard shortcuts called hotkeys.

Table E.2 Annotated Listing of MSCONFIG Startup Entries

Program or File Name	Description
(Default)=%SysDir%\matcher.exe	Virus removal instructions for the virus W32/Matcher@MM.
1on1mail.htm	Virus removal instructions for the virus VBS.1ON1MAIL.
3com Modem Manager or MDMMGR.EXE	Status icon for 3Com modems.
3dfx Task Manager	Configuration applet for Voodoo video cards.
3dfx Tools	Tools applet for Voodoo video cards.
3Dqtl.exe (3Dqtl.exe)	A function of Terratec128i PCI sound card drivers. This loads a sound profile at boot up, restoring volume and other audio settings to a predetermined default. (Not mandatory)
A1000 Settings Utility or CPQA1000.EXE	Compaq A1000Print Fax All-in-One copy scan printer software. Required in the Startup in order to scan, print, copy, and fax.
Access Ramp Monitor or ARMON32.EXE	A program that monitors the status of an Internet connection. (Not mandatory)
Acrobat Assistant or ACROTRAY.EXE or [ACROTRAY]	An Acrobat Reader function that converts Postscript documents to PDF. (Not mandatory)
Active CPU or ACPU.EXE or [ACTIVE CPU]	Generates a graphical representation of CPU activity. (Not mandatory)
Adaptec DirectCD or DIRECTCD.EXE	Allows a formatted CD-RW or CD-R disc to have files written directly to it from Explorer.
Adaware Bootup or AD-AWARE.EXE or [AD-AWARE 5]	Spyware removal utility. (Not mandatory)
Adobe Gamma Loader	Calibrates monitor colors more closely to print colors for Adobe applications. (Not mandatory)
AGSatellite (AGSatellite.exe)	A function of AudioGalaxy software that lets you download MP3 files from their server. (Not mandatory)
AHQTB	Audio Headquarters for a Creative Labs SoundBlaster Live! sound card. (Not mandatory)
AIM Reminder	A function of AOL's Instant Messenger service. (Not mandatory)
AIM Reminder.exe	A virus that mimics the real AIM Reminder.
Alexa	Function of Alexa Toolbar 5.0. An Internet Navigation tool that provides information about the site being viewed. (Not mandatory)

(continued)

Table E.2 Annotated Listing of MSCONFIG Startup Entries (*continued*)

Program or File Name	Description
ALOGSERV.EXE	Function of McAfee Antivirus. Logs scanning activities. (Not mandatory, and has been known to cause issues with some programs.)
AMD POWERNOW! or GEMBACK.EXE	AMD PowerNow! Utility. Maximizes battery life by decreasing CPU speed when the system is running on battery power. (Required on some laptops.)
Anti or anti.exe or [anti]	Automatically clicks AOL's idle/timer popup windows, preventing the user from being forcibly signed off.
anvshell or ANVSHELL.EXE	Puts display properties settings onto an icon in the system tray. (Not mandatory)
AOL Instant Messenger or AIM.EXE	AOL Instant Messenger. (Not mandatory).
AOLTRAY.EXE	Puts AOL icon in system tray. (Not required in startup.)
ARMON32.EXE	Monitors an Internet connection for hang-ups, connection speeds, Internet congestion, and traffic flow. (Not mandatory)
Astro or ATRO.EXE	A utility included with Quicken personal finance software. (Not mandatory)
ASUS Tweak Enable or ASTART.EXE	A utility that is placed on the system tray when the settings for certain ASUS graphics adapters have been configured beyond their normal settings. Allows other changes and/or restoring factory default settings. (Not mandatory)
ATI GART Set-up Utility	Checks the motherboard chipset and determines which drivers to install for certain ATI cards. When the drivers are installed, it should be removed.
ATI Scheduler	Function of ATI driver that remains RAM resident and automatically launches the ATI VIDEO PLAYER at time and date pre-selected by the user. Remove if not being used.
ATI Task Application	Launches display settings for ATI graphics cards. (Not mandatory)
ATI*.* (various different files)	These are associated with an ATI Rage graphics card. (Not mandatory)
AtiCwd32 or ATICWD32.EXE	ATI graphics card system tray. (Not mandatory, but useful)
ATIKEY or ATITASK.EXE or [atitask]	Shortcut to various programs, display settings, and the ATI Desktop online help system. Should not be kept in startup, but rather ran from Start menu when needed.

(*continued*)

Table E.2 Annotated Listing of MSCONFIG Startup Entries (*continued*)

Program or File Name	Description
Attune Download	Monitors PC hardware and provides a shortcut to a PC help network. Use with caution.
AttuneClientEngine or ATTUNE_CE.EXE	Provides a notification service for Attune. (Not mandatory)
AudioHQ	Desktop control panel for the Creative Labs Live card. (Not mandatory)
Aureal 3D Interactive Audio (a3dinit.exe)	3D positional sound controls for Compaq PC's with Aureal-based 3D soundcards. If removed, only standard sound can be obtained.
AutoEA or AHQRUN.EXE	A function of Creative Labs Soundblaster Live! series soundcards. Allows user to specify what audio preset to automatically associate for any audio application. (Not mandatory)
AutoUpdate or XUPDATE.EXE	Function of Mcafee Antivirus that verifies that the software is up to date. (Not mandatory. Can update manually.)
AV Console or AVCONSOL.EXE or [avconsol]	Function of Mcafee Antivirus that scans local or network drives automatically on a user-defined schedule. (Not mandatory)
BACKWEB or USERPROF.EXE	A Compaq service that automatically detects internet connection and downloads any available updates. (Not mandatory)
Battery Bar	Laptop utility that estimates remaining battery power. (Not mandatory, but useful)
BayMgr	Dell laptop utility that allows swapping a battery, DVD, or other item in an accessory bay.
BCDetect or BCDETECT.EXE	A function of Creative Labs that detects when the correct drivers are installed for the video card. It loads the BlasterControl when the drivers are detected. (Not mandatory)
BCMDMMSG or BCMDMMSG.EXE	The modem messaging applet for BCM V.90 56K modems. Required for dial-up if you have one of these modems.
BCMHal or BCMHAL9X.DLL or [bcinit]	Places Display properties for Creative Labs graphics adapters onto system tray. (Not mandatory)
BCTweak or BCTWEAK.EXE	A utility that allows the user to adjust certain settings on Creative Labs graphics adapters. (Not mandatory)

(*continued*)

Table E.2   Annotated Listing of MSCONFIG Startup Entries (*continued*)

Program or File Name	Description
BillMinder or REMIND32	A function of Quicken that reminds the user of due payments. (Not mandatory)
BitMagic or BITLOADER.EXE	A function of Bitmagic's Bitplayer that places the menu options into the toolbar. (Not mandatory)
BlackICE utility or BLACKICE.EXE	A function of Network ICE firewall that places certain menu options on the toolbar. Closing it will close the firewall. No point in removing it. It will reappear on next reboot without editing the registry.
BLSTAPP or BLSTAPP.EXE	Puts access to Creative's BlasterControl in the System Tray. (Not mandatory)
bmlic-1 or LOADER.EXE	A function of Bitmagic's Bitplayer that places certain menu items in the toolbar. Also checks for updates when Internet connection is present. (Not mandatory)
Bonzei Buddy	Talking parrot and monkey. (Neither mandatory or useful and can be quite annoying)
BMO MasterCard Wallet or EWALLET.EXE	Stores your credit card and other personal information in an encrypted file on your PC so that any talented hacker can access it. (Not mandatory)
bombshel or BOMB32.EXE	A function of McAfee Nuts & Bolts. Protects your Windows system from application failure and crashes. (Not mandatory)
BPCPOST or BPCPOST.EXE	Post-setup program for Microsoft TV Viewer. Can be removed after installation is complete.
Cal reminder shortcut	Manages the popups used by MS Works Calendar as reminders. (Not mandatory)
CallControl or FTCTRL32.EXE	A function of FaxTalk Messenger Pro that allows any TAPI-compliant application to access the modem from Windows. (Not mandatory)
Cardscan 300start or CSRESET.EXE	A function of the Cardscan 300 scanner driver that resets the scanner on startup. (Not mandatory)
CBWAttn or CBWATTN.EXE or CBWHost or CBWHOST.EXE	A function of Bitware fax software that answers incoming faxes. Not required for outgoing faxes and has known issues with Windows Power Management.
CC2KUI or COMET.EXE	A program that allows the user to change cursors on the fly. (Not mandatory)
CIJ3P2PSERVER or CIJ3P2PS.EXE	Compaq printer utility. Required for the printer to work correctly.

(*continued*)

Table E.2 Annotated Listing of MSCONFIG Startup Entries (*continued*)

Program or File Name	Description
CISRVR Program or CISRVR.EXE	Compaq Internet setup wizard. (Not mandatory)
CleanSweep or Smart Sweep or Internet Sweep	Function of Norton CleanSweep. Can be started manually. (Not mandatory)
Click The Button or CTB.EXE	A function of Bonzei Buddy. (Neither mandatory nor useful)
ClipMate5x or CLIPMT5X.EXE	A utility that allows the user to maintain multiple items in the Windows Clipboard. (Not mandatory, but can be useful)
Colorific Control Panel (Hgcctl95.exe)	A color-matching utility from E_Color. Ensures accurate gamma and color temperature between your monitor and other still imaging devices. (Not mandatory, but may be useful)
Compaq C3-1000 Settings Utility or cpqc31k.exe or [cpqc31k.exe]	Compaq printer utility. Required in order for the printer to work.
Compaq Internet Setup or INETWIZARD.EXE	Compaq Internet setup wizard. (Not mandatory)
Compaq Knowledge Center or SILENT.EXE & MATCLI.EXE	MATCLI.EXE is the Motive Assistant Command Line Interface that gathers system and personal information into a log file. SILENT.EXE executes matcli.exe quietly in the background. Required for accessing Compaq's Help and Support program.
Compaq Video CD Watcher	Compaq MPEG viewer. (Not mantatory)
CompaqPrinTray or PRINTRAY.EXE	Puts printer icon in toolbar. If disabled, the Control Program or Printer Driver can no longer be directly accessed from your desktop.
CompaqSystray or CPQPSCP.EXE	Compaq Systray icon. (Not mandatory)
COMSMDEXE	3Com utilities. (Not mandatory)
ConfigServices	Part of initial setup. (Not mandatory)
CONMGR.EXE	Connection Manager for Earthlink Internet Services. (Not mandatory)
Controller	Starts WinFax Pro. WinFax will not receive incoming faxes automatically unless running. (Not mandatory)
Cookie Crusher or COOKIE.EXE	A utility that gives the user control over which cookies are accepted by and stored on the system. (Not mandatory)
Cookie Pal or CPBRWTCH.EXE	A utility that gives the user control over which cookies are accepted by and stored on the system. (Not mandatory)

(*continued*)

Table E.2 Annotated Listing of MSCONFIG Startup Entries (*continued*)

Program or File Name	Description
Cool Desk or CDESK.EXE	A virtual desktop manager. (Not mandatory or particularly useful)
Cool Note or COOL.EXE	An electronic sticky-note program. (Not mandatory)
Corel Desktop Application Director	Function of Corel Office Suite that launches its programs from the toolbar. (Not mandatory)
Corel Registration Reminder	Function of Corel software that nags the user to register with Corel. Useful only to Corel.
CountrySelection or PCTPTT.EXE	A function of certain modem drivers. As long as the modem is installed and enabled, this feature will reappear after being disabled.
CPQA1000.EXE	Software for the Compaq A1000 print/fax/scanner. Required for this device to work.
CPQDFWAG	A utility that runs Compaq diagnostics every time the system boots. (Not mandatory)
CPQEASYACC or CPQEADM.EXE or [bttnserv]	Compaq's Easy Access button support. (Not mandatory)
CPQinet or CPQINET.EXE	A function of Compaq Easy Access Button support. Only required if EAB support is desired.
CPQInet Runtime Services	Compaq Easy Access Button support for AOL and CompuServe. (Not mandatory, and useless if you're using another ISP)
CPQINKAG.EXE	Utility for certain Compaq printers that monitors ink usage. (Not mandatory)
cpqns or CPQNPCSS.EXE	A function of Compaq.Net. Not required for those not using this service.
CPQSTUTFIX	A function of certain sound card drivers that cures problems with sound stutter. Required for those sound cards. Do not remove.
CPUFSB or CPUFSB.EXE or [cpufsb]	Utility that allows the user to adjust the motherboard's front side bus speed through the OS. **Caution:** This utility may cause your system to crash or become unstable and may also damage certain components in the system.
CQSCP2PS or CQSCP2P Server	Compaq printer utility. Required for printer to function.
CreateCD or CREATECD.EXE	A function of EZ CD Creator. (Not mandatory)

(*continued*)

Table E.2 Annotated Listing of MSCONFIG Startup Entries (*continued*)

Program or File Name	Description
Creative Lab's AudioHQ or AHQRUN.EXE or AHQTB.EXE	System tray application for SB Live! Environmental Audio Control plug-ins. (Not mandatory)
Creative Lab's Disc Detector	Auto-detects a CD-ROM, DVD-ROM, etc. (Not mandatory)
Creative Lab's Program Launcher	Adds a quick-launch bar to the top of the display and a System Tray icon. (Not mandatory)
Critical Update	Forces frequent visits to Microsoft's Web site, looking for updates. (Not mandatory and can be annoying)
CSInject.exe	A function of Norton CleanSweep (Not mandatory)
CTAVTray or CTAVTRAY.EXE	A function of Creative Labs Soundblaster Live! Soundcard driver. Plays the EAX animation on start-up and adds a System Tray icon for it. (Not mandatory)
CTFMON	Alternative Language input services for Office XP. If you want to disable this in STARTUP, then Text Services and Speech applets in the Control Panel must be disabled. (Not mandatory)
CTRegRun or CTREGRUN.EXE	A nag reminder to register a Creative Labs product. (Not mandatory and can be annoying)
CTSysVol	A function of Creative Labs sound card driver that adds volume controls to the toolbar. (Not mandatory)
Cybermedia Guard Dog or GDLAUNCH.EXE	A function of Mcafee's Internet Guard Dog Software. (Not mandatory)
CyDoor=CD_Load.exe	Spyware. Remove immediately!
Daemon or DAEMON32.EXE	Preloads game profiles for MS Sidewinder game controllers (prior to release 2.0). (Not mandatory)
datcheck or DATCHECK.EXE	Keypanic. Trojan horse that remaps the keyboard. Update your antivirus software and run again.
Dcomcnfg or DCOMCNFG.EXE	A function of Microsoft Basic. (Not mandatory)
Delay or DELAYRUN.EXE	Allows user to configure certain startup items to launch after Windows has loaded. Gives control of the computer to the user more quickly. (Not mandatory)
Description of Shortcut or EZTART.EXE	A function of Mcafee's Utilities that allows the user to customize the appearance of Windows. (Not mandatory)
DEVLDR16.EXE	A function of Creative Labs sound card drivers that provides audio support for DOS applications. (Not mandatory)

(*continued*)

Table E.2 Annotated Listing of MSCONFIG Startup Entries (*continued*)

Program or File Name	Description
DigiGuide or CLIENT.EXE	Electronic TV guide. (Not mandatory)
Digital Dashboard or DEVGULP.EXE	Control panel for a program called Digital Dashboard. (Not mandatory)
Digital River eBot or DOWNLOA~1.EXE	Utility that monitors the system and checks for updates to hardware drivers and software when an Internet connection is present. (Not mandatory)
Disc Detector or CTNOTIFY.EXE	A function of Creative Labs sound card drivers that automatically detects when a CD or DVD has been inserted into the drive. (Not mandatory)
Disknag or DISKNAG.EXE	A Dell utility that reminds the user to make backup diskettes. (Not mandatory)
DkService or DKSERVICE.EXE	A function of Executive Software's Diskeeper (a third-party disk defragmenting utility) that schedules unattended maintenance. (Not mandatory)
DMASwitch or CLDMA.EXE	A function of CyberLink PowerDVD software that allows user to toggle on/off DMA functions for CD devices. (Not mandatory)
DMISL	Desktop Management Software for Intel TokenExpress network card software. (Not mandatory)
DMISTART or WIN32SL.EXE	Dell or Intel utility that collects system information for Client Manager for remote management and/or technical support. (Not mandatory)
DNE Binding Watchdog or RUNDLL DNES.DLL or [DnDneCheckBindings]	Deterministic NDIS Extender. Part of Gilat Communications internet satellite systems. Required if you have this system.
dRMON SmartAgent or SMARTAGT.EXE	A utility that is a part of the 3COM NIC software package. (Not mandatory)
DSS	A function of Broderbund software. Sends information back to manufacturer when Internet connection is detected. (Not mandatory or useful to anyone but Broderbund)
DXM6Patch_981116 or SMARTAGT.EXE	CAB file extractor. (Not mandatory)
EACLEAN.EXE	Compaq Easy Access Button support for the keyboard. (Not mandatory)
Eapcisetup	A function of Rockwell RipTide soundcard application software. (Not mandatory)

(continued)

Table E.2 Annotated Listing of MSCONFIG Startup Entries (*continued*)

Program or File Name	Description
EarthLink ToolBar 5.0 or ETOOLBAR.EXE	A function of EarthLink Internet software. (Not mandatory)
eFax.com Tray Menu or HOTTRAY.EXE	Automatically launches EFAX Messenger software on startup and creates a system tray icon with menu options. (Not mandatory)
EM_EXEC or EM_EXEC.EXE	Advanced features support for a Logitech mouse. (Not mandatory, but removing it will cause certain Logitech features to become disabled.)
EncartaDictionary Quickshelf or QSHLFED.EXE	Quicklaunch for Encarta Dictionary. (Not mandatory)
ENCMON	Keeps track of the time remaining on a factory installed free trial for AT&T internet services. (Not mandatory, and totally useless if you're not using their free trial.)
ENCMONITOR or MONITOR.EXE	A Connect Direct function of the Encompass Monitor. (Not mandatory)
EnsonicMixer STARTER.EXE	A function of Ensonic sound card drivers that puts the Ensonic mixer in system tray. (Not mandatory)
EPSON Background Monitor	Monitors the status of any properly configured Epson printer. Removing does not affect the printer's ability to print. (Not mandatory)
ESSDC.EXE	A function of sound card drivers for sound cards with ESS chipset (notably Ensonic). (Not mandatory)
Etraffic or JAVARUN.EXE	Marketing software installed by a company called TopMoxie. REMOVE.
Event Reminder	A function of Dr. Watson. (Not mandatory)
EWELL.HTM	A virus. Check with your Antivirus vendor for updates and run immediately.
Explorer	System File. Must be running.
FatPipe (DHCP)	Internet connection-sharing and caching software. (Not mandatory)
FaxTalk CallControl 6.X or FTCLCTRL.EXE	A function of FaxTalk Communicator software that handles incoming and outgoing calls. (Not mandatory)
FEELitDeviceManager or FEELITDM.EXE	A function of Immersion TouchSense device drivers. Required for these devices to work.
Filterguard or FILTRGRD.EXE	A function of SOS Internet Filtering Software. Required for this software to function properly.

(*continued*)

Table E.2 Annotated Listing of MSCONFIG Startup Entries (*continued*)

Program or File Name	Description
Find Fast	Function of Microsoft Office. Indexes files for faster searches. (Not mandatory)
Fine Print Dispatcher or FPDISP3.EXE	Function of certain Compaq printer drivers. Required for printer to function properly.
Finish Installing or BBSMAR~1.EXE	A function of Bonzei Buddy that reminds the user that more files are needed to complete installation. (Not mandatory)
Fix-It Av or MEMCHECK.EXE	A function of Trend Micro's Ontrack Antivirus software. Required for software to function properly.
FlyswatDesktop or FLYDESK.EXE	A function of a program called Flyswat. (Not mandatory)
FMLITES or FMLITES.EXE	A function of some modems that puts a visual display similar to the lights of an external modem on the toolbar. (Not mandatory)
FTUNINST or FTUNINST.EXE	Fax Talk Messenger Pro uninstall program. (Not mandatory)
Gator or GATOR.EXE	A function of Gator (a form filler) software that puts menu items on the toolbar. Somewhat resource intensive. Don't use it if you don't need it. (Not mandatory)
GetRight Tray Icon or GETRIGHT.EXE	A download manager that allows the user to resume interrupted downloads and to manage multiple downloads simultaneously. The freeware version adds spyware; the paid version does not. (Not mandatory, but can be useful. Although the spyware isn't.)
Gilat SOM Enumerator or DLLHOST.EXE	A function of Gilat Communications Internet satellite systems—associated with SkyBlaster modem. Required if you have this system.
GilatFTC or FTC.EXE	A function of Gilat Communications Internet satellite systems—associated with SkyBlaster modem. Required if you have this system.
Go!Zilla Monster Downloads	Adds System Tray applet for Go!Zilla.web browser. (Not mandatory)
GuardDogEXE or GDLAUNCH.EXE	A function of Mcafee's Internet Guard Dog software. (Not mandatory)
Guardian or CMGRDIAN.EXE	A function of Mcafee's Guardian software that adds a system tray icon. (Not mandatory)

(*continued*)

Table E.2 Annotated Listing of MSCONFIG Startup Entries (*continued*)

Program or File Name	Description
HC Reminder or HC.EXE	Compaq software. (Not mandatory) (Note that HC.EXE can also be the HumanClick software)
help=3D	This is the VBS/Pleh@MM Virus. Check your antivirus software for updates and run immediately.
Hidserv or HIDSERV.EXE	Human Interface Device Service. Manages devices connected through the USB bus. (Not mandatory, but useful)
HIDSERV.EXE.RUN	Human Interface Device Server, it is required only if you are using USB Audio Devices. (Not mandatory)
Hotbar	Third-party utility that adds new skins for IE. (Not mandatory)
HotSync	Palm Pilot synchronization manager. (Not mandatory and should be launched manually)
HP JetDiscovery	A function of HP JetAdmin software that manages network print jobs.
HP Lamp	Utility for certain HP scanners that controls the light source. Required for these scanners to function properly.
HP ScanPicture	Adds a "Scan Picture" option to the File menu of certain applications. If disabled, the menu option will disappear, but the scanner will still function when accessed through the Start menu. (Not mandatory)
Hpha1mon or HPHA1MON.EXE	Driver for the Media Card reader for certain HP printers that support that function. Required if you wish to use that function.
hppswrsev	Utility for certain HP scanners. (Not mandatory)
hpsysdrv or SPSYSDRV.EXE	A function of the HP keyboard manager that identifies the system as being an HP. On some models, deselecting this function can prevent the system from booting.
HPSCANMonitor or HPSJVXD.EXE	HP scanning software that redirects scanned images from the scanner to the application. Required for the scanner to work properly.
Hpscanpatch or HPSCANFIX.EXE	A driver patch for certain HP scanners. Required for the scanner to work properly.

(*continued*)

Table E.2 Annotated Listing of MSCONFIG Startup Entries (*continued*)

Program or File Name	Description
HumanClick or HC.EXE	A program called HumanClick that allows the user to communicate with visitors on a Web site and to monitor the visitor's activities. (Not mandatory) (Note that HC.EXE can also be the HC Reminder)
HWinst	Gilat rescue (Satellite system restore) For Gilat Communications Internet satellite systems. Required if you have this system. If removed, can cause the system to become unstable and crash unexpectedly.
ICONFIG.EXE or [iconfig]	A function of the Superdisk driver. Required for the device to work properly.
ICQ NetDetect Agent	Periodically checks for Internet connectivity. If found, automatically launches ICQ. (Not mandatory and can be quite annoying)
ICSMGR	Monitors DNS and DHCP requests for Internet Connection Sharing (ICS). Required if ICS is installed.
Image & Restore or IMAGE32.EXE	A function of McAfee Nuts & Bolts. Allows a drive to be recovered after an accidental erasure or formatting. (Not mandatory, but extremely useful when you need it!)
Imesh Auto Update or WISEUPDT.EXE	Checks for downloadable Imesh updates every time an Internet connection is established. Cannot be removed in msconfig. It puts back the checkmark after you try to remove it.
Imesh or IMESHCLIENT.EXE	Utility that allows user to download files from several targets simultaneously. (Not mandatory)
Incontrol Desktop MGR or DMHKEY.EXE	A function of Intouch Control software that adds an extra tab in the Display properties for the Diamond Multimedia video card extra settings. (Not mandatory)
Instant Access	A function of TextBridge Pro OCR software. (Not mandatory)
IntelProcNumUtility	Disables CPU ID. (Not mandatory)
internat or INTERNAT.EXE	Allows user to toggle between installed keyboard languages. (Not mandatory). NOTE: Can also be added by a virus called Netsnake. If languages were not installed, update antivirus software and run immediately!
Introduction-Registration	PC introduction & registration for Compaq computers. Should run only once. Remove if it remains after initial use.

(*continued*)

Table E.2 Annotated Listing of MSCONFIG Startup Entries (*continued*)

Program or File Name	Description
Iomega Disk Icons	Iomega Zip Tools application. Changes the icon and description associated with an Iomega Zip drive from a generic icon to an Iomega Zip drive icon. (Not mandatory, nor is it useful)
Iomega QuickSync 3 or quicksync3.exe or [quicksync3]	A program used with Iomega drives, QuickSync 3 is intended to protect the user from data loss. (Not mandatory)
Iomega Startup Options or IMGSTART.EXE	Adds right-click context menu selections for a Zip drive. (Not mandatory, but useful)
Iomega Watch	Iomega Zip Tools application. Causes your Zip drive to spin down when not in use and prompts the user for a password when trying to access a write-protected disk. (Not mandatory, but useful)
IOMON98.EXE	A function of PCCILIN Antivirus software that performs real-time virus checks. (Not mandatory, but userful)
IPinst	Gilat rescue (Satellite system restore) For Gilat Communications Internet satellite systems. Required if you have this system. If removed, can cause the system to become unstable and crash unexpectedly.
IrMon	Required when an infrared wireless device is installed.
isdbdc or ISDBDC.EXE	A function of the Compaq dial-up networking wizard. (Not mandatory)
K6CPU.EXE	Identifies and authenticates AMD K6 CPU. (Not mandatory)
Kagou	The KAK virus. Update antivirus software and run immediately.
KAK.HTA	The KAK virus. Update antivirus software and run immediately.
KAK.HTML	The KAK virus. Update antivirus software and run immediately.
Kernel16	The SUB Seven Trojan Virus. Update antivirus software and run immediately.
kernel32=kern32.exe	The W32/Badtrans@MM Virus. Update antivirus software and run immediately.
Keyboard Manager or MMKEYBD.EXE	A function of the keyboard driver for certain HP keyboards. (Not mandatory)

(*continued*)

Table E.2 Annotated Listing of MSCONFIG Startup Entries (*continued*)

Program or File Name	Description
Launchboard or LNCHBRD.EXE	A program that allows the user to customize the keyboard to launch programs or Web sites. (Not mandatory)
Lexmark PrinTray or PRINTRAY.EXE	A Lexmark Printer icon. (Not required)
Lexstart or LEXSTART.EXE	Command interpreter for Lexmark printers. Has been known to induce dial-up networking to connect to the Internet. (Not mandatory)
LIU	A function of Logitech Quick Cam driver. (Not mandatory)
Load = OCRAWARE.EXE	A function of OmniPage Limited Edition that allows the user to scan directly into most word processor applications. (Not mandatory)
Load WebCheck or LOADWC.EXE	Program that manages adding, removing, and updating subscriptions. (Not mandatory)
Loadblackd or BLACKD.EXE	A function of BlackICE Defender, an intrusion detection product. Required if you want to use the product.
LoadPowerProfile	Only required if you are using Windows Power Management through Control Panel. If so, there will be two instances. One is loaded by Machine Run and the other by Machines Services. Do not uncheck one unless you uncheck both. (Not mandatory unless Power Management is enabled.)
LOADQM	MSN Explorer Query Manager (Not mandatory)
Loadqm	Loads the MSN Explorer Query Manager. (Not mandatory)
Logitech ImageWare Control Center	Function of Logitech Pagescan scanner driver. (Not mandatory)
Logitech Wakeup or LGWAKEUP.EXE	Function of Logitech autofeed scanners. Detects insertion of paper into scanner and launches scanner software. (Not mandatory, but useful)
Lotus Organizer Easy Clip	Function of Lotus Organizer. Collects information from sources such as email to create an Organizer address, appointment, task, or Notepad page. (Not mandatory)
Lotus Quick Start	Control pad for Lotus SmartSuite. (Not mandatory)
Lotus Suite Start	Start icons for Lotus SmartSuite that appear on the taskbar when you start Windows. Removing this item can result in error messages and prevent SmartSuite from working properly.

(*continued*)

Table E.2 Annotated Listing of MSCONFIG Startup Entries (*continued*)

Program or File Name	Description
LS120 Superdisk	Disk Caching utility for LS-120. (Not mandatory)
LVComs or LVCOMS.EXE	Function of the Logitech QuickCam driver. (Not mandatory)
Lwinst Run Profiler or LWTEST.EXE or LWEMON.EXE	Function of the Logitech Wingman joystick driver. (Not mandatory)
LXSUPMON (LXSUPMON.EXE)	Function of Lexmark Printer driver. (Not mandatory)
Machine Debug Manager or mdm	Part of Visual Studio 6.0. This is required only if a second machine is used to debug programs under development on current computer. (Not mandatory)
MapNDrive or MAPNDRIVE.EXE	A third-party scripting tool that manages mapped network drive. Needed if installed.
Matrox Powerdesk	A function of Matrox graphics card drivers that allows users to adjust display settings on the fly. (Not mandatory)
McAfee Guardian or CMGRDIAN.EXE	A function of McAfee Uninstaller software. Automatically identifies and removes the unnecessary files that remain after a program is removed. (Not mandatory).
McAfee Image or IMAGE32.EXE	A function of McAfee Image that creates an image snapshot of the critical sectors on your hard drive. In the event these sectors become corrupted, Image uses the snapshot to restore data. (Not mandatory)
McAfee VirusScan Registration	Function of McAfee VirusScan that nags the user to register the product. (Not mandatory)
McAfee Wingauge	A McAfee utility that monitors system performance. (Not mandatory)
McAfeeVirusScanService or AVSYNMGR.EXE	A function of McAfee VirusScan version 5.x that runs all the functions under within a single environment. (Not mandatory, but useful)
McAfeeWEbScanX or WEBSCANX.EXE or [Webscanx]	A McAfee utility that monitors Internet activity for possibly harmful events. (Not mandatory, but useful)
MDAC_RUNONCE or RUNONCE.EXE	Microsoft Data Access Components Run Once Wrapper. This is required for Microsoft Data Access Components. Run Once refers to once per session and, therefore, appears any time an MDAC app is running.
MediaRing Talk or MRTALK.EXE	Voice recognition software. Resource intensive. Remove if not needed.

(*continued*)

Table E.2 Annotated Listing of MSCONFIG Startup Entries (*continued*)

Program or File Name	Description
Memturbo	A shareware program that monitors memory usage and dumps code no longer in use. (Not mandatory)
MGAVRTCL.EXE or MGAVRTCL.EXE	A function McAfee Antivirus. Required for real-time virus scanning.
Microangelo Desktop	Preloads certain files critical to MicroAngelo 5.0 to facilitate faster loading. (Not mandatory)
Microsoft Critical Update	Detects and installs critical updates from the Microsoft site when an Internet connection is present. (Not mandatory)
Microsoft Find Fast	A service of Microsoft Office. Indexes files on your hard drive for faster search. (Not mandatory)
Microsoft Greetings Reminders	Reminder of special events like birthdays. (Not mandatory).
Microsoft Office Startup	Preloads certain .DLL files to speed up the launch of Microsoft Office. Also places icon in System Tray. (Not mandatory)
Microsoft Sidewinder Game Controller Software	Preloads profiles for games. (Not mandatory)
Microsoft Webserver	Personal Web server program. (Not mandatory)
Microsoft Works Calendar	MS Works program provides notifications when dates on the MS Works calendar are reached. (Not mandatory)
Microsoft Works Calendar Reminders	MS Works calendar reminder. (Not mandatory)
Microsoft Works Portfolio, WorksFUD, Microsoft Update Detection, Cal reminder shortcut	These are used by Works 2001. Check for updates and announce reminders that were configured in Works programs. (Not mandatory)
Microsoft Works update Detection	Detects and installs MS Works updates from the Microsoft site. (Not mandatory)
MINIFERT.EXE	Electronic distribution software bundled with certain Compaq computers. (Not mandatory)
Minilog or MINILOG.EXE	A function of ZoneAlarm firewall software that maintains the event log. Required for software to function properly.
Mirabilis ICQ	Automatically runs up ICQ when Internet connection is detected. (Not mandatory)
Mixghost	Management utility for Altec Lansing speakers. (Not mandatory)

(*continued*)

Table E.2   Annotated Listing of MSCONFIG Startup Entries (*continued*)

Program or File Name	Description
mmtray	Places a Music Box Jukebox icon in the system tray. (Not mandatory)
MoneyAgent or MONEY EXPRESS.EXE	Function of Microsoft Money. (Not mandatory)
MOSEARCH	Similar to Find Fast feature in Office 2000. Uses the Indexing Services in Office XP to create a catalog of Office files on your computer's hard disk. (Not mandatory)
MotiveMonitor (motmon.exe)	A function of HP Instant Support that watches for errors and collects information useful for resolution through the Internet and email. (Not mandatory, but useful)
Mount Safe & Sound	A function of McAfee VirusScan version 5.x. that creates back-up sets of critical files in a separate area of a hard drive. (Not mandatory)
MS Money Startup	Launches Microsoft Money. (Not mandatory)
MSKernel32 or WINDOWS\SYSTEM\MSKernel32.vbs	The LOVE-LETTER-FOR-YOU virus. Update antivirus software and run immediately.
MSMSGS or MSMSGS.EXE or MSN Messenger	MSN Instant Messenger Service. (Not mandatory)
MSNQuickView	MSN Toolbar that launches at startup.
Mstask	A Microsoft scheduling agent that can be configured to run several applications at specified times. (Not mandatory)
MSUser32 or WINDOWS\SYSTEM\MSUser32.vbs	The LOOK.VBS virus. Update antivirus software and run immediately.
NAV defalert	Norton Antivirus Definitions Alert. A function of Norton Antivirus that warns the user when AV signature files are outdated. (Not mandatory, but useful)
Nav_setup or NAV_SE~1.EXE	McAfee Installation Wizard. Indicates that software installation was not completed. Run Setup program again or remove.
Ndetect	Automatically detects Internet connection and launches ICQ. (Not mandatory)
NeoPlanet or NEO.EXE	Starts Neoplanet web browser automatically when in the startup and creates a system tray icon that allows the user to access it's options. (Not mandatory)
Netsonic or WEBMAIN.EXE	Internet caching program. (Not mandatory)

(*continued*)

Table E.2 Annotated Listing of MSCONFIG Startup Entries (*continued*)

Program or File Name	Description
Netword Agent NWANT33.EXE	Internet browsing utility that allows single-word Web searches. (Not mandatory)
NETWORK.VBS	NETWORK.VBS virus. Update antivirus software and run immediately.
NetworkSetup or DLINK.EXE	A DLink driver utility that provides shortcuts to DLink Web sites. (Not mandatory)
Netzero or NZSTART.EXE	Automatically launches Netzero ISP software at bootup. (Not mandatory)
NetZip Smart Downloader	A download utility that adds Pause, Resume, and Reconnect to your downloads. (Not mandatory)
Norton AutoProtect	Norton Antivirus program. Scans for viruses when you open a program or file. (Not mandatory, but userful)
Norton Crashguard Monitor	Function of Norton Utilities that keeps renegade applications from crashing system. Causes instability with WINMe. (Not mandatory)
Norton Email Protect	Function of Norton Antivirus that sets up a proxy server to isolate the main system from email-borne viruses. (Not mandatory)
Norton System Doctor	Norton program that monitors system configuration and alerts the user when the configuration changes in ways that may cause problems. (Not mandatory)
NovastorSchedulerd	A function of NovaStor NovaBACKUP Software. Required for unattended scheduled backups.
NPROTECT	A function of Norton Utilities. Protects files in Recycle Bin. (Not mandatory)
nscheck or NSCHECK.EXE	Internet caching software. Has been known to cause problems with certain ISPs. (Not mandatory)
oadaemon or OADAEMON.EXE or [oadaemon]	Function of the Compaq C3-1000 printer. Required for printer to function properly.
OEMCLEANUP or OEM_RESET.EXE	Resets OEM installation settings at each bootup. Useful if you want all computers in an organization to be consistent. (Not mandatory)
Office Startup or OSA.EXE	Preloads certain files for quicker launching of Office applications. (Not mandatory)
Onflow or UNISTALL ONFLOW.EXE	Onflow is software that places advertising banners in certain types of software. This program can be run to remove it. (Not mandatory)

(*continued*)

Table E.2 Annotated Listing of MSCONFIG Startup Entries (*continued*)

Program or File Name	Description
Operator	Function of Media Pilot software. Locks port open. (Not mandatory)
Pagekeeper Jobs	Function of Pagekeeper scanner software that manages documents. (Not mandatory)
Password Pal or PASSPAL.EXE	A utility that stores all passwords associated to a specific user in encrypted form. (Not mandatory)
PC Health or PCHSCHD.EXE	WINMe only. Required for the System Restore utility to function properly in Windows Me. The program takes a snapshot of the registry and places the information into data archive.
PCTVOICE or PCTVOICE.EXE	PCTVoice is a program used by certain modems for video conferencing. (Not mandatory)
Pe2ckfnt SE or CHKFONT.EXE	A function of Ulead Photo Express that confirms whether or not fonts are installed properly on a computer. (Not mandatory)
Photo Express Calender Checker SE	A function of Ulead Photo Express that configures Weekly/Monthly/Yearly calendars as wallpaper. (Not mandatory)
PiDunHk or PIDUNHK.EXE	A function of Prodigy Internet services. (Not mandatory)
PiStartup or PISTARTUP.EXE	A function of Prodigy Internet services. (Not mandatory)
Pointer POINT32.EXE	Function of the Microsoft Intellipoint mouse software. If not loaded, then the wheel may not work in certain applications. (Not mandatory, but useful)
Power Meter	Utility on Dell laptop for battery strength and AC power source for batteries. It can be manually launched when it is needed.
Power Panel plus or PANPLUS.EXE or [Panplus]	A function of PowerPanel Plus™ software (included with CyberPower's Power99 and Power2000 models of UPS). Monitors condition and charge of UPS and performs automatic shutdown of system in the event of power failure. Required for full functionality.
Power Reg Scheduler	Software registration reminder. (Not mandatory)
pp5300USB	A function of Paperport software that monitors the status of a Visioneer OneTouch 5300 scanner. (Not mandatory)
Primax 3D Mouse	Driver support for Primax Mouse. (Not mandatory)
PROMON.EXE	Part of Intel NIC diagnostics. (Not mandatory)

(*continued*)

Table E.2 Annotated Listing of MSCONFIG Startup Entries (*continued*)

Program or File Name	Description
Prpcui	Dell utility that manages Intel's Speed-Step functions. (Not mandatory)
Ptsnoop.exe	A function of several modem drivers that monitors the COM port. Will automatically reset itself as long as the modem is enabled.
Q shlf or Quick Shelf or ENCICONS.EXE or [qshlfed]	Launches Encarta dictionary program. (Not mandatory)
Qagent	Quicken Download Manager (also known as Qagent). When the Quicken Download Manager option is enabled, it takes advantage of unused bandwidth on an Internet connection to download current financial information any time your computer is connected to the Internet. (Not mandatory)
QBCD autorun	Automatically launches Quickbooks. (Not mandatory)
QD FastAndSafe	Function of Norton Cleansweep. Deletes unnecessary files. Best if run manually. (Not mandatory)
QuickenSEMessage	A messaging option for Quicken software. (Not mandatory)
QuickShelf 99	Places an icon in the system tray for launching Microsoft Bookshelf. (Not mandatory)
RamBooster or RAMBOOSTER.EXE	A utility that monitors memory usage and dumps unnecessary code. (Not mandatory)
Rave 2 or RAVE.EXE	A Windows application that allows voice communication over an Internet connection. (Not mandatory)
Real Jukebox Systray	Function of Real Jukebox software. Allows user to launch Real Jukebox by double-clicking the icon in the system tray and periodically checks for an Internet connection in order to download updates. (Not mandatory)
RealTray REALPLAY.EXE	Function of Real Audio software. Allows user to launch Real Jukebox by double-clicking the icon in the system tray and periodically checks for an Internet connection in order to download updates. (Not mandatory)
Refresh	A function of Iomega Zip drives. (Not mandatory)
Register Drop Handler	A utility for managing images created by digital cameras or scanners. (Not mandatory)
Regtrk	A function of Norton Utilities that monitors changes to the registry. (Not mandatory, but useful)

(*continued*)

Table E.2 Annotated Listing of MSCONFIG Startup Entries (*continued*)

Program or File Name	Description
Reminder	Bill payment reminder function of MS Money. (Not mandatory)
Reminder-cpqXXXXX or REMIND32.EXE	Reminder to register a Compaq printer. (Not mandatory)
RFTray	Launches the Reality Fusion GameCam Video Interaction Technology Software that ships with the Logitech QuickCam (and other) PC Video Cameras. (Not mandatory)
Ring Central Fax	Utility for allowing PC to answer faxes. (Not mandatory)
rnaapp	Application required by dial-up networking. It loads when a connection is initiated.
Run = (WINDOWS\SYSTEM\list.vbs)	The LIST.VBS virus. Update antivirus software and run immediately.
RUN=	Identifies a specific program to be run during startup. A large number of RUN= statements that are not followed by a specific command may indicate a virus infection.
RUN= (TEMP\LIST.VBS)	The LIST.VBS virus. Update antivirus software and run immediately.
RUN=HPFSCHED	Nags user to register HP printer or scanner. (Not mandatory and can be annoying)
RUNDLL32.EXE	Runs individual routines that have been packaged into a .DLL file. (Not mandatory)
SA3DSRV	Windows 3D sound extension added by Aureal 3D sound cards. (Not mandatory)
SAFEINST.EXE	A utility from Imation that is part of the LS120 Superdisk setup. It checks the parallel port chipset for compatibility. No longer required once software is installed and drive is working.
Savenow or SAVENOW.EXE	A spyware utility that transmits user information to specified locations on the Internet. REMOVE.
SCANREG	Makes a copy of the Windows Registry after attempted startup. Designates whether startup was successful or not. Useful for backing up in the event of a corrupted Registry. Does not remain in memory after the backup has been generated. WHILE NOT MANDATORY, REGISTRY BACKUPS WILL NOT BE GENERATED IF REMOVED. DO NOT REMOVE!

(continued)

Table E.2 Annotated Listing of MSCONFIG Startup Entries (*continued*)

Program or File Name	Description
ScanRegistry (WINDOWS\list.vbs)	The LIST.VBS virus. Update antivirus software and run immediately.
ScanRegistry or SCANREGW.EXE	This is the legitimate Registry scanning utility which must be run at startup. Without it, backup copies of the registry are not completed.
Scheduling Agent	Function of Task Scheduler that automates scheduled events. (Not mandatory if scheduled events are not used)
Service Connection or SCCENTER.EXE	A utility installed by Backweb software for monitoring the connection status. (Not mandatory)
ShockmachineReminder or SMREMINDER.EXE	A utility installed by Shockwave software that monitors the Shockwave Web site for software updates and new content. (Not mandatory)
SHPC32	A function of a Compaq printer driver. Required for the printer to work properly.
SKA.EXE=SKA.EXE	The Happy99.Worm. Not likely to be seen now. If found, run antivirus software immediately.
Sm56acl	System tray icon added by SM56 Modems driver installation. (Not mandatory)
SMS Client Service	Starts the Microsoft Systems Management Server client software. You can remove it, but you might get fired.
SMS Win9x Message Agent	Systems Management Server utility that directs messages to a specific server.
Snsicon or SNSICON.EXE	A utility installed by Second Nature Software, a program that changes background wallpaper based on a preconfigured schedule. Only required if you want the wallpaper to change.
Sonic A3D Control or VRTXCTRL.EXE	Management software for Sonic A3D sound cards. (Not mandatory)
SpeedRacer	A utility installed by Creative Labs sound card software. (Not mandatory).
Spinner Plus or SPINNER.EXE	A utility that provides access to Web-based music broadcasts. (Not mandatory)
SS Runner V3.0 or RUNNER.EXE	Synthesoft screensaver software that creates a system tray icon which enables the screensaver and also from which you can access its option menus. (Not mandatory)

(continued)

Table E.2 Annotated Listing of MSCONFIG Startup Entries (*continued*)

Program or File Name	Description
Sspdsrv or SSDPSRV.EXE	WINMe. Plug and Play function that provides Simple Service Discovery Protocol (SSDP) and General Event Notification Architecture (GENA) support.
Startacc or STARTACC.EXE	Internet caching software. Part of Webroot Accelerate 2000. (Not mandatory)
Startup	A function of Iomega Zip drive software. (Not mandatory)
Startupmonitor	A freeware tool that adds itself to your startup menu so that it can warn you whenever another program tries the same stunt.
State Manager or StateMgr or STATEMGR.EXE	WINMe only. Takes a snapshot of the registry and places the information into data archive. Required for Restore functionality. Do not remove.
Still imageMonitor or STIMON.EXE	A utility that moderates transfer of data between USB still image devices and the application. Consists of two modules, Event Monitor and Control Center. Event Monitor detects events from connected USB scanning devices while Control Center determines how to react to these incoming events. (Not mandatory, but is included with certain HP scanners. If included, then it must be running for your scanning software to work properly.)
Sxgdsenu or SXGDSENU.EXE	On some laptop computers, it is installed to manage sleep or hibernation functions of power management. If your laptop installed it, then you need it.
SymTray - Norton SystemWorks	Collects all Norton SystemWorks system tray icons together into a single icon. (Not mandatory)
SynTPEnh or SYNTPENH.EXE and SynTPLpr or SYNTPLPR.EXE	On some laptop computers, it is installed to manage the touchpad. If your laptop installed it, then you need it.
Sysdoc or SYSDOC32.EXE	Automatic startup for Norton System Doctor. Best if run manually. (Not mandatory)
System DLF or CPQDIAGA.EXE	A Compaq diagnostic utility, which allows the user to view information about your computer's hardware and software configuration. (Not mandatory)
SystemBackup = C:\WINDOWS\MTX_.EXE	The W95.MTX virus/worm. Obsolete, but occasionally reappears. Run antivirus software immediately.
SystemTray or SYSTRAY.EXE	Windows System Tray. This is the system utility that manages all this mess I'm discussing here. Required.

(*continued*)

Table E.2 Annotated Listing of MSCONFIG Startup Entries (*continued*)

Program or File Name	Description
SystemWizard Sniffer	A hardware/software diagnostics utility from SystemSoft. (Not mandatory)
SYSTRAY	Manages the Start button and taskbar region of the screen. No point in removing it. It'll just come back.
T4UMHF5=C:\WINDOWS\ TEMP\T4UMHF5.VBS	The VBS/Anjulie@MM virus. Update antivirus software and run immediately.
Taskbar Display Controls	Appears if the graphics card driver inserts Display Settings icon in the System Tray. (Not mandatory)
TaskMonitor or TASKMON.EXE	Microsoft utility that monitors program usage. (Not mandatory)
TCAUTIEXE or TCAUDIAG	A diagnostics utility for 3com NICs. Monitors status of network connection. (Not mandatory)
Time Sync Add Client	For Palm Pilots and PDA's, needed in the startup in order for those devices to function properly
Timemanager.exe	A utility that monitors how much actual time is spent on any given activity. (Not mandatory)
Tips	Popup pointers for an Intellipoint mouse. (Not mandatory)
Touch Manager	A keyboard utility. (Not mandatory)
Tour or WINCOOL.EXE	WINMe. A popup that nags at the user to watch the Windows Millennium Interactive Video Sampler. (Not mandatory and quite annoying)
Tray Temperature or WEATHERBUG.EXE or [Weatherbug]	A utility that links to the Weatherbug Web site and provides up-to-the-minute weather forecasts. (Not mandatory)
Trayzip or TRAYZIP.EXE	A Zip compression utility that creates a system tray icon. (Not mandatory)
Trickler or FSG.EXE	A spyware program that collects information from the computer and transmits it to a preconfigured Internet location. REMOVE.
TrueVector or VSMON.EXE	A function of ZoneAlarm firewall software. Required for the software to work properly.
TVWakeup	Function of Microsoft Web TV that provides controls on the taskbar. (Not mandatory)
TweakDUN	A utility that finetunes certain Windows settings in order to maximum efficiency of bandwidth usage on a dial-up networking connection. (Not mandatory, but useful)

(*continued*)

Table E.2 Annotated Listing of MSCONFIG Startup Entries (*continued*)

Program or File Name	Description
TweakUI	TweakUI is a program available from Microsoft's Web site that allows a user to adjust many features not otherwise adjustable. Most options require the program to load at startup in order to effect the changes. When TweakUI is used to enter a network password, it will be listed twice. If you remove one, you should remove both. (Not mandatory)
USB Hub Keyboard Patch or SKBPATCH.EXE	WIN95. USB Driver update that extends support to USB keyboards. Required for WIN95 users wanting to use a USB keyboard.
USBMMKBD	Utility that provides USB keyboard support. Required on most systems using USB keyboards.
User32DLL (WINDOWS\User32DLL.vbs)	The LOOK.vbs virus. Update antivirus software and run immediately.
Usrobotics online registration	Registration nag for owners of US Robotics products. (Not mandatory and quite annoying)
VidSvr	TV guide for WEBTV users. (Not mandatory)
VirusScan Console	A function of McAfee VirusScan (through version 4.x) used for scheduling unattended virus scans. Not required if you don't perform regularly scheduled scans.
VirusScan System Scan	A function of McAfee VirusScan (through version 4.x). Known to interfere with certain programs. Scan files manually. (Not mandatory)
VirusScan System Tray	A function of McAfee VirusScan (through version 4.x). Runs if you have any of the VirusScan options running.
Vistascan or VISTASCAN.EXE	Function of VistaScan scanner software. Click this icon and a menu opens. (Not mandatory)
Voodoo2 or 3DFXV2PS.DLL	Function of the Voodoo 2 graphics adapters. Restores Voodoo 2 registry settings that can't be retained normally. Required for 3dfx/Voodoo2 owners.
VortexTray	System tray application for Aureal Vortex-based soundcards. (Not mandatory)
VoyetraTray	Function of Turtle Beach Montego II (and other) sound card drivers. Provides Control Group for the sound functions/associated with AudioStation 3 and 32. (Not mandatory)
VS_STAT.EXE; VSECOMR.EXE; VSHWIN32.EXE; VSSTAT.EXE	Part of McAfee Antivirus program. Required for automated scanning of files and for scheduled system scans.

(*continued*)

Table E.2 Annotated Listing of MSCONFIG Startup Entries (*continued*)

Program or File Name	Description
Vshield	A function of McAfee Antivirus that scans new files as they are added. Not required if manual scans of downloads and disk contents are faithfully done. (Not mandatory, but quite useful)
Vshwin32EXE or VSHWIN32.EXE	A 32-bit function of McAfee Antivirus that scans new files as they are added. Not required if manual scans of downloads and disk contents are faithfully done. (Not mandatory, but quite useful)
VsStatEXE or VSSTAT.EXE	A function of McAfee Antivirus that logs files coming in and actions taken by McAfee on those files. (Not mandatory, but useful)
W3kNETWORK or W3KNET.DLL	A function of advertising-supported software that automatically downloads ads to the users' computers whenever the associated software is run. Quite annoying, but generally required for the associated software to run properly.
Washer or WASHER.EXE	The Windows utility that automatically cleans your browser's cache, cookies, history, mail trash, etc., based on whatever schedule the user has configured in the Clear History function of Internet Options. (Not mandatory, but quite useful)
washindex	A function Webroot Windows Washer, a third-party utility that deletes unnecessary duplicate and temporary files. You can remove it, but as long as the software is installed, it'll just come back.
Watchdog Program or WATCHDOG.EXE	Third-party utility that monitors ISP/dial-up connection. (Not mandatory)
Waterfall Pro 2.99 or WFP.EXE or [wfp]	Waterfall Pro is a utility that monitors CPU temperature and slows CPU speed if it gets too warm. (Not mandatory)
Wcmdmgr.exe	A function of WildTangent software that periodically contacts WildTangent servers to see whether an update is available. (Not mandatory)
Web outfitter tray or STTRAY.EXE	Automatically launches Intel's Web Outfitter software at startup and creates a system tray icon for the option menus.
WebHancer Agent or WHAGENT.EXE	System Tray for Webhancer software, a web caching utility. (Not mandatory and extremely resource intensive)

(continued)

Table E.2 Annotated Listing of MSCONFIG Startup Entries (*continued*)

Program or File Name	Description
Webshots	A utility that automatically downloads screensavers from the Webshots Web site. Useful only if you have Webshots updating your wallpaper on a daily basis.
WhenUstart.exe or WHENU.EXE	An on-line shopping service that automatically launches each time you run Windows. (Not mandatory or useful)
Win32DLL =WINDOWS\Win32DLL.vbs	The LOVE-LETTER-FOR-YOU.TXT.VBS virus. Update antvirus software and run immediately.
WinampAgent or WINAMPA.EXE	Launches a system tray icon for Winamp Player software. (Not mandatory)
WIN-BUGSFIX	LOVE-LETTER-FOR-YOU.TXT.vbs virus removal instructions
WINDLL.EXE	The GirlFriend 1.35 virus. Mostly obsolete but still pops up from time to time. Collects user ID and password information and transmits it to a preconfigured Internet location. Run antivirus software immediately.
Windows Eyes	A utility for blind computer users that replaces common computer responses with speech. (Not mandatory, but useful to those who need it)
Windows=c:\msdos98.exe	The MINE.EXE virus. Update antivirus software and run immediately.
WinFAT32=WinFAT32.EXE	The VBS.Loveletter virus. Update antivirus software and run immediately.
Winkey	Freeware program that allows user to custom-configure Windows hot keys.
WINMGMT.EXE	Enterprise Management software that runs from administrator's machine. Should be removed from client machines.
winmodem or WINMODEM.EXE	Utility installed by a number of software modems. (Not mandatory, but can be useful)
WinPoET or WinPPPoverEthernet.exe or [WinPPPoverEthernet]	Provides end users with authenticated access to high-speed broadband networks using the Microsoft dial-up interface. (Not mandatory)
WKCALREM	Yet another Microsoft Works Calendar reminder. (Not mandatory)
WKDETECT	Automatically looks for updates for Microsoft Works when Internet connection is present. (Not mandatory and can be annoying)

(*continued*)

Table E.2 Annotated Listing of MSCONFIG Startup Entries (*concluded*)

Program or File Name	Description
WKFUD.EXE	Microsoft marketing drivel. (Not mandatory or useful)
Yahoo Pager or YPAGER.EXE	A function of Yahoo! Messenger that allows the user to send instant messages. (Not mandatory)
zBrowser Launcher or COMMANDR.EXE or ITOUCH.EXE	Function of Logitech keyboard software that creates a system tray icon which the can access the menu options. From here, the user can program certain keys on Logitech keyboards. (Not mandatory)
ZipDisk Icons	Related to the Zip drive. (Not mandatory)
ZoneAlarm (zonealarm.exe) Uses 7% resources	Launches ZoneAlarm at startup and creates a system tray icon from which you can access the menu options. Required for ZoneAlarm to function properly.

While not a complete listing (I'm not sure that would be possible), these are some of the more commonly seen entries to the Startup options in MSCONFIG.

BIOS BEEP CODES AND ERROR MESSAGES

While this information is provided in other sections throughout the book, I felt that it would be a good idea to collate it into a single place for quick acquisition. Please note that each version of BIOS by a given manufacturer will change from version to version. Settings described in the Award BIOS setup will also be available in most other brands of BIOS, although they may be located in different sections. Beep codes and error messages are based on information provided by the manufacturers and are subject to change.

BIOS SETUP (AWARD)

Table F.1 Standard CMOS Setup

Setting	Options	Description
Date	Page Up/Page Down	Changes System Date
Time	Page Up/Page Down	Changes System Time
Hard Disks/Type	Auto/User/None	Settings for IDE HDD
Hard Disks/Mode	Normal/LBA/Large/Auto	HDD Translation Method
Drive A	Various Settings	Enables/Disables Floppy A
Drive B	Various Settings	Enables/Disables Floppy B
Video	EGA/VGA, CGA-40, CGA-80, Mono	Establishes type video used
Halt On	Various Options	Stops POST on selected errors

BIOS FEATURES SETUP

Setting	Options	Description
Boot Virus Detection	Enabled/Disabled	Warns of any attempt to write to the boot sector
CPU Level 1 Cache	Enabled/Disabled	Enables read/write operations to L1 cache built into CPU
CPU Level 2 Cache	Enabled/Disabled	Enables read/writer operations to L2 cache built into CPU
CPU Level 2 Cache ECC Check	Enabled/Disabled	Turns on/off ECC Mode
Quick Power On Self Test	Enabled/Disabled	Full Test/Tests only selected system components on cold boot
HDD Sequence	IDE/SCSI	Where to look for MBR
Boot Sequence	Options Vary	Determines the order of devices in which POST looks for the MBR
Boot Up Floppy Seek	Enabled/Disabled	Tests floppy drive to see if it has 40 or 80 tracks
Floppy Disk Access Control	R/W, Read Only	Security Access for floppy drive
HDD Block Mode Sectors	Options Vary	
HDD S.M.A.R.T capability	Enabled/Disabled	IDE SMART Capable?
PS2 Mouse Function Control	Enabled/Auto	Looks to PS2 for mouse
OS2 Onboard Memory	Enabled/Disabled	Use OS2 memory mapping

Setting	Options	Description
PCI/VGA Palette Snoop	Disabled/Enabled	Allows Video adapters to directly access RAM looking for video information
Video ROM/BIOS Shadowing	Enabled/Disabled	Allows copying of BIOS routines to upper memory for enhanced performance
C8000-DFFFF Shadowing (multiple entries)	Enabled/Disabled	Allows copying of Supplemental BIOS to specific addresses
Boot Up NumLock Status	On/Off	Determines whether number lock on keyboard is on or off after system boots
Typomatic Rate Setting	Disabled/Enabled	Disabled turns off *Typomatic Rate* and *Typomatic Delay*
Typomatic Rate	Options vary	Sets speed at which characters repeat when a key on the keyboard is held down
Typomatic Delay	Options vary	Sets time that elapses before keys begin to repeat when a key on the keyboard is held down
Security Option	System/Setup	Determines where security is controlled

CHIPSET FEATURES SETUP

Setting	Options	Description
EDO Autoconfiguration	Enabled/Disabled	Allows chipset to control EDO timing functions
EDO Read Burst Timing	Varies	Sets number of clock cycles for Burst Mode read operations
EDO Write Burst Timing	Varies	Sets number of clock cycles for Burst Mode write operations
EDO RAS Precharge	3T, 4T	Sets number of clock cycles for RAS Precharge
EDO RAS/CAS Delay	2T, 3T	Sets number of clock cycles for RAS/CAS Delay
SDRAM Configuration	Varies	Sets clock speed of SDRAM
SDRAM RAS Precharge	Auto, 3T, 4T	Sets number of clock cycles for RAS Precharge
SDRAM RAS/CAS Delay	Auto, 3T, 2T	Sets number of clock cycles for RAS/CAS Delay
SDRAM Banks Close Policy	Arbitration, Page-Miss	
Graphics Aperture Size	Varies	
Video Memory Cache Mode	UC, USWC	Determines how Video Memory addresses cache
PCI 2.1 Support	Enabled/Disabled	Disabled setting drops system back to PCI Version 1.0
Memory Hole at 15M-16M	Enabled/Disabled	Enables/disables use of these memory addresses
Onboard FDC Controller	Enabled/Disabled	Allows you to disable the floppy disk drive

(Continued)

Table F.1 Standard CMOS Setup *(Continued)*

Setting	Options	Description
	CHIPSET FEATURES SETUP	
Onboard Floppy Swap A/B	Enabled/Disabled	Switches drives A and B
Onboard Serial Port 1	Various settings/Disabled	Allows reconfiguring or disabling Serial Port 1
Onboard Serial Port 2	Various settings/Disabled	Allows reconfiguring or disabling Serial Port 2
Onboard Parallel Port	Various settings/Disabled	Allows reconfiguring or disabling Parallel Port
Parallel Port Mode	Normal, ECC, ECC/ECP	Sets up parallel communications
ECP DMA Select	Varies	Sets DMA channel used by ECP Parallel mode
UART2 Use Infrared	Enabled/Disabled	Sets infrared port to UART2
Onboard PCI/IDE Enable	Both, Primary, Secondary, Disabled	Enables/disables IDE ports
IDE DMA Mode	Auto/Disable	Disables, autoselects Direct Memory Access
IDE 0/1 – Master/Slave	Various	Sets PIO mode and DMA channel for specific device
	POWER MANAGEMENT SETUP	
Power Management	User Defined, Disabled, Min, Max	Determines PM Method
Video Off Option	Suspend ‡ Off, Always On	Determines how the monitor is managed
Video Off Method	Various Options	Determines method by which monitor is shut down
HDD Power Down	Various	How long before hard drive shuts down
Suspend Mode	Various	How long before hard drive goes into suspended mode
PWR Button	Soft-off, Suspend, No Function	Determines how the power button affects power supply
Power Up on Modem ACT	Enabled/Disabled	Modem wakes machine?
AC Power Loss Restart	Enabled/Disabled	Automatically restarts machine when AC power is restored
Wake on LAN	Enabled/Disabled	NIC wakes machine?

PNP AND PCI SETUP

PNP OS Installed?	Yes/No	Is the Operating System PnP Compliant?
Slot 1-? IRQ (several entries)	Auto, various settings	Manually assign an IRQ to a specific slot or let PnP handle allocations?
PCI Latency Timer	Various settings	Number of clock cycles for PCI latency
IRQ 3-15 Used by ISA (several entries)	Yes/No	Is this IRQ assigned to a legacy ISA device?
Force Update ESCD	Enabled/Disabled	Forces reallocation of resources on POST
LOAD BIOS DEFAULTS?	Reloads factory Settings. No internal settings.	
SUPERVISOR PASSWORD	Allows entry of supervisor password	
USER PASSWORD	Allows entry of User password	
IDE HDD AUTODETECT	Automatically detects and configures devices on Primary and Secondary IDE ports	

BIOS BEEP CODES

Beep codes are the distress calls your computer issues when it is unable to start up successfully. Each manufacturer has its own set of codes it uses to translate what's going on during the POST process into something the user can understand, if he or she knows how to translate the code.

Table F.2 Beep Codes for AMI BIOS Chips

	AMI BIOS Codes	
1 short	DRAM refresh error	The programmable interrupt controller or programmable timer has probably failed. Could indicate chipset failure.
2 short	Base 64K Memory parity error	A memory parity error has occurred in the first 64K of RAM. Could be a bad RAM chip.
3 short	Base 64K System memory failure	A memory error has occurred in the first 64K of RAM. Could be a bad RAM chip.
4 short	System timer	The system clock/timer IC has failed. This can also indicate a failure in the first bank of memory.
5 short	Processor	The CPU itself failed.
6 short	Keyboard controller Gate A20 error	The keyboard controller IC has failed. This affects more than the keyboard, because Gate A20 is used to switch the processor to protected mode. Could indicate chipset failure.
7 short	Virtual mode processor error	Either the CPU or the chipset has generated an exception error.
8 short	Display memory R/W test	The system video adapter is either missing or has failed.
9 short	ROM BIOS checksum error	The contents of the system BIOS ROM does not match the value checksum expected. Most likely bad BIOS.
10 short	CMOS shutdown register read/write error	The shutdown for the CMOS has failed
11 short	Cache error	L2 cache is faulty
1 long, 3 short	Cache error	Memory failure above 64K
1 long, 8 short	Display test failure	The system video adapter is either missing or has failed.

The Award BIOS has its own set of beeps and uses the far less than most other brands. Since the Award is one of the most common brands of BIOS out there, if you're going to memorize any codes at all, these are the ones to memorize.

Table F.3 Award BIOS Codes

No Beep	Power Supply, System Board, Speaker	Check power supply for current
Continuous beep	Power Supply, System Board	Power supply is delivering current, but may be bad
Repeating short beeps	Memory Error	Possible bad memory, or poorly seated memory
1 long, 1 short	System Board	
1 long, 2 or 3 short	Display Adapter	Possibly defective video adapter, possibly poorly seated video adapter
1 short	System OK	
2 short	POST Error displayed on monitor	Turns error codes over to display

Phoenix is in the business of making custom BIOSs for different manufacturers. Therefore, its screens show more variance than any other brand. You won't always know that it is actually a Phoenix BIOS. If it doesn't identify itself on boot and resembles nothing in the first section on BIOS settings, it might (or might not) be safe to assume it is Phoenix. In any case, Phoenix uses beep codes more than any other brand. Therefore, its list of codes is much longer.

Table F.4 Phoenix BIOS Codes

1-1-2	CPU test failure	The CPU is faulty. Replace the CPU.
Low 1-1-2	System board select	The motherboard is having an undetermined fault. Replace the motherboard.
1-1-3	CMOS read/write	The real time clock/CMOS is faulty. Replace the CMOS if possible.
Low 1-1-3	Extended CMOS RAM	The extended portion of the CMOS RAM has failed. Replace the CMOS if possible.
1-1-4	BIOS ROM checksum error	The BIOS ROM has failed. Replace the BIOS or upgrade if possible.
1-2-1	PIT failure	The programmable interrupt timer has failed. Replace if possible. Likely chipset failure.
1-2-2	DMA failure	The DMA controller has failed. Likely chipset failure.
1-2-3	DMA read/write failure	The DMA controller has failed. Likely chipset failure.
1-3-1	RAM refresh failure	The RAM refresh controller has failed. Likely chipset failure.
1-3-2	64KB RAM failure	The test of the first 64KB RAM has failed to start.

(Continued)

Table F.4 Phoenix BIOS Codes *(Continued)*

1-3-3	First 64KB RAM failure	The first RAM IC has failed. Likely chipset failure.
1-3-4	First 64KB logic failure	The first RAM control logic has failed.
1-4-1	Address line failure	The address line to the first 64KB RAM has failed.
1-4-2	Parity RAM failure	The first RAM IC has failed. Replace if possible.
1-4-3	EISA failsafe timer test	Replace the motherboard.
1-4-4	EISA NMI port 462 test	Replace the motherboard.
2-1-1	64KB RAM failure	Bit 0; This data bit on the first RAM IC has failed. Likely chipset failure.
2-1-2	64KB RAM failure	Bit 1; This data bit on the first RAM IC has failed. Likely chipset failure.
2-1-3	64KB RAM failure	Bit 2; This data bit on the first RAM IC has failed. Likely chipset failure.
2-1-4	64KB RAM failure	Bit 3; This data bit on the first RAM IC has failed. Likely chipset failure.
2-2-1	64KB RAM failure	Bit 4; This data bit on the first RAM IC has failed. Likely chipset failure.
2-2-2	64KB RAM failure	Bit 5; This data bit on the first RAM IC has failed. Likely chipset failure.
2-2-3	64KB RAM failure	Bit 6; This data bit on the first RAM IC has failed. Likely chipset failure.
2-2-4	64KB RAM failure	Bit 7; This data bit on the first RAM IC has failed. Likely chipset failure.
2-3-1	64KB RAM failure	Bit 8; This data bit on the first RAM IC has failed. Likely chipset failure.
2-3-2	64KB RAM failure	Bit 9; This data bit on the first RAM IC has failed. Likely chipset failure.
2-3-3	64KB RAM failure	Bit 10; This data bit on the first RAM IC has failed. Likely chipset failure.
2-3-4	64KB RAM failure	Bit 11; This data bit on the first RAM IC has failed. Likely chipset failure.
2-4-1	64KB RAM failure	Bit 12; This data bit on the first RAM IC has failed. Likely chipset failure.
2-4-2	64KB RAM failure	Bit 13; This data bit on the first RAM IC has failed. Likely chipset failure.
2-4-3	64KB RAM failure	Bit 14; This data bit on the first RAM IC has failed. Likely chipset failure.
2-4-4	64KB RAM failure	Bit 15; This data bit on the first RAM IC has failed. Likely chipset failure.
3-1-1	Slave DMA register failure	The DMA controller has failed. Replace the controller if possible.

(Continued)

Table F.4 Phoenix BIOS Codes *(Continued)*

3-1-2	Master DMA register failure	The DMA controller has failed. Replace the controller if possible.
3-1-3	Master interrupt mask register failure	The interrupt controller IC has failed.
3-1-4	Slave interrupt mask register failure	The interrupt controller IC has failed.
3-2-2	Interrupt vector error	The BIOS was unable to load the interrupt vectors into memory. Replace the motherboard.
3-2-3	Reserved	
3-2-4	Keyboard controller failure	The keyboard controller has failed. Likely chipset failure.
3-3-1	CMOS RAM power bad	Replace the CMOS battery or CMOS RAM if possible.
3-3-2	CMOS configuration error	The CMOS configuration has failed. Restore the configuration or replace the battery if possible.
3-3-3	Reserved	
3-3-4	Video memory failure	There is a problem with the video memory. Replace the video adapter if possible.
3-4-1	Video initialization failure	There is a problem with the video adapter. Reseat the adapter or replace the adapter if possible.
4-2-1	Timer failure	The system's timer IC has failed. Likely chipset failure.
4-2-2	Shutdown failure	The CMOS has failed. Replace the CMOS IC if possible.
4-2-3	Gate A20 failure	The keyboard controller has failed. Likely chipset failure.
4-2-4	Unexpected interrupt in protected mode	This is a CPU problem. Replace the CPU and retest.
4-3-1	RAM test failure	System RAM addressing circuitry is faulty. Replace the motherboard.
4-3-3	Interval timer channel 2 failure	The system timer IC has failed. Likely chipset failure.
4-3-4	Time of day clock failure	The real time clock/CMOS has failed. Replace the CMOS if possible.
4-4-1	Serial port failure	A error has occurred in the serial port circuitry.
4-4-2	Parallel port failure	A error has occurred in the parallel port circuitry.
4-4-3	Math coprocessor failure	The math coprocessor has failed. If possible, replace the MPU. Most likely a new CPU is needed.

COMMON CHIPSETS

There have been several manufacturers of chipsets over the years, and it is neither my intention nor the publisher's to slight any manufacturer. However, time and space restraints prevent me from publishing every chipset ever seen by man. For the purposes of this section, I have taken the chipsets most commonly seen today and included them in this list.

Table F.5 Intel Chipsets

Chipset Name	Code Name	CPU Supported	Bus	Max RAM	RAM Types	AGP	IDE	USB	PCI	Error Checking	Dual Processors
430LX	Triton	P5	60, 66	192MB	FPM	No	BMIDE	No	2.0	Parity	No
430NX	Neptune	P54	50, 60, 66	512MB	FPM	No	BMIDE	No	2.0	Parity	Yes
430FX	Triton I	P54	60, 66	128MB	FPM/EDO	No	BMIDE	No	2.0	None	No
430HX	Triton II	P54/55	60, 66	512MB	FPM/EDO	No	BMIDE	Yes	2.1	Parity/ECC	Yes
430VX	Triton III	P54/55	50, 60, 66	128MB	EDO/SDRAM	No	BMIDE	Yes	2.1	None	No
430TX	Triton IV (unofficial)	P54/55	50, 60, 66	256MB	EDO/SDRAM	No	UDMA/33	Yes	2.1	None	No
440FX	Natoma	P6/PII	60, 66	1GB	FPM/EDO/BEDO	No	UDMA/33	No	2.1	Parity/ECC	Yes
450GX	Orion	P6	60, 66	4GB	FPM	No	BMIDE	No	2.1	Parity/ECC	QUAD
450KX	Mars	P6	60, 66	1GB	FPM	No	BMIDE	No	2.1	Parity/ECC	Yes
450NX	Deschutes	Xeon	100	8GB	EDO	No	UDMA/33	Yes	2.1	Parity/ECC	Yes
440LX	None	PII/Celeron	66	1GB	EDO/SDRAM	1x	UDMA/33	No	2.1	Parity/ECC	Yes
440EX	None	PII/Celeron	66	256MB	EDO/SDRAM	1x	UDMA/33	Yes	2.1	None	No
440BX	None	PII/PIII/Celeron	66, 100	1GB	EDO/SDRAM	1x, 2x	UDMA/33	Yes	2.1	Parity/ECC	Yes
440GX	None	PII/Xeon	133	1GB	SDRAM	2x	UDMA/33	Yes	2.1	Parity/ECC	No
442ZX	None	PII/Celeron	66, 100	256MB	EDO/SDRAM	1x, 2x	UDMA/33	Yes	2.1	None	No
440ZX66	None	Celeron	66	256	EDO/SDRAM	1x, 2x	UDMA/33	Yes	2.1	None	No
810	Whitney	Celeron	66, 100	512MB	SDRAM	1x, 2x	UDMA/66	Yes	2.2	None	No
810E	Whitney	PII/Celeron	66, 100, 133	512MB	SDRAM	1x, 2x	UDMA/66	Yes	2.2	None	No
815	Solano	PII/Celeron	66, 100, 133	512MB	SDRAM	1x, 2x, 4x	UDMA/66	Yes	2.2	None	No
820	Camino	PII/Celeron	100, 133	1GB	RDRAM[1]	1x, 2x, 4x	UDMA/66	Yes	2.2	ECC	Yes
830	Almador	PII	133	1.5GB	SDRAM	1x, 2x, 4x	UDMA/66	Yes	2.2	ECC	Yes
840	Carmel	PII/Xeon	100, 133	4GB	RDRAM	1x, 2x, 4x	UDMA/66	Yes	2.2	ECC	DUAL PIII QUAD
XEON 850	Willamette	PIV	400	2GB	RDRAM	1x, 2x, 4x	UDMA/100	Yes	2.2	ECC	No

Listing of Intel chipsets since the release of the Pentium CPU

VIA chipsets have long been a standard of the industry. The ones listed here in no way, shape, or form represent every chipset it ever made. Instead I have chosen to provide information on those chipsets that support the most commonly seen CPUs.

Table F.6 VIA Chipsets

Chipset Name	CPU Supported	Bus	Max RAM	RAM Types	AGP	IDE	USB	PCI	Error Checking
VP*	P54	50, 60, 66	512MB	FPM, EDO, BEDO, SDRAM	No	UDMA/33	Yes	2.1	None
VP2*	P54, P55	50, 60, 66	512MB	FPM, EDO, SDRAM	No	UDMA/33	Yes	2.1	ECC
VP2/97*	P54, P55	50, 60, 66	512MB	FPM, EDO, SDRAM	No	UDMA/33	Yes	2.1	ECC
VPX*	P54, P55	66, 75	512MB	FPM, EDO, SDRAM	No	UDMA/33	Yes	2.1	No
VPX/97*	P54, P55	66, 75	512MB	FPM, EDO, SDRAM	No	UDMA/33	Yes	2.1	No
VP3*	P54, P55	50, 60, 66	1GB	FPM, EDO, SDRAM, DDRAM	1x, 2x	UDMA/33	Yes	2.1	ECC/Parity
MVP3*	P54, P55	66, 75, 83, 100	1GB	FPM, EDO, SDRAM	1x, 2x	UDMA/66	Yes	2.1	ECC/Parity
MVP4*	P54, P55	66, 75, 83, 100	768MB	FPM, EDO, SDRAM	1x, 2x	UDMA/66	Yes	2.2	ECC/Parity
Apollo†	P6	66	1GB	FPM, EDO	No	UDMA/33	Yes	2.1	ECC
Apollo PRO*	P6, PII	66, 100	1GB	FPM, EDO, SDRAM, DDRAM, ESDRAM, VC SDRAM	1x, 2x	UDMA/33	Yes	2.1	ECC/Parity
Apollo PRO+*	P6, PII	66, 100	1GB	FPM, EDO, SDRAM, VC SDRAM	1x, 2x	UDMA/33	Yes	2.1	ECC/Parity
Apollo PRO 133*	PIII, Celeron	66, 100, 133	1.5GB	FPM, EDO, SDRAM, VC SDRAM	1x , 2x	UDMA/66	Yes	2.2	ECC/Parity
Apollo PRO 133A†	PIII, Celeron	66, 100, 133	2GB	FPM, EDO, SDRAM, DDRAM, ESDRAM, VC SDRAM	1x, 2x, 4x	UDMA/66	Yes	2.2	ECC/Parity
PM-601*	PIII, Celeron	66, 100, 133	1GB	FPM, EDO, SDRAM, VC SDRAM	1x, 2x	UDMA/66	Yes	2.2	No
PM-133*	PIII, Celeron	66, 100, 133	2GB	FPM, EDO, SDRAM, ESDRAM, VC SDRAM	1x, 2x, 4x	UDMA/66	Yes	2.2	ECC/Parity
Apollo PRO 266†	PIII	66, 100, 133	4GB	SDRAM, VC SDRAM, DDRAM	1x, 2x, 4x	UDMA/66	Yes	2.2	ECC
KX-133*	AMD K7	200	2GB	EDO, SDRAM, VC SDRAM, DDRAM	1x, 2x, 4x	UDMA/66	Yes	2.2	ECC/Parity
KT-133*	AMD K7, Duron	200	2GB	SDRAM, VC SDRAM, DDRAM	1x, 2x, 4x	UDMA/66	Yes	2.2	No
KM-133*	AMD K7, Duron	200, 266	1.5GB	FPM, EDO, SDRAM, VC SDRAM	1x, 2x, 4x	UDMA/66	Yes	2.2	No

List of VIA Chipsets for the K7 and later

* No Dual Processor; † Dual Processor

The Opti chipsets were targeted at the mass-market, lower-priced computers that could be used in schools and corporations or by individuals on a budget. They tend to be problem-free for the most part, but will never win any awards for their blazing performance. Despite that, they still provide more than acceptable system performance, all else being equal.

Table F.7 Opti Chipsets

Chipset Name	CPU Supported	Bus	Max RAM	RAM Types	AGP	IDE	USB	PCI	Error Checking
Python	P5, P54	50, 60, 66	128MB	FPM	No	BMIDE	No	1.0/VLB	Parity
Cobra	P5, P54	50, 60, 66	128MB	FPM	No	BMIDE	No	1.0/VLB	Parity
Viper	P54, P55	50, 60, 66	512MB	FPM, EDO, SDRAM	No	BMIDE	No	2.0	Parity
Viper N	P54, P55	50, 60, 66	512MB	FPM, EDO	No	BMIDE	No	2.0	Parity
Viper N+	P54, P55	50, 60, 66	512MB	FPM, EDO	No	BMIDE	No	2.0	Parity
Viper MAX	P54, P55	50, 60, 66	512MB	FPM, EDO, BEDO, SDRAM	No	BMIDE	Yes	2.0	Parity
Viper Xpress	P54, P55	40, 50, 60, 66	512MB	FPM, EDO	No	BMIDE	Yes	2.1	Parity
Vendetta	P54	50, 60, 66	512MB	FPM, EDO, SDRAM	No	UDMA/33	No	2.1	ECC/Parity
Discovery	P6	60, 66	512MB	FPM, EDO, SDRAM	Yes	UDMA/33	Yes	2.1	ECC/Parity

List of Opti Chipsets

* No Dual Processor; † Dual Processor

Silicon Integrated Systems Corporation specializes in chipsets that support large numbers of onboard peripherals. In this respect, the company has made a very respectable niche for itself in the market. Its chipsets, for the most part, are solid and reliable and provide for reasonably good performance.

Table F.8 SiS Chipsets

Chipset Name	CPU Supported	Bus	Max RAM	RAM Types	AGP	IDE	USB	PCI	Error Checking
501-503*	P54	50, 60, 66	128MB	FPM, EDO	No	BMIDE	No	1.0	No
5511-5513†	P54	50, 60, 66	512MB	FPM, EDO	No	BMIDE	No	2.0	Parity
5571*	P54, P55	50, 60, 66, 75	384MB	FPM, EDO, SDRAM	No	BMIDE	No	2.0	No
5581*	P54, P55	50, 55, 60, 66, 75	384MB	FPM, EDO, SDRAM	No	UDMA/33	Yes	2.0	No
5582*	P54, P55	50, 55, 60, 66, 75	384MB	FPM, EDO, SDRAM	No	UDMA/33	Yes	2.0	No
5591*	P54, P55	50, 55, 60, 66, 75	768MB	FPM, EDO, SDRAM	1x, 2x	UDMA/33	Yes	2.1	No
5592*	P54, P55	50, 55, 60, 66, 75	768MB	FPM, EDO, SDRAM	1x, 2x	UDMA/33	Yes	2.1	No
5596*	P54	50, 60, 66	512MB	FPM, EDO	No	BMIDE	Yes	2.1	No
5597*	P54, P55	50, 55, 60, 66, 75	384	FPM, EDO, SDRAM	No	UDMA/33	Yes	2.1	No
5598*	P54, P55	50, 55, 60, 66, 75	384	FPM, EDO, SDRAM	No	UDMA/33	Yes	2.1	No
530*	P54, P55	66, 75, 83, 95, 100	1.5GB	SDRAM	1x, 2x	UDMA/66	Yes	2.2	No
540*	P54, P55	66, 75, 83, 95, 100	1.5GB	SDRAM, VC SDRAM	1x, 2x, 4x	UDMA/66	Yes	2.2	No
5600†	PII	60, 66, 100	1.5GB	FPM, EDO, SDRAM	1x, 2x	UDMA/33	Yes	2.1	ECC
600†	PII	60, 66, 100	1.5GB	FPM, EDO, SDRAM	1x, 2x	UDMA/33	Yes	2.1	ECC
620*	PII	60, 66, 75, 83, 100	1.5GB	SDRAM	1x, 2x	UDMA/66	Yes	2.2	No
630*	PIII, Celeron	66, 100, 133	3GB	SDRAM, VC SDRAM	1x, 2x, 4x	UDMA/66	Yes	2.2	No
630E*	PIII, Celeron	66, 100, 133	3GB	SDRAM	1x, 2x, 4x	UDMA/66	Yes	2.2	No
730S*	AMD K7, Duron	200	1.5GB	SDRAM	1x, 2x, 4x	UDMA/66	Yes	2.2	No

Listing of SiS Chipsets

* No Dual Processor; † Dual Processor

REFERENCE CHARTS: PINOUTS AND CHARACTER SETS

PINOUTS OF COMMON COMPONENTS

Throughout the book, I discussed in detail some of the different packages used by device manufacturers, both past and present, in assembling their product. For most readers, knowing the actual use of any given pin on a module is of limited use. Someone going into engineering or design, however, might find it useful. Therefore, rather than cluttering up the chapters with the pinouts of specific devices, I have chosen to provide them in the form of an appendix.

Pinouts for 30-pin SIMM

Pin Number	Pin Name	Description
1	VCC	+5VDC
2	/CAS	Column Address Strobe
3	DQ0	Data 0
4	A0	Address 0
5	A1	Address 1
6	DQ1	Data 1
7	A2	Address 2
8	A3	Address 3
9	GND	Ground
10	DQ2	Data 2
11	A4	Address 4
12	A5	Address 5
13	DQ3	Data 3
14	A6	Address 6
15	A7	Address 7
16	DQ4	Data 4
17	A8	Address 8
18	A9	Address 9
19	A10	Address 10
20	DQ5	Data 5
21	/WE	Write Enable
22	GND	Ground
23	DQ6	Data 6
24	A11	Address 11
25	DQ7	Data 7
26	QP	Data Parity Out
27	/RAS	Row Address Strobe
28	/CASP	Parity Bit Column Access Strobe
29	DP	Data Parity In
30	VDC	+5VDC

Pinouts for 72-pin SIMM

Pin Number	Pin Name (Non-parity)	Pin Name (Parity)	Description
1	VSS	VSS	Ground
2	DQ0	DQ0	Data 0
3	DQ16	DQ16	Data 16
4	DQ1	DQ1	Data 1
5	DQ17	DQ17	Data 17
6	DQ2	DQ2	Data 2
7	DQ18	DQ18	Data 18
8	DQ3	DQ3	Data 3
9	DQ19	DQ19	Data 19
10	VCC	VCC	+5VDC
11	Not connected	Not connected	Not connected
12	A0	A0	Address 0
13	A1	A1	Address 1
14	A2	A2	Address 2
15	A3	A3	Address 3
16	A4	A4	Address 4
17	A5	A5	Address 5
18	A6	A6	Address 6
19	A10	A10	Address 10
20	DQ4	DQ4	Data 4
21	DQ20	DQ20	Data 20
22	DQ5	DQ5	Data 5
23	DQ21	DQ21	Data 21
24	DQ6	DQ6	Data 6
25	DQ22	DQ22	Data 22
26	DQ7	DQ7	Data 7
27	DQ23	DQ23	Data 23
28	A7	A7	Address 7
29	A11	A11	Address 11
30	VCC	VCC	+5VDC
31	A8	A8	Address 8
32	A9	A9	Address 9
33	RAS 3	RAS 3	Row Address Strobe 3
34	RAS 2	RAS 2	Row Address Strobe 2
35	Not connected	PQ3	Parity bit 3
36	Not connected	PQ1	Parity bit 1

(Continued)

Pinouts for 72-pin SIMM *(Continued)*

Pin Number	Pin Name (Non-parity)	Pin Name (Parity)	Description
37	Not connected	PQ2	Parity bit 2
38	Not connected	PQ4	Parity bit 4
39	VSS	VSS	Ground
40	CAS 0	CAS 0	Column Address Strobe 0
41	CAS 2	CAS 2	Column Address Strobe 2
42	CAS 3	CAS 3	Column Address Strobe 3
43	CAS 1	CAS 1	Column Address Strobe 1
44	RAS 0	RAS 0	Row Address Strobe 0
45	RAS 1	RAS 1	Row Address Strobe 1
46	Not connected	Not connected	Not connected
47	WE	WE	Read/Write
48	Not connected	Not connected	Not connected
49	DQ8	DQ8	Data 8
50	DQ24	DQ24	Data 24
51	DQ9	DQ9	Data 9
52	DQ25	DQ25	Data 25
53	DQ10	DQ10	Data 10
54	DQ26	DQ26	Data 26
55	DQ11	DQ11	Data 11
56	DQ27	DQ27	Data 27
57	DQ12	DQ12	Data 12
58	DQ28	DQ28	Data 28
59	VCC	VCC	+5 VDC
60	DQ29	DQ29	Data 29
61	DQ13	DQ13	Data 13
62	DQ30	DQ30	Data 30
63	DQ14	DQ14	Data 14
64	DQ31	DQ31	Data 31
65	DQ16	DQ16	Data 16
66	Not connected	Not connected	Not connected
67	PD1	PD1	Presence Detect 1
68	PD2	PD2	Presence Detect 2
69	PD3	PD3	Presence Detect 3
70	PD4	PD4	Presence Detect 4
71	Not connected	Not connected	Not connected
72	VSS	VSS	Ground

Pinouts for 168-pin DIMM

	SIDE ONE				
Pin	Parity	NonParity	72bit	80bit	Description
1	VSS	VSS	VSS	VSS	Ground
2	DQ0	DQ0	DQ0	DQ0	Data 0
3	DQ1	DQ1	DQ1	DQ1	Data 1
4	DQ2	DQ2	DQ2	DQ2	Data 2
5	DQ3	DQ3	DQ3	DQ3	Data 3
6	VCC	VCC	VCC	VCC	+5VDC or +3.3VDC
7	DQ4	DQ4	DQ4	DQ4	Data 4
8	DQ5	DQ5	DQ5	DQ5	Data 5
9	DQ6	DQ6	DQ6	DQ6	Data 6
10	DQ7	DQ7	DQ7	DQ7	Data 7
11	DQ8	DQ8	DQ8	DQ8	Data 8
12	VSS	VSS	VSS	VSS	Ground
13	DQ9	DQ9	DQ9	DQ9	Data 9
14	DQ10	DQ10	DQ10	DQ10	Data 10
15	DQ11	DQ11	DQ11	DQ11	Data 11
16	DQ12	DQ12	DQ12	DQ12	Data 12
17	DQ13	DQ13	DQ13	DQ13	Data 13
18	VCC	VCC	VCC	VCC	+5VDC or +3.3VDC
19	DQ14	DQ14	DQ14	DQ14	Data 14
20	DQ15	DQ15	DQ15	DQ15	Data 15
21	CB0	Not connected	CB0	CB0	Parity Check Bit or Input/Output 0
22	CB1	Not connected	CB1	CB1	Parity Check Bit or Input/Output 1
23	VSS	VSS	VSS	VSS	Ground
24	Not connected	Not connected	Not connected	CB8	Parity Check Bit or Input/Output 8
25	Not connected	Not connected	Not connected	CB9	Parity Check Bit or Input/Output 9
26	VCC	VCC	VCC	VCC	+5VDC or +3.3VDC
27	WE0	WE0	WE0	WE0	Read Write Input
28	CAS0	CAS0	CAS0	CAS0	Column Address Strobe 0
29	CAS1	CAS1	CAS1	CAS1	Column Address Strobe 1
30	RAS0	RAS0	RAS0	RAS0	Row Address Strobe 0
31	OE0	OE0	OE0	OE0	Output Enable
32	VSS	VSS	VSS	VSS	Ground

(Continued)

Pinouts for 168-pin DIMM *(Continued)*

Pin	Parity	NonParity	72bit	80bit	Description
33	A0	A0	A0	A0	Address 0
34	A2	A2	A2	A2	Address 2
35	A4	A4	A4	A4	Address 4
36	A6	A6	A6	A6	Address 6
37	A8	A8	A8	A8	Address 8
38	A10	A10	A10	A10	Address 10
39	A12	A12	A12	A12	Address 12
40	VCC	VCC	VCC	VCC	+5VDC or +3.3VDC
41	VCC	VCC	VCC	VCC	+5VDC or +3.3VDC
42	Not connected	Not connected	Not connected	Not connected	Not connected
43	VSS	VSS	VSS	VSS	Ground
44	OE2	OE2	OE2	OE2	
45	RAS2	RAS2	RAS2	RAS2	Row Address Strobe 2
46	CAS2	CAS2	CAS2	CAS2	Column Address Strobe 2
47	CAS3	CAS3	CAS3	CAS3	Column Address Strobe 3
48	WE2	WE2	WE2	WE2	Read Write Input
49	VCC	VCC	VCC	VCC	+5VDC or +3.3VDC
50	Not connected	Not connected	Not connected	CB10	Parity Check Bit or Input/Output 10
51	Not connected	Not connected	Not connected	CB11	Parity Check Bit or Input/Output 11
52	CB2	Not con-	CB2	CB2	Parity Check Bit or Input/Output 2
53	CB3	Not con-	CB3	CB3	Parity Check Bit or Input/Output 3
54	VSS	VSS	VSS	VSS	Ground
55	DQ16	DQ16	DQ16	DQ16	Data 16
56	DQ17	DQ17	DQ17	DQ17	Data 17
57	DQ18	DQ18	DQ18	DQ18	Data 18
58	DQ19	DQ19	DQ19	DQ19	Data 19
59	VCC	VCC	VCC	VCC	+5VDC or +3.3VDC
60	DQ20	DQ20	DQ20	DQ20	Data 20
61	Not connected	Not connected	Not connected	Not connected	Not connected
62	Not connected	Not connected	Not connected	Not connected	Not connected
63	Not connected	Not connected	Not connected	Not connected	Not connected
64	VSS	VSS	VSS	VSS	Ground

(Continued)

Pinouts for 168-pin DIMM *(Continued)*

Pin	Parity	NonParity	72bit	80bit	Description
65	DQ21	DQ21	DQ21	DQ21	Data 21
66	DQ22	DQ22	DQ22	DQ22	Data 22
67	DQ23	DQ23	DQ23	DQ23	Data 23
68	VSS	VSS	VSS	VSS	Ground
69	DQ24	DQ24	DQ24	DQ24	Data 24
70	DQ25	DQ25	DQ25	DQ25	Data 25
71	DQ26	DQ26	DQ26	DQ26	Data 26
72	DQ27	DQ27	DQ27	DQ27	Data 27
73	VCC	VCC	VCC	VCC	+5VDC or +3.3VDC
74	DQ28	DQ28	DQ28	DQ28	Data 28
75	DQ29	DQ29	DQ29	DQ29	Data 29
76	DQ30	DQ30	DQ30	DQ30	Data 30
77	DQ31	DQ31	DQ31	DQ31	Data 31
78	VSS	VSS	VSS	VSS	Ground
79	Not connected	Not connected	Not connected	Not connected	Not connected
80	Not connected	Not connected	Not connected	Not connected	Not connected
81	Not connected	Not connected	Not connected	Not connected	Not connected
82	SDA	SDA	SDA	SDA	Serial Data
83	SCL	SCL	SCL	SCL	Serial Clock
84	VCC	VCC	VCC	VCC	+5VDC or +3.3VDC

			SIDE TWO		
Pin	Parity	Non-Parity	72-bit ECC	80-bit ECC	Description
85	VSS	VSS	VSS	VSS	Ground
86	DQ32	DQ32	DQ32	DQ32	Data 32
87	DQ33	DQ33	DQ33	DQ33	Data 33
88	DQ34	DQ34	DQ34	DQ34	Data 34
89	DQ35	DQ35	DQ35	DQ35	Data 35
90	VCC	VCC	VCC	VCC	+5VDC or +3.3VDC
91	DQ36	DQ36	DQ36	DQ36	Data 36
92	DQ37	DQ37	DQ37	DQ37	Data 37
93	DQ38	DQ38	DQ38	DQ38	Data 38
94	DQ39	DQ39	DQ39	DQ39	Data 39

(Continued)

Pinouts for 168-pin DIMM *(Continued)*

Pin	Parity	Non-Parity	72-bit ECC	80-bit ECC	Description
95	DQ40	DQ40	DQ40	DQ40	Data 40
96	VSS	VSS	VSS	VSS	Ground
97	DQ41	DQ41	DQ41	DQ41	Data 41
98	DQ42	DQ42	DQ42	DQ42	Data 42
99	DQ43	DQ43	DQ43	DQ43	Data 43
100	DQ44	DQ44	DQ44	DQ44	Data 44
101	DQ45	DQ45	DQ45	DQ45	Data 45
102	VCC	VCC	VCC	VCC	+5VDC or +3.3VDC
103	DQ46	DQ46	DQ46	DQ46	Data 46
104	DQ47	DQ47	DQ47	DQ47	Data 47
105	CB4	Not connected	CB4	CB4	Parity Check Bit or Input/Output 4
106	CB5	Not connected	CB5	CB5	Parity Check Bit or Input/Output 5
107	VSS	VSS	VSS	VSS	Ground
108	Not connected	Not connected	Not connected	CB12	Parity Check Bit or Input/Output 12
109	Not connected	Not connected	Not connected	CB13	Parity Check Bit or Input/Output 13
110	VCC	VCC	VCC	VCC	+5VDC or +3.3VDC
111	Not connected	Not connected	Not connected	Not connected	Not connected
112	CAS4	CAS4	CAS4	CAS4	ColumnAddressStrobe4
113	CAS5	CAS5	CAS5	CAS5	ColumnAddressStrobe5
114	RAS1	RAS1	RAS1	RAS1	Row Address Strobe 1
115	Not connected	Not connected	Not connected	Not connected	Not connected
116	VSS	VSS	VSS	VSS	Ground
117	A1	A1	A1	A1	Address 1
118	A3	A3	A3	A3	Address 3
119	A5	A5	A5	A5	Address 5
120	A7	A7	A7	A7	Address 7
121	A9	A9	A9	A9	Address 9
122	A11	A11	A11	A11	Address 11
123	A13	A13	A13	A13	Address 13
124	VCC	VCC	VCC	VCC	+5VDC or +3.3VDC
125	Not connected	Not connected	Not connected	Not connected	Not connected

(Continued)

Pinouts for 168-pin DIMM *(Continued)*

Pin	Parity	Non-Parity	72-bit ECC	80-bit ECC	Description
126	Not connected	Not connected	Not connected	Not connected	Not connected
127	VSS	VSS	VSS	VSS	Ground
128	Not connected	D not connected	Not connected	Not connected	Not connected
129	RAS3	RAS3	RAS3	RAS3	Column Address Strobe 3
130	CAS6	CAS6	CAS6	CAS6	Column Address Strobe 6
131	CAS7	CAS7	CAS7	CAS7	Column Address Strobe 7
132	Not connected	Not connected	Not connected	Not connected	Not connected
133	VCC	VCC	VCC	VCC	+5VDC or +3.3VDC
134	Not connected	Not connected	Not connected	CB14	Parity Check Bit or Input/Output 14
135	Not connected	Not connected	Not connected	CB15	Parity Check Bit or Input/Output 15
136	CB6	Not connected	CB6	CB6	Parity Check Bit or Input/Output 6
137	CB7	Not connected	CB7	CB7	Parity Check Bit or Input/Output 7
138	VSS	VSS	VSS	VSS	Ground
139	DQ48	DQ48	DQ48	DQ48	Data 48
140	DQ49	DQ49	DQ49	DQ49	Data 49
141	DQ50	DQ50	DQ50	DQ50	Data 50
142	DQ51	DQ51	DQ51	DQ51	Data 51
143	VCC	VCC	VCC	VCC	+5VDC or +3.3VDC
144	DQ52	DQ52	DQ52	DQ52	Data 52
145	Not connected	Not connected	Not connected	Not connected	Not connected
146	Not connected	Not connected	Not connected	Not connected	Not connected
147	Not connected	Not connected	Not connected	Not connected	Notconnected
148	VSS	VSS	VSS	VSS	Ground
149	DQ53	DQ53	DQ53	DQ53	Data 53
150	DQ54	DQ54	DQ54	DQ54	Data 54
151	DQ55	DQ55	DQ55	DQ55	Data 55
152	VSS	VSS	VSS	VSS	Ground
153	DQ56	DQ56	DQ56	DQ56	Data 56
154	DQ57	DQ57	DQ57	DQ57	Data 57

(Continued)

Pinouts for 168-pin DIMM *(Concluded)*

Pin	Parity	Non-Parity	72-bit ECC	80-bit ECC	Description
155	DQ58	DQ58	DQ58	DQ58	Data 58
156	DQ59	DQ59	DQ59	DQ59	Data 59
157	VCC	VCC	VCC	VCC	+5VDC or +3.3VDC
158	DQ60	DQ60	DQ60	DQ60	Data 60
159	DQ61	DQ61	DQ61	DQ61	Data 61
160	DQ62	DQ62	DQ62	DQ62	Data 62
161	DQ63	DQ63	DQ63	DQ63	Data 63
162	VSS	VSS	VSS	VSS	Ground
163	CK3	CK3	CK3	CK3	
164	Not connected	Not connected	Not connected	Not connected	Not connected
165	SA0	SA0	SA0	SA0	Serial Address 0
166	SA1	SA1	SA1	SA1	Serial Address 1
167	SA2	SA2	SA2	SA2	Serial Address 2
168	VCC	VCC	VCC	VCC	+5VDC or +3.3VDC

184-pin Nonregistered DIMM

	SIDE ONE						
PIN	SYMBOL	PIN	SYMBOL	PIN	SYMBOL	PIN	SYMBOL
1	VREF	16	CK1	31	DQ19	46	VDD
2	DQ0	17	CK1#	32	A5	47	DNU
3	VSS	18	VSS	33	DQ24	48	A0
4	DQ1	19	DQ10	34	VSS	49	DNU
5	DQS0	20	DQ11	35	DQ25	50	VSS
6	DQ2	21	CKE0	36	DQS3	51	DNU#
7	VDD	22	VDDQ	37	A4	52	BA1
8	DQ3	23	DQ16	38	VDD	53	DQ32
9	NC	24	DQ17	39	DQ26	54	VDDQ
10	DNU	25	DQS2	40	DQ27	55	DQ33
11	VSS	26	VSS	41	A2	56	DQS4
12	DQ8	27	A9	42	VSS	57	DQ34
13	DQ9	28	DQ18	43	A1	58	VSS
14	DQS1	29	A7	44	DNU	59	BA0
15	VDDQ	30	VDDQ	45	DNU	60	DQ35

(Continued)

184-pin Nonregistered DIMM *(Concluded)*

PIN	SYMBOL	PIN	SYMBOL	PIN	SYMBOL	PIN	SYMBOL
61	DQ40	69	DQ43	77	VDDQ	85	VDD
62	VDDQ	70	VDD	78	DQS6	86	DQS7
63	WE#	71	NC	79	DQ50	87	DQ58
64	DQ41	72	DQ48	80	DQ51	88	DQ59
65	CAS#	73	DQ49	81	VSS	89	VSS
66	VSS	74	VSS	82	NC	90	NC
67	DQS5	75	CK2#	83	DQ56	91	SDA
68	DQ42	76	CK2	84	DQ57	92	SCL

SIDE TWO

PIN	SYMBOL	PIN	SYMBOL	PIN	SYMBOL	PIN	SYMBOL
93	VSS	116	VSS	139	VSS	162	DQ47
94	DQ4	117	DQ21	140	DNU	163	NC
95	DQ5	118	A11	141	A10	164	VDDQ
96	VDDQ	119	DQS11/DM2	142	DNU	165	DQ52
97	DQS9/DM0	120	VDD	143	VDDQ	166	DQ53
98	DQ6	121	DQ22	144	DNU	167	NC
99	DQ7	122	A8	145	VSS	168	VDD
100	VSS	123	DQ23	146	DQ36	169	DQS15/DM6
101	NC	124	VSS	147	DQ37	170	DQ54
102	NC	125	A6	148	VDD	171	DQ55
103	NC	126	DQ28	149	DQS13/DM4	172	VDDQ
104	VDDQ	127	DQ29	150	DQ38	173	NC
105	DQ12	128	VDDQ	151	DQ39	174	DQ60
106	DQ13	129	DQS12/DM3	152	VSS	175	DQ61
107	DQS10/DM1	130	A3	153	DQ44	176	VSS
108	VDD	131	DQ30	154	RAS#	177	DQS16/DM7
109	DQ14	132	VSS	155	DQ45	178	DQ62
110	DQ15	133	DQ31	156	VDDQ	179	DQ63
111	DNU	134	DNU	157	S0#	180	VDDQ
112	VDDQ	135	DNU	158	NC	181	SA0
113	NC	136	VDDQ	159	DQS14/DM5	182	SA1
114	DQ20	137	DNU	160	VSS	183	SA2
115	NC/A12	138	DNU	161	DQ46	184	VDDSPD

Note: Abbreviations in this table are identical to those on other tables. For clarity, due to the number of entries, they have been left out of this table.

Pinouts of 144-pin SO-DIMM

	SIDE ONE		
Pin	Normal	ECC	Description
1	VSS	VSS	Ground
2	VSS	VSS	Ground
3	DQ0	DQ0	Data 0
4	DQ32	DQ32	Data 32
5	DQ1	DQ1	Data 1
6	DQ33	DQ33	Data 33
7	DQ2	DQ2	Data 2
8	DQ34	DQ34	Data 34
9	DQ3	DQ3	Data 3
10	DQ35	DQ35	Data 35
11	VCC	VCC	+5VDC
12	VCC	VCC	+5VDC
13	DQ4	DQ4	Data 4
14	DQ36	DQ36	Data 36
15	DQ5	DQ5	Data 5
16	DQ37	DQ37	Data 37
17	DQ6	DQ6	Data 6
18	DQ38	DQ38	Data 38
19	DQ7	DQ7	Data 7
20	DQ39	DQ39	Data 39
21	VSS	VSS	Ground
22	VSS	VSS	Ground
23	CAS0	CAS0	Column Address Strobe 0
24	CAS4	CAS4	Column Address Strobe 4
25	CAS1	CAS1	Column Address Strobe 1
26	CAS5	CAS5	Column Address Strobe 5
27	VCC	VCC	+5VDC
28	VCC	VCC	+5VDC
29	A0	A0	Address 0
30	A3	A3	Address 3
31	A1	A1	Address 1
32	A4	A4	Address 4
33	A2	A2	Address 2
34	A5	A5	Address 5
35	VSS	VSS	Ground

(Continued)

Pinouts of 144-pin SO-DIMM *(Continued)*

Pin	Normal	ECC	Description
36	VSS	VSS	Ground
37	DQ8	DQ8	Data 8
38	DQ40	DQ40	Data 40
39	DQ9	DQ9	Data 9
40	DQ41	DQ41	Data 41
41	DQ10	DQ10	Data 10
42	DQ42	DQ42	Data 42
43	DQ11	DQ11	Data 11
44	DQ43	DQ43	Data 43
45	VCC	VCC	+5VDC
46	VCC	VCC	+5VDC
47	DQ12	DQ12	Data 12
48	DQ44	DQ44	Data 44
49	DQ13	DQ13	Data 13
50	DQ45	DQ45	Data 45
51	DQ14	DQ14	Data 14
52	DQ46	DQ46	Data 46
53	DQ15	DQ15	Data 15
54	DQ47	DQ47	Data 47
55	VSS	VSS	Ground
56	VSS	VSS	Ground
57	Not connected	CB0	Parity Check Bit 0
58	Not connected	CB4	Parity Check Bit 4
59	Not connected	CB1	Parity Check Bit 1
60	Not connected	CB5	Parity Check Bit 5
61	Not connected	Not connected	Not connected
62	Not connected	Not connected	Not connected
63	VCC	VCC	+5VDC
64	VCC	VCC	+5VDC
65	Not connected	Not connected	Not connected
66	Not connected	Not connected	Not connected
67	WE	WE	Read/Write
68	Not connected	Not connected	Not connected
69	RAS0	RAS0	Row Address Strobe 0
70	Not connected	Not connected	Not connected
71	RAS1	RAS1	Row Address Strobe 1

(Continued)

Pinouts of 144-pin SO-DIMM *(Continued)*

	SIDE TWO		
Pin	Normal	ECC	Description
72	Not connected	Not connected	Not connected
73	OE	OE	Output Enable
74	Not connected	Not connected	Not connected
75	VSS	VSS	Ground
76	VSS	VSS	Ground
77	Not connected	CB2	Parity Check Bit 2
78	Not connected	CB6	Parity Check Bit 6
79	Not connected	CB3	Parity Check Bit 3
80	Not connected	CB7	Parity Check Bit 7
81	VCC	VCC	+5VDC
82	VCC	VCC	+5VDC
83	DQ16	DQ16	Data 16
84	DQ48	DQ48	Data 48
85	DQ17	DQ17	Data 17
86	DQ49	DQ49	Data 49
87	DQ18	DQ18	Data 18
88	DQ50	DQ50	Data 50
89	DQ19	DQ19	Data 19
90	DQ51	DQ51	Data 51
91	VSS	VSS	Ground
92	VSS	VSS	Ground
93	DQ20	DQ20	Data 20
94	DQ52	DQ52	Data 52
95	DQ21	DQ21	Data 21
96	DQ53	DQ53	Data 53
97	DQ22	DQ22	Data 22
98	DQ54	DQ54	Data 54
99	DQ23	DQ23	Data 23
100	DQ55	DQ55	Data 55
101	VCC	VCC	+5VDC
102	VCC	VCC	+5VDC
103	A6	A6	Address 6
104	A7	A7	Address 7
105	A8	A8	Address 8
106	A11	A11	Address 11
107	VSS	VSS	Ground

(Continued)

Pinouts of 144-pin SO-DIMM *(Concluded)*

Pin	Normal	ECC	Description
108	VSS	VSS	Ground
109	A9	A9	Address 9
110	A12	A12	Address 12
111	A10	A10	Address 10
112	A13	A13	Address 13
113	VCC	VCC	+5VDC
114	VCC	VCC	+5VDC
115	CAS2	CAS2	Column Address Strobe 2
116	CAS6	CAS6	Column Address Strobe 6
117	CAS3	CAS3	Column Address Strobe 3
118	CAS7	CAS7	Column Address Strobe 7
119	VSS	VSS	Ground
120	VSS	VSS	Ground
121	DQ24	DQ24	Data 24
122	DQ56	DQ56	Data 56
123	DQ25	DQ25	Data 25
124	DQ57	DQ57	Data 57
125	DQ26	DQ26	Data 26
126	DQ58	DQ58	Data 58
127	DQ27	DQ27	Data 27
128	DQ59	DQ59	Data 59
129	VCC	VCC	+5VDC
130	VCC	VCC	+5VDC
131	DQ28	DQ28	Data 28
132	DQ60	DQ60	Data 60
133	DQ29	DQ29	Data 29
134	DQ61	DQ61	Data 61
135	DQ30	DQ30	Data 30
136	DQ62	DQ62	Data 62
137	DQ31	DQ31	Data 31
138	DQ63	DQ63	Data 63
139	VSS	VSS	Ground
140	VSS	VSS	Ground
141	SDA	SDA	Serial Data
142	SCL	SCL	Serial Clock
143	VCC	VCC	+5VDC
144	VCC	VCC	+5VDC

CABLE PINOUTS

Floppy Disk Cable (nonmedia sense)

Pin	Signal	Pin	Signal	Pin	Signal
1	Ground	13	Ground	25	Ground
2	HD select	14	Reserved	26	Track 0
3	+5v DC	15	Ground	27	Ground
4	Drive Type ID 1	16	Motor enable	28	Write protect
5	Ground	17	Ground	29	Ground
6	+12v DC	18	Direction in	30	Read data
7	Ground	19	Ground	31	Ground
8	Index	20	Step	32	Head 1 Select
9	Ground	21	Ground	33	Ground
10	Reserved	22	Write data	34	Diskette change
11	Ground	23	Ground		
12	Drive select	24	Write enable		

Floppy Disk Cable (media sense)

Pin	Signal	Pin	Signal
1	Ground	18	Direction in
2	Data rate select	19	Ground
3	+5v DC	20	Step
4	Drive type ID 1/Drive Status1	21	Ground
5	Ground	22	Write data
6	+12v DC	23	Ground
7	Ground	24	Write enable
8	Index	25	Ground
9	Drive type ID 0	26	Track 0
10	Reserved	27	Media type ID 0/ Drive status 2
11	Ground	28	Write protect
12	Drive select	29	Ground
13	Ground	30	Read data
14	Security Command	31	Ground
15	Ground	32	Head 1 select
16	Motor enable	33	Data rate select
17	Media type 1/ Drive status 3	34	Diskette change

Serial Cable Pinouts

DB-25	DB-9	Signal Direction	Signal Name
1			Protective Ground
2	3	DTE-to-DCE	Transmitted Data
3	2	DCE-to-DTE	Received Data
4	7	DTE-to-DCE	Request To Send
5	8	DCE-to-DTE	Clear To Send
6	6	DCE-to-DTE	Data Set Ready
7	5		Signal Ground
8	1	DCE-to-DTE	Received Line Signal Detector (Carrier Detect)
20	4	DTE-to-DCE	Data Terminal Ready
22	9	DCE-to-DTE	Ring Indicator

On DB-25 cables, pins 9-19 are not used.

Pinouts for Parallel Cable

PIN	Purpose	PIN	Purpose
Pin 1	-Strobe	Pin 14	Auto Feed -
Pin 2	Data Bit 0 +	Pin 15	Error -
Pin 3	Data Bit 1 +	Pin 16	Initialize Printer -
Pin 4	Data Bit 2 +	Pin 17	Select Input -
Pin 5	Data Bit 3 +	Pin 18	Data Bit 0 Return (ground)
Pin 6	Data Bit 4 +	Pin 19	Data Bit 1 Return (ground)
Pin 7	Data Bit 5 +	Pin 20	Data Bit 2 Return (ground)
Pin 8	Data Bit 6 +	Pin 21	Data Bit 3 Return (ground)
Pin 9	Data Bit 7 +	Pin 22	Data Bit 4 Return (ground)
Pin 10	Acknowledge -	Pin 23	Data Bit 5 Return (ground)
Pin 11	Busy +	Pin 24	Data Bit 6 Return (ground)
Pin 12	Paper End +	Pin 25	Data Bit 7 Return (ground)
Pin 13	Select +		

Pinout Descriptors for Centronics Connector

Pin #	Function	Pin #	Function
1	Strobe	19	Ground
2	Data 0	20	Ground
3	Data 1	21	Ground
4	Data 2	22	Ground
5	Data 3	23	Ground
6	Data 4	24	Ground
7	Data 5	25	Ground
8	Data 6	26	Ground
9	Data 7	27	Ground
10	ACK	28	Ground
11	Busy	29	Ground
12	Paper Out	30	Ground
13	Select	31	Input Prime (Spare)
14	Auto Line Feed	32	Error
15	PI	33	Ground
16	Ground	34	N/C (Spare)
17	Frame Ground	35	+5V
18	+5V	36	Select In (Spare)

EXPANSION BUS PINOUTS

Pinouts for the 8-bit PC Bus

Pin #	Pin Function	Direction	Pin #	Pin Function	Direction
A1:	CHANNEL CHECK	Card-to-PC	B1:	Ground	N/A
A2:	DATA SIGNAL 7	Bidirectional	B2:	RESET DRIVER	PC-to-Card
A3:	DATA SIGNAL 6	Bidirectional	B3:	+5V	N/A
A4:	DATA SIGNAL 5	Bidirectional	B4:	IRQ 2	Card-to-PC
A5:	DATA SIGNAL 4	Bidirectional	B5:	-5V	PC-to-Card
A6:	DATA SIGNAL 3	Bidirectional	B6:	DMA CHANNEL 2	Card-to-PC
A7:	DATA SIGNAL 2	Bidirectional	B7:	-12V	PC-to-Card
A8:	DATA SIGNAL 1	Bidirectional	B8:	NO WAIT STATE	Card-to-PC
A9:	DATA SIGNAL 0	Bidirectional	B9:	+12V	PC-to-Card
A10:	CHANNEL READY	Card-to-PC	B10:	Ground	N/A
A11:	ADDRESS ENABLE	PC-to-Card	B11:	SYSTEM MEMORY WRITE	PC-to-Card
A12:	ADDRESS SIGNAL 19	PC-to-Card	B12:	SYSTEM MEMORY READ	PC-to-Card
A13:	ADDRESS SIGNAL 18	PC-to-Card	B13:	I/O WRITE	PC-to-Card
A14:	ADDRESS SIGNAL 17	PC-to-Card	B14:	I/O READ	PC-to-Card
A15:	ADDRESS SIGNAL 16	PC-to-Card	B15:	DMA ACKNOWLEDGE CHANNEL 3	PC-to-Card
A16:	ADDRESS SIGNAL 15	PC-to-Card	B16:	DMA CHANNEL 3	Card-to-PC
A17:	ADDRESS SIGNAL 14	PC-to-Card	B17:	DMA ACKNOWLEDGE CHANNEL 1	PC-to-Card
A18:	ADDRESS SIGNAL 13	PC-to-Card	B18:	DMA CHANNEL 1	Card-to-PC
A19:	ADDRESS SIGNAL 12	PC-to-Card	B19:	REFRESH	Bidirectional
A20:	ADDRESS SIGNAL 11	PC-to-Card	B20:	BUS CLOCK	PC-to-Card
A21:	ADDRESS SIGNAL 10	PC-to-Card	B21:	IRQ 7	Card-to-PC
A22:	ADDRESS SIGNAL 9	PC-to-Card	B22:	IRQ 6	Card-to-PC
A23:	ADDRESS SIGNAL 8	PC-to-Card	B23:	IRQ 5	Card-to-PC
A24:	ADDRESS SIGNAL 7	PC-to-Card	B24:	IRQ 4	Card-to-PC
A25:	ADDRESS SIGNAL 6	PC-to-Card	B25:	IRQ 3	Card-to-PC
A26:	ADDRESS SIGNAL 5	PC-to-Card	B26:	DMA ACKNOWLEDGE CHANNEL 2	PC-to-Card
A27:	ADDRESS SIGNAL 4	PC-to-Card	B27:	TERMINAL COUNT	PC-to-Card
A28:	ADDRESS SIGNAL 3	PC-to-Card	B28:	BUS ADDRESS LATCH ENABLE	PC-to-Card
A29:	ADDRESS SIGNAL 2	PC-to-Card	B29:	+5V	PC-to-Card
A30:	ADDRESS SIGNAL 1	PC-to-Card	B30:	OSCILLATOR	PC-to-Card
A31:	ADDRESS SIGNAL 0	PC-to-Card	B31:	Ground	N/A

16-bit ISA Extensions

Pin #	Pin Function	Direction	Pin #	Pin Function	Direction
C1	System bus high enable	Bidirectional	D1	Memory 16-bit chip select	Card-to-PC
C2	Address bit 23	Bidirectional	D2	I/O 16-bit chip select	Card-to-PC
C3	Address bit 22	Bidirectional	D3	Interrupt Request 10	Card-to-PC
C4	Address bit 21	Bidirectional	D4	Interrupt Request 11	Card-to-PC
C5	Address bit 20	Bidirectional	D5	Interrupt Request 12	Card-to-PC
C6	Address bit 19	Bidirectional	D6	Interrupt Request 15	Card-to-PC
C7	Address bit 18	Bidirectional	D7	Interrupt Request 14	Card-to-PC
C8	Address bit 17	Bidirectional	D8	DMA Acknowledge 0	PC-to-Card
C9	Memory Read*	Bidirectional	D9	DMA Request 0	Card-to-PC
C10	Memory Write†	Bidirectional	D10	DMA Acknowledge 5	PC-to-Card
C11	Data bit 8	Bidirectional	D11	DMA Request 5	Card-to-PC
C12	Data bit 9	Bidirectional	D12	DMA Acknowledge 6	PC-to-Card
C13	Data bit 10	Bidirectional	D13	DMA Request 6	Card-to-PC
C14	Data bit 11	Bidirectional	D14	DMA Acknowledge 7	PC-to-Card
C15	Data bit 12	Bidirectional	D15	DMA Request 7	Card-to-PC
C16	Data bit 13	Bidirectional	D16	Used with DRQ to gain control of system	PC-to-Card
C17	Data bit 14	Bidirectional	D17		
C18	Data bit 15	Bidirectional	D18	Ground	N/A

*Active on all memory read cycles.
†Active on all memory write cycles.

32-bit PCI Pinouts

Pin	Signal	Description	Pin	Signal	Description
A1	TRST	Test Logic Reset	B1	−12V	−12 VDC
A2	+12V	+12 VDC	B2	TCK	Test Clock
A3	TMS	Test Mode Select	B3	GND	Ground
A4	TDI	Test Data Input	B4	TDO	Test Data Output
A5	+5V	+5 VDC	B5	+5V	+5 VDC
A6	INTA	Interrupt A	B6	+5V	+5 VDC
A7	INTC	Interrupt C	B7	INTB	Interrupt B
A8	+5V	+5 VDC	B8	INTD	Interrupt D
A9	RESV01	Reserved VDC	B9	PRSNT1	Reserved
A10	+5V	+V I/O (+5 V or +3.3 V)	B10	RES	+V I/O (+5 V or +3.3 V)
A11	RESV03	Reserved VDC	B11	PRSNT2	Reserved
A12	GND03	Ground or Open (Key)	B12	GND	Ground or Open (Key)
A13	GND05	Ground or Open (Key)	B13	GND	Ground or Open (Key)
A14	RESV05	Reserved VDC	B14	RES	Reserved VDC
A15	RESET	Reset	B15	GND	Reset
A16	+5V	+V I/O (+5 V or +3.3 V)	B16	CLK	Clock
A17	GNT	Grant PCI use	B17	GND	Ground
A18	GND08	Ground	B18	REQ	Request
A19	RESV06	Reserved VDC	B19	+5V	+V I/O (+5 V or +3.3 V)
A20	AD30	Address/Data 30	B20	AD31	Address/Data 31
A21	+3.3V01	+3.3 VDC	B21	AD29	Address/Data 29
A22	AD28	Address/Data 28	B22	GND	Ground
A23	AD26	Address/Data 26	B23	AD27	Address/Data 27
A24	GND10	Ground	B24	AD25	Address/Data 25
A25	AD24	Address/Data 24	B25	+3.3V	+3.3VDC
A26	IDSEL	Initialization Device Select	B26	C/BE3	Command, Byte Enable 3
A27	+3.3V03	+3.3 VDC	B27	AD23	Address/Data 23
A28	AD22	Address/Data 22	B28	GND	Ground
A29	AD20	Address/Data 20	B29	AD21	Address/Data 21
A30	GND12	Ground	B30	AD19	Address/Data 19
A31	AD18	Address/Data 18	B31	+3.3V	+3.3 VDC
A32	AD16	Address/Data 16	B32	AD17	Address/Data 17
A33	+3.3V05	+3.3 VDC	B33	C/BE2	Command, Byte Enable 2
A34	FRAME	Address or Data phase	B34	GND13	Ground
A35	GND14	Ground	B35	IRDY	Initiator Ready
A36	TRDY	Target Ready	B36	+3.3V06	+3.3 VDC
A37	GND15	Ground	B37	DEVSEL	Device Select

(Continued)

32-bit PCI Pinouts *(Continued)*

Pin	Signal	Description	Pin	Signal	Description
A38	STOP	Stop Transfer Cycle	B38	GND16	Ground
A39	+3.3V07	+3.3 VDC	B39	LOCK	Lock bus
A40	SDONE	Snoop Done	B40	PERR	Parity Error
A41	SBO	Snoop Backoff	B41	+3.3V08	+3.3 VDC
A42	GND17	Ground	B42	SERR	System Error
A43	PAR	Parity	B43	+3.3V09	+3.3 VDC
A44	AD15	Address/Data 15	B44	C/BE1	Command, Byte Enable 1
A45	+3.3V10	+3.3 VDC	B45	AD14	Address/Data 14
A46	AD13	Address/Data 13	B46	GND18	Ground
A47	AD11	Address/Data 11	B47	AD12	Address/Data 12
A48	GND19	Ground	B48	AD10	Address/Data 10
A49	AD9	Address/Data 9	B49	GND20	Ground
A50		Connector Key	B50	(OPEN)	Ground or Open (Key)
A51		Connector Key	B51	(OPEN)	Ground or Open (Key)
A52	C/BE0	Command, Byte Enable 0	B52	AD8	Address/Data 8
A53	+3.3V11	+3.3 VDC	B53	AD7	Address/Data 7
A54	AD6	Address/Data 6	B54	+3.3V12	+3.3 VDC
A55	AD4	Address/Data 4	B55	AD5	Address/Data 5
A56	GND21	Ground	B56	AD3	Address/Data 3
A57	AD2	Address/Data 2	B57	GND22	Ground
A58	AD0	Address/Data 0	B58	AD1	Address/Data 1
A59	+5V	+V I/O (+5 V or +3.3 V)	B59	VCC08	+5 VDC
A60	REQ64	Request 64-bit	B60	ACK64	Acknowledge 64-bit
A61	VCC11	+5 VDC	B61	VCC10	+5 VDC
A62	VCC13	+5 VDC	B62	VCC12	+5 VDC

64-bit PCI Extensions

Pin	Signal	Description	Pin	Signal	Description
A63	GND	Ground	B63	RES	Reserved
A64	C/BE[7]#	Command, Byte Enable 7	B64	GND	Ground
A65	C/BE[5]#	Command, Byte Enable 5	B65	C/BE[6]#	Command, Byte Enable 6
A66	+5V	+V I/O (+5 V or +3.3 V)	B66	C/BE[4]#	Command, Byte Enable 4
A67	PAR64	Parity 64 ???	B67	GND	Ground
A68	AD62	Address/Data 62	B68	AD63	Address/Data 63
A69	GND	Ground	B69	AD61	Address/Data 61
A70	AD60	Address/Data 60	B70	+5V	+V I/O (+5 V or +3.3 V)
A71	AD58	Address/Data 58	B71	AD59	Address/Data 59
A72	GND	Ground	B72	AD57	Address/Data 57
A73	AD56	Address/Data 56	B73	GND	Ground
A74	AD54	Address/Data 54	B74	AD55	Address/Data 55
A75	+5V	+V I/O (+5 V or +3.3 V)	B75	AD53	Address/Data 53
A76	AD52	Address/Data 52	B76	GND	Ground
A77	AD50	Address/Data 50	B77	AD51	Address/Data 51
A78	GND	Ground	B78	AD49	Address/Data 49
A79	AD48	Address/Data 48	B79	+5V	+V I/O (+5 V or +3.3 V)
A80	AD46	Address/Data 46	B80	AD47	Address/Data 47
A81	GND	Ground	B81	AD45	Address/Data 45
A82	AD44	Address/Data 44	B82	GND	Ground
A83	AD42	Address/Data 42	B83	AD43	Address/Data 43
A84	+5V	+V I/O (+5 V or +3.3 V)	B84	AD41	Address/Data 41
A85	AD40	Address/Data 40	B85	GND	Ground
A86	AD38	Address/Data 38	B86	AD39	Address/Data 39
A87	GND	Ground	B87	AD37	Address/Data 37
A88	AD36	Address/Data 36	B88	+5V	+V I/O (+5 V or +3.3 V)
A89	AD34	Address/Data 34	B89	AD35	Address/Data 35
A90	GND	Ground	B90	AD33	Address/Data 33
A91	AD32	Address/Data 32	B91	GND	Ground
A92	RES	Reserved	B92	RES	Reserved
A93	GND	Ground	B93	RES	Reserved
A94	RES	Reserved	B94	GND	Ground

Note: On older 5V PCI systems, there were a few differences. This section concentrates on 3.3V, but points out areas common to both systems.

Character Set Charts

Here is the complete ASCII character set discussed in detail in Chapter One and referred to often in the book. The first chart lists the control characters, and the second lists the printed characters. The third chart lists the Extended Latin Character set.

The ASCII Character Set (Control Characters)

Char	Oct	Dec	Hex	CNTL Key	Control Action
NUL	0	0	0	^@	Null character
SOH	1	1	1	^A	Start of heading, = console interrupt
STX	2	2	2	^B	Start of text (maintenance mode in HP command set)
ETX	3	3	3	^C	End of text
EOT	4	4	4	^D	End of transmission, not the same as ETB
ENQ	5	5	5	^E	Enquiry, goes with ACK (from HP Command Set)
ACK	6	6	6	^F	Acknowledge, clears ENQ logon hand
BEL	7	7	7	^G	Bell, rings the bell...
BS	10	8	8	^H	Backspace (From HP Command Set)
HT	11	9	9	^I	Horizontal tab, move to next tab stop
LF	12	10	a	^J	Line feed
VT	13	11	b	^K	Vertical tab
FF	14	12	c	^L	Form feed, page eject
CR	15	13	d	^M	Carriage return
SO	16	14	e	^N	Shift out, alternate character set
SI	17	15	f	^O	Shift in, resume default character set
DLE	20	16	10	^P	Data link escape
DC1	21	17	11	^Q	XON, with XOFF to pause listings; ":okay to send"
DC2	22	18	12	^R	Device control 2, block-mode flow control
DC3	23	19	13	^S	XOFF, with XON is TERM=18 flow control
DC4	24	20	14	^T	Device control 4
NAK	25	21	15	^U	Negative acknowledge
SYN	26	22	16	^V	Synchronous idle
ETB	27	23	17	^W	End transmission block, not the same as EOT
CAN	30	24	17	^X	Cancel line, MPE echoes
EM	31	25	19	^Y	End of medium, Control-Y interrupt
SUB	32	26	1a	^Z	Substitute
ESC	33	27	1b	^[	Escape, next character is not echoed
FS	34	28	1c	^\	File separator
GS	35	29	1d	^]	Group separator
RS	36	30	1e	^^	Record separator, block-mode terminator
US	37	31	1f	^_	Unit separator

The ASCII Character Set (Printed Characters)

Char	Octal	Dec	Hex	Description
SP	40	32	20	Space
!	41	33	21	Exclamation mark
"	42	34	22	Quotation mark (" in HTML)
#	43	35	23	Crosshatch (number sign)
$	44	36	24	Dollar sign
%	45	37	25	Percent sign
&	46	38	26	Ampersand
'	47	39	27	Closing single quote (apostrophe)
(	50	40	28	Opening parenthesis
)	51	41	29	Closing parenthesis
*	52	42	2a	Asterisk (star, multiply)
+	53	43	2b	Plus
,	54	44	2c	Comma
-	55	45	2d	Hyphen, dash, minus
.	56	46	2e	Period
/	57	47	2f	Slant (forward slash, divide)
0	60	48	30	Zero
1	61	49	31	One
2	62	50	32	Two
3	63	51	33	Three
4	64	52	34	Four
5	65	53	35	Five
6	66	54	36	Six
7	67	55	37	Seven
8	70	56	38	Eight
9	71	57	39	Nine
:	72	58	3a	Colon

Char	Octal	Dec	Hex	Description
;	73	59	3b	Semicolon
<	74	60	3c	Less-than sign (< in HTML)
=	75	61	3d	Equals sign
>	76	62	3e	Greater-than sign (> in HTML)
?	77	63	3f	Question mark
@	100	64	40	At-sign
A	101	65	41	Uppercase A
B	102	66	42	Uppercase B
C	103	67	43	Uppercase C
D	104	68	44	Uppercase D
E	105	69	45	Uppercase E
F	106	70	46	Uppercase F
G	107	71	47	Uppercase G
H	110	72	48	Uppercase H
I	111	73	49	Uppercase I
J	112	74	4a	Uppercase J
K	113	75	4b	Uppercase K
L	114	76	4c	Uppercase L
M	115	77	4d	Uppercase M
N	116	78	4e	Uppercase N
O	117	79	4f	Uppercase O
P	120	80	50	Uppercase P
Q	121	81	51	Uppercase Q
R	122	82	52	Uppercase R
S	123	83	53	Uppercase S

(Continued)

The ASCII Character Set (Printed Characters) *(Concluded)*

Char	Octal	Dec	Hex	Description
T	124	84	54	Uppercase T
U	125	85	55	Uppercase U
V	126	86	56	Uppercase V
W	127	87	57	Uppercase W
X	130	88	58	Uppercase X
Y	131	89	59	Uppercase Y
Z	132	90	5a	Uppercase Z
[	133	91	5b	Opening square bracket
\	134	92	5c	Reverse slant (Backslash)
]	135	93	5d	Closing square bracket
^	136	94	5e	Caret (Circumflex)
_	137	95	5f	Underscore
`	140	96	60	Opening single quote
a	141	97	61	Lowercase a
b	142	98	62	Lowercase b
c	143	99	63	Lowercase c
d	144	100	64	Lowercase d
e	145	101	65	Lowercase e
f	146	102	66	Lowercase f
g	147	103	67	Lowercase g
h	150	104	68	Lowercase h
i	151	105	69	Lowercase i
j	152	106	6a	Lowercase j

Char	Octal	Dec	Hex	Description
k	153	107	6b	Lowercase k
l	154	108	6c	Lowercase l
m	155	109	6d	Lowercase m
n	156	110	6e	Lowercase n
o	157	111	6f	Lowercase o
p	160	112	70	Lowercase p
q	161	113	71	Lowercase q
r	162	114	72	Lowercase r
s	163	115	73	Lowercase s
t	164	116	74	Lowercase t
u	165	117	75	Lowercase u
v	166	118	76	Lowercase v
w	167	119	77	Lowercase w
x	170	120	78	Lowercase x
y	171	121	79	Lowercase y
z	172	122	7a	Lowercase z
{	173	123	7b	Opening curly brace
|	174	124	7c	Vertical line
}	175	125	7d	Closing curly brace
~	176	126	7e	Tilde (approximate)
DEL	177	127	7f	Delete (rubout), cross-hatch box

ISO Latin Character Set

Decimal Value	Character	Description	Decimal Value	Character	Description	Decimal Value	Character	Description
32	Space	Standard space	56	8	Number eight	81	Q	Capital Q
33	!	Exclamation	57	9	Number nine	82	R	Capital R
34	"	Quotation mark	58	:	Colon	83	S	Capital S
35	#	Number sign	59	;	Semicolon	84	T	Capital T
36	$	Dollar sign	60	<	Left carat	85	U	Capital U
37	%	Percent sign	61	=	Equal sign	86	V	Capital V
38	&	Ampersand	62	>	Right carat	87	W	Capital W
39	'	Apostrophe	63	?	Question mark	88	X	Capital X
40	(	Left parenthesis	64	@	At sign	89	Y	Capital Y
41	)	Right parenthesis	65	A	Capital A	90	Z	Capital Z
42	*	Asterisk	66	B	Capital B	91	[	Left bracket
43	+	Plus sign	67	C	Capital C	92	\	Reverse solidus
44	,	Comma	68	D	Capital D	93	]	Right bracket
45	-	Minus sign/dash	69	E	Capital E	94	^	Carat
46	.	Period	70	F	Capital F	95	_	Underscore
47	/	Solidus (slash)	71	G	Capital G	96	`	Acute accent
48	0	Number zero	72	H	Capital H	97	a	Lowercase a
49	1	Number one	73	I	Capital I	98	b	Lowercase b
50	2	Number two	74	J	Capital J	99	c	Lowercase c
51	3	Number three	75	K	Capital K	100	d	Lowercase d
52	4	Number four	76	L	Capital L	101	e	Lowercase e
53	5	Number five	77	M	Capital M	102	f	Lowercase f
54	6	Number six	78	N	Capital N	103	g	Lowercase g
55	7	Number seven	79	O	Capital O	104	h	Lowercase h
			80	P	Capital P	105	i	Lowercase i

(Continued)

ISO Latin Character Set *(Continued)*

Decimal Value	Character	Description
106	j	Lowercase j
107	k	Lowercase k
108	l	Lowercase l
109	m	Lowercase m
110	n	Lowercase n
111	o	Lowercase o
112	p	Lowercase p
113	q	Lowercase q
114	r	Lowercase r
115	s	Lowercase s
116	t	Lowercase t
117	u	Lowercase u
118	v	Lowercase v
119	w	Lowercase w
120	x	Lowercase x
121	y	Lowercase y
122	z	Lowercase z
123	{	Left curly brace
124	|	Vertical bar
125	}	Right curly brace
126	~	Tilde
127-159		Nonprinting
160		Nonbreaking space
161	¡	Inverted exclamation
162	¢	Cent sign

Decimal Value	Character	Description
163	£	Pound sterling
164	¤	General currency sign
165	¥	Yen sign
166	¦	Broken vertical bar
167	§	Section sign
168	¨	Umlaut (dieresis)
169	©	Copyright
170	ª	Feminine ordinal
171	«	Left angle quote, guillemot left
172	¬	Not sign
173		Soft hyphen
174	®	Registered trademark
175	¯	Macron accent
176	°	Degree sign
177	±	Plus or minus
178	²	Superscript two
179	³	Superscript three
180	´	Acute accent
181	µ	Micro sign
182	¶	Paragraph sign
183	·	Middle dot
184	¸	Cedilla
185	¹	Superscript one
186	º	Masculine ordinal
187	»	Right angle quote, guillemot

Code	Char	Description
106	j	Lowercase j
188	¼	Fraction one-fourth
189	½	Fraction one-half
190	¾	Fraction three-fourths
191	¿	Inverted question mark
192	À	Capital A, grave accent (A-grave)
193	Á	Capital A, acute accent (A-acute)
194	Â	Capital A, circumflex accent (A-circ)
195	Ã	Capital A, tilde (A-tilde)
196	Ä	Capital A, dieresis or umlaut mark (A-uml)
197	Å	Capital A, ring (A-ring)
198	Æ	Capital AE dipthong (ligature) (AE-lig)
199	Ç	Capital C, cedilla (C-cedil)
200	È	Capital E, grave accent (E-grave)
201	É	Capital E, acute accent (E-acute)
202	Ê	Capital E, circumflex accent (E-circ)
203	Ë	Capital E, dieresis or umlaut mark (E-uml)
204	Ì	Capital I, grave accent (I-grave)
205	Í	Capital I, acute accent (I-acute)
206	Î	Capital I, circumflex accent (I-circ)
207	Ï	Capital I, dieresis or umlaut mark (I-uml)
208	Ð	Capital Eth, Icelandic (ETH)
209	Ñ	Capital N, tilde (N-tilde)
210	Ò	Capital O, grave accent (O-grave)
211	Ó	Capital O, acute accent (O-acute)
212	Ô	Capital O, circumflex accent (O-circ)
213	Õ	Capital O, tilde (O-tilde)
214	Ö	Capital O, dieresis or umlaut mark (O-uml)
215	×	Multiplication sign
216	Ø	Capital O, slash (O-slash)
217	Ù	Capital U, grave accent (U-grave)
218	Ú	Capital U, acute accent (U-acute)
219	Û	Capital U, circumflex accent (U-circ)
220	Ü	Capital U, dieresis or umlaut mark (U-uml)
221	Ý	Capital Y, acute accent (Y-acute)
222	Þ	Capital THORN, Icelandic (THORN)
223	ß	Small sharp s, German (sz ligature) (szlig)
224	à	Small a, grave accent (a-grave)
225	á	Small a, acute accent (a-acute)
226	â	Small a, circumflex accent (a-circ)
227	ã	Small a, tilde (a-tilde)
228	ä	Small a, dieresis or umlaut mark (a-uml)
229	å	Small a, ring (a-ring)
230	æ	Small ae dipthong (ligature) (ae-lig)
231	ç	Small c, cedilla (c-cedil)
232	è	Small e, grave accent (e-grave)

(Continued)

ISO Latin Character Set *(Concluded)*

Decimal Value	Character	Description	Decimal Value	Character	Description
233	é	Small e, acute accent (e-acute)	245	õ	Small o, tilde (o-tilde)
234	ê	Small e, circumflex accent (e-circ)	246	ö	Small o, dieresis or umlaut mark (o-uml)
235	ë	Small e, dieresis or umlaut mark (e-uml)	247	÷	Division sign
236	ì	Small i, grave accent (i-grave)	248	ø	Small o, slash (o-slash)
237	í	Small i, acute accent (i-acute)	249	ù	Small u, grave accent (u-grave)
238	î	Small i, circumflex accent (i-circ)	250	ú	Small u, acute accent (u-acute)
239	ï	Small i, dieresis or umlaut mark (i-uml)	251	û	Small u, circumflex accent (u-circ)
240	ð	Small eth, Icelandic (eth)	252	ü	Small u, dieresis or umlaut mark (u-uml)
241	ñ	Small n, tilde (n-tilde)	253	ý	Small y, acute accent (y-acute)
242	ò	Small o, grave accent (o-grave)	254	þ	Small thorn, Icelandic (thorn)
243	ó	Small o, acute accent (o-acute)	255	ÿ	Small y, dieresis or umlaut mark (y-uml)
244	ô	Small o, circumflex accent (o-circ)			

INDEX

B

G

H

N

O

P

W